Frommer's®

East Europe

1st Edition

by Mark Baker, Dr. Keith Bain, Angela
Charlton, Heather Coombs, Pippa de Bruyn,
Hana Mastrini, Karen Tormé Olson,
Sanja Bažulić Olson & Andrew Princz

Here's what the critics say about Frommer's:

"Amazingly easy to use. Very portable, very complete."
—*Booklist*

"Detailed, accurate, and easy-to-read information for all price ranges."
—*Glamour Magazine*

"Hotel information is close to encyclopedic."
—*Des Moines Sunday Register*

"Frommer's Guides have a way of giving you a real feel for a place."
—*Knight Ridder Newspapers*

Wiley Publishing, Inc.

Published by:

Wiley Publishing, Inc.
111 River St.
Hoboken, NJ 07030-5774

ISBN: 978-0-470-08958-3
Editors: Caroline Sieg & Margot Weiss
Special thanks to Missy Pluta & Joe Lemaire
Production Editor: M. Faunette Johnston
Cartographer: Andrew Dolan
Photo Editor: Richard Fox
Anniversary Logo Design: Richard Pacifico
Production by Wiley Indianapolis Composition Services

Front cover photo: Slovenia: Bled, Church of the Assumption, Bled Castle with Stol Mountain looming in background.
Back cover photo: Poland, Krakow: Chancel of St. Mary's church

For information on our other products and services or to obtain technical support, please contact our Customer Care Department within the U.S. at 800/762-2974, outside the U.S. at 317/572-3993 or fax 317/572-4002.

Wiley also publishes its books in a variety of electronic formats. Some content that appears in print may not be available in electronic formats.

Manufactured in the United States of America

5 4 3 2 1

Contents

5   Croatia   123

by Karen Olson & Sanja Bažulić Olson

6   The Czech Republic   202

by Hana Mastrini

7 Hungary   270

by Andrew Princz

8 Poland   376

by Mark Baker

9 Romania   471

by Keith Bain

10 Moscow & St. Petersburg

by Angela Charlton & Heather Coombs

11 Slovakia

by Mark Baker

12 Slovenia 643

by Keith Bain

Index 682

List of Maps

About the Authors

Mark Baker is a long-time American expat, living in Prague, and a frequent traveler to both Slovakia and Poland. He's one of the original editors of *The Prague Post* and was for years a foreign correspondent and editor for Radio Free Europe/Radio Liberty, based in Prague. He's now a freelance writer and reporter.

Keith Bain originally hails from the South African coastal city of Durban, where he developed a penchant for the beach, extra-hot curry, and all-night nightlife. He holds a Doctoral degree in contemporary cinema studies and is the co-author of *Frommer's India* and a contributor to *Frommer's Dream Vacations*.

Angela Charlton first went to Russia a few weeks after the collapse of the Soviet Union in 1991, and spent the better part of the ensuing decade living and working there as a journalist. She was a Moscow-based correspondent for the Associated Press for six years and the author of *Frommer's Moscow & St. Petersburg*.

Heather Coombs is a freelance travel writer and translator of Russian and French. She studied languages at Cambridge University while moonlighting as a correspondent for a Russian newspaper before moving to Paris where her credits include work for *Today in English* and *Living in France* magazines, and ForbesTraveler.com.

Pippa de Bruyn is an award-winning journalist based in Cape Town. She is the author of *Frommer's South Africa*, co-author of *Frommer's India*, and a contributor to *Pauline Frommer's Italy*. Her first novel is due for publication in 2008.

Hana Mastrini is a native of the western Czech spa town of Karlovy Vary who became a veteran of the "Velvet Revolution" as a student in Prague in 1989. She is the author of *Frommer's Prague & the Best of the Czech Republic*.

Karen Tormé Olson is the author of *Frommer's Croatia*. Karen, a former news editor for the *Chicago Tribune*, is also a freelance writer/photographer. She works as a high school guidance counselor in Chicago, where she lives with her husband, son, and three large dogs.

Sanja Bažulić Olson is a Croatian national who was born in Denmark but who has lived in Croatia all her life. She graduated from Zagreb University with a degree in agricultural engineering. Sanja is living in Washington, D.C. with her husband Greg, a financial specialist with the U.S. Foreign Service.

Andrew Princz is a freelance culture and travel journalist/consultant. Andrew was the founding editor of *DT – Diplomacy & Trade* magazine in Budapest, and he currently edits the travel and culture website ontheglobe.com. He is a regular contributor to *Wall Street Journal Europe* and recently authored *Bridging the Divide: Canadian and Hungarian stories of the 1956 revolution*.

An Invitation to the Reader

In researching this book, we discovered many wonderful places—hotels, restaurants, shops, and more. We're sure you'll find others. Please tell us about them, so we can share the information with your fellow travelers in upcoming editions. If you were disappointed with a recommendation, we'd love to know that, too. Please write to:

Frommer's Eastern Europe, 1st Edition
Wiley Publishing, Inc. • 111 River St. • Hoboken, NJ 07030-5774

An Additional Note

Please be advised that travel information is subject to change at any time—and this is especially true of prices. We therefore suggest that you write or call ahead for confirmation when making your travel plans. The authors, editors, and publisher cannot be held responsible for the experiences of readers while traveling. Your safety is important to us, however, so we encourage you to stay alert and be aware of your surroundings. Keep a close eye on cameras, purses, and wallets, all favorite targets of thieves and pickpockets.

Other Great Guides for Your Trip:

Frommer's Prague & the Best of the Czech Republic
Frommer's Croatia
Frommer's Budapest & the Best of Hungary
Frommer's Europe
Frommer's Europe by Rail

Frommer's Star Ratings, Icons & Abbreviations

Every hotel, restaurant, and attraction listing in this guide has been ranked for quality, value, service, amenities, and special features using a **star-rating system.** In country, state, and regional guides, we also rate towns and regions to help you narrow down your choices and budget your time accordingly. Hotels and restaurants are rated on a scale of zero (recommended) to three stars (exceptional). Attractions, shopping, nightlife, towns, and regions are rated according to the following scale: zero stars (recommended), one star (highly recommended), two stars (very highly recommended), and three stars (must-see).

In addition to the star-rating system, we also use **seven feature icons** that point you to the great deals, in-the-know advice, and unique experiences that separate travelers from tourists. Throughout the book, look for:

Finds	Special finds—those places only insiders know about
Fun Fact	Fun facts—details that make travelers more informed and their trips more fun
Kids	Best bets for kids and advice for the whole family
Moments	Special moments—those experiences that memories are made of
Overrated	Places or experiences not worth your time or money
Tips	Insider tips—great ways to save time and money
Value	Great values—where to get the best deals

The following **abbreviations** are used for credit cards:

AE	American Express	DISC	Discover	V	Visa
DC	Diners Club	MC	MasterCard		

Frommers.com

Now that you have this guidebook to help you plan a great trip, visit our website at **www.frommers. com** for additional travel information on more than 3,500 destinations. We update features regularly to give you instant access to the most current trip-planning information available. At Frommers.com, you'll find scoops on the best airfares, lodging rates, and car rental bargains. You can even book your travel online through our reliable travel booking partners. Other popular features include:

- Online updates of our most popular guidebooks
- Vacation sweepstakes and contest giveaways
- Newsletters highlighting the hottest travel trends
- Online travel message boards with featured travel discussions

The Best of Eastern Europe

1 The Most Unforgettable Travel Experiences

- **Discovering the Courtyards of Budapest (Hungary).** Budapest's residential streets are truly enchanting, but it is inside the courtyards of the buildings that the city's greatest secret is held: Budapesters are villagers at heart. Fruit trees and flower gardens flourish, cats lounge in the sun, and jars of pickled vegetables line the window ledges. Nearly every apartment building in this city has an open-air courtyard in its center, where pensioners sit on the common balconies smoking cigarettes, gossiping, and watching the children race around the yard, dodging flowerpots and laundry racks. The main entrance doors to many apartment buildings are left unlocked during the daytime hours.

- **Experiencing Time Travel (Country to Coast, Bulgaria).** Lying on an upholstered daybed on the beach, watching bikini-clad waitresses deliver cocktails to a cool house beat, one struggles to comprehend how this sophisticated beach bar could be located just a few hours from villages where people have never heard of the Internet. Bulgaria encloses as many realities as is possible in an MTV world: From its myriad ancient tombs, untouched since they were built more than 2,000 years ago, and its far-flung rural and religious communities, where life is lived as it has been for 100 years, to its dour Communist-era elders and edgy urban youth, Bulgaria is the closest you get to time travel in one country. See chapter 4.

- **Sunset on the Wall (Dubrovnik, Croatia).** When evening approaches Dubrovnik, views from the top of Old Town's protective wall become a kaleidoscope of color and pattern as shifting light and visual perspective change position in tandem. See p. 146.

- **Strolling Across Charles Bridge at Dawn or Dusk (Czech Republic).** The silhouettes of the statues lining the 6-centuries-old crown jewel of Czech heritage hover like ghosts in the still of the sunrise skyline. Early in the morning you can stroll across the bridge without encountering the crowds that appear by midday. With the changing light of dusk, the statues, the bridge, and the city panorama take on a whole different character. See chapter 6.

- **Stepping into History at Karlštejn Castle (Czech Republic).** A 30-minute train ride south of Prague puts you in the most visited Czech landmark in the environs, built by Charles IV (Karel IV in Czech—the namesake of Charles Bridge) in the 14th century to protect the Holy Roman Empire's crown jewels. This Romanesque hilltop bastion fits the image of the castles of medieval lore. See p. 254.

- **Swimming to Bled Island (Slovenia).** Officially the rules say you shouldn't do it, but the most memorable experience of Lake Bled—one of the most beautiful bodies of water in Europe—is a muscle-working swim from the shore to its miniature isle, which has a lovely church dedicated to the Virgin Mary. If you're one of the not-so-brave, you can always hire a boat and row yourself there, or get one of the aspirant gondoliers to take you over in a *pletna,* Bled's very own answer to Venetian gondolas. See chapter 12.
- **Discovering Magnificence in the Bowels of the Earth (Slovenia).** Slovenia has thousands of Karstic caves, but those protected by UNESCO in the Škocjan park are truly unforgettable. Matchless subterranean architecture is built with stalactites, stalagmites, and rim limestone pools not to mention the world's largest underground canyon, stupendous bridges, and drop-away galleries that all work to reconfigure your understanding of life on earth. See chapter 12.
- **Staying in a Village Home in Maramureş (Romania).** The farming villages of Maramureş occupy an idyllic mountainous landscape near Romania's northern border with the Ukraine. Here you'll discover some of the most bucolic communities in all of Europe; there are still more horse-drawn carts than there are motor vehicles, and many households have a cow or two in the backyard. You'll be surrounded by warm, friendly people, many of whom dress only in traditional costume. If you stay with the Pop family in Hoteni, you'll also be introduced to genuine folk music by a genuine Eastern European legend. See p. 544.
- **Traveling by Train through Transylvania (Romania).** You may not have Count Dracula as your guide, but the terrain encompassed by the land "beyond the forest" will set any heart racing. As you wind through vast tracts of forest and pass soaring mountains, often your only reminders of human habitation will be a church steeple peeking through a forest canopy, or a small family of farmers cutting grass with a hand-held scythe. Or the horrifying spectacle of a hideous abandoned industrial complex—built by the Communists—suddenly appearing in the middle of nowhere. See chapter 9.
- **Discovering the Order in the Chaos of an Orthodox Mass in Stavropoleos Church (Bucharest, Romania).** Attending the beautifully sung Mass at this small but delightful church in the very heart of Bucharest will make your spirit soar. Each day, a Byzantine-style chorus draws a dedicated congregation, while during quiet periods one of the five young nuns will happily talk you through the deep spiritual significance of most every aspect of Orthodox faith. See p. 503.
- **Viewing Red Square at Night (Moscow, Russia).** The crimson-and-ivy-colored domes of St. Basil's Cathedral rise in a dizzying welcome to this most majestic of Russian plazas. Stand on the rise in the center of the square and feel a part of Russia's expanse. See chapter 10.
- **Steam Your Stress Away at the Sandunovsky Baths/Sandunovskiye Banyi (Moscow, Russia).** Thaw your eyelashes in January or escape snow flurries in May in the traditional Russian bathhouse, something between a sauna and a Turkish hammam. The pristine Sandunovsky Baths in Moscow are a special treat, with Greek sculptures and marble baths. See p. 582.
- **Watch the Drawbridges Open Along the Neva River (St. Petersburg, Russia).** An unforgettable outing during

White Nights, or anytime, involves perching yourself on the quay at 2am to watch the city's bridges unfold in careful rhythm to allow ships through the Neva.

- **Kraków's Old Town (Kraków, Poland).** Few cities have the sheer knockout attraction of Kraków. And the Old Town is where it delivers the TKO. And the charms are not just skin deep. The Old Town is choked with stunning cafes and restaurants, student clubs, galleries, and shops. Take the day and explore. See p. 427.
- **Długa (Gdańsk, Poland).** Amberphiles will think they died and went to heaven. It's hard to imagine a more beautifully restored pedestrian main street than Gdańsk's main drag. See p. 456.
- **Auschwitz-Birkenau (Oświęcim, Poland).** Words cannot convey what a deeply shocking and moving experience it is to visit what was the largest of the Nazi extermination camps. Plan to spend some time and visit both camps (just a couple of miles apart). Auschwitz is undeniably horrible, but it's at Birkenau where you really grasp the scale of the tragedy. See p. 435.
- **Walking in the High Tatras (High Tatras, Slovakia).** Follow the red-marked Magistrale Trail from one end of the Tatras to the other for some of the most jaw-droppingly beautiful mountain scenery you're likely to see anywhere. The Tatras are not particularly high (most of the peaks are in the 2,400m/8,000-ft. range), but the rocky, snowcapped tops are highly inspiring. The Magistrale takes you around the mountain faces at just above and below the tree line, with incredible views both up and down. See p. 632.

2 The Best Hotel Splurges

- **Hilton Imperial (Dubrovnik, Croatia).** Rather than build a hotel from scratch, Hilton had the wisdom to restore what was salvageable from Dubrovnik's historic 19th-century Imperial and graft a modern hotel onto the base. Every detail has been addressed here, and whether you hail from America or Azerbaijan, you'll be treated as an honored guest. See p. 141.
- **Diamant (Poreč, Croatia).** Though it looks like an impersonal '70s package-style hotel from the outside, it is much more—management has thought of everything, and the hotel has an activity to match guests' every whim. The Diamant deserves special kudos for its efforts to accommodate guests with disabilities. Every part of the hotel can accommodate wheelchairs, even the pool and locker rooms. See p. 175.
- **Hotel Aria (Prague, Czech Republic).** A new luxurious hotel opened in the heart of Malá Strana just around the corner from the St. Nicholas Cathedral. Its melodious theme will especially please music lovers. See p. 224.
- **Four Seasons Hotel (Prague, Czech Republic).** The best luxury Old Town hotel with the best view of Prague Castle and Charles Bridge. If price isn't a concern, choose a room at this new addition to the luxury-hotel list with its unbeatable location. See p. 225.
- **Four Seasons Hotel Gresham Palace (Budapest, Hungary).** The splendid, sprawling hotel is Hungary's foremost hotel. The Art Nouveau architecture is exquisite, and the customer care and attention to detail will leave you feeling pampered. See p. 296.
- **La Residenza (Timişoara, Romania).** One of the most stylish and least

pretentious upmarket hotels in Romania, this is where VIPs visiting the country's most western city stay when they're striking the latest deal or hiding from the press. If you can drag yourself out your plush room, you'll probably get no farther than the lounge or garden—where you'll be tempted to curl up next to the fire or laze beside the pool. It's like being in your favorite uncle's mansion. See p. 538.

- **Staying in Count Kalnoky's Guest-houses (Micloşoara, Romania).** Tudor Kalnoky was born abroad but returned to his Transylvanian homeland after the fall of Communism to reclaim his royal birthright. Having fallen in love with the little Hungarian village once ruled by his forebears, he has set about restoring some of its old houses, and ended up creating one of the most wonderful accommodations opportunities in the whole country. See p. 524.

- **Delta Nature Resort, Danube (Delta, Romania).** This is the first luxury resort in what is widely regarded as the last wilderness in Europe. Guests are ensconced in plush cottages for the night (after enjoying local caviar), while during the day you're given endless options for wildlife encounters (including spying the 300 species of birds that find their way here each year) and cultural exploration (including rubbing shoulders with nuns and members of the small Lipovan communities that have settled in the Delta). See p. 561.

- **Baltschug Kempinski (Moscow, Russia).** The hotel's views of St. Basil's Cathedral and the Kremlin are so breathtaking that TV networks set up here for their stand-ups. The brunch is fit for a czar, and the understated elegance of the rooms complements the facade's pastel ornamentation. See p. 577.

- **Grand Hotel Europe (St. Petersburg, Russia).** This baroque confection in central St. Petersburg charmed Tchaikovsky and Bill Clinton, among other dignitaries. The harpist and the plush furniture of the mezzanine cafe provide respite from a day of touring. See p. 594.

- **Królewski (Gdańsk, Poland).** Rooms to die for just across the canal from Gdańsk's Old Town. Room no. 310 is a corner room, with views over the city in two directions. The breakfast room looks over the river at the town. You'll feel like they've handed you the keys to the city. See p. 453.

- **Grandhotel Praha (High Tatras, Slovakia).** You're in the Tatras, so why not spend a little extra to stay at this beautifully restored turn-of-the-20th-century Alpine manor (that manages to match the mountains for style and grace). The elegantly restored lobby, billiard room, restaurant, and cafe will immediately have you thinking you stepped into *The Great Gatsby* or an Agatha Christie novel. See p. 628.

- **Vila Bled (Slovenia).** It was good enough for Marshall Tito to entertain some of the most powerful men on earth, and now its suites are like miniature museums to the monumental and fatal ambitions of Communism, all preserved like a staid 1950s mausoleum. The lakeside setting may be perfect, but imagine a world in which everything is monogrammed and guests get to lounge on a private lido with a perfect view of a 1,000-year-old hilltop castle. Oh, and the handsome lifeguard doubles as your cocktail waiter! See p. 666.

- **Nebesa (Slovenia).** Anywhere else in the world, this paradisiacal four-cottage "resort" would be considered a bargain. The real splurge is time-related: You'll need to drive several miles to get to this mountainside location, from where you can not only see Italy, but feel the breeze off the ocean, while you're almost eye-level with soaring mountain peaks, often capped with snow. You'll feel like a private guest of the debonair owners as you lounge on your private terrace and conjure up dreams of owning the world as you look down over the beautiful Soča Valley and watch the deer in the adjacent field frolicking at dusk. See p. 672.

- **Kendov Dvorec (Slovenia).** Arguably the finest restored manor in the country, this is an ideal and idyllic retreat filled with antiques and plush furniture. Each meal is a triumph, and while you're pretty much in the country, you're never too far from everywhere else in tiny Slovenia. See p. 675.

3 The Best Hotel Bargains

- **Villa Filipini (Poreč, Croatia).** Despite its location a couple of miles outside Poreč's center and the lack of a beach in the vicinity, the warmth of the hosts, the casual but elegant decor of this tiny inn set in the woods, and the innovative gourmet cuisine in Filipini's restaurant make up for any shortcomings. See p. 176.

- **Hotel Peristil (Split, Croatia).** The Peristil is tucked in a corner inside the walls of Diocletian's palace, and while its facade is respectful of the magnificent Roman ruin, its interior is brand-new (2005) and comfortable. See p. 161.

- **Valsabbion (Pula, Croatia).** The hotel's seven rooms and three suites are decorated with flair in a breezy, romantic style that carries over to its exquisite restaurant, one of the best in Croatia. There is also a spa with a long menu of beauty treatments. See p. 168.

- **Dryanovo Monastery (Near Veliko Tarnovo, Bulgaria).** Many Bulgarian monasteries offer cheap accommodations, but facilities are usually spartan (no hot water, shared toilets) and often less than hygienic. Not so Dryanovo Monastery, where the monks offer spotless en-suite rooms. Admittedly they are tiny, with two single beds, but throw open the window to allow the gushing "prana" of the river coursing past the fortified walls below to lull you asleep, and you'll wake miraculously refreshed. If you'll forego the sight of a long-bearded monk in a black cassock entering your name into a massive leather-bound ledger, you could also opt for a bigger room (and a towel that's larger than the face cloth the monks supply), at Komplex Vodopadi, an independently run hotel within the monastery grounds. See p. 109.

- **Kapsazov's House (Kovachevitsa, Bulgaria).** Located in one of Bulgaria's most attractive heritage mountain villages—all narrow cobbled lanes, and timber homes perched above towering stone walls—this is the classiest guesthouse in the country. Right on the edge of the village, with an immaculate stonewalled garden, you can loll about all day watching swallows dive-bomb the pretty pool, but it is in the evenings, seated at Sofia Kapsazov's table (often with a fascinating mix of expat diplomats and Sofia intelligentsia) that you really know you've landed up in heaven. The angel in charge is Sofia, who hosts regular cooking courses—after one of her meals you'll wish you had time to sign up for one. See p. 99.

- **Pension Větrník (Prague, Czech Republic).** This family-run romantic hideaway is reachable in about 20 minutes by tram from the city center. Its atmosphere and price are unbeatable. See p. 228.

- **Pension Unitas/Art Prison Hostel (Prague, Czech Republic).** An ideal place for budget travelers who want to take advantage of staying in the very center of Prague. See p. 225.

- **Charles Apartment House (Budapest, Hungary).** Comfortable and clean flats—complete with bathrooms and fully equipped kitchens—in Buda apartment buildings. See p. 299.

- **Rembrandt Hotel (Bucharest, Romania).** This chic Dutch-owned boutique hotel embodies the spirit of rejuvenation being experienced in the Romanian capital. It's squeezed into an impossible slither of property in the old quarter, which is steadily coming back to life. Special guests get the small top-floor room with a terrace with views all the way to the Parliamentary Palace built by that madman, Ceauşescu. See p. 496.

- **Casa Rozelor (Braşov, Romania).** With three of the most idiosyncratic guest suites in the country, this guesthouse is a project of love that has taken years of painstaking restoration (now continuing in a similar building nearby), followed by careful detailing with eclectic antiques bought from Gypsies, complemented by some outrageous contemporary art and furniture. And it's right in the heart of Braşov's medieval center. Seldom does the blend of old and new fit so well, and feel so good. See p. 519.

- **Casa Epoca (Sighişoara, Romania).** This recent guesthouse addition to Transylvania's best medieval fortress town occupies a 15th-century Gothic building and comes with few frills. It's done out almost entirely in wood and includes reproduction medieval Saxon beds. Everything is clean, neat,

and stylish, and unlikely to attract a crowd. See p. 526.

- **Pulford Apartments (St. Petersburg, Russia).** Furnished, renovated flats with views of St. Petersburg's greatest monuments. A range of room sizes and services is available, including cleaning and airport transfers. Moscow apartments are also available. See p. 594.

- **G&R Hostels (Moscow, Russia).** Several floors of a drab Soviet hotel have been transformed into clean, comfortable accommodations. Services include cars with drivers and visa support. While the location is not central, it's right next to a metro station. See p. 580.

- **Hotel Karmel (Kraków, Poland).** This lovely family-run inn, tucked away on a quiet street in the former Jewish quarter of Kazimierz, is a total surprise. From the warm and smiling woman at the reception desk to the parquet flooring and the crisp linen on beds, everything about this place says quality. See p. 423.

- **Penzión pod Hradom (Trenčín, Slovakia).** Every town should have a pension as clean, quiet, delightful, and cheap as this one. And the location is ideal, perched on a small lane beside the main square and just below the castle. If the pension is empty, the owners will give you the nicest room in the house for the price of a standard. See p. 623.

- **Hiša Franko Casa (Slovenia).** A treasure just outside Kobarid, near the Italian border in Soča Valley. Beautiful guest rooms are each done out in a unique combination of lively colors and feature such treats as his-and-hers slippers and your personal choice of in-room amenities. It's more pension than hotel, and is something of an afterthought to one of the country's finest restaurants, just downstairs. See p. 671.

- **Antiq Hotel (Ljubljana, Slovenia).** In the heart of Ljubljana's Old Town, right near one of the paths that leads to Castle, this small hotel is brand-new and stuffed full of lovely antique pieces in a wonderful, tasteful jumble that will remind you of the city's excellent Sunday morning market. See p. 656.
- **Max Hotel (Piran, Slovenia).** In this popular destination where Venice is your most obvious point of reference, accommodations are hard to come by during the busy summer season. Affable Max offers just a few simple rooms, but they're bright and tasteful and your life-loving host will do everything to make your stay a pleasurable one (providing you don't interrupt his afternoon siesta). See p. 677.

4 The Best Festivals & Celebrations

- **Festival of the Kukeri (Bulgaria).** During a 30-day period over New Year, known as *"Mrasni Dni"* (Dirty Days), it is said that the gates to heaven and hell are left open, and demons walks the earth. To counter this, villagers don terrifying masks and girdles sagging with huge bells and, armed with wooden weapons, stalk the streets to sound them off. You can see the best examples of the frightening *kukeri* costumes, as well as plenty of photographs, in Sofia's Ethnographic Museum, or plan to visit during an even-numbered year on the last weekend in January when the largest "Festival of the Kukeri" is held in Pernik, and some 3,500 revelers participate in this ancient ritual. See p. 63.
- **Maramureş (Romania).** Countless festivals occur throughout the year, but a favorite is over the Christmas period; the small town of Sighet, near the Ukraine border, comes to life on December 27 when the **Winter Customs Festival** stirs good old-fashioned fun filled with folkloric symbolism. Participants dress up in traditional costumes and young men run around with grotesque masks, cowbells dangling from their waists. See p. 548.
- **New Year's Day (Russia).** This is the major holiday of the Russian year. It's a family event centered around a fir tree, a huge feast, and gift-giving traditions transferred by Soviet leaders from Christmas to the more secular New Year's Day. See p. 571.
- **White Nights in St. Petersburg (Russia).** Two weeks of festivities in late June celebrate the longest day of the year, when the northern sun never dips below the horizon. The White Nights are more than just a party; they're a buoyant, carefree attitude of summer-ness. Take a boat ride through the canals as the sunset melts into a languorous sunrise, and you'll never want to go south again. See p. 571.
- **Jewish Cultural Festival (Kraków, Poland).** Every year in July, Kazimierz opens its doors to Jews and Gentiles from around the world to come and celebrate Jewish culture. The festival has a purpose—it's to promote understanding of Poland's Jewish heritage and to remember what the ghetto once was. Nine days of food, music, and film. See p. 385.
- **Pohoda Music Festival (Trenčín, Slovakia).** Every year in mid-July the normally industrious town of Trenčín lets its hair down for 3 days of independent folk, rock, and pop. The festival has grown in recent years and now lures some of the best bands around. But don't just think traffic jams, mud, and long lines for beer. The atmosphere here is the real draw.

The word "pohoda" means "relax," and that's the whole idea. See p. 610.

- **The Kurentovanje Festival (Slovenia).** Each winter in Ptuj, revelers don crazy masks and take to the streets in a positively pagan celebration that once had some bearing on trying to control the climate. Now it's a spirited reminder that Slovenes love to party. See p. 680.

- **Lent Festival (Maribor, Slovenia).** Maribor's quaint waterfront promenade draws an excellent live music lineup each June, attracting fans and party animals from all over Europe. Right near the main venues is the Stara Trta, apparently the oldest wine-producing vine in the world. See p. 649.

- **Ljubljana Summer Festival (Slovenia)** goes on for several months, during which music, theater, and other types of performances are staged in venues around the city, and also on the streets. Many of the shows are world-class, and some of the most memorable happen in the **Križanke Summer Theater (Slovenia),** a former monastery converted to an outdoor venue in the 1950s by Slovenia's top-rated architect, Joze Plečnik. See p. 664.

5 The Best Outdoor Activities

- **Hiking Rila's Seven Lakes (Rila, Bulgaria).** The most rewarding hike in the country, this is a moderate 2-day (or more) hike from Rila Monastery into Bulgaria's Alps to view the eerily beautiful Seven Lakes. After the first day (a fairly strenuous 6-hr. hike) you reach the Ivan Vazov hut, which you can use as a base to visit the Seven Lakes; better still, push on to one of the *Sedemte ezera* huts, situated on the shores of the lowest lakes—if you can, book the newest, which has the best facilities. See p. 100.

- **Plitvice Lakes National Park (Croatia).** Plitvice is the country's best-known natural wonder. You can choose the difficulty of your exploration, from challenging 8-hour hikes to shorter treks eased by ferry and tram rides. Either way, you'll be rewarded with an infusion of unspoiled nature. The park's 16 crystal-clear turquoise lakes and their countless waterfalls are the marquee attraction and they put on a great show. You'll be fascinated by the lakes, which flow into one another and tumble over deposits of travertine, creating waterfalls that drop a few feet or plunge as much as 64m (210 ft.). All this beauty is set in a dense forest accessed via footpaths, ferries, and fuel-friendly people-movers. See p. 199.

- **Taking a Slow Boat Down the Vltava (Czech Republic).** You can see many of the most striking architectural landmarks from the low-angle and low-stress vantage point of a rowboat you pilot yourself. At night, you can rent a dinghy with lanterns for a very romantic ride.

- **Riding a Faster Boat Down the Vltava (Czech Republic).** For those not willing to test their navigational skills or rowing strength in their own boat, large tour boats offer similar floating views, many with meals. Be sure to check the direction of your voyage to be certain it travels past the castles and palaces.

- **Taking a Walk in the Buda Hills (Hungary).** It's hard to believe that such a large expanse of hilly forest is right here within the capital city. There are hiking trails aplenty; every Budapest native has a favorite. Ask around.

- **Hiking in the Hills Outside Szigliget (Hungary).** You can hike up to the fantastic ruins of a 13th-century castle above this scenic little village in the Lake Balaton region, or go a few miles farther north and hike up into hills covered with vineyards. See p. 362.

- **Swimming in the Thermal Lake at Hévíz (Hungary).** Even in the bitterest spells of winter, the temperature in Europe's largest thermal lake seldom dips below 85°F to 90°F (30°C–32°C). Hungarians swim here year-round, and you can, too! If you're here in winter, it'll be a particularly memorable experience. See p. 360.

- **Climbing the Eger Minaret (Hungary).** Eger, a beautiful, small city in northern Hungary, is home to one of the country's most impressive Turkish ruins: a 14-sided, 33m-tall (110-ft.) minaret. Those who succeed in climbing the steep, cramped, spiral staircase are justly rewarded with a spectacular view. See p. 366.

- **Hiking in the Tatras (Poland).** Zakopane is the jumping-off point to hundreds of kilometers of gorgeous hiking trails. You can choose one of the 2,000m-plus (6,560-ft.) assaults on the peaks, or a more leisurely stroll along breathtaking valleys, carved out by tiny mountain streams. See p. 441.

- **Hiking the Apuseni Mountains (Romania).** Accessible from Oradea in Romania's far west, the Apuseni Mountains are the lowest lying in the Carpathian range. With minimal planning, professional ecofriendly guides can take you caving (in several of over 7,000 caves), skiing, rock-climbing, and even wolf and bear tracking.

You can stay in remote villages and discover a way of life long forgotten by the rest of Europe. See p. 537.

- **Idling Through the Backwaters of the Danube Delta (Romania).** Considered by some to be Europe's most important wildlife sanctuary, the Danube Delta was once threatened by Communism's unchecked industrial program. Now it's once again a haven for bird life, including its famous pelican population, which you can observe while on a boat safari through this unique ecosystem of waterways, lakes, reed-beds, sand dunes, and subtropical forests. See p. 560.

- **Rafting the Dunajec (Slovakia).** This is fun for the whole family. It's not intense white-water rafting, but a gentle group-float down a winding, twisting river that marks the boundary between Poland and Slovakia. The guides are good-natured and all bedecked in the traditional folk costumes of the region. The 13km (8-mile) ride lasts about 90 minutes, after which you can climb a hill to have lunch and ride a rental bike (or take a bus back) to the starting point. See p. 633.

- **Playing in the Great Outdoors of the Soča River Valley (Slovenia).** Whether you're white-water rafting, caving, sky diving, or skiing in winter, the Soča offers great opportunities for inexperienced paddlers and professional adrenaline junkies. No matter where you are or what you're getting up to, the views will take your breath away, again and again. See p. 673.

6 The Best Local Dining Experiences

- **Ego (Veliko Tarnovo, Bulgaria).** Bulgaria's medieval capital comes into its own when the sun goes down. In the languid light the narrow red-roofed buildings that rise precipitously from

the limestone cliffs above the Yantra River start to turn a pale pink, while swallows ride the thermal waves at eye level. Bag a ringside seat on the terrace at Ego—it's not the most atmospheric restaurant in town but food and service are excellent, and the views will have you mesmerized. See p. 110.

- **Krachma (Leshten, Bulgaria).** The most charming restaurant in Bulgaria, Krachma's tables are covered in red-and-white gingham cloth and spread out under the canopy of a magnificent old tree. Beyond are the rolling forested hills of the Rhodope, backdropped by the snowcapped Pirin; behind are a quaint collection of 18th-century timber-and-stone houses, surrounded by lush fecundity. From the tree wine corks dangle; tug one and a tinkling bell summons the waiter. The "Kofte Leshten Style" is superb—a single tender cut of pork rather than the usual patty, delicately flavored—order it with Ljutenitza (mashed red peppers, leek, and spices) and hand-cut potato chips—all "hand-reared" on owner Misho's farm. See p. 100.

- **Kampa Park (Prague, Czech Republic).** This is the best bet for summer outdoor dining in Prague. The restaurant has a riverside view, where you can dine in the shadow of Prague's most famous bridge during the high season. See p. 230.

- **Kavárna Obecní Dům (Prague, Czech Republic).** This reinvigorated Art Nouveau cafe at the **Municipal House** has re-created the grandeur of Jazz Age afternoons. See p. 233.

- **Kisbuda Gyöngye (Budapest, Hungary).** The huge branches of a wonderful old tree create a canopy under which guests dine by candlelight in an interior courtyard.

- **The Aristocratic Atmosphere at Cafe Pushkin (Moscow, Russia).** Plunge into the refined opulence of 19th-century Russia as you spear a bite of suckling pig or sip fine tea from a silver samovar. See p. 581.

- **Fresh Fish at Staraya Tamozhnya (St. Petersburg, Russia).** The spare stone arches of this restaurant evoke the building's history as an 18th-century Customs House. The fish is so fresh you can forget any fears and indulge. See p. 595.

- **Karczma Jana (Olsztyn, Poland).** You'd expect to find excellent food in Warsaw, Kraków, and Gdańsk (and you do), but one place you wouldn't necessarily expect it is in the small city of Olsztyn. Karczma Jana is the best of a new breed of distinctly Polish restaurants, with traditional decor and local specialties done very well—all at a fair price. The riverside location doesn't hurt. See p. 415.

- **Le Colonial (Košice, Slovakia).** There's something to be said for a traditional restaurant that's willing to experiment a bit with the classics. Too many Slovak chefs still follow the old recipes by rote, but here they mix it up a bit, to good effect. For example, the lightly battered and fried chicken breast is a staple on every Slovak menu, but here it comes stuffed with some of that tart sheep's cheese instead and served with freshly cooked string beans. The interior and atmosphere are perfect for a romantic meal or a fun group night out. See p. 640.

- **Planšar (Slovenia).** This is a delightful little pension and restaurant in the bucolic village of Stara Fuzina, not far from Slovenia's magnificent Triglav National Park. Renata Mlakak serves real, traditional Bohinj cuisine, so you can try such delicious down-home specialties as farmer's soup and Bohinj cheese with mashed corn with sour cabbage. But Renata's real talent lies with her perfect homemade *štruklji*—dumplings made with cottage cheese. See p. 667.

7 The Best Museums

- **Varna Archaeological Museum (Bulgaria).** Looking at the small gold figure of Victory—an earring taken from the tomb of a Thracian noblewoman, the detailing so fine it must be appreciated through a magnifying glass—one can't help wonder whether we have progressed much in the 2,400 years since the goldsmith made this exquisite piece. Bulgaria is so laden with Thracian treasure that archaeologists now posit that it the country has, along with Greece and Italy, the most ancient artifacts in Europe, with some 15,000 tombs and 400 ancient settlements scattered throughout the country. Varna's Archaeological Museum is the best place to view the world's oldest gold; Sofia's History Museum is another. See p. 119.

- **Alfons Mucha Museum (Prague, Czech Republic).** Posters, decorative panels, objects, and excerpts from sketchbooks, as well as oil paintings from this well-known Art Nouveau master are displayed at the baroque Kaunický Palace near Václavské náměstí. See p. 242.

- **Resistance, Sighet (Romania).** This evocative memorial to people who died because of Communism in Romania, occupies a chilling former prison in Maramureş, not far from the Ukraine border. Each of the cells—including the one where former Prime Minister Iuliu Maniu died—is an exhibition space. See p. 547.

- **Muzeul Naţional al Satului (Bucharest, Romania).** There are village museums all over Romania, designed to keep the architecture of the country's rural communities within living memory. This one in the capital is so large, it might well be a village unto itself. There's a remarkable range of village houses, churches, and even a windmill, brought from across the country to this outdoor site in the north of the city. See p. 507.

- **Muzeul Naţional de Artă (Romania).** Bucharest's National Museum of Art is an exhaustive (and exhausting) collection of Romanian and European art housed in a wing of the former Royal Palace on Revolution Square. This is the best place to get acquainted with Romanian greats like world-renowned sculptor Constantin Brăncuşi, and treasured Impressionist Nicolae Grigorescu, among many, many others. See p. 503.

- **State Hermitage Museum (St. Petersburg, Russia).** The museum holds one of the world's biggest art collections, from Egyptian carvings to Impressionist masterpieces. The museum is located in the Winter Palace, stormed in 1917 by revolutionaries. See p. 597.

- **Armory Museum (Moscow, Russia).** Fabergé eggs, coronation robes, royal carriages, and jewels have filled what was once the czarist weapons storehouse. See p. 583.

- **Tretyakov Gallery (Moscow, Russia).** The largest collection of Russian art. Chagall and Kandinsky share space with penetrating medieval icons. See p. 584.

- **Museum of the Warsaw Uprising (Warsaw, Poland).** With all of the audiovisual displays and sound effects, it's an assault on the eyes and ears. But when you're done walking through the exhibitions and watching the startling documentaries filmed during the fighting in 1944, you'll understand a lot more about Poles' resolve to preserve their nation. Just the photos alone of Warsaw's total destruction will leave you in awe that a modern city actually exists. See p. 402.

- **Museum of Zakopane Style (Zakopane, Poland).** This low-key museum is dedicated to the fine woodworking craft of the early Zakopane architects of the late 19th and early 20th century. No stunning high-tech visuals, just beautifully carved furnishings and a wonderful aesthetic feel. They took the log cabin and made it a castle. See p. 441.
- **Kobarid Museum (Slovenia).** The Kobarid is Slovenia's best antiwar museum, dedicated to the memory of those who senselessly lost their lives in the fierce battle of Caporetto (Kobarid) which took place around this tiny, peaceful town that's now a center for adventure activities. If the indoor museum doesn't stir your soul, there's an outdoor "walking museum" which you explore with a map over several hours, taking in natural scenery and interesting ruins along the way. See p. 673.

8 The Best Towns & Villages

- **Hum (Istria, Croatia).** It calls itself the smallest town in the world, and population-wise, it might be. But so many people visit this village high in the Istrian interior that it always seems crowded. The village elders have done a wonderful job of restoring the buildings in town to make it tourist-friendly. See p. 178.
- **The Heritage Villages of Pirin, Rhodope, Balkan, and Sredna Gora Mountains (Bulgaria).** Bulgaria has the best-preserved mountain villages in the Balkans. Besides the charm of the 18th and 19th-century stone-and-timber architecture, village life appears untainted by the 21st century, with toothless old-timers in headscarves sunning themselves on benches while young lovers holding hands head off to the fields, hoes casually slung over their shoulders. The most photogenic and evocative villages are hidden deep in the mountains: Kovachevitsa and Dolen are surrounded by the forested flanks of the Rhodope ranges, Zheravna by the lush Balkan foothills, and pretty Koprivishtitsa in the undulating Sredna Gora. See p. 57.
- **Český Krumlov (Czech Republic).** If you have time for only one excursion from Prague, make it Český Krumlov. This living gallery of Renaissance-era buildings housing many galleries, shops, and restaurants is 167km (104 miles) south of Prague. Above it towers the second-largest castle complex in the country, with the Vltava River running underneath. No wonder UNESCO named this town a World Heritage Site. See p. 260.
- **Pécs (Hungary).** This delightful city in southern Hungary is home to one of Hungary's most pleasing central squares and some great examples of Turkish architecture. See p. 368.
- **Sighişoara (Transylvania, Romania).** This medieval citadel, built in the 15th century, was the birthplace of the man who was to inspire Bram Stoker's Count Dracula. Today, it remains inhabited, and despite its compact size, is one of the most gorgeously preserved hilltop fortress cities in Europe, a tiny jumble of ancient nooks and crannies, with cobbled streets, medieval homes, and towers protruding from the battlements. See p. 525.
- **Sibiu (Transylvania, Romania).** Set to be a joint European City of Culture in 2007, Sibiu has received a remarkable makeover, transforming it into a whitewashed version of its

former self: a walled city with bastion towers, large open squares, impossible alleyways, and countless marvelous Gothic, baroque, and Renaissance buildings. See p. 529.

- **Gdańsk (Poland).** If you were expecting a dirty port city on the Baltic, you're in for the surprise of your life. Gdańsk is a beautifully restored old Hanseatic town that's brimming with life. The hotels and restaurants are great; the city couldn't be more inviting. And when you tire of Gdańsk, there's Sopot and the beaches and the nightclubs just up the road. See p. 449.

- **Wrocław (Poland).** This city gets short shrift from Poles—possibly because it still feels, at least in terms of the architecture, very much like a provincial German capital. But don't let that deter you. The Old Town is gorgeous. Those baroque and Renaissance facades sing with color, and will elevate your mood in any season. Wrocław is also filled with students,

ensuring lots of great little clubs tucked away in places you'd least expect. See p. 443.

- **Old Town (Bratislava, Slovakia).** It's hard to imagine a more active, fun, and user-friendly town center than Bratislava's Old Town. The past decade or so has seen a major effort to renovate the facades and bring new life into what was until recently a relatively quiet part of town. The result is a nightly street party. In good weather, the bars and cafes move their tables to the sidewalks and the whole city, it seems, comes out to have a good time. See p. 620.

- **Piran (Slovenia).** Piran is Slovenia's Venice, occupying a sharp promontory on the Istrian Coast. Piran doesn't have canals, but it will make your head spin as you get lost in a jumble of narrow cobblestone streets lined with lovely architecture, some beautifully preserved, some crumbling perfectly. See p. 676.

9 The Best Local Beer & Wine

- **Mitko Manolev (Melnik, Bulgaria).** Mitko, aka "six fingers," may not make the best wine, but he sure offers a great tasting experience. Seated in the cool sandstone cave burrowed into the side of a cliff in the little village of Melnik, Mitko lets you taste his wines direct from the barrel, then bottles your choice (two types of red, both not dissimilar to grape juice, made with no preservatives and slightly sparkling, rather good when served ice cold); worth it if only to watch him personally fill, cork, and label it right in front of you—the most personally handled bottle of wine you're likely to purchase anywhere. See p. 93.

- **Quiet Nest (Black Sea Coast, Bulgaria).** If you want an introduction

to Bulgaria's independent producers, the Queens Winery House, a boutique wine shop on the grounds of the Quiet Nest (the Black Sea Coast palace built by Romania's Queen Marie), is the best place in the country to do so. At the helm is 21-year-old Elleanna, a young winemaker who stocks a superb selection of little-known labels and produces (among others) *Ducessa Aperitiv*, an "Aromatic Wine Drink": Apparently the Romanian queen's favorite tipple, Elleanna managed to pry the recipe from the queen's winemaker before he passed away in 2005. Passionate about the untapped potential of Bulgarian wine, the new queen of the Nest is one to watch. See p. 116.

- **Plzeňské Pivovary/Pilsner Brewery (Prague, Czech Republic).** At U Prazdroje 7, Plzeň will interest anyone who wants to learn more about the brewing process. The brewery actually comprises several breweries, pumping out brands like Pilsner Urquell and Gambrinus, the most widely consumed beer in the Czech Republic. See p. 265.

- **Okocim Beer (Poland).** This is going to generate a lot of controversy. Of the big national beers, Poles seem to favor Żywiec (maybe it's folk dancing on the label that wins them over?). For my money, Okocim is the brew of choice. The slightly sweetish taste is reminiscent of Czech Budvar (Budweiser), and all the other beers more or less taste blandly the same. Drink it straight or add a shot of fruit syrup to the mix (but don't try this if you're male). See p. 382.

- **Ţuică (Romania):** Ţuică (also referred to as Pălinca) is a homemade brandy distilled from plums, pears, apples, or other fruit, and is a popular after-dinner or welcome drink, particularly in Romania's village communities. You'll probably get to taste it whenever you dine or stay with local families, or at traditional restaurants. You can purchase some of the country's best-known Ţuică from Teo Coroian, who runs a small distilling business from his home in the medieval fortress town of Sighişoara. See p. 528.

- **Movia Estate (Slovenia).** You don't even need to visit the wine farm to enjoy tastings of some of Slovenia's favorite vintages. Movia has a wonderful little *vinoteka* right next to the Town Hall on Mestni Square. Luka, your obliging sommelier, will hardly bat an eyelid as you order another glass of something award-winning, but he will certainly remind you just how good it is. See p. 664.

- **The Jeruzalem Wine Route (Slovenia).** In Slovenia's "far" east, this route is perfect for purveyors of fine wine and gentle drives through rambling vineyards. You can stop off at any number of farms, with private tastings usually conducted by one of the owners, and then—should things get out of hand—you can simply stay for the night and pick up where you left off after a scrumptious farm breakfast. See p. 680.

2

Introducing Eastern Europe

If you talk with anyone living in one of the countries included in this guide and refer to his or her homeland's location as Eastern European, you'll quickly be corrected. It's in *central* Europe, you'll be told, whether you are referring to Croatia, Romania, or sometimes even Russia. So why the semantic dispute about geography? Perhaps it's an attempt to shake off the association with persistent suspicions that Eastern Europe is still in the thrall of Soviet socialism. Or perhaps it's just the desire to be accepted without having to deal with the past's unpleasant baggage. Whatever the reason, there is no doubt that this diverse, politically complicated region is coming into its own and creating a new identity.

1 The Region Today

Eastern Europe's many differences translate to a long list of options for vacationers. With so many choices, how can you see everything in a single trip or even decide which is the most worthwhile itinerary? In this chapter, we provide an overall view of the region and explain some of the special features and unique attractions of each country to help you decide what you want to see most. In subsequent chapters, we'll help you plan your trip.

Geographically, the countries of Eastern Europe are diverse and blessed with breathtaking scenery and deep-seated history. Croatia's crystal-blue Adriatic seacoast, Romania's sparkling snowcapped Carpathian peaks, and Poland's lush forests and golden farmland are just three examples of the countless treasures found there. Add Roman ruins, sophisticated metropolitan areas, medieval castles, and Kremlin-era architecture and you have a recipe for a singular adventure.

Culturally Eastern Europe is a cross section of influences from Turkey, Italy, Germany, and other European nations. Many Westerners routinely lump Eastern

European nations under a single umbrella and assume they are interchangeable variations on one depressing theme. Nothing could be further from the truth. If anything, the countries that lie roughly between the Baltic, Adriatic, and Black seas are a remarkably diverse bunch with intersecting but distinct cultures, complicated histories, lusty political traditions, and a list of attractions that run the gamut from religious shrines to opulent palaces to Soviet-era monuments.

But there are similarities among these countries, too. Each has rejected Soviet-style ideology, each is in a different stage of recovery from years of oppression, and each is on a trajectory to become a full member of the global community.

The dilemma lies in the realization that the fate of the Balkan nations depends on the ability of the divergent people who share its history to coexist peacefully. The burden is on each group in the region being strong enough in its own identity and tolerant enough of differences to not feel threatened by any of the other groups.

Serbs and Croats, Hungarians and Soviets, Catholics and Eastern Orthodox—each of these groups has a claim on the culture, and each is in competition with the other for the same piece of real estate. Will they be able to recognize the need for peaceful coexistence and prosper together in peace or will they find they are unable to give up a little to gain a lot?

Even in the face of warring traditions, economic and political developments related to the European Union have transformed Eastern Europe. The road to European Union membership has been difficult for some of the region's countries, but their effort to join the larger European community also reflects a new stability among them. That, in turn, has attracted foreign development and a new tourist demographic.

Bulgaria and Romania in particular are working hard to overcome the offputting perception that they are countries still operating with an iron curtain mentality. Bulgaria's tourism industry hopes that E.U. membership will help dispel those inaccuracies, and its officials are working hard at an image makeover that will more accurately reflect the country as it is today.

The vetting process for E.U. membership has also reduced the shroud of uncertainty surrounding Eastern Europeans' ability to live together peacefully and it has given their citizens—and the world—the hope that the region's future might turn out to be prosperous.

BULGARIA

The fall of the Berlin Wall did little to boost this nation on the Black Sea from its plight as one of the poorest in the old Soviet bloc. In 1999, 10% of the population still lived in impoverished conditions.

The old Communist regime ruled the country until 1997 under the guise of "Socialists," but the state still controlled the economy. The result was hunger, disarray, and eventually an economic collapse.

After the Socialist government fell, there seemed to be little chance that this nation with a heritage dating from Byzantine times would turn around quickly, but governmental and currency reform have moved rapidly.

Situated on the southeastern tip of the Balkans, Bulgaria has pushed hard to become an accepted member of the world cultural and economic community by seeking full membership in the E.U.

Publicity surrounding that effort has put a spotlight on both the good and the bad of Bulgaria's emergence from Communist control.

Tourists are uncovering the complex history of cities like Sofia, which can trace its lineage back 4,000 years. They can savor the mélange of cultures from the Romans to the Ottomans to remnants of the iron curtain years.

The Byzantine Church of St. George, the Sofia Synagogue, and the Ottoman Banya Bashi Mosque all are within easy walking distance of each other.

Skiers are finding banner skiing at bargain prices in resorts such as Borovets and Bansko, while sun worshippers are basking at Black Sea havens like Sunny Beach and Golden Sands.

Right now, Bulgaria is a travel bargain thanks to a relatively low-cost but well-educated workforce. The country's tourism infrastructure still needs a lot of work, but there are signs that the means to improve it are building because investment, construction, and tourism all showed strong growth in 2005.

At press time, Bulgaria had just joined the E.U. and accepted the World Bank's first infusion of cash ($300 million). How the future plays out remains to be seen. The challenge is in putting aside the totalitarian mindset and sustaining reforms that will control corruption and increase the standard of living for Bulgaria's citizens.

Eastern Europe

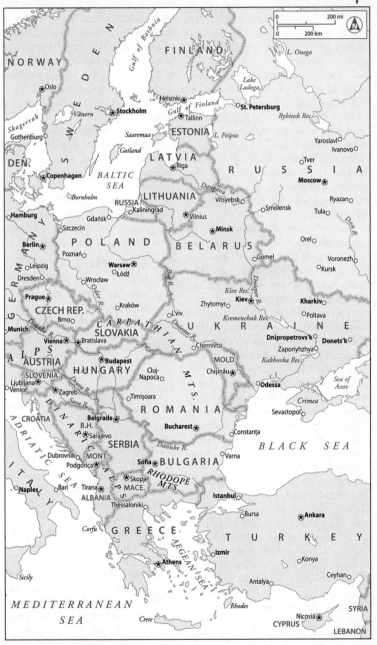

CROATIA

Contemporary Croatia is a land of contrasts and contradictions, a land with diverse geography and cultures that include primitive Stone Age settlements, glittering seaside resorts, vestiges of Greek and Roman antiquity, pristine natural wonders, and newly cosmopolitan cities. It is famous as a sun-drenched tourist destination and infamous as the site of one of the most vicious European wars in modern times.

Croatia has successfully protected its heritage despite invasions by neighboring nations, who played keep-away with the land and pushed aside Croatian culture in favor of their own.

Modern Croats are survivors, fiercely independent people who through the ages again and again emerged from ethnic conflicts and foreign occupations to reassert their national identity. Fortunately, Croatia's wars are in the past and the newly vibrant nation is now solidly in the 21st century poised to embrace progress, global commerce, tourism, and independence as it pushes forward to claim a place in the European Union.

Signs of economic recovery are everywhere, from packed luxury hotels on the Adriatic coast to thriving upscale boutiques and gourmet restaurants in Zagreb. There is no doubt that Croatia is beginning to shake off its down-in-the-mouth persona and present a more sophisticated, savvy face to the world. Tourism is booming, international hoteliers such as Hilton (Dubrovnik) LeMeridien (Split), and Sheraton (Zagreb) have established a presence in the country and local hoteliers especially have been courting an upscale international crowd by upgrading properties on the Dalmatian Coast at a dizzying pace.

Meanwhile, the Croatian government is working to reduce foreign debt, boost the economy, and promote the country's natural treasures while it waits for admittance to the European Union, an event that was stalled until mid-2006 but that is now moving ahead following the arrest of one of Croatia's alleged war criminals. If the process proceeds without any more glitches, E.U. membership could become a reality for Croatia as early as 2010.

Croatian travel professionals are anticipating a healthy increase in tourism when that happens. In the meantime, they are getting the word out about their country's considerable appeal: Croatia's stunning Adriatic seacoast, idyllic islands, cosmopolitan cities, historic sites, and warm-hearted people are the things tour operators' dreams are made of. If Croatia achieves its economic and social goals, there will be no limits to its future.

CZECH REPUBLIC

The landlocked Czech Republic is a crossroads for Eastern Europe thanks to its location in the heart of the region. In some ways the Czech Republic has been the "heart" of the region's emergence from Communist domination, too.

Leaders like Alexander Dubček, who instituted the freedoms that led to the Prague Spring of 1968, and Václav Havel, who engineered the split from Moscow, embody the spirit of the Czech people.

Havel stayed on to lead the new Czech Republic when the former Czechoslovakia split into two nations during the "Velvet Divorce" of 1993.

The two regions that now make up the Czech Republic—Bohemia and Moravia—have fostered a booming tourism industry, especially in Prague, where a multitude of spires punctuate the skyline in the heart of Bohemia.

Visiting **Prague** provides a typical glimpse of the contrasts that exist throughout the country, with designer boutiques and chain restaurants around the corner from ancient cobbled streets and crumbling facades. Prague's timeline is visible in its architecture, from the 9th-century **Prague Castle** to the houses and palaces of **Old Town,** the synagogues of the **Jewish Quarter,** and the **Charles Bridge** where street performers entertain passersby. Visitors to Prague have a lot to take in because the city has a lot to offer. So if you're weary of entertainment delivered by sidewalk violinists and jugglers, take a walk to the **Estates Theater,** formerly Count Nostitz's Theater. If you listen carefully you might pick up the sounds of *Don Giovanni* floating past and the sense that Mozart is smiling.

Prague may be the destination du jour in the Czech Republic, but the country has much more to offer outside the capital. The two major regions are **Bohemia** and **Moravia.** In Bohemia, you can visit the center of the Czech beer-brewing industry and the birthplace of lager. Stop at a tavern in Bohemia, and a beer appears in front of you almost automatically.

In contrast, Moravia's beverage of choice is wine. Moravia's soil is conducive to growing grapes. That fortunate topographical feature supports a robust wine industry that in turn has spawned numerous wine bars serving local vintages.

Both regions are home to numerous **castles** and **châteaux,** which provide visitors with a view into the country's cultural heritage. The state of these architectural treasures varies from pristinely preserved to near-ruins. Those still in good shape offer glimpses into a vanished way of life.

Outdoor enthusiasts have numerous options. Miles of flat, quiet roads await **bicyclists** outside the large cities, and mountainous regions of both Bohemia and Moravia maintain an extensive network of marked trails that connect the smaller towns.

Winter sports enthusiasts in Bohemia can choose between the Alpine resorts of the Giant Mountains of the north and Nordic areas of the Sumava in the south.

And no matter which sport you fancy, at the end of the day you can soothe your muscles at one of the many thermal spas that dot every corner of the country.

At press time, the Czech Republic was in its fifth month without a real government following a deadlocked election, a situation that gave pause to the European Union, which admitted the Czech Republic in 2004. But despite this temporary government in limbo, the Czech Republic is flourishing and keeping in step with its European Union compatriots on the road to prosperity.

HUNGARY

Like many of its neighbors, Hungary has had to battle a series of would-be foreign conquerors on the way to its current state of independence. Hungarians have had to rout occupiers repeatedly over the last 1,000 years or so: They took on the Turks in the 17th century, the Habsburgs in the 19th century, and the Soviets in the 20th century in a 1956 rebellion that is the most infamous of all the country's uprisings.

What began on October 23, 1956, as a student protest to demand the withdrawal of Soviet troops from Hungarian soil ended on November 11, 1956, when the Soviets flexed their military muscle and sent tanks into Budapest to quash the dissidents. When the guns finally fell silent nearly 3 weeks later, more than 25,000 people had died. Shortly afterward, the Soviets arrested or executed thousands of others, and a quarter of a million Hungarians fled to Austria. The last Soviet troops left Hungary in 1991, and this beleaguered nation then began its transformation into an independent citizen of the world community in earnest.

Since then, Hungary has joined NATO (1999), become a member of the the European Union (2004), and experienced a powerful economic growth spurt thanks to investments by foreign companies that amount to billions of dollars.

Hungary has been a free country for more than a decade, and visitors will find a new order softened by courtly old-world customs such as gentlemen kissing their ladies' hands.

Hungary has undergone an image change in the nearly 20 years since the fall of Communism and with it, tourism is has brought hordes of visitors to the country's restored **castles, palaces,** and **museums** and to its **festivals, fairs,** and **harvest celebrations.**

Today Hungary's travel specialists can arrange general or special-interest tours for English speakers, among them a tour with an itinerary that helps visitors research their roots or just walk around the same land where their ancestors once lived.

There is a new national pride evident in big cities and rural villages in Hungary as fear of foreign invasion fades. Many restaurants have revived traditional recipes, museums display artifacts that trace Hungary's turbulent 1,000-year past, and lively Hungarian folk music fills the air wherever you go.

Above all, visitors will feel welcome thanks to the contagious goodwill and optimism of the Hungarian people, who have endured and prospered no matter how high the odds.

POLAND

Since Poland joined the European Union in May 2004, many of its tourist sites have acquired an international reputation as "must-sees" for foreign visitors. **Kraków, Warsaw, Gdańsk, Czestochowa, Auschwitz,** the **Tatra Mountains** are just some of the stops that are attracting large crowds these days, and with good reason.

With a population of more than three-quarters of a million people, **Kraków** is Poland's third-largest city and its former capital. Kraków was left virtually untouched by World War II hostilities, so much of its original architecture and most of its monuments are still intact,

and today it is Poland's unofficial cultural center. Kraków has always been one of Poland's most popular tourist centers, but is also the birthplace of the late Pope John Paul II and as such its popularity with tourists has surged since his death in 2005.

Warsaw is Poland's capital. Unlike Kraków, Warsaw was devastated during World War II and had to be almost totally rebuilt. Today Warsaw is a sophisticated, modern city with a vibrant business district with an Eastern European aura. If you visit, be sure to see **Old Town,** the **Royal Route,** the **Chopin museum,** and the former **Jewish ghetto.**

Gdańsk is a seaport city where in 1978 shipyard electrician **Lech Wałęsa** started the **Solidarity** movement on behalf of workers' rights. Walesa's efforts eventually resulted in the defeat of Communism in Poland and made him a national hero. Gdańsk is also a tourist town thanks to a mild climate, beautiful beaches, and architectural treasures that include the largest brick Gothic church in Europe.

The town of **Czestochowa** is usually associated with **Jasna Gora Monastery,** which is the biggest Marian sanctuary in Poland. For Catholic Poland it is a sacred pilgrimage destination that is home to an icon known as **Black Madonna of Czestochowa.** There are several legends associated with the Black Madonna, but the most common is that the painting saved its church from being destroyed in a fire, but not before the flames darkened the Virgin Mary's flesh tones. Catholics honor the Madonna as Poland's protector and she is credited with many miracles.

The provincial town of **Oświęcim,** aka **Auschwitz,** was the site of the largest Nazi extermination camp during World War II. An estimated 1.5 million people were tortured, starved, and murdered there. Today Auschwitz has been preserved as a monument to man's inhumanity to his fellow man.

The **Tatras** are the highest mountains between the Alps and the Caucasus and the range's rocky peaks are covered with snow year-round. About 250km (150 miles) of trails and ski slopes delight hikers and skiers.

In spite of a turbulent history and dramatic changes in its world standing, Poland has maintained its culture, its faith, and its sense of humor. Coupled with the country's considerable natural wonders, historical sites, and hospitality, these elements are a potent combination for tourists.

ROMANIA

Romania's history is marked by a legacy of bloodthirsty leaders, one of whom inspired the Count Dracula legend (Vlad the Impaler) because of Vlad's cruel method of killing his enemies, and another (Nicolae Ceauşescu) who parlayed personal excesses, repressive policies, and economic miscues to suck a different sort of life force from the people he governed. But the cold-blooded nature of Romania's political leaders has never been able to dull the beauty of the country and the warmth of its people.

Breathtaking scenery and traditional values mark the rural heartland, while **Bucharest** boasts broad boulevards and a sophistication that demonstrate why it was once called the "Paris of the East."

The contrasts between the lavish architecture of the past and the ugly, utilitarian face of the Ceauşescu era are pervasive throughout Bucharest. **Orthodox churches** and **18th-century monasteries** are neighbors to concrete high-rises, a dichotomy that also symbolizes Romania's current state of mind, an attitude that still straddles the chasm between the country's iron curtain past and its 21st-century future.

Hotels in Bucharest are upgrading to accommodate an expected influx of international guests; tour operators are planning ski trips and other excursions to Romania's mountains for 2007 (Poiana Brasov); and budget carrier Wizz Air is planning service to Bucharest from London-Luton three times per week starting in 2007. At the same time, the country's economy is struggling; some of its leaders are under suspicion for war crimes; and the European Union is nervous about the politics of its Balkan member.

Romania's tourism board says the country realized a 40% increase in visitor traffic in 2005. But despite that positive sign, the country has a long way to go to catch up with industry accommodations and service standards appropriate for an international destination.

Romania's modern capital represents just a small portion of this country that covers about the same acreage as the state of Oregon. Actually, most of Romania is a "wild" country, terrain that has pockets of primitive roads that can be difficult to navigate, especially in winter.

Attractions include **Transylvania,** a name that's recognizable to any horror-movie fan because it is the birthplace of the infamous Vlad, and by association the home of filmdom's most famous vampire. The **"Dracula Castle"** there is a popular stop.

Romania is also home to the rugged **Carpathian Mountains,** the **Danube Delta wetland ecosystem,** the amazing **painted monasteries of Bucovina,** countless **rural villages** untouched by time for centuries, and a string of **Black Sea resorts** that have always attracted a crowd.

RUSSIAN FEDERATION (MOSCOW & ST. PETERSBURG)

The Russian landscape depicted in the film *Doctor Zhivago* was characterized by vast expanses of snow-covered land dotted with opulent palaces inhabited by aristocrats and humble homes where ordinary people lived. The discrepancy between the haves and the have-nots in Russia may not be as visual today, but an economic chasm definitely exists in the new Russia.

Oil money has created a superrich class of nouveau riche and at the same time relegated the elderly and longtime patriots to poverty. Perhaps this gap was inevitable: The sheer size of the Russian Federation almost guarantees an adventure in diversity, and the country spreads across 11 time zones and numerous ethnic cultures. But cultural and socioeconomic strata are obvious even in the western portion of the country called "European Russia."

Visits to Russia's two largest cities amplify the differences between the hectic, modern bustle of **Moscow** and the historical, sophisticated aura of imperial **St. Petersburg.**

Moscow flaunts its links to Western culture, with chain restaurants, dance clubs, and a cutthroat club scene. Its residents have discarded the dour, gray mood that characterized the city during the Soviet years in favor of a pursuit of hedonism and wealth.

The city has more billionaires than any other city in the world, but it also is home to vast numbers of beggars, as if to accentuate the city's diversity.

Moscow's economy had been booming since the dissolution of the Soviet Union, opening the door to increased tourism from the West. More than 12 million citizens crowd the subways and clubs. Visitors will find that hotel prices rival or exceed those charged in Paris, and restaurant tabs can run as high or higher than a three-star restaurant in New York. Add to that a rising crime rate and police corruption (tourist shakedowns are common) and you have "big city" problems.

But Moscow is still a fascinating city to explore. Cupolas and cathedrals compete with Soviet-era skyscrapers for visitors' attention, while the brooding specter of the **Kremlin** reminds them of the events from recent history. **Red Square, St. Basil's Cathedral,** and **Lenin's**

Mausoleum all beckon to the tourists, while the **Bolshoi and Chekhov theaters** offer a glimpse into the Russian classical soul.

St. Petersburg is Moscow's cultural counterpoint, a city filled with architectural and artistic wonders. Built by Peter the Great in 1703 on the site of a swamp, St. Petersburg has evolved into the fourth-largest city in Europe. Its role in the arts world solidified by author Fyodor Dostoevski and composer Dmitri Shostakovich.

The **Heritage Museum** in the **Winter Palace** contains one of the world's great collections of art. But intellectual and artistic excellence has not translated into economic progress for St. Petersburg, as it has for Moscow.

SLOVAKIA

Slovakia's tourism industry has burgeoned since that country declared independence in 1993. By the late 1990s Slovakia was receiving more than half a million visitors annually and for the first half of 2006 (Jan–June) the number of visitors was just under 750,000.

Slovakia is situated between Austria, Hungary, and Russia, a position that had a strong influence on its history and architecture. Of the three influential styles, the sensibilities of Austria and Hungary won out. However, in the eastern part of the country the architectural landscape is more Eastern Orthodox than Austro-Hungarian.

Almost every town in Slovakia has a historic church, and each house of worship has something to commend it. However, the most interesting churches in the country are the centuries-old **wooden churches** of northeastern Slovakia. Unfortunately, these are difficult to reach.

Throughout history Slovakia was never a dominant nation and it never became a wealthy nation, either. Consequently the historic sections of Slovak cities are less ornate than those in wealthier countries like Austria.

Slovakian **town squares** deserve special note for their architectural interest. Some have even been designated UNESCO cultural heritage sites (Bardejov, Banska Stiavnica).

Slovak Castles and ruins are another source of interest for architecture buffs. Many have been restored, but even those that have fallen into ruin are notable and every region of the country offers a few examples of each.

If poking around rock piles isn't your passion, check out Slovakia's historic towns and its mountain ski resorts, which seem to ban Westernization and the commercialism that goes hand in hand with capitalism. Here you can comfortably go back in time and experience life as it has been lived in Slovakia for centuries.

Finally, Slovakia's capital city, **Bratislava,** is homey and friendly, but with a surprisingly rich cultural life. Bratislava is a capital city without the usual congestion of most seats of government. Quaint, gentle, and old-world are apt terms to describe this charming city and they extend to food and lodging options, too. Slovakia joined the European Union in 2004, but the country has not yet caught up with its neighbors when it comes to developing a thriving tourism infrastructure. If you visit, don't expect things to be up to Western standards, but that could be a good thing. Instead, luxuriate in an atmosphere that lets you truly experience a bygone era.

SLOVENIA

Slovenia is a country of firsts. As the westernmost country in the region defined as Eastern Europe in this guide, Slovenia was the first to declare its independence (1990). It also was one of the first of this group to join the European Union, and on January 1, 2007, it was the first to adopt the euro as its official currency. Slovenia is definitely the first of this group to boast that it has the lowest crime rate in all of Europe. In fact, this efficient country has moved into the ranks of successful European Union nations with laserlike precision and the result is a country that works. Slovenia has a well-oiled tourism industry with facilities and sites that consistently attract an international crowd. It has even exported its expertise in spa design and management to Croatia, where Slovenian firms are rehabbing that country's aging spa facilities.

Business acumen isn't the only Slovenian virtue. Legend has it that after God created the world he had a fistful of leftover beauty, which he sprinkled over Slovenia. A glimpse of **St. Martin's Pilgrimage Church** rising through the mist from its island perch in the middle of **Lake Bled,** a walk through the subterranean majesty of **Škocjan Caves,** the panoramic view of **Ljubljana** from its namesake castle, or an Adriatic sunset over coastal **Portorož** are enough hard evidence to convince even atheists that the legend is fact.

Slovenia is certainly one of the most easily accessible Eastern European nations from Europe's capitals: It is just 230km (140 miles) from Vienna, 240km (146 miles) from Budapest, and 460km (280 miles) from Milan. It is linked to the world by modern highways, numerous air routes, efficient train service, and even by ferry.

Its position on land surrounded by the mountains of Austria and Italy, Hungary's plains, and the Adriatic makes for a surprisingly diverse landscape. What's even more of a pleasant surprise is that nothing in the country is more than a 2-hour drive from anything else in the country. You can ski an Olympic training run on the slopes above picturesque **Kranjska Gora** in the morning and take a dip in the warm sea at languid Portorož before the sun goes down. You can hike through gorgeous **Triglav National Park** and marvel at its glacial valleys, gorges, and waterfalls. You can even launch your kayak in rushing water that moves fast enough to challenge the most expert white-water fan and finish your run in time for dinner in enchanting Ljubljana the same day.

Of all the countries profiled in this guide, Slovenia has proven to be the most "together" in its plan to become a full member of the global community. Not only has Slovenia's government gone out of its way to attract, and keep, foreign investment since its accession to the E.U. in 2004, it also has shared the resulting wealth with its citizens by taking steps to improve public services and to enhance everyone's everyday life.

3

Planning Your Trip to Eastern Europe

When the Berlin Wall fell in 1989, the iron curtain slowly lifted to give the world its first unobstructed view of Eastern Europe since World War II. What they saw was a region numbed by economic disaster, iron-fisted suppression of the individual, and the neglect of the aesthetic. Almost 2 decades later Eastern Europe's fortunes have changed dramatically, but most North Americans still picture the region east of Berlin and the Adriatic in grim, forbidding Cold War terms and eliminate it from their lists of desirable vacation destinations. Western Europeans, however, have always viewed Eastern European countries as places to explore and relax, and as soon as they were free to travel there without much restriction, they returned in droves to Croatia's Adriatic resorts, the Czech Republic's majestic churches, Hungary's intriguing spa towns, Slovenia's picturesque Alpine villages, Romania's Carpathian mountains, Russia's historic cities, and Poland's bustling markets. North Americans' long-held preconceptions of Eastern Europe are gradually dissipating and more and more English-speaking folks are riding the tourism wave that is sweeping the region. Eastern Europe has finally emerged as a trendy travel frontier where friendly people, stunning natural beauty, compelling history, and relatively low prices are drawing a crowd of savvy travelers. If you go, you'll find an "open" sign on these formerly restricted destinations and you'll wonder why it took you so long to get there.

1 Visitor Information

The country chapters in this guide provide specific information on traveling to and getting around individual Eastern European countries. In this chapter we offer region-wide tips and general information that will help you plan your trip.

2 Entry Requirements & Customs

The information in this section is for quick reference; see individual country chapters for complete details about the entry requirements for your destination.

PASSPORTS & VISAS

For information on how to get a passport, go to "Getting Your Passport in Order" earlier in this chapter—the websites listed provide downloadable passport applications as well as the current fees for processing passport applications. For an up-to-date, country-by-country listing of passport requirements around the world, go to the "Foreign Entry Requirement" Web page of the U.S. State Department at **http://travel.state.gov**. For children under 14, **both** parents/legal guardians must consent to the passport application either in writing or in person. Parents with sole

Destination Eastern Europe: Predeparture Checklist

- Is your passport valid for at least 3 months after the end of your trip?
- Did you check to see if any travel advisories have been issued by the U.S. State Department (http://travel.state.gov) regarding your destination?
- Do you have the address and phone number of your country's embassy or consulate with you?
- Did you notify your credit card issuers that you would be using your credit cards outside your home country? Did you tell them where you will be traveling and for how long?
- Do you have your credit card/ATM PINs? If you have a 5- or 6-digit PIN, did you obtain a 4-digit number from your bank?
- If you purchased traveler's checks, have you recorded the check numbers, and stored the documentation separately from the checks?
- Did you bring your ID cards that could entitle you to discounts, such as AAA and AARP cards, student IDs, and so on?
- Did you leave a copy of your itinerary with someone at home?
- Did you make sure your favorite attraction is open? Call ahead for opening and closing times.

custody must present documentation of their status when applying for a child's passport. Acceptable documentation includes: a court order listing the parent as sole custodian and a court document granting the parent permission to travel with the child, a death certificate for the absent parent, and a certified copy of the child's birth certificate that lists **only** the parent applying for the child's passport. Ask your airline what's required when you book the ticket. Also check the State Department's **Single Parent Travel Forum,** which also has a helpful FAQ section at www.singleparenttravel.net.

Note: See the *"Planning Your Trip to_____"* sections of the individual country chapters for detailed information on entry/visa requirements for each country covered in this book.

MEDICAL REQUIREMENTS

For information on medical requirements and recommendations, see "Health & Safety," p. 34.

CUSTOMS

For information on what you can bring with you upon entry to the countries of Eastern Europe, see the "Customs" section in individual country chapters.

WHAT YOU CAN TAKE HOME
U.S. Citizens

Returning **U.S. citizens** who have been away for at least 48 hours are allowed to bring back, once every 30 days, $800 worth of merchandise duty-free. You'll pay a flat rate of duty on the next $1,000 worth of purchases. Any dollar amount beyond that is subject to duties at whatever rates apply. On mailed gifts, the duty-free limit is $200. Be sure to keep your receipts or purchases accessible to expedite the declaration process. *Note:* If you owe duty, you are required to pay on your arrival in the United States—either by cash, personal check, government or traveler's check, or money order (and, in some locations, a Visa or MasterCard).

To avoid paying duty on foreign-made personal items you owned before your

Getting Your Passport in Order

Allow plenty of time before your trip to apply for a passport; processing normally takes 3 weeks but can take longer during busy periods (especially spring). And keep in mind that if you need a passport in a hurry, you'll pay a higher processing fee.

For Residents of Australia: You can pick up an application from your local post office or any branch of Passports Australia, but you must schedule an interview at the passport office to present your application materials. Call the **Australian Passport Information Service** at © **131-232,** or visit the government website at www.passports.gov.au.

For Residents of Canada: Passport applications are available at travel agencies throughout Canada or from the central **Passport Office,** Department of Foreign Affairs and International Trade, Ottawa, ON K1A 0G3 (© **800/567-6868;** www.ppt.gc.ca).

For Residents of Ireland: You can apply for a 10-year passport at the **Passport Office,** Setanta Centre, Molesworth Street, Dublin 2 (© **01/671-1633;** www.irlgov.ie/iveagh). Those under age 18 and over 65 must apply for a 3-year passport. You can also apply at 1A South Mall, Cork (© **021/272-525**) or at most main post offices.

For Residents of New Zealand: You can pick up a passport application at any New Zealand Passports Office or download it from their website. Contact the **Passports Office** at © **0800/225-050** in New Zealand or 04/474-8100, or log on to www.passports.govt.nz.

For Residents of the United Kingdom: To pick up an application for a standard 10-year passport (5-year passport for children under 16), visit your nearest passport office, major post office, or travel agency or contact the **United Kingdom Passport Service** at © **0870/521-0410** or search its website at www.ukpa.gov.uk.

For Residents of the United States: Whether you're applying in person or by mail, you can download passport applications from the U.S. State Department website at **http://travel.state.gov.** To find your regional passport office, either check the U.S. State Department website or call the **National Passport Information Center** toll-free number (© **877/487-2778**) for automated information.

trip, bring along a bill of sale, insurance policy, jeweler's appraisal, or receipts of purchase. Or you can register items that can be readily identified by a permanently affixed serial number or marking—think laptop computers, cameras, and CD players—with Customs before you leave. Take the items to the nearest Customs office or register them with Customs at the airport from which you're departing. You'll receive, at no cost, a Certificate of Registration, which allows duty-free entry for the life of the item.

With some exceptions, you cannot bring fresh fruits and vegetables into the United States. For specifics on what you can bring back and the corresponding fees, download the invaluable free pamphlet *Know Before You Go!* online at **www.cbp.gov.** (Click on "Travel," and then click on "Know Before You Go! Online Brochure.") Or contact the **U.S. Customs & Border Protection (CBP)**, 1300 Pennsylvania Ave., NW, Washington, DC 20229 (© **877/287-8667**) and request the pamphlet.

Canadian Citizens

Canada allows its citizens a C$750 exemption. Canadians are allowed to bring back duty-free 1 carton of cigarettes, 1 can of tobacco, 40 imperial ounces of liquor, and 50 cigars. In addition, they can mail gifts to Canada valued at less than C$60 a day, provided they're unsolicited and don't contain alcohol or tobacco (write on the package "Unsolicited gift, under $60 value"). All valuables should be declared on the Y-38 form before departure from Canada, including serial numbers of valuables you already own, such as expensive foreign cameras. *Note:* The $750 exemption can only be used once a year and only after an absence of 7 days.

For a clear summary of Canadian rules, write for the booklet *I Declare,* issued by the **Canada Border Services Agency** (© **800/461-9999** in Canada, or 204/983-3500; **www.cbsa-asfc.gc.ca**).

U.K. Citizens

U.K. citizens returning from **a non-E.U. country** have a Customs allowance of: 200 cigarettes; 50 cigars; 250 grams of smoking tobacco; 2 liters of still table wine; 1 liter of spirits or strong liqueurs (over 22% volume); 2 liters of fortified wine, sparkling wine or other liqueurs; 60cc (ml) perfume; 250cc (ml) of toilet water; and £145 worth of all other goods, including gifts and souvenirs. People under 17 cannot have the tobacco or alcohol allowance.

For information, contact **HM Customs & Excise** at © **0845/010-9000** in the U.K., or 020/8929-0152, or consult their website at **www.hmce.gov.uk**.

Australian Citizens

The duty-free allowance in **Australia** is A$400 or, for those under 18, A$200. Citizens can bring in 250 cigarettes or 250 grams of loose tobacco, and 1,125 milliliters of alcohol. If you're returning with valuables you already own, such as foreign-made cameras, you should file form B263. A helpful brochure available from Australian consulates or Customs offices is *Know Before You Go.* For more information, call the **Australian Customs Service** at © **1300/363-263,** or log on to www.customs.gov.au.

New Zealand Citizens

The duty-free allowance for **New Zealand** is NZ$700. Citizens over 17 can bring in 200 cigarettes, 50 cigars, or 250 grams of tobacco (or a mixture of all three if their combined weight doesn't exceed 250 grams); plus 4.5 liters of wine and beer, or 1.125 liters of liquor. New Zealand currency does not carry import or export restrictions. Fill out a certificate of export, listing the valuables you are taking out of the country; that way, you can bring them back without paying duty. Most questions are answered in a free pamphlet available at New Zealand consulates and Customs offices: *New Zealand Customs Guide for Travellers, Notice no. 4.* For more information, contact **New Zealand Customs,** The Customhouse, 17–21 Whitmore St., Box 2218, Wellington (© **04/473-6099** or 0800/428-786; www.customs.govt.nz).

3 Money

CURRENCY

While most of the countries in this guide are in various stages of becoming members of the European Union, Slovenia had replaced its local currency with the euro at publication time. Nonetheless, hotel, attraction, and restaurant prices in Eastern European countries have been quoted in both euros and local currency for years, a practice that sometimes confuses tourists.

Local Currency

For specifics about each country's currency and conversion rates please see the "Money" sections in the individual country chapters.

No matter how prices are listed, most establishments will accept payment in the local currency and you'll get a more favorable conversion rate if you pay with local cash. In addition, **countries such as Bulgaria and Romania are still a mostly cash economy,** so carrying local currency there is a necessity. *Note:* Concessions in most Eastern European airports usually accept U.S. dollars and euros as well as local currency, but it's always useful to have the local currency on hand.

If prices in this book are quoted in the local currency, we provide the conversion rate to U.S. dollars and British pounds; if prices are quoted in euros, we provide the conversion rate in U.S. dollars only. For real-time exchange rates of any currency, check **www.xe.com/ucc** or **www.oanda.com**.

ATMs

In Eastern European cities, the easiest and best way to get cash away from home is from an ATM (automated teller machine), commonly referred to as a "bancomat" in Eastern Europe. The **Cirrus** (© **800/424-7787;** www.mastercard.com) and **PLUS** (© **800/843-7587;** www.visa.com) networks span the globe; look at the back of your bank card to see which network you're on, then call or check online for ATM locations at your destination. Be sure you know your personal identification number (PIN) and daily withdrawal limit before you depart. *Note:* Remember that many banks impose a fee every time you use a card at another bank's ATM, and that fee can be higher for international transactions (up to $5 or more) than for domestic ones (where they're rarely more than $2). In addition, the bank from which you withdraw cash may charge its own fee. For international withdrawal fees, ask your bank. *Note:* In some rural areas, ATMs may not be available and/or reliable. This is especially true in Bulgaria and Romania. For details, please see the "Money" sections in the individual country chapters.

CREDIT CARDS

Credit cards are another safe way to carry money. They also provide a convenient record of all your expenses, and they generally offer relatively good exchange rates. You can withdraw cash advances from your credit cards at banks or ATMs, provided you know your PIN. Keep in mind that you'll pay interest from the moment of your withdrawal, even if you pay your monthly bills on time. Also, note that many banks now assess a 1% to 3% "transaction fee" on *all* charges you incur abroad (whether you're using the local currency or your native currency).

Visa, MasterCard, and Diners Club are the cards commonly accepted in hotels and upscale restaurants in the larger cities of Eastern Europe. Establishments in smaller towns and villages usually require payment in cash, but even if they do accept credit cards, they will often offer a discount for cash payments.

TRAVELER'S CHECKS

You can buy traveler's checks at most banks in the U.S. in denominations of $20, $50, $100, $500, and sometimes $1,000. Generally, you'll pay a service charge ranging from 1% to 5%. However, in most Eastern European countries where mom-and-pop businesses thrive, cash is king and traveler's checks aren't always accepted. Even when they are, a service fee is tacked on them, which makes them a very expensive payment option.

Tips **Easy Money**

You'll avoid lines at airport ATMs by exchanging at least some money—just enough to cover airport incidentals and transportation to your hotel—before you leave home.

When you change money, ask for some small bills or loose change. Petty cash will come in handy for tipping and public transportation. Consider keeping the change separate from your larger bills, so that it's readily accessible and you'll be less of a target for theft.

If you want to use traveler's checks despite the drawbacks, you can buy them at almost any bank. **American Express** offers U.S. dollar denominations of $10, $20, $50, $100, $500, and $1,000 and tacks on service charges ranging from 1% to 4%. By phone, you can buy traveler's checks by calling ℭ **800/807-6233.** American Express card holders should dial ℭ **800/221-7282;** this number accepts collect calls, offers service in several foreign languages, and exempts Amex gold and platinum cardholders from the 1% fee.

Visa offers traveler's checks at Citibank locations nationwide, as well as at several other banks. The service charge ranges between 1.5% and 2%; checks come in denominations of $20, $50, $100, $500, and $1,000. Call ℭ **800/732-1322** for information. AAA members can obtain Visa checks for a $9.95 fee (for checks up to $1,500) at most AAA offices or by calling ℭ **866/339-3378.**

MasterCard also offers traveler's checks. Call ℭ **800/223-9920** for a location near you.

American Express, Thomas Cook, Visa, and **MasterCard** also offer **foreign currency traveler's checks,** which are useful if you're traveling to one country, or to the euro zone; they're accepted at locations where dollar checks may not be.

If you do choose to carry traveler's checks, keep a record of their serial numbers separate from your checks in the event that they are stolen or lost. You'll get a refund faster if you know the numbers.

IF YOUR WALLET IS LOST OR STOLEN Be sure to tell all of your credit card companies the minute you discover your wallet has been lost or stolen, and file a report at the nearest police precinct. Your credit card company or insurer may require a police report number or record of the loss. Most credit card companies have an emergency toll-free number to call if your card is lost or stolen; they may be able to wire you a cash advance immediately or deliver an emergency credit card in a day or two. Emergency numbers for each country are listed in the "Money" section of each individual country chapter.

Note: It's a good idea to photocopy the front and back of the credit cards you carry on a trip and keep them with the photocopy of your passport.

4 When to Go

Eastern Europe sprawls over a huge geographic area with multiple climates that range from Mediterranean to Alpine to something that approaches arctic. In general, the tourist season runs from May through September, with the greatest influx of visitors occurring in July and August, especially in coastal areas, where the weather is sunny and dry almost every day. During these 2 months all sites, attractions, and special events operate at full throttle and charge top dollar. July and August are also when rooms are in shortest supply and when crowds can be overwhelming.

Travelers to Eastern Europe have more elbow room in May and June and from September until mid-October. The weather is more temperate and prices are lower than in the summer months, but some attractions, restaurants, and hotels may operate on reduced schedules during this time. Check ahead if there is something that is a must-see.

During the winter months, tourism shifts to Eastern Europe's mountain ranges and metropolitan areas, leaving coastal areas deserted. In fact, many island and seaside attractions are closed altogether from November to April, and even if they aren't, visitors are few.

Eastern Europe's ski season lasts from December to mid-March (longer in Romania) and except for other snow sports enthusiasts, you won't run into many people outside ski resort areas if you're traveling in the mountains.

Eastern Europe's city dwellers tend to hunker down in winter, when the days can be short, cold, and gray and the nights long, colder, and silent. Concerts and theater productions are in full swing in big cities during the winter but they attract mostly locals, unlike the flamboyant outdoor music festivals that seem to go nonstop in the summer months and attract an international crowd.

Each Eastern European country covered in this guide has its own optimal "season."

HOLIDAYS, CELEBRATIONS & EVENTS

Many of Eastern Europe's holidays and festivals correspond to religious holy days (Catholic and Orthodox) and to national commemorations.

January

New Year's Day. January 1 is the first day of the Gregorian calendar, which is used by most countries in Eastern Europe. This day is both a secular and a religious holiday commemorating the circumcision of Christ. In countries where Eastern Orthodoxy is the predominant religion, many celebrate January 1 as a civic holiday and January 14 as a religious holiday. The Eastern Church in Bulgaria, Romania, and Poland has adopted a modified Julian calendar, which incorporates both religious and civic holidays on January 1. In Russia, January 1 is a civil holiday and the biggest of the year, a holdover from the atheist Soviet government, which banned religious celebrations.

February

Feast of St. Blaise. The patron saint of Dubrovnik (Croatia) is honored each February 3 by Catholics worldwide as a healer of throat ailments. But in Dubrovnik, the saint is also revered as the city's savior, a man who thwarted an attack by invading Turks. He is feted with parades, food, wine, and a workers' day off.

Carnival. This pre-Lenten celebration begins in mid-February and ends at midnight on Shrove Tuesday in cities and villages all over the globe. It is celebrated to various degrees throughout Eastern Europe, but lavishly so in Rijeka, Croatia.

March

National Days. March is a good month for national days in Eastern Europe. **Bulgaria National Day** is March 3 while Hungary's is March 15. Bulgaria also hosts **March Music Days,** a festival of classical music and composers, in March.

April

Easter Sunday and Easter Monday. These movable feasts can fall in March or April, but they are both religious and civic holidays for Catholics and Eastern Rite Christians throughout Eastern Europe whenever they occur.

Eastern Rite Easter is usually 1 or 2 weeks after Catholic/Protestant Easter. The day has taken on greater significance in Russia since the collapse of Soviet atheism. The **International Festival of Ghosts and Phantoms** materializes in Bojnice, Slovakia, at the end of April. On **National Resistance Day** Slovenia stops to remember the movement that stood up to occupying forces during World War II.

May

Labor Day. May 1 is a workers' holiday throughout Eastern Europe.

National Days. Poland's Constitution Day is May 3; Bulgaria has Bulgarian Army Day on May 6; the Czech Republic and Slovakia celebrate Liberation Day on May 8; Hungary commemorates Emancipation Day on May 24; and Croatia celebrates Statehood Day on May 30.

June

Pentecost Sunday. Another movable church feast, Pentecost is celebrated 40 days after Easter throughout Eastern Europe. Pentecost, aka Whit Monday, is also a civic holiday.

Corpus Christi Day. This Catholic holy day also merits some civic closures in Croatia, Poland, Slovakia, and Slovenia. It usually falls in June but can be in late May when Easter falls early in the season.

Summer Festivals. June is the traditional start of the summer festival season in Eastern Europe, which kicks off with dance festivals in Zagreb, Croatia (June 1) and Prague, Czech Republic (June 2).

National Days. Croatia stops everything for **Antifascist Struggle Day** on June 22, and closes down again 3 days later on June 25 for **Statehood Day,** a date it shares with Slovenia's **National Day** holiday. In late June or early July St. Petersburg hosts **White Nights,** a series of concerts, film festivals, all-night boat tours, and other events.

July & August

These 2 months equate with Eastern Europe's high tourism season and the summer festival season all over the region. Choose from **Dubrovnik's (Croatia) Summer Festival,** a 50-year-old theater and music marathon that goes from the second week of July through the third week of August to **Formula I racing** in Budapest (Hungary) at the beginning of August. The **Maiden Festival** in Romania is a vestige of Targu de Fete, a day that guys picked out their brides. Today it is more of a folk festival. Look for single-day or weekend celebrations in specific towns in every country and you can eat, drink, sing, and dance your way across Eastern Europe for 2 months. **Split's Summer Festival** showcases open-air opera, theater, and dance performances and Poreč is the venue for a series of **jazz concerts.** August 15 is the **Feast of the Assumption,** which is a holy day for the world's Catholics, including Eastern Europe's Catholic countries (Croatia, Poland, Slovakia, and Slovenia). See specific country chapters for detailed festival information.

September

The festival season winds down and kids in Eastern Europe go back to school in September. You still can take in a concert or two at the **Prague (Czech Republic) Autumn Music Festival** from mid-September to October or watch a **Marco Polo naval battle reenactment** off Korčula (Croatia) in early September. The **Apollonia Festival of the Arts** takes place in Bulgaria in September and it is followed by the **Golden Rose International Film Festival** at the end of the month.

October

Lots of civic commemorations across Eastern Europe mean plenty of days off work and store closures in October. Croatia, Hungary, the Czech Republic, and Slovenia each close down for a day (Oct 8, 23, 28, and 31 respectively) to celebrate political milestones. The harvest season goes into full swing, too, with village celebrations in progress across the region. Warsaw hosts a **Jazz Jamboree** this month. It is purported to be the oldest jazz festival in Europe.

November

All Saints' Day (Nov 1) is another holy day for Catholics and a day to close up shop in Eastern Europe's Catholic countries (Croatia, Poland, Slovakia, Slovenia). Polish people place lighted candles on the graves of the dearly departed on this day. November 11 is **St. Martin's Day** and the first day of the wine season in grape-growing regions (Croatia, Slovenia) and a day to eat, drink, and be merry.

December

Christmas fairs abound in the Czech Republic in the days leading up to Christmas. Polish children delight on **St. Nicholas Day** (Dec 6) because they receive gifts. Except for Russia, **Christmas Day and St. Stephen's Day** (Dec 25–26) are celebrated throughout Eastern Europe as both religious and civic holidays, as is **New Year's Eve,** aka **St. Sylvester's Day,** on December 31.

5 Travel Insurance

The cost of travel insurance varies widely, depending on the cost and length of your trip, your age and health, and the type of trip you're taking, but expect to pay between 5% and 8% of the vacation itself. You can get estimates from various providers through **InsureMyTrip.com.** Enter your trip cost and dates, your age, and other information, for prices from more than a dozen companies.

TRIP-CANCELLATION INSURANCE

Trip-cancellation insurance will help retrieve your money if you have to back out of a trip or depart early, or if your travel supplier goes bankrupt. Permissible reasons for trip cancellation can range from sickness to natural disasters to the State Department declaring a destination unsafe for travel.

For more information, contact one of the following recommended insurers: **Access America** (☎ 866/807-3982; www.accessamerica.com); **Travel Guard International** (☎ 800/826-4919; www.travelguard.com); **Travel Insured International** (☎ 800/243-3174; www.travelinsured.com); and **Travelex Insurance Services** (☎ 888/457-4602; www.travelex-insurance.com).

Travel in the Age of Bankruptcy

Airlines go bankrupt, so protect yourself by **buying your tickets with a credit card.** The Fair Credit Billing Act guarantees that you can get your money back from the credit card company if a travel supplier goes under (and if you request the refund within 60 days of the bankruptcy). **Travel insurance** can also help, but make sure it covers against "carrier default" for your specific travel provider. And be aware that if a U.S. airline goes bust midtrip, a 2001 federal law requires other carriers to take you to your destination (albeit on a space-available basis) for a fee of no more than $25, provided you rebook within 60 days of the cancellation.

MEDICAL INSURANCE

For travel overseas, most U.S. health plans (including Medicare and Medicaid) do not provide coverage, and the ones that do often require you to pay for services upfront and reimburse you only after you return home. As a safety net, you may want to buy travel medical insurance, particularly if you're traveling to a remote or high-risk area where emergency evacuation might be necessary. If you require additional medical insurance, try **MEDEX Assistance** (✆ 410/453-6300; www.medexassist.com) or **Travel Assistance International** (✆ 800/821-2828; www.travelassistance.com; for general information on services, call the company's Worldwide Assistance Services, Inc., at ✆ 800/777-8710).

LOST-LUGGAGE INSURANCE

On international flights (including U.S. portions of international trips), baggage coverage is limited to approximately $9.07 per pound, up to approximately $635 per checked bag. If you plan to check items more valuable than what's covered by the standard liability, see if your homeowner's policy covers your valuables, get baggage insurance as part of your comprehensive travel-insurance package, or buy Travel Guard's "BagTrak" product.

If your luggage is lost, immediately file a lost-luggage claim at the airport, detailing the luggage contents. Most airlines require that you report delayed, damaged, or lost baggage within 4 hours of arrival. The airlines are required to deliver luggage, once found, directly to your house or destination free of charge.

6 Health & Safety

STAYING HEALTHY

Staying healthy during a trip to Eastern Europe requires common sense and an ounce of prevention. No vaccinations are necessary to visit Eastern Europe and digestive upsets are visitors' biggest health challenges. It is safest to stick with bottled water everywhere.

GENERAL AVAILABILITY OF HEALTHCARE

Hospitals and pharmacies are available in all Eastern European countries, but the quality of treatments and drugs varies widely, even within a single country. Consult individual country chapters for specific information.

If you plan to visit forested areas in the summer or if you choose to consume unpasteurized dairy products, you put yourself at risk for tick-borne infections. According for the Centers for Disease Control (CDC), tick-borne encephalitis, a viral infection of the central nervous system, has been reported in Russia, the Czech Republic, Hungary, Poland, and Slovenia, so take precautions against tick bites if you visit these countries.

In general, the CDC warns travelers not to eat food purchased from street vendors or undercooked food to reduce risk of hepatitis A and typhoid fever. Do not drink beverages with ice if the water supply is suspect. Avoid unpasteurized dairy products. Don't swim in fresh water to avoid exposure to waterborne diseases. Don't handle animals, especially monkeys, dogs, and cats, to avoid bites and rabies and plague. Do not share needles for tattoos, body piercing, or injections. HIV and hepatitis B are global hazards. Avoid poultry farms, bird markets, and other places where live poultry is raised or kept.

Contact the **International Association for Medical Assistance to Travelers (IAMAT)** (✆ 716/754-4883, or 416/652-0137 in Canada; **www.iamat.org**) for tips on travel and health concerns in the countries you're visiting, and for lists of local, English-speaking doctors. The

United States **Centers for Disease Control and Prevention** (☏ 800/311-3435; www.cdc.gov) provides up-to-date information on health hazards by region or country and offers tips on food safety. The website **www.tripprep.com**, sponsored by a consortium of travel-medicine practitioners, may also offer helpful advice on traveling abroad. You can find listings of reliable clinics overseas at the **International Society of Travel Medicine** (www.istm.org).

WHAT TO DO IF YOU GET SICK AWAY FROM HOME

If you suffer from a chronic illness, consult your doctor before your departure. Pack **prescription medications** in your carry-on luggage, and carry them in their original containers, with pharmacy labels—otherwise they won't make it through airport security. Carry the generic name of prescription medicines, in case a local pharmacist is unfamiliar with the brand name. Have prescriptions translated into the local language before you leave home.

For travel abroad, you may have to pay all medical costs upfront and be reimbursed later. See "Medical Insurance," under "Travel Insurance," above.

STAYING SAFE

The U.S. Department of State's Consular Information Program provides Consular Information Sheets, Travel Warnings, and Public Announcements. Travel Warnings are issued when the State Department recommends that Americans avoid travel to a certain country. Public Announcements are issued as a means to disseminate information quickly about terrorist threats and other relatively short-term conditions that pose significant risks to the security of American travelers. Free copies of this information are available by calling the Bureau of Consular Affairs at ☏ **202-647-5225** or via the fax-on-demand system: ☏ **202/647-3000**. Consular Information Sheets and Travel Warnings also are available on the Consular Affairs Internet home page at http://travel.state.gov.

Croatia, the Czech Republic, Hungary, Poland, Slovakia, and Slovenia are generally safe for tourists, though you should exercise the same caution you would in any unfamiliar city and always be aware of your surroundings when walking in less trafficked areas or at night.

Bulgaria, Romania, and Russia are less safe and visitors should take precautions to keep their valuables secure from pickpockets and others who prey on the unaware in major cities. Corruption is widespread in these developing countries and visitors should be skeptical about policemen who stop you and demand payment for fines levied for bogus charges. If you are confronted with a policeman demanding cash on the spot to pay a fine assessed for an alleged infraction, you should insist on going to the nearest police station to pay. But even before you go out, put jewelry and laptops in the hotel safe if you will be gone for the day and don't need them. Never leave any valuables or documents, including passports, in your hotel room when you are gone.

DEALING WITH DISCRIMINATION

Discrimination in Romania is usually reserved for members of the Roma minority (Gypsies) and for children with HIV. Bulgaria is slowly coming into compliance with E.U. antidiscrimination guidelines, but it, too, denies equal treatment to Roma (and women in general). The Russian constitution states that everyone is equal before the law and prohibits discrimination on the basis of race, ethnicity, national origin, or language, but there is no provision for punishment of anyone who breaks the law. In Russia, most discrimination is aimed at former Soviet citizens and select minorities, including the Roma. In the other Eastern European countries covered in this book, discrimination is largely based on internal conflicts and aimed at ethnic groups within the various countries.

ECO-TOURISM

You can find ecofriendly travel tips, statistics, and touring companies and associations—listed by destination under "Travel Choice"—at the TIES website, www.ecotourism.org. **Ecotravel.com** is part online magazine and part ecodirectory that lets you search for touring companies in several categories (water-based, land-based, spiritually oriented, and so on). Also check out **Conservation International** (www.conservation.org), which, with *National Geographic Traveler,* annually presents **World Legacy Awards** (www.wlaward.org) to those travel tour operators, businesses, organizations, and places that have made a significant contribution to sustainable tourism.

7 Specialized Travel Resources

TRAVELERS WITH DISABILITIES

Most disabilities shouldn't stop anyone from traveling. There are more options and resources available than ever before. However, accommodations for disabled travelers in Eastern European countries are sporadic at best and usually concentrated in upscale establishments in larger cities.

If disabled access is a concern, it's best to book through a travel agency that caters to those with this concern. Many travel agencies offer customized tours and itineraries for travelers with disabilities. Among them are **Flying Wheels Travel** (© 507/451-5005; www.flyingwheelstravel.com); **Access-Able Travel Source** (© 303/232-2979; www.access-able.com); and **Accessible Journeys** (© 800/846-4537 or 610/521-0339; www.disabilitytravel.com). **Avis Rent a Car** has an "Avis Access" program that offers such services as a dedicated 24-hour toll-free number (© 888/879-4273) for customers with special travel needs; special car features such as swivel seats, spinner knobs, and hand controls; and accessible bus service.

Organizations that offer assistance to travelers with disabilities include **Moss-Rehab** (www.mossresourcenet.org); the **American Foundation for the Blind (AFB)** (© 800/232-5463; www.afb.org); and **SATH** (Society for Accessible Travel & Hospitality) (© 212/447-7284; www.sath.org). **AirAmbulanceCard.com** is now partnered with SATH and allows you to preselect top-notch hospitals in case of an emergency.

The community website **iCan** (www.icanonline.net/channels/travel) has destination guides and several regular columns on accessible travel. Also check out the quarterly magazine *Emerging Horizons* (www.emerginghorizons.com) and *Open World* magazine, published by SATH.

GAY & LESBIAN TRAVELERS

In the Catholic countries of Eastern Europe (Croatia, Poland, Slovakia, and Slovenia) gay and lesbian travelers won't be hassled, but they won't find many establishments that lay out the welcome mat for them either. Resources for gay and lesbian travelers are few or hidden. For the most part, there is a macho mentality about sexuality in all the countries covered in this guide, and it is a sensibility that is not gay-friendly. The Czech Republic and Slovenia are the most gay-friendly of the countries covered in this book. *Note:* In one recent instance, a hotel owner on the Croatian island of Hvar attempted to promote a week designed to appeal to gay and lesbian travelers much to the chagrin of the local townspeople. The event was marred by many local protests. However, some organized tours to Eastern Europe might exist for this group. **The International Gay and Lesbian Travel Association (IGLTA)** (© 800/448-8550 or 954/776-2626; www.iglta.org) is the trade association for the gay and lesbian travel industry, and offers an online directory of gay- and lesbian-friendly travel businesses; go to their website and click on "Members."

Many agencies offer tours and travel itineraries specifically for gay and lesbian travelers. Among them are **Above and Beyond Tours** (© 800/397-2681; www.abovebeyondtours.com); **Now, Voyager** (© 800/255-6951; www.nowvoyager.com); and **Olivia Cruises & Resorts** (© 800/631-6277; www.olivia.com).

Gay.com Travel (© 800/929-2268 or 415/644-8044; www.gay.com/travel or www.outandabout.com), is an excellent online successor to the popular *Out & About* print magazine. It provides regularly updated information about gay-owned, -oriented, and -friendly lodging, dining, sightseeing, nightlife, and shopping establishments in every important destination worldwide.

The following travel guides are available at many bookstores, or you can order them from any online bookseller: *Frommer's Gay & Lesbian Europe* (www.frommers.com), an excellent travel resource to the top European cities and resorts; *Spartacus International Gay Guide* (Bruno Gmünder Verlag; www.spartacusworld.com/gayguide) and *Odysseus: The International Gay Travel Planner* (Odysseus Enterprises, Ltd.); and the *Damron* guides (www.damron.com), with separate, annual books for gay men and lesbians.

FOR FAMILIES

Families are very important in Eastern Europe, but if you're traveling with children, don't expect any special treatment. You might get reduced rates for children under 12 when you visit museums, a reduced extra-person rate for the child in your hotel room, and a few kiddie menus here and there in restaurants, but other than that there are no financial breaks for the younger set. You'll find most young visitors at the beach, on the ski slopes, or in the museums of Eastern Europe.

Recommended family travel Internet sites include **Family Travel Forum** (www.familytravelforum.com), a comprehensive site that offers customized trip planning; **Family Travel Network** (www.familytravelnetwork.com), a comprehensive site offering sound advice for long-distance and international travel with children; and **Family Travel Files,** which offers an online magazine and a directory of off-the-beaten-path tours and our operators for families.

SENIOR TRAVEL

Many museums and attractions in Eastern Europe offer free or reduced rates to people of retirement age. However, few hotels offer age-based discounts and no restaurants offer the early-bird specials so popular with the over-50 set. However, members of **AARP** (formerly known as the American Association of Retired Persons), 601 E St. NW, Washington, DC 20049 (© 888/687-2277; www.aarp.org), may get discounts on hotels, airfares, and car rentals if these are linked to a U.S.-based company. AARP offers members a wide range of benefits, including *AARP: The Magazine* and a monthly newsletter. Anyone over 50 can join.

Many reliable agencies and organizations target the 50-plus market. **Elderhostel** (© 877/426-8056; www.elderhostel.org) arranges study programs for those aged 55 and over. **ElderTreks** (© 800/741-7956; www.eldertreks.com) offers small-group tours to off-the-beaten-path or adventure-travel locations, restricted to travelers 50 and older. **INTRAV** (© 800/456-8100; www.intrav.com) is a high-end tour operator that caters to the mature, discerning traveler (not specifically seniors), with trips around the world that include guided safaris, polar expeditions, private-jet adventures, and small-boat cruises down jungle rivers.

Recommended publications offering travel resources and discounts for seniors include: the quarterly magazine *Travel 50 & Beyond* (www.travel50andbeyond. com); *Travel Unlimited: Uncommon Adventures for the Mature Traveler* (Avalon); *101 Tips for Mature Travelers,* available from Grand Circle Travel (© 800/221-2610 or 617/350-7500; www.gct.com); and *Unbelievably Good Deals and Great Adventures That You Absolutely Can't Get Unless You're Over 50* (McGraw-Hill), by Joann Rattner Heilman.

WOMEN & SINGLE TRAVELERS

Solo women can travel safely in most of Eastern Europe, but like any other solo traveler, they might find it difficult to book any room at a single-room price. In fact, solo travelers may pay a premium to get a room. On package vacations, single travelers are often hit with a "single supplement" to the base price. To avoid it, you can agree to room with other single travelers or find a compatible roommate before you go, from one of the many roommate-locator agencies.

Travel Buddies Singles Travel Club (© 800/998-9099; www.travelbuddies worldwide.com), based in Canada, runs small, intimate, single-friendly group trips and will match you with a roommate free of charge. **TravelChums** (© 212/787-2621; www.travelchums.com) is an Internet-only travel-companion matching service with elements of an online personals-type site, hosted by the respected New York–based Shaw Guides travel service. **The Single Gourmet Club** (www. singlegourmet.com/chapters.php) is an international social, dining, and travel club for singles of all ages, with club chapters in 21 cities in the U.S. and

Canada. Many reputable tour companies offer singles-only trips. **Singles Travel International** (© 877/765-6874; www. singlestravelintl.com) offers singles-only trips to places like London, Fiji, and the Greek Islands. **Backroads** (© 800/462-2848; www.backroads.com) offers more than 160 active-travel trips to 30 destinations worldwide, including Bali, Morocco, and Costa Rica.

For more information, check out Eleanor Berman's latest edition of *Traveling Solo: Advice and Ideas for More Than 250 Great Vacations* (Globe Pequot), a guide with advice on traveling alone, either solo or as part of a group tour.

Note: In macho countries like Romania, Bulgaria, and the Russian Federation, a woman traveling solo may encounter harassment or other difficulties. In addition, it is not wise for a woman to travel alone at night in these places.

Check out the award-winning website **Journeywoman** (www.journeywoman. com), a "real life" women's travel-information network where you can sign up for a free e-mail newsletter and get advice on everything from etiquette and dress to safety; or the travel guide *Safety and Security for Women Who Travel* by Sheila Swan and Peter Laufer (Travelers' Tales, Inc.), offering common-sense tips on safe travel.

AFRICAN-AMERICAN TRAVELERS

Black Travel Online (www.blacktravel online.com) posts news on upcoming events and includes links to articles and travel-booking sites. **Soul of America** (www.soulofamerica.com) is a comprehensive website, with travel tips, event and family-reunion postings, and sections on historically black beach resorts and active vacations.

Agencies and organizations that provide resources for black travelers include

Rodgers Travel (© 800/825-1775; www. rodgerstravel.com); the **African American Association of Innkeepers International** (© 877/422-5777; www.african americaninns.com); and **Henderson Travel & Tours** (© 800/327-2309 or 301/650-5700; www.hendersontravel. com), which has specialized in trips to Africa since 1957. For more information, check out the following collections and guides: *Go Girl: The Black Woman's Guide to Travel & Adventure* (Eighth Mountain Press), a compilation of travel essays by writers including Jill Nelson and Audre Lorde; *The African American Travel Guide* by Wayne Robinson (Hunter Publishing; www.hunterpublishing.com); *Steppin' Out* by Carla Labat (Avalon); *Travel and Enjoy Magazine* (© 866/ 266-6211; www.travelandenjoy.com); and *Pathfinders Magazine* (© 877/977- PATH; www.pathfinderstravel.com), which includes articles on everything from Rio de Janeiro to Ghana as well as information on upcoming ski, diving, golf, and tennis trips.

STUDENT TRAVEL

If you're a student traveling internationally, you'd be wise to arm yourself with an **International Student Identity Card (ISIC),** which offers substantial savings on rail passes, plane tickets, and entrance fees. It also provides you with basic health and life insurance and a 24-hour help line. The card is available from **STA Travel** (© 800/781-4040 in North America; www.sta.com or www.statravel.com; or www.statravel.co.uk in the U.K.), the biggest student travel agency in the world. If you're no longer a student but are still under 26, you can get an **International Youth Travel Card (IYTC)** from the same people, that entitles you to some discounts (but not on museum admissions). **Travel CUTS** (© 800/667-2887 or 416/614-2887; www.travelcuts.com) offers similar services for both Canadians and U.S. residents. Irish students may prefer to turn to **USIT** (© 01/602-1600; www.usitnow.ie), an Ireland-based specialist in student, youth, and independent travel.

8 Planning Your Trip Online

SURFING FOR AIRFARE

The most popular online travel agencies are **Travelocity** (**www.travelocity.com** or www.travelocity.co.uk); **Expedia** (**www. expedia.com**, www.expedia.co.uk, or www. expedia.ca); and **Orbitz** (www.orbitz.com).

In addition, most airlines now offer online-only fares that even their phone agents know nothing about.

Other helpful websites for booking airline tickets online include:

- www.biddingfortravel.com
- www.cheapflights.com
- www.hotwire.com
- www.kayak.com
- www.lastminutetravel.com
- www.opodo.co.uk
- www.priceline.com
- www.sidestep.com
- www.site59.com
- www.smartertravel.com

SURFING FOR HOTELS

In addition to **Travelocity, Expedia, Orbitz, Priceline,** and **Hotwire** (see above), the following websites will help you with booking hotel rooms online:

- www.hotels.com
- www.quickbook.com
- www.travelaxe.net
- www.travelweb.com
- www.tripadvisor.com

It's a good idea to **get a confirmation number** and **make a printout** of any online booking transaction.

Accommodations in Eastern Europe run the gamut from opulent to awful. See individual country chapters for specific information.

Frommers.com: The Complete Travel Resource

For an excellent travel-planning resource, we highly recommend **Frommers. com** (www.frommers.com), voted Best Travel Site by *PC Magazine*. We're a little biased, of course, but we guarantee that you'll find the travel tips, reviews, monthly vacation giveaways, bookstore, and online-booking capabilities to be thoroughly indispensable. Special features include our popular **Destinations** section, where you can access expert travel tips, hotel and dining recommendations, and advice on the sights to see in more than 3,500 destinations around the globe; the **Frommers.com Newsletter,** with the latest deals, travel trends, and money-saving secrets; and our **Travel Talk** area featuring **Message Boards,** where Frommer's readers post queries and share advice, and where our authors sometimes show up to answer questions. Once you finish your research, the **Book a Trip** area can lead you to Frommer's preferred online partners' websites, where you can book your vacation at affordable prices.

SURFING FOR RENTAL CARS

For booking rental cars online, the best deals are usually found at rental-car company websites, although all the major online travel agencies also offer rental-car reservations services. Priceline and Hotwire work well for rental cars, too; the only "mystery" is which major rental company you get, and for most travelers the difference between Hertz, Avis, and Budget is negligible.

TRAVEL BLOGS & TRAVELOGUES

To read a few blogs about Eastern Europe try www.easterneuropeblog.com. Other blogs include:

- www.gridskipper.com
- www.salon.com/wanderlust
- www.travelblog.com
- www.travelblog.org
- www.worldhum.com
- www.writtenroad.com

---

9 The 21st-Century Traveler

INTERNET ACCESS AWAY FROM HOME
WITHOUT YOUR OWN COMPUTER

To find cybercafes in your destination check **www.cybercaptive.com** and **www.cybercafe.com**.

Aside from formal cybercafes, most **youth hostels** and **public libraries** have Internet access. Avoid **hotel business centers** unless you're willing to pay exorbitant rates. However, some of the better hotels have Wi-Fi throughout or at least in the lobby, as do some coffee shops and bars. In Eastern Europe, you'll find that the connection at Internet cafes can range from fabulous to extremely slow. The best connections are in cities and better hotels, as mentioned above.

Most major airports now have **Internet kiosks** scattered throughout their gates. These give you basic Web access for a per-minute fee that's usually higher than cybercafe prices but very convenient.

WITH YOUR OWN COMPUTER

More and more hotels, cafes, and retailers are signing on as Wi-Fi (wireless fidelity) "hotspots." Mac owners have their own networking technology: Apple AirPort.

T-Mobile Hotspot (www.t-mobile.com/hotspot) serves up wireless connections at more than 1,000 Starbucks coffee shops nationwide. **Boingo** (www.boingo.com) and **Wayport** (www.wayport.com) have set up networks in airports and high-class hotel lobbies. IPass providers (see below) also give you access to a few hundred wireless hotel lobby setups. To locate other hotspots that provide **free wireless networks** in cities around the world, go to **www.personaltelco.net/index.cgi/WirelessCommunities**.

For dial-up access, most business-class hotels throughout the world offer dataports for laptop modems, and a few thousand hotels in the U.S. and Europe now offer free high-speed Internet access. In addition, major Internet service providers (ISPs) have **local access numbers** around the world, allowing you to go online by placing a local call. The **iPass** network also has dial-up numbers around the world. You'll have to sign up with an iPass provider, who will then tell you how to set up your computer for your destination(s). For a list of iPass providers, go to www.ipass.com and click on "Individuals Buy Now." One solid provider is **i2roam** (www.i2roam.com; ✆ **866/811-6209** or 920/235-0475).

Wherever you go, bring a **connection kit** of the right power and phone adapters, a spare phone cord, and a spare Ethernet network cable—or find out whether your hotel supplies them to guests.

Like western Europe, Eastern Europe is on 240V electrical circuits. You'll need at least one two-pronged adaptor plug and a current converter unless your electronic gear operates on dual voltage (120V and 240V).

CELLPHONE USE

The three letters that define much of the world's wireless capabilities are GSM (Global System for Mobiles), a big, seamless network that makes for easy cross-border cellphone use throughout Europe and dozens of other countries worldwide. In the U.S., T-Mobile, AT&T Wireless, and Cingular use this quasi-universal system; in Canada, Microcell and some Rogers customers are GSM, and all Europeans and most Australians use GSM.

If your cellphone is on a GSM system, and you have a world-capable multiband phone such as many Sony Ericsson, Motorola, or Samsung models, you can make and receive calls across civilized areas around much of the globe. Just call your wireless operator and ask for "international roaming" to be activated on your account. Unfortunately, per-minute charges can be high—usually $1 to $1.50 in western Europe and up to $5 in places like Russia and Indonesia. Be sure you bring your AC charger, a converter, and an adaptor plug and check with your provider to be sure your converter is safe for the phone's delicate electrical circuits. A car charger can be useful, too.

It's important to buy an "unlocked" world phone from the get-go. Many cellphone operators sell "locked" phones that restrict you from using any removable SIM card other than the one they supply. Having an unlocked phone allows you to install a cheap, prepaid SIM card that you can purchase and use in your destination country. (Show your phone to the salesperson; not all phones work on all networks.) You'll get a local phone number and dramatically lower calling rates.

Getting a locked phone unlocked can be a hassle, but it can be done. Call your cellular provider before you leave and say you'll be going abroad for several months and want to use the phone with a local provider.

For many, **renting** a phone is a good idea. (Even world phone owners will have to rent new phones if they're traveling to non-GSM regions, such as Japan or Korea.) While you can rent a phone from any number of overseas sites, including kiosks at airports and at car-rental

Online Traveler's Toolbox

Veteran travelers usually carry some essential items to make their trips easier. Following is a selection of handy online tools to bookmark and use.

- **Foreign Languages for Travelers** (www.travlang.com). Learn basic terms in more than 70 languages and click on any underlined phrase to hear what it sounds like.
- **Maps** (www.mapquest.com). This is the best of the mapping sites. It lets you choose a specific address or destination, and in seconds it will return a map and detailed directions.
- **Travel Warnings** (http://travel.state.gov, www.fco.gov.uk/travel, www.voyage.gc.ca, or www.dfat.gov.au/consular/advice). Keep abreast of global developments that affect safe travel.
- **Universal Currency Converter** (www.xe.com/ucc). See what your dollar or pound is worth in more than 100 countries.
- **Visa ATM Locator** (www.visa.com), **MasterCard ATM Locator** (www.mastercard.com). Find an ATM when everything else is closed and you need local currency.
- **Weather** (www.intellicast.com and www.weather.com). Get weather forecasts for cities around the world.

agencies, we suggest renting the phone before you leave home. North Americans can rent one before leaving home from **InTouch USA** (© 800/872-7626; www.intouchglobal.com) or **RoadPost** (© 888/290-1606 or 905/272-5665; www.roadpost.com). InTouch will also, for free, advise you on whether your existing phone will work overseas; simply call © **703/222-7161** between 9am and 4pm EST, or go to **http://intouchglobal.com/travel.htm**.

Buying a phone can be economically attractive, as many nations have cheap prepaid phone systems. Once you arrive at your destination, stop by a local cellphone shop and get the cheapest package; you'll probably pay less than $100 for a phone and a starter calling card. Local

calls may be as low as 10¢ per minute, and in many countries incoming calls are free.

Wilderness adventurers, or those heading to less-developed countries, might consider renting a **satellite phone ("satphone")**. It's different from a cellphone in that it connects to satellites and works where there's no cellular signal or ground-based tower. You can rent satellite phones from RoadPost (see above). InTouch USA (see above) offers a wider range of satphones but at higher rates. Per-minute call charges can be even cheaper than roaming charges with a regular cellphone, but the phone itself is more expensive. As of this writing, satphones were outrageously expensive to buy, so don't even think about it.

10 Getting There

Prague, Warsaw, Zagreb, Budapest, and Moscow receive the greatest number of international flights to Eastern Europe. If you're planning to explore the entire region, you might consider starting at one of these gateways and catching connecting flights to less-serviced destinations. **See the "Getting There" sections of the individual country chapters for detailed information.**

FLYING FOR LESS: TIPS FOR GETTING THE BEST AIRFARE

- Passengers who can book their ticket either **long in advance or at the last minute,** or who **fly midweek** or **at less-trafficked hours** may pay a fraction of the full fare. If your schedule is flexible, say so, and ask if you can secure a cheaper fare by changing your flight plans.
- Search **the Internet** for cheap fares (see "Planning Your Trip Online," above).
- Keep an eye on local newspapers for **promotional specials** or **fare wars,** when airlines lower prices on their most popular routes. You rarely see fare wars offered for peak travel times, but if you can travel in the off-months, you may snag a bargain.
- Try to book a ticket **in its country of origin.** If you're planning a one-way flight from Johannesburg to Bombay, a South Africa–based travel agent will probably have the lowest fares. For multileg trips, book in the country of the first leg; for example, book New York–London–Amsterdam–Rome–New York in the U.S.
- **Consolidators,** also known as bucket shops, are great sources for international tickets, although they usually can't beat Internet fares within North America. Start by looking in Sunday newspaper travel sections; U.S. travelers should focus on the *New York Times, Los Angeles Times,* and *Miami Herald.* U.K. travelers should search in the *Independent, The Guardian,* or *The Observer.* For less-developed destinations, small travel agents who cater to immigrant communities in large cities often have the best deals. *Beware:* Bucket shop tickets are usually nonrefundable or rigged with stiff cancellation penalties, often as high as 50% to 75% of the ticket price, and some put you on charter airlines, which may leave at inconvenient times and experience delays. Several reliable consolidators are worldwide and available online. **STA Travel** has been the world's lead consolidator for students since purchasing Council Travel, but their fares are competitive for travelers of all ages.

Tips Getting Through the Airport

- Arrive at the airport 1 hour before a domestic flight and 2 hours before an international flight; if you show up late, tell an airline employee and he or she will probably expedite you to the front of the line.
- Bring a current, government-issued photo ID such as a driver's license or passport. Children under 18 need government-issued photo IDs for international flights to most countries.
- Speed up security by removing your jacket and shoes before you're screened. In addition, remove metal objects such as big belt buckles. If you've got metallic body parts, a note from your doctor can prevent a long chat with the security screeners.
- Use a TSA-approved lock for your checked luggage. Look for Travel Sentry certified locks at luggage or travel shops and Brookstone stores (or online at www.brookstone.com).

ELTExpress (Flights.com) (© 800/ TRAV-800; www.eltexpress.com) has excellent fares worldwide, particularly to Europe. They also have "local" websites in 12 countries. **FlyCheap** (© 800/FLY-CHEAP; www.1800fly cheap.com), owned by package-holiday megalith MyTravel, has especially good fares to sunny destinations. **Air Tickets Direct** (© 800/778-3447; www.airticketsdirect.com) is based in Montreal and leverages the currently weak Canadian dollar for low fares; they also book trips to places that U.S. travel agents won't touch, such as Cuba.

- Join **frequent-flier clubs.** Frequent-flier membership doesn't cost a cent, but it does entitle you to better seats, faster response to phone inquiries, and prompter service if your luggage is stolen or your flight is canceled or delayed, or if you want to change your seat. And you don't have to fly to earn points; **frequent-flier credit cards** can earn you thousands of miles for doing your everyday shopping. With more than 70 mileage awards programs on the market, consumers have never had more options. Investigate the program details of your favorite airlines before you sink points into any one. Consider which airlines have hubs in the airport nearest you, and, of those carriers, which have the most advantageous alliances, given your most common routes. To play the frequent-flier game to your best advantage, consult Randy Petersen's **Inside Flyer** (www.insideflyer.com). Petersen

and friends review all the programs in detail and post regular updates on changes in policies and trends.

LONG-HAUL FLIGHTS: HOW TO STAY COMFORTABLE

- Your choice of airline and airplane will definitely affect your leg room. Find more details about U.S. airlines at **www.seatguru.com**. For international airlines, the research firm Skytrax has posted a list of average seat pitches at **www.airlinequality.com**.
- Emergency exit seats and bulkhead seats typically have the most legroom. Emergency exit seats are usually left unassigned until the day of a flight (to ensure that someone able-bodied fills the seats); it's worth getting to the ticket counter early to snag one of these spots for a long flight. Many passengers find that bulkhead seating (the row facing the wall at the front of the cabin) offers more legroom, but keep in mind that bulkheads are where airlines often put baby bassinets, so you may be sitting next to an infant.
- To have two seats for yourself in a three-seat row, try for an aisle seat in a center section toward the back of coach. If you're traveling with a companion, book an aisle and a window seat. Middle seats are usually booked last, so chances are good you'll end up with three seats to yourselves.
- Ask about entertainment options. Many airlines offer seatback video systems where you get to choose your movies or play video games—but only on some of their planes. (Boeing 777s are your best bet.)

Tips Don't Stow It—Ship It

Though pricey, it's sometimes worthwhile to travel luggage-free. Specialists in door-to-door luggage delivery include **Virtual Bellhop** (www.virtualbellhop.com), **SkyCap International** (wwww.skycapinternational.com), **Luggage Express** (www.usxpluggageexpress.com), and **Sports Express** (www.sportsexpress.com).

- To sleep, avoid the last row of any section or the row in front of an emergency exit, as these seats are the least likely to recline. Avoid seats near highly trafficked toilet areas. Avoid seats in the back of many jets—these can be narrower than those in the rest of coach. You also may want to reserve a window seat so you can rest your head and avoid being bumped in the aisle.

- Get up, walk around, and stretch every 60 to 90 minutes to keep your blood flowing.
- Drink water before, during, and after your flight to combat the lack of humidity in airplane cabins. Avoid alcohol, which will dehydrate you.
- If you're flying with kids, don't forget to carry on toys, books, pacifiers, and chewing gum to help them relieve ear pressure buildup during ascent and descent.

11 Packages for the Independent Traveler

Package tours are simply a way to buy the airfare, accommodations, and other elements of your trip (such as car rentals, airport transfers, and sometimes even activities) at the same time and often at discounted prices.

One good source of package deals is the airlines themselves. Most major airlines offer air/land packages, including **American Airlines Vacations** (✆ 800/321-2121; www.aavacations.com), **Delta Vacations** (✆ 800/221-6666; www.deltavacations.com), **Continental Airlines Vacations** (✆ 800/301-3800; www.covacations.com), and **United Vacations** (✆ 888/854-3899; www.unitedvacations.com). Several big **online travel agencies**—Expedia, Travelocity, Orbitz, Site59, and Lastminute.com—also do a brisk business in packages.

Travel packages are also listed in the travel section of your local Sunday newspaper. Or check ads in the national travel magazines such as *Arthur Frommer's Budget Travel Magazine*, *Travel + Leisure*, *National Geographic Traveler*, and *Condé Nast Traveler*.

12 Escorted General-Interest Tours

Escorted tours are structured group tours, with a group leader. The price usually includes everything from airfare to hotels, meals, tours, admission costs, and local transportation.

Despite the fact that escorted tours require big deposits and predetermine hotels, restaurants, and itineraries, many people derive security and peace of mind from the structure they offer. Escorted tours—whether they're navigated by bus, motorcoach, train, or boat—let travelers sit back and enjoy the trip without having to drive or worry about details. They take you to the maximum number of sights in the minimum amount of time with the least amount of hassle. They're particularly convenient for people with limited mobility and they can be a great way to make new friends.

On the downside, you'll have little opportunity for serendipitous interactions with locals. The tours can be jam-packed with activities, leaving little room for individual sightseeing, whim, or adventure—plus they often focus on the heavily touristed sites, so you miss out on many a lesser-known gem.

- **Abercrombie & Kent Private Journeys** (✆ 800/554-7016; www.abercrombiekent.com) is U.S.-based and internationally recognized as a luxury travel company. A&K started as an African safari specialist in 1962 and now offers escorted and independent trips to more than 100 countries, including Russia and central and Eastern European nations.

- **Vega International Travel Service** (© 800/FLY-THERE; www.vega travel.net) specializes in travel to Eastern Europe for individuals and corporations. Vega also arranges pilgrimage tours to such popular Catholic

shrines as Međugorje in Bosnia and Czestochowa in Poland.

You can also get recommendations for reputable tour operators with expertise in the area you want to visit from the **American Society of Travel Agents** (© 859/226-4444; www.ntaonline.com).

13 Special-Interest Trips

Here are a couple of companies offering activity-specific opportunities in Eastern Europe.

- **Globus** (© 866/755-8581; www.globus.com) offers vacations to Eastern Europe in a variety of styles. Choose family-oriented, religious, culinary, or vacation styles of your choosing from this 75-year-old company.
- **Smithsonian Journeys** (© 877/338-8687; www.smithsonianjourneys.org) puts together meticulously researched educational trips designed to maximize the time you spend in the places that command the most interest. Itineraries include "behind the scenes"

visits that enhance the cultural and educational experience. Tour leaders are often internationally recognized experts in their fields. Smithsonian's Eastern European destinations include Slovenia, Prague, Budapest, Moscow, and St. Petersburg.

- **The Coordinating Committee for International Voluntary Service** (www.unesco.org/cciv5) is a good place to look for opportunities to immerse yourself in an Eastern European culture and help the people there at the same time. CCIVS helps match aspiring volunteers with organizations that need their help in a country of interest.

Tips **Ask Before You Go**

Before you invest in a package deal or an escorted tour:

- Always ask about the **cancellation policy.** Can you get your money back? Is there a deposit required?
- Ask about the **accommodations choices and prices** for each. Then look up the hotels' reviews in a Frommer's guide and check their rates online for your specific dates of travel. Also find out what types of rooms are offered.
- Request a complete **schedule** (escorted tours only).
- Ask about the **size** and demographics of the group (escorted tours only).
- Discuss what is included in the **price** (transportation, meals, tips, airport transfers, and so on) (escorted tours only).
- Finally, look for **hidden expenses.** Ask whether airport departure fees and taxes, for example, are included in the total cost—they rarely are.

Discovery on Foot

Classic Journeys (℡ 800/200-3887; www.ClassicJourneys.com) is a specialty tour operator that offers unique, upscale escorted vacations to a variety of locations around the world. Their two Eastern Europe excursions run through Croatia's Dalmatian Coast and the area from Prague to Budapest. Airfare from your home country is on your own. The package price is for the in-country experience, though Classic Journeys will help with flight details and extra hotel nights if you ask. The basic fee covers a local guide, first-class hotels, most meals, and all tips, admission fees, tours, and transfers. Tours average 10 people per adventure and the itineraries emphasize culture, history, and walking. We've found that Classic Journeys carefully plans every detail to spare guests unpleasant surprises, but the plan is also flexible in case the group decides there is something they really want to see or do. Classic Journeys can arrange family-oriented experiences or culinary trips, too.

14 Getting Around Eastern Europe

Note: See the "Getting Around" sections of the individual country chapters for more detailed information.

BY CAR

Public transportation in Eastern Europe is generally excellent and a good way to cover a lot of territory inexpensively. However, access to a car is a must if you want to see remote attractions or if you don't have time to wait for train or bus connections. If you plan to rent a car, do it before you leave home. Rates are lower and you are likely to get a better choice of cars. Look for a weekly rate with unlimited mileage. Expect to pay from $50 per day for an economy car with unlimited mileage. Gas, parking, and insurance are necessary.

Note: Be sure you examine and document any scratches, broken equipment, or interior stains when taking possession of your car. You could be charged for the damage when you return the car if you haven't pointed it out ahead of time and noted it on your contract.

BY TRAIN

Train travel in Eastern Europe is comfy, pleasant, and fairly efficient. Almost all major population centers (with the exception of Dubrovnik, Croatia) are linked by rail service. Overnight trains serve a double purpose: They get you to your destination and save the cost of a night in a hotel. If you use this option be sure to ask if you have to make a separate reservation for the bed in addition to the reservation for your transport. The **Thomas Cook European Timetable** (www.thomascook. com) gives an inclusive listing of train schedules and tells you when you have to book in advance or pay extra for things like a pillow. In general, train travel in Eastern Europe is more expensive than bus travel and sometimes fares are comparable with airfares within the country. Not all countries in Eastern Europe honor rail passes. Hungary is the only country covered in this book that accepts Eurailpasses. However, Bulgaria, the Czech Republic, Romania, and Hungary sell single-country rail passes. *Note:* Inter-country rail travel is becoming less of a hassle in Eastern Europe as national rail lines are beginning to align their schedules to make connections and border crossings easier. However, you might run into a glitch (and a long layover) unless you do meticulous planning ahead of time. Intracountry travel is usually problem-free.

BY BUS

Bus travel is a way of life in all of Europe, including Eastern Europe. Usually international buses are equipped with luxuries such as reclining seats, air-conditioning, and even television. Buses tend to be the best for reaching smaller towns and remote sites and sometimes they are the only option for reaching mountainous villages and tiny hamlets. You rarely have to reserve a seat in advance, but you can buy a ticket in advance at a main bus station or from the driver when you board. Buses work well for travel between cities in a single country and for access to areas trains can't access. Every major city in Eastern Europe has a well-developed commuter system that involves buses, trams, and sometimes sophisticated metro systems.

15 Tips on Accommodations

Accommodations in Eastern Europe cover a spectrum as broad as the region is vast. See individual country chapters for specifics on individual accommodations categories for that country.

No matter where you travel in Eastern Europe or what kind of accommodations you plan to use, it is a good idea to make a reservation for your first night in-country well in advance of your arrival.

CAMPING

Pitching a tent is the least expensive accommodations in Eastern Europe and it is also one of the most popular. Campgrounds can range from a monastery backyard (Brač, Croatia) to an elaborate affair with bungalows, cabins, and amenities like a theater, tennis courts, and gourmet restaurants. Camping facilities are also usually away from any town center, but they often have waterfront property. Some camp facilities are set aside for naturists (read: nudists) and others are geared to people who stay for the entire summer. Reservations are accepted at most campgrounds and the better ones fill up quickly. Depending on the country and campground category, these facilities usually close in the winter months and some are open in July and August (high season) only. It's best to make arrangements ahead of your arrival.

Note: In Eastern Europe it is illegal to camp out anyplace but a recognized campground.

PRIVATE ACCOMMODATIONS

Eastern Europe's underground economy runs on the private accommodations industry. You'll find everything from a room in an elderly woman's apartment where you share her bathroom with her to a detached multilevel villa on a family estate when booking this option. It's safest to book a private stay from a local tourist agency, but you will pay a commission. If you use the agency, you will also have the option of inspecting the room and asking for another choice if you don't like it. You can also agree to rent from one of the many "entrepreneurs" who haunt ferry landings and train and bus stations to find guests for their spare rooms. This option is less expensive than an agency-booked place, but you could find that it is inconveniently located or substandard by the time you get there. Almost all private accommodations require cash payment and almost none includes breakfast or any other meals.

Note: If you are staying in a private home in Russia you'll have to pay a rental agency to register your visa with a hotel.

HOSTELS

Most hostels in Eastern Europe are part of the national Youth Hostel Association (YHA), an arm of Hostelling International (HI) (www.iyhf.org), but you don't have to be young to use them. Hostels provide a bed in a dorm-type room, the use of a communal bathroom, and sometimes the use of kitchen facilities. Hostels vary widely in quality and amenities and some even accept reservations.

HOTELS

Eastern Europe rates its hotels via the star method, though there is little consistency within the method or within any given country. A three-star hotel in Slovenia is likely to be much more luxurious and comfortable than a three-star hotel in Bulgaria, for example. Ratings sometimes are ambiguous between cities in the same country, too. However, a few generalizations are possible. Hotels in Eastern Europe almost always include breakfast in the price; single rooms can cost as much as a double because guests are charged by the room, not the number of people and some hotels do not book "singles"); many hotels require multiday bookings and refuse single-night reservations, especially during high season; and many hotels require that you book an all-inclusive room rate and that you take your meals there.

AGRITOURISM

Farmhouse stays are a growing trend in Eastern Europe. In reality these are just a rural version of private accommodations. Usually you'll be staying on a working farm and staying in rooms that mirror the resident family's rooms. Often you can help feed the animals, take a walk in the fields, and enjoy a huge farmer's breakfast made from the earth's bounty. That sometimes means getting up with the chickens, too.

Note: If you stay on a farm in Eastern Europe, you have to identify yourself to Customs when you return to the U.S. to avoid transport of dangerous bacteria.

For apartment, farmhouse, or cottage stays of 2 weeks or more, **Idyll Untours** (© **888/868-6871**; www.untours.com) provides exceptional vacation rentals for a reasonable price—which includes air/ground transportation, cooking facilities, and on-call support from a local resident. Best of all: Untours—named the "Most Generous Company in America" by Newman's Own—donates most profits to provide low-interest loans to underprivileged entrepreneurs around the world (see website for details).

SAVING ON YOUR HOTEL ROOM

The **rack rate** is the maximum rate that a hotel charges for a room. Hardly anybody pays this price, however, except in high season or on holidays. To lower the cost of your room:

- **Ask about special rates or other discounts.** You may qualify for corporate, student, military, senior, frequent flyer, trade union, or other discounts.
- **Dial direct.** When booking a room in a chain hotel, you'll often get a better deal by calling the individual hotel's reservation desk rather than the chain's main number.
- **Book online.** Many hotels offer Internet-only discounts, or supply rooms to Priceline, Hotwire, or Expedia at rates much lower than the ones you can get through the hotel itself.
- **Remember the law of supply and demand.** Resort hotels are most crowded and therefore most expensive on weekends, so discounts are usually available for midweek stays. Business hotels in downtown locations are busiest during the week, so you can expect big discounts over the weekend. Many hotels have high-season and low-season prices, and

booking even 1 day after high season ends can mean big discounts.

- **Look into group or long-stay discounts.** If you come as part of a large group, you should be able to negotiate a bargain rate. Likewise, if you're planning a long stay (at least 5 days), you might qualify for a discount. As a general rule, expect 1 night free after a 7-night stay.

- **Avoid excess charges and hidden costs.** When you book a room, ask whether the hotel charges for parking. Use your own cellphone, pay phones, or prepaid phone cards instead of dialing direct from hotel phones, which usually have exorbitant rates. And don't be tempted by the room's minibar offerings. Finally, ask about local taxes and service charges, which can increase the cost of a room by 15% or more.

- Consider the pros and cons of **all-inclusive** resorts and hotels. The term "all-inclusive" means different things at different hotels. Many all-inclusive hotels will include three meals daily, sports equipment, spa entry, and other amenities; others may include all or most drinks. In general, you'll save money going the "all-inclusive" way—as long as you use the facilities provided. The downside is that your choices are limited and you're stuck eating and playing in one place for the duration of your vacation.

- Carefully consider your hotel's meal plan. If you enjoy eating out and sampling the local cuisine, it makes sense to choose a **Continental Plan (CP),** which includes breakfast only, or a **European Plan (EP),** which doesn't include any meals and allows you maximum flexibility. If you're more interested in saving money, opt for a **Modified American Plan (MAP),** which includes breakfast and one meal, or the **American Plan (AP),** which includes three meals. If you

must choose a MAP, see if you can get a free lunch at your hotel if you decide to do dinner out.

- **Book an efficiency.** A room with a kitchenette allows you to shop for groceries and cook your own meals. This is a big money saver, especially for families on long stays.

- **Consider enrolling in hotel "frequent-stay" programs,** which are upping the ante lately to win the loyalty of repeat customers. Frequent guests can now accumulate points or credits to earn free hotel nights, airline miles, in-room amenities, merchandise, tickets to concerts and events, discounts on sporting facilities—and even credit toward stock in the participating hotel, in the case of the Jameson Inn hotel group. Perks are awarded not only by many chain hotels and motels (Hilton HHonors, Marriott Rewards, Wyndham ByRequest, to name a few), but individual inns and B&Bs. Many chain hotels partner with other hotel chains, car-rental firms, airlines, and credit card companies to give consumers additional incentive to do repeat business.

LANDING THE BEST ROOM

Somebody has to get the best room in the house. It might as well be you. You can start by joining the hotel's frequent-guest program, which may make you eligible for upgrades. A hotel-branded credit card usually gives its owner "silver" or "gold" status in frequent-guest programs for free. Always ask about a corner room. They're often larger and quieter, with more windows and light, and they often cost the same as standard rooms. When you make your reservation, ask if the hotel is renovating; if it is, request a room away from the construction. Ask about nonsmoking rooms, rooms with views, rooms with twin, queen-, or king-size beds. If you're a light sleeper, request a quiet room away from vending machines, elevators, restaurants,

> **Tips Dial E for Easy**
>
> For quick directions on how to call Eastern Europe, see the "Telephone" listing in the "Fast Facts" section of each country chapter.

bars, and discos. Ask for a room that has been most recently renovated or redecorated.

If you aren't happy with your room when you arrive, ask for another one. Most lodgings will be willing to accommodate you.

In resort areas, particularly in seaside locations in Croatia, Slovenia, and along the Black Sea coast, ask the following questions before you book a room:

- What's the view like? Cost-conscious travelers may be willing to pay less for a back room facing the parking lot, especially if they don't plan to spend much time in their room.

- Does the room have air-conditioning or ceiling fans? Do the windows open? If they do, and the nighttime entertainment takes place alfresco, you may want to find out when showtime is over.

- What's included in the price? Your room may be moderately priced, but if you're charged for beach chairs, towels, sports equipment, and other amenities, you could end up spending more than you bargained for.

- How far is the room from the beach and other amenities? If it's far, is there transportation to and from the beach, and is it free?

16 Tips on Dining

Eastern European food is often maligned by Westerners who imagine that they will be dining exclusively on bread, potatoes, meat, and cabbage during a stay in Eastern Europe. Yes, the food in this region can be heavy, especially in places like Russia and Romania where the temperature can fall to arctic levels and stay there for a long time. But Eastern European food can be surprisingly light and sophisticated, like the delicate truffle dishes in Istria (Croatia) and other regional specialties.

When looking for a restaurant, avoid places that display menus translated into seven languages. These are bound to offer diluted versions of wonderful regional foods or awful interpretations of "foreign" dishes. Instead, look for small mom-and-pop

places filled with locals having a good time. Alternatively, you can make quite a good meal from local bakeries and markets where everything from caviar to laundry detergent is sold.

Dining is relatively inexpensive wherever you go in Eastern Europe. You'll find wonderful fish, Italian-style fare, and local wine in Slovenia and Croatia's coastal cities, spicy goulash stews in Hungary, and excellent beer in Poland and the Czech Republic. If you're lucky, you'll also be able to sample a few homemade liqueurs, usually potent brews made from plums, cherries, or other fruits.

One thing is for sure: You won't go hungry in this land where eating is a social event, a sport, and a way to celebrate life.

17 Recommended Books, Films & Music

For an interesting perspective on how Eastern Europe has changed since the Berlin Wall came down, try *The Burdens*

of Freedom: Eastern Europe since 1989 by Padraic Kenney (Fernwood Publishing, 2006). This is part contemporary politics,

Tips for Digital Travel Photography

- **Take along a spare camera—or two.** Even if you've been anointed the "official" photographer of your travel group, encourage others in your party to carry their own cameras and provide fresh perspectives—and backup. Your photographic "second unit" may include you in a few shots so you're not the invisible person of the trip.

- **Stock up on digital film cards.** At home, it's easy to copy pictures from your memory cards to your computer as they fill up. During your travels, cards seem to fill up more quickly. Take along enough digital memory for your entire trip or, at a minimum, enough for at least a few days' of shooting. At intervals, you can copy images to CDs. Many camera stores and souvenir shops offer this service, and a growing number of mass merchandisers have walk-up kiosks you can use to make prints or create CDs while you travel.

- **Share and share alike.** No need to wait until you get home to share your photos. You can upload a gallery's worth to an online photo-sharing service. Just find an Internet cafe where the computers have card readers, or connect your camera to the computer with a cable. You can find online photo sharing services that cost little or nothing at www.clickherefree. com. You can also use America Online's Your Pictures service, or commercial enterprises that give you free or low-cost photo sharing: Kodak's EasyShare gallery (www.kodak.com), Yahoo! Photos (www.photos.yahoo. com), Snapfish (www.snapfish.com), or Shutterfly (www.shutterfly.com).

- **Add voice annotations to your photos.** Many digital cameras allow you to add voice annotations to your shots after they're taken. These serve as excellent reminders and documentation. One castle or cathedral may look like another after a long tour; your voice notes will help you distinguish them.

- **Experiment!** Travel is a great time to try out new techniques. Take photos at night, resting your camera on a handy wall or other support as your self-timer trips the shutter for a long exposure. Try close-ups of flowers, crafts, wildlife, or maybe the exotic cuisine you're about to consume. Discover action photography—shoot the countryside from trains, buses, or cars. With a digital camera, you can experiment and then erase your mistakes.

—*From* Travel Photography Digital Field Guide, 1st edition
(John Wiley & Sons, 2006)

part history, and a lot of insight into the growing pains the region is experiencing. *The Europeanization of Central and Eastern Europe,* edited by Frank Schimmelfennig and Ulrich Sedelmeier (Cornell University Press, 2005), is another book along those lines. The authors discuss the impact of European Union reforms, new laws, and regional social policy on Eastern European culture and traditions. Rebecca West's *Black Lamb and Grey Falcon: A Journey Through Yugoslavia* (Penguin Books, 1994) is considered a seminal work about the region that was the former Yugoslavia. West, who was a journalist, novelist, and critic, began her research in the Balkans with the idea of writing a travel book, but the result turned out to be a significant explanation that illuminates the tangled history of the former Yugoslavia. To gain historical perspective, try *The Balkans Since 1453* by Northwestern University Professor L. S. Stavrianos (Holt, Rinehart and Winston, 1966). It's a bit ponderous but full of little-known facts. *Why Angels Fall: A Journey Through Orthodox Europe from Byzantium to Kosovo,* by Victoria Clark (Macmillan Press, 2000), offers a look at Eastern Europe from a different perspective: Clark interprets the region's recent turmoil in terms of past religious conflicts between Roman Catholic and Eastern Orthodox Christians.

Finally, *Croatia: Travels in Undiscovered Country,* by Tony Fabijančić (University of Alberta Press, 2003), is as entertaining as it is informative. Fabijančić, whose father was born in Croatia, undertakes an epic journey across his father's homeland—on foot. His conversations with people along the way reveal the mindset of a culture and hint at its future direction.

4

Bulgaria

By Pippa de Bruyn

Founded in 681, Bulgaria is the oldest state in Europe, but its roots reach far deeper into history. In the Valley of Kings, in tombs adorned with frescoes and bass reliefs, archaeologists continue to discover mankind's most ancient gold treasures—the beautifully worked objects buried with Bulgaria's Thracian forebears, some dating as far back as 3000 B.C. Uncovering the countless burial mounds dotted throughout Bulgaria's central "belly"—a process only started in earnest less than a decade ago—has revealed that this was home to the world's most sophisticated goldsmiths, and prompted local claims that it was here, in the shadow of the Balkan Mountains, that Europe's first civilization was birthed.

Traversing Bulgaria's mountain ranges—carpeted with ancient forests and carved by mineral-rich rivers—you can see why these sophisticated warrior-artists chose to settle in its fertile plains. It's a magnificent country, rich in natural resources, with a climate that is more southern European than eastern. It is this temperate climate—along with a sweeping coastline of sandy soft beaches, lapped by a gentle, warm Black Sea—that continues to attract new visitors, the vast majority of whom arrive in high summer. Thank heavens. For Bulgaria's treasures lie elsewhere, hidden in the ancient tombs of the Valley of Kings, in the mixture of Bulgarian Renaissance architecture and ancient Roman ruins that line the cobbled streets of Plovdiv, in the views of Bulgaria's medieval capital, the university town Veliko Tarnovo, that rises

precipitously from limestone cliffs that guide the winding Yantra River below, and in the architectural museum towns that lie scattered throughout Bulgaria's mountains. It is particularly the latter, their narrow cobbled lanes and alleys lined with 19th-century stone-and-timber homes, that define Bulgaria as one of the most exciting destinations on the Continent. It's not just exploring the villages themselves, with picture-perfect opportunities around every corner, but getting to them—snaking your way along empty roads, through high embankments laden with red poppies and blowsy white elder flowers; past women in patterned headscarves tilling fields by hand, and toothless old men pulling hillocks of hay so huge you can't see their cart wheels. It's Bulgaria, Eastern Europe even, at its unspoiled best, relatively undiscovered and offering a combination of natural beauty and ancient history, comfortable accommodations, and wonderful fresh cuisine, in surroundings that show little sign of the so-called advances of the 21st century. It's no surprise then that tourism here is on the increase, albeit it slowly, with (at last count) almost 6.5 million visitors now including this rough Balkan jewel in their Eastern European itinerary. With a lack of tourism infrastructure, shocking service levels, and a foreign alphabet, Bulgaria may not be the easiest destination to master, but—armed with this chapter—it will provide you with some of the most authentic experiences that Eastern Europe has to offer.

Bulgaria

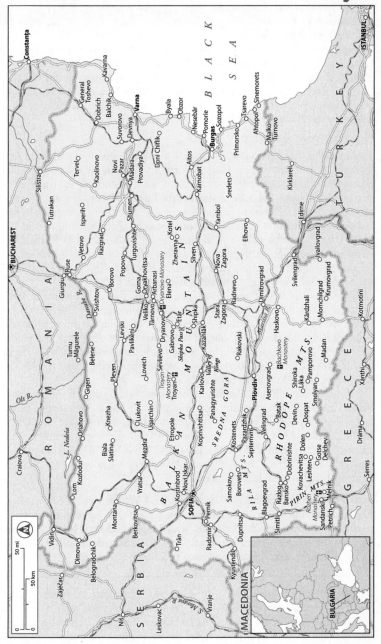

1 Getting to Know Bulgaria

THE LAY OF THE LAND

Situated on the eastern part of the Balkan Peninsula, Bulgaria is sandwiched between Greece and Turkey to the south and the Danube River that denotes most of its border with Romania to the north. West lies Macedonia and Serbia; east the Black Sea. Over half the country is mountainous, with the Sredna Gora and Balkan range slicing the country in half, and the south-central plains (known as the Valley of Kings) flanked by the Pirin, Rila, and Rhodope mountain ranges.

THE REGIONS IN BRIEF

To the west lies the capital **Sofia,** with some 1.2 million citizens, by far the most populous area in the country. But within 90 minutes you are in the southern mountain ranges where the country really starts to strut its stuff. Dominating the region are the eternally snowcapped and majestic peaks of the **Rila** and **Pirin**—stopping just short of 3,000m (9,840 ft.), these mountains are home to the country's most popular hikes and skiing opportunities as well as the hottest mineral spring in Europe—a scalding 216°F (102°C) (though sadly, none of these are well used). East of the Rila and Pirin lie the **Rhodope** range—with riverine gorges and valleys covered in virgin forest, dotted throughout with mountain villages. Touring this region by car is a must for any traveler serious about seeing the best Bulgaria has to offer.

Running east of Sofia, through central Bulgaria, are the gently undulating Sredna Gora and Balkan mountain ranges, creating the Danubian plains of the north (which has no real attractions), while their southern slopes drop into the evocative-sounding **Valley of Kings** (also known as Valley of Roses, after the rose farms here that produce some of the world's best-quality attar). **Kazanluk** is the unofficial capital of the Valley, but **Plovdiv** (pop. 340,000), Bulgaria's second-biggest city, with a gorgeous historic center, makes a far better base.

A short drive north from Plovdiv, in the central Balkan range, is the tiny city of **Veliko Tarnovo,** Bulgaria's medieval capital, less known but as captivating as Plovdiv, and a good stopover on your way to **Varna,** third-biggest city (pop. 300,000, but swelling considerably during summer). This marks the beginning of a highly commercialized concrete ribbon of resorts that line the 380km (236-mile) Black Sea coastline, broken by the UNESCO-listed village of **Nessebar,** with its numerous Byzantine-influenced churches and laid-back **Sozopol.**

SUGGESTED ITINERARY: BULGARIA IN 1 WEEK

The following tour covers the best of Bulgaria, but at a cracking pace. If you want to relax along the way, extend it by 3 days, with 2 nights in Sofia, Plovdiv, and Veliko Tarnovo. If you're really pushed for time, 4 days will have to do; if so, opt for a night in Sofia, Kovachevitsa, Plovdiv, and Veliko Tarnovo.

Day ❶: Arrive in Sofia

Spend the afternoon acclimatizing—have an espresso in one of the open-air bars near the City Garden, and book a table for dinner at Beyond the Alley. If you've got the energy, tackle the walking tour (or at the very least, visit the Russian churches), then spend a few hours in the History Museum (remember that it's closed on Mon). Get back to bed early so you're ready to rise at dawn.

Day ❷: Melnik 🐾🐾

Have your driver pick you up from your hotel at 5:30am (an hour later in winter) to catch the early morning service at Rila Monastery—the best way to experience this UNESCO-listed site, with no tourists to detract from its spirituality. Snack on doughnuts and yogurt from the monk-run bakery outside the gates or take an early lunch at Drushliavitsa (above the monastery), then head south to the tiny winegrowing village of Melnik. Visit Kordopulov's house, sample wine with "six fingers," and dine at Mencheva Kashta. See p. 90.

Day ❸: Leshten/Kovachevitsa 🐾🐾🐾

Visit Rozhen Monastery, then—conditions allowing—head to Leshten via the mountain road that leads to Gotse Delchev, or travel via Bansko. Stop for lunch in Leshten. Stay in one of the Leshten cottages, or head deeper into the mountains to overnight at Kovachevitsa (note that it's worth exploring this heritage village, about a 20-min. drive from Leshten, even if you're not spending the night here). See p. 99.

Day ❹: Plovdiv 🐾🐾🐾

Travel to Plovdiv, stopping to explore the village of Dolen and Bachkovo Monastery along the way. Take a late lunch at Vodopada or push on to Plovdiv. That evening, stroll the cobbled streets of Old Plovdiv. Dine and stay at Hebros.

Day ❺: Veliko Tarnovo 🐾🐾

Set off early for the Kazanluk tomb (make prior arrangements to view the original), then head over the Shipka pass to visit the Icon and Woodcarving museums in Tryavna. Time allowing, visit Etura, the open-air ethnographic museum nearby. Spend the night at Veliko Tarnovo or Dryanovo Monastery.

Day ❻: Varna 🐾

Travel to Varna (about 4 hr. away), via the Madara Horseman. Varna is a party city, so once you've checked out the Thracian treasures in the Archaeological Museum, blow off some steam at one of the many clubs and bars that line the beachfront.

Day ❼: Koprivishtitsa 🐾🐾🐾/Sofia

If you're up for a drive, take the coastal road south (just under 3 hr.) to lunch at a sea-facing restaurant in the fishing port of Sozopol, then head west to overnight at Koprivishtitsa (about 4 hr. from here), one of the country's prettiest heritage villages. Enjoy your last Bulgarian meal "Under the Pear Tree." Ask your driver to drop you off at the airport the following day, allowing around 90 minutes' traveling time, plus check-in time. Alternatively, spend your last night in Sofia and do some last-minute shopping before your flight the next morning.

BULGARIA TODAY

On May 16, 2006, E.U. Enlargement Commissioner Olli Rehn criticized the country's laggard performance on key criteria for joining the E.U. At that stage little progress had been made in the privatization of the national and regional monopolies in the transport and energy sectors, the decommissioning of four nuclear reactors at Kozlodui, agricultural legislation, and—most pressing—no progress at all on dealing with corruption and the powerful underground barons who control as much as 25% of the Bulgarian economy, and wield an equally troubling political influence. Though it's worth noting, as some Bulgarian commentators did, that the E.U. can hardly hold itself up as the purest paragon (at the time 9 out of 10 MPs in Italy were under investigation for fraud or corruption), the ultimatum was clear, and a month later Bulgaria's politicians delivered a task list that promised "zero tolerance."

But while the slap on the wrist evoked much talk, the only zero the public had seen by the end of that year was the percentage of successfully investigated crimes relating to money laundering, forgery, and human and drug trafficking. According to key industry players, some of whom refer to Bulgaria as the "Wild East," levels of corruption are higher here than in Romania, to which it is losing competitive ground due to its poor infrastructure, the shortage of skilled labor, and a dearth of tax incentives. But while Bulgaria has made none of the high-profile arrests brandished by its northern neighbor to E.U. inspectors in 2006 (though it remains to be seen if former Romanian Prime Minister Nastase will ever see a jail term), some Bulgarian commentators argue that real changes *are* taking place, and that it is happening where it matters: far-reaching judicial reforms including a much-needed fostering of judicial independence, and the removal of immunity that members of the legal profession once enjoyed.

The bleating of E.U. members aside (and that includes the U.K., which—having just "welcomed" 500,000 Poles—fears the onslaught of thousands of new immigrants from Bulgaria and Romania), Bulgaria has a strong, stable market economy and, with economic growth around 6%, is the envy of many in the West. It's true that the sluggish coalition government (see "A Look at the Past," below) struggles to respond to private-sector needs, or remove the vestiges of Communist rule, but investment, construction, tourism, property, and banking are all sectors showing strong growth. For now, labor is also relatively cheap, attracting attention as an outsourcing hub for both American and western European companies, though this is likely to take a blow when the youth, said to be of the best educated in Eastern Europe, leave for more lucrative pastures.

On January 1, 2007, Bulgaria joined the E.U., and the World Bank deposited the first $300 million into the country's coffers; whether the resultant industrialization and standardization of key aspects such as agriculture, not to mention the shrinking of an already inadequately sized labor force, will serve Bulgaria as well as is hoped remains to be seen. But the key challenge remains how best to achieve structural reforms that will have a lasting effect, not only on corruption, but productivity and accountability, so that ordinary Bulgarians—too many of whom still live beneath the breadline—can experience the kind of living standards long enjoyed by their wealthier cousins to the west.

A LOOK AT THE PAST

Fragments and tools uncovered near the coast (on view in Varna's fascinating Archaeological Museum) date human habitation here back some 10,000 years, but these pale in significance when viewing Bulgaria's most exhilarating archaeological finds: the Thracian treasures, known as "the oldest gold in the world," proving that a highly sophisticated civilization flourished here from 3000 B.C. to 200 B.C.

What little we know of the Thracian tribes was recorded by the Greeks, who described them as "savage, bloodthirsty warriors," and appropriated a few of the Thracian gods, including Dionysus and Orpheus, for themselves. Weakened by infighting, Thracian numbers were reduced and finally absorbed by the Romans, who arrived in droves in the 1st century, only to be turned out during the 5th century by the Bulgars. In 681 Khan Asparoukh claimed the First Bulgarian Kingdom, a region comprising latter-day Serbia, Macedonia, and parts of northern Greece. But Bulgaria remained a cultural backwater until 855, when the Cyril and Methodius brothers created the Glagolic alphabet (later simplified into Cyrillic) primarily to translate the Bible into their indigenous tongue, but thereby creating an independent literary tradition for Slavic communities as far afield as Russia.

In 1018 Bulgaria fell to the Byzantines, who ruled for almost 170 years before the Bulgarians wrested it back. This launched the second Bulgarian Kingdom in new capital Veliko Tarnovo, from where they ruled the Balkans from the Adriatic to the Aegean. Jealous of its strategic position, the Ottomans invaded in 1398, ushering in a 500-year tenure that came to be known as the "Yoke of Oppression," one that only lifted after the groundswell of nationalism, which spawned the flourishing 19th-century design and art that came to be known as "National Revival" or "Bulgarian Renaissance" style (the best examples found in Plovdiv and Koprivishtitsa) and led to the 1876 April Uprisings. Following its brutal squashing, Russia finally came to the rescue, helping to oust the Ottomans in 1877, an act for which the Bulgarians remained permanently in Russia's debt, erecting numerous monuments and churches, like the Alexander Nevsky in Sofia, as proof of their "special relationship."

This may explain why Bulgaria so meekly accepted the Soviet "invasion" after World War II (during which Bulgaria sided with Hitler in the mistaken hopes of finally reclaiming the territory it lost in World War I). Ostensibly an independent Communist state, Bulgaria in reality once again found itself dominated by an outside power, this time under the "yoke" of the hard-line dictator Todor Zhivkov, who ruled until 1989, when he was quietly removed from power.

Bulgaria's first free elections were held in January 1990, when the Bulgarian Socialist Party was voted into power. Predictably, the poorly managed transition to a free market economy resulted in hyperinflation (579% in 1996), and by the end of the millennia Bulgaria was at the mercy of the IMF, which introduced austere reforms. In 2001 Bulgarians, ill disposed to their fledgling democracy, and overwhelmed by the return of their czar-in-exile, voted with their hearts. Simeon Saxe-Coburg Gotha, who fled after World War II at age 9, was placed at the helm a few months after his return, but the gray, characterless czar did little to improve the fortunes of the country or the average person.

Currently Bulgaria is managed by a fragile coalition between three very disparate parties: the toothless class-based BSP; the hugely resented Movement for Rights and Freedoms, predominantly supported by ethnic Turkish minorities of the south; and the nationalist Movement Simeon II, still headed by the ex-prince who currently stands in the shadow of his Italian cousin's corruption trial for drug and human trafficking. Established to meet the conditions for E.U. accession, the coalition looks unlikely to survive beyond 2007; even if it does, Bulgaria will still lack strong, selfless leadership: the fact that Sofia's current mayor "hardman" Boiko Borissov—Todor Zhivkov's former security chief—enjoys enough popularity for the local press to speculate on his presidential ambitions, does not bode well. The ideal of an accountable, transparent leader with no tentacles into the shadowy past is clearly not one held by all. And without economic prowess, real freedom remains elusive.

BULGARIAN PEOPLE & CULTURE

Gird your loins: Bulgarians can be both insufferably rude and unbelievably charming. According to World Value Surveys (WVS), the Bulgarian culture is "collectivist," meaning that good service and quality goods are traditionally reserved for "in-group" members, and that nepotism may be seen as a value, while individual pride, competitiveness, and initiative may be suppressed. These findings play out in the service industry; you may be shocked by the brusque or downright hostile treatment you'll receive in certain shops, hotels, or restaurants. Ironically, people you meet outside the

When Yes Means No, & No Means Yes

It's worth noting that traditionally Bulgarians shake their heads from side to side when saying yes ("da"), and nod when saying no ("ne"). This quirky characteristic is less apparent among the cool city MTV generation, but definitely worth knowing when asking, or answering, a question.

service industry are often far friendlier. Things improve hugely in the countryside, where curiosity and warmth are the order of the day, and simple requests may not be understood but are met with a wreath of smiles and an invitation to sample a glass of home-brewed rakia. According to the WVS, Bulgarians, like most East Europeans, are also fatalists, which goes some way to understanding their passive attitude to the endemic corruption and political cul-de-sac they seem to find themselves in.

Despite 4 decades of atheist-propagating Communism, 86.6% of Bulgarians are members of the Bulgarian Orthodox Church. There is also a significant minority of Muslims living in the south, including the so-called Pomaks in the Rhodope—Bulgarians forced under the Ottoman rule in the 16th century to convert to the Islamic faith. The tiny minority Gypsies (or Roma, descendants of Indian refugees) are still seriously discriminated against. While sections of the traditional rural society seems unchanged by the advent of the 21st century (at the end of 2005 only 27% of the population had a bank account; over 60% had ever had dealings with a bank), thanks to the ubiquitous TV, Western influences are now exerting pressure, and you'd be hard-pressed to find a bottle of rakia in the hip bars of central Sofia. And while the tradition of the extended family living under one roof is still common, patterns are changing, and young Bulgarians opt to remain childless or migrate west to more lucrative jobs. Most say they have every intention of returning. And despite the problems Bulgaria faces, it's not hard to see why.

BULGARIAN CUISINE

If you're expecting stodgy East European stews, think again: While the pretentious may brand it essentially as "peasant" cuisine, Bulgarian food is the best-kept secret this side of the Balkans, with an emphasis on fresh seasonal produce, and healthy, unfussy preparation methods. Influenced by the 500-year Turkish occupation and its proximity to Greece, it features plenty of spices (many of which are endemic to Bulgaria), and predominantly chicken, pork, and veal, often baked with cheese or yogurt, and piles of fresh and flavorsome vegetables. Perhaps the answer to why Bulgarian fare is so delicious (and hard to export) lies in the quality of the Bulgarian soil, which some say is imbued with a special bio-energy (certainly its herbs are considered of the highest quality in Europe), a result no doubt of its numerous mineral-rich rivers and streams.

Bulgarians almost always start their meal with a fresh simple salad, accompanied by a shot (or two) of rakia, the local grape- or plum-based liquor. Meat—chicken or pork, usually chargrilled over coals or baked in an earthenware pot with vegetables—follows, with a side order of potatoes or bread. Chubritsa—a unique Bulgarian spice—is usually on the table to spice up a meal should you deem it too bland.

Besides the wonderful quality of the cuisine there is the price: you need not pay more than 3€–5€ ($4–$7) for a meal; about as much for a good quality red wine to accompany it; wine lovers will do well to order wine made with Mavrud or Melnik, both grape varieties unique to Bulgaria (white wines fare less well).

LANGUAGE

The biggest challenge for new visitors is that you're not just dealing with a new language but a new alphabet—when trying to find your way around the cities make sure you have a good map. If you're a thin-skinned traveler, you'll want to seek advice or directions from the youngest, hippest person on the street; older citizens tend to speak no English and asking if they do usually affronts. You will find yourself a little more lost outside of the main centers where English speakers are rare. However, this is more than made up with sincere friendliness, and rural folk will usually make a real effort to assist in any way they can. Speaking even just a few phrases can thaw a strained atmosphere or—outside the city—have you seated and trying out a bowl of homemade cabbage soup with your delighted host. Here are a few phrases to help you on your way. (Words, when written with Latin alphabet, are done so phonetically to aid pronunciation, but make for variations in spelling, even in place names (for example, Triavna = Tryavna).

USEFUL WORDS & PHRASES

Bulgarian	English	Pronunciation
Molya	**Please**	*Mall*-ya
Blagodarya	**Thank you**	*Blago*-darya
Mersi	**Thanks (informal)**	*Mer*-see
Dobur-den	**Good day**	*Do*-bar-den
Zdravei!	**Hi! (informal)**	*Zdra*-vay!
Kak si?	**How are you?**	*Kuck*-see?
Az sum dobre	**I am fine**	Az sum-*Dob*-reh
Dobre	**Okay**	*Dob*-reh
Kude . . . ?	**Where is . . . ?**	*Ku*-deh
Kolko struve?	**How much?**	*Kol*-koh *struh*-vah
Prodavate li . . . ?	**Do you sell . . . ?**	*Prodava*-te li

Mozhe li . . . ?/
    Imate li . . . ?
	Can I have . . . /
	    Do you have . . . ?
		Moh-zhe li/*Ima*-teh li

As obicham . . .	**I like/love . . .**	As *obi*-cham
Proshtavaite	**Sorry**	*Proshta*-va-ee-teh
Az iskam . . .	**I want . . .**	Az *is*-kam
Bankata/Bankomata	**Bank/ATM**	*Bunk*-ata/*Banko*-ma-tah
Menu/Smetkata	**Menu/The Bill**	*Men*-u/*Smet*-katah
Café	**Coffee**	*Cah*-feh
Mlyako	**Milk**	*Mlya*-ko
Voda (led)	**Water (ice)**	Vo-*da* (*led*)
Vino(cherveno/byalo)	**Wine (red/white)**	*Vie*-noh(*cherve*-no/*bya*-loh)
Bira	**Beer**	*Bee*-ra
Garnitura	**Side orders**	*Garnee*-too-rah
Hlyab	**Bread**	*Hlya*-b
Apteka	**Pharmacy**	Ap-*tech*-ah
Lekar/Zubolekar	**Doctor/dentist**	*Le*-kar/Za-bo-*le*-kar
Bolen sum	**I am ill**	*Bo*-len *sum*

2 Planning Your Trip to Bulgaria

VISITOR INFO

With limited funds and a (somewhat understandable) suspicion of any centralized bureau, a state-funded tourism body for Bulgaria does not at present exist, nor a tourism-oriented ethos. There are however a number of websites professing to be independent travel advisors; of these www.discover-bulgaria.com is the best for general information. Sofia-based **Zig Zag** (p. 72) is an excellent independent advice bureau and offers a range of services. If you're particularly interested in monasteries, Alder Travel specializes in tours to these (www.alder-travel.com or www.bulgarianmonasteries. com); other recommended tour operators offering general information on their websites are www.study-tours.org, www.andantetravels.co, and www.boroinvest.com. For up-to-date background on the political and economic scene, check out www.sofiaecho. com, Bulgaria's English-language weekly newspaper, staffed by a group of young enthusiastic expats and opinionated Bulgarians. Once there you will struggle to get useful information from "official" bureaus—assuming there is one, and it is open (most offices are understaffed and don't stick to advertised hours). Your best source of information lies with upmarket hotels and, of course, this chapter.

ENTRY REQUIREMENTS

Citizens of the U.S., Canada, Australia, New Zealand, and the U.K. may visit visa-free for 30 days in any 6-month period, as long as your passport is valid for 3 months beyond your stay. Travelers can import an unlimited amount of cash, but if it exceeds 4,000€ the sum must be declared, as you may not export more than imported. The quotas for duty-free import and export of goods for noncommercial use are generally the same as in E.U. countries; note that valuable antiques, artworks, or coins need a permit issued by the Ministry of Culture.

Upon arrival visitors are supposed to register with the local police within 5 days—most hotels will do this paperwork for you, providing you with a registration slip, which you should keep with your passport for when you depart. Officially you are liable to be fined should the authorities demand to see this before you leave the country, but as a short-term visitor you are unlikely to encounter any problems, and there is talk of phasing this out.

MONEY

Regardless of what the tourist literature may tell you about credit cards being widely accepted, please note that outside of Sofia, they certainly are not. Simply put, always carry cash. The local currency is known as the lev or leva (BGN). One lev is made up of 100 stotinki (in denominations of 10, 20, and 50). As the national currency is currently

---

Tour Guides on Call

With English-speaking guides and useful leaflets rather thin on the ground, there is a welcome new initiative launched by local cellphone operator Globul last year. Look out for large brown signboards at popular sites headed with "Call and Learn More About . . . "; dial the number and a recorded voice provides you with background information about the site. Cost of call is 1.20lev ($1.50/40p), 30% of which goes toward upkeep of the site viewed; information lasts about 3 minutes.

Major Festivals in Bulgaria

The Bulgarian calendar features numerous festivals throughout the year, particularly in the rural areas, but the following are worth making a note of: The **Kukeri Festival** is visually arresting: villagers don terrifying outfits to ward of the demons that stalk the earth. It is celebrated in the southwest on **New Year's Eve, January 1** or **14** (and sometimes in Mar; see box "Scary Monsters: Freddy Eat Your Heart Out" on p. 88). **Velikden** (Easter) is the most important holiday in the Orthodox Church, and services with huge attendances are deeply moving—the main service takes place on Saturday night when priests emerge from behind the iconostasis with blazing candelabra and the congregation follows as they perambulate the church three times in celebration of the resurrection. The hugely popular but overrated **Festival of Roses** is celebrated in **early June** in the town of Kazanlak. The **Sofia Music Weeks** usually take place **late May** to **early June** and are a must for classical music lovers, as is the symphonic musical festival held in Plovdiv in **mid-June**. Jazz is added to the line up for the **Varna Summer Festival (mid-June to mid-Aug)** and Sozopol's **Appollonia Festival (early Sept)**.

---

tied to the euro at a fixed rate of almost 2lev = 1€, euros are almost universally accepted; the dollar, being a less stable rate, is less popular (conversions here are worked at a 1€ = $1.27 rate). Banks are the best place to exchange other currency, or draw money on your cards (exchange bureaus charges are usually higher). There are plenty of functioning ATMs in cities and medium-size towns. As credit cards are usually not accepted outside of the big cities (and even where they are, its worth knowing that MasterCard and Visa are more widely so), it is probably ideal to carry a combination of euro traveler's checks and card(s) to make periodic ATM transactions—look out for the latest FNB machines, as these now allow a 400lev ($254/£88) withdrawal in one go (and three in succession). At press time, the exchange rates for 10lev roughly equaled $6.50 or £2. Many hotels list rates in euros—in those instances, we only list euro and U.S. dollar amounts at an exchange of 1€ to $1.27.

WHEN TO GO

With four clearly defined seasons, what you do depends on what time of the year you decide to visit, and—given altitude ranges from sea level to 2,000m (6,560 ft.)—exactly where in Bulgaria you're heading. The best time to visit from a scenic and cuisine point of view is June, when the markets are full of fresh produce, or during September for the fall colors. July and August tend to be hot, sometimes uncomfortably so (average is around 86°F/30°C, but it can be in excess of 104°F/40°C); this is when people traditionally flee Sofia and Plovdiv, seeking respite in the cooler mountain villages and crowded coast. It's not worth visiting in winter unless you're here for the snow; Bulgaria's skiing season runs from December to March.

HOLIDAYS

January 1 (New Year's Day), March 3 (Liberation of Bulgaria), Easter Sunday and Easter Monday, May 1 (Labor Day), May 6 (St. George's Day), May 24 (Saints Cyril and Methodius Day, aka Day of Slavonic Education and Culture), September 6 (Unification Day); September 22 (Independence Day) December 24, 25, and 26 (Christmas). Shops, museums, and banks are closed on all holidays.

GETTING THERE
BY PLANE

Bulgaria has three international airports: Sofia, Varna, and Burgas, but most visitors arrive at Sofia, currently served by 17 airlines from 47 European and Middle Eastern cities, with a brand-new airport terminal that opened in 2006. At present travelers from North America cannot fly direct into Bulgaria; the most frequent connections are usually through London or Frankfurt. *Tip:* Hurrah for the entry of low-cost carrier Wizz Air (www.wizzair.com), which now offers cheap flights from most destinations across Europe into Bulgaria, usually via Budapest. There are also usually cheap charter flights into Varna and Bourgas during the peak summer season; others fly into Plovdiv to coincide with the skiing season.

BY TRAIN

Rail travel is very time-consuming (traveling from Budapest via Serbia takes 17–24 hr.; via Romania closer to 60) and trains and infrastructure in Bulgaria are not well maintained. There is also the wearing potential of a trip ruined by thieves or hustlers. Should you still favor the romance of rail, you will at least (assuming you're a citizen of the U.S., Canada, Australia, New Zealand, or the U.K.) not need a transit visa through Serbia or Romania; for information on a Eurail Selectpass, which allows travel between three to five East European countries, check out www.eurail.net; though note that these passes seldom end up being real value for the money. Popular routes are the Trans-Balkan, which connects Budapest with Thessalonniki, stopping in Sofia (there's also a stop near Veliko Tarnovo); the Bulgaria Express which connects Sofia with Moscow; and the daily Sofia-Belgrade line. In summer you can travel from Bucharest, Budapest, Bratislava, and Prague to Varna and Burgas.

BY BUS

Buses are generally newer and cleaner than trains, and most major cities in Germany, as well as Budapest, Prague, and Vienna, have regular bus service to Sofia. However, due to distances and poor roads (and occasionally tedious and lengthy delays at border crossings), this can be a time-consuming way to get here. Most of the bus journeys from western Europe pass through Serbia; as above, no transit visa is required. For information about bus service from Sofia's relatively slick International Railway Station, call © **02/952-5004.**

BY CAR & FERRY

Visitors traveling from western Europe by car will either take a ferry from Italy to Greece, then head due north, or you will have to pass through Serbia, where you have to pay a special car insurance, or Romania where road conditions are bad, and you will ferry across the Danube from Vidin. Insurance is of course compulsory—it can either be taken out beforehand or on the Bulgarian border.

GETTING AROUND
BY CAR

This is one destination where it is worth getting off the beaten track, and this means— given that most signposts are written in Cyrillic—hiring a car and driver. If you have the time to get lost, there are numerous car-rental companies to choose from (and presently all you'll need is your national driver's license)—to get the best deal, surf around and compare the usual big-name global brands with the highly reputable www.avtorent.com (10-group cars from 14€–52€/$18–$66, including unlimited mileage and insurance), www.md-rent.com, and www.vickyrent.com. The speed limit in the country is 50 to 60kmph (31–37 mph) in populated areas, 80kmph (50 mph) on minor roads, and 120kmph (74 mph) on highways; note that you'll need to display a 5€ ($6.50) per week vignette/decal (from OMV or Shell gas stations).

To rent a car with a driver, contact **Rent-Cars-With-Driver** (✆ **888-68-4848;** http://rentacarsdriver.dir.bg) or **Surprise Tours,** a one-man company run by the amiable and charming Svetlio (✆ **088/7485174;** svelte@mail.bg). Svetlio charges 70€ ($89) per day and 8€ ($10) per 100km (62 miles) to drive you anywhere in his (non-air-conditioned) Passat; while not a qualified guide he is knowledgeable and he is at your beck and call 24 hours. Svetlio will arrange all your accommodations bookings (you can either just specify a budget limitation, or tell him exactly what you want based on the recommendations below). If you want an air-conditioned or 4x4 vehicle, this is hired for an additional fee. Day trips to Rila, Koprovishtitsa, Melnik, Plovdiv, and Veliko Tarnovo cost 80€ to 85€ ($102–$108). A tip is welcome (and usually earned), but not expected.

BY BUS

This is the best way to get around if you have decided against hiring a car, as the proliferation of private companies like ETAP and Grup (www.etapgroup.com) and Biomet (www.biomet-bg.com) has meant that buses are smart, clean, reliable, and user-friendly. This is particularly true if you are traveling and making all your bookings from Sofia. The recently renovated Central bus station (http://tis.centralnaavtogara.bg) has an information desk staffed by helpful English-speakers, and also boasts an easy-to-use, self-help computer system, providing timetables and exact prices charged. There are regular buses (almost hourly) to Plovdiv, Varna, and Veliko Tarnovo; getting to smaller towns like Bansko and Koprivshtitsa will require advance planning.

BY TRAIN

Train travel is not recommended at present: Not only is infrastructure old, leading to potential delays, but cars are often grimy and fellow passengers, usually heavy smokers, are plucked from Sartre's depiction of hell. Bus travel is by comparison well organized, relatively comfortable, and faster. That said, the national train carrier Bulgarian State Railways (BDZh) connects most towns in Bulgaria (with the exception of those located in mountainous Rhodopes and Pirin), and hosts a friendly website, so travelers use the rail system relatively easily (though note that outside of Sofia you'll still have to deal with signboards in Cyrillic, and no on-board indication that you've arrived at your destination); for timetables check http://bdz.creato.biz/en or www.bdz.bg. For information contact Sofia's Central Railway Station at ✆ **02/932-3333.**

BY PLANE

Air travel is a tad indulgent, given that Bulgaria is relatively small (it takes 4–5 hr. to drive from Sofia to the coast), but if you need to get from one side of the country to the other fast, a few airlines connect Sofia with the coast (see Varna "Essentials," later in this chapter).

TIPS ON ACCOMMODATIONS

Unless you're staying in one of the handful of Bulgaria's five-star hotels, do not expect Western standards of service. In small towns you will probably be better off dealing with a family proprietor, but here you'll often struggle to find someone who speaks English. Star ratings are generally misleading; take one off from most establishments and you'll have a much better idea of what you're in for. Decor trends are firmly stuck in the last century (only two or three hotels across the country could be described as modern boutique), and rooms are generally bare, with cheap prefab pine furniture and laminate flooring. Note that Bulgarian hotel descriptions often refer to suites as "apartments," but do not assume that this means a kitchenette or dining area. Bathrooms are usually tiny shower rooms: a large cubicle with a toilet and basin with shower overhead; if you're lucky the toilet paper will remain dry.

On the bright side, places are almost always impeccably clean (certainly so if listed here) and incredibly cheap (hoteliers are incidentally no longer allowed to charge foreigners a higher price; discrepancies can be reported to www.ktzp.bg). Websites worth investigating are www.hotelsbulgaria.com and www.hotels-in-bulgaria.com, though neither features opinionated reviews. If you're more interested in B&B/guesthouses/family hotels, BAAT offers a fabulous booklet with a single photograph and brief description of each entry, along with useful advice on how to plan your trip. To find out where to get a booklet, check www.alternative-tourism.org. *Tip:* In small towns you may have problems making a booking, particularly if you want a particular room, as so few people speak English; use Surprise Tours booking service—send your entire Bulgaria itinerary to svelte@mail.bg and all your bookings will be made for a one-time fee of 20€ ($26).

TIPS ON DINING

Perhaps it is because their food is so good, but Bulgarians are not very adventurous and restaurants, be they upmarket, traditional *mehanas* (taverns), informal diners, or sidewalk cafes, tend to serve the same menu, with small regional differences, throughout the country. Food varies between good and incredibly delicious; location and price gives little indication of the quality of what will finally arrive on the plate. A much better bet is to look for places that attract what is clearly a local clientele—despite the ubiquitous plastic chairs and/or lack of obvious ambience. In fact, the only bad meal you're likely to come across is in an upmarket (and empty) restaurant featuring a fancy fusion menu.

One of the best things about Bulgarian restaurants is that they don't define lunch or dinner time—most open at around 11am and you can order anytime after this. Note that plates are served as they are ready, so don't expect courses to arrive at the same time. Also, if you eat at a mehana, plates are often small; for a full meal, choose a few items. As is the case in hotels, service is sometimes atrocious; don't take it personally, and make sure you check the bill carefully. A 10% tip is expected, but a service charge is often included. Most places have an English translation of the menu, but descriptions are bland, making the choice—given the enormous length of most menus—rather difficult. If lost, order any of the following stalwarts, featured on every menu across the land.

Tarator (cold cucumber and yogurt soup, with chopped garlic, walnuts, and dill); **shopska salad** (cucumber, tomatoes, spring onion, and red pepper, topped with grated white cheese, not unlike feta in taste, and an olive); **kebapche** or **kufte** (respectively finely spiced barbecued sausage or meatball, often cumin-dominated, and prepared over coals), order with "garnish" (potatoes or vegetables, and/or bread), ask for bread grilled, or try parlenka, the local pizza, or patatnik, a Rhodopean specialty in which the potatoes are grated and pan-baked with onions, egg, goat's cheese, and herbs); **shopski cheese** (a creamy cheese, tomato, onion, egg, and mild chile pepper bake); **mish mash** (a surprisingly delicious egg, cheese, and red pepper mix); **burek** (red peppers or zucchini stuffed with a feta-type cheese, spices, and egg). Other typical items on the menu include **kavarma** (individual casseroles of meat, at its best melt-in-the-mouth tender, baked with garlic, onion, peppers, and mushrooms in a traditional earthenware pot), **sarmi** (vine leaves stuffed with rice and tender spicy minced pork and covered in dill-infused strained or thick yogurt) and **moussaka** (a Greek dish of minced meat with eggplant). Bulgarian breakfast is comprised of **banitsa**—a flaky pastry stuffed with salty white cheese—and espresso or **boza,** made from fermented millet; the latter is an acquired taste.

TIPS ON SHOPPING

Bulgarians are gifted artisans; low prices only add to the temptation, so make sure you arrive with plenty of space in your suitcase. Crafts worth looking out for include the uniquely painted earthenware table- and cookware; wooden carvings; spices (chubritsa in particular); rakia (the grape- or plum-based brandy, enjoyed as an aperitif with salad); red wine (even when it's dirt-cheap it's good, but if you're after something special look out for anything produced by Damianitza, particularly Red Ark and No Man's Land), carpets, and embroidered clothing and tablecloths (the traditional red tablecloths you find in almost every restaurant are as cheerful as gingham). Icons are sold on every street corner and in churches, but most are prints pasted on to timber blocks; for a beautifully painted icon you're best off purchasing direct from a master, like the two working out of Etara (see under "Veliko Tarnovo," later in this chapter). Clothing produced locally is very cheap but looks it; better bargains are imported from Turkey. Shops tend to close on Saturday afternoons and on Sundays. Most important (again!), bear in mind that outside of Sofia, shops usually don't accept credit cards. Of those that do, MasterCard and Visa are more widely accepted. A useful website if you're looking for something specific is www.need.bg/en, a comprehensive Bulgarian business catalog.

FAST FACTS: Bulgaria

Addresses Note that streets in Bulgaria are called "ulitsa"; squares are "ploshtad"; "bulevard" is of course a boulevard. "Sveta," usually prefacing a church, means Saint.

Area Code The area code is **+359.**

Banks You'll find banks and ATMs almost everywhere in the city centers and on the main roads running through most towns. As cash is still the most widely used form of payment, make sure you've withdrawn from these before visiting small villages in the mountains.

Business Hours Shops usually open weekdays 9 or 10am to 7pm, and Saturday 9am to 1pm. On Sundays, most shops close. Banks, shops, and sites in rural towns often take a midday break between 12:30 or 1pm and 2pm, and close at 5pm. Most museums close on Mondays.

Car Rentals All major international car hire agencies are represented See "Getting Around: By Car," p. 64.

Climate Summers have a mean maximum temperature of 86°F to 95°F (30°C–35°C), while winters range between mean maximum of 50°F and 59°F (10°C–15°C). Hottest months are July and August. For local weather forecast call © **175.**

Directory Assistance For telephone numbers call © **144** or 02/987-3131; information on long-distance calls © **0123.**

Drugstores While these are found in most towns, most are staffed by people who do not understand English; if you do not have a prescription in Bulgarian or a guide, best to ask your concierge or host to assist you.

Electricity Local current is 220 volts. Outlets take plugs with two round prongs, typical to continental Europe.

Embassies & Consulates **U.S.:** 16 Kozyak St., © 02/937 5100 or 02/963-2022 (www.usembassy.bg); **U.K.:** 9 Moskovska St., © 02/9343-9222 (www.british-embassy.bg); **Canada** (consulate only): © 02/943-370; **Australia:** (consulate only) © 02/946-1334; www.ausemb.gr; **South Africa:** © 02/971-3425; www.africadosulemb.org.br.

Emergencies Ambulance © **150;** fire © **160;** police © **166;** traffic police © **165;** roadside assistance **91 146;** crime hot line © **02/982-2212.**

Hospitals If you are involved in an accident in Sofia, ask to be taken to Hospital Vita (www.vita.bg), located at 9 Dragovitza St. (© **02/943-4398** or 02/846-5376). For nonsurgical procedures head for IMC Medical Centre, located at 28 Gogol St., where staff is on call 24 hours (© **02/944-9326** or 0886 532 551; imc@gbg.bg).

Internet Access Bulgaria has good Internet services in the three major cities; outside of that cybercafes are sparse, so if it's important, choose a hotel that offers this.

Maps See "Lost? Just count the blocks . . .," p. 71.

Newspapers & Books You can pick up the *Sofia Echo,* the weekly English-language paper, at most newspaper stands in Sofia. English books outside of the capital tend to be the schlock crime genre or highbrow classics catering to the student population. When in Sofia, head for the Book Market on pl Slaveikov (open daily weather permitting) for English used novels, or pop into nearby Dom na Knigata (ul Graf Ignatieve; © **02/981 7898;** Mon–Sat 8am–8pm; Sun 9am–6pm).

Police While corruption and Mafiosi-style crime makes headlines, you're unlikely to become a victim. "Politsia" can be contacted at © **166.**

Post Office Post offices are located throughout the country, and usually open from 8:30am to 5:30pm Monday to Saturday, but opening hours can be unpredictable in small towns. The main post office is in Sofia, at 6 Gen Gurko St. (© **02/9496442/46).** There is also an Internet cafe here.

Restrooms Public restrooms are generally not great, and many charge a small fee for their use despite the fact that they are often Turkish-style "squat pots." Better to head into the nearest restaurant.

Telephone Calling home from Bulgaria can be costly. Hotels often quadruple phone charges; pay phones demand a prepaid phone-card, typically sold in small kiosks by a person not likely to speak English (though some hotels stock them). **Intrafonica Bulgaria** offers easy-to-use GSM cellphone rentals; review the packages on the Net (www.intrafonicabulgaria.com), make your choice, and fax the order form and copy of your passport; they will provide you with a local GSM cellphone number within 48 hours, then deliver the phone to your hotel on the first night of arrival. Bulgaria's code is *©* **359.**

Safety & Crime Bulgaria is one of Europe's safest countries, with a below-average crime rate; all you need to guard against is petty theft.

Time Zone Bulgaria is 2 hours ahead of GMT.

Tipping Leave 10% to 15% for all good restaurant and bar service.

Water Bulgaria's tap water is not only potable but delicious. Really—it is the best water I have ever tasted!

3 Sofia

A small group of worshipers stand on a concrete plinth, their heads bowed as a tall man, his long beard a gray rectangle on his black cassock, intones a fervent prayer. Behind this open-air church, flanked by the priest's rusty trailer, children throw themselves about on lurid jumping castles, the generator hum joined by a low thump emanating from a bustling bar-cafe. A group of students approach the central fountain; on each head is perched a large handmade paper hat. They start to dance as a Gypsy busker picks up the pace to serenade this strange parade. It is Sunday, and you could only be in Sofia's overgrown City Garden.

Sofia, capital of Bulgaria, is a fascinating city. It's as run-down as you would expect from a country that has suffered much under Communist rule, and continues to be starved of civic pride due to the high levels of corruption and a poor judicial system. But step away from the traffic-choked boulevards and drab gray concrete edifices, and into the cobbled streets east of the central square, and you find the hard edges of the city softened by untended but verdant parks and towering trees, filled with the unexpected sound of birdsong.

One of the youngest capitals of Europe (it was only declared the administrative center in 1879), Sofia has little to show for its 2,000-year-old origins: Aside from the 4th-century Rotunda of Sveti Georgi, Sofia's oldest building, most of the city's historic buildings date no further than the 18th and 19th century, and even then there is no great architectural beauty; certainly nothing that could be seen as a major tourist draw.

But Sofia's attraction does not lie in checking off a list of must-see attractions, but in wandering its streets at will, stopping to drink the occasional espresso at one of the myriad open-air bars and cafes that have sprung up in and around the parks. While Sofia has traditionally been seen only as a gateway to Bulgaria's beautiful hinterland, itineraries are increasingly featuring 2-night stays in this city, which is gradually evolving into a sexy south-European destination, a testament to the veracity of the city's motto: "Grows but never ages."

GETTING THERE
BY PLANE
Sofia International Airport lies 10km (6¼ miles) east of the city center—to find out times and details of flights from 47 cities across Europe and Middle East on any specific day, take a look at www.sofia-airport.bg, or call ℂ **02/937 2211/12/13.** You can arrange a 10€ ($13) pickup from **Surprise Tours** by sending an e-mail or text message with your flight details to Svetlio to ℂ **088/7485174** or svelte@mail.bg a few days in advance; alternatively exchange a small amount of money (exchange bureau facilities are located in the area before border control in Arrivals Hall; rates are not great) and head for the **OK Supertrans** counters in the Arrivals Hall to book one of their cabs for around 5€ to 7€ ($6.50–$9). If you're on a really tight budget, a mere .50lev (30¢/15p); plus an additional .50lev (30¢/15p) for every suitcase buys you a ticket on bus no. 84, departing every 10 to 15 minutes (5am–11pm) and will drop you at Eagle Bridge on bul Vasil Levski, near Sofia University (a 10-min. walk from the central square, pl Sveta Nedelya). Minibus no. 30 will take you a little closer, to bul Maria Luisa, but drivers may not speak English, and once there you'll probably be stymied by the Cyrillic road signs, so best to fork out for a taxi or transfer.

BY BUS
The new **Central Bus Station** (ℂ **02/813-3202;** www.centralbusstation-sofia.com) is located right next to the train station, but is hugely more sophisticated—we're talking clean toilets, self-help computer terminals, and an information desk at the entrance staffed with efficient English-speakers. **Group** (or Grup), **Biomet,** and **ETAB** are recommended operators but are by no means the only reputable companies; for more information on timetables for buses arriving from abroad and onward internal travel, call ℂ **090021000.** Given that you'll be burdened with luggage, it's a rather long (at least 1.5km/1 mile) walk to where most of the recommended hotels are. Use the taxi booking office at the main exit or catch tram no. 1 or 7 from the platform at the subterranean underpass opposite the train station forecourt (.70lev/45¢/25p), can be purchased from the driver); these will drop you off at **pl Sveta Nedelya,** the central city node (look out for the winged figure of Sofia and the Sheraton on your right), and walk east or west from there.

BY TRAIN
Arriving at the grim Central Railway Station on Maria Luiza Boulevard (ℂ **02/931 1111** or 02/932 3333; www.bdz.bg for train schedule information) is not the best introduction to the city—it's a huge, impersonal, and run-down space offering the usual: coin-operated left luggage lockers, money exchange kiosks, ATMs, dodgy fast food/bar outlets, and ubiquitous station pickpockets.

CITY LAYOUT
Surrounding inner-city "old" Sofia is a large sprawling sea of run-down tenements, Communist-era high-rise buildings, and green suburban areas that lap right up to the foothills of distant Mount Vitosha. Other than two major sites of interest, both located in the hillside suburb of Boyana, there is no real reason to venture beyond the central city; here everything falls within an easy walking-distance radius. Both the central rail and train station are located just over 1km (½ mile) north of **pl Sveta Nedelya,** the traffic-choked central city "square" (it's more of an oval), and the nodus that connects **Bulevard Knyaginya Maria Luiza,** a busy, bustling road, intimidating for pedestrians, with narrower and slightly more laid-back **Bulevard Vitosha,** the city's most renowned

shopping street—together these are the main north-south artery of the city, effectively carving the central city in two. To the east lies the "golden brick road"—historic **Tsar Osvoboditel,** lined with government buildings, including the former Royal Palace, opposite which lies the City Garden, the real heart of the city. In fact the majority of city's sites, and most of the best hotels and restaurants, lie east of bul Maria Luiza. You may be tempted to stick to this side of Sofia, but it's worth crossing bustling Maria Luiza, if only to find yourself in the **Zhenski pazar** ("Ladies' market"), where broad-hipped women pick out the best fruit and vegetables while catching up on the day's gossip— this is the closest Sofia ever gets to Bulgaria's rural roots, and a personal top favorite.

GETTING AROUND
ON FOOT

The best way to get around the city center is on foot. You can walk to every site and restaurant with the exception of the Boyana church and the National History Museum. See the walking tour below. Make sure you have sensible shoes—many of the streets are cobbled; still more are potholed.

BY TAXI

All registered taxis are yellow and must operate by meter. You can hail a taxi from the street or call; make sure the meter is on or ask the price upfront (best to have established with your concierge or host what the going rate should be) as taxi drivers are notorious for charging foreigners up to three times the going rate. Taxi drivers also tend to be quite aggressive, so try not to get into an argument—just take down the license and registration details surreptitiously and ask your embassy to report the driver to ⓒ **0800 18018** or 02/988 5239 (the latter used to report any criminal activity). According to most reliable sources, the best (read honest) taxi service is offered by **OK Taxis,** ⓒ **02/911 19.** Drivers and even dispatchers often speak only Bulgarian, so best to get your concierge or host to assist and have your destination written in Cyrillic.

BY TRAM OR BUS

Traveling by tram, bus, and metro is incredibly cheap—a single ticket (interchangeable for all three) is .70lev/45¢/25p; a day pass is 3lev/$2/£1. Tickets are purchased from newsdealers or booths near stops; remember to validate the ticket once on board or you could be fined 5lev/$4/1£ by a plainclothes official skulking on board. All public transport operates between 5:30am and 11pm. However, the difficulty of traveling by bus or tram (the metro line currently services only the western suburbs; no interest to tourists) is knowing where to get off—unless you have a helpful Bulgarian on board, you may overshoot your stop. Best to stick to a combination of walking and taxis, unless you know your landmarks.

VISITOR INFO

The **National Information and Publicity Centre** (pl Sveta Nedelya; Mon–Fri 9am–5pm; ✆ **02/987 9778;** www.bulgariatravel.org) has plenty of brochures but staff is not trained or well-traveled, so help is pretty substandard. **Zig-Zag** is an independent agency that specializes in good-quality B&B and guesthouse bookings (in Sofia as well as in certain rural destinations) as well car rental (from 25€/$32 per day). They also offer very good value themed trips, including monasteries and mountain village hikes focusing on rare fauna and flora; adventure tours in the mountains; or just a walking tour of Sofia. Staff is intelligent and opinionated. for this valuable attribute you are charged 5lev ($4/1£) ; this can be deducted from any tour you book through them (✆ **02/980 5102;** www.zigzagbg.com; 20V Stamboliyski bul, entrance on Lavele St.; Mon–Fri 9am–6:30pm). For personal advice on an itinerary, contact Nevyana at nevyana@zigzagbg.com.

If you're looking for up-to-date city listings and general information about Sofia, there are three excellent in-depth booklets distributed free through Zig-Zag and a number of hotels: *Sofia in Your Pocket* (www.inyourpocket.com); *The Insider's Guide* (www.insidesofia.com); and *Sofia City Guide* (www.sofiacityguide.com). If you want to know what's on during your stay, take a look at www.programata.bg. Plenty of tour operators offer guided day trips (from 8:30 or 9am–6pm) to the country's top attractions (all remarkably close to the city). **FairPlay International JSC** (✆ **02/943 4574;** www.fpitravel.com) comes highly recommended by concierges; day trips include 3-hour or full-day Sofia tours; Rila Monastery; Koprivishtitsa; Melnik; Plovdiv; and Veliko Tarnovo.

FAST FACTS: Sofia

Banks With some 40 banks now vying for trade, their ATMs are spread throughout the city center and you'll have no problem withdrawing money.

Internet A number of places offer Internet services. **Site** (✆ **02/986-0896**) is conveniently located on 45 Vitosha Blvd., or head for **Internet Café,** Garibaldi on 6 Graf Ignatiev St. (next to KFC; www.garibaldicafe.net).

Medical **IMC International Medical Centre** has English-speaking doctors who will make house calls; also **Pediatricians and Gynecologists** (28 Gogl St; ✆ **0944 9326,** 0944 9317, or 0886 532 551). For dental help: **Dentail Center,** VI 5 Ivan Vazov (✆ **02/987-8422**); or **Denta Plus,** 41 Graf Ignatieff ✆ **02/981-0366.**

Pharmacy For information on the closest pharmacy dial ✆ **178.** A good 24-hour pharmacy is **BD Pharmel-Em** at 10 Yano Sakazov Blvd. (✆ **02/943-3972**); alternatively, try **Apteca** at 160 G. Rakovski (✆ **02/986-7984**).

Restrooms Public restrooms are best avoided. See details in "Restrooms" in "Fast Facts: Bulgaria" (p. 68).

Sofia Lodging, Dining & Attractions

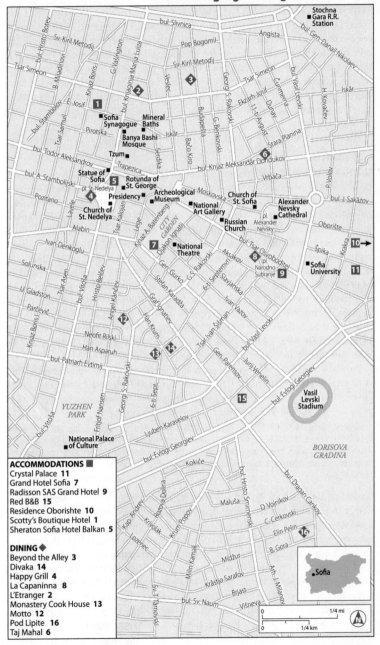

ACCOMMODATIONS ■
Crystal Palace **11**
Grand Hotel Sofia **7**
Radisson SAS Grand Hotel **9**
Red B&B **15**
Residence Oborishte **10**
Scotty's Boutique Hotel **1**
Sheraton Sofia Hotel Balkan **5**

DINING ◆
Beyond the Alley **3**
Divaka **14**
Happy Grill **4**
La Capaninna **8**
L'Etranger **2**
Monastery Cook House **13**
Motto **12**
Pod Lipite **16**
Taj Mahal **6**

WHERE TO STAY

Sofia's hotel scene has come a long way recently with an improved selection across all price categories. Anyone expecting Western standards of service and decor will, however, have to pay more. Of the few five-star hotels, the best are featured below—given that the city center sights are great to see as a walking tour, it makes sense to stay strolling distance from the center, and to this end all the options featured below are exactly that. It's worth bearing in mind that with most hotels aimed at servicing the business community weekend rates are often significantly cheaper than Monday through Thursday.

Note: Ensure that rates quoted include 20% VAT; the city tax is negligible.

EXPENSIVE

Grand Hotel Sofia ★★★ *Value*   This relative newcomer to Sofia's five-star hotels is my top choice, with the best location, neighboring the pretty National Theatre and overlooking the City Park—not only a green lung but the perfect place to watch the full gamut of Bulgarians at play from a number of open-air cafes. It's also extremely luxurious, inspired by the cliché of the grand English gentleman's club, with dark wood-paneled walls throughout, some 400 works of original Bulgarian art, plenty of reproduction leather furniture, and incredibly generous bedrooms (over 50 sq. m/538 sq. ft.). There are three types of rooms all featuring, like the Sheraton, a general sense of opulence; book the entry-level Superior from the third floor up with garden view, or a room on the eighth and ninth floor for great city and Vitosha mountain views. Superior rooms offer good value, particularly over the weekends (165€/$210 double); deluxe and executive rooms are so big one struggles to understand why they bother with suites. The Grand Hotel doesn't exude the sense of gracious history of the Sheraton, but then it doesn't come with the price tag either.

Note that if the Grand is full, a good alternative, opposite leafy Doctor's Gardens, is **Crystal Palace;** room nos. 503 and 504 are a good deal—the only standard-category rooms with a balcony (and views of the gardens) thrown into the 180€ ($229) price tag (© **02/948 9489;** www.crystalpalace-sofia.com).

1 Gurko St., Sofia, 1000. © **02/811-0800.** Fax 02/811-0801. www.grandhotelsofia.bg. 122 units. Weekend: 165€–195€/$210–$248 double; 225€–505€/$286–$641 suite. Weekdays: 185€–215€/$235–$273. AE, DC, MC, V. **Amenities:** 3 restaurants; cafe; 3 bars; 24-hr. room service; executive lounge; business center; conference center; health center; salon; concierge; indoor parking; laundry; dry cleaning. *In room:* A/C, TV, minibar, Internet connection, hair dryer, safe.

Radisson SAS Grand Hotel ★★   This hotel is certainly not grand, but when it comes to personal, sincere service, the Radisson is a hands-down winner—from the chap who opens the door to the mother figure who presides over breakfast (incidentally the biggest and best in Bulgaria), to the wonderful snacks they offer you in the top-floor business center, you'll feel well and truly cosseted. It's an ugly, unprepossessing building—a semicircular embrace on Narodno Sabranie square, but ideally placed—right opposite are the pretty Parliament buildings, which are lit up at night, and a stone's throw farther lies the iconic Alexander Nefski Cathedral. The vibe is both more urban than the Crystal Palace and the Grand, with their leafy surroundings, and more down-home sociable. The reception area spills over into Flannagans, a hugely popular pub that attracts a raucous crowd of expats and Bulgarians on the weekends. The hotel was due to undergo extensive renovations at the end of 2006, with an additional floor being added and decor throughout being overhauled; design proposals looked great—modern and sleek. Pay the extra 10€ ($13) for a Superior Room, identical to a standard but with parliament view—ask for the highest floor available.

4 Narodno Sabranie Sq., Sofia 1000. (C) 02/933 4334 or 02/933 4333. Fax 02/933 4335. www.radissonsas.com. 136 units. Mon–Thurs 210€–230€ ($267–$292) double; Fri–Sun 150€–170€ ($191–$216) double. Suites 230€–290€ ($216–$343). AE, M, V, DISC. Rates include breakfast. **Amenities:** Restaurant; bar; health and fitness center; travel desk; business center; conference center; 24-hr. room service; laundry service; dry cleaning. *In room:* A/C, TV, minibar, Internet connection, hair dryer, safe.

Sheraton Sofia Hotel Balkan ★★★   Housed in one of Sofia's landmarks—part of the Presidency, dating from 1886—this is the only hotel in Sofia with a sense of real history. It has hosted Bulgaria's most important guests for 2 decades, and is the first hotel in Eastern Europe deigned good enough for Sheraton's Luxury Collection. Shadowing the 4th-century Rotunda, and sandwiched between the Presidential Palace and the central square that feeds into Vitosha (the city's best-known shopping street), the Sheraton is also pretty much right in the heart of things—perhaps too much so, given that this means it also overlooks the traffic-choked and alienating intersection between Tsar Osvoboditel and Maria Luiza. The entire hotel has undergone an extensive refurbishment, and the rooms and suites are looking undeniably classy, with decor very much in keeping with the historic nature of the building. Only the rooms on the first floor, with their wonderfully high ceilings, give any real indication of the grand proportions of the building; rooms on the fifth floor have the best views, however. Public spaces were undergoing renovation at press time, but massive chandeliers hanging over vast expanses of marble-inlay flooring remain key features. It's pricey, though, and Sheraton's position as the first choice among well-heeled visitors is slowly being eroded by better-value competitors who know how much guests appreciate such perks as including breakfast with the daily rate.

5 Sveta Nedelya Sq., Sofia, 1000. (C) **02/981 6541** or 02/981 8787. Fax 02/980 6464. www.luxurycollection.com/sofia. 188 units. 315€–365€/$401–$464 double; 390€–800€/$495–$1,016 suite. Breakfast 19€/$24. AE, DC, MC, V. **Amenities:** 2 restaurants; cafe; bar; fitness center; concierge; business center; salon; 24-hr. room service; butler service; executive lounge; laundry; dry cleaning; free airport pickup. *In room:* A/C, TV, minibar, Internet connection, hair dryer, safe.

MODERATE

Residence Oborishte ★★ *Value*   This elegant establishment—a converted private residence dating from the 1930s—is more guesthouse than hotel, with a tiny public area and limited facilities, but the rooms are great. Named after old Bulgarian towns, the seven suites are extremely spacious and tastefully appointed in rich royal colors (pity about laminate floors), and two of them have fireplaces (useful even in June or Sept, when Sofia can have cold bouts). If you're just passing through, Serdica and Sofia (both categorized as rooms rather than suites, the latter with a feminine Juliette balcony overlooking the street), offer excellent value, particularly over the weekend 80(€–90€/$102–$115). Not a huge staff quotient, but there are always at least two persons on hand to offer your complimentary welcome drink, arrange for breakfast to be served in your room (good idea as the breakfast room is poky), or arrange a candlelit dinner (given prior notice); the free pickup service from the airport is also useful. Located near Doctor's Gardens, the most prestigious residential area in Sofia, this is about 10 minutes' walk from Alexander Nevski Cathedral and the city center.

63 Oborishte St., Sofia 1000. (C) **02/814 4888** or 02/814 4878. Fax 02/846 8244. www.residence-oborishte.com. 9 units. Mon–Thurs 90€–160€ ($115–$203) double; weekends 80€–130€ ($102–$165). No credit cards. Rates include breakfast. **Amenities:** Breakfast room; bar; complimentary use of nearby fitness center; laundry; dry cleaning. *In room:* A/C, TV, minibar, Internet connection, safe.

Scotty's Boutique Hotel ✪   It's not really a hotel let alone boutique, but step inside what appears to be a pretty residence—freshly painted in a fetching red—and you've found yourself a really good value B&B/guesthouse (and gay-friendly) with a funky offbeat character. And—as it's diagonally opposite the Old Synagogue—it's right on the walking tour. Rooms are cheaply furnished but with more imagination than anything comparable in this price category. The six double deluxe rooms (75€/$96), named after famous cities, all have balconies with Synagogue views (Sydney and San Francisco are particularly appealing). Double rooms are quite a bit smaller; ask for the one with a balcony. The two singles are predictably tiny, but come with balconies. Bathrooms for all the rooms are appropriately billed as "shower cubicles." There are no real public spaces, and the reception area is up a flight of stairs. Note that breakfast (served only on request, and delivered to the room) costs an additional 5€ ($6); better to head to Zhanski Bazar (this is what it's called) and pick up a banitsa.

11 Ekzarh Iossif St., Sofia, 1000. ⓒ **02/983 6777** or 088/983 6777. Fax 02/983 3229. www.geocities.com/scottys boutiquehotel. 16 units. 55€–75€ ($70–$96) double. AE, DC, MC, V. **Amenities:** Fitness facilities nearby; guided tours; car rental and pickup service on request. *In room:* A/C, TV, minibar, Internet connection, tea- and coffeemaking facilities.

INEXPENSIVE

Red B&B *Finds*   If you're looking to meet the city's intelligentsia rather than foreign hostel dwellers, this B&B is without a doubt the top budget option in Sofia. Once home to one of Bulgaria's most famous sculptors, Andrey Nikolov, it was for 3 decades a meeting place for Bulgarian bohemians, and in the autumn of 2004 again opened its doors as a Centre for Culture and Debate (www.redhouse-sofia.org for information). Accommodations are basic—red-walled rooms have quirky furniture pieces (room nos. 4 and 6 have queen-size beds; nos. 1 and 2 have double beds; the rest are single) but are pretty bare, and none are en-suite. Rooms on the first floor (three bedrooms) share a toilet and bathroom, while those on the third floor (three bedrooms) share two toilets and a shower. Friends traveling together should look at the three-bedroom apartment (sleeps five) for 100€ ($125). The Centre also hosts fascinating debates, dance performances, film screenings, and "freely improvised music experiment." There are shared kitchen facilities and a rooftop terrace where you could eat, but right next door are two cafe/restaurants.

15 Ljuben Karavelov St., Sofia, 1000. ⓒ/fax **02/988 8188.** www.RedBandB.com. 7 units. 40€–50€ ($51–$64) double. No credit cards. **Amenities:** Centre for Culture and Debate.

WHERE TO DINE

Sofia's dining scene is wonderful. You can choose between the fine-dining atmosphere of evocative-sounding places like Beyond the Alley, Behind the Cupboard (Sofia's best restaurant; see below) and House with the Clock (located in the pretty 19th-c. villa at 15 Moskovska St., right next to the British Embassy). Or, if you're in a more laid-back mood, hang out in trendy bar-restaurants like Motto (reviewed below) and watch the city's media and model types schmooze, or go rustic and eat your fill for around 5€ ($6.25) at any number of unpretentious places that fill up in the evenings with students and office workers.

Restaurants that serve Bulgarian food are generally speaking superior to "foreign" cuisine types (with the exception of Turkish, Greek, or Armenian restaurants, like the excellent Egur Egur, where cuisine is very similar to Bulgarian). If you feel like Italian, **La Capaninna,** on Narodno Subranie square (next door to Radisson SAS, with same lovely parliament views; ⓒ **02/980 4438**), is a very good alfresco option, as is the more cafe-style **Club Lavazza** on Vitosha Blvd. (no. 13; ℭ 02/987-3437)—the latter is also the best place in town for a coffee (Lavazza of course), with plenty of cigar-chomping bad boys to make it feel like a truly authentic Italian joint. If you're in the mood for Indian, **Taj Mahal** is rated the best (ℭ 02/987 3632; 11-ti Avgust 11), though newcomer **Awadh** is making real inroads (ℭ 02/943 3001; 41 Cherkovna; www.awadhresetaurant.com). Cozy **Le'Etranger** (ℭ 983 1417; 78 Tsar Simeon St.), the city's best French bistro, in one of Sofia's most cosmopolitan areas, but still a wonderfully intimate affair with only seven tables personally tended by owners Oliver and Mitana. **Tambuktu** (ℭ 02/988 1234; 10 Aksakov St.), a chain specializing in fish dishes, is also highly rated by locals, though the garish signage did not encourage exploration on our part.

With the exception of Pod Lipite and Awadh, all the restaurants listed here are within walking distance of the hotels reviewed above, though you might want to take a cab at night rather than risk getting lost (perfectly safe however). And don't forget to carry cash if credit cards aren't listed—given how inexpensive dining is at these places, it needn't be much.

MODERATE

Beyond the Alley, Behind the Cupboard ★★★ INTERNATIONAL/BULGARIAN   It's not just the name that's quirky; located in an attractive Art Nouveau house, in an interesting up-and-coming area just north of the Cathedral, the decor at this fabled restaurant is equally eccentric. In the lovely garden you are greeted by a classic Bulgarian water fountain, but here sprouting some 20 taps; in the lobby is an antique cupboard filled with childhood mementos (changed seasonally); even the bathroom is a surprise, so don't miss it (and look up)! Food is a mix of international (French/Italian) but with Bulgarian influence—the "village salad," for instance, comprises fresh vegetables topped with Rhodope cheese matured in a juniper casks, while the balls of Itchera goat's cheese, coated and deftly fried in slivered almond coats, is superb; similarly so the oven-baked rabbit, stuffed with sun-dried tomatoes and pine nuts, and served with a potato gratin, and the toasted soda bread stuffed with baked peppers and brie. With a large wine cellar updated annually, the wine list is also a superb introduction to one of Bulgaria's best-kept secrets. Small wonder that this is a personal favorite for the editor of *Bacchus,* Bulgaria's revered food and wine magazine and host to the likes of Bill Clinton and Catherine Deneuve. In short, if you have time for only one restaurant in Sofia, head to Beyond the Alley.

31 Budapeshta St. ℭ 02/983 5545. www.beyond-the-alley.com. Reservations essential at night. 13lev–25lev ($7–$16/£4.50–£8.65). Note that 7% service charge is added to bill. MC, V. Daily noon–midnight.

INEXPENSIVE

Monastery Cook House ★★ BULGARIAN   You need to get here early just to get through the menu—quite the longest we have ever seen, with much of it either mouthwatering or somewhat obscure. Like Pod Lipite, this is thoroughly Bulgarian cuisine, but here the owners have collected traditional recipes from 161 Bulgarian monasteries, and there is plenty on the menu you won't find elsewhere, like "Plakovsjka Hayverna," peeled garlic, mashed with salt and oil, lemon, bread and walnuts; and "Vartyana tarkana," nettle and spinach stew, cooked with walnuts, garlic, cheese, and butter. Like their restaurants, Bulgarians have a real flair for giving dishes amusing names, and Cook House is no exception, with translations like "Thin Waist," "Full Stomach," and "Tasty long-distance runner"—the latter a deboned rabbit leg, marinated in wine and spices, and roasted over coals. Located in an old house on a quiet semiresidential street, every room is decorated with traditional Bulgarian rugs and fabrics, and the atmosphere is wonderfully laid-back—service can be slow, but if Dinev is your waiter it will at least be good. Almost empty at lunch, the Cookhouse is better visited at nights.

67 Hans Asparuh St. © **02/980 3883**. 8lev–12lev ($5–$16/£1.75–£4.15). MC, V. Daily 11am–2am.

Motto CAFE ☞   Motto attracts a really cool crowd, and that includes the staff. If you're not yet in the mood for eating, this is just the place to lounge around with a cocktail or a glass of wine (some of Bulgaria's famous reds are available here by the glass) and the papers (all hanging at the entrance hall, including the *Sofia Echo*). In inclement weather you'll have to sprawl in the stylish dining hall, but if it's balmy head on through to the green garden, furnished with modern timber couches and tables and chairs. Those in search of a romantic tryst be warned: It's laid-back at lunch but can get very crowded at nights, when the DJs can crank it up. Light meals include a tasty avocado and veal salad; chili con carne with tortilla chips, burritos; and spinach rolls with stewed tomatoes and crispy celery. If you really want to fill up, there's a heavier selection (duck breast roasted in red wine and served with forest mushroom jam; chicken breast stuffed with prosciutto, cheese, spinach, and cream). Whether light cafe-style burger, or slightly more challenging main, the kitchen delivers—maybe not immediately when it's at full buzz, but who cares when you're entranced by the crowd, and wondering where all the beautiful people go when the sun comes up.

18 Aksakov St. © **02/987 27 23**. www.motto-bg.com. Main courses 8lev–25lev ($5–$32/£1.75–£8.65). AE, MC, V. Daily 10am–1am.

Pod Lipite ☞☞☞ BULGARIAN   This is possibly the best Bulgarian-themed restaurant in the city—certainly so if you judge a traditionally styled restaurant, geared predominantly to foreigners, by the number of locals who support it. Step inside and you've left the city for a classic timber-beamed rural mehana; four rooms decorated with traditional weavings, musical instruments, and farm implements. Outside in the lovely courtyard (replete with fountain) are more rustic timber tables, each with the traditional ceramic spice dish containing pepper, salt, and other traditional spice mixtures (used regularly in Bulgaria like salt and pepper) such as chubritsa, lyut, and sharena sol, so you can spice up to taste, and a candle lantern to add atmosphere. Then there's the food. If you haven't yet tried Bulgarian cuisine, this is the place to do so. There's a great selection of salads, delicious breads (try the louchnik—a wedge of bread filled with lightly seasoned caramelized onions), followed by a selection of delicately spiced charcoal-grilled meats (or one of the zucchini, eggplant, and or pepper-and-cheese dishes, or "leaf" rolls, if you're no carnivore). The food is excellent, the live music in the evenings is good, and the waiters know what they're talking about. No wonder its been going strong since 1926.

1 Elin Pelin St. © **02/866 5053**. Reservations essential. 8lev–20lev ($5–$13/£1.75–£4.50). No credit cards. Daily noon–1am.

INEXPENSIVE
Divaka ☞☞ *Value* BULGARIAN   Open 24/7, Divaka (meaning "Savage") serves up amazingly large and delicious portions to young Sofians in search of the best bargain this side of the Balkans. The decor is no-nonsense—rough tables and benches in three small rooms with timber archways, as well as a tiny outside area round the back—and service is at best described as indifferent, but the food really is good. The Divaka sarmi

---

Tips Fast Food, Bulgarian Style

Bulgarian men—not known for their liberal views on women—say it's called the **Happy Bar & Grill** because of the uniformed waitstaff—almost all female, with legs apparently vetted before being issued with their micro minis. The food is good, comes fast, and given that you'll spend no more than 6lev to 8lev ($3.80–$5/£2.10–£2.75), Bulgaria's homegrown chain (owned by fast-food entrepreneur Orlin Popov, also responsible for Tambaktu) is understandably a place that makes a population living on an average $100 a month very happy. You'll find one in every major city; if you're keen to try one out in Sofia, head for the huge neon-lit sign located on central Sveta Nedelya Square (✆ **02/980 7353**). Alternatively, if you've wanted a fast-food snack, and not yet enamored with the array of Bulgarian options, head for the recently restored **Halite** (25 Maria Louisa Blvd.), an indoor food market that offers a choice of Chinese, Asian, Italian, Portuguese, and Austrian takeout, all on the mezzanine-level food court.

(3.20€/$4), a deliciously spiced mix of rice and minced pork meat, rolled in vine leaves and covered in a creamy dill and garlic sauce, is simply out of this world, as is the "Hungarian Good Woman," finely spiced strips of grilled pork and sliced vegetables, served with hunks of fresh lemon (note that the latter is big enough for two), or "Savage leg with savage sauce," grilled chicken leg, baked with lukanka, cheese, mushrooms, and onions. There's also a huge choice of Bulgarian salads (big portions), and the vegetarian shish kabob, a hit with noncarnivores.

If you're in the vicinity of Shipka Street, **Veshtitsite**—aka Witches—at no. 9 is, like Divaka, a wonderfully unpretentious restaurant with fabulous food at bargain prices—service is slow but friendly and the kitchen serves the freshest, most delicious salads (the best shopska ever at 3.70lev/£1.30/2.40); and a great plate of Burek (stuffed) peppers (3.90lev/£1.35/$2.55). There's another Divaka branch at 54 Gladston St. (✆ **02/989 9543**); same hours.

41A 6th Septemvri St. ✆ **02/986 6971**. Main courses 5lev–8lev ($3–$5/£1.75–£2.75). No credit cards. Daily 24 hr.

EXPLORING SOFIA

Sofia has enough by way of museums, churches, and street life to plan at least 1 day to explore it. If you're based in the central city, all of its sights can be viewed in a walking tour, outlined below, with only the Boyana Church and National History Museum requiring a 20-minute cab journey. Both are located in the suburb of Boyana; best to hire a cab and travel to Boyana Church, then ask your driver to wait—the viewing of the tiny church won't take a great deal longer than the 10 minutes each visitor is allowed, and he can then drop you off at the National History Museum (just over 2km/1¼ miles away), a visit that could take up 3 hours, depending on your interest.

Today Sophia's population is predominantly geared toward tourism but visitors are still treated to authentic village life as farmers trundle along cobbled lanes in horse-drawn carts, past timber-and-stone houses painted in red, ocher, and royal blue. There are six house museums for which you purchase a single ticket from the museum administration office (daily 10am–6pm) on the main square; note that most of the house museums are closed on Mondays (the exception being Oslekov House, which opens in the morning). Of the six, the most impressive are **Lyutov House** and **Oslekov House,** the latter's grand facade painted with images of Rome, Venice, and Padua. **Kableshkov House** is a far humbler abode, but of historic interest as the birthplace of rebel leader Todor Kableshkov (b. 1851): Todor launched his disastrous Uprising on April 20—ahead of schedule, due to a traitorous spy—by sending the Ottoman authorities notice of their intent in the famous "Bloody Letter," written in the blood of a dead Turk.

There are plenty of places to eat and family-run B&Bs in the village; avoid the well-positioned tourist trap The First Rifle and head across the river to **The Old Pear Tree** (56 Hadjinentso Pavlev; © **0887/733430**)—it's a little off the beaten track (walking distance from Lyutov House) but this is where the locals choose to eat, and serves the best food in town. If you opt to travel to the village by public bus (12lev/$7/£3.75 return; one daily leaving at 1:30pm) rather than an organized tour or hiring a car and driver, you may have to overnight. One of the best B&Bs is the small but efficiently run **Astra** (11 Hadzhi Nencho Palaveev; © **07184/2364;** www.hotelastra.org; from 42lev/$27/£15); Dina Petkova does not speak much English (very few in the village do), but she is warm and welcoming. Equally recommended is pretty **Tryanova kashta** (5 Gereniloto; © **07184/3057** or 0888 427 841; 35lev–60lev/$23–$38/£12–£21, depending on size), offering three rooms in a listed building just up from the main square—try to book the corner "red room," which is delightful; alternatively the "blue room."

National History Museum ★★★ Built by the Communist dictator Todor Zhivkov, the building alone is worth making the journey here: A fabulous brooding presence at the foot of Vitosha, the "Palace" (it has no bedrooms; only huge entrance areas and massive meeting halls) has a wealth of '70s design detailing, and clearly no expense was spared in ensuring that the proportions suitably awed and intimidated all who came to seek an audience. The collection is no less impressive. Founded in 1973, the museum houses more than 650,000 exhibits, the most interesting of which are displayed on the halls on the second floor, dating from "Prehistory: 6th to 2nd millennia B.C." (Hall 1) and "Bulgarian lands from the end 6th century B.C. to 6th century A.D." (Hall 2), to "Bulgarian State during the Middle Ages 7th–14th century" (Hall 3) and "Bulgaria under Ottoman rule 1396–1878" (Hall 4). On the third floor you'll find the

---

Moments **Feeling Devout**

The best time to experience any of Sofia's Orthodox Churches is when the domes are filled with the sonorous sounds of chanting, and the candelabras are ablaze with the flickering flames lit by the devotional for the living and the dead. Religion is alive and thriving in Bulgaria, and the rich ritual and huge and varied community it serves—from young vamps in figure-hugging jeans and snakeskin boots, to aged widowers in black bent over walking sticks—can affect even the most jaded traveler. If you feel moved to participate, purchase a few candles from the booth—note that traditionally candles for the dead are placed on the floor, while candles for the living are around eye-height. Daily liturgy usually takes place at 8am and 5pm; at Alexander Nevsky Saturday the vigil occurs at 6:30pm, while the Sunday evening Mass takes place at 9:30pm.

A Great Day Trip: The Village of Koprivshtitsa

The most popular day trip from Sofia is Rila Monastery (p. 88) but an equally rewarding destination lies 110km (68 miles) east from Sofia (just over 100 min. by car): the architectural museum town **Koprivshtitsa,** one of Bulgaria's most beautiful villages, with almost 400 superb examples of the National Revival building style that swept through the country in the 19th century. Then populated with merchants and tax collectors who imported many of the artisans from Plovdiv to build homes that signified their wealth, tiny Koprivshtitsa also birthed a few of the key revolutionaries who, tired of the living under the corrupt Ottoman Empire, staged the April Uprising of 1876—a rebellion that was brutally squashed but signaled to the rest of Bulgaria, and the Russians, that the country was ready to liberate itself from the "Yoke of Oppression."

slightly dull and badly labeled "Third Bulgarian Kingdom 1878–1946" in Hall 5, and various temporary exhibitions in the remainder—while the carpets and embroidery, showing where elements of the orient start to appear, are very skilled, these are somehow less riveting, though this response may have more to do with sensory overload. If you're pushed for time, head straight for Hall 2 to view the Thracian-era rhytons, armory, and jewelry—the biggest display outside of Varna's Archaeological Museum, then take a look in Hall 3, if only to admire its magnificent ceiling and incredible views of the overgrown yet stylized gardens that flow into the mountain wilderness.

16 Vitoshko Lale St., Boyana (10km/6¼ miles south of town near the ring road/ Okolovrusten put); 20-min. from city or 40-min. journey on trolleybus no. 2. © **02/955 7604.** www.historymuseum.org. 10lev/$6.50/£3.45. Tours 20lev/$13/£6.90. Daily 9:30am–5:30pm.

Boyana Church ⭐⭐⭐   It's an unassuming 11th- and 13th-century building surrounded by lush vegetation, but Boyana Church evokes a great deal of awe in art historians who struggle to explain how realistic aspects such as the three-dimensional facial expressions in the frescoes that cover the interior came to be painted during the 13th century, as this innovation was only ushered in by Italian Renaissance painters over a century later. It's an easy visit, and one of the most tourist-friendly in Bulgaria. Upon payment you are provided with an intelligent English-speaking guide who will accompany you into the church and point out the emotive profiles and movements, and the introduction of realism into the choice of latter-day fashion and fabrics; the guide will also identify the models, including Kalogen and his wife, Desislava, the Sofia landlord and patron who commissioned the building of the 13th-century extension. With any luck you'll be the only person in the church, as tour groups make for a claustrophobic experience. While it is obviously of great historic interest (and the overgrown gardens with their Roman ruins lovely), it's worth noting that this UNESCO-listed site may leave those not fascinated by art history a little cold. The church has, after all, not functioned as such since 1954.

1–3 Boyansko ezero St. (20 min. from the city center, or hour-plus journey on tram 9 to Hladilnika followed by bus 64 to Boyana). © **02/959 0939.** 15lev ($10/£5.20). Daily 9:30am–5:30pm.

Start: Alexander Nevsky Cathedral.
Finish: Zhenski Pazar.
Time: With one or two stops you're looking at around 4 hours.

The best time to do the tour is on a Saturday or Sunday, when the churches are at their most atmospheric, and the City Park is filled with quirky Bulgarians and buzzing cafes. Note that Monday sees most of the museums closed.

❶ Alexander Nevsky Cathedral 🌟🌟 & Icon Museum 🌟🌟🌟

It makes sense to kick off at the gold-domed Alexander Nevski Cathedral, iconic emblem of the capital, and largest in the Balkans. Built in memory of the Russian soldiers who died during the 1877–78 war that helped Bulgaria lift the Ottoman "Yoke of Oppression," it was designed by a Russian architect and named after the patron saint of the Russian "Tsar Liberator." The sheer scale of the richly decorated interior—said to hold 7,000—deserves a visit, particularly during one of the services. Even more so the crypt, which houses the **Icon Museum.** Charting the history of Bulgarian iconography from the end of the 4th century to the end of the 19th century National Revival period, this selection of beautiful paintings—far superior to anything to in the rest of the National Gallery's collection—is an absolute must-see. Also on the A. Nevsky Square (to the right with the cathedral behind you), burns the Eternal Flame of the Unknown Soldier, lit in 1981 in memory of all those who lost their lives in war. Just beyond this is the entrance to:

❷ St. (Sveti) Sofia Church 🌟🌟

Established in the 5th century, St. Sofia (open 9am–6pm) is the city's oldest Eastern Orthodox Church, and gave the city her name during the 15th century. Recently restored, it has undergone various reincarnations (including as a mosque during Ottoman rule, abandoned after two earthquakes toppled the

minaret and cost the then-Imam two sons), but a few remnants of its ancient past remain—look out for the fragment of original Roman mosaic flooring in the right-hand aisle. The simple red brick interior—austere by Orthodox standards—is beautiful, and the church has become a very popular venue for weekend weddings. From here you might want to stroll around the stalls set up on the square (see "Shopping," below), or proceed directly south down Rakovski Street then turn west into Tsar Osvoboditel, turning your back on the statue of the Russian Tsar Alexander II on horseback, and head along its yellow bricks to the:

❸ Russian Church of St. Nicholas 🌟🌟🌟

Hastily built in 1912 to 1914, apparently to serve the needs of a neurotic Russian diplomat who felt that Bulgarian Orthodox traditions bordered on the heretic, the Russian Church (Tsar Osvoboditel 3; 8am–6:30pm) is my favorite in Sofia. It's not as grand as Alexander Nefski, but the small interior is huge on atmosphere, with weekends seeing plenty of devoted worshipers milling around to bow or kiss the various icons. A path to the left leads to the crypt, where Sofians post their prayers into the box next to the marble sarcophagus of Archbishop Serafim, head of the Russian church in Bulgaria in the early 20th century. Continue along Tsar Osvoboditel. The grand building on the right is the former Royal Palace, built in 1873 for the then governor during the Ottoman occupation, and today housing the:

Walking Tour: Cathedrals to Markets

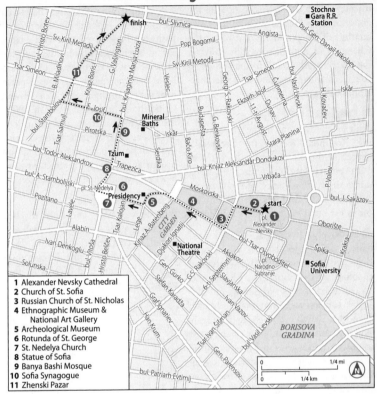

1 Alexander Nevsky Cathedral
2 Church of St. Sofia
3 Russian Church of St. Nicholas
4 Ethnographic Museum &
  National Art Gallery
5 Archeological Museum
6 Rotunda of St. George
7 St. Nedelya Church
8 Statue of Sofia
9 Banya Bashi Mosque
10 Sofia Synagogue
11 Zhenski Pazar

**❹ Ethnographic Museum ✸
and National Art Gallery**

The National Art Gallery (Tues–Sun 10am–6pm) is a real disappointment, with mediocre art and very unfriendly staff—hardly worth the 3lev ($1.95/60p) entry fee; certainly not if Plovdiv—where most of Bulgaria's best artists seems to have originated or congregated—is part of your itinerary. But in the east wing you'll find the Ethnographic Museum (same hours and admission), which has a wonderful display of folk arts and crafts, and explanations on traditional rites. It's a little haphazard, and at times displays look a little like a high-school project, but this is a very worthwhile half-hour, particularly if you want to do a little souvenir shopping (see "Shopping," below).

Opposite the palace is the City Garden, overlooked by the beautiful baroque Ivan Vazov National Theatre. Take a turn in the Gardens and stop at one of the cafe-bars, or keep heading down Tsar Osvoboditel to the:

❺ Archaeological Museum ✸✸

Housed in what used to be the 15th-century "Bujuk" (Big) mosque, this is a lovely light and airy space with well-displayed exhibits, and small enough to tour in 20 minutes. The collection comprises Thracian (don't miss the 400 B.C. gold burial mask upstairs), Greek, Roman, and medieval Bulgarian artifacts, and though not nearly as impressive as the National History Museum, this is a must if you don't have the time to catch a cab to Boyana. Opposite the entrance is the Presidency, administrative quarters of the president (and where the Changing of the Guard occurs daily on the hour); head around to the left into a courtyard where, shadowed by the Sheraton, you'll see the:

❻ Rotunda St. George

Built by the Romans in the 4th century, the Rotunda (8am–5pm) became a church in the 6th century. The 12th- to 14th-century frescoes inside the central dome are worth a glance, but in comparison to Sofia's churches the UNESCO-protected building feels pretty soulless.

❼ St. Ndelya Church ✿

This 19th-century church was largely destroyed by a bomb in 1925—intended to blow up czar Boris III, his life was spared by an accident of timing, but 200 of his subjects were not that fortunate. Like the Russian church it is hugely popular, and as a result one of the most atmospheric churches in Bulgaria during services. From here head north, crossing the "Largo" (use the underpass) to emerge on the other side at TZUM, Sofia's Communist-era shopping mall—surrounded by roads and half submerged is a 14th-century church, the indifference of its location dating back to Ottoman times, when grounds around churches were excavated to symbolically "lower" them. Also surrounded by busy roads is the:

❽ Statue of Sofia

Erected in 2001, the 24m-high (78-ft.) statue—created by Georgi Chapkanov and Stanislav Konstantinov—holds the symbols of fame and wisdom in her hands; her head bears the crown of Tjuhe—Goddess of Fate. Walk north along Maria Luiza Boulevard, and on the right you will see the:

❾ Banya Bashi Mosque

Built in 1576, its minarets still call the city's small Muslim population to prayer.

It is named after the city's Baths, currently being restored; in front of the Baths is a large paved area with a tapped spring where locals fill bottles with fresh mineral water to quench their thirst. Note that the fourth tap runs a permanent supply of piping hot mineral water. Opposite is the Halite, built in 1909 as the city's food market, and useful if you feel like a snack. From here you can either stroll along Pirotska Street, Sofia's only pedestrianized shopping street, or head 2 blocks down Ekzarch Josif Stret to:

❿ Sofia Synagogue

Built between 1905 and 1909, this beautiful synagogue—largest in the Balkans—served a community of some 25,000 descendants of the Sephardic community expelled by the Catholics who found refuge in Bulgaria under the decidedly more tolerant Islamic rulers. Today the community has dwindled to a handful, as most chose to leave for Israel during the Communist era. (The vast majority of Bulgaria's Jews survived World War II despite the fact that czar Boris III sided with Hitler. Under immense pressure from local civic leaders, he refused to deport Bulgarian Jews, fobbing off Nazi demands by forcing the Jews to disperse within the countryside. Many Bulgarian's believe this cost him his life; see Rila Monastery, below.) Having stepped inside to admire the massive Viennese chandelier (weighing in at 1,700 kilograms/3,750 lb.), saunter to the:

⓫ Zhenski Pazar ✿✿✿

This multicultural street (A2, A3 Stefan Stambalov St.), known as "Women's Market," is a world away from the nearby City Garden and its metropolitan pavement cafes. Here heavy-set women in headscarves peruse large piles of colorful fruits and vegetables, bargain for Troyan ceramics (the cheapest prices you'll find anywhere), or simply pick up domestic essentials from the tiny shops, including plenty of Turkish stalls, that line the fresh produce market. It's a great place to wander and pick up a bag of sweet cherries or a freshly baked banitsa, but do watch your bag.

SHOPPING

Most head for **TZUM,** a relatively small modern shopping mall opposite the Sheraton, or the boutiques lining **Vitosha Boulevard**—Sofia's main shopping street. Hristo Botev street runs parallel to Vitosha, and has better bargains, like **Decade** (no. 16) which stocks locally produced cotton leisure wear, and **Rumi Factory Outlet** (no. 23) where you can pick up relatively cheap Bulgarian leather products. Inveterate shoppers should also include a wander down **Graf Ignatief** and **Tsar Ivan Shishman** streets—fashionistas looking for local designs make a beeline for the bohemian creations at **Atelie Mirela Bratova** (no. 4), peruse the collections at **Magazine No 10** (no. 4) or, if you prefer a more quirky take, keep going to **525** (no. 525).

Pirotska (near Tzum, opposite the mosque) is another popular shopping street, and as it's pedestrianized a more pleasant experience than Vitosha Boulevard; stroll down here or head north after a few blocks to get to the **Zhenski Pazar** (see walking tour above)—stepping into this open-air market after Vitosha and Pirotska feels like time travel, with the clientele picking through heaps of fresh produce a century away from their high-heeled counterparts perusing the racks in glitzy boutiques.

BULGARIAN FOLK CRAFTS

Alexander Nevski Square Flea Market   If the weather is fine this open-air arts and crafts flea market in front of the Cathedral and St. Sofia Church is the best place to browse for bargain-priced icons (though not equally so; don't buy at the first stall). Also on offer are embroidered tablecloths, Russian dolls, knitted socks, handmade toys, ceramics, various carved items, and so-called antiques (coins, uniforms, medals), many dating from the Communist era.

Centre of Traditional Folk Arts and Crafts   Conveniently located on the ground floor of the Ethnographic Museum (also an outlet on Paris St.), and open daily, this has the entire range of crafts produced throughout the country. Not always the best prices, but mark-ups aren't huge, and you're sure to find something to suit even the smallest budget—from painted dolls with rose oil capsules to sachets with traditional Bulgarian spices. 2 Aleksandur Batenberg. (C) **989 5210.** A 2nd location at 4 Paris St.; (C) **02/989-6416.** www.bulgariancrafts.hit.bg.

Chushkarcheto Carpet House   Incredibly professional and hard to beat when it comes to selection of predominantly Chiprovtsi carpets. And if none of the ready-made kilims or rugs suit you, you can have one tailor-made to your design and color specifications, then have it shipped over. 38 G.S. Rakovski St. (C) **02/983-6609.** www.tchukilim.com.

Traditzia   This "charity gallery" is a great place to shop for a wide variety of crafts (kilims, knitted or silk accessories, paintings, dolls, tea towels, greeting cards, jewelry, and so on), not least because by shopping at Traditzia you directly support artists that hail from far-flung poverty-stricken regions, as well as the mentally and physically challenged, and staff are friendly. 36 Vasil Levski Blvd. (across the road from Downtown Hotel). (C) **02/981-7765.** www.traditzia.bg.

MUSIC

The Union of Bulgarian Composers *Finds* An unassuming shop with the best selection of folk, devotional, and classical music, all composed and/or recorded by Bulgarian musicians, in the country. Conveniently located opposite the National Theatre. The lady behind the desk is not fluent in English but helpful and will play any number of CDs for you. 2 Ivan Vazov St. *C* **02/988 15 60.**

SOFIA AFTER DARK

Sofia's music, opera, and dance seasons are at their peak during the spring and early summer, but by mid-July most of the city's actors and artists have—like the rest of the population—deserted the sweltering capital and migrated to the coast, taking the city's cultural life with them. This also affects the general nightlife scene, which quiets down considerably in Sofia while taking off on the coast. To find out what's on during your stay, take a look at www.programata.bg (click on "English"), pick up one of the free seasonal or monthly guides, or purchase a copy of the English weekly newspaper, *Sofia Echo.*

Theater performances are almost always in Bulgarian, so best to stick to music concerts or opera; tickets are extremely affordable relative to what you'd pay in a western European city, and while you don't usually have the very top-end performers there are always foreign imports with impeccable credentials. The monolithic **National Palace of Culture** (NDK; 1 Bulgaria Sq.; *C* **02/916 6208;** www.ndk.bg), built in 1981 (ostensibly to mark the year Bulgaria turned 1,300), is the place to be during the Salon Des Arts Sofia, which usually runs mid-May to mid-June; as does the International "Sofia Music Weeks" Festival, hosted in the Bulgaria Hall and Bulgaria Chamber Hall, home to the Bulgarian philharmonic orchestra (1 Aksakov St.; **02/987 7656**). Described as "the jewel in Sofia's cultural crown," the **Sofia National Opera** (1 Vrabcha St., off Rakovski St; *C* **02/981 1549**) is where the city's most talented and guest performers from all over Europe play out the great opera and ballet classics; see what's while you're there by logging onto www.sofiaopera.com. If you're looking for a more avant-garde experience, check out what's happening at hip and happening Red House Centre for Culture and Debate (www.redhouse-sofia.org; see "Where to Stay," earlier in this chapter).

The Sofia nightlife scene is low-key but vibrant, with plenty of nightclubs and trendy bars dotted throughout the city. The following three are personal favorites, but it's worth mentioning that Brilliantine (3 Moskovska St.) is hugely popular, attracting a diverse and interesting crowd, as does gay-friendly Chillout Café (6 Baba Nedelya St., just behind the NDK).

Apartament 52 LOUNGE BAR This is the apartment of Boris, who usually hangs out in the kitchen (he's the one in the easy chair, with the Maltese poodle on his lap). This is also where the drinks are dispensed, including a startling array of freshly squeezed juice combos, most with health-giving additives like ginseng and ginkgo. The rest of the rooms are furnished with comfortable couches on which loners are curled up with books or chatting with virtual friends (there's a free Internet station, as well as a computer with iPod), or cool couples catch up with friends. 52 Parchevich St. *C* **02/887 753454.** 10pm–2am

Chervilo BAR CLUB If you want to know where the Sofian eye candy likes to hang out, head for multiple-bar Chervilo. It's not just that the bargirls and boys are disaffected and gorgeous, or that the interiors are super stylish, or that the music thumps until sunrise, or even that your party "colleagues" are either rich, attractive, or interesting (strict "face control" at the wrought-iron gates, but English-speaking foreigners always welcome) but housed in the attractive buildings that are part of the Military Club on Tsar Osvoboditel, it's easy to find on foot. 9 Tsar Osvoboditel Blvd. 8:30am–6am.

Toba & Co CAFE BAR   If it's a balmy evening, this is a super Parisian-style cafe-bar to hang out before or after supper (House With the Clock is diagonally opposite), with pretty tables and wooden chairs set up in the cast-iron pavilion in the garden behind the Royal Palace. It's principally a bar, but after 10pm a DJ pumps up the atmosphere with groovy sounds, and no one will mind if you raise your hands and sway your hips while sashaying over to the bar. 6 Moskovska St. ℂ **02/989 4696**. 10am until late.

4 The Rila, Pirin & Rhodope Mountains

Sofia might be the country's offbeat heart, but the headiest rush is to be had while traveling into the mountainous landscape that defines much of southwestern Bulgaria. From the soaring snowcapped peaks of the Rila and the Pirin ranges, which flow almost seamlessly into the forested flanks of the Rhodope, the scenery is a balm on the stressed city dwellers' soul: revitalized by icy rivers that charge and tumble through narrow clifflike gorges and lush alpine meadows, and awed by ancient forests, their soft flickering light a proxy of some great cathedral. No wonder then that St. John of Rila, Bulgaria's most famous hermit, holed up in a cave in these mountains for 20 years before stepping out to establish Bulgaria's finest spiritual sanctuary in the shadow of these peaks. Rila Monastery, the physical embodiment of the skills and crafts spawned by Bulgaria's 19th-century renaissance, is the country's most popular inland attraction, and makes a wonderful day trip from Sofia. But the monastery is far from the only or even best attraction in this region.

Farther south, in the foothills of the Pirin's mountainous border with Greece, lies the tiny village of Melnik. This is the country's best-known wine-producing area (Churchill apparently saw through the war armed with cases of Melnik wine), but the village itself, lined with tall whitewashed buildings, is a delight, and the ideal base from which to visit nearby Rozhen monastery—at first glance not as impressive as far larger Rila but perhaps the most atmospheric sanctuary in Bulgaria, where monks still outnumber tourists. Northeast of here lies Bansko, Bulgaria's premier ski resort, but unless you're here for the skiing, head straight through (or, if road surfaces allow, via Melnik) to the real gems of this region: the Rhodopean villages denoted as architectural museums, where cobbled lanes meander past 19th-century stone-and-timber homes, their wrinkled owners basking on benches in the sun. Offering the best places to stay and eat in rural Bulgaria, Kovachevitsa and Leshten in particular are an essential stop on the itinerary.

PLANNING YOUR JOURNEY IN THE SOUTHWEST

Isolated day trips to one or two of the destinations below simply does not do justice to this region, the most beautiful in Bulgaria; there are also very few direct bus or train connections between Sofia and most of these destinations. Here more than anywhere else you simply have to hire a car, preferably with a driver, and traverse the gorgeous mountain passes and villages at your own pace. (See "Getting Around," earlier in this chapter). Ideally you should set aside 3 or 4 nights, though it is possible to cover in 2, overnighting first in Melnik, and the following night in Leshten or Kovachevitsa, before moving on to Plovdiv.

Scary Monsters: Freddy Eat Your Heart Out

While the majority of Bulgarians are traditional Orthodox, plenty still ascribe to more pagan animistic rituals, and nowhere is this more evident than during the annual *kukeri* and *survakari* rites, designed to repel evil spirits and promote fertility, and still practiced in certain villages and cities in the southwest with great fervor on New Year (or Jan 14). During a 30-day period, known as the "dirty days" or *"Mrasni Dni,"* when the days that denote the new and old year mingle, it is believed that the gates to both heaven and hell are temporarily left open, and demons carrying illness and evil walk the earth. A group of selected villagers or townsfolk, each playing specific roles, don terrifying masks and girdles sagging with huge bells. Armed with wooden guns, swords, or axes, they stalk the streets, entering homes to sound off the demons with loud clanging bells and smoke, and "killing" the evil harbingers by sweeping through rooms with their swords. During the fertility rites the kukeri leader, who on occasion carries a large red phallus, simulates sexual encounters with the women in the village to ensure that everything (and everyone) is ready to be "fertilized" in the new year, something that would no doubt see him slapped with a sexual harassment case in the West but accepted here with much hilarity. You can see the best, most frightening, examples of *kukeri* masks, as well as plenty of photographs, in Sofia's ethnographic museum (see above), or arrange to see a real "Festival of the Kukeri"—the largest (and most accessible) is held in Pernik, when some 3,500 revelers dress up to participate in this ancient ritual during the last weekend in January (every even-numbered year). Pernik, 30km (19 miles) southwest of Sofia, is a short bus or train trip away. Alternatively, if you're traveling in March, make sure you're in Shiroka Luka (see below).

RILA MONASTERY ✸✸✸
120km (74 miles) south of Sofia

Bulgarian monks knew how to pick prime real estate, and Rila is no exception. Accosted by the thundering sound of water charging over large boulders—two rivers, the Rilksa and Drushlyavitsa, flank the monastery—and the startling sight of thick alpine forests rising above you like cliffs, their thick triangular fingers clasping snow-capped peaks that sparkle like diamonds, you know you are in one of the most beautiful places in Bulgaria. And that's before you've even stepped inside.

The country's biggest monastery, Rila was included in the UNESCO World Heritage List in 1983 as "a characteristic example of the Bulgarian Renaissance, symbolizing an awareness of a Slavic cultural identity following centuries of occupation." The original sanctuary was founded in the 10th century by the followers of Ivan Rilski "The Miracleworker," aka St. John of Rila, who lived in a tiny cave about a 30-minute walk from the monastery. Revered by kings and subjects alike, the monastery was a cultural and religious refuge during centuries of foreign rule, but it was during the 1830s that the monks gave physical expression to its powerful position within the

Bulgarian psyche, building a four-floor residential building within fortresslike stone walls to house 300 monks, and guest rooms for its many donors. In fact most of what you see today was built between 1834 and 1837 (predated only by the 14th-c. brick tower that rises in the middle of the inner courtyard, and the small 14th-c. church [1343] that stands next to the tower; this had a belfry added in 1844).

Despite the impressive surroundings, it is the church they call "the Nativity of the Virgin" that draws the visitor's eye, with its porch entirely covered in rich decorative frescoes; step inside and the interiors are equally beautiful, with an intricately carved and glittering gilt iconostasis beckoning devotees closer—this is one of the finest examples of the art of the Samokov woodcarvers (a town nearby, like Tryavna famous for producing Bulgaria's finest artists), as are the icons. Here you'll find the silver box with the hand of St. John of Rila (see "Kissing the Bones of a Well-Traveled Saint," below); farther to the left, kept in a drawer, is a 12th-century icon of the Virgin. In a chapel opposite, underneath a simple wooden cross, lies the heart of czar Boris III. The king, who had refused to hand over his Jewish subjects, died on his way back from a trip to Berlin in 1944, prompting speculation that he had been poisoned by the Nazis. The murals were painted by many artists, including Dimitar and Zahari Zograf, the Samokov brothers who were to become the most famous icon painters of the 19th-century National Revival. Zahari is in fact the better known, perhaps because he was arrogant (or sensible) enough to sign his work, and eventually courting enormous controversy by painting himself into some of his murals. The exterior murals are particularly absorbing, with the most awful damnations heaped upon sinners—apocalyptic images that look inspired by the diabolical imagination of Hieronymus Bosch, and must have done plenty to herd the illiterate into the Orthodox fold.

After viewing the church, move on to the monastery museum (daily 8am–5pm; 5lev/$3.50/£1.75), which houses a number of interesting artworks and relics, the most fascinating of which is Raphael's Cross: carved from a single piece of wood, the 81-centimeter-high cross features no less than 104 religious tableaux with 1,500 tiny figures—a 12-year labor of love that cost the monk Raphael his eyesight. After this you can visit one of the monk's cells and the massive cauldrons in the "kitchen"—look up and you realize you've stepped into what is effectively the world's largest chimney. If you have a few hours, set off on the 4km (2.5-mile) walk through the forest above the monastery to Saint John of Rila's original hermitage—a fairly nondescript cave unless you try to work your way up through the fissure known as "Miracle Hole"—in days of yore those who could not achieve this relatively simple feat were thought to be tainted with sin and sent home to atone.

ESSENTIALS: GETTING THERE & GETTING A MEAL

Rila Monastery (✆ **07054/2208**), about 90 minutes south of Sofia, is an easy day trip from the capital by car or tour bus, and serviced by numerous tour operators. **Zig Zag** (✆ **02/980 5102;** www.zigzagbg.com) offers the best-value day trip (58€/$74). The trip is in a private car with a guide, and a maximum of four others. If you don't want to share the experience, book with Surprise Tours (see details below), which will take you to the monastery for 80€ ($102). If you're not hassled by traveling in a large impersonal group book with **FairPlay International JSC** (✆ **02/943 4574;** www.fpitravel.com; 25€/$32, lunch and guide included). Note that there are no direct public buses from Sofia; using this may require an overnight stay; none of the accommodations options,

Kissing the Bones of a Well-Traveled Saint

John of Rila (aka Ivan Rilski) died in 946 at 66. His devoted and grieving follow-ers virtually deified his corpse, which was sent to Sofia. Stolen as plunder by the Hungarian King Bela III in 1183, the relic (or what remained of it) was returned 5 years later (apparently it had made a Catholic bishop blind after the bishop denied the bones were those of a saint) only to then make its way to Veliko Tarnovo in 1194. St. John of Rila finally came home in 1469, but his respite was short; a century later his right hand was removed and toured Russia, distribut-ing miracles and earning funds for the monastery. St. John's left hand is now kept in the church, and is believed to have healing powers—you can ask one of the monks to draw back the velvet cover to reveal the glass box under which the yellowed bones still miraculously gleam, but note that you will then have to kiss it as a sign of respect. Wads of cotton-wool, kept on a pedestal nearby, are said to have become imbued with healing power because of their proxim-ity to the hand—pilgrims who take a piece to place near a source of pain appar-ently experience real relief.

including the spartan and less-than-spotless monastery cells, make for a happy holiday experience. The same is not true for dining; the monk-run bakery just outside the monastery sells the best Bulgarian doughnuts and delicious yogurt. If you're ready for a full meal, keep space for these as a takeout dessert and grab a table at the **Drushliavitsa** restaurant (open daily 8am–11pm), perched above the monastery to the one side of the its namesake river, with a small outdoor terrace. This is by far the best place to eat in the area, serving fresh trout, the mildly spiced local sausage (kebabche), and the most won-derful firm yellow-fleshed potato chips; bread is baked fresh daily by the monastery bak-ery. Despite being next to Bulgaria's top inland attraction, the most expensive item is 5lev/$3.50/£1.75.

Tips: Monastery gates open at dawn and close at dusk; try to get here at 7am (or 8am, depending on time of year) to catch the early morning service; there's a good chance you'll be the only visitor here, watching a ritual that has been witnessed by these walls, every day, for some 200 years. On Thursdays the morning service is dedi-cated to St. John; the beautiful liturgical chanting that accompanies this service dates from the 15th century. Avoid the weekends when the natural tranquillity of the monastery is all but ruined by the huge number of visitors. The same goes for the two main festivals celebrated here on August 18 (St. John's birthday) and October 19 (his feast day).

MELNIK ★★

186km (115 miles) from Sofia

Once a thriving outpost, Melnik boasted a population of 20,000 predominantly Greek citizens (it's a mere 15km/9⅓ miles from the border with Greece) before the Second Balkan War of 1913; hard to believe when you first turn into the sandstone gorge to see the tiny village that is today home to a mere 270.

Set amid numerous pyramid-shaped sandstone outcroppings that create a jagged mountainous backdrop, Melnik is officially designated as a historical Reserve but is atypical of the country's National Revival–era museum towns, with none of the lush fecundity that typifies the rural villages to the north. Semiarid, with a mixed Mediterranean and mountainous climate, this turned out to be ideal winemaking territory, with a *terroir* that nurtures the dusky and robust flavors of the unique Bulgarian red grape variety known as Melnik Broad Vine, and soft sandstone that allows for burrowing cool cave-cellars.

Populated by a handful of born-and-bred locals, the village is admittedly focused on the tourist buck, with at least half the homes transformed into places to stay or eat, but the villagers are justifiably proud of their village, and there's no ugly tourist tat—this, together with the fact that it is not en route to any other major attraction, has left the most popular destination in southern Pirin mercifully unspoiled.

ESSENTIALS: ARRIVING & GETTING AROUND

FairPlay International offer day trips to **Melnik** from Sofia for 49€ ($63), 180€ ($229) with your own car and driver/guide; both prices include lunch. **Surprise Tours** offers a car and driver for 80€ ($102). **Intersport** arranges day trips to Melnik and Rozhen from Bansko for 30€ ($39), lunch included (see "Bansko," below); the same company also offers a 2-day guided walk from Bansko to Melnik, with an overnight stop and dinner on the Tevnoto lake, the highest in Pirin; the price is 50€ ($64) all inclusive. Melnik is not connected by train, and if you travel by public bus you will need to change in Sandanski, a potentially difficult enterprise when drivers and most passengers are unlikely to speak English. Note that Melnik has no information bureau, nor an ATM or bank, so draw enough cash before you leave your last destination, or in Sandanski, the last big town before Melnik.

WHERE TO STAY

Should Bolyarka be full, you'll find that **Despot Slav** a close runner-up; decor is slightly more busy and schizophrenic but room size and rates are virtually identical (© **0743/248** or 089 9984406). A really good alternative if you are watching your budget (and possibly preferable, because it is so personally run that it feels more like a private home than a hotel) is **Uzunova Kushta** (**0889 450849;** 0887 321446, or 07437/270). It's also a mere 20lev ($13/£6.90) per person, breakfast included.

Hotel Bolyarka ★   This humble hotel is the poshest in Melnik, with a stone-walled lobby bar dressed with slightly incongruous faux Regency-style furniture. Rooms are all pretty small, as are the bathrooms but this is as good as it gets in the village; most of the best rooms feature a balcony (the one off room no. 107 has a good view). Alternatively ask for a corner room, like no. 207, which is slightly bigger and has a view (note however that there is no elevator, so if you're carrying heavy luggage the second floor is probably not a good idea for only 1 night). Apartments are slightly larger and worth the extra cost (not so the "luxury" apartments, which are tasteless). The best restaurant in town (see below) is directly opposite.

Main St. © 07437/383, 07437/368, or 0888 455045. Fax 07437369. www.boyarka.hit.bg. 21 units. 60lev ($39/£21) double; 80lev ($51/£28) apt.; 130lev ($83/£45) luxury apt. Rates include breakfast. **Amenities:** Restaurant; bar; sauna; fitness room; cellar; room service; massage; small conference room; laundry. *In room:* TV, minibar, fireplaces (apts. only).

WHERE TO DINE

Ask any local where the best place to eat in town is, and without fail they all answer Mencheva Kashta. Ask Mr. Menchev, the proprietor of Mencheva Kashta, for *his* recommendation, and he points up to **Varvara** (© **088 799 2191** or 07437/388), the bustling mehana just below the Kordopulov House. Views from up here (you look down and across the village) are certainly sublime, as is the smell that wafts across from the terrace as you enter or leave the Kordopulov House, but if you're only in town long enough for one meal, make sure it's the kavarma or meshaniza prepared by Mladen Menchev's women.

Mencheva Kushta ✿✿✿ BULGARIAN   This unassuming little mehana, housed in a 200-year-old listed building, may look unexceptional, but what comes out of the kitchen is. The Mencheva's chicken kavarma is one of the best examples you'll ever taste of this traditional cooking method (essentially slices of chicken, onion, tomatoes, and red pepper, oven-baked with egg in an earthenware ceramic pot), as is the "meshaniza of melnik," which has meat wonderfully tender while vegetables retain their crunch and character. A 100% family affair (patriarch Mladen Menchev is aided by his wife and three children and two daughters-in-law), it was one of the first restaurants to open in Melnik in 1993; before this Mladen was a waiter, unable under the old Communist dispensation to establish his own restaurant. But the years of serving tables paid off; Mladen, the entrepreneur-in-waiting, is now the proud proprietor of Melnik's most successful restaurant. In the evenings Jan and Elana, a young couple dressed in traditional garb, provide wonderful live music, their repertoire based on their travels into the far-flung communities in the Pirin mountains.

Main St. ② 07437/339 or 0889406861. www.melnik-mehana.com. 2.50lev–10lev ($2–$7/85p–£2.40). MC, V. Daily 10am–11pm.

EXPLORING THE VILLAGE & SURROUNDINGS

Featuring a simplified version of the National Revival architectural style you see elsewhere, the 18th and 19th century homes that line the dusty main road are typically built with a fortresslike stone foundation that can stretch as high as two stories, sometimes built into the sandstone slopes, into which the caves were dug to store huge barrels of wine. Above this stone base the whitewashed walls tower, their facades punctuated with shutters, usually closed to ward off the summer heat. It's a lovely look, and quite unique to Melnik.

Once you've strolled along the main street, head uphill to visit the main attraction: the stately home (at least it must have been in 18th-c. Melnik) of the **Kordopulovs** (② 07437/265; daily 10am–9pm; 2lev/$1.50/85p). Said to be the biggest National Revival House in Bulgaria, with a record 24 windows (many of the panes multicolored stained glass, giving it an Eastern-influenced look), Melnik's grandest home was built by Kordopulov, a rich trader of Greek descent, in 1754. After walking through the large airy rooms, you descend into the cool cellar where Kordopulov stored 250 to 300 metric tons of wine in a cave system that took him 12 years to carve. You can do a wine tasting here (not even vaguely in the league of Melnik's finest, but very drinkable and similar in taste to what most of the local villagers produce as their house wine) before exiting and making your way to Mitko's cave (see "Drinking Wine with 'Six Fingers' Manolev," below). Aside from this, and a visit to Rozhen Monastery, perhaps the best reason to venture this far south lies in the middle of Melnik's main road, at the Menchevs (see above), one of the best dining experiences in Bulgaria.

Rozhen Monastery ✿✿   Rozhen is in no way comparable to Rila in terms of size or even grandeur of setting, but approaching the low-slung building there is not a tourist stall in sight (and, if you're lucky, not another tourist either); enter and it is as if you've stepped into another world, a silent, serene place where nothing bad ever

Moments   **Drinking Wine with "Six Fingers" Manolev**

Ironically, given how famous the region is for its red wines, there is no wine shop dedicated to promoting a selection of the winemakers in the village, nor is it possible to arrange a wine tasting (as an individual at any rate) with the region's best cellar—**Damianitza Cellar** (www.melnikwine.bg)—which caters only to groups. If you're not a wine snob, there is, however, a delightful wine-tasting experience to be had in a 250-year-old cave cellar overlooking the village. As you leave Kerdopulova Kushta, take the high path that curves along the hill in the direction of town to find **Mitko Manolev** (*(C)* **0887 545 795**), aka "six fingers," brooding over his barrels. He will offer you a tasting of his wines direct from the barrel (1lev/65¢/35p), all the while ranting about how the E.U. regulations will be the ruin of independent winemakers. Mitko will bottle your wine of choice (two types of red, both not dissimilar to grape juice, made with no preservatives and slightly sparkling, rather good when served ice cold). It may not be entirely to your liking but worth purchasing all the same, if only to watch him personally fill, cork, and label it right in front of you—the most personally handled bottle of wine you're likely to purchase anywhere.

happens. Ironic, given how often the monastery has been pillaged since it was founded by Alexius Slav in 1220. Within the small courtyard, which is surrounded by a two-story structure in timber, is the Church of the Birth of the Holy Virgin. Like Rila, it attracts pilgrims seeking miraculous answers to their prayers all the while educating the illiterate on just how terrifying the wages of sin are, with a florid mural depicting demons tossing those sinners trying to flee into the gaping mouth of the Serpent. While Rozhen is one of the smallest of Bulgaria's monasteries, it is in relatively good condition, with well-tended gardens and orchards—proof of how loved it is by the monks. There is a strong sense here that this is very much a living monastery into which you are intruding as a tourist rather than a pilgrim, so be sensitive to noise levels. Also note that it is strictly forbidden to photograph the monks or the inside of the church.

7km (4½ miles) by road from Melnik, via Karlanovo. Free admission. Daily dawn–dusk.

BANSKO
150km (93 miles) from Sofia

Sprawling at the base of the Pirin, Bansko is Bulgaria's fastest growing winter resort, with a cumulative 65km of marked ski runs and brand-new lifts to ensure that the resort continues to attract the lion's share of foreigners keen to experience conditions on the slopes of "Bulgaria's Alps." Besides the range of runs—ideal for a group comprising beginners, intermediate, and experienced skiers—Bansko is also the only Bulgarian ski resort that is centered around a historic old quarter—a tangle of cobbled streets lined with thick stone walls and metal-studded gates behind which half-timbered double-story homes can be glimpsed. Many of these are now atmospheric *mehanas,* their windows aglow with crackling fires in winter and the sound of lilting traditional songs wafting out along with the delicious aroma of Bulgarian fare, served

---

Fun Fact English Invasion

Get here in high season and you'd be forgiven for thinking that you've somehow taken a wrong turn. Since 2003 some 3,000 Britons have bought homes in
Bansko (over $175 million has been invested in Bulgarian property since 1994),
and in 2005 80% of visitors in town hailed from the U.K. and Ireland.

---

up at such reasonable prices that even those forced to go half- or full-board by hotels
during peak season can afford to junk these (generally awful) meals and head into the
old quarter for a decent spread. But if you're not high up in the mountains or settled
around a table in the village heart, the picture is a little less pretty, as Bansko's innate
charm is increasingly compromised by the unprecedented growth seen in the last few
years—every season sees more concrete poured into foundations that creep beyond the
"official" building line as developers try to deliver on the promise of "uninterrupted
views," with prospects for the hotels left in the wake of their greed ever-diminishing.
The only justice is that 1 year from now, these developers will have to face the butt-
end of the new kids on the block. The exception to this is the pricey Kempinski: situated right on the western edge, where flower-edged balconies provide huge views of
the Pirin, interrupted only by skiers flashing down the final run while others rise to
meet the challenge of its powdered peaks.

ESSENTIALS: GETTING THERE & GETTING AROUND

Surprise Tours offers direct transfers to Bansko (just under 3 hr.) for 75€ ($96). If
you're counting every stotinka, take the **public bus.** The 3-hour journey from Sofia to
Bansko will cost a mere 8lev/$5.20/1.60£, as does the 3½-hour bus trip from Plovdiv.
Buses pull into Ul Patriarh Evitimi, on the northern outskirts; a 10-minute walk from
the old quarter (centered around ploshtad Vazrazhdane) and about 25 to 40 minutes
to the new developments creeping up the slope where most of the "better" hotels are
located. If this is your destination make sure you prearrange a transfer. Around the corner from here you'll find the small **train** station; Bansko's only train connection (via
narrow-gauge track) is with Septemvri, which in turn lies on the Sofia-Plovdiv line. The
journey between Bansko and Septemvri is wonderfully scenic as it trundles through for-
est-clad mountains and valleys of timeless bucolic beauty, but at 5 hours is inconveniently long; that said, if you catch the earliest (there are three a day; get your host to
check most recent times), this could be the best way to reach Plovdiv, allowing you to
take in some Pirin and western Rhodopean scenery without going to the expense of
renting a car. Alternatively, you can experience two-thirds of the journey by booking
with Intersport (see details below), which will put you on the train and pick you up
from the Velingrad station, bringing you back to Bansko by road.

The **tourist information** center is located off the central square (ploshtad Vapt-
sarov) just north of the old quarter, but opening hours are in reality inconveniently
flexible (© **07443/5048;** Mon–Fri 9am–1pm and 2–5pm).

For a wide variety of 1-, 2- and 3-day guided hiking or biking excursions in the Pirin
National Park (ranging from 39lev–149lev/$25–$95/£14–£52), or 1-day rafting
(99lev/$63/£34) and rock-climbing expeditions (49lev/$32/£17), contact **Intersport**
(© **088 878 8859;** www.intersport.bansko.bg). Intersport also offers sightseeing excursions to Melnik and Rozhen Monastery, Leshten and Kovachevitsa, and Dancing Bear

Park; all of these include all transportation, a guide, and lunch, and cost only 59lev ($38/£20).

WHERE TO STAY

Broadly you have two choices in Bansko. You can stay in a B&B in the old quarter, where facilities are basic but a great deal more atmospheric, and you're a stone's throw from the best restaurants in town (note however that these may be a little *too* close in high season, when evening festivities can continue until quite late). Or you can base yourself in the new part of town, where the main benefit is the proximity to the gondola ski lift (a 15- to 25-min. walk if you're based in the old quarter).

The selection below includes the best available in late 2006, but note that developments continue apace. If you're here for an extended skiing trip, you may get a far better package deal in a hotel not listed here; while the hotel will be forgettable, and service nonexistent, the price may be just right. For details on agents who can arrange lodgings, see the last entry of this section. Expect to pay double the summer rate during winter, and triple over the peak time (usually the period just before Christmas and a few days into Jan); hotels and even B&B owners are not keen to divulge these winter rates early (supply and demand being the order of the day), so be prepared for some fluctuations to rates quoted below. Children aged under 5 or 6 usually stay free.

Old Quarter

There are plenty of places to stay in the old quarter, but **Dedo Pene** (✆ **0888 795970,** or 937/299-5643 in the U.S.; www.dedopene.com; 50lev/$32/£17 double) gets my vote. The 1820 home is a bit eclectic, so rooms vary quite a bit, but all share a wonderfully authentic, rustic, and cozy atmosphere, with traditional furnishings and fittings (including the lovely basins—traditionally used to carry water from the well), and wood-and-coal-burning fireplaces. Rooms number 1 and 4 have lovely views of the distant Pirin; others look out onto the red-tiled roofs of the old quarter—make sure you request a room with a view. A close contender, and a tad cheaper (in every way) is **Dvata Smurcha** (2 Velyan Ognev; ✆ **07443/2632;** 16lev–18lev/$11–$12/£5.50–£6.20 per person, including breakfast), located a few steps away from the brilliant **Baryakova mehana** (see "Where to Dine," below). It's named after the two pine trees that stand proud in its well-tended garden. The friendly proprietor speaks virtually no English but is all smiles, and offers five spotless en-suite rooms, most with balconies. The old part of the house (over 100 years) has rooms with balconies that provide lovely views of the Pirin, while rooms in the new part (just over a year old) are slightly bigger and fresher, with garden views. If you fancy staying in a museum of sorts, another good option is **Hadzhiruskovite kushti** (33 Pirin St; ✆ **07443/8422;** 15lev–18lev/$10–$12/£5.20–£4.15 per person). Once home to the man who

---

Missing in Action?

While walking the cobbled streets of the old quarter, you will pass timber doors and stone walls papered with photographs of people, many of them repeated. The notices in fact are of the recently (and not so recently) deceased and advertise dates and times when the family will again be gathering in their memory. This is an integral part of the Orthodox 40-day mourning rite; many gatherings continue after 40 days, hence the many papers.

designed the village church's bell tower (from which the peals still emanate every Sun), and until recently the property of the Union of Bulgarian Architects, it is a truly authentic example of Bansko's 19th-century residences—almost totally unrenovated, with solid stone walls and heavy woodwork. Note though that only the two rooms on the second floor (nos. 5 and 6) are worth booking—these have enough light (rooms below are dark) and open onto a wide veranda with rustic tables and chairs that overlook the untended stone-walled garden. The charming Marin (enough English to get by), makes a delicious home-brewed rakia (brandy); if he knows you know, he's sure to offer.

"NEW" BANSKO

The four-star **Hotel Perun** (© 0749/88477; www.hotelperunbansko.com) is very much a Kempinski wannabe—without the class, staff, or view. But it is a rather smart-looking alpine edifice, a 10-minute walk from the gondola station (or you can use the hotel's shuttle bus service), and has (after Kempinski) the second-best facilities in town (okay, Hotel Strazhite has a bowling alley, but you don't want to be stuck with *that* decor). It's also the best value for your money, even in high season when rooms range between 60€ and 170€ ($77–$216). Families should book the Double Delux Rooms with two separate rooms, each with its own bathroom. If you can forego hotel facilities, and are planning to be here for more than a couple of days, Todorini Kuli apartments (© 0888 441005; www.todorinikuli.com) are the best deal in "new" Bansko, offering excellent value and a great location directly opposite the Kempinski (50m/16 ft. from the Gondola station). Apartments are pretty characterless, but they are brand-new, so finishes look fresh and equipment functions well. Couples should book room no. 2, the biggest; families should opt for a one-bedroom apartment, with separate bedroom and open-plan lounge (with fireplace), dining room, and kitchen—no. 15 is a good option. Rates, depending on size and season, range between 10€ and 140€ ($13–$178).

Kempinski Hotel Grand Arena ★★★ "Excellent position, great staff, pricey though," reads one review, and that just about sums up the Kempinski. This five-star hotel has set the bar high, bringing to Bansko the joys of a grand foyer bar, a wellness center with extensive treatments, and a huge indoor pool. Typical of many chain hotels, rooms are bland and characterless but large and luxurious with balconies from which to enjoy the town's only truly unobstructed mountain views, and various dining options (the latter admittedly overpriced given what's available a 15-min. walk down the hill). The location is unbeatable, and thankfully this is one that will remain so: right on the western edge the hotel is almost butted up against the Gondola station so you can literally ski down the mountain directly into the hotel's "ski room," then stroll over to the bar for a poste-piste celebration. *Note:* Under no circumstances should you get landed with a room facing back into town; book a full mountain-facing room, and stick to your guns; also specify if you want a nonsmoking room.

96 Pirin St., Bansko. © 0749/88888. Fax 0749/88560. www.kempinski-bansko.com. 159 units. Deluxe and executive rooms 220€–270€ ($280–$343) double; 310€–470€ ($394–$597) suite. Rates include breakfast. Check for summer specials. AE, DC, MC, V. Valet parking and garage. **Amenities:** 2 restaurants; bar; 2 lounges; outdoor and indoor pools, tennis court; fitness center; Jacuzzi; steam room and sauna; Kneipp wading basin; conference center; shops; salon; solarium; kids' club; concierge; babysitting; laundry; dry cleaning. *In room:* A/C, TV, minibar, hair dryer, safe, wireless Internet connection.

Roka Villa ★★ *Finds* If you care at all about design, this is without a doubt the top choice in town (though a little far from the gondola station, but the hotel offers a shuttle service). A modern boutique hotel (the likes of which Sofia has yet to see), Roka Villa is clad almost entirely in a mesh of thin gray strips of timber; it's not quite the antithesis of the cutesy alpine chalet look but still alerts the passerby to the fact that within lies something rather different. From the black-walled and gray slate reception, where casually strewn white boulders from the nearby river make a statement both organic and stylish, to the lobby bar, which looks more like a club than a hotel, Roka Villa is as edgy as it gets in Bulgaria, never mind Bansko. Rooms are divided into "small double" (very small, but adequate), "standard double" (some with balconies), "deluxe double" (the best value category; ask for no. 349 or 351, or one with a balcony facing the mountain), double "Brod" room and deluxe maisonette (there is also a standard maisonette, with an unworkable floor plan to be avoided at all costs). Rooms feature red walls against which extratall dark timber headboards are etched; glass dividers are used in the smaller rooms (which incidentally only have one bedside light, which is irritating if you're both readers). The basement spa is equally stylish, though comfort cravers may find the design a little cold.

37B Glazne St., Bansko. ℭ **0749/88337.** Fax 0749/88446. www.villaroka.com 99 units. Summer rates: 56lev–66lev ($36–$42/£19–£23) double; Double Deluxe 76lev ($49/£26); Double "Brod" 84lev ($54/£29); Double "Brod" deluxe and deluxe maisonette 92lev ($59/£32). Winter rates: 150lev–180lev ($96–$115/£52–£62) double; Double Deluxe 210lev ($134/£73); Double "Brod" 213lev ($135/£73); Double "Brod" deluxe and deluxe maisonette 250lev ($159/£86). No credit cards. Rates include breakfast and dinner. **Amenities:** Restaurant; bar; spa center (pool, sauna, steam, solarium, range of treatments); room service; shuttle service to gondola; laundry; Internet access. *In room:* TV, minibar.

WHERE TO DINE

There are more than 40 atmospheric mehanas in the old quarter, all offering basically the same Bulgarian menu, but make sure you don't miss **Baryakova,** generally rated the best in the old quarter (see below). However, **Dedo Pene** is equally so, with a warren of cozy rooms leading out to a small central courtyard (see "Where to Stay," above). If you've covered these two, and looking for something new, another highly rated restaurant, this time just outside the old quarter on Glazne Street (look out for the two large barrels), is **Molerite 1972** (ℭ **07443/8494**).

Baryakova mehana ✸✸✸   Like most mehanas, this is an extended-family affair, in an old 19th-century building covered in traditional decorations (lovely dark timber beams and tables; bright red embroidered table cloths), but the quality of the food sets the standard here. There are a number of specialties—tender pork leg, grilled over coals; ceramic hot plate with sizzling strips of meat and vegetables; the "three meats" (strips of chicken, pork, and veal), cooked with sauerkraut in a pot, and served with rice. The latter is "Banska kapama" a local delicacy, as is "Banski staretz," a local "dry" sausage (like salami, but not as fatty, and uniquely spiced)—order this with white cheese and fresh bread as a starter. Note that Baryakova is usually only open in the evenings, and that the family takes a month off in summer to rest, but cannot say in advance which month this will be.

Velyan Ognev (just off central sq., Vuzrazhdane, in old town). ℭ **0889 534582,** or 0899 670734, or 0899 653377. Main courses 4.80lev–15lev ($3–$10/£1.65–£5.20). No credit cards. Daily 5pm until late.

EXPLORING BANSKO

Bansko's attraction list is predictably small and centered within its old quarter, where cobbled lanes spread out from ploshtad Vuzrazhdane, the square marked by the statue of Father Paisii, author of the *Slav-Bulgarian History*, one of the books that inspired

Cruel Dance

Bear sightings are notoriously rare in the wilds; if you're keen to see one up close, head to the nearby "Dancing Bear Park" (daily 9am–5pm; donations welcome), founded by the *Vier Pfoten* organization, supported by animal rights crusader Brigitte Bardot. Once a widespread source of entertainment, the cruel practice (cubs are placed on a hot plate while music is turned up to make them appear to "dance") was banned in Bulgaria in 2002, but the bears still get up on their paws and dance involuntarily, perhaps associating human visitors with the demands of their (usually) Gypsy owners.

ordinary Bulgarians, and helped launch the National Revival. On the mountain side of the square is the **Church of Sveta Troitsa.** It's pretty unexceptional but note the high walls—erected to hide the major extensions commissioned by the wealthy elite during the early 19th century, a time when the Ottoman rulers had pretty much put a lid on further Orthodox development, the then-mayor of Bansko paid for this defiance with a 5-year tenure in prison. Behind the church is the **Neofit Rilski House Museum** (daily 9am–noon and 2–5pm; 3lev/$2/£1) birthplace of one of Bulgaria's great scholars (he was for instance the first to translate the New Testament into Bulgarian), and another key player in the National Revival. Other than this there is the nearby Rilski Convent, housing a small **Icon Museum** (Yane Sandanski; Mon–Fri 9am–noon and 2–5pm; 3lev/$2/bp]1), and the **Velyanova kushta Museum** (5 Velyan Ognev; same hours as convent), home to the man who carved the iconostasis in the Church of Sveta Troitsa, and today furnished with typical 19th-century items, providing some insight into the relatively humble lifestyle of Bansko's hoi polloi. A little farther north from the old quarter is ploshtad Nikola Vapstarov, where the annual **Bansko International Jazz Festival** is held in August. You can visit the **Nikola Vapstarov House** (same hours as convent; 3lev/$2/£1), where the revolutionary poet was born; it's pretty dull, bar a few crafts on sale in one of the adjacent rooms, and the occasional art exhibition held in the hall downstairs.

THE ARCHITECTURAL RESERVE VILLAGES OF RHODOPE ★★★

If you like your nature served with 18th-century rural architecture, traveling from Bansko through the Rhodope mountains to Plovdiv will more than likely be the highlight of your sojourn in Bulgaria. It's not just the scenic beauty, or the long, empty roads, but the romance of seeing fields tilled by horse-drawn plow, and women and men in traditional garb reaping the produce that will end up delighting your palate at a roadside restaurant. Exploring the mountain villages (the best of which are Leshten, Kovachevitsa, Dolen, and, to a lesser extent, Shiroka Luka and Gela) is like stepping into a living museum, where old folk sit mutely on benches in the sun, against stonewalled and timber-framed homes as their ancestors have for over 300 years. Alleys and lanes in these villages are impassable by car—potholed, and sometimes thick with dung and mud—so you must explore the villages on (well-shod) foot, stumbling onto images of novel beauty: an old woman, walking her goat like a dog, greets another bent double under a huge stack of hay; a gaggle of teenage girls move their hips to a badly tuned radio, giggling at a passing boy on a powder-blue Communist-era motorbike; a girl comes thundering past on horseback, riding with no bridle or saddle, her long brown hair streaming behind her. A camera is essential; spare film or memory card is recommended.

ESSENTIALS: GETTING THERE & GETTING AROUND

Seeing the best this region has to offer involves traveling up roads that are effectively cul-de-sacs. You will have to accept a fair amount of doubling back as you travel east to Pamporovo, one of Bulgaria's top three ski resorts, before heading north to Plovdiv. There only tourism bureau is in Shiroka Luka which has the efficient **Rhodopi tourist center** (daily 8:30am–noon and 1–6:30pm; © **03030/233;** www.shiroka-luka.com) servicing the region; staff provides you with maps and recommendations on places to stay, as well as more information on the annual *kukeri* carnival held here every March, and the **International Bagpipe Festival** (www.gaidaland.com).

WHERE TO STAY & DINE

Kapsazov's kashta ✪✪✪ *Finds*   Relaxing in the immaculate stonewalled garden, watching swallows dive-bomb the pretty pool or just gazing up at the forested slopes that surround the house is a delight; but it is at the dining table that you really know you've landed up in heaven. The angel in the kitchen is Sofia Kapsazov—she has written a cookbook on traditional Bulgarian cooking and also hosts regular cooking courses; after tasting one of her meals you'll wish you had the time to sign up for one. The Kapsazovs were both working as translators in Sofia before they decided to ditch the city and relocate to their weekend getaway, putting the finishing touches on what is a typical Kovachevitsa house from the outside, but a very comfortable, classy guesthouse inside. Today this escape attracts a fascinating mix of expat diplomats, Sofia intelligentsia, and exhausted businessmen, many of them repeat visitors who can't get enough of the utter peace and quiet on offer here, and the wonderful meals of course. As dinners are enjoyed communally, either outside, in the main dining room upstairs or in the huge kitchen (personal favorite, as you can watch Sofia work her magic), there's every chance you'll get a chance to mingle with an interesting crowd, particularly if you're here over weekends—but book months in advance, though the Kapsazovs plan to convert three more houses during the next few years.

15-min. drive north from Leshten. Booking office: P.O. Box 656 BG, Sofia 1000. © **099 403089** or 048/969676. 5 units. 55€ ($70) per person. No credit cards. Rates include breakfast and dinner. **Amenities:** Cooking courses; mushroom and herb picking; hiking.

Leshten Cottages & "Krachma" ✪✪ *Finds*   Leshten, its very name a whispered promise, is where you'll find the little Bulgarian country cottage you never knew you wanted. Built on a steep hillside on a flank of the southwestern Rhodope mountains, Leshten's views—rolling forested hills, backdropped by the snowcapped Pirin range— are the best in Bulgaria, no mean feat given the competition. Once a bustling village, the original population slowly dwindled to nothing, but the village was saved from ruin by the industrious Misho Marinov, who has renovated 15 of the 18th-century houses, retaining their original character, and furnishing them with traditional rugs and blankets. The result is a collection of absolutely charming cottages, with all the creature comforts you need for a thoroughly relaxing stay (if you're looking for a romantic option, book the tiny clay Mali-style en-suite home, the only one Misho has built virtually from scratch). Most have shaded balconies furnished with rustic timber tables and benches from which to drink in the magnificent view; some, like Popskata, even have small walled-off private gardens.

And while it's well equipped for self-catering, why cook, when the best restaurant for miles is a stroll down the lane? **Krachma** ✶✶✶ (literally, "restaurant") is a tiny building on the main road through town, marked by the red-and-white gingham tablecloths you'll see under the spreading canopy of a magnificent old tree. From its branches wine corks dangle; tug one and tinkling bells summon the waiter. The "Kofte Leshten Style" is superb—a single tender cut of pork rather than a patty, delicately flavored—order it with Ljutenitza (mashed red peppers, leek, and spices) and chips—the latter a deep yellow color, waxy and rich in flavor; even the plain cucumber salad, remarkably sweet, is superb. Hardly surprising then to hear that all the produce is hand-grown on Misho's farm. *Tip:* Across the road from the restaurant is a gallery; pop in to see the art on display; with any luck you'll bump into the Bulgarian poet Boris Christov (his wife is the artist), a fascinating character whose eyes are as blue as the horizon behind him, and passionate about Leshten. Boris has a created a photographic catalog of the village history in a small book, *Leshten,* which is on sale here, along with CDs that expound his "personal mythology about the universe."

Leshten is 40km (25 miles) from Bansko (40 min.). ② 07527/552 or 0899 990 776. 15 units. 60lev ($39/£21) room; 120lev ($77/£41) house. No credit cards. **Amenities:** Restaurant. *In room:* TV, kitchen, backgammon, fireplace.

HIKING & SKIING IN THE RILA, PIRIN & RHODOPE MOUNTAINS

Hiking

The most rewarding hike in the country is the "Rila Seven Lakes" trail, a moderate 2- to 4-day walk (walking 5–6 hr. a day). It is well signposted, but if you would prefer an English-speaking guide, with meals and accommodations arranged, the best company to deal with is **Zig Zag** (see Sofia "Visitor Info," earlier in this chapter); their 4-day Rila hike (180€/$231) also includes a visit to Rila Monastery and Mount Malyovitza—at 2,729m (8,951 ft.) not much smaller than nearby Mount Mussala (2,925m/9,594 ft.), the latter the highest summit in southeast Europe. Zig Zag also offer a 4-day guided hike in the Rhodope for 250€ ($318) per person (minimum two participants); as well as hikes that combine kayaking on rivers and dams in the Rhodope.

In Pirin the most highly rated trail is the Bansko-to-Melnik hike; almost on a par is the hike from Mt. Vihren (Pirin's highest point at 2,914m/9,558 ft.) to Tevnoto lake (the highest water in Pirin). Both 2-day hikes are offered by **Intersport** (www.intersport.bansko.bg), which charges 50€/$64 per person, all-inclusive (see "Bansko: Essentials: Getting There & Getting Around," earlier in this chapter, for details).

Skiing

Bulgaria has three main winter resorts: **Borovets,** the oldest, is in the Rila Mountains, but attracts the younger end of the market with the cheapest package deals. Skiing in the Rhodope range is centered around **Pamporovo,** attractively situated in forested surroundings but with no retail or nightlife heart, while in Pirin it is popular **Bansko** that is pulling in the punters, turning it into the fastest developing winter resort in southeastern Europe. Combining the most sophisticated lifts in the country, the longest ski season (mid-Dec to mid-Apr some years) and a characterful 19th-century village heart, Bansko is likely to be your first port of call (see entry above). However, given the uncontrolled development that is slowly ruining this town, less developed Pamporovo may be a better bet; here the best hotel (and with no attractive heart to the resort, you do want to stay in a hotel with the best facilities in town, not least as the rates are currently so favorable) is the new four-star **Hotel Orlovetz** ✹✹ (① **03021/9000** or 03021/8511; pamporovo@bsbg.net). In 2006, 3 nights in a very spacious double room with wonderful mountain views cost a mere 180lev ($115/£62) per night, including breakfast (price reduces with length of stay). The hotel also has an excellent (and equally reasonably priced) range of treatments to deal with aching post-*piste* muscles.

If you would prefer to have everything taken care of by one operator—from accommodations and equipment hire to instructor and passes, take a look at **www.Bulgaria Ski.com**, the biggest source of information on skiing and snowboarding in Bulgaria; booking here is often very cost-effective (6-day "full ski package" including instruction, equipment, and passes costs 263€/$334).

Caveat: While they are cheap, none of Bulgaria's resorts come close to the standards set by European and American resorts, not only from an infrastructure point of view (the reason they didn't make the 2014 Winter Olympics short list), something you will feel keenly if you cannot ski for a day or two due to foul weather.

5 Plovdiv & The Valley of Kings

Plovdiv is 147km (92 miles) from Sofia; 190km (118 miles) from Veliko Tarnovo.

Five thousand years ago the central plains of Bulgaria, stretching from the foothills of the Balkan mountains to the heartlands of the Rhodopes, were once the central home of the Thracian tribes, said to be Europe's first civilization, whose gold and silversmith techniques were the most sophisticated of ancient times. The area, referred to as the "Valley of Kings," is rich in archaeological finds (of which the UNESCO-listed Kanaznluk tomb is the most famous), but the most popular destination in the region is a city. Described during Thracian times as "the biggest and most beautiful towns in all of Thrace," gorgeous Plovdiv is still the jewel in Bulgaria's crown, with a long and varied history that is a great deal more palpable than Sofia's.

Known to the ancient Greek writers as Eumolpiade, the original settlement was invaded by Philip II of Macedon (father of Alexander the Great) in 342 B.C., who renamed it Philippopolis in honor of himself. Initially a frontier town, the city's strategic position on the Belgrade-Constantinople trade route ensured that it flourished under Roman rule (a period of which there is still ample proof, most notably the Roman theater, said to be the largest outside of Italy) but also that it would be invaded (and renamed) no fewer than six times.

The town experienced its second heyday during the late 17th to 19th centuries, when the town's most affluent merchants flashed their wealth by building beautiful town houses. The best urban examples of the style known as National Revival (also referred to as "Bulgarian Baroque'), these richly decorated timber houses showcased the considerable skills of the Bulgarian artisans in their pay.

Declared an architectural-historical reserve in 1956, the cobbled streets of Old Plovdiv—meandering past Roman ruins, imposing mosques, cool church courtyards, and the beautifully painted facades and terraced architecture of these National Revival homes—offer a crash course in local history, while the sheer beauty of the color combinations and geometric lines provide even the most amateur photographer with wonderful images to show off back home.

It may be Bulgaria's second-largest city, but Plovdiv likes to lay claim to the title of "cultural capital'; certainly its art galleries far out-class Sofia's, and in the spring and early summer the Old Town's streets also exude a vibrant, sophisticated atmosphere: from behind the walls of Kuyumdzhioglu House you may hear the tinkling of a piano—a recital in the gardens—while a few blocks farther an orchestra sets up for an evening concert in the ruins of the Roman amphitheater. It's a pleasure to explore, be it for a few hours or over 2 to 3 days, and an ideal base for a trip to nearby Bachkovo Monastery, Bulgaria's second-biggest monastery, or farther south into the Rhodopes to view quaint villages like Shiroka Luka and Gela (see section above), or northeast to the "The Valley of Kings" and the Kazanluk tomb, which can be viewed as a day trip from Plovdiv, or as a staging post in your journey from Plovdiv to Veliko Tarnovo or the Black Sea Coast.

ESSENTIALS

Bulgaria's most beautiful city planned to open the doors to its first tourism bureau only at the end of 2006—proof of just how much Bulgaria's tourism industry still has to grow. At press time no details were available about its location; call © **032/633380** for more information. Alternatively take a look at the semiuseful site www.plovdivcity guide.com. Astral Holidays (www.astralholidays.bg) is one of the city's most established independent travel agencies, but is hopeless when it comes to making astute hotel recommendations. For what's on, pick up the monthly *Plovdiv Visitor's Guide* or *Programata* (www.programata.com)

Plovdiv is best visited in spring and early summer (July–Aug it can get unbearably hot) or autumn; try to avoid the Plovdiv Fairs (early May and mid- to late Sept; for exact dates see www.fair.bg), or at least book your accommodations long in advance as space is limited and prices soar.

GETTING THERE

The Sofia-Istanbul highway that links Sofia with Plovdiv is in tiptop condition, so the journey by car takes 70 to 90 minutes, making it a possible day trip from Sofia (and there are plenty of tour operators that offer this), or even to skip Sofia and treat Plovdiv as your base.

There are three bus terminals. **Yug** is the main terminal on Hristo Botev, where buses connecting Plovdiv with Sofia pull in almost hourly (journey is just over 2 hr.; 10lev/$6.50/£3.50 one-way); also buses that travel to Assenovgrad (from where you can catch another bus to Bachkovo), Varna (7 hr.), Burgas (4 hr.), and Istanbul (6 hr.).

GETTING AROUND

The city is divided into two sections: the 18th- and 19th-century open-air architectural reserve that is Old Plovdiv, sprawled across the three remaining hillocks of ancient Eumolpiade, and "New" Plovdiv, spread around the foothills. With its meandering cobbled lanes, Old Plovdiv—and even the smattering of sites in "New" Plovdiv, essentially ranged along pedestrian Knyaz Aleksandur I Street—is best explored on foot, with all the top sites and hotels listed within walking distance of each other.

WHERE TO STAY

Plovdiv provides ample proof of just how little one can rely on many of Bulgaria's hotel star ratings, with the **Novotel,** the city's only five-star hotel, a dank Communist-era pit, while the zero-rated Hebros is the best option in town. If the hotels below are full (with the exception of the Trimontium, they are after all quite small) look at the following options, all situated near or in the old part of town: **Hotel Bulgaria**

(© **032/633 599;** www.hotelbulgaria.net; Mon–Fri 70€–84€/$89–$107 double; Fri–Sun 65€–74€/$83–$94 double; rates include breakfast) is a business-oriented hotel that also caters for package tourists; rooms are perfectly serviceable and realistically priced. If you don't need the big-hotel vibe, a better deal is the tiny five-roomed hotel right on Old Plovdiv's borders (technically part of it), and a stone's through from the Dzhumaya Mosque: the aptly named **Hotel-Bar Central** (© **032/622 348;** www.hotel-bar-central.com; 40€/$51 double) is wonderfully convenient, albeit apparently staffed by a single disaffected receptionist. It's a slim building, with each room taking up an entire floor, and floor-to-ceiling tinted glass wall providing a sense of space. If you'd prefer to wake up surrounded by the wonderful architecture of Old Plovdiv's National Revival homes, **B&B Old Town** offers a great location and two lovely old-fashioned rooms with carved ceilings and wall frescoes. The surly manageress does not speak English but the website makes for easy bookings, and this is a perfect place to flop into after a hard day's sightseeing—around the corner from Arena, the outdoor cafe/bar overlooking the Roman theater (© **032/265679** or 0887 420 185; www.Bulguide.com/bedbreakfast; 35€–55€/$64–$96 depending on room and season).

Hebros ★★★ *(Value)*   This grand little gem, located on a quiet cobbled street in the heart of Old Plovdiv, is so completely head, shoulders, and feet above the competition that it's almost worth arranging your trip around room availability here. Once the place where top Communist party members relaxed when visiting Plovdiv, the opulence of the materials and craftsmanship displayed in this typical National Revival home are matched by the furnishings. You'll find Bulgarian and Italian antiques throughout; windows draped in heavy velvet or edged with lace; dark varnished floors invariably dressed with rich Oriental rugs; walls decorated with traditional frescoes or timber clad. Book no. 5 if you can (with separate entrance of the courtyard it feels the most private), or no. 3—the latter is the gorgeous room (only the modern-era TV strikes a discordant note) where the dictator Todor Zhivkov liked to dream up more ways to plunder the state coffers. If you're traveling alone, bag the single room, where the bathroom is ingeniously placed in the large cupboard, a very good deal at 69€ ($88); groups or families ask for the apartment that sleeps four and costs 130€ ($166). Despite a lack of hotel facilities, including a proper reception (most just enter through the restaurant), the most important aspects are taken care of: helpful staff, excellent restaurant, and a charming atmosphere and location.

51 A.K Stoilov St., Plovdiv, 4000. © **032/260180** or 625929. Fax 032/260252. www.hebros-hotel.com. 10 units. 95€ ($121) double. Rates include breakfast. MC, V. **Amenities:** Restaurant; Jacuzzi; sauna; room service; laundry. *In room:* A/C, TV, minibar, Internet connection, hair dryer.

Old Town Residence ★★ *(Value)*   If your budget cannot stretch to the Hebros, or it is full, the Residence is the best-value deal in town, but be warned: You may have to put up with some rather surly service. Rumored to be the Plovdiv "holiday home" of some heavies who built it with ill-gotten gains, this custom-built hotel is styled on the neoclassical grand mansions of late-19th-century Old Plovdiv, but there's no mistaking New Money, with its penchant for chandeliers, reproduction furniture, white marble, and bits of gold leaf. Rooms really are quite grand, rates are extremely good, and the location—also in the heart of Old Plovdiv, but here with views of the city sparkling at your feet—unbeatable. Try to book room no. 4 or 3 for the best views; room no. 2 is wonderfully over-the-top (how else to describe a room with three chandeliers) but the bathroom (no tub; cheap fittings) is a bit of a letdown; studio rooms

---

Fun Fact **Pagan Rites & Rituals**

Bulgaria is a wonderful mix of both the Orthodox and the pagan. Besides kukeri, there is "Enyovden," as the summer solstice is known: At dawn families watch their shadows grow; if the shadow is complete, good health is predicted. The night before is also considered the ideal time to pick certain herbs; one, picked by feel, with closed eyes, is used to cure the "half illness" thought to afflict pale and listless youths who have—unbeknownst to them—been mesmerized by an invisible but love-struck dragon.

(nos. 5 and 6) are ideal for single travelers. Popular with the locals as a sundowner venue—so popular in fact that staff deem it unnecessary to woo any new clientele—this is a great place to watch Plovdivians at play. The restaurant is also highly rated.

11 Knyaz Ceretelev St., Plovdiv, 4000. ☎ **032/632389** or 032/620789. residence@abv.bg. 6 units. Double 50€–75€ ($64–$96). Studio rooms 40€ ($52). MC, V. **Amenities:** Restaurant; room service; laundry. *In room:* A/C, TV, hair dryer, fireplace.

Trimontium Princess Hotel ⚷ No list of Plovdiv hotels would be complete without including the Trimontium: A grand structure looming over Tsentralen square, this four-star hotel is rated by some as the city's best hotel, and currently hotel of choice for top-end tour operator Abercrombie & Kent. Which is why it's such a total letdown. No doubt it's a good bet if you have a group too large for the Hebros. Rates are currently rather cheap and it does have all the facilities you'd expect from a large hotel (including a new pool—a great boon in summer, when Plovdiv can be sweltering). But once you see the receptionists wearing pale-blue jackets with padded shoulders and matching miniskirts, and rooms seemingly furnished with items acquired at a bargain sale on office furniture, you can only wonder how it is possible for a hotel that was renovated a decade after the 1980s to be so entirely devoid of taste. Perhaps it will have some ironic appeal, given that reruns of *Dallas* and *Working Girl* are not uncommon; if so, retire to the aptly named Panoramic Floor bar during Happy Hour and sink into the fat rolls of the white leather chairs that teeter on tiny timber feet—this is a marvelous bar, located in the curving roof space of the hotel, and a great place to be when the city lights start to flicker on below.

24 St., Plovdiv, 4000. ☎ **032/605000** or 032/605080. www.trimontium-princess.com. 158 units. 35€–55€ ($45–$51) double; rates vary depending on room size and season (high season June 1–Oct 1). Rates include breakfast. AE, DC, MC, V. **Amenities:** 2 restaurants; bar; fitness room; sauna; hairdresser; business center; casino. *In room:* A/C, TV, minibar, Internet, hair dryer.

WHERE TO DINE

The dining scene is not as stimulating as Sofia, or even Varna, but there is certainly plenty of choice, particularly along pedestrian Knyaz Aleksandur I Street where cafes and pizzerias spill out onto the street. But for a more intimate atmosphere you're better off grabbing a table in one of the cool walled courtyards in Old Plovdiv. Besides the two discussed below you will find two good options on 4th January Street: **Janet** (no. 3; ☎ **032/626 044** or 032/634 149) and **Ulpia** (no 17; ☎ **032/65 3747**), both serving typical Bulgarian fare in wonderful 19th-century National Revival homes.

Hebros ✦✦✦ INTERNATIONAL   Voted the best restaurant in the country a few years back, Hebros restaurant is, like the hotel, a little gem, with a cozy semisubterranean room and pretty stepped courtyard. The menu features a few traditional Bulgarian dishes, like the ubiquitous (and surprisingly delicious) "Mish-Mash"—peppers and tomato baked with egg and white cheese in an earthenware pot—but this is probably a good place to take a break from Bulgarian cuisine. The menu changes regularly but stalwarts include wild mushrooms, simply prepared in butter, foie gras, frogs' legs, and asparagus hollandaise. Leave space for one of the specialties: tender rabbit cooked with plums, tomatoes, and shallots. Local wines are recommended by the glass with each respective dish, so this is also a great place to be introduced to new Bulgarian wines.

51 A.K. Stoilov St., Plovdiv, 4000. ✆ 032/260180 or 032/625929. Main courses 17lev–19lev ($11–$13/£6–£6.50). MC, V. Daily 11am–11pm.

Puldin ✦✦ BULGARIAN   Roman fortifications march through sections of this labyrinthine Revival-era house. Don't dally in the first courtyard you enter, furnished with frilly wrought-iron chairs, nor at the fancy "ritual" dining hall, but descend into the cellarlike basement (where rough-hewn timber tables, covered with traditional red tablecloths, contrast with the rather kitschy lit mural, below which water trickles over large boulders) and step outside into the courtyard that lies beyond, where a violin-and-piano-playing duo are usually entertaining diners, and tables are shaded by trees and vines. If it's hot order a mixture of cold appetizers (their eggplant, roasted peppers, and mushrooms are all delicious); if you're nursing a huge appetite the grilled pork "sword" is big enough for two, or try the pork filet, roasted with peppers, tomatoes, apple, and herbs.

3 Knjaz Tsereletev St. ✆ 032/631 720. Main courses 5.50lev–16lev ($4–$10/£1.90–£5.50). AE, DC, MC, V. 11am–11pm.

EXPLORING PLOVDIV

Given its lack of signposts and meandering layout, with numerous little cul de sac lanes that are well worth exploring, a flexible approach to any walking tour of the architectural-historical reserve is advised. Old Plovdiv is after all the most wonderful place to get lost in; just make sure you're armed with a camera to chart your journey. Below is a tour covering the most important streets and/or sights, which follow on from each other in some topographical order—try to cover a few of these, but follow wherever you're eyes lead you: a street like Kiril Nektariev has no museums per se, but boasts some of the best facades. You can easily cover its prettiest streetscapes in a morning, unless of course you're keen to examine a few of the opulent interiors or view the artworks housed in some of these splendid houses, in which plan a full day or two.

ESSENTIAL DAY TRIPS

Bachkovo Monastery ✦✦✦   Bulgaria's second-largest monastery is, like Rila, a UNESCO-listed monument, and while the natural environment does not impose the sense of grandeur that surrounds the more famous monastery, Bachkovo's artworks alone make this a must-see if you are in the region. Founded in 1083 by two Georgian brothers, the complex was pretty much razed during the Ottoman invasion; today the oldest buildings are the Refectory (1601) and the principal Church of the Assumption of Our Lady (Sveta Bogoroditsa), the latter built in 1604 (though the Sveta Troitsa, a church about 600m/1,968 ft. from the gates, dates from the 14th c., it is usually locked). Sveta Bogoroditsa is filled with beautiful frescoes and murals, but what draws local pilgrims is its 14th-century Virgin Mary icon—said to be a portrait painted by the Apostle Luke, pilgrims believe that it has miraculous properties. Besides Sveta Bogoroditsa, the complex also has two smaller churches: Church of the Archangels (13th–14th c.), located next to the main church, and Church of St. Nikolai (1834–37), in the adjoining courtyard. The latter is worth visiting for the murals, said to be the first documented work by Zahary Zograf and featuring a portrait of the artist in the upper left hand corner of the *Last Judgment* mural that dominates the porch. You can also enter the refectory (4lev/$3/£1.40) where you will find murals of the great Greek philosophers. The monastery is still home to men in flowing black cassocks and gray beards, but today they are vastly outnumbered by tourists and pilgrims lined up to see the icon or to fill their plastic water bottles with the delicious mineral water that runs continuously from the monastery's piped spring.

Tip: The walkway to the monastery gates are lined with dozens of small stalls selling various bits of tourist knickknacks as well as Rhodopean specialties and delicious fast foods; on weekends it can be a bit of a nightmare with blaring music and thronging crowds; for a more convivial atmosphere and decent service, keep heading downhill to **Vodopada.** Principally a huge outdoor terrace situated around a waterfall and trout-filled pond, you can't miss it, and the food here is excellent. Bizarrely there is no English menu, but ask for Lily, the can-do English-speaking waitress, and order the house specialties: marinated mushrooms, followed by charcoal-grilled fresh trout or spit-grilled lamb.

30km/19 miles south of Plovdiv, clearly signposted off the main road connecting Assenovgrad and Smolyan. ✆ 03327/277. Daily 7am–8pm.

Kazanluk Tomb ★★★ *Moments*   Kazanluk, center of the rose-growing plains that surround it, was until recently more strongly associated with the overrated Festival of Roses, which takes place here every June. But the past decade has seen an increasing number of Thracian vaults, hidden beneath the burial mounds scattered throughout the surrounding countryside, excavated, and the area is increasingly referred to as the Valley of Kings (see "Thracian Tombing: Exploring the Graves of Europe's First Civilization"? below). The first to be discovered was in Kazanluk way back in 1944, when soldiers attempted to dig out an air-raid bunker on what was then the outskirts of town. Listed by UNESCO, but off-limits to the general public before 2006, an exact replica was built in 1978. This bizarrely is still the main museum, staffed and open daily; while you need to call ahead to arrange to view the original—be sure to do this, because it is an incredible experience standing in the small domed chamber (approached through a slim corridor-like antechamber—very *Temple of Doom*) to view ceiling frescoes—so close you can almost touch them—dating from the late 4th century B.C. The man seated, his arm entwined around that of a pale women, thought to be his wife, while a servant offers him a plate of pomegranates (traditionally associated with immortality) is thought to be the nobleman who was buried here.

Tip: If all this ancient history has built up an appetite, **Hadji Eminova kushta,** part of the Ethnographic Museum Complex (✆ **0431/62595**)—a short stroll from the tomb—is by far the prettiest spot to lunch in town, with the restaurant comprising a few tables ranged around the verdant and tree-shaded garden, and along the deep timber porch; cuisine—typical Bulgarian—is good, too. For overnight details, see the "Thracian Tombing: Exploring the Graves of Europe's First Civilization" box, below.

Tyulbe Park (300m/984 ft. from town center). Tomb replica May–Oct 9am–5pm; 5lev ($3.50/£1.90). To view the original call ✆ 0431/63762; 20lev ($13/£7).

Thracian Tombing: Exploring the Graves of Europe's First Civilization

The area around the otherwise dull town of Kazanluk is dotted with an esti-mated 1,500 burial mounds, or *mogili;* with each excavation more is revealed about the advanced craftsmanship of the Thracians—the most recent, in August 2006, was a 5,000-year-old dagger, made from a superior alloy of gold and platinum.

You can arrange a private tour of some of these tombs through Kazan-luk-based **Iskra Historical Museum** (Mon–Fri 9am–5:30pm; ℂ **0431/63762**; 15lev/$10/£5.20 per tomb includes and English-speaking guide. If you have problems, ask to speak to Dr. Kosyo Zarev, director of the museum).

If you need to spend the night in Kazanluk (and you will if you're visiting more than one tomb), the most interesting option is the 19th-century **Hadji Eminova kushta** (ℂ **0431/62595**; 25lev–50lev/$16–$32/£8.65–£17). Part of the Ethnographic Museum Complex, it's an authentic house "museum" with a choice of four rooms ranged along the porch. All are traditionally fur-nished and feature wonderful carved ceilings; bathrooms are clean but old, dating from 1976 when the municipal authorities installed them (showers okay; tubs unusable). Ask for no. 11 or no 14, which are both very spacious. Note that Mr. Dimitros, the charming manager, speaks very little English. Alternatively, the best hotel in town is the **Palas,** located right in the center, and the place where the local money celebrates nuptials and the like. Decor is pretty kitsch (how else to describe a plastic rose on pillow) but the staff young and helpful (ℂ **0431/62311**; www.hotel-palas.com; 96lev/$61/£33 double).

6 Veliko Tarnovo & Environs

Veliko Tarnovo 220km (137 miles) from Sofia; 226km (140 miles) from Varna

Veliko Tarnovo, capital of Bulgaria's Second Kingdom from 1185 to 1396, was glori-fied in European circles as "the third city after Rome and the second after Constan-tinople." Today it is more tiny university town than city, and while it does not have the obvious architectural splendors of more famous Plovdiv, it is in some senses an even more charming destination, surrounded by a wild natural environment that remains within view even when you're in its urban heart. The imposing medieval citadel of Tsarevets, perched on its own hill from where it glowers down upon the inhabitants it once enclosed, is the town's top sight. From here the lazy Yantra River curls into the guiding arms of the white limestone cliffs from which narrow red-roofed buildings rise precipitously along one bank to gaze back at the densely vegetated and virtually unpopulated hillsides opposite. It is this undulating green backdrop that gives the place its charm, but it is during the languid summer evenings that the city really comes into its own. Sitting on the cantilevered balcony of one of the city's restaurants as the setting sun turns the narrow dwellings stacked below a soft, pale pink, watching as thousands of birds come out to ride the thermal waves, swooping and diving into the gorge below, you could almost be in a village perched on the sheer cliffs of the Italian Riviera's Cinque Terre—only here the seagulls are swallows, the sea is a tangled forest, and there is hardly a tourist in sight.

The old part of Veliko Tarnovo is pleasant enough to stroll, but besides enjoying the innate beauty of its geography and the town's particular brand of National Revival architecture—dominated here by Viennese Secession-style wrought-iron balconies— Veliko's chief draw is as base for (or stopover to) the many day trips that lie within a comfortable radius from here. They include Tryavna, home to Bulgaria's finest icon and woodcarving museums; Etura, a pretty outdoor ethnographic museum where you can also shop for crafts; the impressive Madara horseman, another of Bulgaria's UNESCO-listed sights; the quaint architectural museum town of Arbanassi; the historic Shipka Pass, gateway to Kazanluk and its famous tomb; as well as 10 nearby monasteries.

ESSENTIALS

GETTING THERE With no stops, Veliko Tarnovo is a 2½-hour drive by **car** from Sofia. It is not really worth traveling by **train** as there is no direct line to the central station (trains from Sofia and Varna pull into Gorna Oryahovitsa, 13km/8 miles north of the city, where scheduled trains then connect you to the city—an unwieldy arrangement); by contrast traveling here by **bus** is fast, convenient, and economical. From Sofia the journey takes no more than 3 hours, costs 11lev ($7/£3.80) one-way (an additional 11lev/$7/£3.80 onward to Varna), with buses departing, on average, every 2 hours. Private buses from Sofia and Varna, including those belonging to highly efficient Etap Adress, pull in at the centrally located tower-block Hotel Etar on Ivailo Street (no matter how convenient the location, do not be tempted to overnight in these overpriced rooms). Buses also arrive here from Plovdiv, a 4-hour bus journey (13lev/$8.50/£4.50).

GETTING AROUND The main sites are centered in the old part, which is tiny— in fact the entire "city" is so small that you can drive from side to side in about 15 minutes. To get to nearby Arbanassi, order a taxi (5lev/$3.50/£1.90). You can get to Tryavna very easily by bus from the Zapad Bus Terminal, 4km (2½ miles) west of the center; the journey takes around 2 hours. For the other recommended day trips it's best to rent a car; the Tourism Information Centre can arrange one for 35lev/$19/£12 day (see below). Bus travel to these destinations is complicated, involving two to three changes with drivers who don't speak English; if you're up for this, speak to the tourism officials for bus schedule details.

VISITOR INFORMATION Veliko Tarnovo has a reasonably helpful tourism information center, with an English-speaking staff that not only dispenses brochures (including the free city guide; www.veliko-tarnovo.net) but can, if pressed, provide reasonably qualitative advice on where to stay and dine. Be sure also to pick up a copy of *The Frontier Times*. The Centre is conveniently located just behind the bus terminal, at Hristo Botev Street (© **062/622148;** www.velikoturnovo.info; Mon–Sat 9am–6pm Apr–Sept, Oct–Mar closed Sat).

WHERE TO STAY

Ironically enough, Veliko Tarnovo has better standards of accommodations than more famous Plovidiv. Besides those reviewed below, the recently renovated **Grand Hotel Yantra** (© **062/600607;** www.yantrabg.com) is definitely worth a look in for its comfortable, tasteful styling and good-value four-star hotel facilities (including a slick spa and wellness center, indoor swimming pool, and wonderful lobby lounge with superb views of the Tsarevets fortress). The only drawback is that, unless you book a **suite with a balcony** overlooking the fortress (these are grand rooms, worth the 180lev/$115/£62 charged, so book if available), most of the rooms only have a small square hole through which to enjoy this picture-perfect view.

Tip: Beget hunters should book a fortress-facing room at **Hotel Comfort** (✆ **062/ 628728;** 55lev–60lev/$35–$39/£19–£21).

Dryanovo Monastery *(Moments* You can stay in most active monasteries for around 10lev ($6.50/£3.50) per person, but while the locations are almost always sublime, living conditions in the monasteries are often austere (no hot water; shared bathrooms) and, well, less than hygienic. Not so at Dryanovo Monastery. Besides the dormitory rooms (open to men only), the monks have renovated a small wing with en-suite rooms for those who expect a little more than a thin mattress—each room has two single beds and a cell-like window that—when open—allows the gushing "prana" of the river coursing past the fortified walls below to lull you to sleep. Shower rooms are clean (if a tad musty), and don't expect more than a bar of soap by way of toiletries, and a towel only slightly larger than a facecloth. But it's a wonderful thing to witness a long-bearded ascetic in a black cassock enter your name into a massive ledger that has the names of countless pilgrims over the years. If you're happy to forgo this sight there is an even better option within the monastery grounds: **Komplex Vodopadi** is a renovated wing that sports larger, more comfortably furnished rooms (and women are allowed here), with balconies overlooking either the monastery or the river—at exactly the same price, this is the bargain of the Balkans. The other reason this monastery stay is so worthwhile is the restaurant, conveniently located just outside the monastery gates, with tables on a terrace right on the river. **Andaka** scores high on service and food too—the chicken kavarma (chicken, onions, mushrooms, and tomatoes roasted and baked in a ceramic dish) is extremely tasty (if on the small side); best of all they also open for breakfast.

Dryanovo, 24km (15 miles) south of Veliko Tarnovo. Monastery rooms ✆ **067/6238.** Komplex Vodopadi ✆ **0899147848.** 25lev ($16/£8.65) double. No credit cards. **Amenities:** Restaurant. *In room:* No phone.

Gurko *(★★* Located on historic Gurko Street (see "Exploring Veliko Tarnovo," p. 111, this geranium- and vine-covered triple-story hotel is as traditional and charming as they come, with almost all rooms opening onto balconies with great views of the hillside opposite, and the Yantra River below. Rooms in this National Revival–era home (so cute you'll want to photograph it even if you don't stay here) are spotless and comfortable, most with double beds, all with en-suite tubs (showers overhead). General use of color and furnishings (plenty of solid timber) is old-fashioned, with some beds covered in traditional bedspreads—if the idea of a boutique hotel leaves you cold, this is the best option in town: an authentic family-run outfit, cheerful and efficient, with a good tavern on the ground floor. Unlike Tsaravets, a lack of fluent English can be a limitation to the tourism assistance available, and the place is very popular with small tour groups, so don't just arrive expecting a room.

33 Gurko St. ✆ **062/627838** or 0888 352 941. www.hotelgurko.hit.bg. 11 units. 55€ ($70) double. No credit cards. **Amenities:** Restaurant/bar; laundry. *In room:* A/C, TV, minibar, Internet, hair dryer, safe.

Studio Hotel *(★★★* *(Value* This ultramodern and stylish hotel is one of the few true boutique hotels in Bulgaria and proves (like the Rako Villa in Bansko) that 21st-century decor and design trends have finally, albeit belatedly (Studio only opened in 2006) arrived in Bulgaria. A stone's throw from the Cathedral and the Tsaravets fortress (of which some of the rooms have great views; book over the weekend in season and catch the light show from your bed), the renovators have very skillfully gutted an old late-19th century building, leaving the exterior intact—it's not a cutting-edge concept, but the combination of old, traditional facade hiding an übermodern interior is as exhilarating as ever. The palette is restrained (predominantly black, white, and gray) but playful, as evidenced by the plentiful touches of red (like the gorgeous '70s-retro bedside lights in bright red, set against baroque-patterned black-and-white wallpaper). Bathroom fittings are predictably sleek and modern (these are quite possibly the best showers to be had in Bulgaria) and the whole experience one of restrained luxury.

4 Todor Lefterov St. ⓒ **062/604010** or 062/604009. www.studiohotel-vt.com. 13 units. 100lev–120lev ($64–$77/£35–£41) double. AE, DC, MC, V. **Amenities:** Restaurant; lobby bar; bar terrace; room service; laundry. *In room:* A/C, TV, minibar, Internet connection.

Tsaravets ⭐⭐   The best thing about the Tsaravets is its owner-manager, the gorgeous Ms. Anguelova, who is not only passionate about her town, but—having spent several years in the hospitality industry in London—a superb hotelier who has grasped that the guest is king. After being "tolerated" by so many Bulgarian hotels it's a breath of fresh air to be welcomed with so much sincerity. The handpicked staff is warm, without being sycophantic, and will take care of your restaurant bookings, discuss with you in detail how to prioritize your time, and provide free transport to anything in town that isn't walking distance. The hotel, built in 1891 for the grand Bulgaria Insurance Company, is also well located in the old part of town—a minute's walk from the Tsaravets fortress gates; 5 minutes from Rakovski Street. It's a small, intimate place, with comfortably furnished, compact rooms (grander than Gurko). Shower rooms are on the small side (it's hard to take a shower without wetting the toilet paper) but Ms. Anguelova plans to update these in 2007.

23 Chitalistna St., Veliko Tarnavo. ⓒ **062/601885** or 062/605655. www.tsarevetshotel.com. 9 units. 65€ ($83) double. MC, V. **Amenities:** Breakfast room/lobby bar; concierge and booking service; room service; Internet access; laundry; dry cleaning. *In room:* A/C, TV, minibar, safe, hair dryer.

WHERE TO DINE

The best restaurants all offer wonderful views of the terraced city as it tumbles down to the Yantra below—to make sure you have a table on the edge of the terrace (and believe us, you do) ask your hotel or driver to book 1 or 2 days in advance, and call again to confirm. If neither Ego or Shtastlivetsa has a table on the terrace, try **Rich** (1 Yantra St., located down a flight of steps opposite the Stambolisky monument; ⓒ 062/27980), owner-managed, exceptionally good value, and superb views on the terrace. Whichever restaurant you choose, make sure you end up on cobbled Rakovski Street at **Stratilat,** Veliko Tarnovo's most happening cafe, and collapse in a wicker chair for a postprandial espresso.

Ego ⭐⭐ *(Value)* BULGARIAN/PIZZA   This large airy space, with large doors that slide away to the outdoor terrace that perches high above the Yantra, its railings decorated with flowering geranium boxes, is just the ticket as the sun goes down. Ego has a huge menu—85 salads alone—and everything is super fresh; waitresses don't speak much English, but service is fast and friendly. If you're here in summer, temperatures will no doubt be sweltering: opt for the refreshing Tambaktu salad—mango with greens, chopped cucumber, and crumbled blue cheese—or the tasty Ego—a bulgur wheat salad served with peeled and roasted tomatoes, peppers, and eggplant, and finely chopped parsley, garlic, onion, garlic, and walnuts. As is the case at Shtastlivetsa, salad portions are huge, so you'll struggle to find the space for the huge array of good pizzas or Bulgarian traditionals offered. But struggle you must: Their "cheese shopski style" is the best ever, and the chicken kavarma—roasted with onion, garlic, tomatoes, corn, peppers, and mushrooms, and served on a tile—equally so.

17 Stefan Stambalov. ⓒ 062/601804. Reservations for the terrace essential. 2.90lev–11lev ($3.50–$10/£1–£3.80). No credit cards. Daily noon–11pm.

Shtastlivetsa ★★ (Value) BULGARIAN/PIZZA   Walk along Stefan Stambolov, the miniboulevard that leads you to the old part of town, and look out for a restaurant where every table is occupied, and you've found Shtastlivetsa. The locals love this place as much for its portions—as huge as they are delicious—as for its prices, so it's hardly surprising that it serves to a packed house almost every day, despite the opening of another branch at 7 Marno Pole St. It's another huge menu, with plenty of pasta and pizza dishes to augment the Bulgarian standards—pizzas are very good (if you want a Bulgarian take on this, try the "country bread" with two types of cheese, walnuts, bacon and apricots); salads are even bigger than Ego's (we're talking half a kilogram minimum). The house specialty is meat cooked "in a sach," which essentially means a variety of meat and vegetable combinations prepared in or on traditional earthenware—opt for one that includes vegetables rather than a pure "mixed meat" dish. Dishes can be ordered as 450 grams or 750 grams (1 lb. or 1½ lb.)—specify the smaller (unless you're sharing) or the waiter, probably with his eye on the service charge included as a percentage on your bill, may "assume" you've ordered the larger portion.

79 Stefan Stambalov. ⓒ 062/600656. Reservations for the terrace essential. 5lev–15lev ($3.50–$10/£1.75–£5.20). AE, DC, MC, V. Daily 11am–11pm.

EXPLORING VELIKO TARNOVO ★★★

Touted as the city's top attraction, **Tsarevets fortress** (ⓒ **062/636 828;** Apr–Sept 8am–7pm; Oct–Mar 9am–5pm; 5lev/$3.50/£1.75) must have been an incredible sight when the medieval walls that girdle the hill enclosed a royal palace, 18 churches, and over 400 houses, but there's not much left of these grand origins. Besides climbing one of the watchtowers for the views, or heading over to Execution Rock to shudder at the hopefully swift justice meted out to the king's itinerant subjects, the main attraction is the hilltop Patriarch's Church of the Ascension. Declared the "mother of all churches" in the Bulgarian Kingdom in 1235, it was restored in 1981 to commemorate Bulgaria's 1,300th birthday. Interiors are covered with interesting modern murals, executed in an almost monochromatic palette by a student of Svetlin Rusev, one of Bulgaria's most influential expressionists—a total contrast to the usual church interior; then again, this is now a monument, not a church. While a daytime wander around the fortress (and do plan to get here early or late, rather than during the draining midday heat) is mildly satisfying, the power that Bulgaria's once-impregnable capital exerted over southeastern Europe for 200 years is better captured by the stunning 40-minute **sound-and-light show** ★★★, when the bathed fortress comes alive in the changing shadows, and stirring music charges through the battlements. The show, held once a week during summer (usually on a weekend night at around 9pm), or whenever a tour group hits town, is best enjoyed from the Assen II square in front of the main entrance.

Once you've explored the Tsarevets Fortress, stroll down to the view the **Churches of Assenova** or "Assen's Quarter," the medieval-era part of town that straddles the banks of the Yantra as it winds through the saddle between Tsarevets and Trapezitsa hills. A tranquil place, the area was pretty much destroyed by an earthquake in 1913, but a few of the churches have been restored, the most impressive being the **Sveti Dimitrius of Thessalonike** ★★, where the *bolyari* Assen and his brother Peter declared war on their Byzantine oppressors. The beautiful brickwork—alternating bands of color, using two kinds of brick, mortar, and stone, with ceramic inlay for additional texture—is typical of the church construction during medieval times (heavily influenced by the Byzantine style), and you'll see plenty more of this if you are pushing on to UNESCO-listed Nessebar on the Black Sea coast. Located on the other side of the river is the recently restored **Church of the 40 Martyrs** ★★. Frescoes here date from the 12th and 14th century, but the two pillars with inscriptions are what fascinate historians: One has an 8th-century inscription that reads: "Man dies, even though he lives nobly, and another is born. Let the latest born, when he examines these records, remember he who made them. The name of the Prince is Omurtag, the Sublime Khan." Four hundred years later, czar Ivan Assen—inspired by the Khan's column—ordered that his many victories be inscribed on one similar, citing here how his "benevolence" spared many.

Heading back into town, you could stop to photograph the pretty facade of the **Museum of the National Revival and Constituent Assembly.** Built in 1872 by the prolific master builder Kolyu Ficheto, who left an indelible imprint on the region (the statue in front is of him), it was ironically enough originally a Turkish police station, where the 1876 April Uprising rebels were tried. A mere 3 years later the Ottomans were finally defeated, and the First Bulgarian Constitution was proclaimed by the Bulgaria's newborn parliament in these halls. As exhibits are in Bulgarian, there is no real reason to enter; even less so the adjacent **Archaeological Museum.** Either take a look at the **Church of SS Konstantin I Elena** (also built by Kolyu Ficheto), or wander picturesque **Gurko Street.** Besides admiring the tall, narrow 18th- and 19th-century homes (you can enter the **Sarafkina House** at no 88; Wed–Mon 9am–6pm, 4lev/$3/£1.40), the street has wonderful river views. On the opposite bank, perched in front of its own tiny hillock, is the **Monument of the Assens**—symbol of the city, this phallic sculpture commemorates the powerful kings of the Second Kingdom: Assen I, Peter, Kaloyan, and Ivan Assen II, under whose reign the Bulgarian Medieval State reached its zenith. Behind it is the 19th-century building that houses the **City Art Museum;** the latter not really worth visiting. The other street worth wandering is **Rakovski Street**—almost as pretty as Gurko, this was once the main trading street and is today still lined with well-preserved shops, now touting tourist souvenirs and various artworks of dubious quality. A short stroll farther is the **House of the Little Monkey,** so named for the stone "monkey" attached to the facade of the first floor (centered between the arches), and another building by Kolyu Ficheto featuring his trademark "Fichevska kobilitsa"—the undulating wave that characterizes the roofline of his domestic architecture.

DAY TRIPS FROM VELIKO TARNOVO

With the exception the Madara Horseman and Zheravna, which can be seen on route to Varna, most of the following can be combined into one day trip (though you'll have to choose one monastery). Note that if you're traveling from Plovdiv, you will be heading up the Shipka Pass to get to Veliko Tarnovo, and could then cover Etura and Tryavna en route, possibly overnighting at Draynovo.

Arbanassi ⚔ Located within sight of Veliko Tarnovo on a high plateau 4km (2½ miles) to the northeast, the village of Arbanassi was settled some 300 years ago, and showcases a rather severe fortified Bulgarian architecture, with solid stone walls and thick nail-studded gates designed to repel accidental fires or planned incursions. The solidity and sheer size of the houses was both a celebration and a display of wealth, albeit here in a rather discreet, austere form. To view the interiors, visit **Kostantsaliev House** (just behind the Kokona fountain; daily 9am–6pm; 4lev/ $3/£1.40). But Arbanassi's main attraction is it's 15th-century **Church of the Nativity** ⚔⚔⚔ (turn left at the fountain; 4lev/$3/£1.40), with its opulent and glittering interior, a stark contrast to the plain exterior.

Despite the heavy fortification, the village was regularly sacked by Turkish outlaws and the inhabitants were gradually forced to ameliorate with the city that lay shimmering below. Today the town, though carefully restored, has a peculiarly dead feel, with most of the houses either owned by wealthy city-dwellers who descend but once a year, or by hoteliers—the streets are thus virtually empty unless swollen by foreign ranks. Views of Veliko Tarnovo from the terrace of Arbanassi "Palace," one of the Communist dictator Todor Zhivkov's many holiday homes, but now a hotel (sadly mismanaged), are worth the trip.

Tryavna & Etura ⚔⚔⚔ Tryavna was established by refugees who escaped from the fall of Tarnovo 400 years ago, but the old town's predominantly timber buildings, 140 of which are listed, date from when the village established the official Guild of Master Builders and Woodcarvers in 1804. Start your wanders from the charming old town square, where village elders play card games under a spreading tree; just off the square is the **tourism office,** useful for a map (22 Angel Kunchev St.; Mon–Fri 9–noon and 2–5pm; note that all the museums, bar the Icon, which opens an hour later, are open daily 9am–6pm in summer and 8am–5pm in winter, and charge 2lev/$1.50/80p). Of interest on the town square are the **Church of Archangel Michael** (the lovely iconostasis was painted by the local Vitanov family, Tryavna's most talented icon painters) and the 1839 **Old School.** But the real reason you're here is to see the **Museum of Woodcarving** so head over the bridge to stroll down gorgeous cobbled **Slaveykov Street.** (Note the house on your right as you cross the bridge; owned by **Zograff Inn,** the two recently renovated rooms overlooking the river are by far the best deal in town; call ⓒ **0677/4970;** ask for "21," a steal at 50lev ($32/£17); www.bgglobe.net/zograf.html). More or less in the center of Slaveykov, clearly marked, is the **Woodcarving Museum,** aka "Daskalov's House." On the first floor you can compare two of the most singularly beautiful ceilings, the result of a competition between Master Dimitur Zlatev and his then apprentice, Ivan Bochukovetsa. Upstairs is another amazing feat: carved portraits by Master Gencho Marangozov of Bulgarian heroes commissioned by another wealthy trader for his "Patriotic Room."

From here it's a bit of a walk uphill to the **Tryavna Icon Museum,** but well worth the effort. The most impressive work is in the first-floor room on the right, which contains the work of the Vitanov and Zachariev families. Inspired by the work on display here, you may suddenly want to take home an icon of commensurate quality. Head for nearby **Etura** ⚔ (9am–6pm; winter 8am–5pm; 6lev/$4/£2), an outdoor ethnographic museum where various crafts are produced by masters using 19th-century traditional methods. The Icon Studio is where you'll find Plamen Malinov and Rossen Donchev plying their trade—you'll pay more for one of their icons than you do for one on the streets, but both are acknowledged to be masters (this is in fact a prerequisite for having any workshop in Etur). In a lovely location on the banks of a burbling stream (which powers much of the equipment), this will be one of the most delightful shopping expeditions ever—unless you don't have cash (no one here takes credit cards).

Surrounding Monasteries ✦✦✦ Twenty monasteries were built around Veliko Tarnovo during its zenith as capital of the Second Kingdom, of which 10 are within a half-hour radius. One of the closest is pretty **Preobrazhenski Monastery.** Follow the winding forest road that branches off the highway heading north to the Danube city of Russe, and suddenly the trees clear to provide glorious uninterrupted views of the hills and valleys beyond. This sublime spot is where the Jewish wife of Ivan Aleksandur decided to celebrate her conversion to Christianity by building **Preobrazhenski,** meaning "Transfiguration," in 1360. Still officially "active," but guarded only by a monk, the monastery itself is largely in ruins, but the church frescoes are undergoing restoration—don't miss Zahari Zograf's *Wheel of Life* on the south wall. Directly across the valley, also surrounded by dense vegetation, you can see the **Sveta Troitsa Convent.** There are other gems, like the **Kapinovo, Kilifarevo** and **Plakovo** monasteries, but if you're looking for a lunch or dinnertime venue, head into the gorge that protects laid-back **Dryanovski Monastery,** as much for its peaceful riverside location and friendly monks, as **Andaka,** the lovely riverside restaurant (see "Where to Stay," above). And if you have decided to include Etura in your itinerary, be sure to fill up a bottle with the sweet-tasting water from nearby **Sokolovski,** meaning "The Falcons"—appropriate, given the views.

Shipka Pass and Church ✦ About 60km (37 miles) south of Veliko Tarnovo, on the road to or from Kazanluk, you will traverse the historic Shipka Pass, scene of the most momentous battle between Russian-Bulgarian and Turkish forces in 1877, a battle that decided the fate of the war, and delivered a cracking blow to the Ottomans. There are two monuments to mark the battle: the rather stern six-story **Freedom Monument** (daily 9am–5pm; 2lev/$1.50/70p), which requires a fair degree of stamina—it's a steep flight of stairs just to the entrance, then many more to reach the top to take in the awesome views of the Balkan Mountains; and the Valley of Kings (including Kazanluk—a tiny, sprawling insect nest below). More accessible is the gold-domed **Church Monument.** Located at the foot of the Pass, this—like Axander Nevsky in Sofia—commemorates the Bulgarian and Russian lives lost during the 1877–78 War of Liberation.

Zheravna ✦✦✦ A total contrast to Arbanassi is the charming architectural museum town of Zheravna, with a great deal more authenticity supplied by a local population (numbering around 700). Depending on road conditions this little-visited village lies 2 to 3 hours from Veliko Tarnovo (a wonderful journey through winding forests and lush pastures), making this more suited as an overnight stop on your way to the coast than a day trip, but if you have not had a chance to explore the little museum towns scattered in the Pirin and Rhodope mountains, then this is a must-see on your itinerary. A hodgepodge of cobbled streets lined with gorgeous 17th-century timber homes shaded by trees and oft covered with vines, their daisy-covered verges cropped by fat goats, it is pure, distilled rural bliss. The most comfortable place to overnight is **Hotel Liv** (© **088 978 3971;** www.hoteliv.com; 50lev/$32.50/£17 double, including breakfast),

THE TRAVELOCITY GUARANTEE

...THAT SAYS EVERYTHING YOU BOOK WILL BE RIGHT, OR WE'LL WORK WITH OUR TRAVEL PARTNERS TO MAKE IT RIGHT, RIGHT AWAY.

To drive home the point,
we're going to use the word "right" in every single sentence.

Let's get right to it. Right to the meat! Only Travelocity guarantees everything about your booking will be right, or we'll work with our travel partners to make it right, right away. Right on!

Here's a picture taken smack dab right in the middle of Antigua, where the Guarantee also covers you.

The Guarantee covers all but one of the items pictured to the right.

For example, what if the ocean view you booked actually looks out at a downright ugly parking lot? You'd be right to call – we're there for you. And no one in their right mind would be pleased to learn the rental car place has closed and left them stranded. Call Travelocity and we'll help get you back on the right track.

Now, you may be thinking, "Yeah, right, I'm so sure." That's OK; you have the right to remain skeptical. That is until we mention help is always right around the corner. Call us right off the bat, knowing our customer service reps are there for you 24/7. Righting wrongs. Left and right.

Now if you're guessing there are some things we can't control, like the weather, well you're right. But we can help you with most things – to get all the details in righting,* visit travelocity.com/guarantee.

*Sorry, spelling things right is one of the few things not covered under the Guarantee.

I'd give my right arm for a guarantee like this, although I'm glad I don't have to.

You'll never roam alone.

two 300-year-old homes recently renovated by Ivan and Vanya, who came here on holiday and fell in love with the village.

Madara Horseman ★★   Lying just over the halfway mark between Veliko Tarnovo and Varna, the UNESCO-listed Madara Horseman, a 95m-high (312 ft.) relief sculpture, was carved into the cliff more than 1,200 years ago. At least, the Greek inscriptions next to the carving date from the 8th century; some believe the horseman predates these by many more hundreds of years, and is in fact the rider-god so revered by the Thracians. The relief is best viewed early morning (opens daily at 8am), or as the suns starts to set (closes 7pm in summer; 5pm in winter) when shadows help delineate the lines of the horseman whose steed appears to be trampling a lion, aided his greyhound. The **Madara National History Archaeological Reserve** (admission 3lev/$2/£1) also comprises the remains of 8th- and 9th-century monasteries (also of a 14th-c. rock monastery), and you can take the cliff path up to the plateau above, where there are more ruins—this time of a 5th-century fortress—and wonderful views.

7 Varna & the Black Sea Coast

449km (278 miles) east of Sofia

Long the premier summer destination for the Eastern bloc, this heavily developed coastline is now also playground to hordes of package tourists from the West, keen to dance the night away to the pulsating beat that emanates from the numerous makeshift summer clubs that seem to range almost continuously along the coast. But when the sun rises, and the shadows draw back to reveal the monstrous hotels that line the beaches, and rows of large pink bodies start to sizzle off their hangovers, it's a far from attractive sight.

Bulgaria's once pristine coastline has largely been ruined. Despite municipal bans stating appropriate distances between beaches and hotels, and specifying the times of the year that building can take place, greedy developers keen to cash in on the huge foreign interest often build year-round, so even those who aren't offended by the existing developments are by noise and dust. But that's not to say that a trip that incorporates a few days on the Black Sea coast is without merit. Besides blowing off steam on the coastal capital's beachfront, it's worth coming this far just to view the "oldest gold in the world" in Varna's Historical Museum, vying with the National History Museum as the most fascinating museum in the country, then heading south to stroll past Byzantine churches and charming 19th-century timber houses in the UNESCO-listed village of Nessebar. Admittedly Nessebar's cobbled streets can get clogged with daytrippers, but this is just the reason to head south to the gorgeous old town of Sozopol, with its plethora of seaside restaurants—time your visit for lunch and, mesmerized by semitranslucent twinkling sea views, you'd be forgiven for thinking you were on the Riviera. Only better, you realize, when the bill arrives.

ESSENTIALS

GETTING THERE   From late April to October you can reach Varna by **plane,** either flying from Sofia or even direct to **Varna airport** (www.varna-airport.bg; 24-hr. flight information ✆ **052 573 323**) or to **Burgas airport** (www.burgas-airport.bg). Most travelers, however, arrive by **road,** traveling from Sofia via Veliko Tarnovo or heading directly east to Burgas and then turning north to Varna or south to Sozopol; bank on spending around 5 hours in a car; 6 if you're traveling by bus

Finds　Quiet Escape to the Queen's Nest

If Varna's cityscape gets too much, take a 45-minute drive north to "Quiet Nest" (© **0579/74452;** 8am–9pm summer; 8lev/$5/£2.80), the modest palace built by the Romanian Queen Marie at the turn of the 20th century just outside the small town of Balchik. The attractive granddaughter of Queen Victoria, Marie had no lack of suitors, including the prince who would be crowned King George V. But Marie's mother, an ambitious royal of Russian descent, did not approve of the British royal bloodline, and sought instead a match in Eastern Europe: Crown Prince Ferdinand of Romania was judged a fitting catch and they duly married in 1893. Described as "a man of no significant character," it is generally agreed that King Ferdinand allowed the more powerful and willful Marie to rule Romania. For her subjects she developed a strong affection, and did much to ease sectarian tensions between Muslims and Christians, but for her husband she felt nothing but "distaste, which grew to revulsion," as she wrote to a friend. An increasingly restless Marie took on a lover, Prince Babu (thought to have influenced her decision to became a devotee of the Baha'i faith, and father of two of her children), and built a retreat on the Black Sea coast, which she called "Quiet Nest." The Palace is unfurnished, and so rather dull, but to the north is a small building in which you'll find a boutique wine shop, **Queens Winery House.** At the helm is 21-year-old Elleanna, a young winemaker who stocks a superb selection of little-known wineries and produces (among other labels) Ducessa Aperitiv, an "Aromatic Wine Drink"—apparently the Romanian queen's favorite drink, the recipe for which Elleanna managed to pry from the queen's winemaker before he passed away in 2005. Passionate about the untapped potential of Bulgarian wine, and a talented maker to boot, the new queen of the Nest is one to watch.

(24lev/$16/£8.50). Buses arrive at the Central Bus Station (© **052/448 349**) on 158 Vladislav Varnenchik Blvd. For **trains** add at another 2 hours (© **052/630 414;** www.bdz.bg).

GETTING AROUND　The easiest way to get around the main attractions in Varna, located within the compact area of its Sea Gardens and Maria Luiza and Suborni streets, is on foot. If you need a cab to explore farther afield, call Lacia at © **052/500-000,** or Maxa at © **052/303 030** or 0888 308 050. If you have flown in, you can rent a car from one of the many reputable car-rental companies in town (www.avis.bg, www.hertz.bg, www.toprentacar.bg). If you wish to catch a bus to or from Nessebar (1½—2 hr. ride south), purchase your ticket from Etap (at Cherno More hotel) then head to 7 Dobrovoltsi St. (© **052/448-349**).

TOURISM INFORMATION　The **Regional Tourism Information Centre** is located at 36 Tsar Osvoboditel Sq. (© **052/602907;** www.tourexpo.bg; Mon–Fri 9am–7pm; Sat 9am–1pm). A useful site (with great shopping and nightlife tips) is www.travel.ciao.co.uk/Varna__Review_5394277).

WHERE TO STAY

Budget travelers need look no further than **Hostel Kashtata** (© **052/639660/1; www.hostelkashtata.com**). Centrally located, with seven bright, light en-suite double rooms in a pale-yellow, century-old house overlooking a quiet leafy lane (only 50m/164 ft. from the beach) it's more B&B than hostel, with added extras like bicycles and room service, and good value at just 30€ ($39) per room. If you want a beachfront recommendation, the new five-story Panorama is bland but comfortable with all rooms featuring sea views—the higher up the better; avoid the first floor (© **052/687-300; www.panoramabg.com**; from 148lev–168lev/$94–$107/£51–£58 double).

Cherno More *(Value)*   A block back from the Sea Gardens, right on buzzing pedestrian Slivnitsa Boulevard, we really like this Communist-era monstrosity. It's an architectural masterpiece if you get the nostalgic charm of brutal fascist '70s-era high-rises, its scale designed to dwarf mere mortals awaiting service in the cavernous entrance lobby. It's a relic from Bulgaria's past that has somehow managed to reinvent itself (at least more so than the nearby similar-era Odessos), though be warned: There are still dank rooms that cower within its 14-floor bulk, replete with Communist-era telephones, old shag carpets, and built-in cabinet radios. Rooms denoted as "deluxe" are the ones to book—almost all on the 7th to 10th floors, these are certainly not "luxe" but renovated and now very bland, very cheap, but functional, and every room has a curved concrete balcony with fabulous city and/or sea views; wonderful, particularly at night. Corner rooms have views both ways—room no. 1014 is a particularly spacious example. (*Note:* In a confusing slight to sensibilities, a "single" room here refers to the fact that a room has *one* bed—even if it is a king, while a "double" room refers to a twin-bedded room.) The dining room—another double-volume area that takes up the entire top floor—has such panoramic views you might not even mind the processed meats and cheese that pass for the breakfast buffet.

33 Slivnitsa., Varna, 9000. © 052/612 or 235/6/7/8. Fax 052/612 243. www.chernomorebg.com. 300 units. 28€ standard (unrenovated) double; 40€–50€ "deluxe" double (referred to as single for double bed; double for twin). Rates include breakfast. MC, V. **Amenities:** Restaurant; bar; fitness and sports center; shops; room service; casino; bingo; beautician; laundry. *In room:* A/C, TV, safe.

Grand Hotel Musala Palace ★★★   A grand old turn-of-the-20th-century hotel, this is a small, intimate boutique option—the top choice in Varna, with every one of its five stars well deserved. Like the Grand in Sofia (no relation) rooms are inspired by the deep, rich comfort of the U.K. gentleman's club, with decor touches ranging from Louis XV–style wingback chairs to Regency-style curtain drapery, plus a few antiques and gilt-framed mirrors thrown in for good measure; bathrooms too reflect the fact that the hotel was recently renovated. Standard rooms are very comfortable, but if it's a special occasion or money is no object, this is one place it's worth splashing out on a deluxe (no. 406 is a great choice) or studio (book no. 102). Located in the center of town, the hotel is strolling distance from the seafront, recommended restaurants, and archaeological museums. The only possible drawback is that—once back and comfortably ensconced in your room you could, given the lack of city or sea views, be in a landlocked capital anywhere in Europe. Then again, this being Varna, with the levels of service and comfort you could only be at the Musala Palace.

3 Musala St., Varna, 9000. © 052/664100. Fax 052/664196. www.musalapalace.bg. 24 units. Fri–Sun 150€–185€ ($191–$235) double; Mon–Thurs 190€–230€ ($261–$318) double. 205€–250€ ($242–$293) suite, depending on

---

Stuck in Burgas?

Burgas does not have the great accommodations options of Varna or Nessebar, but if you find yourself stuck in Burgas, or are here on business, head for the brand-new **Plaza Hotel** on 42 Bogordi St. (✆ **056/846-294**; www.plazahotel-bg. com; from 146lev/$93/£50 double room).

---

day. Rates include breakfast. AE, DC, MC, V. Valet parking. **Amenities:** Restaurant; lobby bar/cafe terrace; wellness center and fitness center; business services; room service; transport services; laundry; dry cleaning. *In room:* A/C, TV, minibar, Internet connection, hair dryer, safe.

WHERE TO DINE IN VARNA

Sofia may be the cuisine capital of Bulgaria, but when it comes to informal dining, Varna blows the socks off its big sister—certainly in the height of summer. Cafes and snack bars line the evening *korso* that stretches from Nezavisimost square to the Slivnitsa before it spills into coast—here, sandwiched between the city's overgrown Sea Gardens and the long curve of its sandy beach, is a seamless "strip mall" of makeshift beach restaurants and bars that curve out from the harbor, finally petering out some 5 to 8km (3–5 miles) north of this. You can wander along here and simply stop at the first place that takes your fancy; the backdrop—a deep sandy beach, lapped by the gentle waters of the Black Sea—is hard to beat. Rated the best fish restaurant by locals, **BM Zaliva** marks the southern tip of the beach. It's a great informal dive (plastic chairs; toes in the sand) where you could opt for a simple sesame-encrusted hake, a hunk of breaded shark, a meaty pan-fried red mullet, or the pricey turbot, fried in garlic and olive oil. But if you've had enough of the thumping beachfront scene, make sure you sample one of the following.

Orient ★★ *Value* TURKISH   "Poor quality prepared food will not be paid" [sic] says the menu, then, "In the event you're met unkindly or without a smile you have the right to require another waiter." This unpretentious restaurant, watched like a hawk by the large and friendly Turkish proprietor, treats the customer as king, and backs it up by the most wonderful food—even the editor of the food and wine mag *Bacchus*, no doubt bored by faddish decor and so-called haute cuisine, rated Orient as a personal Varna favorite after a research trip there in 2006. The array of breads—stuffed or coated like pizzas with cheeses, olives, meats—is fabulous, as are the roasted vegetables, stuffed with delicately spiced meats. Menus are illustrated with clear photographs (with brief English descriptions), so ordering is a relatively easy, though the huge and mouthwatering choice does not preclude this from being a lengthy, drawn-out process.

1 Tzaribrod St. ✆ **052/602 380.** www.orientbg.com. Main courses 2.50lev–10lev ($2–$7/90p–£3.50). No credit cards. Daily 8am–11.30pm.

Prodadena Nevesta ★★★ *Value* BULGARIAN/INTERNATIONAL   Owned by local photographer Nikolai Hristakiev, this restaurant—located opposite the registry office in an old timber house—is a popular choice with Varna foodies who clamber up the staircase to the cozy, wood-paneled rooms, almost every inch covered with bookshelves and wine racks (550 different labels on offer). There is no English menu, but Anna will hopefully be on duty—a great waitress, she is also one of the chefs, and will ask you what you feel like (even if it's not on the menu, Anna knows the chef's unpublished repertoire). Alternatively she'll run through favorites like the bean soup, redolent with Bulgarian mint, and point out rarities like the very traditional but usually homemade "poparasis serena," crusty bread with white cheese, butter, sugar, red pepper, and paprika. If you're hungry, try the mixed grill, served with fresh cucumber and tomato and home-cut potato chips (ask for the latter to be fried with garlic and dill); or the pork loin slow-fried with bacon, gherkins, and mushrooms, then slow-baked with cheese. If you're tiring of Bulgarian, there's a delicious salmon steak, served with carrot puree and broccoli sauce. End with the fried banana and chocolate in filo pastry, and you may roll out rating this the best in Bulgaria.

1 Kralo Marko St. ⓒ 0888 641 440. Main courses 5lev–10lev ($3.50–$8/£1.75–£3.50). MC, V. Daily 11:30am–midnight.

EXPLORING VARNA

Driving into Varna, so-called "pearl" of the Black Sea, you can be forgiven for wondering what the hell you're doing in this run-down port, surrounded by ugly Social-ist-era architecture and visually cut off from the sea by an overgrown and unkempt garden, but stay a day or two and Varna's cosmopolitan vibe starts to creep under your skin. Bulgaria's main naval and commercial shipping port, and adjacent to the coastal resorts of Golden Sands, St. Konstantin and Albena, the city has an interesting edge, made all the more so by the huge annual influx of foreigners and young Sofiates in summer, most here to trawl the overcrowded beaches and pedestrian walkways, and inject more energy into the endless disco beat. This in itself is not reason enough to include the Black Sea capital on your itinerary, but Varna's real draw—even if you're not a history buff—is its Archaeological Museum (see below).

If you still have energy after visiting the museum, you could take the short stroll west to the city's other notable city sight: the huge gold-domed **Assumption of the Holy Virgin Cathedral** (pl Mitropolitska Simeon). From here, you can explore the **Open Market** opposite, coming out at Rousse street where there is incidentally an excellent souvenir shop (**Bulgarian Art Shop; 19 Rousse St.;** ⓒ **052/622299**). Head down Rousse Street to view the neo-baroque **Opera House** (ⓒ **052/650-555;** www.operavarna.bg) on **Nezavisimost Square,** center of the city's cultural life since 1932, and offering a host of shows, including a few modern and traditional ballets, and plenty of operas and operettas during the **International Music Festival Varna Summer,** held at the end of July (though shows start mid-June). Having checked what's showing that night, amble down to view the city's 1,700-year-old **Roman Thermae** (ul Khan Krum and San Stefano; Tues–Sun 10am–5pm; 3lev/$2/£1), one of the largest ancient Roman ruins in Bulgaria.

Varna Archaeological Museum ★★★ Nothing brings home just how ancient the history of Bulgaria is than wandering through the 21 rooms of this museum, view-ing exhibits that are not only inconceivably old but unbelievably sophisticated. Flint tools, some dating from 10,000 B.C., provide proof of just how long ago Bulgaria was inhabited. But it is when you enter the halls in which exhibits from the 294 graves uncovered in the Varna Eneolithic Necropolis that you realize that this region was one of the great cultural centers of the ancient world. Besides the complicated burial ritu-als (corpses were carefully arranged in various positions, and there were also numer-ous "symbolic" graves), there is the sheer quantity of gold found, providing an exceptionally rich inventory of goldsmith techniques 6,200 years ago. But even more jaw-dropping is the gold dating from the 3rd and 4th century B.C., in which the skills of the goldsmiths had developed to the extent that the fine features and billowing drapery of a figurine of Victory so tiny—a gold jewelry item found in the tomb of a Thracian woman—can only fully be appreciated when studied with a magnifying glass.

41 Maria-Luisa Blvd. ⓒ 052/681 030 or 052/681 011. www.varna-bg.com/museums/archaeology/enexhibit. Admission 10lev ($7/£3.50). Summer: Tues–Sun 10am–5pm. Winter: Tues–Sat 10am–5pm.

NESSEBAR ⍟

A rocky "island," connected to the mainland by a short isthmus, Nessebar boasts the finest collection of 19th-century timber homes on the coast, as well as the largest collection of Byzantine-influenced churches. Exploring the tiny port should be a wonderful experience, but it is strangely dissatisfying. Very much a "dead" town, with a mostly nonresident population leeching off the plump and pink tourists that throng its streets (many of them from adjacent Sunny Beach, the largest, cheapest, and most hideous of the Black Sea coast's vast resorts) it is by far the most commercial experience you'll have in Bulgaria (I mean, you know tourism has ruined a town when banners advertising "Roast Beef and Yorkshire Pudding" span its cobbled streets). Still, the architecture is very pretty, and when the hordes have returned to their hutches in Sunny Beach, the Old Town becomes a great deal more pleasant, and is at its best early in the morning, when the cobbled streets are yours to explore virtually on your own. (See overnight options below.)

Only 850m (2,788 ft.) long and 350m (1,148 ft.) long, Nessebar is easy to cover and should take no more than a couple of hours—you can pick up a map from the **Archaeological Museum** (2 Mesembria; Mon–Sat 9am–noon and 1–5pm; 3lev/$2/£1), which is to the right of the Byzantine town gate (A.D. 500); inside you'll find some of the best bits taken from the surrounding churches as well as a few ancient exhibits, like the 3000-year-old stone anchor, and the 200-B.C. statue of Hecate, goddess of witches and fertility. A short stroll down Mesembria brings you to the 14th-century **Pantokrator Church** ⍟⍟. Of the 11 churches, this stone-and-red-brick

---

Moments   Best Lunch on the Black Sea

Take away Nessebar's churches and tourists, and mingle in a few live-in locals, and you have Sozopol—Bulgaria's oldest port, with a fresh produce market and lively lived-in atmosphere. That's not to say Sozopol is devoid of tourists, but these are not the hordes spawned by package tourism. The old town's restaurants are the best along the coast, with sublime views and a serene atmosphere that could have you stopping in for an early snack and leaving in the evening after a long lunch. Add two sandy beaches to cool off on, and Sozopol becomes a really worthwhile lunchtime excursion from Varna or Nessebar (the latter about an hour away). **Ksantana** (7 Morski St., Sozopol; ⓒ 05502/2454), located in an old timber house tucked into the cliffs, and clear views of the glittering sea, is a great option. Succulent langoustines are a highlight, along with the perfectly cooked turbot (their specialty) and meaty Black Sea bluefish—if you've never tried the latter, order the small portion, and augment it with the Ksantana salad—a platter of roast peppers, eggplant purée, shopska salad, and tzatziki.

Paradise Going, Going . . . Found?

The first steps to control the devastating rash of construction on the Black Sea Coast was taken in 2006 when Parliament passed a law setting out new zones (for example, no construction higher than 7.5m/25 ft. on the beach and 100m/328 ft. inland), work restrictions (no work from May–Oct 15), and green/environmental guidelines. A case of closing the door long after the developers have bolted. Or, as Bulgarian proverbs would have it, "putting one's hood up after the rain has stopped."

If you really want to get away from it all, to a beach that isn't overlooked by high-rise hotels, you'll need to travel all the way south to **Sinemorits,** and overnight with the affable Bobby at his **Villa Philadelphia** (www.villa philadelphia.com; ℂ **088 323 391**). Five years ago this little village, almost walking distance from the Turkish border, was off-limits to the public; 3 years later ground was broken by unscrupulous developers, and by end 2006 one of its two beaches had three hideous hotels casting an ominous shadow. To date the long curved beach to the north of the village, a gorgeous much-photographed crescent, flanked by the reed-bordered Veleka River, remains untouched, as does the riverine hinterland. This is the best place (take Bobby with you) from which to witness the Via Pontica, a migratory route that sees thousands of birds from over 300 species migrate via this coast. But developers are chomping at the bit, and while a Thracian gravesite has halted developments on the northern side, this may be temporary. Check on latest developments with Bobby, or ask him to arrange birding or anthropological trips into the interior, where few have as yet ventured.

church is the best preserved and has by far the prettiest, most photogenic exterior but, like most of Nessebar's churches, serves as a gallery showcasing extremely mediocre artists. Take the left-hand fork north to pass Church of St. John the Baptist, stopping to enter **Sveti Spas** (Church of the Saviour; Mon–Fri 10am–5:30pm, Sat–Sun 10am–1:30pm; 3lev/$2/£1). Built in 1609 this is one of only two churches that have frescoes well enough preserved to warrant a small entry fee; the other is **St. Stefan Church** ⟐⟐ (aka New Metropolitan Church; daily 9am–6pm; 3lev/$2/£1). To the north and west of Sveti Spas is a meandering network of narrow cobbled lanes spreads to the shore, along which you'll find the remaining five churches—the only one worth entering is **Sveta Bogoroditsa** for a brief view of its icons and carved bishop's throne. More or less in the center of Old Nessebar you can't miss the ruins of **St. Sofia Church** (Old Metropolitan Church), built in the late 5th and early 6th century, and today surrounded by shops selling tourist tat and tables where you can catch a quick espresso and a sandwich.

There are a plethora of places to eat but be warned: Nessebar's restaurateurs don't have to work at their cuisine standards to fill their tables, and they don't. The most peaceful setting, with the most-photographed view, is **Kapitanska Sreschta** (Captain's Meeting Place) (Chaika St.; ℂ **0554/42124;** 5.90lev–20lev/$2–$14/£2–£7; daily 11am–midnight)—just head for the small fishing boat harbor and look out for the life-size statues in nautical T-shirts at the "Captain's table"; "fish on a tile" is a recommended house specialty, as are mussels, prepared and served in any way you can think of.

If you need to spend the night (and given that Nessebar is only 90 min. from Varna, those who don't want to sample its big-city pulse should choose to base themselves here, covering Varna's Archaeological Museum as a day trip), the most atmospheric places lie within the old quarter. **Trinity** ★★ (© **0554/46700;** www.trinity-nessebar. com), a small custom-built modern hotel built in traditional timber-and-stone style, is the most luxurious option, with professional service standards, and rooms done in tasteful modern neutrals. Ask for a double room (all unfortunately twin-bedded, quashing any romance) with a balcony and sea view, preferably on the second floor— nos. 9 and 10 are best. At 100lev to 150lev ($64–$96/£35–£33) double (studios from 120lev/$77/£41), a good-value option, particularly compared with Varna hotels in the same price category. Virtually neighboring Trinity, cozy **Monte Christo** (© **0554/ 42055;** www.montecristo-bg.com; 95lev–125lev/$61–$80/£33–£28 double) with its more old-fashioned styling, is an equally good choice. For the best views book no. A8.

5

Croatia

by Karen Olson & Sanja Bažulić Olson

Germans, Italians, Austrians, and Hungarians have been aware of Croatia's charms for more than a century and, until very recently, these groups comprised the bulk of the country's summer visitors. That changed after the 1991 war with Serbia. Even after hostilities ended, safety concerns and the notion that there was nothing left worth seeing kept foreign travelers away. Today, tourism is almost back to prewar levels, but negative perceptions persist. The reality is that Croatia is safe and welcoming for tourists, which is clear after the shortest sojourn.

Travelers from the around the world are flocking to the country's miles of coastline, ancient ruins, medieval hilltop castles, and abundant natural wonders, making tourism one of Croatia's most important sources of revenue. That doesn't mean Croatia is overrun with visitors: Even when the foreign influx is at its peak, it still is possible to find a secluded cove where it seems you are the only person on earth. And when hotels are full, there is always a room waiting in a private home where the landlord welcomes you like a long-lost friend.

Croatia's rich and varied natural beauty is reason enough to visit, but for those who want to combine an active vacation with breathtaking scenery, adventure travel options abound. Whether you prefer kayaking on swift rivers, rock climbing

the formidable Velebit limestone walls, windsurfing off islands like Brač, spelunking in the subterranean caves that honeycomb the karstic landscape, or scuba diving off Vis, Croatia is an ideal venue. For those drawn to more sedate pursuits, Croatia offers numerous resorts along its many stretches of "riviera," plus quaint agri-inns in the rural interior, where meandering wine roads are dotted with places to linger over a meal. For those who like to wander, there are leisurely day trips to offshore islands or pilgrimages to a plethora of religious sites. History buffs will revel in the castles, museums, ruins, and churches scattered about the countryside. The past is a living thing in Croatia, where every building, park, and hill has a story that adds to the lore of this ancient land.

Since gaining independence in 1991, Croatia has been working through economic, social, and political issues, and the country hopes to obtain membership in the European Union by 2010. Meanwhile, Croatia is moving ahead with renovation, road building, and restoration, three R's of progress that are closely tied to the current tourism boom. From secluded coves to bustling metropolises, Croatia is the ticket. Be sure to bring a sense of wonder and plenty of film—Croatia is a country of many colors and a magnificent work in progress.

1 Getting to Know Croatia

THE LAY OF THE LAND

Croatia is a crescent-shaped country that borders Slovenia in the northwest, Hungary in the north, Serbia in the northeast, Bosnia-Hercegovina to the east along almost the entire length of the Dalmatian coast, Montenegro in the extreme south, and the Adriatic Sea to the west. Croatia covers about 56,542 sq. km (35,112 sq. miles) and is slightly smaller than West Virginia with a varied topography of mountainous regions, flat plains, lowland basins, and hilly terrain. The country's 1,168 islands account for 4,085 sq. km (2,536 sq. miles) of its 5,835 sq. km. (3,524 sq. miles) of coastline, but just 50 of the islands are inhabited.

THE REGIONS IN BRIEF

DALMATIA   Croatia's southernmost region lies on the eastern Adriatic coast between **Pag Island** in the northwest and the **Bay of Kotor** in the southeast. Dalmatia's climate is Mediterranean with wet, mild winters and long, hot, dry summers. The width of inland Dalmatia ranges from 50km (31 miles) in the north to just a few kilometers wide in the south. Dalmatia is divided into four counties whose capital cities— **Zadar, Split, and Dubrovnik**—are also popular tourist destinations. Dalmatia and its islands account for most of the seacoast, Croatia's main tourist draw.

INLAND CROATIA   From **Zagreb** east to the Danube River, Inland Croatia is home to treasures that include protected nature preserves, picturesque villages, and historic cities. Some like **Mt. Medvednica** north of Zagreb are close to urban areas and public transportation, while others are remote wetlands. The region is dotted with notable castles, cathedrals, and historic sites that are interspersed with villages, rolling wooded hills, long flat plains, lush vineyards, and farmland. Inland Croatia shares a border with Slovenia and Hungary in the north and with Bosnia-Hercegovina in the south. The Danube accounts for much of the eastern border with Serbia.

ISTRIA   Croatia's westernmost region is the country's most visited, perhaps because it is the most accessible to visitors from continental Europe. Istria is a triangular peninsula that juts into the northern Adriatic across the bay from Venice. The region includes the islands of the **Brijuni Archipelago,** made famous by Josip Broz Tito, who received countless celebrities and heads of state at the residence and wildlife park he established there. In addition, clusters of smaller islands and islets lie just off Istria's southeast coast. The region is adjacent to **Rijeka** in the east and is separated by just a few miles of Slovenia from Italy **(Trieste)** at its northwest corner. Istria's west coast is lined with pretty Venetian-influenced towns like **Rovinj** and **Poreč,** while its southernmost city, **Pula,** is home to magnificent Roman ruins. Medieval castles, woodland churches, and charming villages are surrounded by vineyards and olive groves in the interior, where the forests also support thriving hunting and truffle industries.

KVARNER GULF   The northern coastal region that borders the Kvarner Gulf and neighboring islands comprise this region, Croatia's closest to central and western Europe. Location and a mild climate have made Kvarner a popular tourist destination for western Europeans since the heyday of the Austro-Hungarian empire. The Kvarner Gulf region includes the islands of **Krk, Cres, Lošinj, Rab, Unjie,** and **Susak** as well as the **Opatija Riviera,** one of the country's busiest tourist centers.

THE ISLANDS   Croatia's 1,168 islands account for much of its fabled seacoast. Even though just 50 of them are inhabited, each of its Adriatic islands from Istria to

Croatia

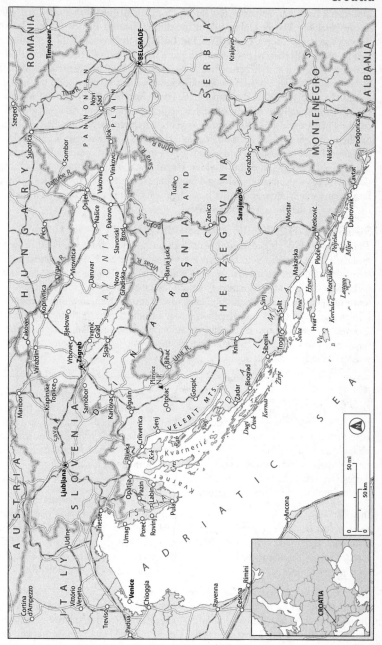

Dubrovnik has a unique personality. From the sultry **Brijuni** cluster off Istria in the north to remote **Vis** off Dubrovnik in the south, Croatia's islands are some of the country's strongest tourist draws. **Cres and Lošinj** in the Kvarner Gulf are characterized by rocky hills that overlook secluded azure bays while to the east, **Rab** is a living museum of Venetian architecture, while its neighbor, **Pag**, is a dichotomy of stark, barren landscape and a bustling weekend-getaway center. Farther south, the **Kornati Archipelago** off Zadar is a diver's paradise. **Hvar, Korčula, Brač, Vis,** and **Mljet** are Croatia's southernmost islands. Hvar has acquired a reputation as a sun-drenched celebrity playground while Korčula is proud of its architecture and art. Brač is notable for the white stone mined in its quarries and the wind–sea collaboration that makes it a Shangri-La for watersports enthusiasts. Brač's major tourist center is **Bol,** which is home to photogenic **Zlatni Rat (Golden Horn)** beach, a thin peninsula that changes shape with the sea current and always draws a huge international crowd. **Vis** is a mecca for extreme watersports, and **Mljet** is the legendary island whose beauty so mesmerized Odysseus that he stayed for 7 years.

SUGGESTED ITINERARIES: THE DUBROVNIK AREA IN 10 DAYS

Tourist routes through Croatia can be as disparate as land is from sea. Don't make the mistake of thinking that you can cover everything in a week or even a month. Rather, start from a hub and concentrate on sites within 161km (100 miles) or so. Save other parts of the country for future trips. Connections, especially along the Dalmatian Coast south of Split and to the southern islands, can be inconvenient and time-consuming, so plan carefully. Here is our suggestion for an introduction to southern Dalmatia.

This tour uses Dubrovnik as a starting point and base and takes 3 days to explore Old Town and the area in its immediate vicinity. Follow that with some island hopping and end your tour in Split.

Day ❶

Start by orienting yourself to Old Town's sites by taking the walking tour detailed later in this section and save taking the walk around the top of Old Town's wall for an early-evening stroll. When you descend, enjoy a fish dinner at a restaurant overlooking the Old Harbor or the sea.

Day ❷

Book an excursion to mystical Mljet and pack wine and cheese for a picnic in the forest. Dinner in Dubrovnik.

Day ❸

Take the bus or water taxi to Cavtat and explore its churches and museums or laze on the beach. Catch any remaining Dubrovnik sites during a predinner walk.

Day ❹

Drive or book an excursion to the Pelješac Peninsula. Stop at Ston to climb the town's 14th-century ramparts and reward yourself with a lunch of oysters from the area's shellfish beds. Continue to Orebič through Pelješac's wine country, stopping to taste new vintages here and there. Dinner/overnight in Orebič.

Day ❺

Book an excursion to Korčula. Spend the day exploring Marco Polo's alleged birthplace and take the late Sem Marina fast boat to Hvar. Have dinner at one of the courtyard restaurants off St. Stephen Square and overnight at Hotel Riva.

Day ❻

Explore Hvar Town and Stari Grad in the afternoon. Return to the Riva and catch a concert at the Franciscan cloister and dinner at a restaurant on the harbor. Overnight at the Riva.

Day ❼

Book transportation to Bol on Brač and spend the day swimming and sunbathing off Zlatni Rat. Tour the waterfront shops before dinner at Taverna Riva off the waterfront. Overnight in Bol.

Day ❽

Book a ferry from Brač to Split. After checking in to the Hotel Peristil or the Vestibul Palace, explore what's left of Diocletian's Palace and the Old Town within its walls. Overnight in Split.

Day ❾

Take a bus 19km (12 miles) northwest to Trogir (or book a guided excursion) and take the day to explore this medieval town on a small island connected to the mainland by a bridge. Return to Split after dinner.

Day ❿

If you have time, take a bus to the Roman ruins of Salona 6.4km (4 miles) outside Split and immerse yourself in the past. Return to Split for the flight home.

CROATIA TODAY

Croatia is still rebuilding its image more than a decade after the end of the Homeland War, and it is determined to take its place at the world table. Signs of economic recovery are everywhere: From packed hotels on the coast to thriving boutiques and restaurants in Zagreb, Croatia is adopting a more sophisticated, savvy posture. Its government is working to reduce foreign debt, boost the economy, and promote the country's natural wonders while it waits for admittance to the European Union.

A LOOK AT THE PAST

Recorded Croatian history begins around 1200 B.C., when people occupying the region that is now Croatia, Bosnia, Albania, and Serbia formed a coalition of tribes known as **Illyrians.** The **Greeks** arrived in the 4th century B.C. and traded oil, wine, salt, metals and other commodities with the Illyrians. In the 3rd century B.C., a 60-year series of wars ended with the Romans on top and the creation of the province of Illyricum.

The spread of Roman colonies across Croatia continued until A.D. 9, when the Adriatic coast and interior lands were annexed by **Tiberius** to create three Roman provinces: **Dalmatia** (Adriatic seacoast), **Noricum** (northern territory/Austria), and **Pannonia** (Hungary), where the Romans built fortresses, roads, bridges, aqueducts, and sparkling new cities—such as Pola (Pula), Jader (Zadar), Salona (Solin) near Split, and Epidaurum (Cavtat). At the end of his reign, Roman Emperor **Diocletian** built his lavish "retirement home" in Split, where it remains as one of the best-preserved vestiges of the Roman era.

From the end of the 4th century until the 7th century, Croatia suffered a series of barbarian invasions. But it was the warlike Asian **Avars** who allegedly brought the **Slavic Croats**—ancestors to today's Croatians—to the area while sacking everything in their path along the way. Eventually the Croats organized into two dukedoms—Pannonia in the north and Dalmatia in the south—which evolved into two distinct cultures—Mediterranean and central European.

Croats continued to live under a series of foreign and Croatian administrations until A.D. 924, when the country was united under **Tomislav I,** the first King of Croatia. He was followed by **King Petar Krešimir IV** and **King Dmitar Zvonimir,** but after Zvonimir's death in the 11th century, the monarchy withered and Croatia and Hungary formed a common kingdom guided by a parliament **(Sabor).** During this time free cities (Dubrovnik, among others) were founded along the coast, increasing trade and political strength in the region.

A **Tatar invasion** in 1242 diverted the government's attention to the country's defense, but ultimately, **Hungarian King Bela IV** outmaneuvered the Tatars and retained control. **Venice,** however, remained determined to control Istria and Dalmatia and ultimately access to the sea; they finally achieved that goal in 1409. During the 15th century the **Ottoman Turks** advanced on Croatian lands and a series of battles and deaths put **Ferdinand I of Habsburg** on Croatia's throne and the Habsburg Empire in control.

In 1808 **Napoleon** captured several coastal towns, uniting Dalmatia with parts of Slovenia and Croatia. When Napoleon was defeated in 1815, the control of Dalmatia once again reverted to the Habsburgs, and **Austria** created the **Kingdom of Illyria,** an administrative unit designed to thwart Hungarian nationalism and unification of the South Slavs. Dalmatia, however, was not part of this reorganization, as Austria decided to keep it as a vacation playground. At the same time, Croatian leaders pushed nationalism by promoting the Croatian language and culture; they formed a Slavic kingdom under the Habsburgs' noses.

Hungary challenged Austria during the revolution that was sweeping across Europe in 1848 and Croatia sided with Austria while calling for self-determination. Austria yielded to the pressure and raised **Josip Jelačić** to the position of ban (viceroy) of Croatia. Jelačić immediately suspended relations with Hungary and declared war, but his Austrian allies reasserted their authority over Croatia after defeating the Hungarians. Austria ended absolute rule over Croatia in 1860. Croatia once again came under Hungarian influence in 1868.

In 1906, Serbs and Croats again came together to create the **Croat-Serb Coalition,** which immediately came under attack by Vienna, which feared that the groups' cooperation with each other would reduce the Austrian influence.

In 1908, Austria-Hungary annexed Bosnia and its diverse population of Catholic Croats, Orthodox Serbs, and Muslims. This move thwarted the Serbian goal of creating a Serbian state and reignited tensions between Croats and Serbs. On June 28, Austrian **Archduke Franz Ferdinand** and his wife were assassinated, and a month later Austria-Hungary declared war on Serbia. Germany sided with Austria; and Russia, France, and Great Britain countered by forming an alliance of their own, putting Croatia and Serbia in opposite corners.

On December 1, 1918, after the Austro-Hungarian Empire had been defeated, the Serb leadership broke rank and created the **Kingdom of Serbs, Croats,** and **Slovenes.** In 1927, its name was changed to the **Kingdom of Yugoslavia** (South Slavia).

Yugoslavia tried to remain neutral at the start of World War II, but pressure to support the Axis side was great, and on March 25, 1941, Yugoslavia's leader aligned the country with the Nazis. Within 2 days the pact was nullified, but Germany would not let the cancellation stand. On April 6, they bombed Belgrade and invaded Yugoslavia. It took them just 10 days to defeat the Yugoslav army.

A resistance movement was organized almost immediately after the German invasion, but it was divided between the **pro-Serbian Četniks** and the **pro-Communist Partisans** led by **Josip Broz "Tito."** The Allies recognized Tito's Partisans as the official resistance and funneled all foreign aid to the Communist group, which helped liberate Belgrade. When the war ended in 1944, more than 1.7 million Yugoslavs had died, about 10% of the country's population.

After the war, Tito's Communist Party won the Yugoslav election, but Tito was not in lockstep with Stalin and declared Yugoslav non-alignment in 1948, which allowed him to function as a **cafeteria Communist.**

The country endured a Soviet blockade in the 1950s under Tito, but Tito's local site-management policy allowed tourism to flourish along the Adriatic coast. He also gave each of Yugoslavia's six republics—**Croatia, Serbia, Slovenia, Bosnia/Herzegovina, Macedonia,** and **Montenegro**—control over its own internal affairs.

Tito died on May 4, 1980, at the age of 88, leaving the Yugoslav state without a strong successor. To complicate matters, the region's economy was deteriorating in the wake of the 1970s oil crisis, a huge national debt, and the disappearance of foreign credit sources. Yugoslavia began to crack along national, religious, and ethnic lines.

In 1987, **Slobodan Milošević** emerged as a proponent of Serb superiority while working toward installing a Communist government in Yugoslavia. Two years after Milošević's debut as a champion of Serbs, the **Berlin Wall** came down, leaving him holding an unpopular position while the rest of Europe raced off in the opposite ideological direction.

In May 1989 the **Croatian Democratic Union (HDZ),** led by former general and historian **Franjo Tuđiman,** became one of the first non-Communist organizations in Croatia, and in less than a year it began campaigning for Croatia's secession from Yugoslavia. By April, free elections were held in Croatia and Tuđman was sworn in as president the next month. He promptly declared Croatian statehood, a preliminary stage before independence, and a constitution was written that declared the Serbs in Croatia a national minority rather than a unique nation within the republic, a move that fomented outrage in the Serb community.

In 1991, Milošević began gathering support for a Greater Serbia, which was to include all the areas of Croatia and Bosnia/Herzegovina where Serbs were in residence. Hostilities broke out in 1991 with Milošević and Serb forces from all over Yugoslavia pouring into Croatia. During the violence, cities such as **Dubrovnik, Vukovar,** and **Osijek** suffered heavy damage; thousands of Croatians were forced to leave their homes; thousands more were killed. Hostilities raged until peace was restored in 1995, but it was 3 more years before the last Serb military units left Croatia.

In April 2001, Slobodan Milošević was arrested and charged with corruption in connection with the war. In November of that year the **UN War Crimes Tribunal** charged him with genocide stemming from his alleged activity during the 1992–95 Bosnian campaign. Milošević died in 2006 while in UN custody at The Hague before his trial could be concluded.

CROATIAN PEOPLE & CULTURE

After centuries of occupation by foreign powers, the 4.5 million citizens of Croatia are embracing their hard-won independence in a big way and reasserting their nationalism. Croatians living on the Venetian-influenced Dalmatian coast and the central European interior are now reveling in their heritage by reviving customs, traditions, and even national dishes that were put aside during the foreign domination. Many of these traditions revolve around religious holidays and saints' feast days and the village church is once again a center of community for Croatians, 90% of whom are Roman Catholic, 4% Serbian Orthodox, and 1% Muslim.

The 1991–95 war devastated Croatia's economy, but the country is no charity case. Croatians see themselves as an active part of modern Europe with ties to western Europe. When Croatia was still part of Yugoslavia, Tito recognized and cultivated global relationships throughout his watch as the country's leader. Unlike other people under Communist influence at the time, Yugoslavians (including Croatians) were allowed to work and travel abroad, and to own property. In addition, they welcomed tourists from all over the world, a tradition that is now one of Croatia's most important sources of income. Modern Croatians value progress, family and friends, good food and wine, nice clothes, vacations on the coast, the environment, the country's historical treasures, and most of all, freedom.

CROATIAN CUISINE

Dining is a national sport in Croatia. Food is good in all regions of the country. However, besides consistent quality and an ever-present offering of grilled meat and fish and pizza from north to south, each part of the country prides itself on specific traditional dishes.

Cuisine in **continental Croatia** is more substantial than in other regions. Smoked meats and cheese *(prgica)* are popular in regional markets, while *sarma* (ground meat in sour cabbage leaves), and *krvavice* (blood sausage with sauerkraut) are main meal staples. *Štrukle* (phyllo filled with fresh cheese, apples, cherries, or other fruit) and *palačinke* (crepes filled with honey and walnuts or jam). In **Gorski Kotar & Lika** in southwest central Croatia, homemade cheeses, fruit brandies, and spit-roasted lamb and pork are favorites. Look for *janjetina* (lamb) baked under a bell-shaped lid *(peka)* or roasted over an open grill.

Istria and the **Kvarner Gulf** regions boast the most diverse cuisine in Croatia. In the Kvarner, try *Creska janjetina* (lamb from the island of Cres) and *škampi* (shrimp dishes) or try any of the game stews infused with bay leaves that grow in the mountainous part of Cres island. On Pag, sample *Paški sir* (Pag cheese), a unique salty sheep cheese infused with herbal notes because of the animals' diet of local vegetation, lamb, and *pršut*. In Istria, any dish with *tartufe* (truffles) is worth a try. *Istarski fuži sa gulasom od divljači* (pasta with game goulash) is sublime. Istria is also the source of some of Croatia's best wines. The main meal in **Dalmatia** typically starts with *pršut* and *Paški sir* scattered with olives and drizzled with oil. *Kamenice* (oysters) from the shellfish beds of Ston on the Pelješac Peninsula are prized, as is anything from the sea.

LANGUAGE

Language can be the most daunting aspect of a trip to Croatia for any English-speaking tourist. Signs in Croatian look like gibberish to English speakers, and conversations sound like it, too. Even with a dictionary, it is difficult to understand what is being said and it is even more difficult to figure out how to form the words for a response. Croatians realize that theirs is a complicated language; consequently, most are fluent in at least one other language, usually German, Italian, or English. However, Croatian words are fairly easy to pronounce if you remember to give sound to every letter, place the accent on the first syllable, and pronounce the letter "j" as a "y," "c" as "ts," "š" as "sh," " ž" as "zhh," and "đ" as "dj." If you try to learn to say and recognize at least a few rudimentary words and phrases in this Slavic variant, you will be richly rewarded for your efforts.

USEFUL WORDS & PHRASES

English	Croatian	Pronunciation
Yes	**Da**	dah
No	**Ne**	nay
good	**dobro**	*doe*-broe
I don't understand.	**Ne razumijem.**	Nay ra-*zoo*-mee-yem.
Where is . . . ?	**Gdje je . . . ?**	*Gd*-yay yay. . .
How much/ How many?	**Koliko?**	*Koe*-lee-koe
Good day.	**Dobar dan.**	*Doe*-bar dahn.
Hi/bye	**Bok**	boke
Thank you.	**Hvalas.**	*Huh*-vah-lah.
Goodbye.	**Doviđenja.**	Doe-vee-*djen*-ya.
Please	**Molim**	*Moe*-leem
I understand.	**Razumijem.**	Rah-*zoo*-mee-yem.
I don't understand.	**Ne razumijem.**	Nay rah-*zoo*-mee-yem.
Where is the . . . ?	**Gdje se nalazi . . . ?**	Ga dyay say *nah*-lah-zee
entry	**ulaz**	*oo*-lahz
exit	**izlaz**	*eez*-lahz
toilets (men)	**toilets (muskarci)**	moosh-*kar*-tsi
toilets (women)	**toilets (žene)**	*zhe*-neh
hospital	**bolnica**	bole-nee-tsu
police	**policija**	poe-*lee*-tsee-yah
prohibited	**zabranjeno**	zah-brah-*nyay*-noe

2 Planning Your Trip to Croatia

VISITOR INFORMATION

The home Web page of the **Republic of Croatia** (www.hr/index.en.shtml) offers potential visitors numerous links to the country. The **Croatian National Tourist Board website** (www.croatia.hr) contributes specifics about trip planning and focuses on transportation and accommodations.

The **Croatian National Tourist Board** has a U.S. office at 350 Fifth Ave., Suite 4003, New York, NY 10118 (© **212/279-8672**); and a U.K. office at 2 Lanchesters, 162–164 Fulham Palace Rd., London W6 9ER (© **020/8563-7979**)

ENTRY REQUIREMENTS

All foreign nationals need a valid passport for entrance to Croatia. Citizens of the U.S., U.K., Australia, Canada, New Zealand, Israel, Ireland, and Singapore do not need visas for tourist/business trips of fewer than 90 days within a 6-month period. For a stay over 90 days, a visa should be obtained in advance. South Africans do require a visa. For more information on visas, go to **www.croatiaemb.org**. For information on getting a passport, see "Getting Your Passport in Order" on p. 27.

Croatian Embassy Locations

In the United States
Croatian Embassy: 2343 Massachusetts Ave. NW, Washington DC 20008 (© 202/588/5899; fax 1 202-588-8937; public@croatiaemb.org).

In Canada
Croatian Embassy: 229 Chapel St., Ottawa, Ontario, K1N 7Y6 (© 613-562-7820; fax 613-562-7821; croemb.ottawa@mvp.hr).

In the United kingdom
Croatian Embassy: 21 Conway St., London, W1P, 5HL, U.K. (© 44 20 7387-2022; fax 44 20 7387-0936; consular.dept.London@mvp.hr).

In Australia
Croatian Embassy: 14 Jindalee Crescent, O'Malley Act, 2606, Canberra (© 61 2 6286-3544; croemb@bigpond.com).

In New Zealand
Consulate General of the Republic of Croatia: 131 Lincoln Rd., Henderson/PO Box 83200 Edmonton, Auckland (© 64 9 836-5581; fax 64 9 836-5481; cro-consulate@xtra.co.nz).

MONEY

The official currency of Croatia is the **kuna (kn),** which comes in notes of 5, 10, 20, 50, 100, 200, 500, and 1000 kn. One kuna equals 100 lipa, and coins with values of 1, 2, 5, 10, 20, and 50 lipa and 1, 2, 5, and 25 kuna are in circulation. To convert prices in kunas to current prices in U.S. dollars, go to www.xe.com/ucc.

EXCHANGE   At press time, the exchange rate was 5.8 Croatian kuna to 1 U.S. dollar. With Croatia's anticipated E.U. membership in progress, many Croatian businesses are beginning to express their prices in euros and kuna, though euros are not yet widely accepted. ATMs (aka Bankomats in Croatia) have been installed in almost all towns and are the most convenient and economical way to obtain Croatian currency. Foreign currency can be changed at post offices, banks, exchange offices, and at some hotels and travel agencies, but beware of service charges, which can be as high as 3%. Any Croatian bank will handle credit card cash advances.

CREDIT CARDS   Most stores, hotels, and upscale restaurants in larger cities accept credit cards, but establishments in small towns generally do not. Most small businesses and market vendors do not accept traveler's checks.

Note: Many restaurants, hotels, and shops offer a discount for cash payments.

WHEN TO GO

July and August are high season on the Croatian coast and islands. This is when the coast is at its best—and worst: Hotel rooms are the priciest, restaurants the busiest, and crowds can be overwhelming. However, Zagreb and other interior cities can be bargains in summer because many citizens head for the coast. The downside is that some Zagreb restaurants and shops may be closed for vacation. In May, June, September, and October, coastal weather is usually mild, the sea warm, and prices lower, but some establishments might be shuttered and some ferry routes might be canceled or on reduced schedules.

Weather in Croatia is divided into two miniclimates. Northern Croatia has a Continental climate, with average temperatures ranging from near freezing in January to about 70°F (21°C) in August. The coastal areas have a more Mediterranean climate, with average temperatures ranging from the mid-40s in January to 100°F (38°C) or above in August. Spring and autumn are pleasant and mild along the coast; inland winters can be cold and snowy.

HOLIDAYS
Public holidays are New Year's Day (Jan 1), Easter (variable), Labor Day (May 1), Corpus Christi (June 15), Anti-Fascist Resistance Day (June 22), Victory Day and National Thanksgiving Day (Aug 5), Assumption Day (Aug 15), Independence Day (Oct 8), All Saints' Day (Nov 1), and Christmas (Dec 25–26). In addition, many towns celebrate their patron saint's day as a public holiday.

GETTING THERE
BY PLANE   The biggest problem for North American tourists visiting Croatia is getting there. At press time, there were no direct flights to Croatia from anywhere in North America. Travelers from this part of the world must make connections to Zagreb, Split, Rijeka, or Dubrovnik with (usually) a Croatia Air (www.croatia airlines.hr) connection from a European hub such as Amsterdam, Berlin, Brussels, Düsseldorf, Frankfurt, Moscow, Munich, Paris, Prague, Rome, Sarajevo, or Vienna. A number of Europe's discount carriers, such as Ryanair, Easyjet, Wizzair, and Sky-Europe, serve Croatia via cities such as London and Venice, but some of these routes are seasonal, always crowded, and heavily taxed.

Note: Airline schedules are not always aligned for Croatia connections and logistics can require an overnight stay in the connecting city. If your itinerary requires an overnight stay, expect to pick up your luggage and go through Customs in the connecting city, then repeat the process when you check in for the second leg of your trip.

BY TRAIN   Croatia has international railway links with Slovenia, Hungary, Italy, Austria, Switzerland, Slovakia, France, Germany, and Bosnia/Hercegovina. There are trains to and from other European countries, but traveling any of these routes can be extremely time-consuming. Traveling from Paris to Zagreb, for example, takes 18-plus hours, while a trip from Frankfurt to Split will take almost 24 hours. If you must get

---

Major Festivals in Croatia
The festivals mentioned here are just a few celebrated every year. Inquire at the Croatian National Tourist Office or at local tourist offices for event contact information and for an updated calendar.

On **January 7,** Croatia's Eastern Orthodox Christians celebrate Christmas and take a day off from work. Dubrovnik celebrates its patron saint on **February 3,** with a parade and lots of revelry to honor St. Blaise. From **mid-July to mid-August,** the Split Summer Festival takes over the city's historic core with exhibitions, concerts, dance, theater, and especially opera performed in the Peristil. Well-known international artists perform during the Dubrovnik Summer Festival, from early July to late August. For **three weekends in October,** Lovran outside Opatija celebrates **Marunada,** a tribute to everything chestnut-related. Martinje (St. Martin's Day) is a church feast day, but **November 11** is also the day when the new wine is blessed and "tested" in unlimited amounts in almost all grape-growing regions of Croatia.

to Croatia from another European city by rail, check schedules and fares and get details on rail passes at **Rail Europe,** www.raileurope.com. Croatian rail travel usually requires train changes because the track gauge is different from that used on Eurail routes. Check **Croatia Railways** (www.hznet.hr).

BY FERRY   Ferry travel is the most common way to access Croatia's islands and coastal towns. Four lines serve major Croatian ports from Bari, Ancona, Pescara, and Venice in Italy. Other lines operate seasonal routes. Information for all ferry lines listed below is available at www.cemar.it.

Note: Not all ferries operate daily routes to all destinations, so you need to check arrival/departure information carefully.

Jadrolinija has three international routes—Ancona-Zadar and Ancona-Split daily, and once-a-week service between Bari and Dubrovnik. Round-trip deck passage for two adults without a vehicle runs 74€ ($88) for the overnight trip between Bari and Dubrovnik, while the fare for two in an external cabin with toilet plus a vehicle is 413€ ($492).

Blue Line International operates daily overnight service between Ancona and Split. Round-trip deck accommodations for two run 160€ ($190) while a deluxe cabin for two with a vehicle runs 525€ ($625) during the summer. For weekend departures from late July through late August add 25%.

SNAV operates several routes between Italy and Croatia and is the only international connection to popular Hvar Island. Prices and schedule information are available from April through September on the cemar.hr website (above).

Venezia Lines travels between Venice and cities such as Rovinj and Pula on Istria's western coast. Schedule and fare information is available at the website listed above or at www.venezialines.com from April through September.

BY CAR   The highways that connect Croatia to Slovenia, Hungary, Bosnia-Hercegovina, and Serbia-Montenegro are good and getting better. This is especially true of the span between Ljubljana and Zagreb, a 2-hour journey. It takes about 5 hours to reach Zagreb (362km/225 miles) from Budapest, Hungary, while visitors from Italy and Austria cross an excellent stretch of road in Slovenia to get to Croatia's borders.

BY BUS   International bus travel in Europe can be comfortable but time-consuming as the escalating price of fuel has catapulted this travel option out of the "cheap" category. Regular international buses connect Croatia with neighboring European countries and those beyond its borders, including the U.K. (www.nationalexpress.com). If time is money for you, consider that while round-trip bus fare between London and Split costs just 171€ ($204), the trip takes about 38 hours and almost 60 hours to return.

GETTING AROUND

BY PLANE   Croatia Air has a near monopoly on flights that travel among Croatia's seven airports (Zagreb, Split, Dubrovnik, Rijeka, Pula, Zadar, and Brač), and unless one of these cities is your final destination, you'll have to transfer to some other mode of transportation to finish your trip.

Note: Domestic flights booked on Croatia Air from outside the country cost nearly twice as much as flights booked at a Croatia Air office in the country unless they are part of a multicity international ticket.

BY BUS   Almost every town in Croatia has a bus station, and the network of bus routes makes this form of transportation an excellent, economical option for travel *within* Croatia. Express routes on updated highways facilitate travel among major cities and buses stop at almost every village in the country, though schedules might be inconvenient for those with limited time.

BY FERRY   Ferry/catamaran travel is a way of life on Croatia's coast. There is no other way to get to the islands (except Pag and Krk, which are linked to the mainland via bridges). Jadrolinija, Sem Marina, and SNAV are the major ferry operators In summer, ferry schedules are beefed up to handle increased traffic, but not necessarily aligned to make connections and island hopping convenient. In winter some lines reduce their schedules. Whenever there is a *bura,* ferries can be sidelined.

Note: When planning your trip, do not underestimate the time it takes to travel by ferry. Besides calculating time for the water crossing, build in time to get to the ferry port, wait in line (which can be hours), and get to your final destination. Check schedules carefully as not all routes operate every day.

BY CAR   Driving is the best method for seeing the real Croatia—even the islands. However, car rental and fuel, with a subcompact starting at about $50 a day and gas selling at unprecedented high prices, can be expensive. During July and August it is important to reserve a rental car before you arrive.

Croatia's main highways (autocestas) are well marked, and well maintained. Secondary roads vary in quality and can range from excellent to unmarked dirt tracts. Gas stations are readily available near the larger cities. They are usually open from 7am to 7pm every day and until 10pm in the summer.

Note: It's a good idea to get a Croatia road map that locates gas stations across the country before you start a long trip. These are usually available at the stations themselves. See www.ina.hr, www.hak.hr, and www.omvistrabenz.hr for details.

BY TRAIN   **Croatian Railways** (www.hznet.hr) is an efficient way to travel between Zagreb and the northern and inland parts of the country. All of Croatia's major cities except Dubrovnik are connected by train service.

TIPS ON ACCOMMODATIONS

Thanks to its longtime popularity as a vacation spot for European travelers, Croatia has an ample supply of accommodations, but the types and quality vary widely. Hotels are the most expensive option, in the shortest supply, and often in need of updating despite labels like "luxury" and "modern." All resort hotels fill up fast, so be sure to reserve early. Some hotels require full-board bookings of no fewer than 7 days in summer and those that do book on a daily B&B basis often tack on a surcharge of as much as 50% per day.

Note: Some hoteliers will offer a discount if you pay with cash.

Private accommodations are an economical alternative and can range from grand apartments to a bed in a dormlike room. Private accommodations can be booked through local agencies, online, or secured through individuals who solicit customers at ferry ports and train and bus stations. Private accommodations often require a minimum multinight stay. Payment is almost always on a cash basis.

Campsites generally have loads of amenities and prime locations near the sea. They can accommodate backpackers or families with RVs, but they fill up quickly in summer and reservations are a must. Croatia also has almost two dozen FKK (nudist) camps as well as some bare-bones hostels in the larger cities. Rates for all kinds of accommodations, including campsites, in the coastal areas are highest in July and August—sometimes double the usual rates.

TIPS ON DINING

Croatian cuisine, like the country itself, is regional in character and divided into coastal and interior styles, with fish and pasta the prevalent offerings in Dalmatia and Istria, grilled meat the entree of choice in the interior, and anything laced with paprika the specialty in Slavonia, the country's easternmost region. Meals at most Croatian restaurants are excellent values, but the smaller, family-run establishments known as konobas generally are the best buy because much of the food and wine is family produced, prepared, and reasonably priced. Whether you choose a restaurant that aspires to be "gourmet," an intimate ma-and-pa place, or a meal cobbled from the town market and corner *pekara* (bakery), you should try local specialties like *čevapčići* (spicy grilled beef or pork meatballs), *blitva* (Swiss chard boiled and served with potatoes, olive oil and garlic), and *burek* (a heavy pastry filled with cheese, meat, or fruit). Fish is often sold by the kilogram in restaurants and the average portion is about 250 grams (9 oz.). Service is almost always included in the menu prices, though leaving loose change as a tip is appreciated. Credit cards are accepted at many upscale restaurants, but even some of the fancier dining rooms offer a discount for cash.

Note: In Dubrovnik, many restaurants no longer build gratuities into the cost of a meal, though almost all charge a couvert, which is a cover charge attached to the bread basket. If you don't want bread, refuse it before it lands on your table and you'll avoid the couvert.

TIPS ON SHOPPING

Unless you are looking for regional items such as Pag lace, Hvar lavender oil, naive art oil-on-glass paintings by artists from the Hlebine school, or Rijeka *Morčići* (ceramic and gold jewelry depicting a black woman in a turban), you'll find that most clothing, shoes, jewelry, and textiles sold in Croatia are imported and expensive. **Town markets** are the best sources for local specialties like homemade *rakija* (brandy), lavender sachets and soap, as well as T-shirts and beachwear. **Grisia Street** in Rovinj and **Tklčićeva Street** in Zagreb are just two examples of town sites where you can find clusters of ateliers, galleries, one-of-a-kind jewelry, crafts, and clothing by Croatian designers. Department stores are open from 8am to 8pm weekdays and 8am to 2 or 3pm Saturdays. Many grocery stores are open Sunday mornings and most town markets are open daily from 7am to noon or beyond.

FAST FACTS: Croatia

American Express **Atlas Travel** (www.atlas-croatia.com) is the agent for American Express in Croatia, with offices in most major cities.

Business Hours Banks and post offices are generally open from 7am to 7pm Monday to Friday without midday breaks. Public offices are open Monday to Friday from 8am to 4pm. During the tourist season, post offices are generally open until 9pm, including Saturday. Shops and department stores stay open from 8am to 8pm and to 2pm Saturday without a break.

Drugstores Ljekarna are open from 8am to 7pm weekdays and until 2pm on Saturday. In larger cities, one pharmacy will be open 24 hours.

Electricity Croatian electricity is 220V, 50 Hz; and the two-prong European plug is standard.

Embassies & Consulates **U.S.:** Andrije Hebranga 2, Zagreb; © 01-66-12-200. **Australia:** Krsnjavoga 1, Zagreb; © 01-48-36-600. **United Kingdom:** Vlaska 121, Zagreb; © 01-45-55-310. Also Obala hrvatskog narodnog preporoda 10, 21000, Split; © 021-341-464.

Emergencies Police © **92**. Fire © **93**. Ambulance © **94**. Roadside assistance © **987**. (When calling from abroad or by cellphone, call © 385 1 987.) General information © **981**. Information about local and intercity numbers © **988**. Information about international numbers, © **902**. Weather forecast and road conditions © **060/520-520**.

Language Most residents of major Croatian cities speak English. Most American movies and programs broadcast on Croatian TV are in English with Croatian subtitles.

Liquor Laws The minimum age for purchasing liquor is 18, but there is no minimum age for consuming it. Croatia has a zero-tolerance law regarding drinking and driving; the legal limit is 0.0% blood alcohol. Package liquor (wine, beer, spirits) can be purchased in markets, wine stores, at some souvenir shops, and at almost every gas station.

Mail It costs 3.50kn (50¢/30p) to send a postcard back to the U.S., and 5kn (a little less than $1/45p) to send a letter weighing up to 20 grams (¾ oz.). It takes 10 days to 2 weeks for postcards to arrive in the U.S. from Croatia and up to a month for regular mail and packages. Other carriers are available (DHL, Fedex, UPS) in major population centers, but the cost is prohibitive (around $50 per pound).

Restrooms There are no free-standing public restrooms in Croatia, but most restaurants and public buildings have them.

Smoking There are no restrictions on smoking in restaurants or public places in Croatia, though many hotels offer nonsmoking guest rooms.

Taxes Croatia's VAT is 22%. Refunds of VAT are made to foreign nationals when they leave the country for goods purchased in Croatia for amounts over 500kn ($86/£46). Salespeople will provide a tax refund form when you make a purchase over 500kn. There is a 10% nonrefundable tax on excursions and hotel rooms. For further information, go to www.carina.hr.

Time Zone Croatia is 1 hour ahead of Greenwich Mean Time, 6 hours ahead of New York (EST), and 9 hours ahead of Los Angeles (PST). Daylight saving time is observed from late March to late September, when clocks are advanced 1 hour.

Tipping Tipping is not yet widely expected in smaller Croatian restaurants, but a 10% to 15% gratuity is often expected at upscale restaurants and larger cities. Otherwise, it is considered polite to leave any coins from your change. A 10% tip for other service providers (taxi drivers, hotel personnel, and others) is the norm, as is a tip for anyone who helps you carry luggage.

Water Tap water is potable throughout Croatia.

3 Dubrovnik

618km (384 miles) S of Zagreb; 213km (132 miles) SE of Split

It would take an army of Hollywood designers to create a set as photogenic as Dubrovnik, and it would take a team of creative stagehands to build it. Yet even after being devastated by Serb shells during the 1991–92 war, this "city made of stone and light" is as strong and magnificent as the shimmering sunsets that ricochet off its 14th-century ramparts. The only telltale reminder of the attack is the brighter color of the terra-cotta roof tiles used to replace those damaged in the war. You might find a few bullet scars, but the "Pearl of the Adriatic" is as lustrous as it was 5 centuries ago when it was a major sea power bustling with prosperous merchants and aristocrats.

Dubrovnik (nee Ragusa) began as a Roman settlement, but from the Middle Ages on it was a prize sought by Venice, Hungary, Turkey, and others who recognized the city's logistical value as a maritime port. *Libertas* (Liberty) has always been uppermost in the minds of Dubrovnik's citizens, and through the ages their thirst for independence kept would-be conquerors at bay.

In 1667, a catastrophic earthquake did to Dubrovnik what the foreign invaders could not: It brought the city to its knees. The quake killed more than 5,000 people and destroyed most of the city's structures. But Dubrovnik recovered and was quickly rebuilt in the new baroque style of the times, only to be shattered again 3 centuries later—this time from the skies in a 1991–92 siege during Croatia's war with Serbia. The hostilities decimated tourism throughout Croatia, but nowhere was the impact more devastating than in Dubrovnik, where visitors vanished. Crowds have once again returned to this charming city nestled between the Adriatic and Dinaric Alps, and it has regained its former status as a vacation destination par excellence.

GETTING THERE

Despite its popularity and position as a tourism mecca, getting to Dubrovnik can be time-consuming and expensive. Even driving there from elsewhere in Croatia is challenging because of the city's position between the mountains and sea and the lack of modern roads leading to it. Ferry routes to Dubrovnik often include multiple stops at various islands, and train service is nonexistent.

BY PLANE   Croatia Airlines (www.croatiaairlines.hr) operates daily flights to Dubrovnik from select European cities. Dubrovnik International Airport (Zračna Luka; www.airport-dubrovnik.hr), is at Čilipi, 18km (11 miles) from the city center.

Croatia Airlines operates shuttle service that is coordinated with incoming Croatia Air flights, though anyone from any flight can ride. Cost is 35kn ($6/£3.25) one-way and it takes about 25 minutes from the airport to the Pile Gate. Buses to the airport leave the main terminal in Dubrovnik at Gruž Port every 90 minutes. Taxis also serve the airport and rides are metered at 25kn ($4.50/£2.30) and 8kn ($1.50/75p) per kilometer. A one-way trip between the airport and Dubrovnik costs about 250kn ($44/£25) one-way but it could be more if you don't settle on the price and terms before you get in the cab. The taxi company's website (www.taxiservicedubrovnik. com) tells you not to pay if the driver doesn't turn on the meter, but arguing about that could get ugly.

BY FERRY   The government-run ferry line Jadrolinija connects Dubrovnik with the islands and cities up and down the coast, including the island of Hvar and the cities of Split and Zadar. Local ferries also run to the Elafiti Islands and Mljet, and excursion boats go just about everywhere. Buy tickets and obtain schedule information at Jadrolinija's Dubrovnik office in Gruž (© **020/418-000**) or at Jadroagent at Radića 32 (© **020/419-000**).

BY CAR   The A-1 autocesta between Zagreb and Split opened in June 2005, reducing travel time between the two cities by an hour. However, the leg of the highway that continues on to Dubrovnik is still in the planning phase and not expected to open until 2010. If you drive to Dubrovnik from Split, you have to take E-65 for the 217km (135-mile) trip, which can take 4 hours. If you drive from Zagreb through to Dubrovnik, it will take a minimum of 7 hours—more during summer gridlock.

BY BUS   Daily buses operate between the Dubrovnik ferry port at Gruž and Zagreb, Zadar, Split, Šibenik, Rijeka, Orebić, and Korčula, as well as Mostar and Sarajevo in Bosnia and Međugorje in Hercegovina. The main Dubrovnik bus terminal is at Put Republike 19 (© **020/357-020**).

BY TRAIN   There is no train service to Dubrovnik.

NEIGHBORHOODS IN BRIEF

The area within Dubrovnik's walls is known as **Old Town,** and most of the city's attractions are there. Besides historic buildings, you will find restaurants, cafes, shops, and services in and around this pedestrians-only zone. **Ploče** is the neighborhood outside Old Town's Eastern Gate. Most of the city's upscale hotels are on beachfront property here, as is Banje, the city's most pleasant beach. **Lapad** is a suburban promenade lined with hotels and restaurants that are backed by a residential area set on a peninsula west of Old Town. Lapad has some beach area, but its main attraction is a cluster of (relatively) moderately priced hotels. A 15-minute ride on the no. 6 bus connects Lapad with Old Town at the Pile Gate. At some indeterminable point, Lapad ends and **Babin Kuk** begins. Babin Kuk has hotels in various price ranges plus access to rocky coves with what optimists call beaches (read: major pebbles/rocks, no sand), scores of restaurants, shops, and public bus routes that connect it to Dubrovnik.

GETTING AROUND

There are no trains or trams in Dubrovnik, but the Libertas city bus system is fairly efficient (www.libertasdubrovnik.hr). If you are staying within comfortable walking distance of Old Town, everything important is accessible on foot.

BY BUS   Buy one-way tickets from a news kiosk or at your hotel for 8kn ($1.40/70p) and save 2kn (35¢/20p). All buses stop at the Pile Gate and continue on to outlying hotels, the ferry port, and beyond. Schedules and route maps are available at the Tourist Information Center in Old Town across from the Franciscan Monastery.

BY TAXI   Taxi stands are at the airport, bus station ,and the Pile Gate. Taxis can be called locally © **020/424-343** (Pile Gate), © **020/423-164** (Ploče), © **020/418-112** (ferry port), © **020/357-044** (bus station), and © **020/435-715** (Lapad). Rides start with 25kn ($4.50/£2.25) on the meter and go up 8kn ($1.40/75p) per kilometer. If you agree to a meterless ride, negotiate a price beforehand to avoid rip-offs and unwanted excursions.

ON FOOT   Negotiating the busy streets outside the walls can be confusing, especially at night. But once you are in the vicinity of Old Town, you can devise your own walking tour using the suggestions in this book. You also can employ a private guide to accompany you on a walk, or you can book a guided Old Town walking tour through the tourist office or through a private tourist agency.

BY CAR   Congestion and parking make driving in Dubrovnik stressful, and Old Town is pedestrianized anyway, but if you rent a car for excursions to nearby Pelješac or Ston, car rental companies at the airport include: **Hertz** (© 01/484-6777; www. hertz.hr), **Budget** (© 020/773-290; www.budget.hr), and **Thrifty** (© 020/773-3588; www.thrifty.com). Be sure to reserve a car in advance to ensure availability.

BY BICYCLE   No companies currently rent bikes in Dubrovnik.

VISITOR INFORMATION

The agencies below represent a partial list that can help with Dubrovnik information and bookings.

Atlas Travel at Ćira Carića 3 (© 020/442-222) operates multiple excursions out of Dubrovnik and can book hotels and private accommodations, air and ferry tickets, adventure sports experiences, and a variety of custom services. **The Dubrovnik Tourist Office** is across the street from the Hilton Imperial on the road leading to the Pile Gate and at several other locations around town. The Pile Gate location at Starčevića 7 (© 020/427-591) is also an Internet center where you can check your e-mail or connect with home. **Elite Travel** at Vukovarska 17 (© 020/358-200) runs specialized tours such as the UNESCO World Heritage Croatia Tour, which visits the country's protected cultural and natural sites, a horseback tour of Konavale, and a canoe safari on the Trebezit River, among others.

Note: If you have the resources, consider booking an English-speaking private guide who not only can plan a custom itinerary for you but also can arrange transport, transfers, and admittance to otherwise inaccessible sites. **Jelena Delić** (© 91/531-8782; damale3@hotmail.com) is one of the best.

FAST FACTS: Dubrovnik

American Express **Atlas Travel** (Ćira Carića 3 © 020/419-119; fax 020/442-645; www.atlas-croatia.com) is the American Express agent in Dubrovnik. Atlas-Amex also has an office at Brsalje 17 (© 020/442-574), open from 8am to 7pm Monday through Saturday.

ATMs Croatian banks operate Bankomats at Stradun, Lapad, Gruž, Cavtat, and the post office across from the Hilton Imperial.

Banks Banks are generally open from 7:30am to 7pm Monday through Friday and from 7:30 to 11:30am Saturday. Some banks close for lunch.

Business Hours Most grocery and department stores are open from 7:30am to 8pm. Nongovernment offices work 8:30am to 5pm Monday through Friday.

Credit Cards Credit cards are generally accepted at hotels and larger restaurants, but be sure to ask before you order.

Emergencies Dial © 94; fire, dial © 93; police, dial © 92.

Hospital Go to the **Dubrovnik General Hospital** (© 020/431-777).

Pharmacy Pharmacies work morning and afternoon Monday through Friday, and Saturday mornings. Almost all accept credit cards.

Telephone Public telephone boxes use phone cards available from newspaper stands and post offices.

Time Zone Dubrovnik is on Central European Time (GMT plus 1 hr.). Daylight saving time starts at the end of March and ends September 30.

Weather Daily forecasts are available at www.dubrovnik-online.com/english/weather.php#general.

WHERE TO STAY IN DUBROVNIK

Note: Some owners refuse to rent for fewer than 3 or 7 days, especially during July and August. If you find one that rents by the night, expect a 20% to 50% surcharge.

VERY EXPENSIVE

Domino Apartments ★   One of these 6 vintage luxury apartments is tucked into a tiny courtyard at the end of Siroko Street. Others are located in nearby historic buildings. All are the equivalent of condo rentals. The "larger" apartments have a tiny living room while the smaller ones are really studios with kitchenettes. Furniture and appliances are new; window views are of neighboring buildings; and the apartments can get noisy when local restaurants are busy. Rental office is in the Fendi store at ground level in the Hliđina Street property.

Hliđina 4. Old Town. ☎ **020/324-940.** Fax 020/324-824. www.dominoapartments.com. 6 units. July 1–Sept. 30 250€ ($335/£171); 200€ ($266/£135) other times. AE, DC, MC, V. *In room:* A/C, TV.

Hilton Imperial ★★★   The Hilton is steps from the Pile Gate and combines the grace of its 1897 predecessor with stylish architectural detail and genteel luxury. The original Imperial (and its guesthouse across the street) sheltered refugees during Croatia's civil war and took direct mortar hits. Hilton wisely preserved what it could from the old Imperial—stone staircases, the lobby footprint—and the result is spectacular. Rooms are spacious and done in earth/sun color schemes with spacious bathrooms that include tubs and showers. Hilton staff members are trained in guest relations and extend the same courtesies to Brioni-suited businesspeople and backpackers alike, an anomaly in Croatia's resident-tourist relationship.

Marijana Blažića 2 (Pile Gate). ☎ **020/320-320.** Fax 020/320-220. www.hilton.com. 147 units. From 265€ ($340) double; from 375€ ($480) executive plus. AE, DC, MC, V. Parking 20€/$25 per day for guests. **Amenities:** Restaurant; piano bar; pool; sauna; steam bath; nonsmoking rooms; room for those w/limited mobility. *In room:* A/C, TV, Internet connection (22€/$28 per day), minibar, hair dryer, safe.

Hotel Excelsior ★★★   The Excelsior enjoys a location that is walking distance from Old Town and steps from the sea. It was built in 1913, expanded in the 1960s, and completely renovated in 1998. Guest rooms, whether in the old or new parts of the hotel, are well appointed, but the rooms overlooking the sea are stunning because they offer breathtaking views of Dubrovnik's wall and lookout towers.

Frana supila 12, Ploče. ☎ **020/353-300.** Fax 020/414-214. www.hotel-excelsior.hr. 164 units. From 359€ ($460) double with sea view and balcony; from 589€ ($754) suite. AE, DC, MC, V. Rates include breakfast. Half-board available. Parking free for hotel guests. **Amenities:** 2 restaurants; piano bar; indoor pool; sauna; Internet access; rooms/facilities for those w/limited mobility. *In room:* A/C, TV, fax, Internet connection, minibar, hair dryer, safe.

Pucić Palace ★ *Overrated*   The legendary haunt of well-heeled visitors to Dubrovnik combines the ambience of a Renaissance palace with contemporary comforts, but it

Coming Attractions

Serb shells destroyed 70% of Dubrovnik's Hotel Libertas during the 1991 war, but now the Rixos Hotel group has begun construction of a 364-unit luxury hotel on the site of the former landmark. Rixos is positioning the new **Libertas Rixos** for a May 2007 opening and an upscale clientele. Besides sumptuously appointed rooms and suites, Libertas will offer three restaurants, including a sushi bar, a spa, a casino, and world-class service. For more information go to www.rixos.com.

falls short of what you'd expect for the stratospheric room rates. Furnishings are top-quality and bathrooms are lined with nonskid tiles and tasteful mosaics and loaded with toiletries, but we're talking tiny showers here. The hotel maintains a yacht in the harbor for guest use; the terrace has a great view of the city; and you *are* staying in a historic monument; but you'll have to decide for yourself if those things offer enough value per dollar.

Ulica Od Puča 1, Old Town. ⓒ 020/326-200, or 020/326-222 reservations. Fax 020/326-223. www.thepucicpalace.com. 19 units. June–Sept from 479€ ($570) double; from 721€ ($858) suite. Other times from 273€ ($325) double; from 515€ ($613) suite. AE, DC, MC, V. Rates include breakfast. **Amenities:** Restaurant; bar; concierge; 24-hr. room service. *In room:* A/C, TV, minibar, safe.

EXPENSIVE

Hotel Perla ⓐ   The Perla opened in April 2005 and it is still evolving. Guest rooms are generous and most have balconies that overlook the hotel's leafy landscaping. Bathrooms are well equipped, but there is no elevator, which makes the trek to the upper floors a pain. Once you check in your location is excellent, but you have to park a couple of blocks away and schlep your luggage because of the Perla's position on the promenade.

Lapad Mali Stradun bb, Lapad. ⓒ 020/438-244. www.perla-dubrovnik.com/index.htm. 20 units. Doubles from 120€ ($142). AE, DC, MC, V. Rates include breakfast. **Amenities:** Restaurant; bar. *In room:* A/C, TV, hair dryer, balcony.

Hotel Stari Grad ⓐⓐ *(Value*   The tiny Stari Grad is a bargain when you consider that, like the pricey Pucić Palace (see above), it is a cultural monument and just one of two hotels within Old Town's walls. The mansion opened as a hotel in 2002 and each room is comfortable, cozy, and augmented by bathrooms equipped with hydromassage showers. The view of Lokrum and Cavtat from the fifth-floor terrace is dynamite.

Od Sigurate br. 4, Old Town. ⓒ 020/322-244. Fax 020/321-256. www.hotelstarigrad.com. 8 units. July 1–Sept 30 from 1,400kn ($242/£128) double; other times from 850kn ($147/£78) double. Rates include breakfast. AE, MC, V. **Amenities:** Restaurant; valet; safe-deposit box; babysitting. *In room:* A/C, TV, dataport, minibar, hair dryer.

Hotel Zagreb ⓐⓐ *(Finds*   Extensive restoration has turned this 19th-century mansion into a salmon-colored showplace on the Lapad promenade. Each guest room is unique, so ask to see yours before you check in. All rooms, whether on the ground floor or on the third level are quiet, spacious, and dripping with character. Some of the staff speak English; all are very helpful.

Šetalište Kralja Zvonimira 27, Lapad. ⓒ 020/436-146. Fax 020/436-006. 24 units. July 1 to mid-Sept from 1,060kn ($186/£97) double; at other times from 700kn ($123/£64) double. AE, DC, MC, V. **Amenities:** Restaurant; bar. *In room:* TV, hair dryer.

Dubrovnik Lodging, Dining & Attractions

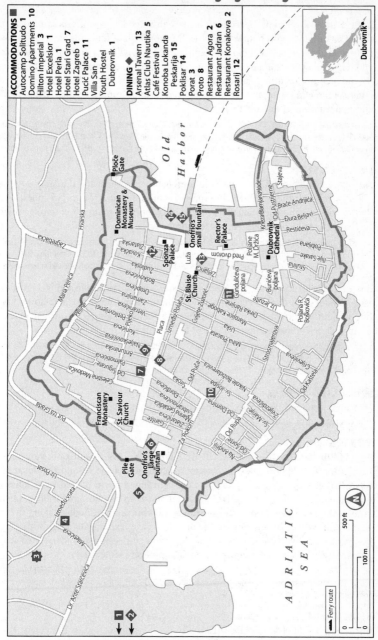

ACCOMMODATIONS ■
Autocamp Solitudo 1
Domino Apartments 10
Hilton Imperial 3
Hotel Excelsior 1
Hotel Perla 1
Hotel Stari Grad 7
Hotel Zagreb 1
Pucić Palace 11
Villa San 4
Youth Hostel
Dubrovnik 1

DINING ◆
Arsenal Tavern 13
Atlas Club Nautika 5
Café Festival 9
Konoba Lokanda
Peskarija 15
Poklisar 14
Porat 3
Proto 8
Restaurant Agora 2
Restaurant Jadran 6
Restaurant Konakova 2
Rosarij 12

Dubrovnik•

MODERATE

Villa San 🏠🏠   Private apartments and rooms are Dubrovnik's best moderately priced accommodations options and Villa San can't be beat for convenience. Villa San is situated above a bank behind the Pile Gate bus stop, 90m (300 ft.) from the beach and steps from the water taxi to Lokrum. The property is managed by the Ahmić family and it comprises four apartments ranging in size from "mini" to "penthouse." The latter is on the top floor and can sleep eight in three bedrooms, kitchen, living room, and two bathrooms, one with a Jacuzzi.

Tiha 2, near Old Town. ℃ 020/411-884. www.villa-san.com. 4 apts. July–Sept from 60€ ($72) double; May–June 50€ ($60) double; Oct–Apr 40€ ($48) double. Penthouse July–Aug and New Year's from 180€ ($215); other times from 120€ ($143). 20% deposit required; cash only, no credit cards. Free parking. *In room:* A/C, TV, some balconies.

INEXPENSIVE

Autocamp Solitudo 🏠🏠   The bathrooms here are excellent and the camp is within .5km (¼ mile) of the sea and many sports facilities, but it is 24km (15 miles) from Dubrovnik proper. Unless you're set on camping, a private room closer to town might be about the same price but a better logistical choice.

Vatroslava Lisinskog 17, Babin Kuk. ℃ 020/448-686. Fax 020/448-688. www.babinkuk.com. 238 campsites. Apr 1–Oct 15 site with electricity and 2 persons 27€ ($35) plus 20€ ($26) tax. AE, DC, MC, V. **Amenities:** Restaurant; market; pool; excursions; facility adaptations for those with limited mobility; laundry; dogs allowed in some areas.

Youth Hostel Dubrovnik 🏠   This hostel stays open all year long and it is just a 10-minute walk from the bus station and 15 minutes from Old Town. The hostel has a fine reputation but you must be a member of a hostelling association to stay in these dorm-style accommodations near one of Dubrovnik's hottest nightlife areas.

Vinka Sagrestana 3, near Old Town. ℃ 020/423-241. Fax 020/412-592. www.hfhs.hr. 19 units with 82 beds. July–Aug bed-and-breakfast 15€ ($18) per person. Other times bed-and-breakfast from 9.35€ ($11) per person. No credit cards. **Amenities:** Restaurant; TV room; membership kitchen.

WHERE TO DINE

It's hard to get a bad meal in Dubrovnik, but it's even more difficult to get a meal that's not overpriced or that bucks the grilled meat/fish or risotto/pasta formula.

VERY EXPENSIVE

Atlas Club Nautika *(Overrated)* GOURMET DALMATIAN   Nautika has one of the best locations in Dubrovnik with its unobstructed view of the sea and the Bokar and Lovrijenac fortresses. Less impressive is the light lunch menu offered from noon to 4pm at 60kn to 120kn ($11–$21/£6–£11) for one of seven uninspired choices. (***Note:*** You get the same view from a table at **Kavana Dubravka** next door or along the rail between the two in **Brsalje Square**.) Dinner is a pricey, extravagant affair, with a tasting menu laden with choices such as sea bass with cuttlefish-ink sauce, stuffed snails Pelješac-style, and excellent vintages from an impressive wine list.

Brsalje 3, Old Town. ℃ 020/442-526. www.esculap-teo.hr. Dinner entrees 148kn–380kn ($26–$66/£14–£35). 7-course degustation menu 99€ ($118) per person without wine. AE, DC, MC, V at dinner only. Daily noon–midnight; light lunch served noon–4pm.

EXPENSIVE

Porat 🏠🏠 CONTINENTAL/DALMATIAN   The Hilton and its Restaurant Porat opened to great fanfare in May 2005, and so far, neither has been a disappointment. Porat's elegant dining room and pretty terrace offer a menu of local dishes enhanced by creative twists and sauces. Try crispy skinned sea bass filet with candied lemon from the lava-stone grill; or beef tenderloin and tomato-shallot marmalade. Duck breast is on the menu, which is unusual in Dalmatia.

In the Hilton Imperial. Marijana Blažića 2. ℭ **020/320-320.** Fax 020/320-220. www.hilton.com. Reservations required for dinner. Entrees 140kn–190kn ($25–$33/£13–£17); lunch and breakfast entrees 70kn–120kn ($12–$22/£6.40–£11). AE, DC, MC, V. Daily 7–10:30am for breakfast; 12:30–2:30pm for lunch; 7–11pm for dinner.

MODERATE

Arsenal Taverna at Gradska Kavana ⭐ CROATIAN   This upscale spot became a delightful addition to Dubrovnik's restaurant scene when it reopened in November 2005 on the Old Harbor near the Ploče Gate. Walk through the Arsenal Wine Bar across from St. Blaise Church off Luža Square and claim a table on the terrace. The menu is typical of Dubrovnik with lots of fish dishes, but it also has a better-than-average selection of grilled meats and an extensive but pricey selection of Croatian wines. A plus: Appetizers include Paški sir, a specialty sheep's milk cheese from the island of Pag, and kulen, a spicy sausage from Slavonia in eastern Croatia. Service can be slow, but who wants to hurry through a meal when the twinkling lights of Dubrovnik are the backdrop?

Pred Dvorom 1. Old Town. ℭ **020/321-065.** Entrees 70kn–140kn ($12–$24/£6.40–£13). AE, DC, MC, V. Daily 9am–2am. Kitchen closes at 11:30pm.

Poklisar ⭐⭐ SEAFOOD/PIZZA   Access this seaside spot on the Old Harbor via the Ploče Gate or just move toward the catchy live music. Poklisar has unabashedly been catering to tourists for 10 years and its extensive menu, friendly waitstaff, and crowded tables are testament to that. The cuisine ranges from pizza to lobster and everything is well prepared and attractively presented. Try the house specialty, skewers of grilled shrimp resting atop blue-cheese risotto, or savor one of the super-thin-crust pizzas while you breathe in the scent of the sea.

Ribarnica 1, Old Town. ℭ **020/322-176.** www.poklisar.com. Pizza 41kn ($7/£3.75); 590kn ($102/£54) for 1 kilo (2.2 lb.) of lobster. AE, DC, MC, V. Daily 9am–midnight.

Proto ⭐⭐ SEAFOOD   The menu says the food is prepared "according to our grandparents' recipes" with local ingredients. Try any of the grilled meats—or even the Dalmatian ham appetizer—to see if either conjures childhood memories. The wine list is full of reds from Pelješac and whites from Korčula. Opt for a table on the second-floor terrace.

Široka 1, Old Town. ℭ **020/323-234.** www.esculap-teo.hr. Reservations recommended. Entrees 74kn–110kn ($13–$19/£6.75–£10). AE, DC, MC, V. Daily 11am–11pm.

Restaurant Agora ⭐ DALMATIAN   Located at the Hotel Perla, Agora's menu lists grilled fish and meats with an unusually high number of steak choices. Preparations are strictly straightforward, which plays up fresh ingredients and cordial service. Filet mignon with baked potato is an excellent choice.

Mali Stradun bb, Lapad. ℭ **020/438-244.** Entrees 50kn–150kn ($9–$26/£4.60–£14), except fish portions in kilos. AE, DC, MC, V. Daily 7am–midnight.

Restaurant Konakova ⭐⭐ *Value* DALMATIAN   This second-floor terrace restaurant packs them in every night. Like most other Dubrovnik dining spots, specialties are seafood, grilled meat, pizza, and pasta, but equal care is given to all dishes. Little touches like complimentary fish pâtés with the bread add value and make Konakova an even bigger bargain.

Šetalište Kralja Zvonimira 38, Lapad. ✆ **020/435-105**. Entrees 45kn–120kn ($8–$21/£4.10–£11). AE, DC, MC, V. Daily noon–midnight.

Rozarij ★★ *(Finds* DALMATIAN SEAFOOD   Rattan tables outside this tiny eatery are arranged on steps around the entrance. Rozarij is on a hard-to-find corner of restaurant-clogged Prijeko (at Zlatarska), but its impeccable seafood is worth searching out. Try shrimp with white risotto or mixed *buzzara,* a combination of mussels and scampi in a fragrant court bouillon.

Prijeko 2, Old Town. ✆ **020/321-257**. Entrees 50kn–120kn ($9–$21/£4.60–£11). No credit cards. Daily 11am–midnight.

INEXPENSIVE

Café Festival ★ SANDWICHES   It can get warm in the afternoon sun at tables under the nautical blue awning outside this smart cafe near the Pile Gate, so go inside to try the salads, pastas, fancy drinks, and homemade pastries. Café Festival is ideal for a light lunch or a cool drink.

Stradun bb, Old Town. ✆ **020/420-888**. www.cafefestival.com. Entrees 15kn–45kn ($3–$8/£1.40–£4.10). AE, DC, MC, V. Daily 8am–11pm.

Konoba Lokanda Peskarija ★ *(Value* FISH/RISOTTO   Turn left from Zlatarska at the east end of the Stradun and go through the wall opening to the Old Harbor. Entertainment is all around you: Watch walkers atop the wall; see boats dock and take off; observe chefs working in an open kitchen that looks like a beach bar; and watch hopeful diners standing around waiting for your table. Prices are low, main courses are limited to a few fish dishes and risottos, but portions are huge. The octopus salad and black risotto are standouts.

Gorica Svetog Vlaha 77. Old Town. ✆ **020/324-750**. Entrees 40kn–65kn ($7–$11/£3.65–£5.95). No credit cards. Daily 8am–2am. Kitchen opens at noon and closes at midnight.

Restaurant Jadran DALMATIAN   Turn right after walking through the Pile Gate to Jadran, a touristy but solid restaurant with both a garden setting and an indoor dining room. The restaurant is in the former Convent of the Poor Clares and the menu has all the usual Dalmatian entrees plus the occasional omelet and salad. Jadran is a good place for a quick bite before or after you embark on the walk around the city wall.

Paska Miličevića 1, Old Town. ✆ **020/323-403**. Fax 020/323-403. Entrees 19kn–49kn ($3.50–$8.50/£1.75–£4.80). AE, DC, MC, V. Daily 10am–midnight.

EXPLORING DUBROVNIK

Dubrovnik sprawls well beyond the city walls, but just about everything worth seeing is within the Old Town enclosure.

City Wall ★★★   No visit to Dubrovnik is complete without a walk along the top of its wall, a work of artful fortification built in medieval times that frames the historic city. As you make the 2km (1¼-mile) circuit around the wall, which is 25m (82 ft.) high and 6m (20 ft.) thick at some points, you'll see greater Dubrovnik and its landmark red-tile rooftops from every conceivable angle. You'll be voyeur to tourists and residents going about their lives, swimming in the Adriatic off the wall's base, or dining at restaurants on rocky outcroppings that abut the wall's foundation.

> ## *Tips* The Heat
>
> When Dubrovnik's temperature is above 80°F (27°C)—the average temperature May through September—tackle the wall when it opens at 9am, or wait until after 5pm. Besides being atop a high roof, you'll be standing on an unshaded stone path that absorbs the sun's heat from dawn to dusk and you'll be "cooked" from above and below. At the very least, take along a large bottle of water.

You can access the wall at three points: just inside the Pile Gate, near the Maritime Museum/John's Fortress, and near the Dominican Monastery at the Ploče Gate. The entire circuit takes about an hour, longer if you're inclined to stop and gape at the spectacular scenery, but you can do a half-walk, too. If you start at the **Pile Gate** entrance, you'll walk up a steep flight of stairs through an arch topped by a statue of St. Blaise. If you want to do the entire 360-degree stroll, continue straight up toward the **Minčeta Tower,** which is recognizable by its distinctive "crown." If you decide on the partial walk, halfway up the stairs you'll have to do a 180 from the stairs via a small landing to reach the wall, and you'll exit near **St. John's Fortress** on the south side. The 16th-century **Revelin Fort** is on the eastern side of the wall above the Ploče Gate; and the 15th-century **Bokar Fortress,** which guarded against sea incursions, is at the southwestern corner across from the 12th-century **Lovrijenac Fortress.**

Old Town. 50kn ($8.60/£4.60) adults 30kn ($3.45/£1.85); children 5-14 10kn ($2/£1); audio rental 40kn ($7/£3.65). July–Aug daily 9am–7:30pm; hours vary other times.

STRADUN DISTRICT

Old Town's western gate, the **Pile Gate** *✸✸✸*, is its busiest point of entry, largely because buses from the city, airport, and ferry terminals deposit their passengers there. A stone bridge leads to the outer gate, guarded by a statue of St. Blaise and during the summer, honor guards in period costume stand there mornings and evenings greeting tourists. The interior gate was built in the 15th century and it, too, has a statue of St. Blaise—this one by Ivan Meštrović, Croatia's premier sculptor.

When you enter Old Town through either the Pile Gate or the Ploče Gate, you will find one of **Onofrio's Fountains** *✸✸✸*. They were constructed in the 15th century so visitors could wash away plague before they entered the city. The fountains provided clean, cold water via an aqueduct from the Dubrovnik River (Rijeka Dubrovačka), 11km (7 miles) away, but their efficacy as germ killers is questionable. The larger fountain at the Pile Gate looks like a domed vat decorated with 16 stone heads, the only ornamentation remaining from the original, thanks to the 1667 quake and the 1991–92 siege. Water from the Luža Square fountain flows through a more

> ## *Warning* Water World
>
> While the water flowing into both Onofrio fountains is pristine and drinkable, beware filling your canteen from the Ploče Gate structure because pigeons habitually perch atop the fountain's top layer, through which the water moves.

ornate device with detailed sculpture work. People fill water bottles and soak bandannas in the cold water, especially in summer when Dubrovnik is steamy.

The Stradun (aka Placa) 🌟🌟🌟 is Dubrovnik's main thoroughfare. It runs from the Pile Gate through Old Town to the Ploče Gate and is paved with limestone buffed to a smooth, shiny surface by tourist footfall. The Stradun is lined with neat, uniform buildings housing shops, restaurants, and entryways to alley-size streets. Historical pictures show that Dubrovnik's pre-1667-earthquake buildings were far more ornate than the present structures.

St. Saviour Church 🌟 The Renaissance-Gothic facade of this small church faces the large Onofrio Fountain inside the Pile Gate. St. Saviour was built in the early 16th century and it is one of the few structures not damaged in the 1667 quake.

Between the Pile Gate and the Franciscan Monastery at Stradun 2. Daily 9am–7pm.

Franciscan Monastery 🌟🌟 A small **apothecary** inside the 14th-century monastery complex has been in business in 1317 and claims to be the oldest working pharmacy in Europe. It has a fascinating display of ancient lab equipment, mortars, measuring implements, and decorative containers used over the centuries. The monastery itself is accessed via a narrow passage from **St. Saviour's Church;** the complex's **Romanesque cloister** is the monastery's most compelling feature (the postquake Renaissance cloister is open to Franciscans only). The lower cloister's open wall of double columns (topped with human, animal, and plant carvings) frame a tranquil open garden area where you can imagine monks enjoying the contemplative life. The complex also is home to a **15th-century well,** the single-nave **St. Francis Church,** a **bell tower,** and the **monastery museum,** whose library contains ancient writings, music manuscripts, gold and silver objets d'art, and other items that illuminate Dubrovnik's history.

Monastery museum 20kn ($3.50/30p) adults; 10kn ($1.75/90p) children. July–Aug 9am–6pm daily. Erratic hours other times of the year.

LUŽA SQUARE

The eastern end of the Stradun opens into busy **Luža Square** 🌟🌟🌟, which is an Old Town crossroads where tourists stop at **Onofrio's Little Fountain,** explore exhibits in **Sponza Palace,** meet friends at the **city bell tower,** take a *bijela* kava break at the **Gradska Kavana,** or sit on the steps of **St. Blaise Church.** Luža Square is also where Dubrovnik's Summer Festival kicks off

The likeness of a warrior is chiseled into the stone **Orlando's Column** 🌟🌟 in the center of Luža Square and represents the legendary hero who reputedly was Charlemagne's nephew. The column was erected in 1419 and once served as the city's forum

---

Fun Fact **Getting Stoned**

When you leave St. Saviour Church for the Franciscan monastery next door, keep your eyes downcast and you'll see a 12×12-inch stone with a carved face and smooth top protruding about 6 inches above the street. You'll also see a crowd watching people attempting to stand on the stone for a few seconds. Legend says that guys who can stay on the stone known as the "Mask" long enough to remove their shirts will have good luck. (Girls also try this but are entitled to the luck without removing their shirts.)

Who Is St. Blaise?

Legend says that St. Blaise once saved a child from choking on a fish bone. Roman Catholics know the Armenian physician and martyr as the patron saint of people with throat problems. However, the people of Dubrovnik revere St. Blaise (Sv. Vlaho) as the hero who saved their city from a sneak attack by Venetian galleys in the 10th century. According to legend, Venetian ships dropped anchor off Lokrum to pick up fresh water for their journey, but the fleet was actually surveying the city in preparation for a takeover. St. Blaise (martyred by Diocletian in 316 B.C.) appeared to the cathedral's priest in a dream and told him about the nefarious plot, thus thwarting the attack. Ever since, St. Blaise has been immortalized in sculpture, art, and other media as the city's protector.

for public proclamations, notices, rallies, and punishments. In 1990 a flag with the city's LIBERTAS motto was flown above the column, which became a rallying point for Dubrovnik's freedom fighters.

As you approach Luža Square from the Stradun, you'll see the arches of the 15th-century **Sponza Palace** ☆☆ (© 020/321-032, free admission) on your left. Today the Sponza is a venue for art exhibits and concerts. A 30m (100-ft.) bell tower next to the palace tolls the hour.

St. Blaise is Dubrovnik's patron saint and **St. Blaise Church** ☆☆☆ on Luža Square, open 8am to 7pm daily, was built between 1706 and 1714 on the site of a ruined 14th-century church. St. Blaise's wide staircase and terrace are popular with weary tourists who settle there for a break, much the same as pigeons congregate on the square itself. Inside, you'll find a silver-plated statue on the main altar depicting St. Blaise holding a 15th-century model of the city as it was before the 1667 earthquake.

The original **Dubrovnik Cathedral (Church of the Assumption)** ☆☆☆ was built between the 12th and 14th centuries atop the ruins of a Byzantine basilica at Poljana Marina Držica. According to legend, a grateful King Richard the Lionhearted financed it to give thanks after being shipwrecked and rescued in Dubrovnik. It was severely damaged in the 1667 earthquake and rebuilt in the au courant baroque style, making it the third church to be constructed on this site. The cathedral's **treasury** (10kn/$1.75/90p; Mon–Sat 9am–5:30pm, Sun 11am–5:30pm) holds the skull, arm, and leg of St. Blaise, plated with gold and stashed behind a marble altar topped by .9m-high (3-ft.) panels of glass.

The original 13th century **Rector's Palace** was destroyed in 1435 when gunpowder stored inside exploded. The palace was rebuilt only to blow up again 28 years later. The current **palace** ☆☆ resides on the original site just south of Luža Square at Pred Dvorom 3 (© 020/321-497; admission 15kn/$3/£1.35). Upstairs rooms now house the **City Museum (Gradski Muzej).** Classical concerts are held in its courtyard during the Summer Festival.

The 14th-century **Dominican Monastery and Museum** ☆☆☆ at Sv. Dominika 4 (Museum admission 10kn/$1.75/90p) are behind the Sponza Palace off a narrow passageway leading to the Ploče Gate. Don't miss the museum, whose art collection includes a reliquary containing the skull of King Stephen I of Hungary.

Fun Fact **It's a Tough Job, But . . .**

Old Ragusa's rectors were elected for a period of 1 month, after which they were sent on a 2-year-long vacation. The reasoning was that the city fathers didn't want anyone to stay in office long enough to accumulate power. Many rectors served their time living in the palace alone, leaving only for official duties, though the rector's family was allowed to accompany him. But if they did, they had to follow the same house rules. The rector could stand for reelection to another month-long term, but not until he completed his 2-year hiatus.

STARA LUKA (OLD HARBOR) DISTRICT

West of St. John's Fortress and to the right of the Rector's Palace is **Gundulić Square,** where a raucous **market** ✿ selling fruits, vegetables, cheeses, homemade wine, recycled water bottles filled with *rakija* (fruit brandy), and other produce is open for business every morning.

The **Jesuit Steps** ✿✿, a long set of baroque stairs off Gundulic market, are reminiscent of Rome's Spanish Steps. They lead up to the **Church of St. Ignatius Loyola** ✿✿✿, Dubrovnik's largest house of worship. The stairs were severely damaged in the 1991–92 siege, but have been restored. They end at the 1658 **Jesuit College** where many of Ragusa's greatest scholars were educated.

The **Ploče Gate** ✿✿✿ is at the eastern end of the Old City and, like the Pile Gate, it has inner and outer sections. The 15th-century portal is approached via a stone bridge.

BEACHES

Croatians loosely define beaches as any place the sea meets the land, and while some beaches may have names, many are little more than rocks used for sunbathing and diving platforms. One "beach" around the corner from the old port is a must-see, if not a must-**swim area** ✿✿✿ where those who are confident swimmers routinely take a dip from a **rocky ledge.** There is even a water polo setup where tournaments are held.

Dubrovnik's main public beach, **Banje,** exists as a beach club (see below). Bobin Kuk's **Copacabana Beach** is a pebble-and-concrete affair with a view of the graceful Dubrovnik bridge and part of the Elafiti Islands. It is one of the few Dubrovnik beaches with facilities for kids, sports enthusiasts, and swimmers with disabilities. A lift on the concrete part of the beach gives seniors and people with disabilities easy access to the water. A beach bar and restaurant provide refreshments and at night the bar becomes a cocktail lounge/disco. **Lapad Bay** is another popular spot for beachgoers and many hotels there have built stairs leading to the flat concrete slabs they call beaches.

The **Eastwest Beach Club** ✿✿✿ at Frana Supila bb. (© **020/412-220**) situated on Dubrovnik's public pebble beach **(Banje)** about 46m (150 ft.) from the entrance to the Ploče (Eastern) Gate. The club has a restaurant with a view, a cocktail bar with dance floor, watersports, a pebble beach with crystal-clear water, attendants, and the unique baldachin, which is a "bed" on the beach that looks like a raised four-poster hung with gauzy curtains. You can rent the baldachin for 200kn ($35/£18) per day.

WALKING TOUR   **DUBROVNIK'S STRADUN**

Start:	Brsalje Square outside the Pile Gate, the west entrance to Old Town.
Finish:	St. Blaise Church/Luža Square.
Time:	Anywhere from 30 minutes to 3 hours, depending on how much time you spend exploring side streets, in churches and museums, shopping, or dining.
Best Times:	Mornings from 8am to noon before the sun is overhead; Evenings after 6pm and until the last bar closes. This when the promenade starts and segues into a fashion show for the young and beautiful.
Worst Times:	Noon to sundown or whenever the temperature rises above 95°F (35°C).

Walking around the top of Dubrovnik's wall is a stroll no visitor should miss, but once you've made the circuit, you'll realize that there's much more to Dubrovnik than the red-tile roofs visible from the ramparts. A walk up and down both sides of the Stradun is an ideal way to become acquainted with the city's charms. Old Town's smooth limestone path originally was a canal separating Old Ragusa from the mainland and walking its length is a good way to get your bearings and become familiar with the attractions between the Pile Gate and the Ploče Gate. There is a high concentration of important sites on and just off the Stradun, and the pedestrian thoroughfare is always crowded. Lots of narrow side streets radiate up and out from the Stradun and intersect with cobbled streets that are packed with religious sites, historic architectural spots, shops, restaurants, a few courtyards, and even some residences.

Start your tour outside the Pile Gate in Brsalje Square next door to the Atlas Travel Agency and between the Nautika restaurant and Dubravka Kavana cafe:

❶ Brsalje Square

Rendezvous in this leafy park, but before you enter Old Town, walk away from the street to the low balustrade. You'll have an unobstructed view of the sea and **Fort Lovrijenac** to the right and the 16th-century **Bokar Fortress** to the left. Lovrijenac is built on a high, rocky peninsula that juts into the sea and it is Dubrovnik's oldest defensive structure. These days it is used as a theater for Shakespearean productions and for performances during **Dubrovnik's Summer Festival.** Croatian native and television star Goran Višjić of *ER* fame is a frequent performer there. Bokar was used as a prison in the 19th century.

Return to the street, turn right, and approach the:

❷ Pile Gate

This is the busiest portal to Old Town and it is really two gates you approach across a wooden drawbridge that once was pulled up each night to protect the city. Note the statue of St. Blaise carved into a niche above the opening of the 16th-century outer gate and another statue of the city's patron (by **Ivan Meštrović**) inside the even older (15th-c.) inner gate. Occasionally musicians and vendors hang out in the courtyard between the gates to catch people on their way out.

Step through the inner gate and stop a moment to orient. Walk through and note:

❸ Onofrio's Large Fountain & the Wall Walk Entrance

Walk inside the Pile Gate and to the left you'll see a steep stairway that leads up to the **Minčeta Tower** at the top of the wall (see p. 147 for details). This is one of three access points to the wall. To the right is **Onofrio's Large Fountain,** a tall concrete dome that during the Middle Ages was a collection point for water that flowed into the city from the **Dubrovnik River** 12km (7½ miles) away via an aqueduct. The fountain was more ornate when it was completed in 1444, but the iron embellishments were destroyed in the 1667 earthquake.

Stay left. The first building on your left is:

❹ Church of Our Saviour

This tiny church was built as a memorial to the victims of a 1520 earthquake, but it became a symbol of strength when it became one of the few buildings to survive the 1667 quake that destroyed most of the city. Today it is used for concerts and exhibits.

Walk on a few steps to:

❺ The Franciscan Monastery/ Museum

Before you explore this building with its columned cloister and ancient pharmacy, note the small stone protruding from the bottom left of the church's front (p. 148) and the people who keep jumping on it. This building, with its garden, architectural features, pharmacy, and museum exhibits is worth a visit (p. 148).

Exit the monastery and begin your Stradun stroll in earnest to investigate the:

❻ Stradun Shops & Side Streets

The Stradun (aka Placa) runs to the clock tower and the **Ploče Gate.** All the buildings along the way are almost identical in style, a result of post-quake construction in the 17th century. Note the arches that frame a combo door and window. The sill was used as a counter over which business was conducted. If you are up for a detour, head up **Žudioska Street** to visit the second-oldest synagogue in Europe and its original 17th-century furnishings.

Continue along the Stradun past Zlatarska Street to the:

❼ Sponza Palace

As you approach Luža Square, note the graceful Renaissance arches of the **Sponza Palace** (p. 149), which used to be Dubrovnik's Customs House. Today it houses the **Memorial Room of the Dubrovnik Defenders,** a visual tribute to the more than 300 people who were

killed from October 1, 1991, to October 26, 1992, while defending Dubrovnik against Serb attacks. Multimedia images of the destruction and photos of the young people who died in the conflict are moving reminders of the devastation that swept Croatia at that time.

Exit the palace and walk up to Orlando's Column in the center of Luža Square and pause at:

❽ Orlando's Column & Onofrio's Small Fountain

Orlando's Column (p. 148) will be in front of you as you exit the Palace and the **Clock Tower** will be to your left. Note the statue's forearm, which was Old Ragusa's standard of measurement (512mm/20 in.). The **Clock Tower** features a pair of bronze men that move up to strike the bell on the hour. The **Town Hall** is the large building to the right of the Clock Tower and **Onofrio's Small Fountain** is in front of that.

Turn left from the front of Orlando's Column and walk through the passageway between the Sponza Palace and the Town Hall. Turn left and head to the Dominican Monastery:

❾ Dominican Monastery, the Old Port & the Ploče Gate

The Dominican Monastery is a complex that includes a large church, cloisters, and a museum. The original 14th-century church was destroyed in the 1667 quake and this one was rebuilt in the 17th century. There are some interesting paintings inside and the church also doubles as a concert venue during the Summer Festival. The cloisters are a must-see with courtyard gardens and interesting stonework (p. 149).

Exit the monastery and left onto Svetoga Dominika. Continue on to explore the Old Harbor, Ploče Gate, and Revelin Fortress and/or retrace your steps and return to Luža Square:

❿ Gradska Kavana & the Rector's Palace

As you return from the Dominican Monastery, the Town Hall and **Gradska Kavana (Town Café)** will be on your left.

Walking Tour: Dubrovnik's Stradun

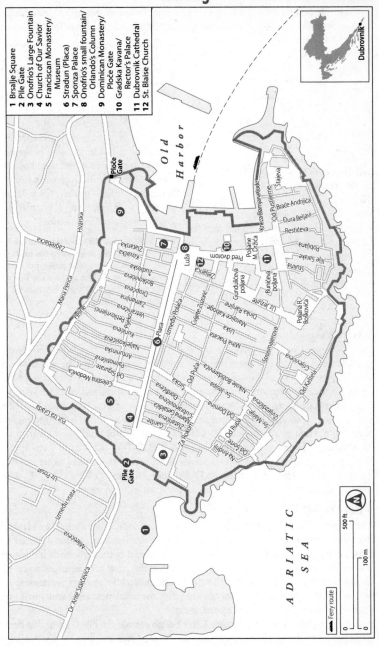

1 Brsalje Square
2 Pile Gate
3 Onofrio's Large Fountain
4 Church of Our Savior
5 Franciscan Monastery/
   Museum
6 Stradun (Placa)
7 Sponza Palace
8 Onofrio's small fountain/
   Orlando's Column
9 Dominican Monastery/
   Ploče Gate
10 Gradska Kavana/
   Rector's Palace
11 Dubrovnik Cathedral
12 St. Blaise Church

Old Harbor

Ploče Gate

Pile Gate

ADRIATIC SEA

Ferry route

N

500 ft
100 m

You can break for a cold drink or coffee and sit at tables facing the square or go inside and grab a spot on the terrace overlooking the Old Harbor. The **Town Theater** is also in this building. The Venetian-Gothic **Rector's Palace** (p. 149) is adjacent to the Gradska Kavana complex fronted by pillars made of marble from Korčula and topped with interesting carvings. The interior is used for summer concerts.

Exit the Rector's Palace and turn left:

⓫ Dubrovnik Cathedral

Note the minimalist gray marble altar that was installed when Roman Catholicism ruled that the priest should face the people during Mass. Its block style is incongruent with the rest of the church's baroque design. Don't miss the church **treasury,** which is loaded with priceless relics, including the skull of St. Blaise and a piece of the True Cross (p. 149).

Exit the cathedral and walk around to the rear and walk up Androvićeva to the Jesuit Steps and Church of St. Ignatius Loyola (p. 150) or turn left and walk past the Rector's Palace to return to Luža Square.

⓬ St. Blaise Church

This 18th-century baroque church (p. 149) is a tribute to Dubrovnik's patron saint. Inside, the altar is the main draw with its statue of the saint holding a model of the city of Dubrovnik as it was before the 1667 quake. Outside, the church's wide steps are a popular resting/meeting place for tourists.

From St. Blaise you can either return to the Pile Gate and inspect the shops along the south side of the Stradun, explore what you've just seen in greater depth, or venture up the steep side streets to discover more sights between the Stradun and the walls.

SHOPPING

You won't need to worry about going over your Customs limit when shopping in Dubrovnik. There are few stores that offer anything uniquely Croatian, and those that do are often overpriced. Goods from Stradun shops are especially costly, so stick to shops on the side streets and limit yourself to souvenir shirts and costume jewelry. If you just can't go home empty-handed, consider a bottle of wine from **Vina Miličić** on the Stradun (ⓒ 020/321-777; open daily 9am–8pm) or a piece of hand-embroidered linen from **Tilda** at Zlatarska 1 (ⓒ 020/321-554). History buffs will want to visit **War Photo Limited** at Antuninska 6 (ⓒ 020/322-166; open daily 9am–9pm), a source for limited-edition prints of scenes from the 1991 war and other conflicts. Don't forget the **Duty Free Shop at Dubrovnik Airport** (ⓒ 020/333-773), where you can get almost everything available in town without paying tax.

DUBROVNIK AFTER DARK

Dubrovnik's after-hours scene has an early and a late shift. From about 8 to 11pm the common activity for babes-in-arms to seniors is strolling the Stradun with an ice-cream cone. But at 11, there's a changing of the crowd as the early birds file out and 18- to 20-somethings flow in, dressed in outfits that rival the costumes worn in a Busby Berkeley musical. Follow the throbbing music blaring from jampacked side streets where nightly block parties convene after the restaurants close and you'll experience Dubrovnik cafe society's second shift.

For a disco experience, try **Latino Club Fuego** outside the Pile Gate at Pile Brsalje 11, open daily 10pm to 4am; or **Labirint Night Club** at Ulica Sv. Dominika bb (ⓒ 020/322-222), open daily 10pm to 4am. There's also the **Night Club Revelin** in the Revelin Fortress at the wall (ⓒ 020/322-164), which was the "in" place of the

2006 season and **Night Club Orlandinjo** in the Dubrovnik Palace in Lapad (⊘ 020/ 430-000). Those with tamer tastes can take in a movie at **Sloboda,** a theater accessed via the mall entrance to the Arsenal Wine Bar (⊘ 020/321-425). Hours vary.

ESCORTED WALKING TOURS
Mediterranean Experience Ltd., at Ćira Carića 3 (⊘ 020/442-201), offers daily 1-hour "Discover Dubrovnik" walks from the Large Onofrio Fountain at 10am and 7pm. The itinerary introduces Dubrovnik's major sights (90kn/$16/£8.20).

DUBROVNIK SUMMER FESTIVAL/LIBERTAS
Almost every Croatian town and village has at least one summer festival, but Dubrovnik's is the largest, running from the second week of July to the third week of August. **Libertas,** as the festival is affectionately named, transforms Sponza Palace, Dubrovnik Cathedral, Lovrijenac Fortress, and other spots all over the city into venues for drama, music, folk, dance, and other performing arts daily at 9:30pm. Dubrovnik is at its most congested during Libertas, so rooms must be booked well in advance. For more information, go to www.dubrovnik-festival.hr.

4 Excursions from Dubrovnik

Dubrovnik may be Croatia's best-known destination, but the islands off its coast and the Pelješac Peninsula have unique charms.

ELAFITI ISLANDS, CAVTAT & LOKRUM
Vivado Travel Agency (⊘ 020/486-471; www.dubrovnik-online.com/vivado) and others operate ticket kiosks at the Old Harbor near the Ploče Gate. They offer daily fish picnic excursions (250kn/$44/£23) to the **Elafiti Islands** (**Koločep, Šipan,** and **Lopud**), sleepy family resorts with minuscule sandy beaches. Koločep has **Hotel Koločep,** a cheerless 118-unit hotel on the water with rooms that go for 149€ ($190) for an air-conditioned double. Lopud's **Grand Hotel** is an abandoned ruin, but the island has a bank of restaurants and several historic churches. Šipan is completely skipable. Consider sampling the Elafitis on a 7-hour boating adventure that includes an onboard grilled-fish lunch followed by a quick post-meal stroll of each island and you'll cover everything worth seeing.

Cavtat (pronounced *sahv*-taht) is (17km/11 miles) southeast of Dubrovnik and reachable by bus, water taxi, or organized tour. Besides its beach and harbor, Cavtat is home to several museums, galleries, and churches. Don't miss the **Račić family mausoleum** in the town graveyard, which is decorated inside and out with pieces sculpted by **Ivan Meštrović,** who worked in Cavtat in the 1920s. To see the artwork inside the mausoleum, call ⊘ 020/478-646 and a custodian will show up to open the tomb for 5kn ($1/45p) per person. Afterward, stop at **Restaurant Leut** (Trumbičev Put II; ⊘ 020/479-050; open daily 9am–midnight) for a light lunch.

Lokrum is the island closest to the Dubrovnik coast (1km/½ mile) and water taxis make the 15-minute crossing every half-hour from the Old Harbor from 9am to 5pm daily for 35kn ($6/£3.20) round-trip. The last boat back to Dubrovnik leaves Lokrum at 6pm. A change of pace is the main reason for visiting Lokrum, and you have your choice of swimming in a small salt lake, sunbathing on a concrete slab "beach," exploring church ruins, or wandering in the woods. The island's nature park was conceived by Archduke Maximilian Habsburg, who bought the island before he became emperor of Mexico in the mid–19th century.

PELJEŠAC PENINSULA

Vineyards, rugged terrain, a few medieval sites, good beaches, and sparse crowds are the draws for this finger of land that protrudes into the sea half an hour north of Dubrovnik. The peninsula is just 65km (40 miles) long, but the roads twist across hills and valleys, making the drive to the peninsula's tip challenging.

Ston and Mali Ston are the peninsula towns closest to the mainland, and if you venture no farther than that, you'll be rewarded with great photo ops, thanks to Ston's 14th-century walls, which snake up the hill behind the town like a mini Great Wall of China. Ston is also the center of Croatia's oyster and mussel production as well as an established working salt pan.

The peninsula beyond is wine country where dozens of family vineyards are terraced onto the hills and planted in the valleys. Mike Grgić of California winemaking fame has a small winery at Trstenik. It is one of many operated by Croatia's big-name vintners. Many vineyards also have tasting rooms, small restaurants, and even retail outlets where you can sample and buy the latest vintages. At the tip of Pelješac, Orebič, is home to one of the country's best beaches and one of its more interesting waterfront promenades. Orebič is also a great spot to set up home base for island hopping.

5 The Rest of Southern Dalmatia

Southern Dalmatia is a relatively narrow expanse of land, but it is fringed by hundreds of islands. To get the most out of a trip to this region, first-time visitors should settle on a few nearby locations that offer multiple attractions—watersports, historic architecture, and/or natural wonders—*after* checking out transportation options and travel times between them.

Warning: Ferry schedules, mountainous roads, and circuitous routes characteristic of this region can make the time it takes to travel even short distances deceiving. Booking a guided tour that hits the highlights while leaving ferry connections and logistical problems to an expert is another option.

HVAR ISLAND/HVAR TOWN

St. Tropez, Majorca, Aspen, and other glamour destinations don't have anything on Hvar, the glitzy island playground patronized by celebrities, the idle rich, and the average visitor.

The island is a hilly piece of real estate with very rocky terrain, a few vineyards, and patches of wild lavender between abandoned stone structures and sparsely populated villages. The island's principal population centers are Hvar Town, Stari Grad, Vrboska, Jelsa, and Sucuraj, towns that have ferry/catamaran ports. Hvar Town is the island's tourism epicenter.

GETTING THERE & GETTING AROUND

Jadrolinija operates service to Stari Grad and Sucuraj and buses connect from there to Hvar Town and Jelsa. Jadrolinija (© 021/741-132) has offices in both Hvar Town and Stari Grad and can provide prices and schedules. Sem Marina runs a daily boat to Hvar Town from Split via Korčula and tourist agencies operate other island hoppers. A bus will take you from Hvar Town to Stari Grad and back, but if you want to see anything else, a car is necessary. Hvar Town is closed to vehicular traffic from the bus station to the Riva, which is clogged with pedestrians until after nightfall when the main square, Trg Sveti Stjepana, becomes the central mob scene.

Tips bb

bb means *bez broja* (without number). This is quite common in Croatia, particularly if the place is a well-known church or restaurant. If you see an address listed with a street name followed by bb, and you are having trouble finding it, simply ask a local for directions.

VISITOR INFORMATION

Hvar Town's principal **tourist office** is at Trg Sv. Stjepana b.b. (© **021/741-059;** fax 021/742-977; www.tzhvar.hr). Stari Grad's is at Nova Riva 2 (© **021/765-763;** www. hvar.hr). Both can provide literature and maps, but if you want accommodations in Hvar Town, go to **Pelegrini Travel,** steps from the boat landing (© **021/742-743;** pelegrini@inet.hr; 8am–10pm Mon–Sat and 6–8pm Sun). Pelegrini also books through travel agencies in Split.

During July and August, there is the potential for a reservation snafu, so be sure you have confirmed—and preferably paid for—accommodations before you arrive. **Atlas Travel** (© **021/741-670**), on the west side of the Hvar Town harbor next to the renovated (Sept 2006) **Adriana Hotel,** is an excellent place to book excursions.

WHERE TO STAY

There are no hotel bargains in Hvar Town. Innkeepers have been scrambling to expand and renovate since the island became all the rage, and the result is that prices are escalating faster than improvements. Moderately priced private accommodations exist, but in the summer especially, you must book 4 days or more just to get a reservation.

Very Expensive

Hotel Podstine ⊛   The Podstine is nestled amid palm and citrus trees next to its own beach, which is a flat concrete strip with a view of the **Pakleni Islands.** The hotel is a 30-minute climb from Hvar Town center, but it offers shuttle service (20kn/$4/£2.15 one-way). Guest rooms are clean and showing their age though most have private balconies. The shaded terrace is a tranquil place to kick back with a glass of wine.

Pod Stine. Hvar Town. © 021/740-400. Fax 021/740-499. www.podstine.com. 40 units. Mid-July to late Aug from 1,900kn ($328/£173) seaside double. Rest of year from 1,085kn ($187/£99) seaside double. AE, DC, MC, V. Guarded parking. **Amenities:** Restaurant; bar; diving center; excursions; bike, scooter, and car rental; room service 11am–11pm. *In room:* A/C, TV, minibar.

Riva (aka Slavija) ⊛⊛   Riva wins our extreme-makeover award. Tourists who stay at the transformed Slavija 9m (30 ft.) from the dock have a bird's-eye view of the waterfront action, and since June 26, 2006, they also have plush surroundings. Rooms are still small because of the building's protected status, but now they are equipped with ultramodern bathrooms, flatscreen TVs, slick designer colors, and patios. The hotel is home to a Mediterranean restaurant and a cocktail lounge where you can schmooze the night away.

Riva bb. Hvar Town. © 021/741-820. Fax 021/741-147. www.suncanihvar.hr. 54 units. Mid-July to Aug double from 275€ ($350); suite from 325€ ($390); Riva suite from 370€ ($475). Rest of year doubles from 214€ ($275); suite from 238€ ($305); Riva suite from 295€ ($378). Rates include breakfast. AE, DC, MC, V. **Amenities:** Restaurant; bar; spa access; Wi-Fi; terrace dancing. *In room:* A/C, SAT/TV, hair dryer, some patios.

Expensive

Hotel Palace *(Overrated)*   Hvar's grande dame is situated behind the 16th-century **loggia** that once graced the town's ducal palace. The Palace was built in the early 20th century, and time has not been kind to its elegant features. Despite soaring ceilings and architectural splendor, guest rooms are small, dated, and without air-conditioning. If you open the window to get a sea breeze, you'll hear the noise on the square or Riva, and that can last until sunrise.

Trg Sveti Stjepana bb. Hvar Town. (℃ 021/741-966. Fax 021/742-240. www.suncanihvar.hr. 73 units. Mid-July to Aug from 125€ ($160) double; from 159€ ($204) suite. Rest of year from 60€ ($77) double. AE, DC, MC, V. Rates include breakfast. **Amenities:** Restaurant; bar; pool. *In room:* TV.

WHERE TO DINE

Most of the restaurants lining Hvar Town's harbor serve pizza, pasta, and grilled fish. However, some dining spots tucked into the narrow, unnamed side streets are bastions of distinctive cuisine.

Very Expensive

Roots ✸ in the Hotel Riva (℃ **021/741-820**) gets points for its casual-chic terrace and creative offerings, but as beautiful as the food and surroundings may be, this brand-new dining room sometimes tries too hard to be "gourmet," especially with its designer pizza toppings: Raspberry vinaigrette, shrimp, and goat cheese might work on salads, but it turns pizza crust into a soggy mess. Roots also offers weekly theme menus (Tex-Mex), and a long list of grossly overpriced wines and exotic cocktails.

Expensive

Lucullus ✸✸✸ off the main square (℃ **021/742-498**) specializes in a light version of slow food, leisurely dining with well-prepared seafood and Dalmatian specialties served in a convivial atmosphere. Wood-grilled pizza is on the menu, but try the island lobster *brodeto* or peka-grilled meat (available if ordered 3 hr. in advance). Lucullus also has a few rooms to rent.

The affable owner of the **Golden Shell** ✸✸ at Petra Hektorovica 8 (℃ **098/1688-797**) cheerfully chortles that slow food is the opposite of fast food, which doesn't begin to explain this Croatian style of dining, which paces courses made from the freshest ingredients to allow diners time to savor their meals. Start with Dalmatian ham and goat cheese in olive oil, and follow with steak stuffed with goat cheese and capers. Food is an art form here.

Moderate

Gostiona Kod Matkovića ✸, at 55 Godina Tradicije (℃ **021/741-854**), is a homey restaurant set in a small courtyard. It has a nice selection of seafood and meats, including spit-roasted lamb, but wine choices are limited to the house white or house red.

Macondo ✸✸, at Groda bb (℃ **021/742-850**), is a seafood restaurant off St. Stephen's Square that spills into a nameless alley. Portions are huge; prices are moderate. You won't be able to resist the *gregada,* a garlicky seafood stew.

EXPLORING HVAR TOWN

Hvar Town is a languid mix of sensual countryside and 13th-century attractions on a harbor where mega-yachts come to mate. Sun, sea, and a trendy social scene pull in a glittering passel of visitors.

The 13th century **St. Stephen's Square (Trg Sveti Stjepan)** ✸✸✸ is Hvar Town's central stage. It is bookended by **St. Stephen's Cathedral** ✸ (daily 7am–noon and

5–7pm) in the east and a small harbor in the west. The square is lined with restaurants, cafes, and galleries, and a **16th-century well** sits in the center of the paved space, which was redone in the late 18th century.

The **Venetian Loggia** ✿✿✿ has suffered several insults to its historical pedigree: It was damaged by the Turks in 1571, repaired, then used as a cafe from the late 19th century to as recently as the early 1970s. The adjacent clock tower was built in the 19th century on the site of a ducal palace that was destroyed in the same assault that damaged the loggia.

The 15th-century **Franciscan Monastery** ✿ is south of the town center along the path skirting the sea. Enter through a cloister, where concerts are held every 2 days during the season. There is also a nice museum with a collection of sacral art and an idyllic garden with a view of the sea. Open daily in summer 10am to noon and 5 to 7pm; winter daily 10am to noon. Performance times and prices vary. The adjacent church, **Our Lady of Mercy,** also dates from the 15th century (✆ 021/741-123; 10kn/$1.75/90p). The 16th-century **Fortress (Fortica)** ✿✿ that overlooks the town offers a sweeping view of Hvar Town's rooftops and its harbor. Inside is a spooky dungeon, displays of amphorae, and a small cafe on the roof (north of Hvar Town center; ✆ 021/741-816; admission 10kn ($1.75/90p). Summer daily 8am to midnight; by appointment only in winter.

Note: The walk up to the fortress is a challenging trek during the day, but at night it can be treacherous because the steps/path leading to the site are not lighted.

Beaches

Hvar Town has both a public pebble beach and a slab beach west of the center that are usually crowded with sunbathers from the nearby package Hotel Amfora. There are also a few small patches of pebbles below the Franciscan church, and lots of flat rocks and concrete slabs at other seaside spots. If you want privacy, for a mere 10kn ($1.75/95p), you can hop a taxi boat to nearby **Pakleni Otoci,** a cluster of pine-forested, uninhabited islands whose coastlines are alternately rimmed with rocks and little pebble beaches.

Watersports

Southern Dalmatia is home to some of the best conditions in Europe for windsurfing, kite boarding, jet-skiing, sailing, diving, and swimming. At the **Viking Diving Center** next to the Podstine Hotel (✆ 021/742-529) you can rent equipment, get instruction, and even book rooms. Cost of single dive is 220kn ($38/£20), a package of 5 days and 10 dives 1,720kn ($300/£157), or a full-day trip with cave diving 490kn ($85/£45). Equipment rental is extra. **Dive Center Hvar** near Hotel Amfora (✆ 021/741-503) runs trips to the island of **Vis,** which recently has become the darling of extreme-sports enthusiasts. DCH also supports other watersports such as water-skiing,

---

Lavender Blues

Hvar is sometimes known as "Lavender Island" because the graceful plant with a hypnotic fragrance once grew in profusion all over the place. Lavender is a native of Hvar's dry Mediterranean climate, and tourist hype says the whole island is enveloped in a cloud of scent in the spring. That may be so, but in July 2006, the only lavender plants we saw were either dried *in situ* by the blistering sun or in sachets sold at kiosks on the Riva.

snorkeling, kite boarding, windsurfing, and banana boating. It rents boats, kayaks, and equipment. Prices run from 250kn ($43/£23) for a single dive including equipment to an all-inclusive certification course for 2,360kn ($405/£215).

6 Split

408km (254 miles) S of Zagreb; 213km (132 miles) NW of Dubrovnik

Split marked its 1,700th birthday and the completion of Diocletian's magnificent palace (A.D. 305) in 2005. Diocletian deliberately chose this site for his retirement home because it provided the best of both country and city. The emperor's Split digs were just 6km (4 miles) from Salona, the provincial center of power, close enough to allow him to periodically stick his finger in affairs of state while living in his seaside palace, which was the size of a small city.

Today's Split is a transportation hub for the Dalmatian coast. Despite Old Town, whose borders are defined by Diocletian's Palace, Split has never had the glamour of other Dalmatian destinations, though most travelers who head for Dubrovnik or the islands pass through or make connections there. Nonetheless, Split has developed into one of the most accessible cities in Croatia.

GETTING THERE

BY PLANE   Split's **airport** (✆ 021/203-171; www.split-airport.tel.hr) is 26km (16 miles) northwest of the city center between Kaštela and Trogir. Flights from cities in Croatia and from many European hubs land there regularly. Service is more frequent in the summer and a shuttle moves passengers between the airport and the bus station (Obala Kneza Domogoja 12; ✆ 021/203-305; 30kn/$5.50/£2.75 each way).

BY CAR   The Zagreb-Split autocesta cuts through mountains and bypasses country roads and has reduced the 5-hour travel time between Zagreb and Split by an hour since it opened in May 2005. Except for weekends in July and August, the 364km (226-mile) drive from Zagreb to Split takes less time than the 213km (132-mile) coastal drive from Split to Dubrovnik.

BY BOAT   International, local, and island carriers move in and out of Split's ferry port almost constantly and daily catamaran service to the islands of Brač, Hvar, Vis, and Korčula originates there. Split is also an international port for ferries making overnight runs to and from Ancona, Italy. Contact the local Jadrolinija office (✆ 021/338-333), Sem Marina (✆ 021/338-292), or Adriatica (✆ 021/338-335) for schedules and prices. **SNAV,** an Italy-based transit company, runs high-speed ferries (4 hr. or less) to Ancona from early June to mid-September (✆ 021/322-252).

BY BUS   Local bus routes include Split and its suburbs, Salona, Klis, Omiš, and Trogir, while multiple lines travel to Zagreb, Zadar, Rijeka, Dubrovnik, and destinations beyond several times a day. International buses provide daily service to Slovenia, Germany, and Italy, and weekly service to Austria and England. Schedule and fare information is available at ✆ 021/338-483.

BY TRAIN   Split's main train station is next to the bus terminal at Obala Kneza Domogoja 10 near the town center. It runs between Split and Zagreb, Knin, and Šibenik. There is also an overnight train between Split and Zagreb. Call the **Split train station** (✆ 021/338-535) or the **national train office** (✆ 060/333-444; www.hznet.hr) for schedule and fare information.

Tips **Taxi Tips**

Be sure to negotiate your taxi fare before getting in the vehicle. Prices for the same ride can vary wildly and cabbies will compete for your business if more than one is available.

CITY LAYOUT & GETTING AROUND

Split's historic core is bounded by Obala Hrvatskog Preporoda (Riva) in the south, Marmontova Street in the west, Kralja Tomislava in the north, and Hrvojeva in the east; Old Town's main square, Narodni Trg, is almost in the center of the rectangle.

Most of Split's important sights are within the palace walls or nearby. The walled city is limited to pedestrians; even the street skirting the Riva outside the walls is closed to motorized vehicles. There are a few sights worth taking in beyond the historic core—the Meštrović Gallery in Marjan, the public beach at Bačvice. Both are reachable via bus or taxi. Taxi stands are at each end of the Riva (in front of the town market and in front of the Bellevue Hotel). If you don't see a cab, call ⓒ **970.**

VISITOR INFORMATION Split's official **Tourist Information Center** is near the Silver Gate/Peristil (ⓒ **021/342-666;** www.visitsplit.com) behind the cathedral in the former chapel of St. Rocco. There is also an information center across from the ferry port at Obala Hrvatskog Narodnog Preporoda 7 (ⓒ **021/348-600**).

WHERE TO STAY

Hotel rooms are scarce in Split, and reasonably priced rooms are almost nonexistent, though private accommodations are fairly easy to secure.

VERY EXPENSIVE

Hotel Vestibul Palace ★★★ Clever 21st-century architects carved this intimate boutique hotel into the space next to what was Diocletian's bedroom. The hotel opened in 2006 and the interior uses high design to meld glass with ancient stone The result is spectacular. Most of the bathrooms have tubs, but those without have high-tech showers. All have flatscreen TVs.

Vestibula 4. ⓒ 021/329-329. www.vestibulpalace.com. 7 units. Doubles July–Aug from 240€ ($295); 190€ ($230) rest of the year. Rates include breakfast. AE, MC, V. **Amenities:** Restaurant; excursions. *In room:* A/C, SAT/TV w/LCD screen, minibar, hair dryer, Wi-Fi.

EXPENSIVE

Hotel Peristil ★★ *Finds*   The Peristil opened in April 2005, putting guests in literal touch with history: The Peristil is just inside the **Silver Gate** and shares a wall with the palace. Outside, guests can breakfast on the limestone terrace; inside, they can listen to music from the annual **Split Summer Festival** from any of the rooms when the windows are open. Guest rooms are comfortably sized and hung with original artwork; most have showers rather than tubs; rooms are equipped with dial-up Internet access; and **Restoran Tifani** ★★ downstairs is a delight.

Note: If you are lucky enough to get room no. 302, you can hear the music *and* see the Silver Gate and Domnius Square below.

Poljana Kraljice Jelene 5. ⓒ 021/329/070. Fax 021/329-088. www.hotelperistil.com. 12 units. July–Aug from 135€ ($173) double; from 108€ ($130) other times. Rates include breakfast. AE, MC, V. **Amenities:** Restaurant; bar. *In room:* A/C, TV, Internet access, hair dryer.

MODERATE

Hotel Adriana ☆☆ The Adriana's accommodations are really rooms over its popular **restaurant** ☆☆. If you can snag a booking, you will be in an ideal location for sightseeing. Guest rooms are plain but comfortable, especially those with a sea view.

Preporoda 8. ℂ **021/340-000.** www.hotel-adriana.hr. 9 units; 2 apts. Mid-Apr to mid-Oct from 850kn ($147/£78) double. 1,400kn ($242/£128) apt. AE, DC, MC, V. **Amenities:** Restaurant. *In room:* A/C, TV, minibar.

Korčula & Brač

The islands of **Korčula** ☆☆☆ and **Brač** ☆☆ are among the most popular day-trip destinations from Split. **Korčula Town** ☆☆☆ is the big draw on Korčula, while **Bol** and **its Zlatni Rat (Golden Horn) beach** ☆☆ pull tourists to Brač. Spend your day exploring Korčula Town's medieval streets, soaking up the sun and international atmosphere on Bol's shape-shifting beach, or riding the waves on a wind board off either island.

Korčula Town: After you climb the **Grand Staircase** that leads across the town's only remaining **wall,** you'll think you've walked through a worm hole to the past. Marco Polo's alleged birthplace is crisscrossed with picturesque stone structures that house restaurants, museums, families, and offices laid out on streets that branch off from the enclave's major north-south thoroughfare (Korčulaskog Statuta). You can spend hours exploring these narrow offshoots and never know exactly where you are in time or space, and you can spend hours more hiking or biking around the island. At its widest point, Korčula is just 8km (5 miles) wide and it is just 32km (20 miles) long.

Note: The approach to Korčula Town from the sea makes for one of the best vacation pictures ever if snapped in the morning.

Korčula Town's well-preserved walled core and medieval attractions, plus the city's claim that it is the birthplace of legendary explorer **Marco Polo,** are the island's main draw. Seasonal visitors also come to Korčula to see the **Moreška Sword Dance,** a summer spectacle that recalls a battle between Christians and "infidels" that was fought over a woman. Finally, the island is an excellent source of olive oil and wine, most notably white wines (Pošip, Grk).

Brač: Croatia's third-largest island (Krk and Cres are nos. 1 and 2 respectively) and its **Zlatni Rat (Golden Horn) beach** ☆☆ are magnets for those who love sun and surf. Brač is one of Croatia's least-developed populated islands, but it is much more than that. This rugged land about an hour's ferry ride from Split is also famous as a windsurfer's paradise, the source of the stone that built Diocletian's palace, the White House in Washington, D.C., and the Reichstag in Berlin. Brač also has a reputation as the source of Bolski Plavac and other highly regarded wines. Brač is really a two-town island because only **Supetar** on the northern shore and **Bol** on the southern shore are easily accessed by tourists.

In the Pipeline

Le Meridien Lav will became the only internationally affiliated hotel in the Split area when it opens in fall 2006 on the site of the former Hotel Lav. The 381-unit hotel is currently being redeveloped as a seafront resort destination with three restaurants, four bars, indoor and outdoor pools, spa facilities, a private beach with watersports and tennis courts. The hotel is 20 minutes from the city center and 40 minutes from Split-Kastela International Airport. Go to www.starwoodhotels.com for more information.

INEXPENSIVE

Hotel Jupiter ☆ *Value*   The Jupiter is located next to the 1,700-year-old Temple of Jupiter near Narodni Trg and in the middle of Split's nightlife action. Jupiter is really a guesthouse, but it is an excellent place to bunk if you don't mind sharing a bathroom. Jupiter had an overhaul for the 2005 season and the spartan rooms and bathrooms now gleam.

Grabovčeva Širina 1. ℭ 021/344-801. www.hotel-jupiter.info. 25 units. 250kn ($43/£23) per person. No credit cards. **Amenities:** Cafe/bar; TV room. *In room:* A/C double and triple rooms, fans in singles.

WHERE TO DINE

It isn't difficult to find a place to eat in Split, but finding a restaurant other than a pizzeria or konoba is challenging. However, Split's dining scene is improving as new hotels open and bring more tourist traffic to town.

VERY EXPENSIVE

Boban ☆☆☆ at Hektorovićeva 49 (ℭ **098/205-575**) has a reputation dating from its founding in 1973. Both the indoor dining room and outdoor terrace are beautiful settings for the chef's consistently excellent creations, which range from seafood preparations to traditional Croatian fare. **Restoran Šumica** ☆☆☆ at Put Firula 6 (ℭ **021/389-897**) is an upscale restaurant near Bačvice Beach southeast of Old Town and one of the most romantic in Split. The house specialty is tagliatelle with scampi and salmon. Pair it with a bottle from Šumica's excellent cellar and enjoy it under pines on the terrace.

EXPENSIVE

Restoran Sarajevo ☆☆, at Domaldova 6 (ℭ **021/347-454**), is an old-style dining room in a space supported by vaulted arches constructed at the beginning of the last millennium. Try the *ražnjići*, chunks of grilled meat skewered on tiny swords and be warned that the mixed-grill plate includes liver. Service can be slow and impersonal. **Restoran Tifani** ☆☆ in Hotel Peristil (ℭ **021/329-070**) is a welcome departure from the same old, same old, that characterizes most of Split's restaurants. Here house-made noodles with mussels, mortadella, and peppers come together in a creamy sauce laced with cheese and sautéed stroganoff is a happy mix of beef, Madeira sauce, mushrooms, gherkins, and cream.

MODERATE

Bistro XVII Stoljeća ☆ at Poljana Grgura Ninskog 7 in Old Town (ℭ **021/314-519**) is an eatery on a courtyard with three others and one of the few places in Split with

Diocletian's Palace ✮✮✮

Historians say Diocletian (A.D. 245–316) was born in a village near Salona, which at the time was the nerve center of the Roman government in Dalmatia. His palace was a heavily protected enclave that included a military installation, and its footprint covered nearly 3 hectares (10 acres) and encompassed the emperor's apartments, several temples, and housing for soldiers and servants.

Diocletian moved into the limestone palace in A.D. 305 after a reign of 21 years, and according to some historians, he had commissioned construction of the palace 8 years earlier in A.D. 293. The names of architects Filotas and Zotikos are engraved on palace foundation stones.

In the years immediately following the emperor's death in A.D. 316, the palace was used as government office space, but it inadvertently became a haven for refugees in the early 7th century when the Avars and Slavs attacked and destroyed Salona, sending that city's citizens to nearby islands and later to the security of the palace walls, which were 2m (6 ft.) thick and nearly 30m (100 ft.) high at points.

This huge influx of refugees overcrowded the palace compound, and the new settlement spread outside its walls. Successive rulers, including the Byzantine emperors, the Croatian kings, the Hungarian-Croatian kings, and the Venetians, accommodated by building structures within and outside the complex, a practice that effectively destroyed the palace's Roman character and left little more than the original walls and vestiges within them.

female waitresses, whose very presence makes dining friendlier for families and solo women. Pasta entrees include noodles Matriciana, wide pasta dressed with tomatoes, bacon, and chile and a Diocletian salad with veggies, squid, and anchovies sprinkled among the greens. **Konoba Varoš** ✮✮ at Ban Mladenova 7 (© **021/396-138**) is a local favorite, which is usually the sign of a good restaurant in Croatia. Tuck into a big plate of lamb or veal hot from the *peka* (grill); or try the blue fish or octopus. Varoš has a long and varied wine list for a simple konoba, which translates to fair bottle prices. **Adriana** ✮✮ at Obala Hrvatskog Preporoda (© **021/344-079**) on the Riva near Old Town is always crowded. Try the seafood risotto or any grilled meat or fish dish. Live music spices up weekends—and sometimes weekdays—during the summer, which is great for restaurant patrons but annoying if you're staying in the Adriana's upstairs rooms.

INEXPENSIVE

Pizzeria Fortuna ✮✮, at Bihačka 2 (© **021/487-202**), offers pastas and salads, too. In a town with so many pizzerias, Fortuna is one of the best. **Caffe/bar Gaga** ✮, at Iza Loža 5 (© **021/342-257**), is where to go after midnight when everything else has closed down. By day Gaga is a popular coffee stop; by night it is a collection of outdoor tables where wall-to-wall people try to relate over throbbing disco music.

Kalumela ✿, at Domaldova 7 (© **021/348-132**), can supply organic whole-grain sandwiches and pastries as well as the usual health-food-store staples.

EXPLORING SPLIT

Diocletian's Palace is Split's marquee attraction, and the **Riva** outside its walls is one of Croatia's busiest promenades.

The **Cathedral of St. Domnius** ✿✿✿, at Kraj Sv. Duje 5 (© **021/342-589;** admission 5kn/$1/55p), was also Diocletian's mausoleum, an elaborate domed structure that Christians converted to a church in the 7th century. The original stone structure was framed by 28 granite and marble columns that Diocletian supposedly looted from Greek and Egyptian temples during one of his campaigns. Because of its proximity to the **Silver Gate,** the cathedral is a popular meeting place and its courtyard is the site of performances during **Split's Summer Festival** ✿✿✿ in July and August.

The **cathedral treasury** ✿ above the sacristy contains a valuable cache of gold and silver in the treasury. From there you can climb the **bell tower** ✿ for 10kn ($1.75/95p) from 8am to 8pm in summer and whenever it is open in winter.

Narodni Trg (People's Square) ✿✿ is west along Krešimirova (formerly the Decumanus) through the Silver Gate. On the north side of the square you'll see the **Town Hall,** now home to the **Ethnographic Museum.** West of Narodni Trg you'll find the indoor fish market (**Ribarnica;** Kraj Sv. Marije; 7am–1pm Mon–Sat; 7–11am Sun). You'll smell it before you see it. Continue west to **Marmontova Street** ✿, a brick-paved pedestrian thoroughfare that forms Old Town's western border. Here you will find international retail outlets (Tommy Hilfiger, Benetton) and a set of McDonald's golden arches. Just south of the walls along Marmontova you'll run into

> ⎛Fun Fact **Mining Silver**
>
> The Silver Gate (Srebrena Vrata), which leads inside from the Pazar market on the palace's eastern side, is a relatively new site in Split's Old Town. For centuries the gate was hidden behind a drab brick wall; it was discovered and excavated just a little over 50 years ago in the 1950s.

the **Bellevue Hotel** and the **Prokurative,** a horseshoe-shaped set of neoclassical government buildings on **Trg Republike.**

Braće Radić Trg (Voćni Trg or Fruit Square) ✿ is smaller than Narodni Trgand and dominated by Ivan Meštrović's sculpture of author **Marko Marulić,** who wrote "Judita," the first narrative poem in Croatian. Marulić (1450–1524) is revered as the father of Croatian literature and his statue shows him with—what else?—a book.

Away from the center, the **Meštrović Gallery** ✿✿✿ at Šetalište Ivana Meštrovića 46, Marjan (© **021/358-450**) was built as a home/atelier for Croatian sculptor Ivan Meštrović and his family. Traveling exhibitions from Croatia and other locations are periodically on display here. Walk up the road to Šetalište Ivana Meštrovića 39 to visit the 16th-century **Kaštelet,** a summer house purchased and remodeled by Meštrović in 1939 as a showcase for his "Life of Christ" reliefs. There is no charge to enter Kaštelet if you have a ticket to the main gallery.

From mid-July to mid-August, the **Split Summer Festival** ✿✿✿ takes place at **Croatian National Theater,** in the **Peristil,** at other Old Town squares, and at other venues. Contact the Croatian National Theater at Gaje Bulata 1 (© **021/585-999**) for information and tickets.

Zipping Through Zadar

During World War II, Zadar was almost destroyed by Allied forces, though it was mostly rebuilt during the postwar Yugoslavia era. The city took another devastating hit when it was isolated by Serb forces and reduced to rubble in the 1991 war. Today, Zadar is fiercely nationalistic, an exceptional mix of new and old architecture, and home to diverse cultures.

Thanks to the new A1 autocesta between Zagreb and Split, it takes just 3 hours to cover the 285km (177 miles) between there and Croatia's capital. Frequent bus service, an airport, a train station, and a generous ferry schedule also make Zadar accessible. However, despite tourist-friendly touches like multilingual signs in front of notable sites, Zadar has not yet become a prime stop for visitors, but its Old Town is worth at least of day of your time.

Start at **St. Donatus Church** ★★★ and the **Roman Forum** ★★★ in its front yard. Look around the St. Donatus's unusual interior with a circular center and watch kids ride their Big Wheels over the Forum's ancient stones. Peek into the 11th-century **Church of St. Mary** ★★ across the street and stop in at the **Benedictine Convent** next door to see its **Gold and Silver of Zadar** exhibit ★★★, one of the best reliquary and religious-art collections anywhere. Have the freshest of fish dinners at **Foša's** ★★★ open-air dining room in the shadow of the city's walls. If you have time (and room), top off the experience with a frozen treat from **Slastičarna Donat** ★★★ off **Obala Kralja Petra Krešimira IV,** the city's promenade, and pause to watch its non-stop street theater. Finally, sit on the marble seaside steps off the promenade and dangle your toes in the sea while you revel in the haunting melody of Zadar's mesmerizing **Sea Organ.** It's an experience you won't soon forget.

7 Istria & the Kvarner Gulf Region

Istria is a triangle-shaped peninsula at the northwestern end of Croatia that protrudes just far enough into the Adriatic to catch the seductive Mediterranean climate while the Kvarner Gulf Region lies directly east of there. Three sides of Istria are lined with beaches and busy marinas, which in turn are festooned with Venetian-style towns that look just as they must have when tall trading ships sailed in and out of their harbors. Kvarner Gulf towns have an Austro-Hungarian bent.

GETTING THERE & GETTING AROUND

BY PLANE   Istria's airport is at Pula, about 5km (3 miles) northwest of the center of town, and it is served by Croatia Airlines (www.croatiaairlines.hr). There is also a smaller airport for private planes and charters near Vrsar in the middle of the western coast. Shuttle buses and taxis (60kn–70kn/$10–$12/£5.50–£6.40) run between Pula's airport and the town center.

BY BOAT   VeneziaLines runs catamarans from Venice to Umag, Poreč, Rovinj, Pula, and Rabac; and from Rimini to Pula. Check the website (www.venezialines.com) or call ℂ **041/24-24-000** from 9am to 6pm Venice time to book tickets or for detailed schedule information. Sem Marina at Boktulijin put bb (© **021/352-444**) runs a ferry between Pula and Zadar with a stop at Mali Losinj.

BY BUS   Autotrans (© **052/741-817;** www.autotrans.hr) runs four daily buses from both Rijeka and Zagreb to Pula, and to major cities such as Umag, Poreč, and Rovinj on the coast. Most interior towns are connected to the coastal cities by at least one bus per day, but travel by bus to inland Istria can be inconvenient.

BY TRAIN   Trains connect Pula to Zagreb (7 hr.) and to Rijeka (2½ hr.) plus other coastal towns. However, if you want to see inland Istria, a car is a necessity.

BY CAR   Auto travel is by far the most flexible way to see Istria beyond the coast and the only sensible way to see the interior. There are car-rental agencies in most of the major population centers.

VISITOR INFORMATION

Istria has an efficient tourist association with information offices in almost every town from Pula on the coast to Oprtalj in the interior highlands. The association and its website (www.istra.com) provide information ranging from maps of the region's olive-oil roads to an up-to-date schedule of events.

PULA

This bustling city of 65,000 people at Istria's southern tip is 265km (165 miles) south-west of Zagreb and 720km (447 miles) northeast of Dubrovnik. Pula is a working port as well as a repository of some of the best Roman ruins in Europe.

GETTING THERE & GETTING AROUND

Tourists can make both regional and international ferry connections in Pula, which has a large number of bus routes to Zagreb and Rijeka, Rovinj, Vrsar, and Poreč, plus the gateway city of Trieste in Italy and coastal towns in Slovenia. Pula is a walkable city and its local bus system can get you almost anywhere you need to go. If you want to explore the hills and valleys of the Istrian interior, you'll need a car, but if you just want a ride past Pula's main sites, catch **Tram Tina,** a bright yellow-and-green mul-ticar vehicle that picks up passengers at the amphitheater or at Forum Square. Tina is run by an enterprising Pula citizen and the tram runs from 9:30am to 10pm. There is no commentary, but for 20kn ($3.45/£1.85) adults and 15kn ($2.60/£1.40) children, you can "skim" 15 sites in 40 minutes.

VISITOR INFORMATION

The **Tourist Information Office** at Forum 2 (© **052/219-197;** www.pulainfo.hr; 9am–8pm Mon–Sat, 10am–6pm Sun and holidays) opposite the Temple of Augustus provides maps, brochures, and lists of events in Pula and around Istria.

Private agencies like **Activatravel Istra** at Scalierova 1 (© **052/215-497**) book spe-cial-interest tours, including truffle-hunting excursions (in season). Several of the Pula's hotels and private accommodations, are handled by **Arena Turist** in the Riviera Hotel at Splitska 1 (© **052/529-400;** www.arenaturist.hr; 7am–8pm Mon–Sat, 8am–1pm Sun). **Atlas Travel** at Starih Statuta 1 (© **052/393-040;** www.atlas-croatia.com) is open from 7am to 8pm Monday to Saturday, 8am to 1pm Sunday. Atlas books excursions, finds private accommodations, and is Pula's American Express agent. **Istra Sun-Way** at Kandlerova 34 (© **052/381-329;** www.istra-sunway.hr) is open from 8am to midnight and books tours to the interior, so you can see some of the smaller inland towns without renting a car.

WHERE TO STAY

There are very few hotels in the center of Pula, but private accommodations are plentiful. Most hotel and beach options are south of the center in on the **Verudela Peninsula,** at **Pješčana Uvala,** or at **Stoja,** reachable on the nos. 1, 3, and 7 buses.

Expensive

Valsabbion ✦✦✦ is a boutique hotel 5.6km (3½ miles) south of the center at Pješå čana Uvala IX/26 (✆ **052/218-033**) with a stylish blend of comfortable rooms, beach, award-winning **restaurant** ✦✦✦, and spa services that help guests switch off stress. Room prices, which start at 166€ ($200) for a double, do not include breakfast, which can be added for 8.30€ ($10). Half-board is pricey, but you'll never forgive yourself if you miss the opportunity to eat as many meals as possible here.

Moderate

Book early because rooms go fast at **Scaletta** ✦✦ at Flavijevska 26 (✆ **052/541-025**), a family-run hotel in central Pula that is one of the cheeriest, best-run hotels in town. Guest rooms start at 750kn ($130/£68) for a double and they are done in soft colors; bathrooms are roomy and gleaming. Scaletta is within walking distance of the Arena and Old Town and its **restaurant** ✦✦ has been recognized as one of the seven best in Istria. The only downside is that access to reception requires some stair-climbing.

Inexpensive

Autocamp Stoja ✦✦ (✆ **052/387-144**) is about 3.2km (2 miles) southwest of the center in suburban Stoja and has 670 spaces for tents plus a bank of mobile homes that sleep up to five people each. A mobile home with air-conditioning starts at 114€ ($136) with a minimum 7-day stay. There are a beach, shops, a market, a restaurant, and sports equipment for use on the property or in the waters off the peninsula, which are some of the best for swimming and watersports.

Pula Youth Hostel ✦ at Zaljev Valsaline 4 (✆ **052/391-133**) is in a tranquil setting 4km (2½ miles) south of the center on Valsaline Bay and reachable via the no. 2 bus from Giardini near the Sergi Arch. Rooms start at 98kn ($17/£8.95) per bed and are dorm-style with four to six beds each; rates include breakfast.

WHERE TO DINE

There is no dearth of decent restaurants in central Pula, but most of the better (upscale) restaurants are in the suburbs south of the center.

Expensive

Valsabbion ✦✦✦ CREATIVE MEDITERRANEAN Unique, superb, a don't-miss experience: This is dining at Valsabbion, where Istrian specialties meet artistic sensibilities and expert preparation. Even a simple lunch can be spectacular with the "Petit Delice" or "Taste of Istria" samplers of Istrian cheeses, tapenades, or fish mousses and olives accompanied by house-made breads. Dinner is the *pièce de résistance* here, and if you can't make up your mind between the scampi rolled in Istrian ham or the chicken breast in vermouth sauce with grapes and artichokes, then try the degustation menu with 11 small portions of Valsabbion's best recipes. Don't miss the olive-oil aperitif either—three cordial glasses filled with Istrian olive oil, olive tapenade, and olive butter, with crusty bread for dipping.

Pjescana Uvala IX/26. ✆ **052/218-033.** Fax 052/383-333. www.valsabbion.net. Reservations required. Entrees 90kn–120kn ($16–$21/£8.20–£11). AE, DC, MC, V. Daily 10am–midnight.

Moderate

Bistro Kupola 🎔 *Value* CROATIAN

A magnificent view of the imposing Sergi Arch dominates the Kupola's second-floor terrace. Music from the street and concerts at the nearby amphitheater float up to the outdoor tables above Pula's T-Mobile headquarters, adding a little extra to the dining experience. Service is polite and helpful, though food is a bit tourist-driven, but why not? This is the kind of spot that demands a look-see from anyone new to Pula. Try tagliatelle Alfredo, which is sprinkled with shaved truffles; or go for spaghetti with a generous helping of seafood. The house red is an excellent Plavac Zlatni.

Trg Portarata 6. ⓒ 098/211-666. Entrees 50kn–140kn ($8.65–$24/£4.60–£13). No credit cards. Daily 8am–midnight.

Scaletta 🎔🎔 *Value* CROATIAN

The lovely Scaletta is a gastronomic delight with surprisingly sophisticated cuisine that incorporates unusual combinations of ingredients like ostrich in orange sauce with mozzarella and potatoes. The dining room has soft lighting, a marble fireplace, an attractive open bar, and a menu with lots of grilled meats and fish.

Flavijevska 26. ⓒ 053/541-025. Fax 052/541-599. www.hotel-scaletta.com. Reservations recommended. Entrees 60kn–220kn ($10–$38/£5.50–£20). AE, DC, MC, V. Mon–Sat 10am–11pm. Closed Sun.

Vela Nera 🎔🎔 CREATIVE SEAFOOD

You can watch your ship come in from Vela Nera's terrace or from the windows of its dining room perched steps away from the Sandy Bay harbor. Either way, you'll be treated to knowledgeable service and inspired cuisine. Vela Nera is more casual than Valsabbion, but no less satisfying. Try the risotto Vela Nero for an unusual taste sensation. It's made with peaches, scampi, and sparkling wine.

Pješčana Uvala bb. ⓒ 052/219-209. Fax 052/215-951. www.velanerahr. Reservations recommended. Entrees 50kn–150kn ($8.60–$26/£4.60–£14). AE, DC, MC, V. Daily 8am–midnight.

Inexpensive

Jupiter 🎔🎔 PIZZA

Pizza is the specialty at this popular place near the Forum. Jupiter has several terrace levels of dining and a huge number of pizza topping choices. Pretty good pasta, too.

Castropola 38. ⓒ 052/214-333. www.planetadria.com/Jupiter. Small pizza 15kn–40kn ($2.60–$7/£1.40–£3.65). No credit cards. Daily 9am–11pm.

EXPLORING PULA

Pula's most interesting sites are its Roman ruins, and of those, the 1st-century **Roman Amphitheater** 🎔🎔🎔 at Flavijevska bb (ⓒ **052/219-028**). Admission is 20kn ($3.45/£1.80) adults, 10kn ($1.75/90p) students, audioguide 30kn ($5.25/£2.75). It's open daily 8am to 9pm. The amphitheater closes at 4pm concert days and is most impressive. The Emperor Augustus (31–14 B.C.) started construction of the amphitheater (aka Arena) in 2 B.C.; it was finished in A.D. 14, during the rule of Vespasianus. Though smaller than Rome's Coliseum, the Arena's outer wall is almost entirely intact. Inside, vestiges of the structure's original fittings are still visible, though its stone seats were removed in medieval times to complete other building projects. The chambers under the Arena have been restored and now house a **museum** 🎔🎔🎔. During the summer, the Arena is a concert site attracting such big-name stars as Andrea Bocelli, and it is the site of the **Croatian Film Festival** (July).

The 1st-century **Temple of Augustus** ★★★ at Trg Republike 3 (no phone; admission 4kn/70¢/40p adults, 2kn/35¢/20p children; open daily in summer 10am–1:30pm and 6–9pm; closed in winter) is dedicated to Octavianus Augustus, the first emperor of Rome. It is on a square that once was the city's Forum, and it was converted to a church after Christianity became the religion of choice in Croatia. It also was used for grain storage and was severely damaged during World War II. A small museum inside has exhibit captions in English, Italian, and Croatian.

The **Sergi Arch** ★★★ opens to Trg Portarata off Sergijevaca and stands in a busy shopping area. Walk through the Sergi Arch and bear left until you get to Carrarina, where you will encounter the **Hercules Gate** ★★, dating from the mid–1st century. It is decorated with a relief of its namesake mythical hero.

Historically significant finds from all over Istria are displayed in Pula's **Archaeological Museum** ★★ at Carrarina 3 (② **052/218-603**; admission 12kn/$2.10/£1.10 adults, 6kn/$1.05/55p children; open 10am–3pm summer, Sun, and holidays; Mon–Fri 9am–3pm; closed Sat–Sun), which once was an Austrian secondary school. Be sure to visit the outdoor sculpture garden decorated with scattered pieces of history. Also note the **Roman Twin Gates** and the **Roman Theater** in back of the garden.

ROVINJ

Rovinj is one of the most photographed cities in Croatia because from the air, its location on a promontory makes it look like a fairy-tale village suspended on a pillow of bright blue sea. In fact, central Rovinj was an islet until the 18th century when the channel separating it from the mainland was filled in. Today, Rovinj's Old Town is a protected monument and one of Istria's most visited sites. The town has preserved the best of its architectural and cultural legacy by allowing development but keeping industry on the mainland, where a tobacco factory and cannery still play major roles in the local economy. Old Town Rovinj is a tangle of steep pedestrian streets that are paved with sea-salt-polished cobblestones and marked with signs in Italian and Croatian. These narrow, winding passages are lined with galleries, quaint shops, and excellent restaurants. Most lead to the town's highest point, where **St. Euphemia Church** and the tallest campanile in Istria dominate the skyline. Add to that a strong Italian personality, a thriving fleet of small fishing boats, a smattering of Venetian-style piazzas and houses, numerous restaurants and cafes with atmospheric rock walls and pounding waves, and you have a town that's both vibrant and historical.

GETTING THERE & GETTING AROUND

Rovinj is half an hour or 25km (16 miles) north of Pula and linked by well-marked roads if you are traveling by car. There is frequent bus service between Rovinj and Pula; service to and from Croatian cities that range from Osijek to Dubrovnik, and international service to select cities in Italy, Germany, and Slovenia. The main bus station is at Trg Na Lokvi 6 (② **052/811-453**; www.tzgrovinj.hr).

Rovinj is a wonderful walking city. To visit the Old Town, you'll have to leave your car in the city lot at the north end of town where fees are a modest 6kn ($1.05/55p) per hour. You can rent a bike at the lot's exit for 100kn ($17/£9.15) per day or 5kn (85¢/50p) per hour if you don't want to rely on walking or if you want to try Rovinj's picturesque bike trail. Local buses serve areas outside the Old Town area, as do taxis.

VISITOR INFORMATION

The **Rovinj Tourist Information Office** is at Pino Budičin 12 (② **052/811-566;** fax 052/816-007; www.tzgrovinj.hr). It is open from 8am to 9pm daily mid-June to mid-September; and from 8am to 3pm Monday to Saturday other times. Located just off the main square at the harbor, it has brochures, maps, and information on accommodations, the town, and its history.

WHERE TO STAY

There are very few hotels in Rovinj's city center and not many in the surrounding area either, considering the number of tourists that visit each year. However, private accommodations are abundant and usually very nice. Stop at any tourist agency, some of which set up kiosks on the road into town so you can book a room on arrival. Not only will these agencies find you a place to sleep, they will lead you to it so you can see if it suits before you pay.

Very Expensive

Eden Hotel ★★   Every room (renovated in 2004) has a couch and a balcony. The balconies overlook green space or lawn where guests can sunbathe or dine. The lunch buffet is set on a terrace under the hotel eaves where there is often live music at night. Bathrooms, balconies, and public spaces were renovated for the 2006 season.

I Adamovića. (C) **052/800-250.** Fax 052/800-215. www.maistra.hr. 325 units. Aug from 192€ ($246) double; rest of year from 82€ ($105) double. 50% reduction for children 2–11; free for children under 2. Rates include breakfast and are based on stays exceeding 3 days. 20% surcharge for stays of 3 or fewer days. Half-board available on request. AE, DC, MC, V. **Amenities:** Restaurant; bar; 2 pools; Internet; babysitting 10am–5pm (included in room rate). *In room:* A/C, TV, minibar, hair dryer, safe.

Villa Angelo d'Oro ★★★   This 17th-century bishop's palace in the Old Town was renovated in 2001 and has been kept in superb condition ever since. Each room is unique in size and decor with plush period furniture and fresh colors. Bathrooms have modern fixtures, though most have showers rather than tubs. Guests can treat themselves to one of the best views in the city from the open-air balcony off the third-floor library before or after they dine in the hotel's **restaurant** ★★★. Parking is .5km (¼ mile) from the hotel, but the staff will pick up and deliver guests from their cars.

Via Svalba 38–42. (C) **052/840-502.** www.rovinj.at. 25 units. Mid-July to mid-Sept from 1,455kn ($251/£136) double. Rest of year from 844kn ($146/£77) double. 50% discount for children 3–11; free for children under 3. Rates include breakfast. Half-board available on request for 185kn ($32/£17) per person. AE, DC, MC, V. Limited free parking. **Amenities:** Restaurant; terrace dining; wine cellar; Jacuzzi; solarium; library. *In room:* A/C, TV, minibar, hair dryer.

Expensive

Hotel Park ★★   From the front, this 1972 structure looks like another impersonal tourist hotel. The Park might offer packages, but it is surprisingly user-friendly. Rooms are done in yellows and blues in modest but comfortable style. The Park also has a long list of guest amenities and services as well as a spectacular view of St. Catherine Island and Old Town Rovinj from the balcony off its lobby. The Park is conveniently located 2 minutes from **Zlatni Rt-Punta Corrente Nature Park** and 5 minutes from Old Town. Despite its size, the hotel fills up from May to October. Call no later than April for reservations.

IM Ronjigova. (C) **052/811-077.** Fax 052/816-977. www.maistra.hr. 237 units. Aug from 164€ ($210) double; rest of year from 73€ ($87) double. 50% discount for children 2–11; free for children under 2. Rates include breakfast and are based on stays exceeding 3 days. 20% surcharge for stays of 3 or fewer days. Half-board available on request. AE, DC, MC, V. Closed 2 months each year, usually mid-Dec to mid-Feb. **Amenities:** Restaurant; bar; ice-cream parlor; 3 pools; excursions; kids' programs; Internet; exchange office; salon; babysitting. *In room:* A/C, TV, hair dryer.

WHERE TO DINE

Restaurants that line the waterfront are touristy and predictable, and prices are a bit inflated. However, all serve respectable seafood and excellent pizza and pasta. Venture a little farther afield for menus that go beyond the expected.

Very Expensive

Amfora ★★★ SEAFOOD   The fish is fresh and the ambience cheerful in this beautiful restaurant that overlooks the marina and Old Town. Amfora is a cut above most waterfront dining both in its cuisine and service—and that is also reflected in its prices. However, if you want first-class seafood, Amfora can't be beat. Try the salted sea bass or a risotto and pair it with one of the restaurant's excellent wines. Closed early January to early March.

A. Rismondo 23. ✆ 052/816-663. Entrees 90kn–175kn ($16–$30/£8.20–£16). AE, DC, MC, V. Daily 11am–midnight.

Angelo d'Oro ★★★ ISTRIAN   During the summer, the restaurant moves to a lovely walled garden, and in winter it settles in an imaginatively styled room inside. Either way, the cuisine is creative and beautifully presented. Try the cream of potato soup with truffles or a grilled fish dish. Don't miss a tour of the stone wine cellar, where you can taste Istrian wines and local specialties such as Istrian ham or cheese.

Via Svalba 38–42. ✆ 052/840-502. www.rovinj.at. Reservations recommended. Entrees 90kn–165kn ($16–$29/£8.20–£15). AE, DC, MC. Daily 7pm–midnight.

Expensive

Konoba Veli Jože ★ ISTRIAN   This rather dark dining room is so loaded with Croatian tchotchkes that they spill over to the outdoor tables, The food is first-rate and really representative of traditional Istrian cuisine. Try the *fuži* with truffles for a taste of the distinctive Istrian pasta and celebrated specialty. Or dig into one of Veli Jože's lamb or fish dishes, which are a bit expensive but worth the extra cost.

Svetog Križa 1. ✆ 052/816-337. Entrees 30kn–120kn ($5.20–$21/£2.75–£11). AE, DC, MC, V. Daily 10am–3am.

Taverna da Baston ★★ ISTRIAN/SEAFOOD   A warm welcome will make you feel at home at this bustling place next door to Rovinj's fish market. Dark brick walls are hung with fishing nets, and local music provides background. Try any of the superfresh fish dishes or the handmade gnocchi with truffles.

Svalba 3. ✆ 098/982-63-95. Entrees 50kn–150kn ($8.65–$26/£4.60–£14). AE, DC, MC, V. Prices include tax, *couvert*, and service. Daily 6am–midnight .

Moderate

Calisona ★ ITALIAN   Calisona, across from the town museum, can get very busy at lunch, partly because of its location and nicely shaded tables, and partly because of its reasonably priced food. Pizza, spaghetti, and risotto are the specialties at Calisona, though there are some grilled fish and meat dishes such as veal medallions, too. The menu is multilingual.

Trg Pignaton 1. ✆ 052/815-313. Entrees 30kn–100kn ($5.20–$17/£2.75–£9.15). AE, MC, V. Daily 8am–midnight.

Gostonica Cisterna ★★ (Value ITALIAN   Inside, stone walls and old farm implements create a rustic ambience. Outside, 12 tables with pink tablecloths beckon passersby to see what smells so good. The seductive aroma will usually be fish on the restaurant's grill or risottos simmering on the stove. Cisterna is in a small courtyard at the bottom of Grisia near the Balbi Arch—easy to miss if you're not looking for it.

Trg Matteotti 3. ℂ 052/811-334. Entrees 35kn–100kn ($6–$17/£3.20–£9.15). AE, DC, MC, V. Daily 8am–3pm and 6pm–midnight.

Inexpensive

Stella di Mare ★★ *(Value* PIZZERIA/SPAGHETTERIA   This laid-back restaurant is so close to the water that sea spray occasionally mists over outdoor tables when waves hit the rocky shoreline. Views of old Rovinj, boats in the harbor, gulls catching dinner, and the roiling sea are incomparable from the restaurant's blue-and-white umbrella tables. A few seafood dishes complement the pizza and pasta offerings. For a local treat, try *koki sa jajem* pizza, a crispy crust topped with cheese, tomato, prosciutto, and an egg (added raw but baked into the mix).

Croche 4. ℂ 091/528-88-83. Pizzas 28kn–45kn ($4.85–$7.75/£2.55–£4.10); pasta from 35kn ($6/£3.20). AE, DC, MC, V. Daily 8am–midnight.

EXPLORING ROVINJ

Rovinj is a browser's paradise, with lots of places to explore on its narrow, winding streets. Rovinj is also an aesthetic gem, and its beauty is readily apparent from a distance and close up. Most sites worth exploring are in the Old Town, plus places farther afield like **Zlatni Rt-Punta Corrente Nature Park** ★★, a densely forested park just steps from the **Hotel Park.** Zlatni Rt is rimmed with rocky beaches and full of hiking paths. **Limska Draga Fjord** ★★★ is a flooded karstic canyon less than 16km (10 miles) north of Rovinj. It looks like a ribbon of clear blue-green water framed with forested walls on two sides. At least two caves with evidence of prehistoric habitation have been discovered there, and several local legends say that pirates used the inlet as a base for surprising merchant ships. Excursions to Limska Draga leave from Rovinj daily and often can be booked directly at seaside or from any travel agency in town for about 190kn ($33/£17) per person.

Balbi Arch ★★   Enter Old Town from the main square through the 17th-century Balbi Arch, which leads up to Grisia, Rovinj's most interesting street. The arch is on the site where one of the town's seven gates once stood; it is carved with a Turk's head on one side and a Venetian's head on the other.

St. Euphemia Church ★★   The baroque church dedicated to Rovinj's co–patron saint is the third iteration of the shrine built in her honor. The present church was built atop Rovinj's highest hill in the early 18th century and the adjacent **bell tower** was built 50 years earlier and is one of the highest campaniles in Istria. It is topped with a copper statue of St. Euphemia that includes a palm and a wheel, symbols of her martyrdom. The people of Rovinj made St. Euphemia a patron saint of the city along with St. George after the stone sarcophagus containing her body mysteriously showed up on their shores following its disappearance from Constantinople in A.D. 800.

Petro Stankovića. ℂ 052/815-615. Daily summer 10am–3pm; only during Mass other times.

POREČ

"Something for everyone" could be Poreč's motto—the seaside resort 67km (42 miles) north of Pula offers everything from a UNESCO World Heritage basilica complex to endless shopping opportunities to slick resort hotels so crammed with activities and services that you think you're in DisneyWorld. Poreč courts tourism, supports tourism, and profits from tourism, but the town and surrounding area still manage to intrigue, perhaps because they are a seamless blend of medieval heritage, a well-oiled

---

Finds **Grisia Street Standouts**

Rovinj's main street is really a steep, cobbled passageway that runs from the main square all the way up to St. Euphemia Church. It is lined with shops and galleries and buildings that still sport vestiges of the town's medieval roots. **Galerija Peti-Božić** at no. 22 is one of the most pleasant and most interesting. This tiny shop specializes in Croatian naive art created by Marija Peti-Božić, who has shown her work in galleries and museums in Zagreb and elsewhere in Europe. Most of Peti-Božić's work is oil on glass, typical of the Hlebine School. The shop is run by the artist's jovial husband, who will proudly rattle off his wife's accomplishments as well as wrap your purchases securely for travel.

Another Grisia Street shop worth a stop is no. 37, where award-winning artist **Olga Vicel** creates naive art in another medium—embroideries using silk thread on linen. Framed pieces run 50€ to 500€ ($60–$600). Galerija Peti-Božić, Grisia 22 (© 091/578-65-28), is usually open Easter through October 8am to 10pm daily. (Call to confirm opening hours.)

August is officially the month of Grisia's art celebration; during this month, shops and restaurants remain open as long as there are people in the streets.

---

service industry, idyllic vineyards and olive groves, and blatant commercialism. Old Town's immaculate cobblestone streets, precisely clipped plantings, multilingual signs, plus enough jewelry stores and gelaterias for every tourist in Croatia are the draw.

It's no mystery why visitors love Poreč: It has a sophisticated tourism infrastructure that lets everyone have a good time without feeling hassled. Poreč is conveniently connected to transportation for exploring the Istrian Riviera or interior.

GETTING THERE & GETTING AROUND
Poreč is just 42km (26 miles) north of Rovinj and a stop on Istria's coastal bus route. (Go to www.autotrans.hr and click on the Istra-Promet button at the bottom of the page for schedules and timetables.) If you are driving, allow 45 minutes for the trip from Rovinj because you will have to go around the Limski Fjord. Poreč's Old Town is easy to navigate on foot, though its end-to-end shopping opportunities might slow you down. City buses serve the Lanterna complex south of town (the bus station is .5km/¼ mile from the town center) as well as nearby spots like Tar, but a car is necessary if you want to stay in one of the charming family-run inns outside the center or if you want to explore the surrounding area.

VISITOR INFORMATION
Poreč knows how to make visitors feel at home. The **Poreč Tourist Information Office** (Zagrebačka 11; © 052/434-983; www.istra.com/porec) can provide maps and brochures as well as leads on available accommodations and events. It is open 8am to 10pm Monday to Saturday all year and 9am to 1pm and 6 to 10pm Sundays during July and August. **Atlas Travel Agency** (Eufrazijeva 63; © 052/434-983; www.atlas.hr) can arrange excursions, hotels, private accommodations, and airline reservations. It is also the local American Express agent. **Di Tours** ⋆⋆ (Prvomajska 2;

© 052/432-100; fax 052/431-300; www.di-tours.com) is one of many private tourist agencies in town, but it has a huge inventory of rooms and apartments in Poreč and vicinity. In August, it offers doubles with shower from 28€ ($34), apartments from 45€ ($54). During the rest of the year, doubles start at 12€ ($15), apartments from 16€ ($19).

WHERE TO STAY
Poreč is the most visited city in Istria, and it has a wide inventory of accommodations. Most hotels are managed by Riviera, but there is a lot of variety available, especially if you opt for a small hotel outside the center.

Expensive
Diamant *★★★* *Value*   Guest rooms are huge and more like suites in this beautifully restored (2003) hotel less than a mile from Poreč's center. Most rooms have balconies and glass doors that are tinted and shaded, plus two bathrooms, one with a tub, and the 10th floor is all suites. The Diamant is also notable for its effort to make the entire hotel accessible to travelers with disabilities. Service is personal and helpful, more typical of small boutique establishments than huge package hotels. The same is true of the hotel's special bike tour that stops at local wineries, farms, olive groves, and monuments, and features a gourmet picnic.

Brulo. *©* 052/400-000. Fax 052/451-206. www.riviera.hr. 244 units. End of July to mid-Aug from 152€ ($181) double; rest of year from 68€ ($81) double. Rates include breakfast and are per person daily based on a stay of 4 or more days. 20% surcharge for stays of 3 days or fewer. AE, DC, MC, V. **Amenities:** 2 restaurants; bar; Internet cafe; juice bar; 2 pools; hot tub; whirlpool; kids' program; excursions; massage; solarium. *In room:* A/C, TV, minibar, hair dryer.

Moderate
Neptun *★*   Neptun has a great location facing the sea. It was built in 1968, renovated in 1995, and improved every year since, though air-conditioning was not part of the plan. Some rooms have dynamite harbor views, as does the rooftop cafe, which is closed during very hot weather. Bathrooms are adequate but have showers and no tubs. Reception is very helpful and pleasant and also handles details for guests of the hotel's two annexes.

Maršala Tita 17. *©* 052/408-800. Fax 052/431-351. www.riviera.hr. 145 units. July 30 to mid-Aug from 96€ ($114) double; rest of year from 68€ ($81) double. Rates include breakfast. AE, DC, MC, V. Half-board available. Discounts for children in the same room as parents. **Amenities:** Restaurant; bar. *In room:* TV, minibar, hair dryer.

Inexpensive
Bijela Uvala *★★★*   Located between Funtana and Poreč, this environment-friendly campground uses solar power and practices ecologically oriented camp management: The camp also offers a large pebble beach with paved sunning areas and lots of programs to amuse the kids.

52440 Poreč. *©* 052/410-551. Fax 052/410-600. www.plavalaguna.hr. July–Aug campsite with tent, car, and 2 people 27€ ($32) per day; rest of year from 14€ ($17). AE, DC, MC. Closed Nov–Mar.

Lanternacamp *★★★*   If you must stay at a huge campground, Lanternacamp is one of the best, with more than 3,000 spaces for tents and/or campers. Lanterna wisely provides plenty of amenities such as electricity and water hookups, superclean bathrooms, supermarkets, a laundry, a pool, and activities for kids. The camp is 13km (8 miles) from Poreč.

52440 Poreč. *©* 052/404-500. Fax 052/404-591. www.riviera.hr. From 35€ ($45) per night for campsite and 2 people. AE, MC, V. Closed Nov–Mar.

Villa Filipini ★★ *Value*   This family-run place 10 minutes from Poreč opened in 2003 and is done in pine to resemble a rustic farmhouse. Mom serves breakfast and Dad is the accountant/handyman, while their son manages the desk and waits on diners in the inn's **restaurant** ★★★. Guest rooms are exceptionally clean and comfy, with French doors that open to the terrace. Upper-floor suites have balconies. You can meet the family's world-champion Istrian hunter in its home at the dog kennel behind the hotel.

Filipini 1B. © 052/463-200. www.istra.com/filipini. 8 units. From 46€ ($55) double; from 92€ ($110) suite. Rates include breakfast. Half-board available. AE, DC, MC, V. Limited free parking. **Amenities:** Restaurant; bar; tennis court; bicycle rental; laundry service. *In room:* A/C, TV, Internet access.

WHERE TO DINE

Dining in Old Town Poreč tends to be a one-note experience: Almost all the restaurants rely on pizza, pasta, and grilled seafood for their menu mainstays. If you want to taste authentic grilled lamb or more unusual Istrian preparations, your best bet is to get out of Old Town.

Very Expensive

Cardo ★★ SEAFOOD   This classy terrace restaurant proudly displays its fish in an outdoor ice case for all to see. A gnarled olive tree and soft lights surrounding the terrace create a romantic mood for diners at the outdoor tables, which are always full. Try the salmon piquant or noodles with mussels, either of which is perfect with a glass of Istrian Malvasia.

Cardo Maximus 6. Old Town. © 052/255-164. Entrees 35kn–330kn ($6–$57/£3.20–£30). AE, DC, MC, V. Daily Apr 1–Nov 1 noon–midnight.

Gostonica Istria ★★   Locals rave about the seafood at Gostonica Istria, a typical indoor/outdoor coastal place where people-watching from the terrace is a side dish. Istria's multi-language menu makes it easy to order. You'll get expertly prepared authentic Istrian cuisine here such as minestrone, fuži, and spiny lobster with noodles. Service is accommodating even if the prices are a little high.

Msgr. Bože Milanovića 30. © 052/434-63. Fax 052/451-482. Entrees 65kn–190kn ($11–$33/£5.95–£17). AE, DC. Daily noon–midnight.

Expensive

Gostonica Gurman ★★★ SEAFOOD   If you order lobster, your waiter will ask you to choose one from a box of live crustaceans. It's not a gimmick for tourists but a sincere effort to give diners the best meal possible. This tiny place in a square off the harbor relies on fresh seafood, steak so tender you can cut it with a butter knife, and one gregarious waiter who has so much energy you'll wonder if he can bilocate.

Trg Frane Supila 5. No phone. Entrees 40kn–130kn ($7–$23/£3.65–£12). AE, DC, MC, V. Daily 11am–midnight.

Restaurant Villa Filipini ★★★ *Finds* ISTRIAN   Pastas are handmade and the kitchen is imaginative in this tiny restaurant in one of Istria's best rural small hotels. Seating on the outdoor terrace gives the impression that you're dining in a forest. The chef bases his dishes on what is fresh in the market and choices can include green gnocchi with mixed cheese and walnut sauce, or ravioli filled with fresh cheese in herb butter. Fish dishes and sauces are particular strengths, as are the excellent wine list and creative sweet treats such as gelato on fresh cheese with sage honey and chocolate sauce.

Filipini 1B. © 052/463-200. www.istra.com/filipini. Entrees 40kn–150kn ($6.90–$26/£3.65–£14). AE, DC, MC, V. Daily noon–11pm.

Moderate

Old Pub Cotton Club ☆ PIZZA/PASTA   The burgundy awnings make Cotton Club look like a tourist trap, but serious food is prepared here. Try the tortellini *mille voglie* (with clams); or the tortellini with pršut, pumpkin, cream, and truffles. Pasta and pizza are emphasized, including nine kinds of tagliatelle, 20 kinds of pizza, risottos, good drinks, ice creams, and live music weekend evenings.

Trg Slobode 5. ℂ **052/453-293**. Fax 052/432-074. Entrees 40kn–110kn ($6.90–$19/£3.65–£10). No credit cards. Daily 9am–1am.

Ulixes ☆ ISTRIAN   The atmosphere at Ulixes is softened by indirect lighting on its courtyard walls, olive trees, soft music, and cats that beg for handouts from diners. When you order, however, stick with fish dishes, which are competently prepared, or try a pasta like fuži with game. Portions are on the small side, even for Croatia.

Decumanus 2. ℂ **052/451-132**. www.istra.com/ulixes. Entrees 40kn–110kn ($7–$19/£3.65–£10). DC, MC, V. Daily noon–midnight.

Inexpensive

Barilla ☆ PIZZA/PASTA   This casual restaurant *is* related to the pasta in the blue box you can get in American grocery stores. There are (understandably) a huge pasta menu and a few grilled meat/fish selections, but dine at Barilla for the 31 kinds of pizza baked in a brick oven.

Eufrazijeva 26. ℂ **052/452-742**. Small pizza 40kn–60kn ($6.90–$10/£3.65–£5.50). DC, MC, V. Daily noon–midnight.

Stari Saloon BISTRO/PIZZERIA ☆☆ 🅥alue   This pizza joint is in a courtyard surrounded by buildings, but that doesn't stop people from jamming the restaurant nightly. Instead of sizing its pizza as small, medium, or large, Stari Saloon lists pie diameters in centimeters. Extra-large pizzas are a whopping 75 centimeters (29 in.) across and served on a wooden disk the size of a small tabletop. Pizza prices start at 55kn ($9.50/£5.15).

Ribarski Trg. ℂ **052/453-228**. Entrees 35kn–110kn ($6–$19/£3.20–£10). AE, DC, MC, V. Daily 10am–11pm.

EXPLORING POREČ

Poreč's Old Town is small but packed with treasures, chief of which is the Euphrasius Basilica and its stunning **mosaics** ☆☆☆. The rest of Old Town's attractions pale in comparison but are interesting enough to warrant a walk-through.

Euphrasian Basilica Complex ☆☆   UNESCO has put this collection of early Christian and Byzantine architecture on its World Heritage List, and you should put them on your "must-see" agenda, too. The basilica is the last of four churches that were built one on top of the other on this site between the 4th and 6th centuries. Besides the basilica, there are an atrium, a baptistery, a bell tower, and a bishop's palace in the complex, which is entered through the arches of the atrium. Even if you aren't into visiting churches, make an effort to see the complex's spectacular **gem-studded mosaics** ☆☆☆ as well as the symbolic early Christian fish mosaic.

Summer daily 7:30am–8pm. Other times during Mass only. Bell tower daily 10am–7pm, 10kn ($1.75/90p).

Trg Marafor ☆☆   The remains of two Roman temples (Mars and Neptune) are the highlight of Marafor, which once was the site of a Roman forum. Today, Marafor is home to several sleek cocktail bars and jazz clubs such as **Lapidarium,** which is tucked into a courtyard strewn with ancient artifacts. Jazz concerts fill the courtyard during the season.

St. Nicholas Island ★★★   Porec's better beaches are off this close-in island, which is a short boat taxi ride away from the harbor.

Taxi boats leave the dock every half-hour.

Baredine Cave ★★★   Excursions to these limestone caverns are among the most popular in Poreč. Just 7km (4½ miles) northeast of town on the road to Višjan, the caves are filled with stalactites and stalagmites. Entry fees cover the services of a guide, who takes you on a 40-minute tour of the underground halls and galleries and tells the story of the cave's legendary ill-fated lovers who died while looking for each other in the subterranean maze.

Nova Vas 52446. ⓒ 052/421-333. www.istra.com/baredine. 45kn ($7.75/£4.10). July–Aug daily 9:30am–6pm; May–June and Sept daily 10am–5pm; Apr and Oct daily 10am–4pm; Nov–Mar for prearranged groups only.

INLAND ISTRIA

It isn't easy being green in a country where seawater blue is the dominant color, but the Istria's emerald interior hints at the unspoiled nature and unique experiences that await those who venture into this often overlooked part of Croatia. As you exit the deep blackness of **Učka Tunnel** in the east or as you drive away from the golden brightness of the **Istrian Coast** in the west, you realize that this is territory that feeds the senses—all of them. In **Green Istria** you can take time to breathe the perfumed air, listen to the bird chatter, touch the rough stone of a medieval castle, or savor the taste of local wines. Here travelers can immerse themselves in the land and the lives of the people who live there. It's a place you can wander through but never feel lost.

GETTING THERE & GETTING AROUND

No matter how you get to Istria, unless you are on a guided excursion, you will need a car to thoroughly explore its inland attractions.

Most towns in inland Istria are small; in fact, one of them, **Hum,** is the smallest town in the world. The main attractions in Istria's inland towns can be readily accessed by walking but many are extremely hilly and must be approached on foot over irregular cobblestone streets, which can be difficult for some. To get to **Motovun,** for example, you have to leave your car at the bottom of a steep street and walk more than a quarter of a mile uphill. Some inland towns are remote, so driving is the only practical way to cover the distance between them.

VISITOR INFORMATION

Every town in Green Istria has its own tourist information center, though those in the smaller towns have very limited hours and are difficult to find. To help visitors get the most out of a trip, the **Istria County Tourist Association** has produced attractive publications on farmhouse stays, cultural itineraries, wine roads, olive-oil roads, and trufflehunting opportunities. These are available through the association, whose main offices are in Poreč at Pionirska 1 (ⓒ **052/452-797;** fax 052/452-796; tzzi-po@pu.hinet.hr), and in Pula at Forum 3 (ⓒ **052/215-799;** fax 052/215-722). The association also maintains a website with English-language links to almost every town: **www.istra.com**.

MOTOVUN, ROČ & HUM

Motovun is one of Istria's better-known interior towns, perhaps because it hosts the **Motovun Film Festival** (www.motovunfilmfestival.com; early Aug, but dates are variable), hot-air balloon competitions, and a festival celebrating truffles and wine. It also doesn't hurt that this hilltop town is just 20 minutes east of Poreč and home to the delightful **Hotel Kaštel** 🏨🏨.

One of the most compelling reasons to stop at nearby **Roč** is its location at one end of the **Glagolitic Alley.** A string of 10 outdoor sculptures that dot the road between Roč and Hum was erected between 1977 and 1981 to celebrate and preserve Glagolitic script. Even though there aren't any explanations on most of them, the sculptures (dedicated to Glagolitic scholars) are interesting to look at. Today Roč is primarily known as a center of Glagolitic literature, and every year the town puts on the **Small Glagolitic Academy** to keep the traditional writing alive. Private rooms are available in Roč (there are signs on the road), and there is a decent konoba. The short strip of road that links Roč and **Hum** is just 6.4km (4 miles) long, but it is a historic corridor because of the commemorative Glagolitic sculptures along the way. Even though Hum's claim to fame is its status as the world's smallest town, from the looks of tourism in the present-day village, that could be changing. Tiny Hum has spiffed up in the last 3 years and is quite appealing. Only about 20 permanent residents live within its well-preserved walls, which enclose two small streets and two churches (one dating from the 12th c.).

GETTING THERE & GETTING AROUND
Istria's inter-city buses (www.autotrans.hr) serve Motuvun, Roc, and Hum, but service can be slow and erratic. Renting a car or booking a guided excursion are the most efficient ways to see these tiny treasures. The important sites in all these towns can be easily accessed on foot.

VISITOR INFORMATION
Information on all three towns and their festivals is available at the **Istria County Tourist Offices** in Pula and Poreč and in each town's local bureau. Motovun's tourist office is at Andrea Antico bb (© 052/681-642); the **Tourist Information Office** in Buzet serves Roč and Hum. It is at Trg Fontana 7/1 in Buzet (© 052/662-343; www.tzg-buje.hr) and can provide information on private accommodations, including farmhouse stays, camping, and events.

WHERE TO STAY & DINE
Besides the Hotel Kaštel in Motovun, the only accommodations in these villages are in private homes, making this an ideal area to try a farmhouse stay and to savor the flavors of Istria at a local dining establishment.

Hotel Kaštel 🏨🏨 in Motovun at Trg Andrea Antico 7 (© 052/681-607) provides panoramic views of the Mirna valley and each guest room offers a different perspective. Guest rooms, which start at 70€ ($84) for a double, were refurbished in 2003 and are equipped with modern bathrooms that don't destroy the character of the 17th-century structure, which once was a palace. If you call ahead, the hotel will pick you up at the bottom of the street leading into Motovun so you don't have to drag your luggage uphill.

Barbacan Enoteque & Restaurant 🏨 on the main walkway into Motovun at Barbakan 1 (© 052/681-791) is pricier than most, but it's also more interesting. Start with the pâté of veal sweetbreads with truffles or the truffled chicken broth. Entrees include filet of beef with black truffle butter, and risotto Montonese with saffron garlic and truffles.

Restoran Kaštel ★★ in Motovun at the Hotel Kaštel at Trg Andrea Antico 7 (© **052/681-607**) serves unusual Istrian dishes as well as a signature dessert that's not on the menu. Try the *frkanci* with venison goulash. The pasta, which is a hybrid gnocchi/noodle, is handmade by Istrian home cooks just for the hotel. Ask for the special chocolate truffle for dessert—it's the size of an egg.

You'll feel like you're in Mom's kitchen in **Ročka Konoba** ★★ in Roč (© **052/660-005**), a rustic dining room with a great view of the rolling countryside. Local specials such as fuži, spicy Istrian sausage, hearty soups, and fragrant homemade bread are on the menu.

Humska Konoba ★★ in tiny Hum at Hum 2 (© **052/660-005**) puts local flavor in the food and atmosphere in this wood-and-stone building. If you dare, sip home-brewed *biska*, a grape brandy–based aperitif flavored with white mistletoe and other herbs. Forget about cholesterol and dig into a meal of home-smoked meat with sauerkraut and have *krostole* (doughnuts) for dessert.

THE KVARNER GULF

It's fairly simple to visit all the major mainland towns that skirt the Kvarner coast by driving Croatia's version of California's Highway 1 from Opatija to Senj, but it's much trickier to coordinate ferry connections to, from, and between the Kvarner islands.

RIJEKA

142km (88 miles) SW of Zagreb; 615km (382 miles) NE of Dubrovnik

No matter which part of the Kvarner Gulf region you choose to explore, you'll probably go through Rijeka, which is at the southern end of the Zagreb-Rijeka autocesta. There are no beaches or resorts on Rijeka's shores, so most people breeze past on their way to somewhere else without a thought to stopping. Rijeka's magnificent collection of 19th-century buildings and monuments *could* use a good power-washing and a little paint, but the city does have attractions worth investigating.

GETTING THERE & GETTING AROUND

BY CAR   Almost all roads in Croatia eventually lead to Rijeka, but you can drive there from Zagreb in less than 2 hours on the Zagreb-Rijeka autocesta (A-6) from the north. A-6 also connects to the A-1 autocesta from Split in the south. From Ljubljana in Slovenia, take E-70 via Postojna and connect with local Route 6 at Illirska Bistrica. You will encounter a border crossing at Rupa (*warning:* Occasionally there is some hassle here, so be sure your documents are in order) and follow E-61 to Rijeka. Ferries from several nearby islands stop at Rijeka and dock near the Riva, south of the center. A schedule and prices can be obtained from www.jadrolinija.hr; or call © **06/032-13-21** for schedule and price info.

BY TRAIN   Except for fast-train service between Zagreb and Split, rail service in Croatia can be cumbersome, but the train stations are usually something to see. That's especially true of the terminal in Rijeka, which is straight out of 19th-century Hungary. Trains that stop there connect with Opatija and other Croatian towns and with some European hubs, too. For a schedule, check the HZ website, www.hznet.hr, which has routes and prices in English. Or you can call the central office (Željeznički Kolodvor; © **060/333444**), though you might not be able to find anyone who speaks English. The station's ticket office is open from 9am to 4pm and from 5:30 to 8:45pm. At other times you can buy tickets on the train.

Rijeka's Morčićl (Moretto, Moro)

This ceramic-and-gold rendering of a black woman in a turban has become a symbol of Rijeka and a distinctive design for jewelry, where the baubles are made. The colorful Mořić is mostly used in earrings, though the image of a Moorish woman is a popular mask worn by revelers during Rijeka's huge pre-Lenten carnival. There are many legends about the Morčić, including tales of victory over the Turks thanks to a woman's prayers, but in reality, the Mořić probably is a vestige of 17th- and 18th-century European fashion, which was mad about anything Asian. As earrings, Morčić were worn by upper-class married women, sailors, fishermen, and only-sons (in the right ear) to ward off evil spirits.

BY BUS   Buses to and from Rijeka connecting with other parts of Croatia run frequently and fares are affordable. A one-way ticket to Zagreb costs $2 to $24 depending on the route. Buses also connect with other cities in Europe. The main bus hub is at Trg Žabica 1 and is open from 5:30am to 9pm (© **060/302 010** reservations and information). You can also buy tickets on board the bus, but getting a seat is uncertain in summer.

BY PLANE   You can get to Rijeka by air, though the airport is actually near **Omišlj** on **Krk Island** 24km (15 miles) south of the city. After you deplane, you can get to town on the Autotrolej bus, which lets you off at the station at Jelačić Square for $3 one-way. Or you can grab a taxi outside the airport and pay as much as $45 for the same ride. Call the Rijeka airport (© **051/842-040**); for flight info, call © **05484-21-32** or check www.rijeka-airport.hr.

GETTING AROUND

Navigating Rijeka and the surrounding area is fairly easy whether you wander around the center or go farther afield. City bus tickets can be purchased at **Tisak** kiosks (newsstands) or from the bus driver, and fares depend on how far you are going. You can go to **Lovran** for $3.60, or to the nearby 'burb of **Trsat** for less than $2. Walking is the favorite travel mode in Rijeka, and maps and other information about restaurants, shows, and monuments can be obtained at the **tourist office** at Korzo 33 (© **051/335-882;** www.tz-rijeka.hr).

Taxis are plentiful and you can hail one off the street that will take you anywhere within the city limits, but you should always confirm the fare with your driver before getting in the car. Buses are also abundant and make regular runs from 5am to 11:30pm daily.

WHERE TO STAY & DINE IN RIJEKA

Despite its position as the third-largest metropolis in Croatia, Rijeka has few standout hotel and dining options.

The 125-year-old **Grand Hotel Bonavia** ✦ at Dolac 4 (© **051/357-100**) in the city's Old Town was completely redone in 2000 with big-city amenities and a covered dining terrace. The standard rooms are a bit tight for 840kn ($145/£77) for a double, but for an extra $30 or so you can get a notably larger space or even a suite with a view. Some rooms have balconies; all have roomy tiled bathrooms.

The **Continental Hotel** at Šetalište Andrije Kačiča-Miošiča (© **051/372-008**) looms over the park in Rijeka's center, but its exterior is far more elegant-looking than the rooms inside. Doubles, while clean and plain, offer few extras and go for 450kn ($78/£41) for a double. Public areas are a bit shabby but the hotel does have a nice terrace, and the coffeehouse serves great desserts.

The ambitious **Bonavia Classic** ◈ at Dolac 4 (© **051/357-100**), in the **Hotel Bonavia** ◈, has a menu that combines the best of Croatian produce with inspired preparations. Begin with piquant octopus soup before you try the Riga, a salad of bitter greens and lobster. Splurge on the Symphony Bonavia, a mélange of beef, veal, and pork filets grilled and accented with Gorgonzola.

Order a *plat du jour* at unpretentious Zalogajnica Grandis Placa at Zagrebačka 16 (© **051/331-981**) and you won't be hungry for a week. ZGP specializes in such classics as stew, goulash, and casseroles. You can see what the locals eat without emptying your wallet.

EXPLORING RIJEKA

The wide pedestrian street called **Korzo** ◈◈ was originally constructed along the path of the town walls and today it is lined with stores, cafes, restaurants, and even an enclosed mall. However, most stores close at 1pm on Saturday and don't reopen until Monday morning, making the area pretty dead on weekends.

The bright yellow **Gradski Toranj (City Tower)** ◈ above the city gate was one of the few structures left standing after the powerful 1750 quake, but it was renovated and tinkered with for 140 years or so after the seismic event, which further altered its appearance. The clock was added in 1873 and the dome on its top in 1890. Walk through the portal below the Tower to **Trg Ivana Koblera,** where you will run into the **Stara Vrata (Roman Gate),** Rijeka's oldest surviving structure. The Stara Vrata once served as the portal to the Roman Praetorium, which was Rijeka's military command center. Much of Rijeka's Old Town (Stari Grad) was demolished to make way for modern infrastructure, but you still can see remnants of the ancient city of **Tarsatica** that once stood in what is now in the vicinity of **St. Vitus Church** ◈◈ at Trg Grivica 11 (© **051/330-879**). According to legend, when a disgruntled 13th-century gambler threw a rock at the crucifix on St. Vitus's main altar, the rendering of Christ's body on the cross began to bleed and the gambler was swallowed up by the earth except for his hand.

OPATIJA

Less than 16km (10 miles) west of Rijeka, Opatija and its adjacent villages are everything Rijeka is not—vibrant, welcoming, clean, and full of clear-water beaches, breathtaking views, comfortable accommodations, and excellent restaurants.

Opatija started as a fishing village with a church and a population in the low double digits. But in the mid–19th century, the mild climate and spectacular seashore caught the fancy of **Iginio Scarpa,** a wealthy Italian businessman who built the lavish **Villa Angiolina** (named after his dead wife), surrounded it with a jungle of exotic flora from around the world, and invited all his aristocratic friends for a visit. Privileged Europeans were so taken with Villa Angiolina and Opatija that one by one they erected villas of their own, each bigger and more ornate than the next, thus cementing Opatija's reputation as a winter playground for the wealthy.

GETTING THERE & GETTING AROUND

BY CAR If you've driven to Rijeka, it's only another 20 minutes to Opatija via the coastal highway.

BY BUS The bus (no. 32) stops in front of the Rijeka train station and travels the length of the Riviera to Lovran every 20 minutes for 10kn ($1.90/90p) one-way.

Once in Opatija, walking throughout the town and to nearby villages is customary.

WHERE TO STAY & DINE

The **Millennium** ☆☆ at Maršala Tita 109 (✆ **051/202-000**) has oversize bathrooms that are better than average, with double marble sinks and little conveniences like retractable clotheslines. The windows have remote-control awnings, but the pillows are flat as pancakes, and the towels are skimpy. Guests have pool and gym privileges, and the staff will make dinner reservations, call a cab, or send your faxes, but doubles that start at 170€ ($217) are steep considering that most other services require an extra fee.

The lemon-drop-yellow **Bristol** ☆☆, at Maršala Tita 108 (✆ **051/706-300**), reopened in late June 2005 after an extensive renovation that ended 15 years of being closed to the public while it sheltered Slavoninan Croats who were displaced by the 1991 war. Happily, the Bristol is now a sophisticated, tasteful showpiece with doubles starting at 156€ ($200). The exceptional English-speaking staff will help guests find a restaurant, book a bike tour/countryside picnic, and everything in between.

The **Hotel Astoria** ☆☆, at Maršala Tita 174 (✆ **051/706-350**), was built in 1904 as Villa Louise in Austrian-Mediterranean style. Today the hotel's atmosphere is more Guggenheim Museum with touches of whimsy. Guest rooms, which start at 150€ ($192) for a double, are sleek and comfortable with artwork, vases filled with lucky bamboo, and a generous-size flat-panel TV.

Despite Viennese architect Carl Seidl's artful 1924 reconstruction of the property, **Villa Ariston's** ☆ guest rooms, which start at 810kn ($139/£74) for a double, are disappointingly cramped, dim, and in need of updating. The presidential suite, however, has a fabulous balcony and an unsurpassed view of the garden. It is rumored that Coco Chanel and JFK slept in the inn at Maršala Tita 179 (✆ **051/271-379**), but not together.

Walking up the long, wide staircase to the **Hotel Imperial**'s front door at Maršala Tita 124/3 (✆ **051/271-577**) makes you feel like you're approaching a monument, and once inside, the impression sticks. The hotel was built in 1885 and resembles a fine old opera house—crystal chandeliers, soaring ceilings, long corridors, heavy velvet curtains, and a dining room fit for a royal banquet. Guest rooms, which start at 585kn ($101/£53) for a double, have updated bathrooms and period furniture, but they are dark and tired-looking even if they have balconies.

Preluk ☆ (✆ **051/622-249**) is a campground 4.8km (3 miles) north of Opatija near Volosko, and for 109kn ($19/£10) for two people and a car and tent site, it is particularly well-situated bargain for those who love watersports.

Amfora ☆☆☆, at Črnikovica 4 (✆ **051/701-222**), in Volosko about 1.6km (1 mile) away from Opatija's main drag, is one of the best restaurants on the Opatija Riviera. Try the savory black risotto done to creamy perfection and full of tender pieces of squid—it's an Adriatic specialty.

Slatina ☆, at Maršala Tita 206 (✆ **051/271-949**), is a local hangout on an enclosed porch, and it dishes up huge portions of Slav specialties like *šopse* salad, a mix of chopped cukes, tomatoes, onions, and peppers covered with shaved sheep cheese and *tavće gravće* (beans in a paprika sauce), a dish that will make you turn up your nose at canned pork and beans forever.

Opatija is also loaded with affordable pizza places and cafes, most of which are along Maršala Tita and the Lungomare.

NIGHTLIFE

Croatia's zero-tolerance law has toned down Opatija's nightlife scene as would-be revelers from Rijeka figured that they could no longer go there to party and risk driving home if they had even a single drink. But even without Rijeka traffic, the town still rocks until around 11pm, which is closing hour for most Opatija restaurants and bars. Until then, you can sip a glass of wine, have a beer, or get rowdy at **Hemingway's** on the promenade or at any restaurant or cafe along the way. However, the most nighttime action is on the **Lungomare** and **Maršala Tita**—and it is alcohol-free. On any given evening it looks like all of Croatia is out taking a stroll, rollerblading, or pausing to watch break dancers and mimes. An ice-cream cone is the party treat of choice.

EXPLORING OPATIJA

Promenading on **Šetalište Franza Josefa** ★★★ in the evening is an art form in Croatia in general and in Opatija in particular, and this 12km (7.2-mile) flagstone walkway along the shore from **Volosko** ★★ (2km/1¼ miles north of Opatija) to **Lovran** ★★ (5.6km/3½ miles south of Opatija) is the granddaddy of them all. It runs past **Villa Angiolina** ★★, the villa that started it all, and that is now a popular venue for weddings when it isn't being used for art exhibits and other cultural events. Open daily June to September from 10am to 9pm.

8 Zagreb

618km (384 miles) N of Dubrovnik; 408km (253 miles) N of Split; 265km (165 miles) NE of Pula

Because visitors to Croatia tend to use Zagreb as a stopover rather than a destination, many of the city's charms are overlooked. It takes patience to discover Zagreb, and it takes knowledge about the past to understand its Balkan soul.

ARRIVING

BY PLANE Zagreb is the entry point for most visitors to Croatia, but there are no direct flights from the U.S., Canada, or Australia. Croatia Air, the national airline company, connects Zagreb with many European hubs as well as with other Croatian cities. **Pleso International Airport** (⊘ **385 01/626-52-22**) is 16km (10 miles) south of the city center, and Croatia Air operates a shuttle every 30 minutes from 5:30am to 7:30pm between the airport and Zagreb's main bus station for 25kn ($4/£2.15) one-way. The ride takes half an hour (⊘ **385 01/615 79 92**). Taxi fares to the city center run between 150kn and 250kn ($26–$45/£14–£23). *Note:* Croatia Air's luggage weight limits may differ from those of other international carriers, so if you are not checking your luggage directly through to Zagreb, you should query Croatia Air on this policy, which is subject to seasonal changes.

Note: When returning to the U.S., be aware that Croatia Air does not allow battery-operated devices in checked luggage, so remove them before checking your bag.

BY BUS Zagreb's bus station is a bright, efficient hub with restaurants, shops, a post office, and local connections to the city center. A 24-hour *garderoba* (luggage storage area) charges 1.20kn (20¢/10p) per hour or $4 per day. ATMs are located near the ticket office as is an exchange that is open from 6am to 10pm daily. Frequent buses link Zagreb and all of Croatia's main cities, which in turn hook up with local lines that run to virtually every village in the country.

BY TRAIN   The 19th-century **Zagreb train station (Glavni Kolodvor)** facing Trg Kralja Tomislava on the city's green horseshoe was renovated in 2004 and is now a pink confection adorned with angels and other statuary. It is close to bus and tram connections into the city center, which is a 10-minute walk with several hotels along the way. A 24-hour *garderoba* is available for 10kn ($1.75/90p) per day. A restaurant with a lovely terrace overlooks the park. There are ATMs, exchange facilities, and an information center (6–10am, 10:30am–6pm, and 6:30–10pm).

Catch the no. 5, 6, or 13 tram in front of the Kralja Tomislav monument to get to Trg Bana Josip Jeličića. Routes may vary, so watch for handwritten signs listing changes taped up at bus stops.

BY CAR   Driving in Zagreb can be nerve-racking. Most streets are marked by small ornamental signs on plaques affixed to building walls at intersections, so you can't see the sign until you're past the intersection. Many buildings in Zagreb do not display street numbers at all or if they do, they can't be read unless you are on top of them. To complicate matters, there is a tangled network of one-way and pedestrian streets. Add to that perpetual street construction and a parking dearth, and you have a driver's nightmare inside the city limits.

VISITOR INFORMATION

The **Zagreb Tourist Information Center** (Trg Bana Jelačića 11; ✆ 01/481-40-51; www.zagreb-touristinfo; 8:30am–8pm Mon–Fri; 9am–5pm Sat; and 10am–2pm Sun and holidays). It sells the **Zagreb Card** for 60kn ($10/£5.50), which covers 72 hours of unlimited city transportation (including the Sjleme cable car), a 50% discount at most museums and galleries, and discounts at participating businesses. There is a second Tourist Information Center at Trg Nikole Šubića Zrinskog 14 (✆ 01/492-16-45).

The **Zagreb County Tourist Association** at Preradovićeva 42 (✆ 01/487-36-65; www.tzzz.hr) is invaluable for information about excursions from Zagreb. Hours are 8am to 4pm Monday to Friday.

Croatia Airlines has an office at Trg Nikole Šubića Zrinskog 17 (✆ 01/481-96-33). It is open 8am to 7pm Monday to Friday and 8am to 3pm Saturday. Tours to sites and cities in Zagreb and throughout Croatia can be arranged through **Atlas Travel** (Zrinjevac 17; ✆ 01/481-39-33), Croatia's largest agency. Atlas is also Croatia's American Express agent. **Generalturist,** at Praška 5 (✆ 01/480-55-55; www.generalturist.com), books flights, excursions, and other trips.

CITY LAYOUT

Zagreb is nestled between **Mount Medvednica** and the **Sava River.** It is a sprawling city, but almost every attraction of note is within 2.4km (1½ miles) of **Trg Bana Jelačića,** the city's main square. The area north of the Trg Jelačića includes **Gornji Grad (Upper Town)** and its Gradec and Kaptol neighborhoods, which are perhaps Zagreb's most picturesque areas. **Donji Grad (Lower Town)** south of Trg Jelačića includes Zagreb's central green spaces known as the Green Horseshoe and runs south to the main train station. You can walk to most points of interest from Trg Jelačića, or hop on the public tram system for 6.50kn ($1.15/60p) per ride. After that, only a

> ### Tips Using Croatian Telephones
>
> To call Zagreb from the United States, dial the **international prefix 011,** then Croatia's country code, **385;** and then Zagreb's city code, **1.** Then dial the actual phone number.
>
> To call the U.S. from Zagreb, dial the **international prefix 00,** then the U.S. country code, **1;** then the area code and number. Other country codes are as follows: Canada, **1;** the United Kingdom, **44;** Ireland **353;** Australia, **61;** New Zealand, **64.**
>
> **To call from one city code to another** within Croatia: Dial the Croatian city code, including the zero, followed by the phone number.
>
> **To make a local call,** simply dial the phone number. No codes necessary. Local calls cost about 5kn ($1/55p) per minute.
>
> **To use a prepaid phone card,** call the service, key in the code on the back of the card, and call the number. It's a good idea to have a prepaid phone card for emergencies because most pay phones don't take money and you'll need a card to use them. You can buy prepaid cards in denominations of 50, 100, 200, and 500 units at most newspaper kiosks, at post offices, and at some tobacconists. Calls are based on unit-per-minute rates, and the farther away you call, the more each unit costs and the faster you use up your units. You can also buy prepaid cards at **Nexcom,** Zavrtnica 17 (℅ **01/606-03-33**); or at **Voicecom,** Ilica 109 (℅ **01/376-01-23;** www.voicecom.hr). Free 0800 access.
>
> **To use a mobile phone,** you can buy a SIM card for 400kn to 600kn ($70–$105/£37–£55) from **VIP** (℅ **091**) or **T-Mobile** (℅ **098**). You can also buy pay-as-you-go SIM cards from news kiosks in smaller denominations. If you have a GSM-equipped phone, it will register and readjust to T-Mobile in Zagreb provided you activate its international capabilities with your service provider in the U.S. before you leave. To call the U.S., hold down the zero key until a plus sign appears in the display. Then dial 1 plus the area code and number. Be aware that you will pay for roaming charges besides the call, which are extremely expensive because the call has to bounce from Croatia to the U.S. and back to Croatia again.

smattering of sights is worth seeking out. **Mount Medvednica Nature Park** and its **Sljeme Peak** in the hills north of town can be accessed from the square by taking tram no. 14 to the end of the line and then tram no. 15 to its terminus. From there you can get a cable car to Sjleme's top. **Mirogoj Cemetery** is also north of the center and can be reached via the no. 106 bus from the cathedral. **Novi Grad (New City)** is an area of bland apartment towers and industry south of the Sava; except for **Jarun Lake** just north of the river and the airport, there isn't much to see here. **Maksimir Park** is an elegant wooded zone east of the center. It can be reached via tram nos. 4, 7, 11, and 12.

GETTING AROUND
BY TRAM OR BUS   Zagreb's electric tram system is quick, efficient, and reliable, and it runs 24/7. Tram routes cover central Zagreb and connect to buses that serve

outlying areas and suburbs. Most lines eventually end up at the main train station, Trg Ban Jelačića, or both.

Tickets can be purchased at Tisak news kiosks for 8kn ($1.40/75p) or on board for 10kn ($1.75/90p). Tickets are good for 90 minutes each way and must be validated with a time stamp at the orange machines on board. Random control checks keep cheaters in check and if you are caught without a ticket or with an unvalidated ticket, the fine is 150kn ($26/£14) on the spot, more if you don't have the money in hand.

Note: Keep a tram/bus route map with you whenever using the system so you can locate the routes' end streets and determine if the vehicle is going in your direction. Almost none of the tram and bus operators speak English.

BY TAXI Taxis are expensive in Zagreb and charge a 25kn ($4.50/£2.40) flat fee plus 7kn ($1) for every ⅗ of a mile. A 20% surcharge is added to that on Sunday and at night, which makes taxis a very expensive way to travel. However, if you must use a cab, you can call one at ℭ **01/668-25-05.** It's a good idea to try to negotiate a price for your trip before you hop in.

ON FOOT Walking is by far the best (and healthiest) way to see Zagreb. Crime is low and you can safely get to almost any museum or restaurant in the central town within half an hour by walking.

FAST FACTS: Zagreb

American Express American Express services are available through **Atlas Travel** at Zrinjevac 17, 10000 Zagreb (ℭ **01/481-39-33**; fax 01/487-30-49). There is also an Amex office at Lastovska 23 (ℭ **01/612-44-22**).

ATMs & Currency Exchange You can withdraw cash using American Express, Diners Club, Maestro/MasterCard, Cirrus, and Visa at ATMs (Bankomats) installed all over Zagreb. Change money or traveler's checks at most banks, exchange offices, and travel agencies for a 1.5% or greater fee. The fee is even higher if you change money at a hotel. **A-Tours** at the main bus station (ℭ **01/ 600-86-66**) is the exchange office with the longest hours. It is open from 6am to 10pm every day.

Business Hours Most banks open at 9am and stay open until 7pm or later Monday to Saturday. The airport branch of Zagrebačka Bank is open on Sunday. Offices generally are open from 8am to 5pm; some have Saturday hours, usually until 1pm. Store hours vary, with many closing from 2 to 5pm or some other interval during the day, but smaller stores open at 9am, and close 8pm Monday to Saturday and all day Sunday. Stores in larger malls are open 7 days a week but most don't reopen after the weekend until 2pm on Monday so employees can restock shelves.

Emergencies For police dial ℭ **92;** for an ambulance, ℭ **94;** and to report a fire, ℭ **93.** For road assistance, dial ℭ **987;** for the **Croatian Auto Club,** dial ℭ **01/464-08-00.**

Internet Access Croatia has embraced computer technology in a big way, and Internet access is easy to find. Try **Ch@rlie's** in the shadow of the Hotel Dubrovnik at Ljudevita Gaja 4a (ℭ **01/488-02-33**). The staff is helpful and you can catch up on e-mail for 10kn ($1.75/95p) per hour while you sip an espresso. Hours are 8am to 10pm daily. **Sublink Cybercafe** is close to Trg Jelačića at Nikole Tesle 12 (© **01/481-13-29**). You can e-mail, print, copy, or scan for 14kn per hour ($2.60/£1.25).

Mail Mail letters at any yellow Posta box, but if you need to buy stamps or send a package, the Central Post Office is at Jurišićeva 13 near the Jadran Hotel (© **01/481-10-90**). Hours are 7 to 9pm Monday to Friday, 8am to 4pm Saturday.

Newspapers & Magazines Very few news kiosks sell English-language newspapers, and those that do sell out quickly. *The International Herald Tribune* is the easiest to find and costs 20kn ($3.50/£1.80). Many hotels print faxed copies of U.S. and other English-language newspapers for a fee.

Pharmacies Need an aspirin? In Zagreb (and all of Croatia) you'll have to go to a pharmacy *(ljekarna)* to buy some. No drugs of any kind are sold anywhere except at a pharmacy. There are several 24-hour ljekarna in Zagreb. Two are at Trg Jelačića (© **01/481-61-54**) and at Ilica 301 (© **01/375-03-21**)

Safety Zagreb enjoys relatively low crime rates, and it's safe to ride public transportation at night and to walk through high-traffic areas. Police presence on Zagreb streets is subtle and you'll rarely see a uniformed officer, but they're there. Exercise the same precautions you'd take in any big city.

WHERE TO STAY

There are few moderately priced and virtually no bargain hotels in Zagreb. In fact, unless you go with private accommodations, most options are at the extreme ends of the price—and quality—list.

VERY EXPENSIVE

Dubrovnik ★★ "Rms w vu" should be the motto of this modern-looking glass-and-metal tower off Trg Jeličića where many of the hotel's rooms look down on the Croatian hero's statue in the main square. Opened in 1929 as the Hotel Milinov, the hotel changed its name to Dubrovnik, added more than 150 rooms in a new glass-and-aluminum wing in 1982, and completed a total renovation in 2003. *Note:* The business suite (210€/$250) includes a rooftop terrace.

Gajeva 1. P.P. 246. 10000 Zagreb. © **01/487-35-55**. Fax 01/486/35-06. www.hotel-dubrovnik.hr. 280 units. From 140€ ($170) double; from 185€ ($220) suite. Rates include breakfast. Special 9-hr. "daily rest" rate 50% the regular room rate. AE, DC, MC, V. Limited free parking. **Amenities:** Restaurant; cafe; bar; business center; salon; room service; nonsmoking rooms; valet; rooms for those w/limited mobility. *In room:* A/C, TV, wireless/dataport, minibar, hair dryer, safe.

Palace ★★ The Secessionist-style hotel just 5 minutes from Trg Jeličića was built as a private palace in 1891 and converted to a hotel in 1907, which makes it the oldest in Zagreb. If you're looking for a comfortable, convenient place to stay that has character and a bit of history, the Palace is the place. Rooms are in tune with 19th-century sensibilities; some have been updated for modern guests.

Trg JJ Strossmayera 10, 10000 Zagreb. © **01/481-46-11**, reservations 01/492-05-30. Fax 01/481-13-58. www.palace.hr. 123 units. From 980kn ($170/£89) double; from 1,200kn ($210/£110) junior suite; from 1,850kn ($320/£169) suite. 20% discount on weekends. Rates include breakfast. AE, DC, MC, V. Limited free parking. **Amenities:** Restaurant; bar; room service; babysitting; nonsmoking rooms. *In room:* A/C, TV, Internet, minibar, hair dryer.

Zagreb Lodging, Dining & Attractions

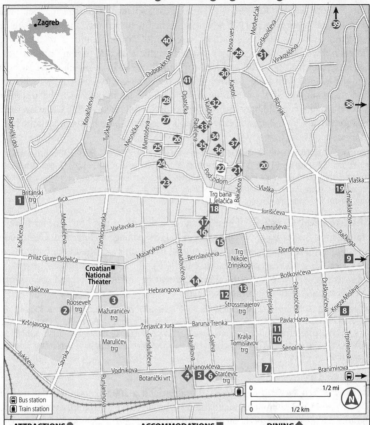

ATTRACTIONS ●
Atelier–Ivan Meštrović
  Foundation **28**
Cathedral of the Assumption
  of the Virgin Mary **20**
Crkva Svetog Marka (St. Mark's
  Church) **27**
Croatian Museum of
  Naive Art **25**
Dolac Market **22**
Ethnographic Museum **3**
Kamenita Vrata (Stone Gate) **26**
Kula Lotrščak
  (Burglars' Tower) **24**
Mimara Museum **2**
Mirogoj Cemetery **38**
Mount Medvednica **39**
Museum of the City of Zagreb **41**
Strossmayer Gallery of
  Old Masters **13**
Tkalčićeva Ulica **34**
Zagreb Archaeological
  Museum **15**

ACCOMMODATIONS ■
Best Western Astoria **11**
Central **7**
Dubrovnik **18**
Ilica **1**
Jadran **19**
Omladinski Hostel **10**
Palace **12**
The Regent Esplanade **5**
Sheraton Zagreb **8**
Sliško **9**

DINING ◆
Bagueri **33**
Baltazar **30**
Boban **17**
Capucine Spaghetteria **37**
Dubrovkin Put **40**
Gallo **14**
Kaptolska Klet **21**
Kod Žaca **31**
LeBistro **6**
Leonardi **35**
Nokturno **36**
Panino **29**
Pinguin Sandwich Bar **16**
Pod Gričkim Topom **23**
Restoran Ivica I Marica **32**
Zinfandel's **4**

The Regent Esplanade ✹✹✹   The elegant Esplanade has attracted well-heeled guests since its opening in 1925 as a stop on the Orient Express, and now a painstaking renovation has seamlessly added New World creature comforts to the historic hotel's old-world opulence. Add to that service that is second to none, and the result is one of the most beautiful and best-run hotels in Croatia. Amenities are first-class and augmented with little luxuries such as fresh flowers, twice-a-day housekeeping, and cushy slippers ideal for padding around on the bathroom's heated marble floor. Liberal use of wood and brass in both private and public areas, a chic **Croatian fusion restaurant** ✹✹✹, and a staff ready to fulfill every need have brought back the hotel's glory days.

Mihanovićeva 1, 10000 Zagreb. ✆ 800/545-4000 from the U.S., or 01/456/66-66. Fax 385 01/66 020. www.regent hotels.com. 209 units. From 149€ ($180) double; from 300€ ($360) suite. AE, DC, MC, V. No pets. **Amenities:** 2 restaurants; terrace dining w/live music; bar; casino; sauna; salon; club floor; concierge; room service; nonsmoking rooms; valet service; 2 rooms for those w/limited mobility. In room: A/C, TV w/pay movies, wireless connection/dataport, minibar, hair dryer, safe, trouser press.

Sheraton Zagreb ✹✹✹   The glass-and-metal front of this hotel not far from the train station makes it easy to spot among Zagreb's vintage architecture. Guest rooms and public spaces are bright and airy, and all bathrooms are fitted with bathtubs and toiletries. Most hotel services are available 24/7 and the restaurant staff is remarkably knowledgeable. There isn't a thing management hasn't thought of, and everything in the Sheraton Zagreb is superbly executed.

Kneza Borne 2, 10000 Zagreb. ✆ 01/455-35-35. Fax 01/455/30/35. www.sheraton.com/zagreb. 306 units. From 145€ ($175) double; from 250€ ($300) suite. AE, DC, MC, V. Guarded parking lot. **Amenities:** 2 restaurants; pastry cafe; piano bar; pool; sauna; concierge; salon; room service; casino; valet service; nonsmoking rooms; rooms for those w/limited mobility. In room: A/C, TV, wireless/dataport, minibar, coffeemaker, hair dryer, iron/ironing board, safe, trouser press.

EXPENSIVE

Best Western Astoria ✹✹ (Value)   Location and a 2005 renovation that took the hotel from frayed to fabulous make the Astoria one of the most underrated in Zagreb. Besides being midway between the train station and Trg Ban Josip Jeličića, guest rooms are loaded with modern amenities like heated bathroom floors and French toiletries. Public spaces have a spiffy, polished look, and service is friendly and efficient.

Petrinjska Ulica 71, 10000 Zagreb. ✆ 01/484-12-22. www.bestwestern.com. 102 units. From 110€ ($135) double; from 175€ ($210) suite. AE, DC, MC, V. Rates include breakfast. **Amenities:** Restaurant; nonsmoking rooms; Internet; rooms for those w/limited mobility. In room: A/C, TV, minibar.

Central   The Central's location across from Zagreb's main train station is convenient to transportation but rooms facing the street can be noisy when trams rumble by. The quality of the Central's rooms' decor is Wal-Mart, and most have showers rather than tubs, but they have a decent number of amenities following a 2002 renovation.

Branimirova 3, PP 97, 10000 Zagreb. ✆ 01/484-11-22. Fax 01/484-13-04. www.hotel-central.hr. 76 units. From 720kn ($125/£66) double; from 1,300kn ($225/£119) suite. AE, DC, MC, V. Rates stay the same all year and include breakfast. **Amenities:** Restaurant (breakfast only); adjacent casino. In room: A/C, TV, dataports and minibars in some rooms, hair dryer, Internet connection.

MODERATE

Ilica   The Ilica is set back from the far end of Zagreb's main shopping street and it is priced lower than almost all other hotels in the central city. Guest rooms are adequate, but the suites are over-the-top kitsch that incorporates a lot of gilt and plastic (there is a full-size refrigerator in the living room of one of them). The no. 6 tram stops in front of the hotel and Britanski Trg and its Sunday antique market are steps away.

Ilica 102, 10000 Zagreb. ✆ **01/377-76-22**. Fax 01/377-77-22. www.hotel-ilica.hrilica.hr. 24 units. From 449kn ($80/£41) double; from 749kn ($130/£68) suite and apt. Rates include breakfast. AE, DC, MC, V. Limited free parking. **Amenities:** Restaurant; nonsmoking rooms; rooms for those w/limited mobility. *In room:* A/C, TV.

Jadran Thanks to a 2003 renovation, the once shabby Jadran is now a pleasant, affordable choice just 5 minutes from the city center. Decor in guest rooms and public areas has been turned up a notch, and both are reasonably modern, though the rooms are not exactly spacious. The Jadran's main advantages are its location and easy access to public transportation.

Vlaška 50, 10000 Zagreb. ✆ **01/455-37-77**. Fax 01/461-21-51. www.hup-zagreb.hr. 48 units. From 726kn ($125/£66) double. AE, DC, MC, V. Rates stay the same all year and include breakfast. Limited free parking. **Amenities:** Restaurant. *In room:* A/C, TV, hair dryer.

Sliško The Sliško is a solid no-frills hotel in back of the main bus station. Opened in the mid-1990s, the Sliško has just enough amenities to make it comfortable and a pricing scale to prevent wallet welts. Rooms are furnished in utilitarian modern and some are small, but all are clean and affordable: Pricing is according to the number of beds used. The first-floor restaurant is thoughtfully glassed off from the smoky bar.

Supilova 13, 10000 Zagreb. ✆ **01/619-42-23**. Fax 385 01/619 42 10. www.slisko.hr. 18 units. From 510kn ($90/£47) double; from 740kn ($130/£68) suite (4 beds). AE, DC, MC, V. 10% discount for cash. Rates include breakfast. **Amenities:** Restaurant; bar. *In room:* A/C, TV.

INEXPENSIVE

Omladinski Hostel The lobby looks like a homeless shelter intake area, and the scent of insecticide is in the air as you approach reception. However, it's one of the few bargain accommodations in Zagreb and as such, its off-putting details can be overlooked. Accommodations range from six-bed, dorm-style rooms to doubles with private bathrooms. The only amenities are vending machines in the lobby, but the Omladinski is 5 minutes from both the city center and the train station.

Petrinjska 77, 10000 Zagreb. ✆ **01/484-12-61**. Fax 01/484-12-69. www.hfhs.hr. 215 beds, most in multibed dorm-style rooms with shared bathrooms. 10 doubles with private bathroom. From 286kn ($50/£4.60) double; from 73kn ($13/£6.70) bed. 5kn ($1/50p) discount for people under 27. AE, DC, MC, V. Check-in is 2pm; checkout is 9pm.

PRIVATE ACCOMMODATIONS

Evistas ✦✦ This accommodations matchmaker is low profile but high on service. Evistas specializes in finding private apartments and sobes (rooms) in private homes for frugal travelers staying in Zagreb, but it also locates and books city youth hostels, rooms on the coast, and suites in posh hotels.

Šenoina 28, 10000 Zagreb. ✆ **01/483-95-54**. evistas@zg.htnet.hr. Mon–Fri 9am–1:30pm and 3–8pm; Sat 9:30am–5pm. Closed Sun.

WHERE TO DINE IN ZAGREB

Eating is a social occasion in Croatia, and Zagreb is full of good restaurants, although the range of cuisine choices is narrow.

VERY EXPENSIVE

Dubrovkin Put ✦✦ SEAFOOD Romantic ambience and pristinely fresh seafood are the standard at this award-winning restaurant in the neighborhood behind Gradec. Service is first-rate and attentive without being obtrusive, and the fish and shellfish preparations are flawless. A full meal is a little pricey but worth it, especially on the relaxing terrace under the stars.

Dubrovkin Put 2. ✆ **01/483-49-70.** Fax 01/482-81-49. Entrees 85kn–150kn ($15–$30/£7.75–£14). AE, DC, MC, V. Daily 10am–midnight.

Zinfandel's ★★★ FUSION By day, diners have a view of lovely Fountain Square through the window-walls of this sophisticated dining room in the Regent Esplanade (see review above), which is the source of the best breakfast buffet on the planet. A little later, Zinfandel serves a casual but wonderfully diverse lunch menu. However, it is at night that things get really creative with dishes such as duck and venison casseroles served with a salad of walnuts, oyster mushrooms, and cranberries; or lamb filet wrapped in zucchini.

Mihanovićeva 1. ✆ **01/456-66-66.** Main courses 65kn–165kn ($15–$30/£5.95–£15). Barbecue is 120kn ($21/£11) per person. AE, DC, MC, V. Dinner daily 6–11pm.

EXPENSIVE

Bagueri ★★★ (Value) ITALIAN A small, understated stucco building painted in shades of cocoa and white and trimmed with gauzy white curtains and geranium window boxes is the setting for one of the best restaurants on Tkalčićeva Street. Entrees such as steak in balsamic sauce, and risotto with greens and prosciutto star here. Add to that a balanced wine list and a competent staff that smiles a lot, and you have the makings of a great meal.

Tkalčićeva 65. ✆ **091/481-38-48.** Reservations recommended. Entrees 45kn–120kn ($8–$21/£4.10–£11). AE, DC, MC, V. Daily 5pm–midnight.

Baltazar ★★ CROATIAN Grilled meat is the focus of this pleasant dining spot with a nice terrace, north of the cathedral on Kaptol. Baltazar is in what may be the city's trendiest neighborhood, but the food holds with tradition. This is the place to try Croatian schnitzel and any other national dish you've been curious about. Service is superb.

Nova Ves 4. ✆ **01/466-69-99.** www.morsko-prase.hr. Entrees 55kn–125kn ($10–$22/£5–£11). AE, DC, MC, V. Mon–Sat noon–midnight. Closed Sun.

Gallo ★★★ ITALIAN Food is art at this beautiful, unpretentious restaurant behind the facade of an unremarkable building a few blocks from the city center. Homemade pasta in countless shapes and a rainbow of colors dries behind glass near the restaurant entrance. The menu is mostly fish with several interesting recipes such as tuna with polenta and red-wine sauce, or beef soup with ravioli. There is a stylish white stone terrace, a casual dining room, and a more formal space where crystal and silver set the tone.

Andrije Hebranga 34. ✆ **01/481-40-14.** Fax 01/481-40-13. www.gallo.castellum.hr. Reservations recommended at dinner. Entrees 60kn–120kn ($11–$21/£4.50–£11). AE, DC, MC, V. Daily 11:30am–midnight.

Kod Žaca ★★ CROATIAN COUNTRY This is a terrific place for veal, beef, ostrich, turkey, pork, horse, and chicken and the sauce of your choice—mushroom, truffle, pepper, or cheese. The portions are generous and all meat dishes are accompanied by either homemade gnocchi or croquettes. With its old-country decor and only 10 small tables inside, Kod Žaca provides a cozy atmosphere in which to dine and feel relaxed.

Grškovićeva 4, just steps up from where Ribnjak changes to Medveščak. ✆ **01/468-4178.** Reservations recommended. Entrees 60kn–120kn ($10–$20/£5.50–£11). No credit cards. Daily noon–2am.

Panino ✦ ITALIAN   You'll forget you're in a shopping mall when seated on the airy green terrace at this spot in Kaptol Center. Breakfast and lunch menus are loaded with affordable options such as prosciutto and asparagus frittata; and the panino sandwich, made with prosciutto, cheese, and egg. At dinner, the restaurant not only has tempting dishes like salmon steak with poppy-seed crust in wine, or dark chicken meat stuffed with prosciutto and radicchio risotto, but suggests complementary wines from its list of boutique vintners.

Nova Ves 11 (Kaptol Centers). ✆ **01/466-90-13.** Fax 01/466-90-14. www.panino.hr. Breakfast entrees 20kn–35kn ($5–$7/£1.85–£3.20); sandwiches 15kn–18kn ($3–$4/£1.40–£1.65); dinner entrees 60kn–120kn ($11–$21/£5.50–£11). AE, DC, MC, V. Daily 9am–midnight.

Pod Gričkim Topom ✦✦✦ CROATIAN   Location, location, location draws a crowd at this traditional-style restaurant on the Strossmayerovo Šetalište, steps midway between Trg Bana Jelačića and Gornji Grad. Bread and tiny balls of Croatian pâté start most meals, which could be anything from grilled meat to pasta. Try the monkfish, which comes with *blitva*, the Croatian version of chopped spinach. Desserts are decadent and the wine list is loaded with fairly priced Croatian choices.

Zakmardijeve Stube 5. ✆ **01/483-36-07.** AE, DC, MC, V. Entrees 65kn–125kn ($12–$22/£5.95–£11). Daily 11am–midnight.

MODERATE

Boban ✦   This boisterous cellar restaurant named after a Croatian soccer star is two flights below Boban's kavana-bar and way below it in noise level. Food is straightforward Italian with a few Croatian-inspired dishes such as venison salami and vegetable-stuffed pancakes with béchamel. The food isn't gourmet and prices won't break your vacation budget, but you won't be wowed by creativity either. Service can be slow when all the tables are full—and that's usually all night, every night.

Gajeva 9. ✆ **01/481-15-49.** www.boban.hr. Entrees 30kn–80kn ($6–$14/£2.75–£7.30). AE, DC, MC, V. Daily 10am–midnight.

Capucine Spaghetteria ✦ *Value* PIZZA/ITALIAN   Endless variations of spaghetti, pizza, and other Italian fare are on the menu at this noisy hangout across the street from Zagreb Cathedral. Pizza is ultrathin-crusted European style, and toppings are mostly fresh ingredients, unless you opt for unusual varieties such as the (untried) Nutella version. The restaurant also has daily blackboard specials for 15kn to 30kn ($2.60–$5.20/£1.40–£2.80), including a horse-meat burger.

Kaptol 6. ✆ **01/481-48-40.** www.capuciner.hr. Entrees including pizza 15kn–60kn ($3–$11/£1.40–£5.50). AE, DC, MC, V. Mon–Sat 10am–1am; Sun noon–1am.

Kaptolska Klet ✦✦ CROATIAN   A huge array of steaks complements an amazing list of Croatian home recipes such as goulash and roasted lamb or pork at this attractive spot across from Zagreb's cathedral. There's a menu for dieters (including ostrich filet) and one for vegetarians, too. The folk-culture ambience on the terrace and inside seems more touristy than functional, but there's nothing ersatz about the food.

Kaptol 5. ✆ **01/481-48-38.** Fax 01/481-43-30. www.mediacaffe.net/kaptolskaklet. Entrees 35kn–80kn ($6–$14/£3.20–£7.30). AE, DC, MC, V. Daily 11am–11pm.

LeBistro ✦✦ FRENCH/CROATIAN   This glassed-in meet-and-eat place in the Regent Esplanade specializes in classic French preparations such as baked escargot, but there is also a touch of nouveau in simple dishes such as bass with wilted Swiss chard and garlic confit. Le Bistro boasts that it serves the best *zagorski štrukli* (cheese baked in phyllo with cream sauce) in town and even offers a frozen version to take home, but we found the dish rather bland, even with sugar on top.

Mihanovićeva 1. ⓒ **01/456-66-66.** Main courses 40kn–100kn ($7–$18/£3.65–£9.15). AE, DC, MC, V. Daily 10am–11pm.

Restoran Ivica I Marica ⭐⭐ CROATIAN VEGETARIAN   The newest kid on busy Tkalčićeva has also introduced a novel concept—traditional Croatian preparations with a healthy twist—whole grains, local products, and no meat. The menu at this woodsy place named after Hansel and Gretel (in Croatian), is no less fascinating. Begin with whole-grain flatbread accompanied by local fresh cheese or olives and tomatoes. Then move to *integral sujnudle* (boiled dumplings with hunter sauce or mushroom sauce). Fish is on the menu, as are moussaka with eggs and soy ham plus four varieties of *štrukli.*

Tkalčićeva 70, 10000 Zagreb. ⓒ **01/481-73-21.** Fax 098/317-092. ivicaimarica@adriazdravahrana.hr. Entrees 39kn–70kn ($7–$12/£3.55–£6.40). AE, DC, MC, V. Daily noon–11pm.

INEXPENSIVE

Nokturno and **Leonardi** ⭐⭐ PIZZA/PASTA   At first glance it's hard to tell where Nokturno begins and its next-door neighbor Leonardi ends. Both are crammed in a space on the side of an alleyway; both have similar menus; and both have the same opening hours. Nokturno is always jammed with patrons, while Leonardi isn't quite so busy, but the pace there is slower, too. It is Nokturno's interpretation of pizza that attracts crowds with its crispy crust and fresh ingredients. Whichever restaurant you choose, you can't miss.

Nokturno: Skalinska 4. ⓒ **01/481-33-94.** Small pizzas 18kn–30kn ($3–$6/£1.62–£3.25); other dishes 20kn–45kn ($4–$8/£3.45–£4.10). AE, DC, MC, V. Daily 9am–1am. **Leonardi:** Skalinska 6. ⓒ **01/487-30-05.** Small pizzas 15kn–35kn ($3–$6/£1.40–£3.20); other dishes 28kn–65kn ($5–$13/£2.55–£5.95). AE, DC, MC, V. Daily 9am–1am.

Pinguin Sandwich Bar ⭐⭐⭐ *Finds* SANDWICHES   Get in line with the locals who mob this tiny made-to-order sandwich shack at all hours. The huge menu is entirely in Croatian, but order-takers understand some English, and most sandwiches are illustrated with color photos. Try the Rustico, a tasty combo of mozzarella, pancetta, oregano, olives, tomatoes, herbed mayo, and any of half a dozen condiments between two fresh-made pitalike rectangles of olive bread. Don't try to eat these Croatian subs while walking down the street or you'll wear them.

Nikola Tesle 7. No phone. Sandwiches 13kn–20kn ($2.25–$3.45/£1.20–£1.85). No credit cards. Mon–Sat 24 hr.; Sun 5pm–midnight.

EXPLORING ZAGREB

The best—and in some cases the only—way to see Zagreb is on foot. Gornji Grad (Upper Town) is full of historic buildings and churches, restaurants, boutiques, monuments, and entertainment venues. Donji Grad (Lower Town) is strong on museums, parks, historic architecture, and shopping. Other sights are a short bus or tram ride from the center of town. Whatever you do, don't miss **Trg Bana Jelačića (Jelačić Square)** ⭐⭐⭐, where the Ban's statue stood for nearly 80 years until World War II, when the square was renamed Republic Square. The statue was removed and stored in pieces after it was determined that the monument had become a rallying point for Croatian nationalists, who were a threat to the ruling Communist Party. It wasn't until 1990 that the statue was returned to its original home, and the square to its original name.

KAPTOL

Dolac ✦✦✦ market at Dolac bb (open Mon–Fri 6am–2pm; Sat 6am–3pm; Sun 6am–noon) is a lively open-air enterprise north of Jelačić, where colorful Croatian products create a vibrant mosaic every day, especially on Friday and Saturday. Opened in 1930, it is Zagreb's most popular open-air market and some say one of the best in Europe. Fruits, vegetables, plants, and textiles are on the upper level, while meat, cheese, olives, herbs, and more are in the covered area below. Fish and cheese are in separate spaces to avoid olfactory over stimulation.

Tkalčićeva Ulica ✦✦✦. To the left of Dolac as you face the stairs leading to it, a cobblestone street winds up a steep incline into the belly of the upper city. It is lined with boutiques, bars, restaurants, galleries in rehabbed 19th-century mansions interspersed with renovation projects. Tkalčićeva is also home to Zagreb's cafe society, and every evening the tables along this thoroughfare are full.

The Cathedral of the Assumption of the Virgin Mary ✦✦✦, at Kaptol 31 (© **01/481-47-27;** free admission) is topped by 105m (345-ft.) twin spires that seem perpetually covered with scaffolding. Work began on the exterior in 1990 and is ongoing, but it can't spoil the grace and beauty of the Herman Bollé masterpiece, which has become a symbol of Zagreb. Inside, the cathedral glows following a refurbishment that was completed in 1988. Note the 18th-century marble pulpit and the sarcophagus of the controversial Blessed Alojzije Stepinac behind the main altar. A Meštrović relief showing Stepanic kneeling before Christ marks the Croatian icon's grave.

GRADEC

Gradec is the second arm of central Zagreb's civic triumvirate. Less commercial than Kaptol, Gradec is packed with interesting museums and monuments.

Kamenita Vrata ✦✦ is a steep walk up a long flight of stairs to Radićeva from Tkalčićeva and a few minutes more up a cobblestone path. Kamenita Vrata was one of four entrances to the walled city of Gradec. Today it is the only gate that survived a devastating 1731 fire. Just inside is a small, dark area that houses the **Chapel of God's Mother** ✦✦ where a **painting of the Virgin and Child** ✦ is installed in an alcove behind a baroque grid. According to legend, the painting is the only thing that survived the fire and it is revered as a miraculous sign. There are a few pews in the dark chapel where people come to pray.

Ivan Meštrović (1883–1962)

Some say Ivan Meštrović is Croatia's greatest sculptor of religious art since the Renaissance. Meštrović was born in 1883 to a peasant family in Vrpolje and spent most of his childhood in Otavice, a tiny, impoverished village in the rocky, mountainous interior of Dalmatia. In the early 1920s, Meštrović settled in Zagreb, where he transformed a 17th-century house (Meštrović Atelier) into his home and studio. After World War II, he immigrated to New York, where he became a professor of sculpture at Syracuse University. In 1955 he moved to a similar position at the University of Notre Dame in South Bend, Indiana, where he lived until his death in 1962. Throughout his career, Meštrović was a prolific artist. His works are on display in museums, public places (including Chicago's Grant Park), and at Notre Dame.

The **tile mosaic** ★★★ depicting the Croatian, Dalmatian, and Slavonian coats of arms is **St. Mark's Church**'s most recognizable feature. Inside, the church at Trg Svetog Marka 5 (℗ **01/485-16-11**) is rather ordinary except for a beautiful Meštrović crucifix. Hours are variable and posted on the door, but not always observed by the folks who have the key to the church. Call to be sure it's open.

Think Grandma Moses interprets Croatia when you approach the **Croatian Museum of Naive Art** ★★ at Ćirilometodska 3 (℗ **01/485-19-11**), a baroque mansion that houses works by such Croatian masters as Ivan Generalić and Ivan Lacković. The enchanting museum focuses on the Hlebine School and its 1,500 colorful, historical, and sometimes irreverent but utterly charming, works.

Atelier-Ivan Meštrović Foundation ★★★ comprises the artist's studio and his 17th-century house at Mletačka 8 (℗ **01/485-11-23**), which are the settings for a vast array of his sculptures and models. Renderings of famous people, religious icons, and just plain folks are exhibited inside and outside in the garden. Not only are finished works on display, but also sketches, models, and photographs, most notably a small study of the Grgur Ninski sculptures in Split and Nin in Dalmatia.

The Museum of the City of Zagreb ★ at Opatička 20 (℗ **01/485-13-64**) is situated in the renovated former convent of the Order of St. Clare. Displays illuminate life in Zagreb from medieval times to the present through weaponry, religious objects, furniture, ethnic costumes, an incredible collection of photographs documenting the city through the years, and scale models of Zagreb at various times in its history. Captions are multilingual. There is also an nice restaurant on the premises open from noon to midnight.

Kula Lotrščak (Burglars' Tower) ★★. A cannon is fired at this vestige of Gradec's fortifications at Strossmayerovo Šetalište 9 (℗ **01/485-17-68**) every day at noon, supposedly to commemorate a Croat victory against the Turks. You can climb the tower to get a fabulous view of the city or just to say you did.

DONJI GRAD (LOWER TOWN)

A mixture of Greek, Macedonian, and Croatian artifacts fills glass cases throughout the **Zagreb Archaeological Museum** ★ at Trg Nikole Šubića Zrinskog 19 (℗ **01/487-31-01**), a monument to prehistoric times. But it is the mummies and funerary exhibits that draw the most oohs and ahs in the northernmost section of Zrinevac. Skeletal remains and the Bronze Age baubles are exhibited as they would have looked *in situ*. There is no museum map or audioguide available, but occasional English-language histories and titles are available. The highlight of the collection is the "Zagreb mummy" and its bandages, which are actually a linen book in Etruscan script.

Heart of the Matter

The shiny red hearts on display in nearly every Zagreb souvenir shop are actually *licitar*, honey-dough similar to gingerbread that is shaped in wooden molds, hardened, and coated with edible red lacquer and decorated with flowers, swirls, and other trim. The colorful hearts traditionally were used as love tokens by young men, who gave them to their girlfriends as an expression of love. Today, the decorated cookies still are given as a sign of affection, but they also are given as special-occasion gifts or as remembrances.

Fun Fact **Color Me Beautiful—and Bizarre**

It may be a case of "If you can't beat 'em, celebrate 'em," but Zagreb has created a venue for graffiti artists who routinely cover the city's buildings with their artwork and commentary. In deference to them, a long wall along Branimirova Ulica has been designated as a public canvas and it is covered with colorful images of everything from portraits to profanity.

Bishop Josip Strossmayer began collecting art when he became bishop of Đakovo. He secured funds to build the beige 19th-century building at Trg Nikole Šubića Zrinskog 11 (© **01/489-51-17**), where the **Strossmayer Gallery of Old Masters** ✹✹ opened in 1884 to house his vast collection of mostly religious art. Today it is also home to the fabled **Baška Tablet,** which is the oldest known example of Glagolitic script in existence and perhaps Croatia's most important artifact. The tablet is displayed under glass in the ground-floor lobby without any conspicuous sign or fanfare. Entry to the gallery is on the third floor, though no signs direct you there.

The **Ethnographic Museum** ✹✹✹ at Mažuranićev Trg 14 (© **01/482-62-20**), south of Trg Maršala Tita, is loaded with a dizzying array of traditional aprons and tunics from all parts of Croatia, as well as collections of agricultural artifacts such as olive- and grape-growing implements and winemaking items. Most of the museum's collections were acquired in the 19th and 20th centuries and cover the full spectrum of how people worked and lived in Old Croatia. Don't miss the gingerbread collection.

Croatian-born Ante Topić Mimara was a lifelong collector who bequeathed his treasures to his country. While there has been some controversy about the provenance of some of the works, the **Mimara Museum**'s vast portfolio is impressive. The museum at Rooseveltov Trg 5 (© **01/482-81-00**) opened in 1987, but displays are surprisingly unsophisticated and the lighting design does not show the works to advantage. Captions are in Croatian only.

FARTHER AFIELD

Ski, hike, or bike on Mount Medvednica (Bear Mountain) 20 minutes north of the Zagreb's center, where cafes, ski rental shops, warming huts, caves, and a **medieval fortress** ✹✹ of Medvedgrad await. If you drive, the turns up to the top are rather steep, but you don't have to worry about oncoming traffic because the road up is one-way, as is the road down. Take the cable car (© **01/458-03-94**) to the top for 11kn ($2/£1) or back down for 17kn ($3/£1.55). Open daily 8am to 8pm.

Note: Be sure you pay attention when driving or biking back to Zagreb: There is a road that goes to the back side of the mountain and ends up in the Zagorje region.

Many of Croatia's heroes and common folk are buried in fascinating **Mirogoj Cemetery** ✹✹✹, but this is no Arlington or Shady Lawn. Mirogoj is a mix of architecture that includes soaring domes; a neo-Renaissance arcade; and trees, flowers, and gravestones adorned with Christian crosses, Jewish six-pointed stars, socialist five-pointed stars, and slender five-sided Muslim headstones because people of all faiths and nationalities are interred here without segregation. To get to Mirogoj, take the no. 106 bus from Kaptol opposite the cathedral for or the no. 14 tram from Trg Jelačića toward Mihaljevac. Exit at the fourth stop. Open daily 8am to 8pm.

ORGANIZED TOURS

Almost everything worth seeing in Zagreb is within walking distance of the main square or a short tram or bus ride away. However, if you want to inject some whimsy into your sightseeing, try one of the city's 2-hour-long costumed walking tours. A guide dressed like a famous person from Zagreb history will show you around and perhaps throw in little-known facts about the city and its sites. You can buy tickets at the Tourist Information Center at Andrijevićeva 12 (© **01/370-35-53**) for 95kn ($16/£8.70) per person. Tours leave from the TIC daily at 10am and 4pm.

SHOPPING IN ZAGREB

Zagreb's economy is recovering after years of being in the dumps following occupations by foreign governments and the 1991 war. But the country has not yet been admitted to the European Union and E.U. investment hasn't kicked in. Except for the action at Dolac market, shopping isn't very exciting in Zagreb, and serious bargain hunters will be disappointed in the prices and what's available. The number of stores that sell good-quality garb is increasing, but as a rule, clothing is either imported and very expensive, or cheaply made and still expensive, depending on its country of origin. However, there are a few retailers worth checking out.

You're likely to need one of **Cerovečki's** (Ilica 50; © **01/484-74-17**) handmade umbrellas if you stay in Zagreb more than a couple of days. Open 8:30am to 8pm Monday to Friday; 8:30am to 3pm Saturday; closed Sunday. **Marks and Spencer** (Nova Ves 11; © **01/468-61-99**) in Kaptol Center specializes in traditional style and conservative casual wear. Hours are 9am to 9pm Monday to Saturday; closed Sunday. Also at King Cross shopping mall in Jankomir. **Algoritam** (Gajeva 1; © **01/481-86-72).** has a large selection of English-language books and magazines as well as reading materials in other languages. Hours are 8am to 9pm Monday to Friday, 8am to 3pm Saturday; closed Sunday. **Muller** fills two floors with everything from high-end French perfume to German-made rubbing liniment and a line of packaged health foods and juices. Tax-free option for purchases over 300kn ($60/£27). Hours are 8am to 8pm Monday to Friday, 8am to 3pm Saturday. Closed Sunday (Trg Jelačaća 8; © **01/489-31-50**). Dalmatian ham, prosciutto, *paški sir* (distinctive cheese made on the island of Pag), and olive oil and wine from Istria and other parts of Croatia are sold At **Pršut Galerija** (Vlaška 7; © **01/481-61-29**). Hours are 8am to 8pm Monday to Friday, 8am to 2pm Saturday; closed Sunday. **Lazer Rok Lumezi** (Tkalčićeva 53; © **01/481-40-30**) likes to collaborate with his customers on designs so he can match his jewelry creations to the personality of the person who will wear them. Hours are 9am to 8pm Monday to Friday, 9am to 3pm Saturday; closed Sunday. The branch of **Turbo Limaž** (Ljudevita Gaja 9a; © **01/481-15-48**) in Zagreb is fine for picking up something to amuse the kids. Think Toys "R" Us, only smaller. Hours are 8am to 8pm Monday to Friday, 8am to 3pm Saturday; closed Sunday.

SHOPPING MALLS

Croatians love to shop, and large, Western-style malls are springing up all over Zagreb. **Kaptol Center** on Nova Ves in Gornji Grad houses upscale retailers; a multiplex cinema; and an assortment of cafes, restaurants, and bars. **Importanne** runs two malls, one under the park across the street from the main train station, and another at Iblerov Trg just west of the center. **Branimir Center** on Branimir just east of the train station also has a multiplex and several restaurants, in addition to shops and the Arcotel Allegra Hotel. **King Cross** at Jankomir southwest of Zagreb is the closest thing to an American mall.

Note: King Cross doesn't open until 2pm on Mondays. It opens at 9am Tuesday to Saturday and stays open until 9pm Sunday.

ZAGREB AFTER DARK

Nightlife in Zagreb is varied but not obvious. Besides the usual complement of bars and cafes, there are casinos, jazz clubs, discos, cinemas, and comedy clubs to occupy even die-hard night owls. Lately, **Jarun Lake,** 4km (2½ miles) southwest of the center, has become hot year-round with "branches" of almost all of Zagreb's popular bars setting up waterside shops there.

Casino City is a comfortable gambling house beneath the Regent Esplanade with roulette tables, card tables, slot machines, and a VIP area for serious gamblers. Free entrance for Esplanade guests. Open daily 8pm to 4am. Mihanovićeva 1. ☎ **01/450-10-00.**

Club Casino Vega is a high-powered establishment in the Sheraton where games include blackjack, roulette, slot machines, and poker. Open daily 8pm to 7am. Draškovićeva 43. ☎ **01/461-18-6.** Fax 01/461-19-25. casinovega@post.htnet.hr.

Bar/restaurant **Boban** is owned by one of Croatia's top soccer players and it's always packed to the max with a noise level to match. There is also outside seating where promenading in resplendent finery is a sport for both sexes. Hours are daily 7am to midnight. Ljudevita Gaja 9. ☎ **01/481-15-49.** www.boban.hr.

Jackie Brown in Kaptol Centar is aimed at a sophisticated crowd that enjoys the finer things in life—cool jazz, vintage Armagnac, and classic cars. Open daily 8am to 1am. Nova Ves 17 (Kaptol Center). ☎ **01/486-0241.**

The decor at **Khala** is reminiscent of a Far Eastern harem and the effect screams "extremely chic and wealthy." Brown wicker chairs and couches fitted with white linen cushions are always filled with beautiful people sipping exotic drinks while murmuring into cellphones and keeping an eye on their Porsches parked at the curb. Open daily 10am to 2am. Nova Ves 11 (Kaptol Center). ☎ **01/486-02-41.**

The music and furniture at **Škola** (next door to the Millennium ice-cream and pastry shop in the center of town), is white-hot, perfect for a first date. Exotic drinks are the specialty; snacks are available, too. Open 9am to 1am Monday to Saturday. Closed Sunday. Bogovićeva 7, 3rd floor. ☎ **01/482-81-96.** www.skolaloungebar.com.

9 Plitvice Lakes National Park

Plitvice Lakes National Park, 137km (85 miles) south of Zagreb, is Croatia's most touted natural wonder: Its majestic waterfalls, lakes, and forests have earned it a place on the UNESCO register of World Heritage Sites and made it Croatia's biggest tourist attraction outside the Adriatic coast and islands. The park's most compelling features are the waterfalls that interconnect 16 clear turquoise lakes, which are set in dense forests of beech, fir, and spruce. Anywhere you go in this nearly 4,800-hectare (12,000-acre) reserve, the water is crystal clear and teeming with fish thanks to deposits of travertine (powdery white limestone rock) under the water. It is the constant distribution of travertine that is responsible for buildups of underwater mounds and thus the waterfalls. The park is also rich with caves, springs, flowering meadows, a gorge that looks like a green branch of the Grand Canyon, and several animal species including deer, wolves, wild boar, and the increasingly rare brown bear.

Plitvice became a national park in 1949. One of the Serb-Croat war's first casualties was a park policeman who was killed in an incident that is sometimes cited as the flashpoint for the 1991 war. The park was occupied for most of the war by Serb troops, and during that time, its offices and hotels were trashed, but the park itself was undamaged. Since then, the hotels and other buildings have been restored and in the last 10 years visitors have returned in droves.

GETTING THERE & GETTING AROUND

By Car   From Zagreb (trip time about 2 hr.), take the Zagreb-Rieka autocesta to Karlovac. Then follow the signs to Plitvice via the old road to Split (E-71).

By Bus   Catch a bus at the main station in Zagreb (2½ hr.), from 8:20am to 1:45am for 48kn to 64kn ($9–$12/£4.40–£6.40) one-way, depending on the time of departure, bus line, and other factors. Check schedules online at www.akz.hr, but you must call for reservations (© 060/313-333) and stop at the main office at Avenue Marin Držića 4 in the town center to get a ticket.

Plitvice is off the old road (E-71) between Split and Zagreb. Almost every town and every hotel in the country either runs tours or connects visitors with tours that include Plitvice or focus on it. There is even a separate **Plitvice Tourism Office** in Zagreb at Trg Kralja Tomislava 19 (© 01/461-3586).

Note: Make sure your bus stops at Plitvice and that it doesn't take the new highway and bypass the park on the way to Split; this is a possibility since the Zagreb-Split leg of the A-1 autocesta opened in June 2005.

VISITOR INFORMATION

There are two entrances to the park, Ulaz 1 and Ulaz 2, each of which has a tourist-info office, gift shop, and snack shop. The tourist office at Ulaz 1 is open daily from 8am to 8pm during July and August, from 9am to 5pm April to June and September, and from 9am to 4pm October to March. The office at Ulaz 2 is open from 8am to 7pm July and August, and from 9am to 5pm April to June and September. Tickets are 85kn ($15/£7.75) per day for adults and about 40kn ($7/£3.65) for seniors and kids 7 to 18. Children under 7 are free. Prices listed here are for high season and are lower other times. Enter at Ulaz (entrance) 2 to begin your tour (if you are visiting anytime except Oct–Mar), because that entrance puts you in the middle of the property and gives you more options for exploring the park. Ulaz 2 is also the site of the park's three hotels (Jezero, Plitvice, and Bellevue).

WHERE TO STAY & DINE

Private accommodations abound all around Plitvice. The hotels below are operated by the park and within walking distance.

Rooms are small, the restaurant is big at the **Hotel Jezero** 🎔 (© 053/751-400), and everything else is generic-looking. However, the food is surprisingly good and the location couldn't be more convenient to the park. Doubles start at 114€ ($135).

The Jezero's sister hotels, **Plitvice** (© 053/751-100) and **Bellevue** (© 053/751-700) are farther away from the park and have fewer services. Doubles at the two start at 82€ ($100) and 75€ ($85) respectively.

Hundreds of dining spots pepper the road to and from Plitvice, most offering spit-roasted lamb or pig and other local specialties. You can stop for a bite or buy your roasted meat by the kilo and picnic in the woods. There are a few sandwich concessions within the park itself as well as hotel restaurants, but there is only one free-standing restaurant within walking distance of the park hotels. But if you stay at one of the park hotels, try **LičKuča** ★★ at Ulaz 1 (© **053/751-023**), a touristy but interesting restaurant with a wood-burning stove large enough to roast a whole cow and a menu laden with authentic Lika dishes.

EXPLORING PLITVICE

Plitvice is hiker heaven, but even couch potatoes can see most of Plitvice's features by combining walking with riding on the park's ferries and buses. Ulaz 2 is roughly in the middle of the park, so if you start there, you can easily get to **Prošćansko,** the park's highest and largest lake, which is ringed by a hilly green landscape. No waterfalls here, as you are at the top of the cascade. From Ulaz 2 it is a quick downhill walk to a ferry, which will take you toward paths flanked by waterfalls you can almost touch. *Note:* Don't try this. Swimming is forbidden, as is walking on the travertine.

Follow the signs to the foot of **Veliki Slap (Big Waterfall),** where slender streams of water zoom off the vertical granite face into **Korana Gorge.** Veliki Slap is the most dramatic waterfall in the park, and sometimes it seems that everyone is rushing to get there. However, there are smaller falls, series of falls, and clusters of falls in other parts of the park that are impressive, too.

6

The Czech Republic

by Hana Mastrini

Here, the last 1,000 years of triumphs in art and architecture have collided, often violently, with power politics and religious conflicts.

1 Getting to Know the Czech Republic

THE LAY OF THE LAND

The Czech Republic borders Germany to the north and west and Austria to the south. Slovakia to the east (which only joined with the Czechs 1918) split with its Slavic neighbor in 1993 to form the independent Czech and Slovak republics in the "Velvet Divorce."

About 10.3 million people inhabit the Czech lands of Bohemia and Moravia, with about 1.2 million living in the districts comprising Prague's metropolitan area.

THE REGIONS IN BRIEF

Of the two regions which make up the Czech Republic, the most well known is Bohemia. This land gave Europe its favorite moniker for a free spirit: "Bohemian." Despite being beaten into submission by successive Austrian, German, and Soviet hegemony, that spirit has lived on. In the 14th century, Prague was the seat of the Holy Roman Empire. So Bohemians maintain their collective historical memory that they too, at least briefly, ruled the world. Even under the domination of the Austrians, Bohemia's industrial base was world-class, and in the peace between the big wars, independent Bohemia, especially Prague, created some of the greatest wealth on earth.

While Bohemia is the traditional home of a beer-favoring populace and the seat of Czech industrial muscle, in Moravia, to the south and east, winemaking is taken as seriously as it is in most other European grape-growing regions. Many wine bars throughout Moravia serve the village's best straight from the cask, usually alongside traditional smoked meats.

SUGGESTED CZECH ITINERARIES

THE BEST OF PRAGUE IN 1 DAY

In order to digest enough of Prague's wonders, do what visiting kings and potentates do on a 1-day visit: Walk the Royal Route (or at least part of it). From the top of the castle hill in Hradčany, tour Prague Castle in the morning. After lunch begin your slow descent through the odd hill-bound architecture of Lesser Town (Malá Strana).

Then stroll across Charles Bridge, on the way to the winding alleys of Old Town (Staré Město). You can happily get lost finding Old Town Square (Staroměstské nám.), stopping at private galleries and cafes along the way. From Old Town Square take

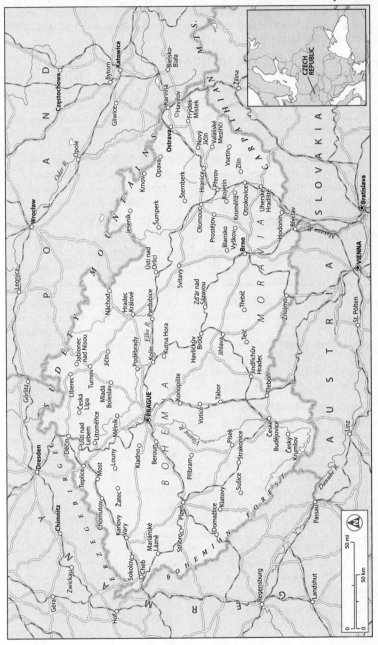

CZECH
REPUBLIC

P O L A N D

Częstochowa
Katowice
Bytom
Bielsko-
Biała
Gliwice
Opole
Żilina
Karviná
Havířov
Frýdek-
Místek
Ostrava
Nový
Jičín
Valašské
Meziříčí
Opava
Vsetín
Krnov
Přerov
Zlín
Šternberk
Hranice
Olomouc
Kojetín
Kroměříž
Otrokovice
Uherské
Hradiště
Prostějov
Jeseník
Šumperk
Blansko
Vyškov
Brno
Hodonín
Břeclav
Ústí nad
Orlicí
Svitavy
Žďár nad
Sázavou
Třebíč
Náchod
Hradec
Králové
Pardubice
Kutná Hora
Znojmo
Telč
Havlíčkův
Brod
Jihlava
Jindřichův
Hradec
St. Pölten
VIENNA
Jablonec
nad Nisou
Jičín
Poděbrady
Kolín
Liberec
Turnov
Mladá
Boleslav
Třeboň
Česká
Lípa
Ústí nad
Labem
Litoměřice
Mělník
PRAGUE
Konopiště
Votice
Tábor
České
Budějovice
Český
Krumlov
Linz
Děčín
Beroun
Kladno
Příbram
Louny
Písek
Louny
Strakonice
Teplice
Most
Žatec
Sušice
Klatovy
Domažlice
Chomutov
Karlovy
Vary
Plzeň
Mariánské
Lázně
Stříbro
Passau
Sokolov
Cheb
Regensburg
Landshut
Zwickau
Hof
Gera
Chemnitz
Zatec
Dresden
Görlitz
Legnica
Wrocław
Oder R.
Elbe R.
Vltava R.
Danube R.
Morava R.

S U D E T Y   M O U N T A I N S

C A R P A T H I A N   M T S.

M O R A V I A

B O H E M I A

B O H E M I A N   F O R E S T

E R Z G E B I R G E

SLOVAKIA

A U S T R I A

Bratislava

50 mi
50 km

Celetná street to Ovocný trh, and you get to Mozart's Prague venue, the Estates' Theater. Dinner and your evening entertainment are all probably within a 10-minute walk from anywhere in this area.

THE BEST OF PRAGUE IN 2 DAYS

On your second day, explore the varied sights of New Town, Old Town, the Jewish Quarter, and Lesser Town—what you didn't have time for the day before. Just wander and browse. Throughout Old Town you'll find numerous shops and galleries offering the finest Bohemian crystal, porcelain, and modern artwork, as well as top fashion boutiques, cafes, and restaurants. While the shops aren't that much different from those in other European cities, the setting is.

From Old Town, it's just a short walk across Charles Bridge to Lesser Town. This was once the neighborhood for diplomats, merchants, and those who served the castle, with narrow houses squeezed between palaces and embassies. Finish the day by getting a riverside view of the city and Charles Bridge from Kampa Park.

THE BEST OF THE CZECH REPUBLIC IN 1 WEEK

The Czech lands offer many historic and cultural monuments. Castles and châteaux dominating the picturesque natural landscape represent the most important part of Czech attractions. Below I give you one example out of many possible itineraries.

Days ❶ & ❷ Arrive in Prague

Spend the first 2 days as recommended above. Then rent a car from one of the rental agencies recommended on p. 218. Keep in mind that the speed limit is 90kmph (56 mph) on two-lane highways and 50kmph (31 mph) in villages.

Day ❸ Český Krumlov 𝒢𝒢𝒢

Leave for this romantic destination in southern Bohemia early in the morning, when the roads aren't too crowded. This will also allow you time to stroll around the city. Take Highway D1 and then E55. The trip takes about 2½ hours. Once there, visit the castle first, then just wander, and finally relax in a local restaurant. Spend the night in one of the recommended hotels or pensions. But book early, as Krumlov is the most popular Czech destination after Prague. See details on p. 260.

Day ❹ České Budějovice, Castle Hluboká nad Vltavou 𝒢𝒢

On this day start heading for Plzeň via České Budějovice, the home of Budvar beer. Upon arrival at České Budějovice,

have a quick stroll and look around one of central Europe's largest squares, where you can also have lunch. In the early afternoon, take Highway E49 and then Highway 105 north for 30 minutes (this includes parking time) to the tiny town Hluboká nad Vltavou, where you'll see a castle fashioned after the Windsor Castle in England towering above the green meadows. For more information see p. 263.

Next, take Highway E49 to Plzeň. You'll get there in about 2 hours. Spend the night there. See p. 264.

Day ❺ Plzeň

Explore Plzeň's center in the morning, when it is the least crowded. If you're interested in the beer-making process, visit the Pilsner Breweries in the early afternoon. Just outside the factory is a restaurant that serves traditional Czech food. See p. 265 for more details.

After your break, hit the road again. Highway E49 will take you to the most popular Czech spa town, Karlovy Vary, in about 1 hour. Spend the night there.

Day ❻ Karlovy Vary ⍟
This town was built for relaxation, which makes it the perfect place to end your Bohemian week.

Start slowly with a stroll around the city's historic center. Then, get your "cup" and taste the mineral waters which make this destination so famous. Finally, book yourself a massage or other individual spa treatment at one of the recommended spa complexes. Find out more about Karlovy Vary on page 256.

Day ❼ Karlovy Vary to Prague
It's time to return to Prague. Take Highway E48. You should reach the capital in 2 hours. Be warned that this two-lane highway is one of the busiest in the country.

THE CZECH REPUBLIC TODAY

Prague was ready for prime time and the First World competitive pressures when the Czechs joined nine other countries to become new members of the European Union in May 2004.

The first decade of a return to capitalism is well past, and the city has taken on the familiar air of a European metropolis that makes a good living from tourism. The most-visited castles and cathedrals are now surrounded by entrepreneurs trying to make back the bucks (or *koruny*) denied to them under Communism—and they're trying to make them back as quickly as possible.

Prague is a city rebuilding its face and its spirit. It's trying to keep up with the massive new flood of cars and visitors and is getting used to the pros and cons of its renewed affluence.

THE CZECH PEOPLE & CULTURE

Prague has once again become a well-heeled business center in the heart of central Europe. Nostalgic and successful Czechs say it's capitalism, not Communism, that comes most naturally here.

If you talk to a Praguer long enough, the conversation will often turn into a lecture about how the country had one of the world's richest economies, per capita, between the world wars. Forty years of Communism, a Praguer will say, was just a detour. The between-wars period, lovingly called the First Republic, recalls a time when democracy and capitalism thrived, and Prague's bistros and dance halls were filled with dandies and flappers swinging the night away, until the Nazi invasion in 1939 spoiled the party.

The First Republic motif has been revived in many clubs and restaurants, and you can see hints of this style in Czech editions of top Western fashion magazines.

Since the 1990 Velvet Revolution, Praguers have been obsessed with style. Many people—especially the *novobohatí* (nouveau riche)—rushed out to buy the flashiest Mercedes or BMW they could find with the quick money gained from the restitution of Communist-seized property.

In the evening, you can find a typical Bohemian playing cards with friends at the neighborhood *hospoda* or *pivnice* (beer hall) or debating at a *kavárna* (cafe). Most likely, though, the typical Czech will be parked in front of the TV, as the country maintains one of the highest per-capita nightly viewing audiences in Europe.

CZECH CUISINE

Czech menus are packed with meat, and the true Czech experience can be summed up in three native words: *vepřo, knedlo, zelo*—pork, dumplings, cabbage. When prepared with care and imagination, Czech food can be hearty and satisfying. Plus, with new restaurants pouring into the city, it's getting easier to eat lighter in Prague.

Besides being the center of extracurricular activity, pubs *(hospody)* are the best places to get fulfilling, inexpensive meals, not to mention the best brews—Pilsner Urquell, Budvar, Staropramen (some call them "liquid bread"). Selections are typically the same: sirloin slices in cream sauce and dumplings *(svíčková na smetaně)*, goulash *(guláš)*, roast beef *(roštěná)*, or breaded, fried *hermelín* cheese *(smažený sýr)*.

Reservations aren't usually accepted, but you might see tables reserved for regulars known as *štamgast.*

LANGUAGE

Bohemia, through good times and bad, has been under a strong Germanic influence, and throughout a great deal of its history, German was the preferred language of the power elite. The Czech language, however, stems from the Slavic family, which includes Polish, Russian, Slovak, and others, though German has altered many Czech words. Czech uses a Latin alphabet with some letters topped by a small hat called a háček to denote Slavic phonic combinations like "sh" for š, "ch" for č, and, everyone's favorite, "rzh" for ř. Slovak differs slightly from Czech, but Czechs and Slovaks understand each other's language.

USEFUL WORDS & PHRASES

English	Czech	Pronunciation
Hello	**Dobrý den**	*Doh*-bree den
Good morning	**Dobré jitro**	*Doh*-breh *yee*-troh
Good evening	**Dobrý večer**	*Doh*-bree *veh*-chair
How are you?	**Jak se máte?**	*Yahk* seh *mah*-teh
Very well	**Velmi dobře**	*Vel*-mee *doh*-brsheh
Thank you	**Děkuji vám**	*Dyek*-ooee vahm
You're welcome	**Prosím**	*Proh*-seem
Please	**Prosím**	*Proh*-seem
Yes	**Ano**	*Ah*-no
No	**Ne**	Neh
Excuse me	**Promiňte**	*Proh*-min-teh
How much does it cost?	**Kolik to stojí?**	*Koh*-leek taw *stoh*-ee
I don't understand.	**Nerozumím.**	*Neh*-roh-zoo-meem
Just a moment.	**Moment, prosím.**	*Moh*-ment, *proh*-seem
Goodbye	**Na shledanou**	*Nah* skleh-dah-noh-oo
I'm looking for . . .	**Hledám . . .**	*Hleh*-dahm . . .
a hotel	**hotel**	*hoh*-tel
a youth hostel	**studentskou ubytovnu**	*stoo*-dent-skoh *oo*-beet-ohv-noo
a bank	**banku**	*bahnk*-oo
the church	**kostel**	*kohs*-tell
the city center	**centrum**	*tsent*-room

the museum	**muzeum**	*moo*-zeh-oom
a pharmacy	**lékárnu**	*lek*-ahr-noo
I have a reservation.	**Mám zamluvený**	
	nocleh.	Mahm *zah*-mloo-veh-ni *nohts*-leh
My name is . . .	**Jmenuji se . . .**	*Meh*-noo-yee seh . . .

2 Planning Your Trip to the Czech Republic

VISITOR INFORMATION

INFORMATION OFFICES   E-Travel, a private Prague-based firm, has developed a fantastic set of websites, including **www.travel.cz** for general Czech tourist and accommodations information and **www.apartments.cz** for booking private apartments online. Start any trip planning here.

The former Communist-era state travel agency, **Čedok,** is now privatized so its only U.S. office has long since closed its doors, but you can contact English-speaking staff through its London or Prague offices or via the Internet. In the United Kingdom, the address is 314–22 Regent St., London W1B 3BG (© **020/7580-3778;** www.cedok. co.uk). You can call the Prague main office for advance bookings at Na Příkopě 18, Praha 1 (© **224-197-632;** www.cedok.cz).

INTERNET INFORMATION   Those hooked up to the Web can find updated information in English on the official Czech Foreign Ministry site at **www.czech.cz.** See above for the **Čedok, AVE,** and **E-Travel** websites. For general tips, check out the Prague Information Service at **www.pis.cz** or **www.prague-info.cz.** And for the latest city lights and sights, try the weekly *Prague Post* website at **www.praguepost.com.**

ENTRY REQUIREMENTS

For an up-to-date, country-by-country listing of passport requirements around the world, go to the "Foreign Entry Requirement" Web page of the U.S. State Department at **http://travel.state.gov.**

DOCUMENTS   American, Canadian, Australian, and New Zealand citizens need only passports and no visa for stays less than 90 days. Their passports must be valid for a period of at least 90 days beyond the expected length of stay in the Czech Republic.

Nationals from the European Union (United Kingdom, Ireland) can travel to the Czech Republic with passports (validity is not limited) and they are allowed to stay for an unlimited period of time.

Children inscribed in their parents' passports can travel with their parents up to the age of 15. Once the child has reached the age of 15, a separate passport is necessary.

For more information, go to **www.czech.cz.** A full list of the Czech embassies and consulates abroad is available on **www.mzv.cz.**

EMBASSIES   The **U.S. Embassy,** Tržiště 15, Praha 1 (© 257-530-663), is open Monday to Friday from 8am to 4:30pm. The **Canadian Embassy,** Muchova 6, Praha 6 (© 272-101-800), is open Monday to Friday from 8:30am to 12:30pm and 1:30 to 4:30pm. The **U.K. Embassy,** Thunovská 14, Praha 1 (© 257-402-111), is open Monday to Friday from 8:30am to 12:30pm and 1:30 to 5pm. You can visit the **Australian Honorary Consul,** Klimentská 10, Praha 1 (© 296-578-350), Monday to Friday from 9am to 1pm and 2 to 5pm. The **Irish Embassy** is at Tržiště 13, Praha 1 (© 257-530-061) and is open Monday to Friday from 9am to 1pm and 2 to 5pm.

The **New Zealand Honorary Consul** is located at Dykova 19, Praha 10 (© 222-514-672), and visits here are by appointment.

MONEY

The basic unit of currency is the **koruna** (plural, **koruny**) or crown, abbreviated **Kč.** Each koruna is divided into 100 **haléřů** or hellers. In this guide, I quote the koruna at about $0.0416 in U.S. dollars: $1 buys 24Kč, and £1 buys 43Kč. Even though the Czech Republic is now a member state of the European Union, it has not accepted the euro as its currency—yet. You will see in Prague's hotels and restaurants prices listed in euros anyway, so European visitors can easily and quickly compare. At this writing, 1 euro buys 30Kč. These rates may vary substantially when you arrive, as the koruna often gyrates wildly in the open economy.

For up-to-the-minute currency conversion go to **www.xe.com/ucc**.

In the Czech Republic, hundreds of new storefront shops provide exchange services but, if possible, use credit cards or bank cards at ATMs (don't forget your PIN). In both cases, rates are better and the commissions are lower. If you must exchange at a storefront shop, beware of fees, which can go as high as 10% of the transaction.

Chequepoint has outlets in heavily touristed areas and keeps long hours, sometimes all night, but their business practices are sometimes questionable. Central Prague locations are 28. října 13 and Staroměstské nám. 21 (both open 24 hr.); Staroměstské nám. 27 (daily 8am–11:30pm); and Václavské nám. 32 (daily 8am–11pm).

If you can't use your credit card at an ATM, stick to larger banks to make your trades; there's usually a 1% to 3% commission.

American Express, MasterCard, and Visa are widely accepted in central Prague, but shopkeepers outside the city center still seem mystified by plastic. The credit card companies bill at a favorable rate of exchange and save you money by eliminating commissions. You can get cash advances on your MasterCard, Visa, or American Express card from **Komerční banka,** at its main branch, Na Příkopě 33, Praha 1 (© **222-432-111**); or at most any of its branches, which now have 24-hour ATMs.

The American Express branch at Václavské nám. 56, Praha 1 provides the lost/stolen card service on © **222-800-237.** For more information and facts go to p. 213.

WHEN TO GO

Spring, which can occasionally bring glorious days, is best known for gray, windy stints with rain. The city and the countryside explode with green around the first of May, so if you're depressed by stark contrasts and cold-weather pollution, plan your trip for between May and October. The high summer season brings a constant flow of tour buses, and people-watching (of practically every culture) is at its best. Most Praguers head for their weekend cottages in high season, so if you're looking for local flavor, try another time.

September into October is one of my favorite periods as cool autumn breezes turn trees on the surrounding hills into a multicolored frame for Prague Castle. The crowds are thinner and the prices are better.

A true lover of Prague's mysticism should aim to come in the dead cold of February. It sounds bizarre, but this is when you can best enjoy the monochrome silhouettes, shadows, and solitude that make Prague unique. You'll never forget a gray, snowy February afternoon on Charles Bridge. The only drawback of a winter visit to Prague,

Major Festivals in the Czech Republic

Febiofest (www.febiofest.cz) is one of the largest noncompetitive film and video festivals in central Europe. Late March. The **Prague Spring Music Festival** is a world-famous 3-week series of symphony, opera, and chamber performances (www.festival.cz). Mid-May to early June. The **Slavnost Pětilisté Růže (Festival of the Five-Petaled Rose)**, held annually to mark the summer solstice gives residents of Český Krumlov the excuse to dress up in Renaissance costumes and parade through the streets. www.ckrumlov.cz. Third weekend in June.

The **Karlovy Vary International Film Festival** (www.iffkv.cz) predates Communism and has regained its "A" rating from the international body governing film festivals. Late June to early July. The **Moravian Autumn International Music Festival** (www.mhf-brno.cz) in Brno is dedicated to symphonic and chamber musical works. Late September/beginning of October.

---

if you forget about the cold and occasional snow, is that castles and other attractions in the provinces are closed (though not Prague Castle).

HOLIDAYS

Official holidays are observed on January 1 (New Year's Day); Easter Monday (Mar/Apr); May 1 (Labor Day); May 8 (Liberation Day, from Fascism); July 5 (Introduction of Christianity); July 6 (Death of Jan Hus); September 28 (St. Wenceslas Day); October 28 (Foundation of the Republic); November 17 (Day of Student Movements in 1939 and 1989); December 24 and 25 (Christmas); and December 26 (St. Stephen's Day).

On these holidays, most businesses and shops (including food shops) are closed, and buses and trams run on Sunday schedules.

GETTING THERE
BY PLANE
The Major Airlines

About two dozen international airlines offer regularly scheduled service into Prague's **Ruzyně Airport.** The only U.S. carrier flying direct to Prague is Continental via its New York/Newark hub using a code-sharing arrangement with the Czech national carrier **ČSA Czech Airlines** (© 800/223-2365; www.czech-airlines.com). ČSA also flies to Prague from Toronto and Montreal. Germany's **Lufthansa** (© 800/645-3880; www.lufthansa-USA.com) has frequent connections to Prague with flights from New York and San Francisco via their Frankfurt hub.

BY TRAIN

Train fares in Europe are lower than those in the United States. Czech tickets are particularly inexpensive but prices are rising. Because European countries are compact, it often takes less time to travel city-to-city by train than by plane. Prague is about 5 hours by train from Munich, Berlin, and Vienna. Direct trains to Prague depart daily from Paris (via Frankfurt) and Berlin (via Dresden).

You should also check the schedule for the ultramodern, high-speed, passenger-only train that travels from London Waterloo International Station to Europe, the **Eurostar,** at www.eurostar.com or by calling © 01777-777-878.

For more information on traveling on České dráhy (Czech Railways) see www.cd.cz.

TRAIN PASSES *Note:* The Czech Republic is not covered by the Eurailpass, though the **European East Pass** and the **Austrian Czech Railpass** are accepted. The Republic does have two country-specific pass options.

CZECH FLEXIPASS   This pass entitles you to any 3 days of unlimited train travel in a 15-day period. It costs $74 for first class and $52 for second class.

PRAGUE EXCURSION PASS   This pass provides one round-trip excursion on the Czech National Railways from any Czech border to Prague (note that you don't have to return to the same border town on the way out from Prague). It is valid for 7 days, and stops in other places in the Czech Republic are allowed on the way to and from Prague but your entire journey must be completed within 1 calendar day. The pass costs $60 for first class or $45 for second class. Travelers 12 to 25 years old can get a **Prague Excursion Youth Pass,** which costs only $50 for first class and $40 for second class.

All of the passes above must be purchased in North America before you leave on your trip. You can buy them on the phone or online from **Rail Europe** (✆ 877/257-2887 in the U.S., or 800/361-RAIL in Canada; www.raileurope.com).

If you're visiting more countries in Eastern Europe, you might want to get the **European East Pass,** which combines travel in Austria, the Czech Republic, Hungary, Poland, and Slovakia. It costs $225 (first class) or $158 (second class), and you can use it for 5 days of unlimited train travel in a 1-month period.

Many rail passes are available in the United Kingdom for travel in Britain and Europe. However, one of the most widely used of these passes, the InterRail card, isn't valid for travel in the Czech Republic.

BY BUS

Throughout Europe, bus transportation is usually less expensive than rail travel and covers a more extensive area. European buses generally outshine their U.S. counterparts. In the Czech Republic, buses cost significantly less than trains and often offer more direct routes. **Europabus,** c/o DER Tours/German Rail, 11933 Wilshire Blvd., Los Angeles, CA 90025 (✆ **800/782-2424** or 310/479-4140), provides information on regular coach service. **Busabout London Traveller's Centre,** 258 Vauxhall Bridge Rd., London, SW 1V 1BS (✆ **0207-950-1661;** www.busabout.com), is a British operator specializing in economical bus tours of Europe. Bookings can be made online.

If you're coming from London, **Eurolines** (✆ **08705-143-219;** www.eurolines.co.uk) runs regular bus service from London to Prague at about £102 round-trip. Coaches are equipped with toilets and reclining seats, and trips take about 30 hours. By law, drivers are required to stop at regular intervals for rest and refreshment.

Kingscourt Express, Havelská 8, Praha 1 (✆ **224-234-583;** www.kce.cz), operates the most popular scheduled bus service between London and Prague, which stops in Prague just across from the Florenc station. The nearly 21-hour trip runs six times weekly, and the round-trip costs 3,100Kč ($129/£62).

BY CAR

You definitely shouldn't rent a car to explore Prague. But if you want to see the countryside, driving can be a fun way to travel. Czechs, who learned to drive in low-powered *Škodas,* still run up your tailpipe before passing, even though many now drive beefier BMWs and Opels. The combination of high-speed muscle cars, rickety Eastern bloc specials, and smoky cargo trucks crawling along can make driving on two-lane highways frustrating. But a car will make it easier to find a budget hotel or a comfortable spot to camp.

GETTING AROUND
BY CAR
A liter of gasoline costs about 30Kč ($1.25/£1), expensive by North American standards but cheaper than in western Europe. Gas stations are plentiful, and most are equipped with small convenience stores.

Except for main highways, which are a seemingly endless parade of construction sites, roads tend to be narrow and in need of repair. Especially at night, you should drive only on major roads. If you must use smaller roads, be careful. For details on car rentals, see p. 218.

If you experience car trouble, major highways have emergency telephones from which you can call for assistance. There's also the **ÚAMK,** a 24-hour motor assistance club that provides service for a fee. They drive bright-yellow pickup trucks and can be summoned on main highways by using the SOS emergency phones located at the side of the road every kilometer or so. If you are not near one of these phones or are on a road that doesn't have them, you can contact ÚAMK at ✆ **1230.** This is a toll-free call.

BY TRAIN
Trains run by České dráhy (Czech Railways) provide a good and less expensive alternative to driving. The fare is determined by how far you travel: 50km (31 miles) cost 64Kč ($2.65/£1) in second class or 96Kč ($4/£2) in first class. First class is not usually available, or needed, on shorter trips.

It's important to find out which Prague station your train departs from, since not all trains leave from the main station, though all major stations are on metro lines. Check when you buy your tickets. Trains heading to destinations in the north usually depart from **Nádraží Holešovice,** Vrbenského ulice, Praha 7 (✆ **224-615-865**), above the Nádraží Holešovice metro stop at the end of the Red metro line (line C). Local trains to the southeast are commonly found at **Smíchovské Nádraží,** Nádražní ulice, Praha 5 (✆ **224-617-686**), on the yellow metro line heading west from the center. Most trains to west and south Bohemia and Moravia leave from **Hlavní Nádraží (Main Station),** Wilsonova 80, Praha 1 (✆ **224-614-071**), at the metro stop of the same name on the red metro (line C) in the center. Train stations in Prague are now better at providing information, especially in English. There are also timetables for public use that allow you to plan your trips.

BY BUS
The Czech Republic operates a pretty decent bus system, and because trains often follow circuitous routes, buses can be a better, though slightly more expensive, option. State-run ČSAD buses are still relatively inexpensive and surprisingly abundant, and

---

⎛Tips⎞ Czech Rail Online
Czech Rail has a useful though somewhat complicated website in English, German, and Czech at **www.cdrail.cz.** To check the timetable, go to **www.jizdnirady. cz** or **www.idos.cz.**

---

they offer terrific coverage of the country. Like train passengers, bus passengers are charged on a kilometer basis, with each kilometer costing about 91 hellers (5¢). Make sure, however, that you buy your tickets early, especially on weekends, and get to the proper boarding area early to ensure you get a seat.

Prague's main bus station, **Central Bus Station—Florenc,** Křižíkova 5, Praha 8 (for bus connections information call ℰ **900-144-444;** www.florenc.cz), is above the Florenc metro stop (line C). Unfortunately, few employees speak English here, making it a bit tricky for non-Czech speakers to obtain schedule information. To find your bus, you can try the large boards just next to the office where all buses are listed. They're in alphabetical order, but sometimes it's tough to find your destination since it may lie in the middle of a route to another place. If you have some time before you depart Prague, your best bet for bus information and tickets is to visit **Čedok,** Na Příkopě 18, Praha 1 (ℰ **800-112-112** or 224-197-111; www.cedok.cz), open Monday to Friday from 9am to 6pm.

BY BIKE

Central European Adventure Tours, Jáchymova 4, Praha 1 (ℰ/fax **222-328-879;** http://cea51.tripod.com), rents touring bikes and arranges whatever transport you need for them. The best biking is outside Prague, on the tertiary roads and paved paths in the provinces. They will suggest routes and provide maps. A 1-day guided biking trip around Karlštejn Castle and Koněpruské Caves costs 680Kč ($28/£14). Call ahead to make arrangements. Tickets and information are also available at the PIS office, Na Příkopě 20, Praha 1.

TIPS ON ACCOMMODATIONS

Note that in Prague you can find the best value in the center of the city by staying in one of the numerous pensions or hotels near náměstí Míru. Don't be afraid to rent a room away from the old quarters of town, especially if it's close to a metro stop. The farther away from the center, the lower the rates will be, and the metro connections are fast and affordable. Always know the latest market exchange rates when budgeting your stay, and build in some padding for any potential surge. The exact rate at many hotels depends on the daily koruna/euro exchange rate.

TIPS ON DINING

Stick to Czech and European cuisines; ingredients for other dishes are more rare and expensive. The more the menu varies from pork, cabbage, and dumplings (with the exception of pizza), the higher the price will be. And remember that the farther from the Castle or Old Town you go, generally the cheaper your meal will be. Go for the beer and eat where you drink it. The food won't be stunning but will be filling and usually cheap. Watch out for on-table treats like almonds, olives, and appetizers. Some restaurants gouge customers by charging exorbitant amounts for them.

BEST BUYS

Fine crystal has been produced in the Bohemian countryside since the 14th century. In the 17th and 18th centuries, it became the preferred glass of the world's elite, drawing royals and the rich to Karlovy Vary to buy straight from the source. Today, the quality remains high, and you can still purchase contemporary glass for prices that are much lower than those in the West. Antiques and antiquarian books and prints are widely available and are distinctive souvenirs, sold by specialist Antikvariáts. Since beer is a little heavy to carry home and the local wine isn't worth it, take home a bottle of **Becherovka,** the nation's popular herbal liqueur from Karlovy Vary. You'll find the distinctive green decanter in shops; it costs about 400Kč ($17/£8) per liter.

FAST FACTS: The Czech Republic

Area Code The area codes for each city are combined with the local numbers. Local phone numbers consist of 9 digits, which must be dialed from anyplace within the Czech Republic.

Business Hours Most **banks** are open Monday to Friday from 8:30am to 6pm. Business **offices** are generally open Monday to Friday from 8am to 6pm. **Pubs** are usually open daily from 11am to midnight. Most **restaurants** open for lunch from noon to 3pm and for dinner from 6 to 11pm; only a few stay open later. **Stores** are typically open Monday to Friday from 9am to 6pm and Saturday from 9am to 1pm, but those in the tourist center keep longer hours and are open Sunday as well.

Currency Exchange Banks generally offer the best exchange rates, but **American Express** is competitive and doesn't charge commission for cashing traveler's checks, regardless of the issuer. Don't hesitate to use a credit card; card exchange rates often work to the traveler's advantage.

Electricity Czech appliances operate on 220 volts and plug into two-pronged outlets that differ from those in America and the United Kingdom. Appliances designed for the U.S. or U.K. markets must use an adapter and a transformer (sometimes incorrectly called a converter). Don't attempt to plug an American appliance directly into a European electrical outlet without a transformer; you'll ruin your appliance and possibly start a fire.

Emergencies Dial the European Emergency Number © **112** or you can reach Prague's **police** at © **158** and **fire** services by dialing © **150** from any phone. To call an **ambulance,** dial © **155.**

Language Berlitz has a comprehensive phrase book in Czech. A clever illustrated **Web tutorial** is found at **www.czechprimer.org.**

Liquor Laws There's no law against teenagers drinking alcohol, but it can only be sold to those who are over 18. Any adult selling liquor to younger person can be prosecuted. Pubs and clubs can stay open 24 hours.

Mail Post offices are plentiful and are normally open Monday to Friday from 8am to 6pm. Mailboxes are orange and are usually attached to the sides of buildings. If you're sending mail overseas, make sure it's marked "Par Avion" so it doesn't go by surface. If you mail your letters at a post office, the clerk will add this stamp for you. Postcards to the U.S. cost 14Kč (60¢/30p), to any E.U. country 9Kč (40¢/20p). Mail can take up to 10 days to reach its destination.

Police Dial the European Emergency Number © **112** from any phone in an emergency. For Czech police dial © **158.**

Restrooms You'll find plenty of public restrooms. Toilets are located in every metro station and are staffed by cleaning personnel who usually charge users 5Kč (20¢/10p) and dispense a precious few sheets of toilet paper.

Be aware—even though restrooms at the city's train stations are staffed, you need to get your toilet paper by yourself from a dispenser situated on the wall before you actually enter the restroom. The charge here is 6Kč (25¢/10p).

Restaurants and pubs around all the major sights are usually kind to nonpatrons who wish to use their facilities. Around the castle and elsewhere, public toilets are clearly marked with the letters wc.

Safety In Prague's center you'll feel generally safer than in most Western cities, but always take common-sense precautions. Be aware of your immediate surroundings. Don't walk alone at night around Wenceslas Square—one of the main areas for prostitution and where a lot of unexplainable loitering takes place. All visitors should be watchful of pickpockets in heavily touristed areas, especially on Charles Bridge, in Old Town Square, and in front of the main train station. Be especially wary on crowded buses, trams, and trains. Don't keep your wallet in a back pocket and don't flash a lot of cash or jewelry. Riding the metro or trams at night feels just as safe as during the day.

Taxes A 19% **value-added tax (VAT)** is built into the price of most goods and services rather than tacked on at the register. Most restaurants also include the VAT in the prices stated on their menus. If they don't, that fact should be stated somewhere on the menu. There are no VAT refunds for the Czech Republic.

Telephone & Fax For **directory inquiries** regarding phone numbers within the Czech Republic, dial ⓒ 1180. For information about services and rates abroad, call ⓒ 1181. Dial tones are continual high-pitched beeps that sound something like busy signals in America. After dialing a number from a pay phone, you might hear a series of very quick beeps that tell you the line is being connected. Busy signals sound like the dial tones, only quicker.

There are two kinds of **pay phones** in normal use. The first accepts coins and the other operates exclusively with a phone card, available from post offices and news agents in denominations ranging from 50Kč to 500Kč ($2.10–$21/£1–£10). The minimum cost of a local call is 4Kč (15¢/8p). Coin-op phones have displays telling you the minimum price for your call, but they don't make change, so don't load more than you have to. You can add more coins as the display gets near zero. Phone-card telephones automatically deduct the price of your call from the card. These cards are especially handy if you want to call abroad, as you don't have to continuously chuck in the change. If you're calling the States, you'd better get a phone card with plenty of points, as calls run about 20Kč (85¢/40p) per minute; calls to the United Kingdom cost 15Kč (60¢/30p) per minute.

A fast, convenient way to call the United States from Europe is via services like AT&T USA Direct. This bypasses the foreign operator and automatically links you to an operator with your long-distance carrier in your home country. The access number in the Czech Republic for **AT&T USA Direct** is ⓒ 00-800-222-55288. For **MCI CALL USA,** dial ⓒ 00-800-001-112. Canadians can connect with **Canada Direct** at ⓒ 00-800-001-115, and Brits can connect with **BT Direct** at ⓒ 00-800-001-144. From a pay phone in the Czech Republic, your local phone card will be debited only for a local call.

Tipping Rules for tipping aren't as strict in the Czech Republic as they are in the United States. At most restaurants and pubs, locals just round the bill up to the nearest few *koruny*. When you're presented with good service at tablecloth places, a 10% tip is proper. Washroom and cloakroom attendants usually expect a couple of koruny, and porters at airports and train stations usually receive 25Kč ($1.05/50p) per bag. Taxi drivers should get about 10%, unless they've already ripped you off, in which case they should get a referral to the police. Check restaurant menus to see if service is included before you leave a tip.

3 Prague

GETTING THERE
BY PLANE

Prague's **Ruzyně Airport** (© 220-113-314; www.prg.aero or www.csl.cz) is located 19km (12 miles) west of the city center. Its new, airy, and efficient departures and arrivals terminals have lost the Communist-era feel and have many added amenities. There's a bank for changing money (usually open daily 7am–11pm), car-rental offices (see "Getting Around," below), and information stands that can help you find accommodations if you've arrived without reservations.

GETTING DOWNTOWN You can make your way from the airport to your hotel by taxi, airport shuttle bus, or city bus.

Official airport taxis are plentiful and line up in front of the arrivals terminal. Alas, the Volkswagen Passats queued directly outside the terminal's main exit all belong to the same cartel sanctioned by the airport authority. (See "Getting Around" below for details.) The drivers are getting more pleasant but are still often arrogant and dishonest. Negotiate the fare in advance and have it written down. Expect to pay about 700Kč to 800Kč ($29–$33/£14–£16) for the 20 or so minutes to the city center, depending on the whims of the syndicate. If you want to save money, find other travelers to share the expense.

CEDAZ (© 220-114-296; www.aas.cz/cedaz) operates an **airport shuttle bus** from the airport to náměstí Republiky in central Prague. It leaves the airport daily every 30 minutes from 5:30am to 9:30pm and stops near the náměstí Republiky metro station. The shuttle costs 90Kč ($3.75/£2) for the 30-minute trip.

Even cheaper is **city bus no. 119,** which takes passengers from the bus stop at the right of the airport exit to the Dejvická metro station (and back). The bus/metro combo costs only 20Kč (85¢/40p), but the bus makes many stops. Travel time is about 40 minutes.

BY TRAIN

Passengers traveling to Prague by train typically pull into one of two central stations: Hlavní nádraží (Main Station) or Nádraží Holešovice (Holešovice Station). Both are on line C of the metro system and offer a number of services, including money exchange, a post office, and a luggage-storage area.

At both terminals you'll find **AVE Ltd.** (© 251-551-011), an accommodations agency that arranges beds in hostels as well as rooms in hotels and apartments. It's open daily from 6am to 11pm. If you arrive without room reservations, this agency is definitely worth a visit.

Hlavní nádraží, Wilsonova třída, Praha 2 (© **224-614-071**), is the grander and more popular station. From the train platform, you'll walk down a flight of stairs and through a tunnel before arriving in the ground-level main hall, which contains ticket windows, a useful **Prague Information Service** office that sells city maps and dispenses information, and restrooms. Also useful is the **ČD center** (© **840-112-113;** www.cd.cz) run by the Czech Railways. It provides domestic and international train information as well as currency exchange and accommodations services. It is open daily 7 to 11am, 11:30am to 2pm, and 2:30 to 5:45pm. Visa and MasterCard are accepted. An information window is open 3:15am to 12:40am (the train station is closed 1–3am). The station's basement holds a left-luggage counter, which is open 24 hours and charges 30Kč ($1.25/£1) per bag per day. The nearby lockers aren't secure and should be avoided.

Nádraží Holešovice, Partyzánská at Vrbenského, Praha 7 (© **224-615-865**), Prague's second train station, is usually the terminus for trains from Berlin and other points north. Although it's not as centrally located as the main station, its more manageable size and location at the end of metro line C make it almost as convenient.

Prague has two smaller train stations. **Masaryk Station,** Hybernská ulice (© **221-111-122**), is primarily for travelers arriving on trains originating from other Bohemian cities or from Brno or Bratislava. Situated about 10 minutes by foot from the main train station, Masaryk is near Staré Město, just a stone's throw from náměstí Republiky metro station. **Smíchov Station,** Nádražní ulice at Rozkošného (© **224-617-686**), is the terminus for commuter trains from western and southern Bohemia, though an occasional international train pulls in here. The station has a 24-hour baggage check and is serviced by metro line B.

BY BUS

The **Central Bus Station–Florenc,** Křižíkova 4–6, Praha 8 (© **900-144-444** for timetable info), is a few blocks north of the main train station. Most local and long-distance buses arrive here. The adjacent Florenc metro station is on both lines B and C. Florenc station is relatively small and doesn't have many visitor services. Even smaller depots are at **Želivského** (metro line A), **Smíchovské nádraží** (metro line B), and **Nádraží Holešovice** (metro line C).

CITY LAYOUT

The **river Vltava** bisects Prague and provides the best line of orientation; you can use **Charles Bridge** as your central point. From the bridge, turn toward **Prague Castle,** the massive complex on the hill with the cathedral thrusting out. Now you're facing west.

Up on the hill is the Castle District known as **Hradčany.** Running up the hill between the bridge and the castle is the district known as **Malá Strana** (literally the "Small Side," but known as Lesser Town in English). Turn around, and behind you on the right (east) bank is **Staré Město** (Old Town), and farther to the south and east **Nové Město** (New Town). The highlands even farther east used to be the royal vineyards, **Vinohrady,** now a popular neighborhood for expatriates with a growing array of accommodations and restaurants. The districts farther out are where most Praguers live, and have few attractions.

MAIN BRIDGES, SQUARES & STREETS You'll best enjoy Prague by walking its narrow streets, busy squares, and scenic bridges. After **Charles Bridge (Karlův most),**

the other two bridges worth walking are **Mánes Bridge (Mánesův most)**, which provides a stunning low-angle view of the castle especially at night, and the **Bridge of the Legions (most Legií)**, which links the National Theater to Petřín Hill.

On the left bank coming off Charles Bridge is **Mostecká Street,** and at the end of it sits the cozy square under the castle hill, **Malostranské náměstí.** On the hill outside the main castle gate is the motorcade-worn **Hradčanské náměstí,** on the city side of which you'll find a spectacular view of spires and red roofs below.

On the east side of Charles Bridge, you can wind through most any of the old alleys leading from the bridge and get pleasantly lost amid the shops and cafes. The tourist-packed route through Old Town is **Karlova Street.** Like Karlova, almost any other route in Old Town will eventually lead you to **Staroměstské náměstí (Old Town Sq.)**, the breathtaking heart of Staré Město. A black monument to Jan Hus, the martyred Czech Protestant leader, dominates the square. The tree-lined boulevard to the right behind Hus is **Pařížská (Parisian Blvd.)** with boutiques and restaurants; it forms the edge of the Jewish Quarter. Over Hus's left shoulder is **Dlouhá Street,** and in front of him to his left is the kitschy shopping zone on **Celetná.** Across the square to Hus's right, past the clock tower of Old Town Hall (Staroměstská radnice), is **Železná Street,** which leads to Mozart's Prague venue, the Estates' Theater. Farther to Hus's right is the narrow alley **Melantrichova,** which winds southeast to **Václavské náměstí (Wenceslas Sq.)**, site of pro-democracy demonstrations in 1968 and 1989.

GETTING AROUND
BY PUBLIC TRANSPORTATION

Prague's public transportation network is one of the few sound Communist-era legacies and is still remarkably affordable. In central Prague, metro (subway) stations abound. Trams and buses offer a cheap sightseeing experience but also require a strong stomach for jostling with fellow passengers in close quarters.

TICKETS & PASSES   For single-use **tickets,** there are two choices. You can ride a maximum of five stations on the metro (not including the station of validation) or 20 minutes on a tram or bus, without transfers (on the metro you can transfer from line A to B to C within 30 min.), for 14Kč (60¢/30p); children 6 and under ride free, 6- to 15-year-olds for 7Kč (30¢/15p). This is usually enough for trips in the historic districts. Rides of more than five stops on the metro, or longer tram or bus rides, with unlimited transfers for up to 75 minutes (90 min. on Sat, Sun, public holidays, and after 8pm on workdays) after your ticket is validated, cost 20Kč (85¢/40p).

A **1-day pass** good for unlimited rides is 80Kč ($3.35/£2), a **3-day pass** 220Kč ($9.15/£4), a **7-day pass** 280Kč ($12/£6), and a **15-day pass** 320Kč ($13/£6).

You can buy tickets from yellow coin-operated machines in metro stations or at most newsstands marked TABÁK or TRAFIKA. Hold on to your validated ticket throughout your ride—you'll need to show it if a ticket collector (be sure to check for his or her badge) asks you. If you're caught without a valid ticket, you'll be asked, and not so kindly, to pay a fine on the spot while all the locals look on, shaking their heads in disgust. The fine is 500Kč ($21/£10).

BY METRO   Metro trains operate daily from 5am to midnight and run every 2 to 6 minutes. On the three lettered lines (A, B, and C, color-coded green, yellow, and red, respectively), the most convenient central stations are Můstek, at the foot of Václavské náměstí (Wenceslas Sq.); Staroměstská, for Old Town Square and Charles

Bridge; and Malostranská, serving Malá Strana and the Castle District. Refer to the metro map for details.

BY ELECTRIC TRAM & BUS   The 24 electric tram (streetcar) lines run practically everywhere, and there's always another tram with the same number traveling back. You never have to hail trams; they make every stop. The most popular trams, nos. 22 and 23 (aka the "tourist trams" and the "pickpocket express"), run past top sights like the National Theater and Prague Castle. Regular bus and tram service stops at midnight, after which selected routes run reduced schedules, usually only once per hour. Schedules are posted at stops. If you miss a night connection, expect a long wait for the next.

Buses tend to be used only outside the older districts of Praha and have 3-digit numbers.

Both the buses and tram lines begin their morning runs around 4:30am.

BY TAXI

I have one word for you: *Beware.*

You can hail taxis in the streets or in front of train stations, large hotels, and popular attractions, but many drivers simply gouge visitors. In the late 1990s, the city canceled price regulations, but instead of creating price competition, it started a turf war between cabbies vying for the best taxi stands. The best fare you can hope for is 22Kč (90¢/40p) per kilometer and 25Kč ($1.05/50p) for the starting rate when you phone a taxi company. It will get more expensive when you stop a taxi on the street. Rates usually aren't posted outside on the taxi's door but on the dashboard—once you're inside it's a bit late to haggle. Try to get the driver to agree to a price and write it down before you get in. Better yet, go by foot or public transport.

If you must go by taxi, call reputable companies with English-speaking dispatchers: **AAA Taxi** (© **14014** or 222-333-222; www.aaataxi.cz); **ProfiTaxi** (© **844-700-800;** www.profitaxi.cz); or **SEDOP** (© **271-722-222;** www.sedop.cz). Demand a receipt for the fare before you start, as it'll keep them a little more honest.

BY CAR

Driving in Prague isn't worth the money or effort. The roads are frustrating and slow, and parking is minimal and expensive. However, a car is a plus if you want to explore other parts of the Czech Republic.

RENTAL COMPANIES   Try **Europcar Czech Rent a Car,** Pařížská 28, Praha 1 (© **224-811-290;** www.europcar.cz), or at Ruzyně Airport, Praha 6 (© 235-364-531). There's also **Hertz,** Karlovo nám. 28, Praha 2 (© **222-231-010;** www.hertz.cz). **Budget** is at Ruzyně Airport (© **220-113-253;** www.budget.cz) and in the Hotel Inter-Continental, náměstí Curieových, Praha 1 (© 222-319-595).

BY BIKE

Though there are no special bike lanes in the city center, and smooth streets are unheard of, Prague is a particularly fun city to bike when the crowds are thin. Vehicular traffic is limited in the city center, where small, winding streets seem especially suited to two-wheeled vehicles. Surprisingly, few people take advantage of this opportunity; cyclists are largely limited to the few foreigners who have imported their own bikes. The city's ubiquitous cobblestones make mountain bikes the natural choice. Check with your hotel about a rental, or try **Dodosport** at Na Zderaze 5 (© **272-769-387**).

> ### Tips   A Warning About Walking
>
> Unless you're in great shape or are a devoted walker, you should gradually prepare for your trip with a walking program to build up the muscles in your legs and feet for the inevitable pounding they'll take. And make sure to do this while wearing the comfortable shoes you plan to bring. Prague is a city of hills, steep staircases, and cobblestone streets that require strong legs and shock-absorbing shoes. Take your time and go at your own pace.

VISITOR INFORMATION

If you want to arrange accommodations before you come, Prague-based **E-travel.cz** offers handy English websites. The general site at www.travel.cz provides booking for hotels and practical touring information, while at www.apartments.cz, you can book a private apartment in a wide range of prices and areas. Once in the city, you can find E-travel.cz near the National Theater at Ostrovní 7; or call their 24-hour call center (© **224-990-990**; fax 224-990-999). Especially for those arriving by train or air, **AVE Travel** (© **251-091-111**; www.avetravel.cz) can arrange accommodations or transfers inside these terminals. It has outlets at the airport, open daily from 7am to 10pm; at the main train station, Hlavní nádraží, open daily from 6am to 11pm; and at the north train station, Nádraží Holešovice, open daily from 7am to 9pm.

The **Prague Information Service (PIS)**, Staroměstské náměstí 1, Praha 1 (© **12-444**; www.pis.cz), at the City Hall, provides tips and tickets for upcoming cultural events and tours. It can also help you find a room. From April to October, it's open Monday to Friday from 9am to 7pm and Saturday and Sunday from 9am to 6pm. During the rest of the year, it's open Monday to Friday from 9am to 6pm and Saturday and Sunday from 9am to 5pm. There is also PIS office inside the main train station.

Čedok, at Na Příkopě 18, Praha 1 (© **800-112-112** or 224-197-111; fax 224-216-324; www.cedok.cz), was once the state travel bureau and is now a privatized agency. Its entrenched position still gives it decent access to tickets and information about domestic events, and the staff can book rail and bus tickets and hotel rooms. Čedok accepts major credit cards and is open Monday to Friday from 9am to 7pm, Saturday 9:30am to 1pm.

FAST FACTS: Prague

American Express For travel arrangements, traveler's checks, currency exchange, and other member services, visit the city's sole American Express office at Václavské nám. 56 (Wenceslas Sq.), Praha 1 (© **222-800-237**). It's open daily from 9am to 7pm.

Bookstores The largest English-language bookshops are **The Globe,** Pštrossova 6, Praha 1 (© **224-934-203**; www.globebookstore.cz), and **Big Ben Bookshop,** Malá Štupartská 5, Praha 1 (© **224-826-565**; www.bigbenbookshop.com).

Currency Exchange There's an American Express office in Prague (see above). **Komerční banka** has three convenient Praha 1 locations with ATMs that accept Visa, MasterCard, and American Express: Na Příkopě 33, Spálená 51, and

Václavské nám. 42 (② **800-111-055,** central switchboard for all branches; www. kb.cz). The exchange offices are open Monday to Friday from 8am to 5pm, but the ATMs are accessible 24 hours.

Živnostenská banka, Na Příkopě 20, Praha 1 (② **224-121-111;** www.ziba.cz), has an exchange office open Monday to Friday from 10am to 9pm and Saturday from 3 to 7pm.

Chequepoint keeps the longest hours but offers the worst exchange rates. Central Prague locations are 28. října 13 and Staroměstské nám. 21 (both open 24 hr.); Staroměstské nám. 27 (open daily 8am–11:30pm); and Václavské nám. 32 (open daily 8am–11pm).

Doctors & Dentists If you need a doctor or dentist and your condition isn't life-threatening, you can visit the Polyclinic at Národní, Národní 9, Praha 1 (② **222-075-120**) during walk-in hours Monday to Friday from 8:30am to 5pm. For emergency medical aid call their mobile phone ② 777-942-270. The **Medicover Clinic,** Vyšehradská 35, Praha 2 (② **224-921-884**), provides EKGs, diagnostics, ophthalmology, house calls, and referrals to specialists. Normal walk-in hours are Monday to Saturday from 7am to 7pm.

For **emergency medical aid,** call the **Foreigners' Medical Clinic,** Na Homolce Hospital, Roentgenova 2, Praha 5 (② **257-272-146,** or 257-272-191 after-hours).

Hospitals Particularly welcoming to foreigners is **Nemocnice Na Homolce,** Roentgenova 2, Praha 5 (② **257-272-146,** or 257-272-191 after-hours). The English-speaking doctors can also make house calls. See "Doctors & Dentists," above, for more information. In an emergency, dial ② **155** for an ambulance.

Internet Access One of Prague's trendiest places is the **Globe** ✮, Pštrossova 6, Praha 1 (② **224-916-264;** www.globebookstore.cz), a cafe-cum-bookstore that provides Internet access. You can browse for 1.50Kč (5¢/2p) per minute. Its new location is open daily from 10am until midnight.

Check your e-mail and surf at the very centrally located new Internet cafe **Inetpoint.cz,** Jungmannova 32, Praha 1 (② **296-245-962;** www.inetpoint.cz). It is open daily 10am to 10pm and the connection charge is 25Kč ($1.05/50p) per 15 minutes. The **Bohemia Bagel,** near the funicular train at Újezd 16 in Malá Strana, Praha 1 (② **257-310-694;** www.bohemiabagel.cz), has about a half-dozen PCs in a pleasant setting for 1Kč (5¢/2p) per minute; it is open daily from 7am to midnight on Monday to Friday, 8am to midnight on Saturday and Sunday. Another place to access the Internet is **Cyber Cafe-Jáma** at V jámě 7, Praha 1 (② **224-222-383;** www.jamapub.cz). It is open daily 11am to 1am.

Laundry & Dry Cleaning **Laundry Kings,** Dejvická 16, Praha 6 (② **233-343-743**) was Prague's first American-style, coin-operated, self-service laundromat. Each small load costs about 70Kč ($2.90/£1). An attendant can do your wash for 180Kč ($7.50/£4) in the same day. Laundry Kings is open Monday to Friday from 7am to 10pm and Saturday and Sunday from 8am to 10pm.

Laundryland, Londýnská 71, Praha 2 (② **222-516-692**), offers dry cleaning as well as laundry service and charges about the same as Laundry Kings. Located 2 blocks from the Náměstí Míru metro station and close to the I. P. Pavlova metro station, it's open daily from 8am to 10pm.

Lost Property If you lose any of your personal property, luggage, or other belongings, try your luck at the Lost Property Office at Karolíny Světlé 5, Praha 1(© **224-235-085**).

Luggage Storage & Lockers The **Ruzyně Airport Luggage Storage Office** never closes and charges 60Kč ($2.50/£1) per item per day. Left-luggage offices are also available at the main train stations, **Hlavní nádraží** and **Nádraží Holešovice**. Both charge 30Kč ($1.25/60p) per bag per day and are technically open 24 hours, but if your train is departing late at night, check to make sure someone will be around. Luggage lockers are available in all of Prague's train stations, but they're not secure and should be avoided.

Mail The **Main Post Office (Hlavní pošta)**, Jindřišská 14, Praha 1 (© **221-131-111**), a few steps from Václavské náměstí, is open 24 hours. You can receive mail, marked "Poste Restante" and addressed to you, care of this post office. If you carry an American Express card or Amex traveler's checks, you would be wiser to receive mail care of **American Express,** Václavské nám. 56 (Wenceslas Sq.), Praha 1 (© **222-800-237**).

Pharmacies The most centrally located pharmacy (*lékárna*) is at Václavské nám. 8, Praha 1 (© **224-227-532**), and is open Monday to Friday from 8am to 6pm. The nearest emergency (24-hr.) pharmacy is at Palackého 5, Praha 1 (© **224-946-982**). If you're in Praha 2, there's an emergency pharmacy on Belgická 37 (© **222-519-731**).

Transport Information The **Prague Information Service,** near Wenceslas Square on Na Příkopě 20, Praha 1 (© **12444**; www.pis.cz), is open Monday to Friday from 9am to 7pm and Saturday and Sunday 9am to 6pm (Apr–Oct), and Monday to Friday 9am to 6pm and Saturday 9am to 3pm (Nov–Mar). PIS can help you get where you are going on local transport (while the travel agencies Čedok, E-Travel.cz, and AVE Travel are all good for intercity connections; see "Visitor Info," above). Train and bus timetables can also be viewed at www.jizdnirady.cz or at www.idos.cz. All metro stations now have much better maps and explanations in English. You will find more on Prague's public transportation at www.dpp.cz.

WHERE TO STAY

The range of accommodations in Prague has widened significantly since the 1989 revolution. Today you can choose the opulence of the Four Seasons Hotel, the coziness of an innovative B&B, or a more spartan stay in a hostel.

Many hotels and pensions are old properties reconstructed to a higher standard, including refined interiors and tiled bathrooms with modern fixtures. The concept of easy access for travelers with disabilities has been slower to emerge, however.

HOTELS Full-service hotels have begun to catch up with Western standards in the face of competition, but rooms are still more expensive than those in many European hotels of similar or better quality. The staff, while much more attentive than they were soon after the revolution, still often act as if you are invading their turf.

The selection is growing, but because there's not much room to build in the historic center, newer properties tend to be farther out. Notable exceptions are given below.

Prague Lodging & Dining

ACCOMMODATIONS ■
Andante **39**
Betlem Club **27**
Corinthia Towers Hotel **46**
Dům krále Jiřího **26**
Flathotel Orion **45**
Four Seasons Hotel **28**
Franz Kafka Museum **24**
Hotel Aria **5**
Hotel Ametyst **44**
Hotel Evropa **31**
Hotel Jalta **32**
Hotel Josef **16**
Hotel Neruda **4**
Hotel Paříž **17**
Hotel Savoy **2**
Palace Hotel **20**
Pension Unitas/Art Prison Hotel **29**
Pension Větrník **1**
Prague Marriott Hotel **19**

DINING ◆
Ambiente Pasta Fresca **21**
Bellevue **25**
Bohemia Bagel **6**
Bonante **41**
Dahab **14**
Don Pedro **36**
Globe **35**
Hergetova Cihelna **10**
Hradčany Restaurant **2**
Grand Café **1**
Kampa Park **9**
Kavárna Medúza **24**
Kavárna Obecní dům **18**
Kavárna Slavia **28**
Kogo **22**
Lahůdky Zlatý kříž **30**
Le Café Colonial **11**
Osmička **42**
Ovocný bar Hájek **33**
Pizzeria Rugantino **12**
Potrefená husa **37**
Radost FX Café **40**
Red Hot & Blues **15**
Restaurant U Čížků **38**
Rybí trh **36**
Saté **3**
U Malířů **8**
U Medvídků **29**
U Modré kachničky **7**
Velryba **34**

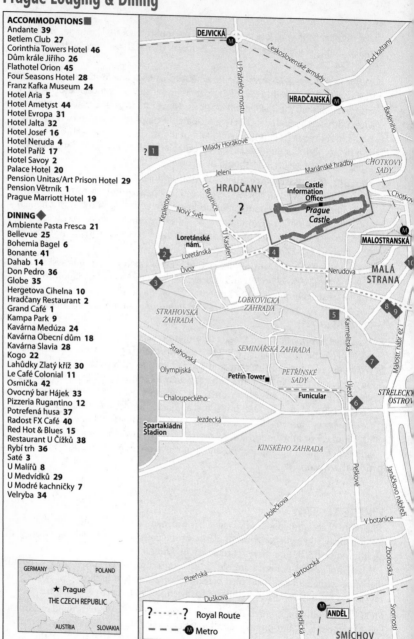

222

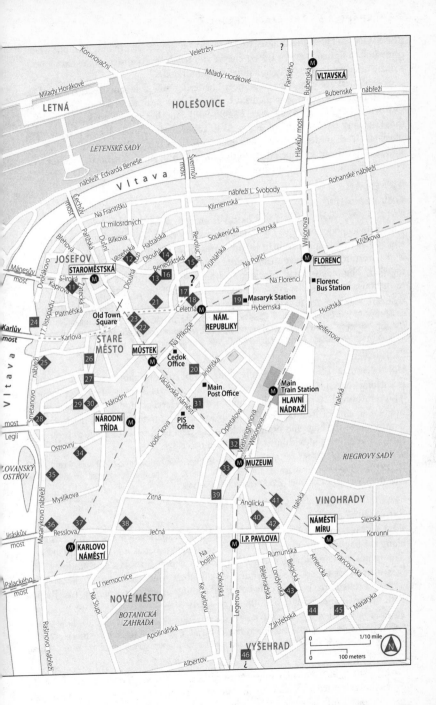

PENSIONS These guesthouses with few services are cheaper than hotels, but when compared to similar Western B&Bs, they're still relatively expensive. Some have found a niche offering a quaint stay in a quiet neighborhood.

Several local agencies offer assistance. The leader now is Prague-based **E-Travel.cz** (www.travel.cz or www.apartments.cz). Its office is near the National Theater at Ostrovní 7 (© **224-990-990;** fax 224-990-999). Another agency, especially good for those arriving late by train or air, is **AVE Travel Ltd.** (© **251-091-111;** www.ave travel.cz). It has outlets at the airport, open daily from 7am to 10pm; at the main train station, Hlavní nádraží, open daily from 6am to 11pm; and at the north train station, Nádraží Holešvice, open daily from 7am to 8:30pm.

HRADČANY
Very Expensive
Hotel Savoy ✸✸✸ Just a few blocks from the castle, the Hotel Savoy welcomes you with a modern lobby. The guest rooms are richly decorated and boast every amenity as well as spacious marble bathrooms. The beds are consistently huge, which is in contrast to the customary central European style of two twin beds shoved together. The pleasant staff provides an attention to detail that's a cut above that at most hotels in Prague. Its Hradčany restaurant is excellent (p. 229).

Keplerova 6, Praha 1. © **224-302-430.** Fax 224-302-128. www.hotel-savoy.cz. 59 units. From 9,600Kč ($399/£223) double; from 12,900Kč ($537/£258) suite. Rates include breakfast. AE, DC, MC, V. Tram: 22 or 23. **Amenities:** Restaurant; bar; "relaxation" center w/small set of exercise machines; sauna; whirlpool; concierge; business services; salon; 24-hr. room service; massage; laundry. *In room:* A/C, TV, VCR, DVD, dataport, minibar, hair dryer, safe.

Expensive
Hotel Neruda ✸✸ Squeezed into a long row of curiosity shops on Nerudova street is a strong contender for the best boutique hotel in Malá Strana—the Hotel Neruda. This refurbished 20-room villa has combined a high level of modern elegance with the original accents of its 14th-century shell. Most of the fixtures—from the fresh new bathrooms to the beds and dining tables—suggest a bold sense of Prague's promising future, but enveloped within its Renaissance past.

Nerudova 44, Praha 1. © **257-535-557.** Fax 257-531-492. www.hotelneruda-praha.cz. 20 units. From 5,550Kč ($231/£110) double. Rates include breakfast. AE, DC, MC, V. Tram: 22 or 23 to Malostranské nám. **Amenities:** Cafe-restaurant; concierge. *In room:* A/C, TV, VCR, minibar, hair dryer, safe.

MALÁ STRANA (LESSER TOWN)
Expensive
Best Western–Hotel Kampa On the edge of the park where troops once camped along the banks of the Vltava, the Kampa occupies what was a 17th-century armory. The rooms are comfortable enough if you don't expect first-class surroundings. The best ones boast a park view—request one of these when booking or checking in. There's a restaurant, but you'd be better off visiting one of those nearby, like Kampa Park under Charles Bridge (p. 230).

Všehrdova 16, Praha 1. © **257-404-444.** Fax 257-404-333. www.euroagentur.cz. 84 units (shower only). From 5,400Kč ($225/£108) double. Rates include breakfast. AE, DC, MC, V. Metro: Malostranská, then tram no. 12, 22, or 23 to the Hellichova stop. **Amenities:** Restaurant w/garden; bar; room service; laundry service; dry cleaning. *In room:* TV, minibar, hair dryer, safe.

Hotel Aria ✸✸ This new music-themed hotel is just around the corner from the St. Nicholas Cathedral. Each of its four floors is tastefully decorated by Versace designers to evoke a different genre of music. The rooms and bathrooms vary in their size and layout, and all are kept to the same exceptionally high standard evident through-out the hotel. There is an impressive library of CDs, DVDs, and books about music off the lobby, and a full-time resident musicologist available to help you choose a concert in the city.

Tržiště 9, Praha 1. ⓒ **225-334-111.** Fax 225-334-666. www.ariahotel.net. 52 units. From 8,010Kč ($333/£160) double; 10,230Kč ($426/£205) suite. Rates include breakfast. AE, MC, V. Metro: Malostranská, then tram no. 12, 22, or 23 to Malostranské nám. **Amenities:** Restaurant; bar; exercise room; courtesy car from the airport; 24-hr. business center; 24-hr. room service. *In room:* A/C, Internet, DVD/CD player, minibar, hair dryer, safe.

STARÉ MĚSTO (OLD TOWN) & JOSEFOV

Very Expensive

Four Seasons Hotel 𝒢𝒢𝒢   This addition to Prague's short list of luxury hotels is its most impressive. Located in an imposing position on the banks of the Vltava River right next to Charles Bridge, the Four Seasons provides an elegant base for exploring Old Town and enjoying the symphonies at the nearby Rudolfinum, while taking in a wonderful panoramic view of Prague Castle across the river.

Its executive suites and guest rooms are nicely appointed. The best have sweeping views and sunken marble tubs. In the tasteful and lower-priced Art Nouveau wing, comfortable doubles can be booked for less than $300, but the street-side views are much less impressive.

All rooms are fitted with fine solid wood furniture, some with antique pieces, others with more modern avant-garde accents.

Veleslavínova 2a, Praha 1. ⓒ **221-427-000.** Fax 221-426-000. www.fourseasons.com. 162 units. From 7,800Kč ($324/£181) double; from 15,600Kč ($649/£363) suite. AE, DC, MC, V. Metro: Staroměstská. **Amenities:** Restaurant; bar; health club; concierge; business services; 24-hr. room service; laundry; dry cleaning overnight. *In room:* A/C, TV, CD, DVD player, dataport, minibar, hair dryer, safe.

Expensive

Hotel Paříž 𝒢𝒢   At the edge of náměstí Republiky and across from the Municipal House, the 100-year-old Paříž provides a rare chance to put yourself back in the gilded First Republic. The high-ceilinged guest rooms are done in a purplish theme; they aren't plush but are comfortable and adequately equipped, with more modern furnishings than the lobby would suggest. It's the ground floor that really maintains an authentic period elegance.

U Obecního domu 1, Praha 1. ⓒ **222-195-195.** Fax 224-225-475. www.hotel-pariz.cz. 94 units (74 with tub/shower combination, 20 with shower only). 4,650Kč ($193/£93) double; 8,250Kč ($343/£165) suite. AE, DC, MC, V. Metro: Náměstí Republiky. **Amenities:** Restaurant; cafe; concierge; business services; 24-hr. room service; babysitting; laundry; dry cleaning. *In room:* A/C, TV, minibar, hair dryer, safe.

Moderate

Dům krále Jiřího   The "House at King George's" perches above two pubs on a narrow side street. The rooms are pretty bare but have a bit more charm than they used to. The ceilings are high, and the dark wooden furniture is another improvement. Ask for a room in back if you want to deaden the clamor of the pubs below. Breakfast is served in the wine cellar, which lacks character despite a recent remodeling.

Liliová 10, Praha 1. ⓒ **353-232-100.** Fax 353-222-999. www.hotel.cz/kraljiri. 11 units. From 2,700Kč ($112/£54) double or suite. Rates include breakfast. AE, MC, V. Metro: Staroměstská. *In room:* TV, fridge.

Inexpensive

Pension Unitas/Art Prison Hostel 𝒱𝒶𝓁𝓊𝑒   With a quirky history (same building complex as Hotel Cloister Inn) and an unbeatable location at this price, the Unitas is great value for the money. On a side street between Old Town Square and the National Theater stands this former convent, which was conveniently seized for use as secret police holding cells under the Communists. One of their most frequent guests, before the place was turned into a postrevolution pension, was none other than the pesky dissident and soon-to-be-president Václav Havel. But once the bizarre allure of staying in Havel's former hoosegow wears off, you realize that this is a pretty artful attempt at providing decent accommodations at a good price. The cells and rooms range from doubles to quads, with comfy mattresses and clean linen provided. There is no curfew, and the complimentary breakfast of cold cuts, rolls, and cheese is fresh and plentiful. The joint bathrooms are clean enough to pass.

Bartolomějská 9, Praha 1. ℂ **224-221-802.** Fax 224-217-555. www.unitas.cz. 36 units (shared bathroom facilities). From 1,200Kč ($50/£24) double in pension; from 490Kč ($20/£10) per person in double room in hostel. Rates include breakfast. AE, MC, V. Metro: Národní třída. **Amenities:** Coin-op laundry.

NOVÉ MĚSTO (NEW TOWN): NEAR WENCESLAS SQUARE
Very Expensive
Palace Hotel ⭐⭐   The Palace has long been the quintessential Prague address for visiting dignitaries and celebrities like Steven Spielberg, the Rolling Stones, and Britain's Prince Charles. The 1903 Art Nouveau building offers a more stoic "Viennese" approach to the era's architectural fashion than the more ornate Paříž (p. 225). The lobby boasts accents like buttery-wood paneling and furniture with subtle flowered upholstery, but the overall effect is that of contemporary wealth sampling the past rather than building a museum to it. The staff makes a point of remembering guests' names and provides excellent service.

The soothing, delicately colored guest rooms are some of the largest luxury accommodations in Prague, each with an Italian marble bathroom.

Panská 12, Praha 1. ℂ **224-093-111.** Fax 224-221-240. www.palacehotel.cz. 124 units (tub/shower combination). From 10,770Kč ($448/£215) double; 11,880Kč ($495/£238) suite. Rates include breakfast. AE, DC, MC, V. Metro: Můstek. **Amenities:** 2 restaurants; cafe; concierge; business services; 24-hr. room service; laundry service. *In room:* A/C, TV, VCR, minibar, safe.

Moderate
Andante *(Value*   This best-value choice near Wenceslas Square is tucked away on a dark side street, about 2 blocks off the top of the square. Despite the less-than-appealing neighborhood, this is the most comfortable property at this price. It lacks the character of the old Hotel Evropa (see below) but is better cared for. With modern beds and good firm mattresses, as well as high-grade Scandinavian furniture and colorful decorations, the rooms gain in comfort what they lose in adventure. They offer plenty of space and white, well-kept bathrooms with tub/shower combinations, some with shower only.

Ve Smečkách 4, Prague 1. ℂ **222-210-021.** Fax 222-210-591. www.andante.cz. 32 units (some with shower only, some with tub only). 3,300Kč ($137/£66) double; 4,560Kč ($190/£91) suite. Rates include breakfast. AE, MC, V. Metro: Muzeum. **Amenities:** Restaurant; tours arranged w/the reception desk; business services; limited room service. *In room:* TV, minibar, hair dryer, iron, safety box available at the reception desk.

Inexpensive
Hotel Evropa   Born in 1889 as the Hotel Archduke Stephan, the Evropa was recast in the early 1900s as an Art Deco hotel. However, this is yet another classic that has seen much better days. Though the statue-studded exterior, still one of the most striking landmarks on Wenceslas Square, has recently been polished, the rooms are aging;

most don't have bathrooms and some are just plain shabby. The best choice is a room facing the square with a balcony.

The hotel's famous cafe, a wood-encased former masterpiece that no longer glows, furthers the theme. Still, this is an affordable way to stay in one of Wenceslas Square's once-grand addresses.

Václavské nám. 25, Praha 1. © **224-215-387.** Fax 224-224-544. www.evropahotel.cz. 90 units, 20 with bathroom (tub only). 2,600Kč ($108/£52) double without bathroom; 4,000Kč ($166/£80) double with bathroom. Rates include continental breakfast. AE, MC, V. Metro: Můstek or Muzeum. **Amenities:** Restaurant; concierge; safe; luggage storage.

NEAR NÁMĚSTÍ REPUBLIKY/BANKING DISTRICT

Expensive

Hotel Josef ★★   The Josef stands as the new home for tasteful minimalism in the new Bohemia. British-based architect Eva Jiřičná brings a new study on the interior use of glass to her native land with its own long history of the glazier's craft.

There is a daring and dramatic effect in every room. Superior rooms are so bold as to offer transparent bathroom nooks, shower stalls, and washrooms with a full view of grooming activities for your partner to absorb in the main sleeping chamber.

Rybná 20, Praha 1. © **221-700-111.** Fax 221-700-999. www.hoteljosef.com. 110 units. From 5,190Kč ($216/£104) double. Rates include breakfast. AE, DC, MC, V. Metro: Náměstí Republiky. **Amenities:** Restaurant; health club; concierge; car rental; courtesy limo; business center; room service; babysitting; laundry. In room: A/C, TV, DVD, CD player, dataport, minibar, hair dryer, safe.

Prague Marriott Hotel ★ (Kids   The Marriott provides just what you would expect—a high standard. The large rooms have bright colors, tasteful, homogenized furniture, and comfortable beds as well as phones, faxes, laptop connections, and other services. The bathrooms are spacious and immaculately maintained. In an effort to attract families, the Marriott offers Sunday family brunches in the Brasserie Praha, where kids are welcome and PC games are available.

V Celnici 8, Praha 1. © **222-888-888.** Fax 222-888-889. www.marriott.com. 328 units. 6,870Kč ($286/£137) double; 8,070Kč ($336/£161) executive-level double; from 8,970Kč ($373/£179) suite. Rates for suites and executive rooms include breakfast. AE, DC, MC, V. Valet parking $31 per day. Metro: Náměstí Republiky. **Amenities:** Restaurant; cafe; bar; indoor swimming pool; well-equipped fitness center; saunas; whirlpools; gym; spa rooms; concierge; fully equipped business center; salon; 24-hr. room service; laundry and dry-cleaning service. In room: A/C, TV, dataport, minibar, hair dryer, safe.

VINOHRADY

Expensive

Hotel Ametyst   The most expensive full-service hotel in an affordable part of town, the Ametyst is less expensive than hotels of similar quality in the older districts, but you can get a better deal at one of the nearby pensions. On a quiet back street about 5 blocks from náměstí Míru, it's spotless and decorated in a warm contemporary style. The top-floor rooms are especially bright and cheery, with pitched ceilings and balconies overlooking the peaceful residential neighborhood.

Jana Masaryka 11, Praha 2. © **222-921-921.** Fax 222-921-999. www.hotelametyst.cz. 84 units (some with tub only, some with shower only). 6,450Kč ($268/£129) double. Rates include breakfast. AE, DC, MC, V. Metro: Náměstí Míru. **Amenities:** 2 restaurants; bar; small fitness center; sauna. In room: TV, minibar, hair dryer, safe.

Inexpensive

Flathotel Orion (Kids   The best family value close to the city center, the Orion is an apartment hotel with each unit sporting a well-equipped kitchen. All accommodations have either one bedroom (sleeps two) or two bedrooms (sleeps up to six). The spacious guest rooms are comfortable but not very imaginative, bordered in pale blue with leather armchairs and dark wooden bed frames without much on the walls. The beds vary in the firmness of their mattresses. The bathrooms are small, basic white, and modern, as are the kitchens. In this friendly neighborhood, fruit and vegetable shops and corner grocery stores can be found around náměstí Míru, just up the street.

Americká 9, Praha 2. © **353-232-100.** Fax 353-222-999. www.hotel.cz/orion. 26 apts with bathroom (tub/shower combination). 2,580Kč ($107/£52) 1 bedroom; 3,320Kč ($138/£66) 2 bedrooms. Breakfast 160Kč ($6.65/£3). AE, MC, V. Metro: Náměstí Míru. **Amenities:** Finnish sauna for 200Kč ($8.30/£4) per hour; tours and activities arrangements at reception; room service; laundry and dry-cleaning service. *In room:* TV, kitchen, fridge, coffeemaker.

ELSEWHERE IN PRAGUE
Expensive
Corinthia Towers Hotel ★ *Kids*   Opened in the mid-1980s, this hotel was one of the last "achievements" of Communist central planners. The medium-size rooms used to be like those in a 1980s upper-middle-range Sheraton, but have undergone renovation. They are fitted with solid furniture and the beds have firm mattresses, but the decoration is pretty bland. The bathrooms are reasonably sized and have tub/shower combinations.

The hotel is American in its approach, with an AMF bowling alley in the basement. Though the city center isn't within walking distance, the Vyšehrad metro station is just below the hotel entrance.

Kongresová 1, Praha 4. © **261-191-111.** Fax 261-225-011. www.corinthia.cz. 583 units. 7,200Kč ($300/£144) double; from 11,850Kč ($493/£237) suite. Rates include breakfast. AE, DC, MC, V. Metro: Vyšehrad. **Amenities:** 2 restaurants; cafe; well-equipped fitness center w/pool, sauna, exercise machines; game room; concierge; activities desk; salon; 24-hr. room service; babysitting; laundry; bowling alley. *In room:* A/C, TV, minibar.

Inexpensive
Pension Větrník *Value* *Kids*   A mostly scenic half-hour tram ride (or metro-tram combo) from the city center takes you to this romantic, secret, country hideaway. After getting off the tram, walk back behind a bunch of large concrete dorms to find a painstakingly restored 18th-century white windmill house. Once you buzz at the metal gate Miloš Opatrný will greet you. Lush gardens and a tennis court lead to a quaint guesthouse with a stone staircase and spacious rooms with big beds, open-beamed ceilings, and modern amenities. The plain bedcovers and odd-shaped table lamps could stand some improvement, however. The bathrooms are roomy, with stand-up showers, and the windows are shuttered and boast flower boxes.

U Větrníku 40, Praha 6. © **220-612-404.** Fax 220-513-390. www.pensionvetrnik.wz.cz. 6 units (4 with shower only, 2 with tub/shower combination). 2,100Kč ($87/£42) double; 3,150Kč ($131/£63) suite. Rates include breakfast. MC. Metro: Line A to Hradčanská station, then tram no. 1 or 18 to Větrník. **Amenities:** Private lighted tennis court in the courtyard. *In room:* TV, hair dryer.

WHERE TO DINE
Whenever someone mentions this country's heavy food, Czechs delight in the fact that obesity is much more of a problem in the United States. Statistically they're right. It seems that the walking-hiking-biking lifestyle of Czechs goes a long way toward keeping their waistlines trim.

As for **main courses,** no self-respecting Czech restaurant could open its doors without serving at least some version of the three national foods: *vepřo, knedlo,* and *zelo* (pork, dumplings, and cabbage). The **pork** *(vepřové maso)* is usually a shoulder or brisket that is baked and lightly seasoned, smoked, or breaded and fried like a schnitzel *(řízek)*. Unlike German sauerkraut, the **cabbage** *(zelí)* is boiled with a light sugar sauce. The **dumplings** are light and spongy if made from flour and bread *(houskové knedlíky)*, or dense and pasty if made from flour and potatoes *(bramborové knedlíky)*. This "VKZ" combo cries out for an original **Budweiser (Budvar), Kozel,** or **Pilsner Urquell** to wash it down.

There's usually a good selection of indigenous freshwater fish, such as trout, perch, and carp, the Christmas favorite. Since the country has no coastline, you'll find most **seafood** at the more expensive restaurants, but a growing selection of salmon, sea bass, shark, and shellfish is shipped in on ice.

As for **dessert,** try a *palačinka,* a crepe-thin pancake filled with chocolate, fruit, or marmalade and whipped cream. Another favorite is *ovocné knedlíky,* whole dumplings filled with strawberries, apricots, or cherries, rolled in butter, topped with powdered sugar and cream.

HRADČANY
Expensive
Hradčany Restaurant ⊛ INTERNATIONAL   Matching the crisp English setting of the hotel in which it resides, the Austrian-managed Hradčany is the most elegant choice this side of the castle. The menu lists vary depending on the season. At this writing, they offer delicious roasted veal with corn or tasty rump steak with pistachio crust.

In the Hotel Savoy, Keplerova 6, Praha 1. ℂ **224-302-150.** Reservations recommended. Main courses lunch 450Kč–650Kč ($19–$27/£9–£13), dinner 590Kč–790Kč ($24–$33/£12–£16). AE, DC, MC, V. Daily noon–3pm and 6–11pm. Tram: 22 or 23, 2 stops past Prague Castle.

Inexpensive
Saté INDONESIAN   The Saté has made quite a business out of simple Indonesian dishes at low prices. It's just down the street from the Castle Square (Hradčanské nám.) and past the massive Černín Palace. The unassuming storefront near the Swedish Embassy doesn't stand out, so look closely. The pork saté comes in a peanut sauce along with a hearty *mie goreng* (traditional Indonesian fried noodles).

Pohořelec 152/3, Praha 1. ℂ **220-514-552.** Main courses 42Kč–220Kč ($1.75–$9.15/£1–£4). No credit cards. Daily 11am–10pm. Tram: 22 or 23.

MALÁ STRANA (LESSER TOWN)
Very Expensive
U Malířů ⊛ *Overrated* FRENCH   Surrounded by Romance-age murals and gorgeously appointed tables in three intimate dining rooms here, you're faced with some tough choices. Half-baked salmon filets swim in caper sauce, tiger shrimps come with oranges, lamb steak is glazed with red-pepper sauce, and baked quail bathes in Sherry. If you want a truly old-world evening of elegant romance and French specialties, U Malířů is worth it.

Maltézské nám. 11, Praha 1. ℂ **257-530-000.** www.umaliru.cz. Reservations necessary. Main courses 480Kč–2,390Kč ($20–$99/£10–£48); fixed-price menus 1,190Kč ($50/£24) and 1,790Kč ($74/£36). AE, DC, MC, V. Daily 7pm–2am. Metro: Malostranská.

Moderate
Hergetova Cihelna ⊛ INTERNATIONAL/PASTA/CZECH   This addition to a list of Prague's top dining experiences quickly became a popular spot on the riverbank. The interior is divided into a restaurant, cocktail bar, cafe, and music lounge, and the

modern furniture is simple and comfortable. From the large summer terrace you can experience one of the most exciting and unforgettable views of the river and Charles Bridge. The food is a good standard; I enjoyed their homemade Czech potato soup with forest mushrooms and garlic called *bramboračka* and Czech *svíčková* (sirloin) served in a cream sauce with dumplings and cranberries.

Cihelná 2b, Praha 1. (© 296-826-103. www.cihelna.com. Main courses 215Kč–695Kč ($8.90–$28/£4–£14). AE, MC, V. Daily 11:30am–1am. Metro: Malostranská.

Kampa Park ★★ CONTINENTAL/SEAFOOD   The best thing about Kampa Park is the summertime riverside view from its patio below Charles Bridge. In high season, the terrace is lively, with grills churning out solid portions of beef, pork, ribs, halibut, sea bass, and other barbecued favorites. Desserts like the fresh strawberry cappuccino have won raves from kids. During colder weather, this left-bank chalet is even more sublime, as candlelit tables provide glimpses of the stone bridge through the windows.

Na Kampě 8b, Praha 1. (© 296-826-102. www.kampagroup.com. Reservations recommended. Main courses 345Kč–795Kč ($14–$33/£7–£16). AE, DC, MC, V. Daily 11:30am–1am. Metro: Malostranská.

U modré kachničky ★ CZECH/CONTINENTAL/WILD GAME   At the "Blue Duckling," on a narrow Malá Strana street, is my choice for the most innovative attempt at refining standard Czech dishes into true Bohemian haute cuisine. The menu is loaded with an array of wild game and quirky spins on Czech village favorites. Starters include lightly spiced venison pâté and gooseliver on toast. You can choose from five different duck specialties. And, the ubiquitous *palačinky* crepes are thin and tender and filled with fruit, nuts, and chocolate. There is an even more popular sister to the first "kachnička," at Michalská 16, Praha 1.

Nebovidská 6, Praha 1. (© 257-320-308. www.umodrekachnicky.cz. Reservations recommended for lunch, required for dinner. Main courses 290Kč–690Kč ($12–$28/£6–£14). AE, MC, V. Daily noon–4pm and 6:30–11:30pm. Metro: Malostranská. Sister restaurant: (© 224-213-418). Reservations recommended. Main courses 240Kč–685Kč ($10–$28/£5–£14). AE, MC, V. Daily 11:30am–11:30pm. Metro: Můstek.

Inexpensive
Bohemia Bagel *Kids* BAGELS/SANDWICHES   Bohemia Bagel emerged in 1997 at the base of Petřín Hill as the answer to the bagel-less morning blues. The roster of golden-brown, hand-rolled, stone-baked bagels is stellar. There's plain, cinnamon raisin, garlic, onion, poppy, tomato basil, cheese, or apple and nut providing a sturdy but tender frame for Scandinavian lox and cream cheese or maybe jalapeño-cheddar cheese.

On the website www.bohemiabagel.cz you can order bagels and other food for at least 500Kč ($20/£10) to be delivered in Praha 1 within an hour.

Újezd 16, Praha 1. (© 257-310-694. Bagels and sandwiches 30Kč–145Kč ($1.25–$6/£1–£3). No credit cards. Mon–Fri 7am–midnight; Sat–Sun 8am–midnight. Tram: 6, 9, 12, 22, or 23 to Újezd stop.

STARÉ MĚSTO (OLD TOWN)
Expensive
Bellevue ★★ INTERNATIONAL   With its excellent view of Prague Castle, the Bellevue is my perennial top choice. The ambitious owners have put all their energy into the intelligent menu: beef, nouvelle sauces, well-dressed fish and duck, delicate pastas, and artistic desserts. For a tamer but extraordinary treat, try the filet of fallow

deer. Al dente pastas share a plate with lobster-and-spinach purée, garlic and herbs, or tomatoes and olives. Desserts feature hot bitter chocolate tart, or wild berries in port and cognac served with vanilla and walnut ice cream.

Smetanovo nábřeží 18, Praha 1. ℂ 222-221-443. www.pfd.cz. Reservations recommended. Main courses 590Kč–890Kč ($24–$37/£12–£18); fixed-price menu 1,990Kč ($82/£40) or 2,290Kč ($95/£46). AE, DC, MC, V. Mon–Sat noon–3pm and 5:30–11pm; Sun 7–11pm (live jazz dinner). Metro: Staroměstská.

Rybí trh SEAFOOD   That strange smell wafting from deep inside the courtyard behind Týn Church is the most extensive selection of fresh seafood in Prague, served at the "Fish Market." From starters like oysters on the half shell and jumbo shrimp to main choices like monkfish, salmon, eel, shark, and many others, you select your favorite fish and method of preparation at the bright counter near the entrance.

Týnský Dvůr 5, Praha 1. ℂ 224-895-447. www.rybitrh.cz. Reservations recommended. Main courses 299Kč–1,500Kč ($12–$62/£6–£30). AE, MC, V. Daily 11am–midnight. Metro: Můstek.

Moderate

Ambiente Pasta Fresca ITALIAN   What this outlet on Celetná offers is location, location, location, and usually enough tables to satisfy the endless tourist rush hour. In a candlelit basement trattoria, the menu is limited to pastas—albeit served about 50 different ways—salads, a few meaty entrees, and garlic bread if you're still hungry.

Celetná 11, Praha 1. ℂ 224-230-244. www.ambi.cz. Reservations recommended. Main courses 158Kč–580Kč ($6.50–$24/£3–£12). AE, MC, V. Daily 11am–midnight. Metro: Můstek.

Kogo 🖈🖈 (Value ITALIAN   This modern, upscale trattoria has become the local Italian favorite for the many brokers and bankers who work nearby. Tucked away on a side street adjacent to the Estates' Theater, Kogo manages to combine the warmth and boisterousness of a family restaurant with a high culinary standard in its pastas, meaty entrees, and desserts.

Kogo has a second location in the atrium of the newly reopened Slovanský Dům shopping and culture center at Na Příkopě 22 (ℂ 221-451-259).

Havelská 27, Praha 1. ℂ 224-214-543. www.kogo.cz. Reservations recommended. Main courses 190Kč–480Kč ($7.90–$20/£4–£10). AE, MC, V. Daily 9am–midnight. Metro: Můstek.

Red Hot & Blues 🖈 (Kids AMERICAN/CAJUN/MEXICAN   Tex-Mex regulars, plus burgers and nachos are on the menu here. Sunday brunch, best enjoyed in the small courtyard, includes tangy huevos rancheros on crispy tortillas. The casual French Quarter feel makes this a family-friendly choice. From 7 to 10:30pm you can hear live jazz.

Jakubská 12, Praha 1. ℂ 222-314-639. www.redhotandblues.com. Main courses 139Kč–499Kč ($5.80–$20/£3–£10). AE, MC, V. Daily 9am–midnight; Sat–Sun brunch 9am–4pm. Metro: Náměstí Republiky.

Inexpensive

Pizzeria Rugantino 🖈 (Kids PIZZA/PASTA   Pizzeria Rugantino serves generous iceberg salads and the best selection of individual pizzas in Prague. Wood-fired stoves and handmade dough result in a crisp and delicate crust. The Diabolo with fresh garlic bits and very hot chiles goes nicely with a salad and a pull of Krušovice beer. The constant buzz, nonsmoking area, heavy childproof wooden tables, and lots of baby chairs make this a family favorite.

Dušní 4, Praha 1. ℂ 222-318-172. Individual pizzas 100Kč–250Kč ($4.15–$10/£2–£5). No credit cards. Mon–Sat 11am–11pm; Sun 5–11pm. Metro: Staroměstská.

Value Inexpensive Meals on the Run

The Czech-style delicatessen **Lahůdky Zlatý Kříž**, Jungmannovo nám. 19 (entrance from Jungmannova 34), Praha 1 (© **221-191-801**), offers the typical Czech snack food *chlebíčky*—a slice of white bread with ham or salami and cheese or potato salad. You have to eat standing up, but prices are pure Czech. Or take it with you and go eat in the cozy garden behind the corner of this building (enter from the square). It's open Monday to Friday from 6:30am to 7pm and Saturday from 9am to 3pm. No credit cards are accepted.

Ovocný bar (fruit bar) Hájek at Václavské nám. 52, Praha 1 (© **222-211-466**), upstairs from an ice-cream stall, welcomes all for coffee and delicious desserts, ice cream, and fruit salads priced from 13Kč to 90Kč (55¢–$3.75/ 25p–£2). This sweet oasis has been popular with the locals for decades. It's open Monday to Saturday 9am to 8pm, Sunday 10am to 8pm.

If you are visiting Prague's Vinohrady quarter, you can't avoid its main square, náměstí Míru, with St. Ludmila's Church. On the right side of the church, when facing it, near the metro entrance, there is usually a stand with the **best hot dog** in Prague. The dog is topped with ketchup or two kinds of tasty Czech mustard and served on a fresh white roll. It costs 14Kč (60¢/30p) and it is available Monday to Friday from 9:30am until the supply for that day lasts.

NOVÉ MĚSTO (NEW TOWN)
Moderate
Restaurant U Čížků ⊕ *Value* CZECH   One of the city's first private restaurants, this cozy cellar–cum–hunting lodge on Charles Square can now be identified by the long line of German tour buses parked outside. The fare is purely Czech, and the massive portions of game, smoked pork, and other meats will stay with you for a while.

Karlovo nám. 34, Praha 2. © **222-232-257**. www.restaurantucizku.cz. Reservations recommended. Main courses 120Kč–290Kč ($5–$12/£2–£6). AE, MC, V. Daily 11:30am–10:30pm. Metro: Karlovo nám.

Inexpensive
Potrefená husa (The Wounded Goose) *Value* CZECH/INTERNATIONAL
This outlet on the river in New Town has its own open fireplace (roaring in the colder months), and discreetly placed TVs. The most interesting offerings on the menu are the thick homemade soups—mainly vegetable-based—served in *chléb* (whole, hollowed-out round bread loaves), and yes, it's cool to eat the bread after the soup is done. There are also standard grilled meats, pastas, salads, and plenty of varieties of beer on draft or in bottles.

Resslova 2, Praha 2. © **224-918-691**. www.pivovary-staropramen.cz. Main courses 100Kč–300Kč ($4.15–$12/ £2–£6). AE, MC, V. Daily 11:30am–1am. Metro: Karlovo nám.

VINOHRADY
Expensive
Bonante *Value* INTERNATIONAL   Bonante is especially great for shunning the cold of an autumn or winter evening near the roaring fire in the brick-cellar dining

room. There are several vegetarian and low-calorie chicken-based selections on the menu. Jazz combos play on most nights from a small stage in the corner. When reserving, ask for a table within view of the fireplace.

Anglická 15, Praha 2. ⓒ 224-221-665. www.bonante-restaurant.cz. Reservations recommended. Main courses 195Kč–695Kč ($8.10–$28/£4–£14). AE, MC, V. Daily 11:30am–11pm. Metro: I. P. Pavlova or Náměstí Míru.

Inexpensive

Osmička ⓡ (Value) (Kids) CZECH/INTERNATIONAL   Osmička is an interesting hybrid in Vinohrady on a side street a few blocks above the National Museum. At first sight, the "Number 8" reveals a tourist-geared cellar restaurant with tawny eclectic colors, local art for sale on the walls, and a menu dominated by Italian standbys, fresh salads, and a variety of sandwiches. But once a Czech sits down, he or she quickly recognizes the neighborhood secret: This is still a good ol' Bohemian *hospoda* with *vepřo-knedlo-zelo* and other indigenous fare at local prices—served on new solid wood furniture by nicer-than-normal staff.

Balbínova 8, Praha 2. ⓒ 222-826-888. www.osmicka.com. Main courses 54Kč–328Kč ($2.15–$14/£1–£7). MC, V. Mon–Fri 11am–midnight; Sat noon–midnight. Metro: I. P. Pavlova or Náměstí Míru.

Radost FX Café ⓡⓡ (Value) VEGETARIAN   *En vogue* and full of vegetarian offerings, Radost is a clubhouse for hip new Bohemians, but it attracts plenty of internanational visitors, too. The veggie burger served on a whole-grain bun is well seasoned and substantial. Sautéed vegetable dishes, tofu, and huge Greek salads round out the health-conscious menu. The dining area is a dark rec room seemingly furnished by a rummage sale of upholstered armchairs, chaise longues, and couches from the 1960s. Guests eat off coffee tables. Too cool.

Bělehradská 120, Praha 2. ⓒ 224-254-776. www.radostfx.cz. Main courses 60Kč–285Kč ($2.50–$11/£1–£6). AE, MC, V. Daily 11:30am–5am. Metro: I. P. Pavlova.

CAFE SOCIETY
Staré Město (Old Town) & Josefov

Today, most of Prague's cafes have lost the indigenous charm of the Jazz Age or, strangely enough, the Communist era. During the Cold War, the venerable Café Slavia, across from the National Theater, became a de facto clubhouse in which dissidents passed the time, often within listening range of the not-so-secret police. It's here that Václav Havel and the arts community often gathered to keep a flicker of the Civic Society alive.

Grand Café CAFE FARE   The biggest draw of this quaint cafe, the former Café Milena, is a great view of the Orloj, an astronomical clock with an hourly parade of saints on the side of Old Town Square's city hall. With a new management came wider selection of main courses as well as higher prices. Make sure you get a table at the window.

Staroměstské nám. 22, Praha 1 (1st floor). ⓒ 221-632-520. www.grandcafe.cz. Cappuccino 89Kč ($3.70/£2); main menu 190Kč–490Kč ($7.90–$20/£4–£10). AE, MC, V. Daily 10am–midnight. Metro: Staroměstská.

Kavárna Obecní dům ⓡⓡ CAFE FARE   An afternoon here feels like a trip back to the time when Art Nouveau was the newest fashion, not history. The reopening of the entire Municipal House in the spring of 1997 was a treat for those who love this style of architecture, and the *kavárna* might be its most spectacular public room. Witness the lofty ceilings, marble wall accents and tables, altarlike mantel at the far end, and huge windows and period chandeliers. Coffee, tea, and other drinks come with pastries and light sandwiches.

In the Municipal House, náměstí Republiky 5, Praha 1. ℂ 222-002-763. www.vysehrad2000.cz. Cakes and coffees from 50Kč–135Kč ($2.10–$5.65/£1–£3). AE, MC, V. Daily 7:30am–11pm. Metro: Náměstí Republiky.

Kavárna Slavia ⍟ CAFE FARE   You'll most certainly walk by this Prague landmark, so why not stop in? The restored crisp Art Deco room recalls the Slavia's 100 years as a meeting place for the city's cultural and intellectual corps. The cafe still has a relatively affordable menu accompanying the gorgeous riverfront panoramic views of Prague Castle.

Národní at Smetanovo nábřeží, Praha 1. ℂ 224-218-493. Coffees and pastries 20Kč–40Kč (85¢–$1.65/40p–£1); salad bar and light menu items 40Kč–120Kč ($1.65–$5/£1–£2). AE, MC, V. Daily 8am–midnight. Metro: Národní třída.

Velryba CAFE FARE   This is the city center's cafe for young intellectuals. Journalists and actors set the mood in this bareish basement on a back street off Národní třída, where the emphasis is on good friends and hard talk. Pretty decent pasta dishes are served.

Opatovická 24, Praha 1. ℂ 224-912-391. Light meals 62Kč–135Kč ($2.50–$5.60/£1–£3). No credit cards. Daily 11am–midnight. Metro: Národní třída.

Nové Město (New Town)

Globe ⍟ LIGHT FARE   A mainstay for younger English-speaking expats, the Globe is split into a fairly well-stocked bookstore and a usually crowded literary cafe serving pastas, sandwiches, salads, and chewy brownies along with stiff espresso. This cafe offers several terminals for Internet connections costing 1.50Kč (5¢/2p) per minute.

Pštrossova 6, Praha 1. ℂ 224-934-203. www.globebookstore.cz. Salads, sandwiches, pastas, and desserts 50Kč–145Kč ($2.10–$6.05/£1–£3). No credit cards. Daily 10am–midnight. Metro: Národní třída.

Vinohrady

Kavárna Medúza CAFE FARE   With the feeling of an old attic, the Medúza, near several Vinohrady hotels and pensions, has a comfortable mix of visitors and students. The cappuccino comes in bowls, not cups, and the garlic bread hits the spot.

Belgická 17, Praha 2. ℂ 222-515-107. Cappuccino 25Kč ($1.05/50p); pastries/light meals 39Kč–95Kč ($1.60–$3.95/£1–£2). No credit cards. Mon–Fri 10am–1am; Sat–Sun noon–1am. Metro: Náměstí Míru.

EXPLORING PRAGUE

While Prague's classical music and the Czech Republic's unmatched beer are among some of the better reasons to visit, the primary pleasure for many is simply strolling

---

⟨**Value**⟩ **Saving Money on Entrance Fees**

If you like museums, galleries, castles, and churches, you may consider getting a **Prague Card**. This pass is valid for 4 days and allows you to visit up to 55 top attractions in the city, including the Prague Castle.

The price is 740Kč ($30/£15) adults and 490Kč ($20/£10) students under 26, and you can buy it at the Čedok office or the PIS information center at Na Příkopě 20, Praha 1. For more information and the whole list of sights go to www.praguecard.biz.

Prague's winding cobblestone streets and enjoying the unique atmosphere. Only by foot can you explore the countless nooks and crannies. It would be hard to think of another world capital where there is so much in such a compact area.

PRAGUE CASTLE (PRAŽSKÝ HRAD) & CHARLES BRIDGE (KARLŮV MOST)

The huge hilltop complex known collectively as **Prague Castle (Pražský Hrad)** ✸✸✸, on Hradčanské náměstí, encompasses dozens of houses, towers, churches, courtyards, and monuments. A visit to the castle can easily take an entire day or more, depending on how thoroughly you explore it. Still, you can see the top sights—St. Vitus Cathedral, the Royal Palace, St. George's Basilica, the Powder Tower, and Golden Lane—in the space of a morning or an afternoon.

If you're feeling particularly fit, you can walk up to the castle, or you can take metro line A to Malostranská or Hradčanská or tram no. 22 or 23.

TICKETS & CASTLE INFORMATION   Tickets are sold at the **Prague Castle Information Center** in the second courtyard after you pass through the main gate from Hradčanské náměstí. The center also arranges tours in various languages and sells tickets for individual concerts and exhibits. The castle is located at Hradčanské náměstí, Hradčany, Praha 1 (✆ **224-373-368;** fax 224-310-896; www.hrad.cz). Admission to the grounds is free. A combination ticket for tour A to six main attractions (St. Vitus Cathedral, Royal Palace including "The Story of Prague Castle" permanent exhibition, St. George's Basilica, Powder Tower, Golden Lane, and Daliborka Tower), without a guide costs 350Kč ($15/£7) adults, 175Kč ($7/£4) students; with an English-speaking guide, 440Kč ($18/£9) adults, 265Kč ($11/£5) students. Tour B (St. Vitus Cathedral, Royal Palace, Golden Lane, and Daliborka Tower) costs 220Kč ($9.20/£4)adults, 110Kč ($5/£2) students; Tour C (only Golden Lane and Daliborka Tower) costs 50Kč ($2/£1) adults and students. For guided tours (groups of five and more), supplement 90Kč ($4/£2) per person (only Tues–Sun 9am–4pm). All tours are free for children under 6. Tickets are valid for 2 days. The castle is open daily 9am to 5pm (to 4pm Nov–Mar). Metro: Malostranská, then tram no. 22 or 23, up the hill two stops.

TOURING ST. VITUS CATHEDRAL (CHRÁM SV. VÍTA) ✸✸✸

St. Vitus Cathedral (Chrám sv. Víta), named for a wealthy 4th-century Sicilian martyr, isn't just the dominant part of the castle, it's the most important section historically.

Built over various phases beginning in A.D. 926 as the court church of the Premyslid princes, the cathedral has long been the center of Prague's religious and political life. The key part of its Gothic construction took place in the 14th century under the direction of Mathias of Arras and Peter Parléř of Gmuend. In the 18th and 19th centuries, subsequent baroque and neo-Gothic additions were made. The **Golden Portal** entrance from the third courtyard is no longer used; however, take a look above the arch. The 1370 mosaic *The Last Judgment* has been painstakingly restored with the help of computer-aided imagery provided by American art researchers.

Of the massive Gothic cathedral's 21 chapels, the **St. Wenceslas Chapel (Svatováclavská kaple)** ✸ stands out as one of Prague's few must-see, indoor sights. Midway toward the high altar on the right, it's encrusted with hundreds of pieces of jasper and amethyst and decorated with paintings from the 14th to the 16th centuries. The chapel sits atop the gravesite of Bohemia's patron saint, St. Wenceslas.

Prague Attractions

Alfons Mucha Museum **30**
Charles Bridge (Karlův most) **14**
Charles Square
  (Karlovo náměstí) **33**
Church of Our Lady Victorious **2**
Church of St. Nicholas
  Malá Strana (Lesser Town) **11**
  Old Town Square **19**
Estates Theater **29**
Franz Kafka Museum **13**
Havel's Market **21**
House at the Black
  Mother of God **28**
Kinský Palace **23**
Maisel Synagogue **18**
Municipal House **32**
Museum Kampa-Sovovy Mlýny **12**
National Theater **32**
Old Jewish Cemetery **16**
Old-New Synagogue **16**
Old Town Hall and
  Astronomical Clock **20**
Old Town Square
  (Staroměstské náměstí) **22**
Pinkas Synagogue **15**
Powder Tower **27**
Prague Castle (Pražský Hrad) **6**
Royal Garden **5**
Royal Palace **8**
St. Agnes Convent **24**
St. George's Convent **9**
St. Vitus Cathedral **7**
State Jewish Museum **16**
Sternberk Palace Art Museum **4**
Strahov Monastery and Library **1**
Týn Church **28**
Veletržní Palác **25**
Vrtbovská Garden **3**
Waldstein Gardens **10**
Wenceslas Square
  (Václavské náměstí) **31**

DEJVICKÁ Ⓜ

Československé armády

Pod kaštany

U Prašného mostu

HRADČANSKÁ Ⓜ

Badeniho

Milady Horákové

Mariánské hradby

CHOTKOVY SADY

Jelení

Chotkov

Castle Information Office **5**

HRADČANY

Keplerova

U Brusnice

Nový Svět

Prague Castle **9**

4 **7** **6** **8**

MALOSTRANSKÁ Ⓜ **10**

Loretánské nám.
Loretánská

U Kasáren

Nerudova **11**

MALÁ STRANA **13**

Úvoz **1**

LOBKOVICKÁ ZAHRADA

STRAHOVSKÁ ZAHRADA

SEMINÁŘSKÁ ZAHRADA **3** **2**

Karmelitská

Malostr. nábřeží

Strahovská

PETŘÍNSKÉ SADY

Olympijská

Petřín Tower ■

Funicular

Újezd **12**

STŘELECKÝ OSTROV

Chaloupeckého

Jezdecká

Spartakiádní Stadion

KINSKÉHO ZAHRADA

Peškové

Janáčkovo nábřeží

Holečkova

V botanice

Plzeňská

Kartouzská

Zborovská

Duškova

ANDĚL Ⓜ

Svornosti

Mozartova

Radlická

SMÍCHOV

GERMANY   POLAND

★Prague
THE CZECH REPUBLIC

AUSTRIA   SLOVAKIA

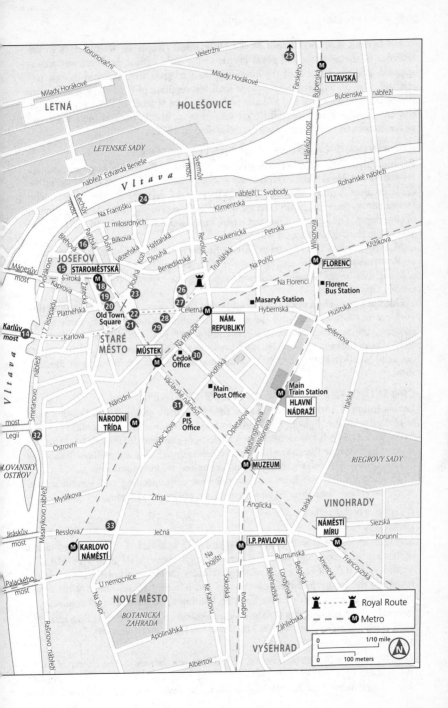

LETNÁ

HOLEŠOVICE

LETENSKÉ SADY

Korunovační

Veletržní

Milady Horákové

Milady Horákové

Farského

Bubenská

M **VLTAVSKÁ**

Bubenské nábřeží

Hlávkův most

Rohanské nábřeží

nábřeží Edvarda Beneše

V l t a v a

Švermův most

Čechův most

Na Františku

U. milosrdných

nábřeží L. Svobody

Klimentská

24

Pařížská

Břehová

Dušní

Bílkova

Vězeňská

Kozí

Haštalská

Dlouhá

Benediktská

Soukenická

Petrská

Revoluční

Na Poříčí

Wilsonova

Křižíkova

16

JOSEFOV

15 **STAROMĚSTSKÁ**

Truhlářská

M **FLORENC**

Mánesův most

Dvořákovo nábřeží

Široká

Kaprova

Žatecká

Maiselova

Platnéřská

18

19

20

M

23

Dlouhá

26

27

Celetná

Na Florenci

■ **Florenc Bus Station**

Husitská

Old Town Square

22

21

28

29

M

NÁM. REPUBLIKY

Hybernská

Masaryk Station

■ **Masaryk Station**

Seifertova

Karlův most

14

17. listopadu

Karlova

STARÉ MĚSTO

Na Příkopě

MŮSTEK

M

Čedok Office

30

Jindřišská

Main Train Station

V l t a v a

Smetanovo nábřeží

Národní

Václavské náměstí

Main Post Office

■ **Main Post Office**

Opletalova

Wilsonova

M **Main Train Station**

HLAVNÍ NÁDRAŽÍ

Italská

most

Legií

32

Ostrovní

NÁRODNÍ TŘÍDA

M

31

PIS Office

■ **PIS Office**

Vodičkova

Washingtonova

RIEGROVY SADY

SLOVANSKÝ OSTROV

Myslíkova

Žitná

Anglická

Italská

VINOHRADY

Jiráskův most

Masarykovo nábřeží

Resslova

Ječná

M **MUZEUM**

Na bojišti

Sokolská

NÁMĚSTÍ MÍRU

M

Slezská

Korunní

33

M **I.P. PAVLOVA**

Rumunská

Legerova

Americká

Francouzská

Palackého most

Rašínovo nábřeží

U nemocnice

KARLOVO NÁMĚSTÍ

M

NOVÉ MĚSTO

Na Slupi

BOTANICKÁ ZAHRADA

Ke Karlovu

Belgická

Londýnská

Bělehradská

Záhřebská

VYŠEHRAD

Apolinářská

Albertov

🏰 .... 🏰 **Royal Route**

--- M **Metro**

0   1/10 mile

0   100 meters

237

Just beyond this, the **Chapel of the Holy Rood (Kaple sv. Kříže)** leads to the entrance of the underground **royal crypt.** In the early 1900s, the crypt was reconstructed, and the remains of the kings and their relatives were replaced in new sarcophagi. The center sarcophagus is the final resting place of Charles IV, the favorite Bohemian king who died in 1378 and is the namesake of much of Prague. In the back row are Charles's four wives (all in one sarcophagus), and in front of them is George of Poděbrady, the last Bohemian king, who died in 1471.

CONTINUING THROUGH THE CASTLE COMPLEX

For more than 700 years, beginning in the 9th century, Bohemian kings and princes resided in the **Royal Palace (Královský palác),** located in the third courtyard of the castle grounds. Vaulted **Vladislav Hall (Vladislavský sál),** the interior's centerpiece, hosted coronations and is still used for special occasions of state such as inaugurations of presidents. The adjacent Diet was where kings and queens met with their advisers and where the Supreme Court was held.

St. George's Basilica (Kostel sv. Jiří), adjacent to the Royal Palace, is Prague's oldest Romanesque structure, dating from the 10th century. It also houses Bohemia's first convent. No longer serving a religious function, the convent contains a gallery of Gothic Czech art.

Golden Lane (Zlatá ulička) and Daliborka Tower ⋆ is a picturesque street of tiny 16th-century houses built into the castle fortifications. Once home to castle sharpshooters, the houses now contain small shops, galleries, and refreshment bars. In 1917, Franz Kafka is said to have lived briefly at no. 22; however, the debate continues as to whether Kafka actually took up residence or just worked in a small office there.

CROSSING THE VLTAVA: CHARLES BRIDGE

Dating from the 14th century, **Charles Bridge (Karlův most)** ⋆⋆⋆, Prague's most celebrated structure, links Prague Castle to Staré Město. For most of its 600 years, the 510m-long (1,673-ft.) span has been a pedestrian promenade, though for centuries walkers had to share the concourse with horse-drawn vehicles and trolleys. Today, the bridge is filled with folks walking among artists and busking musicians.

The best times to stroll across the bridge are early morning and around sunset, when the crowds have thinned and the shadows are more mysterious.

OTHER TOP SIGHTS
Hradčany
Strahov Monastery and Library (Strahovský klášter) ⋆   The second-oldest monastery in Prague, Strahov was founded high above Malá Strana in 1143 by Vladislav II. It's still home to Premonstratensian monks, a scholarly order closely related to the Jesuits, and their dormitories and refectory are off-limits. What draws visitors are the monastery's ornate libraries, holding more than 125,000 volumes.

Strahovské nádvoří 1, Praha 1. ☎ 220-517-278. www.strahovskyklaster.cz. Admission 80Kč ($3.35/£2) adults, 50Kč ($2/£1) students. Daily 9am–noon and 1–5pm. Tram: 22 or 23 from Malostranská metro station.

Malá Strana (Lesser Town)
Church of St. Nicholas (Chrám sv. Mikuláše) ⋆⋆ *Moments*   This church is one of the best examples of high baroque north of the Alps. However, K. I. Dienzenhofer's 1711 design didn't have the massive dome that now dominates the Lesser Town skyline

below Prague Castle. Dienzenhofer's son, Kryštof, added the 78m-high (256-ft.) dome during additional work completed in 1752.

Malostranské nám. 1, Praha 1. ⓒ 257-534-215. www.psalterium.cz. Daily 9am–5pm (4pm in winter); concerts are usually held at 5pm. Admission 50Kč ($2/£1) adults, 25Kč ($1/50p) students. Concerts 390Kč ($16/£8). Metro: Line A to Malostranská.

Staré Město (Old Town)
Estates' Theater (Stavovské divadlo)   Completed in 1783 by wealthy Count F. A. Nostitz, the neoclassical theater became an early symbol of the emerging high Czech culture—with the Greek theme *Patriae et Musis* (the Fatherland and Music) etched above its front columns. In 1799, the wealthy land barons who formed fief-doms known as The Estates gave the theater its current name.

Wolfgang Amadeus Mozart staged the premier of *Don Giovanni* here in 1787 because he said that Vienna's conservative patrons didn't appreciate him or his passion-ate and sometimes shocking work. They also wanted mostly German opera, but Praguers were happy to stage the performance in Italian. "Praguers understand me," Mozart was quoted as saying.

Czech director Miloš Forman returned to his native country to film his Oscar-win-ning *Amadeus*, shooting the scenes of Mozart in Prague with perfect authenticity at the Estates' Theater.

Ovocný trh 1, Praha 1. ⓒ 224-901-448. www.nd.cz. Metro: Line A or B to Můstek.

Old Town Hall (Staroměstská radnice) & Astronomical Clock (Orloj) *Kids*
Crowds congregate in front of Old Town Hall's Astronomical Clock *(orloj)* to watch the glockenspiel spectacle that occurs hourly from 8am to 8pm. Built in 1410, the clock has long been an important symbol of Prague. According to legend, after the timepiece was remodeled at the end of the 15th century, clock artist Master Hanuš was blinded by the Municipal Council so that he couldn't repeat his fine work else-where. In retribution, Hanuš threw himself into the clock mechanism and promptly died. The clock remained out of kilter for almost a century.

Staroměstské nám., Praha 1. ⓒ 724-508-584. www.pis.cz. Admission to tower 50Kč ($2/£1) adults; 40Kč ($1.65/£1) students, children under 10, and seniors. Mar–Oct Mon 11am–6pm, Tues–Sun 9am–6pm; Nov–Feb Mon 11am–5pm, Tues–Sun 9am–5pm. Metro: Line A to Staroměstská.

Josefov
Within Josefov, you'll find a community that for centuries was forced to fend for itself and then experienced horrific purges under Nazi occupation in World War II. Although more than 118,000 Jews were recorded as living in the Czech lands of Bohemia and Moravia in 1939, only 30,000 survived to see the end of the Nazi occu-pation. Today, the Jewish community in the entire country numbers about 3,000 peo-ple, most of whom live in Prague.

The **Jewish Museum in Prague** (www.jewishmuseum.cz) is the name of the organ-ization managing all the Jewish landmarks in Josefov. It provides guided package tours with an English-speaking guide as part of a comprehensive admission price. The pack-age includes the Ceremonial Hall, Old Jewish Cemetery, Old-New Synagogue, Pinkas Synagogue, Klaus Synagogue, Maisel Synagogue, and Spanish Synagogue. From April to October, tours leave on the hour starting at 9am with the last tour at 5pm, but there must be at least 10 people in a group. Off season, the tours are between 9am and

4:30pm. The package costs 500Kč ($20/£10) for adults and 340Kč ($14/£7) for students, free for children under 6.

The Maisel Synagogue now serves as the exhibition space for the **Jewish Museum.** In October 1994, the State Jewish Museum closed; the Torah covers, 100,000 books, and other exhibits once housed there were given to the Jewish community, who then proceeded to return many items to synagogues throughout the country. The Nazis destroyed much of Prague's ancient Judaica during World War II. Ironically, those same Germans constructed an "exotic museum of an extinct race," thus salvaging thousands of objects, such as the valued Torah covers, books, and silver now displayed at the Maisel Synagogue.

Old Jewish Cemetery (Starý židovský hřbitov) ✿ Just 1 block from the Old-New Synagogue, this is one of Europe's oldest Jewish burial grounds, dating from the mid–15th century. Because the local government of the time didn't allow Jews to bury their dead elsewhere, graves were dug deep enough to hold 12 bodies vertically, with each tombstone placed in front of the last. The result is one of the world's most crowded cemeteries: a 1-block area filled with more than 20,000 graves. Among the most famous persons buried here are the celebrated Rabbi Loew (Löw; d. 1609), who created the legend of Golem (a giant clay "monster" to protect Prague's Jews); and banker Markus Mordechai Maisel (d. 1601), then the richest man in Prague and protector of the city's Jewish community during the reign of Rudolf II.

U Starého hřbitova; the entrance is from Široká 3. (☎) 222-317-191. Admission 300Kč ($12/£6) adults, 200Kč ($8.30/£4) students, free for children under 6. Apr–Oct Sun–Fri 9am–6pm; Nov–Mar Sun–Fri 9am–4:30pm. Metro: Line A to Staroměstská.

Old-New Synagogue (Staronová synagóga) ✿ First called the New Synagogue to distinguish it from an even older one that no longer exists, the Old-New Synagogue, built around 1270, is Europe's oldest remaining Jewish house of worship. The faithful have prayed here continuously for more than 700 years, carrying on even after a massive 1389 pogrom in Josefov that killed over 3,000 Jews. Its use as a house of worship was interrupted only between 1941 and 1945 because of the Nazi occupation. The synagogue is also one of Prague's great Gothic buildings, built with vaulted ceilings and retro-fitted with Renaissance-era columns. It is not part of the Jewish Museum, so you can visit this synagogue separately.

Červená 2. (☎) 222-317-191. Admission 200Kč ($8.30/£4) adults, 140Kč ($5.85/£3) students. (If part of the package for Jewish Museum, 500Kč/$20/£12 adults, 340Kč/$14/£7.90 students.) Free for children under 6. Sun–Thurs 9:30am–5pm; Fri 9am–4pm. Metro: Line A to Staroměstská

MUSEUMS & GALLERIES

Many fine private art galleries showing contemporary work by Czech and other artists are in central Prague, within walking distance of Staroměstské náměstí. Although their primary interest is sales, most welcome browsing.

As for public museums and galleries, note that many museums are closed on Monday.

National Gallery Sites

The national collection of fine art is grouped for display in the series of venues known collectively as the **National Gallery (Národní Galerie).** Remember that this term refers to several locations, not just one gallery.

The most extensive collection of classic European works spanning the 14th to the 18th centuries is found at the Archbishop's Palace complex in the **Šternberský palác** across from the main gate to Prague Castle.

Veletržní Palace houses most of the country's 20th-century art collection and now also shows the important national revival works from Czech artists of the 19th century. Much of the rest of the national collection is divided between Kinský Palace on Old Town Square and the Gothic collection at St. Agnes Convent near the river in Old Town.

The key Prague sites within the national gallery system are listed below.

Hradčany
St. Agnes Convent (Klášter sv. Anežky České)
A complex of early Gothic buildings and churches dating from the 13th century, the convent, tucked in a corner of Staré Město, began exhibiting much of the National Gallery's collection of Gothic art in 2000. Once home to the Order of the Poor Clares, it was established in 1234 by St. Agnes of Bohemia, sister of Wenceslas I. The Blessed Agnes became St. Agnes when Pope John Paul II paid his first visit to Prague in 1990 for her canonization.

U Milosrdných 17, Praha 1. ℂ **224-810-628.** www.ngprague.cz. Admission 100Kč ($4.15/£2) adults, 50Kč ($2/£1) children. Tues–Sun 10am–6pm. Metro: Line A to Staroměstská.

St. George's Convent at Prague Castle (Klášter sv. Jiří na Pražském hradě)
Dedicated to displaying traditional Czech art, the castle convent is especially packed with Gothic and baroque Bohemian iconography as well as portraits of patron saints. The most famous among the unique collection of Czech Gothic panel paintings are those by the Master of the Hohenfurth Altarpiece and the Master Theodoricus.

Jiřské nám. 33. ℂ **257-531-644.** www.ngprague.cz. Admission 100Kč ($4.15/£2) adults, 50Kč ($2/£1) students, free for children under 6. Tues–Sun 9am–5pm. Metro: Line A to Malostranská or Hradčanská.

Šternberk Palace (Šternberský palác) ℛ
The jewel in the National Gallery crown (also known casually as the European Art Museum), the gallery at Šternberk Palace, adjacent to the main gate of Prague Castle, displays a wide menu of European art throughout the ages. It features 5 centuries of everything from Orthodox icons to Renaissance oils by Dutch masters.

Hradčanské nám. 15, Praha 1. ℂ **233-090-570.** www.ngprague.cz. Admission 150Kč ($6.25/£3) adults, 70Kč ($2.90/£1) students and children. Tues–Sun 10am–6pm. Metro: Line A to Malostranská or Hradčanská.

Staré Město (Old Town)
Kinský Palace (Palác Kinských)
The reconstructed rococo palace houses graphic works from the National Gallery collection, including pieces by Georges Braque, André Derain, and other modern masters. Pablo Picasso's 1907 *Self-Portrait* is here and has virtually been adopted as the National Gallery's logo.

Staroměstské nám. 12, Praha 1. ℂ **224-810-758.** www.ngprague.cz. Admission is different for each exhibition. Tues–Sun 10am–6pm. Metro: Line A to Staroměstská.

Veletržní Palace (National Gallery)
This 1925 constructivist palace, built for trade fairs, was remodeled and reopened in December 1995 to hold the bulk of the National Gallery's collection of 20th-century works by Czech and other European artists. Three atrium-lit concourses provide a comfortable setting for some catchy and kitschy Czech sculpture and multimedia works. Alas, the best cubist works from

Braque and Picasso, Rodin bronzes, and many other primarily French pieces have been relegated to the second floor.

Veletržní at Dukelských hrdinů 47, Praha 7. © **224-301-111.** www.ngprague.cz. Admission 250Kč ($10/£5) adults, 120Kč ($5/£2) students for 4 floors of the palace; 200Kč ($8.30/£4) adults, 100Kč ($4.15/£2) students for 3 floors; 150Kč ($6.25/£3) adults, 70Kč ($2.90/£1) students for 2 floors; 100Kč ($4.15/£2) adults, 50Kč ($2/£1) students for 1 floor. Free for children under 6. Tues–Sun 10am–6pm. Metro: Line C to Vltavská. Tram: 17.

OTHER MUSEUMS & GALLERIES

MALÁ STRANA

Museum Kampa–Sovovy mlýny ⊛ This building on Kampa island served for most of its history, due to the location, as a mill. Throughout the centuries it was struck by floods, fires, and destructive wars. In September 2003, the Sovovy mlýny was opened as a museum of modern art by Czech-born American Meda Mládková and her foundation. She has been collecting works of Czech and central European artists since the 1950s. Her dream reached its pinnacle when she presented the permanent exhibition of František Kupka's drawings and Otto Gutfreund's sculptures.

U Sovových mlýnů 503/2, Praha 1. © **257-286-147.** www.museumkampa.cz. Admission 120Kč ($5/£2) adults, 60Kč ($2.50/£1) students, free for children under 6. Daily 10am–6pm. Metro: Malostranská.

NOVÉ MĚSTO (NEW TOWN)

Alfons Mucha Museum (Muzeum A. Muchy) ⊛ This museum opened in early 1998 near Wenceslas Square to honor the high priest of Art Nouveau, Alphonse (Alfons in Czech) Mucha. Though the Moravian-born, turn-of-the-20th-century master spent most of his creative years in Paris drawing luminaries like actress Sarah Bernhardt, Mucha's influence can still be seen throughout his home country. The new museum, around the corner from the Palace Hotel, combines examples of his graphic works, posters, and paintings, and highlights his influence in jewelry, fashion, and advertising. Those who remember the 1960s and 1970s will flash back to one of Mucha's most famous works, the sinuous goddess of Job rolling papers.

Panská 7, Praha 1. © **224-216-415.** www.mucha.cz. Admission 120Kč ($5/£2) adults, 60Kč ($2.50/£1) students and children. Daily 10am–6pm. Metro: Můstek.

HISTORIC SQUARES

The most celebrated square in the city, **Old Town Square (Staroměstské nám.)** ⊛⊛⊛ is surrounded by baroque buildings and packed with colorful craftspeople, cafes, and entertainers. In ancient days, the site was a major crossroads on central European merchant routes. In its center stands a memorial to Jan Hus, the 15th-century martyr who crusaded against Prague's German-dominated religious and political establishment. It was unveiled in 1915, on the 500th anniversary of Hus's execution. The monument's most compelling features are the dark asymmetry and fluidity of the figures. Take metro line A to Staroměstská. The square and Staré Město are described in more detail in the Walking Tour on p. 243.

One of the city's most historic squares, **Wenceslas Square (Václavské nám.)** ⊛⊛ was formerly the horse market (Koňský trh). The once muddy swath between the buildings played host to the country's equine auctioneers. The top of the square, where the National Museum now stands, was the outer wall of the New Town fortifications, bordering the Royal Vineyards. Unfortunately, the city's busiest highway now cuts the museum off from the rest of the square it dominates. Trolleys streamed up and down the square until the early 1980s. Today the half-mile-long boulevard is lined with cinemas, shops, hotels, restaurants, casinos, and porn shops.

The square was given its present name in 1848. The pedestal of giant statue of St. Wenceslas has become a popular platform for speakers. Actually, the square has thrice been the site of riots and revolutions—in 1848, 1968, and 1989. At the height of the Velvet Revolution, 250,000 to 300,000 Czechs filled the square during one demonstration. Take metro line A or B to Můstek.

The rapid influx of visitors, the post-Communist wage growth, and a new consumer economy fueled by the shopping habits of the Czech nouveau riche have resulted in expensive boutiques and specialty shops popping up like mushrooms in Prague.

For those looking for a piece of Czech handwork, you can find some of the world's best crystal and glass, often at shockingly low prices. Antiques shops and booksellers abound, and the selection of classical, trendy, and offbeat art is immense at the numerous private galleries. Throughout the city center you'll find quaint, obscure shops, some without phones or advertising.

WALKING TOUR | STARÉ MĚSTO (OLD TOWN)

Although this tour is far from exhaustive, it takes you past some of Old Town's most important buildings and monuments. Go to náměstí Republiky 5, at the metro station. Begin at the:

❶ Municipal House (Obecní dům)

From the beginning, this ornate Art Nouveau building has been an important Czech cultural symbol—the document granting independence to Czechoslovakia was signed here in 1918. The **Prague Symphony** performs in Smetana Hall, the building's most impressive room, with a gorgeous stained-glass ceiling.

With your back to the Municipal House main entrance, walk around to your right under the arch of the:

❷ Powder Tower (Prašná brána, literally Powder Gate)

Once part of Staré Město's system of fortifications, the Powder Tower was built in 1475 as one of the walled city's major gateways. The tower marks the beginning of the **Royal Route,** the traditional path along which medieval Bohemian monarchs paraded on their way to being crowned in Prague Castle's St. Vitus Cathedral.

Continue through the arch down Celetná Street (named after *calt,* a bread baked here in the Middle Ages) to the corner of Ovocný trh, where you'll find the:

❸ House at the Black Mother of God (Dům U Černé Matky boží)

At Celetná 34, this building is important for its cubist architectural style. Cubism, an angular artistic movement, was confined to painting and sculpture in France and most of Europe. As an architectural style, cubism is exclusive to Bohemia.

With your back to the House of the Black Mother of God, cross Celetná into Templová, walk 2 short blocks, and turn left onto Jakubská. At the corner, on your right, you'll see:

❹ St. James's Church (Kostel sv. Jakuba)

Prague's second-longest church contains 21 altars. When you enter, look up just inside the church's front door. The object dangling from above is the shriveled arm of a 16th-century thief.

Return to Celetná and continue walking about 90m (295 ft.). On the right, below the towering spires, is:

❺ Church of Our Lady Before Týn (Kostel paní Marie před Týnem–Týnský chrám)

This is one of the largest and prettiest of Prague's many churches. Famous for its twin spires that loom over nearby Staroměstské náměstí, the church was closely connected to the 14th-century Hussite movement for religious reform. Note the tomb of Danish astronomer Tycho de Brahe (d. 1601), near the high altar.

Exit the church and continue a few more steps along Celetná, which opens up into:

⑥ Old Town Square (Staroměstské náměstí)

Surrounded by baroque buildings and packed with colorful cafes, craftspeople, and entertainers, Staroměstské náměstí looks the way an old European square is supposed to look.

Old Town Square has also seen its share of political protest and punishment. Protestant Hussites rioted here in the 1400s. In the 1620s, the Catholic Habsburg rulers beheaded 27 Protestants here and hung some of the heads in baskets above Charles Bridge. A small white cross has been embedded in the square near the Old Town Hall for each of the beheaded.

To begin your walk around the square, go straight toward the massive black stone monument in the center. Here you'll find the statue of:

⑦ Jan Hus Statue

Jan Hus was a fiery 15th-century preacher who challenged the Roman Catholic hierarchy and was burned at the stake for it. The statue's pedestal has been used as a soapbox by many a populist politician trying to gain points by associating himself with the ill-fated Protestant.

From here, turn around and walk left toward the clock tower.

⑧ Old Town Hall (Staroměstská radnice)

Try to time your walk so you can pass the hall and its **Astronomical Clock** at the top of the hour. It may be an understated show, but each hour a mechanical parade of saints and sinners performs for the crowd watching below (p. 239). If you have time and your knees are up to it, try making the steep, narrow walk up to the

top of the tower for a picturesque view of Old Town's red roofs.

Walking past the right side of the clock tower toward the northwest corner of the square, you'll come to:

⑨ St. Nicholas Church (Kostel sv. Mikuláše)

This is the 1735 design of Prague's baroque master architect K. I. Dienzenhofer. The three-towered edifice isn't as beautiful or as ornate inside as his St. Nicholas Church in Lesser Town, but the crystal fixtures are worth a look.

From the front of the church, walk behind the back of the Hus monument, through the square, to the broad palace with the reddish roof and balcony in front. This is:

⑩ Kinský Palace (Palác Kinských)

From the rococo balcony jutting from the palace's stucco facade, Communist leader Klement Gottwald declared the proletariat takeover of the Czechoslovak government in February 1945. Italian architect Lurago designed the building for Count Goltz. It was later taken over by the Habsburg Prince Rudolf Kinský in 1768. It now houses a fine modern art collection in the **National Gallery** complex of palaces (p. 240).

Next to this is the:

⑪ House at the Stone Bell (Dům U kamenného zvonu)

The medieval Gothic tower was built in the 14th century for the father of Charles IV, John of Luxembourg.

From here, head back toward Old Town Hall, but then about midway to the tower, turn left toward the square's south end and begin walking down Železná. Continue down this car-restricted walking zone about 300m (984 ft.); then, on the left you'll see the pale green:

⑫ Estates' Theater (Stavovské divadlo)

Mozart premiered his opera *Don Giovanni* in this late-18th-century grand hall.

Make sure to walk down Rytířská in front of the theater to get a full view of this beautifully restored building.

Walking Tour: Staré Město (Old Town)

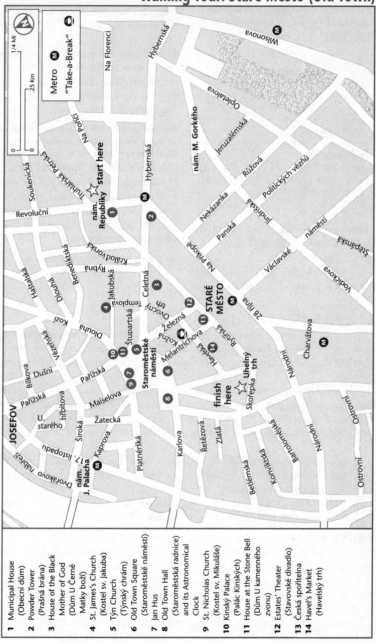

1 Municipal House (Obecní dům)
2 Powder Tower (Prašná brána)
3 House of the Black Mother of God (Dům U Černé Matky boží)
4 St. James's Church (Kostel sv. Jakuba)
5 Týn Church (Týnský chrám)
6 Old Town Square (Staroměstské náměstí)
7 Jan Hus
8 Old Town Hall (Staroměstská radnice) and its Astronomical Clock
9 St. Nicholas Church (Kostel sv. Mikuláše)
10 Kinský Palace (Palác Kinských)
11 House at the Stone Bell (Dům U kamenného zvonu)
12 Estates' Theater (Stavovské divadlo)
13 Česká spořitelna
14 Havel's Market (Havelský trh)

From the front of the theater, walk about 10 steps back up Železná and take the first left on Havelská.

 TAKE A BREAK
At Havelská 27, you can stop for a tasty pasta, lasagna, tiramisu, or thick Italian espresso at the **Kogo** (p. 231). There are tightly packed tables inside, but if the weather is nice, sit in the more comfortable archway. Hours are daily from 9am to midnight. Salads and appetizers from 160Kč ($6.65/£3). You won't be disappointed by their homemade pasta from 192Kč ($8/£4.50).

Continue down Havelská. On the left you'll see:

⓭ Czech Savings Bank (Česká spořitelna)
The 1894 building was originally intended to be a bank, but after the 1948 coup it was seized by the government and turned into a repository for Communist propaganda. After the 1989 revolution, the building was returned to the bank, which restored the intricate friezes and frescoes depicting bankers' propaganda of early Czech capitalism. This is the largest Czech savings bank and worth a peek.

Your next destination is the popular street market that overtakes the remainder of Havelská Street. Simply continue on to:

⓮ Havel's Market (Havelský trh)
At this popular local meeting place, you'll find vegetables, fruit, drinks, soaps, toiletries, artwork, and leather goods. Prices here are generally lower than in most shops. Have fun browsing.

The nearest metro is Můstek, line A or B.

SHOPPING AREAS

The L-shaped half-mile running from the middle of **Wenceslas Square** around the corner to the right on **Na Příkopě** and to the Myslbek Center has become Prague's principal shopping street. In this short distance you'll find three multilevel shopping gallerias.

A handful of fine private **art galleries** is concentrated on the stretch of **Národní třída** running from just east of the National Theater to Wenceslas Square. The wide tree-lined Pařížská, from Old Town Square to the Hotel Inter-Continental, is flanked with top-level boutiques, travel agencies, and airline offices, as well as eclectic local shops.

In the streets surrounding **Old Town Square,** you'll find a wide variety of expensive shops with bizarre nooks offering woodcarvings, garnets, handmade toys, and typical Czech glass and porcelain.

In **Malá Strana,** you'll find artists and craftspeople selling their jewelry, prints, handicrafts, and faux Red Army surplus on Charles Bridge.

HOURS & TAXES

Prague's centrally located shops rely on tourist business and keep fairly long hours. Most are open Monday to Friday from about 9am to 6pm and Saturday from 9am to 1pm, and sometimes much later. Many open on Sunday as well, though usually for a shorter time. Note that some small food shops that keep long hours charge up to 20% more for all their goods.

Prices for goods in shops include the government's 19% **value-added tax (VAT).** All tourists from **outside the E.U.** can save up to 16% of this tax. To make use of this concession, buy from stores with the TAX FREE sign. To qualify, the purchase price must exceed 2,000Kč ($83/£40), including the VAT in 1 day in one store.

SHOPPING A TO Z
ANTIQUES
Antique-Andrle Vladimír   A wide selection of Eastern Orthodox icons distinguishes this shop halfway up on Wenceslas Square. The proprietor produces papers showing that each icon was legitimately obtained (despite heavy restrictions in many countries) and legal for export. There's also a large selection of antique watches and other accessories. Open Monday to Saturday from 10am to 7pm and Sunday from 10am to 6pm. Václavské nám. 17, Praha 1. ✆ **224-009-166.** Metro: Můstek. Also at Křížovnická 1, Praha 1. ✆ **222-311-625.** Metro: Staroměstská. www.antiqueandrle.cz.

ART GALLERIES
The Czech Museum of Fine Arts   This museum presents works of contemporary Czech and other Eastern European artists. Coffee-table books and catalogs with detailed descriptions in English and color reproductions usually accompany well-planned exhibitions. Open Tuesday to Sunday from 10am to 6pm. Husova 19 and 21, Praha 1. ✆ **222-220-218.** www.cmvu.cz. Metro: Národní třída or Můstek.

CRYSTAL & GLASS
Cristallino *⊀*   This store offers one of the largest assortments of Bohemian crystal and glass, as well as some porcelain and jewelry. Designs come from top Czech glass makers and vary from classic patterns to modern glassware. Open daily 9am to 8pm April to December, 9am to 7pm January to March. Celetná 12, Praha 1. ✆ **224-225-173.** www.cristallino.cz. Metro: Můstek.

Moser *⊀⊀⊀* (Value)   The Moser family began selling Bohemia's finest crystal in central Prague in 1857, drawing customers from around the world. Even the king of Siam made a special trip to the Karlovy Vary factory in the 1930s to pick his place settings. The dark-wood showroom upstairs is worth a look if only to get the feeling of Prague at its most elegant. Open Monday to Friday from 9am to 8pm, Saturday and Sunday from 10am to 7pm. Na Příkopě 12, Praha 1. ✆ **224-211-293.** www.moser-glass.com. Metro: Můstek. 2nd Prague shop is at Malé nám. 11, Praha 1. ✆ **224-222-012.** Metro: Můstek.

DEPARTMENT STORES & SHOPPING MALLS
Obchodní Centrum Nový Smíchov *⊀⊀*   This modern shopping mall built on the defunct site of one of the city's most famous factories is Prague's new temple to post-Communist consumption. In just a few minutes' metro ride from Old Town or Malá Strana, you can find many items cheaper than in western Europe or the States. Open daily 9am to 9pm (shops); 7am to midnight (Carrefour); 11am to 11pm (restaurants and entertainment). Plzeňská 8, Praha 5. ✆ **251-511-151.** www.novysmichovoc.cz. Metro: Anděl.

Palác Flora *⊀*   This addition to the city's shopping malls is located in the residential area of Vinohrady. The modern building has been erected right above Flora metro station, so it is easily accessible from the center. Inside you will find a wide selection of shops, restaurants, and cafes and an entertainment center that includes 3-D and 2-D cinemas. Boutiques and fashion shops occupy the second floor. Open Monday to Friday 9am to 9pm, Saturday and Sunday 10am to 10pm. Vinohradská 149, Praha 3. ✆ **255-741-700.** www.edb.cz. Metro: Flora.

Tesco   The best reasons to shop at Tesco are the gifts (including fine Leander rose porcelain), snacks on the ground floor (like a Little Caesar's pizza), and a fine grocery store in the basement. Open Monday to Friday from 8am to 9pm (food department

---

⟨Value⟩ An Open-Air Market

On the short, wide street perpendicular to Melantrichova, between Staroměstské náměstí and Václavské náměstí, **Havel's Market (Havelský trh)**, Havelská
ulice, Praha 1 (named well before Havel became president), features dozens of
private vendors selling seasonal homegrown fruits and vegetables at the best
prices in the city center. Other goods, including detergent, flowers, and cheese,
are also for sale. Open Monday to Friday from 8am to 6pm. Take metro line A
or B to Můstek.

---

from 7am), Saturday from 9am to 8pm (food department from 8am), and Sunday
from 10am to 8pm (food department from 9am). Národní třída 26, Praha 1. ⓒ 222-003-
111. Metro: Národní třída.

GARNETS
Český Granát ⟨Value⟩   This shop has an excellent reputation for good-quality jewelry
at reasonable prices. Traditional, conservative earrings and pendants are spiked with
some interesting and unusual designs. Most pieces are set in 24-karat gold or gold-
plated silver. Open Monday to Saturday from 10am to 7pm and Sunday from 10am
to 7pm. Celetná 4, Praha 1. ⓒ 224-228-281. Metro: Můstek.

GIFTS & SOUVENIRS
Dr. Stuart's Botanicus ⟨★★⟩ ⟨Finds⟩   This chain of natural scent, soap, and herb shops
is an amazing Anglo-Czech success story. Started by a British botanist and Czech partners on a farm northeast of Prague, Dr. Stuart's has found 101 ways to ply a plant into
a sensuous gift and a lucrative trade. There are several outlets throughout Prague, with
this one at the Havelský market probably most convenient for tourists. Open Monday to Friday from 10am to 6pm and Saturday from 10am to 4pm. Michalská 4, Praha 1.
ⓒ 224-212-977. www.botanicus.cz. Metro: Můstek.

Dům Porcelánu Praha ⟨Value⟩   Traditional Czech "onion" *(cibulák)* china is the calling card for this representative shop of the porcelain factory in Dubí near the German
border. The folksy blue-on-bone cobalt onion patterns have become a familiar sight
in country kitchens around the world. Open Monday to Friday from 9am to 7pm,
Saturday from 9am to 2pm, and Sunday from 2 to 5pm. Jugoslávská 16, Praha 2. ⓒ 221-
505-320. www.cibulak.cz. Metro: Náměstí Míru or I. P. Pavlova.

MUSIC
Bontonland Megastore   Selling everything from serious Bohemian classics to
Seattle grunge, the store is in the Koruna Palace, which is open Monday to Saturday
from 9am to 8pm and Sunday from 10am to 7pm. Václavské nám. at Na Příkopě 1, Praha 1.
ⓒ 224-473-080. www.bontonland.cz. Metro: Můstek.

PRAGUE AFTER DARK
For many Czechs, the best nighttime entertainment is boisterous discussion and
world-class brew at a noisy pub. Visitors with a penchant to blend in with the locals
can learn a lot about this part of the world with an evening at the corner *hospoda*.
Many are fascinated just by a quiet stroll over the ancient city's cobblestones lit by the

mellow lamps of Charles Bridge and Malá Strana. Others seek the dark caverns of a fine jazz club or the black light and Day-Glo of a hot dance club.

But Prague's longest entertainment tradition, of course, is classical music.

A safe bet is Mozart's *Don Giovanni,* usually presented about twice a month in its original 2-centuries-old home, the **Estates' Theater.** This production, which has modern accents, can be choppy, but the beautifully restored setting makes even a mediocre performance worth attending.

Serious music lovers are better off at one of the numerous performances of the **Czech Philharmonic** at the Rudolfinum, the **Prague Symphony Orchestra** at Obecní dům, or top **chamber ensembles** at salons and palaces around the city. A pipe organ concert heard while sitting in the pews of one of the city's baroque churches can be inspirational.

TICKETS   Events rarely sell out far in advance, except for major nights during the Prague Spring Music Festival or a staging of *Don Giovanni* in the high season. To secure tickets before arriving, contact the travel bureau **Čedok** in Prague, at Na Příkopě 18, Praha 1 (© **224-197-777;** www.cedok.cz). You can also contact the Prague ticket agency **Ticketpro,** Klimentská 22, Praha 1 (© **296-329-999;** www.ticketpro.cz).

Large, centrally located ticket agencies are **Prague Tourist Center,** Rytířská 12, Praha 1 (© **296-333-333**), open daily from 9am to 8pm; **Bohemia Ticket,** Na Příkopě 16, Praha 1 (© **224-215-031;** www.bohemiaticket.cz), open Monday to Friday from 10am to 7pm, Saturday from 10am to 5pm, and Sunday from 10am to 3pm.

THE PERFORMING ARTS

While performances of Mozart's operas at the Estates' Theater are probably the visitor's best overall choices because of the setting, the **National Opera,** performing in the gold-crowned 19th-century National Theater, remains the country's best-loved company.

The **Prague State Opera (Státní opera Praha),** in the aging State Opera House near the top of Wenceslas Square, has reorganized after its 1992 split with the National Opera and now concentrates primarily on Italian classics, though a few Czech favorites are included each season.

CLASSICAL MUSIC

This small capital boasts three full orchestras, yet all are financially strapped, so the repertoire tends to be conservative, with most concerts providing popular time-tested works. You can get information about all of them at the ticket agencies listed above. Tickets range from 100Kč to 600Kč ($4.15–$25/£2–£12) during the regular season and up to 2,000Kč ($83/£40) for the opening night of the **Prague Spring Festival.** You can find dozens of concerts by the full orchestras or chamber groups each month, but the pickings are thin in July and August, when the musicians are on their holiday.

CLASSICAL CONCERTS AROUND TOWN

When strolling, you'll undoubtedly pick up or be handed lots of leaflets advertising chamber concerts in churches, museums, and other venues. These recitals and choral arrangements usually have programs featuring a classical and baroque repertoire, with an emphasis on pieces by Czech composers. The quality varies, but the results are usually enjoyable. Tickets range from 100Kč to 350Kč ($4.15–$15/£2–£7) and can be purchased at the churches' entrances or sometimes from hotel concierges.

LANDMARK THEATERS & CONCERT HALLS

The Czech Philharmonic at Rudolfinum *(Moments* Named for Prince Rudolf, the beautifully restored Rudolfinum has been one of the city's premier concert venues since it opened in the 19th century. The Rudolfinum's Small Hall mostly presents chamber concerts, while the larger, more celebrated Dvořák Hall is home to the Czech Philharmonic. Alšovo nábřeží 12, Praha 1. © 227-059-352. www.rudolfinum.cz. Metro: Staroměstská.

Estates' Theater (Stavovské divadlo) ⨀⨀ In a city full of spectacularly beautiful theaters, the massive pale-green Estates' still ranks as one of the most awesome. Built in 1783, this is the only theater in the world that's still in its original condition. The Estates' was home to the premiere of Mozart's *Don Giovanni,* which was conducted by the composer himself. Simultaneous English translation, transmitted via headphone, is available for plays staged here. Ovocný trh 1, Praha 1. © 224-902-322. www.nd.cz or www.mozart-praha.cz. Metro: Line A or B to Můstek.

National Theater (Národní divadlo) ⨀⨀ This neo-Renaissance building overlooking the Vltava River was completed in 1881. The theater was built to nurture the Czech National Revival—a grass-roots movement to replace the dominant German culture with that of native Czechs. To finance it, small collection boxes with signs promoting "the prosperity of a dignified national theater" were installed in public places. Almost immediately upon its completion, the building was wrecked by fire; it was rebuilt and opened in 1883 with the premiere of Bedřich Smetana's opera *Libuše.* Národní 2, Praha 1. © 224-901-448. www.nd.cz. Metro: Národní třída.

Prague Symphony Orchestra–Smetana Hall (Smetanova síň) ⨀ Named for the popular composer and fervent Czech nationalist Bedřich Smetana (1824–84), Smetana Hall is located in one of the world's most distinctive Art Nouveau buildings. Since its 1997 reopening after the building's painstaking reconstruction, the ornate and purely exhilarating Smetana Hall has hosted a series of top-notch events. In the Municipal House (Obecní dům), náměstí Republiky 5, Praha 1. © 222-002-336. www.fok.cz. Metro: Náměstí Republiky.

State Opera House (Státní opera) ⨀ First the "New German Theater" and then the "Smetana Theater," the State Opera was built in the 1880s for the purpose of staging Germanic music and drama. Based on a Viennese design, the Renaissance-style theater was rebuilt after suffering serious damage during the bombing of Prague in 1945. Over the years, the auditorium has hosted many great names, including Richard Wagner, Richard Strauss, and Gustav Mahler. Wilsonova 4, Praha 2. © 296-117-111. www.opera.cz. Metro: Muzeum.

THE CLUB & MUSIC SCENE

Where else in the world but Prague can you boogie in a crumbling underground former cinema like the Roxy, then stop off for the herbal wonder liqueur Becherovka in a Romanesque stone cellar? A good source on the latest club spaces, raves, and parties is *"Think"* (www.think.cz), a free monthly usually found at Radost (see below). Also try the Czech Techno site (www.techno.cz/party). Things don't really get started until after 11pm.

Rock & Dance Clubs

Duplex Club & Café ⨀⨀ Located right in the heart of Wenceslas Square, this is one of Prague's more exclusive clubs. From the roof terrace, visitors enjoy a magnificent view of the city's very center. Prague's best DJs perform inside the club itself, where cool lighting and high-tech sound set the right atmosphere. Yes, it was here that Mick Jagger had his 60th birthday party in July 2003 during the Stones' fourth concert in Prague. Prices are reasonable. It's open daily 10:30pm to 3am (Fri–Sat until 5am). Václavské nám. 21, Praha 1. (?) **224-232-319.** www.duplexduplex.cz. Admission 50Kč–150Kč ($2–$6.25/£1.20–£3.40). Metro: Můstek.

Radost FX (✴ (Finds) The Radost tries so hard to catch the retro 1960s and 1970s crowd that it has become a cartoon of itself, yet it remains popular with a mixed straight, gay, and model crowd. The rec-room interior of the ground-floor lounge is great for a chat and a drink. The series of downstairs rooms gets filled with rave and techno mixes. The crowd is very attractive and style-obsessed, and the bouncers have been known to boot those who don't look the part. Open daily from 10pm to 5am. Bělehradská 120, Praha 2. (?) **224-254-776.** www.radostfx.cz. Cover 100Kč–250Kč ($4.15–$10/£2.30–£5.50). Metro: I. P. Pavlova or Náměstí Míru.

Roxy Another reincarnation of a dead cinema, the Roxy pushes the boundaries of bizarre in its dark, stark concrete dance hall down Dlouhá Street near Old Town Square. The balcony allows the art-community crowd to people-watch amid the candlelight. The club is ultra-deconstructionist. Acid jazz, funk, techno, salsa, and reggae are among the tunes on the playlist from the recorded or live acts. The Roxy is the longest late-night romp in town, open daily from 7pm to 5am. Dlouhá 33, Praha 1. (?) **224-826-296.** www.roxy.cz. Cover 50Kč–250Kč ($2–$10/£1.20–£5.40). Metro: Náměstí Republiky.

Jazz

Prague attracts all the serious underground bands you'd expect in a famed capital of Bohemian living. International global fusion groups turn up, and so do some of the top talents of the jazz and funk world, especially during the Prague International Jazz Festival.

AghaRTA Jazz Centrum (✴) Upscale by Czech standards, the AghaRTA regularly features some of the best music in town, from standard acoustic trios and quartets to Dixieland, funk, and fusion. Hot Line, the house band led by AghaRTA part-owner and drummer Michal Hejna, regularly takes the stage. Bands usually begin at 9pm. Open daily from 7pm to midnight. Železná 16, Praha 1. (?) **222-211-275.** www.agharta.cz. Cover 100Kč ($4.15/£2.30). Metro: Můstek.

Metropolitan Jazz Club There never seems to be anyone under 30 in this sophisticated downstairs jazz club, fitted with ceramic-topped tables and red velvet chairs. It's home to a house trio that plays several nights a month, and Dixieland and swing bands fill the rest of the calendar. Concerts begin at 9pm. Open Monday to Friday from 11am to 1am and Saturday and Sunday from 7pm to 1am. Jungmannova 14, Praha 1. (?) **224-347-777.** Cover 100Kč ($4.15/£2.30). Metro: Můstek.

Pubs

Good pub brews and conversations are Prague's preferred late-evening entertainment. Unlike British, Irish, or German beer halls, a true Czech pub ignores accouterments like cushy chairs and warm wooden paneling, and cuts straight to the chase—beer. While some Czech pubs do serve a hearty plate of food alongside the suds, it's the brew, uncommonly cheap at usually less than 30Kč ($1.25/70p) a pint, that keeps people sitting for hours.

U Fleků One of the original microbreweries dating from 1459, U Fleků is Prague's most famous beer hall, one of the few pubs that still serves only its own beer. It's a

Tips   *Není Pivo Jako Pivo:* There's No Beer Like Beer

This seemingly absurd local proverb makes sense when you first taste the cold golden nectar *(pivo)* from its source and realize that you've never really had beer before. While Czechs on the whole aren't religious, *pivo* still elicits a piety unseen in many orthodox countries. The golden Pilsner variety that accounts for most of the beer consumed around the world was born here and has inspired some of the country's most popular fiction, films, poetry, and prayers.

For many Czechs, the corner beer hall *(hospoda* or *pivnice)* is a social and cultural center. Regulars in these smoke-encrusted caves drink beer as lifeblood and seem ill at ease when a foreigner takes their favorite table or disrupts their daily routine. For those wanting to sample the rich, aromatic taste of Czech lagers without ingesting waves of nicotine, dozens of more ventilated pubs and restaurants have emerged since the Velvet Revolution. Alas, the suds in these often cost as much as five times more than those in the standard *hospoda*.

While always informal, Czech pubs observe their own unwritten code of etiquette:

- Large tables are usually shared with strangers.
- When sitting, you should first ask *"Je tu volno?"* ("Is this place taken?"— yeh *two* vohl-no). If it's not, put a cardboard coaster down in front of you to show that you want a beer.
- Don't wave for a waitperson—it'll only delay the process when he or she sees you.
- When the waitperson does finally arrive and sees the coaster in front of you, simply nod or hold up fingers for the number of beers you want for you and your companions.
- If there's a choice, it's usually between size—*malé* (mah-*lay*) is small, *velké* (vel-*kay*) is large—or type—*světlé* (svyet-*lay*) is light, *černé* (cher-*nay*) is dark.
- The waitperson will make pencil marks on a white slip of paper that remains on your table.
- If your waitperson ever comes back for a second round, order enough for the rest of your stay and ask to pay. When he or she returns, say, *"Zaplatíme"* ("We'll pay," zah-plah-*tee*-meh) . . . you might not see him or her again for a long time.

According to brewing industry studies, Czechs drink more beer per capita than any other people. The average Czech downs 320 pints of brew each year; the average American drinks about 190. Of course, a Czech *hospoda* regular will drink the year's average for a family of six. Pub regulars do not

huge place with a maze of timber-lined rooms and a large, loud courtyard where an oompah band performs. The ornate, medieval-style wood ceilings and courtyard columns are charming but not very old. Tourists come here by the busload, but disparaging locals who don't like the German atmosphere avoid the place. The pub's wonder why the Czech national anthem is a song that translates as "Where Is My Home?"

Several widely held Czech superstitions are connected with drinking beer. One says that you should never pour a different kind of beer in a mug holding the remnants of another brew. Bad luck is sure to follow. Some believe that the toast—usually *"Na zdraví!"* ("To your health!")—is negated if anyone fails to clink his or her mug with any of the others at your table and then slams the mug on the table before taking the first chug.

Czech beer comes in various degrees of concentration, usually marked on the label or menu. This is not the amount of alcohol, though the higher degree does carry a higher alcohol content. The standard premium 12-degree brew contains about 5% alcohol, though each label varies. If you want something a little lighter on the head, try a 10-degree, with 3.5% to 4% alcohol content.

The never-ending debate over which Czech beer is best rages on, but here are the top contenders, all readily available in Prague. (Each pub or restaurant will usually flaunt its choice on the front of the building.)

- **Pilsner Urquell:** The original Pilsner lager. A bit bitter but with a smooth texture that comes, the locals say, from the softer alkaline waters that flow under Pilsen. Urquell is mostly packaged for export and often seen at beer boutiques across the Atlantic.
- **Budvar:** The original "Budweiser," this semisweet lager hails from České Budějovice, a town also known by its German name, Budweis. The clash with U.S. giant Anheuser-Busch over the "Budweiser" trademark kept the American giant from selling Bud in much of Europe for years. There's little similarity in the taste of the two—you decide. Busch wanted a stake in the Budvar brewery, but the Czech government balked at a deal in 1996.
- **Staropramen:** The flagship of Prague's home brewery is a solid choice and is easiest to find in the capital. Now that Britain's Bass owns Staropramen, they're marketing a hybrid called Velvet, a cross between a Czech lager and an Irish ale. It's worth a try.
- **Kozel:** This is a favorite with the American expat community, with a distinctive namesake goat on the label. It has a spicy taste and full body. Light beer it is not.
- **Krušovice:** From a tiny brewery in the cradle of the western hop-growing region, this brew, commissioned by Rudolf II 4 centuries ago, used to be hard to find in Prague, but no longer. Lighter but not fizzy, it has just a hint of bitterness.

sweet dark beer is excellent and not available anywhere else; however, the sausages and goulash are overcooked and overpriced. For musical entertainment at the Cabaret Hall (daily from 8pm) there is a cover charge of 100Kč ($4.15/£2). Open daily from 9am to 11pm. Křemencova 11, Praha 2. ℂ 224-934-019. www.ufleku.cz. Metro: Národní třída.

U medvídků (At the Little Bears)   This 5-centuries-old pub off Národní třída was the first in town to serve the original Budweiser, Budvar, on tap. It also serves typical Czech pub food, including *cmunda,* potato pancakes topped with sauerkraut and cured meat. It's smoky inside, but it's easier to breathe here than at most local pubs. Open daily from 11:30am to 11pm. Na Perštýně 7, Praha 1. ✆ **224-211-916.** www.umedvidku. cz. Metro: Národní třída.

The Bar Scene

The city has acquired a much wider selection of bars in recent years to complement its huge array of beer pubs. The competition has brought out a variety of watering holes—from country to French, from straight to gay to mixed—that match the offerings in most any major European capital.

Baráčnická rychta (Small Homeowners Association)   In the heart of Malá Strana, just off Malostranské náměstí, you can find and taste a little bit of old-fashioned good times. Sample good Czech food with Czech beer. Open daily noon until 1am. Tržiště 23, Praha 1. ✆ **257-532-461.** www.baracnickarychta.cz. Metro: Malostranská.

Chateau/Enfer Rouge   Hidden on a small Old Town back street, this loud and lively ground-floor place has twin bars, plank floors, and a good sound system playing contemporary rock. It sells four types of beer on tap and features regular drink specials. It's busy and fun—if you avoid the headache-inducing concoctions from the frozen drink machine. Open Monday to Thursday noon to 3am, Friday noon to 4pm, Saturday 4pm to 4am, Sunday 4pm to 2am. Jakubská 2, Praha 1. ✆ **222-316-328.** Metro: Náměstí Republiky.

Jáma (The Hollow) ✿   This place has been popular for several postrevolutionary years. It feels a lot like an American college pub; Czech and international food is served and Czech beer is on tap. Open daily from 11am to 1am. V Jámě 7, Praha 1. ✆ **224-222-383.** www.jamapub.cz. Metro: Můstek.

Gay & Lesbian Clubs

Prague's small gay and lesbian community is growing in its openness and choices for nightclubs and entertainment. Go to http://prague.gayguide.net for more information. You should also see the review for **Radost FX Café** on p. 251.

Friends   Its atmosphere of an old bar is combined here with a comfortable setting, a super sound and video projection system, new dance floor, and private lounge. Free Wi-Fi Internet connection available. Open Sunday to Thursday 6pm to 3am, Friday and Saturday 6pm to 5am. DJ parties start at 10pm Wednesday through Saturday. Bartolomějská 11, Praha 1. ✆ **224-236-772.** Metro Národní třída.

Tingl Tangl   A popular nightclub attracting a mixed gay, straight, foreign, and local crowd near Charles Bridge, Tingl Tangl offers the most extensive cabaret shows in Old Town, with comical drag queens featured during the weekend and Wednesday shows. Open daily from 8pm to 5am. Karolíny Světlé 12, Praha 1. ✆ **224-238-278.** Cover charges 250Kč ($10/£5.40) for show nights. Metro: Národní třída.

SIDE TRIP TO KARLŠTEJN CASTLE ✿✿✿
29km (18 miles) SW of Prague

By far the most popular destination in the Czech Republic after Prague, Karlštejn Castle is an easy day trip for those interested in getting out of the city. Charles IV built this medieval castle from 1348 to 1357 to safeguard the crown jewels of the Holy Roman Empire. Although the castle had been changed over the years, with such additions as late Gothic staircases and bridges, renovators have removed these additions, restoring the castle to its original medieval state.

ESSENTIALS

GETTING THERE   The best way to get to Karlštejn is by **train** (there's no bus service). Most trains leave from Prague's Main Station (at the Hlavní nádraží metro stop) hourly throughout the day and take about 45 minutes to reach Karlštejn. The one-way, second-class fare is 46Kč ($1.90/£1).

VISITOR INFORMATION   The ticket/castle information booth (© **311-681-370**) can help you, as can any of the restaurants or stores. The castle itself has a website that you can visit at www.hradkarlstejn.cz.

EXPLORING THE CASTLE

Since Karlštejn's beauty lies more in its facade and environs than in the castle itself, the 20- to 30-minute walk up the hill is, along with the view, one of the main features that makes the trip spectacular. It's an excursion well worth making if you can't get farther out of Prague to see some of the other castles. When you finally do reach the top, take some time to look out over the town and down the Well Tower.

To see the interior of the castle, you can choose from two tours. The 50-minute **Tour 1** will take you through the **Imperial Palace, Hall of Knights, Chapel of St. Nicholas, Royal Bedroom,** and **Audience Hall. Tour 2,** which lasts 70 minutes, offers a look at the **Holy Rood Chapel,** famous for the more than 2,000 precious and

---

⟨Moments   A Romantic Getaway

If the air and noise of Prague start to grate on your nerves, or if a quiet, romantic, overnight trip to a castle in the country sounds like the perfect getaway, head for the **Romantic Hotel Mlýn (Mill Hotel)** ⨳, 267 18 Karlštejn (© **311-744-411**; fax 311-744-444; www.hotelmlynkarlstejn.cz).

On the river's edge on the bank opposite the castle, the Mlýn is exactly what its name says—a mill. Converted into a hotel and recently reconstructed, this reasonably priced country inn takes you away from the hustle and bustle of traveling. Its 28 rooms are a little on the small side, but they're quaint and nicely decorated with rustic furniture. At the outdoor patio bar and very good restaurant, you can relax and enjoy the soothing sounds of the river. Service here is a cut above what it is at the other hotels in the area. If you are here for lunch or dinner when the outdoor grill has been fired up, take advantage of it. Use the hotel also as a base for bike and canoe trips along the river. The staff can help you with local tennis courts and reservations for a round of golf.

Rates are 2,500Kč ($104/£50) for a single and 3,100Kč ($129/£62) for a double. MasterCard and Visa are accepted. To get to the hotel, take the bridge across the river that leads to the train station and turn left at the first street. If you cross the rail tracks, you've gone too far.

semiprecious inlaid gems adorning its walls; the **Chapel of St. Catherine,** Karel IV's own private oratory; the **Church of Our Lady;** and the **library.**

Note that you need to make a reservation to visit the Holy Rood Chapel on Tour 2 (© **274-008-154;** fax 274-008-152; www.spusc.cz or www.hradkarlstejn.cz). The shorter Tour 1 costs 200Kč ($8.30/£4) adults, 100Kč ($4.15/£2) students, 20Kč (85¢/40p) children under 6. Tour 2 with the Holy Rood Chapel costs 300Kč ($12/£6) adults, 100Kč ($4.15/£2) students, free for children under 6. The castle is open Tuesday to Sunday: May, June, and September 9am to noon and 12:30 to 5pm; July and August 9am to noon and 12:30 to 6pm; April and October 9am to noon and 1 to 4pm; November, December, and March 9am to noon and 1 to 3pm; closed January and February.

4 Bohemia

Though Bohemia has historically been undivided, there are clear-cut distinctions in the region's geography that make going from town to town easier if you "divide" it into sections. After exploring Prague, decide which area you'd like to see first and then plan accordingly.

Once the religious hotbed of the country, south Bohemia (where you'll find Karlovy Vary) was a focal point of the Hussite wars that eventually ravaged many of its towns and villages. Though the days of war took their toll, the region still features fine examples of architecture from every era. West Bohemia (see Český Krumlov below), home to the country's spa towns, is one of the few places where a full-blown tourist infrastructure is already in place.

KARLOVY VARY (CARLSBAD) ☝
120km (74 miles) W of Prague

The discovery of Karlovy Vary (Carlsbad) by Charles IV reads like a 14th-century episode of the TV show *The Beverly Hillbillies.* According to local lore, the king was out huntin' for some food when up from the ground came a-bubblin' water (though discovered by his dogs and not an errant gunshot). Knowing a good thing when he saw it, Charles immediately set to work building a small castle in the area, naming the town that evolved around it Karlovy Vary, which translates as "Charles's Boiling Place." The first spa buildings were built in 1522, and before long, notables like Albrecht of Wallenstein, Peter the Great, and later Bach, Beethoven, Freud, and Marx all came to Karlovy Vary for a holiday retreat.

After World War II, Eastern bloc travelers discovered the town, and Karlovy Vary became a destination for the proletariat. On doctors' orders, most workers would enjoy regular stays of 2 or 3 weeks, letting the mineral waters ranging from 110°F to 162°F (43°C–72°C) from the town's 12 springs heal their tired and broken bodies. Even now, a large number of spa guests are here by a doctor's prescription.

Today, some 150,000 people, both traditional clientele and newer patrons, travel to the spa resort every year to sip, bathe, and frolic, though most enjoy the "13th spring" (actually a hearty herb-and-mineral liqueur called Becherovka) as much as—if not more than—the 12 nonalcoholic versions. Czechs will tell you that all have medical benefits.

GETTING THERE
At all costs, avoid the train from Prague, which takes over 4 hours on a circuitous route. If you're arriving from another direction, Karlovy Vary's main train station is connected to the town center by bus no. 11.

Taking a bus to Karlovy Vary is much more convenient. Frequent express **buses** make it from Prague's Florenc bus station in 2¼ hours at a cost of 130Kč ($5.40/£3). From Karlovy Vary's Dolní nádraží (bus station) take a 10-minute walk or local bus no. 4 into Karlovy Vary's spa center. Note that you must have a ticket to board local transport. You can buy tickets for 10Kč (40¢/20p) at the bus station stop, or from the bus driver, which will then cost you 15Kč (60¢/30p). For timetable information go to www.jizdnirady.cz.

The nearly 2-hour **drive** from Prague to Karlovy Vary can be very busy and dangerous due to undisciplined Czech drivers. If you're going by car, take Highway E48 from the western end of Prague and follow it straight through to Karlovy Vary.

VISITOR INFORMATION

Infocentrum města Karlovy Vary is located near the main Mlýnská kolonáda, on Lázeňská 1 (© 353-224-097). It's open April to October, Monday to Friday from 7am to 5pm and Saturday and Sunday from 9am to 3pm; November to March, Monday to Friday from 7am to 4pm. Alternatively, you'll find information on www.karlovyvary.cz.

WHERE TO STAY

Some of the town's major spa hotels accommodate only those who are paying for complete treatment, unless for some reason their occupancy rates are particularly low. The hotels I've listed below accept guests for stays of any length.

Expensive

Grandhotel Pupp ☞☞ Well known as one of Karlovy Vary's best hotels, the Pupp, built in 1701, is also one of Europe's oldest hotels. Its public areas boast the expected splendor and charm, as do the renovated guest rooms. The best ones tend to be those facing the town center and are located on the upper floors; these have good views and sturdy wooden furniture. Some rooms have amenities such as air-conditioning, television, minibar, and safe, though not all do. The hotel also has a stylish casino (open midnight–4am).

Mírové nám. 2, 360 91, Karlovy Vary. © 353-109-630. Fax 353-226-638. www.pupp.cz. 110 units. Note that there are no rates in local currency; hotel charges at a converted rate upon checkout. $362 (£181) double deluxe; suite from $437 (£219); $1,625 (£813) presidential apt. Rates include breakfast. AE, DC, MC, V. Valet parking. **Amenities:** 4 restaurants; bar; cafe; pool; tennis courts; golf course; health club; limousine/taxi service; salon; room service (6am–midnight); same-day laundry; casino.

Moderate

Hotel Embassy ☞ On the riverbank across from the Pupp, the Embassy has well-appointed rooms, many with an early-20th-century motif. Set in a historic house, the rooms are medium-size with medium-size bathrooms. The staff here really helps make this hotel worthy of consideration, as does the proximity to the pub, which serves up some of the best goulash and beer in the city.

Nová Louka 21, 360 01 Karlovy Vary. © 353-221-161. Fax 353-223-146. www.embassy.cz. 20 units. 2,595Kč–3,290Kč ($108–$137/£52–£66) double; 3,415Kč–3,830Kč ($142–$159/£69–£77) suite. AE, MC, V. **Amenities:** Pub; lobby bar; indoor golf; pool table. *In room:* TV, minibar, safe.

Inexpensive

Hotel Astoria In the heart of the historic town, the restored Astoria mainly caters to spa guests but, unlike many of its competitors, it is big enough to usually have several rooms available for nontreatment visitors. The staff can be a little gruff at times, but the rooms are big, with satellite TV an added bonus. The restaurant serves standard Czech fare.

Spa Cures & Treatments

Most visitors to Karlovy Vary come for a spa treatment, a therapy that lasts 1 to 3 weeks. After consulting with a spa physician, you're given a specific regimen of activities that may include mineral baths, massages, waxings, mudpacks, electrotherapy, and pure oxygen inhalation. After spending the morning at a spa or sanatorium, you're usually directed to walk the paths of the town's surrounding forest.

The common denominator of all the cures is an ample daily dose of hot mineral water, which bubbles up from 12 springs. This water definitely has a distinct odor and taste. You'll see people chugging it down, but it doesn't necessarily taste very good. Some thermal springs actually taste and smell like rotten eggs. You may want to take a small sip at first. Do keep in mind that the waters are used to treat internal disorders, so the minerals may cleanse the body thoroughly—in other words, they can cause diarrhea.

You'll also notice that almost everyone in town seems to be carrying "the cup." This funny-looking cup is basically a mug with a built-in straw running through the handle. Young and old alike parade around with their mugs, filling and refilling them at each thermal water tap. You can buy these mugs everywhere for as little as 60Kč ($2.50/£1) or as much as 230Kč ($9.55/£5); they make a quirky souvenir. *But be warned:* None of the mugs can make the warmer hot springs taste any better.

The minimum spa treatment lasts 1 week and must be arranged in advance. A spa treatment package traditionally includes room, full board, and complete therapy regimen; the cost varies from about $40 (£22) to $100 (£56) per person per day, depending on season and facilities. Rates are highest from May to September and lowest from November to February.

Vřídelní 92, 360 01 Karlovy Vary. ☎ 353-335-111. Fax 353-224-368. www.astoria-spa.cz. 100 units. Note that there are no rates in local currency; hotel charges at a converted rate upon checkout. $36–$56/£20–£31 double. AE, MC, V. **Amenities:** Restaurant. *In room:* TV, fridge.

WHERE TO DINE
Expensive
Embassy Restaurant CZECH/CONTINENTAL   On the ground floor of the Embassy Hotel, this is one of the oldest restaurants in town. It offers an intimate dining room with historic interior. Here you'll find many traditional Czech dishes with slight twists that make them interesting. The grilled loin of pork covered with a light, creamy, green-pepper sauce makes a nice change from the regular roast pork served by most Czech restaurants.

Nová Louka 21. ☎ 353-221-161. Reservations recommended. Soups 55Kč–85Kč ($2.30–$3.55/£1–£2); main courses 175Kč–985Kč ($7.30–$41/£4–£20). AE, V. Daily 11am–11pm.

Moderate
XXX long ☆ ITALIAN/INTERNATIONAL   The interior of this new addition to the list of local restaurants offers an interesting combination of modern decoration and old furniture. On the large menu is a wide assortment of Italian and international

For information and reservations in Prague, contact **Čedok,** at Na Příkopě 18, and also at Václavské nám. 53, Praha 1 (© **224-197-632;** fax 224-213-786; www.cedok.cz). Many hotels also provide spa and health treatments, so ask when you book your room. Most will happily arrange a treatment if they don't provide them directly.

If you're coming for just a day or two, you can experience the waters on an "outpatient" basis. The largest balneological complex in town (and in the Czech Republic) is the **Alžbětiny Lázně-Lázně V,** Smetanovy sady 1145/1 (© **353-222-536;** www.spa5.cz). On their menu are all kinds of treatments, including water cures, massages, a hot-air bath, a steam bath, a whirlpool, and a pearl bath, as well as use of their swimming pool. You can choose packages of different procedures between 90Kč and 600Kč ($3.75–$25/£2–£12). It's open Monday to Friday 8am to 3pm for spa treatments; the pool is open Saturday and Sunday from 10am to 6pm.

The **Sanatorium Baths III,** Mlýnské nábřeží 7 (© **353-225-641**), welcomes day-trippers with mineral baths, massages, saunas, and a cold pool. It's open Monday to Friday 7am to 2pm for spa treatments; the swimming pool and sauna are open Monday to Friday 3 to 6pm and Saturday 1 to 5pm.

The **Castle Bath (Zámecké Lázně),** Zámecký vrch (© **353-222-649**), is a new spa and wellness house located in a reconstructed site at the foot of the Castle Tower (Zámecká věž) in the old city center. Visitors are welcome daily from 7:30am to 7:30pm to enjoy individual spa treatments. A single entry for 2 to 4 hours costs between $21 and $54 (£12–£30).

meals at reasonable prices. There are several good seafood options. Children will appreciate the extensive pizza menu here. Don't forget to get a good Italian cappuccino served here in funky ceramic cups.

Vřídelní 23. © **353-224-232.** Soups 30Kč ($1.25/£1); main courses 120Kč–350Kč ($5–$15/£2–£7). AE, MC, V. Daily 11am–11pm.

Inexpensive
Cafe Eléfant COFFEE/DESSERT Who needs to travel all the way to Vienna? Since this is a cafe in the true sense of the word, all you'll find are coffee, tea, alcoholic and nonalcoholic drinks, desserts, and enough ambience to satisfy the hordes of Germans who flock to this landmark.

Stará Louka 32. © **353-223-406.** Cakes and desserts 20Kč–120Kč (85¢–$5/40p–£2). AE, MC, V. Daily 10am–10pm.

SHOPPING
Crystal and porcelain are Karlovy Vary's other claims to fame. Dozens of shops throughout town sell everything from plates to chandeliers.

Ludvík Moser founded his first glassware shop in 1857 and became one of this country's foremost names in glass. You can visit the **Moser Factory,** kapitána Jaroše 19 (© **353-449-455;** www.moser-glass.com; bus no. 1, 10, or 22), just west of the town center. Its glass museum is open Monday to Friday 8am to 5:30pm and Saturday 9am to 3pm. There's also a **Moser Store,** on Tržiště 7 (℃ **353-235-303**), right in the heart of new town; it's open daily from 10am to 7pm (Sat–Sun until 6pm). Dozens of other smaller shops also sell the famed glass and are as easy to find in the Old Town as spring water.

ČESKÝ KRUMLOV ✸✸✸
167km (104 miles) S of Prague

If you have time on your visit to the Czech Republic for only one excursion, seriously consider making it **Český Krumlov.** One of Bohemia's prettiest towns, Krumlov is a living gallery of elegant Renaissance-era buildings housing charming cafes, pubs, restaurants, shops, and galleries. In 1992, UNESCO named Český Krumlov a World Heritage Site for its historical importance and physical beauty.

GETTING THERE
From Prague, it's a 2-hour drive down Highway 3 through Tábor.

The only way to reach Český Krumlov by train from Prague is via České Budějovice, a slow ride that deposits you at a station relatively far from the town center (trip time: 3 hr. 50 min.). Six trains leave daily from Prague's Hlavní nádraží; the fare is 336Kč ($14/£7) first class, 224Kč ($9.35/£4) second class. If you are already in České Budějovice and you want to make a trip to Krumlov, several trains connect these two cities throughout the day. The trip takes about 57 minutes and costs 46Kč ($1.90/£1). For timetables, go to **www.jizdnirady.cz**.

The nearly 3-hour **bus** ride from Prague usually involves a transfer in České Budějovice. The fare is 136Kč ($5.65/£3), and the bus station in Český Krumlov is a 15-minute walk from the town's main square.

VISITOR INFORMATION
Right on the main square, the **Information Centrum,** náměstí Svornosti 2, 381 01 Český Krumlov (℃ **380-704-622;** fax 380-704-619; www.ckrumlov.cz), provides a complete array of services, from booking accommodations to reserving tickets for events, as well as a phone and Internet service. It's open daily in July and August from 9am to 8pm; in June and September from 9am to 7pm; in April, May, and October from 9am to 6pm; and from November to March from 9am to 5pm.

EXPLORING THE CHATEAU
Reputedly the second-largest castle in Bohemia (after Prague Castle), **Český Krumlov Château** was constructed in the 13th century as part of a private estate. Throughout the ages, it has been passed on to a variety of private owners, including the Rožmberk family, Bohemia's largest landholders, and the Schwarzenbergs, the Bohemian equivalent of the TV show *Dynasty*'s Carrington family.

There are two guided tours. Tour I begins in the rococo **Chapel of St. George,** and continues through the portrait-packed **Renaissance Rooms,** and the **Schwarzenberg Barogue Suite,** outfitted with ornate furnishings that include Flemish wall tapestries, European paintings, and also the extravagant 17th-century **Golden Carriage.** Tour II includes the **Schwarzenberg portrait gallery** as well as their 19th-century suite. Tours last 1 hour and depart frequently. Most are in Czech or German, however. If you want an English-language tour, arrange it ahead of time (℃ **380-704-721;** www.ckrumlov. cz). The guided tours cost 160Kč ($6.65/£3) adults, 80Kč ($3.35/£2) students (Tour I); 140Kč ($5.85/£3) adults and 70Kč ($2.90/£1) students (Tour II). The tickets are sold separately. The castle hours are from Tuesday to Sunday: June to August 9am to 6pm; April, May, September, and October 9am to 5pm (no Tour II in Apr). The last entrance is 1 hour before closing.

Once past the main castle building, you can see one of the more stunning views of Český Krumlov from **Most Na Plášti,** a walkway that doubles as a belvedere to the Inner Town. Even farther up the hill lie the castle's riding school and gardens.

WHERE TO STAY

With the rise of free enterprise after the fall of Communism, many hotels have sprouted up or are getting a "new" old look. PENSION and ZIMMER FREI signs line Horní and Rooseveltova streets and offer some of the best values in town. For a comprehensive list of area hotels and help with bookings, call or write to the Information Centrum listed above in "Visitor Information."

Expensive
Hotel Růže (Rose Hotel)   Once a Jesuit seminary, this stunning Italian Renaissance building has been turned into a well-appointed hotel. Comfortable in a big-city kind of way, it's packed with amenities and is one of the top places to stay in Český Krumlov. The rooms are clean and spacious, but the promise of a Renaissance stay dissipates quickly. For families or large groups, the larger suites, which have eight beds, provide good value. For the adventurous or those with the right haircut, try one of the cells, where the Jesuit monks used to stay.

Horní 154, 381 01 Český Krumlov. ℅ **380-772-100.** Fax 380-713-146. www.hotelruze.cz. 71 units. 3,800Kč–7,100Kč ($158–$295/£76–£142) double; 5,300Kč–9,600Kč ($220–$400/£106–£192) suite. Rates include breakfast. AE, MC, V. **Amenities:** Restaurant; bar; pool; health club. *In room:* TV, minibar, hair dryer.

Inexpensive
Pension Anna *(Kids)*   Along "pension alley," this is a comfortable and rustic place. What makes the pension a favorite are the friendly management and homey feeling you get as you walk up to your room. Forget hotels—this is the kind of place where you can relax. The owners even let you buy drinks and snacks at the bar downstairs and take them to your room. The suites, with four beds and a living room, are great for families and groups.

Rooseveltova 41, 381 01 Český Krumlov. ℅/fax **380-711-692.** www.pensionanna.euweb.cz. 8 units. 1,250Kč ($52/£25) double; 1,550Kč–2,250Kč ($64–$94/£31–£45) suite. Rates include breakfast. No credit cards. **Amenities:** Bar. *In room:* TV.

Pension Na louži *(Finds)*   Smack-dab in the heart of the Inner Town, the small Na louži, decorated with early-20th-century wooden furniture, is a charming change from many of the bigger, bland rooms found in nearby hotels. If the person at reception starts mentioning names without apparent reason, don't worry; it's not a language problem. Management has given the rooms human names instead of numbers. The only drawback is that the beds (maybe the people for whom the rooms were named were all short) can be a little short for those over 2m (6 ft.).

Kájovská 66, 381 01 Český Krumlov. ℅/fax 380-711-280. www.nalouzi.cz. 7 units. 1,350Kč ($56/£27) double; 1,700Kč ($70/£34) triple; 2,300Kč ($95/£46) suite. No credit cards. **Amenities:** Restaurant/bar.

WHERE TO DINE
Moderate
Krumlovský mlýn CZECH   This restored mill house, which history dates back to the 16th century, is a restaurant, antiques shop, and exhibition in one. Large wooden

Moments   A Renaissance Pub Endures

Most visitors don't venture far enough into the castle to experience this place during the day or night. That's their loss, for I've experienced one of my finest dining experiences in the Czech Republic at **Krčma Markéta**, Zámek 62 (② **380-711-453**).

To get here, walk all the way up the hill through the castle, past the Horní Hrad (Upper Castle) and past the Zámecké divadlo (Castle Theater). Walk through the raised walkway and into the Zámecká zahrada (Castle Garden), where you'll eventually find this Renaissance pub.

When you go inside, you'll feel as if you've left this century. Unfortunately, one of the pub's main draws, former owner Robin Kratochvíl, is gone. The new owners have traded in Kratochvíl's big-enough-to-turn-a-Volkswagen tongs for a set of racks where the meat cooks; they brought in sets of plates, as opposed to the original wooden blocks on which food used to be served; and there is even a menu now. But still go up to the fire and see what's roasting; usually there's a wide variety of meats, including succulent pork cutlets, rabbit, chickens, and pork knees, a Czech delicacy. When the plate comes, don't wait for the vegetables. (Vegetarian dishes are available, however.) Before the night is over, you'll probably find yourself talking to someone else at the pub's large wooden tables.

Krčma Markéta is open April to October, Tuesday to Sunday from 6 to 11pm, and main courses cost 75Kč to 155Kč ($3.10–$6.45/£2–£3).

tables and benches are part of the thematic restaurant on the ground floor, where a traditional Czech menu is served. The terrace on the bank of the Vltava River above the water channel here is a super place to sit in the summer.

Široká 80. ② **380-712-838**. www.krumlovskymlyn.cz. Main courses 150Kč–425Kč ($6.25–$18/£3–£9). No credit cards. Daily 10am–10pm.

Inexpensive

Hospoda Na louži CZECH   The large wooden tables encourage you to get to know your neighbors at this Inner Town pub, located in a 15th-century house. The atmosphere is fun and the food above average. If no table is available, stand and have a drink; tables turn over pretty quickly, and the staff is accommodating. In summer, the terrace seats only six, so dash over if a seat empties.

Kájovská 66. ② **380-711-280**. Main courses 58Kč–158Kč ($2.40–$6.60/£1–£3). No credit cards. Mon–Sat 10am–11pm; Sun 10am–10pm.

ČESKÉ BUDĚJOVICE
147km (91 miles) S of Prague

This fortress town was born in 1265, when Otakar II decided that the intersection of the Vltava and Malše rivers would be the site of a bastion to protect the approaches to southern Bohemia.

Today, České Budějovice, the hometown of the original Budweiser brand beer, is now more a bastion for the beer drinker than a protector of Bohemia.

GETTING THERE

If you're **driving,** leave Prague to the south via the main D1 expressway and take the cutoff for Highway E55, which runs straight to České Budějovice. The trip takes about 1½ hours.

Daily express **trains** from Prague make the trip to České Budějovice in about 2½ hours. The fare is 306Kč ($13/£6) first class or 204Kč ($8.50/£4) second class. Several express **buses** run from Prague's Florenc station each day and take 2½ hours; tickets cost 120Kč ($5/£2).

VISITOR INFORMATION

Tourist Infocentrum, náměstí Přemysla Otakara II. 2 (© **386-801-414**), provides maps and guidebooks and finds lodging. It is open Monday to Friday 8:30am to 6pm, Saturday until 5pm, and Sunday 10am to noon and 12:30 to 4pm. In winter it is open Monday to Friday 9am to 4pm, and Saturday 9am to noon and 12:30 to 3pm. There is a good website about the city; go to **www.c-budejovice.cz** for information.

EXPLORING THE TOWN

You can comfortably see České Budějovice in a day. At its center is one of central Europe's largest squares, the cobblestone **náměstí Přemysla Otakara II**—it may actually be too large, as many of the buildings tend to get lost in all the open space. The

---

Keeping Up with the Schwarzenbergs: Visiting a 141-Room English Castle

Only 8km (5 miles) north of České Budějovice lies **Hluboká nad Vltavou** ✸✸ (© 387-843-911; www.zamekhluboka.cz). Built in the 13th century, this castle has undergone many face-lifts over the years, but none that left as lasting an impression as those ordered by the Schwarzenberg family. As a sign of the region's growing wealth and importance in the mid–19th century, the Schwarzenbergs remodeled the 141-room castle in the neo-Gothic style of England's Windsor Castle. No expense was spared in the quest for opulence. The Schwarzenbergs removed the impressive wooden ceiling from their residence at Český Krumlov and reinstalled it in the large dining room. Other rooms are equally garish in their appointments, making a guided tour worth the time, even though only about a third of the rooms are open to the public.

The castle is open daily May to August from 9am to 5pm (last tour at 4pm); April, September, and October on Tuesday to Sunday from 9am to 4:30pm (last tour at 3pm). There is a lunch break between noon and 12:30pm. Tours in English cost 160Kč ($6.65/£3) adults, 80Kč ($3.35/£2) students.

If you're driving to Hluboká from České Budějovice, take Highway E49 north and then Highway 105 just after leaving the outskirts of České Budějovice.

The town's new **Information Center** at Masarykova 35 (© 387-966-164; www.hluboka.cz) will provide you with maps, souvenirs, and answers to your questions.

square contains the ornate **Fountain of Sampson,** an 18th-century water well that was once the town's principal water supply, plus a mishmash of baroque and Renaissance buildings.

One block northwest of the square is the **Černá věž (Black Tower),** which you can see from almost every point in the city. Consequently, its 360 steps are worth the climb to get a bird's-eye view in all directions. The most famous symbol of České Budějovice, this 70m-tall (236-ft.) 16th-century tower was built as a belfry for the adjacent **St. Nicholas Church.** It is open Tuesday to Sunday from 10am to 6pm; admission is 20Kč (85¢/45p).

WHERE TO STAY

Hotel Bohemia The Bohemia really isn't a hotel but a small pension in the city center, as you'll discover when you walk into the lobby and think that you've stepped into someone's house. The staff makes you feel like one of the family, with their attentive service, and the rooms are pleasant despite being a little small.

Hradební 20, 370 01 České Budějovice. ©/fax **386-360-691.** www.hotel-bohemia-cb.cz. 18 units. 1,790Kč ($74/£36) double. AE, MC, V. **Amenities:** Restaurant. In room: TV, minibar.

WHERE TO DINE

U královské pečeti (At the Royal Seal) ⚑ CZECH This typical Czech-style pub serves up hearty food at reasonable prices. It offers a tasty goulash as well as *svíčková* or game dishes. Located in the Hotel Malý Pivovar, this is a very good choice for a Czech food experience.

In the Hotel Malý Pivovar, ulice Karla IV. 8–10. © **386-360-471.** Soups 25Kč ($1/50p); main courses 65Kč–290Kč ($2.70–$12/£1–£6). AE, DC, MC, V. Daily 10am–11pm.

PLZEŇ (PILSEN)
88km (55 miles) SW of Prague

"Zde se narodilo pivo." The phrase ("the birthplace of beer") greets you at almost every turn. And they aren't kidding. Some 400 years ago, a group of men formed Plzeň's first beer-drinking guild, and today beer is probably the only reason you'll want to stop at this otherwise industrial town. Unfortunately for the town, its prosperity and architecture were ravaged during World War II, and few buildings were left untouched. The main square, náměstí Republiky, is worth a look, but after that there's not much to see.

GETTING THERE

A fast **train** from Prague whisks travelers to Plzeň in just under 2 hours without you having to witness the mayhem caused by Czech drivers. Trains between the two cities are just as plentiful and fit most every schedule. The train costs 210Kč ($8.75/£4) first class or 140Kč ($5.80/£3) second class.

It is an easy 45-minute cruise by **car** on the new Highway D5, which leaves Prague from the west.

VISITOR INFORMATION

Trying to be as visitor-friendly as possible, the **City Information Center Plzeň,** náměstí Republiky 41, 301 16 Plzeň (© **378-035-330;** fax 378-035-332; www.icpilsen.cz or www.plzen-city.cz), is packed with literature to answer your questions. It is open daily April to September 9am to 7pm; October to March Monday to Friday 10am to 5pm, and Saturday and Sunday 10am to 3:30pm.

<Fun Fact> **Plzeň's Claim to Fame**

Founded in 1295 by Václav II, Plzeň was and remains western Bohemia's administrative center. King Václav's real gift to the town, however, wasn't making it an administrative nerve center but granting it brewing rights. So more than 200 microbreweries popped up, one in almost every street-corner basement. Realizing that the brews they were drinking had become mostly inferior by the late 1830s, rebellious beer drinkers demanded quality, forcing the brewers to try harder. "Give us what we want in Plzeň, good and cheap beer!" became the battle cry. In 1842, the brewers combined their expertise to produce a superior brew through what became known as the Pilsner brewing method. If you don't believe it, look in your refrigerator. Most likely, the best beer in there has written somewhere on its label "Pilsner brewed."

TOURING THE BEER SHRINES

Plzeňské Pivovary (Pilsner Brewery), at U Prazdroje 7, actually comprises several breweries, pumping out brands like Pilsner Urquell and Gambrinus, the most widely consumed beer in the Czech Republic. The 1-hour tour of the factory (which has barely changed since its creation) includes a 15-minute film and visits to the fermentation cellars and brewing rooms. The tour starts at 12:30 and 2pm daily. Tours cost 120Kč ($5/£2); the price includes a dozen beer-oriented postcards and a tasting of freshly brewed beer. (For details on other tours, call *Ⓒ* **377-062-888** or log onto www.prazdroj.cz.)

If you didn't get your fill of beer facts at the brewery, the **Pivovarské muzeum (Beer Museum;** *Ⓒ* **377-235-574;** www.prazdroj.cz) is 1 block away on Veleslavínova 6. Inside this former 15th-century house, you'll learn everything there is to know about beer but were afraid to ask. Admission is 60Kč ($2.50/£1), and hours are daily 10am to 6pm (to 5pm Jan–Mar).

WHERE TO STAY

Hotel Central As you look around the historically beautiful old town square, one thing stands out: the Hotel Central. This rather sterile building is across from St. Bartholomew's Church. The surly staff notwithstanding, the hotel is good and surprisingly quiet despite its central location. Ask for one of the rooms facing east; they have a nice view of the church as the sun rises.

Náměstí Republiky 33, 301 00 Plzeň. *Ⓒ* **377-226-757.** Fax 377-226-064. www.central-hotel.cz. 77 units. 1,550Kč–2,390Kč ($64–$99/£31–£48) double. AE, MC, V. **Amenities:** Restaurant; cafe; bar; exercise room; sauna; solarium. *In room:* TV, minibar, safe.

WHERE TO DINE

Moderate

Pilsner Urquell Restaurant CZECH   In the same building that houses the brewery's management, this pub has remained true to those who supply it with beverages by cooking hearty, basic Czech meals, though it is a little pricier than Na Spilce across the way. Because the brewery workers make up the majority of customers here, don't expect a multilingual menu or staff.

U Prazdroje 1 (just outside the brewery gates). © **377-235-608.** Soups 25Kč ($1/50p); main courses 65Kč–219Kč ($2.70–$9.10/£1–£4). AE, MC, V. Mon–Sat 10am–10pm.

5 Moravia

Having seen its fair share of history, Moravia conjures up a different image than Bohemia: Here, too, castles and picture-perfect town squares exist. But the people and slower lifestyle set Moravia apart.

BRNO: THE REGION'S CAPITAL

224km (139 miles) SE of Prague; 128km (79 miles) N of Vienna

Since Brno came of age in the 19th century on the back of its textile industry, the city's architecture, for the most part, lacks the Renaissance facades and meandering alleys of other towns. Indeed, the main square, náměstí Svoboda, bears this out. But spend a day or two here, and the beauty of the old city center will become apparent.

GETTING THERE

Driving to Brno is a trade-off. Take the E50—also named the D1—freeway that leads from the south of Prague all the way. The drive shouldn't take more than 2 hours. But the scenery is little more than one roadside stop after another.

Brno is the focal point for **train** travel in Moravia and most points east, making it an easy 2¾-hour trip from Prague. **Trains** leave almost every hour; the majority leave from Hlavní nádraží (Main Station). The fare is 243Kč ($10/£5) first class or 160Kč ($6.65/£3) second class. **Buses** leave Prague's Florenc station to Brno every hour. The trip takes 2½ hours and costs 140Kč ($5.80/£3).

VISITOR INFORMATION

The **Turistické Informační Centrum (TIC),** Radnická 8, Brno (© **542-211-090;** www.ticbrno.cz), provides a plethora of information on accommodations, plus what's on in Brno and how to see it. It's open Monday to Friday from 9am to 6pm, Saturday 9am to 5:30pm, Sunday 9am to 3pm October to March; April to September Monday to Friday 8:30am to 6pm, Saturday and Sunday 9am to 5:30pm.

STROLLING AROUND BRNO

The Old Town holds most of the attractions you'll want to see, so it's probably best to start at the former seat of government, the Old Town Hall on Radnická 8. Town's oldest secular building, from the 13th century, the **Old Town Hall** is a hodgepodge of styles—Gothic, Renaissance, and baroque elements melding together, demonstrating Brno's development through the ages.

Just south of the Old Town Hall is **Zelný trh (Cabbage Market),** a farmers' market since the 13th century.

Another block closer to the train station, on Kapucínské náměstí, is the **Kostel Nalezení svatého Kříže (Church of the Sacred Cross)** and the **Kapucínský Klášter (Capuchin Monastery;** © 542-213-232).

Dominating **Zelný trh** at its southwest corner is the **Moravian Regional Museum,** Zelný trh 8, Brno (© **542-321-205;** www.mzm.cz), housed in the Dietrichstein Palace. The museum displays a wide array of stuffed birds and wild game, as well as art, coins, and temporary exhibits. Admission is 50Kč ($2/£1) adults, and 25Kč ($1/50p) students and children. It's open Tuesday to Saturday from 9am to 5pm.

From the museum, head up Petrská Street to the **Cathedral of Saints Peter and Paul.**

Take a break at **Denisovy sady,** the park behind the cathedral, and prepare to climb the hill to get to **Špilberk Castle.** It was built in the 13th century, and the Hussites controlled the castle in the 15th century. The Prussians saw the castle's position as an excellent lookout when they occupied it in the early 17th century. And the Nazis turned it into a torture chamber during their stay, executing some 80,000 people deep inside the dungeons. At Špilberk's **Brno City Museum** (© 542-123-611; www.spilberk.cz), you can see several new permanent exhibitions such as "Jail of Nations" or "History of Brno" and others. Admission to all exhibitions, casemates, and the lookout tower is 110Kč ($4.60/£2) adults, 50Kč ($2/£1) students. It's open Tuesday to Sunday from 9am to 6pm May to September, and October and April from 9am to 5pm; and Wednesday to Sunday 10am to 5pm November to March.

WHERE TO STAY

Note that prices, even in the high season, often double for major trade fairs and the Motorcycle Grand Prix.

Expensive

Grandhotel Brno ⊛ Ever since it was taken over by the Austrian chain Austrotel in the mid-1990s, the Grandhotel has lived up to its name. Its rooms are spacious and well appointed, though some located at the front get a little noisy due to the major street running past with its never-ending stream of trams; ask for a room that has windows facing north, away from the commotion.

Benešova 18–20, 657 83 Brno. © **542-518-111.** Fax 542-210-345. www.grandhotelbrno.cz. 110 units. 3,300Kč–5,400Kč ($137–$225/£66–£108) double; 6,150Kč ($256/£123) suite. AE, DC, MC, V. Parking 150Kč ($6.25/£3). **Amenities:** 2 restaurants; nightclub; room service (7am–3am); 24-hr. laundry; casino. *In room:* TV, minibar.

Moderate

Holiday Inn The very modern Holiday Inn Brno, on the fairgrounds, caters mainly to the trade-fair crowd, so be warned that prices may jump steeply when events are scheduled. Everything, from the rooms to the restaurant to the bars, looks eerily similar to their counterparts in other Holiday Inns around the world. Still, the beds are more comfortable than most, and the staff is very friendly and speaks English.

Křížkovského 20, 603 00 Brno. © **543-122-111.** Fax 541-159-081. www.hibrno.cz. 205 units. 3,500Kč ($146/£70) double; 4,600Kč ($191/£92) suite. AE, DC, MC, V. Parking 150Kč ($6.25/£3) per day. **Amenities:** Restaurant; bar; pool; coin-op laundry. *In room:* TV, minibar, hair dryer, iron, trouser press.

Inexpensive

Penzion na Starém Brně Built into the stables below the castle is a restaurant that has now added a small and very cheap pension. Though a little out of the center, lying halfway between the exhibition grounds and the main square, this spot is very clean and quiet. The rooms are sparsely furnished with rustic pieces and hardwood floors, but since they are relatively small, that's okay.

Mendlovo nám. 1, 639 00 Brno. © **543-247-872.** Fax 541-243-738. www.penzion-brno.com. 7 units. 950Kč ($40/£19) double. MC, V. **Amenities:** Restaurant. *In room:* TV.

WHERE TO DINE
Moderate

La Braseria ⓖ ITALIAN   They say that when in Rome, do as the Romans do. So when in Brno, follow this saying and do what the Romans do—come here. Their authentic Italian cuisine (sorry, dumpling aficionados) is too zesty to be passed up. Try the chicken in green-peppercorn sauce for a delicate change. The restaurant is located between the fairgrounds and the center, about a 10-minute walk from either.

Pekařská 80. ⓒ 543-232-042. Reservations recommended. Soups and antipasti 25Kč–210Kč ($1–$8.75/50p–£4); *primi piatti* 55Kč–215Kč ($2.30–$8.95/£1–£4); *secondi* 85Kč–300Kč ($3.55–$12/£2–£6); pizzas 50Kč–150Kč ($2–$6.25/£1–£3). AE, DC, MC, V. Daily noon–midnight.

Modrá Hvězda (Blue Star) CZECH   The Blue Star is one of the few moderately priced restaurants in Brno where you can get good-quality food well into the night. The pepper steak is the favorite and, as you can tell, anything from the grill is your best bet.

Šilingrovo nám. 7. ⓒ 542-215-292. Soups 25Kč–45Kč ($1–$1.85/50–£1); main courses 99Kč–299Kč ($4.10–$12/£2–£6). MC, V. Daily 11am–1am.

TELČ ⓖ

149km (92 miles) SE of Prague; 86km (53 miles) W of Brno

As you pass through towns on your way here, you may be tempted to pass up Telč, dismissing it as yet another "small town with a nice square." Don't. Those who make the trip to Telč strike gold. Telč is one of the few towns in Europe that can boast of not being reconstructed since its original edifices were built. It now enjoys the honor of being a United Nations (UNESCO) World Heritage Site.

GETTING THERE

Located about halfway between České Budějovice and Brno, Telč can be reached by taking Highway 23. **Driving** from Prague, take Highway D1 in the direction of Brno and exit at Jihlava, where you pick up Highway 38 after going through the town. Then head west on Highway 23. It's a 2-hour drive from Prague.

VISITOR INFORMATION

At the **Informační Středisko,** náměstí Zachariáše z Hradce 10 (ⓒ 567-112-407; www.telc-etc.cz or www.telcsko.cz), you'll find a wealth of information concerning accommodations, cultural events, guided tours, and even hunting; brochures are in Czech, German, and English.

SPECIAL EVENTS

The **Prázdniny v Telči (Holidays in Telč),** a season of concerts, recitals, and fairs, runs from the end of July to the middle of August. For details, contact the **Informační Středisko** (or go to www.prazdninyvtelci.cz).

WHERE TO STAY

Hotel Celerin   The most upscale hotel on the square, the Celerin has medium-size rooms; the best ones overlook the square. If you're looking for location, this is the place to stay. Looking out over the square at night when it's bathed in light will remind you why this town is so treasured. Travelers with disabilities will find the staff here helpful, and some rooms are fully accessible.

Náměstí Zachariáše z Hradce 43, 588 56 Telč. ☎ **567-243-477**. Fax 567-213-581. www.hotelcelerin.cz. 12 units. 1,600Kč ($67/£32) double. Rates include continental breakfast. AE, DC, MC, V. **Amenities:** Restaurant; bar. *In room:* TV, fridge.

WHERE TO DINE
U Černého Orla (At the Black Eagle) ⊛ CZECH   If it looks as though all visitors in town are trying to get in here, it's because they are. The Black Eagle is worth the effort. This is one of the few restaurants in Telč that can be trusted to serve good food consistently. Crowd in at any free space and enjoy a wide range of Czech meals.

Náměstí Zachariáše z Hradce 7. ☎ **567-243-222**. Reservations recommended. Soups 20Kč (85¢/40p); main courses 50Kč–190Kč ($2–$7.90/£1–£4). AE, MC, V. June–Sept daily 7am–10pm; Oct–May Tues–Sun 7am–10pm.

7

Hungary

by Andrew Princz

In 1994, I answered an advertisement in the local newspaper in my native Montreal that read, "Seeking a young, well-connected, Hungarian-speaking student for intriguing artistic project." The job was indeed intriguing and artistic: I traveled to Budapest for the summer to help prepare for Canada's participation in the 1996 Expo. The trip started my career as a journalist and, ironically, brought me back to the country my parents had escaped—as young journalists—some 4 decades earlier.

The country I saw that summer—and had occasionally seen as a child—was drastically different from the one my parents knew. They lived in a Hungary that had already lost two-thirds of its territory during World War I. By 1941, the country was plunged into World War II, after which followed the failed 1956 revolution against the Soviet occupation. To this day, bullet holes from the armed insurrection can still be seen on the facades of buildings.

I walked the streets of Budapest that summer and saw a city that was blessedly starting to emerge from the shadows of its past. My Expo gig introduced me to many Hungarian personalities—artists, curators, government officials, and more—and while a few still held onto the mentality of Communist Hungary, many were visionaries trying to break creative barriers and introduce change. Hungary was in the midst of a fierce, lively period of transformation after decades of Communist rule.

Today, Hungary is still eager to move beyond a difficult century and reconnect with the world. After all, this country enjoyed a glorious early history. Budapest once rivaled its neighboring Vienna under the Austro-Hungarian monarchy and enjoyed a flourishing cultural life. In May 2004, Hungary became a member of the European Union and now has an opportunity to be an influential European nation.

Young and old alike, Hungarians love to live, and you'll find lots of friendly locals hanging out in bars and bistros. Explore Budapest, travel the countryside, and take a dip in a relaxing spa. See nature and wildlife at the Tisza Lake, eat exquisite Hungarian fish soup, and venture off to Lake Balaton—their little sea. Get to know Hungary and Hungarians.

1 Getting to Know Hungary

THE LAY OF THE LAND

A member of the European Union since the spring of 2004, Hungary is playing a dynamic game of catch-up. After the systemic changes over 15 years ago, the country did a total turnaround, from a centrally controlled economy under the sphere of influence of the Soviet Union, to almost out-of-control capitalism. Today, the government is trying to find the middle ground and better the lot of the Hungarians as a whole, who have not

Hungary

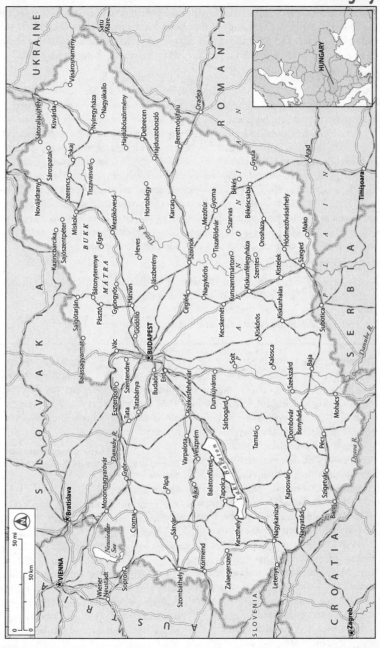

yet seen the fruit of the changes that were promised. Enjoy and learn about Hungary and the Hungarians by traveling outside of the capital. That is where you will find Lake Balaton and vineyards and a Mediterranean lifestyle. Visit the dynamic and young city of Eger, or travel to the Great Hungarian Plain, where Hungary's horsemen once lived.

THE REGIONS IN BRIEF

Life in Hungary revolves around its capital, Budapest. Here, life moves at lightning speed, and sometimes you are taken in by the whirlwind without even noticing it. In order to best appreciate Budapest, give it time, and get to know the people. The best bars or curious hangouts tend to be secretive areas known mostly by word of mouth. The capital is also a romantic feast for the eyes at night, and feast on the beautiful architecture of Andrássy út, which is on the UNESCO world heritage list. After exploring the capital, venture off to the Mátra, Bükk, or Zemplén hills, where you will find the quiet and sleepy village life a welcome change of pace. Hungary's great plain and Tisza lake offer yet another experience: that of an untouched wildlife like the flora and fauna of the dry plain and the marshland of the Tisza Lake. Finally, there is the "Hungarian Sea" of Lake Balaton, where you can swim the shallow shores of the lake, and enjoy horseback riding, vineyards, and traditional restaurants.

SUGGESTED ITINERARIES

Most visits to Hungary center around Budapest, so these itineraries give you a detailed 2-day tour of Budapest, followed by various side-trip options.

Day 1

On your first day in Budapest, start at Deák tér, or anywhere in Inner City.

---

❶ Inner City & Central Pest ⚬⚬

Budapest, a city whose wide boulevards were designed a little over a century ago, is a city that can be walked, so start off in the center city, wander the grand boulevards, and admire the architecture.

Or take a more leisurely stroll around the area and visit a few museums and highlights of the area. You might duck into the **Hungarian National Museum** ⚬⚬ (p. 311), the **Budapest Holocaust Memorial Center** ⚬⚬ (p. 311), or the **Inner City Parish Church** ⚬. As you tour the area, you'll begin to understand the incredible changes that the city has seen in recent years. Many buildings have been completely restored and renovated. Old, decrepit spaces have become complexes, and many more projects are being developed.

Head over to **Váci utca,** which is the main shopping and walking street of Budapest. This booming shopping area developed in Hungary over the past

decade and a half since the systemic changes of 1989. You might try the **Vali Folklór** folk craft shop (p. 336), the **VAM Design Gallery** (p. 334), and various clothing and bookstores (avoid the touristy cafes here).

Walk from Deák tér to the Danube Promenade. Then make your way toward the Kossuth tér metro for:

❷ Parliament ⚬

You can't miss Budapest's grand, eclectic Parliament building, which hugs the Danube. Designed by Imre Steindl and completed in 1902, the building mixes neo-Gothic style with a neo-Renaissance dome. It has been from the outset one of Budapest's symbols, though until 1989 a democratically elected government had convened here exactly once (just after World War II, before the Communist takeover). Since 2000, in addition to its government functions, it has also been home to the fabled Hungarian crown jewels. Unfortunately, you can enter only on guided tours (the half-hour tour is worthwhile for the chance to go inside). See p. 313 for tour times and information.

See p. 313 for tour times and information.

---

3 PARLAMENT KÁVÉHÁZ ℱ

Per Hungarian tradition, sit down in a coffeehouse to read the newspaper, relax, ponder the past, and dream of the future! Situated adjacent to Hungary's parliament buildings, the Parlament Kávéház is decorated with an impressive rounded painting of the parliament buildings, and even a ceiling mural. V. Vértanúk tere 1. ☎ 1/269-4352.

Walk south about .4km (¼ mile) toward the historic Chain Bridge, which you will see in the distance:

4 Chain Bridge ℱ

The Chain Bridge crosses the Danube and empties out into Roosevelt Square. The bridge holds the distinction of being the first permanent crossing to link Buda and Pest. It was initiated at the behest of 19th-century Hungarian reformer Count István Széchenyi after bad weather in 1820 had forced him to wait 8 days before being able to get to his father's funeral. Designed by William Tierney Clark, an Englishman, the bridge was one of the largest suspension bridges of its time when it opened in 1849. According to legend the omission of sculpted tongues on the lions which guard the bridge at either end caused the sculptor to drown himself in the river out of shame. See p. 324. (*Note:* You might duck into the **Four Seasons Hotel Gresham Palace** ℱℱℱ while you're here to view its breathtaking interiors; see p. 296.)

Walk across the Chain Bridge, and take the funicular up to the:

5 Castle District ℱℱ

Castle Hill, a UNESCO World Cultural Heritage site, consists of two parts: the Royal Palace itself and the so-called Castle District, a mostly reconstructed medieval city. For a detailed, 3-hour itinerary of this area, see "Walking Tour: The Castle District," p. 324.

Otherwise, this is a great area for walking and wandering. You might stop into a few highlights, including the **Hungarian National Gallery** ℱ (p. 315), the **Budapest History Museum** ℱ (p. 326), and the **Ludwig Museum of Contemporary Art** ℱ (p. 317).

---

6 RIVALDA CAFÉ & RESTAURANT ℱ

After a long day walking and sightseeing, you might want to have a meal at the Rivalda Café & Restaurant. This restaurant, the brainchild of the Canadian-Hungarian Agnes Weininger, retains the charm of the world of theater that Hungarians love so much. Here, a sole saxophonist plays his lonely tunes, dwarfed by the large yellow backdrop at the far end of the restaurant. Theater lights and riggings adorn the ceilings; the walls are painted with the backdrops of plays and are lined with caricatures of famous Hungarian actors. I. Színház u. 5-9. ☎ 1/489-0236.

After dinner, you might head back to your hotel to relax for a bit so you'll be ready to:

7 Socialize at a Bar, Club, or Bistro

Get a glimpse of Budapest's lively nightlife culture firsthand at a bar, club, or bistro. You'll find all levels of partying available, whether you're looking for hard-core clubbing or just a pub for drinks with the locals. You also might try a hotel bar or a bistro. Bistros are quite popular places for late-night drinks and socializing, and you'll find locals of all ages mingling here. Hungarians can be a bit shy at first, but they open up the more you talk to them. Why not chat them up about your day in the city? See p. 340, "Budapest After Dark."

Day 2

For your second day in Budapest, start at Nyugati Station.

---

❶ Nyugati Railway Station 👁

The historic Nyugati Pályaudvar, or Western Railway Station, was built by Gustave Eiffel's firm, the same company that put up Paris's famous Eiffel Tower. Unfortunately, Budapest doesn't seem to appreciate this monument much. While massive and glorious in its grandeur, the impressive glass structure is notoriously dirty, and the building houses a flashy disco and a McDonald's. Needless to say, both would be well worth moving. Adjacent to the railway station is the **WestEnd City Center**, central Europe's largest shopping center, with over 400 stores.

> Walk toward Oktogon, noting the grand turn-of-the-20th-century Pest architecture, then walk up to Andrássy u. 70:
>
> **❷ LUKÁCS CUKRÁSZDA** 👁
> A faithful reproduction of a vintage coffeehouse, this large, airy establishment was created decades after a coffeehouse of the same name closed its doors. Never too

crowded, it's a great spot for a quiet bite to eat and a cup of joe. Andrássy u. 70. ℭ 1/302-8747.

After lunch, walk a bit down the street to Andrássy u. 60:

❸ Terror Háza (House of Terror) 👁👁

The former headquarters of the AVH secret police, this building is witness to some of the darkest days of 20th-century Hungary. (You will be glad you already ate lunch.) This museum was set up as a memorial to the victims of both Communism and Fascism, and is an attempt to recapture life under successive oppressive regimes in Hungary. The tearing down of the ugly exterior facade has been the subject of much debate, however; for political reasons it has remained the sore

thumb of the grand Andrássy Boulevard. The building was the headquarters of the Nazis in 1944, and many individuals were tortured and murdered in the eerie cellars of this building. The Communist secret police were next to use the venue as a place for their own torture and oppression. See p. 317 for details.

Walk up the majestic Andrássy boulevard toward Heroes' Square and City Park:

❹ Andrássy Boulevard 👁

Lined with trees and a wealth of beautiful apartment buildings, this is *fin de siècle* Pest's greatest boulevard, which is recognized as a World Heritage Site by UNESCO. Andrássy út is the home to a lively cafe and bar scene, as well as a number of small museums. There are colorful terraces, and delicious cakes and ice cream are sold under the shade of the huge trees all the way up to Oktogon.

Once you reach the end of Andrássy boulevard, adjacent to the Museum of Fine Arts, the Múcsarnok, and City Park, you'll find:

❺ Heroes' Square 👁👁

Heroes' Square, built as a project of the millennium over a century ago, celebrates the arrival of the Magyar tribes in the Carpathian Basin. The statues represent the chronology of some 1,000 years of Hungarian history. In 1896 during the famous world exhibition, this space was the apex of some 200 pavilions that made up the festivities.

To your left you will find the **Museum of Fine Arts** 👁 (p. 312). The museum is the main repository of foreign art in Hungary and has one of central Europe's major collections.

Take the Yellow metro line, the oldest in continental Europe until Déak Tér, then take the no. 47 tram to the Gellért Baths:

❻ The Gellért Baths 👁👁

Prepare yourself for a relaxing afternoon, and allow yourself a few hours at

Budapest's most spectacular bathhouse. The Gellért Baths are located in Buda's Hotel Gellért, the oldest Hungarian spa hotel and an Art Nouveau jewel. Enter the baths through the side entrance. The exterior of the building is in need of restoration, but once inside the lobby, you'll be delighted by the details. The unisex indoor pool is without question one of Europe's finest, with marble columns, majolica tiles, and stone lion heads spouting water. The two single-sex Turkish-style thermal baths, off to either side of the pool through badly marked doors, are also glorious, though in need of restoration. See a listing on p. 321, and see the "Thermal Bathing 101" box on p. 323.

After your afternoon of thermal bathing, you may want to head back to your hotel to rest and freshen up for your evening, and then head out to dinner. You'll be going to dinner from your hotel, so it's difficult to recommend a restaurant based on itinerary location. See p. 304 for Budapest dining options.

❼ Attend a Nighttime Concert ✹✹

Spend an evening attending a concert at the **Ferenc Liszt Academy of Music** (p. 343), or the recently opened **National Concert Hall at the Palace of Art** ✹✹, both Budapest's finest concert halls: The first is a more classical hall, while the National Concert Hall is the most modern hall in Budapest. The fine arts are alive and well in Budapest, and a nighttime concert is the perfect cap for your short stint in the city. Note that performances usually start at 7:30 or 8pm.

Side Trips

You've seen Budapest; now its time to get outside of the capital and explore the land of the Magyars. Since the average visitor to Hungary spends less than a week in the country, we've opted to give you a few side-trip options from Budapest, rather than a 1-week or 10-day tour of the entire country. The train system is Budapest-centric, so a full Hungarian tour would be difficult anyway; you'd need several weeks, traveling by bus (time-consuming) or by car (dangerous if you're not used to European driving). But trains, though not quite luxurious, are easy and safe, and they usually cost less than 4,000 Ft ($20/£11) round-trip.

This section lists four options for your Hungarian side trip: **Szentendre** is a charming village and artist colony only 20km (12 miles) from the smog of the capital; **Keszthely** is at the far end of Lake Balaton and away from the throngs of tourists; **Keszthely** is a small scenic town, not far from the beaches, and nearby **Héviz** has lots of recently opened spa-hotels; **Pécs** is a burgeoning cultural center which has lately been attracting many young travelers; and the southern Hungarian city of **Szeged** is another cultural center and Hungary's "spice capital."

Option ❶ A Day in Szentendre ✹✹

After 2 days in Budapest, you might visit Szentendre (pronounced *Sen*-ten-dreh), an artists' colony just north of Budapest and one of the most visited spots in all of Hungary. Take the HÉV (regional train) from Budapest's Batthyány tér metro for a 45-minute ride.

Visit the **Margit Kovács Museum** ✹✹✹ and see a wonderful collection of the late Margit Kovács. Her depictions of peasant life in Hungary are heartwarming. Have a late lunch at the **Aranysárkány Vendéglő** ✹, and take a walk along the river. Then spend your afternoon exploring the many shops, museums, and galleries in town. Fő tér, the main drag, is enticing, but explore all the side streets of this small, manageable town. Try **Régimódi** ✹ for dinner, and stay at the **Róz Panzió**, which overlooks the Danube. (Reserve both several weeks ahead.)

See the "Szentendre" section on p. 352.

Option ❷ 2 Days in Keszthely ⊛ & Héviz ⊛⊛

Keszthely and Héviz are tucked away in a quiet corner of Hungary's very own little "sea," Lake Balaton, almost 200km (125 miles) from Budapest. The towns sit right in a microclimate area, with warm summers, clear skies, and beautiful vistas and hills.

From Budapest, take a 3-hour express (*gyors*) train from Déli Station to Keszthely. Then explore its **Festetics Mansion** ⊛, **Carriage Museum,** or try the puppet museum, the **Babamúzeum.** After roaming around Keszthely, have a traditional Hungarian meal, with a traditional Unicum, at the **Margaréta Étterem.** At night, check out a show at the **Balaton Congress Center and Theater,** and stay either in a "private room" or at the **Danubius Hotel Helikon.**

The next day take a bus to Héviz, 8km (5 miles) northeast of Keszthely, and head straight to the **Rogner Hotel and Spa Therme** ⊛⊛. Take a dip in Europe's largest thermal lake, nearby, for a dip, or spend your whole day unwinding at the hotel. Spa treatments include a selection of health cures, sports, wellness, or even medical treatment programs.

You might shorten this side trip by heading straight to Héviz, then tour Keszthely a bit and relax in the spa hotel at night.

Option ❸ 2 Days in Pécs ⊛⊛⊛

The popular Pécs is the most culturally vibrant Hungarian city outside of the capital—warm and arid, with lots of museums, galleries, and a large student population.

Take an early morning Inter City train from Budapest's Déli Station to Pécs, a 2½-hour ride. Visit the **Tivadar Csontváry Museum** ⊛ and the **Victor Vasarely Museum** ⊛, institutions that celebrate two of Hungary's most notable artists. The **Zsolnay Museum** ⊛⊛⊛ houses a vast collection of vases, plates, cups, figurines, and even ceramic paintings. Then check out the hustle and bustle of the **Pécsi Vásár** ⊛⊛ flea market, where you can find traditional Hungarian wares. Head up on the hill for dinner at the **Bagolyvár Étterem** ⊛, where you can enjoy a fine Hungarian wine before checking in at the fun, centrally located **Hotel Fönix** ⊛⊛.

The next morning, have a coffee and cake at the **Mecsek Cukrászda** before checking out Pécs' houses of worship, the **Pécs Cathedral,** the **Pécs Synagogue** ⊛, and the largest standing Turkish structure, the **Mosque of Pasha Gazi Kassim.**

See the Pécs section on p. 367.

Option ❹ 2 Days in Szeged ⊛

The southern Hungarian town of Szeged gets a lot of traffic from Romanian and Serbian visitors so it's a diverse city, with lots of students. If you're in Hungary in the summer, come here for the **Szeged Summer Festival** ⊛, which offers rock operas, classical music, ballet, and contemporary dance. In July, **Thealter** is a sort of European "fringe festival" of alternative theater.

From Budapest, take the train from Nyugati Station. Start off with a coffee and pastry at the famous **Virág Cukrászda.** Then learn about some local history at the **Móra Ferenc Museum.** Take a walk on the river's edge, then head back to **Kárász utca** ⊛⊛, the main walking street, which is usually bustling with students. Have an upscale dinner at **Zodiákus** or a more casual, boisterous meal at **HBH Bajor Söröző** ⊛. Try to get a room at the reasonably priced and clean **Hotel Matrix,** not far from the center of town.

On your second day here, check out the **Polish Market (Lengyel Piac)** ⊛ on the Southern edge of town and visit the beautiful and historic **Synagogue** ⊛. Then head for some hearty fish stew at **Kiskőrösi Halászcsárda** ⊛.

HUNGARY TODAY

Having acceded to the European Union, Hungary is today going through a series of painful reforms. Because of a continued political polarization of the country between the left- and right-leaning crowds, talking politics in Hungary is a hot potato. While the systemic changes over a decade and a half ago were bloodless, they did not happen without leaving deep scars. Many former Communists remain in the corridors of power on both sides of the political spectrum, to the chagrin of many. In the meantime, Hungary joined the European Union, and the strained political situation has introduced painful reforms. What the result of these will be, and whether they will be successful, is the question of the day.

HUNGARIAN PEOPLE & CULTURE

Ethnic Magyars make up about 94% of the population of Hungary. The population of the Roma (Gypsies) lingers around 2% according to official counts, but numbers of up to 4% have been reported, too. The rest of the population is made up primarily of Germans, Slovaks, Croatians, and Romanians.

Magyars are courteous and generally friendly toward foreigners. If you are invited to someone's home, bring a small gift such as chocolate, wine, or fresh flowers, and learn a few key words of Hungarian—even if your hosts speak English. As always, it is the effort that counts.

Tip: Tread carefully when talking about Hungarian politics. Hungary is politically divided between the conservative and right-wing nationalists, liberals, and the socialists—and opinions can divide families. We advise you start with something light before moving into heated political debates.

HUNGARIAN CUISINE

Hungary's cuisine reflects the rich and varied flavors of four major geographic regions. From Transdanubia, west of the River Danube, come rich mushroom sauces, sorrel soups, cottage cheese and onion dumplings, and high-quality gooseliver. A host of excellent wild-game dishes are prominent in forested northern Hungary. Bucolic Erdély (Transylvania) introduces spices such as tarragon, summer savory, and fresh dill to the palate, and is also known for its lamb dishes and sheep's cheese. And, finally, from the Great Hungarian Plain, the home of Hungary's renowned paprika, come hearty fish, bean, and meat stews all spiced with the red powder ground from different varieties of peppers ranging from *édes* (sweet) to *csípős* (hot).

Lunch, the main meal of the day, begins with soup. *Gyümölcs leves,* a cold fruit soup, is excellent when in season. *Sóskakrém leves,* cream of sorrel soup, is another good seasonal choice. *Babgulyás,* a hearty bean soup, and *halaszle,* a fish soup popular at river- and lakeside spots, constitute meals in themselves.

The main course is generally a meat dish. Try the *paprikás csirke,* chicken cooked in a savory paprika sauce. It's especially good with *galuska,* a pasta dumpling. *Pulykamell,* turkey breast baked with plums and served in a mushroom gravy, is also delicious. Another great choice is *Pörkölt,* a stewed meat dish that comes in many varieties. *Töltött káposzta,* whole cabbage leaves stuffed with rice, meat, and spices, is another favorite.

LANGUAGE

Part of Budapest's mystery stems from the complex and unusual language of the Hungarians, Magyar. Magyar originated on the eastern side of the Ural Mountains: Along with Finnish and Estonian, it's one of Europe's few representatives of the Finno-Ugric family of languages. The Hungarian language has long been one of the country's greatest obstacles; nevertheless, the Hungarian people are intensely proud of their language and its charms. Our transcription of Hungarian pronunciations is of necessity approximate.

USEFUL WORDS & PHRASES

English	Hungarian	Pronunciation
Good day/Hello	**Jó napot**	*Yoh* napoht
Good morning	**Jó reggelt**	*Yoh* reg-gelt
Good evening	**Jó estét**	*Yoh* esh-tayt
Goodbye	**Viszontlátásra**	*Vee*-sont-lah-tahsh-ra
My name is . . .	**vagyok . . .**	*Vodge*-yohk
Thank you	**Köszönöm**	*Kuh*-suh-nuhm
You're welcome	**Kérem**	*Kay*-rem
Please	**Legyen szíves**	*Ledge*-yen *see*-vesh
Yes	**Igen**	*Ee*-gen
No	**Nem**	*Nem*
Good/Okay	**Jó**	*Yo*
Excuse me	**Bocsánat**	*Boh*-chahnat
How much does it cost?	**Mennyi bekerül?**	*Men*-yee *beh*-keh-roohl?
I don't understand	**Nem értem**	*Nem* ayr-tem
I don't know	**Nem tudom**	*Nem too*-dum
Where is the . . . ?	**Hol van a . . . ?**	*Hohl* von a . . . ?
bus station	**busz állomás**	*boos ahh*-loh-mahsh
train station	**vonatállomás**	*vah*-not-*ahh*-loh-mahsh
bank	**bank**	*bahnk*
pharmacy	**patiká**	*paw*-tee-kah
tourist office	**turista iroda**	*too*-reesh-ta *eer*-ohda
restroom/toilet	**wc**	*vayt*-say

2 Planning Your Trip to Hungary

VISITOR INFORMATION

Tourism infrastructure has been developing at a furious pace in Hungary, be it through the development of high-quality hotels and restaurants, and even improvements to the service sector. In most cities you will find tourism-related information offices called **Tourinform** (© 1/438-8080; www.tourinform.hu), a branch of the Hungarian National Tourist Office. In Budapest, the location is at Sütő u. 2, 1052 Budapest (© 1/438-8080 or 06/80-630800; www.tourinform.hu), open daily from 8am to 8pm. You'll also find a branch office in the heart of Budapest's Broadway, at Liszt Ferenc tér 11 (© 1/322-4098; fax 1/342-2541), open daily from 9am to 7pm. These offices will distribute pamphlets on events and attractions that can be found in the area that you are visiting, and help you with finding appropriate accommodations and restaurants. The tourism authority, **Magyar Turizmus Rt** (© 1/488-8701;

www.hugarytourism.hu), also has offices throughout the world, and it is their mandate to promote Hungary as a destination for tourism.

For general country information and a variety of pamphlets and maps before you leave, contact the government-sponsored **Hungarian National Tourist Office,** 150 E. 58th St., New York, NY 10155 (© **212/355-0240;** www.gotohungary.com). In London the **Hungarian National Tourist Office** is at 46 Eaton Place, London SW1X 8AL (© **020/7823-1032**). The Hungarian National Tourist Office's main website, a great source of information, is **www.gotohungary.com.**

Another site with lots of helpful information for visitors is **www.vista.hu.** Find general city information at **www.budapest.com.** Current local news, entertainment listings, and the like can be found at either **www.budapestsun.com, www. budapesttimes.hu,** or **www.ontheglobe.com.**

ENTRY REQUIREMENTS

Embassies   The embassy of **Australia** is at XII. Királyhágó tér 8–9 (© **1/457-9777**); the embassy of **Canada** is at II. Ganz u. 12–14 (© **1/392-3360**); the embassy of the **Republic of Ireland** is at V. Szabadság tér 7 (© **1/302-9600**); the embassy of the **United Kingdom** is at V. Harmincad u. 6 (© **1/266-2888**); and the embassy of the **United States** is at V. Szabadság tér 12 (© **1/475-4400**). New Zealand does not have an embassy in Budapest, but the U.K. embassy can handle passport matters for New Zealand citizens.

MONEY

The basic unit of currency in Hungary is the **forint (Ft).** Coins come in denominations of 1, 2, 5, 10, 20, 50, and 100 Ft. Banknotes come in denominations of 200, 500, 1,000, 5,000, 10,000, and 20,000 Ft.

The U.S. dollar has weakened over the past several years, but Hungary continues to be considerably less expensive for travelers than most Western countries. Labor-intensive services, such as picture framing, tailoring, shoe and watch repair, and the like, are particularly inexpensive.

As of this writing, the rate of exchange is $1 = 200 Ft (50p) (or 100 Ft = 50¢/25p), and this is the rate used to calculate all the U.S. dollar prices in this book. Of course, exchange rates fluctuate over time.

The best official rates for both cash and traveler's checks are obtained at banks. Exchange booths are also located throughout the city center, in train stations, and in most luxury hotels, but exchange booths almost uniformly offer less favorable rates than banks. ATMs are found in front of banks throughout the city or in major shopping malls. You may withdraw forints at the daily exchange rate from your home account through the Cirrus and PLUS networks. At some banks and at all exchange booths, you will get a better rate when exchanging cash.

You should regard with extreme suspicion anyone who accosts you on the street wanting to change money, especially someone offering you a rate more than 2% to 3% better than the official one. Such a person is certainly out to cheat you. It is not recommended to exchange money in anything but a bank or a registered exchange booth.

The Hungarian forint, fully convertible, leaves no restrictions regarding re-exchange of forints back into your currency. Consequently, unlike in the past, you need not retain your currency exchange receipts as proof of exchange.

You'll avoid lines at airport ATMs (automated teller machines) by exchanging at least some money—just enough to cover airport incidentals and transportation to your hotel—before you leave home (though don't expect the exchange rate to be ideal). You can exchange money at your local American Express or Thomas Cook office or at your bank. American Express also dispenses traveler's checks and foreign currency via www.americanexpress.com or ✆ 800/807-6233, but they'll charge a $15 order fee and additional shipping costs. American Express cardholders should dial ✆ 800/221-7282; this number accepts collect calls, offers service in several foreign languages, and exempts Amex gold and platinum cardholders from the 1% fee.

WHEN TO GO

Budapest has a relatively mild climate—the annual mean temperature in Hungary is 50°F (10°C). Nevertheless, summer temperatures often exceed 80°F to 85°F (27°C–29°C), and sweltering hot, humid days are typical in July and August. January and February are the coldest months, averaging 30°F (–1°C), though temperatures can dip well below that on any given day. Be prepared for damp and chilly weather in winter. Spring is usually mild and, especially in May, wet. Autumn is usually quite pleasant, with mild, cooler weather through October.

HOLIDAYS

Hungarian holidays are: January 1 (New Year's Day), March 15 (National Holiday), Easter Sunday and Easter Monday, May 1 (May Day), Whit Monday, August 20 (St. Stephen's Day), October 23 (Republic Day), November 1 (All Saints' Day), and December 25 and 26 (Christmas). Shops, museums, and banks are closed on all holidays.

GETTING THERE & GETTING AROUND
BY PLANE

Northwest Airlines (✆ 800/447-4747) and **Malév** (✆ 800/877-5429, 800/262-5380, or 800/223-6884), the former Hungarian state airline, offer nonstop service between North America and Budapest. Other leading carriers include **Lufthansa** (✆ 800/645-3880), **British Airways** (✆ 800/247-9297), **Delta Airlines** (✆ 800/241-4141), and **Austrian Air** (✆ 800/843-0002).

Budapest is served by two adjacent airports, **Ferihegy I** and **Ferihegy II,** located in the XVIII district in southeastern Pest. Generally, Ferihegy I serves low-cost carriers, while Ferihegy II (which has a **Terminal A** and a **Terminal B**) serves the flagship carrier and other traditional airlines. There are several main information numbers: For arrivals, try ✆ 1/296-5052; for departures, call ✆ 1/296-5883; and for general information, call ✆ 1/296-7155. Make sure you pick up a copy of the free *LRI Airport Budapest Magazine* while at the airport, as it contains a wealth of valuable phone numbers and transportation-related information, as well as articles on Hungary.

All arriving flights are international since there is no domestic air service in Hungary. All arriving passengers pass through the same Customs gate and emerge into the bustling arrivals hall of the airport.

Though extended and modernized over the past few years, the airport remains quite small. In each terminal, you will find several accommodations offices, rental-car agencies, shops, and exchange booths. Note that exchange rates are generally less favorable here than in the city, so you may not want to change very much money at the airport. Twenty-four-hour left-luggage service is available at Terminal B (✆ 1/296-8802).

BY TRAIN

Countless trains arrive in Budapest from most corners of Europe. Many connect through Vienna, where 11 daily trains depart for Budapest from either the Westbahnhof or Sudbahnhof station. Six daily trains connect Prague and Budapest, while one connects Berlin with Budapest and two connect Warsaw with Budapest.

The train trip between Vienna and Budapest takes about 3½ hours. Hungarian railway offers a great deal for short-term visitors coming from Vienna: a round-trip second-class ticket, valid up to 4 days, that includes a free pass for all public transport in Budapest. For more information on Vienna trains, contact the **Austrian National Tourist Board,** 500 Fifth Ave., Suite 800, New York, NY 10110 (℃ **212/944-6885**); 11601 Wilshire Blvd., Suite 2480, Los Angeles, CA 90025 (℃ **310/477-3332**); 30 St. George St., London W1R 0AL (℃ **020/7629-0461**); 2 Bloor St. E., Suite 3330, Toronto, ON M4W 1A8 (℃ **416/967-3381**); or 1010 Sherbrooke St. W., Suite 1410, Montreal, PQ H3A 2R7 (℃ **514/849-3708**).

Train travel within Hungary is generally very efficient; trains almost always depart right on time and usually arrive on time. You can access a full, user-friendly timetable on the Web at **www.elvira.hu**.

Hungarian ticket agents speak little English, so you will need to know some basic terminology in Hungarian. *Indul* means "departure" and *érkezik* means "arrival." The timetables for arrivals are displayed in big white posters *(érkező vonatok)*, while departures *(induló vonatok)* are on yellow posters. The relevant terms in the timetables are *honnan* (from where), *hova* (to where), *vágány* (platform), *munkanap* (weekdays), *hétvége* (weekend), *munkaszüneti nap* (Sat), *ünnepnap* (holiday), *gyors* (fast train)—stops only at major cities, as posted, and *IC* (inter city)—stops only once or twice en route; you must reserve a seat for IC trains. Ticket terminology is as follows: *jegy* (ticket), *oda* (one-way), *oda-vissza* (round-trip), *helyjegy* (reservation), *első osztály* (first class), *másodosztály* (second class), *nem dohányzó* (nonsmoking), *ma* (today), and *holnap* (tomorrow).

A train posted as *személy* is a local train, which stops at every single village and town on its route. Always opt for a *gyors* (fast) or Intercity train to get to your destination in a timely manner. All Intercity trains (but no other domestic trains) require a *helyjegy* (seat reservation); ask for the reservation when purchasing your ticket. On Intercity trains, you must sit in your assigned seat. All Intercity trains now comply strictly with a new law imposing constraints on smoking in public spaces; they have a single car designated for smokers, while the rest of the train is nonsmoking. If you want a seat in the smoking car, you need to ask for *dohányzó* when buying your ticket. The gyors train is typically an old, gritty, rumbling train with the classic eight-seat compartments. The Intercity, a state-of-the-art, clean, modern train without compartments, is said to travel faster, but our experience has shown us that there's seldom more than 30 minutes difference between the two in terms of speed.

During the day, obtain **domestic train information** over the phone by dialing ℃ **1/461-5400** and **international train information** at ℃ **1/461-5500.** Purchase tickets at train station ticket windows or from the MÁV Service Office, VI. Andrássy út 35 (℃ **1/322-8405,** open Monday through Friday 9am to 6pm in summer, 9am to 5pm in winter. You need at least half an hour before departure time to make a reservation.

BY BUS

Buses to and from western and Eastern Europe and points in Hungary west of the Danube call at **Népliget.** You reach this station by getting off at the Népliget metro stop on the Red line. Buses to and from the Danube Bend and other points north of Budapest call at the **Árpád híd bus station** (✆ **1/320-9229** or 1/317-9886). Take the Blue line metro to Árpád híd. For domestic and international bus information, call ✆ **1/219-8080,** though you should be aware that it can be rather difficult to get through to the bus stations over the telephone and to reach an English speaker. Your best bet is perhaps to gather your information in person or ask for assistance at the Tourinform office (p. 278).

BY CAR

Several major highways link Hungary to nearby European capitals. The recently modernized **E60** (or M1) connects Budapest with Vienna and points west; it is a toll road from the Austrian border to the city of Györ. The **E65** connects Budapest with Prague and points north.

The **border crossings** from Austria and Slovakia (from which countries most Westerners enter Hungary) are hassle-free. In addition to your passport, you may be requested to present your driver's license, vehicle registration, and proof of insurance (the number plate and symbol indicating country of origin are acceptable proof). A green card is required of vehicles bearing license plates of Bulgaria, France, the former USSR, Greece, Poland, Italy, Romania, and Israel. Hungary no longer requires the International Driver's License. Cars entering Hungary are required to have a decal indicating country of registration, a first-aid kit, and an emergency triangle.

Driving distances are: from Vienna, 248km (154 miles); from Prague, 560km (347 miles); from Frankfurt, 952km (590 miles); and from Rome, 1,294km (802 miles).

BY HYDROFOIL

The Hungarian state shipping company **MAHART** operates hydrofoils on the Danube between Vienna and Budapest in the spring and summer months. It's an extremely popular route, so you should book your tickets well in advance. In North America or Britain, contact the Austrian National Tourist Board (see "By Train," above). In Vienna contact MAHART, Handelskai 265 (✆ **43/729-2161;** fax 43/729-2163). Or visit this website: www.besthotelz.com/hungary/hydrofoil/hydrofoil.htm.

From April 3 through July 2 the MAHART hydrofoil departs Vienna at 9am daily, arriving in Budapest at 2:30pm, with a stop in Bratislava when necessary (passengers getting on or off). From July 3 to August 29, two hydrofoils make the daily passage, departing Vienna at 8am and 1pm, arriving in Budapest at 1:30 and 6:30pm, respectively. From August 30 to November 1, the schedule returns to one hydrofoil daily, departing Vienna at 9am and arriving in Budapest at 2:30pm. Customs and passport control begin 1 hour prior to departure. Eurailpass holders also receive a discount, as long as they buy the ticket before boarding. ISIC holders also receive a discount. The Budapest office of **MAHART** is at V. Belgrád rakpart (✆ **1/318-1880**). Boats and hydrofoils from Vienna arrive at the international boat station next door to the MAHART office on the **Belgrád rakpart,** which is on the Pest side of the Danube, between the Szabadság and Erzsébet bridges.

TIPS ON ACCOMMODATIONS

In Budapest, accommodations range from beautiful, historic gems that were built in the early 20th century, to drab, utilitarian establishments that are products of the city's Warsaw Pact days. Rates in Budapest, however, remain relatively palatable compared to the rates of other European capitals. Competition, also, has resulted in the prices for hotel rooms remaining stable in recent years.

With the addition of many new hotels and pensions (small innlike hotels) that have opened in recent years, Budapest has been playing catch-up, and as a result is not a city lacking in guest beds, as it once was. This said, in high season—or, say, during the Formula 1 weekend in August—it can still be quite difficult to secure a hotel or pension room or a hostel bed, so make reservations and get written confirmation well in advance of your stay.

In Budapest and the rest of Hungary, keep in mind that if you want a room with a double bed, you should specifically request it; otherwise, you are likely to get a room with twin beds. Single rooms are generally available, as are extra beds or cots. Hungarian hotels often use the word "apartment" to describe connected rooms without a kitchen. In these listings, we have referred to such rooms as "suites," reserving the term "apartment" for accommodations with kitchen facilities.

Most accommodations agencies can secure private room rentals in private homes and help reserve hotel and pension rooms. The most established agencies are the former state-owned travel agents **Ibusz** (see below), **MÁV Tours** (© 1/182-9011), and **Budapest Tourist** (© 1/117-3555). Although newer private agencies continue to bloom, the older agencies tend to have the greatest number of rooms listed. There are agencies at the airport, in all three major train stations, throughout central Pest, and along the main roads into Budapest for travelers arriving by car. You can also reserve online through many of the agencies listed below.

The main **Ibusz reservations office** is at Ferenciek tere 10 (© 1/485-2700; fax 1/318-2805; www.ibusz.hu), accessible by the Blue metro line. This office is open year-round Monday through Friday 9am to 6pm.

TIPS ON DINING

Étterem is the most common Hungarian word for restaurant and is applied to everything from cafeteria-style eateries to first-class restaurants. A *vendéglő*, or guesthouse, is a smaller, more intimate restaurant (literally an "inn"), often with a Hungarian folk motif; a *csárda* is a countryside *vendéglő* (often built on major motorways and frequently found around Lake Balaton and other holiday areas). An *étkezde* is an informal lunchroom open only in the daytime, while an *önkiszolgáló* means self-service cafeteria; these are typically open only for lunch. Stand-up *büfés* (snack counters) are often found in bus stations and near busy transportation hubs. A *cukrászda* or *kávéház* is a classic central European coffeehouse, where lingering over a beverage and pastry has developed into an art form.

There are also a variety of establishments that, though primarily designed for drinking, also serve meals. A *borozó* is a wine bar; these are often found in cellars (they are likely to include in their name the word *pince* [cellar] or *barlang* [cave]), and generally feature a house wine. A *söröző* is a beer bar; these places, too, are often found in cellars. Sandwiches are usually available in *borozós* and *sörözős*. Finally, a *kocsma* is a sort of roadside tavern. Kocsmas are found on side streets in residential neighborhoods; the Buda Hills are filled with them. Most kocsmas serve a full dinner, but the kitchens close early.

Warning: While this country is landlocked, many restaurants pride themselves of their fresh seafood delights. Many Hungarians probably hark back to a time when the sea was a part of this land, and some even think that the sea is closer than it actually is. The fact is, such a promise is hard to keep; **we recommend staying away from imported seafood.** At traditional Hungarian restaurants you will find delightful local fish: **Szeged** or **Tisza** fish soups are delicious, and far better than a far-from-fresh seafood platter.

FAST FACTS: Budapest

American Express The American Express office is in Budapest between Vörösmarty tér and Deák tér in central Pest, at V. Deák Ferenc u. 10 (© 1/235-4330 or 1/235-4300; fax 1/267-2028). It's open Monday through Friday from 9am to 5pm. There's an American Express cash ATM on the street in front of the office.

Business Hours In Budapest, most **stores** are open Monday through Friday from 10am to 6pm and Saturday from 9 or 10am to 1 or 2pm. Some shops close for an hour at lunchtime, and most stores are closed Sunday, except those in the central tourist areas. Some shop owners and restaurateurs also close for 2 weeks in August. On weekdays, food stores open early, at around 6 or 7am, and close at around 6 or 7pm. Certain grocery stores, called "nonstops," are open 24 hours (however, a growing number of shops call themselves "nonstop" even if they close for the night at 10 or 11pm). **Banks** are usually open Monday through Thursday from 8am to 3pm and Friday from 8am to 2pm.

Doctors For a list of English-speaking doctors in Hungary (most will be located in Budapest), call your embassy (see "Embassies," below).

Electricity Hungarian electricity is 220 volts, AC.

Embassies The embassy of **Australia** is at XII. Királyhágó tér 8–9 (© 1/457-9777); the embassy of **Canada** is at II. Ganz u. 12–14 (© 1/392-3360); the embassy of the **Republic of Ireland** is at V. Szabadság tér 7 (© 1/302-9600); the embassy of the **United Kingdom** is at V. Harmincad u. 6 (© 1/266-2888); and the embassy of the **United States** is at V. Szabadság tér 12 (© 1/475-4400). New Zealand does not have an embassy in Budapest, but the U.K. embassy can handle matters for New Zealand citizens.

Emergencies Dial © **104** for an ambulance, © **105** for the fire department, and © **107** for the police. © **1/438-8080** is a 24-hour hot line in English for reporting crime.

Etiquette & Customs Old-world etiquette is still very much alive in Hungary. People speak very politely, hold doors open for women, readily give up seats on the bus for those who need them, and so on.

Internet Access In larger towns, Internet cafes are readily available but connection speeds and service may be spotty at times. Be patient.

Liquor Laws The legal drinking age in Hungary is 18.

Newspapers & Magazines For English-language articles on current events and politics in Hungary, pick up the *Budapest Sun* or the *Budapest Times*, both weeklies.

Police Dial © **107** for the police.

Restrooms The word for toilet in Hungarian is *WC* (pronounced *vay*-tsay). *Női* means "women's"; *férfi* means "men's."

Safety Hungary is fairly safe, and violent street crime is far less common than in similar-sized U.S. cities. However, you should always be on the lookout for pickpockets, especially on crowded buses, trains, and trams. In Budapest, there is no shortage of rambunctious drunks at night, but they don't seem to pose much danger to others. (**Note:** Budapest is filled with underpasses. Be careful at night; you can always choose to cross a street aboveground if an underpass appears deserted.)

Smoking Smoking is forbidden in all public places (including all public transportation), except in most restaurants and pubs, where smoking is considered to be an indispensable part of the ambience. Although a 1999 law requires all restaurants to have a nonsmoking section, the fact is that most barely comply. Expect most restaurants to be smoky places. *Tilos a dohányzás* or *Dohányozni tilos* means "No Smoking."

Taxes Taxes are included in restaurant and hotel rates, and in shop purchases. International travelers are entitled, upon leaving the country, to a refund of the 25% VAT on certain purchases.

Telephone The country code for Hungary is 36. **To call to Hungary from abroad:** Dial the appropriate numbers to get an international dial tone (011 from the U.S.), then dial 36 (Hungary country code), followed by the appropriate city code (for Budapest, 1), followed by the six- or seven-digit telephone number. **To make international calls:** To make international calls from Hungary, dial 00 and then the country code (U.S. or Canada 1, U.K. 44, Ireland 353, Australia 61, New Zealand 64). Next you dial the area code and number. **To make a call from one Hungary area code to another,** first dial 06; when you hear a tone, dial the area code and number.

Time Zone Hungary is on Central European time, 2 hours ahead of Greenwich Mean Time and 6 hours ahead of Eastern Standard Time from March 26 to October 26; from October 27 to March 25 (during the equivalent of daylight saving time), the difference is 1 hour and 5 hours, respectively.

Tipping If a restaurant bill includes a service fee, as some restaurants do (be sure to ask), there is no need to tip; if not, add 15% to 20% to the bill.

Water Tap water is generally considered safe for drinking. Mineral water, which many Hungarians prefer to tap water, is called *ásványvíz*. Purified bottled water has pink labels for identification.

3 Budapest

Living and working in Budapest today, I see a buzzing culture that is becoming more and more dynamically European. A vibrant young generation is proof of this. While the political elite continue to argue about the past, the youth are concentrating on the future. They're becoming multilingual; they're creating new film festivals and fashion shows. The scene they're developing is vibrant and fun—if a bit secretive and cliquish. While it might take some time to enter into their world, it's a fun journey in the end. They are playing catch-up, living off the seat of their pants.

ARRIVING

BY PLANE The easiest way into the city is probably the **Airport Minibus** (© 1/296-8555; www.bud.hu), a public service of the LRI (Budapest Airport Authority). The minibus, which leaves every 10 or 15 minutes throughout the day, takes you directly to any address in the city. From either terminal, it costs 2,300 Ft ($12/£6.50);

the price includes luggage transport. The trip takes from 30 minutes to an hour, depending on how many stops are made. The Airport Minibus desk is easily found in the main hall of both terminals. Minibuses also provide the same efficient service returning to the airport; arrange for your pickup from your hotel *1 full day in advance* by calling the number above. The minibus will pick up passengers virtually anywhere in the Budapest area.

We strongly discourage the use of cabs from the **Airport Taxi** fleet (© 1/296-6534), which are generally overpriced. A ride downtown from one of these cabs might cost significantly more than a recommended fleet (see "Getting Around," later in this chapter, for names and contact information). Unfortunately, for reasons no one has been able to explain to us with a straight face, cabs from the Airport Taxi fleet are the only cabs permitted to wait for fares on the airport grounds. However, dozens of cabs from the cheaper fleets that we recommend are stationed at all times at roadside pullouts just off the airport property, a stone's throw from the terminal, waiting for radio calls from their dispatchers. All it takes is a phone call from the terminal and a cab will be there for you in a matter of minutes (see "Getting Around" and "By Taxi," later in this chapter). For three or more people traveling together (and maybe even two people), a taxi from a recommended fleet to the city, at approximately 4,500 Ft ($23/£12), will be substantially cheaper than the combined minibus fares. A taxi from the airport to downtown takes about 20 to 30 minutes.

It's also possible to get to the city by public transportation; the trip takes about 1 hour total. Take the red-lettered **bus no. 93** to the last stop, Kőbánya-Kispest. From there, the Blue metro line runs to the Inner City of Pest. The cost is two transit tickets, which is 290 Ft ($1.45/75p) altogether; tickets can be bought from the automated vending machine at the bus stop (coins only) or from any newsstand in the airport.

BY TRAIN Budapest has three major train stations: Keleti pályaudvar (Eastern Station), Nyugati pályaudvar (Western Station), and Déli pályaudvar (Southern Station). The stations' names, curiously, correspond neither to their geographical location in the city nor to the origins or destinations of trains serving them. Each has a metro station beneath it and an array of accommodations offices, currency-exchange booths, and other services.

Most international trains pull into bustling **Keleti Station** (© 1/314-5010), a classic steel-girdered European train station located in Pest's seedy Baross tér, beyond the Outer Ring on the border of the VII and VIII districts. Various hustlers offering rooms and taxis woo travelers here. The Red line of the metro is below the station; numerous bus, tram, and trolleybus lines serve Baross tér as well.

Some international trains arrive at **Nyugati Station** (© 1/349-0115), another classic designed by the Eiffel company and built in the 1870s. It's located on the Outer Ring, at the border of the V, VI, and XIII districts. A station for the Blue line of the metro is beneath Nyugati, and numerous tram and bus lines serve busy Nyugati tér.

Few international trains arrive at **Déli Station** (© 1/375-6293), an ugly run-down modern building in central Buda; the terminus of the Red metro line is beneath this train station.

MÁV operates a minibus that will take you from any of the three stations to the airport for 2,000 Ft ($10/£5.15) per person (minimum two persons), or between stations for 1,000 Ft ($5/£2.60) per person (minimum two persons), with further discounts available for larger groups. To order the minibus, call © **1/353-2722.**

Often, however, a taxi fare will be cheaper, especially for groups of two or more travelers (see "Getting Around," below).

BY BUS The Népliget Bus Station is the city's recently opened modern main bus terminal on the Red metro line at the **Stadionok** stop. The Blue line goes to the much smaller **Árpád híd bus station** that caters to domestic bus service only.

CITY LAYOUT

You'll follow this section much better with a map in hand. The city of Budapest came into being in 1873, the result of a union of three separate cities: **Buda, Pest,** and **Óbuda.** Budapest, like Hungary itself, is defined by the **River Danube (Duna).** The stretch of the Danube flowing through the capital is fairly wide (the average width is 400m/1,325 ft.), and most of the city's historic sites are on or near the river. Eight bridges connect the two banks, including five in the city center. The Széchenyi Chain Bridge (Lánchíd), built in 1849, was the first permanent bridge across the Danube. Although it was blown up by the Nazis, it was rebuilt after the war.

GETTING AROUND
BY PUBLIC TRANSPORTATION

Budapest has an extensive, efficient, and inexpensive public transportation system. If you have some patience and enjoy reading maps, you can easily learn the system well enough to use it wisely. Public transportation, however, is not without its drawbacks. The biggest disadvantage is that except for 17 well-traveled bus and tram routes, all forms of transport shut down for the night at around 11:30pm (see "Night Service," below). Certain areas of the city, most notably the Buda Hills, are beyond the reach of this night service, and taxis are thus required for late-night journeys. Another problem with the system is that travel can be quite slow, especially during rush hour. A third disadvantage, pertinent mostly to travelers, is that Castle Hill can be reached in only three ways by public transportation and all of these modes of transportation are quite crowded in the high seasons. Finally, and perhaps most importantly, crowded public transport is the place where you are most likely to be targeted by Budapest's professional pickpockets.

FARES **All forms of public transportation** (metro, bus, tram, trolleybus, some HÉV railway lines, and cogwheel railway) in Budapest require the self-validation of prepurchased tickets *(vonaljegy),* which cost 170 Ft (85¢/45p) apiece (children under 6 travel free); single tickets can be bought at metro ticket windows, newspaper kiosks, and the occasional tobacco shop. There are also automated machines in most metro stations and at major transportation hubs, most of which have been recently modernized or installed and provide reliable service. We recommend that you buy a handful of tickets in advance so that you can avoid the trouble of constantly having to replenish your stock with the appropriate coins for the vending machines. For 1,450 Ft ($7.25/£3.75) you can get a 10-pack *(tizes csomag),* and for 2,800 Ft ($14/£7.20), you can get a 20-pack *(huszas csomag).*

While this standard ticket is valid on the metro, three types of optional single-ride metro tickets were introduced several years ago, making ticket buying a bit more complicated for those who are inclined to try to buy the most appropriate ticket for their journey. A "metro section ticket" *(metrószakaszjegy),* at 120 Ft (60¢/32p), is valid for a single metro trip stopping at three stations or less. A "metro transfer ticket" *(metróátszállójegy),* at 270 Ft ($1.35/72p), allows you to transfer from one metro line to another on the same ticket, without any limit to the number of stations that the train stops at during your journey. And a "metro section transfer ticket" (metró-szakaszát-szállójegy), at 185 Ft (90¢/49p), allows you to transfer from one metro line to another, but only for a trip totaling five or fewer stops.

For convenience, we recommend that you purchase a day pass or multiday pass while in Budapest. Passes need only be validated once, saving you the hassle of having to validate a ticket every time you board the metro. A pass will probably save you some money, too, as you are likely to be getting on and off public transportation all day long. Day passes (napijegy) cost 1,350 Ft ($6.75/£3.50) and are valid until midnight of the day of purchase. Buy them from metro ticket windows; the clerk validates the pass at the time of purchase. A 3-day pass (turistajegy) costs 2,700 Ft ($14/£6.95) and a 7-day travel-card (hetijegy) costs 3,100 Ft ($16/£8); these have the same validation procedure as the day pass.

For longer stays in Budapest, consider a 2-week pass (kéthétibérlet) at 4,050 Ft ($20/£10), or a monthly pass (havibérlet) or 30-day pass (30 napos bérlet), both at 6,250 Ft ($31/£16). These two passes are available only at major metro stations, and you need to bring a regulation passport photo.

Dark-blue-uniformed inspectors (who even now flip out a hidden red armband when approaching you—a remnant of the not-too-distant past when they traveled the metro in plain clothes) frequently come around checking for valid tickets, particularly at the top or bottom of the escalators to metro platforms. On-the-spot fines of 2,000 Ft ($10/£5.15) are assessed to fare dodgers; pleading ignorance generally doesn't work. Given how inexpensive public transport is, risking a time-consuming altercation with metro inspectors is probably not worth it. Metro tickets are good for 1 hour for any distance along the line you're riding, except for metro section tickets (metrószakasz-jegy), which are valid only for 30 minutes. You may get off and reboard with the same ticket within the valid time period.

The **Budapest Card,** a tourist card that we do not particularly recommend (it does not pack any value), combines a 3-day turistajegy (transportation pass) with free entry to certain museums and other discounts.

SCHEDULES & MAPS All public transport operates on rough schedules, posted at bus and tram shelters and in metro stations. The schedules are a little confusing at first, but you'll get used to them. The most important thing to note, perhaps, is when the last ride of the night departs: Many a luckless traveler has waited late at night for a bus that won't be calling until 6am!

The transportation map produced by the Budapest Transport Authority (BKV térkép) is available at most metro ticket windows for a small fee. Since transportation routes are extremely difficult to read on most city maps, we suggest that you buy one of these handy maps if you plan to spend more than a few days in the city. In addition, on the map's reverse side is a full listing of routes, including the all-important night-bus routes.

NIGHT SERVICE Most of the Budapest transportation system closes down between 11:30pm or midnight and 5am. There are, however, 17 night routes (13 bus and 4 tram), and they're generally quite safe. A map of night routes is posted at many central tram and bus stops, and a full listing appears on the BKV transportation map. The no. 78É night bus follows the route of the Red metro line, while the no. 14É night bus follows the route of the Blue metro line. Though night buses often share the same numbers as buses on daytime routes (though with an É suffix, meaning éjszaka, or night), they may actually run different routes. Night buses require the standard, self-validated ticket. Many night buses skip stops, so pay attention.

UNDERPASSES   Underpasses are found beneath most major boulevards in Budapest. Underpasses are often crowded with vendors, shops, and the like, and many of them have as many as five or six different exits, each letting you out onto a different part of the square or street. Signs direct you to bus, tram, trolleybus, and metro stops, often using the word *fele,* meaning "toward." *Note:* Although Budapest is a very safe city, especially when compared to American cities of comparable size, underpasses tend to be among the more menacing places late at night, as various lowlifes enjoy hanging out in these subterranean confines.

Directions given throughout this book use a metro station as a starting point whenever possible. In cases where that's simply impossible, other major transportation hubs, such as Móricz Zsigmond körtér in southern Buda, are used as starting points.

BY METRO
You'll no doubt spend a lot of time in the Budapest metro. The system is clean and efficient, with trains running every 3 to 5 minutes from about 4:30am until about 11:30pm. The main shortcoming is that there are just three lines, only one of which crosses under the Danube to Buda. (A fourth line has long been planned, but it will be several years before it becomes a reality.) The three lines are universally known by color—Yellow, Red, and Blue. Officially, they have numbers as well (1, 2, and 3, respectively), but all Hungarians refer to them by color, and all signs are color coded. All three lines converge at **Deák tér**, the only point where any lines meet.

The **Yellow (1) line** is the oldest metro on the European continent. Built in 1894 as part of the Hungarian millennial celebration, it has been refurbished and restored to its original splendor. Signs for the Yellow line, lacking the distinctive colored M, are harder to spot than signs for the Blue and Red lines. Look for signs saying *földalatti* (underground). Each station has two separate entrances, one for each direction. The Yellow line runs from Vörösmarty tér, site of Gerbeaud's Cukrászda in the heart of central Pest, out the length of Andrássy út, past the Városliget (City Park), ending at Mexikói út, in a trendy residential part of Pest known as Zugló. So, depending on the direction you're heading, enter either the side marked IRÁNY MEXIKÓI ÚT or IRÁNY VÖRÖSMARTY TÉR. Incidentally, somewhere in the middle of the line is a stop called Vörösmarty utca; this is a small street running off Andrássy út and should not be confused with the terminus, Vörösmarty tér. (However, at each of these stops you will find a splendid traditional coffeehouse, Gerbaud and Lukács, respectively.) It's worth taking a ride on this line, with its distinct 19th-century atmosphere.

The **Red (2)** and **Blue (3) lines** are modern metros and to reach them you descend long, steep escalators. The Red line runs from Örs vezér tere in eastern Pest, through the center, and across the Danube to Batthyány tér, Moszkva tér, and finally Déli Station. Keleti Station is also along the Red line. The Blue line runs from Kőbánya-Kispest, in southeastern Pest, through the center, and out to Újpest-Központ in northern Pest. Nyugati Station is along the Blue line.

On the street above stations of both the Red and Blue lines are distinctive colored M signs. Tickets should be validated at automated boxes before you descend the escalator. When changing lines at Deák tér, you're required to validate another ticket (unless you have a special "metro transfer ticket"). The orange validating machines are in the hallways between lines but are easy to miss, particularly if there are big crowds.

BY BUS

There are about 200 different bus *(busz)* lines in greater Budapest. Many parts of the city, most notably the Buda Hills, are best accessed by bus. Although buses are the most difficult to use of Budapest's transportation choices, with patience (and a BKV map) you'll be able to get around in no time. With the exception of night buses, most lines are in service from about 4:30am to about 11:30pm. Some bus lines run far less frequently (or not at all) on weekends, while others run far more frequently (or only) on weekends. This information is both on the reverse of the BKV transportation map and on the schedules posted at every bus stop.

Black-numbered local buses constitute the majority of the city's lines. Red-numbered buses are express; generally, but not always, the express buses follow the same routes as local buses with the same number, simply skipping certain stops along the way. If the red number on the bus is followed by an *E,* the bus runs nonstop between terminals (whereas an *É*—with an accent mark—signifies *éjszaka,* meaning night). Depending on your destination, an express bus may be a much faster way of traveling. A few buses are labeled by something other than a number; one you'll probably use is the *Várbusz* (Palace Bus), a minibus that runs between Várfok utca, up the steep hillside from Buda's Moszkva tér, and the Castle District. The buses themselves have always been blue, though now some express buses are beginning to appear in red.

Tickets are self-validated onboard the bus by the mechanical red box found by each door. You can board the bus by any door. Unlike metro tickets, bus tickets are valid not for the line, but for the individual bus; you're not allowed to get off and reboard another bus going in the same direction without a new ticket. Tickets cannot be purchased from the driver; see "Fares" on p. 287 for information on where to purchase public transportation tickets.

The biggest problem for bus-riding travelers is the drivers' practice of skipping stops when no one is waiting to get on and no one has signaled to get off. To signal your intention to get off at the next stop, press the button above the door (beware—some drivers open only the doors that have been signaled). Most stops don't have their names posted; a list of stops is posted inside all buses, but if stops are skipped, you may lose track. Chances are, though, that the locals riding a given bus will know exactly where your stop is, and will kindly help you to reach your stop. You can also ask the driver to let you know when he has reached your stop.

Avoid buses in central areas during rush hours, since traffic tends to be quite bad. It pays to go a bit out of your way to use a metro or tram at these times instead, or simply to walk.

BY TRAM

You'll find Budapest's 34 bright-yellow tram lines (known as *villamos* in Hungarian) very useful, particularly nos. 4 and 6, which travel along the Outer Ring (Nagykörút), and nos. 47 and 49, which run along the Inner Ring. Tram no. 2, which travels along the Danube on the Pest side between Margit híd and Boráros tér, provides an incredible view of the Buda Hills, including the Castle District, and is far better than any sightseeing tour on a bus.

Tickets are self-validated onboard. As with buses, tickets are valid for one ride, not for the line itself. Trams stop at every station, and all doors open, regardless of whether anyone is waiting to get on. *Important:* The buttons near the tram doors are for emergency stops, not stop requests.

When a tram line is closed for maintenance, replacement buses ply the tram route. They go by the same number as the tram, with a V (for *villamos*) preceding the number. See "Fares" on p. 287 for information on where to purchase public transportation tickets.

BY TROLLEYBUS

Red trolleybuses are electric buses that receive power from a cable above the street. There are only 14 trolleybus lines in Budapest, all in Pest. Of particular interest to train travelers is no. 73, the fastest route between Keleti Station and Nyugati Station. All the information in the "By Bus" section above regarding boarding, ticket validation, and stop-skipping applies to trolleybuses as well. See "Fares" on p. 287 for information on where to purchase public transportation tickets.

BY HÉV

The **HÉV** is a suburban railway network that connects Budapest to various points along the city's outskirts. There are four HÉV lines; only one, the Szentendre line, is of serious interest to visitors (see "The Danube Bend," later in this chapter).

The terminus for the Szentendre HÉV line is Buda's Batthyány tér, also a station on the Red metro line. The train makes 10 stops in northern Buda and Óbuda en route to Szentendre. Most hotels, restaurants, and sights in northern Buda and Óbuda are best reached by the HÉV (so indicated in the directions given throughout this book). To reach Óbuda's Fő tér (Main Sq.), get off at the Árpád híd (Árpád Bridge) stop.

The HÉV runs regularly between 4am and 11:30pm. For trips within the city limits, the cost is one transit ticket, self-validated as on a bus or tram. Tickets to Szentendre cost 452 Ft ($2.25) (minus 170 Ft/85¢ for the portion of the trip within city limits if you have a valid day pass). HÉV tickets to destinations beyond the city limits are available at HÉV ticket windows at the Batthyány tér station, at the Margit híd station, or from the conductor onboard (no penalty assessed for such purchase).

BY COGWHEEL RAILWAY & FUNICULAR

Budapest's **cogwheel railway** *(fogaskerekű)* runs from Városmajor, across the street from the Hotel Budapest on Szilágyi Erzsébet fasor in Buda, to Széchenyi-hegy, one terminus of the Children's Railway (Gyermek Vasút) and site of Hotel Panoráma. The cogwheel railway runs from 5am to 11pm, and normal transportation tickets (see "Fares," above; self-validated onboard) are used. The pleasant route twists high into the Buda Hills; at 170 Ft (55¢/45p), it is well worth taking just for the ride.

The **funicular** *(sikló)* connects Buda's Clark Ádám tér, at the head of the Széchenyi Chain Bridge, with Dísz tér, just outside the Buda Castle. The funicular is one of only two forms of public transportation serving the Castle District (the **Várbusz** and bus no. 16 are the other possibilities; see "By Bus," above). An extremely steep and short ride (and greenhouse-hot on sunny days), the funicular runs at frequent intervals from 7:30am to 10pm (closed on alternate Mon). Tickets cost 650 Ft ($3.25/£1.65) to go up, and 550 Ft ($3/£1.40) on the way down for adults and 350 Ft ($1.75/90p) for children regardless of direction.

BY TAXI

We divide Budapest taxis into two general categories: large organized fleets and private fleets or privately owned taxis. If you only follow one piece of advice in this book, it's this: Do business with the former and avoid the latter. Because taxi regulations permit fleets (or private drivers) to establish their own rates (within certain parameters), fares vary greatly between the different fleets and among the private unaffiliated drivers.

The best rates are invariably those of the larger fleet companies. We particularly recommended **City Taxi** (© 1/211-1111). Other reliable fleets include **Volántaxi** (© 1/466-6666), **Rádió Taxi** (© 1/377-7777), **Fő Taxi** (© 1/222-2222), Tele5 (© 1/355-5555), 6×6 (© 1/266-6666), and **Budataxi** (© 1/233-3333). You can call one of these companies from your hotel or from a restaurant—or ask whomever is in charge to call for you—even if there are other private taxis waiting around outside. You will seldom, if ever, wait more than 5 minutes for a fleet taxi unless you're in an extremely remote neighborhood (or in bad weather).

Finally, you are most likely dealing with a dishonest driver if he asks you to pay for his return trip, asks to be paid in anything but forints, or quotes you a "flat rate" in lieu of running the meter. If you desire a station wagon, ask for a *"kombi"* when calling for your taxi, and in the summer you can also request an air-conditioned vehicle.

Tipping is usually not more than 10%. Hungarians usually round the bill up. If you think the driver has cheated you, then you certainly should not tip. In fact, it is recommended that you call the company and complain, as most will punish their members for untoward behavior.

Though most people call for a taxi or pick one up at a taxi stand (a stand is basically any piece of sidewalk or street where one or more drivers congregate), it is possible to hail one on the street, though the base rate will be substantially higher. At taxi stands in Budapest, the customer chooses with whom to do business; as we said before, go with a cab from one of the recommended fleets, even if it's not the first in line.

Additional pointers are found in the brochure *Taking a Taxi in Budapest,* available at Tourinform and elsewhere.

BY CAR

There's no reason to use a car for sightseeing in Budapest. You may, however, wish to rent a car for trips out of the city. Although Hertz, Avis, National, and Budget offices can be found in town and at the airport, marginally better deals can be had from some of the smaller companies. You are urged to reserve a rental car as early as possible. If you reserve from abroad, ask for written confirmation by fax or e-mail. If you don't receive a confirmation, it's wise to assume that the reservation has not been properly made.

We have quoted rates for the least expensive car type currently listed by each of the following recommended agencies:

We recommend **Fox Auto Rent,** XXII. Nagytétényi út 48–50, 1222 Budapest (© 1/382-9000; fax 1/382-9003; www.fox-autorent.com), which rents the Fiat Panda for 44€ ($55) per day for a rental of 1 to 3 days, and 223€ ($279) for a week, insurance and mileage included. They also require a deposit of 400€ ($500) on a credit card. Though located far from the city center, Fox will deliver the car to you at your hotel without charge between 8am and 6pm.

The more expensive **Denzel Europcar InterRent,** VIII. Üllöi út 60–62, 1082 Budapest (© 1/477-1080; fax 1/477-1099; www.nationalcar.hu), offers the Opel Corza or Fiat Punto for 55€ ($69) per day plus 9€ ($11) for insurance, or 46€ ($58) per day for 3 to 4 days. They also have a rental counter at the airport (© 1/296-6610), but here you pay an additional 12% airport tax.

VISITOR INFORMATION

Since Budapest continues to undergo rapid changes, published tourist information is often out-of-date. The best information source in the city is **Tourinform** (© 1/317-8992; www.hungarytourism.hu), the office of the Hungarian Tourist Board. Centrally located at V. Sütő u. 2, just off Deák tér (reached by all three metro lines) in Pest, the main office is open daily from 8am to 8pm. There is now another Tourinform office in the bustling entertainment district of Liszt Ferenc tér, open daily from 9am to 7pm in the high season (Liszt Ferenc tér is just down the street from Oktogon, reached by the Yellow line of the metro or tram no. 4 or 6). The staffs in both offices speak English and dispense advice on all tourist-related subjects, from concert tickets to pension rooms, from train schedules to horseback riding.

You can also access city information through the **"Touch Info"** user-friendly computer terminals located at the airport, at Déli Railway Station, at several of the larger metro stations, and in the market hall at Fővám tér.

The *Budapest Sun* (www.budapestsun.com) and *Budapest Times* (www.budapest times.hu), both English-language weekly newspapers, also have listings for concerts, theater, dance, film, and other events, along with restaurant reviews and the occasional interesting article; they are available at most hotels and many newsstands. *Budapest Week,* once a weekly magazine, is now strictly a website, **www.budapestweek.com**, which has a handy restaurant reservation network that lets you book your table online for free. **Ontheglobe.com** is another Web-based resource that provides articles about Hungary and previews of cultural events. (Full disclosure: We write and edit ontheglobe.com, so we're a bit biased.) **Xpatloop.com** and **pestiside.hu** also attempt to map out Budapest's cultural and social scene.

WHERE TO STAY

SEASONS

Most hotels and pensions in Budapest divide the year into three seasons. **High season** is roughly from March or April through September or October. (The weekend of the Grand Prix, which is the second weekend in Aug, is especially tight.) The week between Christmas and New Year's, Easter week, and the period of the Budapest Spring Festival (mid- to late Mar) are also considered high season. The months of March (excepting the Budapest Spring Festival in mid- to late Mar) and October and/or November are usually considered **midseason. Low season** is roughly November through February, except Christmas week. Some hotels discount as much as 30% in low season, while others offer no winter discounts—be sure to inquire.

PRICE CATEGORIES

Most hotels and pensions in Budapest list their prices in euros. Listing rates in euros is not just intended as a means of transition to the E.U. currency (Hungary is expected to adopt the euro sometime after 2010), it is also a hedge against forint inflation (though the forint has been surprisingly strong over the past few years). All hotels in Budapest accept payment in Hungarian forints as well as in foreign currencies. Where prices are quoted in euros, we provide a dollar conversion. The exchange rate used for this chapter is 1€ equals $1.20. When we list prices in forints, we provide U.S. dollar and British pound conversion rates, at a rate of 500 forint to $2.50 to £1.30.

All hotels are required to charge a 12% value-added tax (VAT). Most build the tax into their rates, while a few tack it on top of their rates. When booking a room, ask

Budapest Lodging, Dining & Attractions

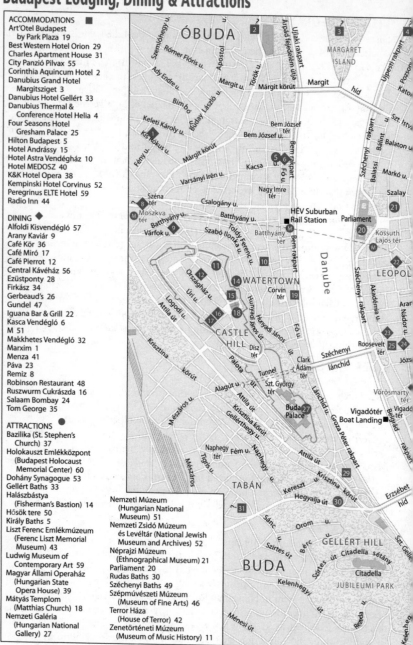

ACCOMMODATIONS ■
Art'Otel Budapest
  by Park Plaza 19
Best Western Hotel Orion 29
Charles Apartment House 31
City Panzió Pilvax 55
Corinthia Aquincum Hotel 2
Danubius Grand Hotel
  Margitsziget 3
Danubius Hotel Gellért 33
Danubius Thermal &
  Conference Hotel Helia 4
Four Seasons Hotel
  Gresham Palace 25
Hilton Budapest 5
Hotel Andrássy 1
Hotel Astra Vendégház 10
Hotel MEDOSZ 40
K&K Hotel Opera 38
Kempinski Hotel Corvinus 52
Peregrinus ELTE Hotel 59
Radio Inn 44

DINING ◆
Alföldi Kisvendéglő 57
Arany Kaviár 9
Café Kör 36
Café Miró 17
Café Pierrot 12
Central Kávéház 56
Ezüstponty 28
Firkász 34
Gerbeaud's 26
Gundel 47
Iguana Bar & Grill 22
Kasca Vendéglő 6
M 51
Makkhetes Vendéglő 32
Marxim 1
Menza 41
Páva 23
Remiz 8
Robinson Restaurant 48
Ruszwurm Cukrászda 16
Salaam Bombay 24
Tom George 35

ATTRACTIONS ●
Bazilika (St. Stephen's
  Church) 37
Holokauszt Emlékközpont
  (Budapest Holocaust
  Memorial Center) 60
Dohány Synagogue 53
Gellért Baths 33
Halászbástya
  (Fisherman's Bastion) 14
Hősök tere 50
Király Baths 5
Liszt Ferenc Emlékmúzeum
  (Ferenc Liszt Memorial
  Museum) 43
Ludwig Museum of
  Contemporary Art 59
Magyar Állami Operaház
  (Hungarian State
  Opera House) 39
Mátyás Templom
  (Matthias Church) 18
Nemzeti Galéria
  (Hungarian National
  Gallery) 27

Nemzeti Múzeum
  (Hungarian National
  Museum) 51
Nemzeti Zsidó Múzeum
  és Levéltár (National Jewish
  Museum and Archives) 52
Néprajzi Múzeum
  (Ethnographical Museum) 21
Parliament 20
Rudas Baths 30
Széchenyi Baths 49
Szépművészeti Múzeum
  (Museum of Fine Arts) 46
Terror Háza
  (House of Terror) 42
Zenetörténeti Múzeum
  (Museum of Music History) 11

whether the VAT is included in the quoted price. Unless otherwise indicated, prices in this book include the VAT.

Note: We have found that the websites of hotels are frequently inaccurate with respect to rates, so make sure to call the hotel to confirm.

THE INNER CITY & CENTRAL PEST
Very Expensive

Art'Otel Budapest by Park Plaza ★★   Opened in 2000 by a German chain, this is the first Art'Otel outside of Germany. The premise behind the concept is that each hotel spotlights the work of a single artist. In this case, the artist is Donald Sultan. There are more than 600 of his works in the hotel and he designed everything from the furniture and the carpets to the silverware. The modern side of the hotel is a seven-story building facing the Danube, while the rear comprises of four two-story baroque town houses, which now serve as rooms, suites, and the Chelsea Restaurant. Rooms on the top three floors of the new building facing the Danube command the best views, while rooms in the old houses have higher ceilings, some original fittings and features, but no view. Three floors are smoke-free.

I. bem rakpart 16–19, 1011 Budapest. © **800/814-7000** in North America, 0800/169-6128 in Britain, or 1/487-9487-5500. Fax 1/487-9488. www.artotels.com. 164 units. 198€–228€ ($237–$273) double; 100€ ($120) extra for suite; 20€ ($24) Danube view supplement. Lower weekend and Internet rates. VAT included. Children 12 and under stay free in parent's room. Rates include breakfast. AE, MC, V. Parking 3,000 Ft ($15/£7.70) per day. Metro: Batthyány tér (Red line). **Amenities:** Restaurant; bar; sauna; exercise room; concierge; valet parking; business center; art shop; salon; limited room service; wireless Internet in public areas; rooms for those w/limited mobility. *In room:* A/C, TV w/pay movies, dataport w/ISDN, wireless Internet, minibar, coffeemaker (in suites and executive rooms), hair dryer, iron/ironing board on request, safe, voice mail, robe.

Four Seasons Hotel Gresham Palace ★★★   Prepare to have your breath taken away as you step into the Art Nouveau entrance of this elegant, palatial property, on par with the finest in the world. Directly opposite the Chain Bridge and a postcardlike view of the Buda Castle, the Four Seasons has the most picturesque location of any hotel in town, and rooms overlooking the Danube can rightfully claim to have the best views in the city. Opened in June 2004, the hotel was originally completed in 1906, and was nearly destroyed in World War II. It has now been painstakingly restored—in a 5-year, $110-million renovation—down to the last detail. Like all Four Seasons' properties, this hotel strives to pamper guests in every way. From the lobby topped with a glass cupola and the chandelier made from clear glass leaves hanging in front of the reception desk to the fitness center and spa spanning the entire top "attic" floor of the hotel and bathrooms fitted with Spanish marble and deep-soak bathtubs, attention to detail here is strong. While all rooms are beautiful, the most expensive suites are equipped with bedroom sets made of mother of pearl. The restaurant Pava serves Italian cuisine and is one of the best in town, and the Gresham Kávéház is located on the site of a popular 1930s cafe and is a bit less formal. The Bar and Lobby Lounge is located below another glass cupola, serving light snacks, a large selection of wine, and an extensive martini list (rare in Hungary), along with live nightly piano music.

V. Roosevelt tér 5–6, 1051 Budapest. © **800/819-5053** in North America, or 1/268-6000. Fax 1/268-5000. www.fourseasons.com/budapest. 179 units. 280€–830€ ($336–$996) double; 950€–4,500€ ($1,140–$5,400) suite. VAT not included. Children stay free in parent's room. Breakfast 26€ ($31) extra. AE, DC, MC, V. Parking 39€ ($45) per day. Metro: Vörösmarty tér (all lines). **Amenities:** 2 restaurants; bar; indoor swimming pool; sauna; exercise room; concierge; business center; salon; airport transfer; 24-hr. room service; massage; laundry service; dry cleaning. *In room:* A/C, satellite TV w/pay movies, fax machine available, high-speed Internet access, minibar, hair dryer, safe, robe, newspapers, voice mail.

Kempinski Hotel Corvinus 🎔🎔 Located in the heart of Pest, just off Deák tér, this slick German-run hotel, opened in 1992, has quickly earned a reputation as the hotel of choice for corporate visitors to Budapest (and also big-act musicians—Madonna, Michael Jackson, the Rolling Stones, and Bob Dylan have all stayed here). The building itself is, at least from the outside, a cement behemoth, one of a number of ugly new buildings marring this neighborhood (though the recent reconstruction of nearby Erzsébet tér has made the immediate neighborhood a lot nicer). On the inside, however, the decor is modern sleek German and everything is quietly and unmistakably luxurious. The rooms are as well appointed as one might expect from such a hotel, and soundproof windows shield guests from the noise of the busy traffic below. Temporary art exhibitions line the walls, and the hotel has an impressive art and antiques collection. The impressive spa was renovated in early 2005, and transports guests to Asia with its authentic Tjai masseuses and Asian-accented rooms. It includes a fitness room, massage rooms, a solarium, steam baths, a sauna, a pool, and a number of other features. Rooms are equipped with up-to-date technology, including mobile Internet connections. The hotel has a number of excellent restaurants and its American-style buffet breakfast (not included in the rate) is exceptional. Almost half the rooms are smoke-free.

V. Erzsébet tér 7–8, 1051 Budapest. ℂ **800/426-3135** in North America, 00800/426-313-55 in Britain, or 1/429-3777. Fax 1/429-4777. www.kempinski-budapest.com. 365 units. 260€–450€ ($312–$540) double; 570€–2,600€ ($684–$3,120) suite. VAT not included. Children 12 and under stay free in parent's room. Breakfast 27€ ($32) extra. AE, MC, V. Parking 7,000 Ft ($35/£18) per day. Metro: Deák tér (all lines). **Amenities:** 3 restaurants; 2 bars; indoor swimming pool; sauna; exercise room; concierge; car-rental desk; business center; conference facilities; shops; salon; 24-hr. room service; massage; laundry service; dry cleaning; rooms for those w/limited mobility. *In room:* A/C, satellite TV w/pay movies, high-speed Internet access, minibar, hair dryer, safe, separate shower, robe, 2 phones.

Expensive

K & K Hotel Opera 🎔 🅥🅐🅛🅤🅔 Operated by the Austrian K & K hotel chain, this tasteful, elegant establishment opened in 1994 and expanded in 1998. A complete renovation was completed in September 2005, and the hotel is a few steps above most of the city's other four-star hotels. Directly across the street from the Opera House in central Pest, the hotel building blends nicely with the surrounding architecture. The interior design is now even pleasing, with an understated elegance. The hotel is on a quiet residential street, and the soundproof windows in the guest rooms keep out street noise. A tastefully decorated bar/cafe/restaurant echoes the Asian touches found throughout the hotel. The staff is uniformly friendly and helpful, even when inundated with groups. This hotel is not only within close proximity of the Opera House, but is also right near Budapest's theater district. Half of the rooms are now nonsmoking, but there are no wheelchair-accessible rooms.

VI. Révay u. 24, 1065 Budapest. ℂ **1/269-0222.** Fax 1/269-0230. www.kkhotels.com. 205 units. 168€ ($201) single; 209€ ($250) double; 336€ ($403) suite. Rates include breakfast. VAT included. AE, DC, MC, V. Parking 15€ ($12). Metro: Opera (Yellow line). **Amenities:** Exercise room; sauna; tour desk; car rental; business center; massage; babysitting; laundry service; currency exchange; Internet corner. *In room:* A/C, TV, high-speed Internet connection, minibar, coffeemaker, hair dryer, safe.

Moderate

City Panzió Pilvax 🎔 Opened in 1997, this is one of three Inner City pensions owned by the Taverna Hotel group, which also owns the large Hotel Taverna on Váci utca. The staff is friendly and the rooms are clean and functional, but this place lacks the charm found in many of the pensions in the Buda Hills. It costs a bit more than the Buda Hills pensions, too, but the location is obviously what you are paying for.

The pension is on a narrow, quiet street just a few minutes by foot from the hubbub of central Pest.

V. Pilvax köz 1–3, 1052 Budapest. ✆ **1/266-7660.** Fax 1/317-6396. www.taverna.hu. 32 units. 79€ ($94) single; 99€ ($118) double. Rates 20% lower in low season. Rates include breakfast. AE, DC, MC, V. Metro: Ferenciek tere (Blue line). **Amenities:** 2 restaurants; bar; bike rental; business center; laundry service. *In room:* A/C, TV w/pay movies, minibar, hair dryer, safe.

Peregrinus ELTE Hotel *(Value)*   Peregrinus ELTE Hotel is ideally situated in the heart of the Inner City of Pest, across the street from a historic Serbian church on a small side street half a block from Váci utca, the popular pedestrian-only street. This is the guesthouse of Pest's ELTE University. While many guests are affiliated with the university, the hotel is open to the public as well. The building dates from the turn of the 20th century and was renovated before the hotel was opened in 1994. The rooms are simple but comfortable. You should reserve well in advance. Payment must be in cash in Hungarian forints.

V. Szerb u. 3, 1056 Budapest. ✆ **1/266-4911.** Fax 1/266-4913. 26 units. 24,000 Ft ($120/£62) double; 18,000 Ft ($90/£46) in high season. Rates include breakfast. No credit cards. No parking. Metro: Kálvin tér (Blue line). *In room:* A/C in the attic units, TV, minibar.

Inexpensive

Hotel MEDOSZ ★ *(Value)*   The MEDOSZ was formerly a trade-union hotel for agricultural workers. It is located on Jókai tér, in the heart of Pest's theater district, just across the street from the bustling Liszt Ferenc tér. The neighborhood surrounding the hotels is also one of Pest's centers of nightlife. A couple of blocks from the Opera House, this is as good as it gets off the river in central Pest. The rooms are simple but clean. The hotel remains a great value given its location. Unfortunately, this hotel maintains discriminative pricing, with a separate pricing structure for Hungarians than for international guests. Next door to Hotel MEDOSZ is one of Budapest's special treats for children: a puppet theater *(bábszínház)*.

VI. Jókai tér 9, 1061 Budapest. ✆ **1/374-3000.** Fax 1/332-4316. www.medoszhotel.hu. 67 units. 55€ ($66) double. Rates are 20% lower in low season. Rates include breakfast. DC, MC, V. Metered on-street parking difficult in neighborhood; there is an indoor garage in nearby Aradi utca. Metro: Oktogon (Yellow line). **Amenities:** Restaurant; bar; laundry service. *In room:* TV.

CENTRAL BUDA
Very Expensive

Danubius Hotel Gellért ★ *(Kids)*   This splendid, sprawling Art Nouveau hotel first opened in 1918. Much of it is run down now, but 38 rooms were refurbished in 2000, and there are tentative plans for more renovations. It's still one of the most charming hotels in Budapest, and the spa is among Budapest's most famous. Located at the base of Gellért Hill in Buda, on the bank of the Danube, the Gellért is one of several thermal bath hotels in Budapest that are managed or owned by Danubius Hotels. The circular hotel lobby has marble columns and a mezzanine level. The quality and size of the rooms vary greatly—it seems to be hit-or-miss. Only 29 rooms have air-conditioning and 38 rooms don't have tubs. Some rooms with balconies offer great views over the Danube, but these can be noisy since the hotel fronts loud and busy Gellért Square. Many of the back-facing rooms afford nice views of the baths and the neighboring gardens and buildings. For the best rooms, ask for a Danube-facing king-size refurbished room.

While the majority of guests don't come for the official spa treatment, there are a number of spa-related facilities that all guests can use free of charge: two pools (one indoor, and one outdoor with child-pleasing artificial waves), a steam room, and the Art Nouveau Gellért Baths, perhaps the most popular of Budapest's thermal baths (most travelers visit them at least once during their stay). If you come in the summer, a nighttime plunge under the stars is a must.

XI. Gellért tér 1, 1111 Budapest. ⓒ 1/889-5500. Fax 1/889-5505. www.danubiusgroup.com/gellert. 234 units. 130€–210€ ($156–$252) double; 270€ ($324) suite. Rates include breakfast and use of the spa. AE, DC, MC, V. Parking 8€ ($9.60) per night. Tram: 47 or 49 from Deák tér. **Amenities:** 3 restaurants; bar; 2 swimming pools (1 indoor, 1 outdoor) and thermal pools; sauna; tour desk; car rental; business center; shops; limited room service; massage; babysitting; laundry service. *In room:* A/C (some rooms), TV, minibar, hair dryers (in refurbished rooms), robe, safe.

Expensive

Hotel Astra Vendégház *Finds* This little gem of a hotel opened in 1996 in a renovated 300-year-old building on a quiet side street in Buda's lovely Watertown neighborhood. The rooms are large, with wood floors and classic Hungarian-style furniture; the overall effect is a far more homey and pleasant space than is found in most Budapest hotel rooms. Indeed, the hotel is tasteful through and through, and the staff is friendly. Some rooms overlook the inner courtyard, while others face the street. There is a dark cellar bar with a pool table, and a simple, unadorned breakfast room.

I. Vám u. 6, 1011 Budapest. ⓒ 1/214-1906. Fax 1/214-1907. www.hotelastra.hu. 12 units. All units are doubles and cost 150€ ($180) for 2 people and 90€ ($108) for 1. No credit cards. Rates include breakfast. Rates 10% lower in low season. Only meter parking is available on street. Metro: Batthyány tér (Red line). **Amenities:** Restaurant; bar; car-rental desk; babysitting (upon request). *In room:* A/C, TV, minibar.

Moderate

Best Western Hotel Orion Conveniently located in Buda's Watertown neighborhood, between Castle Hill and the Danube, this small five-story hotel is tucked away on a relatively quiet street near many of the city's best sights. Though the rooms are bright and cheerful enough, and five have balconies, they unfortunately lack castle and river views. Döbrentei tér, a messy but convenient transportation hub, is a few minutes away by foot. Pets are welcome.

I. Döbrentei u. 13, 1013 Budapest. ⓒ 1/356-8933 or 1/356-8583. Fax 1/375-5418. www.hotels.hu/orion. 30 units. 88€ ($105) single; 112€ ($134) double. Rates include breakfast. Rates lower in low season. AE, DC, MC, V. Free parking on street. Tram: 19 from Batthyány tér to Döbrentei tér. Pets welcome. **Amenities:** Restaurant; sauna; tour desk; car-rental desk; limited room service; nonsmoking floors. *In room:* A/C, TV, dataport, minibar.

Inexpensive

Charles Apartment House *Value* This is one of the better housing deals in Budapest. Owner Károly Szombati has gradually amassed 70 apartments in a group of apartment buildings in a dull but convenient Buda neighborhood (near the Hotel Novotel). The apartments are a 30-minute walk or a 5-minute bus ride from downtown Pest. All accommodations are ordinary Budapest apartments in ordinary residential buildings. The furnishings are comfortable and clean, and all apartments have full bathrooms and kitchens. Hegyalja út is a very busy street, but only two apartments face out onto it; the rest are in the interior or on the side of the building. A nearby park has tennis courts and a track. There is a new restaurant in the apartment complex, and a pub and grocery store nearby. The friendly, English-speaking reception is open 24 hours.

I. Hegyalja út 23, 1016 Budapest. ⓒ 1/212-9169. Fax 1/202-2984. www.charleshotel.hu. 70 units. 48€–136€ ($57–$163) apt for 1–4. Rates include breakfast. Rates approximately 5% lower in low season. AE, DC, MC, V. Parking 8.50€ ($10) per day. Bus: 78 from Keleti pu. to Mészáros utca. **Amenities:** Restaurant; bar; bike rental; tour desk; business center; babysitting; laundry service. *In room:* A/C, TV, kitchen, minibar, hair dryer, safe.

THE CASTLE DISTRICT
Very Expensive

Hilton Budapest   One of only two hotels in Buda's charming Castle District (the other is Hotel Kulturinnov), the Hilton, built in 1977, was widely considered to be the city's classiest hotel at the time. Its location, on Hess András tér, next door to Matthias Church and the Fisherman's Bastion, is no less than spectacular, but these days the Hilton lags behind many of its competitors in terms of service and facilities. The hotel's award-winning design incorporates both the ruins of a 13th-century Dominican church (the church tower rises above the hotel) and the baroque facade of a 17th-century Jesuit college, which makes up the hotel's main entrance. The ruins were carefully restored during the hotel's construction, and the results are uniformly magnificent. The building is clearly modern, and its exterior tends to stand out from the old surrounding Castle District architecture. The hotel has been undergoing renovations since 2000, and nearly everything but the restaurant has been refurbished. More expensive rooms have views over the Danube, with a full vista of the Pest skyline; rooms on the other side of the hotel overlook the delightful streets of the Castle District. Rooms are handsomely furnished and are equipped with such amenities as two-line telephones, WebTV, and bathrobes. The luxurious Dominican Restaurant has an international menu; dinner is accompanied by piano music. The more traditional Corvina Restaurant has a Hungarian menu and nightly Gypsy music. Drinks are served in the tiny Faust Wine Cellar in the abbey and the Lobby Bar, which has outdoor tables behind the hotel by the Fisherman's Bastion. The lovely Dominican Courtyard is the site of summer concerts. There are 122 smoke-free rooms.

I. Hess András tér 1–3, 1014 Budapest. ⓒ 1/488-6600. Fax 1/488-6644. www.hilton.com. 322 units. 140€–260€ ($168–$312) double; 450€–2,000€ ($540–$2,400) suite. VAT not included. Children stay free in parent's room. Breakfast 25€ ($30) extra. AE, DC, MC, V. Parking for 26€ ($31) per day in garage. Bus: Várbusz from Moszkva tér or no. 16 from Deák tér. **Amenities:** 2 restaurants; 2 bars; exercise room; sauna; concierge; tour desk; free airport minibus; shops; business center; meeting facilities; salon; 24-hr. room service; babysitting; laundry service; rooms for those w/limited mobility. *In room:* A/C, TV w/pay movies, WebTV, dataport, minibar, coffeemaker, hair dryer, iron/ironing board (on request), safe.

OUTER PEST
Very Expensive

Danubius Thermal & Conference Hotel Helia 🏃🏃 *Kids*   The Thermal Hotel Helia is one of several so-called "thermal" hotels in Budapest now managed and owned by Danubius Hotels. The hotel originally opened in 1990 as a Hungarian-Finnish joint venture. Despite the change in ownership, it continues to provide all the spa- and sauna-related amenities of the two cultures. While the majority of guests do not come for the official spa treatment, there are a number of spa-related facilities that all guests can use free of charge: thermal baths, a swimming pool, a sauna, a Jacuzzi, steam baths, more than a dozen types of massages, and a fitness room. The bright, sunny guest rooms sport tall windows. Some rooms have balconies, and four suites have private saunas. Four of the six floors have been refurbished and offer high-speed Internet access, while the others only offer dial-up. The Jupiter Restaurant offers international cuisine with live music at dinner and serves both buffet and a la carte lunches and dinners.

XIII. Kárpát u. 62–64, 1133 Budapest. ⓒ 1/889-5800. Fax 1/889-5801. www.danubiushotels.com/helia. 262 units (5 with wheelchair access). 135€–145€ ($162–$174) single; 154€–164€ ($185–$197) double; 266€–388€ ($319–$465) suite. VAT included. Danube view 10€ ($12) extra. Rates include breakfast and use of spa facilities. AE, MC, V. Trolleybus: 79 from Keleti Station. **Amenities:** 2 restaurants; indoor pool; thermal baths; health club; spa; business center; conference facilities; various shops; salon/barber; room service (6am–10pm); massage; babysitting;

same-day laundry service; dry cleaning; nonsmoking rooms; dentist; rooms for those w/limited mobility. *In room:* A/C, TV, dataport, minibar, iron/ironing board.

Expensive

Hotel Andrássy ★★ *Finds*   The Hotel Andrássy is a little gem of a hotel, located in an exclusive embassy neighborhood just off Pest's Andrássy út, a minute's journey on foot from Heroes' Square and the City Park, and a 25-minute walk from the center of Pest. The lobby is spacious and tasteful, with marble columns. The enormous suites are marvelous, featuring luxuriously large double beds, spacious bathrooms with massage showers, and vintage Hungarian furniture, carpets, and prints. There's a safe in each suite and at the reception desk. The standard rooms, although quite nice and also furnished with vintage Hungarian furniture, carpets, and prints, can't compare with the suites in spaciousness, so a splurge is recommended here. Half of the guest rooms come with a terrace.

VI. Munkácsy Mihály u. 5–7, 1063 Budapest. © **1/321-2000.** Fax 1/322-9445. www.andrassyhotel.com. 70 units. 271€ ($325) double; 407€ ($488) suite. AE, MC, V. Parking 17€ ($20) per day. Metro: Bajza utca (Yellow line). **Amenities:** Restaurant; indoor heated swimming pool; exercise room; sauna; concierge; business center; 24-hr. room service. *In room:* TV/VCR, dataport, minibar, safe.

Moderate

Radio Inn ★ *Value*   As the official guesthouse of Hungarian National Radio, the Radio Inn houses many visiting dignitaries, though it is also open to the public. The inn is in an exclusive embassy neighborhood (it's located next door to the embassy of the People's Republic of China), a stone's throw from City Park, and a block from Pest's grand Andrássy út. The metro's Yellow line takes you into the center of Pest in 5 minutes; alternatively, it's a 30-minute walk. Behind the building, there's an enormous private courtyard full of flowers. The huge apartments (all with fully equipped, spacious kitchens) are comfortably furnished and painstakingly clean. Note that the toilets and bathrooms are separate, European-style. The management is somewhat old-system (read: begrudging with information, slightly suspicious of foreigners), yet cordial enough. Make sure you reserve well ahead of arrival. The restaurant housed in the same building is a superb place for dinner.

VI. Benczúr u. 19, 1068 Budapest. © **1/342-8347** or 1/322-8284. Fax 1/322-8284. www.radioinn.hu. 36 units. 52€ ($62), 75€ ($90), and 92€ ($110) for 1-, 2-, and 3-person apts, respectively. Rates about 10%–20% lower in low season. Breakfast 7€ ($8.40) extra. AE, MC, V. Limited parking available on street. Metro: Bajza utca (Yellow line). **Amenities:** Restaurant; bar; 24-hr. room service; laundry service; nonsmoking rooms. *In room:* TV, kitchen (apts only), minibar, fridge.

ÓBUDA
Very Expensive

Corinthia Aquincum Hotel ★ *Kids*   Located on the banks of the Danube, just minutes from Óbuda's lovely Old City center, the Corinthia Aquincum Hotel was opened in 1991. This is a "thermal" hotel, though not all guests come for the spa facilities. Spa-related facilities that all guests can use free of charge include a swimming pool, a sauna, thermal baths, a Jacuzzi, a kneipp pool, a steam bath, a hydromassage shower (in which you control the directions and strengths of the many jets), and a fitness room. This delightful, modern hotel is built on the site of a Roman spa, hence its Roman theme. The rooms are cheerful, with soundproof windows and complimentary bathrobes. The spa facilities are really the main attraction here, and water is pumped in from Margit Island. The Restaurant Apicius serves both lunch and dinner, with a salad bar and buffet lunch. The chef has been named the best young chef by the Hungarian Society of

Restaurateurs, and the Sunday wellness brunch is popular with locals. There's live piano or Gypsy music nightly. The Iris Night Club has live music and shows nightly, and the Calix Bar on the ground level is a more relaxed place for drinks and light snacks.

III. Árpád fejedelem útja 94, 1036 Budapest. ℂ **1/436-4100.** Fax 1/436-4156. www.corinthia.hu. 310 units. 220€ ($264) single; 230€ ($276) double; 410€ ($492) suite. 25€ ($30) executive room supplement. Rates include breakfast, spa facilities usage, and VAT. Children 12 and under stay free in parent's room. DC, MC, V. Parking available for 12€ ($14) in garage. Train: HÉV suburban railway from Batthyány tér to Árpád híd. Small pets allowed. **Amenities:** Restaurant; 2 bars; indoor heated pool; health club; spa; Jacuzzi; sauna; bike rental; concierge; car-rental desk; currency exchange; meeting facilities; shops; business center; salon; 24-hr. room service; babysitting; laundry service; dry cleaning (weekdays only); executive rooms. *In room:* A/C, TV, dataport, minibar, hair dryer, robe, safe (executive rooms), trouser press (executive rooms).

Moderate

Hotel Római ✦ *Finds* A former resort for minor Communist Party officials, this hotel is a bit off the beaten track, but its location in the Római Fürdő section of Óbuda, on the banks of the Danube, is refreshingly peaceful. The lobby is spacious and comfortable, equipped with pool tables and a bar. The rooms were recently renovated and refurbished, though they are pretty generic in design. Each room has a balcony. There's an outdoor swimming pool and a large garden. It takes a while to get here from the center of Budapest (especially if you do not have a car), but you will feel as if you are staying in the countryside.

III. Szent János u. 16, 1039 Budapest. ℂ/fax **1/388-6167.** 24 units; 12 apts. 56€ ($67) double; 82€ ($98) apt (sleeps 4). Breakfast included. V. Ample free parking. Train: Suburban HÉV line from Batthyány tér to Római Fürdő; then bus no. 34 to Szent János utca. **Amenities:** Restaurant; bar; outdoor pool; car-rental desk. *In room:* TV, fridge.

MARGARET ISLAND
Expensive

Danubius Grand Hotel Margitsziget ✦✦ This is one of only two hotels on Margaret Island, Budapest's most popular park. Though two bridges connect the island with the rest of the city, vehicular traffic (except one city bus) is forbidden except for access to the hotels. Located on the northern tip of lovely Margaret Island, in the middle of the Danube, this hotel was originally built in 1873. Destroyed in World War II, it was restored and reopened in 1987, and has a Bauhaus style and a lovely country hunting-lodge feel to it, with lots of dark wood, green leather chairs, and marble floors and columns. An underground tunnel connects the hotel to the adjacent Thermal Hotel Margitsziget. While the majority of guests don't come for the official spa treatment, a number of spa-related facilities at the Thermal Hotel can be used free of charge, including the swimming pool, the sauna, and the thermal bath. The rooms are standard for a four-star hotel, and each is slightly different, some with balconies. Many of the rooms have retained the original light fittings and other features, but a few of them only have showers. The fitness room, sauna, and pools were recently modernized to meet the highest standards. The formal Széchenyi Restaurant serves international/Hungarian cuisine, including special diet dishes and kosher meals on request, along with live Gypsy music. There is also terrace dining. There are several bars, including the lively Dreher Bierstube. The hotel is smoke-free.

XIII. Margitsziget, 1138 Budapest. ℂ **800/448-4321** in North America, or 1/889-4700. Fax 1/889-4939. www.danubius hotels.com. 164 units. 135€–148€ ($162–$177) single; 154€–168€ ($184–$201) double; 178€–228€ ($213–$273) suite. Rates include breakfast, VAT, and spa facilities. AE, DC, MC, V. Parking 13€ ($16) per day. **Amenities:** Restaurant; 3 bars; access to Thermal Hotel's swimming pool, thermal bath, spa, and sauna; shops; Jacuzzi; car rental; business center; salon; 24-hr. room service; laundry service; dry-cleaning service; travel agency; wireless Internet in public areas; rooms for those w/limited mobility. *In room:* A/C, TV, dataport, minibar, coffeemaker, safe, phone.

WHERE TO DINE

Budapest features an increasingly diverse range of restaurants to go along with those more traditional eateries that have stood the test of time. Ethnic restaurants have appeared on the scene in the last decade; you'll find Japanese, Korean, Indian, Middle Eastern, Greek, and Mexican restaurants in the city. Of course, most tourists understandably want to sample authentic Hungarian food while in Budapest. Each restaurant has its own story and character. In this city, traditional fare runs the gamut from greasy to gourmet; there are few palates that can't be pleased here. Budapest has gained a reputation for good dining at reasonable prices, so live it up.

However, one warning: While this country is landlocked, many restaurants pride themselves of their fresh seafood delights. Many Hungarians probably hark back to a time when the sea was a part of this land, and some even think that the sea is closer than it actually is. The fact is, such a promise is hard to keep; **we recommend staying away from imported seafood.** At traditional Hungarian restaurants you will find delightful local fish: **Szeged** or **Tisza** fish soups are delicious, and far better than a far-from-fresh seafood platter.

WARNING   The U.S. Embassy circulates a list of restaurants that engage in "unethical business practices" such as "excessive billing," using "physical intimidation" to compel payment of excessive bills, and "assaulting customers" for nonpayment of excessive bills. If you don't want to encounter the "restaurant mafia," avoid these places. The current list includes **Városközpont** (accessible by outside elevator), Budapest V district, Váci utca 16; **La Dolce Vita,** Október 6. utca 8; **Nirvana Night Club,** Szent István krt. 13; **Ti'Amo Bar,** Budapest IX district, Ferenc körút 19–21; **Diamond Club,** Budapest II district, Bimbó út 3; and **Pigalle Night Club,** Budapest VIII district, Kiss József utca 1–3.

You can always check the embassy website for updated information: visit http://budapest.usembassy.gov/tourist_advisory.html.

THE INNER CITY & CENTRAL PEST
Expensive

Páva 𝒢𝒢 ITALIAN   The restaurant of Budapest's truly world-class hotel must be elegant and suave at the same time, and this one is both. While the atmosphere here is a tad stiff, the dining experience is memorable. Make sure you leave yourself a lot of time to enjoy the Páva, however, which serves really great Italian cuisine: this is a 3-hour, six-course meal, and if you are lucky the friendly Italian restaurant manager Andrea Colla will guide you through a dinner in which four kinds of wines are served. We started with warm baby artichoke with provolone cheese and arugula served with a light balsamic dressing. Then came the best part of the feast: a porcini and truffle cappuccino with wild mushrooms and taleggio toast which was basically a mushroom soup, but exquisite and truly memorable. Next was a pumpkin and scampi risotto, which was followed by a bitter and truly unsavory grenade apple and Campari gratiné. It was supposed to guide us into the main course, but it just didn't work. The roasted duck breast with wild mushrooms served with folded ravioli was excellent, however, and it was a pleasure just dining in this building, one of Budapest's most beautiful.

Roosevelt tér 5–6. ℂ 1/268-5100. Reservations recommended. 6-course menu 9,800 Ft ($49/£25), with wines 18,000 Ft ($90/£46). AE, DC, MC, V. Mon–Sat 6–10pm. Metro: Deák tér (all lines) or Kossuth tér (Red line).

Moderate

Café Kör ✿ HUNGARIAN CONTEMPORARY   This centrally located restaurant began as a coffeehouse in 1995, and in subsequent years it developed both in terms of its space and in cuisine to the comfortable and reliable restaurant that it is today. Just a stone's throw away from the Basilica, the owners developed Café Kör based on models of simple decor and attentive cuisine seen in other international capitals. The restaurant has become increasingly popular due to its proximity to four- and five-star hotels, notably the Hotel Four Seasons Gresham Palace. We recommend this restaurant because you will always be satisfied, although not necessarily overly impressed.

V. Sas u. 17. ✆ 1/311-0053. Reservations recommended. Soup 490 Ft–680 Ft ($2.50–$3.50/£1.30–£1.75); starters 730 Ft–2,300 Ft ($4.95–$9.95/£1.90–£5.90); main courses 1,600 Ft–3,580 Ft ($8.45–$25/£4.10–£9.20). No credit cards. Mon–Sat 10am–11pm. Metro: Bajcsy-Zsilinszky út (Yellow line).

Firkász ✿✿ *Value* HUNGARIAN CONTEMPORARY   A reminder that traditions can live on and become reborn in the form of new and lively places like Firkász. "Tradition is our future" is their motto of sorts, one that the immaculately dressed manager Gergely Sallai takes very seriously. There is a turn-of-the-20th-century feeling to the restaurant, and yet it remains contemporary. This place has the roots of a magical place that keeps old-style traditions alive. The eatery is decorated with a wealth of wine bottles, and the walls are pasted with early-20th-century newspapers, old pictures, telephones, or clocks. It is the favorite eatery of the finest young Hungarian film-director, the 30-year-old Kornél Mundruczó, who is an almost daily regular here, in the old-world style. Some regulars venture in for a drink or meal at the bar, while others are seated and watch the lively accordion player, or a tad tipsy or more gathering of tourists. The restaurant serves a wide selection—60 to 80 strong—of Hungarian wines. We had a tender and rich deer ragout with mashed potatoes, but choose from a vast selection of Hungarian specialties like Szeged Goulash, gooseliver, or wild game.

XIII. Tátra u. 18. ✆ 1/450-1118. Reservations recommended. Soup 590 Ft–1,390 Ft ($2.95–$6.95/£1.50–£3.60); starters 990 Ft–2,390 Ft ($4.95–$12/£2.55–£6.15); main courses 1,999 Ft–4,690 Ft ($10–$23/£5.15–£12). MC, V. Daily noon–midnight. Tram: 4 or 6 to Jászai Mari tér.

Iguana Bar & Grill ✿✿ *Kids* MEXICAN   Colorfully decorated and always buzzing with activity, you might have trouble finding a seat at this buzzing restaurant. This is a real hangout for Budapest expatriates, but also draws younger crowds and families. The decor includes a fare of old Mexican posters, reproductions from Diego Rivera oddities, and strangely, even a reproduction of an old master painting of the Last Supper. Iguana is known for home-style service and reliable, good-ol' Mexican food: quesadillas, chiles, fajitas, burritos, enchiladas, plus vegetarian options. For those who are adventuresome, try the enticing fajitas made of marinated strips of tenderloin, chicken, and shrimp. The fajitas are grilled on a sizzling hot steamy iron platter with onions and peppers. Jenő's Quesadilla (formerly Gino's) is my special treat, which includes a red pepper next to it on the menu and is purportedly named after a Budapest expatriate. You might also try the Iguana Beer, made especially for the restaurant by a small Csepel Island brewery.

Zóltán u. 16. ✆ 1/331-4352. www.iguana.hu. Reservations recommended. Appetizers 600 Ft–1,200 Ft ($3–$6/£1.55–£3.10); main courses 1,800 Ft–3,300 Ft ($9–$17/£4.65–£8.50). AE, DISC, MC, V. Daily 11:30am–12:30am (Fri–Sat until 1:30am). Metro: Kossuth tér (Red line).

M ✿✿ HUNGARIAN CONTEMPORARY   French cuisine and atmosphere are blended with Hungarian flavors in this restaurant that serves its water in Communist-era jugs—and what it saves on the furnishings, it invests in good, simple, and fresh foods. The decor here is as simple as it gets, with curtains and flowers literally drawn on the walls in simple lines. Next to the popular cafe square at Liszt Ferenc Tér, the atmosphere is homelike with Spanish or French music playing quietly in the background. Miklós Sulyok, the owner of this restaurant, is well known in the liberal circles of Budapest politics and has cohorts among the poets, writers, and artists of the capital. This small two-floor restaurant has a very snug atmosphere and even serves homemade bread. The menu changes on a daily basis, and let this be a surprise for the visitors. We enjoyed a grilled Viking steak served with sausages and potatoes on a large wooden plate. The chef makes a point of creating meals on a whim, based on what he finds fresh at the market. Because of the home-style nature of this restaurant, some of the plates may not always be available . . . but the chef will always be able to dream something up for you.

VII. Kertész utca 48. ⓒ 1/342-8991. www.rajzoltetterem.hu. Soups 650 Ft–750 Ft ($3.25–$3.75/£1.70–£1.95); starters 1,350 Ft–1,550 Ft ($6.75–$7.75/£3.50–£4); main courses 1,250 Ft–2,550 Ft ($6.25–$13/£3.20–£6.55). No credit cards. Daily noon–midnight. Metro: Oktogon.

Menza 🐾 *Value* HUNGARIAN CONTEMPORARY   It's not surprising that this restaurant is the brainchild of the same team that started exporting Communist-era shoes to Europe as a kind of nostalgia item. The place, decorated in pastel orange and greens, exudes creativity, which is probably why Hungarian experimental theater's true star Anna-Maria Láng of the Krétakör group once recommended it as her top pick. Run by the youngish entrepreneur Roland Radványi, the decor here is decidedly retro and reminiscent of the '60s or '70s without the accompanying disco beats. The food, on the other hand, is traditional but sumptuous. We started with the clear beef soup with carrots, vegetables, and dumplings (surprisingly not served with horseradish). The appetizers were more exciting: duck liver pâté or the adventuresome bone marrow—taken right out of the bone in front of you—served with a salad and garlic toast. For the main course, we tried the exquisite chicken breast with plums and red onions, as well as the divine duck breast with cabbage pasta: We recommend both.

VI. Liszt Ferenc tér 2. ⓒ 1/413-1482. Reservations recommended. Soups 560 Ft–690 Ft ($2.80–$3.45/£1.45–£1.80); starters 850 Ft–1,190 Ft ($4.25–$5.95/£2.20–£3); main courses 1,390 Ft–2,790 Ft ($6.95–$14/£3.60–£7.15). AE, MC, V. Daily 10am–midnight. Metro: Oktogon (Yellow line).

Salaam Bombay 🐾🐾 INDIAN   "I wanted to create an Indian restaurant . . . but in Europe, without emphasizing the typical statues, tandoori, or butter chicken . . ." said the ambitious Firdosh Irani, the managing director of this recently opened restaurant. And this is exactly what he did. Irani came to Budapest in 1994 via New York, and has been in the Indian cuisine business for over 30 years. And it shows, since this restaurant probably gives you the best value that your money can buy in Budapest, as well as a unique look at a more contemporary and varied Indian menu than we are accustomed to. The interior of the restaurant was designed in India, and created in Budapest. Psychedelic colors pervade the space, with shells, sand, and bamboo sticks leaving it both exotic and sparsely contemporary at the same time. We started with the unusual and sumptuous chicken momo, which was basically steamed dumplings stuffed with chicken and served with a spicy sauce. The chicken rolls cooked in a creamy almond sauce were also the favorite of this gourmet taster. As the food kept on coming, the many varied hot and piquant tastes melded one after another into a crescendo. Irani, who is emphatic and passionate about introducing a new look to Indian dining, emphasizes that times are changing, and he is changing with them.

V. Mérleg u. 6. © 1/411-1252. www.salaambombay.hu. Soups 500 Ft–600 Ft ($2.50–$3/£1.30–£1.50); starters 700 Ft–950 Ft ($3.50–$4.75/£1.80–£2.45); main courses 1,500 Ft–3,200 Ft ($7.50–$16/£3.80–£8.20). MC, V. Daily noon–3pm and 6–11:30pm. Metro: Deák tér (Red line).

Tom George ⭐ *Overrated* HUNGARIAN CONTEMPORARY   One of Budapest's most trendy restaurants is frequented by both suave Hungarians and visitors as well, particularly the English crowds. The palette runs from contemporary Indian to Japanese, with a generous selection of sushi. The interior is spacious, the lighting atmospheric, and the general feeling emanates "coolness." If you are with a small group, reserve the rounded tables at the far end of the restaurant that seat eight comfortably. While we do recommend this restaurant, the only problem is the service. Despite a high proportion of waiters, the service can be gruelingly slow and the waiters less than enlightening. We started with an Indian lentil soup with creamy veggies, followed by a fresh, light green salad. We finished our meal with a tender Argentine sirloin steak, and watched enviously as a variety of beautiful-looking sushi was served to the next table!

V. Október 6 utca 8. © 1/266-3525. Reservations recommended. Soups 680 Ft–1,650 Ft ($3.40–$8.25/£1.75–£4.25); starters 1,650 Ft–3,580 Ft ($8.25–$18/£4.25–£9.20); main courses 2,500 Ft–7,600 Ft ($13–$38/£6.40–£20). AE, MC, V. Daily noon–midnight. Metro: Ferenciek tere (Blue line).

Inexpensive

Alföldi Kisvendéglő ⭐ HUNGARIAN TRADITIONAL   The spicy, paprika-laced tastes of the Hungarian Plain are presented well in this time-tested Pest eatery. There is a comprehensive menu of traditional Hungarian fare, which is in English but continues to have lots of funny mistakes. Our host explained, "We are not linguists!" They concentrate on true Hungarian cuisine. When we visited, waiter Imre Bárkovits was celebrating 31 years working at the restaurant. He recommended the classic Szeged fisherman's soup, which is a meal in and of itself, containing three different kinds of fish. They serve Balaton fish, white sea fish, lamb, and the age-old specialties, chicken and veal paprikas. Choose between the rustic interior or weather permitting, sidewalk tables on a busy road. The waiters are formal, and can be a bit old school. As per tradition.

V. Kecskeméti u. 4. © 1/267-0224. Soup 720 Ft–950 Ft ($3.60–$4.75/£1.85–£2.45); starters 575 Ft–1,776 Ft ($3.40–$7.50/£1.50–£4.60); main courses 990 Ft–1,640 Ft ($4.95–$8.20/£2.55–£4.20). MC, V. Daily 11am–midnight. Metro: Kálvin tér (Blue line).

BEYOND CENTRAL PEST
Very Expensive

Gundel ⭐⭐ *Moments* HUNGARIAN TRADITIONAL   Budapest's fanciest and most famous restaurant, Gundel was reopened in 1992 under the auspices of the well-known restaurateur George Lang, owner of New York's Café des Artistes. The Hungarian-born Lang, author of *The Cuisine of Hungary,* and his partner Ronald Lauder, son of Estée Lauder and a one-time New York gubernatorial candidate, spared no effort in attempting to re-create the original splendor for which Gundel, founded in 1894, achieved its international reputation. Located in City Park, Gundel has an opulent dining room adorned with 19th-century paintings and a large, magnificent floral centerpiece. The kitchen prides itself on preparing traditional dishes in an innovative fashion. Lamb and wild-game entrees are house specialties. Gundel is also a place to be seen, and it is a very serious tradition in Budapest: many notable characters or dignitaries make a point of having at least one meal in Gundel's when visiting the Hungarian capital.

XIV. Állatkerti út 2. © **1/468-4040**. www.gundel.hu. Reservations highly recommended. Soup 1,350 Ft–1,860 Ft ($6.75–$9.30/£3.50–£4.80); starters 3,350 Ft–17,300 Ft ($17–$87/£8.60–£44); main courses 4,980 Ft–9,740 Ft ($25–$49/£13–£25); prix-fixe menu 17,500 Ft–36,000 Ft ($88–$180/£45–£92). AE, DC, MC, V. Daily noon–4pm and 6:30pm–midnight. Metro: Hősök tere (Yellow line).

Expensive

Robinson Restaurant ★★ HUNGARIAN CONTEMPORARY The setting could not be more romantic and harmonious, with live music and tasteful decor around you as you dine overlooking the small but tranquil lake in City Park. Robinson is one of Budapest's most dynamic and well-situated restaurants, near both Heroes' Square and the Museum of Fine Arts. The food is varied, ranging from traditional classics like chicken paprika served with egg dumplings, to more exotic seafood dishes like the savory giant prawn on garlic-spinach bed with green curry. We had a perfectly done, tender ripened Angus sirloin steak with onion rings and French potato hot-pot, which was on the daily menu. Vegetarian and children's menus are available, and a coffee shop (also overlooking the lake) is on the second floor.

XIV. Városligeti tó. © **1/422-0224**. www.robinsonrestaurant.hu. Reservations recommended. Soup 790 Ft–890 Ft ($3.95–$4.45/£2–£2.30); starters 1,990 Ft–2,890 Ft ($9.95–$14/£5.10–£7.40); main courses 2,790 Ft–5,980 Ft ($14–$30/£7.15–£15). AE, DC, MC, V. Daily noon–4pm and 6pm–midnight. Metro: Hősök tere (Yellow line).

CENTRAL BUDA
Very Expensive

Kacsa Vendéglő ★★★ HUNGARIAN TRADITIONAL Translated as "Duck Inn," this elegant, charming restaurant gives you a first-rate dining experience that feels both luxurious and homey. The space is located on Fő utca, the main street of Watertown, the Buda neighborhood that lies between Castle Hill and the Danube. Enticing main courses include roast duck with morello cherries, haunch of venison with grapes, and fresh pikeperch from Balaton. Other enticing dishes on the menu include grilled frogs' legs on a bed of vegetables with white wine, smoked salmon, or the delicious grilled forest mushrooms with cognac sauce and wild rice. The restaurant, which has functioned as an eatery for some 160 years, is run by Áron Rozsnyai, who obviously loves what he does, and he does it well. A trio of string players in the space completes a perfectly choreographed dining experience.

Fő u. 75. © **1/201-9992**. Reservations recommended. Soup 800 Ft–1,300 Ft ($4–$6.50/£2–£3.30); starters 1,800 Ft–4,100 Ft ($9–$21/£4.60–£11); main courses 1,600 Ft–6,500 Ft ($8–$33/£4.10–£17). AE, MC, V. Daily noon–1am. Metro: Batthyány tér (Red line).

Inexpensive

Marxim (Kids PIZZA On a gritty industrial street near Moszkva tér, Marxim's chief appeal lies not in its cuisine but in its decor, which attracts visitors from far and wide. The motif is Marxist nostalgia (the entrance is marked by a small neon red flag), but with a nod to the macabre side of the old system. The cellar space is a virtual museum of barbed wire, red flags, banners, posters, and cartoons recalling Hungary's dark past. Several years ago, Marxim was unsuccessfully prosecuted under a controversial law banning the display of the symbols of "hateful" political organizations. Amazingly, this is one of very few places in Budapest where you can still see this kind of stuff, so thoroughly have symbols of the Communist period been erased. This loud, very smoky cellar space is more of a bar than a restaurant. A number of draft beers are available on tap.

II. Kisrókus u. 23. © **1/316-0231**. Pizza 590 Ft–1,290 Ft ($2.95–$6.45/£1.50–£3.30); pasta 520 Ft–890 Ft ($2.60–$4.45/£1.35–£2.30). No credit cards. Mon–Thurs noon–1am; Fri–Sat noon–2am; Sun 6pm–1am. Metro: Moszkva tér (Red line).

THE CASTLE DISTRICT

Very Expensive

Arany Kaviár ★★ RUSSIAN   This venue is a lavishly decorated Russian restaurant that brings back memories of the Belle Epoque Russia of the time of the czars. Serving truly magnificent caviar, we think that this is the kind of place the characters of Tolstoy could have frolicked, feasted, sang, and danced in. The plush interior is decorated with Russian samovars, icons, and paintings depicting cold winter landscapes. If your pocketbook can afford it, treat yourself to a wide variety of rather pricey caviars, including Russian Astrakhan Beluga Caviar, or even more exotic Iranian varieties. Meals take a long time, and are interrupted by swigs of fine vodka, which you should only drink cold. We had a lavish cold-starter plate, rich with fish, caviar, king prawns, and other seafood delights. The strips of beef prepared to Count Stroganoff's original recipe, which served as our main dish, was almost an aside. By the time it was served, our spirits were deep in the cool Russian interior. The slowly served starters, drinks, and sumptuous fireworks of different tastes served as appetizers fulfilled its mission: to serve delicate foods as a hardy meal.

I. Ostrom u. 19. ✆ 1/201-6737. www.aranykaviar.hu. Reservations required. Soup 850 Ft–1,800 Ft ($4.25–$9/£2.20–£4.60); starters 1,050 Ft–3,500 Ft ($5.25–$18/£2.70–£9); main courses 3,500 Ft–9,500 Ft ($18–$48/£9–£24). AE, DC, DISC, MC, V. Daily noon–midnight. Bus: Várbusz from Moszkva tér.

Expensive

Café Pierrot ★★ HUNGARIAN CONTEMPORARY   This intimate, comfortable restaurant serving excellent cuisine was originally established as a real coffeehouse-style cafe, while over the years it developed to become the elegant establishment that it is today. Following recent renovations, the atmosphere feels like a high-class wine cellar decorated with contemporary artworks, soft lighting, and fresh orchids. We started with a gooseliver trilogy, which included a brûlée, a liver terrine, and grilled. If the Gundel's grilled gooseliver is the barometer by which to be measured, then Pierrot lost out, being less tender and a little bit chunky. The marinated venison steak, however, was truly delicious, and the place was also beautifully presented. The menu also includes tempting dishes like oven-roasted duck breast or roasted guinea fowl breast. The back part of the restaurant is more intimate, while the frontal area is closer to the action. A pianist plays every evening after 6pm.

I. Fortuna u. 14. ✆ 1/375-6971. www.pierrot.hu. Reservations recommended. Soups 990 Ft–1,190 Ft ($4.95–$5.95/£2.50–£3); starters 1,590 Ft–3,290 Ft ($7.95–$16/£4.10–£8.45); main courses 2,690 Ft–5,890 Ft ($13–$29/£6.90–£15). AE, DC, MC, V. Daily 11am–midnight. Bus: Várbusz from Moszkva tér.

Inexpensive

Café Miró ★ HUNGARIAN CONTEMPORARY   Located in the heart of the castle area, this restaurant and coffee and pastry shop is an ideal place to stop in between visiting museums and getting to know the area. Miró, named affectionately after the 20th-century surrealist painter, also serves an assortment of salads and warm dishes, the most popular being a spring salad with chicken, Roquefort cheese, and avocado slices. We had the mozzarella and spinach turkey breast served with potato croquettes, which was palatable. The service here is not top-notch either; being either slow (we waited more than three-quarters of an hour for our meal), or without a smile. It is, however, the most convenient and comfortable place for a brief respite in this area.

I. Úri u. 30. ✆ 1/201-5573. Soups 790 Ft–990 Ft ($3.95–$4.95/£2–£2.50); starters 1,390 Ft–1,590 Ft ($6.95–$7.95/£3.60–£4.10); main courses 1,790 Ft–2,890 Ft ($8.95–$14/£4.60–£7.40). No credit cards. Daily 9am–midnight. Bus: Várbusz from Moszkva tér.

THE BUDA HILLS
Expensive
Remiz ★★ (Value) HUNGARIAN CONTEMPORARY   Remiz was born at a time when many entrepreneurs were opening little food shops, while others, like Remiz owner Alice Meződi, wanted to bring dining out of the Socialist era. The "Remiz" is literally the place where trams spend the night, and the venue for this restaurant that was opened in 1992. Meződi and her husband, József, the lead singer of the classic Hungarian rock band Apostol, are also magnets for creative dinner guests, including Hungarian actor András Kern, actress Enikő Eszenyi, choreographer Iván Markó, and the elder-statesman Hungarian film director Miklós Jancsó. A pianist and trumpet player effortlessly play melodies in the tram-shaped restaurant, which is decorated with early-20th-century posters. Try an assortment of gooseliver specialties, classic chicken paprikas, or a tender veal filet with bolete mushrooms that will leave you satisfied, and just curious enough to ask Alice to tell you some stories.

II. Budakeszi út 5. © **1/275-1396.** www.remiz.hu. Reservations recommended. Soup 780 Ft–1,240 Ft ($3.90–$6.20/£2–£3.20); starters 980 Ft–2,620 Ft ($4.90–$13/£2.50–£6.75); main courses 1,980 Ft–3,520 Ft ($9.90–$18/£5.10–£9). AE, DC, MC, V. Daily 9am–midnight. Bus: 158 from Moszkva tér (departs from Csaba utca, at the top of the stairs, near the stop from which the Várbusz departs for the Castle District).

Moderate
Ezüstponty ★★★ (Finds) HUNGARIAN TRADITIONAL   A true and tested traditional Hungarian fish and game restaurant that enjoys a history of some 150 years on the very same spot. The author's favorite Hungarian restaurant, this unassuming and magical place allows you to enjoy a wide variety of home-style dishes served in an old-world atmosphere. The building itself feels like a rustic woodsy country house that is awakened nightly with live traditional Hungarian music played on the violin and guitar. It is decorated with paintings of sailboats, old photographs, and Budapest street scenes. Austere waiters serve a menu that is long and varied, but the true specialty remains the heavy but sumptuous carp soup Szeged-style with haslets, served in a small stew pot. Best consumed with fresh hot peppers, toast, and butter, the soup is rich, textured, and always fresh. The no-nonsense manager recommended a Wels goulash (basically, very rich fish paprikas) served with galuska, sour cream, and bacon bits. No visitor should come to Budapest without visiting this place at least once, because then—and only then—can you truly return knowing that you have tasted authentic, traditional, and hardy Hungarian cuisine.

XII. Némethvölgy út 96. © **1/319-1632.** Reservations recommended. Soup 480 Ft–750 Ft ($2.40–$3.75/£1.25–£1.95); starters 940 Ft–2,350 Ft ($4.70–$12/£2.40–£6); main courses 1,580 Ft–3,450 Ft ($7.90–$17/£4–£8.90). AE, DC, MC, V. Daily 11am–11pm. Tram: 59 from Déli Pályaudvar.

Inexpensive
Makkhetes Vendéglő ★ (Finds) HUNGARIAN TRADITIONAL   In the lower part of the Buda Hills, Makkhetes (the name means "7 of Acorns," a Hungarian playing card) is a rustic little neighborhood eatery. The crude wood paneling and absence of ornamentation give it a distinctly country atmosphere. The regulars (the waiters seem to know everyone who enters) start filing in at 11:30am for lunch. The food is good and the portions are large. You won't go wrong with the *paprika csirke galuskával* (chicken paprika with dumplings). Outdoor dining is available.

XII. Németvölgyi út 56. © **1/355-7330.** Soup 420 Ft–760 Ft ($1.65–$3.10/£1.10–£1.95); main courses 990 Ft–2,400 Ft ($3.80–$9.90/£2.55–£6.15). No credit cards. Daily 11am–10pm. Tram: 59 from Moszkva tér to Kiss János altábornagy utca stop (then walk up hill to the right on Kiss János altábornagy utca).

TRADITIONAL COFFEEHOUSES

Like Vienna, imperial Budapest was famous for its coffeehouse culture. Literary movements and political circles alike were identified in large part by which coffeehouse they met in. Sándor Petőfi, the revolutionary poet of 1848 fame, is said to have instructed his friend János Arany, another leading Hungarian poet of the day, to write to him in care of the Pilvax Coffee House, as he spent more time there than at home. Although Communism managed to dull this cherished institution, a handful of classic coffeehouses miraculously survived the tangled tragedies of the 20th century, and, with just a few exceptions, all have been carefully restored to their original splendor.

All the classic coffeehouses offer delicious pastries and coffee in an atmosphere of luxurious—if occasionally faded—splendor. Many offer small sandwiches, some serve ice cream, and some feature bar drinks. Pastries are displayed in a glass. Table sharing is common, and lingering for hours over a single cup of coffee or a pastry is perfectly acceptable, and is in fact encouraged by the free daily papers provided by the house.

THE INNER CITY & CENTRAL PEST

Centrál Kávéház 𝕉𝕉𝕉   This is the closest to the Viennese coffeehouse culture in Budapest, and is a perfect replica of the original establishment that stood on the premises from 1887. Although there is a superb restaurant here as well, this place is best known as a coffeehouse. The house was restored by one of Hungary's own homegrown successful businessman, Imre Somody—one of the country's very few new millionaires who seem willing to recycle profits by investing in the country's general wealth. This place is perfectly located in the Inner City, and is always busy with an interesting mix of the local university crowd from ELTE and CEU, celebrity intellectuals, and the ever-present travelers, who have taken to the place immediately. Watch at the right end of the smoky section as you enter where a table is perpetually reserved for local writer Géza Csemer, who is more than a regular here. The coffeehouse's calm green interior also allows you to check out the free copies of various newspapers over a coffee and a fresh croissant. You can visit as early as 8am; this is the only place open at that time of the day in the area. A simple espresso at Centrál costs 310 Ft ($1.60/80p).

V. Károlyi Mihály u. 9. 𝄪 1/266-2110. www.centralkavehaz.hu. AE, DISC, MC, V. Daily 8am–midnight. Metro: Ferenciek tere (Blue line).

Gerbeaud's 𝕉𝕉 *Kids*   Gerbeaud's is probably Budapest's most famous coffeehouse. Founded in 1858, it has stood on its current spot since 1870. Whether you sit inside amid the splendor of the late-19th-century furnishings, or outside on one of Pest's liveliest pedestrian-only squares, you will surely enjoy the fine pastries that made the name Gerbeaud famous; we especially recommend their moist plum pies *(szilvás lepény)*. Gerbeaud's reputation and location ensure that it's filled to capacity throughout the year, although many locals complain that the value-for-money ratio has become disappointing. Given its history, however, you cannot afford not to have at least one coffee here during your stay. In good weather, try getting a table outside on bustling Vörösmarty tér where you can watch kids (yours perhaps?) play around (and on) the square's fountain.

V. Vörösmarty tér 7. 𝄪 1/429-9000. www.gerbeaud.hu. AE, DISC, MC, V. Daily 9am–9pm. Metro: Vörösmarty tér (Yellow line).

CENTRAL BUDA

Auguszt Cukrászda 𝕉𝕉   We highly recommend this true and tested coffeehouse, established in 1870 and remarkably still run by the family of the founder. The latest of four generations of confectioners, József Auguszt, who now runs the coffee shop, came to greet us with his chef's hat eager explain his family's long-standing Budapest tradition. The coffeehouse even existed in various locations and in some form or another during the Communist era, save for the harshest years of the 1950s. In 1951 it was nationalized, the same year that József was born. As was the tradition of the Communists with entrepreneurial types, they sent the family off to the countryside, in their case, a small town in northeastern Hungary called Taktaszada. A year after Hungary's 1956 revolution things became easier; they returned to Budapest and the family opened the coffeehouse in its current location. József continues the family tradition of creating a new cake for his father's birthday. Some years, they work, some years they don't. The E-80, named after his father Elemér Auguszt, was created on his father's 80th birthday, and has become a staple of the shop. József is now working on the King's Cake, or the cake of Kings! His father will be 93 years old. . . .

II. Fény utca 8. (① 1/316-3817. www.ausztcukraszda.hu. No credit cards. Tues–Sat 10am–6pm. Metro: Batthyány tér (Red line).

THE CASTLE DISTRICT

Ruszwurm Cukrászda 🍴🍴 *Kids*   More than a century old, the Ruszwurm is an utterly charming little place, with two rooms outfitted with small tables and chairs, and shelves lined with antiques. It is owned by the Szamos dynasty of pastry and marzipan chefs. It can be very difficult to find a free table here, and the four out front on the sidewalk seem forever occupied. You must try the unsurpassable *krémes,* a two-layered crisp pastry confection with vanilla cream filling. Another favorite here is the Dobos torta, a multilayered cake with a thin caramel crust on top.

I. Szentháromság u. 7. (① 1/375-5284. No credit cards. Daily 9am–8pm in high season, 10am–7pm in low season. Bus: Várbusz from Moszkva tér or no. 16 from Deák tér to Castle Hill. Funicular: From Clark Ádám tér to Castle Hill.

EXPLORING BUDAPEST

Historic Budapest is surprisingly small, and many sights listed in the following pages can be reached by foot from the city center. Take the time to stroll from one place to the next—you'll find yourself passing magnificent, if often run-down, examples of the city's distinctive architecture.

PEST: THE TOP ATTRACTIONS
Museums

Museums are closed on Mondays, except where noted. Most museums offer substantial student and senior discounts. Many also offer a family rate. Inquire at the ticket window.

Holokauszt Emlékközpont (Budapest Holocaust Memorial Center) 🍴🍴
This center, a beautiful and moving memorial to the Jews murdered during World War II, opened in 2004 and became the first government-funded Holocaust Memorial Center in central Europe. The center is built around an old, eclectic-style synagogue building that was designed by Leopold Baumhorn (1860–1932), the most prolific architect of synagogues at the turn of the 20th century. The space has a permanent exhibition and a research center. The temporary exhibitions tend to be small or multimedia photography exhibitions. A memorial wall lists the names of Holocaust victims.

IX. Páva u. 39. (① 1/455-3333. www.hdke.hu. Free admission. Tues–Sun 10am–6pm. Metro: Ferenc körut (Blue line).

Nemzeti Múzeum (Hungarian National Museum) 🍴🍴   The Hungarian National Museum, an enormous neoclassical structure built from 1837 to 1847, was one of the great projects of the early-19th-century Age of Reform, a period that also saw the construction of the Chain Bridge and the National Theater (no longer standing), as well as the development of the modern Hungarian national identity. The museum was a major site during the beginning of the Hungarian Revolution of 1848 and 1849; on its wide steps on March 15, 1848, the poet Sándor Petőfi and other young radicals are said to have exhorted the people of Pest to revolt against the Habsburgs. The very presence of such an imposing structure in the capital of Hungary, and its exhibits, which proudly detail the accomplishments of the Magyars, played a significant role in the development of 19th-century Hungarian nationalism.

VIII. Múzeum krt. 14. ℭ 1/338-2122. www.hnm.hu. Free admission. Tues–Sun 10am–6pm (to 5pm in winter). Metro: Kálvin tér (Blue line).

Néprajzi Múzeum (Ethnographical Museum)   Directly across Kossuth tér from the House of Parliament, the vast Ethnographical Museum is located in the stately neo-Renaissance/eclectic former Hungarian Supreme Court building. The ornate interior rivals that of the Opera House. A ceiling fresco of Justitia, the goddess of justice, by the well-known artist Károly Lotz, dominates the lobby. Although a third of the museum's holdings are from outside Hungary, you'll want to concentrate on the Hungarian items. The fascinating permanent exhibition, "From Ancient Times to Civilization," features everything from drinking jugs to razor cases to chairs to clothing.

V. Kossuth tér 12. ℭ 1/473-2400. www.neprajz.hu. Free admission for permanent exhibits. 1,200 Ft ($6/£3.10) for temporary shows. Tues–Sun 10am–6pm. Metro: Kossuth tér (Red line).

Szépművészeti Múzeum (Museum of Fine Arts) 𝒜𝒜   Planned at the time of the 1896 millennial celebration of the Magyar Conquest, the Museum of Fine Arts opened 10 years later in this neoclassical behemoth on the left side of huge Heroes' Square, at the edge of City Park. The museum is the main repository of foreign art in Hungary and it houses one of central Europe's major collections of such works. A significant part of the collection was acquired in 1871 from the Esterházys, an enormously wealthy noble family who spent centuries amassing great art. There are eight sections in the museum: Egyptian Art, Antiquities, Baroque Sculpture, Old Masters, Drawings and Prints, 19th-Century Masters, 20th-Century Masters, and Modern Sculpture. Most great names associated with the old masters—Tiepolo, Tintoretto, Veronese, Titian, Raphael, Van Dyck, Bruegel, Rembrandt, Rubens, Hals, Hogarth, Dürer, Cranach, Holbein, Goya, Velázquez, El Greco, and others—are represented here. It has been said, though, that while the museum suffers no shortage of works by the old masters, it can boast precious few outright masterpieces. Delacroix, Corot, and Manet are the best-represented 19th-century French artists in the museum.

XIV. Hősök tere. ℭ 1/469-7100. Free admission for permanent collection; other exhibits 1,000 Ft–1,800 Ft ($5–$9/£2.60–£4.65). Tues–Sun 10am–5:30pm. Free guided tours in English at 11am Tues–Fri, Sat 11am and 3pm. Metro: Hősök tere (Yellow line).

Historic Squares & Buildings

Hősök tere (Heroes' Square) 𝒜𝒜 𝘒𝘪𝘥𝘴   Situated at the end of Pest's great boulevard, Andrássy út, and at the entrance to its most famous park, City Park (Városliget), the wide-open plaza of Hősök tere (Heroes' Square) is one of the symbols of the city. During the country's Communist era, Socialist holidays were invariably celebrated with huge military reviews in the square. In 1989 a rally here on the day of the reburial of Imre Nagy (who was the prime minister of Hungary during the Hungarian Revolution and who was executed after the 1956 uprising against the Soviet-backed regime) attracted 300,000 people to the square.

The square, like the park beyond it, was laid out for the 1896 Magyar Conquest millennial celebration. In its center stands the 35m-high (118-ft.) Millennial Column; arrayed around the base of the column are equestrian statues of Árpád and the six other Magyar tribal leaders who led the conquest. Behind the column, arrayed along a colonnade, are 14 heroes of Hungarian history, including King Stephen I, the country's first Christian king (first on left); King Matthias Corvinus, who presided over Buda's golden age in the 15th century (sixth from right); and Lajos Kossuth, leader of the 1848–49 War of Independence (first on right). The statues were restored in 1996 in honor of the 1,100th anniversary of the Magyar Conquest. Kids adore looking at the equestrian statues, and the square is close to many kid-friendly activities. Two of Budapest's major museums, the Museum of Fine Arts and the Exhibition Hall, flank Heroes' Square.

Take the metro to Hősök tere (Yellow line).

Magyar Állami Operaház (Hungarian State Opera House) 𝕂𝕂   Completed in 1884, the Opera House, on Pest's elegant Andrássy út, is the crowning achievement of famous Hungarian architect Miklós Ybl. Budapest's most celebrated performance hall, the opera house boasts a fantastically ornate interior featuring frescoes by two of the best-known Hungarian artists of the day, Bertalan Székely and Károly Lotz. Both inside and outside are dozens of statues of such greats as Beethoven, Mozart, Verdi, Wagner, Smetana, Tchaikovsky, and Monteverdi. Home to both the State Opera and the State Ballet, the Opera House has a rich and evocative history, which is related on the guided tours given daily at 3 and 4pm (these can be arranged in English). Well-known directors of the Opera House have included Gustav Mahler and Ferenc Erkel. See p. 341 for information on performances. The only way to tour the interior is on a guided tour, which costs 2,400 Ft ($12/£6.15). The blatant discrimination here is that if you have the same tour in Hungarian, the price is a mere 500 Ft ($2.50/£1.30). They claim it is because of the translation, but with the plethora of young language speakers, this is a weak excuse. After all, travel to other European cities, and most would condemn this practice.

VI. Andrássy út 22. 🕐 **1/331-2550**. www.opera.hu. Tour 2,400 Ft ($12/£6.15). Tours given daily at 3 and 4pm (available in English). Metro: Opera (Yellow line).

Parliament 𝕂   Budapest's great Parliament building, completed in 1902, was built to the eclectic design of Imre Steindl. It mixes a predominant neo-Gothic style with a neo-Renaissance dome. Standing proudly on the Danube bank, visible from almost any riverside vantage point, it has been from the outset one of Budapest's symbols, though until 1989 a democratically elected government had convened here exactly once (just after World War II, before the Communist takeover). Built at a time of extreme optimism and national purpose, the building was self-consciously intended to be one of the world's great houses of Parliament, and it remains one of the largest state buildings in Europe. The main cupola is decorated with statues of Hungarian kings.

On either side of the cupola are waiting rooms leading into the respective houses of Parliament. The members of Parliament are said to gather in these waiting rooms during breaks in the session to smoke and chat—note the cigar holders on the side of the doors. The waiting room on the Senate side (blue carpet) is adorned with statues of farmers, peasants, tradesmen, and workers. The figures that decorate the waiting room on the Representatives' side (red carpet) are of sailors, soldiers, and postal officials. The interior decor is predominantly neo-Gothic. The ceiling frescoes are by Károly Lotz,

Hungary's best-known fresco artist. Note the large carpet from the small Hungarian village of Békésszentandrás, which is purportedly the biggest handmade carpet in Europe. The Parliament is also home to the legendary crown jewels of St. Stephen, which were moved here from the National Museum as part of the Hungarian millennium celebration.

V. Kossuth tér. (℡ 1/441-4415. www.parlament.hu. Admission (by guided tour only): 60-min. tour in English 2,300 Ft ($12/£5.90), 1,150 Ft ($5.75/£2.95) students. Tickets are available at Gate X. Tours are given Mon–Fri 10am and noon, 2pm (but not on days in which Parliament is in session, which are usually Tues and Wed, or during protocol events); Sat 4pm; Sun 2pm. Metro: Kossuth tér (Red line).

Churches & Synagogues

Bazilika (St. Stephen's Church) ⟨★⟩   Although not a basilica in the technical sense of the word, Hungarians like to call St. Stephen's "the Basilica" in honor of its sheer size: It's the largest church in the country. It took over 50 years to build the Bazilika (the collapse of the dome in 1868 caused significant delays); three leading architects, two of whom (József Hild and Miklós Ybl) died before work was finished, presided over its construction. The church was considered so sturdy that important documents and artworks were stored in it during the World War II bombings. In 2003 a full-scale renovation of the church and neighboring square was completed, and now the cleaned-up front of the church graces the colorful and grand Szent István tér (St. Stephen's Sq.), where travelers sip their coffee in open-air cafes. The bust above the main entrance is of King Stephen, Hungary's first Christian king. Inside the church, in the Chapel of the Holy Right (Szent Jobb Kápolna), you can see Hungarian Catholicism's most cherished—and bizarre—holy relic: Stephen's preserved right hand. Organ concerts are sometimes held here, although repairs to the organ have made them intermittent. Daily Mass is held at 7am and 8am at the Szent Jobb Chapel, and 5:30 and 6pm in the Basilica; Sunday Mass at 8, 9, and 10am, noon, and 6 and 7:30pm.

V. Szent István tér 33. (℡ 1/317-2859. www.basilica.hu. Church free; treasury 300 Ft ($1.50/80p); tower 500 Ft ($2.50/£1.30). Church daily 7am–6pm, except during services; treasury daily 9am–5pm (10am–4pm in winter); Szent Jobb Chapel Mon–Sat 9am–5pm (10am–4pm in winter), Sun 1–5pm; tower Apr–Oct Mon–Sat 10am–6pm (closed Nov–Mar). Metro: Arany János utca (Blue line) or Bajcsy-Zsilinszky út (Yellow line).

Dohány Synagogue ⟨★⟩   Built in 1859, this is Europe's largest synagogue and the world's second-largest synagogue. Budapest's Jewish community still uses it. The architecture has striking Byzantine and Moorish elements; the interior is vast and ornate, with two balconies and the unusual presence of an organ. An ambitious restoration was completed in recent years, funded in large part by a foundation set up by the American actor Tony Curtis, who is of Hungarian-Jewish descent. The building's original splendor is now apparent.

The synagogue has a rich but tragic history. Adolf Eichmann arrived with the occupying Nazi forces in March 1944 to supervise the establishment of the Jewish ghetto and the subsequent deportations. Up to 20,000 Jews took refuge inside the synagogue complex, but 7,000 did not survive the bleak winter of 1944 and 1945. These victims are buried in the courtyard, where you can also see a piece of the original brick ghetto wall. The National Jewish Museum is inside the synagogue complex (see p. 317 for information on the museum).

VII. Dohány u. 2–8. Admission 600 Ft ($3/£1.55). Mon–Thurs 10am–5pm; Fri 10am–2pm; Sun 10am–2pm. Services are held Fri 6pm and Sat 9am. Metro: Astoria (Red line) or Deák tér (all lines).

BUDA: THE TOP ATTRACTIONS
Museums
Nemzeti Galéria (Hungarian National Gallery) ⊛ A repository of Hungarian art from medieval times through the 20th century, the Hungarian National Gallery is an enormous museum—you couldn't possibly view the entire collection during a single visit. The museum was founded during the great reform period of the mid–19th century and was moved to its present location in Buda Palace in 1975. Hungary has produced some fine artists, particularly in the late 19th century, and this is the place to view their work. The giants of the time are the brilliant **Mihály Munkácsy** ⊛⊛, whose masterpieces include *The Lintmakers, Condemned Cell,* and *Woman Carrying Wood;* László Paál, a painter of village scenes, including *Village Road in Berzova, Path in the Forest at Fontainbleau,* and *Depth of the Forest;* **Károly Ferenczy** ⊛⊛, whose mastery of light is seen in *Morning Sunshine* and *Evening in March;* and Pál Szinyei Merse, a plein-air artist whose own artistic developments paralleled those of the early French Impressionists (check out *Picnic in May*). Some other artists to look for are Gyula Benczúr, who painted grand historical scenes; Károly Lotz, best known as a fresco painter (you can see his creations at the Opera House and Matthias Church), who is represented at the museum by a number of nudes and several fine thunderstorm paintings; and Bertalan Székely, a painter of historical scenes and landscapes. József Rippl-Rónai's canvases are premier examples of Hungarian post-Impressionism and Art Nouveau (see *Father and Uncle Piacsek Drinking Red Wine* and *My Grandmother*), while Tivadar Csontváry Kosztka, the "Rousseau of the Danube," is considered by some critics to be a genius of early modern art.

I. In Buda Palace, Wings B, C, and D, on Castle Hill. ℂ 1/375-5567. Free admission to permanent collection. Variable entrance for temporary exhibitions. Tues–Sun 10am–6pm. Bus: Várbusz from Moszkva tér or 16 from Deák tér to Castle Hill. Funicular: From Clark Ádám tér to Castle Hill.

A Famous Church
Mátyás Templom (Matthias Church) ⊛ Officially named the Church of Our Lady, this symbol of Buda's Castle District is popularly known as Matthias Church after the much-loved 15th-century Renaissance king who was the main donor of the building and who was twice married here. The structure that originally stood here dates from the mid–13th century. However, like other old churches in Budapest, Matthias Church has an interesting history of destruction and reconstruction, and was constantly being refashioned in the architectural style that was popular at the time of reconstruction. The last two Hungarian kings (Habsburgs) were crowned in this church: Franz Joseph in 1867 (Liszt wrote and performed his *Coronation Mass* for the occasion) and Charles IV in 1916. The church interior is decorated with works by two outstanding 19th-century Hungarian painters, Károly Lotz and Bertalan Székely. Organ concerts are held here every other Friday evening in July and August at 8pm. Daily Mass is held at 8:30am, 12:30pm, and 6pm; Sunday Mass at 8:30am, 9:30am, noon, and 6pm.

I. Szentháromság tér 2. ℂ 1/355-5657. Admission 600 Ft ($3/£1.55). Daily 9am–6pm. Bus: Várbusz from Moszkva tér or 16 from Deák tér Castle Hill. Funicular: From Clark Ádám tér to Castle Hill.

ÓBUDA
Roman Ruins
The **ruins of Aquincum** ⊛, the once-bustling capital of the Roman province of Pannonia, are spread throughout the southern part of Óbuda. Unfortunately, the various sites are far away from one another, and the layout of modern Óbuda is quite

Gellért Hegy (Gellért Hill)

Gellért Hill, towering 230m (754 ft.) above the Danube, offers the single best panorama of the city. The hill is named after the iron-fisted Italian Bishop Gellért, who assisted Hungary's first Christian king, Stephen I, in converting the Magyars. Gellért became a martyr when vengeful pagans killed him by rolling him down the side of this hill in a barrel. An enormous statue of Gellért now stands on the hill, with the bishop defiantly holding a cross in his outstretched hand.

On top of Gellért Hill you'll find the **Liberation Monument,** built in 1947 supposedly to commemorate the Red Army's liberation of Budapest from Nazi occupation, though many believe that Admiral Horthy, Hungary's wartime leader, had planned the statue prior to the liberation to honor his fighter-pilot son, who was killed in the war. A mammoth statue, it's one of the last Socialist Realist memorials you'll find in Hungary. The statue's centerpiece, a giant female figure holding a leaf aloft, is affectionately known as *Kiflis Zsuzsa* (*kifli* is a crescent-shaped roll eaten daily by many Hungarians, while Zsuzsa, or Susie, is a common girl's name). Hungarian children like to call the smaller flame-holding figure at her side *Fagylaltos fiú* (the boy with the ice-cream cone).

Also atop Gellért Hill is the **Citadella** (© 1/365-6076), a symbol of power built for military control by the Austrians in 1851, shortly after they crushed the Hungarian War of Independence of 1848 and 1849. It costs 1,200 Ft ($6/£3.10) to enter the Citadella, which is open daily from 9am to 7pm. There are several exhibitions to see here, but the main attraction is the great view. To get here, take bus no. 27 from Móricz Zsigmond körtér or hike up on any of the various paved pathways that originate at the base of the hill.

antipedestrian (the main Budapest-Szentendre highway cuts right through Óbuda), so it's difficult to see everything. Fortunately, two major sites are right across the road from one another, near the Aquincum station of the suburban HÉV railroad. The ruined **Amphitheater of the Civilian Town** is directly beside the HÉV station. It's open all the time and you're free to wander through (you should be aware that homeless people sometimes set up shelter within the walls). Across the highway from the amphitheater stand the ruins of the Civilian Town. Everything is visible from the roadside, except for the collection at the **Aquincum Museum,** which is located at III. Szentendrei u. 139 (© 1/250-1650; www.aquincum.hu). This neoclassical structure was built at the end of the 19th century in harmony with its surroundings. The museum exhibits coins, utensils, jewelry, and pottery from Roman times. Its most unique exhibit is a portable water organ (a rare and precious musical instrument) from A.D. 228. Entry to the museum is 700 Ft ($3.50/£1.80). It's open from May to September, Tuesday through Sunday from 10am to 5pm, and from October to April, Tuesday through Sunday 9am to 5pm. Take the HÉV suburban railroad from Batthyány tér to Aquincum.

MORE MUSEUMS & SIGHTS

PEST

Ludwig Múzeum (Ludwig Museum of Contemporary Art) ⊛ Located in the recently opened Palace of Art, overlooking the Danube, this was formerly the Museum of the Hungarian Workers' Movement. Now converted to a more politically correct purpose, it houses a less-than-inspiring and poorly curated permanent exhibition of contemporary Hungarian and international art. The collection consists primarily of American pop art and central European contemporary works. It includes several late Picassos, Andy Warhol's *Single Elvis,* and a still functional Jean Tinguely, as well as an eclectic mix of Hungarian works by artists like Imre Bukta, Beáta Veszely, and Imre Bak. Like the Kunsthalle in Vienna, this museum is sometimes worth visiting for the various temporary exhibitions of contemporary works, mostly by alternative European artists.

IX. Komor Marcell u. 1. ⓒ 1/555-3444. www.ludwigmuseum.hu. Free admission for permanent collection. Sun, Tues, Fri 10am–6pm; Wed noon–6pm; Thurs noon–8pm; Sat 10am–8pm; closed Mon. Tram: 2 or 2A.

Nemzeti Zsidó Múzeum és Levéltár (National Jewish Museum and Archives) This museum is located in the Dohány Synagogue complex (p. 314). A tablet outside informs visitors that Theodor Herzl, the founder of Zionism, was born on this spot. The four-room museum is devoted to the long history of Jews in Hungary. Displays include Sabbath and holiday items (including some gorgeous examples of the famous Herend porcelain company's Passover plates), and ritual and everyday artifacts. The last room contains a small, moving exhibit on the Holocaust in Hungary.

VII. Dohány u. 2–8. ⓒ 1/342-8942. Admission 1,000 Ft ($5/£2.60). Mon–Thurs 10am–5pm; Fri and Sun 10am–2pm. Metro: Astoria (Red line) or Deák tér (all lines).

Terror Háza (House of Terror) ⊛⊛ The former headquarters of the ÁVH secret police, this building is witness to some of the darkest days of 20th-century Hungary and is now a chilling museum, one of the best in Hungary. It was set up as a memorial to the victims of both Communism and Fascism, and is an attempt to recapture life under successive oppressive regimes in Hungary. The building was the headquarters of the Nazis in 1944, and many individuals were tortured and murdered in the eerie cellars of this building. The Communist secret police were next to use the venue as a place for their own torture and oppression. The tearing down of the ugly exterior facade has been the subject of much debate, however, and for political reasons it has remained the sore thumb of the grand Andrássy boulevard.

VI. Andrássy út 60. ⓒ 1/374-2600. www.houseofterror.hu. Admission 1,200 Ft ($6/£3.10). Tues–Fri 10am–6pm; Sat–Sun 10am–7:30pm. Metro: Oktogon (Yellow line).

PARKS & GARDENS

Hungarians love to stroll in the park, and on weekends and summer afternoons, it seems as if the whole of Budapest is out enjoying what Hungarians lovingly refer to as "the nature."

Popular **Margaret Island (Margit-sziget)** ⊛⊛ has been a public park since 1908. The long, narrow island, connected to both Buda and Pest via the Margaret and Árpád bridges, is barred to most vehicular traffic. In addition to three important ruins—the Dominican Convent, a 13th- to 14th-century Franciscan church, and a 12th-century Premonstratensian chapel—attractions on the island include the Palatinus Strand open-air baths ,hich draw upon the famous thermal waters under Margaret Island; the Alfréd Hajós Sport Pool; and the Open-Air Theater. Sunbathers line the steep

Where Have All the Statues Gone?

Ever wonder where all the vanished Communist statues went after the fall? Over 15 years ago, Budapest and the rest of Hungary were filled with monuments to Lenin, to Marx and Engels, to the Red Army, and to the many lesser-known figures of Hungarian and international Communism. Torn rudely from their pedestals in the aftermath of 1989, they sat in warehouses for a few years gathering dust, until a controversial plan for a **Socialist Statue Park (Szoborpark Múzeum)** was realized. The park's inconvenient location and the relatively small number of statues on display (reflecting nothing of their former ubiquity) make the park less enticing than it could be. In addition, the best examples of the genre, dating from the Stalinist period of the late 1940s and 1950s, were removed from public view long before 1989 and were presumably destroyed long ago.

Located in the XXII district (extreme Southern Buda) on Balatoni út (② 1/424-7500; www.szoborpark.hu), the park is a memorial to an era, to despotism, and to bad taste. The museum gift shop sells all sorts of Communist-era memorabilia, such as T-shirts, medals, and cassettes of Red Army marching songs. The park is open daily from 10am to dusk and admission is 600 Ft ($3/£1.55). To get to the park, take the black-lettered bus no. 7 from Ferenciek tere to Etele tér. Board a yellow Volán bus (to Érd) for a 20-minute ride to the park. Or, for a premium, you can take the new and convenient direct bus service from Deák tér for 2,450 Ft ($12/£6.30) (admission ticket to the park included). The timetable varies almost monthly, but 11am and 3pm departures remain constant for July and August.

embankments along the river, and bikes are available for rent. There are several snack bars, open-air restaurants, and even clubs. Despite all this, Margaret Island remains a quiet, tranquil place. In any direction off the main road, you can find well-tended gardens or a patch of grass under the shade of a willow tree for a private picnic. Margaret Island is best reached by bus no. 26 from Nyugati tér, which runs the length of the island, or tram no. 4 or 6, which stops at the entrance to the island midway across the Margaret Bridge. *Warning:* These are popular metro lines for pickpockets.

City Park (Városliget) ⟨★⟩ is an equally popular place to spend a summer day, and families are everywhere. Heroes' Square, at the end of Andrássy út, is the most logical starting point for a walk in City Park. Built in 1896 as part of the Hungarian millennial celebrations, the square has been the site of some important moments in Hungarian history. The lake behind the square is used for boating in summer and for ice-skating in winter (p. 322). The Vajdahunyad Castle, located by the lake, is an architectural mishmash if there ever was one. The castle was built as a temporary structure in 1896 for the millennial celebration in order to demonstrate the different architectural styles in Hungary; it was so popular that a permanent structure was eventually designed to replace it. It is now home to the **Agricultural Museum,** the largest of its kind in Europe, which has especially interesting exhibitions on Hungary's grape and wine industries. Admission to the museum is 900 Ft ($4.50/£2.30); it's open in summer, early fall, and late spring Tuesday through Friday and Sunday from 10am to

5pm, Saturday 10am to 6pm; in late fall, winter, and early spring Monday through Friday 10am to 4pm, Saturday and Sunday to 5pm. Take the Yellow line of the metro to Széchenyi fürdő to get to the museum. The Yellow metro line makes stops at Hősök tere (Heroes' Sq.), at the edge of the park, and at Széchenyi fürdő, in the middle of the park.

FOR THE MUSIC LOVER

Liszt Ferenc Emlékmúzeum (Ferenc Liszt Memorial Museum)   Located in the apartment in which Liszt spent his last years, this modest museum features several of the composer's pianos, including a child's Bachmann piano and two Chickering & Sons grand pianos. Also noteworthy are the many portraits of Liszt done by the leading Austrian and Hungarian artists of his time, including two busts by the Hungarian sculptor Alajos Stróbl. Concerts are performed here on Saturdays at 11am.

VI. Vörösmarty u. 35. ⓒ 1/322-9804. Admission 400 Ft ($1.60/85p). Guided group tours in English for a whopping 7,200 Ft ($36/£18), if arranged in advance. Mon–Fri 10am–6pm; Sat 9am–5pm. Metro: Vörösmarty utca (Yellow line).

Zenetörténeti Múzeum (Museum of Music History)   Various instruments and manuscripts are displayed in this museum, which is housed in a historic building in Buda's Castle District. You'll find a reproduction of Béla Bartók's workshop as well as the Bartók Archives. For lack of sponsorship, this gorgeous concert venue has been silent since mid-2000, to the deep regret of local music aficionados. Perhaps by the time you arrive, the museum will again be hosting concerts.

I. Táncsics M. u. 7. ⓒ 1/214-6770, ext. 250. Admission 400 Ft ($2/£1). Tues–Sun 10am–6pm. Bus: Várbusz from Moszkva tér or 16 from Deák tér to Castle Hill. Funicular: From Clark Ádám tér to Castle Hill.

ORGANIZED TOURS
BUS TOURS
Ibusz (ⓒ 1/485-2700; www.ibusz.hu), with decades of experience, offers 11 different boat and bus tours, ranging from basic city tours to special folklore-oriented tours. Unfortunately, the tours are pretty sterile and boring, and we actually think you're better off taking a walking tour or a different boat tour (see below). Ibusz operates year-round, with an abbreviated schedule in the off season. All buses are air-conditioned, and all guides speak English. Some sample offerings are a 3-hour **Budapest City Tour** for 5,000 Ft to 10,000 Ft ($25–$50/£13–£26); free for children under 12, and a 2-hour Parliament Tour (you'll be inside the building for 2 hr.) for 7,500 Ft ($38/£19). There's a free hotel pickup service that will pick you up 30 minutes before departure time. For a full list of tours, pick up the Ibusz *Budapest Sightseeing* catalog, available at all Ibusz offices, Tourinform, and most hotels. Tours can be booked at any Ibusz office and at most major hotels, or by calling Ibusz directly at ⓒ 1/485-2700. All major credit cards are accepted.

BOAT TOURS
A boat tour is a great way to absorb the scope and scale of the Hungarian capital, and a majority of the city's grand sights can be seen from the river. The Hungarian state company **MAHART** operates daily 2-hour sightseeing cruises on the Danube, using two-story steamboats. The Budapest office of MAHART is at V. Belgrád rakpart (ⓒ 1/318-1704; www.mahartpassnave.hu). Boats depart frequently from Vigadó tér (on the Pest waterfront, between the Erzsébet Bridge and the Chain Bridge, near the Budapest Marriott hotel) on weekends and holidays in the spring and every day in summer. Additionally, MAHART offers chartered boat tours (for large groups) up and

down the Tisza River in eastern Hungary from April 1 to October 15. These tours are booked through separate agencies in the towns of departure (Tokaj, Kisköre, Tiszac-sege, Szolnok, Szeged, and many others along the river). Ask at MAHART for further information and for the telephone numbers necessary for booking.

Legenda, at XI. Fraknó u. 4 (② **1/266-4190;** www.legenda.hu), a private company founded in 1990, offers several boat tours on the Danube, using two-story steam-boats. The daytime tour, called "Duna Bella," operates daily at 2:30pm, year-round, with additional daily trips during the summer. The 2-hour ride includes a stop at Mar-garet Island, with a walk on the island. Tickets cost 3,600 Ft ($18/£9.25). The night-time tour, departing daily at 8:15pm, is called "Danube Legend" and is more than a bit hokey, but worth it for the view of the city all lit up. "Danube Legend" tickets cost 4,200 Ft ($21/£11). On both trips your ticket entitles you to two free glasses of wine or beer and unlimited soft drinks. A shorter variation of the daytime tour, without the stop on the island, runs from mid-April to mid-October. All boats leave from the Vigadó tér port, Pier 7. Tickets are available through most major hotels, at the dock, and through the Legenda office. Look for the company's brochure at Tourinform.

The **Operetta Ship,** departing from at Vigadó tér (② **20/332-9116,** 1/318-1223, or 1/488-0475; www.operetthajo.hu), offers a unique candlelit boat tour that includes performers of the Hungarian State Opera House singing famous operas, operettas, Italian and Spanish songs, musicals, instrumental solos, and Hungarian folklore. Dur-ing the tours, you will hear famous excerpts from Strauss, Mozart, Lehar, Gershwin, Puccini, and more. The boat tour runs from April until October, and operates Mon-day to Wednesday, Friday, and Sunday from 8 to 10pm. The boat tour with a dinner included costs 12,500 Ft ($63/£32), or 8,500 Ft ($43/£22) without the meal. There is also a "music" sightseeing tour guided in English, German, or Hungarian, that costs 4,000 Ft ($20/£10).

SPECIALTY TOURS

Chosen Tours (②/fax **1/355-2202**) specializes in tours related to Jewish life and her-itage in Budapest. The 11/2- to 2-hour guided walking tour of Pest's historic Jewish Quarter is a good introduction to that fascinating neighborhood. Tours are conducted from April through October and run Monday through Friday and Sunday, beginning at 10am in front of the Dohány Synagogue, on Dohány utca. The walking tour costs 2,420 Ft ($11/£6.20). You should reserve a space on the tour ahead of time. Chosen Tours offers a 1-hour, air-conditioned bus tour of Jewish sights in Buda as an add-on to the walking tour. Called "Budapest Through Jewish Eyes," the combination tour ticket costs 3,740 Ft ($17/£9.60). Reserve your space early. Other tours, available for private bookings, include a tour of Jewish art and a trip to Szentendre, as well as tours catering to individual needs and interests (such as Jewish "roots" tours). The company offers a free pickup service from select hotel locations.

SPA BATHING & SWIMMING: BUDAPEST'S MOST POPULAR THERMAL BATHS

Hungarians are great believers in the medicinal powers of thermal bathing. Even if you are unsure about the health benefits, it's hard to deny that time spent in thermal baths is enjoyable and relaxing. The baths of Budapest have a long and proud history, stretching back to Roman times. The bath culture flourished while the city was under Turkish occupation, and several still-functioning bathhouses—Király, Rudas, and Rácz—are among the architectural relics of the Turkish period. In the late 19th and early 20th centuries—Budapest's "golden age"—several fabulous bathhouses were built: the extravagant and eclectic Széchenyi Baths in City Park, the splendid Art Nouveau Gellért Baths, and the solid neoclassical Lukács Baths. All of these bathhouses are still in use and are worth a look even for nonbathers. Most baths in Budapest have recently instituted a complicated new pricing system (dubbed the "refund system") that charges according to the time that you have spent in the baths. Previously, a single admission ticket bought you an unlimited visit. Now, you are generally required to pay for the longest possible duration (4 hr. or more) when you enter the bathhouse and you are refunded on the basis of the actual time that you spent on the premises when you exit. You are given a chip card upon entry; keep careful track of the card because if you lose it you are assumed to have stayed for the maximum time and you will not receive a refund.

THE BEST BATHHOUSES

Gellért Baths 🌟🌟 Budapest's most spectacular bathhouse, the Gellért Baths are located in Buda's Hotel Gellért, the oldest Hungarian spa hotel and an Art Nouveau jewel. Enter the baths through the side entrance. The exterior of the building is in need of restoration, but once inside the lobby, you'll be delighted by the details. The unisex indoor pool is without question one of Europe's finest, with marble columns, majolica tiles, and stone lion heads spouting water. The two single-sex Turkish-style thermal baths, off to either side of the pool through badly marked doors, are also glorious, though in need of restoration. In the summer months, the outdoor roof pool attracts a lot of attention for 10 minutes every hour on the hour, when the artificial wave machine is turned on. There are separate nude sunbathing decks for men and women, but you'll have to figure out where they are. In general, you need patience to navigate this place.

XI. Kelenhegyi út 4. 📞 1/466-6166. Admission to the thermal bath costs 3,000 Ft ($15/£7.70) for 4 hr. or more; a 15-min. massage is 2,300 Ft ($12/£5.90). Lockers or cabins are included. Admission to all pools and baths, without a cabin and only communal dressing rooms, is 2,500 Ft ($13/£6.40) adults and children, for 4 hr. or more. Prices and the lengthy list of services, including the complicated refund system, are posted in English. The thermal baths are open in summer daily 6am–7pm; in winter Mon–Fri 6am–7pm, Sat–Sun 6am–5pm, with the last entrance an hour before closing. Take tram 47 or 49 from Deák tér to Szent Gellért tér.

Király Baths 🌟🌟 The Király Baths are one of Budapest's most important architectural monuments to Turkish rule. This is a place where Hungarian culture meets the Eastern culture that influenced it. The bath itself, built in the late 16th century, is housed under an octagonal domed roof. Sunlight filters through small round windows in the ceiling. The water glows. The effect is perfectly tranquil. In addition to the thermal baths, there are sauna and steam room facilities. Bring a towel if you like, since you will not receive one until the end of your treatment. Upon exiting the baths, help yourself to a cotton sheet from the pile near the base of the stairs. Wrap yourself up and lounge with a cup of tea in the relaxation room, where you can also receive a pedicure or massage.

Women can use the baths on Monday, Wednesday, and Friday from 7am to 5pm. Men are welcome on Tuesday, Thursday, and Saturday from 9am to 7pm.

I. Fő u. 84. 📞 1/201-4392. Admission to baths 1,100 Ft ($5.50/£2.80) for 1½ hr. only. Metro: Batthyány tér (Red line).

Rudas Baths 🌟🌟 Near the Erzsébet Bridge, on the Buda side of the city, is another of Budapest's classic Turkish baths. These baths are for men only, though both sexes are admitted to the swimming pool. During early mornings the crowd is predominantly composed of older men, and according to local lore, the place becomes something of a pickup spot after 9am. The first baths were built on this site in the 14th century, although the Rudas Bathhouse itself dates to the late 16th century. It boasts an octagonal pool and domed roof; some of the small window holes in the cupola have stained glass, while others are open to the sky, allowing diffused light to stream in. You'll find most of the same services and facilities here that you would at Király: a thermal bath, a sauna, and a steam bath.

I. Döbrentei tér 9. © **1/356-1322.** Admission to thermal baths 1,000 Ft ($5/£2.60) for 1½ hr. only, swimming pool 800 Ft ($4/£2). Weekdays 6am–8pm; weekends 6am–1pm. Bus: 7; get off at the Buda side of the Erzsébet Bridge, turn left, and walk down to the riverside.

Széchenyi Baths ★★   Part of an immense health spa located in the City Park, the Széchenyi Baths are perhaps second only to the Gellért Baths in terms of facilities and popular appeal. Ivy climbs the walls of the sprawling pool complex here. On a nice day, crowds of bathers, including many families and tourists, visit the palatial unisex outdoor swimming pool. Turkish-style thermal baths are segregated and are located off to the sides of the pool. Look for the older gentlemen concentrating intently on their chess games, half-immersed in the steaming pool. Prices are all posted in English, and the refund system is described.

XIV. Állatkerti út 11–14, in City Park. © **1/363-3210.** www.szechenzifurdo.hu. Admission to the thermal baths is 2,000 Ft ($10/£5.15), dressing cabins are extra. Daily 6am–7pm, except Sat–Sun in winter, when the complex closes at 5pm. Metro: Széchenyi fürdő (Yellow line).

OUTDOOR ACTIVITIES & SPORTS

GOLF   For information, contact the **Hungarian Golf Club,** V. Bécsi út 5 (© **1/ 317-6025;** www.golfhungary.hu). The nearest course is located on Szentendre Island, 25 minutes north of Budapest by car. Call the course directly at © **26/392-465.** For putting practice, the **19th Hole Golf Driving Range** is located at II. Adyliget, Feketefej u. 6 (© **1/354-1510**).

HORSEBACK RIDING   Riding remains a popular activity in Hungary, land of the widely feared Magyar horsemen of a bygone era. A good place to mount up is the **Petneházy Lovasiskola (Riding School),** at II. Feketefej u. 2 (© **1/397-5048;** www. petnehazy-lovascentrum.hu). As far out in the Buda Hills as you can go without leaving the city limits, the school is located in open country, with trails in the hills. Riding on the track with a trainer costs 2,500 Ft ($13/£6.40) for 30 minutes; open riding with a guide is 4,500 Ft ($23/£12). There are also pony rides for children at 1,500 Ft ($7.50/£3.85) for 15 minutes, and there are 30-minute horse-cart rides at 10,000 Ft ($50/£26) for a group of up to 10 people. The Petneházy Country Club is down the road. At the stable is a great little *csárda* (inn/restaurant), recently renovated; you might want to have lunch here. The stable is open year-round Friday, Saturday, and Sunday from 9am to 5pm. Take bus no. 56 (56E is fastest) from Moszkva tér to the last stop, then bus no. 63 to Feketefej utca, followed by a 10-minute walk.

The **Hungarian Equestrian Tourism Association,** located at V. Ferenciek tere 4 (© **1/317-1644;** fax 1/267-0171; www.equi.hu), might also serve your riding interests.

IN-LINE SKATING & ICE-SKATING   There are several options for both in Budapest. The oldest and most popular ice rink is in Városliget, on the lake next to Vajdahunyad castle. However, since it is an open-air facility, it is open only from mid-October until the end of February. Hours are Monday through Friday 9am to 1pm

Tips Thermal Bathing 101

Thermal bathing is an activity steeped in ritual. For this reason, and because bathhouse employees tend to be unfriendly relics of the old system, many foreigners find a trip to the baths stressful or confusing at first. As with any ritualistic activity, it helps to spend some time observing before joining in. Even then, you are likely not to know what to do or where to go. The best advice is to try to enjoy the foreignness of the experience—why else do we leave home?

The most confusing step may well be the first: the ticket window, with its endless list of prices for different facilities and services, often without English translations. Chances are you're coming to use one of the following facilities or services: *uszoda* (pool); *termál* (thermal pool); *fürdő* (bath); *gőzfürdő* (steam bath); massage; and/or sauna. There is no particular order in which people move from one facility to the next; do whatever feels most comfortable. Towel rental is *törülköző* or *lepedő*. An entry ticket generally entitles you to a free locker in the locker room *(öltöző);* or, at some bathhouses, you can opt to pay an additional fee for a private cabin *(kabin).* At the Király, everyone gets a private dressing room and an employee locks and unlocks the rooms (p. 321).

Remember to pack a bathing suit—and a bathing cap, if you wish to swim in the pools—so you won't have to rent vintage 1970 models. In the single-sex baths, nude bathing is the custom and the norm. Towels are provided, but usually as you reenter the locker area after bathing. You may want to bring your own towel with you into the bathing areas if this makes you uncomfortable. Flip-flops are also a good idea. Soap and shampoo are only allowed in the showers, but should be brought out to the bath area so that you can avoid having to return to the comparatively cold locker room prematurely. You will, most likely, want to wash your hair after soaking in the sulfuric waters. Long hair must be tied back when bathing. Leave your eyeglasses in your locker as they will get fogged up in the baths.

Generally, extra services (massage, pedicure) are received after a bath. Tipping is tricky; locker room attendants do not expect tips (except perhaps at the Gellért) but would welcome a tip in the 200 Ft to 400 Ft range ($1–$2/50p–£1) while masseurs and manicurists expect a tip in the 200 Ft to 600 Ft range ($1–$3/50p–£1.55).

There are drinking fountains in the bath areas, and it's a good idea to drink plenty of water before a bath. And don't bathe on an empty stomach; the hot water and steam take a heavy toll on the unfortified body, especially for those unaccustomed to the baths. Most bathhouses have snack bars in the lobbies where you can pick up a cold juice or sandwich on your way out. After the baths, you will be thirsty and hungry. Be sure to replenish yourself.

and 4 to 8pm; Saturday 9am to 1pm, 2 to 6pm, and 7 to 10pm; Sunday 10am to 1pm and 4 to 8pm. The fee is 300 Ft ($1.50/80p) on weekdays and 600 Ft ($3/£1.55) on weekends. Skates rent for 500 Ft ($2.50/£1.30) an hour. International visitors should also have their passports for ID when renting. Adults and children can rent in-line and ice skates at all the rinks.

TENNIS   If you plan to play tennis in Budapest, bring your own racquet along since most courts don't rent equipment; when it is available, it's usually primitive.

Many of Budapest's luxury hotels, particularly those removed from the city center, have tennis courts that nonguests can rent. The **MTK Sport Complex,** in Buda at XI. Bartók Béla út 63 (© **1/209-1595**), boasts 13 outdoor clay courts. The fee is a very reasonable 500 Ft ($2.50/£1.30) per hour during the day or 1,200 Ft ($6/£3.10) per hour at night, under floodlights. Three outdoor courts are covered by a tent year-round; from October through April, all courts are covered and the price of play throughout the day is 2,200 Ft ($11/£5.65) per hour. Equipment is not available for rental. The facility is open daily from 6am to 10pm. Móricz Zsigmond körtér, a transportation hub served by countless buses and trams, is only 5 minutes from the center by foot.

WALKING TOUR   THE CASTLE DISTRICT

Start:	Roosevelt tér, Pest side of Chain Bridge.
Finish:	Tóth Árpád sétány, Castle District.
Time:	3 to 4 hours (excluding museum visits).
Best Times:	Tuesday through Sunday.
Worst Time:	Monday, when museums are closed.

A limestone-capped plateau rising impressively above the Danube, Castle Hill was first settled in the 13th century; it remains the spiritual capital of Hungary. The district has been leveled more than once, most recently by the 1945 Soviet shelling of Nazi forces. It was always painstakingly rebuilt in the prevailing style of the day, shifting from Gothic to baroque to Renaissance. After World War II, an attempt was made to incorporate various elements of the district's historic appearance into the general restoration. Castle Hill, a UNESCO World Cultural Heritage site, consists of two parts: the Royal Palace itself and the so-called Castle District, a mostly reconstructed medieval city. The Royal Palace now houses a number of museums, including the Hungarian National Gallery. The adjoining Castle District is a compact, narrow neighborhood of cobblestone lanes and twisting alleys; restrictions on vehicular traffic enhance the tranquillity and the old-world feel. Prime examples of every type of Hungarian architecture, from early Gothic to neo-Romanesque, can be seen. A leisurely walk in the Castle District will be a warmly remembered experience.

To get an accurate picture of the dimensions and grandeur of Castle Hill, start the walking tour in Pest's Roosevelt tér, on the:

❶ Széchenyi Chain Bridge

One of the outstanding landmarks of Budapest, the first permanent bridge across the Danube was originally built in 1849. Sadly, that first bridge was destroyed by Nazi dynamite during World War II. The 1949 opening ceremony for the

reconstructed bridge was held 100 years to the day after its original inauguration.

Walk across the bridge. Arriving in Buda, you're now in:

❷ Clark Ádám tér

This square was named for the Scottish engineer who supervised the building of the bridge and afterward made Budapest his home.

Walking Tour: The Castle District

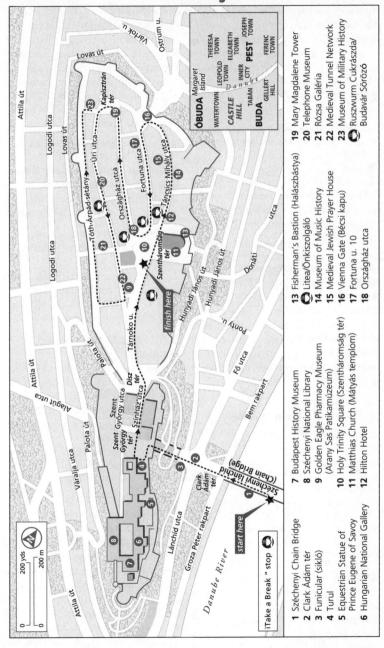

1 Széchenyi Chain Bridge
2 Clark Ádám tér
3 Funicular (sikló)
4 Turul
5 Equestrian Statue of Prince Eugene of Savoy
6 Hungarian National Gallery
7 Budapest History Museum
8 Széchenyi National Library
9 Golden Eagle Pharmacy Museum (Arany Sas Patikamúzeum)
10 Holy Trinity Square (Szentháromság tér)
11 Matthias Church (Mátyás templom)
12 Hilton Hotel
13 Fisherman's Bastion (Halászbástya)
⓵ Litea/Önkiszolgáló
14 Museum of Music History
15 Medieval Jewish Prayer House
16 Vienna Gate (Bécsi kapu)
17 Fortuna u. 10
18 Országház utca
19 Mary Magdalene Tower
20 Telephone Museum
21 Rózsa Galéria
22 Medieval Tunnel Network
23 Museum of Military History
⓵ Ruszwurm Cukrászda/ Budavár Söröző

ⓘ "Take a Break" stop

start here

finish here

325

From Clark Ádám tér, take the:

➌ Funicular *(sikló)*

The funicular will transport you up to the Royal Palace in just a minute or two. Dating from 1870, it too was destroyed in World War II and was not rebuilt until 1986. You can also walk up the steep stairs to Castle Hill.

Whichever method of ascent you choose, when you arrive at the top, turn and look left at the statue of the:

➍ Turul

This mythical eagle is perched on the wall looking out over the Danube to Pest. The eagle is said to have guided the ancient Magyars in their westward migration.

The main courtyard of the palace, from which the museums are entered, is on the building's far side, but first go down the nearby stairs to see the:

➎ Equestrian Statue of Prince Eugene of Savoy

Prince Eugene was one of the leaders of the united Christian armies that ousted the Turks from Hungary in the late 17th century. Inside the palace are a number of museums. You might want to visit them now or return after the walking tour.

The first museum is the:

➏ Hungarian National Gallery

This museum houses much of the greatest art ever produced by Hungarians. Don't miss the works of the 19th-century artists Mihály Munkácsy, László Paál, Károly Ferenczy, Pál Szinyei Merse, Gyula Benczúr, and Károly Lotz. Nor should you overlook József Rippl-Rónai, the great Art Nouveau painter of the turn-of-the-20th-century period.

Proceed to the:

➐ Budapest History Museum

The highlights here are the Gothic rooms and statues that were uncovered during the post–World War II excavation and rebuilding of the Royal Palace. The rooms and all their contents, dating from as far as the 14th century, were buried for hundreds of years.

Next we have the:

➑ Széchenyi National Library

The library is named for Ferenc Széchenyi (not his more famous son István, after whom the Chain Bridge is named), who founded the institution in 1802. It now houses the world's greatest collection of "Hungarica," with some four million holdings.

Now proceed to Wing A of the Buda Palace, where you'll find the:

➒ Golden Eagle Pharmacy Museum (Arany Sas Patikamúzeum)

Renaissance and baroque pharmacy relics are displayed in this odd little museum.

Just ahead on Tárnok utca is:

➓ Holy Trinity Square (Szentháromság tér)

This central square of the Castle District is where you'll find the Holy Trinity Column, or Plague Column, dating from the early 18th century, and the:

⓫ Matthias Church (Mátyás templom)

Officially called the Church of Our Lady, this symbol of the Castle District is universally known as Matthias Church because the Renaissance monarch, Matthias Corvinus, one of Hungary's most revered kings, was the major donor of the church and was married twice inside it. There's an ecclesiastical art collection inside. Organ concerts are held Tuesday and Friday evenings in the summer.

Next door to the church is the:

⓬ Hilton Hotel

The Castle District's only major hotel, the Hilton tastefully incorporates two ruins into its award-winning design: a 13th-century Dominican church, with a tower rising above the hotel, and the baroque facade of a 17th-century Jesuit college, which makes up the hotel's main entrance. During the Socialist years, this was one of the very few Western-style hotels accompanied by a casino. Summer concerts are held in the Dominican Courtyard.

Behind the Hilton is the:

⑬ Fisherman's Bastion (Halászbástya)

This sprawling neo-Romanesque structure was built in 1905 on the site of an old fish market (hence the name), and affords a marvelous panorama of Pest. Looking out over the Danube to Pest, you can see (from left to right): Margaret Island and the Margaret Bridge, Parliament, St. Stephen's Basilica, the Chain Bridge, the Vigadó Concert Hall, the Inner City Parish Church, the Erzsébet Bridge, and the Szabadság Bridge. Avoid the overpriced restaurant inside the Fisherman's Bastion.

TAKE A BREAK
You may want to stop at **Litea,** a bookstore and tearoom located in the Fortuna Passage, opposite the Hilton. You can browse, then sit and enjoy a cup of tea while looking over your selections. If it is lunch you desire, head to the **Café Miró,** opposite the Matthias Church on Úri utca (p. 308), where you can have a light lunch, coffee, tea, or a sumptuous pastry.

Because the entire length of each of the Castle District's north-south streets is worth seeing, the tour will now take you back and forth between the immediate area of Szentháromság tér and the northern end of the district. First, head down Táncsics Mihály utca, to Táncsics Mihály u. 7, the:

⑭ Museum of Music History

Beethoven stayed here for a spell in 1800, when this structure was a private home. The museum now houses the archives of the great composer Bartók. The building next door, at Táncsics Mihály u. 9, served for many years as a prison. Among those incarcerated here were Mihály Táncsics, the 19th-century champion of free press after whom the street is named, and Lajos Kossuth, the leader of the 1848-to-1849 anti-Habsburg revolution. Táncsics utca was the center of Buda's Jewish community during medieval times. During general postwar reconstruction work in the 1960s, the remains of several synagogues were uncovered.

Continue walking down the street to Táncsics Mihály u. 26, where you'll find the:

⑮ Medieval Jewish Prayer House

This building dates from the 14th century. In the 15th and 16th centuries, the Jews of Buda thrived under Turkish rule. The 1686 Christian reconquest of Buda was soon followed by a massacre of Jews. Many survivors fled Buda; this tiny Sephardic synagogue was turned into an apartment.

After exiting the synagogue, retrace your steps about 9m (30 ft.) back on Táncsics Mihály utca, turn left onto Babits Mihály köz, and then turn left onto Babits Mihály sétány. This path will take you onto the top of the:

⑯ Vienna Gate (Bécsi kapu)

This is one of the main entrances to the Castle District. From the top of the gate, you can look out onto the fashionable Rose Hill (Rózsadomb) neighborhood in the Buda Hills. The enormous neo-Romanesque building towering above Bécsi kapu tér houses the National Archives. Bécsi kapu tér is also home to a lovely row of houses (nos. 5–8).

From here, head up Fortuna utca to the house at:

⑰ Fortuna u. 10

This is certainly one of the district's most photographed houses. It dates from the 13th century but has been restored in Louis XVI style. The facade incorporates medieval details.

Continue to Fortuna u. 4, where you'll find the charming, unassuming:

⑱ Országház utca

This is one of two streets in the Castle District that are best suited for viewing a mysterious Hungarian contribution to Gothic architecture: niches of unknown function that were built into the entryways of medieval buildings. When uncovered during reconstruction, the niches were either preserved or incorporated into the designs of new, modern structures. Niches can be seen in Országház u. nos. 9 and 20, while no. 28 has enormous wooden doors.

Walk down Országház utca until it ends in Kapisztrán tér, site of the:

⑲ Mary Magdalene Tower

Once part of a large 13th-century church, the tower is the only section that survived World War II.

Now take Úri utca back in the direction of the Royal Palace. In a corner of the courtyard of Úri u. 49, a vast former cloister, stands the small:

⑳ Telephone Museum

The museum's prime attraction is the actual telephone exchange (7A1-type rotary system) that was in use in the city from 1928 to 1985.

Continue down Úri u. and make a right onto Szentháromság u., and walk to no. 13 where you'll see:

㉑ Rózsa Galéria

No doubt you've noticed the presence in the Castle District of a large number of art galleries. Hungarian naive and primitive art is on display at this gallery. Works of art can be had for, on average, 100,000 Ft ($100/£257).

Head back to Úri u. and find no. 9, the entrance to the:

㉒ Medieval Tunnel Network

The network weaves its way through the almost 15km (9 miles) of rock beneath the Castle District. The only part of this network that you can actually see is home to the Buda Wax Works, an unimpressive, tacky exhibit on the "legends" of early Hungarian history.

Úri utca ends back in Dísz tér. Take tiny Móra Ferenc utca (to the right) to Tóth Árpád sétány, the promenade that runs the length of the western rampart of the Castle District. This is a shady road with numerous benches. At its northern end, appropriately housed in the former barracks at Tóth Árpád sétány 40, is the:

㉓ Museum of Military History

This museum is dedicated to the history of Hungary's military endeavors, including World War I and World War II. For those looking for the exhibits on the 1956 Revolution, many of these exhibits have been transferred to the Terror House museum.

The walking tour ends back near Szentháromság tér, where you can catch the Várbusz down to Moszkva tér. Alternatively, from Dísz tér you can get bus no. 16 to Deák tér.

WINDING DOWN

The **Ruszwurm Cukrászda,** Szentháromság u. 7, has been here since 1827. This little coffeehouse and pastry shop is the only one of its kind in the Castle District. Its pastries are among the city's best. Just down the street, at Úri u. 13, is **Budavár Söröző,** a good spot for a snack, espresso, or beer. It has just two tiny tables inside and three or four outside on the sidewalk.

MAIN SHOPPING STREETS   The hub of the tourist-packed capital is the first pedestrian shopping street in Budapest, Váci utca. It runs from the stately Vörösmarty tér in the center of Pest, across Kossuth Lajos utca, all the way to Vámház krt. High-end locals and travelers alike throng Váci utca as well as the boutique- and shop-filled roads bisecting pedestrian streets and courtyards. Váci utca was formerly known throughout the country as *the* street for good bookshops. Sadly, only one remains. The street is now largely occupied by Euro-fashion clothing boutiques (where high prices prevail) and an overwhelming number of folklore/souvenir shops, as well as cafes and bars (many of which are overpriced tourist traps).

Another popular shopping area for travelers is the **Castle District** in Buda, with its abundance of overpriced folk-art boutiques and art galleries. A healthy selection of

Hungarian wines from historical local viticulture regions can also be found in the intimate labyrinthine cellar of the **House of Hungarian Wines.**

While Hungarians might window-shop in these two neighborhoods, they tend to do their serious shopping elsewhere. One of their favorite streets is Pest's **Outer Ring (Nagykörút),** which extends into **West End Center,** central Europe's largest multifunction shopping mall, located just behind the Nyugati Railway Station. Another bustling shopping street is Pest's **Kossuth Lajos utca,** off the Erzsébet Bridge, and its continuation, **Rákóczi út,** which extends all the way out to Keleti Railway Station. **Andrássy út,** from Deák tér to Oktogon, is also a popular, though much more upscale, shopping street. Together with the adjacent **Liszt Ferenc tér** and **Nagymező utca,** Andrássy út is also the most popular hub for nightlife, with numerous coffee shops, bars, and restaurants. In Buda, Hungarian crowds visit the shops of **Margit körút** and the neighborhood around the transportation hub **Móricz Zsigmond körtér,** where the Buda Skála department store is located. Hidden among the herd of cafes and restaurants of the lively **Ráday utca,** small interior design boutiques and shops present unique presents and doodads. You can often pay by credit card in the most popular shopping areas.

HOURS   Most stores are open Monday through Friday from 10am to 6pm and Saturday from 9am or 10am to about 1pm. Some stores stay open an hour or two later on Thursday or Friday, and some close for an hour at lunchtime. Most shops are closed on Sunday, except for those in downtown Pest. Shopping malls are open on weekends, sometimes as late as 9pm or 10pm.

TAXES & REFUNDS   Refunds on the 10%-to-25% **value-added tax (VAT),** which is built into all prices, are available for most consumer goods purchases of more than 50,000 Ft ($250/£128), VAT included (look for stores with the "Tax-Free" logo in the window). The refund process, however, is elaborate and confusing. In most shops, the salesperson can provide you with the necessary documents: the store receipt, a separate receipt indicating the VAT amount on your purchase, the VAT reclaim form, and the mailing envelope. The salesperson should also be able to help you fill out the paperwork. Use a separate claim form for each applicable purchase. If you are departing Hungary by plane, you can collect your refund at the **IBUSZ Agency** at Ferihegy Airport. You have to do this right after checking in but *before* you pass security control. Otherwise, hold on to the full packet until you leave Hungary and get your forms certified by Customs when you land. Then, mail in your envelope and wait for your refund. Two wrinkles: You must get your forms certified by Customs within 90 days of the purchase, and you must mail in your forms within 183 days of the date of export certification on the refund claim form. For further information, contact **Global Refund (Innova-Invest Pénzügyi Rt.),** IV. Ferenciek tere 10, 1053 Budapest (✆ **1/411-0157;** fax 1/411-0159; www.globalrefund.com).

SHIPPING & CUSTOMS   You can ship a box to yourself from any post office, but the rules on packing boxes are as strict as they are arcane. The Hungarian postal authorities prefer that you use one of their official shipping boxes, for sale at all post offices. They're quite flimsy, however, and have been known to break open in transit.

Very few shops will organize shipping for you. Exceptions to this rule include most Herend and Zsolnay porcelain shops, Ajka crystal shops, and certain art galleries, which employ the services of a packing-and-shipping company, Touristpost. Touristpost offers three kinds of delivery: express, airmail, and surface. At the moment, it seems that the service is not available directly to the public but functions only through these particular shops. You may inquire further at **Touristpost,** III. Meggyfa u. 31 (✆ **1/388-7465;**

www.touristpost.hu). Though the service is costly (for example, 30,000 Ft/$135/£77 for 60 lb.), you will still likely be paying less for fine porcelain and crystal purchased in Hungary than you would at home.

Hungarian Customs regulations do not limit the export of noncommercial quantities of most goods. However, the export of some food staples, like coffee (1 kilogram) is strictly regulated (but rarely enforced). The limit on wine and spirits is 1 liter each, and 500 cigarettes may be exported. For more on Customs, see p. 25.

SHOPPING A TO Z
Antiques
With a rich selection of specialized shops carrying antique artifacts from keys to precious furniture, Budapest will please all bric-a-brac-adoring travelers. Nevertheless, when shopping for antiques, you should know that Hungary forbids the export of items that are designated "cultural treasures." Some purchases come with a certificate allowing export; with other purchases, the buyer has the responsibility of going to the correct office (in the Museum of Applied Arts) and applying for the certificate. Our advice is to buy only from those shops that supply the certificate for you; a journey through Hungarian bureaucracy—like any other bureaucracy—can be a withering experience.

Although it no longer has a monopoly on the sale of antiques, the state-owned trading house contingent **BÁV** (Bizományi Kereskedőház és Záloghitel Rt.; www.bav.hu) continues to control the lion's share of the antiques market in Hungary. Here's a partial list of addresses, contact information, and products for BÁV shops:

- The shop at II. Franken Leo u. 13 (© **1/315-0417**) specializes in vintage paintings, jewelry, and furniture.
- The shop at V. Bécsi u. 1 (© **1/266-2087**; fax 1/317-2548), near Deák tér, is the largest of the shops, specializing in antique furniture, chandeliers, carpets, and paintings.
- The shop at V. Ferenciek tere 10 (© **1/318-3733**) specializes in carpets and jewelry.
- The shop at V. Szent István körút 3 (© **1/473-0666**), on Pest's shopping Outer Ring, showcases antique furniture, carpets, and jewelry.
- The shop at VI. Andrássy út 43 (© **1/342-9143**), near the Opera House, specializes in antique art, furniture, carpets, porcelain, and silver.
- The shop at V. Párizsi u. 2 (© **1/318-6217**) stocks rare jewelry gems.
- The shop at IX. Tűzoltó u. 14 (© **1/215-6657**) specializes in furniture.

Anna Antiques   Carefully packed from wall to wall, this beautiful shop presents a nice selection of furniture and pottery while also excelling in hand-embroidered textiles. Take your time and find out more about the objects on display from the charming shop owner. Open Monday through Friday 10am to 6pm, Saturday 10am to 3pm. V. Falk Miksa u. 18–20. © 1/302-5461. Tram: 4 or 6.

Bardoni Eurostyle Antiques   With its stay-awhile atmosphere, the store is decorated as a chic but congested living room. Bardoni carries characteristic Art Nouveau, Bauhaus, and Art Deco furniture and decorations. Open Monday through Friday 10am to 6pm, and Saturday 10am to 2pm. V. Falk Miksa u. 12. © 1/269-0090. www.bardoni.hu. Tram: 4 or 6.

Mihálka Gallery   In this centrally located cramped gallery you'll find a wide array of 18th- and 19th-century vintage furniture, paintings, objets d'art, and interior decorations. Open Monday through Friday 10am to 6pm, Saturday 10am to 2pm. V. Bajcsy Zsilinszky út 20. © 1/302-8650. www.mihalka.hu. Metro: Arany János u. (Blue line).

The **Ecseri Flea Market** (see "Markets," later in this chapter) also deserves mention here, as numerous private antiques dealers operate booths at this one-of-a-kind open-air market.

Art Galleries

Budapest is home to a developing—and still fairly quick-changing—art gallery scene. Uniquely, many art galleries are also auction houses, and vice versa. A new generation of Hungarian collectors has developed, and significant interest from European and international collectors has really fueled the development of the Hungarian modern-art market. The market for antiques is also dynamic as many objects that gathered dust over the Communist era have once again entered the market. Contemporary art, meanwhile, has made less headway in the past few years, and remains an area for future development.

Galleries tend to keep normal store hours (Mon–Fri 10am–6pm and Sat 10am–1 or 2pm, sometimes as late as 6pm). They're concentrated in two areas: the Inner City of Pest and Buda's Castle District. If you want to browse, the art and antiques area of Budapest runs along Falk Miksa, from Jászai Mari tér down to the parliament. A host of art galleries and antiques shops can be found along this route. The art gallery with the best taste in furniture and modern paintings is the Ernst Gallery, located adjacent to Budapest's best coffeehouse, the Central Coffee House.

Ernst Gallery   The gallery features fine and applied arts from Hungary and around Europe. The Ernst Gallery, the most posh gallery in town, is run by a dynamic duo of the Austrian-born Ernst Wastl and his Greek-born wife, Eleni Korani. They put together exhibitions, discover "unknown" Hungarian artists, and whatever they put their hands onto ends up being the talk of the town. The gallery also exhibits and sells fine furniture and a wealthy collection of rarities including vintage art books, posters, and other curiosities. Open Monday through Friday 10am to 7pm, and Saturday 10am to 2pm. V. Irányi u. 27. ℂ **1/266-4016** or 1/266-4017. www.ernstgaleria.hu. Metro: Ferenciek tér (Blue line).

Godot Gallery   Located beside the cafe of the same name, Godot opened its door to the arty crowd in 1999 in order to present a new, dynamic space for contemporary Hungarian art. Exhibitions follow distinctly anti-mainstream themes, and this is reflected in the uneven quality of the works displayed. Open Monday through Friday 10am to 6pm. VII. Madách I. u. 8. ℂ **1/322-5272**. www.godot.hu. Metro: Deák tér (all lines).

Kieselbach Gallery and Auction House   Established and directed by art historian Tamás Kieselbach, the Kieselbach gallery functions as a gallery and auction house. It also puts on museum-type shows that present artworks from private collections at biannual non-selling exhibitions. The gallery specializes in paintings from Hungarian artists between 1850 and 1950. Auctions are held twice a year. Open Monday through Friday 10am to 6pm, and Saturday and Sunday 10am to 1pm. V. Szent István körút 5. ℂ **1/269-3148** or 1/269-2210. www.kieselbach.hu. Tram: 4 or 6 to Jászai Mari tér.

Mû-terem Gallery and Auction House   Established and directed by art historian Judit Virág and her husband, István Törö, this gallery also functions as an auction house. Similar to their main competitors, the Kieselbach Gallery, this gallery also puts on museum-type shows presenting artworks from private collections. Paintings by 19th- and 20th-century Hungarian artists are found here, a gallery that regularly produces record-setting prices for artists. Auctions are held twice a year. Open Monday through Friday 10am to 6pm, and Saturday and Sunday 10am to 1pm. V. Falk Miksa u. 30. ℂ **1/269-3148** or 1/269-2210. www.mu-terem.hu. Tram: 4 or 6 to Jászai Mari tér.

(Finds) Hungarian Art Market: From Bust to Boom

Over the past 15 years, Hungarian artworks, including those of modern Hungarian masters such as Jószef Rippl-Ronai, Béla Iványi Grünwald, Béla Kádár, and Armand Shöenberger, have been gaining popularity among both Hungarian and international collectors.

As a result after a decade-old transition from Communism to a market-driven economy in Hungary, the art market has gone from bust to boom as collectors discover the works of classical and modern Hungarian artists. Even in the U.S., paintings are fetching record-breaking prices. In the spring of 2005, a József Rippl-Ronai (1861–1927) painting called *Girl with a Cage* (1891–92) was auctioned off to Budapest-based art dealer Ernst Wastl of Ernst Gallery (see listing in this section) for a whopping $590,400.

The market within Hungary itself has been particularly active. Many art-works are returning to Hungary after having been dispersed during World War II, or the subsequent Communist era. Before World War II, Hungarian private collectors amassed notable collections, although many of these were pillaged by Nazi Germany and later Soviet Russia after the war. (Many of Hungary's prewar cultural treasures to this day are thought to be in Russia, and their return is the subject of protracted and heated negotiations between the two countries, which seem to be getting nowhere.)

You can see this feeding frenzy for Hungarian art at spring and fall auctions in Budapest, which fill to capacity (with some also bidding on the phone from international locations). Visitors watch in awe as records are broken almost on a yearly basis. Paintings that only a decade ago may have fetched $15,000, can now fetch 10 times that, especially if you are talking about internationally renowned artists like Mihály Munkácsy.

The auction-house scene in Hungary has become so popular that in contrast to North America or Europe, most of the important private galleries have created a dual system of being both auction houses and galleries. See the art galleries listed in this section, and call or inquire in person for their auction schedules.

Bookstores

Bestsellers   Bestsellers is Budapest's first English-language bookstore (opened in 1992). With its spacious and bright interior, the shop is a popular meeting spot for English-speaking travelers. The store has a wide selection of fiction, as well as a reasonably good collection of travel books, including books on Hungary. A wide selection of newspapers and magazines is also available. (**Note:** The owner also runs **Király Books,** at I. Fő u. 79, which has a fair selection of guidebooks, maps, and language books in mostly English and French; call ✆ **1/214-0972.**) Open Monday through Friday 9am to 6:30pm, Saturday 10am to 5pm, Sunday 10am to 4pm. V. Október 6 u. 11. ✆ **1/312-1295.** Metro: Arany János utca (Blue line).

Central European University Bookstore   This store features books covering a wide variety of disciplines. The selection of books on central and Eastern European politics and history is particularly notable since the Central European University Press publishes a great variety of books on all topics central European (visit www.ceupress.com). Open Monday through Friday 10am to 6pm. V. Nádor utca 9. ℭ 1/327-3097. Metro: Kossuth tér (Red line) or Arany János utca (Blue line).

Írók Boltja ⭐⭐ The "Writers' Bookshop"—a true literary center with a rich history, first-rate literary events, and inspired window displays—is a mecca for writers, readers, and curious bystanders. In the first half of the last century the store was the popular Japanese Coffee House, a popular literary coffee shop, then became the Spark Bookstore around 1955, during the Communist era. The shop's name was changed around 1958, and was state-run until 1991, when 14 employees became the co-owners during the privatization of state-owned business. It is now practically an institution, and Hungarian authors such as Péter Nádas, Péter Eszterházy, and Nobel prize–winner Imre Kertész have read here. Almost all events are held in Hungarian, but the store has a nice selection of English-language books, plus a cozy in-store coffee corner. Open Monday through Friday 10am to 6pm, Saturday 10am to 1pm. VI. Andrássy út 45. ℭ 1/322-1645. www.irokboltja.hu. Metro: Oktogon (Yellow line).

Litea: Literature & Tea Bookshop Situated in the Fortuna courtyard, opposite the Hilton Hotel, this bookshop/teahouse stocks a wide range of books on Hungary; CDs and cassettes of the works of Hungarian composers; and cards, maps, and other quality souvenirs for serious enthusiasts of Hungarian culture. Take your time browsing, order a cup of tea, sit, and have a closer look at the books that interest you. This calm, no-obligation-to-buy atmosphere is a rare find. Open daily 10am to 6pm. I. Hess András tér 4. ℭ 1/375-6987. www.litea.hu. Bus: Várbusz from Moszkva tér, bus 16 from Deák tér, or funicular from Clark Ádám tér, to Castle Hill.

Fashion & Shoes

We list just a few options, assuming that you'll discover the rest on your own. For discount clothes, see "Markets," p. 336.

Ciánkáli Called the Anti-Fashion Shop, this "high-quality" secondhand shop chain sells vintage junk and alternative-punk modish collections and accessories. They also display a large selection of funky brand-new items. Look for the wide selection of leather clothing. Open Monday through Friday 10am to 7pm, Saturday 10am to 2pm. VII. Dohány u. 68. ℭ 1/341-0540. Metro: Blaha Lujza tér (Red line).

Emilia Anda Mixing organic materials like silk with plastic or paper, the noted young designer Emilia Anda's clothes make heads turn. Her studies in architecture paved the way for creating her inimitable lustrous get-ups, one that stands out in the Hungarian fashion world. Open Monday through Friday noon to 6pm, Saturday 11am to 2pm. V. Váci u. 16/b. No phone. Metro: Vörösmarty tér (Yellow line).

Iguana Looking for some sparkling oversize grandma-glasses or perhaps crazy '60s or '70s cult accessories? A shrine for retro-rats, the shop stocks rows of peace jackets, trousers, bags, and jewelry. Listen to or purchase some of their all-star euphoric secondhand CDs. Open Monday through Friday 11am to 7pm, Saturday 10am to 2pm. VIII. Krúdy Gyula u. 9. No phone. www.iguanaretro.hu. Metro: Kálvin tér (Blue line). There is a 2nd store at XI. Tompa u. 1. No phone. Tram: 4 or 6.

Katti Zoób Celebrated Hungarian fashion designer Zoób's high-end couture ranges from slick, eccentric, yet harmonious businesswomen's outfits to smart and naughty on-the-go-wear and accessories. The shop, located in the capacious MOM Park, is open Monday through Saturday 10am to 8pm, Sunday 10am to 6pm. XII. Alkotás u. 53. ℭ 1/487-5609. www.kattizoob.com. Tram: 59 or 61.

Katalin Hampel   Put on the Hungarian design map with her unique marriage of traditional Hungarian clothing with a modern flair, Katalin Hampel designs women's clothing marked by delicate precision of handmade embroidery. Open Monday through Friday 10am to 6pm, Saturday 10am to 1pm. V. Váci u. 8. ⓒ **1/318-9741.** www.tangoantique.com. Metro: Vörösmarty tér (Yellow line).

La Boutique   Showcasing the products of significant high-end shoe designers, the shop specializes in men's shoes and the prices match Western designer label prices. Open Monday through Friday 10am to 7pm, and Saturday 10am to 4pm. VI. Andrássy út 16. ⓒ **1/302-5646.** Metro: Opera (Yellow line).

Látomás   Run by 25 suave creative designers, the shop is a fresh addition to the growing Hungarian fashion marketplace. The sexy, chic, and unique hats, jewelry, and accessories are intended mostly for women—although men might find some must-have's as well. Browse through their spicy secondhand clothing stock as well. Open Monday through Friday 11 to 7pm, Saturday 11am to 3pm. VII. Dohány u. 20. No phone. Tram: 4 or 6.

Manu-Art   Handmade by local designers, these warm clothes are likely to cheer up those who work in the cool outdoors. Odd fluffy sheep, crazy snails, or curlicue nonfigurative designs suit all ages. Open Monday through Friday 10am to 7pm, Saturday 10am to 2pm. V. Károly krt. 10 ⓒ **1/266-8136.** Metro: Astoria (Red line). There is a 2nd store in the busy Mammut mall (same phone).

Náray Tamás   Situated in the posh Ybl Palace, across from the Central Kávéház, this elegant and spacious shop sells the creations of one of Hungary's most celebrated designers, Tamás Náray. The clothes are tasteful, yet the materials used have much to be desired. The cutting-edge status of the collection is reflected in the extreme price range. Monday through Friday noon to 8pm, Saturday 10am to 2pm. V. Károlyi M. u. 12. ⓒ **1/266-2473.** Metro: Ferenciek tere (Blue line).

Retrock   A group of young contemporary designers swimming against the mainstream fashion-current established this colorful boutique comprising one-of-a-kind clothes and accessories. Sanctuary for extreme fashion aficionados. Open Monday through Friday 10:30am to 7:30pm, Saturday 10:30am to 4:30pm. V. Ferenczy István u. 28. ⓒ **1/318-1007.** www.retrock.com. Metro: Astoria (Red line).

Tisza Cipő   A former Soviet-era brand, Tisza Shoes has been smartly resuscitated into a retro shoe brand that shot up on the must-have shoes in Hungary. It is now enjoying its laid-back, high-end segment market position. Open Monday through Friday 10am to 6pm, Saturday 10am to 2pm. VII. Károly körút 1. ⓒ **1/266-3055.** www.tiszacipo. hu. Metro: Astoria (Red line).

The Art of MAG Design Jewelry

Nine gifted jewelry artists joined forces in 2001 and now offer quality jewelry under the label **MAG Design,** managed and directed by the friendly Péter Lipták. Best in show: Klára Abaffy combines silver with various exotic materials; Eszter Zámori works with gold, silver, and colorful precious stones (and some pieces make slight sounds as you move); and Gyöngyvér Gaál once combined miniature flowers with silver, coral, and polyester. See the MAG Design wares and talk to Peter in the **VAM Design Gallery,** which is open Monday to Friday from 8am to 6pm (Tues 1–4pm), at Váci utca 62–64 (ⓒ **30/984-3616**).

Extreme Fashion! Budapest's Avant-Garde Designers

While Hungary can't compete with the fashion capitals of Paris, New York, or Milan, some trailblazers in the Hungarian fashion world are setting the foundations again. They remember Hungary's prewar glamour, when Budapest was termed the "Paris of Eastern Europe," a notion quashed by years of Communism and its attacks on creative self-expression. Now, several established designers like **Tamás Náray** and **Katti Zoób** are catering to the new upper class with some posh, pricey designs.

Tamás Király, meanwhile, is a true creative visionary who puts on shows everywhere from New York to London—including several with the noted designer Vivienne Westwood. Király is more of a fashion artist than a "label" designer. He creates designs that could come out of some fantasy dreamscape, and he takes part in numerous "performances." Don't be surprised if you see a model walking around Budapest with bizarre metallic structures, followed by another in a costume and on crutches, with another eating cotton candy off of the body of yet another model. If you see one of these avant-garde fashion performances, it is likely that the event was dreamed up by Tamás Király. If you decide to buy one of the creations, though, you may be disappointed. They are probably not for sale. Király truly lives on the outer edges of the classical "fashion world," all while being in the center of a unique creative world. He considers himself, meanwhile, the "most free designer in the universe."

For more on the Budapest fashion scene, visit Pep! Magazine's website, **www.pepmagazin.hu** (click "English").

For information on Budapest Fashion Weeks, see **www.budapestfashion week.com** and **www.fashionweek.hu**.

Vakondgyár   Offering Hungarian youth fashion, this T-shirt boutique chain features outrageous shirts designed by a whimsical young artist. Starting with the mole figure—the cute key character that gave the brand its name—the shirts' self-indulgent designs include fanciful insects, goofy Hungarian cartoon characters, and other New Age logolike creations in a cacophony of color. Open Monday through Friday 10am to 6pm, Saturday 10am to 1pm. V. Magyar u. 52. © **20/222-5295**. Metro: Kálvin tér (Blue line).

V50 Design Art Studio ℛ   Fashion designer Valeria Fazekas has an eye for clothes that are both eye-catching and elegant. Her hats are works of art. Prices are reasonable, but she does not accept credit cards. She has a second shop at V. Belgrád rakpart 16, where she can often be found working late into the night in the upstairs studio. Both shops are open Monday through Friday 10am to 6pm, Saturday 10am to 2pm. V. Váci u. 50. © **1/337-5320**. Metro: Ferenciek tere (Blue line).

Folk Crafts

Except for a few specialty shops like the ones listed below, the stores of the formerly state-owned **Folkart Háziipar** should be your main source for Hungary's justly famous folk items. Almost everything sold at these stores is handmade—from tablecloths to miniature dolls, from ceramic dishes to sheepskin vests. You can shop with the knowledge that a jury has examined all items for authenticity. Look for the distinctive label (or sticker) that will let you know that you are looking at a Folkart product: a circle with a bird in the center, surrounded by the words FOLKART/NÉPMŰVÉSZETI HUNGARY. The private folk-art shops lining Váci utca and the streets of the Castle District tend to be much more expensive than Folkart, and their products, unlike Folkart's, often tend toward the kitschy (though with some notable exceptions). Folkart's main store, **Folkart Centrum,** has been relocated to the upper end of the mall at V. Váci u. 58 (© **1/318-4697**) and is open daily 10am to 7pm.

One outstanding private shop on Váci utca is **Vali Folklór,** in the courtyard of Váci u. 23 (© **1/337-6301**). A soft-spoken man named Bálint Ács runs this cluttered shop. Ács travels through the villages of Hungary and neighboring countries buying up authentic folk items. He's extremely knowledgeable about the products he sells, and he enjoys speaking with customers (in German or English). When he is not around, his elderly mother keeps shop (she doesn't speak English). The most appealing items here are the traditional women's clothing and the jewelry boxes. From time to time, the store features marvelous, genuine Russian icons. The store has recently expanded its collection to include a great variety of now-hard-to-find Soviet and Eastern European Communist-era pins, medals, and badges, with fair prices. Bálint Ács' mother can tailor clothing for your size in 3 to 4 days. Open Monday through Friday 10am to 6pm, Saturday and Sunday 10am to 7pm (sometimes closed on weekends; call ahead).

Holló Folkart Gallery, at V. Vitkovics Mihály u. 12 (© **1/317-8103**), is an unusual gallery selling handcrafted reproductions of original folk-art pieces from various regions of the country. Beautiful carved and painted furniture is for sale, as are small mirrors, decorative boxes, traditional decorative pottery, and wooden candlesticks. Open Monday through Friday from 10am to 6pm, Saturday 10am to 2pm.

Markets

Warning: Markets in Budapest are very crowded, bustling places. Beware of pickpockets; carry your valuables under your clothing in a money belt rather than in a wallet.

Ecseri Flea Market   According to a local rumor you can find anything at this busy flea market—from eviscerated bombshells to dinosaur eggs. True? Well, you seem to believe it once inside. You are greeted by rows of wooden tables chock-full of old dishes, toys, linens, and bric-a-brac as you enter this market at Nagykőrösi út 156. From the tiny cubicles in the narrow corridors, serious dealers market their wares: Herend and Zsolnay porcelain, Bulgarian and Russian icons, silverware, paintings, furniture, clocks, rugs, prewar dolls and stuffed animals, antique clothing, and jewelry. Due to all the tourist attention—mostly during the weekend—the prices of the market have increased severely although some bargains can still be made. Antiques buyers: Be aware that you'll need permission from the Museum of Applied Arts to take your purchases out of the country (p. 330). Haggling is standard and necessary. Purchases are in cash only. The market runs Monday through Friday 8am to 2pm, Saturday 6am to 2pm, Sunday 8am to 1pm. XIX. Nagykőrösi út. © **1/280-8840.** Take bus 54 from Boráros tér.

FRUIT & VEGETABLE MARKETS (*CSARNOK* OR *PIAC*)   There are five vintage market halls *(vásárcsarnok)* in Budapest. These vast cavernous spaces, architectural wonders of steel and glass, were built in the 1890s in the ambitious grandiose style of the time. Three are still in use as markets and provide a measure of local color you certainly won't find in the grocery store. Hungarian produce in season is sensational, and you'll seldom go wrong with a pound of strawberries, a cup of raspberries, or a couple of peaches.

The **Központi Vásárcsarnok (Central Market Hall)**, at IX. Vámház körút 1–3 (© 1/217-6067), is the largest and most spectacular market hall. Located on the Inner Ring (Kiskörút), just on the Pest side of the Szabadság Bridge, it was impeccably reconstructed in 1995. This bright, three-level market hall is a pleasure to visit. Fresh produce, meat, and cheese vendors dominate the space. Keep your eyes open for inexpensive saffron and dried mushrooms. The mezzanine level features folk-art booths, coffee and drink bars, and fast-food booths. The basement level houses fishmongers, pickled goods, a complete selection of spices, and Asian import foods, along with a large grocery store. The market is open Monday 6am to 5pm, Tuesday through Friday 6am to 6pm, Saturday 6am to 2pm. The nearest metro station is Kálvin tér (Blue line).

The recently restored **Belvárosi Vásárcsarnok (Inner City Market Hall)**, at V. Hold utca 13 (© 1/476-3952), is located in central Pest in the heart of the Lipótváros (Leopold Town), behind the Hungarian National Band at Szabadság tér. It houses a large supermarket and several cheesy discount clothing shops, in addition to a handful of independent fruit-and-vegetable vendors. The market is open Monday 6:30am to 5pm, Tuesday through Friday 6:30am to 6pm, Saturday from 6:30am to 2pm. Take the metro either to Kossuth tér (Red line) or to Arany János utca (Blue line).

The **Rákóczi téri Vásárcsarnok,** at VIII. Rákóczi tér 7–9 (© 1/313-8442), was badly damaged by fire in 1988 but was restored to its original splendor and reopened in 1991. There's only a small area of private vendors; the rest of the hall is filled with retail booths. Open Monday 6am to 4pm, Tuesday through Friday 6am to 6pm, Saturday 6am to 1pm. Take the metro to Blaha Lujza tér (Red line) or tram no. 4 or 6 directly to Rákóczi tér.

In addition to these three large classic market halls, Budapest has a number of neighborhood produce markets. The **Fehérvári úti Vásárcsarnok,** at XI. Kőrösi J. u. 7–9 (© 1/385-6563), in front of the Buda Skála department store, is the latest classic food market in Budapest to be renovated. Some of the charm is lost, but such is progress. Just a block from the Móricz Zsigmond körtér transportation hub, it's open Monday 6:30am to 5pm, Tuesday through Friday from 6:30am to 6pm, Saturday 6:30am to 1pm. Take tram no. 47 from Deák tér to Fehérvári út, or any tram or bus to Móricz Zsigmond körtér.

The **Fény utca Piac,** on II. Fény utca, just off Moszkva tér in Buda, formerly a nondescript neighborhood market, underwent an ambitious reconstruction in 1998 in connection with the building of the Mammut shopping mall, to which it is now attached. Unfortunately, the renovation has meant higher rental fees, which have driven out most of the small independent vendors. Except for a small area on the first floor designated for vendors, the new market retains little of the old atmosphere. Open Monday 6am to 5pm, Tuesday through Friday 6am to 6pm, Saturday 6:30am to 1pm. Take the metro to Moszkva tér (Red line).

Lehel tér Piac, at VI. Lehel tér (© 1/288-6898), is another neighborhood market, whose reconstruction was completed in 2003. The market features a wide selection of fresh food and meats, cheap Hungarian trademark products as well as rinky-dink clothing, kitchen appliances, and flowers. Unfortunately, the reconstruction, as in the other cases, has diminished the neighborhood charm we used to love so much. Interestingly for history buffs, the designer of the controversial architecture—resembling a tacky, colorful adventure park—is none other than László Rajk, the son of the

Communist Party official of the same name whose trial and execution for conspiracy in 1949 represented the beginning of the dark era of Stalinist paranoia and terror in postwar Hungary. The market is open Monday through Friday 6am to 6pm, Saturday 6am to 2pm. Take the metro to Lehel tér (Blue line).

Music

Akt.Records   Once known as Afrofilia, this cozy shop in the heart of Budapest stocks an impressive collection of minimal, hip-hop, electro, jazz, and folklore records. Open Monday through Friday 11am to 7pm, Saturday 11am to 4pm. V. Múzeum körút 7. ℂ 1/266-3080. www.manamana.hu. Metro: Astoria (Red line).

Fonó Budai Zeneház   The Fonó Budai Zeneház entertainment complex is your source for Hungarian folk music. The complex features a folk music store and an auditorium for live folk performances *(táncház)*. It's open Monday and Tuesday 2 to 5pm, Wednesday through Friday 2 to 10pm, Saturday 7 to 10pm. Closed in July and August. I. Sztregova u. 3. ℂ 1/206-5300. www.fono.hu. Tram: 47 or 49 from Deák tér (5 stops past Móricz Zsigmond körtér).

Hungaroton   The factory outlet of the Hungarian record company of the same name, this is definitely *the* place for classical-music buffs looking for Hungarian composers' recordings by contemporary Hungarian artists such as Zoltán Kocsis, Dezső Ránki, and András Schiff. Reasonable CD prices keep the Hungarian music alive. Open Monday through Friday 8am to 3:30pm. VII. Rottenbiller utca 47. ℂ 1/322-8839. www.hungaroton.hu. Tram: 4 or 6 to Király utca.

Indie-Go   Developing independent artists, this head-twisting music shop features a wide selection of world music, alternative, break beat, hip-hop, jazz, and down tempo genres. The collections here provide a solid base for several alternative radio stations. Open Monday through Friday 11am to 8pm, Saturday 11am to 4pm. VIII. Krúdy Gyula u. 7. ℂ 1/486-2927. www.indiego.com. Metro: Kálvin tér (Blue line) or tram 4 or 6 to Baross u.

Liszt Ferenc Zeneműbolt (Ferenc Liszt Music Shop)   Budapest's musical crowd frequents this shop, located near both the State Opera House and the Ferenc Liszt Academy of Music. Sheet music, scores, records, tapes, CDs, and books are available. The store carries an excellent selection of classical music, composed and performed by Hungarian artists. The store is open Monday through Friday 10am to 6pm, Saturday 10am to 1pm. VI. Andrássy út 45. ℂ 1/322-4091. Metro: Oktogon (Yellow line).

Selekta   Located behind the impressive Opera House, this shop—with an enticing chill-out interior—presents a broad spectrum of rhythmic Jamaican music, current dance-hall, ska, hip-hop, and roots grooves. Open Monday through Friday noon to 8pm, Saturday noon to 4pm. VI. Lázár u. 7. No phone. Metro: Opera (Yellow line).

Trancewave Records   This store specializes in alternative and punk music, although the selection is scrimpy. They also sell secondhand CDs, LPs, and vinyl. Party and concert information is available. Open Monday through Friday 11am to 8pm, Saturday noon to 4pm. VI. Révay köz 2. ℂ 1/302-2927. www.trancewave.hu. Metro: Arany János utca (Blue line).

Wave   On a small side street off Bajcsy-Zsilinszky út, directly across the street from the rear of St. Stephen's Basilica, Wave is a popular spot among young Hungarians looking for acid rock, rap, techno, and world music. Open Monday through Friday 11am to 7pm, Saturday 11am to 3pm. Révay utca 4. ℂ 1/331-0718. Metro: Arany János utca (Blue line).

Porcelain, Pottery & Crystal

Ajka Crystal Hungary's renowned crystal producer from the Lake Balaton Region sells fine stemware and other crystal at great prices. Founded by Bernát Neumann in 1878, the company was privatized by FOTEX Rt. in 1990. Showcased are the company's brilliant yet simple crystal glasses, chalices, and crystal artwork. V. József Attila u. 7. ℂ 1/317-8133. Metro: Deák tér (all lines).

Herend Shop Hand-painted Herend porcelain, first produced in 1826 in the town of Herend near Veszprém in western Hungary, is world-renowned (check it out at www.herend.com). This shop, the oldest and largest Herend shop in Budapest, has the widest selection in the capital. They can arrange shipping (visit www.tourist post.hu). Even if you don't intend to buy, come just to see some gorgeous examples of Hungary's most famous product. The store is located in Pest's Inner City, on quiet József nádor tér, just a few minutes' walk from Vörösmarty tér. Open Monday through Friday from 10am to 6pm, Saturday from 9am to 1pm. There is also a Herend shop at V. Kigyó u. 5 (ℂ **1/318-3439**) that also offers shipping. If you're planning a trip to Veszprém or Lake Balaton, don't miss the Herend Museum in the town of Herend (p. 358 in "The Lake Balaton Region"). V. József nádor tér 11. ℂ 1/318-9200. www.herend.hu. Metro: Vörösmarty tér (Yellow line) or Deák tér (all lines).

Herend Village Pottery If the formal Herend porcelain isn't your style (or in your price range), this delightful, casual pottery might be just the thing. The *majolika* (village pottery) is a hand-painted folklore-inspired way of making pottery. Various patterns and solid colors are available; all are dishwasher and oven safe. Because everything is handcrafted, it's possible to order and reorder particular pieces at a later time. Prices are reasonable here. The owners are very knowledgeable and eager to assist, but not pushy. Open Tuesday through Friday 9am to 5pm, Saturday 9am to noon. II. Fő utca 61. ℂ 1/356-7899. Metro: Batthyány tér (Red line).

Zsolnay Márkabolt Delightfully gaudy Zsolnay porcelain, from the southern city of Pécs, is Hungary's second-most-celebrated brand of porcelain, and this shop has Budapest's widest selection. They arrange shipping through Touristpost (p. 329). Even if you don't intend to buy, come just to see some fabulous examples of Hungary's other internationally known porcelain. Check out examples of the pottery at www.zsolnay usa.com. The store is open Monday through Friday 10am to 6pm, Saturday 10am to 1pm. V. Kígyó u. 4. ℂ 1/318-3712. Metro: Vörösmarty tér (Yellow line) or Deák tér (all lines).

Wine, Spirits & Cheese

Budapest Wine Society Truly among the experts in wine, the Wine Society operates in four shops in Budapest. Founded by Tom Howells and Attila Tálos, the shop sells an immense number of wines produced by over 50 local wine-growers. Drop in for free samples on Saturday. Open from Monday to Friday noon to 8pm, Saturday 10am to 3pm. XI. Ráday u. 7. ℂ 1/219-5647. Metro: Kálvin tér (Blue line). www.bortarsasag.hu. Also: Batthyány u. 59. ℂ 1/212-2569. Metro: Batthyány tér (Red line).

The House of Hungarian Pálinka Locals say that good Pálinka (a traditional form of brandy) should warm the stomach, not burn the throat, a common side effect of strong brandy. This shop offers the finest selection of Pálinka—distilled from everything from plums, pears, apples, and walnuts to honey-paprika—that will indeed delight both stomach and throat. Watch out for the head-spinning effect. Open Monday through Saturday 9am to 7pm. VIII. Rákóczi Street 17. ℂ 1/338-4219. www. magyarpalinkahaza.hu. Metro: Blaha Lujza tér (Red line) or bus 7.

Présház   This tasteful wine store—named after the "press room," or the room where the grapes are rammed to extract the sweet nectar—is located in the Inner City area. They offer over 300 types of Hungarian wine and have a knowledgeable staff that is fluent in English. You can have your order delivered within Budapest if you purchase a crate. Open Monday through Friday 10am to 6pm, Saturday 10am to 4pm. The second shop is at V. Váci u. 10 (© **1/266-1100**). V. Párizsi utca 1–3. © **1/266-0636**. www. preshaz.hu. Metro: Vörösmarty tér (Yellow line).

Wine & Arts Decanter Borszaküzlet   A club of wine-lovers, this shop features elegant wines from hidden provincial Hungarian wine-growers, top-notch award-wining wine-masters in addition to Italian and Spanish wines. Open Tuesday through Friday 6 to 8pm, Saturday 10am to 2pm. MOM Park, XII. Kléh István u. 3. © **1/201-9029**. www.grandvin.hu. Tram: 59 or 61.

BUDAPEST AFTER DARK

Budapest is blessed with a rich and varied cultural life. And there is no event that is unaffordable to the average tourist. In fact, you can still go to the Opera House, one of Europe's finest, for less than 800 Ft ($4/£2). (The most expensive tickets in the house, for the fabulously ornate royal box once used by the Habsburgs, still go for less than 10,000 Ft, or $50/£26.) Almost all of the city's theaters and concert halls, with the exception of those hosting internationally touring rock groups, offer tickets for 800 Ft to 4,000 Ft ($4–$20/£2–£10). (Of course, you can also get 5,000 Ft–8,000 Ft/$25–$40/£13–£21 tickets at the same venue if you wish.) It makes sense in Budapest (as elsewhere, of course) to select a performance based as much on the venue as on the program. If, for example, the Great Hall of the Academy of Music is presenting a program that you wouldn't ordinarily attend, it might be worth your while to reconsider due to the splendor of the venue.

The opera, ballet, and theater seasons run from September through May or June, but most theaters and halls also host performances during the summer festivals. A number of lovely churches and stunning halls offer concerts exclusively in the summer. While classical music has a long and proud tradition in Budapest, jazz, blues, rock, disco, and the world of DJs have exploded in the past couple of decades. Herds of stylish, unique new clubs and bars have opened up everywhere; the parties start late and last until morning. So put on your dancing shoes or slip your opera glasses into your pocket; whatever your entertainment preference, Budapest nights offer plenty to choose from.

PROGRAM LISTINGS   The most complete schedule of mainstream performing arts is found in the free bimonthly *Koncert Kalendárium,* available at the Central Philharmonic Ticket Office on Madách utca. The *Budapest Sun* has comprehensive events calendars; the weekly *Budapest Times* includes cultural listings. *Budapest Panorama,* a free monthly tourist booklet, offers only partial entertainment listings, featuring what the editors consider the monthly highlights. All of the publications mentioned above are in English.

TICKET OFFICES   When purchasing opera, ballet, theater, or concert tickets in advance, you're better off going to one of the commission-free state-run ticket offices than to the individual box offices. There are always schedules posted, and you'll have a variety of choices. If none of the cashiers speaks English, find a helpful customer who can translate for you. On the day of the performance, though, you might have better luck at the box office. The **Cultur-Comfort Ticket Office (Cultur-Comfort**

Központi Jegyiroda), VI. Paulay Ede u. 31 (𝒞 **1/322-0000;** www.cultur-comfort. hu), sells tickets to just about everything, from theater and operettas to sports events and rock concerts. The office is open Monday through Friday 9am to 6pm. For **opera and ballet,** go to the **Hungarian State Opera Ticket Office (Magyar Állami Opera Jegyiroda),** VI. Andrássy út 22 (𝒞 **1/353-0170**), open Monday through Friday 11am to 5pm. Try **Concert & Media,** XI. Üllői út 11–13 (𝒞 **1/455-9000;** www. jegyelado.hu.), for classical performances as well as pop, jazz, and rock concerts. For just about everything from rock and jazz concert, opera, ballet performances, and theater tickets, try **Ticket Express,** VI. Jókai u. 40 (𝒞 **1/353-0692;** www.tex.hu), open Monday through Saturday from 10am to 7pm. Additional Ticket Express offices can be found at V. Deák Ferenc u. 19 (𝒞 **1/266-7070**), open Monday through Saturday from 10am to 9pm; VI. Andrássy út 18 (𝒞 **1/312-0000**), open Monday through Friday 9:30am to 6:30pm; and VIII. József krt. 50 (𝒞 **1/344-0369**), open Monday through Friday 9:30am to 6:30pm.

Note: For cheaper tickets, try going to the actual box office of the venue, as the ticket agencies may not carry the entire price range of tickets. You may also find that agencies charge a commission (usually about 4%), especially for a hit show.

THE PERFORMING ARTS

The major symphony orchestras in Budapest are the Budapest Festival Orchestra, the Philharmonic Society Orchestra, the Hungarian State Symphony Orchestra, the Budapest Symphony Orchestra, and the Hungarian Railway Workers' (MÁV) Symphony Orchestra. The major chamber orchestras include the Hungarian Chamber Orchestra, the Ferenc Liszt Chamber Orchestra, the Budapest String Players, and the newly established Hungarian Virtuosi. Major choirs include the Budapest Chorus, the Hungarian State Choir, the Hungarian Radio and Television Choir, the Budapest Madrigal Choir, and the University Choir.

Budapest is now on the touring route of dozens of major European ensembles and virtuosos. Keep your eyes open for well-known touring artists.

Note: Most Budapesters tend to dress more formally than casually when attending performances.

OPERA, OPERETTA & BALLET

Budapesti Operettszínház (Budapest Operetta Theater)   Referred to as the "palace of entertainment" in its incipient times, the building was designed by two acclaimed Viennese architects, Fellner and Helmer, in 1894. In the heart of Budapest's theater district, the recently renovated Budapest Operetta Theater is not only the site of operetta, but also of musicals and rock operas. Restored seating boxes, antique chandeliers, and period-style furnishings are paired with state-of-the-art stage equipment—an enchanting, quality experience is guaranteed. A highlight among Art Nouveau style buildings, the theater hosts exquisite banquettes and balls—among which is opulent Operetta Ball. Performances of *Romeo and Juliette, Baroness Lili,* and *Ball in the Savoy* are the order of the day here. However, the greatest musical hits, like *Cats* and *The Phantom of the Opera,* whose European world premier outside England took place in Hungary in the spring of 2003, are shown in **Madách Theater** (p. 344) on the Outer Ring. The off season is mid-July to mid-August. The box office is open Monday through Friday 10am to 7pm, and Saturday 1 to 7pm. VI. Nagymező u. 17. 𝒞 1/312-4866. www.operettszinhaz.hu. Tickets 2,000 Ft–5,000 Ft ($10–$25/£5.20–£13). Metro: Opera or Oktogon (Yellow line).

Erkel Színház (Erkel Theater)   Named the "People's Opera," the Erkel Theater is the second home of the State Opera and Ballet. The largest theater in Hungary, it seats as many as 2,400 people. Though it was built in Art Nouveau style in 1911, little of its original character is apparent because of the various renovations it has undergone. If you have a choice, go to the Opera House instead (their seasons—mid-Sept to mid-June—are the same). Chamber orchestra concerts are also performed here. The box office is open Tuesday through Saturday from 11am until the beginning of the performance, or to 5pm, Sunday from 11am to 1pm and 4pm until the beginning of the performance. VIII. Köztársaság tér 30. (ⓒ) 1/333-0540. www.opera.hu. Tickets 800 Ft–4,000 Ft ($4–$20/£2.10–£11). Metro: Keleti pu. (Red line).

Magyar Állami Operaház (Hungarian State Opera House)   Completed in 1884, the Opera House is the crowning achievement of the famous Hungarian architect Miklós Ybl. It's easily Budapest's most famous performance hall and an attraction in its own right. The lobby is adorned with Bertalan Székely's frescoes; the ceiling frescoes in the concert hall itself are by Károly Lotz. **Guided tours** of the Opera House leave daily at 3 and 4pm; the cost is 2,000 Ft ($9/£5.15).

The splendid Opera House, home to both the State Opera and the State Ballet, possesses a rich history. A political scandal marked the opening performance in 1884: Ferenc Liszt had written a piece to be performed especially for the event, but when it was discovered that he had incorporated elements of the *Rákóczi March,* a patriotic Hungarian (and anti-Habsburg) melody, he was prevented from playing it. Gustav Mahler and Ferenc Erkel rank as the Opera House's most famous directors.

Hungarians adore opera, and a large percentage of seats are sold on a subscription basis; buy your tickets a few days ahead of time if you can. The season runs from mid-September to mid-June. Summer visitors, however, can take in the approximately 10 performances (both opera and ballet) during the Summer Operafest, in July or August. Seating capacity is 1,260. The box office is open Tuesday through Saturday from 11am until the beginning of the performance, or to 5pm, Sunday from 11am to 1pm and 4pm until the beginning of the performances. There are occasional weekend matinees selling for 300 Ft to 3,500 Ft ($1.50–$18/80p–£9). VI. Andrássy út 22. (ⓒ) 1/335-0170. www.opera.hu. Tickets 800 Ft–10,000 Ft ($4–$50/£2.10–£27). Metro: Opera (Yellow line).

CLASSICAL MUSIC

Matthias Church   A Budapest icon in the center of the historic Castle district, this church is a neo-Gothic classic, named after Matthias Corvinus, the Renaissance king who was married here. The church is a key location for excellent organ recitals, sacred music concerts for a cappella choir, or orchestras. The box office is open Wednesday through Sunday 1 to 5:30pm. I. Szentháromság tér 2. (ⓒ) 1/355-5657. Tickets 1,000 Ft–7,000 Ft ($5–$35/£2.70–£19). Take the Castle minibus from Moszkva tér (Red line).

Palace of Art (ⓐⓐ)   The Palace of Art's National Concert Hall and Festival Theater are the latest concert and performing arts venues: This is a must-see venue for visitors to Budapest. The theaters are situated in the Millennium City Center, which seems to grow every year. The main concert hall is the finest contemporary classical-music venue in Budapest, and now hosts concerts from the most important orchestras from around the world. The concert schedule varies; check out their website which has excellent search features. IX. Komor Marcell u. 1. (ⓒ) 1/555-3000. www.mupa.hu. Take tram 2 from downtown toward the Lágymányos bridge.

The Birth of the Palace of Art

Hungary welcomed the opening of the **Palace of Art** ⍟⍟ in early 2005, the latest cultural complex created in the Hungarian capital, which includes a National Concert Hall, a new home for the Ludwig Museum of Contemporary Art, and the smaller Festival Theater.

The jewel of the crown in this gargantuan complex, situated on the Danube adjacent to Hungary's National Theater, is the National Concert Hall, the largest of its kind in Hungary, seating 1,699 with standing room for an additional 200. The room itself was sealed sonorously from the outside world and sits in a gargantuan box floating on steel and rubber springs. There are 66 resonant chambers around the walls, and a 40-ton canopy above the podium to make sure that listeners hear only the music. Previously unable to host larger symphonic orchestras in a world-class venue, Hungary now boasts a truly top-quality contemporary space able to welcome the most notable international orchestras—putting the country on the international classical music map.

The adjacent **Ludwig Museum** hosts temporary exhibitions on the first floor, while the two above will feature works from the Ludwig collection—largely American pop art and central European contemporary. The smaller **Festival Theater** hosts contemporary dance and other performing arts events. The $160-million project was created in a public-private partnership agreement between the Hungarian government and developer TriGránit Development Corporation, spearheaded by central European real estate tycoon Sándor Demján. The developer is using the complex as a template for cultural and entertainment centers to be built in other central European cities.

The complex is housed in the **Millennium City Center,** a space that promises to be more than merely a cultural space. Plans dictate the creation of a conference and tourism-related hub here, of which the Palace of Art and Hungary's National Theater are the first two main attractions. The same developers have plans for a convention center, five hotels, office buildings, a casino and exhibition pavilion, and even a spa.

Zeneakadémia (Ferenc Liszt Academy of Music)   The Great Hall (Nagyterem) of the Academy of Music, with a seating capacity of 1,200 is—next to the recently opened National Concert Hall—Budapest's premier concert hall. Hungary's leading center of musical education, the Academy was built in the early years of the 20th century; the building's interior is decorated in lavish Art Nouveau style. If you go to only one performance in Budapest, it should be at the Opera House, the National Convert Hall, or here. Unfortunately, the Great Hall is not used in the summer months; the smaller Kisterem, also a fine hall, is used at that time. Home to the renowned Franz Liszt Academy of Music since 1907, student recitals can be attended here sometimes even for free, although the main attractions are major Hungarian and international performances. A weekly schedule is posted outside the Király utca entrance to the academy. The box office is open Monday through Friday from 10am to 8pm, and weekends 2 to 8pm. Performances are frequent. VI. Liszt Ferenc tér 8. © 1/462-4600. www.liszt.hu. Tickets 1,000 Ft–8,000 Ft ($5–$40/£2.55-£20). Metro: Oktogon (Yellow line) or Nyugati Pályaudvar (Blue line).

THEATER & DANCE

Budapest has an extremely lively theater season from September through June. For productions in English, there are still some at the **Merlin Theater,** V. Gerlóczy u. 4 (© **1/317-9338** or 1/318-9844; www.merlinszinhaz.hu), located on a quiet street in the heart of the Inner City. The Merlin now programs about 40% English-language shows, but somehow these efforts have never really resulted in a great following. In the productions, however, both Hungarian and foreign actors are featured. Tickets cost 600 Ft to 2,000 Ft ($3–$20/£1.55–£5.15); the box office is open Monday through Friday noon to 7pm, Saturday and Sunday 2 to 7pm. Take the metro to Astoria (Red line) or Deák tér (all lines).

If you are looking for the best of international dance, music, or theater, head to the **Trafó House of Contemporary Art,** IX. Liliom utca 41 (© **1/215-1600** or 1/456-2040; www.trafo.hu), which has the aura of the Joyce Theatre in New York. This venue was once a building that housed a giant transformer (which connects it to the western European tradition of settling artistic centers and institutions in empty industrial buildings). Since it opened in 1998, this venue has introduced some bold programming (which occasionally upsets traditional-minded Hungarians). This is truly a place to go for intellectually adventurous and risky work. Prepare to gasp occasionally. We especially recommend the dance works debuted here by groups such as the French-Hungarian **Compagnie Pál Frenák** (www.ciefrenak.org); don't miss them if they're in town. Tickets cost 800 Ft to 2,000 Ft ($4–$20/£2.10–£11); box office is open Monday through Saturday from 5 until about 8pm. Reserve tickets in advance. Take tram no. 4 or 6, or go by metro to Ferenc Körut (Blue line).

For musical productions, especially those by Andrew Lloyd Webber, go to the **Madách Theater,** VII. Erzsébet krt. 29–33 (© **1/478-2041;** www.madachszinhaz.hu), built in 1961 on the site of the famous Royal Orpheum Theater and beautifully restored in 1999. Their hit production—since spring 2003—is *The Phantom of the Opera;* Budapest is the only place in Europe outside of London where you can see the original production. Ticket prices are 800 Ft to 10,000 Ft ($4–$50/£2–£26). The box office is open daily from 3 to 7pm; performances are usually at 7pm. Take tram no. 4 or 6 to Wesselényi utca. Also staging musical performances, mostly by Hungarian authors, is the **Vígszínház (Comedy Theatre of Budapest),** XIII. Szent István krt. 14 (© **1/329-2340;** www.vigszinhaz.hu), which was recently restored to its original, delightfully gaudy, neo-baroque splendor. In the 1950s the Vígszínház served as the venue for the Hungarian Communist Party's New Year's Eve balls, hosted by Stalinist-era dictator Mátyás Rákosi. With a show every night, the theater stages numerous audience-drawing plays by foreign and local writers. The box office is open daily 11am to 7pm. Ticket prices are 1,200 Ft to 3,000 Ft ($6–$15/£3.20–£8). Take the metro to Nyugati pu. (Blue line).

The **International Buda Stage,** II. Tárogató út 2–4 (© **1/391-2525;** www. ibs-b.hu), hosts local and international theater performances. The box office is open Monday through Friday 10am to noon, 1 to 6pm, and on weekends 1 hour before the start of the performance. Tickets cost 1,200 Ft to 2,500 Ft ($6–$13/£3.10–£6.40).

An important venue of the world of contemporary performing arts in Budapest is the **MU Theatre,** XI. Körösy József u. 17 (℃ **1/209-4014;** www.mu.hu). This theater is becoming increasingly dynamic, with many young dancers and choreographers starting off their careers in this experimental, cozy environment. The box office is open Monday through Thursday 5pm until the beginning of the performance, and Friday through Sunday an hour before the start of the performance. Tickets cost 800 Ft to 1,500 Ft ($3.80–$7.20/£2–£3.85). Take bus no. 86 or tram no. 4 to Moricz Zsigmond körtér.

THE CLUB SCENE

Buzzing day and night, Budapest bars are present in cacophony of styles and music. Due to their constantly changing events, you'd be wise to check out *Pesti Est*—the largest free weekly program magazine listing all events from movies, theater offerings, and classical ballet performances to daily nightlife activities. Newcomers *Flyerz* and *Exit* also offer a less complete yet well-edited selection of events. English-language publications **Budapest Sun** (www.budapestsun.com) and **Budapest Times** (www. budapesttimes.hu) also list highlights. In order to help define the different categories of nightlife, we have tried to define an "average-age" guideline for the venues. Opening hours vary, but most clubs start dancing around 11pm and stay lively until closing time.

A38 Boat 𝒦𝒦   A former Ukrainian stone-carrying ship anchored at the Buda-side foot of the Petőfi Bridge. As soon as it appeared on the Danube, it struck a chord with the local youth, competing for the title of "hippest disco in town." Since its opening in 2003 it lost some of its allure, however. Taking place on the lower deck, feet-thumping crowds enjoy the city's best mainstream and alternative, underground live shows. The terrace is open only in the summer while the concert hall downstairs is open year-round. Open daily 11am to 4am, with crowds generally in their 20s and 30s. XI. Pázmány Péter sétány. ℃ 1/464-3940. www.a38.hu. Cover: mostly free, concerts 1,000 Ft–6,000 Ft ($5–$30/£2.60–£15). Tram: 4 or 6 to the Buda side of Petőfi bridge.

Chachacha Underground Café 𝒦   A retro-funky world beneath the ground, this cafe/club was built in the metro underpass of Kalvin Square; it's a glass-covered human boutique. The casino-bar lounge is decorated with zebra-striped couches and armchairs, with an oddly painted ceiling. Late night, this turns into an insane dance arena, with the drunken crowds overflowing into the underpass. The music typically brings back the hits of the '70s and '80s while also spinning some spaced-out tracks. Visit the bar's classy summer location on Margaret Island. Open daily 11am to 5am. Crowd: 30s. Metro underpass, Kalvin Sq. No phone. www.chachacha.hu. Metro: Kálvin tér (Blue line).

Fat Mo's Music Club 𝒦𝒦   This divey supper club is always crowded. Live jazz concerts start at 9pm and dancing starts at 11pm. The best night is definitely Monday, with the Hot Jazz Band performing in the style of the '20s and '30s. Make sure to book a table if you wish to enjoy the club's superb food, including the best succulent American-style steaks in town. Open Monday through Wednesday noon to 2am, Thursday and Friday noon to 4am, Saturday 6pm to 4am, and Sunday 6pm to 2am. Crowd: 30s. V. Nyári Pál u. 11. ℃ 1/267-3199. Metro: Kálvin tér (Blue line).

Home   Posh trance-dance fanatics line up at this massive 2,000-sq.-m (22,000-sq.-ft.) dance hall, located in the hills of Óbuda, for some of the city's best electronic music. The expensive bar, solarium-tanned go-go dancers, and renowned local and international DJs attract a wide clientele of platform-heeled, underdressed girls and Mafiosa-type sporty tomcats—a lavish meat market. Bouncers have a reputation of being on the doggy side. Crowd: 20s and 30s. III. Harsány lejtő 6. No phone. www.homeclub. hu. Cover: 2,000 Ft–3,000 Ft ($10–$15/£5.15–£7.70).Bus: 18.

Közgáz Cellar   Beneath the massive Budapest University of Economic Science lies this student-filled disco where dance floors are packed solid during weekends. Laid-back atmosphere, supreme happy hours, and a cheerful karaoke and dance crowd, in addition to groovy disco tunes on the main dance floor offer bundles of fun. Open Tuesday through Saturday 9:30pm to 5am. Crowd: 20s and 30s. IX. Fővám tér 8. ✆ 1/215-4359. Cover: 500 Ft ($2.50/£1.30) for men, free for women. Metro: Kálvin tér (Blue line) or tram 2, 47, or 49 to Fővám tér.

Kultiplex 🏰🏰   A bohemian two-story club, Kultiplex—an alternative cultural multiplex—was converted from the Blue Box cinema, although a small art-movie house still operates within. Hosting the best local alternative beats, funky arty crowds rule the place. The summer cafe in the back is a pleasant, wallet-friendly place to unwind. Open daily 10am to 4:30am. Crowd: 20s and 30s. IX. Kinizsi u. 28. ✆ 1/219-0706. Cover: 500 Ft–6,000 Ft ($2.50–$30/£1.30–£15). Metro: Ferenc körút (Blue line).

Living Room 🏰   While couples socialize in the loungelike atmosphere during daytime, this roomy classic disco-club becomes full with scores of dancers during weekends. Be careful of the all-you-can-drink university parties. Opening hours vary. Crowd: 20s and 30s. IV. Kossuth Lajos u. 17. No phone. Cover: 500 Ft–2,000 Ft ($2.50–$10/£1.30–£5.15). Metro: Astoria (Red line).

Old Man's Music Pub 🏰🏰   Old Man's offers the best jazz and blues in Hungary. The Pege Quartet plays here, as does Hobo and his blues band. A very hip spot. Open daily 3pm until the crowd leaves. Crowd: 30s and 40s. Akácfa u. 13. ✆ 1/322-7645. www.oldmans.hu. Metro: Blaha Luzja tér (Red line).

Piaf   Named after the remarkably soulful French singer, Piaf is renowned for its bohemian-like late-night, after-hours parties. Once inside the heavy iron door—guarded by a feisty woman—you'll find yourself among seductive red velvet furnishings in a distinct '80s Parisian-style bar. In the downstairs dance floor the spinning of oldies can get pretty heated, and the crowds can be quite wild. Open daily 10pm to 6am. Crowd: varied. VI. Nagymező u. 25. ✆ 1/312-3823. Cover: 800 Ft ($4/£2). Metro: Oktogon or Opera (Yellow line).

Süss Fel Nap 🏰🏰   Fittingly titled "Sunrise," this newly expanded bar—a favorite among university students during the weekend—rocks the dancing crowd until dawn with punk and alternative music. Superb DJs and live bands provide the tunes. Open daily 5pm until dawn. Crowd: 20s and 30s. V. Szent István körút 11. ✆ 1/374-3329. www.sussfelnap.hu. Cover: 500 Ft–2,000 Ft ($2.50–$10/£1.30–£5.15). Metro: Nyugati pu. (Blue line).

Trafó Bar Tango   A cultural center for young, alternative artists, this club is housed in an old electric power station that has been renovated. Trafó hosts the hippest selection of alternative artists, from reggae to classic Indian music. The small dance floor and scant bar area are supplemented by the relaxed, easygoing, loungelike chill-out area. Open daily 6pm to 4am. Crowd: varied. IX. Liliom u. 41. ✆ 1/215-1600. www.trafo.hu. Cover: 500 Ft–2,000 Ft ($2.50–$10/£1.30–£5.15). Metro: Ferenc körút (Blue line) or tram 4 or 6 to Üllöi út.

Underground   An oldie among clubs, Underground was initially built as an homage to Bosnian-born Emir Kusturica's film of the same name. Today, after a series of rebirths, the place has turned into a welcoming, red-dominant interior with a dance floor in the back where karaoke awaits visitors on Tuesday, Wednesday, and Sunday. A minimalist selection of homemade-style specialties is served during the day. Crowd: 20s and 30s. VI. Teréz körút 30. ℂ **1/269-5566.** www.underground-budapest.hu. Metro: Oktogon (Yellow line) or tram 4 or 6.

THE BAR SCENE

Aloe   A sizzling bar filled with long-legged lovelies with warm-brown eyes, and powerful yet remarkably cheap drinks prepared by attentive bar staff. This place is known among locals as the temple of good, inexpensive cocktails. Open daily 5pm to 2am. VI. Zichy Jenő u. 34. ℂ **1/269-4536.** Metro: Nyugati pu. (Blue line).

Balettcipő   A colorful, cheerful coffeehouse/bar in the heart of the theater district—behind the Opera house, "Ballet shoe" has a laid-back, open atmosphere—great for catching up with a longtime friend. A largely Hungarian client base and a simple yet refreshing cafe-style menu. Open Monday through Friday 8am to midnight, and Saturday and Sunday 10am to midnight. VI. Hajós u. 14. ℂ **1/269-3114.** Metro: Opera (Yellow line).

Becketts   A lively authentic Irish pub, Becketts serves the best Guinness in the city to the crowd of expats and local high-class yuppies. The cheerful staff—some with a clear Irish accent—the spacious bar, a cozy restaurant, live music, and/or the lively sport telecasts pack the pub throughout the week. Open Monday through Friday noon to 1am, and Saturday and Sunday noon to 3am. V. Bajcsy-Zsilinszky út 72. ℂ **1/311-1033.** www.budapestsun.com/becketts. Metro: Nyugati pu. (Blue line).

Fregatt   This was the first English-style pub in Hungary, though now it's too crowded and noisy to really feel like one. Hungarians make up the better half of the clientele, but American and other English-speaking expats also frequent this place. Guinness stout is on draft. Live jazz is performed on Thursday and Sunday. Open Monday through Friday 3pm to 1am, and Saturday and Sunday 5pm to 1am. V. Molnár u. 26. ℂ **1/318-9997.** Metro: Ferenciek tere (Blue line) or tram 2, 47, or 49.

Irish Cat Pub   This was the first Irish-style pub in Budapest; there's Guinness on tap and a well-equipped whiskey bar. It's a popular meeting place for expats and travelers. The pub features a full menu. Open daily 11am to 2am. V. Múzeum krt. 41. ℂ **1/266-4085.** www.irishcat.hu. Metro: Kálvin tér (Blue line).

Janis Pub   Named and decorated after the illustrious wild-child Janis Joplin, this easily accessible pub features a fine selection of alcohols at moderate prices, '70s and '80s hits, and the occasional live concert. Open Monday through Thursday 4pm to 2am, Friday and Saturday 4pm to 3am, and Sunday 6pm to 2am. V. Királyi Pál u. 8. ℂ **1/266-7364.** www.janispub.hu. Metro: Kálvin tér or Ferenciek tere (Blue line).

Kuplung   Located in a former warehouse, Kuplung (Clutch) packs a lively, young crowd in its stony interior. In a squat-like atmosphere, table football *(csocsó)* fans spin away on one of the many tables, while loud groovy sounds fill this vast hangar. Cheap drinks might just make you "clutch" onto your chair. Open daily 6pm to 5am. VI. Király u. 46. No phone. Tram: 4 or 6 to Király u.

Picasso Point   This cafe-bar-restaurant joint is a popular hangout among the local youth, which is understandable knowing that Picasso Point has a downright warm, welcoming atmosphere which is only underlined by the ever-smiling staff. By day the restaurant offers a wide selection of local specialties, while adventure-seekers find pleasure in the basement party-arena during nights. Open Monday through Wednesday noon to midnight, Thursday noon to 3am, Friday noon to 4am, and Saturday 6pm to 4am. VI. Hajós u. 31. ✆ 1/312-1727. www.picassopoint.hu. Metro: Nyugati pu. (Blue line).

Pótkulcs   A bohemian bar, Pótkulcs (Spare Key) draws an artsy-looking crowd of travelers and locals alike. Beyond the rusty metal entrance, this large pub is filled with rickety chairs, couches, and tables—a great place to socialize. The friendly yet crazy-looking chef prepares tasty and ample meals. Presenting the local artists-to-be, the pub features an eclectic mix of temporary art exhibitions and unique concerts. Open daily 5pm to 2:30am. VI. Csengery u. 65/b. ✆ 1/269-1050. www.potkulcs.hu. Metro: Nyugati pu. (Blue line).

Sark   Located on a corner—hence the name—Sark has three levels filled with utter coolness. On the gallery, powerful black-and-white prints of characteristic faces gaze at you from the walls, the bustling bar surroundings on the main floor are usually crammed, while the blank basement dance floor hosts occasional concerts and dance crazes. Open Monday through Wednesday noon to 3am, Thursday through Saturday noon to 5pm, and Sunday 5pm to 2am. VII. Klauzál tér 14. ✆ 1/328-0752. www.sark.hu. Tram: 4 or 6 to Wesselényi u.

Szilvuplé   Lounge/cafe/restaurant/bar compacted into one, Szilvuplé's attractiveness lies in its steady, calm, welcoming atmosphere. The secession-style indoor design, colorful cocktail bar, attentive staff, moderate prices, and talented DJs create the buzz each night. Open Thursday through Saturday 6pm to 4am, and Sunday through Wednesday 6pm to 2am. VI. Ó u. 33. ✆ 1/302-2499. www.szilvuple.hu. Metro: Opera (Yellow line).

Szimpla   A wholly unpretentious bohemian bar packed with ramshackle antique furniture, a favorite of the local arty and adventure-seeking traveler crowd. The dimly lit, couch-packed underground cellar is a relaxing, pleasant place to unwind. Open daily noon to 2am. VII. Kertész u. 48. ✆ 1/342-1034. Metro: Oktogon (Yellow line) or tram 4 or 6 to Király u.

Szóda   The red-dominant retro-futuristic design with snug leather couches is coupled with fitting rows of empty soda bottles. The underground bar and dance floor is shelter for the whacky all-night dance-rats. Open Monday through Friday 9am to daybreak, and Saturday and Sunday 2pm to daybreak. VII. Wesselényi u. 18. ✆ 1/461-0007. www.szoda.com. Tram: 4 or 6 to Wesselényi u.

Vittula   A hidden small and new-wave-intimate cellar bar for travelers, expatriates, and locals alike who squeeze in to listen to retro-funky vibes or live music by local youth talents. Consistently busy and almost always unbearably smoky. Open daily 6pm until dawn. VII. Kertész u. 4. No phone. Metro: Blaha Lujza tér (Red line).

HUNGARIAN DANCE HOUSES

Although Hungarian folk music is no longer a key characteristic of rural life (except, perhaps, in Transylvania, now part of Romania), recent years have seen the growth of an urban-centered folk revival movement known as the *táncház* (dance house). An interactive evening of folk music and folk dancing, in a neighborhood community center, might just rank as one of the best and most authentic cultural experiences you can have in Budapest. We've listed a few of the best-known dance houses below. The format usually consists of about an hour of dance-step instruction followed by several hours of dancing accompanied by a live band, which might include some of Hungary's best folk musicians, in an authentic, casual atmosphere. You can come just to watch and listen if you're nervous about dancing.

The leading Hungarian folk band, Muzsikás, whose lead singer is the incomparable Márta Sebestyén (they have toured the U.S., playing to great acclaim), hosts a táncház every Thursday (Sept–May only) from 8pm to midnight (500 Ft/$2.50/£1.30) at the **Marczibányi Square Cultural House (Marczibányi tér Művelődési Ház)**, II. Marczibányi tér 5/a (© **1/212-2820**). Take the Red line metro to Moszkva tér. If you're in town during a Muzsikás performance, don't miss it. The **FMH Cultural House (Szakszervezetek Fővárosi Művelődési Ház)**, XI. Fehérvári út 47 (© **1/203-3868**), hosts activities from various yoga genres, creative dance, Irish tap dancing, dance therapy, and belly dancing to arts and craft clubs like painting, sewing, and basketwork. Folk bands that perform on traditional instruments play every Thursday or Friday evening, September through May, for 500 Ft ($2.50/£1.30). The evening kicks off with a táncház hour at 7pm. Also at the FMH Cultural House, *csángó táncház,* the oldest and most authentic type of traditional Hungarian folk dance, is danced Friday or Saturday from 7 to 11pm, for 500 Ft ($2.50/£1.30). On the first Saturday of each month, you can enjoy the best klezmer bands in town. Tram no. 47 from Deák tér gets you to FMH Cultural House.

The founder of the Dance House movement in the early 1970s, Béla Halmos leads the crazed Kalamajka (Ruckus) band and weekend dance houses in the **Downtown Cultural House (Belvárosi Ifjúsági Műelődési Ház)**, V. Molnár u. 9 (© **1/371-5928**). Take the Blue metro to Ferenciek tere.

An important heritage-preserving center, the **Almássy Square Culture Center (Almássy téri Művelődési Központ)**, VII. Almássy tér 6 (© **1/352-1572**), stages some of the best folk-dance dance houses in a relaxed, easygoing atmosphere on its multilevel complex. Traditional Hungarian dances, Transylvanian "moldova" dances, Sirtos—Greek dances and native Brazilian dances are taught throughout weekdays. For the specific monthly plan check out www.almassy.hu. Entrance fees vary, averaging around 500 Ft to 1,000 Ft ($2.50–$5/£1.30–£2.60). A short walk from Blaha Lujza tér (Blue line or tram no. 4 or 6) gets you to this folk center.

GAY & LESBIAN BARS

As with the capricious dance club scene, gay "in" bars become "out," or even close down, at a moment's notice. The gay bar scene in Budapest is largely male-oriented at this point, though this is starting to change. For reliable and up-to-date information, visit **www.budapestgaycity.net** or **http://budapest.gayguide.net**.

Angel A nondescript basement establishment with a bar, a restaurant, and a huge dance floor, Angel has been around for a while now and is here to stay. The clientele is not exclusively gay, especially on Friday and Saturday nights, when Angel hosts its now-famous transvestite show starting at 11:45pm. Saturday nights are men only. Sunday is an "open day" (meaning straight folks are welcome). Open Thursday through Sunday 10am to dawn. VII. Szövetség u. 33. © 1/351-6490. Cover 800 Ft ($4/£2). Metro: Blaha Lujza tér (Red line).

Árkádia In the heart of downtown this small, intimate yet crammed bar is the perfect place to meet, dance, or get cozy with an attractive stranger, with a popular backroom. Open daily 8pm to 5am. V. Türr István u. 5. No phone. www.arkadiagaybar.hu. Metro: Vörösmarty tér (Yellow line).

Capella This trendy and fashionable bar is one of the most popular homosexual clubs in the city, though we're not fans. The funky cabaret-style shows and extravagant drag shows and the house-centered music draw a rather hectic mixture of homo- and heterosexuals. Open Wednesday through Sunday 9pm to 4am. V. Belgrád rkp. 23. ℂ **1/328-6231.** Cover: 1,000 Ft ($5/£2.60) Metro: Fereciek tere (Blue line)

CoXx Club   A sizzling gay men-only bar in the underground shelter and an Internet cafe rolled into one, CoXx—formerly known as Chaos—has a large art gallery on the main level. Open daily 9pm to 4am. VII. Dohány u. 38. ℂ **1/344-4884.** www.coxx.hu. Drink minimum 1,000 Ft ($5/£2.60). Metro: Astoria or Blaha Lujza tér (Red line).

Mystery Bar   The first gay bar in the city, Mystery Bar is a very small but cozy place that draws a large foreign clientele and is perfect for conversation and meeting new people. Open Monday through Friday 4pm to 4am, and Saturday and Sunday 6pm to 4am. V. Nagysándor József u. 3. ℂ **1/312-1436.** www.mysterybar.hu. Metro: Arany János utca (Blue line).

UpSide Down   An elegant basement bar—formerly operated as a public bathroom—UpSide Down's clientele is mostly straight. Rather pricey, its laid-back loungelike stylish decor is a suitable place to wind down at the end of the day. Monday and Wednesday night features gay and lesbian Karaoke. Open daily 8am to 5am. V. Podmaniczky tér 1. No phone. Metro: Arany János u. (Blue line).

MORE ENTERTAINMENT

CASINOS   Budapest has couple dozen casinos. Many are located in luxury hotels: **Casino Budapest Hilton,** I. Hess András tér 1–3 (ℂ **1/375-1001**); **Las Vegas Casino,** in the Atrium Hyatt Hotel, V. Roosevelt tér 2 (ℂ **1/317-6022;** www.lasvegas casino.hu); and **Orfeum Casino,** in the Hotel Béke Radisson, VI. Teréz krt. 43 (ℂ **1/301-1600**). Formal dress is required. Other popular casinos include: **Grand Casino Budapest,** V. Deák Ferenc u. 13 (ℂ **1/483-0170**), **Tropicana Casino,** V. Vigadó u. 2 (ℂ **1/327-7250;** www.tropicanacasino.hu), and the elegant **Várkert Casino** on the Danube side, Ybl Miklós tér 9 (ℂ **1/202-4244;** www.varkert.com).

MOVIES   A healthy number of English-language movies are always playing in Budapest. The best source of listings and addresses is either the **Budapest Sun,** or the free weekly, **Pesti Est,** which has an English-language section for movies. Movies labeled *szinkronizált, m.b.,* or *magyarul beszél* mean that the movie has been dubbed into Hungarian; *feliratos* means subtitled. Tickets cost around 600 Ft to 1,500 Ft ($3–$7.50/£1.55–£3.85). Most multiplexes provide the option of seeing movies in their original language (even if the movie itself was dubbed) while art movies are a bit more difficult. The two main art cinemas (www.artmozi.hu) that play daily English-language features are **Művész,** VI. Teréz krt. 30 (ℂ **1/332-6726;** tram no. 4 or 6), and **Puskin,** V. Kossuth L. u. 18 (ℂ **1/429-6080;** Red line metro to Astoria).

4 The Danube Bend

The Danube Bend (Dunakanyar), a string of small riverside towns just north of Budapest, is a popular excursion spot for both international travelers and Hungarians. The name "Danube Bend" is actually a misnomer, since the river doesn't actually change direction at this point. The Danube, which enters Hungary from the northwest, flows in a southeasterly direction for a while, forming the border with Hungary's northern neighbor, Slovakia. Just after Esztergom, about 40km (25 miles) north of Budapest, the river swings abruptly south. This is the start of the Danube Bend region. The river then swings sharply north again just before Visegrád, and then heads south again before reaching Vác. From Vác, it flows more or less directly south, through Budapest and down toward the country's Serbian and Croatian borders.

The delightful towns along the snaking Bend—in particular, Szentendre, Visegrád, and Esztergom—can easily be seen on day trips from Budapest since they're all within a couple of hours of the city. The great natural beauty of the area, where forested hills loom over the river, makes it a welcome haven for those weary of the city. Travelers with more time in Budapest can easily make a long weekend out of a visit to the Bend.

GETTING THERE

BY BOAT   From April to September, boats run between Budapest and the towns of the Danube Bend. A leisurely boat ride through the countryside is one of the highlights of an excursion. All boats depart Budapest's Vigadó tér boat landing, which is located in Pest between Erzsébet Bridge and Szabadság Bridge, stopping to pick up passengers 5 minutes later at Buda's Batthyány tér landing, which is in Buda and is also a Red line metro stop, before continuing up the river.

Schedules and towns served are complicated, so contact **MAHART,** the state shipping company, at the Vigadó tér landing (*©* **1/318-1704;** www.mahartpassnave.hu, click on the British flag) for information. You can also get MAHART information from Tourinform.

Round-trip prices are 1,330 Ft ($6/£3.40) to Szentendre, 1,390 Ft ($6.25/£3.40) to Visegrád, and 1,460 Ft ($6.60/£3.75) to Esztergom. Children up to age 14 receive a 50% discount, and children under 4 can travel free if they don't require their own seats.

The approximate travel time from Budapest is 2 hours to Szentendre, 3½ hours to Visegrád, and 5 hours to Esztergom. If time is tight, consider the train or bus (both of which are also considerably cheaper).

BY TRAIN   For information and details on traveling by Budapest rail, see p. 281.

To Szentendre   The HÉV suburban railroad connects Budapest's Batthyány tér with Szentendre. Trains leave daily, year-round, every 20 minutes or so from 4am to 11:30pm. The one-way fare is 320 Ft ($1.45/85p); subtract 125 Ft (55¢/35p) if you have a valid Budapest public transportation pass. The trip takes 45 minutes.

To Visegrád   There's no direct train service to Visegrád. Instead, take the train departing from Nyugati Station to Nagymaros. The trip takes 1 hour, and there are 20 daily trains. From Nagymaros, take a **ferry** (**RÉV;** *©* **06/80/406-611**) across the river to Visegrád. The ferry dock is a 5-minute walk from the train station. A ferry leaves every hour throughout the day. The train ticket to Nagymaros costs 436 Ft ($1.95/£1.10); the ferry ticket to Visegrád costs 200 Ft (90¢/50p). The train-to-ferry trip is much more enjoyable than the long, slow bus ride.

BY BUS   Approximately 30 daily buses travel the same route to Szentendre, Visegrád, and Esztergom, departing from **Budapest's Árpád híd bus station** (*©* **1/329-1450;** at the Blue line metro station of the same name). The one-way fare to Szentendre is 282 Ft ($1.25/75p); the trip takes about 30 minutes. The fare to Visegrád is 451 Ft ($2/£1.05), and the trip takes 1¼ hours. To Esztergom, take the bus that travels via a town called Dorog; it costs 563 Ft ($2.55/£1.45) and takes 1¼ hours. The bus that goes to Esztergom via Visegrád takes 2 hours and costs 732 Ft ($3.30/£1.90) (fare is determined by mileage of travel, and this is a longer route). Keep in mind, of course, that all travel by bus is subject to occasional traffic delays, especially during rush hour.

BY CAR   From Budapest, Route 11 hugs the west bank of the Danube, taking you to Szentendre, Visegrád, and Esztergom. Alternatively, you could head "overland" to Esztergom by Route 10, switching to Route 111 at Dorog.

SZENTENDRE

21km (13 miles) N of Budapest

The center of Szentendre (pronounced *Sen*-ten-dreh) must rank with Pest's Váci utca and Buda's Castle District as one of the most heavily visited spots in all of Hungary. In the summer, it becomes one huge handicraft and souvenir marketplace. Despite the excess of vendors, Szentendre remains a gorgeous little town. In medieval times, Serbian settlers fleeing Turkish northward expansion populated Szentendre, which counts half a dozen Serbian churches among its rich collection of historic buildings. The town retains a distinctively Mediterranean flavor that's rare this far north in Europe.

Since the early 1900s, Szentendre has been home to an artists' colony. Today, about 100 artists live and work here. As a result, the town has a wealth of museums and galleries, the best of which are listed below. Surprisingly few people visit the museums, however, distracted perhaps by the shopping opportunities. We recommend that you explore more than the main drag, Fő tér. After the almost-suffocating hubbub of the center of the city, we're pretty sure you'll appreciate the peace and quiet of the many exhibition halls and the winding cobblestone streets that lead to a Roman Catholic churchyard at the top of the hill, with lovely views of the red-tile rooftops. Wander down side streets; Szentendre is too small for you to get lost in and too beautiful for a less-than-thorough exploration.

ESSENTIALS

For information on getting to Szentendre. One of Szentendre's information offices, **Tourinform,** is at Dumtsa Jenő u. 22 (© **26/317-965**), with maps of Szentendre (and the Danube Bend region), as well as concert and exhibition schedules. The office can also provide accommodations information. The office is open April through October Monday to Friday from 9am to 7pm, and weekends from 9am to 2pm; the office is closed on weekends in the off season but is open weekdays from 9am to 5pm. If you arrive in Szentendre by train or bus, you'll come upon this office as you follow the flow of pedestrian traffic into town on Kossuth Lajos utca. If you arrive by boat, you may find the **Ibusz** office sooner, located on the corner of Bogdányi út and Gőzhajó utca (© **26/310-181**). This office is open April to October Monday through Friday from 9am to 5pm and weekends 10am to 2pm. From November to March, it's open weekdays only, 9am to 4pm.

Another good source of information, particularly if you are planning to stay in the region more than a day, is **Jági Utazás,** at Kucsera F. u. 15 (©/fax **26/310-030**). The staff here is extremely knowledgeable and dedicated. From planning hunting or horseback-riding excursions to helping you find the right pension room to recommending the best *palacsinta* (crepe) place in town, they seem to know it all. The office is open weekdays 10am to 6pm in summer and 9am to 5pm in winter.

WHERE TO STAY

Róz Panzió, Pannónia utca 6/b (© **26/311-737;** fax 26/310-979; www.hotelroz szentendre.hu) has 10 units and a nice garden overlooking the Danube for breakfast when weather permits. Rooms are 40€ ($46) for a double during off season, 50€ ($63) in high season, breakfast included. Parking is available.

EXPLORING THE MUSEUMS & CHURCHES

Ámos and Anna Múzeum ✦ *Finds*   This exceptional museum was the former home of artist couple Imre Ámos and Margit Anna, whose work represents the beginning of expressionist painting in Hungary. Opened after Anna's death in 1991, the collection is Szentendre's best-kept secret. Particularly engaging are the drawings Ámos did between periods of forced labor on the Russian front, where he eventually died of typhus. On a lighter note are Anna's wonderful puppets. Ámos's art seems influenced by Chagall, whereas Anna's work invokes Miró and Klee.

Outside the museum, in the courtyard, is Anna's gravesite, around which visitors have left wishing stones from the garden as tokens of respect.

Bogdányi u. 10. ℰ **26/310-790**. Admission 500 Ft ($2.25/£1.30). Summer daily 10am–6pm; winter daily 1–5pm.

Barcsay Museum   The conservative Socialist dictates of the day restricted the work of artist Jenő Barcsay (1900–88). Nevertheless, in his anatomical drawings, etchings, and charcoal and ink drawings, Barcsay's genius shines through. We particularly like his pastel drawings of Szentendre street scenes.

Dumtsa Jenő u. 10. ℰ **26/310-244**. Admission 500 Ft ($2.25/£1.30). Tues–Sun 10am–6pm.

Blagovestenska Church   The Blagovestenska church is the only one of the town's several Serbian Orthodox churches that you can be fairly sure to find open. The tiny church, dating from 1752, was built on the site of a wooden church from the Serbian migration of 1690. A rococo iconostasis features paintings by Mihailo Zivkovic; notice that the eyes of all the icons are upon you.

Fő tér 4. Admission 200 Ft (90¢/50p). Tues–Sun 10am–5pm.

Ferenczy Museum ℰℰ   Next door to the Blagovestenska in Main Square (Fő tér), the Ferenczy Museum is dedicated to the art of the extraordinary Ferenczy family. The featured artist is Károly Ferenczy, one of Hungary's leading Impressionists—you can see more of his work in Budapest's National Museum. Works by Ferenczy's lesser-known children—Noémi (tapestry maker), Valér (painter), and Beni (sculptor and medallion maker)—are also on display.

Fő tér 6. ℰ **26/310-244**. Admission 500 Ft ($2.25/£1.30). Wed–Sun 10am–5pm.

Margit Kovács Museum ℰℰℰ   This expansive museum features the work of Hungary's best-known ceramic artist, Margit Kovács, who died in 1977. This museum displays the breadth of Kovács's talents. We were especially moved by her sculptures of elderly women and by her folk art–influenced friezes of village life. When the museum is full, people are required to wait outside before entering.

Vastagh György u. 1. ℰ **26/310-244**. Admission 600 Ft ($2.70/£1.55). Apr–Oct Tues–Sun 10am–6pm; Nov–Mar Tues–Sun 10am–4pm. Walk east from Fő tér on Görög utca.

Serbian Orthodox Museum   The Serbian Orthodox Museum is housed next door to a Serbian Orthodox church (services are at 10am Sun) in one of the buildings of the former episcopate, just north of Fő tér. The collection here—one of the most extensive of its kind in predominantly Catholic Hungary—features exceptional 16th- through 19th-century icons, liturgical vessels, scrolls in Arabic from the Ottoman period, and other types of ecclesiastical art. Informative labels are in Hungarian and English.

Pátriárka u. 5. ℰ **26/312-399**. Admission 400 Ft ($1.80/£1). Apr–Oct Tues–Sun 10am–5pm; Nov–Mar Fri–Sun 10am–4pm. Walk north from Fő tér on Alkotmány utca.

WHERE TO DINE
Aranysárkány Vendéglő (Golden Dragon Inn) ℰ HUNGARIAN   Located just east of Fő tér on Hunyadi utca, which leads into Alkotmány utca, the Golden Dragon is always filled to capacity. The crowd includes a good percentage of Hungarians, definitely a good sign in a heavily visited town like Szentendre.

Long wooden tables set with sterling cutlery provide a relaxed but tasteful atmosphere in this air-conditioned restaurant. You can choose from such enticing offerings as alpine lamb, roast leg of goose, Székely-style stuffed cabbage (the Székely are a Hungarian ethnic group native to Transylvania), spinach cream, and venison steak. Vegetarians can order the vegetable plate, a respectable presentation of grilled and steamed vegetables in season. The cheese dumplings do a good job of rounding out the meal. Various traditional Hungarian beers are on draft, and the wine list features selections from 22 regions of the country.

Alkotmány u. 1/a. ℂ 26/301-479. www.aranysarkany.hu. Reservations recommended. Soup 700 Ft–800 Ft ($3.15–$3.60/£1.80–£1.85); main courses 1,900 Ft–2,600 Ft ($8.55–$12/£4.90–£6.70). AE, DC, MC, V. Daily noon–10pm.

Régimódi ✸ HUNGARIAN   If you walk directly south from Fő tér, you'll find this excellent choice for dining. An elegant restaurant in a former private home, Régimódi is furnished with antique Hungarian carpets and chandeliers. Original artworks decorate the walls. Limited terrace dining is available, though you might not want to miss out on eating amid the rich interior decor. The menu offers a wide range of Hungarian specialties, with an emphasis on game dishes. The wild-deer stew in red wine is particularly sumptuous, while less adventurous diners might opt for the turkey breast stuffed with stewed fruit in cheese sauce. The menu also features numerous salad options. There's an extensive wine list.

Futó u. 3. ℂ 26/311-105. Reservations recommended. Soup 400 Ft–500 Ft ($1.80–$2.25/£1–£1.30); main courses 1,200 Ft–3,000 Ft ($5.40–$14/£3.10–£7.70). DC, MC, V. Daily 9am–11pm.

VISEGRÁD

45km (28 miles) NW of Budapest

Halfway between Szentendre and Esztergom, Visegrád (pronounced *Vee*-sheh-grod) is a sparsely populated, sleepy riverside village, which makes its history all the more fascinating and hard to believe: The Romans built a fort here, which was still standing when Slovak settlers gave the town its present name (meaning "High Castle") in the 9th or 10th century. After the Mongol invasion (1241–42), construction began on both the present ruined hilltop citadel and the former riverside palace. Eventually, Visegrád boasted one of the finest royal palaces ever built in Hungary. Only one king, Charles Robert (1307–42), actually used it as his primary residence, but monarchs from Béla IV, in the 13th century, through Matthias Corvinus, in the late 15th century, spent time in Visegrád and contributed to its development, the latter expanding the palace into a great Renaissance center known throughout Europe.

ESSENTIALS

For information on getting to **Visegrád,** The information center, **Visegrád Tours,** RÉV u. 15 (ℂ **26/398-160**), is located across the road from the RÉV ferryboat landing (not to be confused with the MAHART boat landing, which is about .8km/½ mile down the road). It is open daily from April through October 9am to 6pm, from November through March weekdays 10am to 4pm.

WHERE TO STAY

Good accommodations can be found at **Honti Panzió,** Fő utca 66 (ℂ **26/398-120;** www.hotels.hu/honti), which has 7 units. Double rooms are 40€ ($46) year-round, breakfast included; parking is provided.

EXPLORING THE PALACE & THE CITADEL

The **Royal Palace** once covered much of the area where the MAHART boat landing and Fő utca (Main St.) are now found. Indeed, the entrance to the palace's open-air ruins, called the **King Matthias Museum,** is at Fő u. 29 (© **26/398-126**). Admission is 400 Ft ($1.80/£1). The museum is open Tuesday through Sunday 9am to 4:30pm. The buried ruins of the palace, having achieved a near-mythical status, were discovered only recently. Almost all of what you see is the result of ongoing reconstruction, which has been vigorous in recent years. Aside from the general atmosphere of ruined grandeur, the main attractions are the red-marble base of the Hercules Fountain in the Ornamental Courtyard and the reconstructed Gothic arcaded hallway down below. Exhibit descriptions are in English. Because of the under-construction aspect of the place, you need to keep a close eye on the kids here.

The **Citadel** ★★ (© **26/398-101**), situated on the hilltop above Visegrád, affords one of the finest views you'll find over the Danube. Off to your left you can see the site of the controversial Nagymaros Dam, an abandoned Hungarian-Czechoslovak hydroelectric project. Admission to the Citadel is 400 Ft ($1.80/£1). It is open daily in summer 9am to 6pm, in winter on weekends only from 9:30am to 6pm. There are three buses a day to the Citadel, departing from the RÉV ferryboat terminal at 9:26am, 12:26pm, and 3:26pm, respectively. Otherwise, "City Bus," an inappropriately named van taxi that awaits passengers outside Visegrád Tours, takes people up the steep incline to the Citadel for the equally steep fare of 2,500 Ft ($11/£6.40) apiece. If you decide to go on foot, keep in mind that it's more than a casual walk to the Citadel; the journey up the hill takes about 2 hours. There may be snack and ice-cream carts along the way, but there are no permanent establishments, so you many want to pack some snacks and drinks.

WHERE TO DINE

Don Vito Pizzeria & Ristorante ★ (Kids PIZZA   Don Vito Pizzeria serves very good pizza in a pleasant, relaxed atmosphere. It's a good option if you're traveling with kids. Try the "Don Vito," a delicious and very Hungarian mushroom, gooseliver, and apple pizza, or the beautiful "Albino," which is great for vegetarians with a ricotta, garlic, and herb topping. Beer and wine are served.

Fő u. 83. © **26/397-230**. Individual pizzas 600 Ft–1,400 Ft ($2.70–$6.30/£1.55–£3.60). No credit cards. Daily 11am–midnight.

Renaissance Restaurant ★★ (Kids HUNGARIAN   This restaurant specializes in authentic medieval cuisine. Food is served in clay crockery without silverware (you only get a wooden spoon) and guests are offered Burger King–like paper crowns to wear. The decor and the lyre music enhance the fun, openly kitschy atmosphere. This is perhaps the only restaurant in the whole country where you won't find something on the menu spiced with paprika, since the spice wasn't around in medieval Hungary. If you're big on the medieval theme, come for dinner on a Thursday (July–Aug), when a six-course "Royal Feast" is served following a 45-minute duel between knights. No vegetarians, please! Tickets for this special evening are handled by Visegrád Tours (p. 354). The duel gets underway at 6pm sharp.

Fő u. 11 (across the street from the MAHART boat landing). © **26/398-081**. Main courses 1,900 Ft–3,200 Ft ($8.55–$14/£4.90–£8.20). V. Daily noon–10pm.

5 The Lake Balaton Region

Lake Balaton may not be the Mediterranean, but don't tell that to Hungarians. Somehow, over the years, Hungarians have managed to create their own central European version of a Mediterranean culture along the shores of their long, shallow, milky-white lake. Throughout the long summer, swimmers, windsurfers, sailors, kayakers, and cruisers fill the warm and silky smooth lake, Europe's largest at 80km (50 miles) long and 15km (10 miles) wide at its broadest point. Around the lake's 197km (315 miles) of shoreline, vacationers cast their reels for pike; play tennis, soccer, and volleyball; ride horses; and hike in the hills.

First settled in the Iron Age, the Balaton region has been a recreation spot since at least Roman times. From the 18th century onward, the upper classes erected spas and villas along the shoreline. Not until the post–World War II Communist era did the lake open up to a wider tourist base. Many large hotels along the lake are former trade union resorts built under the previous regime.

Lake Balaton seems to have something for everyone. Teenagers, students, and young travelers tend to congregate in the hedonistic towns on the south shore, where the land is as flat as it is in Pest. Here, huge 1970s-style beachside hotels are filled to capacity all summer long, and disco music pulsates into the early morning hours. From these resorts, you can walk for 10 minutes and find yourself deep in farm country. The air here is still and quiet; in summer the sun hangs heavily in the sky.

Adult travelers and families tend to spend more time on the hillier, more graceful, north shore. There, little villages are neatly tucked away in the rolling countryside, where the grapes of the popular Balaton wines ripen in the strong southern sun. If you're coming from Budapest, the northern shore of the lake at first appears every bit as built up and crowded as the southern shore. Beyond Balatonfüred, however, this impression begins to fade. You'll discover the Tihany Peninsula, a protected area whose 12 sq. km (4¾ sq. miles) jut out into the lake like a knob. Moving westward along the coast, passing from one lakeside settlement to the next, you can make forays inland into the rolling hills of the Balaton wine country. Stop for a swim—or for the night— in a small town like Szigliget. The city of Keszthely, sitting at the lake's western edge, marks the end of the northern shore area. All towns on the lake are within 1½ to 4 hours from Budapest by an InterCity, a *gyors* (fast) train, or a much longer journey on a *személy* (local) train (see below).

Since the summer of 2000, a cultural event called "The Valley of Arts" has been held on the northern side of the lake, near **Kapolcs,** attracting thousands of local and international artists and travelers. It was started as a local project by a handful of Hungarian contemporary artists who settled down in Kapolcs, the center of six little adjacent villages in the gorgeous Káli valley. The 10-day-long arts event includes film, music, theater, visual art exhibits, and literature readings, and is held at the end of July, running through the beginning of August. Visit www.kapolcs.hu for information on exact dates. For general information on programs and services of just about any area of Balaton, see www.balaton-tourism.hu.

EXPLORING THE LAKE BALATON REGION
GETTING THERE & GETTING AROUND
BY TRAIN   From Budapest, trains to the various towns along the lake depart from Déli Station. The local *(személy)* trains are interminably slow, stopping at each village along the lake. Unless you're going to a tiny village (sometimes a good idea), try to get

on an express *(gyors)* train. To Keszthely, the trip takes about 3 hours and costs 2,030 Ft ($10/£5.20). To reach Tihany, take a train to Balatonfüred for 1,420 Ft ($7.10/£3.65; travel time 2 hr.), and then a local bus to Tihany.

BY CAR   From Budapest, take the M7 motorway south through Székesfehérvár until you hit the lake. Route 71 circles the lake.

If you're planning to visit Lake Balaton for more than a day or two, you should consider renting a car, which will give you much greater mobility. The various towns differ enough from one another that you may want to keep driving until you find a place that really speaks to you. Without a car, this is obviously more difficult. Also, wherever you go in the region, you'll find that private rooms are both cheaper and easier to get if you travel a few miles off the lake. Driving directly to the lake from Budapest will take about an hour and 15 minutes.

BY BOAT & FERRY   Passenger boats on Lake Balaton let you travel across the lake as well as between towns on the same shore. The boat routes are extensive, and the rates are cheap, but the boats are considerably slower than surface transportation. All major towns have docks with departures and arrivals. Children 3 and under travel free, and those 13 and under get half-price tickets. A single ferry *(komp)* running between Tihany and Szántód lets you transport a car across the width of the lake.

All boat and ferry information is available from the **BAHART** office in Siófok (© **84/310-050** or 84/312-144; www.balatonihajozas.hu). Local tourist offices all along the lake (several listed below) also have schedules and other information.

BY BUS   Once at the lake, you might find that buses are the best way of getting around locally. Buses will be indispensable, of course, if you take private-room lodging a few miles away from the lake.

WHERE TO STAY IN THE AREA

Because hotel prices are unusually high in the Balaton region, and since just about every local family rents out a room or two in summer, we especially recommend private rooms as the lodging of choice in this area. You can reserve a room through a local tourist office or you can just look for the ubiquitous SZOBA KIADÓ (or ZIMMER FREI) signs that decorate most front gates in the region. When you take a room without using a tourist agency as the intermediary, prices are generally negotiable. (Owners sometimes prefer hard currency.) In the height of the season, you shouldn't have to pay more than 6,000 Ft ($30/£15) for a double room within reasonable proximity of the lake.

Many budget travelers pitch their tents in **lakeside campgrounds** all around the lake. Campgrounds are generally quite inexpensive, and their locations are well marked on maps.

All the campgrounds have working facilities, but are probably not as clean as many people are accustomed to.

THE TIHANY PENINSULA

The Tihany (pronounced *Tee*-hine) Peninsula, a national park since 1952, has several towns on it, the most notable of which is called, appropriately, **Tihany** (or Tihany Village). Because the peninsula is a protected area, building is heavily restricted; consequently, this area maintains a rustic charm that's unusual in the Balaton region.

The Tihany Peninsula also features a lush, protected interior, accessible by a trail from Tihany Village, with several little inland lakes—including the aptly named **Inner**

Herend: Home of Hungary's Finest Porcelain

About 16km (10 miles) west of Veszprém lies the sleepy village of Herend. What distinguishes this village from other villages in the area is the presence of the Herend Porcelain factory, where Hungary's finest porcelain has been made since 1826.

Herend Porcelain began to establish its international reputation as far back as 1851, when a dinner set was displayed at the Great Exhibition in London. Artists hand-paint every piece, from tableware to decorative accessories. Patterns include delicate flowers, butterflies, and birds.

The recently opened **Porcelanium Visitors Center,** at Kossuth Lajos utca 140 in Herend, features the newly expanded Herend Museum (© **88/261-801**), which displays a dazzling collection of Herend porcelain. A minitour of the factory and a porcelain-making demonstration film are also part of the visitor center offerings. The Porcelanium is open daily from May to October, 9am to 5:30pm; Tuesday to Saturday only, from November to April, 9am to 3:30pm. Admission is 400 Ft ($1.80/£1). At the **factory store** (© **88/523-223**), which accepts credit cards, you might find patterns that are unavailable in Budapest's Herend Shop (p. 339). Prices will be comparable to those in Budapest, but much less than what Herend costs in the United States. The factory store is open in summer Monday through Saturday from 9:30am to 6pm, Sunday until 4pm; in winter Monday through Friday from 9:30am to 4pm, Saturday 9:30am to 2pm. The Porcelanium Visitors Center also has a coffeehouse and upscale restaurant. Food is served on Herend china, naturally. Herend is easily accessible via bus from Veszprém.

Lake and **Outer Lake**—as well as a lookout tower offering views out over the Balaton. Give yourself at least an hour or two to explore the interior.

As you travel west from the Tihany Peninsula, the landscape begins to get hillier.

ESSENTIALS

GETTING THERE   The rail line that circles Lake Balaton does not serve the Tihany Peninsula. The nearest railway station is in Aszófő, about 5km (3 miles) from Tihany Village. A local bus to Tihany, synchronized to the rail timetable, departs from just outside the railway station in Aszófő and from just outside the railway station in the larger nearby town of Balatonfüred. You can also go by ferry from Szántód or Balatonföldvár, or by boat from Balatonfüred.

VISITOR INFORMATION   Visitor information and private-room bookings for the Tihany Peninsula are available in Tihany Village at **Tourinform,** Kossuth u. 20 (©/fax **87/448-804;** www.tourinform.hu). The office is open May through October only, Monday through Friday from 8:30am to 7pm and on weekends from 8:30am to 12:30pm.

EXPLORING TIHANY VILLAGE

The 18th-century baroque **Abbey Church** ✿ is, undoubtedly, Tihany Village's main attraction. The church stands on the site of an earlier 11th-century Romanesque church (the charter for which contains the first words ever written in Hungarian), around whose remains the crypt of the current church was built. These remains include the marble gravestone of King Andrew, who died in 1060; this is the sole Hungarian royal tomb that remains in its original location. A resident Austrian-born monk carved the exquisite wooden altar and pulpit in the 18th century. The frescoes in the church are by three of Hungary's better-known 19th-century painters, whose work can be viewed throughout the country: Károly Lotz, Bertalan Székely, and Lajos Deák-Ébner.

Next door to the Abbey Church is the **Tihany Museum** (✆ **87/448-650**), housed in an 18th-century baroque structure, like the church. The museum features exhibitions on the surrounding region's history and culture. You pay a single entry fee of 500 Ft ($2.50/£1.30) for both the church and museum. Both are open daily from 9am to 5:30pm.

Tihany Village is also the site of the legendary **Echo Hill,** a scenic spot overlooking the lake (near the Echo Restaurant), which is reached via a winding path that starts from the left side of the Abbey Church. Voices on Echo Hill reverberate back from the side of the church. See for yourself.

Some say the best ice cream on Lake Balaton is to be had at the shop on the road between the Abbey Church and Echo Hill.

BADACSONY & SZIGLIGET ★★
160km (100 miles) SW of Budapest

BADACSONY
Nestled in one of the most picturesque corners of Lake Balaton is Badacsony, an area which includes four villages noted for their beautiful vistas and some of the best wines of Hungary. The Badacsony area is dotted with wine cellars, and the tradition of viticulture and winegrowing dates from the Celtic and Roman times. Other than wine tasting, Badacsony boasts walking trails where you can study the diverse basalt forms and the former quarry walls. You'll also find a 4km-long (2.5-mile) circular trail, starting from the Kisfaludy House on the southern side of Badacsony Hill. Contact **Botanikai tanösvény Badacsony** (✆ **87/461-069;** www.bfnpi.hu) for guided tours.

One of the better-known vintners in Hungary is Huba Szeremley, whose Badacsony wines have consistently been winners in Italy, France, and Hungary. The best way to find out about Szeremley's regular wine tastings is to visit his restaurant, **Szent Orbán Borház és Étterem,** Badacsonytomaj, Kisfaludy S. u. 5 (✆ **87/432-382;** www.szeremley.com), open daily from noon to 10pm.

The **Borbarátok Panzió** ★★, Badacsonytomaj, Római út. 78 (✆ **87/471-000;** www.borbaratok.hu), is a family-operated restaurant and hotel. They serve traditional Hungarian fare and also offer a wide variety of programs including wine tasting, harvest, fishing, and walking tours. Main courses at the restaurant run from 1,200 Ft to 2,700 Ft ($6–$14/£3.10–£7). The restaurant is open daily 11:30am to 11pm in high season, and in low season, daily 11:30am to 10pm.

SZIGLIGET
Halfway between Tihany and Keszthely is the lovely village of Szigliget (pronounced *Sig*-lee-get). If you are as taken as we were by the thatched-roof houses, the lush vineyards, and the sunny Mediterranean feel of Szigliget, you might consider spending the night. There are also the ubiquitous ZIMMER FREI signs indicating the presence of a private room,

---

Kids   **An Excursion to the Thermal Lake in Hévíz**

If you think the water of Lake Balaton is warm, just wait until you jump into the lake at **Hévíz** ✸✸ (pronounced *Hay*-veez), a resort town about 8km (5 miles) northwest of Keszthely. Here you'll find the largest thermal lake in Europe and the second largest in the world (the largest is in New Zealand), covering 50,000 sq. m (538,195 sq. ft.).

The lake's water temperature seldom dips below 85°F to 90°F (29°C–32°C)—even in the most bitter spell of winter. Consequently, people swim in the lake year-round. You are bound to notice the huge numbers of German travelers taking advantage of the waters. Hévíz has been one of Hungary's leading spa resorts for over 100 years, and it retains a distinct 19th-century atmosphere.

While the lakeside area is suitable for ambling, no visit to Hévíz would be complete without a swim. An enclosed causeway leads out into the center of the lake, where locker rooms and the requisite services, including massage, float rental, and a *palacsinta* (crepe) bar are housed (✆ 83/501-700).

You can easily reach Hévíz by bus from Keszthely. Buses depart every half-hour or so from the bus station (conveniently stopping to pick up passengers in front of the church on Fő tér). The entrance to the lake is just opposite the bus station. You'll see a whimsical wooden facade and the words TÓ FÜRDŐ (Bathing Lake). Tickets cost 900 Ft ($4.50/£2.30) for up to 3 hours or 1,600 Ft ($8/£4.10) for a day pass; however, the latter is not available from November through March. The lake is open daily 8:30am to 5pm in the summer and 9am to 4:30pm in winter. Your ticket entitles you to a locker; insert the ticket into the slot in the locker and the key will come out of the lock. Keep the ticket until exiting, as the attendant needs to see it to determine whether you've stayed a half-day or a full day.

There is no shallow water in the lake, so use discretion when bringing children. However, there is a nice small playground on the grounds that they will enjoy.

If you want to stay in the town of Hévíz at a wellness hotel, in walking distance of the lake, we recommend **Rogner Hotel and Spa Therme** ✸✸, Lótusvirág u. (✆ 83/501-700; www.lotustherme.com). Open year-round, this 230-room hotel is located in what feels like a secluded wooded area and includes health cures, sports, medical treatments, and evening programs. A double room in high season is 81€ ($97).

---

along the roads. **Szőlőskert Panzió** (✆ 87/461-264), on Vadrózsa utca, might be the best option, given its close proximity to the beach. Situated on the hillside amid lush terraces of grapes, the pension is open only in summer. A double is 9,000 Ft ($41/£23).

Szigliget is home to the fantastic ruins of the 13th-century **Szigliget Castle,** Kossuth u. 54 (✆ 87/461-069; www.szigligetivar.hu), which stand above the town on **Várhegy (Castle Hill).** In the days of the Turkish invasions, the Hungarian Balaton fleet, protected by the high castle, called Szigliget home. You can hike up to the ruins for a splendid view of the lake and the surrounding countryside; look for the path behind the white 18th-century church, which stands on the highest spot in the village.

A good place to fortify yourself for the hike is the **Vár Vendéglő** ⚔, Kisfaludy u. 30 (*C* **87/461-040**), on the road up to the castle. It's a casual restaurant with plenty of outdoor seating, serving traditional Hungarian fare. Main courses run from 1,000 Ft to 1,800 Ft ($5–$9/£2.60–£4.65). It's open daily 11am to 11pm in the high season.

The lively **beach** at Szigliget provides a striking contrast to the quiet village and is a good place to take kids. In summer, buses from neighboring towns drop off hordes of beachgoers. The beach area is crowded with fried-food and beer stands, ice-cream vendors, a swing set, and a volleyball net.

Szigliget is also home to the **Eszterházy Wine Cellar,** Kossuth u. 3 (*C* **87/461-044**), the largest wine cellar in the region. After a hike in the hills or a day in the sun, a little wine tasting just might be in order.

If you really enjoy hiking, you might want to take a local bus from Szigliget to the nondescript nearby village of **Hegymagas,** about 5km (3 miles) to the north along the Szigliget-Tapolca bus route. The town's name means "Tall Hill," and from here you can hike up **Szent György-hegy (St. George Hill).** This marvelous vineyard-covered hill has several hiking trails, the most strenuous of which goes up and over the rocky summit.

LAKE BALATON'S SOUTHERN SHORE

If you're looking for long days at the beach followed by long nights out on the town, the southern shore of Lake Balaton may be the place for you. After all, a million Hungarian students can't be wrong. Or could they?

Siófok, the largest resort town on Lake Balaton, is at the lake's southeastern end. Its growth dates back to the 1860s, when Budapest was first connected to the southern shore of the lake by rail. Thus, we suppose, nobody alive can remember a time (other than the war years) when Siófok was not overrun by summertime revelers. Many of the majestic old villas along the large plane tree–lined streets have been restored or renovated, and can even be rented in the summer months.

The bustling Siófok caters largely to a young, active crowd of students and teenagers who fill every inch of the town's beaches all day long and then pack their sunburned bodies into the town's discos until the early morning hours. Large, modern, expensive hotels line the shore in Siófok. You'll find no empty stretches of beach here, but you will find windsurfing, tennis, and boating.

While this city is no cultural capital, the architecture of some of the older buildings is impressive. Note the old railway station, and the many villas around the Gold Coast (Aranypart). You will also find some important contemporary buildings, notably the Evangelical Church, designed by one of Hungary's most appreciated architects, **Imre Makovecz**—who is known for his use of wood and light in his structures that dot the country. Most of the wood used for the building was imported from Finland.

Siófok is also trying to attract visitors to recently constructed wellness centers, open year-round, which offer an assortment of facilities plus the added benefit of Hungary's warm-water springs.

For more information on the southern shore, contact the **Tourinform** (*C*/fax **84/310-117;** www.siofokportal.com) office in Siófok, right below the immense water tower in the center of town.

WHERE TO STAY

Siófok is basically plastered with tourists during the summer months, and there are a wide variety of options from large hotels or resorts on the Gold Coast to the east of the center of town, or the Silver Coast (Ezüstpart), to the west. Additional accommodations can be found on the city's website at www.siofokportal.com.

We recommend pampering yourself at a "wellness center" for a few days. The **Hotel Azúr** ★★, Vitorlás u. 11 (✆ **84/501-400;** www.hotelazur.hu) is the most comfortable, plush, and welcoming hotel and wellness center in town. The pools are large, it has a nice fitness room, and the whole complex is extremely tasteful. During the summer months, the hotel facilities look directly onto Lake Balaton. Rates are 135€ ($162) in summer and 85€ ($102) in winter for a double room, and breakfast is included. The hotel has a good-size indoor swimming pool, a sauna, a massage club, Finnish saunas, a beauty salon, and thermal pools.

The **Hotel Residence** ★, Erkel Ferenc u. 49 (✆ **84/506-840;** www.hotel-residence. hu) also has an extensive list of services, including massages, gyms, baths, and aromatherapy. There is a private beach on the shores of Lake Balaton reserved for the hotel, but it is located several hundred meters away. Rates are 107€ ($128) in summer and 87€ ($105) in winter for a double room, and breakfast is included. The hotel has a good-size indoor swimming pool, a sauna, a massage club, Finnish saunas, a beauty salon, and thermal pools.

WHERE TO DINE

Try the **Sándor Restaurant** (✆ **84/312-829;** www.sandorrestaurant.hu), on Erkel F. utca 30, popular with locals for large portions of contemporary Hungarian food. If you're looking for more traditional Hungarian fare, occasionally with live Gypsy music, try the **Csárdás Restaurant,** at Fő u. 105 (✆ **84/310-642**).

6 Northeastern Hungary

Northeast of the Danube Bend is Hungary's hilliest region, where the country's highest peak—Matra Hill, at 998m (3,327 ft.)—can be found. Here you can visit the preserved medieval village of Hollókő; see remnants of the country's Turkish heritage in Eger, also known for its regional wines; and explore the 23km (14-mile) cave system in Aggtelek.

HOLLÓKŐ: A PRESERVED PALÓC VILLAGE ★
102km (63 miles) NE of Budapest

The village of Hollókő (pronounced *Ho*-low-koo) is one of the most charming spots in Hungary. This UNESCO World Heritage Site is a perfectly preserved but still vibrant Palóc village. The rural Palóc people speak an unusual Hungarian dialect, and they have some of the more colorful folk customs and costumes in Hungary. If you're in Hungary at Easter time, by all means consider spending the holiday in Hollókő. Hollókő's traditional Easter celebration features townspeople in traditional dress and Masses in the town church.

ESSENTIALS

GETTING THERE   The only direct **bus** to Hollókő departs from Budapest's central bus station, Stadionok Bus Station (✆ **1/382-0888**). It departs daily at 8:30am and takes about 2½ hours to reach the town. The fare is 1,400 Ft ($5.60/£3.60).

Alternatively, you can take a bus from Árpád híd bus station in Budapest (© 1/412-2597) to Szécsény or Pásztó, where you switch to a local bus to Hollókő, of which there are four daily.

If you're **driving** from Budapest, take the M3 motorway to Hatvan, the M21 from Hatvan to Pásztó, and local roads from Pásztó to Hollókő.

VISITOR INFORMATION The best information office is the **Foundation of Hollókő,** at Kossuth Lajos út. 68 (© **32/579-010;** www.holloko.hu). It's open in summer Monday to Friday 8am to 8pm and weekends 10am to 6pm; in winter, it's open Monday to Friday 8am to 5pm and weekends 10am to 4pm. You can also get information through **Nograd Tourist** in Salgótarján (© **32/310-660**) or through **Tourinform** in Szécsény, at Ady Endre u. 12 (© **32/370-777;** www.szecseny.hu).

SEASONAL EVENTS

At **Easter time** ⍟, villagers wear national costumes and participate in a folk festival. Traditional song, dance, and foods are featured. On the last weekend in July, the **Palóc Szőttes Festival** ⍟ is held in Hollókő. Folk dance troupes from Nógrád county as well as international folk dance troupes perform on an open-air stage. Folk art by local artisans is also on display. In the winter, groups visiting Hollókő can participate in a **wild-pig hunt** and subsequent roast.

EXPLORING THE VILLAGE

A one-street town, Hollókő is idyllically set in a quiet, green valley, with **hiking trails** all around. A restored 14th-century **castle** is perched on a hilltop over the village.

In the village itself you can admire the 14th-century wooden-towered church and the sturdy, traditional peasant architecture and observe the elderly women at work on their embroidery (samples are for sale). You can also visit the **Village Museum** at Kossuth Lajos u. 82, where exhibits detail everyday Palóc life starting in the early 20th century. Official hours are Tuesday through Sunday from 10am to 4pm; closed in winter. Like everything else in town, though, the museum's opening times are flexible. Entry is 100 Ft (50¢/25p).

WHERE TO STAY

In Hollókő, traditionally furnished thatch-roofed **peasant houses** are available for rent on a nightly or longer basis. You can rent a **room in a shared house** (with shared facilities), or rent an **entire house.** The prices vary depending on the size of the room or house and the number of people in your party, but 8,500 Ft ($43/£22) for a double room is average. Standard **private rooms** are also available in Hollókő. All accommodations can be booked in advance through the tourist offices in Hollókő or Salgótarján (see "Essentials," above). If you arrive without reservations (which is not advised), the address and phone number of a room finder are posted on the door of the **Foundation of Hollókő** at Kossuth Lajos u. 68 (© **32/579-011**).

WHERE TO DINE

Dining options are limited in tiny Hollókő. The **Vár Étterem,** Kossuth Lajos u. 95 (© **32/379-029**), serves decent Hungarian food at very low prices. Try a dish prepared with the "treasure of the local forests," porcini mushrooms. There is indoor and outdoor seating. The menu is available in English, and the waiters are patient. The restaurant is open daily noon to 8pm, except Christmas Day.

EGER

126km (78 miles) NE of Budapest

Eger (pronounced *Egg*-air), a small baroque city lying in a valley between the Matra and Bükk mountains, is best known for three things: its castle, its wine, and its women—the women of the 16th century, that is. In that dark era of Turkish invasions, the women of Eger claimed their place in the Hungarian national consciousness by bravely fighting alongside István Dobó's army in defense of Eger's castle in 1552. Greatly outnumbered by the invaders, the defenders of Eger fought off the Turks for 38 grueling days, achieving a momentous victory that would stall the Turkish advance into Hungary for nearly half a century. Forty-four years later, in 1596, the sultan's forces attacked Eger again, this time taking the castle without great difficulty. Dobó's initial victory, though, and particularly the role of the women defenders, is a much cherished and mythologized historical event, recalled in numerous paintings, poems, and monuments.

As for the wine, the area around Eger is known for producing some fine vintages. Most famous among the regional potions is undoubtedly the heavily marketed *Egri bikavér* (Eger Bull's Blood), a strong dark-red wine. There are many other wines that are worth sampling as well—and no shortage of places in Eger to sample them.

Today Eger's landscape presents a harmonious blend of old and new. The ruined castle, one of Hungary's proudest symbols, dominates the skyline; throughout the summer huge groups of Hungarian children visit the castle. Eger is also home to one of Hungary's most impressive Turkish ruins: a single, tall, slender minaret. The view from the top of the minaret affords a wonderful vista of the town's surroundings. If you wander beyond the confines of the old section, you'll find a small modern city.

ESSENTIALS

GETTING THERE   Eger is a 2-hour direct **train** ride from Budapest. Sixteen daily trains depart Budapest's Keleti Station. Tickets cost 1,624 Ft ($8.10/£4.20).

If you're **driving** from Budapest, take the M3 motorway east to Kerecsend, where you pick up Route 25 north to Eger. There is a 1,400 Ft ($7/£3.60) toll; a toll ticket, valid for a week, is available at all MOL Petrol stations.

VISITOR INFORMATION   For information, visit or contact **Tourinform,** at Bajcsy-Zsilinszky u. 9 (© **36/517-715;** www.eger.hu). The office is open in summer Monday through Friday from 9am to 6pm and on weekends from 10am to 1pm; off season, the office closes an hour earlier and is closed on Sunday. For private-room booking, try **Egertourist,** at Bajcsy-Zsilinszky u. 9 (© **36/510-270;** www.egertourist. hu). This office is open Monday through Saturday from 10am to 6pm.

EXPLORING OLD EGER

All of Eger's main sites are within easy walking distance of **Dobó István tér** ✮✮, the lovely, dignified square that's the center of old Eger. Dobó István tér is home to the **Minorite Church,** a fine 18th-century baroque church. You'll also find a statue of town defender Dobó, flanked by a knight and a woman, by Alajos Strobl, one of the country's leading turn-of-the-20th-century sculptors. Strobl's other work includes the statue of King Stephen on Buda's Castle Hill and the statue of poet János Arany in front of the National Museum in Pest. The larger statue in the square, erected in the 1960s, is a more recent—and less subtle—rendition of the fight against the Turks.

The reconstructed ruins of **Eger Castle,** visible from just about anywhere in the city, can be reached by walking northeast out of the square; take the path out of Dózsa

György tér. You can wander around the grounds free of charge daily from 8am to 8pm in summer and daily 8am to 6pm in winter, or you can explore the two museums on the premises. The **István Dobó Castle Museum** (© 36/312-744) relates the history of the castle and displays some Turkish artifacts. The **Eger Picture Gallery** is particularly worth a visit for those who have not yet seen the Hungarian National Gallery in Buda; the same fine 19th-century Hungarian artists are featured in both museums. The museums are open Tuesday through Sunday from 10am to 5pm, until 4pm in winter. Admission to each museum is 800 Ft ($4/£2); separate admission for each museum.

Just to the west of the castle, on Harangöntő utca, is Eger's most visible reminder of the Turkish period, its **Minaret** (© 36/410-233). Though the mosque that held the minaret was destroyed in 1841, the 14-sided, 33m-tall (110-ft.) minaret survives to this day in remarkably good condition. For 100 Ft (50¢/25p), you can ascend its narrow height. It's a terrifying journey up a steep, cramped spiral staircase; because the space is so narrow, you can't turn back if anyone is behind you. Consequently, the ascent is not recommended for the weak-kneed or weak-hearted. Those who do make the climb, however, are justly rewarded with a spectacular view. Officially, the Minaret is open daily from 10am to 6pm, to 4pm in winter, but the ticket taker in the little booth at the Minaret's base is not always faithful to these hours; depending on the weather conditions, the hours may be longer or shorter. If no one is there, you should ask at the nearby Minaret Hotel.

Moving from the graceful to the overpowering, you'll find the massive **Basilica**— the second-largest church in Hungary (after Esztergom's Basilica)—a few blocks to the south on Eszterházy tér. József Hild, who was one of the architects of St. Stephen's Basilica in Pest, built this church in the 1830s in the grandiose neoclassical style of the time. It's open daily from 6am to 7pm. Thirty-minute organ concerts are held in the church in summer, beginning at 11:30am Monday through Saturday and at 12:45pm on Sunday. These times are subject to change; check at Tourinform. Admission is free.

Opposite the cathedral is the **Lyceum** ⚘⚘ (© 36/520-400), perhaps Eger's finest example of 18th-century architecture. The **library** *(kö nyvtár)* ⚘ on the first floor is the highlight of a visit to the Lyceum; the ceiling fresco of the Council of Trent by Johann Lukas Kracker and József Zach ranks among the greatest pieces of Hungarian art. The baroque carved bookshelves are magnificent. The library has a letter written by Mozart, the only one of its kind in the country. The Lyceum is open to the public in summer Tuesday through Sunday from 9:30am to 3pm; in winter Saturday and Sunday from 9:30am to 1pm. Admission is 350 Ft ($1.75/90p). In July and August, concerts are frequently performed in the yard of the Lyceum. Ask at Tourinform for the schedule and ticket information.

If you missed visiting a spa or bathhouse in Budapest, try Eger's own Turkish bath at Fürdő u. 1–3 (© 36/413-356). The bath is mixed sex, open only on Saturday from 2 to 6pm and Sunday from 8am to 6pm. The rate is 700 Ft ($3.50/£1.80) for an hour. Spa services are posted in English. Northeastern Hungary is rich in thermal waters; ask at Tourinform for a list of spas in the region.

WHERE TO STAY

Eger is blessed with several fine little hotels right in the center of town. Two stand out in particular: The **Hotel Korona** ⚘, Tündérpart 5, 3300 Eger (© 36/310-287; fax 36/310-261), is a clean, cozy establishment on an extremely quiet residential street just a few blocks west of Dobó István tér. The hotel has a shaded patio, where breakfast is served, and a wine cellar. There are 40 rooms, all with private bathrooms. A double room goes for 60€ to 90€ ($72–$108) in summer, with prices about 15% lower off season. Rates include breakfast and sauna. Credit cards are accepted. Bus no. 11, 12, or 14 will get you there from the train station; get off at Csiky Sándor utca and you're practically at the doorstep.

Another guesthouse is right by the Beautiful Women's Valley and only a 15-minute walk from the historic center of the town, the **Bacchus Panzio** ✛, located at Szépasszony völgy utca 29 (© **36/428-950;** www.bacchuspanzio.hu). This hotel offers double rooms for 10,000 Ft to 14,000 Ft ($50–$70/£26–£36) in high season and 8,500 Ft to 12,000 Ft ($43–$60/£22–£31) in low season. Rates include breakfast.

For something peacefully removed from the downtown, try the **Garten Vendégház,** Legányi u. 6, 3300 Eger (© **36/320-371**). Operated by the Zsemlye family, this guesthouse is located on a quiet residential street in the hills overlooking the city. The view from the gorgeous garden is splendid. The price of a double room is 10,000 Ft ($50/£26) in high season and 8,000 Ft ($40/£21) in low season. Rates include breakfast.

Travelers on a tighter budget should consider renting a private room through **Egertourist** (see above) or **Tourinform.** Rates in Eger are as low as 2,500 Ft ($13/£6.40) for a bed with a shared bathroom and as high as 6,500 Ft ($33/£17) for an apartment with bathroom and kitchen.

WHERE TO DINE

The **Fehér Szarvas Vadásztanya (White Stag Hunting Inn)** ✛, located next door to the Park Hotel at Klapka u. 8 (© **36/411-129**), a few blocks south of Dobó István tér, is one of Eger's best-known and best-loved restaurants. The menu offers a full range of Hungarian wild-game specialties. The hearty, paprika-laced stews are especially good. Award-winning regional wines are featured. A piano and bass duet plays nightly amid the kitschy hunting lodge decor. The restaurant is open daily from noon to 11pm, and reservations are recommended. Credit cards are accepted.

WHERE TO SAMPLE LOCAL WINE

The best place to sample local wines is in the vineyard country just west of Eger, in the wine cellars of the **Szépasszony-völgy (Valley of the Beautiful Women).** More than 200 wine cellars are here, each offering its own vintage. Some cellars have live music. Although the wine cellars don't serve food, you can grab a meal at one of the local restaurants. Generally, the cellars open at 10am and close by 9 or 10pm.

The easiest way to get to the Szépasszony-völgy is by taxi, though you can also walk there from the center of town in 30 or 40 minutes. You could also take bus no. 13 to the Hatvani Temető (Hatvan Cemetery) and walk from there; it's a 10- to 15-minute walk.

AGGTELEK: AN ENTRANCE TO THE CAVES ✛
224km (139 miles) NE of Budapest

Tucked away beneath the Slovak border in northernmost Hungary, about 80km (50 miles) north of Eger, **Aggtelek National Park (Aggteleki Nemzeti Park)** is home to the extensive **Baradla cave network,** one of Europe's most spectacular cave systems. Although the remote and sparsely populated Aggtelek region is also suitable for hiking, people tend to travel to Aggtelek primarily to explore the caves.

You can enter the Baradla cave system on guided tours from either of two villages: Aggtelek or Jósvafő, which is on the other side of the mountain. The tours are a lot of fun. The caves are open daily 8am to 6pm in summer, to 4pm in winter. Call Aggtelek National Park (© **48/350-006**) for tour information. If this is your first time in a cave, you'll be astounded by the magical subterranean world of stalactites, stalagmites, and other bizarre formations. Three different guided tours—appropriately called short *(rövid)*, which is 1 or 2 hours long; medium *(közép)*, which is 5 hours long; and long *(hosszú)*, which is 7 hours long—depart at different times throughout the day.

The **Hotel Cseppkő** (© **48/343-075**), in the village of Aggtelek, is a popular place to crash after a day in the caves. Double rooms start at 8,400 Ft ($36/£22), breakfast included. Though it's nothing to write home about, the Cseppkő is clean and conveniently located. Camping is also popular in the area.

Travelers without cars can get to Aggtelek by bus from Eger. The trip takes 3 hours. From Miskolc, the trip takes 2 hours. Ask about transportation at the local tourist office (such as Eger's Tourinform or Egertourist), where you can also ask for help booking a room in the Hotel Cseppkő. Off season there is no need to book in advance.

7 Southern Hungary

The mainly agricultural region of the Alföld (Great Plain), including the last remnants of the Puszta, Hungary's prairie, lies south and east of the Danube River. The main cities here are Kecskemét and Szeged. The Great Plain comprises approximately 51,800 sq. km (20,000 sq. miles). On the other side of the river, in southwestern Hungary, are the verdant Mecsek Hills. The city of Pécs is the focal point of this hilly region.

THE 2,000-YEAR-OLD CITY OF PÉCS ✸✸✸
197km (123 miles) SW of Budapest

Pécs (pronounced *Paych*) is a delightful, exuberant place, the largest and loveliest city in the Mecsek Hill region. Situated 32km (20 miles) or so from the Croatian border, the city enjoys a particularly warm and arid climate; in fact, the rolling hills around Pécs are the source of some of Hungary's finest fresh fruit. Few places in Hungary possess a more Mediterranean quality than Pécs, the city that was recently named to share the title of Cultural Capital of Europe in 2010.

Known as the "2,000-year-old city," Pécs was a major settlement in Roman times, when it was called Sopianae. It was later the site of Hungary's first university, founded in 1367. While that university no longer exists, Pécs remains one of the country's most important centers of learning. The city's present university, Janus Pannonius University (named for a local ecclesiastical poet of the 15th c.) was moved here from Bratislava after that city (known as Pozsony to Hungarians) was allocated to Czechoslovakia when Czechoslovakia was created after World War I.

Pécs thrived during the almost-150-year Turkish occupation, and reminders of this period fill the city. Although Pécs (like much of Hungary) was almost completely destroyed during the bloody liberation battles between the Ottoman and Christian armies, what did survive—particularly the Mosque of Pasha Gazi Kassim—may well be the best examples of Turkish architecture in the country.

The people of Pécs are proud of their city. If you travel just a block or two outside the historic core, you'll see that the city is booming: People throng the shops and streets, and buses thunder past in every direction. Pécs is a city on the move. It exhibits none of the torpor you might notice on a hot summer afternoon in Great Plain towns like Kecskemét or Szeged.

If you walk up Janus Pannonius utca toward Széchenyi tér, about a block up the street, you'll notice on your left a small metal fence covered with padlocks. Young lovers visiting Pécs have left these locks as a token of their desire to live in this beautiful city.

ESSENTIALS

GETTING THERE   Ten **trains** depart daily from Budapest's Déli Station; four of these are InterCity trains, which are quicker than the so-called "fast" trains. The fare is 4,060 Ft ($20/£10). On an InterCity train the journey takes about 2½ hours and you are required to pay an additional fee for a seat reservation. On a "fast" train *(gyors)*, the trip is around 3 hours, but you don't need a reservation.

If you are **driving** from Budapest, take the M6 south for approximately 3 hours (the distance is 210km/130 miles).

VISITOR INFORMATION   The best source of information in Pécs is **Tourinform,** at Széchenyi tér 9 (✆ **72/213-315;** www.tourinform.hu). Tourinform is open April through October, Monday through Friday from 9am to 7pm and on weekends from 9am to 6pm; in winter Monday through Friday from 8am to 4pm. Tourinform can provide a list of local private-room accommodations, though you'll have to reserve the room yourself.

If you want to have a room reserved for you, visit **Mecsek Tourist,** at Széchenyi tér 1 (✆ **72/513-372;** www.mecsektours.hu). The office is open Monday through Friday from 9am to 5pm; and on Saturday from 9am to 1pm in summer.

A free weekly magazine called ***Pécsi Est*** contains lots of useful information; pick it up anywhere. You can also get city information online at **www.pecs.hu**.

EXPLORING OLD PÉCS

Today the old section of Pécs captivates visitors. One of Hungary's most pleasing central squares is here—**Széchenyi tér** ⟨★★★⟩, which is set on an incline with a mosque at the top and a powerful equestrian statue of János Hunyadi at the bottom. Hunyadi defeated the Turks in the 1456 Battle of Nándorfehérvár (present-day Belgrade), thus forestalling their northward advance by nearly a century. Grand pastel-colored buildings line the cobblestone streets that border the square.

Old Pécs is known for its many museums and galleries; after Budapest, Pécs is perhaps the biggest center of the arts in Hungary. The large student population contributes greatly to this creative state of affairs. We list several museums below, but there are many more, some containing works by contemporary and student artists. Pécs is also home to the Zsolnay ceramics factory. Zsolnay porcelain, though lesser known internationally than its rival Herend, may be more popular domestically. The Zsolnay Museum, also listed below, is a must-see in Pécs.

MUSEUMS

Jakawali Hassan Museum   This museum is housed inside a 16th-century mosque that has the distinction of being the only mosque in Hungary with a minaret still intact (though, unfortunately, you can't ascend the minaret as you can Eger's mosqueless minaret). Like the much larger mosque up in Széchenyi tér, this mosque was converted to a church after the Turks were driven from Pécs; however, in the 1950s the mosque was restored to its original form. The museum's main attraction is the building itself, although various Muslim religious artifacts are on display as well.

Rákóczi út 2. ✆ **72/313-853.** Admission 150 Ft (70¢/40p). Apr–Sept Thurs–Sun 10am–6pm (closed 1–2pm for lunch). Closed Oct–Mar.

Tivadar Csontváry Museum ⟨★⟩   Tivadar Csontváry Kosztka (1853–1919), today one of Hungary's most beloved artists, remained unknown during his lifetime, scorned by the art establishment. His mystical post-Impressionist landscapes suggest a unique vision of the world—one that is both tormented and idyllic, an atmosphere attributed by some to the artist's schizophrenia. Hungarians like to point out that some time after Csontváry's death, Picasso saw an exhibition of his work and referred to him as the "other" artistic genius of the 20th century. This little museum houses an impressive collection of his work. Across the street from the museum, in the park beneath Pécs Cathedral, is a statue of Csontváry.

Janus Pannonius u. 11. ⒞ **72/310-544.** Admission 600 Ft ($3/£1.55). Summer Tues–Sun 10am–6pm; winter Tues–Sun 10am–4pm.

Victor Vasarely Museum ⋆ The late Victor Vasarely, internationally known father of "op art," was born in the house that this museum now occupies. This is one of two museums in the country devoted solely to Vasarely's work. While Vasarely's fame was achieved abroad, Pécs proudly considers him a native son.

Kaptalan u. 3. ⒞ **72/324-822.** Admission 600 Ft ($3/£1.55). Tues–Sat 10am–6pm; Sun 10am–4pm.

Zsolnay Museum ⋆⋆⋆ This is one of five museums on Kaptalan utca, Pécs's "street of museums," and you shouldn't miss it. The Zsolnay Museum displays some of the best examples of Zsolnay porcelain, produced locally since 1852. There are vases, plates, cups, figurines, and even ceramic paintings. Once you've seen the museum, check out the Zsolnay fountain at the lower end of Széchenyi tér.

Kaptalan u. 2. ⒞ **72/324-822.** Admission 700 Ft ($3.50/£1.80). Tues–Sat 10am–6pm, to 4pm in winter; Sun 10am–4pm.

HOUSES OF WORSHIP
Mosque of Pasha Gazi Kassim The largest Turkish structure still standing in Hungary, this former mosque now houses a Catholic church. It was built in the late 16th century, during the Turkish occupation, on the site of an earlier church. The mix of religious traditions is evident everywhere you look, and the effect is rather pleasing. An English-language description of the building's history is posted on a bulletin board on the left-hand wall.

At the top of Széchenyi tér. ⒞ **72/227-166.** Free admission. High season Mon–Sat 10am–3pm, Sun 11:30am–3pm; winter Mon–Sat 10am–2pm, Sun 11:30am–2pm.

Pécs Cathedral Dating from the 11th century, this four-towered cathedral has been destroyed and rebuilt on several occasions. During the Turkish occupation it was used as a mosque and sported a minaret. The neoclassical exterior is the work of the early-19th-century architect Mihály Pollack. The interior remains primarily Gothic, with some baroque additions and furnishings. Various paintings and murals by leading 19th-century artists Károly Lotz and Bertalan Székely are inside. Organ concerts are performed in the cathedral throughout the year; inquire at the cathedral or at Tourinform for the schedule.

The square in front of the cathedral—as well as the little park beneath it—is a popular gathering place, and occasionally the site of folk concerts or dances.

On Dóm tér. ⒞ **72/513-030.** Cathedral admission (includes treasury and crypt) 800 Ft ($4/£2). Apr–Oct Mon–Sat 9am–5pm, Sun 1–5pm; Nov–Mar Mon–Sat 10am–4pm, Sun 1–4pm. The church is not open to the public during weddings, which are often on Sat afternoons.

Pécs Synagogue ⋆ Pécs's grand old synagogue is incongruously situated in what is now one of the city's busiest shopping squares, Kossuth tér. Nevertheless, once inside you'll find it to be a quiet, cool place far removed from the bustle outside. The synagogue was built in 1869, and the original rich oak interior survives to this day. Next door is the former Jewish school of Pécs, now a Croatian school. Before World War II, the synagogue had over 4,000 members, of whom only 464 survived the Holocaust. Every year, Pécs's small Jewish community commemorates the 1944 deportations to Auschwitz on the first Sunday after July 4.

Regular services are held in the smaller temple next door at Fürdő 1 (there isn't a sign; go through the building into the courtyard and cross diagonally to the right) on Friday at 6:30pm.

Kossuth tér. 1–3. © 72/315-881. Admission 200 Ft ($1/50p). May–Oct Sun–Fri 10am–5pm. Closed Nov–Feb.

SHOPPING

A short stroll through the center of town makes it clear that Pécs is prospering. Several pedestrian-only streets make shopping in Pécs a favorite activity. For a more exotic shopping experience, visit the **Pécsi Vásár (Pécs Flea Market)** ★★. At this crowded, bustling, open-air market you can find everything from antique china and silver to Turkish T-shirts and Chinese baby booties. Tables of homemade preserves and honey stand alongside boxes of used car parts. The main attraction, however, is the animal market, where people sell puppies and kittens out of the trunks of their cars. You might also find chickens, rabbits, and even pigs and horses for sale. The market is open every day, though Sunday is the biggest and best day (particularly for the animal market).

To get to the flea market, take a special bus, marked VÁSÁR, which departs from the Konsum shopping center in the center of downtown Pécs regularly. You need two standard city bus tickets for this bus; these are available at newsstands and kiosks or ask the bus driver. You can also take the no. 3 bus from the Konsum (only one ticket required), but you'll have to walk some distance from the stop to the entrance of the flea market.

OUTDOOR ACTIVITIES

If you are visiting Pécs in the summer, you are bound to feel the heat. Cool off in the waves at **Hullám uszoda (Wave Swimming Pool)** on Szendrey Júlia utca (© 72/512-936). Admission is 600 Ft ($3/£1.55). The pool is open daily from 6am to 10pm. Another swimming pool complex, which belongs to the university, is at Ifjúság útja 6 (© 72/501-519, ext. 4195). There is a wading pool for kids as well as a 25m (82-ft.) lap pool. Admission is 300 Ft ($1.50/80p). After swimming, treat yourself to some of the best ice cream in town, right down the street at Egerszegi Cukrászda.

Pécs is home to perhaps one of the most appealing neighborhood playgrounds in all of Hungary. **Napsugár Játszókert (Sunshine Playground)** is on Vadász utca, a short bus ride from the city center. Built in 1997 by a foundation and with donations from the community, this small grassy playground has a quaint, friendly appeal. There are chunky wooden climbing structures, slides, seesaws, swings (including an infant swing), a sandbox, and picnic tables. To get there, take bus no. 27 from the Konsum to the "Ledina" stop.

WHERE TO STAY

You can book a private room through **Mecsek Tourist** (see "Essentials," above) or **Ibusz,** Király u. 11. (© 72/212-157; www.ibusz.hu).

If you're in the mood for a funky little hotel right in the center of town, try the popular **Hotel Fönix** ★★, at Hunyadi út 2 (© 72/311-682). This unique hotel, just off the top of Széchenyi tér, has 14 rooms and 3 apartments, each one with oddly angled walls and sloped ceilings. The rooms are a bit cramped, but all are clean and have refrigerators and TVs. Each room has a private shower, but only eight have their own toilets; the common facilities are well maintained. The three apartments have full facilities and their own entrance off the street. A double room costs 11,000 Ft ($55/£28), a room without a private toilet is 9,500 Ft ($48/£24), and apartments go for 19,000 Ft ($95/£49). Rates include breakfast. Call several days ahead to reserve a room. Credit cards are accepted.

If the Hotel Fönix is full, the management can book a room for you at a pension that they operate called **Kertész Panzió,** at Sáfrány u. 42 (© **72/327-551**).

WHERE TO DINE
Bagolyvár Étterem ⑧ HUNGARIAN   Bagolyvár, a large, classy restaurant, serves delicious, hearty food in a fabulous setting, high in the hills overlooking the city. The view is excellent, the service is equally good, and there's a well-stocked wine cellar. *Note:* The same owner operates a second restaurant, **Dóm Vendéglő,** in the city center, at Király u. 3 (© **72/210-088** or 72/310-736). Dóm Vendéglő was recently expanded to include a fine pizzeria building (© **72/310-736**).

Felsőhavi Dűlő 6/1. © **72/211-333.** Reservations recommended in summer. Main courses 1,000 Ft–3,000 Ft ($5–$15/£2.60–£7.70). AE, DC, MC, V. Daily noon–midnight. Bus: 33 from in front of the Konsum shopping center to the last stop.

COFFEEHOUSES & ICE-CREAM PARLORS
Pécs offers numerous places to enjoy coffee and sweets. Try **Mecsek Cukrászda,** on Széchenyi tér 16 (© **72/315-444**), for a quick jolt of espresso and any number of sinfully good and inexpensive pastries. For a more leisurely coffeehouse experience, try the **Royal Kávéház,** at the corner of Király utca and Széchenyi tér (© **72/210-683**). There's outdoor seating, but the renovated Art Deco interior makes sitting inside worthwhile.

For ice cream, **Capri,** a very popular shop at Citrom u. 7 (© **72/333-658**), 3 blocks south of Széchenyi tér, serves various sundaes as well as cones. Some locals, however, claim that the ice cream at Capri is inferior to that of the **Egerszegi Fagylaltozó,** on Rókusalja utca (© **72/256-660**), a 15-minute walk from the center. The owners of Egerszegi also own a second, easier-to-reach place at Bajcsy-Zsilinszky u. 5 (© **72/327-540**). Our favorite for sweets and ice cream is **Magda Cukrászda** ⑧⑧, at Kandó Kálmán u. 4 (© **72/511-055**). This is a bright, bustling neighborhood *cukrászda,* where the selection and quality of cakes and ice creams is superb (though ice cream is not sold during the winter). Notable ice-cream flavors include poppy seed, chestnut, blueberry cream, cherry cream, and cinnamon. The slightly out-of-the-way location (near the train station) apparently hasn't deterred customers at all. The store is open daily from 10am to 8pm, in winter to 7pm.

SZEGED: HUNGARY'S SPICE CAPITAL ⑧⑧
168km (105 miles) SE of Budapest

Szeged (pronounced *Seh*-ged), the proud capital of the Great Plain, is a hot and dusty but hospitable town. World famous for its paprika and salami *(Pick Szalami),* Szeged is also home to one of Hungary's major universities, named after Attila József, the brilliant but disturbed interwar poet who rose to artistic heights from a childhood of desperate poverty. As a young man, he was expelled from the university that would later change its name to honor him. Driven by private demons, Hungary's great "proletarian poet" committed suicide at the age of 32 by hurling himself under a train at Balatonszárszó, by Lake Balaton. József failed to achieve wide recognition during his lifetime; today, though, he is adored in Hungary, particularly by teenagers and students drawn to his rebellious, nonconformist, irreverent spirit. The national book fair is traditionally opened on his birthday, April 11, each year. A wonderfully unassuming statue of the poet stands in front of the university's main building on Dugonics tér. The only other statue of him that we know of is next to the Parliament Building in Budapest, sitting on the steps of the embankment, evoking thoughts of one of József's famous poems, about the multicultural Danube, written against the specter of nationalism in the 1930s.

In addition to its status as a center of learning and culture, Szeged is the industrial capital of the Great Plain (Alföld), though you wouldn't know it by spending a day or two in the city center. The Tisza River splits the city in two, with the historic center lying, Pest-style, within a series of concentric ring boulevards on the left bank. Indeed, the river looms large in Szeged's history: The city was almost completely destroyed when the Tisza flooded in 1879. With financial assistance from a number of European cities—Brussels, Berlin, Rome, London, and Paris—the city was rebuilt in the characteristic ring style of the time. The postflood reconstruction explains why Szeged's finest architecture is of the *fin de siècle* Art Nouveau style. Don't miss the synagogue (see "Exploring the Historic Center," below) and the recently restored Reök Building (now a bank) on the corner of Kölcsey utca and Feketesas utca.

The people of Szegend, many of whom are students, love to stroll along the riverside, sit in cafes, and window-shop on the just reconstructed elegant **Karász utca** ⊛⊛, the town's main pedestrian-only street. Dóm tér, a beautiful, wide square, is home to the **Szeged Summer Festival** ⊛, a popular summer-long series of cultural events. At the end of July, Szeged also plays host to a theater festival known as **Thealter** for its focus on alternative performances. An international festival, Thealter was founded by drama students from the university and draws theater troupes from all over Europe. In 2003 Thealter celebrated its 13th season. Ask about both of these festivals at **Tourinform** or Szeged Tourist.

ESSENTIALS

GETTING THERE   Twelve daily **trains** depart Budapest's Nyugati Station, of which four are InterCity. The fare for all is 2,030 Ft ($10/£5.20). On an InterCity train the journey takes about 2¼ hours, and you are required to pay an additional fee for a seat reservation. On a fast train *(gyors)*, the trip is more like 3 hours, but you don't need a reservation. (Travel times by trains generally seem to have slowed down in the past several years due to the poor conditions of the tracks all over the country.)

If you're **driving** from Budapest, take the M5 motorway south through Kecskemét and Kiskunfélegyháza.

VISITOR INFORMATION   The best source of information, as usual, is **Tourinform,** at Dugonics tér 2 (© 62/488-690; www.szeged.hu), located in the recently renovated 19th-century courtyard of the fine pastry shop Z. Nagy Cukrászda (reviewed below). The office is open Monday through Friday from 9am to 5pm. If you wish to book a private room, try **Szeged Tourist,** at Klauzál tér 7 (© 62/420-428), open Monday through Friday from 9am to 5pm.

Pick up *Szegedi Est,* a free weekly magazine with lots of useful information.

MAHART, the Hungarian ferry line company, organizes boat tours up and down the Tisza River from the first of April through mid-October. For information, contact the MAHART boat station in Szeged at © 62/425-834.

EXPLORING THE HISTORIC CENTER

Móra Ferenc Museum   Located near the river's edge, this imposing structure houses a varied collection of exhibits that relate to local history. Of particular note is the display of local folk costumes and the exhibit that reconstructs the nomadic lifestyle of the early Hungarian settlers.

Roosevelt tér 1–3. ℂ **62/549-040**. www.mfm.u-szeged.hu. Admission 400 Ft ($2/£1). Tues–Sun 10am–5pm.

Synagogue ⚅   A relic of Szeged's once-thriving Jewish community, the synagogue was completed in 1903. Considered the masterpiece of architect Lipot Baumhorn, who was a disciple of Ödön Lechner and the most prolific and renowned synagogue architect in modern Europe, the great synagogue in Szeged exemplifies a confident eclecticism. The building mixes cupolas, turrets, tracery, and other ornamental effects. It occupies a full block in an otherwise sleepy, tree-lined residential neighborhood just west of the city center. The synagogue is fully functioning and holds services at 6pm every Friday.

Inside the vestibule is a series of marble plaques, listing by name the local victims of the Holocaust. Behind the synagogue, at Hajnóczy u. 12, stands the Old Synagogue, built in 1843 and badly damaged in the flood of 1879. Its reconstruction was completed in 1998. It serves as a cultural center and a venue for alternative theater groups and chamber-music concerts.

If you find the synagogue closed when it should be open, go to the address that's posted near the entrance and the caretaker will open the synagogue for you.

Jósika utca. ℂ **62/423-849**. Admission 300 Ft ($1.50/80p). Summer Sun–Fri 9am–noon and 1–5pm; winter Sun–Fri 10am–2pm. Services at 6pm every Fri. From Dugonics tér, walk right on Tisza Lajos körút, and turn left on Gutenberg utca.

Votive Church   The symbol of Szeged's post-flood revitalization, this church, with its two tall, slender clock towers, was built in 1912. Its elaborately painted neo-Renaissance interior suggests a much older structure. Inside the church is one of Europe's largest organs, with over 9,000 pipes. Ask at Tourinform or Szeged Tourist (p. 372) about organ recitals.

In front of the church is the Broken Tower, a remnant of the 13th-century Romanesque church that stood on this spot. Across from the church, there is a wall clock from which wooden figures emerge on the hour to play a Kodály tune. Masses are held here at 6:30am, 7:30am, and 6pm every day.

On Dóm tér. Free admission. Mon–Sat 9am–6pm; Sun 9:30–10am, 11–11:30am, and 12:30–6pm. Masses take place at 6:30am, 7:30am, and 6pm daily.

OPEN-AIR MARKETS

Situated within 32km (20 miles) of two international borders (Romanian and Serbian), Szeged has long attracted shoppers and vendors from a variety of countries. If open-air markets interest you, check out the **Polish Market (Lengyel Piac)** ⚅ at the southwestern edge of town. Once filled with Polish smugglers (the name has stuck), this dusty flea market is now home to Vietnamese, Chinese, Romanian, Serbian, Uzbeki, and other vendors. You never know what kind of junk you might find here—it all depends on what's "in season." Unfortunately, the Cold War souvenirs that once attracted Westerners to markets like this are seldom displayed any longer. The market is open Monday through Saturday from dawn to midafternoon. To get to the Polish Market, located in a dusty field at the corner of Petőfi Sándor sugárút and Rákóczi utca, walk straight out Petőfi Sándor sugárút from the center of town or take tram no. 4.

Szeged's **main fruit-and-vegetable market** ✯ is located behind the bus station on Mars tér (formerly Marx tér, and still known to many as such). The vendors are local Hungarian farmers. If you haven't tried any Hungarian produce yet, you're missing out on something wonderful. You won't be disappointed with the peaches, apricots, watermelons, cherries, strawberries, plums, or pears. The market is open Monday through Saturday from dawn until midafternoon—arrive early for the best selection. Fresh flowers and dried paprika wreathes are also sold here.

You can buy Szeged's signature paprika and salami anywhere food is sold.

WHERE TO STAY

Private rooms can be booked through **Szeged Tourist** (see "Essentials," above) or **Ibusz** at Oroszlán u. 3 (📞 **62/471-177**).

Hotel Matrix   This fairly new choice is about 10 minutes from the central Dugonics tér by tram no. 4 or trolleybus no. 9. The tasteful, small hotel is clean and pleasant, with a friendly and professional management. Its pleasant rooms all have showers.

Zárda u. 8, 6720 Szeged. 📞 **62/556-000.** Fax 62/420-827. 10 units. 9,600 Ft ($48/£25) double. Breakfast 900 Ft ($4.50/£2.30) extra. AE, V. **Amenities:** Laundry service. *In room:* TV.

Kata Panzió ✯   We highly recommend this lovely little pension, which opened in 1995 in a quiet residential neighborhood a 10-minute walk from central Klauzál tér. It features plenty of common space, sunny balconies on each floor, an enchanting terrace garden, and a friendly German shepherd named Ivan. Four double rooms, one triple, and one quad are available; all have private bathrooms.

Bolyai János u. 15 (between Gogol u. and Kálvária sgt.), 6720 Szeged. 📞 **62/311-258.** 6 units. 9,600 Ft ($48/£25) double. Rates include breakfast. 600 Ft ($3/£ 1.55) VAT extra. No credit cards. Free parking. *In room:* TV.

WHERE TO DINE

Gödör ✯ HUNGARIAN   Gödör is the local university's restaurant; faculty members pack it at lunchtime. The extensive menu of Hungarian specialties (including many vegetarian options) is very reasonably priced.

Tisza Lajos krt. 103 (next to the Hero's Gate). 📞 **62/420-130.** Main courses 650 Ft–1,500 Ft ($3.25–$7.50/£1.70–£3.85). No credit cards. Daily 11am–10pm.

Kiskőrösi Halászcsárda ✯ HUNGARIAN   You'd do well to sample local fish at this authentic riverside restaurant. Paprika and onions are the spices of choice for hearty fish stews and bisques alike.

Felső Tisza-part 336. 📞 **62/495-480.** Reservations recommended. Main courses 700 Ft–1,200 Ft ($3.50–$6/£1.80–£3.10). AE, DC, DISC, MC, V. Sun–Thurs 11am–midnight; Fri–Sat 11am–2am.

Pagoda Étterem ✯ CHINESE   This is our favorite Chinese restaurant in all of Hungary. The menu is extensive and the dishes are delicious. The Chinese lanterns and dragon-red tablecloths add to the appeal.

Zrinyi u. 5. 📞 **62/312-490.** Main courses from 1,000 Ft ($5/£2.60). AE, V. Tues–Sat noon–midnight; Sun–Mon noon–10pm.

Zodiákus HUNGARIAN/EUROPEAN   Zodiákus, formerly known as Alabárdos, is *the* choice for an elegant, upscale dining experience. It is more cheerful than its predecessor, with the previous cellarlike design replaced by a lighter and airier arrangement. Hungarian cuisine is served on Herend porcelain; the cutlery is sterling. Locals consider this the town's finest restaurant. We recommend all of the poultry dishes here, especially the chicken breast with zucchini in a creamy cheese sauce. There is a pub right next door, open 10am to 2am. The pub menu is small but wholesome: salads and cheese-based dishes. Draft beer is available. It's a popular place with Szeged's large foreign student population.

Oskola u. 13. (© **62/420-914**. Reservations recommended. Main courses 790 Ft–2,500 Ft ($3.95–$13/£2–£6.40). No credit cards. Mon–Thurs 11am–midnight; Fri–Sat 11am–1am.

COFFEEHOUSES & ICE-CREAM PARLORS

Szeged is famous for its **Virág Cukrászda,** an old-world coffeehouse on Klauzál tér. A local petition in the early 1990s prevented this Szeged institution from being turned into a car showroom. It is open daily from 8am to 10pm. The **Kis Virág (Little Flower)** *★★*, across the square, is the Virág Cukrászda's takeout place, where you can pick up a wide variety of delicious pastries for a lower price and sample the best ice cream in town (in winter there is service inside the Kis Virág). Their specialty is *rakott rétes* (layered strudel), which is the divine local version of the traditional Jewish pastry *flodni.* In our opinion, it's the best we've tried anywhere in the country. Kis Virág is open daily from 8am to 8pm.

Rivaling (and some say surpassing in the realm of traditional pastries) the Kis Virág for takeout pastries and cakes is the tiny **Z. Nagy Cukrászda** *★*, located on József Attila sgt. 24 (just off of Tisza Lajos krt. by the river). It's a good walk from the center of town but it's well worth it. If you're being lazy, there is a more spacious Z. Nagy shop, with a terrace in its courtyard, right in the center of town, on Dugonics tér, just off Karász utca (the pedestrian-only street). Z. Nagy dispenses a scrumptious *Erzsi kocka,* walnut paste sandwiched between two shortbread cookies, dipped in dark chocolate. On hot, dusty summer days, the line at the most popular ice-cream shop, **Palánk** (on the corner of Tömörkény utca and Oskola utca), snakes out the door and down the street. By all means, join the queue.

SZEGED AFTER DARK

Jazz Kocsma, at Kálmány L. u. 14 (© **62/326-680**), is the place for live jazz. Local bands play on Sunday. It's a groovy, smoky, student scene. The kitchen serves Mexican food. Open daily 11am to 2am; no cover. **Mojo Club,** Alföldi utca 1 (© **62/ 426-606**), next to the university building for the arts, is another jazz club. As the posters in the window proudly advertise (you will see the posters of OTPOR, the pioneering Serbian youth organization that successfully organized resistance to the Belgrade university collectives), the owners of this place have maintained their close links with their former country of residence, Serbia. The sunken rooms here have a distinctly bohemian appeal. There's a full bar and decent pizza and pasta on the menu. It's open Monday through Saturday from 11am to 2am, Sunday from 6pm to midnight; in summer open daily from 6pm only. There's no cover. Reservations are highly recommended at both these clubs.

8

Poland

by Mark Baker

Poland is coming into its own as a vacation destination. During the first years after the 1989 democratic revolutions in Eastern Europe, it seemed Prague and Budapest grabbed all the headlines. Now, travelers are looking for something farther afield, and with the advent of budget air carriers in Europe, travel to countries like Poland has never been cheaper or easier.

For some, a trip to Poland is an opportunity to reconnect with their Polish roots, a chance, perhaps, to sample some of their grandmother's pierogies in their natural setting. Others are attracted to the unique beauty of Kraków, which has rightfully joined Prague and Budapest as part of the trinity of must-sees in central Europe. Still others are drawn by Poland's dramatic and often tragic history. The absolute horrors of World War II, followed by the decades of Communist rule, have etched painful and moving monuments in the landscape. No country, with the possible exception of Russia, suffered as much as Poland during World War II. Millions of Poles, and nearly the entire prewar Jewish population of 1.2 million, were killed in fighting or in concentration camps. The deeply affecting and sobering thoughts on seeing the camps at Auschwitz and Birkenau, near Kraków, will last a

lifetime. Nearly equally moving are the stories of the Łódź and Warsaw Jewish ghettos, or the story of the Warsaw uprising of 1944, when the city's residents rose up courageously and futilely against their Nazi oppressors.

There are many uplifting moments of history, too. In Warsaw, the entire Old Town has been rebuilt brick by brick in an emotional show of a city reclaiming its history. In Gdańsk, you can visit the shipyards where Lech Wałęsa and his Solidarity trade union first rose to power to oppose Poland's Communist government in 1980. It was the rise of Solidarity that helped to bring down Communism in Poland, and arguably sparked the revolutions that swept the region in 1989.

And Poland is not only history. To the south, below Kraków, rise the majestic High Tatras, one of Europe's most starkly beautiful ranges. To the north, the Baltic seacoast, with its pristine beaches, stretches for miles. The northeast is covered with lakes that run to the borderlands with Lithuania and Belarus. In the east of the country, you'll find patches of some Europe's last-remaining primeval forest, and a small existing herd of indigenous bison that once covered large parts of the Continent.

1 Getting to Know Poland

THE LAY OF THE LAND

Poland is a mostly flat, sprawling country, covering some 312,000 sq. km (around 100,000 sq. miles). Its historical position, between Germany in the west and Russia in the east, has caused no end of hardship. Following World War II, the country's borders

Poland

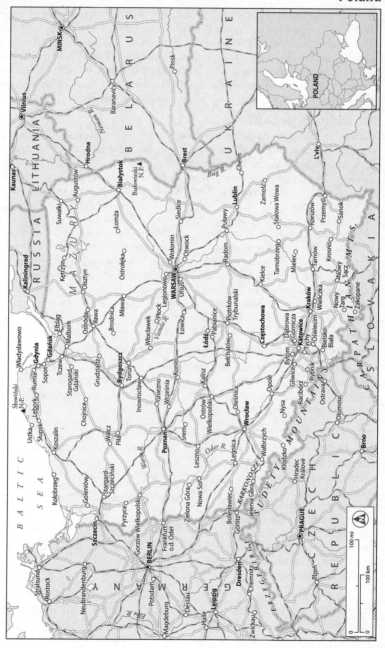

were shifted approximately 200km (120 miles) to the west, gaining territory at the expense of Germany and losing it to the then-Soviet Union. The country shares borders with the Czech Republic and Slovakia in the south, and Belarus and Ukraine to the south and east. Germany lies to the west. To the north, Poland borders the Baltic Sea and Lithuania. Poland also shares a long northern border with the Russian enclave of Kaliningrad, part of former German East Prussia that the Soviet Union claimed after World War II, but which does not connect to the Russian homeland.

THE REGIONS IN BRIEF

Warsaw, the capital, lies in the easterly center of the country, the main city of a relatively flat region known as Mazovia. To the northeast, an interconnected series of rivers and lakes, known as the Mazurian lakes, stretches out to Kaliningrad and Lithuania. Much of this land was part of the German province of East Prussia and belonged to Germany as recently as World War II. South of Warsaw and Mazovia are the regions of Małopolska (Little Poland), often seen as the Polish heartland, and Kraków. Under Austrian occupation, Kraków was a leading city of the province of Galicia, which spreads east into present-day Ukraine. Below Kraków begins an area known as the Podhale, the foothills of the Tatras, and then farther south the mountains themselves. To the immediate west of Kraków lies the immense industrial region of Upper Silesia, including the central city of Katowice. Farther west, to Lower Silesia, the region becomes more agricultural. The capital of this area is Wrocław, the former German city of Breslau. North of Wrocław, starts the enormous regions of Wielkopolska (Greater Poland) and Pomorze (Pomerania)—the ancient borderlands between Germany and Poland and rich with the legacy of the Teutonic Knights.

SUGGESTED ITINERARY: POLAND IN 10 DAYS

Poland is a large country with small roads and generally slow trains. That means it's hard to cover ground quickly and best to keep travel plans relatively modest. The following itinerary is laid out for car travel but with a little effort can be adapted to train and/or bus travel.

Days ❶ & ❷ Arrive in Warsaw

Get settled in and if you've got the energy, try to arrange for a city tour in the afternoon. Warsaw is sprawling and even if you're not an "organized tour" type of person, this is one place where it makes sense. Spend the second day with a more leisurely stroll of the Old Town. Don't pass up the chance to see the Museum of the Warsaw Uprising.

Days ❸ & ❹ Kraków

Drive or take the train to Kraków—either way it will take about 4 hours. Give yourself plenty of time to enjoy Poland's most popular travel destination. Dedicate at least a day for the Old Town and the

Wawel castle area, and another for Kazimierz and the sights of the former Jewish quarter.

Day ❺ Kraków Day Trip

The former Nazi extermination camp at Auschwitz/Birkenau lies about 90 minutes west of Kraków by car; alternatively, you can book one of several Auschwitz day tours through the tourist information office. It's a must, particularly if you have never had the chance to visit a Holocaust site in the past. If you're traveling with small children and looking for a more cheerful day trip, try the Wieliczka Salt Mines, easily reachable from Kraków by bus or train.

Day ⑥ Wrocław

This formerly German city—and now firmly Polish—is a delight. Spend the day on the square and walking along the little lanes near the river. Unlike Kraków, there are no real must-sees here; simply take in the town at your own pace and recharge your batteries.

Day ⑦ Poznań or Toruń

You choose. Both are about 2 hours north of Wrocław on the way to Gdańsk. Poznań is a bustling, medium-size city with great restaurants and decent nightlife. Toruń is tinier, with a beautiful, small square and a couple of great boutique hotels, though the options in the evening are limited.

Days ⑧ & ⑨ Gdańsk

This Baltic seaport is one of the real highlights of any trip to Poland: a beautifully restored city, rich with history and natural beauty. Try to squeeze out an extra day if you can. Sopot makes an easy day trip (and especially good in hot weather since there's a beach). If you've got more time, visit the enormous Teutonic Knights' castle at Malbork to the south or the sand dunes at Słowiński National Park to the northwest.

Day ⑩ Warsaw

Warsaw and your gateway home is an easy few hours train journey from Gdańsk. By road, plan on at least 5 or 6 hours, owing to bad roads and heavy traffic. But if you've come this far by car, you know by now that it always takes a lot longer than it looks on the map!

POLAND TODAY

Poland's transformation since the fall of Communism in 1989 has been nothing short of phenomenal. What was until not long ago a downtrodden, debt-ridden, basket case of a country has turned itself around 180 degrees. Today, Poland is a proud member of the European Union and NATO. Its currency is stable, and its economy is one of the fastest growing in Europe. You'll see gleaming new office towers on the ever-changing Warsaw skyline. And throughout the country, you'll see evidence of an emerging prosperity that was unthinkable 10 to 15 years ago.

To be sure, alongside this newly emerging wealth, you'll run across many still very depressed areas—particularly in industrial cities like Łódź and in large parts of Warsaw itself. You'll also see greater numbers than you might expect of homeless people, public drunks, beggars, and simply those who have fallen through the cracks. Not everyone has benefited equally from the country's rapid transformation to a democratic political system and a free-market economy. Industrial workers, particularly those over the age of 50 for whom adapting to the changes proved more difficult, have been hardest hit. Young people, too, have found it difficult to cope with ever-rising living costs on very low wages. Many are now leaving the country for places like the U.K. and Ireland, where they can earn more tending bar than they can working as young professionals at home.

But it's important to put this into some perspective. Just a little more than a decade and a half ago, Poland was falling apart. The country was $30 billion in debt to international lenders. The air was unbreatheable—particularly in Kraków, downwind from the enormous steel mill complex at Nowa Huta. It wasn't unusual for Poles to spend hours standing in line simply to buy a piece of fruit or a bottle of imported shampoo. And membership in the European Union was unthinkable. Worst of all perhaps was the feeling of utter hopelessness, as if it were somehow Poland's fate to end up on the wrong side of history every time. That's been replaced by something better and infectious: a cautious optimism that maybe this time around the better times are here to stay.

A LOOK AT THE PAST

Nowhere in Europe will you feel history more strongly than in Poland. The country's unenviable position though the ages, between Germany in the west and Russia to the east, and without defensible natural borders, has meant Polish history has been one long struggle for survival.

The Poles first established themselves in the areas to the west of Warsaw around the turn of the first millennium, descendants of migrant Slav tribes that came to Eastern Europe around A.D. 800. In the centuries following the first millennium, the early nobility forged a strategic union with an order of crusaders, the Teutonic Knights, to defend Polish interests from pagan Prussians to the west. The Knights built enormous castles over a wide swath of western Poland, and the Poles soon found themselves with a cunning and ruthless rival on their hands for the spoils of the Baltic Sea trade. In 1410, the Poles joined forces with the Lithuanians and others and managed to defeat the Teutonic Knights at Grünwald, in one of the great epic battles of the late Middle Ages. That battle is still fondly remembered in Polish history books.

Poland's early capital was Kraków, but the seat of government was moved to Warsaw in the 16th century after union with Lithuania greatly expanded Poland's territory. In the 17th century, the Poles are generally credited with saving Europe in another epic battle, this one against the Ottoman Turks. Commander Jan Sobieski saved the day for Christian Europe, repelling the Turks at the gates of Vienna in 1683.

From this point on, Polish history runs mostly downhill. Poland was unable to resist the gradual rise of Prussia in the west and Tsarist Russia in the east as great powers. The result was a series of partitions of Poland in the late 18th century, with parts of Polish territory eventually going to Prussia, Russia, and Habsburg Austria. For 125 years, Poland disappeared from the map of Europe.

Independent Poland was restored in 1918 after the collapse of Austria-Hungary and Germany in World War I. The interwar period was relatively rocky, but World War II was Poland's worst nightmare come true. Nazi Germany fired the first shot from Gdańsk harbor on September 1, 1939. Russia, under terms of a nonaggression pact with Germany, seized the eastern part of the country. In the ensuing battle between fascism and Communism, Poland was caught in the middle. Nearly a quarter of all Poles died in the war, including more than a million Polish Jews. The Nazis used Polish soil for the worst of their extermination camps, at Auschwitz-Birkenau and Treblinka, among others. Poland's once-handsome capital of Warsaw was ordered razed to the ground by a Nazi leadership enraged by Polish resistance there. By the end of the war, nearly every one of the city's million inhabitants had been killed or expelled, and 85% of the city lay in ruins.

Poland was reconstituted at the end of the war, but with radically different borders. Bowing to Stalin's demands, the U.S. and U.K. ceded vast tracts of formerly Polish territory in the east to the Soviet Union. In turn, the new Poland was compensated with former German territory in the west. The Polish borders were shifted some 200km (120 miles) westward. The ethnic German population was expelled and replaced by Poles transferred from the east of the country.

But the end of the war brought little relief. Poland was given over to the Soviet sphere of influence, and though Communism held little appeal for most Poles, a series of Soviet-backed Communist governments uneasily led the country for the next four decades. The government managed to maintain order through massive borrowing on international financial markets, but mismanagement of the economy led to one crisis after another. In the end it was this desire for higher living standards—perhaps even more than a desire for political freedom—that led to the creation of the Solidarity trade union and the genesis of the anti-Communist movement. Solidarity began at the shipyards in Gdańsk, but eventually spread to the rest of the country. The initial demands were for higher wages and more influence in managing the economy, but the challenge to the Communist leadership was clear. At around the same time, the Catholic Church had elevated a cardinal from Kraków, Karol Woytyła, to be pope. If Solidarity provided the organizational framework for Poles to resist, Pope John Paul provided the moral inspiration. In early 1989, the Poles held their first semi-free election—a landmark vote that bolstered anti-Communist activists across Eastern Europe. By the end of that epic year, the Eastern bloc was free.

Since the end of Communism, Poland has made great strides, reducing its international debt, while living standards have continued to rise. In 1999 Poland realized a longtime goal of joining the NATO military alliance, and in 2004 entered the European Union.

POLISH PEOPLE & CULTURE

Poles are typically highly educated and highly cultured, with a firm grasp of their country's long and rich tradition in literature, poetry, performing arts, and film. The strong role of culture in everyday life is not surprising given the country's tragic history. For the 125 years, until 1918, that Poland ceased to exist as a country, it was quite literally a shared culture that held the people together. In modern times, it was this common cultural heritage that helped people to weather the Nazi and Soviet occupations, and to endure 40 years of Communist rule after World War II. Don't be surprised if your Polish hosts ask you if you've ever heard of this or that Polish romantic poet or postwar film director. And don't be surprised if they appear disappointed if you can't immediately come up with some insightful comment. Part of this disappointment is the feeling that if Polish history hadn't been so brutal, many of these writers and intellectuals would be as well known today as their counterparts in western Europe.

You'll sense too a strong feeling of national pride. Poles are proud of their history. They're proud of their resistance, however futile, to the Nazi invasion in 1939, and of the tragic Warsaw uprising in 1944. And they're proud of their country's leading role in ending Communism in the 1980s. And today this pride extends to Poland's membership in the European Union. Poland was the largest of the new countries to enter the E.U. in 2004, and Poland has effectively used its size to carve out an influential role for itself in Brussels.

Americans are likely to feel particularly welcome. Poland's ties to the United States go back all the way to Tadeusz Kościuszko and the Revolutionary War. Today, Poles proudly cite Chicago as the second-biggest Polish city in the world after Warsaw (even though these days more young Poles are emigrating to Ireland and the U.K. than to the U.S.). Just about everyone has a cousin, uncle, or grandparent who lives or used to live in one of the 50 states.

POLISH CUISINE

Polish food has a hearty, homemade feel, and when it's done well, it can be delicious. The staple of Polish cuisine is probably the **pierogi,** a pocket of dough stuffed with anything from potato meal, cottage cheese, or cabbage to ground beef or even raspberries or strawberries. Pierogies are traditionally prepared boiled and served with fried onions (except of course the fruit-filled ones), though you may also find them baked or fried and topped with anything from sour cream to garlic sauce. Pierogies are extremely flexible. They can be eaten as a snack or as a main course, for lunch or for dinner. They also make a great option for vegetarians; just be sure to tell them to hold the bacon bits they sometimes pour on top. Pierogies prepared "Ruskie" style are meatless, stuffed with potatoes and cottage cheese. **Placki,** potato pancakes, are nearly as ubiquitous and delicious, and are often cooked with mushrooms or smoked meat.

Meals generally begin with an appetizer, cold **(przekąski zimne)** or hot **(przekąski gorące).** Among the former, herring **(śledż),** usually served in a sour cream sauce and piled with chopped onions, is my favorite. Other popular cold starters include stuffed fish or paté (pasztet). Hot starters can include pierogies or a piece of homemade sausage **(kiełbasa).**

Soups **(zupy)** are a mainstay. **Żurek** is a filling, sourish rye broth, seasoned with dill and usually served with sausage and egg. **Barszcz** is a clear, red-beet soup, often served with a little pastry on the side. **Bigos,** known on menus in English as "hunter's stew," another national mania, is made from sauerkraut, and is something between a soup and a main course. Every Polish grandmother has her own version, and local lore says the homemade variety tastes best on the seventh reheating!

Main courses are less original, and often revolve around chicken, pork, or beef, though game (venison or boar usually) and fish (pike and trout are popular) are also common. Sides **(dodatki)** usually involve some form of potato, fried or boiled, or sometimes fried potato dumplings. More creative sides include buckwheat groats or beets, the latter sometimes flavored with apple. Desserts include fruit pierogies, the ubiquitous ice cream **(lody),** and pancakes, sometimes filled with cottage cheese and served with fruit sauce.

Mealtimes adhere to the Continental standard. Breakfast is usually taken early, and is often no more than a cup of tea or coffee and a bread roll. Hotels usually lay on the traditional buffet-style breakfast, centered on cold cuts, cheeses, yogurts, and cereals, but this is more than what a Pole would normally eat. Lunch is served from about noon to 2pm, though restaurants don't usually get rolling until about 1pm. Dinner starts around 6pm and can go until 9 or 10pm. After that, kitchens start closing down.

Snack foods run the gamut from Western fast-food outlets (McDonald's, KFC, and Pizza Hut are the most common) to kabob stands and pizza parlors. You'll find decent pizza in nearly every Polish city and town of any size. Look especially for **zapiekanki,** foot-long, open-faced baguettes, topped with sauce and cheese and baked.

As for drinking, Poles are best known for their vodka, but it's beer in fact that's the national drink. You'll find the major brands, Okocim, Lech, Tyskie, and Żywiec, just about everywhere. There's little difference among the majors, though Okocim might get the nod—its slightly sweetish taste reminiscent of Czech Budvar. Men take theirs straight up. Women frequently sweeten their beer with fruit syrup (raspberry is the most common) and drink it through a straw! Among the most popular vodkas, Belvedere and Chopin are considered top shelf, though increasingly imported vodkas are squeezing out the local brands. In addition, you'll find a range of flavored vodkas. Żubrówka is slightly greenish, owing to a long blade of bison grass from the east of the country in every bottle. Miodówka, honey-flavored and easy to drink in large quantity, is worth a try. Wine is much less common, and nearly always imported.

As for nonalcoholic drinks, Poles are traditionally tea drinkers, though coffee, increasingly sold as espressos and lattes in trendy coffee shops, is making inroads. Tea is normally drunk in a glass with sugar. The quality of the coffee has greatly improved in the past decade, but for some reason the dark, bitter liquid called "coffee" served at hotel and pension breakfasts is still often undrinkable.

LANGUAGE

Unless you're a scholar of Slavic languages (or you already speak some Polish), you'll find Polish nearly incomprehensible. There are relatively few English cognates, and the vexing combinations of consonants—"szcz" comes to mind—and accent marks (z's with dots and l's with lines through them?) will have you shaking your head after a couple of minutes of trying to puzzle it out. Fortunately, there are a fair amount of English speakers around, and nearly all hotels, tourist offices, and restaurants will be able to manage some English. German will also help, especially in areas of the south and west, close to the German border.

USEFUL WORDS & PHRASES

English	Polish	Pronunciation
Hello/Good Day	**Dzień dobry**	Djeen *doh*-bree
Yes	**Tak**	*Tahk*
No	**Nie**	Nee-yeh
Hi! or Bye! (informal)	**Cześć!**	*Chesh*-ch
Good evening	**Dobry wieczór**	*Doh*-bree *vyeh*-choor
Goodbye	**Do widzenia**	*Doh* vee-*djen*-ya
Good night	**Dobranoc**	Doh-*brah*-nohts
Thank you	**Dziękuję**	Djen-*koo*-yeh
Please/you're welcome	**Proszę**	*Proh*-sheh
How are you? (informal)	**Jak sie masz?**	*Yahk* sheh mahsh?
How are you? (formal)	**Jak sie pan (to a man)/pani (to a woman) ma?**	*Yahk* sheh pahn/pahn-ee mah?
Fine	**Dobrze**	*Dohb*-zheh
Do you speak English?	**Czy pan/pani mówi po angielsku?**	Chee pahn/pahn-ee *moo*-vee poh ahng-*yel*-skoo?
I don't understand	**Nie rozumiem**	Ne-yeh roh-*zoom*-yem
How much is it?	**Ile kosztuje?**	Eel-eh kosh-*too*-yeh?
Menu	**Jadłospis**	*Jahd*-woe-spees
The bill, please	**Proszę o rachunek**	*Proh*-sheh oh *rahk*-oo-nek
Cheers!	**Na zdrowie**	Nah-*zdroh*-vyeh

English	Polish	Pronunciation
Bon appétit!	**Smacznego**	Smahch-*neh*-go
Open	**Otwarty**	*Oh*-twar-tee
Closed	**Zamkniety**	*Zahm*-knyeh-tee

2 Planning Your Trip to Poland

VISITOR INFORMATION
ENTRY REQUIREMENTS

There are no special requirements for entering Poland. Passport holders from the U.S., Canada, and Australia can enter the country without a visa and stay for 90 days. Passport holders from E.U. member countries, including the U.K., do not need a visa.

MONEY

The main unit of currency is the **złoty** (zł), which is divided into 100 **groszy** (gr). Bills come in denominations of 10 zł, 20 zł, 50 zł, 100 zł, and 200 zł. The most useful coins are the 5 zł, 2 zł, and 1 zł. You'll also see coins of 50 gr, 10 gr, 2 gr, and rarely 1 gr. At the time of this writing, 1 U.S. dollar was worth a little under 3 zł, and 1 British pound about 5.7 zł.

As a member of the European Union, Poland will someday adopt the euro, but that's not likely to happen until 2009 or 2010. In the meantime, some establishments catering to visitors, including many hotels, will quote rates in euros and accept them as payment. Some hotels quote exclusively in euros.

You can change money in nearly any bank or exchange office, identified in Polish as "kantor." You'll see them everywhere. You'll get the best rate, however, simply using your credit or debit card in an ATM. In large cities and towns you'll see an ATM on nearly every block.

WHEN TO GO

Poland's climate is characterized by hot summers and dark, cold winters. Unless you're heading to the Tatras to ski, avoid travel from January to March. Many of the attractions are closed for the season, and the cold and snow make getting around difficult. Note that Kraków and Zakopane are both popular Christmas and New Year's destinations and hotel prices rise accordingly. Summer brings good weather, but more crowds as Poles take to the roads on their summer holidays. September and October are ideal with fewer crowds and usually reliably good weather.

HOLIDAYS

January 1 (New Year's Day), Easter Sunday and Monday, May 1 (State Holiday), May 3 (Constitution Day), Corpus Christi (falls on 9th Thurs following Easter Sunday), August 15 (Assumption), November 1 (All Saints' Day), November 11 (Independence Day), and December 25 and 26 (Christmas Day). Offices, banks, museums, and many stores are closed on holidays, though some stores and restaurants remain open.

GETTING THERE

BY PLANE   Warsaw remains the major air gateway to Poland, with extensive connections throughout Europe, and some nonstop flights to North America. See Warsaw, "Getting There," below for more details. Kraków's Jan Pavel II Airport is also easy to reach from nearly any large airport in Europe. The advent of low-cost budget carriers

Major Festivals in Poland

The calendar is filled with festivals of all kinds, with the most popular celebrations connected to religious dates or Poland's folk or cultural traditions. The annual Marian pilgrimages culminate in August at the Jasna Góra shrine in Częstochowa for the Feast of the Assumption on August 15. Warsaw, Kraków, Wrocław, and Poznań all host jazz, contemporary, and classical music festivals throughout the year. The best idea is to check in with the local tourist information offices when you arrive to see what's going on during the time you're there. Kraków's Kazimierz district hosts the increasingly popular Jewish Cultural Festival every year in July. Klezmer music concerts, films, and cultural discussions highlight the agenda. Zakopane and the surrounding area is the epicenter of the country's folk fests, with the biggest draw being Zakopane's Mountain Folklore Festival in August.

in Europe in recent years has also opened up several other cities to regular and convenient air travel, including Łódź, Poznań, Wrocław, and Gdańsk.

BY TRAIN   The national rail network, PKP, is well integrated into the Europe-wide rail system. Warsaw lies on the main east-west line running from Berlin to Moscow. Kraków is accessible from Prague, Vienna, and points south, though connections require a change of trains at Katowice.

BY BUS   International bus travel has become less popular in recent years due to the arrival of the budget air carriers, which often match the buses for ticket prices, but naturally get you there much quicker. Nevertheless, the Polish national bus carrier works in cooperation with Eurolines, and large Polish cities are easy to reach by bus.

BY CAR   Poland is easily accessible by car. From the west, there are several international border crossings along the German, Czech, and Slovak frontiers. Note that some smaller border crossings may operate only in daylight hours.

BY SHIP   It's possible to travel to Poland by ferry from two ports in Sweden, putting in at Gdańsk and Gdynia on the Baltic coast. See Gdańsk, "Getting There," later in this chapter for more details.

GETTING AROUND

BY CAR   Car travel offers flexibility but can be slow and highly frustrating. Most Polish highways—even those connecting major cities—are of the narrow, two-lane variety and are usually clogged with trucks, buses, tractors, and even occasionally horse-drawn carts. For most stretches, plan on at least 2 hours driving time per 100km (60 miles) distance. And drive defensively. Polish drivers have an abysmal record when it comes to per capita accidents and fatalities. Poland follows normal Continental rules of the road, with priority given to cars on roundabouts and vehicles coming from the right at unmarked intersections. The speed limit on (the few) four-lane freeways is 130kmph (78 mph). This drops to 90kmph (54 mph) on two-lane highways outside urban areas, and 50kmph (30 mph) or slower in built-up areas. Speed checks are common. Spot alcohol checks are also frequent. The blood/alcohol limit is 0.2%—one beer.

BY TRAIN   The Polish state railroad, PKP, has improved its service in recent years, and train travel is usually the quickest and best way to move between big cities or to cover long distances. The best trains are the intercity (IC) trains, which link nearly all of the country's biggest cities. You'll see IC trains marked in red on timetables; these are more expensive than regular trains and require an obligatory seat reservation. Next best are express trains (Ex), which also require a reservation. Avoid other types of trains for longer distances. Fares are relatively low by Western standards, with journeys between major cities rarely over $30. For overnight trips, you can book a couchette in a six-bunk car for around 90 zł ($30/£16) or a sleeper in a three-bunk car for 120 zł ($40/£22). Be sure to book these in advance if possible.

BY BUS   Buses are the preferred means of travel to smaller towns and villages, or for traveling within regions. The country's national carrier, PKS, maintains an extensive network of routes linking nearly all cities and towns of any size at all. On popular runs, such as between Kraków and Zakopane, private bus lines have emerged to supplement the public network. These private lines may cost a little more but are worth it since they are not obligated to stop at every small town and village along the way. Bus stations are almost always located near the main train stations. You can usually buy tickets in advance or from the driver, but watch to have exact change, since the driver may not have enough cash on hand to deal with large bills.

TIPS ON ACCOMMODATIONS
The past decade has seen a boom in hotel construction, but most of that has come in the high and high-middle ends of the market in order to cater to the growing amount of business travel to Poland. That means rates will probably be higher than you expect. On the good side, this dependence on the business traveler means that hotels often cut rates on the weekends to fill beds. "Standard double rooms" are usually understood to mean twin beds; rooms with queen-size beds are often classified as "deluxe" and cost more. Most places now have nonsmoking accommodations, and a growing number of hotels are now mostly or entirely smoke-free. If you're traveling by car, note that parking is often not included in the price. Hotels will frequently offer guarded parking for a fee, usually 30 zł ($10/£5.50). In urban areas this is definitely the way to go.

In addition to hotels and pensions ("pensjonaty"), there's no shortage of people offering private accommodations in their homes or flats. This is more common in heavily touristed areas away from larger cities—in places like Zakopane, for example. Look for the signs saying "wolny pokoj" (free room) or "noclegi" (lodging) hanging from outside houses. Prices are much lower than hotels, but standards vary considerably. Always take a look at the room first before accepting.

TIPS ON DINING
Restaurant meals have greatly improved in the past decade. It used to be nearly impossible to find decent food outside of a private home, but entrepreneurs have seized on the growing numbers of businessmen and tourists. In addition to standard restaurants ("restauracja"), look for places with the word "karczma" (literally "inn") in the name. These are often done up in traditional, peasant style, with simpler cooking and a warmer atmosphere. Here and there you'll still see the occasional "bar mleczny," or milk bar; these self-service canteens traditionally cater to students and are great for simple Polish meals like pierogies, potato pancakes, soups, and some meat dishes. Milk bars often have shorter opening hours, are nonsmoking, and don't serve alcohol.

FAST FACTS: Poland

American Express Warsaw Lim Center, Al Jerozolimskie 65/79 (© 022/630–69–52; open Mon–Fri 9am–7pm, Sat 10am–6pm).

Business Hours Stores and offices are generally open Monday to Friday 9am to 6pm. Banks are open Monday to Friday 9am to 4pm. Some larger stores have limited Saturday hours, usually 9am to noon. Museums and other tourist attractions are often closed on Mondays.

Doctors & Dentists In Warsaw, the **LIM Medical Center** is centrally located in the Marriott complex and staffs a full range of English-speaking doctors and specialists (al. Jerozolimskie 65/79; © 022/458–70–00). For dentists, the **Austrian Dental Center** (Zelazna 54; © 022/654–21–16) comes highly recommended.

Electricity Polish outlets follow the Continental norm (220v, 50hz) with two round plugs. Most appliances that run on 110v will require a transformer.

Embassies **U.S.:** ul. Ujadowskie 29/31, © 022/502–20–00; **Canada:** ul. Matejki 1/5, © 022/584–31–00; **U.K.:** al. Róż 1, © 022/311–00–00.

Emergencies In an emergency, dial the following numbers: police © 997, fire © 998, ambulance © 999, road assistance © 981 or 9637 (Polish motoring association/PZM). The general emergency number if using a cellphone is © 112.

Internet & E-mail Internet cafes are ubiquitous throughout Warsaw, Kraków, and other large cities. Internet cafes generally charge around 2 zł (65¢/40p) per half-hour of Internet use. Many better hotels now set aside at least one public computer for guests to use. A growing number of better hotels and cafes now offer wireless Internet access.

Post Offices & Mail The rate for mailing a postcard abroad is 2.50 zł (about 80¢/45p) and a first-class letter 3.20 zł ($1.05/60p).

Safety Violent crime is relatively rare, but theft is a serious problem. Don't leave valuables in cars overnight. Watch your pockets and purses carefully. If you're traveling with a bike, don't leave it outside unattended (even if it's firmly locked). Many hotels and pensions will allow you to take your bicycle in with you to your room.

Telephones & Fax Poland's country code is 48. To dial Poland from abroad, dial the international access code (for example, 011 in the U.S.), plus 48 and then the local Poland area code (minus the zero). The area code for Warsaw is 02. To call long distance within Poland, dial the area code (retaining the zero) plus the number. To dial abroad from Poland, dial 00 and then the country code and area code to where you are calling. A call to the U.S. or Canada would begin 00-1.

Time Zone Poland is in the Central European Time zone (CET), 1 hour ahead of GMT and 6 hours ahead of the eastern United States.

Tipping In restaurants, round up the bill by 10% to reward good service. Bellhops, taxi drivers, and tour guides will also expect a small amount in return for services rendered. Around 5 zł ($1.70/£1) is usually enough under any circumstance.

Toilets Public toilets are a relative rarity, so you'll find yourself seeking out nearby restaurants or hotels and asking to use the facilities. This is usually not a problem. Some establishments will ask for 1 zł (35¢/20p) for the privilege. Service stations and other places sometimes have pay toilets. The fee is usually a one-złoty coin. Some public toilets still use the older symbols to designate men's and women's facilities; for the record, men are upside-down triangles; women are circles (don't ask me why).

Water Tap water is generally potable and there are no specific health concerns. If in doubt, buy bottled water, which is cheap and widely available.

3 Warsaw

Poland's capital city—not often included on many tourist itineraries—deserves a fresh look. While it will never have the charm of Kraków or Gdańsk, there's a spirit of rebirth here that's immediately contagious. Some 85% of the city was destroyed during World War II, and nearly everything you see, including the charming and very "old" looking **Old Town (Stare Miasto),** has been around only for a few decades. The Old Town was faithfully rebuilt, brick by brick, in the aftermath of the war, according to paintings, photographs, architectural sketches, and personal memories. The reconstruction was so good that in 1980 UNESCO included the Old Town on its list of World Cultural Heritage sites.

Warsaw started life as a relatively small river town in the 14th century, but within a century it had become the capital city of the Duchy of Mazovia, ruling over small fiefdoms in central Poland. The city's fortunes steadily improved in the 16th century after the duchy was incorporated into the Polish crown and Poland formed a union with Lithuania. The union greatly expanded the amount of territory under Polish influence. In 1596, King Sigismund III decided to move the capital to Warsaw from Kraków, mainly because it was easier for noblemen to travel to more centrally situated Warsaw. The subsequent centuries brought the usual mix of prosperity and disaster; the Swedes sacked the city in the 17th century, but in spite of it all Warsaw continued to grow wealthier.

The Polish partitions at the end of the 18th century relegated Warsaw to the status of a provincial town for the next 125 years. Initially, the Prussians ruled over the city, but the Congress of Vienna, in 1815, placed czarist Russia in firm control. Despite the occupation, Warsaw thrived in the 19th century as a western outpost of the Russian empire. Finally, in 1918, after Germany's defeat and Russia's collapse in World War I, Warsaw was reconstituted as the capital of newly independent Poland.

Things went reasonably well for a time until World War II, when the city—like the rest of the country—was plunged into a modern-day Dante's Inferno. The Nazis occupied the city in 1939 and held it for nearly the entire course of the war. The occupation was brutal; thousands of Warsaw residents were imprisoned or killed. Initially, it was the Jews who bore the brunt. The Nazis herded the city's entire Jewish population of about 300,000, as well as around 100,000 Jews from elsewhere around Poland, into a small ghetto area west of the Old Town. Nearly all of them eventually lost their lives to sickness, starvation, or—mainly—the gas chambers at Treblinka. In 1943, the Jews heroically rose up against their oppressors in the first of two wartime Warsaw uprisings. The uprising was quickly put down and what remained of the ghetto was completely destroyed.

A year later, in 1944, with the war going badly for the Germans, the Polish resistance fighters, the Home Army, called for a general uprising against the German occupiers. For weeks in August and September of that year, Warsaw residents fought pitched battles with the Germans throughout the city, initially recording some heroic victories. Part of the plan was to enlist the assistance of the approaching Soviet Red Army, who had advanced to the Warsaw suburb of Praga across the river. That assistance never came, and the Germans eventually crushed the uprising. Hitler was so enraged that he ordered the remaining population expelled and the city razed to the ground. By the end of the war, 85% of Warsaw lay in ruins, and two out of every three residents—nearly 900,000 people—had died or were missing.

The postwar years were bleak ones. Poland was cut off from Marshall Plan aid and the bulk of the reconstruction assistance initially came from the Soviet Union. With so much of the city destroyed, the Soviet-inspired planners could start from scratch. They widened the avenues to the proportions you see today and filled them with drab "Socialist-Realist"-style offices and apartment blocks. To be fair, some of these buildings aren't so awful. The area around the Plac Konstytucji, in particular, has some handsome postwar buildings. And of course the unmissable Palace of Culture and Science is the granddaddy of them all. It's a strictly love-it-or-hate-it affair, with many city residents falling squarely into the latter camp.

One notable exception to the postwar reconstruction was the Old Town. Instead of rebuilding it in modern Socialist style, Warsaw residents overwhelmingly chose to reconstruct exactly what they had lost. It's a moving story of reclaiming identity from history, and the results are phenomenal.

Since the fall of Communism, the city's fortunes have improved immensely. Warsaw, as the capital city, has grabbed more than its share of the country's newfound wealth and the city skyline is looking more and more like a sun-belt boomtown every day. The changes are every bit as dramatic on the cultural front. New clubs, theaters, performance spaces, and restaurants have opened their doors, and the city feels more vital now than it has in many, many decades.

GETTING THERE

BY PLANE   Warsaw's Okęcie airport (© **022/650 42 20;** www.lotnisko-chopina. pl), sometimes called by its formal name, Frederyk Chopin Airport, is 10km (6 miles) from the city center. Most major international carriers use the main terminal, while budget airlines arrive and depart from a separate but nearby terminal. The main terminal is well served by a tourist information office, automated teller machines, and a Ruch kiosk where you can buy tickets for the trams and buses. To get to the center of the city, take bus no. 175, which makes the run in about half an hour. During the night, bus no. 611 makes a similar run. Tickets cost 2.40 zł (80¢/45p). You'll need to buy an extra ticket for your bags. Taxis make the run to the center for around 40 zł ($13/£7)—the exact fare depending on the destination.

BY TRAIN   Major international and domestic trains arrive and depart from Warsaw's Central Station (Warszawa Centralna, Al. Jerozolimskie 54; © **022/620 45 12;** www.pkp.com.pl), located in the heart of the city in Śródmieście (just across the street from the Marriott Hotel). Centralna is, to put it mildly, confusing. It's a vast 1970s concrete jungle, filled with underground passageways that seemingly lead nowhere and misleadingly marked stairways that will have you coming and going, and getting no place at all. Fortunately, the officials at Polish rail have cleaned up the station in recent years, and they've even added some English-speaking ticket sellers to the international ticketing counter. Centralna is well served by taxis, tram lines, and buses; the only trick is finding which stairway to use to locate the tram going in the direction you want to travel.

BY BUS   Warsaw's main bus station (Dworzec Centralny PKS; © 022/94 33) is situated in the city center (Śródmieście), about 1km (½ mile) to the west of the Centralna train station along Al. Jerozolimskie. The station handles all of the bus traffic to and from western Europe as well as most major Polish routes. The station is well served by tram, bus, or taxi to anywhere in the city. The easiest way to get between the bus and train stations is to grab any tram heading in the direction you want to go and ride three stops.

BY CAR   As Poland's capital city, all roads lead to Warsaw. You'll have no problem finding your way here. You may be surprised, though, by how long it takes to get here, and once you're here by the sheer volume of traffic. Once you've found your hotel, stow the car and use the trams and taxis.

CITY LAYOUT

Warsaw is cut in two by the Vistula River (Wisła), but nearly all of the interesting things to see and do lie on the river's western side. The heart of the city, and where you'll find most of the hotels, restaurants, and nightlife, is the central district known as Śródmieście. With its huge avenues and acres of space between buildings, it's not particularly pedestrian-friendly. But trams scoot down the rails at an impressive speed and can whisk you around in a few minutes. The center of Śródmieście is the intersection of Aleje Jerozolimskie (Jerusalem Avenue) and Marszałkowska street. The Old Town (Stare Miasto) lies about 1km (½ mile) to the north. The best way to find it on foot is to follow the street Nowy Świat, which intersects with Al. Jerozolimskie, and continue along the "Royal Route," Krakowskie Przedmieście, which brings you to the Royal Castle, and the start of the Old Town. To the south of Jerozolimskie, along the Al. Ujazdowski, beginning at Plac Trzech Krzyży, you'll find Warsaw's embassy district, and some of the city's swankiest shops, cafes, restaurants, and nightclubs. Farther to the south lies the enormous residential district of Mokotów, home to some half of the city's two million people. Across the Vistula from the Old Town is the up-and-coming residential district of Praga. This area has long been one of the poorest districts in Warsaw, but is starting to see something of a revival, primarily led by artists attracted by Praga's rock-bottom rents.

GETTING AROUND

ON FOOT   Warsaw is a big city, so walking is only an option within specific areas, such as the Old Town or in Śródmieście. For longer distances, you'll want to use public transportation or taxis.

BY TRAM   Trams trundle down Warsaw's enormous avenues regularly from about 5am to 11pm, and are the best means for covering large distances quickly and cheaply. Tickets costs 2.40 zł (80¢/45p), and you can buy them from Ruch kiosks around town or almost any place near a tram stop that sells newspapers and cigarettes. You may have a hard time finding a place to buy a ticket in the evening, so buy several during the day and stock up. You can also buy reasonably priced long-term tickets: for 1 day (7 zł/$2.30/£1.20), 3 days (12 zł/$4/£2.20), and 1 week (24 zł/$8/£4.30). The tram

EXPENSIVE

Grand Hotel Orbis ★★   This used to be a reliably cheap if grim relic from Communist times with an absolutely unbeatable location. Now, thanks to an injection of cash from the Mercure chain, it's been thoroughly renovated inside and out. The rooms are bright and sunny and the public areas tidy if a bit on the formal side. The facade has gotten a sandblasting, and looks as good as the day it opened. The problem is the improvements have come at a cost, and sadly the Grand is no longer the bargain it once was. Still, it's a nice choice because of its location near the trendy embassy district, with some of the city's best cafes, shops, and nightlife a 5-minute walk away. As of this writing the hotel was contemplating a name change in 2007 to the "Mercure Grand" (which will no doubt add a few more złoty to the final tab).

Krucza 28. ⓒ **022/583-21-00.** Fax 022/621-97-24. www.orbisonline.pl. 355 units. 400 zł ($133/£70) double. AE, DC, MC, V. **Amenities:** Restaurant; spa; limited room service; nonsmoking rooms. *In room:* A/C, TV, dataport, minibar, hair dryer.

Hotel Jan III Sobieski ★   This is a slightly cheaper version of the upscale business hotels, but still offering very high-quality accommodations. The lower prices are probably due to the hotel's location, slightly down from the heart of Śródmieście (but still an easy tram jaunt away). The hotel was one of the first luxury properties to open up after the fall of Communism in 1989 and as such is showing its age a little. That said the rooms are very nicely done in muted contemporary look and soundproofed against the busy street below. The guest list includes Art Garfunkel, Carlos Santana, and Herbie Hancock (which shows they must be doing something right here).

Plac A. Zawiszy 1. ⓒ **022/579-10-00.** www.sobieski.com.pl. 427 units. 560 zł ($186/£95) double. AE, DC, MC, V. **Amenities:** 2 restaurants; health club and spa; concierge; business center; 24-hr. room service; dry cleaning; nonsmoking rooms. *In room:* A/C, TV, dataport, minibar, hair dryer.

Marriott ★★   Of the big chains in town, this one offers arguably the best location and the best value. Maybe because the hotel has been established here the longest, since 1989, its rack rates are among the lowest of the four-star hotels. It is every bit as posh and comfortable as any of the others, and the hotel has worked hard in recent years to upgrade the rooms (and improve the bedding). Former guests include U.S. President George W. Bush. For years, Warsaw residents have admired the hotel's rectangular skyscraper—like something out of the Dallas or Denver skyline—as a fitting capitalist foil to the Socialist-Realist wedding cake Palace of Culture just across the street.

Al. Jerozolimskie 65/79. ⓒ **022/630-63-06.** Fax 022/630–03–11. www.marriott.com/wawpl. 518 units. 520 zł ($173/£90) double. AE, DC, MC, V. **Amenities:** 3 restaurants; indoor pool; health club and spa; concierge; business center; 24-hr. room service; dry cleaning; nonsmoking rooms. *In room:* A/C, TV, dataport, minibar, coffeemaker, hair dryer, iron, safe.

Moderate

Boutique Bed & Breakfast ★★   This unique B&B was the dream of a Polish expat living in Chicago who returned home after 1989. He wanted to create the best small hotel experience he could think of and has mostly succeeded. Each of the five rooms is done up differently, but the emphasis is on high-quality traditional furniture and a decidedly homey ambience. The "Queen" and "King" apartments come with full kitchens and Wi-Fi Internet access. "Prince" is my favorite, with a beautiful high-backed bed and light hardwood floors. Don't come expecting anonymity. Jacek, the owner, likes to take an interest in his guests and wax enthusiastically about his hometown. If you're looking for something more interactive than the standard hotel, this may be just right. Excellent Old Town location.

Smolna 14/7. © 022/829-48-01. www.bedandbreakfast.pl. 5 units. 270 zł ($90/£50) double. AE, DC, MC, V. **Amenities:** Business center; nonsmoking rooms. *In room:* TV, kitchen (some rooms), fridge (some rooms), coffeemaker (some rooms), hair dryer.

IBIS Hotel-Stare Miasto 𝒜𝒜　Sometimes the IBIS hotel chain is a real lifesaver. The philosophy of a clean, modern, stripped-down business hotel at tourist rates is especially welcome in a city like Warsaw, where every other place seems to assume that Payroll is footing the bill. The rooms and public areas are stark in keeping with the IBIS idea, but you won't find a nicer room at this price so close to the Old Town.

Muranowska 2. © 022/310-10-00. Fax 022/310-10-10. www.ibishotel.com. 330 units. 259 zł ($87/£48) double. AE, DC, MC, V. **Amenities:** Restaurant; nonsmoking rooms. *In room:* A/C, TV, dataport.

Kyriad Prestige 𝒜𝒜　This hotel is owned by the same chain as the Premiere Classe (see below), but the philosophy here is to offer top-end business services at moderate prices. Travelers accustomed to four-star luxuries can save substantial cash over the likes of the InterContinental and Marriott. The neighborhood is on the gray side, but a nearby tram can get you to the center in about 5 minutes. The rooms are large and comfortably furnished in contemporary styles. Excellent business services, including several conference rooms, if you happen to be mixing business with pleasure.

Towarowa 2. © 022/582-75-00. Fax 022/582-75-01. www.kyriadprestige.com.pl. 133 units. 359 zł ($120/£65) double. AE, DC, MC, V. **Amenities:** Restaurant; spa; room service; nonsmoking rooms. *In room:* A/C, TV, dataport, minibar, hair dryer.

Maria 𝒜　Arguably the best of the smaller, family-run hotels in town. The rooms are on the austere side of modern, but several have hardwood floors and these tend to be smarter looking and more comfortable. The restaurant is light and cheerful, and the staff couldn't be more welcoming. The in-town location is convenient to the sights, especially to the former Jewish ghetto. The Old Town is about a 20-minute walk. The location, just off a major artery, is easy to get to if you're coming by car.

Jana Pawla II 71. © 022/838-40-62. Fax 022/838-38-40. www.hotelmaria.pl. 24 units. 380 zł ($127/£70) double. AE, DC, MC, V. **Amenities:** Restaurant; nonsmoking rooms. *In room:* A/C, TV, dataport, minibar, hair dryer.

Zajazd Napoleoński 𝒜𝒜　There's been an inn on this site on the eastern side of the Vistula since at least the 18th century when the location was ideal for the incoming carriage trade. The current building dates from the 19th century and is rich in period detail, including elegant crystal chandeliers and tiled flooring. One of the dining areas is done up in Biedermeier. The rooms can't match the style of the public areas but are large, with high ceilings and a solid feel. The location, a bit out of the action, helps to keep prices in check, yet the center is an easy tram ride away. A nice choice if you're looking for something other than an international chain and don't want to shell out for the Rialto.

Płowiecka 83. © 022/815-30-68. www.napoleon.waw.pl. 24 units. 310 zł ($103/£55) double. AE, DC, MC, V. **Amenities:** Restaurant; concierge; courtesy car; business center; dry cleaning; nonsmoking rooms. *In room:* A/C, TV, dataport, minibar, hair dryer.

INEXPENSIVE
Nathan's Villa Hostel 𝒜𝒜　The same owner/philosophy as the Nathan's hostel in Kraków. The idea is to combine some of the amenities of a decent hotel with the

sociability of a hostel. Nathan is a likable American expat who wants to provide high standards at a fair price. Most of the clientele falls into the standard backpacker category, but the doors are open to all comers, young, old, and in-between. Several private double rooms are on offer, so you don't have to sleep *en groupe*. Free laundry is one of several perks that you wouldn't normally expect at a hostel, and the central city location is ideal.

Piękna 24/26. ✆ 022/622-29-46. Fax 022/622-29-46. www.nathansvilla.com. 14 units. 170 zł ($56/£30) double. AE, DC, MC, V. **Amenities:** Laundry; nonsmoking rooms.

Premiere Classe ★★ *Value* The theory behind this French hotel chain is to offer spotless, modern rooms with absolutely no frills at cut-rate prices. It's found a real niche in Warsaw, where decent, affordable rooms in the center are in short supply. The rooms themselves are microscopic—and I've seen Winnebagoes with bigger bathrooms—but they're very clean, cozy, and comfortable. Watch the add-on prices. Room rates do not include breakfast (18 zł/$6/£3.15), parking (30 zł/$10/£5.25 a day), or in-room Wi-Fi (10 zł/$3.30/£1.75 for 2 hours).

Towarowa 2. ✆ 022/624-08-00. Fax 022/620-26-29. www.premiereclasse.com.pl. 126 units. 179 zł ($60/£32) double. AE, DC, MC, V. **Amenities:** Restaurant; nonsmoking rooms. *In room:* A/C, TV.

WHERE TO DINE

The dining scene is exploding. Warsaw is great for Polish food, and as a bustling city of two million, also good for just about any international cuisine you can think of. The best places tend to be in the central city, Śródmieście, especially south of Al. Jerozolimskie. Dress is casual to neat-casual except in the more expensive places (where snappier dress is more appropriate, though rarely required).

VERY EXPENSIVE

Ale Gloria ★★ POLISH Fusion food is catching on in Poland, but here it's defined a little differently. Instead of the usual "Asia meets the West" concept common in other places, in Poland it often means "traditional Polish food plus something whacky tossed in." For starters try wild game pâté served with bitter orange sauce or stuffed carp in a raisin wine gelatin (get the idea?). The mains are more down-to-earth, but still exhibit an occasional flight of fancy. One of the best is boar roulade served in a Bombay gin and honey sauce. The service is top-notch and the crowd is a mix of beautiful people and embassy types who can afford to dabble.

Plac Trzech Krzyży 3. ✆ 022/584-70-80. Reservations recommended. Lunch and dinner items 45 zł–66 zł ($15–$22/£8–£12). AE, DC, MC, V. Daily noon–11pm.

U Fukiera ★ POLISH One of the fanciest meals in the city, served in an overwrought but undeniably intimate and romantic space on the Old Town's main square. Antique crystal, fresh flowers, and original art on the walls lend a special feel. The quality of the food is disputed. Some say it's the best in town, others that it's slightly overrated (but still *quite* good). Not surprisingly for a traditional restaurant, the menu is heavy on game. For a different kind of starter try the white borscht with porcini mushrooms. The roast leg of venison in cream sauce won't disappoint. Dress up for this one.

Rynek Starego Miasta 27. ✆ 022/831-10-13. Reservations recommended. Lunch and dinner items 30 zł–60 zł ($10–$20/£5.50–£11). AE, DC, MC, V. Daily noon–10pm.

EXPENSIVE

Delicja Polska ★★ POLISH   Cozy, inviting space with excellent Polish food. The menu leans toward the traditional, but with the addition of something slightly unexpected. For a warm starter, try the pierogies stuffed with veal. Two of the best main course selections include the boar tenderloin with juniper sauce and beet root, and the veal cutlets marinated in bison grass. The intimate dining room makes it a destination choice for an evening meal. Easy-to-reach location near Pl. Konstytucji.

Koszykowa 54. (C) 022/630-88-50. Reservations recommended. Lunch and dinner items 30 zł–60 zł ($10–$20/ £5.50–£11). AE, DC, MC, V. Daily noon–10pm.

Polski Smak POLISH   A great place to sample some excellent Polish cooking without having to deal with pretentious settings and wallet-busting prices. For starters go for the herring in three sauces: curry; sour cream and onion; and tomato. For mains, they're all recommendable, but the house specialty of roast duck served with cranberries and baked apple is excellent. Try it with a side of fried potato dumplings. The neighborhood, on a small side street off of Nowy Świat, is a delight. After your meal take a stroll and a glass of wine at one of the many little bars and cafes in the area.

Galczyńskiego 3. (C) 022/826-59-67. Lunch and dinner items 27 zł–36 zł ($9–$12/£5–£7). AE, DC, MC, V. Daily noon–11pm.

Tandoori Palace INDIAN   One of the pleasures of a big city like Warsaw is the chance to branch out culinarily speaking. This popular little place calls itself the "best Indian food in Poland," a claim of dubious merit (like boasting the "best burritos in Saskatchewan"). But no matter, the Indian food here is very good. I usually order the yellow lentils with nan bread as a starter followed by a spicy lamb curry. It's not exactly cheap, though beloved by Warsaw's expats.

Marszałkowska 21/25. (C) 022/825-23-75. Lunch and dinner items 27 zł–36 zł ($9–$12/£5–£7). AE, DC, MC, V. Daily noon–10pm.

MODERATE

Chłopskie Jadło POLISH   I hesitated dropping this one in, but if you're dying to try decent Polish food and don't have a lot of cash to spare, this might be your best option. Chłopskie Jadło is a Polish chain, with locations in Kraków and Gdańsk. The idea is the same everywhere: good-to-very-good traditional Polish food served with all the trimmings in a lively, clean, cottage-style atmosphere. It's a lot of fun, and the cost-value ratio may be the best in town.

Pl. Konstytucji 1. (C) 022/339-17-15. Lunch and dinner items 21 zł–30 zł ($7–$10/£4–£5.50). AE, DC, MC, V. Daily noon–11pm.

Restauracja Świętojańska POLISH   Nice alternative to the high-priced U Fukiera in the Old Town. The menus are similar, but the prices here are around half and the quality of the food is comparable. What you'll miss is the unique atmosphere; this place favors the homey and traditional. A great spot for lunch if you happen to be in the area.

Świętojańska 2. (C) 022/635-35-35. Lunch and dinner items 15 zł–30 zł ($5–$10/£2.60–£6). AE, DC, MC, V. Daily noon–10pm.

INEXPENSIVE

Champion's Sports Bar AMERICAN   An American-style sports bar run by the Marriott hotel group and one of the best spots around for burgers and ribs, or even the odd chance to catch a football or baseball game on one of the large-screen TVs scattered around. Cheerful service and beer "by the pitcher" complete the picture. If you're tired of pierogies on the road, or perhaps a wee bit homesick, this place will set you straight.

Al. Jerozolimskie 65/79. ✆ 022/630-51-19. Lunch and dinner items 18 zł–27 zł ($6–$9/£3.30–£5). AE, DC, MC, V. Daily 11am–midnight.

Nonsolo Pizza ⟨★★⟩ ITALIAN   This small, austere, Italian-run pizzeria uses traditional wood-fired ovens and, złoty-for-złoty, may be the best pizza in the city. The atmosphere is informal, and not a particularly great choice for a special night out, but it's fine for lunch or a quick meal before going out. Has great pasta too (my favorite is "Ovoletti," with fresh tomatoes, basil, and mozzarella). It's especially convenient if you happen to be staying at the Sobieski, Premiere Classe, or Kyriad Prestige hotels (see "Where to Stay," earlier in this chapter); it's an easy 5-minute walk from all of these along Al. Jerozolimskie in the direction heading away from the center.

Grojecka 20c. ✆ 022/824-12-73. Lunch and dinner items 15 zł–21 zł ($5–$7/£2.60–£3.80). AE, DC, MC, V. Daily 10am–9pm.

Pierrogeria ⟨★★⟩ POLISH   Newly opened and fast becoming *the* spot for pierogies and simple Polish food (great barszcz, too!) in the Old Town. Order your pierogies traditionally boiled or fried, and choose from a variety of sauces, including relative rarities like dill or garlic. The Old Town location makes it a great stop for an easy lunch while taking in the sights.

Ul. Krzywe Kolo 30. ✆ 022/654-88-44. Lunch and dinner items 12 zł–18 zł ($4–$6/£2.20–£3.30). MC, V. Daily noon–10pm.

Warsaw Tortilla Factory ⟨★★⟩ MEXICAN   I know it's dangerous to recommend a burrito joint in a pierogi town, but this place delivers the goods. All of the usual Tex-Mex staples, including excellent burritos, fajitas, and hot chicken wings. The atmosphere is casual, and the clientele is mostly young professionals and expats out for a fun night. Strong cocktails!

Wilcza 46. ✆ 022/621-86-22. Lunch and dinner items 15 zł–30 zł ($5–$10/£2.60–£6). AE, DC, MC, V. Daily noon–10pm.

EXPLORING WARSAW

Warsaw is a large city, so plan your exploration in pieces at a time, moving between areas with trams or taxis. A good place to start a walking tour of the city is the **Old Town (Stare Miasto).** The beautiful baroque and Renaissance-style burghers' houses would be remarkable in their own right for their beauty and period detailing, but what makes these houses truly astounding is that they're only a few decades old. As one of the main centers of the 1944 Warsaw Uprising (see below), the Old Town bore the brunt of German reprisal attacks and the entire area, save for one building, was blown to bits at the end of 1944. After the war, to reclaim their heritage, the Polish people launched an enormous project to rebuild the Old Town, exactly as it was, brick-by-brick. Many of the original architectural sketches were destroyed in the war, so the town was rebuilt from paintings, photographs, drawings, and people's memories. The reconstruction was so authentic that UNESCO in 1980 listed the Old Town as a World Heritage Site. Today, the Old Town is given over mostly to touts and tourists, but still rewards a couple of hours of strolling. Behind the old-world facades, the buildings themselves are modern apartment blocks. Spend a couple of hours walking here, taking in the central square, and the adjoining streets and alleyways. The **Royal Castle,** at the entrance to the Old Town, is also a replica, having been completed only in the 1980s. It's worth a stop to admire some rich period interiors and an excellent permanent art collection.

Continue your tour south along what's been known for centuries as Warsaw's Royal Route, following the now-swanky, cafe-lined streets of **Krakowskie Przedmieście** and **Nowy Świat.** As you walk, bear in the mind that these streets too saw intense fighting during World War II and were completely rebuilt from rubble after the war. Much of this area is dominated by Warsaw University, and the streets are often filled with students. By day, it's a great place to stroll and have a coffee; by night, you'll find plenty of clubs, bars, and restaurants.

Nowy Świat eventually empties into **Aleje Jerozolimskie (Jerusalem Ave.),** one of the main arteries of Warsaw's central city, **Śródmieście.** This is the heart of the city, and you'll find yourself spending a lot of time on this avenue, and the giant avenue that bisects it at the geographic center of Śródmieście, **Marszałkowska.** Heading west on Jerozolimskie, just beyond Marszałkowska, you can't miss the giant Stalinist wedding-cake **Palace of Culture and Science,** for years a symbol of the city's subjugation, firmly under the thumb of the Soviet Union. The 60-story "palace" was built in the 1950s as a gift to the Polish people from Josef Stalin. What to do with the tower has bedeviled city planners since the fall of Communism in 1989. Suggestions have ranged from demolishing it to rehabbing it to its original purpose as a house of culture. The latter alternative appears to be winning out, and it looks as if the palace is here to stay. You can take an elevator to the 30th floor for some nice views of the city.

North of Jerozolimskie, following Marszałkowska, leads to a highly interesting complex of buildings built in the 1950s in an austere but still striking Socialist-Realist style. The most impressive, or hideous (depending on your taste in architecture), cluster of buildings lies on and just to the north of **Constitution Place (Plac Konstytucji).** Before the war, Marszałkowska was arguably the most fashionable avenue in Warsaw. It was totally destroyed by the Germans in reprisals for the Warsaw Uprising, and in the 1950s was widened and rebuilt in Stalinist style. Take a while to explore the area and the streets that branch off on both sides, noting the oversize reliefs of the proletariat heroes on the buildings. These days, this neighborhood is one of the trendiest in Warsaw and you'll see, sprouting here and there, hipster cafes and pubs that use the architecture in a newly ironic and humorous way.

South of Jerozolimskie, near the intersection with Nowy Świat, lies the city's most exclusive quarter and home to many government buildings, including the parliament (Sejm) and foreign embassies. It's also the preferred neighborhood for exclusive boutiques and fashion houses. Head south to the **Three Crosses Square (Plac Trzech Krzyży)** and then down the main boutique shopping street of **Mokotowska.** Make a note to come back here during the evening, when the street-side cafes start filling with life. A little farther on you'll find the city's favorite park for a stroll: **Łazienki Park.** The park is filled with little treasures, including a lake, lots of nice footpaths, and an overblown Art Deco statue honoring Poland's most famous composer, Frederyk Chopin (cultural aside: Chopin was born in Poland to a French father and a Polish mother). On Sundays in nice weather you'll find a regular Chopin-in-the-park concert; the music starts around noon. You'll also find here the very fine neoclassical summer palace of Poland's last king, Stanisław August Poniatowski.

The former **Jewish Ghetto** lies to the north of the city center, just to the west of the Old Town. Most of the ghetto, which in the early years of World War II held some 400,000 Jews, was destroyed in the war, and walking around today you'll find few clues to its former role. There are plans to build a Jewish cultural center and museum here, but those are still some years away. For now, the main sights are an evocative **Monument to the Ghetto Heroes** (ul. Zamenhofe), which recalls the heroic Jewish uprising in 1943, and a concrete-bunker-type memorial at the "**Umschlagplatz**" (ul. Stawki near the corner with ul. Dzika), the place where Jews were rounded up for train transports to the Treblinka extermination camp in the east of the country.

As in Kraków, Łódź, and other Polish cities, the tragedy of the Jews here is one of the most poignant stories of the war. Here in Warsaw, the Germans first started rounding up the city's enormous Jewish population toward the end of 1940. The ghetto's population swelled to some 400,000 to 450,000 residents and conditions were appalling. An elaborate system of gates and staircases was built to allow Jews inside to move within the ghetto, but no one was permitted to enter or leave. The first deportations and mass killings began about a year later, at the end of 1941. The Jews rebelled in 1943 as news of the gas chambers reached the ghetto and the residents realized they had no choice but to fight. The heroic rebellion, the "first" Warsaw uprising, not to be confused with the general Warsaw uprising a year later, was brutally put down by the Germans. The ghetto was liquidated shortly thereafter, and what remained was destroyed in the general uprising the next year. Nearly all of the city's Jews were killed in the uprising or the extermination camps, and today only around 5,000 Jews remain in Warsaw. Roman Polański's Oscar-winning film, *The Pianist*, recounts the story of the ghetto through the eyes of Władysław Szpilman, an accomplished piano player and one of the ghetto's best-known residents. Szpilman eventually escaped during a transport to the concentration camp and survived the war. He even returned to live out his life in Warsaw.

In addition to the major sights listed below, there are smaller museums to suit every interest, including, among others, one dedicated to Polish Romantic poet Adam Mickiewicz (Rynek Starego Miasta; ✆ **022/831-76-91**), to composer Frederyk Chopin (Okólnik 1; ✆ **022/827-54-71**), and to the horrific Katyń massacre in which an entire generation of Polish army officers—some 20,000 in all—were shot and killed by the Soviet Red Army in the Katyń woods (ul. Powsińska 13; ✆ **022/842-66-11**).

Royal Castle (Zamek Królewski) ✸✸   The original residence of Polish kings and dating from the 14th and later the seat of the Polish parliament, the castle was completely destroyed in the Warsaw uprising and its aftermath. What you see today is a painstaking reconstruction that was finished only in 1984. Two tours are offered: "Route I" and "Route II." Of the two, the second is more interesting, passing through the regal apartments of Poland's last monarch, King Stanisław August Poniatowski, and to the Canaletto room, where the famed cityscapes of Warsaw by the Italian painter Bernardo Bellotto hang. These paintings, and others not on display, were of extreme value in rebuilding the Old Town from scratch after the war. The tour ends in the lavish ballroom, the largest room in the castle.

Pl. Zamkovy 4. ✆ 022/657-21-70. Tues–Sat 10am–6pm; Sun–Mon 11am–6pm Regular ticket for Route 1 is 10 zł ($3.30/£1.70) and Route II is 18 zl ($6/£3). (Sun free admission).

The Palace of Culture and Science (Palac Kultury i Nauki) ✸   Warsaw's landmark tower is a building many residents would like to see knocked down. The 1950s

Socialist-Realist wedding cake was originally a gift from former Soviet leader Josef Stalin, but the symbolic intention was clear from the start. Stalin was marking his turf, and Poland was part of the Eastern bloc. Today, with Poland firmly within the European Union and the Soviet Union a distant nightmare, public attitudes toward the "palace" have softened somewhat. What used to look tragic, now looks undeniably comic, and it seems the building will continue in its role as a cultural venue for some time to come. You can ride to the top—30 stories—for a fine view over the city (but let's be honest here, 30 stories is not really that dramatic). The humdrum interior is also a bit of a disappointment. Save yourself the admission and, instead, admire the amazing exterior for free. You won't be able to take your eyes off of it.

Pl Defilad. ✆ **022/656-76-00.** www.pkin.pl. Daily 9am–8pm. Admission 20 zł ($6.65/£3.50), reduced for groups of 10 or more.

The Museum of the Warsaw Uprising (Muzeum Powstania Warszawskiego)

This relatively new museum, with its hands-on exhibits and high-tech imagery, has emerged as one of Warsaw's main tourist attractions. The museum, housed in a former transformer station for the trams, is a large and confusing space to navigate once inside. Try to follow the arrows on the suggested route, but don't despair if you find yourself ambling from one display case to another. Everyone else is doing the same.

A little history will help you to get your bearings. On August 1, 1944, at precisely 5pm, the commanders of the Polish insurgent Home Army, loyal to Poland's government-in-exile in London, called for a general uprising throughout the Nazi-occupied city. The Germans, at the time, were in retreat on all sides, having suffered reversals on the Western front, in France and Italy, and in the East, at the hands of the Soviet Red Army. By the end of July that year, the Red Army had moved to within the city limits of Warsaw and were camped on the eastern bank of the Vistula in the suburb of Praga. With the combined forces of the Home Army and the Red Army, it seemed the right moment to drive the Germans out and liberate Warsaw. Alas, it was not to be. The first few happy days of the uprising saw the Polish insurgents capture pockets of the city, including the Old Town and adjacent suburbs. But the Germans resisted fiercely, and the Red Army, for reasons that are not entirely clear to this day, never stepped in to help. The resistance lasted several weeks before Polish commanders were forced to capitulate in the face of rapidly escalating civilian casualties. Thousands of Warsaw residents died in the fighting and the subsequent reprisal attacks by German forces. The uprising so infuriated Hitler that he ordered the complete annihilation of the city. In the weeks following the uprising, Warsaw's buildings were listed in terms of their cultural significance and dynamited one by one. Some 85% of the city was eventually destroyed. As for the Russians, the accepted theory is that they viewed the Polish Home Army as a potential enemy and preferred simply to watch the Germans and Poles kill each other. To this day, many Poles have never forgiven the Russians this decision.

The museum charts the full course of the uprising starting from the German invasion in 1939, through life in occupied Warsaw, and the events of 1944 and their aftermath. Don't miss the harrowing documentary films shown on the upper floors, with English subtitles, that tell the story from the inside. They were made by Polish journalists during the occupation and were shown in Warsaw cinemas while the fighting was going on.

Grzybowska 79. ✆ **022/626-95-06.** Mon, Wed, Fri 8am–6pm, Thurs 8am–8pm, Sat–Sun 10am–6pm; Closed Tues. Admission 4 zł ($1.30/70p). Free Sun.

Gestapo Headquarters (Mauzoleum Walki i Męczeństwa)   Currently housing the Ministry of Education, from 1939 to 1945 this was the one place in town you absolutely didn't want to be summoned to for questioning. A small museum in the building's lower reaches shows the cells and interrogation rooms nearly untouched from how they were at the end of the war. The displays paint a vivid picture of the torture and killing that went on here—and the lengths to which the Nazis went to break the back of the Polish opposition.

Szucha 25. ✆ **022/629-49-19**. Free admission. Wed–Sun 10am–4pm.

Pawiak Prison ★★   Another frightening reminder of the horrific times of World War II. Something like 100,000 prisoners passed through the gates here during the nearly years of the Nazi occupation, when the prison was run by the Gestapo. Among the prisoners were political activists, members of the clergy, university professors, or simply anyone who could be suspected of opposing the Germans. Very few of the people imprisoned here got out alive. Most were sent to extermination camps, while around 40,000 people were actually executed on the grounds.

Dzielna 24/26. ✆ **022/831-92-89**. Free admission. Wed–Sun 10am–4pm.

Historical Museum of Warsaw ★★   A fascinating tour through the capital's ups and downs through the centuries. The exhibits paint an amazing contrast between the richness of the city up until World War II and the often-starker reality you see today. There are good displays on the Warsaw Uprising (though not as thorough as at the Warsaw Uprising museum). A moving film (English showings at noon) documents the destruction of the city during the war.

Rynek Starego Miasta 42. ✆ **022/635-16-25**. Free admission. Tues 10am–4pm; Wed–Fri 11am–5pm; Sat–Sun 10am–4pm.

Outside of Warsaw
Wilanów Palace ★★   Poles are rightfully proud of this baroque-era palace built to honor King Jan Sobieski. If you've seen Versailles near Paris or Schoenbruenn in Vienna you'll get the idea immediately: Size matters. This enormous building has no less than 60 rooms, most stuffed with royal memorabilia and portraits of Polish monarchs and heavyweights—though some rooms, like the Etruscan Room, display oddities such as vases dating from the 4th century B.C. The garden surrounding the palace is a delight and well worth a walk around. The palace can only be seen with a guided tour. Take the hourly Polish tour if you're not particularly interested in all the details of all of the portraits; otherwise try to book an English tour in advance by calling the number below, or once there try to latch onto any English-speaking group you happen to see.

Ul. Stanisława Kostki Potockiego 10/16. ✆ **022/842-25-09** (to arrange tours). www.wilanow-palac.art.pl. Admission to the palace 16 zł ($5.33/£2.70); to the park 5 zł ($1.66/90p); free Sat. Mid-May to mid–Sept: Wed 9am–6pm, Thurs–Fri 9am–4pm, Sat 10am–4pm, Sun 9:30am–7pm, Mon 9am–6pm. Mid–Sept to mid–May: Wed–Fri 9am–4pm, Sat 10am–4pm, Mon 9am–4pm.

SHOPPING
Not so long ago the idea of a shopping trip to Warsaw would have drawn laughs, with images of standing in line for bananas and knockoff jeans. But these days Warsaw can hold its own with any European capital, East or West, for food, fashion, or whatever you've got in mind. For clothing, most of the big international retail chains are clustered

in **Śródmieście**—look especially along **Al. Jerozolimskie** and **Marszałkowska.** South of Jerozolimskie, especially in the area around the **Plac Trzech Krzyży,** you'll find the best of boutique shopping, with local Polish designers rubbing elbows with the likes of Escada and Hugo Boss. Trailing south from the Plac Trzech Krzyży you'll find the über-trendiest of Warsaw shopping streets, **Mokotowska,** with its low-rise mix of international boutiques, fashionable home furnishing stores, and here and there still the occasional Polish deli or bakery. Mokotowska is currently home to the local branch of names like Commes des Garcons and Burberry, but check out also Polish shops and designers like Odzieżowe Pole (Mokotowska 51/53) and Finezja Studio (Mokotowska 65).

For more everyday shopping and particularly for picking up anything you might have forgotten at home, try the **Arkadia** mall (Ul. Jana Pawla II; 🕿 022/331-34-00; www.arkadia.com.pl), hailed locally as the biggest indoor shopping center in central Europe. Hundreds of stores, with everything from high- and low-end fashions, home electronics, furnishings, and food. You're not likely to find many surprises, but the sheer scale of the place will shock. The mall also has a 15-cinema multiplex with a good bet to have several films in English—in case you trapped inside on a rainy or snowy day.

For English-language books, try looking at **American Bookstore,** with a couple of central locations (Koszykowa 55, Nowy Świat 61; 🕿 022/660-56-37; www.american bookstore.pl). This place stocks a nice selection of Polish authors in translation, as well as books about the Holocaust, World War II, Solidarity, the fall of Communism, and other interesting topics.

For cheaper Polish-made products and low-cost souvenirs, try **Cepelia** (Marszałkowska 99/101; 🕿 022/628-77-57), the local branch of a national group selling folk art, traditional fabrics, leather goods, ceramics, and woodworking. Nice place for a "Made in Poland" gift, though you may have to pick through some obviously touristy dross.

One of the oddest shopping experiences in Warsaw takes place every day in a sports stadium across the river in Praga. Check out the **Dziesięciolecia Stadium** (take any tram heading east along Al. Jerozolimskie across the Poniatowski bridge). This is home to Poland's vast open-air Russian market, possibly the biggest of its kind in Europe. It's doubtful you'll find a lot worth buying—most of the stuff tends to be aimed at low-income families trying to make ends meet on Polish salaries—but the atmosphere is unique.

WARSAW AFTER DARK

Warsaw is a great "after dark" town. The city's opera and classical music offerings are some of the best in the country, and the availability of relatively cheap tickets means the performances are accessible to just about anyone. The main opera venue is the **Teatr Wielki** (Plac Teatralny 1; 🕿 022/692-02-00; www.teatrwielki.pl). Here you'll find everything from the Italian classics to occasionally bolder works featuring Polish avant-garde composers. The theater box office is open Monday to Saturday 9am to 7pm, Sunday 10am to 7pm. For classical music, the first address is the **Filharmonia Narodowa,** the home of the National Philharmonic (Jasna 5; 🕿 022/551-71-30; www.filharmonia.pl). The box office is located at Sienkiewicza 10 and is open Monday to Saturday 10am to 2pm and 3 to 7pm. Try timing your arrival just before show-time to get cheaper last-minutes tickets.

There's no shortage of cafes, bars, and dance clubs. For cafes and little cocktail bars, try the strip along Krakowskie Przedmieście, Nowy Świat, and south of Al. Jerozolimskie to the area around Plac Trzech Krzyży. For clubs, most of the action is still in the central city, Śródmieście, though some of the trendier places are pioneering areas farther afield, like the still-somewhat-dingy (but getting cooler) suburb of Praga.

The Cinnamon   Stylish, high-powered disco/dance club, complete with velvet ropes and monkeys guarding the door. Draws a well-dressed, good-looking crowd, from 20s to 40s, with thick wallets (for him) and slinky dresses (for her). The party doesn't usually get rolling until after midnight. Plac Piłsudskiego 1. *C* 022/323-76-00. www.thecinnamon.pl.

Foksal 19   A truly beautiful cocktail bar with drinking the main pursuit on the main level and a "Boogie Nights"-inspired dance club upstairs. Similar in vibe and clientele to "The Cinnamon," but the music is more interesting—not just the standard Ibiza dance tunes, but eclectic house and funk. Foksal 19. *C* 022/829-29-55. www.foksal19.com.

Jazz HotL   Relatively recently opened jazz club, with a growing repertoire of good shows and a great location between Old Town and the central city. Decent choice for a low-key but enjoyable evening of music and conversation. The restaurant is on the pricey side. Krakowskie Przedmieście 13. *C* 022/826-74-66. www.jazzhotl.pl.

Melodia   A former swanky haunt in Communist times, it's now a dark-wood, upscale bar and restaurant, popular with the business crowd. Decent food and occasional jazz and other live performances. Good spot for a quiet drink. Nowy Świat 3/5. *C* 022/583-01-80. www.klubmelodia.pl.

Opium Pleasure Lounge   A popular chill-out bar and music club, with a vaguely Middle Eastern, Persian theme. Popular with the beautiful crowd, and it doesn't really get going until very late. Open until 4am (closed Sun–Tues). Wierzbowa 9/11. *C* 022/827-71-61.

Pewex   A kind of Commie-throwback experience. Pewex stores, in the bad old days, were state-run hard-currency stores, where imported goods—everything from "Lee Cooper" jeans to bottles of "Fa" shampoo—were priced in dollars and available only to the lucky few. Pewex is filled with kitschy '70s memorabilia and lots of good-natured irony. Closes at 11pm, so a better place to start an evening than to end one. Nowy Świat 22/28. *C* 022/826-54-81.

Sheesha Bar   Yet another late-night drinking spot offering those ubiquitous hookahs, and with a strong Middle Eastern, North African theme. Popular with students, and a nice spot to relax and converse. Sienkiewicza 3. *C* 022/828-25-25.

Trakt Fabryczny   Funky performance art space in the down-at-heel Warsaw suburb of Praga (on the right side of the Vistula River). Praga is slowly, slowly gentrifying and places like this are drawing people here from all parts of the city. There's no regular program, and the opening hours are spotty, but Friday and Saturday nights usually offer something interesting in the form of DJs or live music. Otwocka 14. No phone.

ŁÓDŹ
110km (65 miles) SW of Warsaw

Poland's second-largest city's nickname is the "Manchester of Poland," a reference to Łódź's rise in the 19th century as an industrial powerhouse, and to the vast textile mills here that employed tens of thousands of workers at the turn of the 20th century. For Americans, the hulking relics and depressed housing stock of a bygone industrial era will bring to mind the inner cities of Detroit, Buffalo, and Cleveland. Still, there's an energy and vitality here that many Polish cities lack, and if you're passing by, Łódź certainly merits a full day of exploration. The city can be visited as a long day trip from Warsaw, but it's better approached as a destination in its own right. The prospect of some excellent restaurants and a couple of nice hotels sweetens the deal.

Łódź is relatively young as Polish cities go. It only came into its own in the 19th century, when German and later Jewish industrialists built large textile mills to exploit access to the vast Russian and Chinese markets to the east. Unlike Kraków or Wrocław, you'll search in vain here for a large market square, a Rynek, surrounded by gabled baroque and Renaissance houses. Instead, you'll find—amid the tenements and badly neglected housing stock—fine examples of the sumptuous neo-baroque and neoclassical mansions and town palaces favored by the wealthy 19th-century bourgeoisie.

By the start of the 20th century Łódź had grown from a village just a few decades earlier to a city of more than 300,000 people, and its factories, mansions, and civic institutions were among the finest in the country. It was a magnet for poor Poles from around the country, but above all it attracted Jews, drawn here by the relatively tolerant social climate and economic opportunity. At its height, the Jewish community numbered some 230,000 people, around a third of the city's immediate pre–World War II population.

But if the city's economic rise was rapid, its decline was precipitous as well. At the end of World War I, with the establishment of independent Poland, the city lost its privileged access to the Russian and Far Eastern markets. World War II, and the Nazi occupation, was an unmitigated disaster. While many of the buildings survived the war intact, nearly the entire Jewish population was wiped out—first herded into a massive ghetto north of the city center, and then shipped off train by train to the death camps at Chełmo and Auschwitz-Birkenau. For decades after the war, the story of the "Litzmannstadt" ghetto, as it was known at the time, was little known outside of Poland. Now, Jewish groups from around the world are getting the word out. You can tour much of the former ghetto as well as visit the Jewish cemetery, the largest of its kind in Europe.

The Communist period brought more ruin to the city. The once-profitable mills were run into the ground by inept state ownership. The city was blighted by some of the most insensitive Communist-era planning to ever come off the drawing board. The period since 1989 has seen a massive effort to transform the bleak postindustrial cityscape into a lively cultural center. And that effort is partially succeeding. The heart of the transformation is the city's main drag, Piotrkowska, a nearly 4km-long (2½-mile) pedestrianized strip, lined with restaurants, cafes, bars, clubs, and shops. By day, it's a place to stroll, window-shop, and take an open-air coffee. By night, it's arguably Poland's most intense street party, filled with raucous revelers swilling beer from cans as club music blares from behind nearly every door. Just to the north of the city center, the huge complex of former textile mills has now been transformed into Europe's biggest shopping and entertainment complex, Manufaktura.

Łódź also boasts one of Poland's best museums of modern art, and a clutch of other interesting museums, many housed in the mansions of the old industrial elite. For fans of international film, Łódź is home to the Poland's most highly regarded film school and the country's only Museum of Cinematography. Legendary Polish film directors Andrzej Wajda, Krzysztof Kieslowski, and Roman Polański, among others, all learned their craft here.

ESSENTIALS
GETTING THERE   Łódź lies at the geographic center of modern Poland and is well-served by roads, trains, and buses from around the country. Trains from Warsaw arrive and depart from the central Fabryczna station, a 10-minute walk from the center of town. Trains to other destination use Kaliska station (Ul. Unii Lubelskiej 3/5; ✆ 042/205-44-08). The main bus station (Pl. Salacińskiego 1; ✆ 042/631-97-06; www.pks.lodz.pl) is situated just behind Fabryczna train station.

VISITOR INFORMATION   The city of Łódź Tourist Information Center (Piotrkowska 87; ✆ 042/638-59-55; www.cityoflodz.pl) is one-stop shopping for all you'll ever need to know. Here you'll find two helpful pamphlets for negotiating the city: *Łódź Tourist Attractions* and the *Łódź City Guide,* as well as the essential *Jewish Landmarks in Łódź.* The latter includes a (long) self-guided walking tour of the Łódź (Litzmannstadt) ghetto. The staff maintains a complete list of hotels and can help arrange transportation and restaurant reservations.

GETTING AROUND   Łódź is a large city, with attractions clustered on both ends of the pedestrian strip, Piotrkowska. To walk its length takes about 45 minutes at a comfortable pace. You can also hire a pedicab driver, who will whisk you end to end in about 10 minutes for 5 zł ($1.65/90p). Piotrkowski is perfect for cycling, but rentals can be hard to find. Ask at the tourist information center. To reach the Jewish Cemetery and the Radegast station, take tram no. 1 or no. 6 to the end, or hail a cab. The taxi ride will cost about 12 zł ($4/£2.20).

WHERE TO STAY
The better places are all clustered around the center at Piotrkowska, but the area can get noisy at night. Ask for a room away from the main street. Rates are generally high for what's offered, but many hotels offer steep discounts on weekends.

Grand Hotel ⟨ If you're coming from Wrocław and you've seen the Monopol, this is Łódź's version: a faded turn-of-the-20th-century grande dame of a hotel that has fallen into benign neglect under the management of the former state-owned Orbis hotel chain. If you love those period Art Nouveau details, wide sweeping corridors, and generously sized rooms with high ceilings—and don't mind antiquated plumbing, indifferent service, and an inedible breakfast—then this is your place. The location is right at the heart of the pedestrian zone.

Piotrkowska 72. ✆ 042/633-99-20. Fax 042/633-78-76. www.orbis.pl. 161 units. 360 zł ($120/£65) double. AE, DC, MC, V. **Amenities:** Restaurant; limited room service; nonsmoking rooms. *In room:* TV, dataport, minibar, hair dryer.

Hotel Savoy ⟨⟨ This likably run-down turn-of-the-20th-century hotel is just down the street from the similar, but more expensive Grand Hotel. The Savoy feels smaller than the Grand and more intimate, though it's plainer. Many of the older period elements have been stripped away through wars and countless, often thoughtless, renovations. Ask to see several rooms, since they all differ slightly in furnishings. Some are jewels of the schlock 1960s and 1970s, while others try to re-create a 1920s feel. Choose your mood. Ask for a room away from the deceptively quiet-looking courtyard. At 6am, it becomes a veritable beehive of heavy construction work.

Traugutta 6. ✆ 042/632-93-60. Fax 042/632–93–68. 70 units. 250 zł ($83/£45) double. AE, DC, MC, V. **Amenities:** Restaurant; limited room service; nonsmoking rooms. *In room:* Some A/C, TV, hair dryer.

IBIS ✮✮ Łódź's most modern hotel and probably the best choice if you're mixing business with pleasure. The hotel offers relatively rare local amenities like full conference facilities, Internet access, and a dedicated business center. It's also a good choice in midsummer, since it's one of a handful of hotels in town to offer in-room air-conditioning. This is a standard IBIS hotel, meaning boxy, prefab rooms and sterile, impersonal lobby and reception area. Big weekend discounts.

Piłsudskiego 11. © 042/638-67-00. www.ibishotel.com. 208 units. Weekdays 270 zł ($90/£50) double; weekends 175 zł ($58/£46) double. AE, DC, MC, V. **Amenities:** Restaurant; limited room service; nonsmoking rooms. *In room:* A/C, TV, dataport, minibar, hair dryer.

WHERE TO DINE

You'll find most of the restaurants, including all of the big Polish chains like Rooster, Sphinx, and Sioux, grouped along Piotrkowska. Skip the chains and try one of the special places listed below.

Anatewka ✮✮ JEWISH Fun, informal Jewish-themed restaurant; the kind of place where the chef comes out halfway through the meal to pour you a shot of kosher vodka on the house. The two tiny, crowded dining rooms feel more like the parlor of a Jewish aunt, with overstuffed chairs and walls crammed with Jewish bric-a-brac. A fiddler, while not quite on the roof, plays nightly from a little perch just below the ceiling. The food is very good. The signature "Duck Rubenstein" comes served in a tart sauce of cherries, seasoned with clove.

Ul. 6 Sierpnia 2/4. © 042/630-36-35. Lunch and dinner items 18 zł–36 zł ($6–$12/£3.30–£6.50). AE, DC, MC, V. Daily noon–11pm.

Ciągoty i tęsknoty ✮✮✮ *Finds* INTERNATIONAL Don't despair as the taxi heads out of town, past row after row of falling-down, Socialist-era housing projects. You're headed toward one of the best meals in Łódź, and one of the city's best-kept dining secrets. Perched between two ghastly apartment blocks is a little oasis of '50s jazz and fresh flowers. The menu is perched somewhere between home cooking and haute cuisine, with salads, pierogies, pasta dishes, and some seriously good mains centered on pork, chicken, and boiled beef. The tagliatelle with brie and fresh tomatoes is a creative vegetarian option. It's about 3km (2 miles) from the center of town, so a taxi (12 zł/$4/£2) each way is the sanest option.

Wojska Polskiego 144a. © 042/650-87-94. Lunch and dinner items 18 zł–36 zł ($6–$12/£3.30–£6.50). AE, DC, MC, V. Mon–Fri noon–10pm; Sat–Sun 1–10pm.

Presto ✮✮ ITALIAN Much-better-than-average pizzeria, serving doughy pies topped with a slightly sweetish red sauce and cooked in a traditional wood-fired oven. The menu includes the usual suspects, but pizza "San Francisco" breaks new ground with bananas, pineapples, and curry sauce. A more reliable choice might be "Sparare," with bacon, mushrooms, and onions. Also offers a good range of salads and pasta dishes. Popular on Friday and Saturday nights because of its location in a little passageway just off of Łódź's main pedestrian walk. Service can be slow, so plan on a long evening.

Piotrkowska 67 (in the passageway). © 042/630-88-83. Lunch and dinner items 12 zł–21 zł ($4–$7/£2.20–£3.80). No credit cards. Daily noon–10pm.

Varoska ✮ HUNGARIAN What could be better than having a traditional Hungarian poerkoelt (a thick stew) or a chicken paprikas smack dab in the geographic center of Poland? If your taste buds need awakening after all of those pierogies, bite into one of those little red peppers that accompany every dish. The Hungarian "potato pancake" is a great and filling mix of pork goulash, sour cream, and snips of red pepper wrapped up in a fresh-baked potato pancake. The service is friendly, and the atmosphere somewhere between homey and intimate.

Traugutta 4. ⓒ **042/632-45-46.** Lunch and dinner items 18 zł–30 zł ($6–$10/£3.30–£5.50). No credit cards. Daily noon–10pm.

ŁÓDŹ

To get your bearings, start out at one end of Piotrkowska (it doesn't matter which) and walk from end to end. This is where it all happens in Łódź. Feel free to meander down the various side streets. You'll find houses and buildings in all states of repair and disrepair. It's an urban-rehabbers dream, and someday this all might be trendy shops and boutiques. In addition to the numerous pubs, restaurants, and coffee bars, Piotrkowska is lined up and down with turn-of-the-last-century *neo*-this, *neo*-that architectural gems. The house at no. 78 marks the birthplace of renowned pianist Artur Rubinstein, the city's most famous local son.

The former textile mills, now the Manufaktura shopping mall, as well as the History of Łódź museum and the former Jewish ghetto all lie to the north of the city center, beyond the terminus of Piotrkowska at the Plac Wolności, easily identified by the statue of Polish national hero Tadeusz Kościuszko at the center.

The Łódź Ghetto (Litzmannstadt) ☆☆ If one of your reasons for visiting Poland is to trace Jewish heritage, then you'll certainly want to explore what remains of the Łódź ghetto (known by its German name of Litzmannstadt), once the second-biggest urban concentration of Jews in Europe after the Warsaw ghetto. But be forewarned, not much of the former ghetto survived World War II and the area has been rebuilt with mostly prefab Communist housing blocks and shops. Much of a walking tour of the ghetto consists of weaving through drab and depressed streets, looking for hard-to-find memorial plaques and trying to imagine what life must have been like during what was a much different era.

The Litzmannstadt ghetto is one of the saddest and least-well-known stories of the war. The Germans first formed the ghetto in 1940, after invading Poland and incorporating the Łódź area into the German Reich. In all some 230,000 Jews from Łódź and around Europe were eventually moved here to live in cramped, appalling conditions. Next to the Jewish ghetto, the Nazis formed a second camp for several thousand Gypsies (Roma) brought here from Austria's Burgenland province. High walls and a system of heavily guarded steps and pathways allowed the detainees to move between various parts of the ghetto, but prevented anyone from entering or leaving. For a time, the ghetto functioned as a quasi-normal city, with the Jews more or less allowed to administer their own affairs in exchange for forced labor that contributed to the Nazi war effort. In 1944, with the approach of the end of the war, the Nazis stepped up their extermination campaign and began regular large-scale transports to death camps at Chełmno and Auschwitz. Some 200,000 Jews were eventually killed.

Begin the tour by picking up a copy of the brochure *Jewish Landmarks in Łódź*, available at the tourist information office on Piotrkowska. The walk starts north of the city center at the **Bałucki Rynek,** once the city's main market and the site of the German administration of the ghetto. You can find it by walking north along Piotrkowski, crossing the Plac Wolności, and continuing on through the park. From here the trail snakes along about 10km (6 miles), ending at the **Jewish Cemetery (Cmentarz Zły-dowski)**, the largest of its kind in Europe, and the **Radegast** train station, from where the transports to the extermination camps departed. The cemetery is open daily except Saturdays and has a small exhibition of photographs of Jewish life in Łódź and the ghetto. The Radegast station (about 15-min. walk north of the Jewish cemetery) has been restored to its appearance during the war, with three Deutsche Reichsbahn cattle cars ominously left standing on the tracks, the doors wide open.

After the war, a scattering of Jews returned to the city to try to rebuild a fraction of what they lost. Today, the Jewish population numbers around 5,000 from a pre–World War II population of nearly a quarter-million.

Jewish Cemetery (Cmentarz Złydowski). Ul. Bracka. Free admission. Sun–Fri 10am–4pm.

Łódź Art Museum (Muzeum Sztuki w Łódźi) ★★   A must for fans of modern art, from the functionalist, constructivist 1920s to the abstract 1950s and pop-art, op-art 1960s. The collection includes works by Marc Chagall and Max Ernst. Skip the first two floors and head straight for the museum's prize pieces on the third floor, including several of the young rake Witkacy's amazing society sketches from the 1920s.

Więckowskiego 36. ☎ 042/633-97-90. Admission 7 zł ($2.30/£1.25), free Thurs. Tues–Fri 10am–5pm; Sat–Sun 10am–4pm.

History of Łódź Museum ★   If you're intrigued by the city and want to know more, this is where to come. All about textiles, the history of the city's barons, a bit about Artur Rubinstein, and even information on Jewish Łódź, all housed in the sumptuous neo-baroque palace of Łódź industrialist par excellence, Izrael Kalmanowicz Poznański.

Ogrodowa 15. ☎ 042/633-97-90. www.poznanskipalace.muzeum-lodz.pl. Daily 10am–2pm; Wed 2–6pm.

Museum of Cinematography ★★   If you're a fan of international film, you'll want to stop by to pay tribute to Poland's panoply of great directors, including Roman Polański, Andrzej Wajda, and Krzysztof Kieslowski, all of whom studied and worked in Łódź. The museum's annual rotating exhibitions highlight the work of one of the directors, including stills and posters from the films and various memorabilia (2006 was Kieslowski's year, being the 10th anniversary of his death). The museum is housed in the former residence of one of the city's great capitalist barons, Karol Scheibler, and part of the fun is just poking around this incredible neo-baroque mansion.

Pl. Zwycięstwa 1. ☎ 042/674-09-57. www.kinomuzeum.pl. Admission 7 zł ($2.30/£1.25), free on Tues. Tues–Fri 10am–4pm; Sat–Sun 9am–4pm.

SHOPPING

Łódź offers one of the most unusual shopping opportunities in Poland and possibly all of Europe. In an effort to revitalize the city, the former textile mills have been reconstructed and converted into an enormous shopping mall and entertainment facility, **Manufaktura** (Jana Karskiego 5; ☎ 042/654-03-08; open daily 10am–9pm), complete with a 15-screen multiplex, a climbing wall, Europe's longest fountain at 300m (984 ft.), and an on-site sandpit for beach volleyball. The 19th-century redbrick factory architecture is stunning and the restoration work a model for similar reconstruction efforts around the country. If you're a fan of urban rehab or just want to spend the day at the mall, stop by and take a look.

AFTER DARK

Łódź is a shot-and-a-beer town in the best sense of the term, and if you're looking for a spot to drink, carouse, and club, you needn't go any farther than Piotrkowska: 4 km of restaurants, cafes, and bars that open early and close late. It might be the only city in Europe where you won't notice groups of drunken Brits on a stag party. The whole town, it seems, is on a stag-night blitz.

OLSZTYN & THE MAZURIAN LAKES
200km (120 miles) N of Warsaw

To the northeast of Warsaw, and stretching to the border with Russia (Kaliningrad) and Lithuania, lies an enormous expanse of lakes and interconnected waterways, the Mazurian lakes, that form one of the most popular summer vacation destinations for Poles. The medium-size city of Olsztyn (www.miasto.olsztyn.pl) is a pretty place in its own right, and makes for a good base for starting exploration of the lakes.

Olsztyn was founded in the 14th century by the Teutonic Knights, but passed into Polish hands a century later. It fell under Prussian control at the end of the 18th century and until World War II, the population was mostly German. Much of the city was destroyed during the war and its ethnic-German population expelled.

The lake district proper begins in Mrągowo, about 50km (30 miles) east of Olsztyn. The most popular, and arguably the nicest, lakeside town is Mikołajki (70km/42 miles from Olsztyn), just above Lake Śniardwy. Giżycko and Węgorzewo, to the north, are also comfortable lakeside resorts. One of the most popular activities in the lakes region is canoeing, and several organizers run multiday (1- and 2-week) paddle trips throughout the region, with the day spent out on the water and accommodations at night in simple bunks at canoe-rental outlets along the way. In summer, regular ferries also glide between the resorts.

ESSENTIALS

GETTING THERE   Olsztyn lies on major Polish rail and bus lines and is easily accessible from nearly anywhere in the country. Figure on about 2 to 3 hours by bus or train from Warsaw. It's also a relatively easy, though often crowded drive from the capital. Figure on 3 hours behind the wheel.

VISITOR INFORMATION   Olsztyn's indispensable tourist information office (Staromiejska 1; ✆ **089/5353-5-65;** www.warmia-mazury-rot.pl; daily 9am–5pm) is the first port of call for all kinds of information on exploring the lakes region. The office provides city and regional maps, as well as can help advise on where to stay and find rooms. They can also help arrange canoe and other boat trips, and bike trips around the lakes. Unfortunately, the staff speaks only halting English; German is more useful in this part of the country owing to the area's historical ties to Germany. You'll find the office just to the left of the big gate before you enter the Old Town.

GETTING AROUND   Olsztyn's Old Town (Stare Miasto) is small, and once you've arrived from the bus or train station, walking is the best option. The bus and train stations are located about 1.6km (1 mile) from town. You can walk into town in about 20 minutes, or grab nearly any public bus, or a taxi (about 10 zł/$3.30/£1.80).

For travel farther on to the lakes in the east, you have the option of taking either the train or the bus to resorts like Mrągowo and Mikołajki. Buses are often but not always the quickest option. The tourist information office can help with the latest

The Wolf's Lair

Hidden among the beautiful Mazurian lakes is a fascinating and creepy place that you should certainly seek out if you're in the area. Near the little town of Kętrzyn, north of Mrągowo, lies the bombed-out remains of Hitler's eastern command base, the "Wolf's Lair." It's best known as the site of a 1944 attempt on Hitler's life that very nearly succeeded and might well have changed the course of history.

The Wolf's Lair was in fact a large camp of reinforced-concrete bunkers, some with walls as thick as 8m (25 ft.). The top Nazi leadership, including Hitler and Hermann Goering, maintained their own personal bunkers. Additionally, there were bunkers for communications and troop commands, a train station, an airstrip, and even a casino bunker. Hitler was a frequent visitor to the Wolf's Lair from its initial construction in 1941 until 1944, when it was abandoned just ahead of the Russian advance as the war drew to a close. In January 1945, the Germans dynamited the bunkers to prevent them from falling into enemy hands. This is what you see today. The bunkers have been preserved in their original "destroyed" state, and you're more or less free to walk among the jarring, jagged concrete ruins sitting incongruously amid beautiful forest.

The details of the assassination read like a spy thriller. The would-be assassin, an officer of aristocratic bearing named Claus Schenk von Stauffenberg, by 1944 had come to see the war as unwinnable. He and other likeminded officers believed that if Germany had any hope of avoiding total annihilation, Hitler had to be stopped. On July 20, 1944, Von Stauffenberg was dispatched to the Wolf's Lair to brief the *Fuehrer* and other top Nazi leaders on troop levels on the Eastern Front. He arrived at the meeting with a time bomb hidden in his briefcase. Just before the meeting started, he placed the briefcase near Hitler, activated the bomb, and immediately left

transportation advice. The bus station itself maintains a relatively user-friendly timetable.

WHERE TO STAY

Olsztyn has a range of nice hotels, with most concentrated in and around the Old Town.

Expensive

Hotel Warmiński ★★   A crisp and clean, high-rise business hotel, nicely situated between the train station and the Old Town, about a 10- to 15-minute walk from both. The service is impersonal but efficient. Amenities include local rarities like a massage and fitness room, covered parking (for a fee), and in-room Internet access (LAN connection). The buffet breakfast is a treat, with a full range of Polish appetizers like salted herring, pâté, and homemade sausage on hand. The chef will whip up an omelet on the spot. The hotel occasionally runs special offers that include a buffet supper in the room price.

the room. The resulting explosion eventually killed four people, but not Hitler. One of the generals had moved the briefcase just before it exploded, unwittingly saving the *Fuehrer's* life.

Von Stauffenberg quickly flew back to Berlin believing the assassination attempt had succeeded. Once Hitler recovered from his minor injuries, he ordered Von Stauffenberg's arrest and the rounding up of anyone and everyone who might have been involved in the plot. Von Stauffenberg was executed by firing squad later that night. The Nazis eventually arrested some 7,000 people on suspected involvement in the coup attempt, though many of these people had no prior knowledge of the plot and nothing to do it. Some 5,000 people were executed.

From Olsztyn you can get to the Wolf's Lair by taking a bus or train (about an hour in summer) to Kętrzyn, and then taking a bus from the combined bus/train station there 8km (5 miles) to the village of Gierłoż. You can also take a taxi from Kętrzyn station to Gierłoż. The fare will run about 25 zł ($8.35/£4.75) one-way. If you're driving, follow the signs to Kętrzyn and then farther to Gierłoż. If you get lost, ask for directions at the Kętrzyn tourist information office (Pl. Piłsudskiego 1; © 089/751-47-65; daily 9am–6pm). They maintain a mimeographed map with driving directions (it's the most frequent question they handle).

Once there you can buy a map of the grounds for 5 zł ($1.70/90p) and walk the red- and yellow-marked paths that connect the bunker ruins. If you're really interested in the history, hire a private guide to take you around. Guides start at around 50 zł ($17/£9).

Wolf's Lair ("Wolfschanze" in German, "Wilczy Szaniec" in Polish). Gierłoż (8km/5 miles east of Kętrzyn). Open Tuesday to Sunday 9am to 6pm. Admission 8 zł ($2.65/£1.40), parking 8 zł ($2.65/£1.40).

Kolobrzeska 1. © **089/522-14-00.** Fax 089/533-67-63. www.hotel-warminski.com.pl. 135 units. 290 zł ($96/£50) double. AE, DC, MC, V. **Amenities:** Restaurant; exercise room; limited room service; massage; dry cleaning; nonsmoking rooms. *In room:* TV, dataport, minibar, hair dryer.

Moderate

Hotel Kopernik ⭐ Nicer than the Gromada, and a decent low-budget pick if you can't get in at the Hotel Pod Zamkiem. The Kopernik began life as a Socialist-era block of houses or apartments, but a total makeover and a fresh coat of paint have given it a modern, efficient feel. The rooms are small, but are clean and the mattresses thicker than government-issue. The location is a bit out-of-the-way, beyond the Old Town if you are approaching from the train and bus stations. Take a bus into the center and walk a couple of minutes, or take a taxi from the station for about 10 zł ($3.30/£1.75).

Warszawska 37. © **089/522-99-29.** Fax 089/527-93-92. www.kopernik.olsztyn.pl. 62 units. 195 zł ($65/£35) double. AE, DC, MC, V. **Amenities:** Restaurant; nonsmoking rooms. *In room:* TV, hair dryer.

Hotel Pod Zamkiem ★★ *(Finds)* This is a nicely restored three-story, *Jugendstil* villa, just a short walk from the castle. The villa once belonged to the head of the local stonemasons, and since 1989 has been on the registry of historic places. You'll love the high-beam ceilings, the dark wood trim and the Secessionist/Art Nouveau detailing carved into the wood. The rooms can't match the high styling, but are cozy, and some are filled with antique wardrobes and beds. Once you've checked in, have a drink in the garden under 100-year-old trees.

Nowowiejskiego 10. © **089/535-12-87**. Fax 089/534-09-40. www.hotel-olsztyn.com.pl. 15 units. 190 zł ($63/£35) double. AE, DC, MC, V. **Amenities:** Restaurant. *In room:* TV.

Inexpensive

Hotel Gromada A tired-looking, 1970s-era high-rise, just across from the train and bus stations, this is nevertheless an acceptable option if you're just passing through or arriving late and don't want to deal with transportation into the city. The inside is sterile, but cheerier and better maintained than the outside. The rooms are modern, small, and clean, with a kind of dormitory-for-grown-ups feel about the place.

Pl. Konstytucji 3. © **089/534-63-30**. Fax 089/534-58-64. 96 units. 168 zł ($56/£30) double. AE, DC, MC, V. **Amenities:** Restaurant. *In room:* TV.

WHERE TO DINE

The Old Town is filled with quick-bite and fast-food options, but if you have time for a real meal, try one of the places below.

Oh Give Me a Home, Where the Bison Still Roam . . .

Primeval forests and wild herds of bison in Poland? That's right. Those buffalo heads on the sides of bottles of Żubr beer and fifths of Żubrówka vodka are not just marketing ploys. Poland is home to Europe's largest surviving herd of ancient bison. As in North America, bison were once ubiquitous on the landscape of Europe, but through overhunting and habitat encroachment, their numbers were sharply reduced. Now it's estimated Europe's herd has no more than a thousand or so animals—and many of them call Poland home.

You can see the bison at a remarkable national park that also holds some of Europe's last remaining parcels of primeval forest. The Białowieża National Park (Białowieski Park Narodowy; www.bpn.com.pl) covers some 1,000 sq. km (390 sq. miles) and since 1980 has been on the UNESCO list of World Natural Heritage sites. In addition to around 250 head of bison, the park shelters large populations of deer, boar, elk, beaver, and wolf, as well as hundreds of species of birds and countless numbers of species of plant life. Something like 400 different types of lichen alone have been found in the park.

The park makes for a remarkable side trip. A separate nearby bison reserve (see location details below), also has on display large populations of horses, boar, and deer, and is great for kids.

Karczma Jana ✸✸✸ POLISH   Outstanding Polish food is served in a lovely cottage-style atmosphere in the Old Town just at the foot of the river. Don't expect lightning service, especially on the terrace in summer, but you wouldn't want to rush anyway. For something a little different, try the beef rolls, served with sides of spiced beets and buckwheat groats. The kind of place where the waiter might bring a plate of pâtés as an *amuse-bouche*.

Kołłątaja 11. ✆ **089/522-29-46**. Lunch and dinner items 18 zł–27 zł ($6–$9/£3.30–£5). AE, DC, MC, V. Daily 11am–10pm.

Via Napoli ✸ ITALIAN   Very unlike your typical Polish pizza joint—meaning it's much more upscale (but not more expensive), with a clean, modern decor and a nicer range of salads, pizzas, and pastas. At the same time, the attitude is casual and reservations don't seem to be a problem. In summer, sit on the terrace in the back overlooking the river.

Okopowa 21. ✆ **089/522-99-99**. Lunch and dinner items 15 zł–21 zł ($5–$7/£2.70–£3.70). AE, DC, MC, V. Daily 11am–10pm.

EXPLORING

Much of the Old Town, Stare Miasto, was destroyed during World War II. Though it was rebuilt in a traditional style, it retains a modern, 1960s-to-1970s feel. That's not to say it's not a pleasant place to linger for a few hours. The streets toward the Łyna river are particularly nice and atmospheric. Most of the sites in town center on the 14th-century **Castle** (Zamkowa 2; ✆ **089/527-95-96**; www.muzeum.olsztyn.pl), originally built by the Teutonic Knights but thoroughly rebuilt since, tucked in behind the Old Town. You can climb to the top of the tower for a commanding view of the town and surroundings. A small museum (June–Sept Tues–Sun 9am–5pm; Oct–May Tues–Sun 10am–4pm) can fill you in on the region's Polish history, and there's a small room in the castle where the astronomer and jack-of-all-trades Copernicus once lived. He once apparently commanded a Polish garrison here while under siege by the Teutonic Knights.

AFTER DARK

For a relatively small city Olsztyn has a lively nightlife. Most of the better clubs and cafes are in the Old Town, on the streets just along the riverbank and near the castle. The area is pretty small, so just take a walk and see if any places appeal. For music and occasionally live acts, try the **Bohema Jazz Club** (Targ Rybny 15; ✆ **0604/483-789**). For coffee or a quiet drink, head for the **Awangarda** (Stare Miasto 23; ✆ **089/527-28-27**) coffee bar, next to the cinema of the same name. The cozy "retro-rialto" interior, done up to look like an old cinema, is fun. One wall is given over to photos of Marilyn Monroe.

The center of the action is the village of Białowieża, about 80km (50 miles) southeast of the industrial city of Białystok. Here you'll find the main park office as well as several decent hotels and restaurants for an overnight stay.

While much of the park is open to the public, some of the more valuable areas of primeval forest are restricted and can only be visited with a registered guide. You can hire guides (165 zł/$55/£30 per group of up to 20 people) at the main park office. The tour, on foot, takes about 3 hours and covers 3km to 4km (about 2 miles) of ground (liberally interspersed with lively stories about the park's origins and animal and plant life). You can also enter the park via horse-drawn cart. Expect to pay up to 145 zł ($48/£25) for a cart that holds four people.

The forest at Białowieża was known through the centuries as a prized hunting ground, and survived relatively intact for this very reason. It was a favored spot of the Polish and Russian nobility. The park had some rough years during World War II and immediately after, but appears to be thriving now.

Park Palacowy (to enter the park and hire a guide), Białowieża (entrance near the Best Western hotel). ✆ 085/ 681-22-5. Mon–Fri 8am–4pm; Sat–Sun 8am–3pm. Rezerwat Pokazowy Żubrów (the entrance to the bison reserve), Białowieża (entrance 4km/2 miles from town along the road to Hajnówka). Tues–Sun 9am–5pm.

4 Kraków

300km (180 miles) S of Warsaw

Kraków, the capital of the Polish region of Małopolska, is one of the most beautiful cities in central Europe and a highlight on any tour of the region. The city escaped serious damage during World War II and its only real regional rival for pure drop-dead beauty is the Czech capital, Prague. The formal perfection of its enormous central square, the Rynek Główny, as well as the charm of the surrounding streets and Wawel Castle have always been known to Poles. (In fact, Kraków remains the number-one domestic tourist destination). But now the word on Kraków has spread far and wide, and the city is firmly (and justifiably) established on the main central European tourism axis that includes Vienna, Budapest, and Prague.

That's good news for visitors. It means decent plane, rail, and bus connections from any point north, south, or west of the city (although to be honest, the rail connection from the south would be much better if you didn't have to change trains in Katowice). It also means some of the best restaurants and hotels in Poland, and a city that's fully accustomed to catering to the needs of visitors.

Kraków's precise origins are unclear, but the city first rose to prominence at the turn of the first millennium as a thriving market town. The enormous size of the Rynek attests to Kraków's early importance, even if its exact origins are unknown. One story about Kraków's founding has it that a poor man named "Krak" started the whole thing by slaying a dragon that was ravaging the early inhabitants. Krak allegedly felled the beast by filling an animal carcass with sulfur (or lye) and tricking the beast to eat it. Naturally, so the story goes, he was awarded great wealth and a city, "Krak-ów," named after him.

But frankly, I'm a bit skeptical. The city of Brno, in the Czech Republic, has a similar myth about *its* early days. And it's hard to imagine there were that many beasts running around, as well as clever men with bags of sulfur on hand to the job. What is clear is that by the time of the early Piast dynasty in the 11th century, Kraków was booming, and Wawel Hill, with its commanding view of the Vistula River, was a natural setting for a capital.

As befitting any medieval city, Kraków had its ups and downs. In the 13th century, the city was razed to the ground by the central Asian Tartars, but was quickly rebuilt (and parts remain remarkably unchanged to this day). Kraków's heyday was arguably the mid–14th century when King Kazimierz the Great commissioned many of the city's finest buildings and established Jagellonian University, the second university to be founded in central Europe after Prague's Charles University. For more than 5 centuries,

Kraków served as the seat of the Polish kingdom (it only lost out to the usurper Warsaw in 1596 after the union with Lithuania made the Polish-Lithuanian kingdom so large that it became difficult for distant noblemen to travel here).

Kraków started to decline around this time. Following the Polish partitions at the end of the 18th century, Kraków eventually fell under the domination of Austria-Hungary, and was ruled from Vienna. It became the main city in the new Austrian province of Galicia, but had to share some of the administrative duties with the eastern city of Lwów (which must have quite a climb down for a former Polish capital!).

Viennese rule proved to be a boon in its own right. The Habsburgs were far more liberal in their views than either the Prussians or czarist Russia, and the relative tolerance here fostered a Polish cultural renaissance that lasted well into the 20th century. Kraków was the base of the late-19th and early-20th-century Młoda Polska (Young Poland) movement, a revival of literature, art, and architecture (often likened to "Art Nouveau") that is still fondly remembered to this day.

Kraków had traditionally been viewed as a haven for Jews ever since the 14th century when King Kazimierz first opened Poland to Jewish settlement. The Kraków district named for the king, Kazimierz, began life as a separate Polish town, but through the centuries slowly acquired the characteristics of a traditional Jewish quarter. By the 19th and early 20th centuries Kazimierz was one of the leading Jewish settlements in central Europe, lending Kraków a unique dimension as a center of both Catholic and Jewish scholarship.

World War II drastically altered the city and for all intents and purposes ended this Jewish cultural legacy. The Nazis made Kraków the nominal capital of their rump Polish state: the "General Gouvernement." The Nazi governor, and later war criminal, Hans Frank, ruled brutally from atop Wawel Castle. One of the first Nazi atrocities was to arrest and eventually execute the Polish faculty of Jagellonian University. Not long after the start of the war, the Nazis expelled the Jews from Kazimierz, first placing them in a confined ghetto space at Podgórze, about a mile south of Kazimierz, and later deporting nearly all of them to death camps. (As a historical aside: Frank was prosecuted at the Nuremburg trials and executed in 1946.)

Kraków luckily escaped destruction at the end of the war, but fared poorly in the postwar decades under the Communist leadership. The Communists never liked the city, probably because of its royal roots and intellectual and Catholic pretensions. For whatever reason they decided to place their biggest postwar industrial project, the enormous Nowa Huta steelworks, just a couple of miles upwind from the Old Town. Many argue the intention was to win over the skeptical Kraków intellectuals to the Communist side, but the noise, dirt, and smoke from the mills, not surprisingly, had the opposite effect. The new workers were slow to embrace Communism, and during those wretched days of the 1970s, when a series of food price hikes galvanized workers around the country, the city was suddenly transformed into a hotbed of anti-Communist activism.

Kraków will be forever linked with its most famous favorite son, Pope John Paul II. The pope, Karol Woytyła, was born not far from Kraków, in the town of Wadowice, and rose up through the church hierarchy here, serving for many years as the archbishop of the Kraków diocese before being elevated to pope in 1978. If Gdańsk and the Solidarity trade union provided the industrial might of the anti-Communist movement, then Kraków and Pope John Paul II were the movement's spiritual heart.

The pope's landmark trip to Poland in 1979, shortly after being elected pontiff, ignited a long-dormant Polish spirit and united the country in opposition to the Soviet-imposed government.

Kraków's charms are multidimensional. In addition to the beautifully restored Old Town, complete with its fairy-tale castle, there's the former Jewish quarter of Kazimierz. If you've seen Steven Spielberg's Oscar-winning movie *Schindler's List,* you'll recognize many of the film locations as you walk around Kazimierz. For anyone unfamiliar with the film (or the book on which it was based, Thomas Keneally's *Schindler's Ark*), Oskar Schindler was a German industrialist who operated an enamel factory during World War II. By employing Jews from the nearby ghetto, he managed to spare the lives of 1,100 people who otherwise would have gone to the death camps at Auschwitz. Schindler's factory, now closed down, is still standing (there are plans afoot eventually to open a museum). At the moment it's derelict and perhaps all the more fascinating for that. You can poke your nose in and wander around; occasionally kids are on hand to take visitors on an impromptu tour.

Outside of central Kraków, there are several trips that merit a few hours or a full day of sightseeing. The most important of these is the former Nazi extermination camp at Auschwitz-Birkenau (in the town of Oświęcim, about 81km/50 miles to the west of the city). Also recommended is a trip to the unusual and unforgettable Wieliczka salt mines. And if you've got time and a penchant for modern architecture, check out the Nowa Huta steelworks and the amazing Socialist-Realist housing project built around the mills.

GETTING THERE

BY PLANE   John Paul II International Airport (© **012/639-30-00;** www.lotnisko-balice.pl) is located in the suburb of Balice, about 10km (6 miles) from town. The airport is easily reachable by bus or taxi. Radtur (© **012/423-5499;** www.radtur.pl) operates a shuttle in summer between the airport and the bus station for 7 zł ($2.30/£1.20) each way. The shuttle runs each way about once an hour between 10am and 8pm. For a taxi, expect to pay about 50 zł–60 zł ($20/£11) for a ride into town.

BY TRAIN   Kraków's main train station, the Dworzec Główny (pl. Kolejowy; © 012/393-11-11; www.pkp.Kraków.pl) is about 20 minutes' walk from the center of the city. Kraków is well served by rail and departures for Warsaw and other major cities are frequent. The rail distance from Warsaw is about 5 hours. Note that travel to international destinations like Prague often require you to change trains in Katowice.

BY BUS   Kraków's newly opened central bus station (ul. Bosacka) is located just behind the main train station and is an easy walk or relatively cheap taxi ride to the center of town.

BY CAR   Kraków lies on the main east-west highway, the A4, running through southern Poland. It's nearly a straight 3-hour shot on mostly four-lane highway from the German border, through the cities of Wrocław and Katowice. You'll have to pay a toll of 6 zł from Katowice, but for the speed and convenience (compared to other roads in Poland) it's a bargain at twice the price. From other directions, including from Warsaw or points south, you'll have to contend with much smaller roads and longer drive times. Once in Kraków, stow the car since it's unlikely to help you navigate the city's small, tram-clogged roads.

CITY LAYOUT

Kraków's Old Town is relatively compact and comprised of the main square (Rynek Główny) and the streets that radiate from it in all directions (bordered by what remains of the medieval town walls and the circular park, the Planty). Most of the main tourist sites are situated within a 10- or 15-minute walk from the square.

The Wawel castle district comprises a second major tourist destination and is a 10-minute walk south of the main square, following Grodzka street.

The former Jewish ghetto of Kazimierz lies about a 20-minute walk south of the main square beyond the castle. To save time, it's possible to take a taxi from the Old Town to Kazimierz. Expect to pay about 15 zł ($5/£2.60). A number of trams also make the run between the two.

GETTING AROUND

ON FOOT   Much of Kraków is closed to traffic, so walking is often the only option. Distances are manageable.

BY TRAM   Kraków is well served by a comprehensive tram network, and this is a quick and easy way to reach more far-flung destinations. Try to avoid tram travel at rush hour unless you enjoy getting pressed up against the doors like you're in the Tokyo subway. A ticket costs 2.50 zł (80¢/45p) and can be bought at newspaper kiosks around town. Validate your ticket on entering the tram and hold onto it until the end of the ride.

BY BUS   Like trams, buses ply Kraków's streets from early morning until after 11pm or so and are a vital part of the city's transit network. You probably won't need to use the buses unless your hotel is well outside the city center. A ticket costs 2.50 zł (80¢/45p) and can be bought at newspaper kiosks around town. Validate your ticket on entering the tram and hold onto it until the end of the ride.

BY TAXI   Taxis are relatively cheap and a dependable means of getting around. You can hail taxis on the street or at special taxi stands around town. The fare for a typical hop, such as from the Old Town to Kazimierz, will average 15 zł to 20 zł ($5–$6.80/£2.60–£3.60).

BY BIKE   Biking is becoming increasingly popular, and there are now bike lanes scattered around town, including a nice run along the Vistula river and through the park, the Planty, that rings the main square. That said, biking is a better bet for an hour or two of sightseeing rather than as a practical means for getting around. Kraków Bike Tours (© **0663/731-515**) offers fun and instructional 2-hour bike tours in season in the afternoons and evenings.

VISITOR INFORMATION

The city of Kraków maintains an extensive and helpful network of tourist information offices around town in all of the tourist hot spots, including an office in the former Jewish quarter of Kazimierz. Here you'll find some excellent brochures, including one called the *Tourist Information Compendium* and another *Two Days in Kraków*. They also have excellent free maps, a wealth of suggestions, and can help find and book hotel rooms. Note that the Kazimierz office is (inexplicably) closed on weekends. The main offices are located at the following addresses:

Town Hall Tower (Main Square) (© 012/433-73-10; daily 9am–7pm)
Św. Jana 2 (Old Town) (© 012/421-77-87; Mon–Sat 10am–6pm)

John Paul II International Airport (© 012/285–53–41; daily 10am–6pm)
Szpitalna 25 (Old Town) (© 012/432–01–10; Mon–Sat 9am–7pm, Sun 9am–5pm)
Józefa 7 (Kazimierz) (© 012/422–04–71; Mon–Fri 10am–4pm)

WHERE TO STAY

Kraków has some beautiful hotels, and if you've got the cash and want to splurge, you can do so in real style. Most of the stunning properties are located in the Old Town, along the streets running off the Main Square or tucked in a quiet park location off the Planty. A second cluster of decent places to stay is in Kazimierz. You won't find the five-star luxury class here like in the Old Town, but there are a number of nice three- and four-star properties that are, on balance, a little cheaper and quieter than their Old Town counterparts. As for location, both are excellent. An Old Town property puts you just a few steps away from the restaurants and cafes around the square, as well as Kraków's main museums and sites. On the other hand, if you're into bars, clubs, and trendy restaurants, then Kazimierz is where you want to be. Either way, the distances between the two are not great, just a 15-minute walk or short cab ride.

Rates are generally highest between April 1 and October 31, as well as over the Christmas and New Year's holidays. Room prices drop by 10% to 20% from November through March. The prices below are for a standard double room (twin beds) in high season (outside of the Christmas and New Year's holiday season).

VERY EXPENSIVE

Amadeus ★★★ A fully modern hotel, working hard—and succeeding—at re-creating an 18th-century feel. For the room interiors, think Colonial Williamsburg, with intricately carved white woodworking in the beds and nightstands, chandeliers, and floor-to-ceiling floral print drapes. Mozart could actually drop by and feel quite at home. The service is top-notch and the location, just a couple feet off the main square, is ideal. A perfect choice if you want a hotel that will stick in your mind as long as Kraków's main square does.

Mikołajska 20. © **012/429-60-70.** Fax 012/429-60-72. www.hotel-amadeus.pl. 22 units. 540 zł ($180/£95) double. AE, DC, MC, V. **Amenities:** Restaurant; fitness club; sauna; limited room service; nonsmoking rooms. *In room:* A/C, TV, dataport, minibar, hair dryer.

Copernicus ★★★ Widely considered the best address in town; certainly the best of the boutique-size properties. Managed by the international Relais & Châteaux chain, and the polish shows. You'll be charmed immediately by the enormous Renaissance atrium shooting to the ceiling, and the period detailing—from the 16th century—that extends throughout the hotel and to the wood-beamed ceilings in the rooms on the first and second floors. A fresco, the *Four Fathers of the Church,* dating from the year 1500, covers the wall in room no. 101. U.S. President George W. Bush and his wife, Laura, stayed here in 2003.

Kanonicza 16. © **012/424-34-00.** Fax 012/424-34-05. www.hotel.com.pl. 29 units. 850 zł ($283/£150) double. AE, DC, MC, V. **Amenities:** Restaurant; indoor pool; sauna; room service; nonsmoking rooms. *In room:* A/C, TV, dataport, minibar, hair dryer, safe.

Sheraton Kraków ★★★ This is a relatively recent addition to the high-end corporate market, but is already setting standards as arguably the best business hotel in the city. Everything is conceived with comfort and convenience in mind all the way

Grodzka 9. ℭ **012/429-54-10.** Fax 012/429-55-76. www.rthotels.pl. 59 units. 400 zł ($133/£70) double. MC, V. **Amenities:** Nonsmoking rooms. *In room:* Some A/C, TV, dataport, minibar, hair dryer.

MODERATE

Hotel Eden ⭐⭐   A good second choice in Kazimierz at this price level if you can't get in at the Karmel (see below). It's similar in many ways, well maintained and quiet, but not quite as immediately charming. The rooms are modestly furnished and on the plain side, more functional than inspiring. Uniquely, the Eden has a "salt grotto" spa in the basement, using salt brought in from Pakistan. The idea is for you to sit in the special saline air for 45 minutes to reduce stress and heal a multitude of ills, ranging from asthma to tonsillitis to acne. Once you've cured whatever ails you, head around the corner to the local pub called (not kidding): "Ye Olde Goat."

Ciemna 15. ℭ **012/430-65-65.** Fax 012/430-67-67. www.hoteleden.pl. 15 units. 350 zł ($117/£65) double. AE, DC, MC, V. **Amenities:** Restaurant; spa; room service; nonsmoking rooms. *In room:* A/C, TV, dataport, minibar, hair dryer.

Hotel Karmel ⭐⭐⭐ *Finds*   By far the most charming and inviting of Kazimierz's hotels and pensions. Maybe it's the quiet location, in a forgotten spot in the former ghetto, or the flowers hanging off the house windows, or the cute Italian restaurant on the ground floor. Something about the hotel says "home." Parquet flooring throughout. Splurge on a "comfort" room, with a big double bed and a couple of sofas in the room.

Kupa 15. ℭ **012/430-66-97.** Fax 012/430-67-26. www.karmel.com.pl. 15 units. 300 zł ($100/£55) double; 360 zł ($120/£65) double "comfort." AE, DC, MC, V. **Amenities:** Restaurant; room service; nonsmoking rooms. *In room:* A/C, TV, dataport, minibar, hair dryer.

Hotel Kazimierz ⭐   Probably the most popular hotel in Kraków's former Jewish quarter, but not necessarily the best. The plain lobby and public areas are redeemed somewhat by a beautiful, enclosed inner courtyard. The rooms too are nothing special, but are clean and comfortable. The location is superb, near the entrance to the former Jewish quarter, but also not far from Wawel and the Old Town. They sometimes lower the rates on weekends, so ask when you book.

Miodowo 16. ℭ **012/421-66-29.** Fax 012/422-28-84. www.hk.com.pl. 35 units. 280 zł ($93/£48) double. AE, DC, MC, V. **Amenities:** Restaurant; room service; nonsmoking rooms. *In room:* Some A/C, TV, dataport, minibar, hair dryer.

Hotel Saski ⭐⭐ *Finds*   Kraków residents might laugh at this hotel being labeled a "find" since it's one of the best-known hotels in the city, right off the main square. But what many don't realize is that it's at least 100 zł ($33/£18) a night less than other hotels in its class and location. So if you're looking for a glorious old hotel, with a tiled-floor lobby and chandeliers, in the center of town and don't want to shell out major cash, this your place. Ask to see several rooms since they are all different—some are quite modern and border on the plain, while others are in high period style with quaint, old-fashioned beds and tables.

Sławkowska 3. ℭ **012/421-42-22.** Fax 012/421-48-30. www.hotel-saski.com.pl. 20 units. 265 zł ($88/£48) double without bathroom; 360 zł ($120/£65) with bathroom. AE, DC, MC, V. **Amenities:** Restaurant; room service; nonsmoking rooms. *In room:* Some A/C, TV, dataport, minibar, hair dryer.

INEXPENSIVE

Nathan's Villa Hostel ⭐⭐   The American owner of this well-run and highly regarded hostel just across from Wawel Castle says his aim is to combine the social aspects of a hostel with the amenities you'd expect from a hotel. And at this price he definitely gets it right. In addition to the standard 8- and 10-bed rooms typical for a hostel, Nathan's rents out private doubles. In summer most of the guests are backpackers, but during the rest of the year, the hostel fills up with people of all age groups looking to save money while not sacrificing on location or cleanliness. Perks include free laundry, an Internet room, and a DVD movie room in case you get a rainy day.

Sw. Agnieszki 1. © 012/422-35-45. www.nathansvilla.com. 20 units. 160 zł ($53/£30) double. MC, V. **Amenities:** Bar; laundry service; nonsmoking rooms.

U Pana Cogito ★★ *Value* If you don't mind walking, this renovated villa complex, about 15 to 20 minutes by foot from the city center, represents real value. The modern rooms, done up in neutral beige and gold, have all of the personality of a standard Holiday Inn, but they're clean and quiet, with nicely done bathrooms and unexpected touches at this price point like air-conditioning in the rooms and full Internet access (LAN connection).

Bałuckiego 6. © 012/269-72-00. Fax 012/269-72-02. www.pcogito.pl. 14 units. 250 zł ($83/£45) double. AE, DC, MC, V. **Amenities:** Restaurant; nonsmoking rooms. *In room:* A/C, TV, dataport, minibar, hair dryer.

WHERE TO DINE

Most of the fancier and more established restaurants are in the Old Town on the main square or along the streets running off the square, particularly to the south. The newer, trendier, and sometimes better places are located in Kazimierz. One area in the former ghetto to look is along Plac Nowy; the other dining cluster, including most of the Jewish-themed restaurants, is along Szeroka. Except for the very pricey places in the Old Town, dress is mostly casual. That's particularly true of the Kazimierz locales, which cater to a largely student and young professional crowd. Note that though many restaurants claim to stay open until 11pm or midnight, on slow nights it's not unusual for kitchens to start closing down at 10pm. Go early to avoid disappointment.

VERY EXPENSIVE

Cyrano de Bergerac ★★ FRENCH It's such a pleasure to taste Polish food with a French twist when it's done this well. That means staples like game, pork, and duck, but with a nuance. The duck, for example, isn't served with apple or cranberry, but caramelized peach and cardamom instead. The pork knuckle is candied in honey—the glazing giving it a sweetish barbecue flavor. The brick exposed interior is stunning, with candlelight and white linens on the table. The service is polished, but can be slow on busy nights. Beware the prices on wines, with many bottles pushing the $60-to-$90 range. Dress for this one and reserve in advance.

Sławkowska 26. © 012/411-72-88. Lunch and dinner items 42 zł–90 zł ($14–$30/£7.50–£16). AE, DC, MC, V. Mon–Sat noon–midnight.

Edo Sushi Bar ★★★ JAPANESE One of the best sushi restaurants in central Europe is on a quiet corner in Kazimierz. The hushed, spare, modern decor puts the emphasis firmly on the food. Very fresh nigiri sushi and some creative maki rolls keep the crowds happy. My favorite is the "rainbow roll"—an all-in-one sushi medley—washed down with a glass of Polish beer, which pairs surprisingly well with the fish.

Bożego Ciała 3. © 0661/316-607. Lunch and dinner items 30 zł–48 zł ($10–$16/£5.50–£9). AE, DC, MC, V. Daily 11am–10pm.

EXPENSIVE

Klezmer Hois ✸✸ JEWISH   Arguably the best of the Jewish-themed restaurants that line Szeroka in Kazimierz. The "Fiddler on the Roof" motif has become big business in the former Jewish quarter in recent years, and what often happens is that the food part gets lost in the klezmer shuffle. Luckily that's not happened here. There's not much recognizably Jewish or kosher on the menu, with the exception of appetizers like gefilte fish and carp "Jewish style," but everything is creatively prepared and done well. My favorite is the beef casserole in a spicy sauce of garlic and cumin. The party atmosphere on crowded night is infectious, as the wine pours and the fiddlers fiddle. Good for groups, but probably too boisterous for singles dining alone.

Szeroka 6. ✆ 012/411-12-45. Lunch and dinner items 24 zł–36 zł ($8–$12/£4.40–£7). AE, DC, MC, V. Daily 9am–11pm.

Nostalgia ✸✸ POLISH   A meal here is like dining in the country home of a well-to-do friend—warm and inviting yet somehow still refined and special. The atmosphere extends to the cooking as well: Polish staples like pierogies, pork, and game, but well turned out and served on fine china. This is a perfect balance between something like Cyrano de Bergerac (see above) and CK Dezerterzy (below). The same attention to detail as the former, but with the more relaxed feel and prices of the latter. Excellent selection of meatless entrees for vegetarians. Reserve in advance to be on the safe side.

Karmelicka 10. ✆ 012/425-42-60. Reservations recommended. Lunch and dinner items 24 zł–36 zł ($8–$12/£4.40–£7). AE, DC, MC, V. Daily noon–11pm.

MODERATE

CK Dezerterzy ✸✸ POLISH   A cozy, family-style tavern serving well-prepared traditional Polish cooking, in a warm setting down a small side street just off the Rynek Główny. It's perfect if you've just arrived and want a hassle-free, very good meal, and don't want to stray too far from the hotel. The only possible drawback is that it's popular with guidebooks (like this one), so while you'll probably find many Poles on the night you're here and tucking into your bigos or pierogies, you may wind up next to a table of guests from your own hometown.

Bracka 6. ✆ 012/422-79-31. Lunch and dinner items 18 zł–27 zł ($6–$9/£3.30–£5). AE, DC, MC, V. Daily 10am–10pm.

Flower Power ✸ INTERNATIONAL   The grooviest little nook in Kazimierz. Exotic, Moroccan-inspired dishes like chicken tajine, served with lemon and olives (just like in Marrakech). The front room is more like a standard coffee shop, complete with free Wi-Fi. The back room is more relaxed, with embroidered cushions on the floor for sitting and water pipes for hire. The sign at the backroom sums it up: PLEASE REMOVE YOUR SHOES, PEACE AND LOVE. Excellent coffees and a nice range of special teas.

Nova (just off Plac Nowy). ✆ 012/430-64-78. Lunch and dinner items 15 zł–24 zł ($5–$8/£2.60–£4.50). No credit cards. Daily 10am–9pm.

Le Scandale ✸ INTERNATIONAL   Great breakfast or light lunch spot right on Plac Nowy in Kazimierz. Decent bagels, eggs, and coffee served from 8am. On weekends, arrive early to snag one of those highly coveted square-side tables, perfect for people-watching while sipping your espresso. The menu is heavy on international munchies, like quesadillas, simple pastas, and sandwiches, but also does well with steaks and seafood.

Plac Nowy 9. ⟨ **012/430-68-55.** Lunch and dinner items 15 zł–24 zł ($5–$8/£2.60–£4.50). AE, DC, MC, V. Daily 8am–11pm.

INEXPENSIVE

Any Time 🐥🐥 INTERNATIONAL   I love this little place just down from the Plac Nowy in Kazimierz. If you're looking for simple sandwiches, fresh ingredients, and homesick-curing desserts like chocolate cake and apple pie, definitely stop by. It's ideal for a late lunch after a long slog through the Jewish quarter. Possibly too informal for a special dinner, but not bad for a quick bite if other plans are on the evening card.

Estery 16. ⟨ **012/625-60-61.** Lunch and dinner items 12 zł–18 zł ($4–$6/£2.20–£3.30). No credit cards. Daily 10am–10pm.

Bagelmama 🐥🐥 INTERNATIONAL   Great bagels, as well as very good lentil soup, and even decent burritos, in a tiny shop just near to where Kazimierz starts if you're walking from Wawel and the Old Town. This is *the* place to go for that classic bagel breakfast with smoked lox, onions, and capers (so good in fact it's worth skipping the pension's spread of tired cheese and cold cuts for). *Be forewarned:* There are only three tables, so be prepared to wait or get takeout.

Estery 16. ⟨ **012/431-19-42.** Lunch and dinner items 12 zł–18 zł ($4–$6/£2.20–£3.30). No credit cards. Tues–Sun 10am–9pm.

Fabryka Pizza 🐥 ITALIAN   The pizza standards in Poland continue to rise and this new Kazimierz spot is widely considered to be the new pace-setter. The excellent pizzas are cooked in a wood-fired oven. You can order "small" or "large," with small being enough for two normal-size appetites. The interior is stark, dark, and highly trendy. The names of the pizzas are especially amusing. "Hog on Vacation" is ham with pineapple—get the idea?

Józefa 34. ⟨ **012/433-80-80.** Lunch and dinner items 12 zł–21 zł ($4–$7/£2.20–£4). No credit cards. Mon–Sat 10am–10pm; Sun noon–10.

Pierożki U Vincenta 🐥🐥🐥 POLISH   This tiny and highly inviting little pierogi stand just off of Józefa in Kazimierz serves every style of pierogi imaginable. The house version, "Vincent," is stuffed with minced meat and spicy lentils, served with fried onions and little bits of bacon. Other concoctions include Moroccan-inspired couscous pierogies, "Górale" pierogies, stuffed with sheep's cheese, and dozens of others. Try it with a cup of beet soup. The four tables hold about 12 diners in all.

Józefa 11. ⟨ **012/430-68-34.** Lunch and dinner items 9 zł–12 zł ($3–$4/£1.60–£2.20). No credit cards. Sun–Thurs noon–9pm; Fri–Sat noon–10pm.

U Babci Maliny 🐥🐥 POLISH   This is Kraków's answer to the "Neptun" in Gdańsk, in other words a decent "milk bar," serving not-bad-at-all Polish standards like bigos, pork dishes, and pierogies at prices that make it hard to believe they can pay the rent. It's a little tricky to find. Walk into the building and through some rooms and down some stairs. Usually you can follow the crowd, since this place is justifiably popular. Order your food, get a number, and then wait around until your order is called. As is customary with milk bars, watch the early closing times and smoking is not permitted.

Sławkowska 17. ✆ **012/422-76-01.** Lunch and dinner items 6 zł–15 zł ($2–$5/£1.60–£2.70). No credit cards. Mon–Fri 11am–8pm; Sat–Sun noon–8pm.

Cafes

Jama Michalika ⭐ CAFE   In the early decades of the 20th century, this was the epicenter of all things cool and a major meeting point for the Młoda Polska crowd. Alas, those days are gone, and now it's largely given over to tourists. The incredible Art Nouveau interior and the evocative period paintings on the wall are definitely worth poking your nose in for a look. Beware the unfriendly cloakroom attendants (coat and hat check mandatory). You may have to wrestle a waiter to the ground to take your order.

Floriańska 45. ✆ **012/422-15-61.** Lunch and dinner items 12 zł–27 zł ($4–$9/£2.20–£5). AE, DC, MC, V. Daily 9am–midnight.

Noworolski ⭐⭐ CAFE   Lovingly restored Art Nouveau interior recalls Kraków's elegant past. The perfect spot for a leisurely coffee and cake.

Rynek Główny 1. ✆ **012/422-47-71.** Lunch and dinner items 12 zł–27 zł ($4–$9/£2.20–£5). AE, DC, MC, V. Daily 9am–midnight.

EXPLORING KRAKÓW

A sensible plan for sightseeing in Kraków is to divide the city into three basic areas: the Old Town, including the Rynek Główny; the Wawel Castle compound (with its many rooms and museums); and "Jewish" Kraków, including the former Jewish quarter of Kazimierz and the wartime Jewish ghetto of Podgórze farther south. Ideally, leave a day devoted to each. If you're pressed for time, you could conceivably link the Old Town and Wawel in 1 day, while leaving Kazimierz for the next.

EXPLORING THE OLD TOWN

Kraków's Old Town is a pedestrian's paradise. It's hard to imagine a more attractive town core. It's a powerful argument for historical preservation and the value of vital urban spaces. The **Rynek Główny** by all accounts is a remarkable public space. Measuring some 200m (600 ft.) square and ringed around by stately buildings, it creates a natural arena for public performances of all stripes.

The most striking building on the square is the beautiful Gothic cathedral of **St. Mary's**—its uneven towers evoking for Poles the very essence of the city. Be sure to stop here at some point precisely on the hour to hear a lone trumpeter play his plaintive wail from the open window of the highest tower. As you listen to him play, you'll hear the last note cut off in midblow. That's intentional and meant to recall the assault on the city by the Tartars in the 13th century. Legend has it that as the trumpeter at the time was calling the city's residents to arms, a Tartar marksman caught the trumpeter with an arrow right through his throat. (I admit I'm a little skeptical of this story, too. Judging from the height and size of the window, that Tartar must have been an excellent shot!)

At the center of the square is the **Cloth Hall,** the Sukiennice, which dates from the 14th century and served as the stalls of the town's original merchants. The original Cloth Hall burned down in the 16th century, and what you see today is a mostly Renaissance building, with neo-Gothic flourishes added in the 19th century. Today, it's still filled with marketers, hawking (mostly) cheap Polish souvenirs to the throngs of visitors. Just near the Cloth Hall stands the enormous **Town Hall Tower.** It's the last surviving piece of Kraków's original town hall, which was demolished in the early 19th century in an apparent bid to clean up the square. Today the tower houses a branch of the tourist information office, and you can climb to the top for a view over the Old Town.

Streets and alleys lead off the square in all directions. Of these the most important are **ul. Floriańska** and **ul. Grodzka,** both part of the famed Royal Route of Polish kings. Floriańska leads to the Floriańska Gate, dating back to the start of the 14th century. The gate was once the main entryway to the Old Town and part of the original medieval fortification system. Grodzka flows out of the square at the square's southern end and leads to the ancient Wawel Castle.

Archdiocesan Museum   This is essential viewing for fans of the late Pope John Paul II. John Paul lived here as the archbishop of the Kraków diocese until his elevation to pope in 1978. Today, the museum has largely been given over to his legacy, with a fine collection of gifts presented to the pope by heads of state from around the world. You'll also see a nice collection of sacral painting and sculpture dating from the 13th century.

Kanonicza 19. ℂ 012/421-89-63. Tues–Fri 10am–4pm; Sat–Sun 10am–3pm.

Church of Saints Peter and Paul   One of the most evocative of Kraków's many churches, chiefly because of the statues of the 12 disciples lining the front entrance. It's said that the Jesuits spent so much money building the front and facade that they ran out of money to finish the rest of the building (which if you look behind the facade you'll see is constructed from ordinary brick). The interior is less impressive, though still worth a peek in.

Grodzka 54. ℂ 012/422-65-73.

Czartoryski Museum   The Czartoryski family members were gifted art collectors, and this collection is one of the finest in central Europe. Two international masterpieces are on display: Leonardo da Vinci's *Lady with an Ermine* and Rembrandt's *Landscape with the Good Samaritan.* A third masterpiece, Raphael's *Portrait of a Young Man,* was sadly taken away by the Nazis and never recovered. The museum also houses a sizable collection of ancient art from the Middle East, Greece, and Egypt.

Sw. Jana 19. ℂ 012/422-55-66. www.muzeum-czartoryskich.krakow.pl. Admission 9 zł ($3/£1.60); free Thurs. Tues 10am–4pm; Wed 10am–7pm; Thurs 10am–4pm; Fri–Sat 10am–7pm; Sun 10am–3pm.

St. Andrew's Church   It's hard to imagine a more perfect foil to the attention-grabbing Church of Saints Peter and Paul across the street. This humble, handsome church dates from the 11th century and has been part of the city's history for some 900 years. Its simple Romanesque exterior is a tonic to the eyes. The interior, on the other hand, borders on the jarring, remodeled in baroque style in the 18th century.

Grodzka 56. ℂ 012/422-16-12.

St. Mary's Cathedral   The original church was destroyed in the Tartar raids of the 13th century, and rebuilding began relatively soon after. The hushed interior makes for essential viewing. The elaborately carved 15th-century wooden altarpiece, by the master carver Veit Stoss, is the immediate crowd-pleaser. But the highlight of this church, at least for me, is not inside at all. It's the forlorn trumpeter in the high tower, playing his lonely hourly dirge to the defenders of the Kraków from the Tartar hordes—in order that the people below know the correct time.

Rynek Główny 4. ℂ **012/422-05-21**. Mon–Sat 11:30am–6pm; Sun 2–6pm.

Wyspiański Museum   Fans of Polish art will have heard of Stanisław Wyspiański, one of the originators of a turn-of-the-20th-century art movement known as Młoda Polska (Young Poland). The Młoda Polska movement, based largely here in Kraków and Zakopane, reinvigorated Polish culture in the years before World War I. You'll note parallels between Wyspiański's paintings and drawings and the Art Nouveau movement in Paris and Brussels, and *Jugendstil* in Vienna.

Szczepańska 11. ℂ **012/422-70-21**. www.muzeum.krakow.pl. Admission 6 zł ($2/£1); free Thurs. Tues 10am–4pm; Wed 10am–7pm; Thurs 10am–4pm; Fri–Sat 10am–7pm; Sun 10am–3pm.

EXPLORING WAWEL CASTLE

Wawel Castle (www.wawel.krakow.pl) is Poland's pride and joy. With Warsaw having been flattened by the Nazis, this ancient castle, and former capital, rising 45m (150 ft.) above the Vistula, has become something of a symbol of the survival of the Polish nation. Understandably, for non-Poles, Wawel has less symbolic significance, but is still a handsome castle in its own right and well worth an extended visit.

The original castle dates from around the 10th century, when the area was first chosen as the seat of Polish kings. For more than 5 centuries, the castle stood as the home of Polish royalty. The original castle was built in a Romanesque style, and subsequently remodeled over the centuries, depending on the architectural fashions of the day. What you see today is a mix of Romanesque, Gothic, Renaissance, and baroque.

The castle fell into disrepair after the Polish capital was moved to Warsaw at the end of the 16th century, but its darkest days came during World War II, when it was occupied by the Nazi governor of the wartime rump Polish state, Hans Frank. The castle luckily escaped serious damage during the war.

Aside from the castle, the complex comprises a **Cathedral,** including the **Royal Tombs,** the **Cathedral Museum,** the **Royal Chambers,** with an impressive collection of tapestries, and the **Treasury and Armory.** (There are actually more things to see than this, but these are the highlights.) It's a lot to see and the tourist office and guides will recommend putting in a whole day. But if castles are not your thing, or if your interest in Polish history leaves something to be desired, don't overdo it. Two to 3 hours is usually enough to see the main castle and cathedral complex.

The grounds are open to the public free of charge, but entry to the castle and various other sites requires buying separate tickets. Note that in high season, the number of visitors is restricted. To ensure you get to see what you want, phone ahead to the main ticket office (ℂ **012/422-16-97**) to reserve. The castle hours are: Tuesday 9:30am to 4pm, Wednesday and Thursday 9:30am to 3pm, Friday 9:30am to 4pm, Saturday 9:30am to 3pm, and Sunday 10am to 3pm. Admission is 15 zł ($5/£2.60) (and 75 zł/$25/£14 for an English-speaking guide).

Wawel Cathedral and Cathedral Museum   This is the spiritual home of the Polish state, testifying to the strong historical link between the Polish royalty and the Catholic Church. The chapels here, and the Royal Tombs below, hold the remains of all but four of Poland's 45 rulers (King Kazimierz the Great's tomb is in red marble to the right of the main altar.) Admission includes the tombs and the climb to the top of the Zygmunt Bell, which dates from the early 16th century. The bell is rung only occasionally to mark highly significant moments, such as the death of Pope John Paul II in 2005.

Wawel Hill. ℂ 012/422-26-43. Admission 10 zł ($3.30/£1.75); museum 5 zł ($1.65/90p). Mon–Sat 9am–5pm; Sun 12:15–5pm. Museum closed Mon.

Lost Wawel ✿   A high-tech exhibition to give visitors a feel for how Wawel castle looked in its very earliest days. The exhibit includes parts of the Rotunda of the Virgin Mary, which was the first church to be built in Kraków.

Wawel Hill. ℂ 012/422-51-55. Free admission. Tues 9:30am–4pm; Wed 9:30am–3pm; Thurs 9am–3pm; Fri 9:30am–4pm; Sat 11am–5pm; Sun 10am–3pm.

Royal Chambers ✿✿   The highlight of a visit here is 136 Flemish tapestries commissioned by King Sigismund August. The rooms hold vast collections of paintings, sketches, frescoes, and period furnishings. One of the more memorable rooms, on the top floor, is the Assembly Room, complete with the king's throne and a wooden ceiling carved with the likenesses of Kraków residents of the time.

Wawel Hill. ℂ 012/422-51-55. Free admission. Tues 9:30am–4pm; Wed 9:30am–3pm; Thurs 9am–3pm; Fri 9:30am–4pm; Sat 11am–5pm; Sun 10am–3pm.

Treasury and Armory ✿   Exhibitions of what's left of the Polish royal jewels, including the coronation sword. An impressive show of medieval fighting instruments, including swords and full complements of knights' armor.

Wawel Hill. No phone. Free admission. Tues–Sat 9:30am–3pm.

EXPLORING KAZIMIERZ

Kazimierz, the former Jewish quarter, is an absolute must that defies easy description. It's at once a tumbled-down, decrepit former ghetto, filled with the haunting artifacts of a culture that was brutally uprooted and destroyed a generation ago. It also happens to be Kraków's coolest nightclub district, filled with cafes, cocktail bars, and trendy eateries that would not be out of place in New York's Soho or East Village. The juxtaposition is enlivening and jarring at the same time. To their credit, the Kraków city authorities have resisted the temptation to clean up the area to make it more presentable to visitors. Don't expect an easy, tourist-friendly experience. It's dirty, down at the heel, and at the same time thoroughly engaging.

Kazimierz began life as a Polish city in the 14th century, but starting from around 1500 onward it took on an increasingly Jewish character as Jews first decided to live here and then were forced to by edict. The original Jewish ghetto incorporated about the northern half of modern-day Kazimierz, bounded by a stone wall along today's Józefa street. In the 19th century, the Jews won the right of abode and the walls were eventually torn down. Many elected to stay in Kazimierz, and the 19th century, through World War I and the start of World War II, is regarded as the quarter's heyday.

The Nazi invasion put an end to centuries of Jewish life here. The Nazis first imposed a series of harsh measures on Jewish life, and in 1941 forcibly expelled the residents across the river to the newly constructed ghetto at Podgórze. At the Isaak Synagogue you can see special films of this deportation shot by the Germans themselves for propaganda purposes. By 1943 and 1944, with the liquidation of the Podgórze ghetto, nearly all of Kazimierz's 60,000 Jews had been killed or died of starvation or exhaustion.

There's no prescribed plan for visiting the former Jewish quarter. The natural point of departure is the central **Plac Nowy,** once the quarter's main market and now given over to a depressing combination of fruit and flea market (no doubt with real fleas). The **tourist information center** maintains an office at Józefa 7 (*C* **012/422-04-71;** Mon–Fri 10am–4pm), and can provide maps and information. Look too for sign-posted routes marked **"Trasa zabytków żydowskych,"** which includes all of the major sites. Visit the synagogues individually; each costs about 7 zł ($2.30/£1.20) to enter. Don't expect gorgeous interiors; it's fortunate enough that these buildings are still standing.

After you've toured the major sites, don't overlook the **Galicia Jewish Museum** on Dajwór street, just beyond the main ghetto area. Check out too the **New Cemetery (Nowy Cmentarz)** at the far end of Miodowa street, walking below a railroad under-pass. This became the main Jewish cemetery in the 19th century, and the thousands of headstones are silent testimony to the former size of this community.

Galicia Jewish Museum ✿✿   This often-overlooked museum, in a far corner of Kazimierz, is almost a must-see. The main exhibition features contemporary and often very beautiful photographs of important Jewish sites throughout southern Poland with an explanation of what happened there. The effect works beautifully. So much of the experience of visiting Poland is running across sites very much like these pictures and trying to piece together the history behind it. The lesson here is that nearly every place has a tragic story.

Dajwór 18. *C* **012/421-68-42.** Daily 10am–4:30pm.

Isaak Synagogue ✿✿✿   This is widely considered the most beautiful synagogue in Kazimierz, dating from 1664. It was badly damaged during the Nazi occupation and has only been partially restored. The rooms hold moving photographs of former Kazimierz residents and their families, but the highlights are several older documen-tary films on Kazimierz that run continuously during the day. One film is French from the late 1930s, narrated in German, on health conditions in the ghetto; another is a U.S. film from earlier in the decade about Jewish life here. The most haunting of all are the silent newsreels filmed by the Germans themselves of the clearing of the Jewish quarter in 1941.

Kupa 16. *C* **012/430-55-77.** Sun–Fri 9am–7pm.

Old Synagogue ✿✿   Home to an educational set of exhibitions of Jewish life in Poland. Dating from the early 16th century, this is the oldest surviving example of Jewish architecture in the country.

Szeroka 24. *C* **012/422-09-62.** Tues–Sun 9am–5pm; Mon 10am–2pm.

Remuh Synagogue and Cemetery ✿✿   This is still in active use as a synagogue. You can walk through cemetery, which was used until the start of the 19th century, when the New Cemetery was opened.

Szeroka 40. *C* **012/422-12-74.** Sun–Fri 10am–4pm.

Temple Synagogue ✿✿   The relative grandeur of this synagogue best captures the wealth of Jewish life here before the war.

Miodowa 24. *C* **012/423-20-97.** Sun–Fri 10am–6pm.

PODGÓRZE

South of Kazimierz, across the Vistula River, lies the wartime Jewish ghetto of Podgórze. It was here, at today's **Plac Bohaterów Getta,** where thousands of the city's Jews were forcibly moved and incarcerated in March 1941. Much of the area has since been rebuilt, and walking the depressed streets today, you'll be hard-pressed to imagine what it must have been like for thousands of Jews to be pent up here with only the prospect of eventually being sent to the camps at Auschwitz or, more nearby, Płaszów. The ghetto was eventually razed in 1943 and the inhabitants killed. Look for the **Apteka Pod Orłem** on the Plac Bohaterów Getta, which today houses a small but fascinating museum on the history of the ghetto. About 15-minute walk from the square brings you to **Oskar Schindler's former enamel factory.** At press time, this was still abandoned, but open to the public to walk around (this may change soon if plans go forward to open a museum or art gallery here).

Apteka Pod Orłem ✴✴   You'll find an enthralling collection of photographs and documents from life in the Podgórze ghetto, from its inception 1941 to its eventual liquidation 2 years later.

Plac Bohaterów Getta 18. ℂ 012/656-56-25. Admission 4 zł ($2/£1); free Mon. May–Oct Mon 10am–2pm, Tues–Sun 9:30am–5pm; Nov–Apr Mon 10am–2pm, Tues–Thurs 9am–4pm, Fri 11am–6pm, Sat 9am–4pm.

Oskar Schindler's Emalia Factory ✴✴   An essential stop for anyone interested in the history of the Podgórze ghetto or in the film *Schindler's List.* Many of the scenes were filmed here and you'll have the distinct sense of déjà vu just arriving at the depressing scene. The factory is closed down, but occasionally the gates are open for an impromptu "museum," complete with English-speaking students who offer themselves as guides. Be sure to look through the guest book. More than once you'll see the signature of a former worker here along with the words "because of Oskar Schindler I am still alive." Gripping.

Lipowa 4. No phone. Hours vary.

OUTSIDE OF KRAKÓW

Wieliczka Salt Mines ✴✴   I must confess to a touch of claustrophobia and for that reason I don't get much out of this trip to a subterranean salt mine, about 16km (10 miles) southeast of Kraków. But many people—including the folks at the UNESCO cultural heritage office—absolutely love it, so I'm bowing to popular will and giving it two stars. Salt has been mined in the area for centuries, and talented miners and artisans through the ages here have crafted some incredible chambers, bas reliefs, and statues from that once highly coveted white powder. The mine covers nine floors and goes to a depth of some 300m (nearly 1,000 ft.). The highlights include an enormous salt lake as well as St. Anthony's Chapel and the larger Chapel of St. Kinga. You can only the visit the mine via a guided tour. Polish language tours run throughout the day; English-language tours are less frequent, but still often enough (at least in summer) that you won't have to wait long (last English tour is at 5pm). In winter, it's best to time your arrival to the tour schedule (10am and 12:30pm). The tours cover three levels of the mine and take about 2 hours. Be sure to pack a sweater since it's cool down there, and wear comfortable shoes. You can reach Wieliczka easily by train or a special minibus that leaves from the main train station. Several travel agencies in Kraków also offer guided tours as a day trip.

Daniłowicza 10 (Wieliczka). ℂ 012/278-73-02. www.kopalnia.pl. Admission 60 zł ($20/£11). Mid-Apr to mid-Oct daily 7:30am–7:30pm; mid-Oct to mid-Apr Tues–Sun 8am–4pm.

Nowa Huta 𝄞𝄞   In the 1950s, the Communist authorities decided to try to win over the hearts and minds of skeptical Cracovians by building this model Socialist community, just a tram ride away the Rynek Główny. They built an enormous steel mill (the name Nowa Huta means "new mill"), as well as rows of carefully constructed worker housing, shops, and recreational facilities for what was conceived of as the city of the future. It didn't quite work out as planned; Kraków intellectuals were never impressed by a steel mill, and the workers never really cottoned on to the Communist cause. But Nowa Huta is still standing and in its own way looks absolutely fabulous. Any fan of urban design or anyone with a penchant for Communist history will enjoy a couple of hours of walking around, admiring the buildings, the broad avenues, and the parks and squares. The structures have held up remarkably well, and indeed the area looks better now than it ever has. Part of the reason is that the mills are no longer running at anywhere near capacity, so the air is cleaner. And, ironically, capitalism has added a touch of badly needed prosperity, meaning the residents have a little money to maintain the buildings. On the other hand, there's something undeniably sad too; this grandiose project in social engineering has been reduced to little more than a curiosity (though more than 100,000 people still call Nowa Huta home). The shops that line the magnificent boulevards—once conceived to sell everything a typical family would need (even if the shops rarely had anything worth buying)—look forlorn; and many of them are empty. Aside from walking, there's not much to do, and little provision has been made for the visitor. You'll search in vain for a decent restaurant, so plan on eating back in Kraków. The easiest way to reach Nowa Huta is take tram no. 4 or 15 from the train station about 20 minutes to the stop "Plac Centralny." From here it's a short walk to the main square, renamed to honor former U.S. President Ronald Reagan. If you'd like a more in-depth tour, **Crazy Guides** (Floriańska 38; ℂ **0888/68-68-71;** www.crazyguides.com) offers guided visits to Nowa Huta, including travel in a Communist-era Trabant for about 120 zł ($40/£22) per person.

SHOPPING

Warsaw is better when it comes to high-end design and fashion, and Gdańsk is a better place to buy amber and jewelry. Kraków is filled with interesting shops to peruse, especially for art, antiques, and trinkets. Most of the better stores are concentrated in the Old Town along the streets that radiate from the Main Square. Kazimierz has emerged as a second shopping mecca; here, the emphasis understandably is on Judaica, but the little streets are filled with shops selling everything from trendy art and design to out-and-out junk.

For classic Polish souvenirs, including handicrafts, woodcarving, and (naturally) amber, first try the stalls at the **Cloth Hall (Sukiennice)** in the middle of the Rynek Główny. You'll have to pick through lots of dross, but hidden among the "Poland" T-shirts and mass-produced icons, you'll find some beautifully carved wood and amber chess sets, as well as locally produced cloth, lace, and leather goods.

Sławkowska Street in the Old Town has a nice grouping of art and antiques stores. For some unusual modern Polish painting and sculpture, stop by **Galeria AG** (Sławkowska 10; ℂ **012/429-51-78;** www.galeriaag.art.pl). **Atest** (Sławkowska 14; ℂ **012/421-95-19**), just down the street, is one of the better places for antiques.

For English-language books, Kraków is blessed with at least two treasures. The first is undeniably **Massolit** books (Felicjanek 4; ℂ **012/432-41-50;** www.massolit.com), easily one of the best new and used English bookshops in central Europe. Massolit is especially strong on Polish authors in translation, but has thousands of titles under all conceivable categories (plus a very cute cafe and a quiet, contemplative ambience highly conducive to reading and thinking). The other is **Austeria** in Kazimierz, next to the High Synagogue (Józefa 38; ✆ **012/430-68-89**). Here you'll find hundreds of titles on Judaica, Polish history, and the Holocaust, as well as some incredibly beautiful photographs, posters, CDs, and reproductions of old maps.

Kraków is a good place to find that exclusive bottle of Polish vodka. Two stores stand out. **Szambelan** (Gołebia 2; ✆ **012/430-2409;** www.szambelan.com.pl) and **F. H. Herbert** (Grodzka 59; no phone). Szambelan is best known for its exotic bottle shapes, but both stores carry a nice range of the best straight and flavored vodkas, as well as an excellent selection of wines and other beverages.

KRAKÓW AFTER DARK

Kraków is the cultural hub of southern Poland, and as such supports an active program of live theater, dance, classical music, and opera. The **Cultural Information Center** (Św. Jana 2; ✆ **012/421-77-87**) is the first stop to find out what's on and seeing if tickets are available. The friendly staff can help guide you to the best events. The center for classical music is the **Philharmonic Hall** (Zwierzyniecka 1; ✆ **012/422-43-12;** box office Tues—Sat noon–7pm). The city supports several opera companies, including the very good **Opera in Słowacki Theater** (Pl. Św Ducha 1; ✆ **012/422-78-07;** www.opera.krakow.pl).

For drinking, dancing, and clubbing both the Old Town and Kazimierz are natural areas to start a night crawl. The Old Town caters more to tourists and students from nearby Jagellonian University; in Kazimierz the scene is more diverse and a little older, with young professionals, artists, and hipsters of all sorts attracted to some of the best clubs in central Europe.

Old Town

Ministerstwo   Emerging as probably Kraków's best venue for DJs and house music (not to mention, the essential lava lamp decor!). The action starts late and runs until dawn. Good location, just off the Main Square. Szpitalna 1. ✆ **012/429-67-90.** www.klub ministerstwo.pl. Tues–Sat 11pm–5am.

Nic Nowego   I hesitated before including this modern Irish-themed bar since it's so popular with tourists and is in every other guidebook. But if you're looking for a visitor-friendly place where English is spoken and the menu looks comforting and familiar, you could do far worse. In addition to decent cocktails and conversation, you'll find a nice array of burgers and sandwiches on the munchie menu. Breakfast is served daily, and the scrambled eggs and coffee here are probably a lot better than what your pension has planned for you. Św. Krzyże. ✆ **012/421-61-88.** Mon–Fri 7am–3am; Sat–Sun 10am–3am.

Pauza   You'll have to look around a bit for this moody little cocktail bar, which now numbers among coolest drinking spots in the city despite few clues that it's even there. Order at the bar and head for the chill-out lounge in the back. Floriańska 18/3. ✆ **0602/63-78-33.** Daily noon–midnight.

Rdza   Another contender for best dance club in the Old Town. Choose fashionable dress to make it past the guys at the door, and then enjoy the trance, dance, and mood tunes, served up by some of the best Polish and imported DJs on offer. Attracts an early-20s to 30s crowd. Bracka 3-5. ⓒ **0600/39-55-41**. Daily 9pm–4am.

Kazimierz

Alchemia   One of the original bars/clubs to lead the Kazimierz renaissance in the late 1990s, when the former Jewish quarter morphed from a forgotten corner of Kraków to its current "party amid the past" feel. The old furniture, faded photos, and frayed carpets set a design tone that's still going strong. It's no longer the bar of the moment, but still a great place to get a feel for what Kazimierz is all about. Estery 5. ⓒ **012/421-22-00**. Daily 9am–4am.

Les Couleurs   By day, an innocent French-themed cafe, complete with very good espresso and 1960s, arty French posters on the wall. By night, a great little bar to drop by for an after-dinner beer or cocktail. Just boisterous enough to feel lively, but still quiet enough to hear yourself talk. Estery 10. ⓒ **012/429-42-70**. Mon–Fri 7am–2am; Sat–Sun 9am–2am.

Moment   New and trendy; one the coolest spots these days to have a drink. Clocks on the wall to remind you of the inexorable passage of time, and encouraging you to make this your moment. Popular with the newly moneyed, postcollege crowd. Worth seeking out. Józefa 32. No phone. Daily noon–2am.

Opium   It seems like every Polish city these days has a club named Opium. This popular bar and dance club fits right in. You're not likely to find any real opium, but you will find lots of beautiful people and good cocktails. Come early to grab a coveted sofa seat, since this place fills up fast after 11pm. Jakuba 19. ⓒ **012/421-94-61**. Sun–Thurs 4pm–1am; Fri–Sat 4pm–5am.

DAY TRIP: AUSCHWITZ-BIRKENAU

The concentration and extermination camps of Auschwitz and Birkenau lie about 80km (50 miles) to the west of Kraków, and can be seen visited in a day trip from the city. Several travel agencies run guided coach tours of the death camps; these usually include transportation from Kraków's main square and an English-language guide once you've arrived at the camps. It's also easy to visit the camps on your own. Several trains make the run daily to Auschwitz/Oświęcim from Kraków's main station. By car it's an easy 90-minute drive along the main highway to Katowice, turning south at the Czarnów exit and following the signs first to Oświęcim and once in town to the "Auschwitz Museum."

Whatever you've heard or read about the death camps, nothing is likely to prepare you for the shock of seeing them in person. Auschwitz is the better known of the two, though it's at Birkenau, south of Auschwitz, where you see and really feel the sheer scale of the atrocities. The precise number of deaths at the camps is disputed, but well over a million people died in the gas chambers, or were hanged or shot or died of disease or exhaustion. Most of the victims were Jews, brought here from 1942 to 1944 from all around Europe stuffed in rail cattle cars. In addition to Jews, thousands of POWs, including many Poles, Russians, and Gypsies (Roma), were exterminated here as well.

Most visitors start their exploration of the camps at Auschwitz, the first of three concentration/extermination camps built in the area (the third, Monowice, is in a suburb of Oświęcim and not included on most itineraries).

Auschwitz got its start in 1940, when the Germans requisitioned a former Polish garrison town, Oświęcim, for the purpose of establishing a prisoner-of-war camp. The first groups of detainees included Polish political prisoners and Russian POWs. Conditions were appalling and in the first year alone, nearly all of the several thousand Russian POWs died of exhaustion and malnutrition. It was only later—in 1942 after the Germans adopted a formal policy of exterminating Europe's Jewish population—that Auschwitz became primarily a death camp for Europe's Jewry.

Admission to the Auschwitz museum is free, and you're allowed to roam the camp grounds at will, taking in the atrocities at your own pace. On entering the museum, you'll first have the chance of seeing a horrific 15-minute film of the liberation of the camp by the Soviet soldiers in early 1945. The film is offered in several languages, with English showings once every 90 minutes or so (if you miss a showing, you can always come back to see it later). After that, you walk through the camp gates passing below Auschwitz's infamous motto "Arbeit Macht Frei" (Through Work, Freedom). Once inside, the buildings and barracks are given over to various exhibitions and displays. Don't miss the exhibition at Block No. 4, "On Extermination." It's here where you'll see the whole system of rail transports, the brutal "selection" process to see which of the new arrivals would go straight to the gas chambers and which would get a temporary reprieve to work, as well as the mechanics of the gas chambers, the canisters of the Zyklon-B gas used, and, in one particularly gruesome window display, yards and yards of human hair used to make rugs and textiles.

Birkenau, also known as Auschwitz II, lies about 2km (1¼ miles) to the south. It's larger, more open, and even (if possible) more ghastly than Auschwitz. It's here where most of the mass gas-chamber exterminations took place at one of the five gas chambers located at the back of the camp. You can walk the distance between Auschwitz and Birkenau in about 30 minutes; alternatively take one of the museum shuttle buses that run on every hour on the half-hour from the front of the museum. A cab ride between the two camps will cost you about 10 zł ($3.30/£1.90).

Birkenau appears almost untouched from how it looked in 1945. Your first sight of the camp will be of the main gate, the "Gate of Death." The orderly process of the arrival of Jews and other prisoners by train, the confiscation of their belongings, the "selection" process of internment or immediate death, and finally the gas chambers are horrific in their efficiency. And the scale is shocking—stark brick prisoner blocks laid out as far as the eye can see. There are no films here and few resources for the visitor. Instead set aside an hour or so to stroll the camp to take it in. Don't miss the remains of the gas chambers situated toward the back, not far from the memorial to Holocaust victims. The Germans themselves destroyed four of the gas chambers at the end of 1944 and early 1945 to cover up their crimes once it was apparent the war could not be won. Now, little of the gas chambers remain. You can return to the main Auschwitz museum by foot, shuttle bus, or taxi, and from Auschwitz back to Kraków by bus or train.

5 The Rest of Malopolska

ZAKOPANE

100km (60 miles) S of Kraków

Zakopane is a surprisingly likable, sprawling mountain village that serves as the hub of the Polish side of the High Tatras. With its array of accommodations, including some very beautiful hotels, restaurants, and attractions, it's a sensible base for any exploration of the region.

Zakopane plays a role in Poland's literary and cultural history that may be unprecedented as far as mountain resorts go. Certainly there is no equivalent on the Slovak side of the Tatras, where the resorts are simply resorts, and the mountains, though lovely places to hike or ski, are still only mountains. In the 19th and early 20th centuries, a swath of Poland's intellectual elite decamped here in a bid no less ambitious than to reinvent, or at least reinterpret, Polish culture. The country's best writers, poets, artists, musicians, and architects gathered here and found something uniquely Polish in the unspoiled nature and solid mountain cottages of simple people.

The two world wars and the decades of Communism that followed put an end to the Zakopane art colony, but a special, funky feeling remains. Certainly the wooden houses here are some of the most beautiful you'll see anywhere, and in and among the trees and the gardens—and away from the crowds—you'll find a stimulating, uniquely Polish resort that feels very much of a different age.

At the height of the summer or winter season—when the main street, Krupówki, is filled to bursting with vacationers—it may take awhile to find that special feeling. After you've had your fill of the "Main Street" scene, branch off among the neighborhoods, where a more relaxed and pleasing aesthetic takes hold.

ESSENTIALS

GETTING THERE   Zakopane is well served by rail and bus lines. Private bus is the easiest way to move between Kraków and Zakopane; several private lines make the trip for about 15 zł ($5/£2.60) each way. In Zakopane, Szwagropol (ul. Kościuszki 19a; ℭ 018/20-17-123; www.szwagropol.pl) offers 14 departures daily to and from Kraków's main bus station to just in front of Zakopane's Tourist Information Center. The last bus leaves Kraków at 8:10pm.

GETTING AROUND   Central Zakopane is fairly compact and partly closed to car traffic, so walking is really the only option for getting around. The town itself, though, spreads out a couple of miles in both directions, so if you're staying outside of the center (and don't have a car), you'll have to rely on taxis or local buses to get around. The main taxi stand is conveniently located just outside the main bus and train terminals. Bikes are another option, but ask at the Tourist Information Office, since rental agencies change from season to season.

VISITOR INFORMATION   You'll be a little confused when you arrive by the sheer number of private tourist agencies offering everything from information to accommodations, lift tickets, and day trips. Zakopane's small Tourist Information Center (Centrum Informacji Turystycznej) (Kościuszki 17; ℭ 018/201-22-11; www.zakopane.pl) can help with general orientation questions and provide maps, but that's about it. For more hands-on service, including booking hotel rooms, walk across the street to Tourist

Punkt (Kościuszki 17; ℂ **018/200-01-77**; www.tourist-punkt.pl). The helpful staff maintains lists of dozens of private rooms, pensions, and hotels at every price point. Simply describe what you're looking for and they will fix you up. Another private agency, Zwyrtołka, two doors down toward town (Kościuszki 15; ℂ **018/201-52-12**), maintains a list of rooms. Both agencies can help arrange day trips, including excursions to Slovakia, as well as sell lift passes and advise on things like ski and bike rental.

WHERE TO STAY

Hotel rates in Zakopane are high, and this is one town where you may want to consider staying in a pension or private room. These abound. If you arrive in town early, simply walk around and inquire where you see signs saying WOLNY POKOJE or NOCLEGI. Or to save time, try Tourist Punkt (see above). They maintain an extensive database of private accommodations (with photos) and will happily book you a room. Make sure to specify that you want to be in the center, otherwise they may try to place you in a far-flung corner of town. Expect to pay about 50 zł ($17/£9) a person for a private room. Hotel and room rates rise considerably in the week between Christmas and New Year's. Aside from that, January, February, and August are the busiest times of the year, and pre-booking is essential. The rates below are for summer and winter season, outside of the Christmas and New Year period.

Very Expensive

Hotel Belvedere 🏵🏵   At the moment, the classiest place to stay in Zakopane. The ambience here is the 1920s, but updated with extras like a Roman spa and a game room, with a bowling alley and other more-modern pursuits. The in-house restaurant is top-notch. The real advantage is location, about 2km (1¼ miles) outside of the center. That makes it a 10- to 15-minute walk to Krupówki, but means you can also escape the masses and enjoy the mountains if you want. One of the nicest hiking trails along the Biała river valley starts just above the hotel's doors.

Droga do Białego 3. ℂ **018/202-12-00.** Fax 018/202–12–50. www.belvederehotel.pl. 175 units. 690 zł ($230/£140) double. AE, DC, MC, V. **Amenities:** Restaurant; indoor swimming pool; spa; bike and ski rental; concierge; business center; shopping arcade; salon; room service; dry cleaning; nonsmoking rooms. *In room:* A/C, TV, dataport, minibar, hair dryer, safe.

Hotel Litwor 🏵   This luxury hotel occupying a handsome mountain chalet admittedly looks a little out of place in the middle of busy Krupówki street. When it opened in 1999, the hotel claimed to be the first four-star hotel in this part of Poland. Certainly it's still one of the best in town, but the Belvedere offers more of a feeling of exclusivity, and when reconstruction is finished at the Grand Hotel Stamary, *it* may be better than both. The rooms are well proportioned and furnished in contemporary browns and blues. Ask for one with a view to the mountains. Wi-Fi Internet access is available throughout the hotel.

Krupówki 40. ℂ **018/202-42-00.** Fax 018/202-42-05. www.litwor.pl. 63 units. 575 zł ($192/£100) double. AE, DC, MC, V. **Amenities:** Restaurant; indoor swimming pool; fitness room; spa; bike and ski rental; concierge; salon; limited room service; dry cleaning; nonsmoking rooms. *In room:* A/C, TV, minibar, hair dryer.

Expensive

Grand Hotel Stamary 🏵🏵🏵 *(Finds)*   This beautifully restored turn-of-the-20th-century manor hotel whisks you away to those stylish 1920s and 1930s with its elegant lobby and cocktail bar, and wide corridors with dark-wood flooring. The period detailing extends to the rooms, furnished in browns and golds. The location is superb, just where the bus from Kraków drops you off, and a short walk down from the main train and bus terminals. The main pedestrian street, Krupówki, is about 180m (600 ft.) down the street—near enough to be convenient but far enough from the commotion. The restoration process is still underway and the spa and wellness facilities were not open at this writing (though the owners say all will be ready for 2007).

Kościuszki 19. ℂ 018/201-91-00. www.stamary.pl. 53 units. www.stamary.pl. 450 zł ($150/£80) double. AE, DC, MC, V. **Amenities:** Restaurant; fitness center; spa; dry cleaning; nonsmoking rooms. *In room:* A/C, TV, dataport, minibar, hair dryer.

Hotel Villa Marilor 𝕱𝕱   Occupying a sprawling Kaiser yellow villa just across the street from the Grand Hotel Stamary, this is another contender for "nicest place to stay in Zakopane." Peace and quiet is what the hotel is offering here, and once you step onto the beautiful grounds you won't hear a sound. Everything feels refined, from the chandeliers and marble-topped desks in the lobby to the nicely sized rooms, furnished in late-19th-century style. The hotel offers special rooms for disabled persons. Wi-Fi Internet access available throughout the hotel and on the garden terrace.

Kościuszki 18. ℂ 018/206-44-11. Fax 018/206-44-10. www.hotele-marilor.com.pl. 20 units. 480 zł ($160/£85) double. AE, DC, MC, V. **Amenities:** Restaurant; outdoor tennis court; fitness center, spa; concierge; business center; room service; dry cleaning; nonsmoking rooms. *In room:* A/C, TV, dataport, minibar, hair dryer.

Moderate
Hotel Gromada 𝕱   This utilitarian, 1960s high-rise offers amenities like a spa and fitness room at rates about half the competition. The rooms are boxy but clean and comfortable. Ask for a room away from the busy street. The location is central, just a couple of steps off Krupówki. The location means it tends to fill up fast, so try booking in advance. The receptionist says the hotel is due for a makeover, so some of the facilities may be updated by the time you arrive.

Zaruskiego 2. ℂ 018/201-50-11. Fax 018/201-53-30. 55 units. 220 zł ($73/£40) double. AE, DC, MC, V. **Amenities:** Restaurant; fitness room; sauna (with salt grotto); nonsmoking rooms. *In room:* TV, hair dryer.

Inexpensive
Pensjonat Szarotka 𝕱𝕱   This smallish, eccentric 1930s villa feels more in harmony with Zakopane's artistic past. The pension is not far from the Belvedere, about two kilometers out of the center of town, and close to the Biała valley hiking trail. The squeaky stairways, the cozy little reading room with a fireplace, and the evocative black-and-white photos on the wall all scream "Grandma's house." The lovely 1930s breakfast nook is a real treat. On the downside, the rooms are tiny and crammed together (how did they carve 17 rooms out of this house?) Still, for the money, the atmosphere, and the location, it can't be beat.

Male Żywczańskie 16a. ℂ 018/206-40-50. Fax 018/201-48-02. www.szarotka.pl. 17 units. 180 zł ($60/£32) double. No credit cards. **Amenities:** Restaurant; nonsmoking rooms. *In room:* TV.

WHERE TO DINE
Most of the restaurants are clustered along the main pedestrian area, Krupówki. The lower stretch is the loudest and most congested. If you're looking for something a little quieter, walk uphill along the street a couple of blocks and the crowds start to thin out. Restaurant meals are relatively cheap, and most of what's on offer in town is broadly the same. In addition to the places listed here, the restaurants in the Hotel

Belvedere and Hotel Litwor are both highly regarded locally, though are somewhat more expensive.

Very Expensive

Otwarcze ⓕ POLISH   The loudest and most popular of a number of similar faux-folk-style grill restaurants along the main pedestrian street. Rack after rack of yard-long shish kabobs on the grill, an ensemble of highlander musicians to set the mood, and waitstaff decked out like a Polish episode of *Little House on the Prairie*. Don't panic. It's just as kitschy for Poles as it is for everyone else, and the mood is definitely fun. The menu runs several pages long, but most people simply order the "szaszlyk" (shish kabob), a mix of grilled pork, sausage, and onions, served with grilled potatoes and a self-serve salad.

Krupówki 26–28 (just around the corner from the Kolorowe.) No phone. Lunch and dinner items 27 zł–36 zł ($9–$12/£5–£7). No credit cards. Daily 11am–10pm.

Expensive

Kolorowe ⓕ POLISH   Similar in attitude but perhaps slightly quieter and more civilized than the Otwarcze next door. A similar card, with mostly pork shish kabobs on the grill, and accompanying live music and waitresses in full peasant regalia. They also offer pizza, but that's more of an afterthought. Stick with the grilled meats and enjoy.

Krupówki 26. ⓒ 018/150-55. Lunch and dinner items 21 zł–30 zł ($7–$10/£3.60–£6). No credit cards. Daily 11am–10pm.

Moderate

Kalina ⓕⓕ POLISH   The quietest and altogether most pleasant of the Polish-style restaurants on Krupówki and certainly worth seeking out. Here the folklore element is low-key. You won't always find live music, but as compensation you'll get a cook who pays more attention to what's on the plate and some alternatives to grilled pork, like decent pierogies and roast duck. The interior is done up in traditional cottage style, meaning intricately carved woodworking, wood-beamed ceilings, and a nice warm fire.

Krupówki 46. ⓒ 018/201-26-50. Lunch and dinner items 18 zł27 zł ($6–$9/£3.30–£4.80). No credit cards. Daily 11am–10pm.

Pstrag Górski ⓕ SEAFOOD   Popular little spot just off the main drag that special-izes in grilled river fish, especially—as the name suggests—trout (pstrag). Good choice for a nice lunch or a light early meal. In addition to fish dishes, they also have a full range of grilled meats. In summer, eat on the covered terrace overlooking the throngs on Krupówki,

Krupówki 6. ⓒ 018/206-41-63. Lunch and dinner items 18 zł–24 zł ($6–$9/£3.30–£4.80). AE, DC, MC, V. Daily 11am–10pm.

Soprano ⓕⓕ ITALIAN   Hard to believe, but you can actually find outstanding pizza in the middle of the kitschiest street in Poland. Soprano offers most of the stan-dard combinations, but also has healthier options like broccoli and fresh spinach top-pings. Sit out on the terrace and enjoy the view, or have a quieter, candlelit pizza in the back.

Krupówki 49. ⓒ 018/201-54-43. Lunch and dinner items 21 zł–27 zł ($7–$9/£3.60–£4.80). No credit cards. Daily 11am–10pm.

Inexpensive

Pizza Dominium ITALIAN   Not as good as Soprano, but cheaper and quicker. Dominium is a popular and successful Polish pizza chain going head-to-head with Pizza Hut. The locals may have the advantage with thick-crust pizzas and usually fresh ingredients. This branch is on Krupówki, but they also have a restaurant at 2,000m (6,560 ft.) on the peak at Kasprowy Wierch, if you happen to be in the neighborhood.

Krupówki 51. © 018/206-42-11. Lunch and dinner items 12 zł–18 zł ($4–$6/£2.20–£3.30). No credit cards. Daily 11am–10pm.

EXPLORING

Krupówki merits about an hour's stroll end to end. Toward the northern end of Krupówki (downhill), follow Ko1cieliska to the left for a couple of blocks to see two of the town's most interesting sites. One is a tiny wooden church, the **Church of St. Clement;** the other is the adjoining **cemetery,** with some of the most ornately carved headstones you're likely ever to see. Look especially for the highly stylized totem pole that marks the grave of Stanisław Witkiewicz (see below), the architect who first set off the local craze for all things wooden.

Tatra Museum (Muzeum Tatrzańskie)   There's not much information in English, so you're not likely to get much out of this exhibition of the personalities and events that have shaped Zakopane and the Tatras down through the ages. Still, there are some interesting stands of folk architecture and costumes on the ground floor. Children will like the stuffed animals on the second floor, showing the diversity of the flora and fauna in the mountain regions. Be sure to stow your camera safely out of sight from the museum guards. They are paranoid you might want to photograph something (a stuffed beaver maybe?). If they see you have a camera, they will follow you around the entire museum.

Krupówki 10. www.muzeumtatrzanskie.com.pl. Tues–Fri 9am–4:30pm; Sun 9am–3pm.

Museum of Zakopane Style (Muzeum Stylu Zakopańskiego) ✵✵   More interesting than the Tatra Museum is this tribute to the work of groundbreaking Polish architect Stanisław Witkiewicz, the originator of the fabled wooden houses that came to be known as the "Zakopane style." The mansion that houses the museum, the Willa Koliba, dating from 1894, was the first to be built in this style, roughly Poland's equivalent of the Arts and Crafts movement. One of the draws is simply the chance to walk around one of these big old houses, but there are plenty of interesting examples of ornately carved furniture and accessories. Upstairs, there's a small gallery of the freaky and fascinating 1920s society portraits by Witkiewicz's son, Witkacy. He was portraitist of choice for Poland's Lost Generation.

Kościeliska 18. Wed–Sat 9:30am–4:30pm; Sun 9am–3pm.

OUTSIDE OF ZAKOPANE

Zakopane is a natural jumping-off point for active pursuits of all sorts. In summer, the activity of choice is hiking in the mountains. Good hiking maps are available at the tourist information offices and at nearly any hotel or kiosk. Many of the best trails begin just a short walk from town.

A good hike of about 4 hours of moderate to heavy exertion and some awesome views begins from the Hotel Belvedere and follows the yellow trail along the Biała Valley (Dolina Białego). After a 90-minute ascent, turn onto the black trail, following the signs for Stążyska Polana, and returning to Zakopane via the red trail along the Stążyska Valley. Another popular hike to a different part of the mountains is to follow the red trail to Morskie Oko, an Alpine lake in the far southern corner of Poland's share of the High Tatras. Most travel agencies in town offer packages that include transportation to the trail head to the east of Zakopane, but once you get off the bus you'll have to walk or take a horse cart (40 zl/$13/£7) the 9km (5½ miles) uphill to the lake.

In winter, the most popular hill for skiing is Kasprowy Wierch, with several slopes of all difficulty levels starting from here. To reach it, take a bus from Zakopane to Kuźnice, and then by cable car to the peak.

Zakopane is also a good base for a rafting the Dunajec River, east of the Tatras along Poland's border with Slovakia. In nice weather, this is a fabulous day out, especially for kids, on traditional timber boats, led by Górale mountain men kitted out in their folk garb. (For a longer description of the trip, see "Slovakia," p. 633.) The boating center on the Polish side is at Sromowce Kąty. The Świat travel agency (Zamoyskiego 12; *☎* 018/210-31-99) is one of several agencies in Zakopane that arrange trips, including transportation, for about 120 zł ($40/£22) a person.

SHOPPING

Krupówki is jammed wall-to-wall with souvenir shops, gold and silver dealers, and outdoor outfitters, all competing for your attention with a jumble of cafes, restaurants, pizza joints, and refreshment stands. Just about everything you might need, you'll find along this busy 5 or 6 blocks. Most of the gift and souvenir stores peddle in the same sorts of imported, mass-produced junk—wooden toys, T-shirts, hats and scarves, and mock traditional clothing that sadly have little connection to Zakopane. For something more authentic, try looking in at **Cepelia,** with two locations on Krupówki (nos. 2 and 48; *☎* 018/201-50-48). Here you'll find locally produced carved wooden boxes, animal pelts, leather goods, and the odd knickknack or two. **Art Gallery Yam** (Krupówki 63; *☎* 018/206-69-84) is about as funky as it gets in Zakopane. Check out the rotating exhibitions of contemporary Polish painters. Some riveting modern Tatra landscapes, and other works that draw on the absurdist visual style of Polish art in the '70s and '80s.

One souvenir you won't be able to miss are those little rounds of sheep's milk cheese, **Oscypek,** that you see everywhere around town. The recipe apparently goes back some 500 years. The salty taste goes great with beer.

AFTER DARK

Paparazzi   The local version of a regional chain of cocktail bar/nightclubs occupies a beautiful creek-side location that is *the* after-hours spot in town for a cold beer or glass of wine. Also offers passable versions of international dishes like chicken burritos and Caesar salads. Ul. Gen. Galicy 8. *☎* 018/206-32-51. Daily noon–1am.

Piano Bar   Just next to Art Gallery Yam and draws on its artistic funkiness for a laid-back, hipster feel. Though it's just down a small alley from the Krupówki throng, it's a world away in attitude. Krupówki 63 (in the little alleyway). Daily 4pm–midnight.

6 Silesia

WROCŁAW

300km (180 miles) E of Kraków

Wrocław, the capital of Lower Silesia, known as Dolny Śląsk in Polish, is a surprisingly likable big city. Although it was extensively damaged during World War II and stagnated under Communism, it's bounced back in a big way. Part of the reason has been its western location, near the German border. This has made it easily accessible to prosperous German day-trippers, who pour over the border for a coffee and a strudel. It's also drawn outside investment, particularly from the Japanese, who are eager to reach the rich markets of western Europe while producing in low-wage Poland.

The heart of the city is a beautifully restored central square, the Rynek, and the playfully colorful baroque and Renaissance houses that line the square on all sides. On a warm summer's evening, the square comes to life, as it seems the entire city descends for a glass of beer or a cup of coffee. Most of this area lay in ruins in 1945, when the Germans held out here for months against an intense Russian barrage. But all that seems forgotten now. Only the presence of the surviving red-brick Gothic churches, now mostly restored, but here and there still showing some of their wartime wounds, evokes a sense of the scale of the destruction.

Wrocław was founded some 1,000 years ago by Slavs, but its population had become increasingly Germanized throughout the centuries. Until the end of World War II Wrocław was known as the German city of Breslau. The city came under Polish control with the defeat of Nazi Germany and the shifting of Poland's borders hundreds of kilometers to the West. The surviving Germans were driven out of the city and Wrocław was repopulated by Poles—many coming from the east of the country, particularly the city of Lwów, which came under Soviet domination. Although the city was overwhelmingly German just a generation ago, about the only German you're likely to hear now are from the day-trippers ordering their coffee.

In spite of the border change and population shift, the city retains the unmistakable feel of a German provincial town, especially in the Rynek and the streets of the Old Town. Spend time as well along the Odra River, which passes the town just to the north of the Rynek. It's said there are more bridges here than any other city in Europe. The river area was under heavy reconstruction in 2006, but the city authorities have promised to have things ready by 2007.

ESSENTIALS

GETTING THERE   Wrocław lies on the main four-lane highway (A4) linking the German border with the city of Kraków, so getting here from Germany or Kraków is easy. The stretch from Kraków to Katowice will cost a toll of 6.50 zł ($2.20/£1.15) but is well worth the money. Rail and bus links are good between Wrocław and major Polish towns and cities. The train and bus stations are situated together, about 2km (1 mile) south of the central city. The main train station, Główny, is a spooky-looking multiturreted castle and a tourist site in its own right. To get to town from the station, walk 15 minutes or take a taxi.

GETTING AROUND   You'll find yourself doing a lot of walking. The Old Town is relatively small and closed off to cars. Outside of the Old Town, tram and bus lines are extensive. Tickets cost 2 zł (65¢/35p) and are available from vending machines around town or newspaper kiosks. As for taxis, dishonest drivers have sometimes been a problem. Never get into a unlicensed taxi and use reputable firms when possible. **Lux** (© **9623**) and **Hallo** (© **9621**) are two of the best.

VISITOR INFORMATION   Wrocław's helpful tourist information center is situated on the Rynek (Rynek 14; © **071/344-31-11;** www.itwroclaw.pl; daily 9am– 9pm). In addition to the usual services of handing out maps and selling postcards, the staff can help arrange tours of the city, book hotel and restaurant reservations, help to sort out bus and train tickets, and even rent bikes. The office is also a good source of cultural information. To see what's on, pick up a free copy of *The Visitor,* updated every 2 months, at the tourist information office.

WHERE TO STAY

Hotel prices have been rising in recent years in step with the growing economy and rising accommodations standards. You can beat the high cost by planning your visit on a weekend, when rates are cut by as much as 30%. There's a good cluster of hotels along Kiełbaśnicza, in the northern part of the Old Town near the university.

Very Expensive

Holiday Inn 🐾🐾   Not long ago, this was arguably the best place to stay in Wrocław. It's still an exceptionally nice hotel, but for the money there are now equally comfortable places closer to the Rynek. The outlying location, however, is excellent if you are arriving by train or bus, since the hotel is just a short hop from both. For business, this is probably still the best address in town, given the extensive business center and conference facilities. And it's certainly still one of the few places around offering warmed bathroom tiles and bathtubs as standard.

Piłsudskiego 49/57. © **071/787-00-00,** or 44-870-400-91-21 (U.K.-based central reservation service). Fax 071/ 787-00-01. www.wroclaw.globalhotels.pl or www.holiday-inn.com. 164 units. 520 zł ($173/£90). AE, DC, MC, V. **Amenities:** Restaurant; exercise room; sauna; concierge car-rental desk; business center; salon; room service; massage; executive-level rooms; nonsmoking rooms. *In room:* A/C, TV, dataport, minibar, hair dryer, trouser press (executive rooms only).

Hotel Prima/Best Western 🐾   To be sure, a clean and well-managed hotel, but feels overpriced given some of the newer properties on the market. Everything you would expect from the Best Western chain. The staff training is evident from the first encounter with the helpful reception desk. The rooms are upscale middle-market, with carpets and floral prints on the bedspreads (like a well-furnished suburban home). The hotel's Sir William restaurant is a nice choice for vegetarians.

Kiełbaśnicza 16/19. © **071/782-55-55.** Fax 071/342-67-32. www.bestwestern-prima.pl. 79 units. 420 zł ($140/£75) double. AE, DC, MC, V. **Amenities:** Restaurant; exercise room; sauna; limited room service; nonsmoking rooms. *In room:* A/C, TV, dataport, minibar, hair dryer.

Expensive

Art Hotel 🐾   Occupying two renovated burghers' houses in Wrocław's art (and hotel) quarter, this is a welcome alternative to the chains. The funky, bright orange exterior will draw you in. The reception area is sleek and cool. Each room has been furnished individually in an eclectic mix of modern and traditional. The restaurant gets high marks from local critics.

Kiełbaśnicza 20. ☎ **071/787-71-00.** Fax 071/342-39-29. www.arthotel.pl 77 units. 360 zł ($120/£65) small double, 410 zł ($133/£70) standard double. AE, DC, MC, V. **Amenities:** Restaurant; exercise room; business center; salon; room service; massage; nonsmoking rooms. *In room:* A/C, TV, dataport, minibar, hair dryer.

Hotel Patio 🌟🌟   Another renovated Burgher's house on Kiełbaśnicza, but slightly cheaper than its rivals. The Patio is every bit as inviting as the Art and Prima hotels, but what you don't get for the price are a fitness room, sauna, and air-conditioning. The rooms, done in fresh colors, light woods, and whites, are a notch more inviting than the competition.

Kiełbaśnicza 24/25. ☎ **071/375-04-00.** Fax 071/343-91-49. www.hotelpatio.pl. 49 units. 360 zł ($120/£65) double. AE, DC, MC, V. **Amenities:** Restaurant; limited room service; nonsmoking rooms. *In room:* TV, dataport, minibar, hair dryer.

Qubus Hotel 🌟🌟🌟   This smallish and smart hotel just a short walk from the Rynek is oriented more toward visiting businessmen. Rates are discounted 25% for weekend stays. Competes head-to-head with the Prima/Best Western, but gets the nod for slightly lower prices, a swimming pool, and a more modern feel throughout. Qubus is a growing chain of high-quality hotels.

Sw. Marii Magdaleny 2. ☎ **071/341-09-20.** Fax 071/375–29–47. www.qubushotel.com. 87 units. 400 zł ($133/£70) double. AE, DC, MC, V. **Amenities:** Restaurant; indoor pool; sauna; limited room service; nonsmoking rooms. *In room:* A/C, TV, dataport, minibar, hair dryer.

Moderate

Hotel Zaułek 🌟   Decent in-town choice, given the excellent location and relatively low price. The hotel is run by a foundation for the university of Wrocław and does double-duty hosting visiting professors and university guests. From the outside, the hotel looks like an aging housing complex, but on the inside it's neat, clean, and quiet. The rooms are modestly furnished but perfect for a short stay.

Garbary 11. ☎ **071/341-00-46.** Fax 071/375-29-47. 15 units. 290 zł ($93/£50) double. AE, DC, MC, V. **Amenities:** Restaurant; nonsmoking rooms. *In room:* TV, minibar, hair dryer.

Inexpensive

Hotel Monopol 🌟🌟 *Value*   This glorious, turn-of-the-20th-century Art Nouveau hotel, right on the approach to the Rynek, has definitely seen better days. It's the perfect throwback experience, but it's not clear whether you're going back to the glory days when Marlene Dietrich stayed here or to the Communist 1970s and 1980s, when the receptionist was obviously trained. The rugs are a little frayed and the plumbing fixtures could use an update, but the atmosphere remains special. A plaque on the first floor says Pablo Picasso stayed here after World War II to attend an international conference of intellectuals. Don't bother with the breakfast buffet; it's inedible. Instead walk toward the Rynek and have a coffee at Coffee Heaven (Świdnicka 3), a decent Polish incarnation of Starbucks.

Heleny Modrzejewskiej 2. ☎ **071/343-70-41.** Fax 071/343–51–03. 70 units. 264 zł ($88/£45) double. AE, DC, MC, V. **Amenities:** Restaurant; shopping arcade; salon; limited room service; nonsmoking rooms. *In room:* TV, hair dryer.

WHERE TO DINE

The Rynek is lined with restaurants, cafes, and bars from corner to corner. Most restaurants post their menus out front, so peruse the square and see what you're hungry for.

Very Expensive

Sakana Sushi Bar ✦✦✦ JAPANESE   A standout Japanese sushi bar of the kind where you sit on stools and watch little boats of delicacies float by, selecting this one or that depending on your appetite—or if you're like me, your wallet. Each plate has a different color, with white being the cheapest (starting at around 9 zł/$3/£1.60) and heading due north from there. Three plates makes for a filling meal, so if you choose carefully you can still keep it under budget, but what's the fun of that when the food is this fantastic?

Odrazańska 17/1a. ✆ **071/343-37-10.** Lunch and dinner items 42 zł–60 zł ($14–$20/£7.50–£11). AE, DC, MC, V. Mon–Sat noon–10pm; Sun 1–10pm.

Expensive

Karczma Lwowska ✦✦ POLISH/UKRAINIAN   Named for the former Polish, now Ukrainian, city from where many current Wrocław residents originally hail. The menu features many hard-to-find specialties from eastern Poland, including Gołąbki Kresówki, stuffed peppers stuffed with spiced minced meat and mushrooms. In summer, dine on the terrace, or in winter in the evocative, tavern-style interior. Best to book ahead to avoid disappointment, especially on a warm summer's evening, when the terrace is filled to brimming.

Rynek 4. ✆ **071/343-98-87.** Lunch and dinner items 21 zł–42 zł ($7–$14/£3.60–£7.50). AE, DC, MC, V. Daily 11am–11pm.

Pani Dulska ✦✦ POLISH   Very good Polish restaurant in an elegant, subdued setting that's faithful both to Poland's traditional tavern decor and modern style at the same time. Daily luncheon specials are good value, but it's also a nice splurge at night. Try the grilled pork served in a sauce of juniper berries. The location, just down from "hotel row," Kiełbaśnicza, makes getting here just a 2-minute walk away.

Kiełbaśnicza 13. ✆ **071/793-37-22.** Lunch and dinner items 27 zł–36 zł ($9–$12/£4.70–£6.50). AE, DC, MC, V. Daily 11am–11pm.

Moderate

Novocaina ✦✦ ITALIAN   A trendy new entry on the Rynek that promises only the freshest ingredients, without preservatives or additives. And the Italian-influenced menu mostly delivers. The pizzas are cooked in a traditional cherrywood-fired oven and come out just right. The high points are the salads and sandwiches, making this a good lunchtime pick and popular with Wrocław's young professional crowd. Very good coffee and free Wi-Fi are two more good reasons to visit.

Rynek 13. ✆ **071/343-69-15.** Lunch and dinner items 21 zł–30 zł ($7–$10/£3.60–£5.50). AE, DC, MC, V. Daily 9am–11pm.

Inexpensive

Alladin's ✦ MIDDLE EASTERN   A rarity in Poland is a decent Middle Eastern restaurant, and this one is one of the best you'll find. The hummus and falafel make for a welcome departure from heavier Polish food. Alladin's is close to the university and attracts an informal student crowd for both lunches and dinners.

Odrazańska 23. ✆ **071/796-73-27.** Lunch and dinner items 18 zł–24 zł ($6–$8/£3.20–£4.30). No credit cards. Daily 11:30am–10pm.

Rodeo Drive ✦ TEX-MEX   One of the better Polish chain restaurants to emerge in the last few years; this one features "Texas-style" steaks, ribs, and burgers. Ordinarily, you could skip the America-themed restaurants in favor of more exotic Polish fare, but in a land of mediocre burgers, this place really does stand out if you're in the mood. The portions are enormous, so even 6-foot-2 cowboys might be content with a "cowgirl" portion—even if the waitress does raise an eyebrow when you order it. The corner Rynek location is one of the better spots to people-watch.

Rynek18/21. ✆ 071/343-96-15. Lunch and dinner items 18 zł–24 zł ($6–$8/£3.20–£4.30). AE, DC, MC, V. Daily 11am–10pm.

EXPLORING

The main tourist attractions can be seen in a few hours of leisurely strolling. The natural place to start, and the best place to get your bearings, is the enormous **Rynek.** The Rynek is dominated (and that really *is* the right word in this case) by the enormous Town Hall, the Ratusz, at the center of the square. The Rynek is lined some of the most cheerful baroque and Renaissance facades to grace a Polish town square. On the northwest corner of the square is the foreboding, Gothic red-brick **St. Elizabeth Church (Kościół Św. Elżbiety),** Wrocław's most impressive. You can climb the tower, but keep in mind it's over 90m (280 ft.) high. To the east of the Rynek is another evocative and beautiful church, the **Church of Mary Magdalene (Kościół Św. Marii Magdaleny).** Just to the west of the Rynek, past the Tourist Information Office, is the smaller **Plac Solny,** the former salt market that's now given over to an enormous flower market. Off the square, the side streets in all directions merit a couple of hours of ambling. North of the Rynek, and along the Odra River, is the university district, where you'll find some of best nightspots. To the northwest of the Rynek, around Kiełbaśnicza, is Wrocław's arty district—formed amid some weathered but pretty blocks of buildings that survived the onslaught of World War II. Here you'll find a small street called the Old Shambles, "Stare Jatki." This was formerly the butchers' quarter, and is now filled with art galleries and coffee bars.

From the university district, follow the Odra River to right over a series of small, picturesque islands to the **Ostrów Tumski,** with another clutch of medieval churches. Much of the river area was under heavy construction in 2006, and once it's all finished, this will be wonderful place to spend time.

Town Hall (Ratusz) ✦✦   One of Poland's largest and most awe-inspiring town halls. It was originally built in the late 13th century, but added on to and renovated time and time again down through the centuries. It's lost its administrative function and now serves a mostly decorative role—a place to situate a huge tower and hang an astronomical clock. The city museum inside is worth a quick peek, but more to see the inside of the building than to peruse the exhibits at length.

Rynek. ✆ 071/347-16-93. Wed–Sun 10am–5pm.

Panorama of the Battle of Racławice (Panorama Racławicka) ✦✦   This enormous 360-degree "panorama" painting dates from the late 19th century and depicts the battle of Racławice on April 4, 1794, when a Polish force led by national hero Tadeusz Kościuszko defeated the Russian army. The battle came at a time when Poland faced threats from the east, west, and south, and aroused hopes that Poland might survive as a nation. Those hopes proved short-lived. A few months later, in November 1794, the Polish uprising was crushed, and Poland was later divided among Prussia, Russia, and Austria in the infamous Polish partition. The painting itself, executed while Poland was still partitioned, was a bold national statement at the time, and still evokes strong national sentiment. In the years following World War II, the painting was hidden from view lest its anti-Russian sentiments offend the Soviet overlords. After the rise of the Solidarity in the 1980s, the painting was finally unveiled to the general public in 1985.

Purkyniego 11. ⓒ 071/344-16-61. Daily 9am–5pm.

National Museum (Muzeum Narodowe) ⌖   The National Museum is located just down from the Panorama Racławicka and you can use the same admission ticket for entry to both. This museum is interesting primarily because it combines the collections of both the cities of Wrocław and Lwów, and is very strong on medieval painting and sculpture from both eastern and western Poland. That said, unless you're particularly interested in Poland or have some very specific historical knowledge, you're unlikely to get much from the very detailed holdings here.

Pl. Powstancow Warszawy 5. ⓒ 071/343-88-30. Wed–Sun 10am–4pm.

OUTSIDE OF WROCŁAW

If you have a couple of days to spare and are seeking relief from the city, Wrocław is a good jumping-off spot for exploring the Polish side of the **Sudeten (Sudety) mountains** that form the country's southern border with the Czech Republic. Both sides of the border are lined with little resort towns for hiking in summer and skiing in winter. The tallest peaks are in the 1,600m (5,000-ft.) range; most of the area is covered by the Karkonosze National Park, with its miles and miles of restorative hiking trails. The largest town in the region is picturesque **Jelenia Góra,** about 100km (60 miles) southwest of Wrocław. From Jelenia Góra it's just a short bus ride to the resorts of **Szklarska Poręba** and **Karpacz.** Of the two, Szklarska Poręba is prettier, but Karpacz is closer to the trails. Several buses and trains daily make the trip from Wrocław to Jelenia Góra, with buses being slightly faster. By car, it's a 2-hour drive. If you're driving to the Czech Republic, the area is an easy stopover. The main Czech border crossing is only about 30km (18 miles) down the road from Jelenia Góra.

WROCŁAW AFTER DARK

Wrocław is renowned for its theater, long regarded as some of the most daring and experimental in the country. But for non-Polish speakers, this is likely to be of little interest. The Tourist Information Office at the Rynek is a good source of information on more accessible performances of classical music and opera. The **Wrocław Philharmonic** (Piłsudskiego 19; ⓒ **071/343-85-28**) is a good bet for an excellent concert in season on a Friday or Saturday night. The **Lower Silesian Opera** (Opera Dolnośląska, Świdnicka 35; ⓒ **071/372-43-57**) is one of the country's leading companies.

For culture of the lower-brow sort, Wrocław is a great drinking and party town. Its festive spirit, not surprisingly, is bolstered by the tens of thousands of college students here. The university area has more than its fair share of beer gardens, cafes, and cocktail bars. Try the places along Ruska and Kuźnica. Naturally, the Rynek itself is a major draw. What appear to be normal restaurants and cafes during the day transmogrify into everything from rowdy beer halls to ultrachill dance clubs after sunset.

Graciarnia 🌟🌟 This is a good spot if you're looking for a quiet beer or drink in the evening, a little bit away from the action. A self-described "chill zone" features antique furniture, a laid-back clientele, and very friendly servers. Ul. K. Wielkiego 39. No phone. Daily noon–1am.

7 Gdańsk & the Baltic Seacoast

GDAŃSK
420km (250 miles) N of Wrocław

Gdańsk (www.Gdańsk.pl or http://guide.trojmiasto.pl) is a pleasant surprise. If you were expecting a dingy Baltic seaport, maybe reinforced by those foggy, black-and-white TV memories of Lech Wałęsa and embattled Solidarity dockworkers, you'll be in for a shock. Modern-day Gdańsk is a beautiful seaside town, with a lovingly restored Old Town and an easy, laid-back feel. On arrival, you'll immediately want to extend your stay, so plan on spending at least an extra day longer than budgeted.

Even for Poland, Gdańsk has a particularly twisted history that will play havoc with anyone who is even mildly geographically challenged. The city rose to prominence in the 16th and 17th centuries as one of the most important towns of the Hanseatic League, a grouping of prosperous seaport cities that controlled much of the trade in the North and Baltic seas. Because of its wealth, Gdańsk was hotly contested between German and Polish interests, though it managed to retain its status as a semi-autonomous city-state. After the Polish partition at the end of the 18th century, the city fell under Prussian rule and became firmly identified as "Danzig," its German name. Following Germany's defeat in World War I, the city's status became one of the thorniest issues facing the drafters of the Treaty of Versailles. They opted to create what they called the "Free City of Danzig"—neither German nor Polish—alongside a Polish-ruled strip of land that would effectively cut off mainland Germany from its East Prussian hinterland. Hitler was able to exploit very effectively the existence of this Polish "corridor" as part of his argument that the Treaty of Versailles was highly unfair to Germany. He even chose the port of Gdańsk to launch his war on Poland on Sept. 1, 1939, when German gunboats fired on the Polish garrison at Westerplatte.

Gdańsk was thoroughly destroyed in World War II, with the Russians and Allied bombers effectively finishing off any destruction the Germans weren't able to complete themselves. But Gdańsk was luckier than many Polish cities in that the reconstruction after the war was uncommonly sensitive. And unlike the reconstruction of Warsaw's Old Town (which seemed mostly to benefit the tourists), Gdańsk's newly built Old Town feels thoroughly lived in and authentic. The main drag, Długa ulica, is gorgeous and the streets radiating from it are filled with life.

During the Communist period, Gdańsk rose to fame as the home of the Lenin Shipyards and the Solidarity Trade Union. It was here, now known as the Gdańsk shipyards, where very tense negotiations in August 1980 between Solidarity, led by a youngish Lech Wałęsa, and the government resulted in official recognition of the first independent trade union in Communist Eastern Europe. The government later reneged on the agreement and imposed martial law, but Gdańsk continued as a hotbed of labor unrest and strikes. Roundtable talks in the late 1980s saw the government agree to a power-sharing arrangement that in 1989 led to the first semifree elections and a nationwide political triumph for Solidarity. You can still see the shipyards, about a 15-minute walk north of the Old Town, and visit an inspirational museum, the "Road to Freedom" (Drogi do Wolności), that details those tense moments in 1980 and the eventual overthrow of Communism.

Gdańsk is the largest and southernmost of a string of three Baltic resorts known as the "Trójmiasto" (Tri-Cities). Sopot, about 6km (4 miles) farther along the coast, is smaller, quieter, and more exclusive. Sopot was traditionally a retreat for the very wealthy, and while today it's probably better known as the Baltic party town par excellence, it still retains a whiff of old money. It's here too where you'll find the most easily accessible, and acceptably clean, beaches in summer. Gdynia, about 15km (10 miles) to the north, is the least impressive of the three. Not that long ago Gdynia was a relatively quiet coastal village, but it was built up in a hurry after World War I, when Polish authorities fashioned it into the country's busiest Baltic seaport. A convenient rail line links all three towns, with departures in all directions several times an hour during the day.

GETTING THERE

BY PLANE Port Lotniczy Gdańsk (also known as Lech Wałęsa International Airport) (Slowackiego 200; ℂ **058/348-11-11**) is about 10km (6 miles) west of the city. The airport has added several flights in recent years, and now has good direct connections to major European cities like London (Luton and Stansted) and Frankfurt, and several Scandinavian cities, among others. To get to town from the airport, take bus B, which runs twice hourly during daylight hours to Gdańsk's central Główny train station. The trip takes three 1.40 zł (50¢/30p) tickets. Leave about 30 minutes for the journey (more during rush hour). A taxi into town will cost about 40 zł ($13/£7). A taxi to Sopot will run about 50 zł ($17/£9) and to Gdynia about 70 zł ($23/£12).

BY TRAIN For most arrivals, Gdańsk's Główny train station (Dworzec PKP) (Podwale Grodzkie 1l; ℂ **058/721-94-36**) is the first port of a call. The station is just 5 minutes' walk (below a major highway) from the center of the city. Gdańsk is well served by the Polish state railroad, and departures to Warsaw and other major cities are frequent. Local trains to Sopot and Gdynia (see below) also depart from here. Buy domestic tickets at the ground-floor ticket windows; purchase international tickets upstairs.

BY BUS The main bus station, Dworzec PKS (ul. 3 Maje 12; ℂ **058/302-15-32**), is located just behind the train station. The Old Town is an easy walk, passing through the train station and then below the highway using the underpass. As Poland's Baltic hub, the city is a primary destination for domestic and international bus lines.

BY CAR Gdańsk is a traffic nightmare, so leave plenty of time to get here. The first problem is the major and seemingly permanent road construction, which has badly tied up routes coming from all directions. The main roads running south are the E75 to Toruń and the E77 to Warsaw. The E28 is the main route west toward Germany. Coming from the west, it skirts Gdańsk as it heads south. The E28 is someday planned to be a major four-lane north-south artery, but certainly not any time in the lifetime of this book. Once you arrive in the city, brace yourself for hour-long jams during the morning and evening rush hours. The drive from Warsaw, with traffic, may take as long 5 to 6 hours.

BY BOAT   It is possible to arrive in Gdańsk by ferry from Sweden. Polferries (www.polferries.pl) offers regular service between the Swedish port of Nynaeshamm (60km/36 miles south of Stockholm) and Gdańsk's Nowy Port (Przemyslowa 1; 7km north of the center; © **058/343-00-78**). The ferries depart every second or third day at 6pm and arrive at noon. Returns from Gdańsk follow the same schedule. Tickets (one adult without car) run about $80 each way. Sleeping berths are extra and start at $10 for a modest bunk to $150 for luxury cabin for two. Stena Line (www.stenaline.pl) runs a similar service from the southern Swedish city of Karlskrona (500km/300 miles south of Stockholm) to Gdynia's passenger ferry port. In summer, the ferries make the 10-hour journey twice daily at 9am and 9pm. Tickets (without car) run about $80 each way.

CITY LAYOUT

Confusingly, unlike other Polish cities, the heart of Gdańsk is technically not called the "Old Town," or **Stare Miasto.** There is a Stare Miasto, but it lies just to the north of the main center, the **Główne Miasto.** The Główne Miasto is where you'll find the main pedestrian walk, **ul. Długa (Long St.),** its extension, the **Długi Targ (the Long Market),** as well as the most interesting side streets, and the main pedestrian walk along the **Motława Canal.** Stare Miasto is about a 15-minute walk north, and it's here where you'll find the **Gdańsk shipyards,** the **Solidarity memorial,** and the **Road to Freedom** exhibit. Farther to the north, in the direction of Sopot, lies the still-skuzzy **Nowy Port,** as well as the far-nicer suburbs of **Wrzeszcz** and **Oliwa.** The former is home to many of the city's more affordable hotels and pensions. The heart of **Sopot** is about 6km (4 miles) to the north of Gdańsk's city center. **Gdynia** is about 15km (10 miles) to the north.

GETTING AROUND

ON FOOT   Much of central Gdańsk, including ul. Długa and the walkway along the canal, is closed to motor vehicles, so walking is the best option. The center is compact and easily walkable. To get to Sopot or Gdynia or places farther afield, however, you'll need to use public transportation.

BY TRAM   Gdańsk has an efficient network of trams that whisk you from the center of the city to the suburbs of Wrzeszcz and Oliwa in a few minutes. Note that trams do not run to Sopot and Gdynia. Tickets cost 1.40 zł (50¢/30p) for a short 10-minute ride. Buy and validate three tickets (4.20 zl/$1.40/75p) for longer rides of up to 30 minutes. You can buy tickets at Ruch kiosks, magazine counters, and from special vending machines.

BY BUS   City buses are useful for getting to some of the pensions on Beethovena ul., but otherwise walking, trams, trains, and taxis should be sufficient. Ticketing is the same as for trams, with a single short journey of 10 minutes costing 1.40 zł (50¢/30p).

BY TRAIN   A quick and reliable local train service, the SKM (Szybka Kolej Miejska), links the main cities of the Tri-Cities, Gdańsk, Sopot, and Gdynia. Several trains an hour during the day depart from Gdańsk's main train station. The full journey up to Gdynia will take a little more than half an hour and cost 4 zł ($1.35/70p). Buy your tickets in the hallway below the main station and validate them before you board the train.

BY TAXI   A good way to get to your hotel on arrival at the bus or train station, but you won't need taxis much once you've sorted out the public transportation system. Figure on fares of around 20 zł ($6.65/£3.60) for journeys in town.

BY FERRY   It's possible to go by ferry from Gdańsk to several local and regional destinations, including Westerplatte, Sopot, and Gdynia, as well as to the beaches on the Hel Peninsula farther afield. The main ferry landing (Długie Pobrzeże; ℂ **058/301-49-26**) is just near the intersection of the Długi Targ and the waterway, outside the Green Gate.

BY BIKE   Gdańsk is navigable by bicycle, and several new bike lanes now connect the center with the suburb of Wrzeszcz and beyond toward Sopot. That said, the network is spotty and there are plenty of places where you'll still have to contend with stairways, sidewalks, heavy traffic, and clueless Polish drivers. Bikes, however, are a good way of getting around Sopot. An easy and tranquil 10km (6-mile) bike lane skirts the beaches from Sopot to the northern Gdańsk suburbs.

VISITOR INFORMATION

The city's main tourist information office (ul. Długa 45; ℂ **058/301-91-51**) is conveniently situated in the heart of the Główne Miasto on the pedestrianized ul. Długa. The office is badly overburdened in summer, but nevertheless an essential stop for maps, lists of hotels and pensions, and ideas of what to see and do. Pick up a copy of the map "Gdańsk, Stare Miasto," a large-format, easy-to-read guide to all of the major sights in the center of town. Also look for the free brochure *The Best of Gdańsk*, a comprehensive, self-guided walking tour, with explanations in English. The tourist office also sells copies of *Gdańsk, In Your Pocket* (5 zl/$1.65/85p), an excellent overview of the city, including sections on Sopot and Gdynia.

WHERE TO STAY

The lodging situation has improved in recent years, but accommodations are still tight in July and August, so pre-booking is essential. Most of the expensive places, not surprisingly, are in the center, and you'll usually have to pay a premium for location. The cheaper places and pensions tend to be in the suburbs, like Wrzeszcz, about 3km (1¾ miles) north of the center toward Sopot.

Very Expensive

Hanza 👁👁   This is a clean, modern, privately owned hotel right along the river promenade, boasting an impressive roster of actors and politicians who regularly book here. The lobby and public areas have an understated, contemporary look. The rooms, in blue carpet and dark wood, are on the plain side, but very comfortable. Be sure to ask for a room with a view over the canal and the old town in the background (though these tend to fill up first). One big perk: It's one of the few hotels in the center to offer a full-service fitness club and sauna.

Tokarska 6. ℂ **058/305-34-27.** Fax 058/305-33-86. www.hotelhanza.pl. 60 units. 600 zł ($200/£110) double. AE, DC, MC, V. **Amenities:** Restaurant; health club and spa; concierge; business center; limited room service; nonsmoking rooms. *In room:* A/C, TV, dataport, minibar, hair dryer.

Podewils 👁👁   This relatively small, old-fashioned villa across the river from the town center is widely regarded as the city's finest hotel, though for less money you get more amenities at the Hanza and a better view at the Królewski. The Podewils's location will be much improved once the apartment buildings under construction next door are finished. Be sure to ask for a city view—not one that looks out onto the building site. That said, each of the rooms is meticulously decorated in beautiful antiques, and the professional staff will look after your every whim. Don't pass up the chance to have a meal or a glass of wine on the terrace overlooking the canal and the Old Town.

Szafarnia 2. © **058/300-95-60.** Fax 058/300-95-70. www.podewils.pl. 10 units. 800 zł ($266/£140) double. AE, DC, MC, V. **Amenities:** Restaurant; sauna; concierge; room service; nonsmoking rooms. *In room:* A/C, TV, dataport, minibar, hair dryer, safe.

Expensive

Kamienica Goldwasser 👁👁👁 *Value*   You couldn't ask for a better location at a better price. Seven nicely furnished apartments, right on the waterfront and above one of the city's nicest restaurants. Each room is furnished individually, in a tasteful mix of modern and traditional styles. Some rooms have fireplaces; ask to see a couple before choosing. That said there isn't much in the way of amenities or facilities. The reception is located inside the restaurant.

Długie Pobrzeże 22. © **058/301-88-78.** Fax 058/301-12-44. www.goldwasser.pl. 7 units. 340 zł ($113/£60) double. AE, DC, MC, V. **Amenities:** Restaurant. *In room:* TV, hair dryer.

Królewski 👁👁👁   This sleek, modern hotel is in a tastefully remodeled former granary just across the canal from Gdańsk's town center. If you can get it, ask for room no. 310—a corner double with drop-dead views of the riverside and all of Gdańsk's spires and gables. The rooms are tastefully modern, some with hardwood floors and bathtubs. The restaurant and breakfast room look out over the river, through a round little window like you're on a cruise. A special place.

Ołowianka 1. © **058/326-11-11.** Fax 058/326-11-10. www.hotelkrolewski.pl. 30 units. 360 zł ($120/£65) double. AE, DC, MC, V. **Amenities:** Restaurant. *In room:* A/C, TV, dataport, minibar, hair dryer.

Villa Eva 👁   Overpriced for what it is, but nevertheless a clean, comfortable hotel within relatively easy reach, via tram, of the Old Town. The owners seem to be going for a "boutique hotel" ambience, but little things like the sparsely furnished rooms and the lack of hair dryers in the bathrooms make it feel more like a high-end pension. The restaurant downstairs is very good, and a nice welcome if you arrive late and tired. The location, in the tony suburb of Wrzeszcz, is about 3km (1¾ miles) from the center (a 20–30-min. walk or a 10-min. tram ride from the train station).

Batorego 28. © **058/341-67-85.** Fax 058/341-67-85. www.villaeva.pl. 15 units. 360 zł ($120/£65) double. AE, DC, MC, V. **Amenities:** Restaurant. *In room:* TV, dataport.

Wolne Miasto 👁   The first thing you'll notice is the beautiful antique reception desk. That sets the tone for a well-run, attractively appointed in-town hotel. The decor is a restrained traditional look, with rooms fitted out with red carpets and antique wardrobes. The restaurant dabbles in relative exotica like tapas dishes and gets good marks from local critics.

Św. Ducha 2. © **058/305-22-55.** Fax 058/322-24-47. www.hotelwm.pl. 43 units. 340 zł ($113/£60) double. AE, DC, MC, V. **Amenities:** Restaurant. *In room:* TV, dataport, minibar.

Moderate

Biała Lilia ★★   This lodging is somewhere between a small hotel and a pension. It offers excellent value, given the crisp modern furnishings and the in-town location, just across the bridge from the Green Door and the delights of Długa. After so many sterile contemporary rooms, it's nice to see one that actually looks inviting. The cream walls and dark green carpeting lend a warmth that makes you want to linger. Ask the staff to show you the unique second-floor garden terrace out the back.

Spichrzowa 16. ℭ 058/301-70-74. Fax 058/320-14-73. www.bialalilia.pl. 16 units. 245 zł ($85/£45) double. AE, DC, MC, V. **Amenities:** Restaurant. *In room:* TV, dataport, minibar.

Kamienica Gotyk ★★ *(Finds* Ordinarily, you'd expect to pay a fortune for the location—in Gdańsk's oldest house on its loveliest street—but by some quirk of fate this charming little guesthouse is one of the least expensive hotels in town. I guess the owners like to feel virtuous. Admittedly, there's not much in the way of services or amenities, and the room furnishings feel like an afterthought, but the location is unbeatable. If you can get in, don't hesitate to book it.

Mariacka 1. ℭ **058/301-85-67.** www.gotykhouse.eu. 5 units. 250 zł ($83/£45) double. AE, DC, MC, V. *In room:* TV.

Inexpensive

Angela ★★   Quieter than it looks, since the pension is perched back away from the busy suburban street. Once you walk back to where the house is you see a lovely garden setting and a very clean and well-run pension. The rooms are basic, but good value in Gdańsk's overpriced hotel market. It's not far from the similar Stemp-Tur pension, so you might try taking a look at both before choosing. Take a cab on arrival to find the place; once you've checked in and gotten situated the receptionist can help you with the buses in and out of the center.

Beethovena 12. ℭ **058/302-23-15.** www.villaangela.pl. 18 units. 210 zł ($70/£40) double. AE, DC, MC, V. **Amenities:** Restaurant. *In room:* TV.

Stemp-Tur ★★   Not as nice on the inside as the Angela (and no English spoken), but the garden is an absolute delight. Johann Sebastien Bach Street, where the pension is located, is right out of a page of *Better Homes and Gardens* magazine. If Beaver Cleaver had been raised in Gdańsk, he would have lived here. Take a taxi to get here, and then use the bus for getting around.

Bacha 45. ℭ **058/306-35-30.** www.stemptur.com.pl. 5 units. 160 zł ($53/£30) double. AE, DC, MC, V.

WHERE TO DINE

With the possible exception of Kraków/Kazimierz, Gdańsk has some of the best restaurants in Poland. You'll find a mix of cuisines and some great Polish places at all price levels. Most are just a short walk from Długa.

Very Expensive

Goldwasser ★★ INTERNATIONAL   A local institution and well worth a splurge as much for the food as for the unbeatable riverside location and gorgeous interior. Here's also the place to sample "Goldwasser," a slightly sweetish vodka flavored with, among other things, flakes of gold. Everything gets the thumbs up, but the fresh fish dishes come highly recommended, as do the homemade pierogies. In summer, sit outside on the terrace. In winter, warm yourself up in cozy, tavernlike surroundings.

Długie Pobrzeże. © **058/301-88-78**. Lunch and dinner items 24 zł–48 zł ($8–$16/£4.20–£9). AE, DC, MC, V. Daily 11am–11pm.

Salonik ★★ POLISH   Gdańsk is blessed with two natural "splurge" choices. The Goldwasser is one, and this elegant, upmarket "Salon," just down from the Neptune fountain on Długa, is the other. The sign out front calls this a "Polish" restaurant, but they're not talking about pierogies and potato pancakes. Think more along the lines of "duck breast in plum sauce" or "lamb medallions." The mood at lunch is less formal, and the street-side terrace is makes for a very memorable midday meal. In the evenings, you'll want to dress up a little to match the surroundings.

Długa 18/21. © **058/322-00-44**. Lunch and dinner items 30 zł–54 zł ($10–$18/£5.50–£10). AE, DC, MC, V. Daily 11am–midnight.

Expensive

Barracuda ★ SEAFOOD   From the outside, you could mistake this for a nightclub (something about the way the sign BARRACUDA looks), but it's serious fish food at very reasonable prices. Try the combined sole and salmon entree with spinach in crème sauce. Good central location, just a block over from Długa ulica. It also does a nice range of steaks and pork dishes.

Piwna 61/63. © **058/301-49-62**. Lunch and dinner items 21 zł–30 zł ($7–$10/£4–£5.50). AE, DC, MC, V. Daily 11am–midnight.

Kansai ★ JAPANESE   Sushi hit the big time in Poland a couple of years ago, and it seems every large Polish city now has a decent sushi joint. Kansai is one of the best. Maybe it's the proximity to the sea and the high standards for seafood here generally, but the sushi tastes fresher than most, and the maki rolls go far beyond the standard tuna and salmon. The only drawbacks are the cost—but that goes with the territory— and the early closing time. Like most Japanese restaurants, however, the atmosphere is stark bordering on sterile, and you wouldn't want to linger long after your sake anyway.

Oganta 124. © **058/324-08-88**. Lunch and dinner items 24 zł–48 zł ($8–$16/£4.40–£9). AE, DC, MC, V. Daily noon–9pm.

Moderate

Estragon ★ INTERNATIONAL   Newly opened eatery just off Długa, combining high-quality international dishes and a stylish yet unpretentious atmosphere. The menu is a strong on what you might call the new "Continental" cuisine: steaks, pork chops, and stuffed chicken breasts. The chicken stuffed with spinach is very nice and a lighter alternative to heavy Polish cooking. Vegetarians will welcome the soy burger on the menu. The unfussy presentation is reminiscent of something you might see in New York's East Village, and the cook serves up a reasonable and recommendable facsimile of a New York–style cheesecake.

Chlebnicka 26. © **058/309-17-00**. Lunch and dinner items 21 zł–27 zł ($7–$9/£4–£5). AE, DC, MC, V. Daily 11am–11pm.

Kreska INTERNATIONAL   A trendy and highly regarded modern restaurant, specializing in what it calls "fusion" food. In this case, judging by the menu, fusion refers to nothing more exotic than vegetarian lasagna, but no matter, the kitchen is trying and the results are mostly good. The stark and stylish decor draws a good-looking crowd in the evening. The kitchen really shines at lunch, though, when its freshly made sandwiches and salads are just what the doctor ordered. Kreska opens early (10am) for breakfast and offers a classic three eggs, toast, and hot beverage for 11 zł ($3.65/£1.90).

Sw. Ducha 2. © 058/300-05-94. Lunch and dinner items 18 zł–27 zł ($6–$9/£3.20–£5). AE, DC, MC, V. Daily 10am–11pm.

Restauracja Targ Rybny ★★ SEAFOOD   The new kid in town, and quickly emerging as one of the best places for fish—both grilled and fried. The location, a bit out of the center, about 15 minutes walk from Długa ulica, helps keep prices down. For something different, try the pierogies stuffed with white fish. In summer, sit on the terrace overlooking the square called—appropriately enough—the "fish market." Reservations are not needed at the moment, but that could change once this place hits the big time.

Targ Rybny 6c. © 058/320-90-11. Lunch and dinner items 18 zł–27 zł ($6–$9/£3.20–£5). AE, DC, MC, V. Daily 11am–10pm.

Inexpensive
Neptun POLISH   This traditional milk bar, on Długa, just a few doors down from the ultraposh Salonik, is probably the cheapest meal in central Gdańsk. Don't expect anything fancy, just take a place in line with everyone else and point to the dish you want when you get to the counter. The big portions of cabbage rolls, bigos, pork chops, and other typical cafeteria items are good value for money. The prices are still marked in groszy!

Długa 33/34. © 058/301-49-88. Lunch and dinner items 6 zł–9 zł ($2–$3/£1.10–£1.60). No credit cards. Mon–Fri 8am–7pm; Sat 10am–6pm.

Pieregarnia U Dzika ★★ POLISH   "Pieregarnias," as the word suggests, are restaurants that specialize in pierogies and are relative late-comers to the Polish dining scene. This one, centrally located around the corner from busy Mariacka street, is better than most and a good place to sample those little dumplings and, naturally, a glass of beer to wash them down. The menu includes both the standard stuffings liked ground beef, potato, and cottage cheese, and also a few more inventive varieties. Pierogies "Wileńskie" are a nice change of pace, with buckwheat groats and bacon instead of the usual potatoes and cottage cheese. Servings are a large 10 pieces, enough for a full meal and then some.

Piwna 59/60. © 058/305-26-76. Lunch and dinner items 15 zł–21 zł ($5–$7/£2.70–£4). AE, DC, MC, V. Daily 11am–11pm.

EXPLORING GDAŃSK
Central Gdańsk is one of the most pleasantly walkable cities in central Europe. You couldn't ask for a more strikingly beautiful and colorful main street than **ul. Długa,** the heart of the Główne Miasto. As you walk its length, from the **Golden Gate** at one end to **Długi Targ** and the magnificent **Green Gate** at the other, bear in mind that nearly everything you see was rebuilt after World War II. The focal point of Długa is the fountain of **Neptune,** the god of the sea. The fountain dates from 1549. You'll find the main tourist information office just opposite the fountain. The Green Gate was originally meant to house visiting royalty, but now it serves as an exhibition space

and houses the houses of former president and Solidarity leader Lech Wałęsa. Walk through the Green Gate and you'll find the **Motława canal** and a picture-perfect seaside promenade. Turn left on **Długie Pobrzeże** and continue up a few blocks, turning back into the city through St. Mary's Gate to **ul. Mariacka.** This is one of the most picturesque of the side streets that flank Długa and it's the heart of "Amberville." In nearly every shop on the street you'll find gold, brown, and green amber broaches, pendants, necklaces, and earrings. At the western end of Mariacka you'll find the imposing red-brick monolith of the **Church of St. Mary,** reputedly the largest red-brick church in the world.

The Gdańsk shipyards and the Solidarity memorial are located north of the central city, about 15 minutes' walk from Długa. You'll need a map or at least some perseverance as you meander along the old streets until you see the big 38m-high (125-ft.) piece of steel that marks the **Monument to the Fallen Shipyard Workers.**

Town Hall ☆☆☆   One of the country's finest town halls; the original building dates from the 14th century, but it was badly damaged during World War II and what you see today is a very nicely turned out reconstruction. The building is beautiful inside and out. One of the highlights inside is the Red Room (Sala Czerwona), truly red, with its sumptuous furniture and ceiling and wall paintings. At the center is a painting entitled *The Glorification of the Unity of Gdańsk with Poland.* Take a stroll through the city's historical museum here, noting the black-and-white photographs of Gdańsk in 1945 and its near total destruction in the war.

Długa 47. © **058/767-91-00.** Free admission. May–Sept Tues–Sat 10am–6pm, Sun 11am–6pm, Mon 10am–3pm; Oct–Apr closed Mon.

Arthur's Court (Dwór Artusa) ☆☆   One of the most impressive houses in the city was recently opened to the public after extensive renovation. The "Arthur's Court," named for King Arthur, was founded as a meeting place for the town's wealthiest businessmen and leading dignitaries. The house dates from the 14th century, but was remodeled several times, including once in the 19th century when it was given its neo-Gothic look following the vogue of the time. One of the highlights inside is a 9m-high (30-ft.) Renaissance tiled oven. The exterior was demolished in World War II, but many of the interior pieces had been removed beforehand and survived the fighting.

Długi Targ 43/44. © **058/767-91-00.** Free admission. May–Sept Tues—Sat 10am–6pm, Sun 11am–6pm; Oct–Apr shorter opening hours, closed Mon.

St. Mary's Church ☆☆   This enormous red-brick church is reputedly the largest of its kind in the world. Its nave and 31 chapels can hold more 20,000 people. The church endeared itself to the people of Gdańsk in the years after the imposition of martial law in 1981 when members of the Solidarity trade union sheltered here. The church is more impressive from the outside than in; it was badly damaged during World War II and the frescoes inside were covered over in white. Note the astronomical clock on the outside; it not only tells time, but gives the phases of moon, and shows the position of the sun and the moon in relation to the signs of the zodiac. If you're feeling up to it climb the 402 steps to top of the tower for an unparalleled view over the city.

Podkramarksa 5. Daily 9am–6pm.

Amber Museum   A must for all fans of that beautiful ossified pine resin that helped make Gdańsk wealthy. On six floors of exhibits, you'll learn everything you'll ever need to know about amber, including how it's mined and processed, what it looks like under a microscope, and how it was used through ages, not just as jewelry but in art and medicine. If you're thinking of buying some amber while you're in Gdańsk, you might want to stop here first for an educational primer. One part of the exhibition is given over to fake amber, and how to identify the genuine article.

Targ Węglowy. www.mhmg.gda.pl. From May to Sept, open daily 10am–6pm, Sun 11am–6pm, Mon 10am–3pm; from Sept–May, closed Mon.

Central Maritime Museum   The best of four separate museums that highlight Gdańsk's history as a port city. Here you'll find more or less the A-to-Z compendium on Polish maritime history, from the turn of the first millennium to modern times. Some of the best exhibits are the detailed models of the ships, lots of old weaponry, and at the top some oil paintings of old boats. The museum is housed in three Renaissance-era granaries.

Ołowianka 9/13. ℂ 058/310-86-11. www.cmm.pl. Tues–Sun 10am–4pm.

Monument to the Fallen Shipyard Workers   This enormous steel monument, some 40m (125 ft.) high, was built in 1980 to remember the 44 people who died during bloody anti-Communist riots of 1970. Its construction was one of the demands put forward by the striking workers in August 1980. The presence of the monument was keenly embarrassing to the Communist authorities, and Solidarity leader Lech Wałęsa even likened it to a harpoon driven into the side of a whale.

Plac Solidarności (near the entrance to the Roads to Freedom exhibit).

Roads to Freedom   A strange but ultimately highly worthwhile trip down the road of the anti-Communist struggle in Poland, from the riots in 1970 that tore the country apart to the rise of the Solidarity trade union later that decade and finally to the historic agreement in August 1980 that led to the union's official recognition by the Communist government. Solidarity was the first independent trade union to be recognized in the Eastern bloc; the move eventually paved the way for the first semi-free elections in 1989 and finally the toppling of Communist regimes in Poland and throughout Eastern Europe. The exhibition is strange because it's confusingly laid out. The entrance is to the side of the actual factory gate to the Gdańsk shipyards. There are no ticket-takers in sight; simply walk through the gates and look for the mostly likely building to hold a museum. Once inside, things become a little clearer. One room is given over to a mock-up of a typical empty grocery store during Communist times. The real draws, however, are the moving newsreels of events as they unfolded during those tense times. One room features a short documentary film of the days leading up to the August agreement and then to the very tense times a year later when the government reneged on the deal and imposed martial law. Another shows a newsreel from the violent 1970 riots, which few outside of Poland have ever heard of. Another film looks at all of the revolutions in Eastern Europe. And at the back, you can see the actual room where the August Accords were signed. An inspiration.

Doki1. ℂ 058/769-29-20. www.fcs.org.pl. May–Sept Tues–Sun 10am–5pm; Oct–Apr 10am–4pm.

Westerplatte ★★   Westerplatte is known to Poles as the place where World War II began. It was here on this peninsula on Sept. 1, 1939, that the German gunboat *Schleswig-Holstein* first fired on a small garrison of about 180 Polish troops. The Poles, though badly outnumbered, held out valiantly, repelling 3,000 German soldiers for 7 days. The buildings have been left pretty much as they were after the battle, and you can walk past the badly damaged guardhouse and barracks. A small museum outlines the history of those first few days of the war.

Sucharskiego 1. ⓒ **058/343-69-72**. Tues–Sun 9am–4pm.

OUTSIDE OF GDAŃSK

Hel Peninsula ★★   The first question in summer visitors usually ask is "Where are the beaches?" If you've got little time, the best choice is probably Sopot, but if you've got a day to spare and the sun is shining, why not go for something a little more remote? The Hel Peninsula is a pencil-thin strip of land that juts into the Baltic north of Gdynia. It's far enough away from industrial Gdańsk to ensure some of the Baltic's cleanest water, and the sleepy fishing town of Hel is a delight in its own right. In summer, you can take the ferry out to Hel from Gdańsk, Sopot, or Gdynia. From Gdańsk, ferries depart from main ferry port along the Motława canal; figure on about 2 hours for the trip each way. Alternatively, there's train service from Gdańsk and Gdynia, and a quicker minibus from Gdynia's bus station.

SHOPPING

For centuries the center of the Baltic amber trade, Gdańsk is still *the* place to buy it. You'll find no shortage of amber dealers in town. The biggest concentrations are on the main street Długa and along quieter Mariacka, a couple of streets over. Before buying try to educate yourself a bit about quality amber. While the majority of the dealers are reputable, amber fakes abound so always watch carefully that you're buying the real deal. The **Amber Museum** (see "Exploring Gdańsk," above) is a good place to start to learn about amber. One legitimate gallery with some beautiful pieces is **L Galeria** (Mariacka 23/24; ⓒ **0501/338-770**).

Another purely "I got it in Gdańsk" gift is **Goldwasser** vodka. While the sweetish taste is not to everyone's liking, who could pass up flakes of gold in their cocktail? You can buy a gift box at the Goldwasser restaurant (see earlier in this chapter).

GDAŃSK AFTER DARK

Most of the serious culture revolves around two venues: The **Frederyk Chopin Baltic Philharmonic** (Ołowianka 1; ⓒ **058/320-62-62**; www.filharmonia.gda.pl) and the **State Baltic Opera** (Al. Zwycięstwa 15; ⓒ **058/763-49-12**; www.operabaltycka.pl). The Philharmonic's main home is right across the Motława canal from the center of the city. Check the website (Polish only, but easy enough to sort out basic information) or ask at the tourist information office on Długa. You can buy tickets at the Motława box office or at the specific performance venue up to 2 hours before the show. The opera maintains a lively program in season, with visiting and local companies. The quirky website (with English translation) is a good place to buy tickets to performances, or try the box office during office hours. Gdańsk's **Miniatura Theater** (Grunwaldszka 16; ⓒ **058/341-01-23**; www.miniatura.prv.pl) maintains a lively and excellent repertoire of puppet shows and fairy tales aimed at children, but shows are almost exclusively in Polish.

Sopot

Don't pass up the chance to see Sopot, Gdańsk's answer to the Hamptons and Atlantic City all rolled up into one. Before World War II, Sopot was the haunt of the moneyed classes—a place where in order to properly summer you had to be somebody. After the war, during the Communist period, the resort lost some of its sheen. It was still regarded as exclusive, but the idea of a decadent seaside resort didn't fit well with the reigning ideological aesthetic. Since 1989, Sopot has mounted something of a comeback, cashing in on both its former allure and affirming its identity as Poland's top summertime party town.

Sopot's an easy 25-minute train ride from Gdańsk's main station. From the station, head down the steps to ul. Kościuszki, which leads you to town's main drag, ul. Bohaterów Monte Cassino, a long, sloping pedestrianized walk that takes you all the way to the pier.

From here there are several things to do. You can stroll the pier, the longest along the Baltic coast. It's possible to catch the ferry here to the Hel Peninsula or over to Gdańsk as alternative way to get back. Sopot's beaches, some of the nicest and most accessible in the Gdańsk area, fan off on both sides of the pier. To the right, a long, tree-lined walk, with a very nice bike path, skirts the beach and will take you all the back to the suburbs of Gdańsk. Should you feel the urge to cycle, Rowerownia (ul. Bitwa Pod Płowcami 39; ℂ 058/551-11-76) rents by the hour or the day.

Bohaterów Monte Cassino is lined on both sides with restaurants and cafes; sometime around midevening—10pm or so—the mood shifts into party drive, and these very same places transform themselves into some of the Tri-Cities' most happening clubs.

The Główne Miasto is filled with cafes, bars, and clubs, with the best of these not necessarily on Długa, but on the side streets that parallel. Try the streets Św. Ducha, Piwna, and Chlebnicka. The embankment along Długie Pobrzeże is a nice spot for an evening stroll, with plenty of places along the way for a drink, a coffee, or a meal. That said, for serious partying, particularly in summer, Sopot is the place to be. Centrally located between Gdańsk and Gdynia, and with that whole seaside-chic thing going on anyway, it's a natural draw at night for the whole region.

Café Absinthe   Fun and highly recommended bar where the emphasis is definitely on drinking, though not necessarily absinthe. Draws an eclectic crowd that seems to shares a love of chaos. Św. Ducha 2. ℂ 058/320-37-84.

Faktoria   In Sopot, probably the best gay dance club in the Tri-Cities. Draws a mix of gay and straight men and women for a big night out. Karaoke nights, special fashion shows, and the usual mix of disco, pop, and glam. Rzemieślnicza 26. ℂ 058/555-00-86.

Ferber Café   Another central Gdańsk coffee bar that does double duty: a respectable "Clark Kent" by day serving tourists their espressos, and morphing into a party animal "Superman" at night, serving cocktails to the local glitterati. Długa 77/78. ℭ 058/301-55-66.

Kamienica   By day, the best place on Mariacka for that much-needed coffee or tea break. By night, a great little bar with a cozy feel and more-than-decent food. Mariacka 37/39. ℭ 058/301-12-30.

Ksantypa   One of the most popular clubs in town for techno, trance, drum and bass, or whatever happens to be on the DJ's mind that night. Draws a young crowd who come mainly for the chemicals and the beat. Piastowka 210. ℭ 058/553-14-59.

Papryka   Thoroughly enjoyable night out at a relatively laid-back Sopot bar and nightclub, where nearly everything—from the leather sofas to the walls—is bathed in warm, red hues. Great DJs and usually just quiet enough to converse under the music. Grunwaldzka 11. ℭ 058/551-74-76.

Słowiński National Park

There's a remarkable landscape of wetlands and giant sand dunes, butted up against the Baltic Sea, about 2 hour's ride or drive northwest of the Tri-Cities. The Słowiński National Park is unique enough to be included on the UNESCO's list of protected biospheres, and makes for nice day out away from the bustle of Gdańsk and the Tri-Cities' crowded beaches.

The park begins about 2km (1 mile) west of the seaside resort of Łeba. Łeba itself is not much, but keep pressing on to see the park's two lakes and the enormous, shifting sand dunes that rise to a height of some 40m (125 ft.).

The park has something for everyone. The protected wetlands make it a great spot for birders, and in and among the more common species, you'll find rarer sorts like cranes and black storks. World War II history buffs will be interested in hearing how the Nazis used the unique sandy landscape as a training ground for Rommel's Afrika Korps. The Germans also conducted early experiments in rocketry here, and just west of the hamlet of Rabka, you'll find an early and eerie-looking launchpad and a small museum. And of course there's the amazing giant dunes themselves, stretching for a length of about 5km (3 miles). The dunes migrate up to 10m (30 ft.) every year. After you've hiked awhile into the center of the dunes, you'll swear you're in the Sahara. Poland feels far, far away.

Cars are restricted from entering the park area. In nice weather, walking is a pleasant option. But you can also rent bikes by hour, or hitch a ride on a horse-drawn cart, electric trolley, or even a golf cart. To get here from the Tri-Cities, make your way north to Gdynia and take the bus (15 zł/$5/£2.75) for Łeba. If you're driving, follow the E28 highway in the direction of Słupsk, bearing right at Lębork. Allow at least 2 hours by bus or car along often-difficult roads.

Słowiński National Park. Admission 4 zł ($1.35/£0.75). Daily 8am to dark.

DAY TRIP TO MALBORK CASTLE

The monumental Teutonic Knights castle at Malbork (or Marienburg, as it's known in German) lies just 60km (36 miles) south of Gdańsk and is an easy day trip by train or car. The castle, a UNESCO World Heritage Site, is a jaw-dropper—the biggest brick-built castle in the world.

The castle dates from the beginning of the 14th century and was intended to mark the capital of the Teutonic Knights' new northern European home. At the time, the Knights, an order of Christian crusaders fighting in the Holy Lands, had suffered a string of military defeats and were forced to retreat to Europe. They accepted an offer of land by a Polish duke, who was hoping to use the Knights' power to subdue pagan Prussians in the West. The Knights, always eager to subdue pagans, began construction of the Malbork castle in 1309. They were ruthless and highly disciplined, and soon came to rival the Polish kings for control over the vital Baltic Sea trade, including trade in amber. A century later, in 1410, the Poles—along with the Lithuanians and troops from other lands—joined forces to defeat the Knights at the epic Battle of Grünwald (sometimes called the "Battle of Tannenberg" in history books). This marked the beginning of the end of the Knights' reign in western Poland. They were eventually forced to abandon the Malbork castle and were dispatched to East Prussia. (As a side note, the Knights still exist, but are devoted to wholly—and *holy*—peaceful pursuits, like running schools and hospitals.)

Following the Knights' defeat, the castle fell to the Polish kings, who used it as an occasional residence. After the Polish partition at the end of the 18th century the Prussians took control of Malbork and the castle, turning it into a military barracks. German control lasted until the end of World War II, when heavy fighting between Germans and Russians destroyed the town and left the castle in ruins. What you see today is the result of a long and steady restoration process that was only completed about a decade ago.

You can tour the castle individually or with a guide. There's an impressive amber display, lots of information about the Teutonic Knights and their militaristic lifestyle, and of course displays of medieval weaponry. Allow yourself 3 hours or more to give this incredible castle complex at least a cursory once-over.

By train, Malbork lies on the main Gdańsk–Warsaw line, meaning that departures from Gdańsk are frequent. By car, figure on about 45 minutes drive south along the E75 highway.

Malbork Castle. ℭ **055/647-09-78.** www.zamek.malbork.pl. Admission 30 zł ($10/£5.50). May–Sept daily 9am–7pm; Oct–Apr daily 10am–3pm.

TORUŃ

150km (90 miles) S of Gdańsk

Toruń is an exceedingly charming university town with at least three things going for it. One, obviously, is its claim to fame as the birthplace of Nicholas Copernicus in 1473. He was the first to postulate that the earth revolves around the sun (and not vice versa), setting the stage for later major advances in astronomy (and greatly ruffling the feathers of the Catholic Church in the process!). The second is Toruń's unrivaled stock of original baroque and Renaissance buildings. Unlike many Polish towns of its size, Toruń escaped major damage in World War II. This is a chance to see what Poland might have looked like had history turned out differently. The third is a number of very nice hotels, with at least one in each price category, including possibly the choicest boutique hotel in the country.

As with many cities in this part of Poland, Toruń began life as a stronghold for the Teutonic Knights, a German order that was originally invited by the Polish kings to secure the area, but later turned on its hosts and amassed its own empire. Tensions between the Knights and Toruń residents traditionally ran high, culminating in a moment of what must have been sheer madness in 1454, when the citizens stormed the Knights' castle just outside the Old Town and tore it apart brick by brick. Amazingly, the rubble is still there (looking not unlike it must have looked 550 years ago), and for the price of 1 zł (30¢/20p) you're free to walk around the ruins. The siege effectively ended the Knights' domination of the city.

Toruń grew prosperous as a member of the Hanseatic League and trade along the Wisła River, but the town fell to the Prussians following the Polish partition at the end of the 18th century. Toruń was under German rule for the next 125 years, until the end of World War I. German troops occupied the city in September 1939 and stayed until February 1945, driven out by the Polish army. Thankfully, the town escaped heavy damage during the fighting.

ESSENTIALS
GETTING THERE   Toruń lies on major bus and rail links, with frequent daily service to major cities. By road, it's equidistant from Poznań, Gdańsk, and Warsaw. Figure on 2 to 3 hours' driving time from each.

GETTING AROUND   Toruń's historic area, comprising the Old and New Towns, is largely closed off to motor vehicles, so walking is the only option.

VISITOR INFORMATION   The Toruń Tourist Information Center (Rynek Staromiejski 25; ✆ **056/621-09-31**) is centrally located on the Old Town Square and staffed by young, friendly English speakers. They can help find hotels, suggest restaurants, and bring you up-to-date on anything that might be going on in town of special interest.

WHERE TO STAY
Toruń has some very nice hotels scattered in and around the Old and New Towns. Finding a room is usually not a problem outside of the busy summer months of July and August.

Expensive
Hotel Heban   Occupying two renovated town houses in the area just between the Old and New Towns. One building, much more atmospheric, dates from the 17th century, the other, across the street, from the 19th century. The latter, more modern building is pitched more toward business clients. Ask for room no. 3 in the older building—a picture-perfect double with hardwood floors and wood-beamed ceilings, and just waiting for a vase of beautiful flowers to complete the picture.

Małe Garbary 7. ✆ **056/652-15-55.** Fax 056/652-15-65. www.hotel-heban.com.pl. 20 units. 300 zł ($100/£55) double. AE, DC, MC, V. **Amenities:** Restaurant. *In room:* TV, dataport, hair dryer.

Moderate
Hotel Petite Fleur   A boutique hotel occupying two stunningly renovated centuries-old burghers' houses. The reception area and cozy little reading room off to the

side mix modern flair and traditional furnishings to good effect. The rooms on the top floor have wood-beamed ceilings. The chef in the hotel restaurant is French-trained and serves up a mix of French and Polish specialties. You won't find this level of style and comfort at this price anywhere else in Poland.

Piekary 25. ✆ **056/663-44-00.** Fax 056/663-54-54. www.petitefleur.pl. 16 units. 250 zł ($83/£45) double. AE, DC, MC, V. **Amenities:** Restaurant. *In room:* TV, dataport, hair dryer.

Inexpensive

Hotel Retman   Clean, quiet, family-run inn about a block away from the Old Town square. Rooms are on the small side, but nicely finished with dark woods and scrubbed clean. Unexpected amenities include in-room Wi-Fi. Skip the mediocre breakfast unless you wake up starving.

Rabiańska 15. ✆ **056/657-44-60.** Fax 056/657-44-61. www.hotelretman.pl. 15 units. 210 zł ($70/£40) double. AE, DC, MC, V. **Amenities:** Restaurant. *In room:* TV, dataport.

WHERE TO DINE

Manekin ⋆   Sweet and savory crepes offer a nice budget alternative to pizzas and kabobs. The pancake with chicken, beans, and onions, topped with spicy tomato sauce, is filling without going overboard. Service is friendly and efficient. In summer you can eat on the terrace overlooking the Old Town Square.

Stary Rynek 16. ✆ **056/621-05-04.** Lunch and dinner items 9 zł–15 zł ($3–$5/£1.60–£2.80). No credit cards. Daily 11:30am–10pm.

Pizzeria Browarna   Exceedingly popular pizza joint, with good, filling pies and pasta dishes on offer. Friday and Saturday night finds the place crammed with teens and students; at other times, families predominate. Not great for a romantic dinner for two, but ideal for a quick, cheap bite on the run.

Mostowa 17. ✆ **056/622-66-74.** Lunch and dinner items 12 zł–15 zł ($4–$5/£2.20–£2.75). No credit cards. Daily 11:30am–10pm.

Pod Modrym Fartuchem ⋆⋆   This pleasant, traditional Polish inn is in a tiny baroque-facaded house on a corner just off the New Town Square. All of the classic Polish dishes, served in a refined but casual space. Sit outside near the square in nice weather.

Rynek Nowomiejski 8. ✆ **056/622-26-26.** Lunch and dinner items 21 zł–27 zł ($7–$9/£3.70–£5). AE, DC, MC, V. Daily 11:30am–10pm.

EXPLORING

Toruń is divided into a historic core and a modern city, comprising an Old Town (Stare Miasto) and a New Town (Nowe Miasto), each having its own square and connected to the other by the long Szeroka ul. You can easily take in the town in a couple of hours of leisurely walking. In addition to the sights below, be sure to stroll along the river for a great view of the town walls (especially pretty at night) and stop by the ruins of the former castle of the Teutonic Knights (ul. Predzamcze, between the Old and New Towns).

The Old Town Hall (Ratusz Staromiejski) ⋆   Right in the center of the Rynek and the most impressive of a series of beautiful buildings that line the Old Town Square. You can climb the 42m (130-ft.) tower for a view over the city and across the river, and take in the town museum. Here you'll find a nice collection of stained glass and other crafts through the ages and paintings of former prominent residents.

Rynek Staromiejski 1. May–Sept Tues–Sun 10am–6pm; Oct–Apr Tues–Sun 10am–4pm.

Nicholas Copernicus Museum (Muzeum Mikolaja Kopernika) ★★★   If you're in Toruń, you've got to pay a visit to the birthplace of the man who banished the earth from the center of the universe. Copernicus's major work, "De revolutionibus orbium coelestium" (On the Revolutions of the Heavenly Spheres), was initially viewed as blasphemy by the Catholic Church, and it wasn't until his death in 1543 that the work was published. Copernicus's theories paved the way for a series of astronomical break-throughs in the 16th and 17th centuries, including the work of Galileo, Tycho Brahe, Johannes Kepler, and Sir Isaac Newton. Copernicus was a jack-of-all-trades, and when he wasn't theorizing about the earth and the sun, he was working as a physician, a local administrator, and even as a commander defending Olsztyn castle against an onslaught of Teutonic Knights. You won't find an original copy of "De revolutionibus" here, but several rooms filled with period artifacts and pictures.

Ul. M. Kopernika 15/17. ✆ 056/267-48. Tues–Sun 10am–5pm.

SHOPPING

Toruń is famous throughout Poland for its gingerbread (piernik). You'll find it available at shops around town. One excellent place to try is **Emporium** (ul. Piekarny 28; ✆ **056/657-61-08**). The young, English-speaking owner is more than happy to tell you all about the history of gingerbread-making in Toruń, and can even give you the recipe if you want to make it at home. He also stocks a range of other souvenirs unique to Toruń (T-shirts, statues of Copernicus, and so on) and runs a bicycle rental.

AFTER DARK

After sunset it seems the whole town descends on the Old Town Square, near the Copernicus statue, and starts the evening promenade through the square and then down Szeroka, and then back. Most of the better clubs, bars, and cafes are along the strip. They're all fun and pretty much the same.

POZNAŃ

120km (75 miles) S of Toruń

Poznań, the main center of the province of Wielkopolska (Greater Poland), is a bustling city of 600,000 people. To Poles, it's regarded as the legendary birthplace of Poland, but to outsiders it's known more for its many annual trade fairs (making Poznań a cousin of sorts to Leipzig in Germany and Brno in the Czech Republic). The city lies on one of Europe's main east-west train lines, stretching from Paris and Berlin to Warsaw and Moscow, which makes getting here a snap. The city's principal attraction is its enormous and beautiful town square, the Stary Rynek, which when filled to brimming on a warm summer evening looks and feels not unlike Kraków's Rynek Główny or Prague's Old Town Square.

Poznań owes its traditional prosperity to its position along main transportation routes and astride the Warta River. During the Prussian occupation, when the town was known as Posen, it became one of the region's leading industrial centers, a position it retains until this day. The prosperity is evident in the sheer size of the square and in the many handsome buildings that stretch out in all directions.

In more modern times, Poznań has been known to Poles as the home of the 1956 anti-Communist riots, the first-ever show of resistance in the country to the Communist authorities. At the time, tens of the thousands of workers took to the streets to demand better working conditions and higher pay. The strikes turned violent and the government responded by calling in the soldiers and tanks. In all some 76 civilians and 8 soldiers died in the fighting. The strikes were a major embarrassment throughout Communist Eastern Europe and pierced the veil of the Communist Poland as a "workers'" state.

Most of the major sights can be seen in a few hours, but the presence of some nice hotels and good restaurants invites an overnight stay.

ESSENTIALS

GETTING THERE Poznań's **Ławica International Airport** (Bukowska 285; ℰ **061/849-23-44;** www.airport-Poznań.com.pl) is 5km (3 miles) west of the city center. It's grown in importance recently, and now has direct flights to a number of major European cities, including London's Stansted airport, Brussels, Frankfurt, Munich, and Vienna. There's regular bus service (no. 78) to and from the airport to the city center. By rail, Poznań lies on the main line connecting Berlin to Warsaw and points east. It's easy to hop off at Poznań in the morning, tour the town for a few hours, and then catch a later train in either direction. The **train station** (Dworcowa 1; ℰ **061/866-12-12**) is 2km (1 mile) from the town center, near the fairgrounds. It's a15-minute walk, or a short tram or bus ride to the center. The **main bus station** (Dworzec Autobusowy, Towarova 17/19; ℰ **061/664-25-25**) is near the train station. Poznań lies on major national and international bus routes. By car, Poznań lies on the main Berlin-Warsaw highway, the E30. Figure on about 3 hours or so to drive from Warsaw in normal traffic, and a little more than 2 hours from Wrocław if you're coming up from the south.

GETTING AROUND Poznań has an efficient public transportation system of buses and trams, but if you're staying near the Stary Rynek, you'll be doing most of your travel by foot. Tickets can be bought at Ruch kiosks (or nearly anywhere they sell newspapers and tobacco) and cost 2.40 zł (80¢/45p) for a trip of 30 minutes.

VISITOR INFORMATION The city's main **Tourist Information Center** (Stary Rynek 59/60; ℰ **061/852-61-56**) is conveniently located on the Old Town Square. The helpful staff gives out maps and brochures and can advise on rooms. Another good source of information is the **City Information Center** (Ratajczaka 44; ℰ **061/ 851-96-45;** www.cim.poznan.pl.) The CIM is good on cultural activities and can sell tickets for concerts and performances.

WHERE TO STAY

Poznań's hotel rates are reasonable, except when an international trade fair is going on in town. Then hotels unabashedly jack up the prices 30% to 40%. The summer months are normally safe, but during the rest of the year, there's usually a trade fair going on at least 1 week a month. The rates listed below are for standard doubles outside of fair times. Note that many hotels offer reduced weekend rates.

Very Expensive

Domina Prestige ⟨★ Designed more for corporate travelers than individuals, this hotel features 41 fully equipped apartments, complete with bedroom, living room, and kitchen. The kitchens haves fridges, stoves, microwaves, and full sets of pots and pans if you'd ever want to whip up a meal during your stay. The presentation is high-end, with sleek modern furnishings, crisp uniforms for the staff, and lots of high-tech gadgetry throughout. But some of the suites are already showing a little wear and tear, so ask to see a couple before deciding on one. Popular during fair time.

Sw. Marcin 2. © **061/859-05-90.** Fax 0061/859-05-91. www.dominahotels.com. 41 units. 450 zł ($150/£80) double. AE, DC, MC, V. **Amenities:** Concierge; business services; salon; nonsmoking rooms. *In room:* A/C, TV, fax, dataport, kitchen, fridge, coffeemaker, hair dryer, iron, safe.

Hotel Royal ⋆ The Royal is widely considered one of Poznań's best hotels, though with the option of the Brovaria (see below), the rates look a little high for what's on offer. The location is excellent, on one of the city's main arteries not far from the Stary Rynek. The hotel is tucked away in a little courtyard away from the street, so noise is not a problem. The Royal has a distinguished pedigree, dating from the turn of the 20th century, and was the first hotel in the city to open for business following World War II. Now under new management, the rooms are classy looking, with floral-print spreads and high-quality woods throughout. The reception desk is more than happy to book restaurant reservations or advise on city tours.

Sw. Marcin 71. © **061/858-23-00.** Fax 0061/858–23–06. www.hotel-royal.com.pl. 31 units. 420 zł ($140/£75) double. AE, DC, MC, V. **Amenities:** Restaurant; concierge; business center; limited room service, dry cleaning; nonsmoking rooms. *In room:* TV, dataport, hair dryer.

Expensive

Hotel Brovaria ⋆⋆⋆ For the money, probably the best bed (with a view) in town. The hotel's location, occupying three tastefully renovated town houses on the Stary Rynek, cannot be beat. The decor is a restrained modern—somewhere between 1930s "modern" and contemporary—with beige bedspreads and dark woods. The hotel's restaurant is one of the finest in the city, and the in-house pub even brews its own beer.

Stary Rynek 73/74. © **061/858-68-68.** Fax 0061/858-68-69. www.brovaria.pl. 22 units. 300 zł ($100/£55) double. AE, DC, MC, V. **Amenities:** 2 restaurants; limited room service; nonsmoking rooms. *In room:* TV, dataport, hair dryer.

Moderate

Hotel Stare Miasto ⋆⋆ *(Finds)* A new hotel and a great choice for the price; the rates are lower than you might expect for the quality of the facilities because of the hotel's location in a slightly dodgy, but still safe neighborhood, about 10 minutes' walk from the Stary Rynek. The stylish reception area is open and airy. The rooms are on the small side, but nicely furnished in a contemporary look. The inevitable breakfast buffet is more inventive than most, and the chef will cook some eggs on the spot on request. The doubles are not uniformly furnished, so ask to see a couple of different styles before choosing.

Rybaki 36. © **061/663-62-42.** Fax 0061/659-00-43. www.hotelstaremiasto.pl. 23 units. 295 zł ($98/£55) double. AE, DC, MC, V. **Amenities:** Restaurant. *In room:* A/C, TV, dataport.

Inexpensive

Hotel Lech A modern high-rise on a busy street, not far from the central square. The rooms are plain but clean. Not a bad deal, given the location and in-room amenities like free Internet access. Pulls in a lot of bus-tour packages, and even offers reduced rates for students. Avoid the restaurant downstairs; there's much better food just a short walk away.

Sw. Marcin 74. © **061/853-01-51.** Fax 0061/853-08-80. www.hotel-lech.poznan.pl. 80 units. 244 zł ($81/£45) double. AE, DC, MC, V. **Amenities:** Restaurant. *In room:* TV, dataport, hair dryer.

WHERE TO DINE

There's no shortage of restaurants along the Stary Rynek. Nearly every house along the perimeter of the enormous square offers some kind of food or drink, usually both.

Very Expensive

Kresowa 🌾🌾 POLISH   A little hard to find, tucked away in the maze of buildings at the center of the Stary Rynek, but well worth the effort. This is widely considered one of the top Polish restaurants in town, and a superb choice for the celebratory "we've arrived in Poznań" evening meal. The atmosphere is more formal than most, so smart-casual is the way to dress. The clientele includes a mix of businessmen, private parties, and Poles out for a special evening. The menu is heavy on Polish standards and meat dishes. The grilled salmon comes highly recommended. Try to book beforehand for Friday and Saturday nights.

Stary Rynek 3. © **061/853-12-91.** Lunch and dinner items 21 zł–42 zł ($7–$14/£4–£8). AE, DC, MC, V. Mon–Sat 1–11pm; Sun noon–6pm.

Expensive

Brovaria 🌾🌾🌾 POLISH/INTERNATIONAL   The first-floor restaurant of the Hotel Brovaria is one of the hippest spots in town and a real draw for locals and visitors alike. Many come for the home-brewed beer, which is hoppier and tangier than traditional Polish beer, and comes as both a standard Pilsner and recommendable honey-flavored lager. The menu is a balance of inventive international dishes and Polish standards with a view toward presentation and use of fresh ingredients. The roast duck with apple comes nicely crisped with a side of beets and potatoes, and is absolutely delicious.

Stary Rynek 73/74. © **061/858-68-68.** Lunch and dinner items 21 zł–36 zł ($7–$12/£4–£7). AE, DC, MC, V. Daily noon–11pm.

Dom Vikingów 🌾🌾 INTERNATIONAL   Similar in style and appearance to Bee Jay's (see below), but more upmarket and with more attention paid to the food. Danish ownership explains the "House of Vikings" name, and also the appearance of Danish herring on the menu. The steaks are the draw here. The interior is divided into several different themes, including a cafe and sports bar. During the summer, the outdoor terrace is the place for afternoon coffee. The early opening hours are good to keep in mind if you're staying somewhere that serves inedible breakfast or no breakfast at all.

Stary Rynek 62. © **061/852-71-53.** Lunch and dinner items 21 zł–36 zł ($7–$12/£4–£7). AE, DC, MC, V. Daily 9am–11pm.

Moderate

Markowa Knajpa 🌾   Less formal than the Kresowa, but with similarly well-prepared local dishes. The decor is simple in keeping with the "knajpa" (bistro) theme, with stark, white walls, dark woods, and hardwood floors. The customer base includes mostly businessmen and young professionals. Czech Pilsner Urquell beer on tap. Just a couple of blocks off the Stary Rynek.

Kramarska 15. © **061/853-01-78.** Lunch and dinner items 15 zł–30 zł ($5–$10/£2.70–£5.50). AE, DC, MC, V. Daily 9am–11pm.

Inexpensive

Bee Jay's 🌾   An enormous watering hole, sports-bar complex on the Stary Rynek. It's a popular spot for salads, sandwiches, quesadillas, and also the odd Indian entree.

This food is more stick-to-your-ribs, than stick-in-your-mind as a great meal, but if you're looking for something easy and relatively cheap, this is one of the best spots on the square. Not a bad choice too if you're only in for drinks; the bar is so large there's always room for a few more people.

Stary Rynek 87. ⓒ 061/853-11-15. Lunch and dinner items 15 zł–21 zł ($5–$7/£2.70–£3.75). AE, DC, MC, V. Daily 11:30am–11pm.

Exploring

Naturally, any exploration of Poznań must start at the Stary Rynek, the city's cultural and commercial center for centuries. It's hard to find a livelier and sunnier town square than Poznań's—filled with color, people, and a range of performance art from early morning to late at night. At night, it's particularly beguiling. Most of the square is kept dark, with only the statues and some of the buildings lit up. Much of the square, and indeed much of the city proper, was destroyed in World War II, so many of the buildings here are faithful reconstructions of the originals.

West of the Stary Rynek, at the Warta River, is the small holy island of **Ostrów Tumski.** Legend has it this was the birthplace of the Polish nation. This is where Poland first accepted Catholic baptism in the 10th century; and one of the country's most celebrated cathedrals still stands here. You can walk to the island from the Stary Rynek or take tram no. 1, 4, or 8 over the bridge.

Poznań's unofficial nickname could well be the "Museum City." In addition to the major museums noted below, the city has smaller museums dedicated to musical instruments, vintage cars, the Poznań army, and the work of Polish writer Henryk Sienkiewicz, who won the Nobel Prize for Literature in 1905, among others.

Old Town Hall (Ratusz) ⓐ   Originally dates from the 14th century but extensively renovated in the 16th century in Renaissance style by the Italian architect Giovanni Quadro. Unfortunately, much of the building was destroyed in World War II, and little of the original structure remains. The best example of what remains is the early Gothic cellars, which today house the Historical Museum of Poznań. The museum is worth a look if you're interested in Poznań's development from the 10th century on. Entry to the museum also allows you to see the rich interior of the building itself. Outside the Town Hall, at noon, take a look at the clock to the see two mechanical goats butt heads. The goats apparently refer to a town myth that two animals once locked horns and drew the townspeople's attention to a fire that might have burned down the city.

Stary Rynek 1. ⓒ 061/856-81-91. Sun–Tues and Fri 9am–4pm; Wed 11am–5pm

Zamek ⓐ   This fascinating building will appeal to World War II buffs. The "castle" actually only dates from the beginning of the 20th century, and was built by the Germans to serve as a residence for the kaiser on trips to the area (when Poznań, as Posen, was a German city). Between the two world wars, it was used by Poznań University, but after the Nazi invasion of 1939, work quickly began to refashion the building into an office for Adolf Hitler and a residence for the Nazi governor of this part of occupied Poland. The architect for the project was none other than Albert Speer. Work was completed in 1944, just shortly before the Germans were driven out of Poznań. For years, there was talk of tearing down the "castle" but today it's used as a cultural center. Visitors are free to walk the corridors during open hours.

Sw. Marcin 80/82. Daily 9am–5pm.

Cathedral 𝒓𝒓 The Basilica of Saints Peter and Paul retains its importance as one of the most revered churches in Poland. Excavations have revealed the presence of a church on this site for more than 1,000 years, since the Polish kings first accepted Catholicism in the 10th century. Architectural tinkering and rebuilding through the years, and the burning of the cathedral in 1945, have greatly altered its appearance, with the current appearance a mix of neo-Gothic and baroque. The remains of Poland's first kings, Mieszko I and Boleslaw the Brave, are in a chapel at the back of the altar.

Ostrów Tumski 17. ℂ **061/852-96-42**. Mon–Sat 9am–6pm.

National Museum 𝒓𝒓 An impressive art collection that's particularly strong on examples of the "Młoda Polska" art movement from the early years of the 20th century and some riveting abstracts from the 1950s and 1960s. An older wing holds extensive collections of Italian, Dutch, Flemish, and Spanish paintings.

Marcinkowskiego 9. ℂ **061/852-59-69**. Admission 4 zł ($2/£1); free Sat. Tues–Sat 10am–5pm (Thurs 4pm); Sun 11am–3pm.

AFTER DARK

The Zamek Cultural Center (Św. Marcin 80/82; ℂ **061/646-52-60;** www.zamek. poznan.pl) is a good first stop to check on what's on in Poznań. For events, buy tickets at the City Information Center/CIM (Ratajczaka 44; ℂ **061/851-96-45;** www. cim.poznan.pl).

For drinking and clubbing you won't have to venture far from the Stary Rynek. To get started, check out **Dom Vikingów** or **Bee Jay's** (see "Where to Dine," above). For dancing, **Cute** (Stary Rynek 37; ℂ **061/851-91-37**) is one of the city's best-known venues for house, techno, trance, and just plain dance. For a quieter night in summer, do like the locals and simply choose a table on the Rynek and watch the city walk by.

9

Romania

by Keith Bain

When Tolstoy visited Bucharest, he commented that Romanians had a "sad destiny," based no doubt on a strong sense of their troubled past—Romania's soul is tormented by history, its loveliness overshadowed by the reputations of malevolent personalities like Vlad the Impaler and Nicolae Ceauşescu. But while bloodthirsty men have worked their ugly politics here (and left their ruinous marks on the land), it remains a country of great beauty; one that (unlike its biggest cultural export, Count Dracula) has shed its curse and pulses with life and fascinating diversity.

While Bucharest buzzes with the energy of a world capital, somewhere in a field, a lone farmer wields a scythe, harvesting the grass his livestock will eat during the cold winters. In the context of the Europe Union (Romania becomes a full-fledged member in 2007) the contrast between urban and rural life is staggering. It is a country coated in forest and defined by the curved backbone of Carpathian peaks. Its natural treasures include the Alpine splendor of snowcapped mountains like Moldoveanu and the vast frontier wetlands of the Danube Delta, mildly comparable to the Okavango in Africa. And along with the rolling hills and soaring Alps, swathes of forest and vast tracts of preindustrial landscape, there are enchanting castles and richly decorated churches reflecting the varied histories of a people who, for centuries, have struggled to create and hold onto a single, united state.

Part of what makes Romania special has to do with the apparent newness of it all. During its isolation under Communism, many of Romania's great treasures were unknown to the world, and were considered unimportant by a leadership hellbent on fulfilling its sociopolitical master plan. To the outside world, this was a dark and foreboding place, haunted by Dracula's eternal ghost, and tormented by Ceauşescu's living one. But while Ceauşescu's program of systemization tried to squash the past, many lovely centuries-old towns and cities have maintained their historic grandeur, albeit faded and crumbling. Retaining their historic core, often centered on dramatic fortresses and fleshed out by rambling cobblestone streets and narrow alleyways or ancient gateways leading to secret courtyards, Romania's baroque, Gothic, and Secessionist cities are a delight to explore, and while much work is needed to improve tourism infrastructure, the time to visit Romania is now. For Romania is on the verge of yet another revolution, this time one that will not only launch it into the European Union, bolstering the economy and signaling new opportunities for the younger generation, but a revolution that will in all probability finally take its toll on the medieval lifestyle of many of its backwater communities. Romania, once a country weighed down by its troubled past, is poised for a formidable future.

1 Getting to Know Romania

THE LAY OF THE LAND

Romania—just a bit smaller than the United Kingdom and roughly the size of the state of Oregon—is situated in the southeastern part of central Europe, and is made up, in roughly equal measures, of lowland, hilly, and mountainous terrain. It borders Hungary and Serbia to the west, Moldova and the Ukraine to the north and east, and Bulgaria to the south, with whom it shares, along with its northern neighbor Ukraine, a slither of Black Sea coastline to the east. Forming much of the border with Bulgaria and Serbia is the River Danube as it makes its way toward the Black Sea, where it forms one of Europe's largest wetlands, the Danube Delta. Perpetually expanding, the Delta is effectively increasing Romania's surface area; in the last 40 years, it has expanded by almost 1,000 sq. km (390 sq. miles).

THE REGIONS IN BRIEF

About one-third of the country comprises the **Carpathian Mountains,** or "Transylvanian Alps," a soaring back-to-front Nike swish that separates Transylvania from the country's two other main provinces, Wallachia, to the south, and Moldavia, to the east. Through the centuries, these three historically distinct regions have been fought over by invaders from all quarters, and they now make up the bulk of Romania, a unified nation for fewer than 100 years.

Transylvania has always been a great prize, ruled largely by the Hungarian Empire and also settled by Saxon immigrants who came to protect it on behalf of the Hungarians. Here, along with splendid medieval villages centered on fortified churches, are the country's most popular tourist destinations, located at the foothills of the Carpathians. **Wallachia** was the first Romanian province to gain independence from Hungary, and is known as the "Heart of Romania," with the centrally located capital, Bucharest, rapidly reestablishing itself in a bid to reclaim its former moniker as the "Paris of the East." **Moldavia,** which once included Bessarabia (which now makes up parts of the Ukraine and the Republic of Moldova), was another former Hungarian principality, which achieved independence in the mid–14th century. Known primarily for its beautiful painted monasteries, Moldavia's sylvan scenery is a backdrop for rural villages trapped in time and imbued with great folkloric traditions.

Even better known for its ancient village life is the small region of **Maramureş,** in the northern part of Transylvania on the border with the Ukraine. Here, the sublime, unspoiled scenery shelters stunning wooden churches and a bucolic way of life. Occupying the western fringe of the country are **Crişana and Banat,** former Austro-Hungarian strongholds that now border Hungary and Serbia respectively. Overdevelopment has blighted the Black Sea coastal resorts of the easternmost region of **Northern Dobrogea,** so much so that vacation bookings fell by about 50% in 2006, many sun-seekers heading instead to the pristine coast of Croatia. Visitors still seeking a coastal sojourn should make for the Danube Delta where the unique wetland ecosystem is emerging as an enchanting destination.

SUGGESTED ITINERARY: ROMANIA IN 10 TO 12 DAYS

The following itinerary can be adapted according to your preferences. For example, you can skip the Delta, or Maramureş, if you'd prefer just exploring Romania's cities

Romania

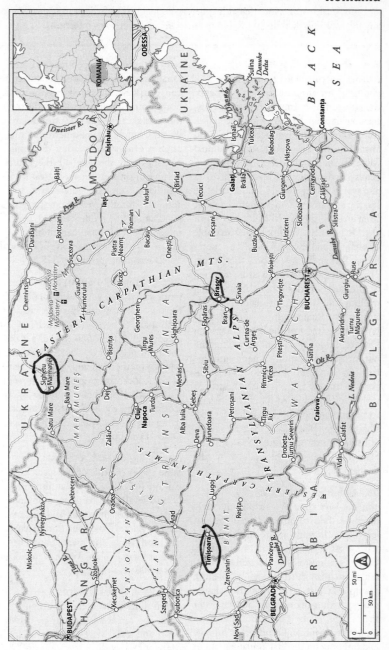

and medieval towns. Note that this itinerary is designed to make a tour possible for anyone traveling by train (try Rapid or InterCity trains at www.infofer.ro).

Days ❶ & ❷ Bucharest

Arrange for your hotel to have a taxi pick you up at the airport and then experience the intoxicating energy of this heady, combustible capital: It's a city on the move. Make time for the Cotroceni Palace (call ahead to book a tour), the National Museum of Art, and the small but gorgeous Stavreolpolous Church, where it's also worth calling ahead if you'd prefer to learn something meaningful about Romanian Orthodox faith. It's also worth checking out the world's biggest example of architectural excess, Ceaușescu's megalithic Parliamentary Palace, but you'll probably need to devote an entire morning or afternoon, thanks to a rather annoying queuing-and-waiting procedure. Try to stay at the Rembrandt, a fabulous little hotel in the midst of the historic Lipscani District, or—if you don't mind forking out considerably more—check into the friendly, plush, no-nonsense K+K Elisabeta, right near the National Theater. At night, you'll be spoiled for choice—classy restaurants are opening faster than it's possible to keep track of, and there are dozens of bars that stay open until the wee hours. Start the night in the vicinity of the Romanian Athenaeum.

Day ❸ Sinaia & Brașov

You can save time by catching the early morning train to Sinaia, where you can leave your luggage at the station before setting off for the guided tour of Peleș Castle, a fantastic introduction to modern Romanian history and a splendid example of just how far interior design can go with a big enough budget. After the castle, you can visit the local monastery before collecting your luggage and hopping on the first available train to Brașov, about an hour away. Brașov is

centered on a wide-open medieval public square, surrounded by lovely architecture. You can view the whole historic center from Mount Tampa, getting to the top in the cable car. Visit the world-famous Black Church; in summer, you might catch a concert showcasing the brilliant acoustics and showing off the church's massive organ. But Brașov is great for just wandering around; there are lovely antiques stores, several fantastic restaurants, and great hidden alleyways. Don't miss the historic Schei neighborhood. Be sure to reserve a room in one of the small hotels recommended on p. 518.

Day ❹ Brașov to Sighișoara

Once you've had your fill of Brașov, take the train to the World Heritage citadel of Sighișoara. There's not much to do, except soak up the ambience of a walled, cobblestone, hilltop city. Explore its Church on the Hill, and climb to the top of the Clock Tower above the museum. Taste *tuică* (fruit brandy) made by Teo Coroian, and eat in the restaurant occupying the house where the real Count Dracula was born.

Day ❺ Sighișoara to Sibiu

Sibiu shares the title of European City of Culture in 2007—it's a beautiful mélange of medieval and baroque monuments, with churches, museums and pedestrian squares galore. Take your time exploring, and don't miss the great Transylvanian food at Crama Sibiul Vechi, which occupies a 500-year-old cellar.

Days ❻ & ❼ Maramureș

If you don't fancy spending 6 hours in a train, you can break the journey between Sibiu and Baia Mare—the main city in Maramureș—with a stop-over in Cluj-Napoca, a prosperous city with a large student population and modern aspirations; explore the cafes around the lively town square, and visit the church lording over it.

The trip into Maramureş will take you back a hundred years or so. Arrange to stay with a local family for 1 or 2 nights to experience village life; with advance planning, DiscoveRomania (p. 488) will organize a driver to pick you up at the train station (or the airport) and can ensure that you have a guide throughout your stay in this, Romania's most bucolic region. Explore the gorgeous wooden churches scattered throughout the region, then visit the Merry Cemetery at Săpânţa and the anti-Communist museum in nearby Sighet.

Days ❽ & ❾ Moldavia's painted monasteries

From Maramureş, arrange to be driven all the way to Suceava in the neighboring province of Moldavia, beyond the northern edge of the Carpathian Mountains. Spend the night at one of the recommended hotels in Guru Humorului. The following day, you can take your time exploring the best of the painted monasteries of southern Bucovina—Voronet, Moldoviţa, Suceaviţa, and Humor.

Days ❿ & ⓬ Danube Delta

End your Romanian tour by getting back to nature. The Danube Delta is now home to the smartest resort in the whole country: organize well in advance for staff at the Delta Nature Resort to arrange a road transfer from Suceava. Two nights in the Delta will charge your batteries and prepare you for the trip back to Bucharest and then home.

ROMANIA TODAY

Existing impressions of Romania are usually a hangover from Ceauşescu's iron-fisted stranglehold, with strong memories of starving orphans, destruction of cultural monuments, and industrial plants spilling toxic waste. Indeed, Communism did a great deal to break the spirit of this nation. But the Romanian people broke the back of the regime in a small but bloody revolution that, back in 1989, was only the start of a long road to recovery.

Chat with the locals, and you'll hear much about a country beleaguered by corruption (a 2006 World Bank report stated that 50% of businesses are troubled by the level of graft) and a general lack of confidence in political leaders, underscored by schizophrenic election results. And while minister-level officials play dirty-tactic politics, people on the ground continue to experience widespread economic impoverishment, particularly in rural areas—about one-third of the workforce continues to earn a living through agriculture. Romania is seen as a source of cheap labor, and a number of foreign companies have set up shop here mainly to take advantage of these low-wage expectations. Many young people with skills and education, as well as those disheartened by limited work prospects at home, cross the border for better wages and opportunities; with E.U. accession, the drain of human resources is likely to be substantial, at least for a time. Equally, locals complain, it is impossible to "get things done" in Romania, as a stultifying bureaucracy strangles entrepreneurial efforts.

In some ways, these ongoing problems are a residue of Communism, where the regime primarily served those who were connected to the seat of power, and a centralized public sector tended to curb anything resembling entrepreneurship. There was no such thing as foreign tourism, and therefore a general absence of service-industry culture. Jobs were there to be filled, not necessarily performed with any aplomb (if, indeed, at all), so the status quo—no matter how frustrating and dehumanizing—was fastidiously maintained.

In 2007, Traian Băsescu enters his third year as president of Romania. Heading a large coalition, Băsescu professes to hold real democratic ideals and genuinely oppose corruption; as such the E.U. views his leadership as critical for the country's future. While Romania remains one of Europe's poorest nations, there has after all been steady reform; the new government has imposed one of Europe's most liberal tax systems and wages are steadily arising. The spirit of development that has slowly gripped the nation may not necessarily have the entire population hopping at the pace set by Bucharest, but it clearly signals the aspirations for a prosperous future and—despite ongoing public and media aspersions about corruption and political bungling—urban Romania seems hellbent on careening into full-blown capitalism and reaping the fruits of free-market enterprise.

A LOOK AT THE PAST

Romania's past is defined by violent conflict and war. Peace—and indeed nationhood—is new to a region that has been perpetually invaded for well over a millennium.

While Thracian tribes settled here about 3,000 years ago, Romanians trace their culture back to the Dacians. They were a highly regarded race, referred to by Herodotus as "the fairest and most courageous of men" because of their fearlessness in the face of death. Greeks colonized the territory near the Black Sea coast and developed the cities of Tomis (now Constanta), Istria, and Callatis (now Mangalia) from around 700 B.C., while the Dacian king Burebista controlled most of what is now Romania; he established a powerful kingdom between 70 and 44 B.C. By A.D. 100, the Dacian civilization had reached its zenith and the Romans now moved in, forcing its inhabitants to adopt the language of the conquerors. Rome was to rule Dacia for nearly 200 years before Christianity was adopted in the 4th century by the Daco-Romans who fell subject to invasion by assorted European and Asian tribes for the next 6 centuries. By the 11th century, when Magyar (Hungarian) armies invaded and occupied Transylvania, Romanians were the only Latin-speaking people in the eastern quadrant of the former Roman Empire. They were also the only Latin people still practicing the Orthodox faith.

While Transylvania's Romanian population was almost entirely subjugated by ruling Hungarians and their Saxon allies, the Middle Ages saw great (and bloodthirsty) local warriors in Moldavia and Wallachia—men like Stephen the Great, Vlad the Impaler, and Michael the Brave—fighting to maintain their sovereignty in the face of the ongoing Hungarian and Ottoman threat. In 1600, the Wallachian prince, Michael the Brave (Mihai Viteazul), even briefly united the three provinces, only to be defeated by the Turkish and Habsburg armies; Transylvania became a jewel in the burgeoning Austro-Hungarian Empire while other bits of Romania were carved up and divided between different powers.

In 1848, Hungary took complete control of Transylvania, while Moldavia and Wallachia, headed for unification, finally merging to become a fledgling Romania in the 1860s. A decision was made to give the new country a nonpartisan ruler, and so a German blue blood, Prince Karl of Hohenzollern-Sigmaringen, was chosen to sit on the throne of the new Romanian kingdom, created in 1881. He ruled as King Carol I until 1914 when he was succeeded by his nephew and adopted son, Ferdinand. During Ferdinand's rule, Romania joined World War I on the side of the Triple Entente in a successful effort to incorporate the lost Romanian provinces of Transylvania,

Bucovina, and Bessarabia. In 1930, King Ferdinand I was succeeded by his son, Carol II. Ten years later, the Soviet Union annexed Bessarabia as well as northern Bucovina, while Germany and Italy forced Romania to give northern Transylvania to Hungary and southern Dobrogea to Bulgaria. Massive political turmoil and nationwide demonstrations caused the abdication of Carol II, leaving his 19-year-old son, Michael, to sit on the throne. With Carol II in exile, Marshall Ion Antonescu imposed a military dictatorship and Romania joined the Nazis but the young Michael staged a royal coup in 1944, and quickly changed sides against the Germans.

In 1945, as part of the Yalta Agreement, Romania fell under direct Soviet influence; Red Army presence enabled the rapid strengthening of the country's Communists, who forced King Michael to abdicate in 1947. Less than 70 years after becoming a kingdom, Romania became a People's Republic and was under the direct, often excruciating, economic control of the USSR until 1958. The notorious SovRom agreements exhausted the country's already limited resources, and Big Brother made taxing war-reparation demands. But the devastation was not limited to financial resources; during this time an estimated two million Romanians were imprisoned, mostly on spurious charges, and between 1948 and 1964, over 200,000 citizens died in Communist-related "incidents."

In 1968, an upstart Communist named Nicolae Ceauşescu publicly condemned Soviet intervention in Czechoslovakia, thereafter receiving kudos and economic assistance from the West. Apparently nobody noticed Ceauşescu's burgeoning megalomania until it was too late, when his obsessions turned toward national debt repayment and a catastrophic systemization of the economic and social structure with rapid industrial development, replete with concrete apartment blocks and toxic factories.

Amid the economic gloom, Ceauşescu created a monstrous police state, and embarked on a program of cultlike self-glorification, which included the silencing of opponents and extreme and violent violations of human rights and civil liberties. So terrifying and pervasive was the dictatorship that women who suffered miscarriages were subjected to tormenting interrogation sessions as an inability to carry full term was seen as an attempt to stymie Ceauşescu's plan to "grow" the nation's workforce.

Life increasingly unbearable, 1989 saw furious anti-Communist protests—sparked in Timişoara and then across the country—and Ceauşescu and his regime were finally toppled. Two years later a new democratic constitution was adopted, and the difficult transition toward a free-market economy was underway. But the road to recovery has been rocky due to the instability created by successive governments, a result of schizophrenic public support, marked by corrupt politicians, many of whom were active in the former regime. But after more than a decade of economic instability and decline, the new millennium finally seems to have ushered in an era of transformation, economic growth, and foreign investment: In October 2004, months before the E.U.-accession treaty was signed, the country was granted "functional market economy" status.

ROMANIAN PEOPLE & CULTURE

Many Romanians take pride in being "a Latin island in a Slavic sea," thinking of themselves as the most eastern Romance people, completely surrounded by non-Latin peoples. While often under the political and cultural dominance of the Ottoman Empire, it is Western culture that has come to predominate.

While Romanians are proud of their heritage, and take delight in recounting the names of great individuals—inventors, scientists, poets, discoverers and leaders—they

Roma: Dancing to Their Own Tune

If there's one topic that stirs considerable debate and even anger among Romanians, it's the status of the Roma—or Gypsy—population, believed to be a widely disenfranchised 1.8 to 2 million, but counted at the polls as a mere 535,140 people at the last census. Many are overtly intolerant toward the Roma community, largely because of their associations with crime, vagrancy, and social disharmony. Many Roma live in ghetto-style environments at the fringes of villages and towns, earning a living through informal trade and begging. They are also held accountable for most of the petty crime in Romania. Hatred on both sides has sparked occasional violence. Nevertheless, the Gypsies are widely known for their savvy as well as their musical talent; although generally uneducated and unemployed, they carve out an existence and maintain strong cultural traditions; a few standout Gypsy musicians and bands have become international successes, for example. It's unfortunate that your strongest associations with this minority will most likely be through bright-eyed children asking for money or food on trains or selling kitsch at tourist hot spots.

are not afraid to engage honestly with strangers about the challenges Romania faces, from unmet soccer aspirations to the trials of E.U. accession. In fact you'll hear a great deal on Romania's problems—its politics, its police, and in more or less the same breath, its rampant corruption—than about its burgeoning promise. Life under Ceauşescu may be a harder topic to broach, though, and use your own discretion when discussing matters such as religion and views on homosexuality. Almost 87% of the population belongs to the Romanian Orthodox Church, so exercise a basic respect for Christian values. Faith is very much a way of life rather than a once-a-week affair; many Romanians live a deeply religious life and you'll see Orthodox believers of all ages crossing themselves—passionately or casually—as they pass churches and other sacred places.

LANGUAGE

In all cities and towns you should have little trouble communicating in English, although Italian will occasionally serve you better. In villages, you may have difficulty communicating with older people, but young people who have attended school in the post-Communist dispensation usually understand English. Don't shy away from conversations that hinge on a vocabulary of just a few words.

Although there is a fairly sizeable Hungarian minority that continues to use its own language in schools and civil administration, a small Gypsy community that speaks Roma, and a few dwindling communities descended from the Saxons who settled in Transylvania centuries ago that speak German, Romanian is the official language.

Romanian is a Romance language, evolved from the Latin spoken in ancient times by the people in the eastern provinces of the Roman Empire. Structurally complex, it will sound familiar to if you speak or understand Italian, Spanish, French or Portuguese. The language uses a Latin alphabet, with a few modified characters; these are

out for periodic publications by local publishers, **igloo media;** their monthly magazine *igloo habitat & arhitectură* is a chic survey of contemporary trends, both locally and internationally; you can also visit their website, www.igloo.ro.

Police You can contact the police anywhere in Romania by dialing ℂ **955.** Be aware that there are abundant complaints by locals about police corruption and also a somewhat laissez-faire attitude toward certain types of crime; bribes are often expected. Generally, the same attitude is not extended to foreigners; a more likely problem may be an inability or unwillingness to understand English. If you have a police-related emergency, consider also contacting your embassy.

Restrooms Your general reaction to public toilets will be "yuck"; try to avoid these. In Bucharest, paid-for toilets in public gardens are increasingly acceptable.

Safety & Crime There is relatively little violent crime in Romania. Pickpockets may operate in crowded areas, and tend to target the country's tourist hot spots. When sitting in bars, cafes, and restaurants take care not to leave your handbag on the floor or over the back of your seat; similarly, don't leave valuables lying around. Campers are vulnerable. Stray dogs pose a threat when hungry or provoked; some are infected with rabies; if bitten, seek medical assistance immediately.

Taxes & Service Charges An assortment of taxes may be added to your hotel bill; this will be clearly advertised and more often than not is included in the published tariff. VAT is mandatory, while there are a few state and local taxes which may apply, depending on where in the country you are. In a few towns, a small tax is added to the cost of museum tickets, sometimes pushing the cost from L3 ($1.10/55p) to L3.05 ($1.10/60p), for example; while this is a minuscule amount, it does provide headaches for whoever is trying to find change for you.

Telephones Romania's telecommunications have received a great deal of attention in recent years and there is hardly an unconnected spot in the country. Mobile telephones have also made a considerable impact. For an international operator, dial ℂ **951.** Public pay phones are orange and use magnetic cards, which can be bought from post offices and some hotels; you can purchase L10 ($3.60/£1.90) and L20 ($7.20/£3.85) cards. Most hotels now have direct international dialing from your room, although this is extremely pricey; those that have the facility usually have detailed dialing instructions in-room. Finally, for domestic calls, you can expect to hear a bizarre range of dialing tones, many of which sound convincingly like engaged or dead signals; often you should just wait to hear if your call is likely to be answered.

Time Zone During winter, Romania is 7 hours ahead of U.S. Eastern Standard Time; or 2 hours ahead of Greenwich Mean Time. During summer, daylight saving time puts Romanian clocks 1 hour forward, along with the rest of Europe.

Tipping Gratuities are neither mandatory nor expected in the majority of situations; expensive establishments are the exception. Bear in mind, though, that many services remain inexpensive relative to the rest of Europe, and that Romanians are paid appallingly. Consider giving a 10% tip in restaurants, and round up the fare for taxi drivers, if you feel you've been decently treated. Be aware of certain city taxi drivers who will just as soon assume that they can do the rounding up themselves; insist on getting your change, and then hand over whatever tip amount you've decided on.

Water One-third of Europe's naturally occurring mineral springs are found in Romania. Officially, tap water is potable and safe to drink.

2 Planning Your Trip to Romania

VISITOR INFORMATION

Romania's **National Authority for Tourism** operates a website (www.romaniatravel. com) with extensive information about the country and latest developments. You can visit the website of the **Romanian National Tourist Office**, alternatively, try contacting their representatives in the **U.S.** (355 Lexington Ave., 19th Floor, New York, NY 10017; ✆ **212/545-8484;** fax 212/251-0429; www.romaniatourism.com), or in the **United Kingdom** (22 New Cavendish St., London WIM7LH; ✆ **020/7224-3692;** fax 020/7935-6435; www.VisitRomania.com).

ENTRY REQUIREMENTS

American, Canadian, and British citizens require only a valid passport if intending to visit for 90 days or less. Holders of Australian and New Zealand passports require a visa; you'll need to complete the required form and submit this, together with a fee of approximately 35€ ($44), a passport valid for at least 6 months beyond the final date of your visit, medical insurance, proof of accommodations, and proof that you have funds amounting to 100€ ($125) for each day of your visit. Note that Romanian visa laws change regularly, so it's worth getting the up-to-date scoop by contacting their embassy or consulate near you. There is no entry or departure tax. Extensions of stays beyond 90 days can be obtained from the local passport office. No vaccinations are required.

EMBASSIES & CONSULATES

In the U.S.   1607 23rd St. NW, Washington DC 20008-2809; ✆ **202/232-3694,** 202/332-4846, or 202/332-4848; fax 202/232-4748; www.roembus.org. 200 East 38th St., New York, NY 10016; ✆ **212-682-9122.** 11766 Wilshire Blvd., Los Angeles, CA 90025; ✆ **310/444-0043.**

In Canada   655 Rideau St., Ottawa, Ontario, K1N 6A3; ✆ **613/789-3709,** ext. 119; fax 613/789-4365; www.cyberus.ca/~romania.

In the U.K.   Arundel House, 4 Palace Green, Kensington, London W84QD; ✆ 020/ **7937-9666/7** or 020/7376-0683; fax 020/7937-8069; www.roemb.co.uk.

In Australia   4 Dalman Crescent, O'Malley, Canberra ACT 2606; ✆ **02/6290-2442** or 02/6286-2343; fax 02/6286-2433; http://canberra.mae.ro.

In New Zealand   There's an Honorary Consulate in Wellington: 53 Homewood Ave., Karori; ✆ **04/476-6883;** fax 04/476-6512; giffpip@xtra.co.nz.

CUSTOMS REGULATIONS

You are entitled to carry the equivalent of $10,000 cash or traveler's checks on your person when entering Romania; any excess amount must be declared to Customs authorities. You may also bring personal goods and medicines, as well as publications, records and DVDs, slides, and other photographic materials, so long as these are for your personal use. In addition, you may freely carry other goods to the value of 100€ ($125).

MONEY

At press time, Romania had only just entered into the European Union (exact date: Jan 1, 2007); consequently, it is still common to hear price quotes in three different currencies, namely Romanian *leu* (plural *lei*), New Romanian *leu* (RON), and euros. For the most part, however, it is the *new* leu that is important, bearing in mind that 1 *new* leu is the equivalent of the outdated 10,000 *old* lei; four zeros were simply dropped from the currency on July 1, 2005.

Since January 1, 2007, the new *lei* has officially been the only official currency. Where prices are quoted in *lei,* the symbol "L" is used throughout this chapter (note that some establishments prefer euros). However, old habits persist, and many Romanians will still quote in the old currency, but will tell you the cost in thousands; thus, "40" will refer to "40,000 *old* lei," which is actually only 4 *new* lei, at press time $1.44. It pays to be on your toes. Until December 2006, both old and new coins and notes remained in circulation and were accepted; starting in January 2007, old currency was withdrawn. Romanian New Lei notes come in denominations of 1, 5, 10, 50, 100, and 500. One *leu* is divided into 100 *bani,* and these come in coin denominations of 1, 5, 10, and 50 *bani.*

Although Romania is not expected to adopt the euro until after 2010, many hotels prefer to give a straight euro quote; all such establishments accept credit cards. MasterCard and Visa are accepted at just about all city hotels, restaurants, and shops, while American Express and Diners Club are less useful. Many outlets can only accept cards (credit cards, included) for which you have a PIN, which you'll be asked to punch in at the cash register; you'll then sign for the transaction as you would for a standard credit card purchase. Keep an eye on your credit card while it is being used for payment; there are frequent reports of illegal imprints being made by restaurant and store employees.

WHEN TO GO

Season, more than anything, is likely to influence the timing of your visit to Romania. Here, temperatures can be extreme; winters get nasty, with closure of certain attractions during the most bitterly cold times of the year, while ski destinations kick into gear from December to mid-March. If you fancy a white Christmas, December is a great time to experience a host of traditional celebrations, particularly in rural communities such as those found in Maramureş and Moldavia, as well as Transylvania. At the other extreme, mid-summer can be grueling, with global warming taking its toll here (July 2006 saw temperatures in some cities hit a stupefying 104°F/40°C). May and October are possibly the most beautiful months, unencumbered by extreme heat.

HOLIDAYS

New Year (*Revelion*) is celebrated on January 1 and 2, while National Day—commemorating Transylvania's inclusion into greater Romania in 1918—is celebrated on December 1. Christmas (*Crăciun*) is officially observed on December 25 and 26, and both days are public holidays. Labor Day is celebrated on May 1, but businesses may shut down for more than just the 1 day. Determined according to the Julian calendar, Orthodox Easter is closely observed and while not an official public holiday,

Major Festivals in Romania

Romanians love to party and have traditionally found many endearing reasons to celebrate; many of these celebrations are no longer observed, however. Festivals are generally determined by traditional folklore as well as by the Orthodox Church's important feasts; numerous local celebrations also add color to the lineup of festivals around the country. On **March 9, Forty Saints' Day** is celebrated as part of Lent in some rural communities where villagers bake colaci, special loaves of bread that are blessed and handed out as an act of charity. A popular Spring festival is the **National Festival of Spring Agriculture Customs (Tanjaua de pe Marna)** held in **April/early May** in the Maramureş village of Hoteni; it remains a lively local party opportunity, with folk music, dancing, and much drinking. Also in **early May** (usually the first or second Sun), are the **Measuring of the Milk Festivals,** in the Apuseni Mountains, where shepherds compete to see whose sheep and goats are the biggest producers of milk; great carousing follows the ritual milking. On the **first Sunday in May,** the **Pageant of the Juni** in Braşov is one of the most accessible and splendid city festivals, drawing large crowds to see costumed youths parading with brass bands and culminating in spectacular Horăs (Round Dances). In summer, the **Girl Fair (Târgul de fete)** of Mount Găina takes place near Avram Iancu, in the Apuseni Mountains **(last Sun before July 20).** Traditionally an opportunity for shepherds to meet prospective brides, the festival is now a great opportunity to hear the country's finest traditional folk musicians perform live.

On **August 15,** Orthodox believers observe the **Feast of the Assumption of the Virgin Mary,** while in September it is the time of harvest festivals in numerous villages across the country. Saxons celebrate their heritage in the fortified town of Biertan, in Transylvania, on the **second Saturday of September.** The annual **Roma Festival** (a time of impressive celebration that draws Gypsies from across the country) is held in the Wallachia village of Costeşti **(first week of Sept).**

Braşov hosts an **International Jazz Festival** in **mid-May.** Pop fans can look out for **The Golden Stag Festival,** also in Braşov, in **mid-September;** running since 1968, the festival launched the international career of Julio Iglesias and has showcased the talents of Christina Aguillera and Ricky Martin. Drawing some major international film personalities, **TIFF (Transylvania International Film Festival)** happens in Cluj in **early June.**

---

may influence opening and closing times. Most businesses and attractions are closed on these days.

HEALTH CONCERNS

Romania is free of risk when it comes to infectious diseases, malaria, and poisonous insects. Officially, tap water is potable and safe to drink, but there are accounts of water supplies in some areas being compromised, so check with your host or hotel. Mosquitoes frequent the Danube Delta as well as other low-lying areas during the hot summer months; bring insect repellent. Good medical facilities are available in cities and towns, but the quality of medical practitioners varies considerably; only visit a physician who has been recommended to you.

Smoking is now banned in public spaces in Romania, but this law is vehemently ignored; there's no smoking on planes, but there's plenty on trains and other enclosed spaces, including restaurants. Most high-end hotels now have nonsmoking rooms.

GETTING THERE
BY PLANE

Many national airlines, including Romania's official carrier, **Tarom** (www.tarom.ro) have direct flights from London and other major western European centers, including Amsterdam (KLM only), Athens, Bologna (Alitalia only), Düsseldorf (Lufthansa only), Frankfurt, Madrid, Milan, Munich, Paris, Rome, Vienna, and Zurich. Eastern European capitals that are connected by air include Budapest, Prague, Sofia, and Warsaw. Where possible, if you're traveling from North America, Australia, or New Zealand, you should shop around for an airline that offers direct connections from your country of origin through one of the European capitals; many of the bigger airlines have code-share agreements with Tarom, which means that times between connecting flights are reduced. If you're traveling from New York or Sydney, you are able to book your entire journey through Tarom, but departure dates are limited by the availability of partner airlines. For these ultralong-haul journeys, you are best off with **British Airways** (www.british-airways.com) via London, **Air France** (www.airfrance.com) via Paris, **Swiss** (www.swiss.com) via Zurich, or **KLM** (www.klm.com), via Amsterdam.

Most international flights arrive at Bucharest's **Henri Coanda International Airport** (generally known by its pre-2006 name, Otopeni); however, Romania does have a number of other international airports receiving a few flights from a handful of European national and regional airlines. These airports are small and hassle-free and located in tourist-friendly destinations such as Timisoara, Cluj-Napoca, Iaşi, and Constanta.

BY TRAIN

Trains are viable, but not necessarily cheap or speedy. **Romania's National Railway service** (www.infofer.ro) operates services, many of which include overnight sleepers in first- and second-class carriages. Visit www.raileurope.com for details of schedules and reservations.

BY BUS

The size of the country along with the condition of most Romanian roads makes the thought of traveling overland in a large vehicle nothing short of nightmarish. Nevertheless, Romania's principal cities are connected by bus services to most important European centers, including London, Paris, Rome, Frankfurt, Berlin, Budapest, Sofia, Vienna, Milan, Istanbul, and Athens.

BY CAR

If you drive a rental car into Romania, you will require a *RoVinieta* road toll license; these are available at border crossings, and can also be purchased at many gas stations. Expect to pay $5 for a 7-day license or $8 for a 30-day version. You will require proof that you have insurance for the car and you must carry all the vehicle registration documentation with you. U.S., Canadian, and E.U. driver's licenses are acceptable for driving in Romania. Note that Romanian roads are often in a very dismal condition and driving is not recommended unless you have off-road capability.

GETTING AROUND
BY PLANE
Tarom, the national carrier, operates a timetable of flights between Bucharest and the country's smaller airports; the best deals can only be purchased online (www.tarom. ro). Romania's domestic airports are generally quiet and (with the exception of taxis) hassle-free; you can usually arrive for check-in within 30 minutes of your flight and have plenty of time to spare before takeoff.

BY TRAIN
Romania's rail network (CFR) is extensive and quite exhaustive. Trains are relatively comfortable and generally safe (although there are regular accounts of luggage being stolen from sleeping or incautious passengers); in many of the newer trains, there is almost no difference between first and second class. In the majority of cases, you will be assigned a specific carriage and seat. It's quite possible to plan all rail travel before leaving home. Go to the online timetable at www.infofer.ro or go to www.cfr.ro; click on "Train Schedule" to begin searching, bearing in mind that you must enter the Romanian spelling of your departure and destination cities. CFR's services are categorized by the speed of the journey; the fastest trips are on InterCity (IC) trains; these are the most expensive. Next down the rung are Rapid (R) trains—slightly more economical but not quite as fast. Avoid Personal (P) trains, which stop at practically every village. While you can book your tickets online, nearly every town and city has a CFR office located in the center, where you can purchase domestic and international tickets in advance. Traditionally, tickets bought at the train station have only been made available 1 hour before the scheduled journey; this bureaucratic tradition seems to be fading, however, with tickets increasingly available several hours ahead of schedule. With the exception of very popular routes—such as those linking Bucharest with the coast during summer—it is relatively easy obtain train tickets even minutes before departure. The problem is that ticketing lines can be exasperating, with long waits (many travelers need to make elaborate purchases using state-discounted discounted schemes that require time-consuming paperwork); you are advised to purchase tickets in a timely fashion.

In Bucharest, you can make advance train bookings at either the **Agentia de Voiaj SNCFR** (Str. Domnita Anastasia 10–14; © **021/313-2643;** www.cfr.ro) but only up to 24 hours before departure, or at **Wasteels** (Gara du Nord; © **021/317-0369;** www. wasteels.ro/en; Mon–Fri 8am–7pm, Sat 8am–2pm), which is good for domestic as well as international trains.

BY CAR
You'll need nerves of steel to surrender to Romania's roads and culture of high-speed, aggressive driving; tarmac in some areas is in an unpredictable state of repair, signage is less than desirable, and local drivers are in a terrible hurry. Distances between some destinations, combined with heavy traffic, is another deterrent. You may however want to hire a car with a driver in order to get to attractions in some areas; to explore the villages of Maramures and the painted monasteries in Moldavia, for example, this is a necessity, unless you are with an organized tour. If you have car trouble, contact the **Automobil Clubul Roman (ACR;** © **9271**), Romania's version of the Automobile Association.

TIPS ON ACCOMMODATIONS

In a country where the service industry was for a long time associated with spying on guests for the Communist government, service does not always meet expectations, but accommodations are steadily improving. Hotels are rated according to a star system, which is a moderately informative guide to the type of facilities you can expect to find. However, genuine quality often hides in the details, and there are many three-star properties that are more intimate and classy than their four- or even five-star neighbors. Most *Pensiunea* (basically, a family-run guesthouse or scaled-down version of a hotel) are rated two or three stars, because they offer meals and bedrooms with en-suite facilities; in the same price category, however, you may find a very much better villa which simply doesn't have an elevator.

Home stays are an excellent way of getting to grips with village or community life; in rural areas, there are an unprecedented number of "agritourism" schemes enabling you to stay with local families at low cost. Be warned, however, that life for some of these families may be fairly simple; you'll be expected to put up with similar conditions. Always check if there is regular hot water, electricity supply, and bathroom facilities (in this chapter, you'll find mention of any problems in this regard). For extensive home-stay options across the country, contact **A.N.T.R.E.C.** (National Association of Rural, Ecological and Cultural Tourism; Str. Maica Alexandra 7, Bucharest; ℂ **021/ 223-7024;** fax 021/222-8001; www.antrec.ro), which has an excellent online booking system with helpful details of its network of guesthouses.

When booking a room, note that a "double" usually refers to a twin-bedded unit; double-bedded guest rooms are frequently referred to as "matrimonials." To eliminate any misunderstanding, it's best to request a "matrimonial double," and top this with a request for a "king-size" bed, which will not really impact the size of the bed, but will ensure that you don't have two singles. And be suspicious of accepting accommodations when you're told that only the expensive suite is available; this is usually pure nonsense.

TIPS ON DINING

Meat is big in Romania, and you're generally expected to be a carnivore to cope with traditional "Romanian" cuisine that favors pork, but includes plenty of fish, widely considered a vegetable in these parts. Traditional staples include *mămăligă*, a polenta-type pottage made from cornmeal, and *sarmale*, parcels made with cabbage or vine leaves, stuffed with rice or meat. Specialties will vary from region to region, as will the tastes of similar dishes, prepared according to local traditions. Generally, most places you visit will have restaurants, bistros, less formal taverns *(tavernă)*, and wine cellars *(crama)* that double as atmospheric dining halls. Some of these places will have the formal stuffiness preferred in certain Eastern European circles, while down-home-looking eateries are often just fine for a homey, affordable meal. Most restaurants will also have a terrace *(terasă)*, ideal in summer. Romania is also known for its potent homemade brandies, made from plums and other fruit; don't pass up the offer of a tot of *țuică* (sometimes called *palinca*), sure to raise your body temperature.

TOURS & TRAVEL AGENTS

The best-known company for Romania is U.K.-based **Transylvania Uncovered** ⟨★★★⟩ (1 Atkinson Court, Fell Foot, Newby Bridge, Cumbria, United Kingdom LA128NW; ℂ **0044-1539-531258;** www.beyondtheforest.com) which offers dozens of specialized trips, mostly with a specific area of interest, such as the brand-new "Raggle-Taggle" tour, which focuses on Gypsy culture. The company offers different travel and flight options, so you can match trips to your budget, and accommodations range from top hotels to stays on organic farms. **DiscoveRomania** ☆☆☆ (Str. Paul Richter 1/1, 500025 Braşov, Romania; © **0722-74-6262;** www.discoveromania.ro) is another excellent tour company that is also a founder member of the Association of Eco-Tourism in Romania (www.eco-romania.ro); hands-on owner Laura Vesa has a range of interesting and varied packages for travelers keen to discover the "real" Romania. To this end accommodations are generally with local families in small villages, and Laura can plan your visit around special festivals and events to deepen the experience. Nature lovers should inquire after the tour that combines 3 days animal tracking in the Carpathian Mountains with a night in a Moldavian wine-producing village and 2 nights in the Delta, in the fishing village of Uzlina.

For adventure tours and mountain activities, **Apuseni Experience** ☆☆☆ (© **0259/ 47-2434;** www.apuseniexperience.ro) is one of the best outfits in Romania, based in the city of Oradea. **Abercombie & Kent** (© **800/554-7016;** www.abercrombieand kent.com) offers a 14-day "Highlights of Romania & Bulgaria" tour. The online **Romanian Travel Guide** (www.rotravel.com) is a resource for virtual planners with links to local tour operators. You can book discounted accommodations at discounted rates through this service. U.S.-based **Quest Tours & Adventures** (© **800/621-8687;** www.romtour.com) has specialist tours to Romania, ranging in duration from the 2-day "Touch of Transylvania" tour to the 11-day "World Heritage" tour.

GAY ROMANIA

Homosexuality is no longer illegal in Romania, thanks largely to pressure from the E.U. to bring human rights practices in line with the rest of Europe. This represents the end of a long battle against nasty discrimination in legislation, but does not solve the problem of an inherently homophobic society. When the first Romanian gay pride march took place in Bucharest in 2005, it was in the face of tremendous, vocal opposition from the church, government, and the police, not to mention the city mayor. Slowly, gay-friendly or exclusively gay clubs are emerging, but this is only in the larger cities; public displays of homosexual affection are not likely to attract a positive response.

3 Bucharest

Caught up in a necromantic adventure with its elegant, faded past, Bucharest may not be to every traveler's taste, but for those interested in experiencing the fast-paced, idio-syncratic flashiness of a city that's clearly on the edge of a tidal wave of change, it is certainly worth planning a few days here. A heady mix of beautifully old, blandly new, and somewhere ambiguously in-between (the latter defined by the brash architecture of Ceauşescu-era behemoths), Bucharest seems to know that it's the capital of a nation on the move, a country finally ready to take its place in the European brotherhood.

Legend tells that Bucharest was named after a young shepherd, Bucur, who was so moved by the beauty of this spot on the eastern bank of the Dâmboviţa River that he built a church here, but these humble origins are since long lost in the shrouds of history. Strategically located, Bucharest grew wealthy off trade between the East and West, and entered its swinging heyday after it was crowned the nation's capital in 1862. Then came the World War II bombings, devastating earthquakes in 1940 and

1977, and Ceauşescu. The capital limped its way out of the 20th century, burdened with memories of devouring bulldozers, violent protests, and state-sanctioned massacres. Hard to believe that a mere decade later the pride and promise of the entire nation can be gauged in the strut and swagger of the city's youthful student population, their stride (and blood) quickened by new prospects and fortunes to be made with E.U. ascension.

Bucharest today is once again a vibrant, culturally astute capital. Besides a sustained program of theater, music, and opera, it draws major international music acts that fill up the city's stadiums with up-for-it crowds: Within 1 month in 2006, Billy Idol, 50 Cent, Depeche Mode, and the Deftones all performed here, attracting energetic crowds, bound up in a perhaps worrisome embrace of all things Western. But while Ceauşescu might have torn out much of its antiquity, replacing century-old winding roads with pencil-straight boulevards, you can still get lost in the old soul of this riveting city. Playful curiosities, in which the past tangles with the future, remain—nuns reach into their habits to answer ringing cellphones. Mafioso-wannabes show off in flashy new cars, racing past street-side Gypsies selling flowers. Men on the sidewalks offer their services as talking scales. And in antiques stores, treasures gather dust while locals stock up on symbols of modern consumerism. The signs are all there; unsuppressible Bucharest is shedding its skin and edging its way into a prosperous future.

GETTING THERE

BY PLANE   International flights arrive at **Henri Coanda International Airport** (Şos. Bucureşti-Ploieşti; ✆ **021/201-4050** or 021/204-1423), still generally referred to by its former name, Otopeni, which lies 16km (10 miles) north of the city and has a relatively small, but moderately chaotic international terminal; the **information desk** (✆ **021/204-1000**) is located in the departures lounge. Note that all the taxis and even the shuttle services at the airport will overcharge you (20€–25€/$25–$31 instead of around 10€–12€/$13–$15) for the trip into the city; if you have a hotel reservation, have them arrange a transfer. A reliable airport service is **Fly Taxi Company** (✆ **021/9440**), which charges L1.50 (55¢) per kilometer, or try one of the companies listed under "Getting Around," below. Every 15 minutes, **bus** no. 783 stops at Terminal A (arrivals) and heads into the city (40 min.); buy tickets from the driver.

BY TRAIN   Trains from various European capitals arrive at Bucharest's **Gara de Nord** (Piaţa Gară de Nord 1; ✆ **021/223-2060;** www.cfr.ro), a large, well-organized station that also has connections with almost every destination around the country.

BY BUS   Think twice before tackling long-distance trips through Romania, and that includes any international journey toward Bucharest. If you must, then **Eurolines** (Str. Buzeşti 44; ✆ **021/230-5489;** www.eurolines.ro) is your best for the long, arduous journey from Paris, Madrid, Brussels, or Frankfurt.

CITY LAYOUT & NEIGHBORHOODS IN BRIEF

To the **north** of the city, broad tree-lined boulevards are home to fantastic, crumbling mansions, including foreign embassies and important diplomatic residences. Cobblestone side streets shelter gorgeous homes, many clad in layers of ivy and tucked behind overgrown gardens. It's a neighborhood with an opulent shabbiness, unencumbered by drab apartment blocks or concrete monstrosities; if there's one area in the city that's good for cycling or jogging, this is it. Two major roads, Şoseaua Kiseleff and Bulevard Aviatorilor, stretch from the lakes at the northern extremity of the city to **Piaţa Victoriei,** where security officers protect Government building. The square is also close to the main train station, Gara de Nord, and near the important Museum of the Romanian Peasant.

From Piaţa Victoriei, **Calea Victoriei** leads southeast into the heart of **downtown Bucharest** with its heady urban feel; monuments and historic buildings stand cheek-by-jowl with more modern edifices and there's a constant surge of energy.

Downtown has two notable centers. The first is **Piaţa Revolutiei,** bisected by Calea Victoriei; this where you'll find the Royal Palace (now the National Art Museum), and the Romanian Athenaeum, as well as smaller streets leading to all manner of restaurants, bars, and terraces. Southeast of here is **Piaţa Universitatii,** identifiable by the monstrous Intercontinental Hotel and the austere National Theater building, both on one side of the busy intersection. Bulevard Regina Elisabeta becomes Bulevard Carol I as it slices through this point from west to east, while Bulevard Nicolae Bălcescu cuts through from the north. Farther south, **Strada Lipscani** is the main (now pedestrian) road of the city's historic district, known simply as Lipscani. To the east of Piaţa Universitatii are the lovely Cişmigiu Gardens, a small oasis in the middle of the big city.

South of the gardens is the notorious Palace of Parliament and the Centru Civic, where Ceauşescu demolished one-sixth of the old city to make way for a curtain of concrete blocks and pencil-straight boulevards. Principal among these is long, fat Champs-Élysées-style Unirii Boulevard, linking the parliamentary palace with Piaţa Unirii and studded with fountains, one for each county in Romania.

GETTING AROUND

BY TAXI   Renowned for their unflinching rip-off tactics, Bucharest's taxis are actually a very affordable way of getting around the city. The onus is on you, however, to check that the fare is clearly displayed on the side of the vehicle (generally, L1–L3/35¢/20p–$1.10/60p is acceptable; although some charge up to L5/$1.80/£1 for an air-conditioned ride); then make sure the driver uses the meter. A rated taxi company is **Grant** (© 021/9433), upfront and honest; it's a good idea to call them well ahead of any important trips you need to make. Also reliable are Prof Taxi (© **021/9422**), Meridian (© **021/9444**), CrisTaxi (© **021/9461** or 021/9466), and Perrozzi (© **021/9631**).

BY METRO   Completely underutilized by locals, the Metro can be a rather dull way to get around the city. Nevertheless, it is cheap and the network is simple enough to figure out with a brief glance at one of the maps posted in the underground stations. Buy tickets (each one is valid for two trips) at the booths adjacent to the passenger gates. Trains run between 5:30am and 11:30pm, arriving every 5 minutes at busy times, but only three times an hour in slow periods.

ON FOOT   In summer it's a punishing walk from one end of the city to the other but if you're energetic, you'll get a much better sense of the city and its people by strolling the sidewalks. This is also a great way to make architectural discoveries and find back-street neighborhoods that nobody ever mentions.

BY TRAM, BUS & TROLLEYBUS   Public transport operates between 5am and 11:30pm, with shorter hours on Sunday, but you really need to know where you're going and get to grips with the network to make the trams and trolleybuses work for you. Bucharest's buses are cramped, hot, and stuffy, and you'll be more likely to fall prey to pickpockets on one of them than anywhere else. Tickets for all services can be purchased at any of the many RATB kiosks around the city (look for BILETE signs), where you can also pick up a timetable (purchase Amco's *Public Ground Transport*

Map if you're going to use public transport); timetables are also posted on streetlamps near bus stops (the central "station" is across the road from Hotel Ibis on Calea Griviţei). Remember to use the self-service machine to validate your ticket once you're on board.

VISITOR INFORMATION

There is no official tourist information service in Bucharest; in most cases, your hotel will be able to point you in the right direction, and provide you with a map. Ask specifically for the listings publication, *Bucharest in your Pocket,* which has maps as well as details of hotels, restaurants, and attractions. Bucharest's bookstores stock some good publications on the city and on major points of interest around the country. The **European Union Information Center** (✆ **021/315-3470;** www.infoeuropa.ro) on Piaţa Revoluţiei, can also help you get your bearings.

FAST FACTS: Bucharest

Airlines The headquarters of the national carrier, **Tarom** (Spl. Independenţei 17; ✆ **021/337-0400;** www.tarom.ro; Mon–Fri 9am–7pm, Sat 9am–1pm), are at the **airport** (✆ **021/204-1355** or 021/201-4979). **British Airways:** Calea Victoriei 15; ✆ **021/303-2222;** Mon–Fri 9am–5pm. **Air France:** Str. General Proporgescu 1-5; ✆ **021/312-0085.**

Ambulance In emergencies, dial ✆ **973** or 021/243-1333, to summon **Puls,** a private ambulance service; otherwise, dial ✆ **021/224-0187** (Mon–Sat 7:30am–7:30pm; Sun 7:30am–1:30pm).

American Express Represented by Marshal Turism (www.marshal.ro), at B-dul Unirii 20 (✆ **021/335-1224**), and B-dul Magheru 43 (✆ **021/223-1204**). Open Monday to Friday 9am to 6pm and Saturday 9am to 1pm.

Area Codes For Bucharest dial ✆ **021.**

Banks & Currency Exchange Banks are the best place to exchange foreign currency. ATMs are everywhere and are the best way to obtain local currency, assuming that your credit card has a PIN, or that your cash card has been enabled for international use. Open round-the-clock is **Alliance Exchange** (B-dul Bălcescu 30).

Car Rentals **Avis** (various branches; ✆ 021/210-4344; www.avis.ro), **Hertz** (✆ 021/222-1256; www.hertz.com.ro), and **Europcar** (B-dul General Magheru; (✆ 021/313-1540). Standard car rental is now as low as €29 ($36) per day for a cheap model with unlimited mileage. If you prefer something classier, try **Bavaria Rent a Car** (www.bavariarent.ro; ✆ 021/201-4534), specializing in BMWs, with tough models that will better handle some of Romania's more treacherous roads.

Drugstores Open round-the-clock, **Help Net** has branches at B-dul Unirii 24 (✆ **021/335-7425**), Calea 13 Septembrie 126 (✆ **021/411-9574**), Şos. Mihai Bravu 128, bl. D24 (✆ **021/252-7266**), and Str. Av. Radu Beller 8 (✆ **021/233-8984**).

Embassies The Consular Section of the **U.S. Embassy** (Mon–Fri 8am–5pm) is at Str. N. Filipescu 26; ✆ **021/200-3300;** www.usembassy.ro. The **Canadian Embassy**

(Mon–Thurs 9am–5pm; Fri 8.30am–2pm) is at Str. Nicolae Iorga 36; ✆ 021/307-5000; www.dfait-maeci.gc.ca. The **U.K. Embassy** (Mon–Thurs 8:30am–1pm and 2–5pm; Fri 8:30am–2:30pm) is at Str. Jules Michelet 24; ✆ 021/210-7300; www.britishembassy.gov.uk/romania. Contact the **Australian Embassy** (B-dul Unirii 74; www.romaniaaustralia.ro) at ✆ 021/320-9802. There is no New Zealand Embassy in Bucharest; your best contact is in Vienna (✆ 0043/1/318-8505).

Emergencies Dial ✆ 961 in case of emergencies; for an ambulance, dial ✆ 961 or **973**; and contact ✆ 981 in case of fire. See "Police," below.

Hospital Romania's best state-run facility is **Emergency Clinic Hospital (Spitalul de Urgenta Floreasca;** Calea Floreasca 8; ✆ 021/317-0121). A good private service is **Victor Babes** (Str. Mihai Bravu 281; ✆ 021/317-9503), which is also open 24 hours a day, and has a price list for all services on its website, www.cdt-babes.ro. A good chain of clinics is **Medicover** (emergency number ✆ 021/310-4040), with three branches, at Calea Plevnei 96 (✆ 021/310-4410), Str. Dr. Grozovici 6 (✆ 021/310-1599), and Str. Grigore Alexandrescu 16-20 (✆ 021/310-1688); they're open 8am to 8pm weekdays and also Saturday morning.

Internet Access Most hotels now have Internet, and many have Wi-Fi.

Police Dial ✆ 955. The most central police station is at Calea Victoriei 17; ✆ 021/311-2021.

Post Office Bucharest's **main post office** is located at Str. Matei Millo 10, and is open Monday to Friday 7:30am to 8pm and Saturday 8am to 2pm.

WHERE TO STAY

Bucharest is well geared to receive visitors with company expense accounts, with respected western chains all represented here and offering most of the luxuries and comforts you might expect in other parts of the world. An increasing number of modest and better-priced accommodations are available, although you may miss some of the amenities offered by similarly priced properties back home (few have pools, for example). Budget hotels leave much to be desired.

Hotels are spread across the city, but there are only about 4km (2½ miles) between the northernmost (Sofitel) and southernmost (Marriott Grand) hotels mentioned here. If you want to be in the heart of the city, there are plenty of hotels across the quality spectrum right in the center, within walking distance of major attractions. But bear in mind that Bucharest's attractions are spread out enough to make proximity to the center only a minor consideration when choosing your hotel.

VERY EXPENSIVE

If you want to be near Ceaușescu's Palace of the People and, in fact, stay in the hotel he conjured up to accommodate his guests, consider reserving a room at the **JW Marriott Bucharest Grand Hotel** ℛ (Calea 13 Septembrie 90; ✆ 021/403-0000; fax 021/403-0001; www.marriott.com/buhro; from 290€/$363 double, without breakfast or taxes), where you can expect the usual standard in-room amenities and hotel services. There's also the good chance of having any number of important dignitaries as fellow guests; the Marriott is a typically huge and luxurious complex with myriad

EXPENSIVE

Hotel Capşa ⚑⚑★ Beautiful chandeliers sparkle in the all-marble lobby of this historic hotel, signaling to all its long and distinguished pedigree. Established by Grigore Capşa in 1852, it was here that the first U.S. Embassy was housed between 1880 and 1884. Emperors, kings, statesmen, and Francis Ford Coppola have been guests here, and it still bears discreet references to significant political events that were decided in meetings held here by the country's leaders in times gone by. More gracious and better priced than a number of similarly comfortable Bucharest hotels, its guest rooms are spacious, with high ceilings and carpets, wall-mounted chandeliers, antique armoires, and plaster molded detailing. If it's important, specify whether you'd like a tub or shower. And bear in mind that Capşa has excellent specials during quiet periods, so look out for last-minute deals.

Calea Victoriei 36, Bucharest. ✆ 021/313-4038. Fax 021/313-5999. www.capsa.ro. 61 units. 200€ ($250) double; 225€–450€ ($282–$563) suite; 490€ ($613) apt; 600€ ($750) imperial suite. Breakfast 15€ ($19) per person. MC, V. **Amenities:** Restaurant; bar; fitness center; sauna; massage; hairdresser; room service; laundry; courier. *In room:* A/C, TV, minibar.

Lido Hotel ⚑ Operating since 1930, this grand old hotel is a good alternative if the Hotel Capsa is full, or has suddenly raised its rates substantially. Guest rooms, done out in faux-Venetian style with painted wood and a pale color palette, are comfortable enough but have a slightly faded feel; while these could do with a refurb the bathrooms are looking good, with combination tub/shower. One of the best reasons to stay here is the spectacle of city life from the tiny balconies overlooking busy General Mageru Boulevard—pure Bucharest (depending on your fancy, the housekeepers, who all seem to resemble supermodels and work in ridiculously short skirts, are another).

B-dul General Magheru 5, Bucharest. ✆ 021/314-4930. Fax 021/312-1414. www.lido.ro. 119 units. 240€ ($300) double; 345€ ($431) suite. AE, MC, V. **Amenities:** Restaurant; brasserie; breakfast room; bar; fitness center; massage; sauna; Jacuzzi; salon; room service; laundry. *In room:* A/C, TV, minibar, hair dryer.

MODERATE

Hotel Opera ⚑ After a major renovation in 2002, this small hotel—right in the center of town—has emerged as one of the best options in the city, given its location and price. Decorated with an assortment of music-related items, antiques, and lovely sepia photos of '50s Bucharest, Opera offers smart yet sensible lodgings, with spacious guest rooms. Bathrooms are equally comfortable; standard doubles have showers, so you'll need to book a suite if you prefer a tub. At weekends, when rates are reduced, it may be worth forking out a little extra for one of the junior suites, each named for a different opera. There's no in-house restaurant, but staff can point you in the direction of something suitable, or you can order meals to your room. If you're in the mood for company, you can join the locals who while away their time playing backgammon in the lobby bar.

Str. Ion Brezoianu 37, Bucharest. ✆ 021/312-4855/7. Fax 021/312-4858. www.hotelopera.ro. 33 units. Weekday/weekend: 150€/130€ ($188/$163) double; 175€/150€ ($219/$188) executive double; 195€/150€ ($244/$188) junior suite. Rates include breakfast and VAT. AE, MC, V. **Amenities:** Breakfast room; lobby bar; fitness room (from 2007); car rental; business lounge; room service; laundry; airport transfers at 20€ ($25). *In room:* A/C, TV, Internet, minibar, tea- and coffeemaking facility, hair dryer, safe.

Hotel Unique ⚑⚑ *Finds* Small, intimate, and contemporary, this boutique hotel opened in 2006, but looks set to join the ranks of the city's best. There are just four guest rooms and one suite per floor, all with sleek, contemporary styling (white and blonde wood dramatically offset by touches of red or orange). It's worth paying the little extra for suites that come with balconies or splash out on the sumptuous penthouse apartment, which affords a panoramic view of the surrounding neighborhood. If that's taken, never mind; all the accommodations are still wonderfully spacious. Not a huge array of facilities but the small, smart breakfast room and tiny garden terrace should suffice.

Piața Romana, Str. Caderea Bastiliei 35, 010615 Bucharest. ©/fax **021/319-4591** or 021/311-8196. www.hotel unique.ro. 15 units. 124€ ($155) double; 139€ ($174) junior suite. Rates include breakfast and taxes. Weekend rates may be cheaper. Internet may offer lower rates. MC, V. **Amenities:** Breakfast room; coffee bar; terrace; limited room service; laundry; airport transfers. *In room:* A/C, TV, Internet, minibar, tea- and coffeemaking facility, hair dryer, safe, DVD on request.

Rembrandt Hotel ★★★ *Value*   Compact and utterly chic, this Dutch-owned boutique hotel is the personal top choice in the city, with gorgeous contemporary guest rooms, comfortable beds, and welcoming staff. It's also located slap-bang in the center of the city, across the road from the National Bank of Romania, another gorgeous city monument. Just 15 rooms are squeezed into an almost impossibly narrow slither of carefully restored downtown real estate, but the Rembrandt has, in just a few years, come to define the spirit of renewal and rejuvenation that Bucharest's historic Lipscani District has been crying out for. Accommodations are beautiful; simple and sleek, they're done out with wooden floors, fabulous white linens, and Art Nouveau light fittings. When Ethan Hawke was in town to support his mother's local charity organization, he'd checked into the Rembrandt before the media were even aware of his arrival—it's *that* discreet and unpretentious. If you don't mind having a slightly smaller room, note that there's one top-floor unit with a private balcony from which the spectacular views of the city stretch as far as the Parliamentary Palace. Rembrandt is near a wide range of lovely restaurants, and is perfect for exploring the city on foot. Note that rates are more than 10% lower at weekends.

Str. Smârdan 11, Bucharest. © **021/313-9315.** Fax 021/313-9316. www.rembrandt.ro. 15 units. 81€–91€ ($101–$114) tourist double; 93€–113€ ($116–$141) standard double; 123€–143€ ($154–$179) business double. Rates include breakfast and taxes. MC, V. **Amenities:** Bistro; bar; laundry. *In room:* A/C, TV, DVD and CD player, Internet, minibar, hair dryer.

Residence ★★ *Value*   Location aside (Residence is in the north of the city, within walking distance of the Arcul d'Triumf, but you will have to catch a cab to see other top sights), this is one of the best small hotels in Bucharest. Wood floor passages lead to carpeted guest rooms decked out in smart bamboo furniture (making them thoroughly unique in Bucharest) with wrought-iron beds; they're spacious and, by local standards, lovely. Public spaces are an eclectic combination of contemporary and neo-classical elements; there's a relaxed atmosphere that makes this Residence feel homey and inviting. Note that the "Garden Restaurant" is actually indoors, and there is no garden; the terrazzo-style dining area at the front of the hotel is a popular meeting spot for locals and visitors.

Str. Clucerului 19, Bucharest. © **021/223-1978.** Fax 021/222-9046. www.residence.com.ro. 35 units. 90€ ($113) double; 100€ ($125) studio; 120€ ($150) suite. Rates include breakfast. MC, V. **Amenities:** 2 restaurants; bar; fitness center; travel services; airport transfers; laundry. *In room:* A/C, TV, Internet, minibar.

INEXPENSIVE

If you don't mind foregoing room service and the like, a good way to save money is to rent an apartment; just make sure you're not located too far from the action.

Room with a View

At the climax of the December 1989 Revolution, students from the **University of Bucharest** were among those who sat on busy University Square in protest, only to be driven over by tanks still loyal to Ceauşescu. The square is today still lorded over by the ugly frame of the **Intercontinental Hotel** (B-dul Nicolae Bălcescu 4; © 021/310-2020; www.intercontinental.com), from where you can share the same view as the international press who witnessed the wholesale massacre of ordinary citizens barricaded in by the military. On the night of December 21, 1,000 helpless victims were killed here; a black cross marks the spot where the first victim fell in the early evening. Today, the areas in front of the **National Theater (Teatrul Naţional)** and the fountain in front of the University building are once again popular meeting points for students who find many diversions around or near this great physical and symbolic crossroads.

Bucharest Comfort Suites (www.comfortsuites.ro) and **City Comfort** (www.city comfort.ro) both offer rentals that work out far cheaper than hotel stays; rates start at 35€ ($44) per night, including central locations. Apartments are clean, modestly furnished, and include occasional cleaning service and air-conditioning; some have free Internet access.

Hotel Carpaţi *(Value*   Built in the 1920s, this six-floor hotel has assorted clean guest rooms, with or without en-suite bathrooms; some have private showers but no toilet (and vice versa), while a few have their own bathroom *and* separate toilet. Rates vary according to the level of privacy and in-room amenities. If you're splurging, the suites represent unbelievable value; they're disproportionately spacious, with old, leather sofas, chandeliers, antique telephones, and bathtubs. They're let down by extremely soft mattresses, though. Rates include a simple breakfast and moody reception staff. This is one of Bucharest's most popular budget hotels, often filled with last-minute arrivals leading to complaints of reservations not being honored; if you decide to stay here, get your booking confirmation in triplicate. *A final warning:* Mind your head on the stairs.

Str. Matei Millo 16, Bucharest. © 021/315-0140. Fax 021/312-1857. www.hotelcarpatibucuresti.ro. 40 units. 22€ ($28) double with shared bathroom; 40€ ($50) twin with shared shower; 63€ ($79) en-suite double; 71€ ($89) suite. MC, V. **Amenities:** Breakfast area. *In room:* TV, some A/C, fridge.

WHERE TO DINE

If you just want to wander around looking for a restaurant head for Str. Episcopiei, where the streets are lined with cafes and restaurants, including the charming Bistro Atheneu (reviewed below). A short stroll from here is **Byblos Bar & Restaurant,** a great place to grab a drink and light lunch, like pizza, panini, bruschetta, and salad (including the delectable Byblos salad—spinach leaves, pine-nut kernels, and Parmesan in a garlicky olive-oil dressing); at night Byblos transforms itself into an altogether more classy dining experience (Nicolae Golescu 14–16; © 021/313-2091). Back down Str. Episcopiei you might want to take a look at popular tourist haunt, **La Mama** (Str. Episcopiei 7; © 021/312-9797; www.lamama.ro). Something of a

Bucharest institution, La Mama is now a chain of restaurants known for their dangerously large (and inexpensive) portions of definitively Romanian meat dishes. While the country-style soup, *sarmale,* and *tochiturǎ* (stew made with chunks of meat, sausage, and liver) all seem to emulate village cooking, there's an overwhelming lack of imagination, and the food while filling is never memorable.

EXPENSIVE

Balthazar 🍴🍴🍴 FRENCH-ASIAN   One of the city's finest restaurants, this is a stunning example of Bucharest's contemporary aspirations; the owners describe the atmosphere as "sensual-chic," which pretty much describes the elegant rusticity of the place. Start with Peking duck *blinis* (small Eastern European pancakes), tuna "cigars," or smoked eel on a bed of cheese. Mains include beef *pavé* smothered in the chef's secret "Balthazar" sauce and served with stuffed artichokes and tomatoes, lamb rib chops served with bamboo and a cherry sauce, and blue fin tuna steak with pineapple carpaccio, fennel, and bamboo salad. There's also sea bream with spinach mousse served with black tiger shrimp sauce. If you're after a lighter meal, opt for the Asian salad with black tiger shrimps and ginger sauce. The dessert menu is almost an occasion on its own: Who can decide between wild berry sorbet, chocolate surprise, and cheesecake served with ginger ice cream?

Str. Dumbrava Roșie 2. ⓒ **021/212-1460.** www.balthazar.ro. Reservations essential. Main courses L33–L74 ($12–$27/£6.30–£14). MC, V. Daily noon–midnight.

Casa Doina 🍴🍴 ROMANIAN/MEDITERRANEAN   In Bucharest's leafy north, among the embassies and mansions, this classy establishment occupies a fine 18th-century villa with a gorgeous garden terrace for summer dining (which is also heated in winter); this is a favored place for the old school air-kissing crowd, where foreigners hobnob with the rich while chef Doru Dobre cooks up a storm for his sophisticated clientele. Start with polenta topped with bacon and shaved cheese, topped with an egg and served with sour cream, or have the in-house version of *sarmale,* sour cabbage leaves stuffed with meat and served (of course) with polenta. The menu is not too complicated, with plenty to keep both unadventurous and keen-to-experiment taste buds happy; chicken filet is stuffed with Roquefort and finished off with bacon and Parmesan; braised ducking is served with sauerkraut and grilled duck liver with cherry sauce. Fresh fish is available at the daily market price; their swordfish is gently fried in olive oil. Finish off with nougat glace with egg custard and maple syrup.

Șos. Kiseleff 4. ⓒ **021/222-6717.** www.casadoina.ro. Reservations recommended. Main courses L25–L70 ($9–$25/£5–£13). MC, V. Daily 11am–1am.

MODERATE

Bistro Atheneu 🍴 ROMANIAN/ECLECTIC   This atmospheric bistro, going strong since 1924, features an indoor fountain and bohemian decor that could be culled from a flea market, with expired antique clocks, dangling bells, violins, and framed mirrors, even an ancient cash register. The kitchen may be relying a bit on its reputation, but it remains a reliable choice for wholesome, tasty meals at equally reliable prices. Seating is scattered around a rambling warren of spaces, and the menu is chalked up daily; on offer will be the usual mainstays like grilled pork, grilled chicken, beef entrecôte, chicken livers, and lasagna. Romanian specialties include *sarmale* and *tochitura* (pork stew); if you're lucky (or you could inquire if the chef will prepare it), the delectable chicken breast, wrapped in bacon and prepared with smoked plum, cinnamon, red wine, and a secret brown sauce, and finished with green basil, will be available.

Str. Episcopiei 3. © 021/313-4900. Main courses L24 ($8.60/£4.60). MC, V. Daily noon–1am.

Burebista Vanatoresc ⚔ ROMANIAN   This is pure unadulterated Romanian cuisine, but animal-lovers (and vegetarians) should steer clear of this medieval-themed meat temple with decor straight out of a natural history museum. Animal trophies and stuffed birds peer down from the walls as you feast on dishes straight from the hunt: specialties include bear paws and civet. Some more palatable items include spicy, crispy pork ribs, filet of wild boar in red-wine sauce, roasted wild pheasant with currant sauce, and flame-grilled beef filet with a red-wine and brandy sauce. While there are promises of musical performances most evenings, it's not unlikely that you'll be listening to awful Western pop songs; be warned also that service can get extremely surly and sluggish.

Str. Batistei 14. © 021/211-8929. www.restaurantburebista.ro. Main courses L10–L70 ($3.60–$26/£1.90–£13); bear paws L450 ($162/£86) each. MC, V. Daily 11am–midnight.

Charme ⚔ ITALIAN/ECLECTIC   New, favored hangout of Bucharest's entrepreneurial brat-pack, this pleasant restaurant centers on a long, lovely bar counter, and offers relaxed dining in a bright space in the Lipscani District. A self-consciously contemporary atmosphere (most of the seating is on sofas or awkward, modish swivel chairs) is enhanced by good lounge music, and tall, friendly waiters in Dunhill-sponsored uniforms. Dishes are simple, wholesome and tasty: take your pick of grilled lamb, *osso buco,* grilled swordfish, calamari with spicy ricotta cheese, lamb chops with black beer sauce, pasta with porcini mushrooms, or beef filet with a choice of mustard sauce, a rich Gorgonzola sauce, or fresh asparagus. Most of what's on the menu is under €10 ($13), and your table will be supplied with fresh bread and olives to nibble on. It may be flavor of the month (it only opened mid-2006), but the location lends it great charm; grab a seat on the small wooden terrace and you'll easily spend an afternoon watching pedestrians come and go.

Smardan 12. © 021/3111-1619. Main courses L12–L45 ($4.30–$16/£2.30–£8.60). Cover L2.50 (90¢/50p). MC, V. Daily 9am–11pm; lounge and bar until late.

Il Gattopardo Blu ITALIAN/ROMANIAN   The setting is the thing here, inside the mournfully atmospheric Casa Scriitorilor (HQ of the Writers' Union), a perfectly crumbling pile that's ripe for restoration (and certainly worth exploring before or after your meal). Once inside the monument, look through the cobwebs for the little red sign on a mezzanine-level door; it reads "restaurant 12-24," and behind the door is the "Blue Leopard" restaurant (named for Visconti's famous film *The Leopard*). A lovely place for a relaxed lunch in summer, when you should head straight for the leafy terrace garden. Grilled sturgeon and trout are popular, as is the escallop of beef, but to be honest you're not here for the food, but to imbibe in a naive romantic fantasy, with birds twittering in the trees above, while canned Romanian love songs are belted out by operatic voices.

Calea Victoriei 115. © 021/319-6595. Main courses L11–L58 ($3.95–$21/£2.10–£11). MC, V. Sun–Fri noon–midnight.

La Mandragora ⚔⚔⚔ FRENCH FUSION   Decadent decor and smart ideas about food have inspired a classy, edgy ambience at this lovely new restaurant that opened in a renovated house in June 2006. Lilac-colored walls, a glittering bar, and gathered drapes are the opening gambit for an evening of superb food. French dishes with a twist is how you might describe the divine creations of German chef Paul Peter Kopij, who plans seasonal innovations and additions to a cleverly sophisticated, yet simple menu. Cream of carrot or shiitake mushroom soup, and beef carpaccio with beet and pine-nut salad are some of the starters likely to be on offer. Then there's breast of duck cooked in Guinness ale, while whatever fish is freshest from the daily market will be the favored seafood option. Best are the homemade ice creams; choose either La Mandragora's ice cream assortment, or crème brûlée with green apple ice cream.

Str. Mendeleev 29. (© 072-280-6187. Reservations essential. Main courses L24–L49 ($8.60–$18/£4.60–£9.40). MC, V. Mon–Sat 6pm–late; kitchen closes 11pm.

INEXPENSIVE

La Taifas (★ (Value ROMANIAN/INTERNATIONAL   Restaurateur Gibi Anghelescu's atmospheric venture (this is the younger sibling of Bistro Atheneu) seems like the work of an Arabian Nights fantasist, with brightly colored walls and plenty of silver, copper, onion-domes, and filigree motifs; the name means "having a chat" and that seems to be what the cushioned, carpeted seating areas encourage you to do. All in all, an atmospheric, fun venue where there's often live music. The kitchen changes its mind daily, and items are chalked up on a board; best to simply ask for the favored dish of the day, but do ask about the mint cod *(cod cu mentă)*, which is filleted and allowed to soak up the flavor from a bed of mint for 24 hours. La Taifas is also fairly good value, with a fabulous lunchtime special: 6€ ($7.50) for a three-course meal with a glass of wine (12:30–2:30pm).

Str. Gheorghe Manu 16. (© 021/212-7788. Main courses L7–L30 ($2.50–$11/£1.30–£5.80). MC, V. Noon–1am.

Market 8 (★★ DELI   Superbly styled with a designer's eye for contemporary flair, this lovely deli occupies a sidewalk corner in the Lipscani District. It opened mid-2005 to instant popularity, welcomed for its artful integration of lounge-bar with cafe-style delicatessen, brought to life with fanciful furniture (assorted, clever armchairs), a small gallery of carefully chosen books, paintings, and other objects d'arts, and purple walls painted with what can only be described as alien plant life. You can pop in to buy take-home eats, but you'd be missing out: Grab a seat in the eclectic-smart restaurant and be prepared to be charmed by your waiter. Beers are served in frosted glasses, best with simple sandwiches (try olive-encrusted ciabatta with eggplant, feta, crème fraîche, bacon, and mozzarella). There's a simple, ever-changing menu of wholesome meals, such as pastas, pork schnitzel, or fragrant chicken prepared with cashews.

Str. Stavropoleos 8. (© 021/313-4167. dom@digi.ro. Main courses L14–L28 ($5–$10/£2.70–£5.40); sandwiches L10–L14 ($3.60–$5/£1.90–£2.70). No credit cards. Mon–Sat 8am–10pm.

EXPLORING BUCHAREST
CITY TOURS & GUIDED WALKS

CRIF Tours (© 021/444-0164; www.discoverromania.ro) is owned by Cristian Florea, an English-speaking guide who leads groups and individuals not only through Bucharest, but also to other parts of the country. His knowledge of Romanian history alone is reason enough to get in contact with him. **Cultural Travel & Tours** (© 021/336-3163; www.cttours.ro) offer exactly what their name suggests. Tailor-made tours of Bucharest start at 29€ ($36) per person, and you can also arrange guided tours of any part of the country. Also offering personalized, culturally geared itineraries is the

happened in 1989 still lingers, when Ceaușescu gave his last speech to an angry crowd from the balcony of the **Communist Party Central Committee building** before ordering soldiers to open fire and fleeing in his helicopter. To the far north of the square is the city's landmark hotel, the **Athénée Palace Hilton** (see "Where to Stay," earlier in this chapter); also looking onto the square are the **Ateneul Roman** and **National Museum of Art** (see below). At the southern end of the square is the early-18th-century **Crețulescu Church;** behind it, look for the headless statue commemorating heroes lost to the revolution.

Biserica Stavropoleos ⭑⭑⭑ Dedicated to the archangels Michael and Gabriel, Stavropoleos (running parallel with Lipscani St.) is one of Romania's most atmospheric churches, a small and gracious place of worship that is especially loved by its dedicated congregation, drawn by the enlightened and charismatic priest. Now restored as a monastery, Stavropoleos was built in 1724 by Ioanikie Stratonikeas (frescoed on the left as you enter the church), a Greek monk who came to Bucharest to raise funds for his hometown monastery. Today, it's in the hands of five hardworking nuns; they look after an impressive library with a collection of old manuscripts and spend time transcribing Cyrillic musical scores electronically. For one of the best introductions to Orthodox church symbolism, ask to see the exhibition of icons and liturgical objects which the nuns have laid out to simulate a traditional church plan; your guiding nun will explain the meaning of each icon and elaborate on its particular significance. Try to attend Mass here at least once; rites are held every morning (7:30am) when the choir consists of female voices, while on Wednesdays at 4:30pm, it's an all-male performance of the Byzantine-style chorus.

Str. Stavropoleos. ✆ 021/313-4747. Free admission. Daily 7:30am–6pm.

Ateneul Român (Romanian Athenaeum) ⭑⭑ Recognized as one of the loveliest architectural works in Bucharest, the Romanian Athenaeum is something of an urban fulcrum, marking out the cultural and social center of the city; inaugurated in 1888, it was designed by French architect Albert Galleron (who also conceived the shapely National Bank of Romania in the Lipscani District). Facing the Royal Palace and standing adjacent the **Athénée Palace Hilton** hotel, the lovely exterior is matched by interior frescoes and mosaics. The most wonderful way to experience the Athenaeum is to attend a concert in the 1,000-seat auditorium; intensify the experience by choosing a performance of the Philharmonic George Enescu, the city's premiere orchestra, named for the nation's greatest composer who debuted here in 1898.

Entrance Str. Benjamin Franklin 1–3. ✆ 021/315-2567 or 021/315-8798. Daily 1:30–4pm.

Muzeul Național de Artă ⭑⭑⭑ Romania's National Museum of Art, opposite the Ateneul Roman, consists of three different collections, exhibited in part of the expansive former **Royal Palace** on Piața Revoluției. Of these, the most important are the **Gallery of Romanian Medieval Art** (almost exclusively devoted to icons, images, and carved objects related to religious pursuits), on the first floor, and the **Gallery of Romanian Modern Art,** above it. The latter provides a thorough overview of the evolution of 19th- and 20th-century painting and sculpture, working almost chronologically over two floors. It's an excellent place to discover the work of Gheorghe Tattarescu (1818–94), Theodor Aman (whose 19th-c. street scenes of popular tourist towns provide an excellent comparative study for some of the places you might visit), Karl Storck, Ioan Andreescu, sculptor Frederick Storck (look out for his fabulous *The Mystery,* 1925), the marvelous Impressionist Ștefan Luchian (1868–1916), and Theodor

Pallady, who painted a great number of naked ladies. There's a lively selection of works by the Impressionists, abstract expressionists, and Cubists; Marcel Iancu's *Portrait of a Man* is a brilliant Cubist-inspired work, worth seeking out, as is—for different reasons—Jean Davis's *Portrait of a Woman*, which looks like a precursor for *Beavis and Butthead*. The most important work here is the handful of otherworldly sculptures by Constantin Brâncuși (1876–1953); spend some time studying *Sleep* (1908), and then give your

Understanding the Orthodox Church

As you wander into an Orthodox church, you may think that the mass of beautiful frescoes and icons, and liturgical rites in which a priest keeps disappearing and reappearing from behind the iconostasis are nothing short of chaotic. You'd be wrong. There is meaning encoded in the design and layout of the artful interiors and rituals. Before entering, look above the door. You'll see Christ and several angels, along with the patron saint for whom the church is usually named. As you enter the *pronaos,* on the left are images of the church's builders and financiers, while on the right are frescoes of the leaders and royalty during the church's inception. Various important saints will occur throughout; those who practiced healing during their lifetimes will be holding a spoon, while those who were martyred are depicted with a cross. Humans painted with wings are said to have lived their lives like angels. In the dome above the *pronaos,* you'll see the Holy Mother praying for you, watching you as you enter; prophets of the Old Testament surround her. Also in the *pronaos* is a free-standing icon depicting Romanian saints; worshipers press their lips to this upon arrival. Typically, men occupy the right side of the church, while women are on the left. The angels painted on the inside of the main dome over the *naos* are said to come down from the heavens to take part in the service. The altar at the front of the church is the reserve of the priest, and sometimes other men are permitted to enter; the altar is screened off from public view by an iconostasis, with a number of painted doors. The Royal Door is in the center, and is painted with the Annunciation (Gabriel, carrying a flower, informing Mary that she will be the mother of God); the emperor who was permitted to approach the altar traditionally used this door.

From left to right across the iconostasis are the four royal icons: the saintly church protector, then the Holy Virgin, Jesus Christ, and finally the patron saint, after whom the church is named. At Mass, the priest will repeatedly disappear through these doors, returning with different icons and incense burners strung with bells; the bells emulate the sounds of the cherubim, while some say the incense denotes Christ in the Virgin's womb (incense holder). Above the royal icons, a series of smaller panels depicts major Christian celebrations, or events from the life of Christ; the row above that depicts Jesus, flanked by Mary, St. John the Baptist, and all the Apostles. Above that is a row of prophets. The nuns at Stavropoleos will happily elaborate on details of their faith, should you show an interest.

attention to *The Prayer* (1907), in which he renders a young female subject in an impossible kneeling position to stupendous effect. More wonderful sculpture includes Oscar Han's *The Kiss* (1924), and the only male nude on display, *Study of a Male Nude,* by Alexandru Plămădeală.

From the Romanian art collections, cross the courtyard to get to the less gripping **Gallery of European Art,** with its collection of 2,233 paintings, 578 sculptures, and 9,189 pieces of decorative art. Some astonishing lithographs are kept here, depicting amusing historical scenes as well as quite terrible images of death and disease.

Calea Victoriei 49–53. (✆) 021/313-3030. European Gallery: 021/314-8119. http://art.museum.ro. Admission L9 ($3.25/£1.75). Combined ticket with Museum of Art Collections (see below) L16 ($5.75/£3). Free 1st Wed of each month. Oct–Apr Wed–Sun 10am–6pm; May–Sept Wed–Sun 11am–7pm; last entry 30 min. before closing.

Muzeul Colecțiilor de Artă

North of the Ateneul Roman is the Museum of Art Collections, occupying the Ghica Palace, or Casa Romanit, an early-19th-century building that housed the country's supreme court from 1883 until the Communist takeover. The art collections of the bourgeoisie were stored here during the time when wealth was dangerously unfashionable. Today, the museum offers a condensed, manageable version of the extensive National Art Museum farther south, enjoyed in peace—don't be surprised if you are alone among a group of 20 museum attendants. The collection includes a rich survey of notable 19th- and 20th-century Romanian artists, together with some good, if anachronistic, religious icons. Particularly lovely are sculptures by Bucharest-born artist Oscar Han (1891–1976), and the paintings by Nicolae Grigorescu (1838–1907). Other favorites include fabulous nudes by Nicolae Tonzita (1886–1940), Theodor Pallady's *Femei în peisaj* (six pale naked maidens frolicking in the bushes, 1920), and Iosif Iser's intense, yet playful *Dancer in an Armchair,* directly opposite a series of cartoons by Marcel Iancu (1895–1984). (Next door to the museum is the atmospheric restaurant, Il Gattopardo Blu; see above.)

Calea Victoriei 111. (✆) 021/659-6693. Ticket for individual collection: L7 ($2.50/£1.35). Combined ticket for the collections of the National Art Museum (see above): L16 ($5.75/£3). Free admission on first Wed of each month. Oct–Apr Fri–Weds 10am–6pm; May–Sept Fri–Wed 11am–7pm; last entry 30 min. before closing.

Muzeul Țăranului Român

Occupying an early-20th-century building by Nicolae Ghica-Budești, the **Museum of the Romanian Peasant** is stocked full of furniture, farming equipment, costumes, crucifixes, tapestries, textiles, and some very beautiful religious icons; surprisingly, a great deal of the seemingly primitive technology on the first floor is what continues to be used—along with many of the lifestyle objects kept here—by rural communities to this day. During the Communist years, the building housed the Museum of the Communist Party and Romanian Revolutionary Workers Movement. On your way out, don't miss the basement exhibition (accessed via stairs next to the entrance) devoted to that time; the smell of mothballs adds a strangely appropriate atmosphere to a stirring display remembering Communism's collectivization scheme, highlighted by numerous unattractive busts of Lenin. Entitled "The Pest," the exhibit is a "memorial of the pain and hurt land-collectivization caused to the peasant world." Oddly, the main exhibit is a desk (from which collective control was exercised) littered with nutshells and onion peels. *Tip:* The souvenir shop here is worth browsing.

Șos. Kiseleff 3. (✆) 021/650-5360. Admission L6 ($2.15/£1.15) adults; L2 (70¢/40p) seniors and students; audioguide L10 ($3.60/£4.60). Tues–Sun 10am–6pm; last entry at 5pm.

SOUTHERN BUCHAREST

Mănăstirea Radu Vodă   On a hill at the edge of the Dâmbovița River, the church of the **Prince Radu Monastery** is set in a serene garden; built in 1613 and 1614, it replaced an earlier wooden structure. Bright, immaculate frescoes by Gheorghe Tattarescu were added in the 19th century. For a sublime experience, come for the liturgy, when worshipers kneel at the feet of the priest; as Mass is read and sung, you'll be hard-pressed to imagine that the Romanian language was not developed precisely for such heavenly devotions. Across the road from the monastery is the mid-18th-century **Biserica Orthodoxă "Bucur Ciobanul"** (𝒞 **0724-506-843;** 8am–6pm daily), reached via a steep stairway. Dedicated to the shepherd Bucur, attributed with the founding of Bucharest, the walls of this tiny church are covered in icons, executed in various styles and rendered on wood and glass.

Str. Radu Vodă 24A. Free admission. Daily 8am–1am. Liturgy: Mon–Fri 8am; Sat–Sun 8:30am; Daily 6pm and 10:30pm, each service lasts between 1½ and 4½ hours.

Muzeul de Istorie al Evreilor din România   The Romanian military is known to have played a devastating role in the Holocaust, and this Jewish History Museum is a good lest-we-forget reminder of Bucharest's once-prominent Jewish community. The museum occupies a synagogue built in 1850 and is centered on a statue mournfully remembering the 350,000 Romanians who perished at Auschwitz. Today, you can still visit the **Choral Temple** (𝒞 **021/312-2169;** services), a red-brick synagogue on Strada Vineri to the east of the Old Town; built in 1857, it stands at the edge of an elegant neighborhood touched by the hand of 19th-century architect Marcel Iancu. Attended by the city's tiny, dwindling Jewish community, services are held 8am and 7pm Sunday to Friday, and at 8:30am and 7pm Saturdays.

Str. Mămulari 3. 𝒞 021/311-0870. Free admission. Sun–Wed and Fri 9am–1pm; Thurs 9am–4pm.

Palatul Cotroceni   If you visit just one secular attraction in Bucharest, make it this one; the guided tour provides excellent historical insights and is a worthwhile survey of architectural trends in Romania. **Cotroceni Palace** (the official residence of the president, hence the tight security) was built by Carol I in the late 19th century. It became the loveless home of Ferdinand, his nephew and adopted heir, and the young Queen Marie (see "Quiet Escape to the Queen's Nest," p. 116), but has undergone many transformations since the initial designs were executed. During Ceaușescu's dictatorship it was used as the "Pioneer's Palace," where young leaders were schooled in the ways of Communism, and—after the devastating earthquake of 1977—restored as a guesthouse, although it never served this function. You will pass through a host of reception rooms, sleeping quarters, and private chambers, each styled to a particular theme: the German New Renaissance dining room, private dining quarters of Carol I in Florentine style; Oriental painting room used by Queen Marie and her children; the hunting room which showcases trophies hunted by King Ferdinand, as well as bearskin rugs hunted by Ceaușescu. Interestingly King Ferdinand's apartments are done out in a far more dainty, feminine style than Queen Marie's, whose quarters are quite austere—living proof of who wore the pants in this relationship. **Note:** You need to phone ahead and book one of the tours, and you must bring your passport as a security deposit; ask your taxi driver to wait for you, or order a cab in advance, as the museum entrance is on a busy road in the middle of nowhere.

B-dul Geniului 1. 𝒞 021/317-3107/6. Fax 021/312-1618. Admission L20 ($7.20/£3.85). Tues–Sun 10am–5pm.

Taking a Breather in the Big City

Bucharest has a number of lovely parks offering a few simple distractions from the mayhem of city life. Slap bang in the center are the **Cişmigiu Gardens** (between B-dul Regina Elisabeta, Calea Victoriei, Str. Stirbei Vodă and B-dul Schitu Măgureanu), developed in the mid-1800s when indigenous Romanian flora was collected along with exotic varieties from Vienna. Hire a boat and row yourself around the miniature lake, or grab a table under one of the Heineken-sponsored umbrellas at **Ristorante Debarcader Cişmigiu** (© 021/25-8479), where the food is expensive, but the views are free.

Palatul Parlamentului (Parliamentary Palace)   No matter how much you prepare yourself for it, your first glimpse of this square concrete bulk with its classical facade and escutcheoned gateways is a jaw-dropper. Ceauşescu infamously had a sixth of Bucharest flattened to make space for this project, and it kept 20,000 workers and 700 architects busy round-the-clock for 5 years during the main period of construction—visiting the "House of the People," as it's known locally, is effectively to gaze at the physical manifestation of Ceauşescu's unyielding attempt to monumentalize his regime. Visitors buy a ticket from the tiny souvenir shop at the entrance; be prepared to wait for an English guide to appear and initiate a thoroughly long-winded security check. The tour is fascinating: You'll wander through redundantly spacious Soviet-style halls, passageways, and ballrooms, eyeing as you go an eye-popping collection of hand-woven carpets, miles of silk drapery, and patterned walls, floors, and ceilings fashioned from a million cubic meters of marble and tons of oak and cherrywood; all testament to massive squandering of the national coffers. Curiously, there is no air-conditioning (apparently Ceauşescu had a phobia in this regard), and the building is still only 90% complete; hysterically, Ceauşescu had a serious size complex; he had one of the stairways replaced several times because he found the steps too big for his little feet. By the way, don't believe all your guide tells you; one popular anecdote is that the balcony that looks toward Piaţa Unirii is where Michael Jackson greeted fans with the words "Hello Budapest"; Jackson actually performed at the National Stadium.

Calea 13 Septembrie 1. © 021/311-3611 or 021/402-1426. Admission L20 ($7.20/£2.50) adults, L10 ($3.60/£1.25) children/students; photography L30 ($11/£5.75). Daily 10am–4pm. May close unexpectedly due to state functions.

NORTHERN CITY SIGHTS

Muzeul Naţional al Satului   Showcasing Romanian rural architecture since 1936, the open-air National Village Museum is frequently referred to as one of the country's best; if you're not visiting any rural regions, it may well provide some insight into the simple, unencumbered lives led by those living in Romania's bucolic communities. Visitors roam through a selection of 85 different houses, huts, windmills, churches, and outhouses that have been collected from around the country to showcase the depth of variety and architectural beauty of ordinary homesteads and dwelling; most of the constructions are thatch-roofed and built of wood, clay, or mud. Divided by region, the museum's overgrown lawn-fringed concrete pathways take you from Transylvania to Dobrogea to Oltenia and Moldavia in a relatively short space of time. The audioguide is a useful tool for making sense of the different architectural styles, even if the voice recording is rushed. Be warned that although the museum opens at 9am, this is also the time for staff to start cleaning, and the majority of houses are only unlocked for the public after around 11am. Note that the souvenir shop is not as good as the one at the Peasant Museum.

Şos. Kiseleff 28–30. ℂ 021/222-9106. www.muzeul-satului.ro. Adults L5 ($1.80/£1). Students and children L2.50 (90¢/50p). Audioguide L7 ($2.50/£1.35), plus ID as deposit. Tues–Sun 9am–7pm; Mon 10am–5pm.

SHOPPING

Keep your eyes open on the streets; on the steps of old monuments and around inner city sidewalks, you'll spot casual traders selling collectibles, including books and old Romanian LP records. You'll also be amazed at the number of shops beneath the city surface in its subways; there are at least four or five bookstores under the ground at the intersection at Piaţa Universităţii.

Antiques lovers can have a lot of fun poking through Bucharest's innumerable *"antichităţi"* stores. Typically, you'll find a mix of furniture, ornaments, knickknacks, and artworks that vary dramatically in value. You'll come across items that were salvaged during the Communist era, when homes and neighborhoods were destroyed, or things that have been kept in basements out of harm's way for decades. Start at **Hanul cu Tei** (Str. Lipscani 63–65; ℂ 021/313-0181; www.hanulcutei.ro; Mon–Fri 10am–7pm, Sat 10am–2pm), an arcade in the heart of the Lipscani District; there's a range of antiques stores and a extensive selection of artworks. Around here, you've every chance of finding street traders with something worthwhile to sell. Also in the Lipscani area, you can admire antique furniture as well as smaller decorative items at **European Heritage** (Str. Şepcari 16; ℂ 021/315-9537; www.european-heritage.com; Mon–Sat 10am–7pm, Sun noon–5pm). Stefan Vezure sells bronzes, porcelain, paintings, and sculptures as well as religious icons from his store, **Stef Art** (Str. Buzeşti 19; ℂ 0720/32-7338; vezure_stefan@yahoo.com). For paintings, rare maps, and manuscripts, as well as antique photographs, visit **Galeria de Artă Zambaccian** (Str. Blănari 12; ℂ 021/315-3485; galeriazambaccian@yahoo.com). For an upmarket spend, visit **Galeria Valore Antiques** (ℂ 021/224-4182; galeriavalore@yahoo.com) in the Plaza of the World Trade Center-Sofitel complex. If you'd like to visit an artist's studio, try **Iuliana Vîlsan** (Lascăr Catargiu 45; ℂ 0722/69-2892; www.iuliana-vilsan. net), but call first to make an appointment.

For all sorts of upmarket retail therapy, head for Calea Victoriei, where you'll find **Hugo Boss, Stefanel,** and **Guess,** next door to which is **Lamoda** with an exclusive and expensive range of men's and women's clothing. Directly across the road from these, is **Naracamicie,** with fantastic European-style shirts and blouses for men and women, and next door is **Musette** with fabulous ladies shoes and accessories. The best boutique we came across in Bucharest is **Zebra Society** (ℂ 0744-339-163), tucked away in a small arcade at Calea Victoriei 122; two young fashionistas create imaginative designs for men and women. Calea Victoriei is also good for art purchases; you could pick up an interesting canvas or two at **Galateea** (Calea Victoriei 132; ℂ 021/317-3814; Mon–Sat 11am–7pm), a contemporary space hosting provocative exhibitions with work for sale.

Occupying the same building as the Hotel Lido is **Ania Handicraft** (daily 9am–9pm) which has well-made traditional dresses, blouses, and other garments, as well as religious icons, brought in from villages around the country.

A great memento for anyone with an interest in sports is a branded Steaua Bucharest football shirt from the country's most important club, at one of the **Nike** outlets in either the Unirea or Bucureşti mall.

Getting a Handle on Romanian Wine

Romania's best wine growing regions are Dogrogea and Oltenia, a region of Wallachia. A good everyday red is Fetească Neagră, from the Banat's Val Duna region; similar to Shiraz, it has the taste of dry, spicy plums. The "La Cetate" merlot is a reliable variety from Oltenia region; there's a hint of honey on the palate, accompanied by a lively, ripe tartness. But the very best red is a cabernet sauvignon called La Catate Tezaur (or "treasure"); especially stunning is the 2002 vintage, which is remarkably light despite being a big, robust, full-bodied wine. Although there's now a small chain of wine outlets, **Vinexpert** *experience* (Pasaj Vilacrosse, Calea Victoriei 16-18-20; ℂ **021/313-4480;** 021/326-8539/40; www.vinexpert.info) is a relaxed lounge-style tasting venue near Lipscani, and the place to arrange an afternoon or evening Romanian wine tasting. Book ahead if you want a specialized tasting session with a dedicated sommelier.

Cărturești   A fabulous bookstore chain with the best music collection in the city; head straight for the branch located on Strada Pictor Arthur Verona; you'll find brilliant art books, coffee-table glossies, and also the most relaxingly atmospheric tea shop in town. Branches: Pictor Arthur Verona 13, Edgar Quinet 9, and Anador Center. ℂ **021/317-3459.** info@carturesi.ro. Mon–Fri 10am–9pm; Sat 11am–8pm; Sun 1–7pm.

Cotroceni Magazin de Arta   Rather pricey souvenirs and books can be purchased from this small shop at the end of your tour of the Cotroceni Palace. Consider buying one of Ana Ponta's Dolls of Romania, lovely soft toys dressed in traditional costumes that are perfect as gifts for young children, or for collectors. Muzeul Cotroceni, B-dul Geniului 1. ℂ **021/317-3107/6.** Tues–Sun 10am–5pm.

Libraria Noi 🟊🟊   Excellent, well-stocked bookstore with an extensive range of English books, including fashionable publications about Romania. You can also buy DVDs and CDs here (admittedly the selection is limited), but the real find is the little side-outlet with old maps, out-of-date prints, and lithographs, which you can paw through to discover that something special. B-dul. Nicolae Bălecescu 18. ℂ **021/311-0700.** www.librarianoi.ro. Mon–Sat 9:30am–8:30pm; Sun 11am–9pm.

Museum of the Romanian Peasant Shop 🟊🟊   The best place in the country to pick up authentic, yet well-made handicrafts, traditional costumes, and folk art. Şos. Kiseleff 3. ℂ **021/650-5360.** Tues–Sun 10am–6pm.

BUCHAREST AFTER DARK

The best source for all entertainment happenings is *Time Out Bucureşti* 🟊🟊🟊 (www.timeoutbucuresti.ro), which carries extensive listings and information; though published only in Romanian, with a little savvy you can figure it out and certainly make sense of the dates, times, and venues. The fortnightly publication is available at newsagents and bookstores for a mere L2.90 ($1/55p). The other fairly reliable information source is the useful English-language *Bucharest in Your Pocket* 🟊, though it only highlights major events. You can pick it up from the larger hotels, either for free or for the cover price of L8 ($2.90/£1.55); note that stock is often depleted early.

LIVE MUSIC, THEATER & OPERA

Catch **classical concerts** by, among others, the George Enescu Philharmonic Orchestra at the sublime **Romanian Athenaeum**⍣⍣⍣ (Str. Benjamin Franklin 1-3; ℂ 021/315-8798); the box office (ℂ 021/315-6875) operates Tuesday to Friday noon to 7pm, and before evening shows on Saturday and Sunday (4–7pm), and Sunday matinees (10–11am).

Opera buffs can take in occasional performances at the Opera Română (B-dul Mihail Kogălniceanu 70–72; ℂ 021/314-6980); note that the box office is closed Monday.

There's **jazz** at several venues around the city; one of the best-known spots is **Green Hours 22 Jazz Café** (Calea Victoriei 120; ℂ 021/314-5751; www.green-hours.ro; open 24 hr.), which has even spawned its own alternative record label; call beforehand to check what's on the program.

Major concerts, often by visiting international stars, are usually held at one of the city's two football stadiums, **Stadionul Dinamo** or **Stadionul National,** while slightly more intimate events are held at the **Arenele Romane** in Parcul Libertăţii (also called Parcul Carol I).

To find out what's showing (and whether its in English) at the **Ion Luca Caragiale National Theater** ⍣, visit the box office (B-dul Nicolae Bălcescu 2; ℂ 021/314-7171; Mon 10am–4pm, Tues–Sun 10am–7pm). Other theaters worth checking out are **Teatrul Odeon**⍣⍣ (Calea Victoriei 40-42; ℂ 021/314-7234; www.teatrul-odeon.ro); **Teatrul Bulandra** (B-dul. Schitu Măgureanu 1; ℂ 021/314-7546; www.bulandra.ro); and Lipscani's **Teatrul du Comedie** (Sf. Dumitru 2; ℂ 021/315-9137).

Note that you can buy tickets for most live events by visiting **Bilete Online (Online Tickets)** at www.bilete.ro.

BARS & CLUBS

Bucharest loves to party, and you'll find a busy watering hole any time, night or day. Cafes and bars are often interchangeable, adapting to the vicissitudes of the crowd or the time of day; the same place you visit for an early-morning espresso could turn out to be your late-night cocktail venue. **Horeca 100%** is published by the Romanian listing group, 24-Fun (www.24fun.ro); it includes an extensive list of bars and clubs.

Club Bamboo   Grab a supermodel under each arm and strike a bourgeois pose; you'll probably need to drop names to get through the front door, but inside it's an

---

Vice Advice for Guys

It's 10pm; the sun has just disappeared. You've finished a meal at a classy restaurant. Venturing onto the sidewalk, you're waiting while your partner powders her nose. Out of nowhere, a friendly, energetic man, no more than 22 years old, materializes: "Girls? You want girls? Wanna party with young girls?" Flabbergasted, you decline. "Not tonight? Take my number. Maybe tomorrow." Prostitution is rife in Bucharest; the number of erotic clubs tucked between the churches and monuments is staggering, so it's easy to assume that anything and everything is up for grabs. Be warned: prostitution is illegal. A system of bribes allows prostitutes to ply their trade even in top hotels; not surprisingly, the cops get the largest cut.

anthropological study in excess and wealth. Apart from the unnaturally upmarket crowd, things are pretty mellow, with just enough action on the dance floor to keep things interesting. Str. Rămuri Tei 39. ℂ 0788-296-776. Thurs–Sat 11:30pm–6am.

EXIT 𝒜𝒜   Who said you had to be a teenager to have fun in Bucharest; this swinging club beneath Amsterdam Grand Café offers a refreshing take on the smoother rhythms of New Jazz, Bosa Nova, and chill-out music, studiously mixed by knowing DJs. Str. Covaci 6. ℂ 021/313-7580. Fri–Sat 9pm–4am.

Impact Club   Hard, sweaty club with a hot DJ lineup, this is Bucharest's most perceptibly gay dance venue. Str. Viitorului 26. ℂ 021/212-0620. www.go2impact.ro.

Lăptăria Enache 𝒜   Smart and wild, the National Theater bar attracts a swinging following (mostly from among the university crowd). It's on the fourth floor of the theater building, and you'll have to search for the anonymous entrance near the Dominusart Gallery. Musical entertainments include good jazz. It's rooftop neighbor is called **La Motoare,** great during summer. B-dul Nicolae Balcescu 2. ℂ 021/315-8508. www.laptaria.totalnet.ro. Mon–Thurs noon–2am; Fri–Sat noon–4am; Sun 1pm–2am.

The Office 𝒜   With a name this pretentious, you'd better dress for success; the crowd is hot and eager and you'd best come armed with plenty of cash (credit cards also accepted). Str. Tache Ionescu 2. ℂ 021/211-6748. www.theoffice.ro. 8pm until late.

Salsa III 𝒜   Want to see how Romanians tune in to their Latino roots? The dedicated salsa crowd (which seems to follow this club around as it reincarnates in different venues) certainly knows a thing or two about getting its groove on. Str. Mihai Eminescu 89. ℂ 0723-531-841. Mon–Sat 8pm–last guest.

Tempo 𝒜   One of the swanky new places attracting Bucharest's chic crowd, Tempo is actually a restaurant, but its eye-catching decor: padded bar, glass tabletops balanced on short classical fluted columns, and trendy white-and-red theme make it a good for a sundowner or perpetual people-watching any time of day. Str. George Enescu 10. ℂ 021/313-1228. cafetempo@xnet.ro. Daily 8am–late.

Tonka Soul Café 𝒜   Open round-the-clock, the vibe changes according to the hour; great for early-morning coffee, it becomes a groovy hangout after dark and peaks after midnight when tunes get loud and the youngish crowd gets wild, ordering from a menu of cocktails and exclusively imported beers. Wooden deck chairs, orange cushions, flatscreen TVs, and contemporary art combine in a relaxed haven near the Amzei Market. Piaţa Amzei, Str. Biserica Amzei 19. ℂ 021/317-8342. www.tonka.ro. Open all hours.

4 Wallachia

Wallachia, of which Bucharest is now the capital, is the traditional heart of Romania; in fact, locals refer to it as Ţară Românească—"The Romanian Land." Named for the landowner princes, the Wallachs (or Vlachs), who ruled southern Romania from the 14th to the 18th century, its key historical figures (including notorious Vlad Ţepeş) were committed to defying Turkish control in one way or another. Proud claims insist that Wallachia was never actually part of the Ottoman Empire, enabling a distinctive post-Byzantine evolution in the arts and architecture that set it apart from the rest of the Balkans. Indeed, it was here that the uniquely Romanian architectural movement— known as the Brâncovenesc style—was developed by Constantin Brâncoveanu in the latter part of the 17th century; the best example of this being the beautifully frescoed Great Church at the Horezu Monastery.

Wallachia remains largely undiscovered, losing out to its famous northerly neighbor; most travelers get their "facts" directly from Dracula movies, associating the thrills of vampire tourism with Transylvania, whereas the "real" Count Dracula actually ruled Wallachia. Vlad the Impaler had his princely court in the city of Târgovişte, and any claims to a "Castle Dracula" really belong to the awesomely situated citadel at Poienari, north of the little town of Curtea de Arges, where there's another beautiful cathedral. Finally, north of Bucharest, on Wallachia-Transylvania border, there is the ski resort of Sinaia, which boasts one of Europe's most beautiful palaces, Peleş, now the finest museum in the country.

SINAIA

Sinaia is 135km (84 miles) N of Bucharest

Right near the Wallachian border with Transylvania, in the beautiful Prahova Valley at the foot of the Bucegi Mountains, Sinaia is regarded as the Pearl of the Carpathians. When Romania became a kingdom in the late 19th century, this was chosen as the site of the royal summer palace, an absolute must-see on any Romanian itinerary. It's also an extremely popular weekend getaway for well-to-do city folk, and one of the country's most popular ski destinations, centered on Mt. Furnica.

ESSENTIALS

Sinaia is on a busy rail line between Bucharest (126km/78 miles) and Braşov (48km/30 miles); there are regular connections with both. If you plan a day trip from Bucharest, catch the morning InterCity train (between 9:45am and 10:15am) to Sinaia, and return to Bucharest on the 5:48pm. Another possibility is to stop in Sinaia and continue to Braşov by fast train at 3 or 6pm.

Sinaia is pretty much a walker's town. If you're self-driving, ensure that your hotel has parking (those reviewed here do), as traffic can get frustrating in busy periods. Taxis, buses, and maxitaxis are available for trips into the hills.

At the town hall, you'll find the **tourist information center** (B-dul Carol I 14; ✆ **0244/31-5656;** www.infosinaia.ro). You can procure more information about the town from **Dracula's Land** (B-dul Carol I 14; ✆ **0244/31-1441;** daily 9am–6pm), which also offers accommodations deals with sizable discounts. Adventurous types can ask after hikes into the surrounding mountains; it may be worth hiring the services of a guide.

In winter, you can get information and hire equipment for winter activities from the aptly named ski school and shop, **Snow** (Str. Cuza Voda 2a; ✆ **0244/31-1198);** beginners can sign up for inexpensive private lessons. Experienced skiers have only to join the queues for the **cable car** (✆ **0244/31-1674)** behind Hotel New Montana.

WHERE TO STAY & DINE

Despite the influx of Bucharest's wealthy weekend-getaway crowd, there are sadly no really good accommodations options in Sinaia. There's also really only one noteworthy restaurant in town, and that's **Taverna Sarbului** (Calea Codrului; ✆ **0244/ 31-4400;** daily noon–1am) which has the monopoly on satisfying hungry, ravenous carnivores. Things get incredibly busy—even medieval—as the waitstaff swoops around with feast-size portions of legendary meat dishes.

Caraiman   Conveniently situated across the road from the train station (up a steep pedestrian embankment), this has been operating since 1881. Guest rooms still exhibit some signs of its former glory; although certainly no longer luxurious; they're spacious and generally comfortable, although beds are merely adequate and bathrooms on the small side. Units on the first floor have views from private balconies that stick out over the park; note that third-floor rooms have shared balconies.

4 B-dul Carol I, Sinaia. © **0244/31-3551.** Fax 0244/31-0625. 72 units. L154 ($55/£30) double; L212 ($76/£41) suite. MC, V. **Amenities:** Restaurant; bar; dining terrace; salon; room service; laundry. *In room:* TV, minibar.

New Montana ⟨ A hefty bouncer stands watch at the entrance to this, Sinaia's smartest hotel; big, brash, and right in the center, New Montana seems a little out of place in this small town with its crumbling houses and mountain scenery. Built for Bucharest's wealthy weekend-getaway crowd, it's popular with loads of tourists who are bussed off for sightseeing trips from the front door. Inside, everything is shiny and modern, and more often than not it's western hip-hop music that's playing in the bright lobby bar. Tight, gold-trimmed elevators whisk you up to your room, which are quite ordinary, despite soothing white cotton linens; bathrooms are slightly larger than the elevators, though. Ask for a room overlooking the main road; oddly, these are your best bet, since dogs bark perpetually at night round the back, where rooms don't have balconies.

24 B-dul Carol I, Sinaia. © **0244/31-2751/2/3.** Fax 0244/31-2754. www.newmontana.ro. 177 units. 99€ ($124) double; 195€ ($244) junior suite; 244€–254€ ($305–$318) suite. **Amenities:** Restaurant; lobby lounge and pub; bar; health center. *In room:* TV, Internet, minibar, hair dryer.

WHAT TO DO & SIGHTS TO SEE

In addition to the top sights in town, Sinaia is just 1.2 miles (2km) from the **George Enescu Memorial House (Casa Memorială George Enescu;** Cumpătu; © **0244/31-1753;** Tues–Sun 9am–3pm; L6/$2.15/£1.15 adults), worth a visit if you have time. Built in the 1920s as a summer home for the country's great composer, it preserves antique furnishings, Enescu's piano, and also some poignant memorabilia; best of all, you'll get to hear recordings of his music as your explore the house, which surprisingly given that the Ottomans never got a look in, echoes the style of a Turkish Conac. On the way to or from the castle grounds you might want to take a brief look at **Sinaia Monastery** ⟨ (Str. Mănăstirii 2; © **0244/31-4917;** daily 9:30am–6pm; donation expected), where almost two dozen monks still actively worship at the two Orthodox churches, the smaller of which dates from 1695. The first Romanian-language Bible, written in Cyrillic script in 1668, is the prize exhibit in the monastery's little history museum.

Muzeul Naţional Peleş ⟨⟨⟨ Easily the most beautiful palace in Romania, and one of the finest in Europe, magnificent Peleş Castle—the summer residence of Romania's first king, Carol I (it's his statue at the entrance)—looks from a distance like something out of *Harry Potter*. Begun in 1875 and inaugurated in 1883, it's a triumph of German neo-Renaissance architecture, with various modern conveniences added over time: this was the first palace in Europe to be completely served by electricity; the first to be centrally heated, and the first castle with a central vacuum-cleaning system. Peleş sports around 170 rooms, and the handful on public display are spectacular examples of "tasteful opulence"; the reception rooms, libraries, studies, bedrooms, and ballrooms are decorated with carefully selected works of extreme quality and value. Alongside the 2,000-strong collection of paintings are imported statues, chandeliers, exotic furniture, gigantic mirrors, and phenomenal hand-woven carpets; each room suggesting the ambience of a different country or region, and perfectly preserved. Although Ceauşescu claimed to have little regard for Peleş, he did use the palace to entertain; Nixon, Gaddafi, Ford, and Arafat were some of his notable guests here. While they no doubt got to experience the palace in a completely different light (you may for instance have to wait for the next available English tour), you will almost certainly be delighted by the guided hour-long tour, the best in the country.

Str. Peleşului 2. ✆ **0244/31-0918.** www.peles.ro. Adults L12 ($4.30/£2.30); seniors and students L5 ($1.80/£1). Purchase a ticket and then ring the bell at the visitor's entrance. Tues 11am–5pm; Wed–Sun 9am–5pm; last ticket sold at 4pm.

Pelişor Palace ⊀   The name literally means "Little Peleş," and a visit here really does pale in comparison to the sensory overload at Peleş. It's said that Ferdinand (1865–1927), Carol's nephew and adopted son, commissioned this castle because he found Peleş too overwhelming; another, more likely story is that it was built for Marie, who didn't see eye to eye with the king. Built in German faux-medieval style in 1892, it's 200m (656 ft.) from Peleş, and its 70 rooms are filled with evidence of Marie's then-personal taste; a pastel-infused mixture of Celtic and Byzantine elements with an Art Nouveau sensibility and plenty of turn-of-the-20th-century Viennese furniture and Tiffany glassware thrown into the mix.

Str. Peleşului. ✆ **0244/31-2184.** www.peles.ro. Adults L9 ($3.25/£1.75), seniors and students L3 ($1/60p). Tues 11am–5pm; Wed–Sun 9am–5pm; last ticket sold at 4pm.

CURTEA DE ARGEŞ, POIENARI CITADEL & BEYOND

Although not all that easy to get to, Curtea de Argeş is worth the effort for its magnificent monastery as well as being home to Wallachia's oldest surviving church, built by the princes who ruled Wallachia from the adjacent palace during the 14th century. From **Curtea de Argeş,** heading north through the Argeş Valley, you'll come to the **Citadel of Poienari,** where you'll be able to say that you've finally caught up with the actual castle of "Count Dracula," or at least, what's left of it. From here, self-driving brave hearts can tackle the extraordinary **Tranfăgăraşan Highway,** a magnificent and challenging mountain pass (supposedly Europe's highest, reaching 2,034m/6,672 ft.) that wends its way over the Făgăraş Mountains and into Transylvania; due to extreme weather conditions the route is only open for 3 months of the year.

If you have the time and your own transport, it's worthwhile heading farther west to see the UNESCO-listed **Horezu Monastery,** particularly if you're here during the first week of September when the nearby village of **Costeşti** livens up for its annual **Roma Festival.** Attended by the self-proclaimed "emperor" of all the Roma people, it's a time of fierce celebration and deal-making that draws Gypsies from across the country.

Some 200km (124 miles) west of Curtea de Argeş is **Târgu Jiu,** an unspectacular place were it not home to some of the great outdoor sculpture of the great modernist, Constantin Brancuşi, who was born in a nearby village in 1876. The collection includes Brancuşi's most significant work, the *Endless Column,* considered one of the world's most important sculptures.

ESSENTIALS

There are daily fast InterCity trains from Bucharest to Piteşti; from there, change for one of six connections to Curtea de Argeş. State buses and maxitaxis connect Bucharest and Curtea de Argeş more directly, if you're up for a bumpy ride. The town has been generously signposted, so it's easy to get to the sights. **Posada Tourism**

Agency (℃ **0248/72-1109** or 0248/72-1451/2) in the Posada Hotel is your best bet for local information and for accommodations bookings.

WHERE TO STAY & DINE

Besides offering the only **tourist information office** (℃ **0248/72-2530;** Mon–Fri 8am–4pm, Sat 10am–12:30pm) in town, **Hotel Posada** (B-dul Basarabilor 27–29; ℃ **0248/72-1451/2;** fax 0248/50-6047; office@posada.ro) is about your best bet for a decent night's stay in Curtea de Argeş; the best doubles cost L140 to L170 ($50–$61/£27–£33), but there cheaper options, and three marginally pricier suites. Romanian dishes are served at the simple **Restaurant Capra Neagră** (Str. Alexandru Lahovary; ℃ **0248/72-1619**). If you're self-driving, however, rather consider bedding down at **Cabana Valea Cu Peşti** (Tranfâgăraşan, Arefu, jud. Argeş; ℃ **0788-361-021;** L140–L165/$50–$59/£27–£32 double), beyond Poienari, on lovely Lake Vidraru; it's easily the more atmospheric and interesting option, having served as one of Ceauşescu's hunting lodges. Reservations can be made through Hotel Posada's website, or by calling ℃ **0747-119-901** (Mon–Fri 8:30am–6pm); it's worth calling ahead since there is only one double-bedded guest room, and the hotel is often taken up by groups. Note that the Posada group is planning a motel closer to Poienari Castle set to echo some of the style and traditions of the time when it was built.

WHAT TO SEE & DO

The cathedral is the principal reason to be here, but time allowing you might want to take a wander through the ruins of the **Argeş Palace**—originally built in the 1300s by Wallachia's Hungarian founder, Radu Negru (or Basarab I)—and the **Princely Church;** the latter is in fairly good shape and work has been done to reveal fantastic Byzantine frescoes long hidden under centuries of tacky restoration (Curtea Domnească; Tues–Sun 9am–5pm; L6/$2.15/£1.15).

Mănăstirea Curtea de Argeş ★★★   This 16th-century Episcopal cathedral is considered one of the loveliest religious monuments in Wallachia, frequently compared to an elaborately decorated cake, made with marble and studded with mosaics. Several nasty stories surround the master builder and stonemason, Manole, responsible for the project. Tricked into building his own wife (who was very much alive at the time) into the walls of the church (a tradition meant to ensure that the victim's ghost would forever protect the building) Manole was left on the roof without means of escape, as the king wanted to ensure that no other similar church would ever be built. Insane with grief the poor man apparently tried to fly from the roof, only to crash and die on the spot now marked by the famous **Manole's Well.** The church was greatly restored and rebuilt in the late 19th century, and several members of the Romanian royal family, including Carol I and his wife, Elizabeth, are buried inside. B-dul. Basarabilor. Daily 8am–7pm.

Poienari Castle   Here's a cliff-top location to fuel the Dracula-obsessed imagination. The citadel—built by Vlad "The Impaler" Tepeş, inspiration for the mythic bloodthirsty count (see "Vlad & the Epic Mythology of Count Dracula," below)—is about 5km (3 miles) north of the little village of **Arefu,** allegedly inhabited exclusively by descendants of villagers who long ago helped Vlad Tepeş escape a decisive Turkish siege of the castle. Follow the road north out of Arefu (there is no public transport, by the way) until you come to a hydroelectric plant, next to which is the start of an exhausting 1,480-step climb up to the castle; be sure to buy something to drink at the little stall, since you'll be climbing for about half an hour. Ţepeş built the castle as a defensive fortress against intruders from Transylvania; to save costs and punish his mortal enemies, the Turks, he had Turkish prisoners of war do all the work, subjecting them to hideous conditions as they toiled endlessly, often dying in the process. Clearly the enterprise was cursed, and a large chunk of the castle dropped off the cliff back in 1888; the same fate that befell Vlad's wife 400 years earlier when she allegedly jumped to her death, Lady Macbeth–style, during the Turkish siege.

Cetatea Poienari. Admission L6 ($2.15/£1.15). Daily 9am–5pm.

5 Transylvania

For horror fans, the name sits in the throat and is urged out with an unholy drawl, but—aside from the sheer Gothic drama of medieval towns and hilltop citadels—there's very little to evoke Transylvania's ominous association. Yes, Vlad Ţepeş was born in the fortress city of Sighişoara, and wolves do roam the Carpathians (in fact, they're considered a protective force in Romanian culture), but Transylvania's reality is more one of fairy-tale forests surrounding charming Saxon towns and fortified church steeples poking through the treetops.

A possession of the Hungarian king from the 10th century, Transylvania has been the source of a power struggle for 1,000 years. Hungary only gave up its territorial claims in 1996. Legend tells how the lost children of Hamelin emerged from a cave here; of course, that's a fanciful account of the arrival of Transylvania's Aryan German-speaking population, the Saxons. Settlers from the Lower Rhine, Flanders, and the Moselle region, these blue-eyed blondes were lured here in the 12th century by the Hungarian monarchy who promised them land and other liberties in return for protection against the Ottoman and Tartar threat. The Saxons established seven fortified cities, the *Siebenbürgen,* with outlying villages centered on fortified churches, serving as both spiritual and military protection. Today the major settlements of Braşov, Sighisoara, and Sibiu remain popular destinations, but there are dozens more Saxon villages throughout Transylvania that are remarkably untouched by modern life. The Saxon community has dwindled over the centuries, but Transylvania still includes a sizeable Hungarian minority tracing its ancestry to the Széklers, a clan of warriors accorded noble privileges for defending Hungary's eastern frontier.

Separating Transylvania from Wallachia in the south and Moldavia to the east are the Carpathian Mountains, where Anthony Minghella filmed *Cold Mountain,* a movie shot through with images of a sublime, beautiful wilderness. While you won't encounter any wolves, were or otherwise, you will—as many trekkers discover—come across the odd shepherd or remote mountain village where smiles and frowns are your only tools of communication.

Near Braşov is Bran Castle, touted by the ill-informed as "Dracula's Castle." With a gorgeous medieval Saxon center Braşov is also home to the ominously pretty Black Church, the biggest Gothic cathedral between Istanbul and Vienna. And if you are pining to rub shoulders with a real count, Transylvania may have the answer: Count Tudor Kalnoky offers some of the best lodgings in the country in the Hungarian farming community of Micloşoara.

Vlad & the Epic Mythology of Count Dracula

Etched into popular consciousness by countless horror films, Count Dracula is best described as a mythical figure loosely based on blood-drinking rituals known to have occurred in certain Balkanic regions. However, Bram Stoker's anemic somnambulist is most fittingly linked with a Wallachian warlord nicknamed Vlad Tepeş—Vlad the Impaler—in honor of his penchant for bloodletting and cruel tortures. In fact, his real-life atrocities were far more terrifying than anything conjured up by Bela Lugosi or Gary Oldman. As young boys, Vlad and his brother, Radu the Handsome, were sent to the Turks as hostages by their own father, who *was* nicknamed Dracul, or "Devil," because of a knightly order to which he belonged.

Undoubtedly witnessing all sorts of terrible tortures and abuses, and living in fear of his young life, Vlad remained in Adrianople until he was 17, when his father was assassinated by the Hungarians, and the Turks gave him an army in order to reclaim the Wallachian throne. It took him almost 10 years to finally capture the Wallachian throne convincingly and establish his court in Târgoviste. There he earned his reputation for dire cruelty; in one popular story, he set fire to a sealed castle filled with sick, poor, and destitute people, "to rid them of their troubles," as he callously put it. He ruthlessly did away with any perceived threat and enjoyed watching his victims die, often setting up banquets from which to observe the spectacle of suffering. Impalement was favored because the torment could go on for days, and he took great pleasure in mass executions; some estimates place the number of men, women, and children who died at his hands at 500,000. Eventually, it was his brother, Radu the Handsome, who caused Vlad to flee to Hungary where he was first imprisoned but then converted to Catholicism. After Radu's death, he once again took control of Wallachia, but was killed in 1476 in a battle with the Turks who displayed his head in Constantinople to prove to the world that he was indeed dead, while his body was supposedly buried at a monastery on the island of Snagov near Bucharest. Apparently, excavations there in 1931 found no sign of his coffin.

BRAŞOV ⭐⭐⭐
Braşov is 168km (104 miles) NW of Bucharest

Also known by its Saxon name Kronstadt, Braşov grew to prominence from the 13th century when Germanic knights arrived and fortified their settlement with walls and watchtowers and it became a prosperous trade center for the Austro-Hungarian Empire. Although it's hemmed in by the thick outer layer of a modern, industrial city, Braşov's medieval and baroque heart is gorgeously well preserved, and seemingly sequestered from the world by mountains that surround it on three sides. A popular base for exploring legendary Bran Castle and hilltop Rasnov Fortress, Braşov also has its own ski resort, Poiana Braşov, which is a wonderful setting for summer hikes in the lovely, practically untouched Ardeal mountains.

ARRIVAL, ORIENTATION & GETTING AROUND

Braşov has no airport but the city is extremely well served by trains from across the country; there are almost 20 per day pulling in from Bucharest, only 3 hours away on an InterCity train. The **train station** (© **0268/41-0233**) is about 3.5km (2 miles) from the heart of Braşov's old city; a taxi into town should cost around L5 ($1.80/£1). You can purchase onward tickets from **CFR Agenţie de Voiaj** (Str. Republicii 53; © **0268/47-0696;** Mon–Fri 8am–6pm, Sat 9am–1pm). Once you're in the historic part of the city, you should manage everything by foot or bus; you can get information on bus routes from the **tourist office** (© **0268/41-9078;** Mon–Sat 9am–5pm), conveniently located in the former **Council House (Casa Sfantului)** in the center of Piaţa Sfatului. Staff will also supply you with maps and information about the city, as well as advising on excursions to neighboring attractions, like Bran (just 30km/19 miles from Braşov) and Râşnov. A good introduction to the city as well as Romania itself is found at www.brasov.ro, well worth investigating before you leave home. To get to **Poiana Braşov,** take bus no. 20 from the Livada Postei stop; it leaves every half-hour and is a comfortable 20-minute journey.

Reserve at least 24 hours in advance to join **Braşov Walking Tours** (© **0727/38-1478;** www.brasovwalkingtours.com) which has a 2-hour guided exploration of the city setting off from the tourist office; available in English, the tour costs 5€ ($6.25) per person, minimum of three people.

WHERE TO STAY

For details of Braşov's brand-new **Casa Wagner**—situated on Piaţa Sfatului with just 12 guest rooms—which was due to open by late 2006, visit www.casa-wagner.eu. Another hotel you may want to investigate is **Hotel Aro Palace** (© **0268/47-8800;** www.aro-palace.ro; from 148€/$185 double), which was undergoing the final phases of a major renovation, including a new wellness spa (due to be completed in 2007); however, what this ugly modern edifice really needs is a total redesign, and no amount of face-saving refurbishment will change the fact that it lacks the intimacy and personal touch you'll find at either Bella Muzica or Casa Rozelor.

Bella Muzica 🏠🏠   Right on Piaţa Sfatului, in a 400-year-old building, Bella Muzica is everything you want from a small hotel in a medieval town: Atmosphere, charm, and comfort are all here in equal measure. The designers used soothing earth tones punctuated by wood-framed watercolor paintings of buildings around Braşov, and ensured that contemporary comforts are combined seamlessly with the historical

---

The Bear Necessities

Unfortunately you're unlikely to spot any of the 6,000 or so brown bears that roam wild in the Carpathians (nor wolves or lynx for that matter). Where bears do appear, however, are around the dustbins of certain Braşov suburbs, where they've learned to scavenge. This is partly out of laziness, and partly due to past environmental mismanagement. While the Carpathians can comfortably support 5,000 to 6,000 bears, during the Ceauşescu regime, the population was purposefully grown to 10,000—to make the dictator's hunting trips more fruitful. Today, licensed hunting of around 600 bears per year helps keep numbers in check.

ambience. Furnishings are luxurious, but never grandiose, and while there's an antique theme, there's no sign of frilly excess. Guest rooms are carpeted and decently laid out in an approximation of what might be called "country antique style" and there's some exposed brickwork to remind you of the building's pedigree. Mattresses are on the thin side, and bathrooms aren't exactly enormous; if you want the tasteful ambience, but also value your space, opt for one of the apartments, or—even better—try getting a suite at Casa Rozelor (reviewed below). Note that there's no elevator, but there are rooms on the ground level if you'd prefer not to deal with stairs; the upstairs doubles are also smaller than those on the lower floor.

Piața Sfantului 19, Brașov. © 0268/47-7956. www.bellamuzica.ro. 22 units. L270 ($97/£52) double; L440–L540 ($158–$194/£84–£104) suite. Rates include breakfast. AE, MC, V. **Amenities:** Restaurant; bar; breakfast room; room service; laundry. *In room:* A/C (suites only), TV, Internet, minibar, safe, Jacuzzi (suites only).

Casa Rozelor ★★★ (Finds)

Book now to stay in one of the three beautifully idiosyncratic, design-conscious apartments that have been fashioned from the hull of a 15th-century national monument, just a few steps from the center of the city. You'll not only enjoy absolute comfort, surrounded by a glorious collection of antiques, artworks, and bric-a-brac, but have a great deal of fun discovering the details of the interior design, executed by the artist-designer Mihai Alexadru. Incredibly spacious, yet made to feel like home, these apartments all have their own kitchen, dining area, lounge, and bedroom; each of the spaces—including the fabulous bathrooms—is unique and refreshingly original, an artful blend of classic or Deco elements with modern artworks and contemporary details (wonderful bathroom fittings, flatscreen TVs). They also have parquet flooring and exposed wood beam ceilings; suite no. 6 is an upstairs-downstairs unit with its own spiral staircase leading to the bedroom where there's also a private terrace, while suite no. 5 is a massive second-floor open-plan space with another lovely balcony. Only opened in January 2006, Rozelor remains a well-kept secret, but word is sure to get out, so don't dally with that reservation.

Str. Michael Weiss 20, Brașov. © 0268/47-5212 or 0747/49-0727. Fax 0268/47-5212. www.casarozelor.ro. 3 units. 100€ ($125) double. Rates include breakfast and all taxes. MC, V. **Amenities:** Room service; breakfast served in room; laundry room. *In room:* TV, kitchenette, hair dryer.

Residence Hirscher ★ (Finds)

As if concealing its identity, this alternative to the traditional hotel is identified by nothing other than a single brass sign at the entrance of a stately late-19th-century Austro-Hungarian building; it's on Apollonia Hirscher Street, just a short stroll from the historic center of town, but feels far away from it all. Opened in late 2005, the sober neoclassical facade conceals modern interiors; with just 12 large apartments, each with a lounge, bedroom, kitchen, and dining area, it really is a "residence" rather than a hotel. With parquet flooring, decent furniture, and relaxed, neutral tones, this is a great option for anyone who values space, peace, and quiet. There are no hotel amenities, just a friendly full-time reception; apartments are serviced daily.

Reședința Hirscher, Str. Apollonia Hirscher 14, Brașov. © 0368/40-1212 or 0726/74-6402. Fax 0368/40-1213. www.residence-hirscher.com. 12 units. 80€ ($100) double; 90€ ($113) double with 1 or 2 extra persons. DC, MC, V. *In room:* TV, Internet, kitchen, tea- and coffeemaking facilities.

WHERE TO DINE

Bella Muzica ★★ MEXICAN/HUNGARIAN/ECLECTIC

With a menu stretching the gamut of the globe—from fajitas and burritos to Romanian pork dishes—you'll be excused from initial confusion. Added to the dilemma of trying to figure out what inspired the kitchen's bold eclecticism is the setting—an underground cellar of beautiful vaulted brickwork, decorated with lanterns, bits of pottery, and lengths of rope, and each table outfitted with a red buzzer to alert your waiter. Accept the paradox and move on to the house specialties like the popular "Outlaw's Steak" *(friptura haiduceasca)*, Banat-style escalopes of pork (served with egg and a tangy "brown" sauce); paprikash stew, made with chicken, pork and bacon; or the Kronstadt ragout. If you're lucky (and use your buzzer judiciously), you'll be offered free shots of Romanian plum moonshine *(palincă)*.

Piaţa Sfatului 19. © 0268/47-7946. Reservations essential. Main courses L9.50–L44 ($3.40–$16/£1.85–£3.10). MC, V. Daily noon–11pm.

Butoiul Sasului ✦✦✦ SAXON TRANSYLVANIAN/ECLECTIC   In many ways, the "Saxon Barrel" may just be Braşov's least pretentious restaurant; the waiters are always smiling and helpful, and at night there's bound to be some great local music performed live (sit in the off-street courtyard to best appreciate this). The food is traditional Saxon Transylvanian, so there's plenty of sauerkraut and pork. Also available are two-person platters with hearty portions of spareribs *and* pork chops, or a mix grill plate of chops, smoked and salted meats, and sausages. If you want something cheap and down-home, ask for the leg of pork with beans—it's simple, succulent, and very filling. There's also filet of cod and grilled trout if you're looking for something a little lighter. You can order a liter of house wine for L18 ($6.50/£3.50), and there are some pricier vintages from the Prahova Valley, which are well worth sampling.

Str. Republicii 53–55. © 0268/41-0499 or 0745-315-936. Reservations recommended. Main courses L9–L20 ($3.25–$7.20/£1.75–£3.85); platters for 2 L33–L39 ($12–$14/£6.35–£7.50). MC, V. Daily 11am–midnight.

Casa Hirscher ✦✦ ITALIAN   Occupying the back end of the famous "House of Trade" established by Apollonia Hirscher in 1545, this is a slightly upmarket bistro, with an outdoor courtyard. Outdoing the multifarious nearby venues flaunting Italian cuisine, dishes here are authentic and excellent. Try their homemade specialties: *tortelloni ripieni con melanzane* (pasta stuffed with eggplant, mussels, and pesto), or *tagliolini san Daniele,* made with sliced Italian ham, cream, Parmesan, and poppies. Fish lovers can choose from dorado, sole, trout, and pikeperch, all perfectly prepared, as is the beef filet with a cabernet sauce. There's also tasty roast deer, and melt-in-the-mouth oven-baked lamb, served with seasonal vegetables.

Piaţa Sfatului 12–14, entrance on Str. Apollonia Hirscher. © 0268/41-0533. www.casahirscher.ro. Main courses L9.90–L43 ($3.50–$15/£1.90–£8.25). MC, V. Daily noon–midnight.

Sergiana ✦ TRANSYLVANIAN   Diners can choose from a variety of nooks and crannies in this cozy underground eatery; waiters are decked out in camp Germanic outfits, while at night there's a roaming ensemble serenading with old peasant tunes. Topping the list of popular dishes is deer calf with wildberry and hazelnut sauce, served with rice. Other recommendations for staunch meat-eaters is the *Ceaunu lu Tuşa proptit în varză şi mălai,* a hearty plate of smoked sausages, ribs, and pork pastrami, served with polenta and sauerkraut, and all smothered with a healthy amount of freshly sliced garlic. You can forgo the sauerkraut in favor of a fresh salad. There's good wild boar stew, salmon prepared in wine, and a tasty pastry of pikeperch, served with grape and lemon sauce. Leave space for the sweet cheese dumplings, served with sour cream and jam. Order a bottle from the Murfatlar Winery from the fair-priced wine list.

The ground-level entrance to this subterranean restaurant is marked by **Vinalia wine boutique** (© 0746-213-300; www.vinalia.ro; daily 10am–10pm), which is an excellent place to buy Romanian vintages, including offerings from the Prince Ştirbey estate (www.stirbey.com) in Wallachia's prestigious Drăgăşani region.

Str. Mureşenilor 27. © 0268/41-9775. www.sergiana.ro. Main courses L9–L20 ($3.25–$7.20/£3.25–£3.85). MC, V; PIN required for your credit card. Daily 11am–midnight.

EXPLORING BRAŞOV

The city is centered on **Piaţa Sfatului** ✸✸, on which the city's most imposing monument, the **Black Church** (reviewed below), backs. A wide-open medieval square, Sfatului is the best place to succumb to Braşov's salubrious charms; throughout the day, people meet to plot their next move, be it dining at one of the always-packed restaurants, exploring the city's architectural heritage, or people-watching and chasing pigeons. Around the square a range of attractive Saxon buildings vie for attention. In the center of the square is the 15th-century yellow-and-white **Casa Sfatului (Council House),** now home to the city's tourist office as well as the **Braşov Historical Museum** (Muzeul Judetean de Istorie Braşov; © 0268/47-2363; Tues–Sun 10am–6pm; L3.05/$1.10/60p adults, L2.05/75¢/40p seniors and students); capping the building is the 58m-high (190 ft.) **Trumpeter's Tower,** originally used for meetings. West of the Council House, amid a long row of fabulous buildings, is **Casa Mureşenilor (Piaţa Sfatului 25;** © 0268/47-7864; Tues–Sat 9am–3pm), now memorializing the 19th-century political journalist and editor, Iacob Mureşianu. On the eastern side of the square is **Casa Hirscher.** Built between 1539 and 1545 by Apollonia Hirscher, the widow of one of the city's mayors, it was set up as a trading house for the merchant community, but is now a tourist restaurant, **Cerbul Carpaţin (Carpathian Stag;** © 0268/44-3981). And at the northern end of the square, next to the shamelessly located KFC, is a passage leading to **The Church of the Assumption of the Virgin,** tucked well away from public view; completed in 1899, the church tower was destroyed by earthquake in 1940, and only rebuilt in 1972.

From Piaţa Sfatului you can either wander south through the **Schei District** (described below), or head for the northwestern corner to take Strada Mureşenilor, which stretches past a number of restaurants and bars and soon reaches B-dul. Eroilor, with the leafy expanse of Parcul Central on the far side. Turn right along B-dul. Eroilor, passing the ugly facade of the Aro Palace Hotel to reach **Braşov's Art Museum** (no. 21; Tues–Sun 10am–6pm; L3/$1.10/60p), which includes a sizable collection of works by notable 19th- and 20th-century Romanian artists. Farther on is a **Memorial to the Victims of the 1989 Revolution;** behind this you'll see the bulky **District Council** building. Eroilor becomes B-dul 15 Novembrie, with Piaţa Teatrului spreading out in front of the **Sică Alexandrescu Drama Theater.** Turning right in front of the memorial cross, however, you'll head into **Str. Republicii,** a charming car-free promenade lined with the city's most alluring shops and cafes, and a few decent restaurants; of particular note are the many antiques stores (the best being **Rams Antik** and **Antique Edy,** which has two branches). Although there are a few interesting diversions up the various side streets, Republicii eventually lands you back on Piaţa Sfatului.

For more great photographic vantages of the city, head for the **Black Tower (Turnul Neagru),** part of the defensive walls, which once protected Brastov and which still hold vigil over the city from the face of Warthe Hill, west of Piaţa Sfantului (Tues–Sun

---

Tips **Bird's-Eye View**

Locals like to take romantic strolls along the promenade above the long section of defensive walls that still remains on the eastern edge of the city, at the foot of Mount Tâmpa. Midway along the promenade is the **Telecabina Tâmpa,** a cable car that delivers passengers to the top of the mountain, 995m (295 ft.) up, in 140 seconds (Mon noon–5pm, Tues–Fri 9:30am–6pm, Sat–Sun 9:30am–8pm; last ticket sold 30 min. before closing; L7/$2.50/£1.35 return). Ignore the restaurant (expensive and soulless) and take the path to the right and walk for around 10 minutes to the recently built **Terasa Belvedere** lookout point.

10am–6pm; last tickets 5:30pm; admission L3.05/$1.10/60p; photography L19/$6.70/£3.55). The tower includes a pretty drab medieval display; ignore this and take the steps leading to the top levels; the **view** ★★ from the top of the Black Tower is spectacular (you can happily pass on the White Tower). Take the pathway behind the Black Tower up to **Promenade Warthe** for more great city views. And if you're still not satisfied, organize a helicopter tour with **Brextrans** (Str. Dealul Spirii 53; ⓒ **0268/44-3666**).

Biserica Neagrã ★★★   The 90m-long (295 ft.) and 21m-high (69-ft.) "Black Church" is the biggest Gothic cathedral between Istanbul and Vienna. Work started in 1383, but the building was destroyed during the Ottoman invasion of 1421 before it could be completed. It was finally finished in 1480, although there was more destruction between 1530 and 1630, when a total of 40 earthquakes hit the region. Originally a Catholic church, it became Lutheran during the Reformation. When a tragic fire swept through Braşov on April 21, 1689, the charred remains of the church (the baptismal font at the front of the church is one of the few thing that survived) afforded it its ghoulish name; today there is nothing dark about it, although the exterior is slightly ominous, even haunting. Inside, however, the church is overwhelmingly white and now horribly illuminated by awful modern light fittings. The 180 rugs you see hanging from the balconies—given to the church by merchants who returned after successful trade missions in the Middle East—make up the second-largest collection of its kind in the world; the bell in the clock tower is also the largest in Romania, weighing in at 6 tons. If you are a fan of church or choral music, look out for summer concerts (select evenings mid-June through Aug); this will be the best opportunity to hear the colossal 4,000-pipe organ and much-vaunted acoustics in action.

Biserica Neagrã. Admission L4 ($1.45/75p). Mon–Sat 10am–6pm. Mass is held on Sun 10am.

Schei District ★★   Follow Strada Porta Schei south and pass through the **Schei Gate** (1828), an archway leading to Braşov's oldest area, the neighborhood where the subservient Romanian community was sequestered during the racist rule of the Saxons. The neighborhood retains much of its historical character, defined by narrow streets and unimposing buildings; one of the loveliest is the Orthodox **Cathedral of St. Nicholas** (Piaţa Unirii; Mon–Sat 8am–6pm, Sun 9am–6pm), an eclectic merging of Gothic, Renaissance and baroque elements. Established by the *voivodes* (landowners) of Wallachia, this is Transylvania's first Orthodox church, built 1493 to 1564 on the site of an earlier wooden building; it's lavishly adorned with frescoes and rugs. Near the church, behind the statue of an intellectual-looking man holding a scroll, is the **First Romanian School Museum (Muzeul Prima Şcuală Românească;** Piaţa Unirii 1-2; *©* **0268/44-3879;** 9am–5pm), where the first Romanian Bible is kept, along with the first Romanian letter written using the Latin alphabet, and the country's first press, used in this building when it was a printing house. From the square, head farther along Str. Prof. Vasile Saftu until you get to lovely **Biserica Sfânta Treime (Church of the Holy Trinity),** well off the beaten track, but memorable for its early-morning Mass (from 7:30am), attended by a congregation of retired locals; the interior is fantastically frescoed, and there's a small museum. The cemetery is where the city's Romanian serfs are buried. Schei also shelters the country's original **Romanian lyceum** (Str. Prundului), which hosted the first vernacular opera in 1882.

Schei, via Str. Porta Schei, south of Piaţa Sfatului.

POIANA BRAŞOV

Braşov's fabulous little forest-fringed ski resort, **Poiana Braşov,** is situated on the slopes of the Postăvarul Massif, a fine year-round Carpathian Mountain getaway. It's beautiful in summer, when the mountains are perfect for extended hikes and when Romania's athletes come to train in open space and clean air. From December through March, it fills up with skiers; casual winter-sports enthusiasts will have an easy time of it. Experienced skiers won't be challenged, however; this is generally for beginners and anyone looking for a relaxing time on the slopes, although some of the pistes are rated "difficult." There is limited off-piste skiing. There's a gondola service as well as two cable cars to get you to the summit of Cristianul Mave (1,690m/5,543 ft.) and Mt. Postavarul (1,802m/5,911 ft.), the two peaks here. Poiana Braşov offers ski instruction as well as a range of slope activities; for all the information you might need, visit www.ana.ro; alternatively try www.skiresorts.ro. The best restaurant in town is **Coliba Haiducilor** (Str. Drumul Sulinarului; *©* **0268/26-2137**), with a lovely country atmosphere, warm log fire, and home-style cooking. If the salubrious atmosphere works its charms on you, ask the owners about their accommodations at **Casa Viorel** (Str. Poiana lui Stechil; *©* **0268/26-2431**). You can also organize accommodations through many agencies in Braşov; try to avoid staying at the larger hotels, which are soulless.

Bran Castle *(Overrated*   Part medieval fortress, part tourist con, Bran Castle is probably the best-known attraction in Romania. Most people arrive in modest Bran village, just 30km (19 miles) from Braşov, expecting to find "Dracula's Castle," and many suckers leave oblivious to the truth: Vlad Tepeş may have passed through Bran at some stage of his violent career, but he certainly never lived here (see "Vlad & the Epic Mythology of Count Dracula," earlier in this chapter). If anything, Bran Castle is very much a fairy-tale castle; perched upon a cliff, with whitewashed turrets and defensive bastions, it is somehow too quaint, too fragile, too pretty, to entertain thoughts of bats or monsters. Completed in record time, between 1377 and 1382, Bran was built as a defensive outpost to protect Hungary's Transylvanian interests against the expanding Ottoman Empire; it also collected customs on goods moving between Wallachia and Transylvania. Control of the castle changed repeatedly over the centuries, until the people of Braşov gave it to the Romanian Royal family in 1920. At the request of Queen Marie, chief architect Karl Liman (who also worked for her at Pelişor in Sinaia) transformed the defensive fortress into a modern summer residence fit for royalty, complete with electric lighting and running water. Marie, who features in many photographic displays, undertook the interior design, styling the rooms much as they look today. There's certainly nothing scary here, unless you have a fear of crowds; try to arrive as early as possible to avoid the masses and walk through the castle at your leisure, enjoying the fantastic views from the balconies, windows, and battlements. Included in your ticket is an ethnographic display of well-maintained (and usually locked) peasant homes at the foot of the castle hill. Not included is a visit to the super-revolting Haunted Castle and Skeleton's Tavern (L7/$2.50/£1.35) for kids that forms part of the tourist clutter of souvenir stalls near the ticket office. In 2006, the Castle was officially returned to Princess Ileana's son, Dominic, a New York City architect. The jury is still out on what he will do with his inheritance, but we're hoping he'll clear out the kitsch flea market around the entrance to Bran's extensive ground and restore some of the property's grandeur.

Muzeul Bran, Bran. ⓒ **0268/23-8333.** wwwbrancastlemuseum.ro. Admission L12 ($4.30/£2.30) adults, L6 ($2.20/£1.15) seniors and students, free for children under 5; L10 ($3.60/£1.90) photography, L18 ($6.50/£3.45) video camera use. English guided tours are available; ask for availability. Mon noon–6pm; Tues–Sun 9am–6pm.

BRAŞOV AFTER DARK

With its wooden floors and exposed brickwork walls, **Festival '39** ⓡⓡ (Str. Mureşenilor 23; ⓒ **0268/47-8664;** www.festival39.com; daily 10am–2am) is a classy little all-day bar; beautiful and unpretentious, it's decorated with dozens of framed antique photos and large picture windows that open onto a sidewalk—great for people-watching. For an evening drink, call to reserve a table. Another place for a relaxed drink is nearby **Hypnose** in an arcade off Strada Mureşenilor, across from Piaţa Sfatului; it's an above-ground cellar-style space with vaulted ceilings, comfortable armchairs, and a simple, smart bar. It's not for nothing that **Opium** ⓡ (Str. Republicii 2; ⓒ **0722-397-887;** daily 10am–late) calls itself "the chill-out caffe"; it's a chicly decorated lounge-bar with an umbrella-shaded terrace on the city's premiere pedestrian mall. This is prime people-watching real estate; you can start your day here with a caffeine fix, and return at the end of the night for great tunes and fast-flowing cocktails. Finally, there's a sophisticated atmosphere at the less-than-traditional **Auld Scottish Pub** (Str. Apollonia Hirscher 10; ⓒ **0268/47-0183;** daily 11am–3am), which has embraced leather sofas, pop music, and a big, upmarket crowd.

Braşov's up-for-it party venue is marvelously called **Theatre** (Str. Lunga 1; ⓒ **0721-972-224;** www.theatreclub.ro), which pulls a dedicated crowd with its regular lineup of international DJs; keep your eyes peeled for posters and flyers (always available at Opium), or consult the latest edition of the free listings guide, *SapteSeri* (available almost everywhere). Inquire at the tourist office about festivals, theater, and music events.

HOBNOBBING WITH ROYALTY: ROMANIA'S FINEST VILLAGE STAY ⓡⓡⓡ

In the predominantly Hungarian village of Micloşoara (known as Miklósvár in Hungarian), **Count Kalnoky's Guesthouses** offers some of the finest accommodations in the country. The project is the brainchild of born-in-exile Count Tudor Kalnoky (a dead ringer for Ralph Fiennes), whose family left Romania in 1939 with the rise of fascism; after the fall of Communism, he spent nearly a decade in court fighting to get his family properties back from the government and has since set to work reclaiming his 750-year-old aristocratic heritage by restoring a series of houses scattered around the rural village; they've become luxurious and lovely cottagey guest rooms for visitors seeking an authentic treat in the heart of Transylvania. With a population of 500, Micloşoara's village life is confined to old people sitting on benches outside their homes, literally waiting for the cows to come home. These villagers are descendants of the Szeklers who came to Transylvania to defend the eastern border of their empire.

At the main house—or "Hunting Manor"—there's a lounge with fireplace, and drawing rooms with books and antiques. There's also a 17th-century wine cellar, where dinners are usually served. Guest quarters are spread around the village, although you can stay in the old "serfs' house," near the main kitchen. Painted a fantastic blue, it's a favorite of regular visitors, so you'll need to reserve it in advance. Not that it really matters: Lodgings are all immaculate, with solid wooden floors, antique furniture, ceramic wood-burning fires, good lighting, comfortable beds, and wonderful modern bathrooms. There are no televisions or radios; instead, there's plenty of atmosphere and an in-room sauna.

To keep you busy between breakfast and dinnertime, the Count offers scheduled activities; spend the day with a shepherd, or hang with a villager, ride on a cart, go horseback riding, or milk the cows; there are visits to neighboring villages, and the option of fishing or hiking. Tudor himself studied to be a vet, and birders should ask if he's available for a specialized tour. There are also various cultural excursions and explorations of local natural phenomena, including the nearby cave where the lost children of Hamelin supposedly made their reappearance. One drawback may be adhering to the daily program of organized events, so it's worth asking for a detailed schedule well in advance so you can request any tailor-made changes. Also note that dinner is communal; if you'd prefer privacy, make prior arrangements. In summer, it's worth requesting at least one outdoor dinner. If you've got your own car, this is a fantastic base from which to explore southern Transylvania, the only problem being the treacherous potholed road leading to the village itself.

Micloşoara. © **0267/31-4088** or 0742-202-586 for reservations. Fax 0267/31-4088. www.transylvaniancastle.com. 8 units. 90€ ($113) double. Rates include breakfast. Lunch or dinner: 18€ ($23) per person, including wine. All-inclusive rate: 230€ ($288) double. Last-minute deals and long-stay discounts available. MC, V. Credit card payment incurs 3% penalty. **Amenities:** Dining areas; wine cellar; airport and train station transfers from Bucharest or Braşov; wide range of excursions and experiential adventures; horseback riding; laundry. *In room:* A/C, tea- and coffeemaking facility, hair dryer, sauna.

SIGHIŞOARA ✦✦✦
Sighişoara is 221km (137 miles) NW of Bucharest

Medieval Sighişoara is the only inhabited citadel of its kind in Europe; remarkably preserved, it's earned its place on UNESCO's World Heritage list. Of course there's also plenty of hype around the fact that Vlad Ţepeş (aka Count Dracula) was born here, but that's not the reason to make this excursion. Built in the 15th century, this hilltop fortress town is a gorgeous, tiny jumble of cobbled streets lined with medieval houses and towers jutting menacingly from the battlements—compact, yet with a myriad ancient nooks and crannies, this is a wonderful place to explore, and easily better than the more popular Bran Castle.

ARRIVAL, ORIENTATION & GETTING AROUND
Sighişoara has a fairly good run of train connections with Braşov and Bucharest, and there is a fairly extensive range of services to and from other towns likely to be on your

itinerary; you can for instance get a direct train here from Budapest, Vienna, and Prague. Sighişoara's **train station** is about 1km (⅔ mile) from the old city, at one end of a quiet residential neighborhood outside the medieval center. When trains arrive, taxis turn up to drive visitors to their hotels; there is an access road leading from the lower city into the citadel. Although your hotel should be able to organize any onward travel, you can buy train tickets from the **CFR Agenţie de Voiaj** (Str. O. Goga 6A; ℂ **0265/77-1820;** Mon–Fri 8am–4pm), in the lower part of town.

The **information center** (ℂ **0265/77-7844**) of the charitable organization on the town square (**Piaţa Cetăţii**) organizes tours, bike rentals, and Internet access.

WHERE TO STAY & DINE

Part of the **Burg Hostel** (Str. Bastionului 4–6; ℂ **0265/77-8489;** fax 0265/50-6086; www.ibz.org.ro) occupies the only building in the citadel with a wooden roof, built in the early 14th century, and right near the town square. Thoroughly clean and reasonably comfortable, sleeping quarters include large dorm rooms (with seven beds at L30/$11/£5.75 per night), and a few en-suite doubles (around 30€/$38). Popular with locals and travelers alike, the restaurant and bar get very busy (although the food is uninspired). A fair step up from the hostel is a comfortable private room, with modern en-suite shower, in the home of **Teo Coroian,** the local *palinca* distiller (Str. Şcolii 14; ℂ **0265/77-1677;** www.delateo.com); 40€ ($50) gets you a good double room with breakfast and a help-yourself bar fridge filled with mineral water, beer, and—of course—plenty of homemade plum, pear, and apple brandy; also included are coffee and snacks, and the comfortable vibe of a small home.

Of the hotel restaurants, **Casa Wagner** (daily 8am–11pm) is the best, with a lovely wine cellar as well as a sheltered courtyard terrace round the back. If you've left Bran Castle disappointed, you may be interested in dining at **Casa Vlad Dracul,** the only restaurant in the country with any authentic link to the legend. History claims that Vlad Tepiş was born in this house in 1431. The medieval decor and candlelit tavern atmosphere do little to render the place "spooky" but the menu does however offer an unforgiving vampire bent: "Dracula House medallions," for example, are slithers of pork on bread, covered with a slop of garlic, mushroom, and tomato ketchup, that popular stand-in for blood.

Casa Epoca ✸✸ *(Finds* A stylishly spick-and-span guesthouse occupying a 15th-century Gothic building, Epoca has timbered floors, exposed wood-beam ceilings, and wrought-iron, wall-mounted electric candelabras. The gracious owner has gone to lengths to give character to the rooms, which are furnished with lovely wooden items, including reproduction medieval Saxon beds with firm mattresses and clean white linens (televisions are hidden away in a cupboard). All bathrooms have showers, except the apartment, which has a corner tub. The attic rooms are especially lovely. Breakfast is served in a fine vaulted brick cellar.

Str. Tamplarilor 4, Sighişoara 545400. ℂ **0265/77-3232.** Fax 0265/77-2237. www.casaepoca.ro. 11 units. 45€–50€ ($56–$63) double; 68€–75€ ($85–$94) suite; 90€–100€ ($113–$125) apt. Rates include breakfast. No credit cards. **Amenities:** Bar; laundry; 24-hr. medical assistance; car rental; massage. *In room:* TV, minibar.

Casa Wagner ✸ Perfectly sited in the center of the citadel, this intimate hotel is defined by its tasteful layout and Saxon antiques. While it doesn't have the long list of amenities offered at Hotel Sighişoara (virtually neighboring Wagner), you're likely to enjoy more personal attention from the staff. White-walled guest rooms are spacious, with wooden floors and simple, carefully selected furnishings. The stairs to the upper floors can be a bit taxing, so ask for a first-floor unit if possible if you're not keen to lug luggage. Bathrooms are modern with a tub/shower combo. This hotel also has the best in-house dining options: Choose between the cozy cellar beneath the hotel, the courtyard-terrace round the back, or the cafe-lounge-bar area just off the lobby.

Piaţa Cetăţii 7, Sighişoara. ⓒ 0265/50-6014. Fax 0265/50-6015. www.casa-wagner.com. 22 units (10 new units planned for 2007). Oct 15–Apr 15 45€ ($56) double, 65€ ($81) suite; Apr 16–Oct 14 60€ ($75) double, 80€ ($100) suite; 10€ ($13) extra bed. Rates include breakfast and VAT. MC, V. **Amenities:** Restaurant; bar; business services; room service; laundry. *In room:* TV, minibar.

Hotel Sighişoara ☆
With its timbered ceilings, wooden floors, and occasional original frescoes, the citadel's largest hotel is also charming. There's also a great lineup of amenities, including a vaulted cellar-restaurant that practically doubles as a museum of curious antiques. Guest rooms are decorated to conjure up a mild sense of the medieval, particularly those with vaulted ceilings; they're all different sizes, but are fairly spacious, with large windows and flower boxes framing views of the cobbled streets; those on the top floor provide great rooftop views through angled ceilings. Not all rooms have air-conditioning. The biggest drawback here is the good likelihood that a busload of tourists will turn up at any moment.

Str. Şcolii 4–6, 545400 Sighişoara. ⓒ/fax 0265/77-1000. hotelsighisoara@elsig.ro. 32 units. L190 ($68/£36) double; L300 ($108/£58) apt. Rates include breakfast. Rates higher during Medieval Festival. MC, V. **Amenities:** Restaurant; bar; fitness room; sauna; massage; room service; laundry. *In room:* A/C (some), TV, minibar, hair dryer.

WHAT TO DO & SIGHTS TO SEE

Part of its charm is that there's not much to do in Sighişoara; the citadel itself is the attraction. As you roam the streets, don't be surprised if déjà vu sets in; the town is tiny enough to be covered on foot in just a few minutes, but there's joy to be had in retracing your steps, as the architecture is affected by even the subtlest changes in light. Spend some time visiting the citadel's few churches and museums, which add context to the broader picture; try to climb the Clock Tower as early as possible, taking in the fantastic view of the city before the tourist hordes arrive (in fact, from up there you'll see the buses making their way up Strada Turnului signaling that the historic town is open for business). Then visit the Church on the Hill, which seems ordinary from the outside, but is imbued with a fascinating energy. Besides the sights reviewed below, you can also take in the 15th-century Gothic-style **Church of the Dominican Monastery,** adjacent the Clock Tower. Don't forget to wind down the day by grabbing a beer on Piaţa Cetăţii; there's sometimes a craft market and usually a lively atmosphere.

The Clock Tower & City Museums ☆☆
Surmounting the main entrance to the city, the whole **Muzeul de Istorie (History Museum)** is a tower climb, so be prepared for some legwork. It's one of the more useful history museums, starting with a model of the town as it was in 1735. There is also a collection of surgical instruments that includes a bloodcurdling array of knives and saws, not to mention enema syringes that will make you grateful for being born into an enlightened age. The best exhibition room (reached via the short stairway next to the display of Dr. Josef Bacon, who founded the museum in 1899) includes several chromo-engravings of everyday life in 18th- and 19th-century Sighişoara. As you ascend the clock tower, you can check out different components of the elaborate clock mechanism, straining your neck along the way to get views of the city. From the top, the magical 360-degree view includes shingled rooftops, fairy-tale steeples, turreted guard towers, and—in the near distance—the encroachment of modern apartments. Polished metal plaques indicate distances to

---

Tips **Getting Fortified in the Citadel**

Palinca—homemade plum, apple, and pear brandy—is a fine Transylvanian tradition. In the heart of Sighişoara, you'll soon find your way to homey little **Teo's
Cellar** (Str. Şcolii 14; © **0265/77-1677**; www.delateo.com), where you can sample the powerful distillations and learn about the process from the man himself. Teo has hundreds of potent vintages for you to take home, and he's
enlisted the help of various artisans to create bottles in an astounding range of
shapes and sizes; combined with their spirited contents, they make good gifts.
Teo also has a very comfortable en-suite guest room in his home (see "Where
to Stay," p. 526).

---

various capitals around the world; at this point, you're 7,431km (4,607 miles) from
New York.

Back down on the ground, your combination ticket includes entrance to the tiny
one-room **Torture Chamber Museum** (nearby, tucked into the city wall), which once
served as the citadel's prison. Also nearby is the **Museum of Medieval Arms,** a curiously curated exhibition that includes African daggers and arrows among the more traditional assortment of European killing machines.

Piaţa Muzeului 1. © **0265/77-1108**. History Museum and Clock Tower entry: L4.10 ($1.50/80p); combined ticket for
all museums: L7 ($2.50/£1.35). Mon 10am–4:30pm; Tues–Fri 9am–6:30pm; Sat–Sun 9am–4:30pm.

Church on the Hill & Cemetery ★★   A covered stairway with nearly 180 steps
leads up the hill to the Gothic-style *Biserica din Deal,* allegedly built in 1345 for the
Saxon community; local guides will dispute this, however, claiming that this is simply
the year when the church was converted to its Gothic form. There are a few unexpected surprises here, including a unique fresco in one of the archways in which the
Holy Trinity is depicted as a three-faced entity, with the Holy Ghost depicted as
female. Also unique is the Last Judgment fresco without any depiction of purgatory.
Take the time to venture into the crypt beneath the church, where 30 tombs are
cloaked in a cool atmosphere of vampiric calm.

Worth exploring for its weathered charm is the Saxon cemetery opposite the church
doorway; strangely, the positioning of some of the gravestones clearly suggests that
some of the dead have made attempts to escape. To the right of the cemetery entrance
is the **Goldsmiths' Tower.**

Biserica din Deal. L2 (70¢/40p) admission. Times vary; usually 8am–8pm in summer.

The Saxon church of Biertan

Fortified churches were the norm in medieval Europe, with the architectural form
reaching its apotheosis in Transylvania under Saxon architects. The Saxon village of
Biertan (Birthälm) is home to one of the finest and largest of these. Situated within
sylvan surroundings—low hills carpeted with orchards and vineyards—this
UNESCO-listed church was built in the late-Gothic style during the first part of the
16th century; the village itself dates from 1283. The church occupies a hill in the center of town, its solid periphery walls and four watchtowers a reminder of how these
religious buildings served a dual function as places of worship and defense against
marauding enemies. At the foot of the hill, walls and archways and towers mark out
further protective fortifications. A covered stairway allows access to the church, most

of which is made of brick, plastered and painted throughout; 20th-century restoration work has revealed frescoes that have been partially restored. The stone pulpit, probably carved by a Braşovian named Ullricus, suggests a transition between Gothic and Renaissance periods. Between 1572 and 1867, Biertan was the residence of Transylvania's evangelical bishops, many of whose tombstones can be found inside the church. Getting to Biertan is a bit of a chore by public transport; hire a taxi from Sighişoara if you don't have your own vehicle, and expect to pay between 12€ and 15€ ($15–$19) one-way. The church can be visited Tuesday through Saturday, 9am to noon and 1 to 7pm, and on Sunday 9 to 11am and 2 to 7pm; there's usually a helpful guide inside the church who will show you around; be sure to ask about the medieval lock mechanism of the vestry door. Biertan comes to life once a year in September when it plays host to a Saxon reunion drawing a festive crowd of Transylvanian-born Germans.

Biertan. www.biertan.com. Tues–Fri and Sun 9am–noon and 1–7pm; Sat 9am–noon and 1–4pm.

SIBIU ✸✸✸
Sibiu is 274km (170 miles) NW of Bucharest

Sibiu is on the verge of being discovered: In 2007, it shares the "European City of Culture" title with Luxembourg. Undergoing a thorough big-budget makeover, its large medieval squares and gorgeous buildings have been extensively rejuvenated with repairs, fresh coats of paint, and a good spring-cleaning. An excellent example of the (usually smaller) fortified Saxon towns that dot the Transylvanian landscape, Sibiu was saved from destruction during the Communist era largely because Ceauşescu's son, Nicu, was the city's mayor. The medieval heart, surrounded by a sprawling city, is held together by stone-walled fortifications and the remains of the 39 guild towers that served as defensive watchtowers; within lie cobblestone streets, secret back-alleys, crumbling stairways, and elegant monuments.

Built by the Saxons in the 12th century on the site of the Roman village of Cibinium, Sibiu is known to Germans as Hermannstadt and it remains home to Romania's largest German-speaking community, though now a meager 5,500. Originally designed to a concentric circular plan, with four walls dividing the residential zones according to class, this was Transylvania's ancient capital, with the Saxons ruling from the center and Romanians occupying the outermost ring. While it's often thought of as Romania's most welcoming and laid-back city, its worth remembering that it was here, in the second half of the 19th century, that the Romanian nationalist movement first stirred, agitating against Transylvania's Magyarization; today, vestiges of Astra (the Transylvanian Association from Romanian Literature and Culture) can still be found, particularly at the Folk Museum just outside the city.

ARRIVAL, ORIENTATION & GETTING AROUND
Tarom (Str. Nicolae Bălcescu 10; ✆ **0269/21-1604;** Mon–Fri 8am–6pm) flies from Bucharest to Sibiu on Wednesday, Thursday, and Sunday at 9:30pm. Both Tarom and **Carpatair** (✆ **0269/22-9161**) have connections with German destinations, and Carpatair flies to Timişoara. Extensive work on Sibu's **railway station** (Piaţa 1 Decembrie) should have it in a user-friendly condition by 2007; it's about 650m (2,132 ft.) from Piaţa Mare, and is directly opposite the **bus station.** For years, the problem has been finding connections to the city, but train access is likely to be much improved as Sibiu is thrust into the European limelight. From the station, catch trolleybus no. 1 to get to the center, or use a **taxi** (✆ **0269/44-4444**). You can buy

onward train tickets from **CFR's Agenţie de Voiaj office** (Str. Nicolae Bălcescu 6; ℂ **0269/21-6441;** Mon–Fri 7:30am–7:30pm).

For information and sightseeing services, head directly to **Kultours** on the ground floor of Casa Luxemburg (Piaţa Mica 16; ℂ **0269/21-6854;** www.kultours.ro). They hand out a useful map, offer sightseeing trips, rent bicycles, rent rooms, and sell books, souvenirs, and postcards; their 1-day tour of the city is the best on offer. Set to be a worthy source of information from 2007 is the **Tourist Information Office** (Piaţa Mare 7; ℂ **0269/21-1110;** Mon–Sat 9am–5pm, Sun 10am–1pm); visit their website (www.sibiu.ro) before your trip.

WHERE TO STAY

Given the expected influx of visitors, it is remarkable that Sibiu has a dearth of good accommodations options, with the "Roman Emperor" being the top choice only because there is no strong competition. If you're on a budget (or just not keen to waste your money), take a look at **The Old Town Hostel** (Piaţa Mică 26, Sibiu; ℂ **0269/21-6445;** www.hostelsibiu.ro), run by the same people who own Casa Luxemburg (reviewed below). Occupying a 450-year-old monument and former pharmacy, it's an excellent-value hostel with one double room for 20€ to 25€ ($25–$31) per night (dorm beds go for 10€/$13). The premises are neat, clean, and often empty, and staff are eager to help where they can.

✗ **Casa Luxemburg** *(Value (Kids*   Run by Sibiu's best tourist agency, Luxemburg House occupies a great location in one of Sibiu's famous original monuments at one end of Piaţa Mică—the city's medieval heart. You need to climb a tricky wooden stairway to get to the large rooms and suites on the second floor; these have modern furniture, parquet floors, and en-suite showers. There is also an apartment with a kitchenette, but without the view over the square. Ironically, mattresses here are better than those at the Împăratul Romanilor, and this is a good option if you're traveling with children since it's possible to book a three- or four-bedded unit. There has been no attempt to capitalize on the history, and it's not luxurious, but a stay here does represent very good value, better certainly than the Emperor.

Piaţa Miă 16, Sibiu. ℂ/fax **0269/21-6854.** www.casaluxemburg.ro. 6 units. L190 ($68/£36) double; L270 ($97/£52) triple; L310 ($112/£59) apt. MC, V. **Amenities:** Breakfast buffet; 24-hr. reception and tourist agency; sightseeing; car rental; souvenir shop. *In room:* TV.

Hotel Împăratul Romanilor *(✦*   Renovated extensively in 2003 and with plans for further improvements before the City of Culture festivities commence in 2007, the "Roman Emperor" hotel traces its history from 1555, when the city's first inn stood on this site in the heart of the medieval town. It is the supposed pride of Sibiu's hospitality industry, listing Johann Strauss, Franz Liszt, and various heads of state and royals among its guests, but this is a position it has earned more by default than anything else. There are enough pieces of antique and reproduction furniture to evoke a sense of gracious living, but it lacks the bells and whistles of a definitively luxurious hotel, with long passageways with much-scrubbed but still grubby-looking carpets and mixed-bag guest rooms that combine faux-antique and modern to create a rather bland look. And in many respects, given the price, service is lax and e-mail bookings are unreliable. Time for a newcomer to shake up the scene.

Str. Nicolae Balcescu 2-4, Sibiu. ℂ **0269/21-6500.** Fax 0269/21-3278. www.aurelius.compace.ro. 95 units. L280 ($101/£54) double with tub; L270 ($97/£52) double with shower; L320 ($115/£61) studio; L400–L460

($144–$166/£77–£32) apt. Rates include breakfast. MC, V. **Amenities:** Restaurant; bar; lounge; fitness center; sauna; massage; 24-hr. room service; laundry. *In room:* TV, minibar.

WHERE TO DINE

Built into the side of one of the city walls, reached via a set of steps between Str. Turnului and Piaţa Huet, is **Pivnita de vinuri "Weinkeller"** (Str. Tunrului 2; ⓒ **0269/ 21-0319;** Tues–Sun noon–midnight), a wine cellar-cum-restaurant with traditional German dishes and light meals (like quiche Lorraine and cold meat-and-cheese platters) and an extensive wine list with vintage indicated on a map, so you'll learn a bit about where they've come from.

✗ Crama Sibiul Vechi ✗✗✗ *(Value* TRANSYLVANIAN   One of the top places in the country for authentic Transylvanian food, this unpretentious 100-year-old restaurant is loved by locals—and for good reason. Hidden away on a side street off Str. Nicolae Bălcescu, Sibiul Vechi occupies a late-15th-century cellar decorated in traditional "village style" and prides itself on the authenticity of the experience; waiters are in traditional costume getup, and even the plates and wine goblets are handcrafted. There's not much reason to study the menu: Without any hesitation (unless you're vegetarian), order the Shepard's Bag *(traista ciobanului),* a chicken breast parcel stuffed full of sliced sausage, salami, and cheese, and served with grilled polenta—it's fantastic. Alternatives are more or less all meaty: peasant's stew (ladled into your bowl at the table), *muşchi de pork Sibiu* (pork filet, Sibiu-style), Transylvanian mixed grill, or even *creier pane* (deep fried brains in a light batter).

Str. Papiu Ilarian 3. ⓒ **0269/21-3985.** www.sibiulvechi.ro. Main courses L8.50–L21.50 ($3.05–$7.75/£1.65–£4.10). MC, V. Daily 11am–midnight.

EXPLORING SIBIU

Sibiu's interesting bits stretch between **Piaţă Mică** in what is known as "**Lower Town,**" and **Piaţa Unirii,** situated at the junction of Sibiu's charming medieval heart and pulsing modern city. **Piaţă Mică** ("small" square), once the commercial center of the city—**Casa Artelor** at the northern end of the square originally dates from 1370 when it was a market hall—is surrounded on all sides by a lovely collection of buildings freshly coated in a palette of flash pastels. Of the prettiest is **Casa Luxemburg,** now occupied by several decent bars, a tourist shop, and guesthouse (see "Where to Stay," above), and right near the famous **Liar's Bridge**—so named because (among other fanciful reasons) it will apparently collapse if you tell a fib while standing on it; apparently no one has dared test the theory since it was constructed in 1859. The bridge links Piaţa Mică to adjacent **Piaţa Huet,** at the center of which stands the monumental **Evangelical Cathedral** (reviewed below). Piaţă Huet's southern end is in turn linked with **Piaţa Mare,** the "big" town square and once the social hub of the original walled city, where—among other crowd-pulling activities—executions were carried out. This marks the end of "Lower Town."

Set aside an hour to explore the city's top attraction, located on Piaţa Mare—the **Brukenthal Palace,** with its famous art museum (reviewed below)—as well as the **Roman Catholic Cathedral,** built by the Jesuits (1726–33), in the baroque style (the statue out front memorializes the peasants who fought in the uprisings of 1848). Between the palace and the church is the gorgeously impressive headquarters of the **Banca Agricola,** and in the northwestern corner of the square, the **Council Tower** (1588).

Stretching southwest of Piaţa Mare is pedestrianized **Strada Nicolae Bălcescu,** established in 1492 and lined with shops, cafes, galleries, and a couple of side streets worth wandering for a sense of medieval back-alley life. Lined with Renaissance-style architecture, Str. Bălcescu eventually collides with modern Sibiu, a sudden time-shifting shock as you hit newly restored **Piaţa Unirii** (where you'll find Crama Sibiul Vechi, the city's highly rated restaurant). Along the southeastern periphery of the old center, much of the original defensive wall still stands, dotted with a few of its guild-sponsored watchtowers.

Upper Town's most attractive stretch is **Str. Avram Iancu,** which runs between the Council Tower building and the **Ursuline Church;** along the road is Sibiu's oldest residence, known as **Casa Bobel,** which has apparently retained the same appearance for half a millennium. Midway between the square and the church, you should come upon the steep **Pasajul Scolii (School Passage),** which leads to the cobbled depths of Str. Movilei.

The **Ursuline Church** is a huge edifice with a sculpted effigy of St. Ursula above the entrance; it was built in 1474 and was originally a Dominican monastery, but was closed in 1543 when the Reformation converted the Saxon population to Lutheranism; in 1733 it was taken over by the Ursuline nuns who converted the original Gothic interiors to the baroque—get here at 8am to hear women in the church singing and chanting with great solemnity. Near the church, on the corner of Filarmonicii and Strada General Magheru, you'll find **Teea,** a charming place for flavored teas (and coffee); upstairs is **Galeria Art-Vo** (Mon–Fri 10am–6pm; Sat 10am–1pm). Baroque flourishes define the city's **Franciscan Church** (Str. Şelarilor) situated in a quiet corner, and linked to Strada General Magheru by a narrow passageway. It was built in 1716 and the white-and-pastel interior includes such high kitsch as a Madonna statue framed by a rockery Liturgical Mass is held on Sundays at 9am, and on Tuesday and Thursday at 5pm.

At the edge of the old city near the **Powder Tower** is the neoclassical **Sala Thalia** (Str. Cetăţii), the new home of the State Philharmonic (established in 1788), likely to have a busy season during the Cultural Capital celebrations. Farther along Str. Cetăţii is the **Natural History Museum** (Tues–Sun 9am–5pm), founded in 1895.

Brukenthal Museum ✸✸   Baron Samuel von Brukenthal was an Austrian governor who played a significant role in Transylvanian history, and was also a significant patron for the development of homeopathic medicine. His Sibiu palace is of interest architecturally—it is one of Romania's great baroque monuments, built between 1778 and 1788—but it also hosts the country's oldest art gallery, with an extensive collection of works from the German, Austrian, and Flemish schools under stucco ceiling and chandeliers; vestiges of the original baroque styling remain, along with silk walls, white rococo stoves, and 18th-century Transylvanian marquetry furniture. Open to the public since 1817, the galleries are in dire need of better lighting (some of the paintings are almost nothing but glare and shadow). Nevertheless, there are a few good impressions of Transylvanian cities through the ages.

Also part of the National Brukenthal Museum are satellite galleries and exhibits, including the **Contemporary Art Gallery** (accessed on Str. Tribunei), and the **History Museum (Muzeul de Istorie)** (Str. Mitropoliei 2; ✆ **0269/21-8143;** Tues–Sun 8:30am–4:30pm; L4/$1.45/75p adults, L2/70¢/40p discount), with a collection of just about anything and everything stored up from Sibiu's historical heyday, housed in the 15th-century Primăriă Municipiului (also thoroughly renovated in 2006). There are no English explanations, but you can just about follow the logic; the views from the windows do beat the displays, however.

Piaţa Mare 4–5. ℭ **0269/21-7691**. www.brukenthalmuseum.ro. Summer Tues–Sun 9am–5pm; winter Tues–Sun 10am–4pm. Adults L6 ($2.15/£1.15), seniors and students L3 ($1.10/60p).

Evangelical Cathedral ⊛⊛

Work on this late-Gothic church began in 1320, and continued for 200 years. Gray-stone walls with curved vaulting form the interior stark; at the back of the church, the 6,000-pipe organ is the biggest in the country. The north wall of the nave is studded with stone epitaphs, including that of Prince Mihnea the Bad (Vodă cel Rău), the son of Vlad the Impaler, who was assassinated on the church square in 1510 just after attending a service here. Also don't miss the fantastic 9m (30-ft.) fresco in the choir; known as the "Rosenauer Painting," it is a superb crucifixion scene rendered in 1445; above this, note the Hungarian royal insignia featuring a lion and Bohemian vulture; below the fresco are the first Christian Hungarian kings (Ludovic with an ax and Stephen with scepter). Rising to a height of 73m (239 ft.), the bell tower was built as part of the city's defense system when a pair of guards would keep watch and use flags to signal the arrival of enemy armies. You can join a **tower tour,** offered by a Kultours guide who'll be hanging around the entrance (in summer, daily 9am–7pm; L3/$1.10/60p), climbing a steep 192 steps to get to the top, but it's worth it for the views.

Piaţa Huet. Open daily, summer 10am–6pm; winter 11am–4pm. Organ concerts on Wed evenings June–Sept.

Orthodox Church ⊛

Marked by a pair of entrance towers, Romania's second-largest Orthodox church was built between 1902 and 1906; its sandy yellow and ocher-colored brickwork apparently a miniature copy of the cathedral of St. Sophia in Istanbul. The huge carved door bears a German symbol, while inside, incense wafts through a majestic space hung with fantastic chandeliers and glorious frescoes cover almost every inch.

Str. Mitropoliei 35. Daily 6am–8pm.

Astra Museum of Traditional Folk Civilization

Rent a bicycle from Kultours and get directions for the 5km (3-mile) ride to this pleasant and fairly well-organized outdoor exhibition that doubles as sociopolitical demonstration. It's all about hanging on to traditional heritage, with the emphasis on village homesteads as well as folk pastimes. And it's decidedly pro-Romanian.

Calea Răşinarilor 14. ℭ **0269/24-2599**. 2€ ($2.50) adults; 1€ ($1.25) children. June–Sept Tues–Sun 10am–6pm; Oct–May Tues–Sun 9am–4pm.

SIBIU AFTER DARK

Most fun for idling at a terrace cafe is probably Piaţa Mică, and there are always watchable people trundling between Piaţa Mare and Lower Town. With its warren of nooks and crannies, **Kulturcafe** ⊛⊛ (Piaţa Mică 16; ℭ **0788-154-475;** daily 9am–3am) is an atmospheric cellar-style venue in the basement of Casa Luxemburg; exhibitions of photographs or installation art often set the mood, while the music ranges from jazz or blues to retro and experimental electronica. German beer is served along with tequilas, cocktails, and "absolutely anything." In summer, there's a terrace out on Piaţa Mică. **Art Café** ⊛ (Str Filarmonicii 2; ℭ **0722-265-992;** daily 11am–midnight) is inside the building of the philharmonic; graffiti and musical instruments decorate the walls that embrace a bohemian bonhomie well into the night. The **Philharmonic** (ℭ **0269/21-0264**) itself has been going since 1949, and lends the city of Sibiu a culturally glamorous air.

En Route to Maramureş

There's a long stretch between southern Transylvania and the northern frontier region of Maramureş; consider cutting the journey by stopping in Transylvania's capital city, **Cluj-Napoca**. A smart university town believed to be the most expensive place in the country to live, it's a cosmopolitan place, best measured by the popularity of its cafe culture; grab a seat at a venue around Piaţa Unirii and you'll find the place filled with supercool posers wearing D&G apparel and tearing around in sports cars, their faces hidden behind massive sunglasses. The best place to stay is **Déjà Vu** ⚇ (Str. Ion Ghica 2, Cluj-Napoca; ⓒ/fax **0264/35-4941/61**; www.deja-vu.ro; 80€–88€/$100–$110 double with breakfast), a great little Art Nouveau–style hotel in a quiet residential neighborhood near the historical center. The restaurant here is one of the best in town, and the staff extremely helpful.

HIKING & CLIMBING IN THE FĂGĂRAŞ MOUNTAINS

Between Braşov and Sibiu lie the lovely Făgăraş Mountains, a popular Carpathian hiking region, studded with glacial lakes and soaring peaks. Reachable during peak summer months from Wallachia along the high-altitude Transfăgărăşan Highway, there are other, less daunting routes accessed via Highway 1, running between Braşov and Sibiu. The region has plenty of overnight "cabanas," making the massif well suited to independent hikers. The main towns in the region are **Făgăraş** and **Victoria,** the latter the principal starting point for most hikers; it's just 10km (6¼ miles) south of the highway. There are great hikes toward Mount Moldeveanu (Romania's highest point at 2,543m/8,341 ft.), which is popular with climbers who can settle in for the night at **Cabana Podragu.** About 10km (6¼ miles) east of Victoria is the 17th-century **Brâncoveanu Monastery;** from the monastery, you can hike south, more or less along the Sâmbăta River, to reach **Cabana Valea Sambetei** (ⓒ **0269/31-5756**).

From **Cabana Cascadă Bâlea,** there's a cable car to take you up to 1,968m (6,560 ft.), where you can explore glacial Lake Balea, where **Villa Paltinul** (ⓒ **269-524277;** www.balea-lac.ro; try to book the main bedroom), once a small hunting lodge for Nicolae Ceauşescu, is a convenient stopover for hikers, and well-managed by Olaru Marius. From the lake, you can also follow a trail to Negoiu Peak, the region's second-highest mountain.

In winter, there's now also novelty accommodations available at the eight-roomed, highly seasonal **Bâlea Lac Ice Hotel.** Situated at an altitude of 2,040m (6,500 ft.) and created with ice from Lake Bâlea, the star-shaped igloo of a hotel takes about 1 month to build and requires an indoor temperature of 37°F (–3°C). First built in early 2006 and only available until May (at the latest), the hotel's guest rooms feature sheepskin-covered ice beds and ice versions of Brancusi sculptures. Doubles are a mere 37€ ($46); book through Meridian Travel (www.ice.hotel.balea.lac.en.meridian-travel.ro).

6 Crişana & the Banat

Romania's westernmost regions, Crişana and the Banat, only became part of Romania in 1918, before which they formed part of a unique entity in the Austro-Hungarian crown. Many visitors who travel over land from Hungary drift in through the border at Borş to stop at Oradea, capital of Bihor county in the northern part of Romanian Crişana, before taking highway E671 to the Habsburg city of Timişoara. The principal city of the Banat, this is considered the country's most forward-thinking metropole— after all it was here, in Timişoara, that the great Revolution of December 1989 was ignited, changing the course of Romanian history forever.

ORADEA

Oradea is 592km (367 miles) NW of Bucharest and 152km (94 miles) W of Cluj-Napoca

A small, prosperous city at the western limits of Romania, Oradea benefits from the marks left by the Austro-Hungarian Empire, best evidenced in the elaborate and sometimes dainty Secessionist architecture fringing its avenues and squares. A whiff of its former *fin de siècle* cosmopolitanism still hangs in the air, and the city awaits its tourist renaissance as workers restore much of the visual glory of its historic center, a program already well underway in mid-2006. While Oradea is lovely for its restrained ambience (best experienced on foot), it is also convenient for adventures into the Apuseni Mountains, with its seamless meadows, karstic formations, spectacular caves, wildlife, and traditional communities.

ARRIVAL, ORIENTATION & GETTING AROUND

Tarom (Piaţa Republicii 2; ☎ **0259/23-1918;** Mon–Fri 6:30am–8pm, Sat 10am–1pm) has early-morning weekday flights from Bucharest to Oradea's **airport** (Calea Aradului; ☎ **0259/41-6082**), situated 6km (3¾ miles) from the center. Shuttle buses run Tarom passengers to and from the airport free of charge.

Oradea's **train station** (Piaţa Bucureşti) is 1km (⅔ mile) north of the center; there are always taxis out front. Book onward travel at the **CFR office** (Mon–Fri 7am–7pm) on the corner of Calea Republicii and Piaţa Ferdinand.

Oradea operates its own (though at research time somewhat out-of-date) website, www.oradea.ro. For the real lowdown on the city, visit the offices of **Apuseni Experience,** specializing in adventure tours, but happy to help visitors find their feet (1st Floor, Piaţa Decembrie 4-6; ☎ **0259/47-2434**).

WHERE TO STAY

A slightly cheaper alternative, Hotel Scorilo (☎ **0259/47-0910;** www.hotelscorilo.ro; L200/$72/£38 double) scores low on taste (linoleum-covered headboards, melamine furniture, and wood-and-leatherette sofas) but high on service; it is situated in an old (1703) building near the Catholic Cathedral (and train station), and its in-house restaurant is the best dining option in town (see "Where to Dine," below).

Hotel Elite   It doesn't quite live up to its name, but this is Oradea's classiest hotel, situated in a residential neighborhood, just a short distance from the historic center. Guest rooms are spacious, with simple, neat furnishings, decent-size bathrooms (with tub/shower combo), and comfortable beds; the best units enjoy views onto a tree-lined park. While the atmosphere is generally tranquil and laid-back (a waistcoated barman hovering in the lobby all day waiting to take your order), handfuls of festive guests do sometimes occupy the terrace until the small hours. Helpful staff offers discreet service, and the restaurant is one of the best in town.

Str. I.C. Bratianu 26, 410051 Oradea. ☎/fax **0259/41-4924** or 0259/41-9759. www.hotelelite.ro. 30 units. 85€ ($106) double; 99€ ($124) deluxe. Rates include breakfast. MC, V. **Amenities:** Restaurant; breakfast room; 24-hr. bar;

sauna; Jacuzzi; 24-hr. room service; airport and train station transfers; car rental; laundry; medic-on-call. *In room:* A/C, TV, Internet, minibar, hair dryer, safe.

WHERE TO DINE

If you've tired of East European meat, and looking for a light southern Europe touch, **La Galleria** (© **0259/47-5490;** www.wpg.ro; Mon–Sat noon–3pm and 7–11:30pm) is the best Italian joint in town (you'll find it right near the State Theater). If not you'll find plenty of low-key, down-home Romanian/Hungarian options along or around Strada Republicii. Alternatively, head for the small, agreeable restaurant at centrally located **Hotel Elite** (see details above) where you could start with a salad of forest mushrooms with marinated vegetables, then move on to Moldavian-style pork, or the Mediterranean-style orata fish, baked with tomato, olives, and oregano.

Scorilo's ★★ ROMANIAN/HUNGARIAN   There's a stellar menu at this wonderful hotel restaurant just north of the center, and the venue is good too: In winter you can dine in the cellar, while the summer terrace is lovely, and there's live music on weekday evenings. You will however have to come well prepared to eat meat: Wild boar, goose legs cooked in champagne, and traditional Hungarian stew made with pork *and* bacon, and prepared with garlic and golden potatoes, are just a few of the favorites. If you can't decide, go all out and order the "Hunter's Plate," and sample a large array of venison.

Hotel Scorilo, Parcul Petőfi 16. © **0259/47-0910** or 0259/41-4681. Main courses L14–L63 ($5–$23/£2.65–£12). MC, V. Daily 11:30am–midnight.

EXPLORING ORADEA

Oradea has a fairly manageable center, its north and south divided by the Crişul Repede River, which flows through the city. The two main points of focus—Piaţa Republicii (north) and Piaţa Unirii (south)—lie on either side of the river, linked by one of several bridges. Running northeast from one corner of Piaţa Republicii is Calea Republicii, a long pedestrianized road lined with lovely buildings. Oradea's **Citadel** lies east of Piaţa Unirii, beyond the large Parcul Central, and behind a blight of modern concrete blocks.

Take a casual stroll down pedestrianized **Strada Republicii,** recently revamped and lined on both sides by an endless succession of Secessionist buildings, and you'll wish you were spending more time in the city, if only to browse the numerous shops and take plentiful breaks at the cafes. Don't miss a short detour down Str. Roman Ciorogariu to look at the colorful and extremely ornate facade of the **Episcopia Ortodoxâ Română (Romanian Orthodox Bishopric);** behind you is a citrus yellow building housing **Stones & Antique Consignatie** (© **0722-823-189;** Mon–Fri 10am–1pm and 4–6pm), which sells all manner of antique kitsch, and well worth a look.

At its southern end, Republicii joins **Piaţa Regele Ferdinand,** where the **State Theater (Teatrul de Stat;** © **0259/41-7864;** www.oradeatheatre.com) has been undergoing a much-needed revamp to return its facade to the original neoclassical splendor designed by Helmer and Fellner in 1900. Also worth a gander on this square is the facade of the **Art School (Scoala de Arte Oradea),** now the seat of the Philharmonic Orchestra.

Head south across the bridge over River Crişul Repede to reach wide-open and startlingly empty **Piaţa Unirii;** directly in front of you as you cross the river, is a Catholic Church obscuring the view of a **statue of Mihai Viteazul,** the great Wallachian prince said to have passed through the city before the end of his reign (1593–1601). On your right is the **City Hall,** built in 1902 and 1903, and source of the hourly tolling of the city's bell. On your left, in the distance beyond the **statue of Mihai Eminescu,** you'll see the **Synagogue.** Beyond the City Hall is the **Library,** built in 1905; opposite is the newly renovated Secessionist-style "Black Vulture Palace," or **Palatul Vulturul Negru** (1907–09), which conceals a mall-like arcade and namesake hotel; bars, restaurants, and casinos occupy the warren-like passageway under a wonderful stained-glass ceiling. Just down from the Black Eagle is Oradea's Orthodox **Moon Church (Biserica cu Lună);** built between 1784 and 1790, it is named for its unique mechanical lunar phase indicator.

To the east of Piaţa Unirii—beyond the central park, apartment blocks, and busy main road intersection—is Oradea's 13th-century **Citadel,** much expanded in the 18th century, when it took its present five-cornered bastion-enhanced proportions. Situated just south of the Criul Repede, the crumbling fortress—home the university's art department—is used for the odd upbeat event. Look out especially for medieval festivals held here in early July, when the citadel becomes a playground: there's a mix of folk, contemporary, and hard-core medieval music, and the best archers in the region compete in a serious test of mettle, dressed in Knights of the Round Table costumes of varying degrees of authenticity.

Roman Catholic Cathedral   Looking more like an administrative building than the country's largest baroque church, this imposing edifice was built between 1752 and 1780; the attractive interiors are best experienced during Mass or when organ recitals are held here. Just next-door is the **Episcopal Palace** (built in 1770) which, until January 2006, housed the regional **Museum of the Crişana;** the museum will reopen at Strada Armatei Româna 1/A as soon as the 400,000 artifacts have been relocated.

Str. Şirul Canoncilor.

ADVENTURES IN THE APUSENI MOUNTAINS

The Apuseni Mountains (the lowest-lying of the Carpathian range) are one of Romania's great adventure destinations, with opportunities not only for trekking and caving (there are some 7,000 caves in the region), but also river-based adventures, cycling, rock-climbing, bird-watching, cross-country skiing, horse-riding, and even dog-sledding. The best way to experience this region—home to steadily increasingly lynx and wolf populations, and high-altitude wetlands with carnivorous plants and rare orchid species—is with **Apuseni Experience** ★★★ (no. 8, 1st floor, Piaţa Decembrie 4–6, Oradea; © **0259/47-2434;** www.apuseniexperience.ro), probably Romania's top mountain-adventure company. The company employs mostly specialists in their field, who will lead you on a variety of treks and caving adventures, including a visit to the country's longest (Vantului) cave and the Ciur Ponor cave system, with preserved prehistoric human footprints and a 3,500-year-old subterranean glacier. Experienced cavers can arrange trips to underground waterfalls and lakes (including the Avenul din Sesuri, 217m/712 ft. below ground); less extreme treks, hikes, and bike trips take you into the heart of the so-called "Lost World" plateau to try your hand at shepherding, or tracking wolves and bears. During all of their trips, Apuseni Experience will introduce you to the culture of the local communities, or you can focus entirely on a cultural tour. Apuseni Experience is also involved in various internationally recognized projects aiming to preserve the region's unique heritage. While you can tailor-make your adventure, combining activities, there are also predetermined programs, with costs per head starting at 53€ ($66) per day, all-inclusive. Accommodations are in mountain guesthouses, family homes, and rustic mountain chalets, or there's always the option of camping under the stars. To design an adventure that's to your taste, contact Paul Iacobaş (© **0745-602-301;** paul@apuseniexperience.ro), who started Apuseni Experience after 3 years with the U.S. Peace Corps.

TIMIŞOARA ✶✶✶
Timişoara is 562km (348 miles) W of Bucharest

Timişoara (pronounced tim-*uh*-schwara, and called "Temesvar" by Hungarians) is considered Romania's most cosmopolitan city, defined by its strong associations with western European culture and progressive aspirations: This was the first European city to install street lighting, and the first to run off hydroelectric power. You'd never guess that this peaceful place, with its languid parks and gardens and gorgeous, lively squares, was once a hotbed of military and political violence: Timişoara, regarded as the first free city of Romania, was for a long time one of the major military bases against the Ottoman Empire in its ongoing advance on central Europe. When the citadel did finally fall to the Turkish armies, it took 164 years of planned invasions, and more than one army, before the Habsburgs finally managed to toss out the Turkish occupiers. The Austrian stamp remains clearly evident in the city's urban design, appealing for its voluminous parks and squares, and mix of baroque, neoclassical, and Art Nouveau buildings.

ARRIVAL, ORIENTATION & GETTING AROUND

Tarom (B-dul Revoluţiei 3–5; © **0256/49-0150;** Mon–Fri 7am–7pm, Sat 7am–1pm) flies from Bucharest to Timişoara each weekday at 9am. **Carpat Air** (www.carpatair.ro) flies the same route Monday through Saturday. You can skip Bucharest entirely by flying straight to Timişoara from London with a number of airlines, including Tarom, Malev, Austrian, Lufthansa, Alitalia, and low-cost carrier Easyjet. There are also flights from other European cities, so it's worth investigating before booking yourself directly to the capital. Situated 13km (8 miles) from the city center, the **airport** (Calea Lugojului; © **0256/49-1637**) has a free shuttle service into town for Tarom passengers; taxis and public buses are also available. **Avis** rents cars at the airport (© **0256/20-3234**) or in town (© **0256/30-9425**).

Trains from practically anywhere in Romania and a number of European cities pull in at **Gară Timişoara-Nord** (Str. Gării 2; © **0256/49-1696**). Onward tickets can be purchased at the **CFR Agenţie de Voiaj** (Piaţa Vitoriei 2; © **0256/49-1889**) on weekdays, but be warned that there is almost always a queue with lengthy waits.

WHERE TO STAY

La Residenza ✶✶✶ *(Value* This is one of the best hotels in Romania (and the country's only member of Small Elegant Hotels of the World); the preferred destination for business bigwigs and visiting celebs (this is where Shakira bedded down when she rocked the city in 2006). Behind the shuttered walls is a family of hoteliers with a discreet sense of luxury; you're made to feel as though you are in your very own intimate and stylish home, with plenty of added comforts. Accommodations are elegant, combining distinctive old-world styling with Italian mattresses, Spanish drapes, and Belgian carpets; select antiques and lovely decorative elements work to create a remarkably unaffected sense of luxury. Standard (comfort) rooms are quite spacious (and a steal at just under 100€/$120), but for an extra 30€ ($36) you can book the 28-sq.-m (301-sq.-ft.) deluxe unit; if you're up for a splurge the Garden suite is tops.

Public spaces are like an old country mansion; along with the fine furniture and art-works, the "living room" has a small library, plasma TV, chess set, fireplace, and piano. The garden, centered on a pool with its own pavilion, features apricot, fig, and quince trees that provide fruit for the homemade jams served at breakfast. The charming German owners (very much a family affair) are a great source on the city's best places to dine or shop.

Str Independenței 14, Timişoara. © **0256/40-1080.** Fax 0256/40-1079. www.laresidenza.ro. 20 units. L370 ($133/ £71) double; L450 ($162/£86) deluxe; L470 ($169/£90) superior deluxe; L530 ($191/£102) suite; L570 ($205/£109) garden suite; L620 ($223/£119) executive suite. Rates include breakfast and taxes. MC, V. **Amenities:** Restaurant; bar; lounge; swimming pool; sauna; massage; library; room service; laundry; beauty treatments; car rental. *In room:* A/C, TV, Internet, minibar, hair dryer, safe.

Rhegina Blue ⟨★⟩   This is a pretty reasonable four-floor hotel, with contemporary, modernist styling (though not that much cheaper than the entry level rooms at the vastly superior La Residenza). Guest rooms are functional, comfortable, and continue the modernist theme—plenty of straight, clean lines, offset by soft fabrics and the odd floral arrangement; they're carpeted with small balconies. Best of all, near the koi pond and Japanese garden (replete with white rabbits and turtles) is a gorgeous pool surrounded by a luxurious wooden deck. Staff can help with sightseeing. Its sister establishment, **Hotel Reghina** (Str. Cozia 91; © **0256/49-1166;** www.hotel-reghina.ro) is an award-winning, slightly cheaper option with similar service standards and comfortable, if somewhat kitschy guest rooms; there are six doubles (L240/$86/£44) and six suites (L300–L400/$108–$144/£58–£77).

Str. Cozia 51–53, Timişoara. © **0256/40-7299.** Fax 0256/40-7298. www.reghina-blue.ro. 50 units. 85€ ($106) double; 171€ ($214) penthouse apt. Rates include breakfast. AE, DC, MC, V. **Amenities:** Restaurant; bar; swimming pool; fitness center, sauna; business center, room service; laundry; airport transfers; Wi-Fi. *In room:* A/C, TV, Internet, minibar, hair dryer.

Savoy Hotel ⟨★⟩   Built in 1935, the Savoy recently underwent a complete renovation, much touted in the Romanian design media, in which the original Art Deco facade was retained while creating a contemporary, minimalist interior. Designers have successfully restored the exclusive, tasteful ambience for which the property was once known but the public spaces are thoroughly modernized, with huge walls of glass to let in loads of light and elegant, spacious guest rooms imbued with a similarly minimalist aesthetic. With a fresh, modern makeover, the Savoy is one of the nicest places in the city, and isn't too far from the center. Service is friendly and professional, and there's good dining in chef Gabriel Cretu's intimate restaurant.

Spl. Tudor Vladimirescu 2, Timisoara 300193. © **0256/24-9900.** Fax 0256/27-5500. www.hotelsavoy-tm.com. 55 units. 77€ ($96) double; 97€ ($121) studio; 180€ ($225) suite. MC, V. **Amenities:** Restaurant; bar; fitness center, sauna; conferencing; room service; laundry; information desk. *In room:* A/C, TV, Internet, minibar, safe.

WHERE TO DINE

While the most popular restaurant in town is the tourist-friendly **Lloyd's** (© **0256/ 20-3752**) on Piaţa Victoriei, the highly visible location comes at a cost: besides the average food (which often arrives cold), there are frequent bag-snatchings by petty criminals and prostitutes. Give it a miss as Timişoara has a wide range of excellent restaurants, many of which were established by members of the city's Italian expat community. Da Toni is our top choice but for high-profile dining (and celebrity prices), head to **Ristorante Al Duomo** ⟨★⟩ (Str. Paul Chinezu 2; © **0256/43-7199**), near the Opera; the Italian chef has not only worked his way into the hearts of local diners, but also onto national television. Also worth a mention is **Pozzo dei Desideri** ✶✶ (Str. E. Gojdu 6; ✆ **0256/22-9170**), owned by affable restaurateur Dana, who cooks a melt-in-the-mouth lamb. But if you want to be right near the action, head for **Casa cu flori** ✶ **(House of Flowers;** Str. Alba Iulia 1; ✆ **0256/43-5080;** www.casacuflori.ro), an elegant restaurant serving Romanian specialties on the first floor of a house on the road linking Piaţa Victoriei with Piaţa Liberatii; the small terrace downstairs is ideal for watching the constant ebb of human traffic between these two popular spaces.

Da Toni ✶✶✶ ITALIAN   If you want to know where the Italian ambassador and his wife get a taste of home, come to this wonderfully relaxed and always bustling Tuscan eatery. A magnetic Italian named Toni, whose robust charms keep this lively eatery packed to bursting, serves authentic pizza and pasta. Toni's son, Oliviero, sells the best ice cream in town, so you know what to do for dessert.

Str. Daliei 14. ✆ **0256/49-0298.** Main courses L9–L28 ($3.25–$10/£1.70–£5.40). MC, V. Daily noon–midnight.

EXPLORING TIMIŞOARA

To the southern end of the center, the Bega Canal forms a natural boundary between the old and newer parts of the city, surrounded on both banks by expansive **Parcul Central (Central Park),** favored by amorous students from the University of West Timişoara. North of the center are the **Botanical Gardens,** and nearby, tucked behind remnants of the city's ancient bastion walls, is the city's subdued open-air **market,** selling fresh farm consumables; visit the stalls in the middle for excellent honey as well as traditional herbal medicines. Near the market is Str. Gheorghe Lazăr, for a selection of good fashion outlets. Also in the vicinity is the **Great Synagogue** (Str. Mărăşeşti 6), which is under renovation until October 2008, but worth a look for the lovely facade.

The city's main areas of interest, however, are its squares and pedestrianized boulevards, surrounded on all sides by architecturally idiosyncratic buildings that form an elegant backdrop to the public lives on display. All day long, people gather for drinks and gossip energetically; it's an atmosphere of complete civil flamboyance in a city largely remembered as the site of some of the most brutal political martyrdoms in recent Romanian history.

Piaţa Victoriei—lorded over by the delightful **Metropolitan Orthodox Cathedral** (reviewed below) at its southern end—is where the first blows of the great December 1989 Revolution were struck; you can still see bullet holes in some of the buildings, bizarre given the exuberant atmosphere of the square's high-society life. At the southern end, in front of the Orthodox Cathedral, is the **Luna Capitolina,** a monument to the victims of the revolution. At the north end is the city's 18th-century **National Theater and Opera House (Teatrul Naţional şi Opera Română;** Str. Mărăşeşti 2; ✆ **0256/20-1284)** not much to look at, but a fine place for an evening of culture (see "Timişoara After Dark," below). From the Orthodox Cathedral, it's an almost straight route north through Piaţa Victoriei, past the Opera House and then along Alba Iulia into **Piaţa Libertăţii,** "Liberty Square," the small square that is the city's historical center. This is where, in the early 16th century, the leader of the peasant uprising then raging across Transylvania was executed in public view before his followers were forced to eat pieces of his burned flesh. Now the public view is of languid sessions on cafe terraces, in full view of the baroque **Old Town Hall** (1734), housing the university's music school. Following the road north past the Town Hall, you will soon arrive at Piaţa Unirii, a large square surrounded by monumental, colorful baroque buildings and centered on a **column** erected in memory of victims of plague which struck in the

1730s. While you'll have your work cut out for you choosing which cafe or lounge-style terrace bar to arrange yourself at, its worth first taking in some of the more note-worthy monuments, particularly the pale yellow **Serbian Orthodox Church** across the road from the Sinatra Club (a popular place for a midday drink), and—on the other side of the square—the **Roman Catholic Cathedral,** both built in the mid-1700s. At the southern edge of Piața Unirii, Strada Palanca leads east past the **Art Museum,** the **Dicasterial Palace,** and then finally to the **Banat Ethnographic Museum.**

Metropolitan Orthodox Cathedral ⟨★★⟩ One of Romania's loveliest cathedrals, the 83m (272-ft.) towering Catedrala Mitropolitana Ortodoxa adds color to the sky-line at the southern end of Piața Victoriei; combining neo-Byzantine and Moldavian architectural elements, it's brick walls are an ornate patchwork of ocher and yellow

---

Touring the Revolution

In December 1989, after 45 years of Communism, ordinary Romanians had tired of the oppression, poverty, and enforced slavery to a system that con-trolled all facets of life. Ceaușescu had effectively cut his country off from the outside world, supplying citizens with only what little propaganda he deemed appropriate. While official reports spoke of industrial might and technological progress, in reality ordinary people were starving and those who spoke out were quickly silenced. In western frontier cities like Timișoara, however, media reports seeping in from nearby Hungary prob-ably contributed to a more cantankerous social atmosphere. As the country prepared to celebrate another morbid Christmas, the long-awaited cries for change suddenly became roaring protests. Over a period of 10 days, begin-ning with urgent gatherings in Timișoara, protestors demonstrated their opposition to the regime, destroying its symbols and burning effigies of Ceaușescu, and chanting "Down with Ceaușescu! Down with Communism! We want liberty!" The revolution is believed to have been sparked by a gathering at the **Tökes Reform Church (Biserica Reformată Tökés;** Str. Tim-otei Cipariu 1; ℭ **0256/49-2992),** south of the Bega Canal; here, on Decem-ber 15, thousands of protestors rallied together to oppose the Securitate's planned eviction of Pastor Lászlo Tökes, a known opponent of the Ceaușescu regime. In what many believe was a calculated opportunity, the small uprising quickly escalated, gaining momentum as it heaved toward **Piața Victoriei (Victory Square).** For 3 days, the rally continued, culminating in Ceaușescu's order to open fire. Look carefully for evidence of the event; you'll find bullet holes and plaques around the long, broad square now sur-rounded by relaxed cafes and boutiques. At one end of the square, across a busy road, the **Orthodox Cathedral** is where many young protestors lost their lives. Near Piața Unirii is the **Museum of the December 1989 Uprising** (Str. Emanuil Ungureanu 8; daily 9am–5pm; donations expected) which charts the events of the Revolution through detailed exhibits, including photographs, paintings, and a video, and dutifully looked after by Dr. Traian Orban, himself a survivor who was shot during the uprising.

bands, while the colored mosaic-style shingles on the turreted spires create dynamic geometric patterns. It's a young church (built 1936–46), but the atmosphere generated by its strong associations with the 1989 Revolution complements the somber spirituality of the interior, dominated by three gigantic chandeliers that float above the regular stream of worshipers. Since 1956, the cathedral has held the relics of St. Joseph the New (in a box to the right of the entrance). Joseph, the patron saint of the Banat, was born in Dalmatia in 1568 and became Metropolitan of Timişoara in 1658; he apparently had the gift of prophesy and could perform miracles, bringing on the rains which quelled a great fire that once threatened the city. In the basement, there's a **museum** (with irregular hours), exhibiting religious icons, some 500 years old.

B-dul 16 Decembrie 1989 and B-dul Regele Ferdinand I.

TIMIŞOARA AFTER DARK

For event listings, pick up a free issue of *24-Fun Timişoara,* in Romanian with fragments of English, but which gives a fairly good idea of what's on and where.

Timişoara enjoys strong cultural associations and is proud of having independent German, Hungarian, and Romanian theaters; first up on the list of highlights is an opera or drama at the **National Theater and Opera House** (Str. Mărăşeşti 2; © **0256/20-1284**) For an evening of classical music, head to the other end of Piaţa Victoriei to find the **State Philharmonic Theater (Filharmonia de Stat Banatul;** B-dul C.D. Loga 2; © **0256/49-2521**) to the left of the Cathedral. Tickets for both venues are available at **Agenţia Teatrală** (Str. Maraşe şti; © **0256/49-9908;** Tues–Sun 10am–1pm and 5–7pm) just around the corner from the Opera House entrance. For jazz, the best place is **Jazz Club Pod 16** 🎭🎭 (Pod Piaţa Maria; © **0729-945-397;** www.jazzclubpod16.ro), which has something to look forward to every night of the week; look out especially for an outfit named Ţapinarii.

Komodo 🎭🎭 (Str. Gheorghe Lazăr; © **0722-279-177;** 9am–late) is the city's best lounge bar, slickly designed for a chic crowd; there's a dance floor downstairs and the music varies from retro to house, but the atmosphere in the cocktail lounge is decidedly "Buddha Bar." To get your spirits up, order a Velvet Hammer or Playa Azul; caipirinhas and caipiroskas are the best in the Banat. Komodo occupies an unmarked building; look out for the round streetlights out front.

7 Maramureş

The northern county of Maramureş (pronounced mah-rah-*moo*-resh), situated on the Ukraine border, is widely regarded as a kind of living museum; lifestyles and culture have changed little in well over a century. Village life is surreal, defined by working horses, carts laden with hay, elaborately carved wooden gates, and people in traditional costumes. Aside from an otherworldly way of life, the most celebrated of the attractions here are the famous Maramureş wooden churches, a number of which are now inscribed on UNESCO's World Heritage List. And as if wood-hewn churches in time-forgotten villages were not enough, Maramureş is also blessed with an idyllic setting, its backcountry roads providing surrender-to-the-moment journeys through valleys torn through majestic mountainscapes, the most famous perhaps being the Rodna Mountains, good for hiking and adventures far away from humanity.

Described here is a plan for exploration of the loveliest parts of Maramureş, discovering its traditional villages, a selection of churches, and two of the most idiosyncratic attractions in Romania, the Merry Cemetery of Săpânţa, and the Prison Museum in

Sighet. Enchanting as the region is, it's bucolic rhythms won't be around forever, so prioritize a visit here soon.

ARRIVAL, ORIENTATION & GETTING AROUND

Tarom (B-dul Bucureşti 5; ✆ 0262/22-1624) flies from Bucharest to **Baia Mare,** the main city, on Tuesday (7am), Thursday (4:25pm), and Friday (8:45am). The **airport** (✆ 0262/22-2245; www.baiamareairport.po.ro) is 10km (6¼ miles) from the city at Tautii Magheraus village; a free shuttle will take you into town. There are also daily **train connections** from the capital and most other major centers, including Cluj, Oradea, Braşov, and Suceava; Baia Mare's **train station** is at Str. Gării 4 (✆ 0262/22-0995). One train per day pulls in from Budapest. It's also possible to catch a train directly to **Sighetu Marmaţiei,** near the Ukraine border, although you're looking at a much longer journey. You can purchase onward tickets at the **CFR** office (Str. Victoriei 57; ✆ 0262/21-9113).

Maramureş is best explored by car, and you are better off having a driver who knows their way around; the region may be small, but it is certainly not signposted to make life easy for outsiders. If you need a taxi in Baia Mare, call **Stotax** (✆ 0262/953) or **Gallant** (✆ 0262/942); rates are .25€ (30¢) per kilometer.

All the villages are situated in two valleys in the eastern part of Maramureş, occupying a fairly compact region. These are the **Mara Valley** and the **Izei Valley,** both northeast of the district capital, **Baia Mare,** which is likely to be your point of arrival in Maramureş. Three days in the region, using a car and driver and staying at private homes in the villages (avoid the larger towns, which have little to recommend them aside from their small historic centers) will give you ample time. Like the larger towns, Baia Mare is disappointing; arrange to be met at the airport or station by your driver, and head immediately for the Mara Valley and beyond (perhaps stopping briefly at Baia Mare's colorful outdoor market to pick up some fresh fruit, and perhaps a cheese that you can give to your host as a gift).

ORGANIZING YOUR MARAMUREŞ EXPERIENCE

For complete peace of mind, contact **DiscoveRomania** ✮✮✮ (see "Tours & Travel Agents," at the beginning of this chapter). Laura Vesa will tailor-make a Maramureş holiday for you, arranging transport (about 50€/$63 per day) and accommodations (20€–25€/$25–$31 per person per day, half board) and incorporating fabulous experiences along the way. You can arrange everything via e-mail, and know that there's nothing to worry about; she will also let you know about local festivals so that you can plan your trip accordingly. DiscoveRomania is dedicated to eco-sensible sustainable tourism, so accommodations are mostly in village homes (three of these are reviewed below); if you insist on being in a city hotel, ask for one of the options in Baia Mare or Sighet that are suggested below. Iron out the details of your itinerary with Laura well in advance since your hosts may not speak English; this won't be a problem if you've arranged for a guide to accompany you, but if you're doing without a guide, it's best that your hosts understand all your needs while you're there.

If you leave your planning until your arrival in Maramureş, head for the **Mara Holiday Travel Agency** inside Baia Mare's Mara Hotel (B-dul. Unirii 11; ✆ 062/22-6656; mara@sintec.ro); on fairly short notice, they'll put together an itinerary and set you up with transport (70€–80€/$88–$100 per day) and village accommodations (20€–25€/$25–$31 per person per night) in the Iza Valley.

WHERE TO STAY & DINE
VILLAGE STAYS

Home stays are a fine way of discovering the region and its people, and locals have discovered that they are an excellent way to supplement their incomes—in some villages, it seems as though every second house is open for business, offering beds and home-cooked meals. The quality of the experience may differ from home to home (a firmer mattress here, a larger shower room there), but ultimately, it is dealings with your convivial hosts that translate into memories. The three options described below can all be arranged as part of a tour with DiscoveRomania; each is in a unique village environment.

Casa Popicu ★★   The pace of life in Hoteni village is as relaxed and charmed as the couple who own this homestead; Ion Pop, nicknamed "Popicu" by his enchanting wife, Geţa, is one of Romania's most sought-after folk musicians, and is acknowledged internationally for his contribution to the preservation of traditional music. Popicu and Geţa have two wooden houses (including their original 150-year-old home) and a modern cottage each with guest accommodations; here, at the foot of the Gutai Mountains, they farm with bees, fish and chickens, and share their garden with three lawn-mowing sheep and an obedient shepherd dog. Lodging options range from en-suite rooms in the modern cottage, to rooms with shared bathrooms, and two-bedroom suites with private facilities. Most of the rooms enjoy a view over the surrounding farm landscape; some have private balconies. Geţa prepares hearty meals, served in the traditional dining room of the main house; she's also mastering English, and loves taking guests out on the road to see the sights, crossing herself meaningfully each time she starts the car. Some units have en-suite bathroom.

Hoteni Village 37A, Mara Valley. ✆ **0722-979-048** or 0262/37-4546. 11 units. 20€–25€ ($25–$31) per person per night. No credit cards. **Amenities:** Kitchen; dining room; living room w/TV stereo.

Pensiunea Ileana Teleptean ★   Vadu Izea is practically on the southern edge of Sighet; development here has benefited tremendously from Belgian and French economic support, and you're likely to witness a blurring of traditional and contemporary lifestyles. Arguably the best guesthouse here is Casa Teleptean, owned and run by vivacious Illeana who doesn't speak English, but is permanently beaming and busy. You'll recognize the house by its superb carved gateway and the collection of red pots that decorate the tree next to it. Topped by a beautifully carved roof, the three-story house offers neatly appointed, simple guest rooms with wooden floors, rugs, and beds covered with clean, patterned linens. Most of these have one bathroom between two rooms. On the second floor there are two carpeted rooms with en-suite bathrooms (showers only); these also share a terrace with wonderful views. Also on the property is a traditional "honeymoon" apartment, filled with woolen blankets and tapestries. There's also a garden terrace area where Ileana serves excellent home-cooked meals; her children (who speak some English) are part of a traditional music group who often put on entertainment for guests. While here, visit the local **museum,** which is also the oldest house in the village, built in 1750; you can also arrange private tours of the area by contacting Ramona Ardelean (✆ **0744/82-7829**).

Vadu Izei 506. ✆ **0262/33-0474** or 0742-492-240. 9 units. 20€–25€ ($25–$31) per person per night. No credit cards. *In room:* TV.

The Priest's House, Botiza (Pensiunea Bebecaru) ★   Although it's known as the "Priest's House," these accommodations are firmly under the management of the priest's delightful wife, Victoria Bebecaru. The couple may not speak a word of English

(Victoria does speak French), but they are warm and welcoming, and it's a bizarre honor to spend time with the village's spiritual leader (a man who incidentally also makes a potent plum *tuica,* which you'll sample at mealtimes). There are three upstairs rooms available in the priest's private home, a brick house stuffed full of books, handicrafts, animal skins, and family photos, but you'll probably want to opt for a room in their nearby guesthouse, fashioned out of wood in traditional Maramureş style. There are four twin-bedded rooms sharing three bathrooms. Accommodations are on the first floor, reached via a spiral staircase, while downstairs are themed artisan studios where Victoria works on her woolen handicrafts. You'll have just about everything you need for a relaxed escape from modernity.

No. 743, Botiza. (✆ **0262/33-4207** or 0262/33-4107. 6 units. 20€–25€ ($25–$31) per person per night. **Amenities:** TV; fishing; horseback riding.

IN SIGHETU MARMAŢIEI

Casa Iurca de Câlineşti ★★   This gorgeous *pensiune,* next door to the Elie Wiesel Museum, is owned and operated by a noble family whose members trace their lineage from 1374; they've combined traditional elements such as carved doorways and craftwork furniture with modern comforts to create the best accommodations in Sighet. Neatly appointed twin-bedded guest rooms (there are no double beds) feature wooden floors and attractive country-style wooden furniture; they also have large bathrooms with showers. Room no. 5 has a small porch overlooking the wood-beam courtyard where costumed waiters serve local cuisine. There's also a themed indoor restaurant with a quaint fireplace and decorative touches, like exposed brick, clay jugs, and traditional cloth hangings, to create a village dining room atmosphere; this is easily the best place to dine anywhere in the region. Ask the titled owners about their swanky country house, where you can also arrange to stay.

Str. Dragoş Vodă, Sighetu Marmaţiei. (✆ **0262/31-8882.** Fax 0262/31-8885. www.casaiurca.com. 5 units. L150 ($54/£29) double. MC, V. **Amenities:** Restaurant; bar; traditional performances; laundry. *In room:* A/C, TV, Internet, minibar, hair dryer.

IN BAIA MARE

If you must stay in Baia Mare because of an early or late departure or arrival, there's a clutch of relatively decent hotels. Recently renovated, **Hotel Rivulus** (Str. Culturii 3, Baia Mare; (✆ **0262/21-6302;** www.hotelrivulus.ro; 57€/$71 double with breakfast) is right in the center of town. It's a slightly stiff business hotel with a no-nonsense atmosphere; nevertheless, the refurbished rooms are smart and comfortable (beware of the cheaper two-star rooms, though), and have small private balconies. There's a decent restaurant and a popular terrace-cafe. Alternatively **Pensiune Union** (Str. Crisan 9, Baia Mare; (✆ **0262/21-5752;** L130–L160/$47–$58/£25–£31) offers good value—book the massive honeymoon suite, featuring a four-poster bed and football-stadium bathroom with sunken tub. There are also two smaller rooms in this mustard-and-green colored mansion, but rates are so similar that you might as well take the more romantic option. Styling is eclectic at best; elaborate chandeliers, leather sofas, and wooden headboards combine in a garish approximation of Maramureş city-style.

There's a variety of popular cafes and bars around the cobblestone town center, **Piaţa Libertăţii**—you could do a lot worse than **Corvin Medieval Restaurant,** worth a visit for the refreshingly naive-kitsch design (the whole place is decked out in faux-medieval memorabilia in a series of brick-vaulted rooms, with mannequins dressed in period costume; even the waitresses are styled as serving wenches) as well as the good

Hungarian food. You'll sit on stiff Knights of the Round Table chairs and drink from large wine goblets as a bib is tied around your neck in true medieval feast style. After, shimmy on over to the **Barbarossa;** marked by two pirate statues at the entrance, this is possibly the most popular bar in town, with a hip, sexy crowd filling its outdoor tables.

WHAT TO SEE & DO

BAIA MARE & THE MARA VALLEY

Tracing its history from the early 1300s, when it grew as a gold-mining center and became a prized possession of the Hungarian royal family, Baia Mare (which means "Big Mine") is today better known for a range of 20th-century industrial-chemical disasters. Most recently, in January 2000, the Maramureş district capital was the site of the devastating Aurul Gold Mine cyanine-spill disaster, from which the greater European region is yet to recover. Baia Mare has for a long time had little to recommend it; there is a revolution afoot, however, and the town appears to be preparing for a revival. Keenest evidence of this is in and around its large cobblestone town center, **Piaţa Libertăţii,** which is now a perfectly pleasant place from which to admire the surrounding medieval and classical architecture, some of which dates from the 14th and 15th centuries.

That said, it's only once you've left Baia Mare, and passed through the dying mining town of Baia Sprie, that you'll lose your heart to Maramureş. Named for the Mara River, which runs from Baia Mare to Sighetu Marmaţiei, the **Mara Valley** is dotted with villages that epitomize the tranquil spirit of Maramureş, and where you'll discover many of the unique wooden churches that have brought architectural renown to the region. From Baia Sprie, the road forks; head south to reach the villages of **Plopiş** and **Surdeşti,** both with UNESCO-protected wooden churches. From Surdeşti, the road continues north through Cavnic and over the **Neteda Pass,** affording terrific mountainous views from 1,040m (3,411 ft.). The next village, also with a famous church, is **Budeşti.** From here, one of two northerly roads leads to **Ocna Şugatag,** a tiny former spa village, where salt was mined until 50 years ago. Most appealing of the villages in the vicinity is **Hoteni,** a total escape from the world and a perfectly positioned base from which to explore other parts of the Mara Valley. Be sure to visit Hoteni's wooden church and the nearby church at **Deseşti.** It's also worth making the effort to visit the hillside church in the village of **Călineşti.**

SIGHETU MARMAŢIEI & SĂPÂNŢA

Sighet is 67km (42 miles) N of Baia Mare; Săpânţa is 12km (7½ miles) NW of Sighet

Close to the Ukraine border, Sighetu Marmaţiei (usually referred to as "Sighet") is a relatively quiet market town, and the cultural center of Maramureş. Sighet is also home to one of the world's finest anti-Communism museums (reviewed below), also referred to as the Prison Museum; if you see only one thing here, make this it. Parts of the midtown **Ethnographic Museum** (Piaţa Libertăţii 15) pertain to the local way of life in a vaguely informative manner; included is a cornucopia of traditional costumes, exhibited alongside scarecrowlike effigies (one of which even has an erect corn cob phallus). Sighet is also remembered as the birthplace of Elie Wiesel, the Jewish writer who coined the termed "Holocaust" and won the 1986 Nobel Peace Prize. Wiesel himself now lives in Boston, but the house where he lived before the war has been converted into a rather unexciting museum known as **Casa Elie Wiesel** (corner of Str. Dragoş Vodă and Str. Tudor Vladimirescu). Only one of the eight synagogues still exists, serving the tiny (30) population; it's at Str. Bessarabia, number 10. For more information about the synagogue and other aspects of Maramureş's Jewish history, visit the adjacent **Jewish Community Center** (✆ **0262/31-1652**; Tues–Sun 10am–4pm). Just outside of town, Sighet's **Village Museum** is another of Romania's many open-air exhibitions curating compendium-size collections of traditional homesteads; you'll get far more pleasure out of experiencing the villages firsthand.

Sighet is also very convenient for the nearby village of Săpânţa, where one of the country's most imaginative and unlikely attractions—a colorful cemetery (reviewed below)—is located.

Memorial Museum of the Victims of Communism and the Resistance ★★★

One of the most evocative museums in Romania, Sighet's Memorial Museum was built as a prison in 1897; in 1948 it became a political prison and remained as such until 1955. During that time, around 200 political prisoners—former leaders, academics, Catholic priests and bishops, and other enemies of the state—were detained, tortured, and kept hidden from public view; a quarter of these men died during their imprisonment. In 1997, the prison became a museum—alongside similar projects at Auschwitz and Normandy—dedicated to the memory of those who became victims of an authoritarian political regime. The 80 or so cells serve as exhibition rooms, each one shedding light on a different aspect of the tyrannies of Romania's 20th-century history, with particular focus on the atrocities of Ceauşescu as well as the abuses wrought on individuals and groups during the transition to Communism in the wake of World War II. Among the stirring exhibits is a corridor wall lined with 3,000 photographs of Romanian political prisoners. You'll see the tiny cell where 80-year-old former Prime Minister Iuliu Maniu died in 1953. Less important prisoners shared larger cells with up to 80 inmates. The so-called Black Cell was used for punishing inmates, who were often forced to stand chained and naked for "offenses" such as talking or looking at one another. The courtyard, one of two spaces where prisoners were allowed outside for 10 minutes per week, now houses a memorial chamber inscribed with the names of thousands of victims of Communism.

Str. Cornelieu Corposcu 4, Sighet. ✆ **0262/31-9424.** www.memorialsighet.ro. L5 ($1.80/£1) adults; L2 (70¢/40p) students, children, and seniors; L3 ($1.10/60p) photography. Apr 15–Oct 15 Daily 9:30am–6:30pm; Oct 16–Apr 14 Tues–Sun 10am–4pm. Last entry 30 min. before closing.

Săpânţa's Merry Cemetery ★★★

Apparently, the genealogical line from the ancient Dacians and the people of Maramureş is purer than elsewhere in Romania, as is evidenced in their cultural attitude toward death. The Dacians were often praised for their fearlessness in battle, which was linked to their belief in their supreme god, Zalmoxis, and in the afterlife. In contemporary Maramureş, villagers still don't see death as a tragedy; this pragmatic understanding of the relationship between life and the hereafter is exemplified in the unusual artistry practiced at Săpânţa's **Cimitirul Vesel,** or "Cheerful Cemetery," a zany collection of over 800 carved and colorfully painted wooden headstones surrounding the village church (built in 1886). The idea of marking the graves with anecdotal images and amusing epitaphs was that of Stan Ioan Pâtras, who died in 1977 and now occupying his own blue-marked grave facing the church entrance. Pătraş dedicated himself to creating grave markings that truly served the purpose of remembering those who lie buried here; the dedications either encapsulate the spirit of the life or describe the moment of death of the individual buried beneath it. Some simply describe the occupation of the buried person, while others come across as damning messages from beyond the grave; the poem on the tombstone of a baby girl reads: "Burn in hell, you damn taxi that came from Sibiu. As large as Romania is, you couldn't find another place to stop. Only in front of my house, to kill me." Pătraş's legacy continues today through Dumitru Pop who has been responsible for the headstones for 3 decades now; Pop runs a small **museum** dedicated to Pătraş, not far from the cemetery, where he will also demonstrate how the headstones are created.

Cimitirul Vesel, Săpânţa, 12km (7½ miles) northwest of Sighet. ℂ 0262/37-2127. Cemetery and museum admission each L3 ($1.10/60p). Daily sunrise–sunset.

IZEI VALLEY

Gorgeous Valea Izei is a hypnotically bucolic world between Sighet and the village of Moisei, farther east. Starting with **Vadu Izei,** 5km (3 miles) southeast of Sighet, an exploration of this lovely valley will transport you back in time where horse carts outnumber cars, traditional dress is more pervasive than modern attire, and lining the roads are beautiful houses with thatched roofs and fantastic carved wooden gates, filled with elegant folkloric details. Practically every village also has its own exquisite wooden church worthy of exploration (although hunting down the key is often an adventure on its own). Beyond Vadu Izei are the villages of Onceşti and then **Bârsana,** site of a popular monastery and fabulous wooden church (see below). Farther south and east, the valley road passes through Roza Vlea and then splits; head southwest to the sprawling village of **Botiza,** where you can stay in the home of the local priest (see above), and hike (or drive) to the church of Poienile Izei, painted with horrific images of damnation and punishment. Back along the main road, it's a short journey to Ieud, known for the famous **Church on the Hill,** originally established in 1364, but rebuilt in the mid–18th century after destruction at the hands of the Tartars. Ieud's other, "lower" church is also worth a visit.

Each village usually has a dedicated market day, when everyone heads for the center to buy necessities and exchange gossip. You'll probably also encounter villagers practicing traditional crafts; here the age-old pastime of sitting on a bench in front of the house watching the world go by while spinning wool or simply waiting for the daily gossip is still in evidence. Of course, things are changing; satellite dishes signal a time when simple entertainments are being replaced by the tedium of television, and younger generations who set off to earn their fortunes in other parts of Europe are

Festival Fever

Maramureş villagers are known for their traditional weekly neighborhood parties, known as *băută*. Of course, in the age of television, the party spirit is harder to sustain, but some traditional village festivals continue to hold out. In early May, Hoteni Village hosts the 2-week **Tânjaua de pe Mara** fertility festival to celebrate the completion of the spring plowing; folk music and dancing mark the occasion. In mid-July, Vadu Izea hosts the spectacular **Maramizical Festival,** a 4-day celebration of international folk music. In winter, it's Sighet that comes to life when the **Winter Customs Festival** hits town on December 27. The day is imbued with folkloric symbolism and good old-fashioned fun, and everyone dresses in traditional costumes and young men run through the streets wearing grotesque masks while cowbells dangle from their waists. For the when and where of Maramureş festivals, contact DiscoveRomania (see "Organizing Your Maramureş Experience," earlier in this chapter).

returning to build ugly concrete houses that will, if unchecked, blight this idyllic world forever.

THE WOODEN CHURCHES OF MARAMUREŞ

Traditional timber architecture defines the unique churches of Maramureş; built on a pebble-filled stone block base, they are a peculiar evolution of the Gothic style, based on the *Blockbau* system, using traditional techniques developed over generations by the stone- and woodcutters of the region. Oak or pine beams are assembled using V-, U-, or T-shaped joints, allowing solid, but flexible constructions, with a high, steep double-pitched roof. That's the technical detail, anyway. In truth, their beauty lies in the organic textures of their darkly weathered wood, which have an almost liquid appearance; a shock of finely crafted dark chocolate assuming the shape of a church amid overgrown cemeteries. These churches are particularly loved for their soaring bell towers, one of which has long been recognized as the tallest wooden structure in Europe. The churches were built to replace earlier constructions destroyed in 1717 during the Tartar invasions; barred from building permanent churches, their architects decided on the wooden solutions seen today. They may not be ancient, but their survival over the last few centuries does make them special, since they are without any real fortification. Briefly described here are a handful of the 93 wooden churches in Maramureş; each listed under the village in which it is found. All of these churches can be visited as excursions from accommodations recommended in either the Mara or Izei valleys. You'll more than likely find the churches locked; even if you are visiting without a guide, it should be quite easy to track down the key. Don't be afraid to approach one of the locals and then hint that you're looking for the key by saying "chiea?" (kay-yah) while indicating the church. You'll almost certainly receive a positive response. Although nobody will say anything, it's only reasonable to leave a small donation (L5–L10/$1.80–$3.60/£1–£1.90) at each church you visit.

Bârsana 👁👁 Smaller than most of the churches, this was built in 1720 and was initially part of the Bârsana monastery. It was transferred to the present hilltop site in 1806, when a two-level portico was also added and the painter Hodor Toader added to the original interior frescoes, demonstrating distinct baroque and rococo influences on his work. A few kilometers from the village are the salubrious grounds of the **Bârsana Monastery,** easily mistaken for Maramureş's very own Orthodox Disneyland. Take a few minutes to wander around the manicured gardens and take a peek at the 16th-century church; most of the other monastic buildings were constructed after the fall of Communism.

Bârsana, 19km (12 miles) SE of Sighet, Izei Valley.

Budeşti 👁👁👁 The village of Budeşti is charming; children charge around on bicycles, while grown-ups in traditional attire make conversation in the streets. Your only problem might be finding the local priest who has the key to the Church of St. Nicholas; he'll require some tracking down if you want to see the frescoed interior. This is one of the most celebrated examples of the Maramureş style, built of oak in 1643; it is considered large—18m (59 ft.) long and 8m (26 ft.) wide. The earliest paintings are by Alexandru Ponehalski, rendered in 1762; while the work in the sanctuary is by Ioan Opris, and dates from 1832.

Budeşti, Mara Valley.

Călineşti ★★ This church is not part of the World Heritage List consignment, and is fairly well off the beaten track; it's also harder to locate, but is well known to—and loved by—locals (like the Pop family who run Casa Popicu; see "Where to Stay & Dine," earlier in this chapter). Apparently the 14th-century church was relocated to this site in 1665 because of a legend involving a girl named Călina; whenever she passed this spot her candle would start burning spontaneously, indicating that this was a place of miracles. Getting to the church involves a fairly stiff walk, possibly escorted by one of the ancient villagers. Once you're admitted to the church and the wooden shutters are opened, look out for the "Road to Heaven" fresco, represented by a ladder on which souls descend in order to be reunited with their bodies before the final judgment. Also look above the iconostasis for the slightly personified images of the sun and moon watching over Christ on the cross; the frescoes are the work of muralist Alexandru Ponehalski executed almost 30 years before he rendered the exquisite frescoes in Ieud.
Călineşti, Mara Valley.

Deseşti ★★★ Decorative motifs are cut into the wood of the exterior of the Church of the Holy Paraskeva, creating something of a sculptural artwork of the entire construction. It was built in 1770 and is now surrounded by tombstones in an overgrown graveyard. The interior walls and curved ceiling are covered in frescoes executed in 1780 by the celebrated artist Radu Munteanu, then considered a leader in religious painting. For a better view at the paintings, climb the stairs to the balcony from where you can study the particularly splendid crucifixion scene at the front of the church.
Deseşti, Mara Valley.

Ieud Deal ★★★ Ieud's hilltop Church of the Nativity of the Virgin is highly regarded for the spectacularly rich iconography in the frescoes of Alexandru Ponehalski (1782); his work here is considered the best in all of Maramureş. According to the UNESCO reports, the original structure, built in 1364, was completely destroyed by the Tartars in 1717, and the present church went up in the middle of the 18th century. Uniquely, this church is complemented by a free-standing bell tower.
Ieud, Izei Valley. Obtain the key from the shop opposite the church entrance.

Poienile Izei ★★★ You can walk to the Church of Saint Paraskeva in the Meadows of Iza from the village of Botiza (about an hour each way). One of the oldest wooden churches, it was constructed in 1604, yet it is far more fascinating (and famous) for its late-18th-century interior frescoes, alive with terrible images of hell.
Poienile Izei, 6km (3¾ miles) north of Botiza, Izei Valley.

Şurdeşti ★★★ Built at the pinnacle of the Maramureş architectural evolution (in 1767), the Church of the Holy Archangels is a must-see because of its exemplary synthesis of all the elements associated with the wooden churches; the interior was decorated by a team of three painters who worked here in 1783. To get here, you need to cross the dramatic Neteda Pass (which reaches 1,040m/3,411 ft.) south of Budeşti, passing through the town of Cavnic along the way.
Şurdeşti, on the road between Cavnic and Plopiş.

8 Moldavia & the Painted Churches of Southern Bucovina

Achieving independence in the 14th century, Moldavia achieved its apogee during the anti-Ottoman crusades with great defensive battles fought and won by Stephen the

Great (who ruled 1457–1504) and his successor, Petrus Rareş. Military success ensured a cultural renaissance, evidenced in Moldavia's beautiful painted monasteries that have earned great artistic acclaim, and attract visitors from around the world. The most precious of these churches are all with a 60km (37-mile) radius of the city of Suceava; once the princely seat of the Moldavian rulers, but thoroughly ruined during Ceasc's reign, this is still a useful base from which to explore the churches. Mostly situated in remote rural villages in lush landscapes, the churches of these monastic complexes have almost all been painted—inside and out—with such astonishingly unique and vivid frescoes that they have been accorded UNESCO World Heritage status and are considered one of the great artistic treasures of Romania.

Today, Moldavia's capital is Iaşi, the country's second-largest city, with an important university. While it's not an obvious travel destination, it has some significant urban architecture, and enjoys a lively cultural scene complemented by a cosmopolitan vibe that points to the aspirations of its highly visible student population. Iaşi is a good place to wander, popping in to churches and wandering through squares as you discover its diverse inhabitants and their preferred spaces. It's also filled with reminders of much-loved Mihai Eminescu, a lovesick poet whose tragic life perhaps epitomizes Romania's notion of romance.

ESSENTIALS

Tarom (Str. Arcu 3–5; ✆ **0232/26-7768**) flies from Bucharest to Iaşi every evening at 8:45pm, and has additional daytime flights most weekdays. The **airport** is 5km (3 miles) from the center; call **Delta Taxi** (✆ **0232/22-2222**) or have your hotel send a vehicle to pick you up. To explore the monasteries, you need to get to Suceava or the nearby town of Guru Humorului (referred to as "GH" by locals). There are fewer flights per week from Bucharest to Suceava, so you might want to consider flying to Iaşi and then taking a train to Suceava. The InterCity train from Bucharest to Iaşi takes between 6 and 7 hours. There are two IC trains daily, at 6:35am and at 5:19pm, and several other slower options. From Iaşi, Suceava is just 2 hours away.

To rent a car, contact **Autonom Rent-a-Car** (www.autonom.ro) in Iaşi (Str. Ştefan cel Mare 8–12; ✆ **0232/22-0504**) or Suceava (Str. Nicolae Bălcescu 2; ✆ **0230/52-1101**); you'll pay 30€ ($38) per day for a cheap model with unlimited mileage.

SUCEAVA & THE MONASTERIES OF SOUTHERN BUCOVINA
Suceava is 439km (272 miles) NE of Bucharest and 150km (93 miles) NW of Iaşi

Once an important Moldavian city, Suceava is one of those more severely impacted by Ceauşescu's industrialization program, its river poisoned by factory waste and its air polluted by unsavory gases, yet it remains an important tourism hub for excursions to the elegant painted monasteries in the surrounding countryside. Alternatively you could base yourself in nearby Gura Humorului, a small town, well geared for travelers, with privately run *pensiunes* by the bucket load.

WHERE TO STAY
In Suceava
Hotel Balada   It may not be luxurious or even particularly inspiring, but the Balada is generally considered to be the best hotel in town. Guest rooms are clean and tidy, and while not especially attractive, they are functional in an old-fashioned sort of way. Unless you're dead set on the anonymity of a hotel, you'll have a better experience at Villa Alice, at less than half the price.

Str Mitropiliei 3, Suceava. ℂ **0230/52-2146** or 0230/52-0408. Fax 0230/52-0087. www.balada.ro. 19 units. L246 ($89/£47) double; L390 ($140/£85) suite; L62 ($22/£12) extra bed. Rates include breakfast, but exclude 2% tax. AE, MC, V. **Amenities:** Restaurant; laundry. *In room:* A/C, TV, Internet, minibar.

Villa Alice *(Value)*   This family-run establishment offers great value and a central location in a quiet neighborhood. Hospitality here is a notch above that in the city's larger hotels; most importantly, it offers private tours to the monasteries. Guest rooms are simple, exceptionally clean, and have private balconies; they're also relatively comfortable, despite the kitschy gold bedspreads (and, in some cases, lime-green walls). In summer, it's worth paying a bit extra for a so-called "luxury room," which includes air-conditioning (and free Internet).

Str Simion Florea Marian 1, Suceava. ℂ/fax **0230/52-2254.** www.villaalice.ro. 16 units. L100–L150 ($36–$54/ £6.90–£10) double. Rates exclude 2% tax. **Amenities:** Restaurant; bar; fitness room; sauna; room service; medical facility on call. *In room:* A/C (luxury rooms), TV, Internet, minibar, hair dryer.

Gura Humorului & Environs

Best Western Bucovina Club de Munte *(★)*   While lacking any real sophistication or class, this thoroughly Western franchisee provides a range of comforts and is the best-positioned hotel for exploring the painted churches. Capped by a wood-timbered roof, meant to echo traditional Bucovine architectural elements, it enjoys a commanding position overlooking Guru Humorului's main square. From the mezzanine, with its lobby bar, pool table, and token village souvenir-ornaments, tiny elevators rise through eight floors of accommodations. Guest rooms are carpeted and decorated in unusual color combinations (yellow and green, or lime and ocher) and dark wood furniture (including four-poster beds); bathrooms have showers and are on the small side. Ensure that you reserve a Deluxe Room with Mountain View, and check twice (before arriving) that you have an upper-floor unit with balcony. Views from this—the closest thing to a skyscraper in these parts—are simply splendid.

Piaţa Republicii 18, Gura Humorului. ℂ **0230/20-7000.** Fax 0230/20-7001. www.bestwesternbucovina.ro. 130 units. L285 ($103/£55) double; L314 ($113/£60) deluxe with mountain view; L438 ($158/£84) junior suite; L548 ($197/£105) VIP suite; L639 ($230/£123) presidential suite. AE, DC, MC, V. **Amenities:** 2 restaurants; bar; terrace; fitness center, sauna, Turkish bath, massage; concierge; room service; wireless Internet; airport transfers; mountain biking, hunting, fishing, horseback riding, skiing, rafting; business facilities; safe. *In room:* TV, minibar, hair dryer.

Casa Elena   A short drive from Guru Humorului, right near Voronet Monastery, Casa Elena is set in well-tended grounds with panoramic views of the Bucovina hillscape. Reckoned to offer the best pensiune-style accommodations in the region (famous for having hosted three former presidents, including Iliescu, since it opened in 1999), the complex comprises five different "villas," each featuring a variety of rooms in different configurations. A stay here is pleasant enough, although—as with the Best Western in Guru Humorului—you may find it packed out with tour groups, and the guest rooms are unspectacular, done out in a countrified approximation of modest luxury with strange color schemes and cheap wood furniture. Traditional touches have been used almost perfunctorily to develop some sort of aesthetic in the numerous public spaces (it's all built to quite a convoluted plan), but it's the convenience of the location rather than the design of the place that should draw you here. Be warned that the hot water supply is inconsistent, and if you dine in one of the restaurants, you may find some of your choices unavailable. But if you succumb to the beauty of the surrounding lush landscape, you should soon forget its shortcomings.

Voronet, 3.5km (2 miles) from Guru Humorului. (℃ **0230/23-0651.** Fax 0230/23-5326. www.casaelena.ro. 35 units. 58€ ($73) double; 71€ ($89) apt. Rates include breakfast and taxes. MC, V. **Amenities:** 2 restaurants; bar; sauna; meeting rooms; room service; laundry; airport transfers; cart and sleigh rides; billiard table; traditional performances; Internet; children's playground. *In room:* TV, minibar, hair dryer.

WHERE TO DINE

Latino ⚓ ITALIAN/INTERNATIONAL   Across the road from the Armenian Monastery, this is Suceava's best bet for either a drink or a meal. Young waiters with Latin looks, long red aprons, and a willingness to go through the entire menu with you make this place a delight. Start by sharing an "Aperitiv Latino"—a platter of cheeses, Parma ham, and Italian salami, served with fresh bread. There's fine selection of pastas and pizzas, but those with a real appetite should consider splashing out for one of the duck *(rață)* dishes, especially good with wild mushrooms.

Str Curtea Domnească. (℃ **0230/52-3627.** Main courses L11–L29.50 ($4–$11/£2.10–£2.65). MC, V. Daily 10am–midnight.

EXPLORING MOLDAVIA'S PAINTED MONASTERIES ⚓⚓⚓

Among the great delights Romania has to offer (for some the greatest) are the monastic churches in the southern Bucovina region of Moldavia. With exteriors and interiors almost entirely covered in vivid frescoes of biblical tales—images rendering the word of God (and the clergy) accessible to the illiterate masses—these are considered so unique that the best preserved have been accorded UNESCO World Heritage status. Bluntly put, these well-preserved examples are nothing short of miraculous, given that their painted exteriors have faced exposure to extreme conditions, including snow and blinding sun, for 400 to 500 years.

Located within fortified monastic complexes designed to stave off enemy attacks, the churches were erected to thank God for victories in battles against the Turkish invaders; the frescoes that adorn the churches thus also honor their founders and ironically enough pay tribute to the violent warrior-leaders and womanizers, like Ștefan cel Mare (Stephen the Great), who fought to protect the land from marauding invaders. A cousin of Vlad the Impaler, Ștefan cel Mare was responsible for commissioning many of the churches; canonized in 1992, he not only slaughtered countless Turks, but left a trail of illegitimate children born of his voracious appetite for women.

Five monastic complexes are reviewed below, but there are many more that might be explored during a longer visit to the region; if you don't want to join an organized tour you will need to hire a car and driver or an English-speaking guide (see recommendations below). Note, too, that the five "monasteries" described here are actually inhabited by nuns rather than monks; nevertheless, they are all living religious monuments, and visitors should dress accordingly; don't show up with bare legs or shoulders (wraparound skirts are available for those ignorant of these strictly enforced rules). There's a small fee for photography (L6/$2.15/£1.15) within the monastic grounds, but cameras may not be used inside the churches. Opening times given here are for the summer; times may vary during colder periods, when monasteries close earlier. Admission is L4 ($1.45/75p).

Without too much of a rush, you can comfortably see all five monasteries reviewed below in 1 day. For a top-notch monastery tour, look no further than knowledgeable **Ciprian Șlenku** (℃ **0744-292-588;** monasetrytour@yahoo.com), who will talk you through the history and cultural significance of each of the monuments you visit, tailoring an outing to match your schedule. If he's not available, an equally rated guide is **Monica** (© **0230/52-5213;** www.classhostel.home.ro). Besides operating a local hostel, this bright-eyed entrepreneur is on good terms with many of the nuns, which makes the visits even more special. Monica is also the most careful driver in Romania. Trips to the monasteries can also be arranged through **Icar Tours** (Str. Ştefan cel Mare 24, Suceava; © **0230/52-4894;** www.icar.ro), an agency that's also useful for other travel needs. **DiscoveRomania** (see "Tours & Travel Agents," earlier in this chapter) includes the Moldavian churches on one of its itineraries.

Dragomirna Monastery ★★ (Moments) Fabulously situated amid rolling fields (a mere 15 min. by car from Suceava), these monumental defensive walls secured one of Bucovina's most elegant churches. While it's not on the UNESCO list and does not feature exterior frescoes, the combination of Georgian, Armenian, and Byzantine architectural elements has created a building that is akin to a beautiful stone space-ship, graced by a 42m (138 ft.) tower (undergoing many years of restoration). Pay your entry fee to the nun behind the souvenir counter in the entryway, where you can buy a decorative egg covered with beads studiously applied with beeswax by one of the 60 nuns who live here. Then venture into the nave. Unlike the other monastic churches, this one is very active, with Mass held from 8:30am until noon; try to come for this beautiful Orthodox ritual. Before leaving, ask the ticketing nun to show you the **museum of medieval art,** reached via the stairway near the entrance to the complex. Among various religious relics is the rather phallic **candle of consecration,** made from beeswax by Bishop Anastasie Crimca, who established the church between 1602 and 1609, when the candle was first lit.

Dragomirna, 4km (2½ miles) from Mitocul Drogomirnei, 12km (7½ miles) from Suceava. Admission L4 ($1.45). Daily 8am–7pm.

Voronet ★★★ Revered for its *Last Judgment* fresco, Voronet is regarded by Romanians as the "Sistine Chapel of the East"; it remains marvelously preserved, despite being in disuse from the start of Habsburg rule in 1785 until 1991. Built by Ştefan cel Mare in 1488 after a victorious battle against the Turks, the construction took just 3 months and 3 weeks; frescoes were added in 1534 and 1535, during the reign of Stephen's illegitimate son Petru Rareş. The paintings here epitomize a Moldavian innovation in Byzantine painting, exemplified by the degree of chromatic harmony and a new humanism with religious scenes featuring recognizable aspects of the Moldavian people of the time, like the faces of the angels, purportedly based on Moldavian women. Look out also for archangels blowing the *bucium,* an instrument used by Romanian shepherds, and the portrayals of doomed souls—all have fierce faces and wear turbans, characterizing them as Turks. The exterior fresco work is characterized by the use of a spectacular blue, said to be of such originality that it has earned the sobriquet "Voronet blue."

But it is the marvelously preserved *Last Judgment* on the western facade that leaves you breathless; it's an excellent example of Christian art as a dire warning against paganism and wickedness. It's also a fascinating marriage of biblical and secular symbolism. Notice, for example, the inclusion of the wild animals being judged for tearing apart their human victims, pieces of which they now return, while among them a lone deer stands empty-handed since this animal represents innocence in Romanian folklore. Notice also how, at Christ's feet, important figures—kings and popes—struggle to get out of hell, while elsewhere people clamber to enter the Gates of Heaven. Near the seat of Judgment, Adam and Eve are depicted alongside various prophets and martyrs;

they're separated from the "wicked" by a dove representing the Holy Spirit, while Moses (holding a scroll) points out their misdeeds. Below the dove, ugly demons try to steal souls, fighting among themselves as they torture sinners. On the southern wall is the *Tree of Jesse,* recounting Christ's genealogy. As you enter the church, you'll see the martyrdom of St. Sebastian, above you on your left; you'll also see numerous other martyrs suffering terrible tortures. Inside the church, the frescoes have been revitalized thanks to a thorough restoration job; works worth looking out for include *The Last Supper,* and, in the nave, a painting of Ştefan cel Mare with his wife and legitimate son, Bogdan.

Voronet is 4km (2½ miles) from Guru Humorului. Admission L4 ($1.45). Tues–Sun 10am–7pm.

Humor *(★★★* Humor was built in 1530, the absence of a tower suggesting that it was not built by a royal leader but by High Chancellor Theodor Bubuiog at the request of Voivode Petru Rareş. Standout architectural elements include the floating Byzantine vault and the inclusion of Gothic window frames; the arcaded open porch was another innovation for the time, apparently inspired by local building traditions. Smaller than the other monastic churches, Humor's paintings are Byzantine, but include Gothic and Roman elements; the predominant color here is a dark red, made from the madder pigment. The exterior frescoes are less well preserved than those at Voronet, but what does remain is quite lovely. Badly faded on the southern wall is the siege of Constantinople, with the Virgin answering the prayers of the besieged. As you enter the church, angels peer down at you from above, perhaps preparing you for the sight of more horrors being visited upon the martyrs. In the adjacent "Woman's Room" there are numerous depictions of female saints. For spectacular views of the surrounding countryside and the village of Mănăstirea Humor, climb the fantastically narrow stairs in the tower (built in 1641) attached to the complex outer wall; the trip up is more fun than the Tower of London. Like Humor, this church was only brought back into service after the fall of Communism.

Mănăstirea Humor is roughly 5km (3 miles) north of Guru Humorului. Admission L4 ($1.45). Daily 10am–6pm.

Moldoviţa *(★★★* While it's a little harder to get here than to the slightly more commercial monasteries at Voronet and Humor, it's worth the extra effort to view some of the best preserved of all the monastery frescoes. Looked after by a group of 42 exceedingly friendly nuns (the oldest of whom, Mica Marina, is approaching 85, and has been here since she was 14), the church was built by Petra Rareş, the illegitimate son of Stephen the Great, between 1532 and 1537, to replace an earlier church erected by Alexander the Good (Alexandru cel Bun). Notable here is the distinctive narrative style of the Byzantine technique; in many of the frescoes, you can discern two different points in time within a single frame. In other words, a single image is used to tell a story. Moldovita's exterior has been badly defaced—first by Turkish invaders who carved out the eyes of the frescoed characters in order to spare being judged by them, and later during the Austro-Hungarian occupation by Germanic visitors who carved their names into the porch walls. Inside, the first two rooms of the church are covered in representations of each day of the church calendar; if you can find a nun who speaks English, she may help you find the day of your birth and so identify the patron saint of your birthday. The museum, in one corner of the complex, houses Petru Rareş's throne, as well as the monastery's prized "Pomme d'Or" (Golden Apple) award from UNESCO.

Moldoviţa. Admission L4 ($1.45). Daily 10am–6pm.

Sucevița ✫✫✫   A host of angels greets you from the well-preserved southern wall of this gorgeously painted church, situated 32km (20 miles) north of Moldovița. Built a mere 410 years ago, Sucevita once served as a fortified city-in-miniature for villagers who'd hide behind its massive walls during attacks; the fortifications and monastery grounds are certainly the largest. On the northern wall, Greek philosophers are represented as kings of knowledge; try to locate Plato—the coffin on his head symbolizes the fact that he was the first philosopher to speak about the soul, considered a Christian concept. The enclosed porch around the entrance is the most elaborately painted of all the churches. Pay attention to the zodiac signs above you as you enter, and notice the angels at the edges of the cycles, rolling up time. Inside, bloody accounts of the life, torture, and death of various saints—notably St. George, are depicted. In the second room, notice the Star of David on the lower curtainlike portion of the frescoes, an unusual symbolic reference to the Old Testament, not found in the three previous churches. Here, in the center of the iconostasis, is an exceptionally lifelike rendition of Christ. Another highlight is a curious tapestry woven by Ieremia Movila (whose father built the monastery); there are 10,000 pearls woven into the piece. The monastery is apparently haunted by the ghost of the artist who, while working on the western wall, tragically fell from the scaffolding; the frustrated spirit has since prevented the fresco from being completed.

Sucevița. Admission L4 ($1.45). Daily 8am–8pm.

IAȘI

Iași is 393km (244 miles) NE of Bucharest

Some of Iași's most vivid associations are with the country's literary superhero, Mihai Eminescu, who lived, loved, and wrote poetry here for a good part of his highly romanticized life. But the city is much older than Eminescu, of course; founded in the 14th century, it usurped Suceava as Moldavia's capital in 1565. As the seat of power, the city experienced a long-term renaissance in cultural activity and architectural development, culminating in its being declared the first capital of Romania (for a brief spell between 1859–62), and the establishment of the first Romanian university here in 1860. The resultant tide of cosmopolitanism is still evident today, albeit tucked between uglier relics of 20th-century construction, notably in the form of concrete blocks that blight the city's neoclassical center.

But Iași, like so much of Romania, is on the rebound, with plenty of restoration and renovation programs up and running. The city may be Bucharest extra-light, but the pulse is growing.

WHERE TO STAY

If the idea of staying in a Wild West–themed hotel in Eastern Europe gives you the heebie-jeebies (see Little Texas review, below), recent newcomer **Majestic** is a welcome addition to Iași's burgeoning accommodations scene (© **0232/25-5557**; www.pensiuneamajestic.ro; from L195/$70/£37 double). It's smart, low-key, and intimate; it's also just a short walk from the center of town. Guest rooms feature some of the city's most comfortable beds, and bathrooms are decent-size. You could also check out what's happening behind the beautiful facade of the **Traian Hotel,** located on historic Piața Unirii. The neoclassical building was designed by Gustave Eiffel in 1882; in 2006 it was undergoing much-needed renovations (reports prior to this were of totally substandard accommodations); to find out whether these have finally been completed (and how these have affected rates) call © **0232/14-3330.**

Little Texas ☆☆   An oasis in a desert of drab hotel options, this American-run place overlooking Iaşi offers the most pleasant accommodations anywhere in the region, with a genuinely warm design aesthetic, and more in-room comfort than you'll find elsewhere in the city. Although it's themed on Wild West iconography (framed images of John Wayne, saddlebags, six-shooters, and Texan paraphernalia), and country tunes form a perpetual backdrop to the public areas, the blend of American kitsch and Romanian staff somehow works. Set in beautifully tended grounds with a rock-built waterfall, fountain, cherry trees, and an old ox-wagon (no escaping the Western frontier theme), this small hotel is a short cab ride from the city, which it overlooks; reserve a room with a view of Iaşi, which also includes a panorama of the surrounding hills from your small private porch (if you don't mind the stairs, ask for room no. 43). Rooms on the lower floor open directly onto the lawn. Breakfasts are strictly American, and the restaurant serves up Tex-Mex dishes with a Romanian twist; locals flock here for the food, so in summer the dining terrace is often abuzz, and the saloon-style indoor area is ideal for winter.

Moara de Vânt 31–33, Iaşi. © **0232/21-6995.** Fax 0232/27-2545. www.littletexas.org. 31 units. L270–L290 ($97–$104/£52–£56) double; L310 ($112/£59) suite. Rates include breakfast. **Amenities:** Restaurant; outdoor terrace; bar; room service; laundry; travel assistance. *In room:* A/C, TV, minibar, hair dryer.

WHERE TO DINE

Casa Pogor ROMANIAN   Fringing the gardens of Pogor House Literary Museum, the summer terrace at this historic venue is always abuzz. It's so popular in fact, that getting the attention of one of the overworked waiters can by frustrating; nevertheless, if you've got patience and fancy a fairly wide-ranging selection of traditional fish and meat dishes, it's not half bad. The menu is strictly in Romanian, but you can't go wrong if you order trout (or *păstrăv*) which—like everything on the menu—is prepared to order, and served on plates featuring quotes by Eminescu, who would meet here to debate fellow writers. In cooler months, the musty cellar becomes the most atmospheric space in town.

Str Vasile Pagov 4. © **0232/24-3006.** Main courses L3.50–L21 ($1.25–$7.40/£70–£6.95). MC, V. Daily 10am–2am.

GinGer Ale ☆☆ INTERNATIONAL   Odd though the name may be, the food and service here are wonderful in equal measure; in summer, sit on the upstairs terrace, where grape vines and a guava tree shelter you from the heat. Strangely, the Irish dishes are specialties of the house; there's a delicious mutton hot pot (prepared with *pulpa de batal, sos rosu ciuperci,* and *cartofi*), but you could as easily have Irish ragout or leg of mutton in ginger sauce. Steaks can be ordered with a rich Gorgonzola sauce, and fish recommendations run the gamut from grilled pike to carp or salmon. New dishes appear regularly; successful experiments include Thai salad with roasted veal, salmon and spinach salad, and an excellent risotto with chicken livers and mushrooms. Note that GinGer Ale offers great discounts for daytime diners; weekdays between 11am and 4pm, they take 20% off your food bill; on weekends up to 50%.

Str. Săulescu 23. © **0232/27-6017.** www.gingerale.ro. Main courses L5–L29 ($1.80–$10/£1–£5.60). AE, DC, MC, V. Daily 11am–1am.

EXPLORING IAŞI

Iaşi's heart is **Piaţa Unirii,** overlooked by both the beautiful Hotel Traian and the monstrous Hotel Unirea, the two buildings forming a binary representation of how modernization has afflicted many parts of Romania. Centered on a **statue of Prince Alexandru Ioan Cuza,** Paiţa Unirii is surrounded by restaurants, shops, and bars. B-dul Ştefan cel Mare şi Sfânt links Piaţa Unirii with the Palace of Culture (reviewed below), about 1km (½ mile) away. Along this boulevard, you'll find the difficult-to-miss Metropolitan Cathedral, across from the city's **Central Park,** a remarkably peaceful place filled with busts of Romanian writers. Music often fills the evening air, making the park a lovely place to visit; this is where locals come to relax, lovers meet to swoon, and friends gather before taking in a show at the **National Theater** (designed by Viennese duo Helmer and Fellner), on the other end of the park.

Heading northwest from Piaţa Unirii, Str. Alexandru Lăpuşneanu passes by **Piaţa Mihai Eminescu,** from where **B-dul Carol I** continues into the heart of the energetic **University District,** alive with scholarly pursuits. On Piaţa Mihai Eminescu is the Student Cultural House and a little park with the **Voievodes Statuary,** representations of eight great Moldavian leaders, including Dragoş, the first prince (who ruled from 1352–53), and mighty Ştefan cel Mare, considered one of the Romania's all-time greatest leaders (he ruled for almost 50 years, 1457–1504).

A bit farther along B-dul Carol I, you can veer down tree-sheltered Str. Vasile Pogor, where you can visit **Casă Pogor** (© **0232/31-2830;** Tues–Sun 10am–5pm), which houses the **Pogor House Literary Museum,** a tribute to the nation's writing fraternity, members of which assembled here for gatherings of Pogor's celebrated literary society during the latter part of the 19th century. Consider stopping for lunch at the popular restaurant here (see "Where to Dine," above).

Heading farther north along B-dul Carol I, you'll pass the large building of **Alexandru Ioan Cuza University,** on your left, and eventually reach **Copou Park,** a lovely 19th-century garden, famous for a linden tree under which love-torn Eminescu would

Eminescu, Romania's 19th-Century Eminem

One of the best films to come out of Romania in recent years is *Eminescu vs. Eminem,* a clever exploration of youth culture in relation to the nation's most highly revered poet, Mihai Eminescu. Many young Romanians, even in this popular-culture era, adore Eminescu and will go to any lengths to convince you of his talent and great genius; one student told me that an autopsy found Eminescu's brain to be heavier than average. But like many great geniuses, Eminescu was greatly troubled by affairs of the heart. While married, he fell head-over-heels with Veronica Micle, whose husband was an important clergyman. Brokenhearted by his love, Eminescu was convinced that Veronica was in fact too good for him and that he could never make her happy with his limited financial means; even when both their spouses had died, he refused to ask for Veronica's hand in marriage. True to the tragic romance of their ill-fated love, Veronica committed suicide shortly after Eminescu's death.

sit and compose his finest poems; look for a bust of the writer near the main entrance, and then find that of his lover, Veronica, facing him from a distance.

Palatul Culturii (Palace of Culture) ⚐   Formerly housing the city's government, this massive neo-Gothic fairy-tale castle was built between 1906 and 1925; on this site are also some of the remains of the 15th-century princely court. The palace entrance is marked by a late-19th-century equestrian statue of Ştefan cel Mare, and there's a memorial to local heroes who died in the 1989 revolution. Fabulously ornate balconies, stairways guarded by stone-sculpted birds of prey, stained-glass windows, and massive tapestries (look for those by Liviu Suhor) make the Palace worth a visit in its own right, but it also hosts a number of museums, galleries, and temporary exhibitions. Prioritize the **Muzeul de Arta (Art Museum),** with its fine survey of several important Romanian artists, notably Nicolae Grigorescu, who excelled at rendering pale, impressionistic scenes of village life. More modern works include those by Nicolae Tonzita (1886–1940), Ştefan Dimitrescu (1886–1933), and the fabulous Theodor Pallady (1871–1956), who seems to have favored nudes and still-life paintings. Also in this building are an **Ethnographic Museum,** dealing with aspects of village life, and a **History Museum,** which focuses on Moldavia's past.

B-dul Ştefan cel Mare şi Sfânt. ✆ 0232/21-8383. Art Museum entrance is L2.50 (90¢/50p). Fri–Wed 10am–5pm.

Metropolitan Cathedral ⚐   Completed as recently as 1839 (although started in 1761), Catedrale Metropolitana Sf. Parascheva—the country's biggest Orthodox cathedral—is virtually always busy with believers who've come to worship, receive blessings, or meditate; never more so than in October on the day of its patron saint, Paraschiva, when many complete the journey on their knees or lie completely prostrate. Paintings by Gheorghe Tattarescu adorn the vast interior.

B-dul Ştefan cel Mare şi Sfânt.

Biserica Sfinţilor Trei Ierarhi ⚐⚐   Dedicated to three saints, the vividly decorated Church of the Three Hierarchs mingles various architectural styles—eastern elements play off against Renaissance and western Gothic forebears, generating a look that is quite original and fantastic. Prince Vasile Lupu built it between 1637 and 1639; to make doubly certain of his place in heaven, he adorned the exterior with silver, gold, and lapis lazuli. In the church are the tombs of Lupu and his family, as well as the Moldavian princes Dimitrie Cantemir and Alexandru Ioan Cuza, who first unified Moldavia and Wallachia in 1859. Now part of a monastic complex, the church grounds include a museum featuring frescoes of the 17th century.

B-dul Ştefan cel Mare şi Sfânt. Admission L2 (70¢/40p). Museum Tues–Sun 10am–4pm.

WINE-TASTING NEAR IAŞI

Another reason to be in Iaşi is to visit the 15th-century vineyards of **Cotnari,** just 54km (33 miles) away. Home to some of the country's most famous grapes, Cotnari produces huge quantities of a dessert wine that was much loved by Stephen the Great. Visit **Cotnari Winery** (✆ 0232/73-0393; www.cotnari.ro) for wine-tastings, tours, and—on September 14—harvest celebrations. **Bucium winery** is only 7km (4⅓ miles) south of Iaşi and is popular for its champagne.

9 Northern Dobrogea: Romania's Black Sea Coast & the Danube Delta

Ancient Greek colonies were established in Dobrogea in the 7th century B.C., with the founding of Histria, 70km (43 miles) north of the regional capital Constanţa, Romania's major port city. Later, this became a Roman province, and a base for conquering the Dacians. From 1418, the region fell to the Turks and remained under Ottoman rule until they were expelled in 1878; Dobrogea was divided in two, the southern portion going to Bulgaria and Northern Dobrogea becoming part of Romania.

Today, there are two distinct regions comprising Northern Dobrogea. Like Bulgaria, the southern fringes along the Black Sea Coast have been totally colonized, turning the country's Riviera to near-ruin. Now overdeveloped or steeped by the summer rush of both the moneyed elite and an unruly neobohemian crowd, there are few stretches of sand left unspoiled by tourist exploitation. The northern part of Dobrogea is known for its bird colonies, inhabiting the expansive Danube Delta, a wetland biosphere widely considered one of Europe's last true wildernesses.

BLACK SEA COASTAL RESORTS

Unfortunately, Romania's once lovely and fairly untouched seaside Riviera on the Black Sea has become developed and exploited to the point where domestic holiday-makers finally decided to boycott it, and visitor numbers dropped by about 50% in 2006. If you like getting caught up in the mayhem of a noisy, bloated string of resorts and beaches strewn with empty liquor bottles, music blaring from speakers across once-serene getaways, then by all means set off for one of the tiny villages within striking distance of Constanţa. Or you can join the bourgeoisie in their upmarket playground of Mamaia, a fanciful collection of fancy hotels and designer luggage leaving almost no room to erect your beach umbrella. Beach reforms are planned, but they will take a few years to kick in; until such time, you're advised to save your sun-worshipping for elsewhere.

THE DANUBE DELTA ✦✦✦

Heralded by some as the last great wilderness in Europe and the Continent's greatest wildlife sanctuary, the Danube Delta is a unique destination, affording nature experiences usually associated with Africa or South America. Only now showing on the international tourist radar, this well-kept secret is developing into a top-class conservation area, protected by UNESCO as a World Heritage Site. Diversity is key; while there isn't the vast assortment of land animals and predator activity that one finds in Botswana's Okavango Delta, for example, the Danube is heaven for birders. Over 300 species of birds make their home in this unique ecosystem consisting of almost 250,000 hectares of waterways, lakes, reed-beds, sand dunes, and subtropical forests as the 2,860km (1,773-mile) river splits into three main branches and gushes into the Black Sea. And among the birdlife and the 1,150 species of flora are small fishing and farming communities that remain steeped in the culture of another, forgotten time. These include Russian and Lipovan communities with cultures and practices that are distinct from anywhere else in Romania.

ESSENTIALS

On the banks of the Danube, the ancient Greek port town of **Tulcea** might be considered the headquarters of the Delta; although there's nothing in the town itself that's should detain you, you're likely to pass through en route to destinations in the Delta proper. The fastest way to get to Tulcea from Bucharest is by **chartered plane,** which can be organized through Delta Nature Resort if you intend staying there. Alternatively you can catch one of two daily InterCity **trains;** these leave Bucharest at 6:55am and 5:26pm and the journey is 5 hours. Tulcea's **train station** (Str. Potului; ✆ **0240/ 51-3706**) is right near the **bus station** (✆ **024051-3304**), which is attached to the **Navrom ferry terminal.**

Tulcea hosts the **Danube Delta Research Institute** (Str. Babadag 165; ✆ **0240/ 52-4550;** www.indd.tim.ro), useful if you're after hard facts about this unique biosphere. Tulcea is also home to the **Danube Delta Biosphere Reserve Headquarters** (Str. Portului 34A; ✆ **0240/51-8945/24;** www.ddbra.ro), which hosts the **Information and Ecological Education Centre** (✆ **0240/51-9214;** www.deltaturism.ro), which can provide you with local and Delta-related information; staff can also help you with accommodations, but note that they're only open weekdays.

If you want to stay in Tulcea itself, **Hotel Rex** (Str. Toamnei 1; ✆ **0240/51-1351**) is the classiest option, with air-conditioned guest rooms for under 100€ ($125) double.

ALL-INCLUSIVE DELTA EXPERIENCES

Until recently, visitor numbers were severely limited by the lack of decent lodging options; today, in addition to the possibility of staying in small village guesthouses, there are a number of newly developed upmarket resorts that, mercifully, are striving to protect the natural resources of the region.

Delta Nature Resort ✺✺✺   Established in 2005, Romania's finest resort not only situates you in the heart of one of Europe's most beautiful natural environments, but cushions you in luxury and offers a smorgasbord of activities to keep you entertained. Designed to echo the style of the Delta's fishing villages, there are 30 luxurious villas spread along the banks of Lake Somova, an ideal location. Built from local wood and stone, each villa has a porch overlooking the wide-open expanse of the Delta. Inside you have a private living room, plush bedroom, and fine contemporary bathrooms to match. Besides birding expeditions, some of the best cultural experiences in the country are to be had at a nearby convent, where the nuns serve up delicious organic lunches, while traditional Delta soups are served on some of the longer fishing and water-based excursions. More energetic guests can kayak or canoe their way across the waters, getting close to the pelicans and cormorants with one of the resident rangers, botanists, or naturalists.

Luxury road transfers from Bucharest to the resort cost 300€ ($375) round-trip, for up to five guests; this is the most convenient way of traveling, and cost-effective provided there are other passengers to share the expense. If you're feeling particularly glamorous, ask for a helicopter transfer.

Complex Turistic, Somova-Parches, km 3, Jud. Tulcea. ✆ **866/322-7199** in the U.S., 020/7924-5834 in the U.K., 0725-408-000, or 021/311-4532 reservations. Fax 0725-408-001. www.deltaresort.com. 30 units. 200€ ($250) double; rate includes breakfast; 130€ ($163) double, full board; taxes extra. MC, V. **Amenities:** Restaurant; bar; pool; business center; gift shop; room service; various boating; fishing; birding; nature walks; cultural tours; wine-tasting; traditional performances; airport transfers (from Bucharest); massage center; laundry. *In room:* Fireplace, TV, Internet, tea- and coffeemaking facility, minibar, hair dryer, safe.

Enisala Safari Village ✺✺   Not in quite the same league as Delta Resort, this rustic, smart little guest resort is in the old fortress village of Enisala, about 30km (19 miles) south of Tulcea, and less than 30 minutes from Black Sea Coast. Enisala ("new village") was once Byzantine outpost, later colonized by the Genoese and the Ottomans. It's right near vast Lake Razim, and a couple of hours by motorboat from the very heart of the Danube Delta. Different itineraries allow guests to get a varied experience of the region. Accommodations comprise thatch- or clay-tile roof cottages with whitewashed walls and blue wooden shutters to mimic the rusticity of local village houses. Guest rooms are simple and bright, with patterned stone-tile floors and roll-down straw blinds. Boats are available for lake and Delta excursions, and guides take you hiking, bird-watching, and fishing. You can also explore the region by bike or motorbike. Staff will also arrange visits to the nearby Babadag mosque, the vineyards of Niculiţel, the ruins of the ancient Greek city of Histria, off-road trips to the Russian village of Slava Rusa, and the Slavonic monastery of Vovidenia, where you can arrange for a picnic. At night, fires are lit, and rugged types can opt to camp outdoors (in military tents). Dine outdoors at an open barbecue or experience a Byzantine-style evening in the wine cellar or in the intimate dinner lounge. It's small enough for guests to make the decisions, and pleasant enough to spend a couple of days.

Safari Village: Enisala, nr. 94 A, jud. Tulcea. Bucharest office: Str. Episcopiei 5, apt 18, Bucharest. © **0722-300-200.** Fax 021/314-5837. safari@safari.ro. 4 doubles, 2 family rooms. 110€ ($138) double, includes all meals; children under 14 pay half. MC, V. **Amenities:** Dinner lounge; wine cellar; 2 terraces; barbecue area; camping; sightseeing and organized trips; bird-watching; photo safaris; Danube cruise; 4x4 trips; mountain biking; motor biking; airport transfers; Internet; small archaeological museum. *In room:* A/C.

10

Moscow & St. Petersburg

by Angela Charlton & Heather Coombs

Russia breathes superlatives: the world's biggest country; its largest supplier of natural gas and second-largest oil producer; and home of the planet's longest railroads, busiest subway system (Moscow's), and one of its deepest, biggest, and oldest lakes (Baikal, in Siberia). It even boasts balmy beach resorts (on the Black Sea), though the Kremlin and the snowcapped cupolas of its cathedrals seem truer reflections of this northern nation's might and mysticism.

There is much for travelers to experience in Russia's two most popular cities.

In Moscow, the traditions of the Bolshoi Theater coexist with some of Europe's most cutting-edge DJs. In St. Petersburg, the Hermitage Museum is a fortress of fine art from around the world, and the Russian Museum overflows with works by local artists. Russia's tourism infrastructure is still underdeveloped, but Moscow and St. Petersburg are fast catching up with the changes brought by capitalism. Take along some pluck and flexibility and have a look at the best Russia has to offer.

1 Getting to Know Moscow & St. Petersburg

MOSCOW & ST. PETERSBURG ORIENTATION

At Moscow's heart lies the Kremlin, from which the rest of the city has expanded in roughly concentric circles: the Boulevard Ring, the Garden Ring, and the Third Ring. The last circle, the Moscow Ring Road, is the bypass around the city limits. The Moscow and Yauza rivers curve through the city, delineating neighborhoods. Visitors are often struck by Moscow's broad boulevards and large swaths of green space.

St. Petersburg, like Moscow, is dense and territorially large, but not as unwieldy or overwhelming as its southern sister. Peter the Great built his dream city on a cluster of islands in the marshland of the Gulf of Finland. To make sense of this boggy site, he designed a network of canals and bridges, resulting in a city of remarkable logic and beauty. The Neva River folds around the city center, taking in water from the city's canals before flowing out to the Baltic Sea. The city's main land artery is Nevsky Prospekt, a 4km-long (2½-mile) avenue that slices across the city center.

MOSCOW & ST. PETERSBURG TODAY

Moscow is almost a country unto itself, a metropolis of 12 million people enjoying the fruits of Russia's booming oil economy. Despite Russians' innate conservatism, today's Moscow is a 24-hour city that pulses with change, from the ruthlessly competitive restaurant and club scenes to the volatile financial markets and the clamor for the latest top-of-the-line cellphone.

St. Petersburg's reputation as Russia's intellectual and cultural center has not brought the city the prosperity that today's Moscow enjoys, but Petersburg has better hotel choices and a restaurant scene nearly as vibrant as the capital's. The vision of the city's founder, Peter the Great, lives on—even new buildings adhere to the symmetry and classicism of Peter's day.

Although Russia as a whole is a graying country with a relatively low standard of living, Moscow and St. Petersburg are its glaring exceptions, and are experiencing a genuine economic boom that has brought them in line with the world's richest cities.

For tourists there's never been a better time to visit Russia. Surly Soviet service is giving way to smiling efficiency, new restaurants open in Moscow almost daily, and fashions are as fresh as in Milan. Cash machines are ubiquitous and English is increasingly widespread. Russia has, at last, opened its doors to the world.

A LOOK AT THE PAST

Russia's struggle for identity, association, and empire has defined it since the Vikings formed the state of Rus nearly 1,200 years ago. Blood and repression have marred this struggle, right up to today.

Moscow has dominated the country's political, economic, and cultural life for most of the past 900 years; St. Petersburg, during the 2 centuries when it assumed the role of Russia's capital, plunged Russia at long last into the modern world.

The first Russian state was founded in Novgorod in the 9th century, and later shifted to Kiev, now the capital of Ukraine. The era of **Kievan Rus,** as it was called, saw the flowering of a major European entity, whose territories stretched across present-day Belarus, Ukraine, and much of western Russia. As Kievan Rus, the country gained a religion and an official language and developed the distinctive architectural styles seen across the region today.

Moscow became the seat of Russian authority in 1326. The Russian state was feeble, however, and fell to repeated invasion by Mongol Tatars from the east. The Tatars kept Russia's princes under their thumbs until Ivan III (Ivan the Great) came to power in the late 1400s. His reign saw Muscovite-controlled lands spread north to the Arctic and east to the Urals. Ivan the Great launched construction of the Kremlin's magnificent cathedrals and its current walls.

His grandson Ivan IV, the first Russian crowned "czar," became better known as **Ivan the Terrible.** He instituted Russia's first secret police force, persecuted former friends as enemies, and killed his own son and pregnant daughter-in-law in a fit of rage. The country and his dynasty were devastated by the time Ivan IV died in 1584.

The ensuing decades were wrought with bloody, corrupt struggles that came to be known as the **"Time of Troubles."** At last the 16-year-old Mikhail Romanov, a distant relative of Ivan the Terrible, was elected czar in 1613. Mikhail established a dynasty that would last until czar Nicholas II was executed by Bolsheviks 300 years later.

Although Russians through the ages have debated whether to look to western Europe or to their Slavic roots for inspiration, **Peter the Great** had no doubts. Peter traveled to western Europe and upon his return moved to a swamp on the Baltic Sea, transforming it into a capital of columned, Italian-designed palaces along broad avenues and canals. St. Petersburg's beauty came at a great price: Thousands of people died fulfilling Peter's sometimes impossible building orders.

Russia's next exceptional leader was **Catherine the Great** (1762–96), a German princess who married into the Romanov family and conspired to oust her husband to attain the throne. She greatly expanded Russia's territory to the east and south, and her foreign policies won her and Russia great respect in the rest of Europe. Russia's aristocracy came to speak French better than Russian.

Russia's love affair with France collapsed under Napoleon, who gave Russia its biggest military challenge in centuries. The French made it into **Moscow in 1812**— but only after the Russians had set fires in the city, stripped it bare, and fled, leaving Napoleon's army without food and shelter on the eve of winter. The *Grande Armée* retreated, and the Russians' victorious drive into Paris 2 years later was immortalized in poems, songs, and children's rhymes.

Much of Russia's 19th century was defined by **prerevolutionary struggle,** and the czars sought to stamp out dissent even where it didn't exist. The 1825 Decembrist uprising, led by reformist generals in the royal army, was quashed by czar Nicholas I, who then bolstered the secret police. Czar Alexander II freed the serfs in 1861, but society remained unequal and most of the population was still poor and uneducated.

Nicholas II—the last of the Romanov czars—assumed the throne in 1894 with few plans for reform. He stifled an uprising of striking workers in January 1905 on what is known as **Russia's Bloody Sunday.** Under pressure from the population, the czar allowed the creation of a limited parliament, Russia's first ever, elected in 1906.

Fighting the Germans in World War I further weakened Nicholas's shaky hold on the country, and with revolution in the air, he abdicated in February 1917. An aristocrat-led provisional government jockeyed for power with revolutionary parties. Lenin's extremist **Bolshevik Party** emerged the victor. Nicholas, his wife Alexandra, and their five children were exiled to Siberia and then executed in 1918, as civil war engulfed the nation. Years of chaos, famine, and bloodshed followed, before the Union of Soviet Socialist Republics was born.

After Lenin died in 1924, **Stalin** worked his way to the top of the Communist Party leadership. Stalin crafted a dictatorship by gradually purging his rivals, real and imagined. His repression reached a peak in the late 1930s, with millions executed or exiled to prison camps across Siberia and the Arctic, referred to by their Russian initials GULAG, or State Agency for Labor Camps.

Stalin tried to head off war with Germany, but Hitler invaded anyway, plunging the Soviet Union into a war that cost the country 27 million lives, more losses than any nation suffered in World War II.

Genuine grief mixed with nervous relief gripped the country when Stalin died in 1953, as many feared that life without this frightening father figure would be even worse than with him. Nikita Khrushchev's eventual rise to power brought a **thaw;** political prisoners were released and there was a slight relaxation of censorship amid continued postwar economic growth. Soviet space successes during this time—including sending the first satellite, first man, and first woman to space—awed the world and fueled the Cold War arms race.

From the mid-1980s, Gorbachev's name became synonymous with the policies of *glasnost* **(openness)** and *perestroika* **(restructuring)** that he tried to apply to the Soviet system. But he underestimated how deeply the country's economy and political legitimacy had decayed. The reforms he introduced took on a momentum that doomed him and the Soviet Union.

Russia under **Putin,** who was overwhelmingly elected president in 2000 and just as enthusiastically reelected in 2004, is undoubtedly a calmer and richer place than it was in the chaotic 1990s. Putin cut taxes, allowed the sale of land for the first time since Lenin's days, and has presided over the greatest growth in Russia's economy in decades. However, his achievements have been due largely to the fact that he's disabled the political opposition.

PEOPLE & CULTURE

Russians are among the most festive and giving people on the planet, always ready to put their last morsel of food and last drop of drink on the table to honor an unexpected late-night guest with toasts, more toasts, and laughter. Although the changes of the past decade have been rough on Russians, they've adapted quickly—today's Russian university graduates know more languages, and more about financial markets and text messaging than many of their Western counterparts.

Despite Russia's bloody history, the country is succeeding in producing some of the world's best science, music, and literature. In the 19th century, **Pushkin** became Russians' best-loved poet, with his direct, melodic use of the Russian language. Dostoevski's fiction delved into innermost existential depths, and Tchaikovsky's symphonies gave voice to the terror and triumph of war with France. They are just a few of the legions of cultural heroes who found success in their uniquely Russian ways of expression.

Russians take great pride in their cultural heritage, and in the Soviet era nearly everyone, factory worker and collective farmer included, made regular visits to theater, concert hall, or opera house. Russia's rigorous **ballet** traditions have relaxed little in the past 200 years, and that commitment to physical perfection carries over into every form of dance represented in today's Russia. For **classical music** fans, there's no better way to pay tribute to the homeland of Tchaikovsky, Rachmaninoff, Mussorgsky, Scriabin, Shostakovich, and Rimsky-Korsakov than to hear their works played in a Russian conservatory by their dedicated heirs.

CUISINE

Russia's culinary traditions run from the daylong, table-crushing feasts of the 19th-century aristocracy to the cabbage soup and potatoes on which generations of ordinary Russians were raised. Russian food is generally rich and well-salted.

Traditional dishes include the Siberian specialty *Pelmeni,* which are dumplings filled with ground beef, pork, or lamb and spices and boiled in broth (a bit like overstuffed ravioli). *Varenniki* are a larger, flatter version of these dumplings, filled with potatoes or berries. *Piroshki* are small baked pies filled with ground meat, cabbage, or fruit, and are eaten with your hands; *pirogi* are large dessert pies. Buttery *bliny,* thin crepelike pancakes, are spread with jam or savory fillings such as ham and cheese and rolled up. Tiny round *olady* are the pancakes eaten with caviar. Russian soups include the refreshing summer soup *zelyoniye shchi* or the winter stew *solyanka.*

Your trip to Russia will invariably involve a taste of **vodka,** the national drink. Most vodkas are distilled from wheat, rye, or barley malt or some combination of the three. The Stolichnaya, Russky Standart, and Flagman brands are excellent choices. If you want to appreciate a good vodka the way Russians do, you should drink it well chilled and straight, preferably in 50-gram shots. Down it in one gulp, and always chase it with something to eat. Russians prefer pickles, marinated herring, or a slice of lard.

Local beers are improving rapidly; Baltika and Nevskoye are cheap and tasty choices. If you're feeling adventurous, try *kvas,* a thirst-quenching beverage made from fermented bread. Russians' drink of choice, however, is **tea** *(chai),* ideally served from a samovar: a small pot of strong tea base *(zavarka)* sits brewing on top and is diluted to taste with the hot water from the belly of the samovar *(kipitok).*

LANGUAGE

The Cyrillic alphabet scares off most tourists from trying to pick up any Russian, and that's a great shame. The 33-letter alphabet is not hard to learn, since many of the letters are the same as in English. Knowing how to read those dizzying signs will make your trip through Russia less mysterious and more comfortable.

Most Russians in hotels, restaurants, and shops will speak some English, especially those of the younger generations. Any effort to speak Russian will be welcomed, and in smaller establishments even a few words of Russian may get you out of a bind or improve service. Below are some useful words and phrases.

USEFUL RUSSIAN PHRASES

English	Russian	Pronunciation
Yes/No	Да, нет	Da, Nyet
Hello	здравствуйте	*Zdras*-tvoo-tye
Goodbye	до свидания	Da svi-*da*-nya
Thank you	спасибо	Spa-*see*-ba
Please/You're welcome	пожалуйста	Pa-*zha*-li-sta
Excuse me	извините	Eez-vee-*nee*-tye
Sorry	простите, пожалуйста	Prah-*stee*-tye, pa-*zha*-li-sta
How are you?	Как дела?	Kak deh-*la*
Fine, good	Хорошо	Kho-ro-*show*
Bad	плохо	*Plo*-kha
Do you speak English?	вы говорите по-английски?	Vy go-vo-*ree*-te po ang-*lee*-skee?
I don't speak Russian	Я не говорю по-русски	Ya nee guh-vuh-*ryoo* pa-*roo*-skee
I speak a little Russian	Я немного говорю по-русски	Ya ne-*mno*-go guh-vuh-*ryoo* pa-*roo*-skee
How much does it cost?	сколько стоит?	*Skol*-ka *sto*-eet?
Where is . . .	где находится . . .	Gde na-*kho*-dee-tsa . . .
the metro station	станция метро	*stan*-tsee-ya me-*tro*
the restroom/WC	туалет	tua-*let*
Pharmacy	аптека	Ap-*teh*-ka
Currency exchange	обмен валюты	Ob-*men* vah-*lyoo*-tee
ATM/cash machine	банкомат	Bahnk-o-*mat*
Help!	помогите	Pa-ma-*gee*-tye

2 Planning Your Trip to Moscow & St. Petersburg

VISITOR INFORMATION

Hotels and tour desks are likely to have as much information as the official tourist offices (for addresses, see section 3, "Moscow" and section 4, "St. Petersburg").

Most hotels and many newspaper kiosks sell maps in English (ask for a Karta na angliiskom, pronounced *kar*-ta na ahn-*glees*-kom). See **www.yell.ru/map** for interactive maps of Moscow and St. Petersburg.

Useful websites include **www.infoservices.com**, featuring the Travelers' Yellow Pages for Moscow and St. Petersburg, with searchable telephone and address listings in English, including nearest metro station and opening hours.

There are numerous free listings magazines at nearly all hotels and many restaurants. Most are in English and Russian and are full of information.

ENTRY REQUIREMENTS

All visitors to Russia need a visa. Package tours usually take care of this, though you will need to give the travel agency your passport for submission to the Russian embassy. For independent travelers, visa applicants must provide proof of hotel reservations in an official letter from a hotel or travel agency. Travelers staying in private homes need an invitation from a Russian organization. Two places that offer this service for a fee are **www.waytorussia.net**; and Sindbad's Hostel, **www.sindbad.ru** (© **812/331-2020**). Start the process several weeks before you leave. If you apply by mail, you will have to send your passport to the embassy.

While in Russia you need to **register your visa**. Most hotels will do this for you. If they don't offer this service, check with the visa agencies above.

RUSSIAN EMBASSY LOCATIONS OVERSEAS

United States: Embassy: 2641 Tunlaw Rd. NW, Washington, DC (© 202/939-8907, 202/939-8913, or 202/939-8918; www.russianembassy.org).

Consulates: 9 E. 91 St., New York, NY (© 212/348-0926); 2790 Green St., San Francisco, CA (© 415/928-6878); 2322 Westin Building, 2001 6th Ave., Seattle, WA (© 206/728-1910).

Britain: 5 Kensington Palace Gardens, London W8 4QS (© 0870/005-6972).

Canada: 52 Range Rd., Ottawa, Ontario K1N 8G5 (© 613/594-8488).

Australia: 78 Canberra Ave., Griffith, Canberra, ACT 2603 (© 02/6295-9474).

Ireland: 186 Orwell Rd., Rathgar, Dublin (© 01/492-3492).

CUSTOMS REGULATIONS

WHAT YOU CAN BRING INTO RUSSIA

Visitors can bring in most things other than weapons, drugs, and livestock. If you have cash in any currency worth more than $1,500; anything antique; or valuable jewelry, laptop computers, cameras, or other electronics, then fill out a Customs declaration form upon entry and go through the **Red Channel** at airport Customs. The declaration form will be stamped and returned to you, and you must present it again upon departure. You can take up to $10,000 if you declare it.

WHAT YOU CAN TAKE HOME FROM RUSSIA

Most souvenirs are safe to take home, except antiques, artwork, and caviar. Travelers are currently allowed to take 250 grams (10 oz.) out of the country. The rules on artwork and antiques change frequently; they most often affect religious icons, old samovars, and artwork worth over $1,000. In some cases, the item cannot be exported; in others, export is permitted but only with Culture Ministry certification. Most vendors can complete the export certification for you. Tourists wishing to export anything valuable or anything made before 1960 (including books or Soviet memorabilia) should have the store certify it or clear it themselves with the **Russian Ministry of Culture's Assessment Committee** (in Moscow, © 095/921-3258; in St. Petersburg, © 812/310-1454). Applications are cheap (about $10), but export duties can run up to 100% and the process is tedious.

MONEY

Russia's **ruble** is still not technically a "hard" currency, which means very few banks abroad will exchange them. The U.S. dollar was the de facto second currency in the

---

Currency Confusion

Many hotels, restaurants, and chic shops list their prices in "monetary units" (abbreviated Y.E. in Russian). The unit was essentially another way of saying "dollars" while adhering to the Russian law that forbids businesses from trading in any currency other than the ruble. Today the monetary unit is either pegged to the dollar, the euro, or somewhere in between. Restaurants and hotels will have a note at the front desk and on the menus or price lists indicating the current "monetary unit exchange rate" (for example: 28 rubles = 1 Y.E.). It's a good idea to have a small calculator handy for times like this. Even if the price is listed in dollar-pegged "units," however, you have to pay your bill in rubles.

1990s. If you're not queasy about carrying cash from home, change it at currency exchange booths. Booths in town offer more competitive rates than do hotels and airports and do not charge commissions, though most buy only U.S. dollars and euros. Be sure to have crisp, new bills, as exchange booths often refuse well-worn notes or those printed pre-1995.

The easiest way to get **cash** in Moscow and St. Petersburg is from an ATM. The **Cirrus** (© 800/424-7787; www.mastercard.com) and **PLUS** (© 800/843-7587; www.visa.com) networks span the globe. Most Russian ATMs accept both.

Credit cards are welcome in nearly all Russian hotels and many restaurants, but many museums and train stations take only cash. Cards most commonly accepted in Russia are American Express, Visa, MasterCard, and Eurocard.

Few places in Russia accept **traveler's checks** outside major hotels and restaurants, and those that do usually only accept American Express.

Current exchange rates are around 28 rubles to the U.S. dollar and 50 rubles to the British pound.

WHEN TO GO

Frost-tinged, wind-whipped, ice-glazed. Snow blankets much of Russia for most of the year, and Moscow and St. Petersburg usually see flurries in May and September. Understandably, prices are lower September through May and tourist sites less crowded. Hotel and airline rates spike around the New Year's holiday.

Most visitors favor **summer,** both in Moscow and subarctic St. Petersburg, with sunsets that linger until sunrise, balmy temperatures, and all-night activity that makes you forget it's 3am and you haven't slept. Summer weather in both cities can be unpredictable, though, with spells of heavy heat (and rare air-conditioning) or drizzly cold. Bring layers and an umbrella no matter when you go.

Autumn is a few idyllic weeks in late September and early October when the poplars and oaks shed their leaves and the afternoon sun warms you enough to help you through the cooling nights. Spring, a few weeks in April, is slushy and succinct.

If a **winter wonderland** is your fantasy, Russia in December won't disappoint you. The northern sun shines softly low on the horizon, and snow masks garbage-strewn courtyards. Cross-country skiing fans can wind through forests within Moscow city limits or skate-ski along the frozen Gulf of Finland in St. Petersburg. However, many country palaces and other outdoor sites close in winter.

Businesses and government agencies slow down considerably because of vacations the first 2 weeks of January, the first 2 weeks of May, and much of August. These are calmer times to visit Russia but can prove a nightmare if you have visa problems or other administrative needs.

Average temperatures in Moscow and St. Petersburg range from around 12°F (–11°C) in January to 66°F (19°C) in July.

HOLIDAYS

January 1 (New Year's Day), January 2, January 7 (Russian Orthodox Christmas), February 23 (Armed Forces Day), March 8 (International Women's Day), Monday following Orthodox Easter (which is usually 1 or 2 weeks after Catholic/Protestant Easter), May 1 and 2 (Labor Day/Spring Festival), May 9 (Victory Day), June 12 (Russian Independence Day), November 7 (Day of Reconciliation and Accord), and December 12 (Constitution Day). December 25 is not a holiday in Russia. Commerce slows down during holidays but doesn't shut down. Many museums and restaurants remain open but with limited hours.

HEALTH CONCERNS

No vaccinations are necessary to visit Russia, though there have been cases of diphtheria and cholera in provincial areas in recent years. Most visitors' biggest health challenges are digestive, either from St. Petersburg's bacteria-ridden water or dubiously prepared street food. Bottled water is cheap and widely available. HIV is a growing problem.

GETTING THERE
BY PLANE

Russia's chief international carrier remains Aeroflot. Delta is the only major U.S. airline that flies into Russia, though all major European carriers serve Moscow and St. Petersburg. You can often find good deals through British Airways, BMI, Air France,

---

Major Festivals in Russia

The biggest party of the year is undoubtedly **New Year's Eve.** After the Communists wiped Christmas off the official calendar, this date became the focus for gift-giving and family celebrations. Since the fall of Communism, **Orthodox Christmas (January 7)** and **Easter** have reemerged as major religious holidays, marked by feasts and church services. **Maslenitsa** or Butter week in **February/March** is traditionally a time to eat lots of buttery *bliny* and other rich foods before Orthodox Lent begins, and many towns stage raucous Maslenitsa festivals. Many still celebrate **Labor Day (May 1)** with parades under red Communist banners. **Victory Day** on **May 9** is still a major Russian holiday commemorating Hitler's defeat in World War II.

Cultural festivals include Moscow's **Easter Arts Festival** in **April/May,** featuring choral ensembles and bell-ringing. St. Petersburg's **White Nights** in **late June/early July** is 2 weeks of all-night concerts, film festivals, and boat tours to celebrate the northern lights, when the sun never sets. The city's **White Days** festival in **late December** includes winter carnivals and a dense program of dance, opera, and orchestral performances.

and KLM. For a cheaper option, try the Eastern European airlines, such as Poland's LOT, or Hungary's Malév; or Asian carriers such as Air India. For contact information for airlines serving Moscow and/or St. Petersburg, see p. 575.

BY TRAIN

Rail travel into and around Russia is romantic and often comfortable, but time-consuming. The most direct train route from London to Moscow, for example, takes 48 hours. Customs procedures are unpredictable on trains. If you're traveling through Belarus or Ukraine you will need a transit visa; contact your nearest embassy or consulate for details.

BY CAR

The country's vast expanse makes arriving by car a daunting proposition. Roads outside central Moscow and St. Petersburg are dismal, signage is poor and often only in the Cyrillic alphabet, and roadside services—including gas stations—are scarce. Be sure you have international documentation, including car registration and insurance, and an international driver's license. Your visa should indicate you are bringing a car into the country. Renting a car once you arrive is a more reliable and pleasant option.

BY BUS

Several European tour companies offer bus trips to Moscow, usually from Germany; or to St. Petersburg, usually from Finland. The journey from Berlin to Moscow is long, about 2 days, and involves poorly maintained Russian highways and long waits at the borders. You will need transit visas if you travel through Belarus, as most Moscow-bound routes go. The Helsinki-to-St. Petersburg journey takes about 7 hours and is often included on Scandinavian-based tours.

PACKAGES FOR THE INDEPENDENT TRAVELER

Package tours are simply a way to buy the airfare, accommodations, and other elements of your trip at the same time and often at discounted prices. Tour companies to try are **Eastern Tours,** focusing on reasonably priced tours to Moscow, St. Petersburg, and Kiev (© 800/339-6967; www.traveltorussia.com); and **Cosmos Tours** (© 800/276-1241; www.cosmos.com). Most major airlines offer air/land packages, and several big online travel agencies—Expedia, Travelocity, Orbitz, Site59, and Lastminute.com—also do a brisk business in packages.

ESCORTED TOURS

Russia's tourism industry is only beginning to tap the travel possibilities across the world's largest country, and this makes an escorted tour—with a group leader, including airfare, hotels, meals, admission costs, and local transportation—quite appealing. The main drawback of an escorted tour is its high cost.

For general-interest tours, **Escorted Russian Tours** (© 800/942-3301; www.escortedrussiantours.com) provides a range of offerings focusing on Moscow and St. Petersburg, as do the U.K.-based **Russian Gateway** (© 07050-803-160; www.russiangateway.co.uk) and the Russian-based **www.tourstorussia.com**.

One popular excursion is a **cruise from St. Petersburg to Moscow.** It takes your boat about 10 days to wind through rivers and canals, with stops at the island monastery at Valaam, the fairy tale–like wooden village of Kizhi, lakes Ladoga and Onega, and the Volga river towns of Yaroslavl and Kostroma. **Russian Tours** (www.rus-tours.com) and **Russiana** (www.russiana.co.uk) are two places to start.

GETTING AROUND RUSSIA
BY TRAIN

The most pleasant, romantic, and historical way to travel around Russia is by train. The Moscow–St. Petersburg route is the most frequented and best maintained. Travelers choose between a 8-hour night trip in a comfortable sleeping compartment, and a 5-hour day trip (prices run from $45–$85). Arranging train tickets before you arrive, for example through a travel agent, is the safest way to go. Most hotels can arrange train tickets to major cities.

Commuter trains (called *elektrichki*) with hard benches and rock-bottom prices serve many of the country estates and other sights just outside the big cities.

BY PLANE

Given Russia's size, plane travel is crucial for reaching more distant destinations. The Russian airlines Aeroflot and Rossiya (formerly Pulkovo) dominate the Moscow–St. Petersburg route, and prices for a one-way ticket run $60 to $100. Flights on this route are nearly all on large, sturdy, and reliable Soviet-era jets, and the service is steadily improving. See **www.aeroflot.ru**, **www.pulkovo.ru**, or **www.eastline-tour.ru**.

BY CAR

Renting a car can be a reasonable way to get around, but a strongly recommended alternative is to rent a car with a driver. It can cost no more than a standard rental. Companies to try for Avis (www.avis.com), Hertz (www.hertz.com), or Europcar (www.europcar.com).

BY BUS

Russian-run tourist buses offer day trips to cities on the Golden Ring outside Moscow and several sights around St. Petersburg, and are generally comfortable. Vendors often hawk tours on loudspeakers at central spots such as St. Petersburg's Nevsky Prospekt metro station and Moscow's Red Square. Hotels can often arrange bus tours.

TIPS ON ACCOMMODATIONS

Luxury chains are well represented, and include Marriott, InterContinental, and Sheraton. Holiday Inn and Best Western are somewhat cheaper, but Moscow in particular has too few midrange hotel rooms to satisfy demand. Russia's star-rating system is an unreliable indicator of quality.

Several **Soviet-era hotels** used by package tours are undergoing renovations, and the increased price for these rooms is worth it for the improved plumbing and service.

Russian **bed-and-breakfasts** usually occupy a single floor of an apartment building. Some were once communal apartments, but today they are renovated and quite comfortable. In St. Petersburg, **"minihotels"** are often a renovated floor of an apartment building, and they offer more services than most bed-and-breakfasts.

Renting a **private apartment** for your stay is also popular, opening up more options in price and location than the hotel industry can. This is especially convenient during high seasons. The safest bet is to use a real-estate agency that services the apartment and is available for assistance at all hours in case of emergency.

If you're seeking a closer look at day-to-day Russian existence, or want to learn or practice Russian, a **home stay** can be a good option. The ideal home stay is an apartment with a family history and a family member eager to tell you about it. The best way to determine what you're getting into is to call your hosts before you reserve.

Shopping online for hotels is generally done by booking through the hotel's own website or through an independent hotel agency. Prices can vary considerably from site to site and it pays to shop around. Three Russian-specialty sites to try are **www.hotels-russia.net**, **www.bnb.ru**, and **www.waytorussia.net**. Even the highest-end locations sometimes offer deep discounts through online or traditional travel agencies or their own websites, up to 60% off the official rate.

Neither Moscow nor St. Petersburg offers an official reservations service, and your chances of just showing up and getting a room are slim, even in hostels. You are strongly recommended to reserve in advance by phone or online.

Be sure to find out *before you reserve* whether your hotel or host can arrange your **visa invitation.** If not, you'll need to find a reputable travel agency to do that for you, which could cost up to $100 more and takes at least 2 weeks.

TIPS ON DINING

Restaurants generally serve continuously from lunch through dinner, and few are open before noon. Keep an eye out for **"business lunches,"** a good way to get a reasonably priced meal and quick service at midday.

Top-end hotels offer elaborate, all-you-can-eat **Sunday brunches,** replete with caviar and Russian delicacies. These hotels often offer a pleasant afternoon tea.

Try restaurants that specialize in Russian or fusion Russian-European cuisine, or sample the cuisines from other former Soviet republics: the Caucasus Mountains spices of Georgia, Azerbaijan, and Armenia. These cuisines have worked their way into Russian cooking over the centuries, and they boast a much richer selection of fruits, vegetables, and spices than Russia's cold climate can produce.

International chain restaurants, hotel restaurants, and those in the top price categories all have nonsmoking sections; elsewhere it's hit-or-miss.

TIPS ON SHOPPING

The chief challenge in finding unique souvenirs and gifts in Russia is determining whether you can export them. See "Customs Regulations," above, for the regulations of Russia's Culture Ministry, which affect Orthodox icons, samovars, and many artworks. Demand receipts when buying anything valuable, even items from open-air markets.

Moscow and St. Petersburg have no sales tax, but be clear with the vendor about what currency is being cited (see "Money," above). VAT is included in the price, but it is not refundable at the border as it is in some European countries.

Hotel gift shops are the most expensive places in town for souvenirs, and heavily touristed areas are a close second. Better bets are small crafts shops or **outdoor markets** farther from the center of town. For Orthodox icons and other church-related paraphernalia, the monasteries have the most authentic and attractive selection.

In general, vendors have become much more market-savvy after a decade of capitalism. That means the shocking bargains of black market days are long gone, but it also means that quality is more reliable and competition has livened up the selection of products available. Beware, as in all big cities, of con artists on the street trying to sell a "real" silver fox hat or czarist medal hat for a suspiciously low price. Finally, avoid purchasing vodka from street kiosks—the rock-bottom prices often conceal liquids of dubious quality.

3 Moscow

Moscow has matured over a millennium into a richly layered, ever-expanding, and never-sleeping metropolis. Its sporadic growth has left it without a compact down-town, which means that great sights, hotels, and restaurants can be found in nearly any corner of the city. Its vast territory requires plenty of walking and rides on public transport.

VISITOR INFORMATION

Hotels or tour desks are generally the best source of information, although **Intourist,** formerly the government tourist agency, still has Moscow offices in the Kosmos Hotel at 150 Prospekt Mira (℃ **095/730-1919;** www.intourist.ru) and 15 Stoleshnikov Pereulok (℃ **095/925-3434**). Pick up a copy of the free English-language daily *The Moscow Times* for weather, exchange rates, and entertainment listings. Most of the hotels listed carry copies. See also "Visitor Information" in section 2 in this chapter.

For general city tours and Kremlin tours, **Capital Tours** (4 Ilinka Ulitsa, inside Gostiny Dvor; ℃ **095/232-2442;** www.capitaltours.ru) is the best equipped and most friendly. Its Kremlin tours include the Armory and run 6 days a week at 10:30am and at 3pm, for $20 plus admission. City bus tours run daily at 11am and 2:30pm for $20.

GETTING THERE

BY PLANE   Most international flights arrive at **Sheremetevo-2 Airport** (℃ **095/ 956-4666** or 095/578-4727; www.sheremetyevo-airport.ru), 30km (18 miles) north of downtown. Taxis to the city center run at around $30 (£15). **Moscow Taxi** (www. moscow-taxi.com) and **Taxi Blues** (℃ **095/789-6654**) offer good English-speaking services. Buses from Sheremetevo-2 stop at Rechnoi Vokzal metro station (bus no. 551) or Planernaya metro station (bus no. 517). A few European airlines now arrive at the bright, renovated **Domodedovo Airport** (℃ **095/933-6666** or 095/363-3064; www.domodedovo.ru), 50km (28 miles) south of the center. It runs a train direct to Paveletsky station, just south of the city center. Taxis from Domodedovo to the cen-ter take about an hour and cost 856 rubles–1,427 rubles ($30–$50/£15–£25), payable in rubles.

BY TRAIN   The St. Petersburg–Moscow train route brings you into Leningradsky station, conveniently located on the Circle Line of the metro. Western European trains generally arrive in Belorussky station, barely north of the city center and within walk-ing distance of the hotels on busy Tverskaya street.

BY BUS   Buses arrive at **Tsentralny Avtovokzal (Central Bus Terminal)** at 2 Ural-skaya Ulitsa (℃ **095/468-0400**). The Shcholkovskaya metro station is adjacent. Taxis from the terminal take about 30 minutes to reach the center at a rate of $15 (£8).

BY CAR   Take the vehicle to your hotel and inquire about secure parking. Don't drive around Moscow.

GETTING AROUND

BY PUBLIC TRANSPORTATION   The **Moscow Metro** is an attraction unto itself (p. 584), and well worth a visit just to view a few stations. Station entrances are marked with a letter M. Opening and closing times are roughly 5:30am to 1am. Tick-ets are sold in each station; 10 trips cost 105 rubles ($3.80/£2).

Three of the best **tram** lines (A, 3, and 39) run along the Boulevard Ring before crossing the Moscow River, offering a stunning view of the Kremlin. **Trolleybuses** are a good option for travel around the Garden Ring Road or along Novy Arbat Street. Trolley stops are marked with the letter T, and tram stops with the letters TP. Trams and trolleybuses run from 6am to midnight. Tickets for trams and trolleybuses cost 11 rubles (40¢/20p) from the driver.

BY TAXI   Official taxis are hard to come by in Moscow, except at train stations and major hotels. Try Moscow Taxi (online only at www.moscow-taxi.com) or City Taxi (① 095/789-3232).

BY CAR   The following agencies rent cars with and without drivers: **AM Rent** at 65 Dubininskaya Ulitsa, ① 095/952-9658, www.amrent.ru; **Budget Rent-a-Car** at Sheremetevo-2 Airport, ① 095/578-7344; and 23 1-aya Tverskaya-Yamskaya Ulitsa, ① 095/931-9700; www.budgetrentacar.com.

FAST FACTS: Moscow

American Express   The main local office is at 21a Sadovo-Kudrinskaya Ulitsa (① 095/755-9001), open from 9am to 7pm Monday through Friday, from 9am to 2pm Saturday.

Currency Exchange   Exchange booths *(obmen valyuty)* are found in every hotel, at many restaurants, and near all major metro stations. Many are open 24 hours. Banks can give cash advances on a credit card in rubles.

Doctor   The **American Medical Center Moscow**, 1 Grokholsky Pereulok (① 095/933-7700), has Western-standard medical care and English-speaking staff.

Embassies   **United States:** 19/23 Novinsky Bulvar; ① 095/256-4261; **Britain:** 10 Smolenskaya Naberezhnaya; ① 095/956-7301; **Canada:** 23 Starokonyushenniy Pereulok; ① 095/956-6666; **Australia:** 13 Kropotkinskiy Pereulok; ① 095/956-6070; **Ireland:** 5 Grokholsky Pereulok; ① 095/288-4101.

Emergencies   For fire, dial ① **01**; police ① **02**; ambulance ① **03**.

Internet Access   Most hotel business centers offer Wi-Fi or online access. For Internet cafes, try 24-hour **Time Online** at Okhotny Ryad shopping center next to the Kremlin (1 Manezhnaya Ploshchad; www.timeonline.ru), or **CafeMax** (see www.cafemax.ru for locations).

Postal Services   The main international post office is at 26 Myasnitskaya (① 095/928-6311). It's open daily 8am to 7:45pm. Several international shipping companies serve Russia, such as **FedEx** (① 095/234-3400) and **UPS** (① 095/961-2211), though their services are not cheap.

Telephone   The city code for Moscow is 095. For international calls from Russia, dial 8, wait for a tone, then dial 10, then dial the country code. Access numbers for AT&T in Moscow are ① **755-5042** and **325-5042**; MCI is ① **747-3322**; BT Direct is ① **10-80-01-10-1044**; Canada Direct is ① **755-5045**.

WHERE TO STAY

The boom in Moscow hotel space since the Soviet Union's collapse has focused on luxury or business-class accommodations, and demand is high for midrange hotels.

Most of the better deals on hotels are found beyond the Garden Ring Road, well away from the main sights. If your hotel is near a metro station, that can reduce travel time considerably. Rack rates listed here are in U.S. dollars, and do **not** include breakfast and the 18% VAT, unless noted.

VERY EXPENSIVE

Baltschug Kempinski ✸✸✸   The Baltschug led the post-Soviet transformation of this district across the Moscow River from the Kremlin. Its pristine, buttercup-yellow facade immediately altered the neglected neighborhood of canals and abandoned churches. Just over the bridge is Red Square and its attendant activity; the bohemian bustle of Pyatnitskaya Street spreads out in the other direction, to the south. Don't miss the sumptuous brunch of prerevolutionary Russian delicacies and all the caviar you could want.

1 Ulitsa Balchug. © **800/426-3135** or 095/230-6500. Fax 095/230-6502. www.kempinski-moscow.com. 232 units. $360 (£180) double; from $800 (£400) suite; $65 (£33) extra bed. AE, DC, MC, V. Metro: Teatralnaya, Kuznetsky Most, or Lubyanka. **Amenities:** 3 restaurants; 2 bars; indoor heated pool; health club; spa; Jacuzzi; 2 saunas; children's center; game room; concierge; tour desk; car-rental desk; limo; 24-hr. business center; Wi-Fi; shopping arcade; salon; 24-hr. room service; massage; babysitting; laundry service; same-day dry cleaning; nonsmoking rooms; executive rooms. *In room:* A/C, TV w/satellite, dataport, minibar, fridge, coffeemaker, hair dryer, iron, safe.

EXPENSIVE

Holiday Inn Vinogradovo ✸ *Kids*   This resort-type facility is unlike anything else Moscow has to offer. Well removed from the city, it's tucked in a forest 4km (2½ miles) beyond the bypass marking the city limits, not too far from the airport. The free shuttle to and from town takes awhile but makes the hotel feel less remote. The plus side of such a distant locale is the availability of outdoor amenities unheard of at other Moscow hotels: horseback riding, and cross-country skiing in winter; watersports in summer. Guest rooms are generous in size. Kids eat free.

Dmitrovskoye Shosse, Estate 171. © **877/477-4674** or 095/937-0670. www.ichotels.com. 154 units. $200–$270 (£100–£135) double, depending on when you reserve; from $300 (£150) suite. AE, DC, MC, V. 4km (2½ miles) north of Moscow Ring Rd. along Dmitrovskoye Shosse (visible from the highway). **Amenities:** 2 restaurants; 2 bars; indoor pool; health club; sauna; tour desk; transport desk; 24-hr. business center; salon; 24-hr. room service; massage; laundry room; same-day dry cleaning; nonsmoking rooms; executive rooms; bowling alley. *In room:* TV w/satellite, fridge, coffeemaker, iron.

Marco Polo Presnja ✸✸   A rare example of style, service, and affordability when it opened in 1993, the Marco Polo now faces greater competition in its category, and its prices have risen accordingly. Yet it remains one of Moscow's most coveted places to stay. The leafy neighborhood between the Boulevard Ring and the Garden Ring is ideal for strolling, and nearby Malaya Bronnaya Street offers several unusual shopping and dining finds you won't encounter on the city's main drags. The main attraction nearby is the park at Patriarchs' Ponds. Despite the hotel's relatively modest size, its guest rooms, bathrooms, closets, and corridors are spacious and airy.

4 Spiridonevsky Pereulok. © **095/244-3631**. Fax 095/926-5402. www.presnja.ru. 72 units. $300 (£150) double; from $370 (£185) suite; $48 (£24) extra bed. AE, DC, MC, V. Metro: Pushkinskaya, Tverskaya, or Mayakovskaya. **Amenities:** 2 restaurants; bar and lounge; sauna; concierge; tour desk; transport desk; business center; room service; massage; laundry service; dry cleaning; executive rooms. *In room:* A/C, TV w/satellite and pay movies, minibar, fridge, hair dryer, iron.

Metropol ✸✸   The Art Nouveau mosaic by Mikhail Vrubel that tops the Metropol's facade sets it apart in era and in style from other hotels of its class. Some

Moscow Lodging, Dining & Attractions

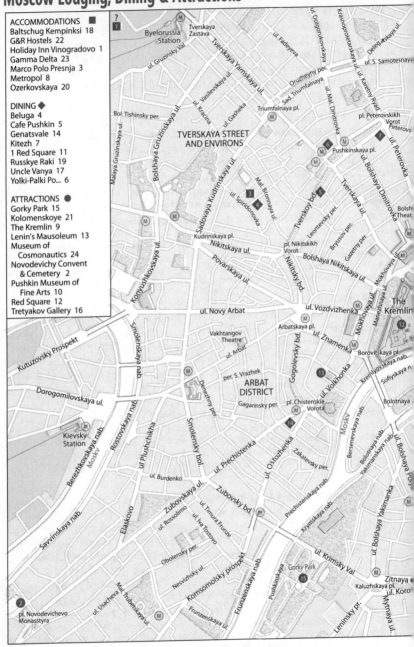

ACCOMMODATIONS ■
Baltschug Kempinksi 18
G&R Hostels 22
Holiday Inn Vinogradovo 1
Gamma Delta 23
Marco Polo Presnja 3
Metropol 8
Ozerkovskaya 20

DINING ◆
Beluga 4
Cafe Pushkin 5
Genatsvale 14
Kitezh 7
1 Red Square 11
Russkye Raki 19
Uncle Vanya 17
Yolki-Palki Po... 6

ATTRACTIONS ●
Gorky Park 15
Kolomenskoye 21
The Kremlin 9
Lenin's Mausoleum 13
Museum of
    Cosmonautics 24
Novodevichy Convent
    & Cemetery 2
Pushkin Museum of
    Fine Arts 10
Red Square 12
Tretyakov Gallery 16

Common terms and abbreviations

prospekt/pr.	Avenue
ulitsa/ul.	Street
naberezhnaya/nab.	Embankment
most	Bridge
ploshchad/pl.	Square or plaza
sad	Garden
ostrov	Island

of its grandeur has faded in comparison to the newer luxury hotels in the neighborhood, but the Metropol, built in 1901 and last renovated in 1991, remains a historic and visual treasure. The rooms are compact for the price, but several offer antique writing tables or armchairs once belonging to aristocratic Russian families. The Metropol's western wall is still etched with stylistic letters reading: THE DICTATORSHIP OF THE PROLETARIAT IS READY TO FREE HUMANITY FROM THE YOKE OF CAPITAL.

1/4 Teatralny Proyezd. ☎ 095/927-6040. www.metropol-moscow.ru. 365 units. $350 (£175) double; from $500 (£250) suite. AE, DC, MC, V. Metro: Teatralnaya or Lubyanka. **Amenities:** 3 restaurants; nightclub and casino; health club; spa; Jacuzzi; sauna; concierge; tour desk; transport desk; limo; 24-hr. business center; shopping arcade; salon; 24-hr. room service; massage; laundry service; same-day dry cleaning; nonsmoking rooms; executive rooms. *In room:* A/C, TV w/satellite, dataport, minibar, fridge, coffeemaker, hair dryer, iron, safe.

MODERATE

Gamma-Delta (★) (*Value*)   This is the closest to a Western-standard facility in this price range. Lobby computer screens tastefully and helpfully display prices and services in Russian and English. Staff is accustomed to international travelers.

71 Izmailovskoye Shosse. ☎ 095/737-7055. Fax 095/166-7486. www.izmailovo.ru. More than 1,000 units. $60 (£30) unrenovated double, $80 (£40) renovated double; from $80 (£40) suite. AE, DC, MC, V. Metro: Izmailovsky Park. **Amenities:** 9 restaurants and bars; sauna; game room; concierge; tour desk; transport desk; business center; shopping arcade; salon; room service; laundry and ironing service. *In room:* TV w/cable, fridge, hair dryer.

Ozerkovskaya (★★) (*Value*)   A welcome addition to the hotel scene south of the Moscow River, the Ozerkovskaya occupies a new brick building set off from the road along one of the canals in the picturesque Zamoskvarechye. Eager staff and cozy yet spacious rooms make the Ozerkovskaya one of Moscow's best hotels in this category. Its location, deep in a residential neighborhood, is not exactly central, but it's certainly quiet. Tretyakov Gallery can be reached on foot; and the Paveletskaya metro station is about a 10-minute walk away. Rates include VAT and breakfast.

50 Ozerkovskaya Naberezhnaya, building 2. ☎ 095/951-9582. Fax 095/951-9753. ozerkovskaya@bk.ru. 25 units. $170 (£85) double; from $210 (£105) suite. AE, DC, MC, V. Metro: Paveletskaya. **Amenities:** Restaurant and bar; health club with very small pool; sauna; billiard room; tour desk; transport desk; business center; salon; room service; laundry and ironing service; dry cleaning; executive rooms. *In room:* TV w/satellite, dataport, kitchen, minibar, fridge, hair dryer.

INEXPENSIVE

G&R Hostels   Though Moscow lacks hostels of the traditional sort, several independent entrepreneurs have taken over a floor or more of existing buildings and converted them into low-budget accommodations. G&R is one of the more pleasant and reliable in this category, and offers family-style units with private bathrooms and telephones, in addition to singles and doubles with shared bathrooms. The hostel can arrange for visas, a big plus in this price category. G&R is almost on top of a metro station (Ryazansky Prospekt), and the ride to the center takes about 15 minutes. Prices include VAT and breakfast, and discounts are available.

3/2 Zelenodolskaya St. ☎ 095/378-0001. www.hostels.ru. 15 units. $30 (£15) single with shared bathroom; $48 (£24) double with shared bathroom; $70–$95 (£35–£48) family suite. MC, V. Metro: Ryazansky Prospekt. **Amenities:** Tour and transport desk; visa support; common kitchen; business center. *In room:* Some rooms with cable TV, fridge.

WHERE TO DINE

In today's Moscow you can find food to satisfy any palate, in marked contrast to the decades of Soviet shortages. There are now restaurants to suit any pocketbook or craving—at any time of day or night. See also "Tips on Dining" on p. 574.

VERY EXPENSIVE

Beluga ✸✸ RUSSIAN   The haute couture attitudes, decor, and clientele of this caviar bar fit perfectly with the luxuriousness of its specialty, pearly sturgeon eggs. The caviar is excellent and expensive, though not necessarily better than what you find in other top Russian restaurants. Caviar is served straight, in set quantities by the gram, and accompanied by a generous array of rich dark breads, pasta, and grilled vegetables.

12/9 Spiridonevsky Pereulok. ✆ 095/411-4444. Reservations recommended. Main courses $20–$100 (£10–£50). AE, DC, MC, V. Daily noon–midnight. Metro: Pushkinskaya.

1 Red Square (Krasnaya Ploshchad, 1) ✸✸✸ RUSSIAN   The name says it all. From the top floor of the National History Museum on the north side of Red Square, you can enjoy a meal as you gaze directly across the cobblestone expanse leading to St. Basil's Cathedral on the opposite end. The museum's neo-Gothic turrets and the location's historical significance imbue the restaurant staff and the Russian clientele with a sense of national importance. The menu is Russian and traditional, including a re-creation of the "czar's menu" of a century ago.

1 Red Square (enter through Historical Museum). ✆ 095/925-3600. http://redsquare.ru/english. Reservations recommended. Main courses $20 (£10) and up; business lunch $19 (£10). AE, MC, V. Daily noon–midnight. Metro: Ploshchad Revolutsii or Okhotny Ryad.

EXPENSIVE

Cafe Pushkin ✸✸✸ RUSSIAN   Perhaps Moscow's most sophisticated 24-hour restaurant, the three-story Cafe Pushkin has the feel of an 18th-century mansion but dates from the late 1990s. Each of the floors has a different thrust, with a cherrywood bar and well-lit cafe on the first floor, a more formal dining room on the second, and a decadent and breezy summer cafe on the top. Standouts are *ukha,* a creamy, spiced fish soup; and grilled sterlet (sturgeon) with forest mushrooms.

26a Tverskoi Bulvar. ✆ 095/229-5590. Reservations required for restaurant and summer terrace. Main courses $15–$40 (£8–£20). AE, DC, MC, V. 1st floor open daily 24 hr., top floors daily noon–midnight. Metro: Pushkinskaya.

Kitezh ✸✸✸ RUSSIAN   Kitezh sees its purpose as upholding tradition and legend. If you have just one real Russian meal in Moscow, make it here. The restaurant is poised in a stone basement that re-creates a 17th-century farmhouse atmosphere, across from a 14th-century monastery on a quiet stretch of historic Petrovka Street, a great district for a postmeal stroll. Sauces are rich, divine, and heavy. This is one of the few Russian restaurants that does justice to beef stroganoff. Desserts include thick, Jell-O-like *kisel,* and light and buttery *bliny* with homemade jam.

23/10 Ulitsa Petrovka. ✆ 095/209-6685. Reservations recommended. Main courses $12–$25 (£6–£13). AE, MC, V. Daily noon–midnight. Metro: Kuznetsky Most.

MODERATE

Genatsvale ✸✸ GEORGIAN   This family-run restaurant—whose name means "comrade" in Georgian—is Moscow's best introduction to the colorful and flavorful cuisine of Georgia. The country-style dining hall is a welcome dose of earthiness on this street of chic restaurants. Try the finely ground lamb kabob, or the garlic-walnut paste rolled in thinly sliced eggplant.

12/1 Ostozhenka. ✆ 095/202-0445. Main courses $8–$20 (£4–£10). MC, V. Daily noon–midnight. Metro: Kropotkinskaya.

Uncle Vanya ✸✸ RUSSIAN   This cozy, artsy treasure left its original location in a theater basement to relocate to another basement in this even more cozy, artsy section of town. The restaurant takes its name from one of Anton Chekhov's plays. The menu of Russian favorites is accessible and safe, with highlights including cold sorrel soup (*zelyoniye shchi*), wild mushrooms, and buckwheat kasha.

16 Pyatnitskaya (entrance in courtyard). © **095/951-0586**. Main courses $5–$15 (£3–£8). MC, V. Daily 8:30am–midnight. Metro: Novokuznetskaya.

INEXPENSIVE

Russkye Raki (Russian Crayfish) ⊛ RUSSIAN   To a Russian, the crayfish is a summertime staple as crucial to the national cuisine as caviar, and much more accessible. Bright red, just-boiled crayfish are the main draw, with variations such as boiled in beer, spiced, or doused in cream sauce.

11/4 Maroseika, building 1. © **095/921-8545**. Main courses $3–$8 (£2–£4). No credit cards. Daily 11am–11pm. Metro: Kitai-Gorod.

Moments Banya Bliss

It's not on most tourist itineraries, but if you can squeeze it in, there's no better way to shed city grime and immerse yourself in Russian culture than to visit a banya. Something between a steam bath and a sauna, the banya has been an important cleansing and resting ritual for centuries. Traditional banyas are huts built alongside rural houses, where families take turns steaming themselves clean, then plunge into a tub of cool water or a nearby stream, or roll in the snow to cool off. In Moscow, banya culture ranges from elite spa-type facilities with expensive body masks and luxurious pedicures (for both sexes) to more proletarian facilities used by residents of communal apartments tired of waiting in line for the shower at home. Thought to cure many ills, the banya is a great rainy-day activity for tourists, too, if you pick one with a bit of history. In the women's halls, bathers treat the steam water with eucalyptus oil and coat their skin with honey, coffee grounds, or whatever other remedy they learned from grandma. In the men's halls, business deals are often made over copious beer and snacks. In both halls you're likely to see bathers beating each other (gently) with birch branches; the practice is believed to enhance the cleansing process.

Sandunovskiye Banyi, an ornate and cheerful 19th-century bathhouse, is a favorite with "new Russians" and Moscow-based expatriates. They have two levels of service for each gender. A 2-hour deluxe-level session costs $22 (£11); a 2-hour standard-level session costs $14 (£7). The differences between the deluxe and standard sessions are minimal; a "deluxe" session basically translates into more elegant furnishings and a larger steam room. Sheets, towels, and slippers can be rented for $1 to $4 (£80–£3.35), or you can bring your own. The deluxe level is offered Tuesday through Sunday from 8am to 10pm; the standard level is offered Wednesday through Monday from 8am to 10pm. You'll find the baths at 14 Neglinnaya St., buildings 3 to 7; the entrance is on Zvonarsky Pereulok (© **095/925-4631**; www.sanduny.ru).

S lyokhim parom, as the Russians say, or "Good steam to you."

Yolki-Palki Po . . . ✻ ⟨*Value*⟩ CENTRAL ASIAN As soon as you shed your coat, you'll be greeted by a row of fresh ingredients that you heap into a bowl according to your mood and hand to the chef at the center of an enormous circular grill. The Mongolian barbecue–style concept is adapted with central Asian ingredients and Russian side dishes, and it has found huge success in Moscow.

18a Tverskaya Ulitsa. ⟨𝒞⟩ 095/200-3920. Main courses $7 (£4). No credit cards. Daily 11am–5am. Metro: Pushkin-skaya or Tverskaya.

EXPLORING MOSCOW

Moscow is less a beautiful city than a collection of beautiful sights, many of them hidden beyond the expansive modern boulevards that Soviet governments bulldozed through town. The key to delighting in Moscow is to not let it overwhelm you. The things to see fall roughly into four categories: church-related, art-related, Soviet-related, and everything else. Try to get a taste of each, regardless of your interests.

SUGGESTED ITINERARIES

If You Have ❶ Day
Capturing Moscow in 1 day means hitting the **Kremlin** and **Red Square** early and branching out from there (see the **"Walking Tour"** below). In the evening, explore the artsy **Arbat** neighborhood.

If You Have ❷ Days
Use your second day to immerse yourself in Russian art at the **Tretyakov Gallery,** wander the canals of **Zamoskvarechye.** Reserve the evening for **Pushkin Square** and lively **Tverskaya Street.**

If You Have ❸ Days
On the third day in Moscow, spend the morning at **Novodevichy Convent and Cemetery,** a secluded spot that feels miles from the downtown rush. Then take a car or the metro to **Gorky Park.** After lunch, head to the **Pushkin Museum of Fine Arts,** and spend the evening on a bus tour that hits sights farther afield.

THE TOP ATTRACTIONS

The Kremlin This 28-hectare (130-acre) fortress emerged in the 12th century as a wooden encampment, and survived many an invader to become synonymous with modern totalitarianism in the 20th century. Physically it's still a citadel, surrounded by unscalable red-brick walls and tightly guarded gates, though the moat that protected its north and east sides were filled in nearly 200 years ago. Its oak walls were replaced with white stone ones in the 1360s, which were replaced again by 2.2km (1½ miles) of red-brick ramparts in the 1490s. Much of that brick remains standing.

Cathedral Square (Sobornaya Ploshchad) ✻✻✻ forms a monument to Russian architecture of the 15th and 16th centuries, and its cathedrals deserve a thorough tour inside and out. The most prominent building on the square is the **Cathedral of the Assumption** ✻✻, a white limestone building with scalloped arches topped by almost chunky golden domes. Started in 1475 by Italian architect Aristotle Fioravanti, this church is the most tourist-friendly of the cathedrals on the square, with detailed English labels on icons and architectural details.

The Armory Museum ✻✻ (⟨𝒞⟩ 095/302-3776), despite its name, holds much more than guns. The Russo-Byzantine building, dating from the 19th century, occupies the spot where royal treasures were housed since the 14th century and offers a sweeping introduction to Russian history. Exhibits include the Fabergé eggs exchanged by Russia's last royal couple, czar Nicholas II and empress Alexandra.

Kremlin tickets available at Kutafya Tower in Alexander Gardens (© 095/203-0349). Access to the grounds costs $3 (£2) for adults, $2 (75p) for students with ID and for children 7 and up. Admission to the grounds and the Cathedral Square complex costs $12 (£6) for adults, $69 (£35) for students with ID and for children 7 and up. Admission to the Armory costs $14 (£7) for adults, $7 (£4) for students and for children 7 and up.

Red Square (Krasnaya Ploshchad) ★★★

One of the world's most recognizable public spaces, Red Square is as impressive in reality as it is on screen. The square was already famous by 1434, when it was dubbed "Trading Square." Its current name appeared in the 1660s, when the word *krasnaya* meant "beautiful" or "important" as well as "red." The name took on different connotations in the 20th century, when the red flag–bearing Communists staged massive parades and demonstrations on the aptly titled square.

Red Square (Krasnaya Ploshchad). No phone. Free admission. Metro: Ploshchad Revolutsii or Okhotny Ryad.

Lenin's Mausoleum (Mavzolei Lenina)

The embalmed body of the founder of the Soviet state is still on display in a mausoleum on Red Square. The stark Constructivist pyramid of red granite and gray and black labradorite was built in 1930, 6 years after Vladimir Lenin's death. Backpacks are forbidden; they must be left at the bag check by the Kremlin's Borovitsky. Visit after seeing the Kremlin, and then get your bags.

Red Square. No phone. Free admission. Tues, Thurs, and Sat–Sun 10am–1pm. Metro: Ploshchad Revolutsii, Teatralnaya, or Okhotny Ryad.

Novodevichy Convent & Cemetery (Novodevichy Monastyr i Kladbishche) ★★

If you visit only one holy site in Moscow, make it this one. The convent, founded in 1524, became over ensuing eras a carefully arranged complex of churches in a variety of architectural styles. Don't miss the **cemetery** behind the convent, which bears the unique gravestones of many Russian literary, musical, and scientific heroes.

Novodevichy Proyezd. © 095/246-8526. Admission to the grounds $2 (£1); a combined ticket including churches and exhibits $7 (£4). Cemetery admission $2 (£1). Cathedrals may be closed to tourists on Easter and feast days. Wed–Sun 10am–5pm. Metro: Sportivnaya.

The Moscow Metro ★★ (Value)

Most cities' public transit systems are eyesores. Moscow's is a masterpiece. Today it's the world's busiest subway system. Its oldest stations, dating from the 1930s and 1940s, are its grandest. Highlights include Ploshchad Revolutsii, with its bronze sculptures of Soviet swimmers and sailors holding up the marble columns; Kievskaya, with its mosaics portraying Ukrainian-Russian friendship; and Novoslobodskaya, with its Art Nouveau stained glass.

Museum of Cosmonautics (Muzei Kosmonavtiki) ★ (Kids) (Value)

Housed beneath a giant aluminum monument of a rocket soaring into space, this museum is a tribute to the minds and might that put the Soviet Union head-to-head with the United States in the Space Race. It's far from the center (but right on top of a metro station).

Prospekt Mira 111. © 095/283-7914. Admission $1.50 (75p) adults, 75¢ (40p) children over 7. Audioguide in English $3.50 (£2). Tues–Sun 10am–6pm; closed last Fri of each month. Metro: VDNKh.

Tretyakov Gallery (Tretyakovskaya Galereya) ★★★

Newcomers to Russian art and connoisseurs alike leave awed by this collection of masterpieces. The gallery was Russia's first public art museum, and remains the premier repository of Russian art, starting with Orthodox icons dating from Russia's conversion in the 9th century, through to the naturalism of the 19th century, the Art Nouveau works of Mikhail Vrubel, and the 20th-century avant-garde works of Malevich and Kandinsky.

10 Lavrushinsky Pereulok. ℭ **095/230-7788**. Admission $8 (£4) adults, $4.50 (£2) students and children over 7. Audioguide $10 (£5). No credit cards, but there's an ATM. Small group tours in English $35 (£18) plus admission. Tues–Sun 10am–7:30pm. Metro: Tretyakovskaya or Novokuznetskaya.

Pushkin Museum of Fine Arts (Muzei Izobratitelnykh Isskustv imeni Pushkina) ✸✸

An impressive collection of French Impressionist works, ancient Greek sculptures, and Egyptian bronzes, as well as works by Rembrandt, Rubens, and the Italian Renaissance masters. Be sure to view the exhibition of controversial paintings stolen from European Jews by the Nazis and later seized by Soviet troops (Russians call them "rescued" artworks), including pieces by Renoir and van Gogh.

12 Volkhonka. ℭ **095/203-7998**. Admission $11 (£6) adults, $5.25 (£3) students and children 7 and up. Exhibits $3.50 (£2). Audioguides $7 (£4); available at the coat check downstairs. Tues–Sun 10am–7pm. Metro: Kropotkinskaya.

Gorky Park ✸

The most visited part of the park is near the entrance, where an amusement park, ponds, and street performers compete for attention. A space shuttle, designed for space flight but scrapped for lack of funding, is now parked along the river and open to visitors. Note the Lenin carving over the park's columned entrance.

Krymsky Val. Admission $1.75 (90p). Daily 9am–9pm. Metro: Oktyabrskaya or Park Kultury.

Kolomenskoye ✸✸✸ Kids

This park, museum, festival site, and religious-history tour is the jewel of Moscow's estate museums. Kolomenskoye gathers churches and historic buildings from the 15th to the 20th centuries in a huge green space perfect for picnicking, sledding, or lounging in the grass.

39 Prospekt Andropova. ℭ **095/112-5217**. Admission to the park $1.75 (£1). Daily 9am–9pm; museums Tues–Sun 10am–5:30pm. Metro: Kolomenskaya.

WALKING TOUR   HISTORIC MOSCOW

This walk covers several centuries of Moscow's history, and provides a sense of how the eras blend to make modern Moscow. It begins at Red Square, and continues through the neighborhood of **Kitai-Gorod,** with its showcase of Russian architecture from the 15th to 17th centuries. A good time to take this tour is a morning from Wednesday to Sunday when crowds are thinner and exhibits open. Allow 2 to 3 hours.

---

❶ St. Basil's Cathedral

The oldest building on this tour, this 16th-century cathedral has come to symbolize Russia to the rest of the world, but it was almost torn down by Stalin as an anachronistic eyesore. Legend has it that a favorite architect rescued the cathedral by threatening to take his own life on its stairs.

When leaving the cathedral, turn right, away from the Kremlin, down Varvarka Street. Take the stairs on the right-hand side of the street down to the path that runs alongside a string of churches and mansions. This is one of the few sections of Moscow preserved as it was in centuries past. Continue to no. 4:

❷ English Courtyard (Angliisky Podvorye)

This wooden-roofed building is one of the oldest civilian structures in Moscow, a 16th-century merchant's center granted to English traders by Ivan the Terrible. The small exhibit inside is worth a visit for the building's interior and artifacts (labeled in English). It's open Tuesday through Sunday from 10am to 6pm (ℭ **095/298-3952**).

Continue up the path, noting the yellow-and-white (and no longer functioning) Church of St. Maxim the Blessed. The next few buildings were once part of the Znamensky Monastery. No. 10 houses:

❸ The Museum of the Romanov Boyars

The Romanov Boyars (nobles) lived here before Mikhail Romanov was crowned czar in 1613, launching the Romanov dynasty. The only original part of this building is the basement; the rest was added later to re-create conditions of 16th-century Moscow. The building was once part of a minicity that stretched to the Moscow River. The museum is open Wednesday from 11am to 7pm, and Thursday to Sunday from 10am to 6pm (📞 **095/298-3706**). Closed the first Monday of the month.

Head to the building next door, the last one along the row, just beneath the hotel driveway:

❹ St. George's Church

This church was built in two different eras, the 16th and 18th centuries, and its two parts remain different colors. It stills hold regular services.

Head up the stairs to Varvarka proper, and continue down the hill. The street opens onto an intersection that can only be crossed by underground walkway. The sole remaining part of the 16th-century Varvarka gate tower is the white stone base, still visible in the underground passage. Once you're underground, continue straight along your trajectory from Varvarka. Take the first stairwell on your left aboveground. You should emerge in front of:

❺ Cyril and Methodius Monument

Perched in the middle of Slavic Square, this monument portrays the two 9th-century monks credited with inventing the Cyrillic alphabet, used in Russia and many Slavic countries to this day. Up the hill behind the monument stretch the leafy slopes of Novaya Ploshchad (New Square), crisscrossed by shaded paths lined with benches.

Head to the plaza on the far side of Novaya Ploshchad, and look across it at a building that no Russian feels indifferent to:

❻ Lubyanka

The Bolshevik secret police seized this granite-and-sandstone building from an insurance company in 1918, and its residents have spied on Russians ever since. Now it's the headquarters of the Federal Security Service, once led by President Putin.

Head back into the capitalist rush of modern Moscow by crossing over to Myasnitskaya Ulitsa, to the right of Lubyanka. Follow the street past a string of bookshops and cafes until you see Krivokolyonny Pereulok off to the right. Take this street (which translates as "Crooked Knee Lane") past the 18th- and 19th-century mansions now housing offices and apartments, until you reach two churches clustered together:

❼ Church of the Archangel Gabriel & Church of St. Theodore Stratilites

The twisting gold dome of the Church of the Archangel Gabriel is the most noticeable of its nontraditional architectural features. Commissioned in 1705, the church is a clear example of the period when European classicism overrode Russian architecture, with grand buttresses and cornices not seen on most Orthodox churches.

Continue a few yards to the end of Krivokolyonny Pereulok. You'll emerge onto Chistoprudny Bulvar, a boulevard with a green space running down its center. Enter the park and head right, until you reach:

❽ Chistiye Prudy

This area was referred to as "Dirty Ponds" in the days when it housed a meat market, whose refuse ran into the murky pools. The 19th-century city government cleaned it up and rechristened it "Clean Ponds," or Chistiye Prudy. Only one pond remains; it's a mecca for skaters and toddlers on sleds in winter, and for rental boats in summer.

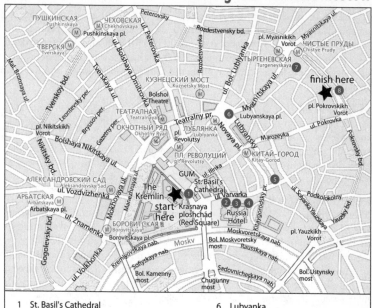

1 St. Basil's Cathedral	6 Lubyanka
2 English Courtyard	7 Church of the Archangel Gabriel &
3 The Museum of the Romanov Boyars	Church of St. Theodore Stratilites
4 St. George's Church	8 Chistye Prudy
5 Cyril and Methodius Monument	

SHOPPING

Just about any souvenir, bauble, or item of clothing can be found just off Red Square, at the two major shopping centers: **GUM** and **Okhotny Ryad**. Moscow's shopping mecca is the huge open-air bazaar open daily at **Izmailovsky Park** (near the metro station of the same name), in eastern Moscow outside the Garden Ring. It has a huge selection of *matryoshka* nesting dolls, plus Russian space-program memorabilia, intricate and original jewelry, blue-hued Uzbek plates, lacquer boxes, and much more.

Kupina's (© 095/202 4100) two stores on the Arbat offer Russian and European art and antiques, and **Alfa-Art** (© 095/230 0091), an established gallery inside the New Tretyakov Modern Art Museum, holds regular auctions for its most valuable works as well as regular sales of its icons, paintings, and other items. For a great introduction to the Russian ceramic style known as Gzhel, with delicate blue designs painted on white porcelain and occasionally trimmed in gold, try **Gzhel** (© 095/299 2953) on Sadoyaya Samotechnaya near Mayakovskaya metro. Hand-embroidered linens from the textile-producing towns along the Volga are a good buy, and can be found at **Vologodsky Len** (© 095/232 9463) near Red Square.

The ornate **Eliseyevsky Gastronom** (*C* **095/209 0760**) on Tverskaya Street has an abundant collection of teas, sweets, and other Russian goods on display beneath its soaring ceilings, while **Aromatny Mir** (*C* **095/917 1160**) on Ulitsa Pokrovka near Kitai Gorod metro features a broad selection of vodkas you won't find at home, as well as wines from the former Soviet republics of Georgia and Moldova, and rich Armenian brandies.

MOSCOW AFTER DARK

A large proportion of Moscow's tourists come primarily for its performing arts or, increasingly, its nightlife. Its reputation in both departments is well-deserved. The most thorough English-language listings for theater, music, and movies are found in the Friday edition of *The Moscow Times* (www.themoscowtimes.com). Check *eXile* newspaper (www.exile.ru) for the latest hot clubs and bars.

PERFORMING ARTS

Bolshoi Theater　Moscow's top dance venue remains the Bolshoi, the showcase for several generations of internationally adored ballet stars. Tchaikovsky's classics still form its backbone. Operas at the Bolshoi stick to the classics, such as *The Marriage of Figaro, The Barber of Seville,* and *Carmen.* Tickets must be purchased at least a week in advance. The Bolshoi is currently undergoing extensive renovations, expected to take until at least 2008. The second stage is still open, hosting the main company and all the same performances. 1 Teatralnaya Sq. *C* **095/292-9986** or 095/250-7317. www.bolshoi.ru. Metro: Teatralnaya.

Chaliapin House Museum　You'll really feel transported to prerevolutionary Russia during a concert in this house, where opera singer Fyodor Chaliapin lived and performed for friends and family. A cluster of chairs around the piano ensures intimacy with the soloists and small ensembles who perform here a few nights a week. 25 Novinsky Bulvar (next to the U.S. Embassy). *C* **095/205-6236.** Metro: Barrikadnaya.

Maly Theater　The theater is called "Maly" (small) only because it's across from the Bolshoi (which means "big" or "grand"), but the Maly's hall is full-size and its performances top-quality. Most shows are in Russian, with an emphasis on classics from Chekhov, Ostrovsky, and Griboyedov. 1/6 Teatralnaya Sq. (across from the Bolshoi). *C* **095/923-2521.** Metro: Teatralnaya.

Moiseyev Ballet　Founded in 1937 by Bolshoi Theater choreographer Igor Moiseyev, this company sought to break free from the restraints of classical dance and has been putting on brilliant performances of their mixture of ballet and folk dance ever since. 31 Tverskaya St. *C* **095/299-5372.** www.moiseyev.org. Metro: Pushkinskaya.

Moscow Conservatory (Konservatoria)　This is the most popular and most historic place to hear Russian and international classical music performed by the country's top orchestras and soloists. The conservatory, housed in an 18th-century mansion now fronted by a statue of Tchaikovsky, is still the premier training ground for Russian musicians. 13 Bolshaya Nikitskaya St. *C* **095/299-8183.** Metro: Arbatskaya.

DANCE CLUBS & BARS

Conservatory　This atrium bar on the top floor of the Ararat Park Hyatt Hotel is one of the few elegant and accessible places to watch Red Square at night. The ergonomic design and gorgeous customers are as eye-catching as the view from the wraparound windows. 4 Neglinnaya Ulitsa. *C* **095/783-1234.** Metro: Teatralnaya or Kuznetsky Most.

Modest Charm of the Bourgeoisie (Skromnoye Oboyaniye Burzhuazi)
This compact hall is the favored "preparty" spot of Moscow clubbers. It features lounge music in a mellow atmosphere to get you in the mood before the real party-hopping begins. It's open daily 24 hours. 24 Bolshaya Lubyanka. (℃ 095/923-0848. Metro: Lubyanka.

Propaganda   House, trance, and techno, popular with students, expats, straights, gays, artists, and young capitalists. Try to get a table upstairs for a little more space and a perfect people-watching angle. Open daily from noon to 6am. 7 Bolshoi Zlatoustinsky Pereulok. (℃ 095/924-5732. Cover Sat only, $3. Metro: Lubyanka or Kitai-Gorod.

Shtolnaya   With beer taps at nearly every table, this is a fun but dangerous drinking hole. The taps are metered, but you always end up drinking more than you intended. 6 Zatsepsky Val. (℃ 095/953-4268. Metro: Paveletskaya.

4 St. Petersburg

St. Petersburg is Russia's principal port, and its geography and history make it immediately distinguishable from Moscow. St. Petersburg did not grow gradually from provincial backwater to major metropolis like its southern rival—this city was built up from the bogs, fast and furious, to be an imperial capital. Museums, palaces, and ballet and opera houses are where St. Petersburgs's strengths lie.

VISITOR INFORMATION

The **St. Petersburg City Tourist Office** at 54 Sadovaya Ulitsa (℃ 812/453-2121) does not have much more to offer than most hotels, but is worth a visit to find out about festivals or special events. An easy-to-read and detailed **map** is the bilingual "St. Petersburg Guide to the City." Look out for the twice-weekly *The St. Petersburg Times,* and *Afisha Petersburg,* which is the best weekly magazine for entertainment, dining, and shopping advice. See also "Visitor Information" in section 2 of this chapter.

The best tours of St. Petersburg are those done by **boat.** The smaller boats that cruise the canals give a closer view of the city's insides than the ferries that go up and down the Neva River. You can pick up a canal tour on Griboyedov Canal just north of Nevsky Prospekt, and on the Fontanka River just north of Nevsky Prospekt; prices run $3.50 to $7 (£2–£4) for a 1-hour tour.

GETTING THERE

BY PLANE   International flights into St. Petersburg land at the renovated **Pulkovo-2 Airport** (℃ 812/104-3444; http://eng.pulkovo.ru), 16km (10 miles) south of the city limits or about a 30-minute ride to the center of town. You can arrange a taxi in advance by calling the **official airport cab company** at ℃ 812/312-0022. Public bus no. 13 takes you to Moskovskaya metro station for a few rubles.

BY TRAIN   Trains from Moscow arrive at Moskovsky (Moscow) Station, on Nevsky Prospekt and within walking distance of several hotels. From Helsinki, the trip ends at Finland Station (Finlandsky Vokzal; 6 Ploshchad Lenina). Other European trains arrive at Warsaw Station (Varshavsky Vokzal; 118 Naberezhnaya Obvodnogo Kanala).

BY BUS   A few tour companies offer bus tours to St. Petersburg from Scandinavia on top-class Finnish coaches. Buses arrive at **St. Petersburg Bus Station (Avtobusny Vokzal;** 36 Naberezhnaya Obvodonovo Kanala; ℃ 812/166-5777).

BY BOAT The port is 20 minutes south of the center. Most cruises include a bus trip to the center. Authorized taxis (regular taxis are not allowed into the port) cost around $20 each way. Return trips leave from Kazansky Cathedral on Nevsky Prospekt.

BY CAR Not including the long lines for Customs at the border, the 370km (230-mile) drive from Helsinki is about 6 hours. Once in St. Petersburg, head straight to your hotel and settle the parking question.

GETTING AROUND
BY PUBLIC TRANSPORTATION

The **St. Petersburg Metro** is a fast, cheap, and extraordinarily deep subway system that every visitor should try out at least once. Station entrances are marked with a blue letter "M." The four-line system is easy to follow, with each line color-coded and transfers clearly marked. Trains run from 5:45am to 12:15am. Tokens cost 5 rubles (about 20 ¢/1p) for one trip, or magnetic cards for 1, 2, 5, or 10 trips.

Two **tram** lines worth trying are the no. 14, which runs from the Mariinsky Theater up through the center of town and across the Neva; another is the no. 1, which runs through Vasilevsky Island, including a stop just outside the Vasileostrovskaya metro station. **Trolleybuses** run along Nevsky Prospekt and some other large avenues. Tickets for trams and trolleybuses cost 11 rubles (40¢) and are available from the driver.

BY TAXI Reliable companies to try are the official **Petersburg Taxi** (© **068**-that's right, just 3 digits) or **Taxi Park** (© **812/265-1333**).

BY CAR Some rental companies to try are **Hertz/Travel Rent** (© **812/324-3242;** www.hertz.com) or **Europecar** (© **812/380-1662;** www.europcar.com). Both have offices at Pulkovo airport and rent cars with or without drivers.

FAST FACTS: St. Petersburg

American Express The main local office is in the Grand Hotel Europe (1 Mikhailovskaya Ulitsa; © 812/326-4500), open daily from 9am to 6pm.

Currency Exchange Every St. Petersburg hotel, many restaurants, and all major streets have exchange booths *(obmen valyuty)*, many open 24 hours. They have signs out front with the buy-and-sell rate for dollars and euros. For other currencies, try the booths in the underground walkway at Gostiny Dvor.

Doctor **American Medical Center St. Petersburg,** 10 Serpukhovskaya Ulitsa (© 812/326-1730) has Western-standard medical care and English-speaking staff.

Embassies The following addresses are for consulates based in St. Petersburg (embassies are in Moscow, see "Fast Facts: Moscow" in section 3).
United States: 15 Furshtadskaya Ulitsa (© 812/275-1701); **Britain:** 5 Ploshchad Proletarskoi Diktatury (© 812/320-3200); **Canada:** 32 Malodetskoselsky Prospekt (© 812/325-8448).

Emergencies For fire, dial © **01**; police © **02**; ambulance © **03**.

Internet Access Most hotel business centers offer online access, though at steeper rates than the Internet cafes popping up around the center of town.

Try **Quo Vadis**, at 24 Nevsky Prospekt; or **Café Max** at 90/92 Nevsky Prospekt. Both are open 24 hours.

Postal Services The main city post office (Glavny Pochtamt) is at 9 Pochtamt-skaya Ulitsa (✆ **812/312-8302**). Several international shipping companies serve Russia, such as **FedEx** (✆ **812/379-9040**) and **DHL** (✆ **812/318-4472**).

Telephone The city code for St. Petersburg is 812. For international calls from Russia, dial 8, wait for a tone, dial 10, then dial the country code. Access numbers in St. Petersburg are AT&T **325-5042**; MCI **747-3322**; BT Direct 8 (tone) **10-80-01-10-1044**; Canada Direct **755-5045** or **747-3325**.

WHERE TO STAY

Variation and innovation characterize St. Petersburg's hotel scene. The nicest and priciest hotels, and nearly all of the international chains, are clustered on upper Nevsky Prospekt. The huge Soviet-era hotel towers are farther from the center, and sometimes quite far from the metro. They offer better prices, but their quality is variable. The best price-to-quality ratio is found in the "minihotels" springing up around town. When choosing accommodations in St. Petersburg, bear in mind that it's a city of bridges that are drawn up in the wee hours to allow shipping traffic through. This means that if your late-night plans involve something on the other side of the Neva River from your hotel, you may be in for a long wait or a detour to get back.

Prices below are in U.S. dollars and British Pounds and do *not* include breakfast or 18% VAT unless noted.

VERY EXPENSIVE

Astoria 🏵🏵🏵 An example of Art Nouveau at its apex, the five-star Astoria offers 21st-century decadence in a pre-revolutionary setting, overlooking St. Isaac's Cathedral with the Neva River in the background. The Astoria and adjacent Angleterre (see next listing) opened in 1912 on the site of a 19th-century English/Russian hotel venture. Unfortunately, the mirrored, Art Nouveau Winter Garden is open only for special events—peek inside and imagine the balls held here a century ago. The Astoria is an excellent stop for tea even if you're not staying overnight.

39 Ulitsa Bolshaya Morskaya. ✆ 812/313-5757. Fax 812/313-5059. www.astoria.spb.ru. 220 units. From $380 (£190) double; from $700 (£350) suite. Rates 10% higher May–July. AE, DC, MC, V. Metro: Nevsky Prospekt. **Amenities:** 2 restaurants; bar and lounge; pool; health club; spa; Jacuzzi; sauna; billiard room; concierge; tour desk; car-rental desk; limo; 24-hr. business center; shopping arcade; salon; 24-hr. room service; laundry service; same-day dry cleaning; non-smoking rooms; executive rooms. *In room:* A/C, TV w/satellite, dataport, minibar, fridge, hair dryer, iron, safe.

EXPENSIVE

Angleterre 🏵🏵 Initially a wing of the Astoria, the four-star Angleterre shares a designer and a kitchen with its "sister hotel," though they're now under separate management. Today the Angleterre is a slightly less expensive, less well-preserved neighbor of the Astoria, but it is still a luxurious place to stay. The spacious guest rooms, many boasting wide windows, are decorated in warm woods that differ little from the Astoria's. The view of St. Isaac's makes a street-facing room worthwhile.

39 Bolshaya Morskaya Ulitsa. ✆ 812/313-5787. Fax 812/313-5118. www.angleterrehotel.com. 193 units. $260 (£130) double; from $400 (£200) suite. Mid-May to mid-July $330 (£165) double. AE, DC, MC, V. Metro: Nevsky

St. Petersburg Lodging, Dining & Attractions

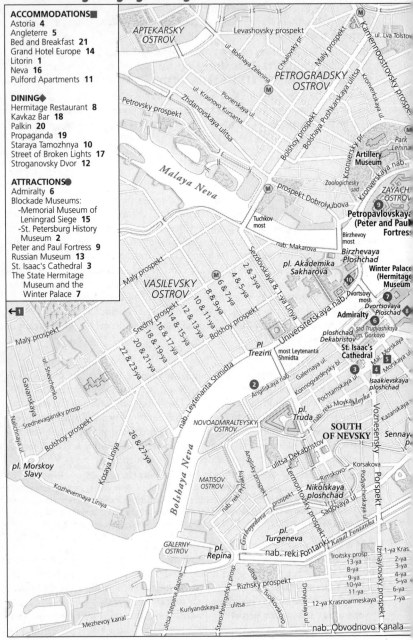

ACCOMMODATIONS
Astoria **4**
Angleterre **5**
Bed and Breakfast **21**
Grand Hotel Europe **14**
Litorin **1**
Neva **16**
Pulford Apartments **11**

DINING
Hermitage Restaurant **8**
Kavkaz Bar **18**
Palkin **20**
Propaganda **19**
Staraya Tamozhnya **10**
Street of Broken Lights **17**
Stroganovsky Dvor **12**

ATTRACTIONS
Admiralty **6**
Blockade Museums:
  -Memorial Museum of
    Leningrad Siege **15**
  -St. Petersburg History
    Museum **2**
Peter and Paul Fortress **9**
Russian Museum **13**
St. Isaac's Cathedral **3**
The State Hermitage
  Museum and the
  Winter Palace **7**

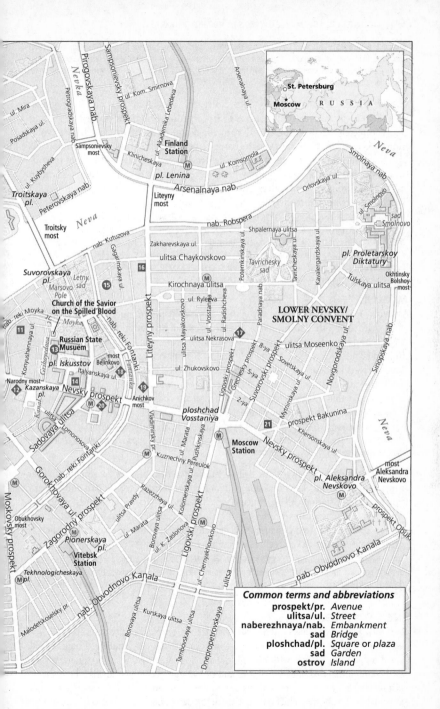

Prospekt. **Amenities:** Restaurant w/live jazz pianist every evening; small indoor pool; health club; spa; sauna; concierge; tour desk; car-rental desk; limo; 24-hr. business center; salon; 24-hr. room service; laundry service; same-day dry cleaning; nonsmoking rooms; executive rooms. *In room:* A/C, TV w/pay movies and satellite, dataport, mini-bar, fridge, coffeemaker, hair dryer, iron, safe.

Grand Hotel Europe 𝒞✮✮✮ This hotel has every right to call itself grand. Grandeur seeps from its ceiling friezes to its carpeting. Originally opened in 1875, it was completely rehauled for a 1991 reopening, and much of what seems prerevolutionary is recent re-creation, from the baroque facade to the Art Nouveau interiors. Its five floors surround a luscious winter garden and mezzanine cafe visible from inward-facing rooms. Even if you don't stay here, spend a lazy morning or rainy afternoon savoring tea from a silver samovar and listening to the harpist on the mezzanine. Guest rooms are elegant and modern.

1 Mikhailovskaya Ulitsa. 𝒞 **800/426-3135** or 812/329-6000. Fax 812/329-6001. www.grandhoteleurope.com. 300 units. From $310 (£105) double; from $790 (£395) suite. Rates 20% higher May–July. $40 (£20) extra bed. AE, DC, MC, V. Metro: Gostiny Dvor or Nevsky Prospekt. **Amenities:** 5 restaurants; 2 bars; health club; Jacuzzi; sauna; concierge; tour desk; car-rental desk; limos; 24-hr. business center; shopping arcade; salon; 24-hr. room service; massage; babysitting; laundry service; same-day dry cleaning; nonsmoking rooms; executive rooms. *In room:* A/C, TV w/satellite and pay movies, dataport, minibar, fridge, hair dryer, iron, safe.

MODERATE

Litorin 𝒞✮✮ One of many appealing, reasonably priced minihotels opening on Vasilevsky Island, the Litorin stands out for its careful juxtaposition of modern art and 19th-century fireplaces. The hotel opened in 2003 and is still expanding. The staff pays individual attention to guests and to detail, which makes up for some of the standard hotel services it doesn't provide, such as laundry facilities. The bathrooms are large and fully renovated. It's a long walk to the nearest metro, though compensation is the less-frequented sights nearby, such as the cathedral on the embankment; the icebreaker *Krasin* docked nearby; and the Mining Institute, one of Russia's first universities.

12 Liniya 27 (Vasilevsky Island). 𝒞/fax **095/328-1946.** www.litorin.ru. 12 units. $125–$140 (£63–£70) double. AE, MC, V. Metro: Vasileostrovskaya. **Amenities:** Restaurant; sauna; tour desk; transport desk; business center; Wi-Fi; room service. *In room:* A/C, TV w/satellite, dataport, safe.

Pulford Apartments 𝒞✮ This British-Russian company offers apartments all over town, but its prime spots are along the lanes between Palace Square and Nevsky Prospekt metro station. All apartments are renovated to Western standards, with fully equipped kitchens and bathrooms, and from one to several bedrooms. Maid service can be arranged as often as you like, as can any number of hotel-like services such as extra towels, theater tickets, cellphone rental, and visa help.

Main office: 6 Moika Embankment. 𝒞 **812/325-6277.** Fax 812/320-7561. www.pulford.com. From $130 (£65) double for 1-bedroom apt. AE, DC, MC, V. **Amenities:** Tour arrangements and personal guides; transport services; laundry service; dry cleaning; nonsmoking rooms; executive rooms. *In room:* A/C, TV w/satellite, dataport, kitchen, fridge, coffeemaker, hair dryer, iron, safe.

INEXPENSIVE

Bed and Breakfast 𝒞*Value* The only true bargain on Nevsky, this seven-room hostel was once a communal apartment in an imposing Stalin-era building. Rooms in the B&B range from a single with no window to a spacious triple with an expansive view. Bathrooms are shared but have shower and tub and are well-maintained. A basic breakfast is offered—or can be made yourself—in the common kitchen. A washing machine is available. The hostel's chief drawbacks are the dank and foreboding stairwell and the lack of an elevator to the third floor. Otherwise, this is an excellent, low-priced option.

74 Nevsky Prospekt. ① **812/315-1917** or 812/315-0495. www.bednbreakfast.sp.ru. 7 units at Nevsky location, but other locations around town. $30 (£15) single; $40 (£20) double; $50 (£25) triple. No credit cards. Metro: Gostiny Dvor. **Amenities:** Tour and transport assistance; laundry service; common kitchen w/fridge. *In room:* Coffeemaker, hair dryer, iron, safe on request.

Neva ⍟ The heavy wooden door opens onto a mirrored, marble staircase that dates back to the 1860s, when the hotel was built. The guest rooms have soaring ceilings and intricate molding, though beds are often creaky and windows lack modern insulation from street noise and drafts. The less-expensive rooms have showers with no stalls; the suites all have modern bathrooms. The second-floor cafe serves breakfast in style. Several rooms have views of the Neva.

17 Ulitsa Chaikovskogo. ① **812/278-0500.** Fax 812/273-2593. www.nevahotel.spb.ru. 133 units. From $80 (£40) double; from $130 (£65) suite. AE, MC, V. Metro: Chernyshevskaya or Gorkovskaya. **Amenities:** Restaurant and bar; sauna and very small pool; tour and transport desk; business center; salon; room service; laundry and ironing service. *In room:* TV w/cable, fridge.

WHERE TO DINE

St. Petersburg's current dining scene reflects its seaside and river-crossed geography, with fresh- and saltwater fish on every menu. Its eye-on-Europe heritage means that traditional Russian dishes are often upstaged by French-inspired terrines and roasts, or by pastas and pizza. St. Petersburg restaurants have a very good quality-to-price ratio.

VERY EXPENSIVE

Palkin ⍟⍟⍟ RUSSIAN If you want to splurge just once in St. Petersburg, do it here. The original Palkin opened in 1785 and became a mecca for aristocrats and intellectuals; today's reincarnation opened in 2002 on the same spot. The interior today is at least as sumptuous as in the decadent days of Catherine the Great. Today, members of Russia's 21st-century elite make it a frequent stop, including friends of St. Petersburg native (and Russian president) Vladimir Putin. Chefs research menus of past centuries, including wedding feasts for grand princes, to create dishes like sterlet baked in white wine with a sauce of cèpes and crayfish.

47 Nevsky Prospekt. ① **812/103-5371.** Reservations required. Jackets preferred for men. Main courses $40–$60 (£20–£30). AE, DC, MC, V. Daily 11am until last guest leaves. Metro: Nevsky Prospekt.

EXPENSIVE

Hermitage Restaurant ⍟⍟⍟ RUSSIAN/FRENCH The location right on Palace Square is what draws people here, but the inventive cuisine and atmosphere are what keep them coming back. Above a labyrinth of dining halls, the vaulted stone ceilings give the place the feel of a secret treasure cavern; works by local artists hang in the corridors. Each dining room is distinct in style, from the table sizes and shapes to the silverware and window coverings. The menu combines imperial-era favorites like pikeperch grilled with cèpe mushrooms from the surrounding forests, and more modern French-inspired favorites such as a delicately seasoned veal tartare.

8 Dvortsovaya Ploshchad (Palace Sq.). ① **812/314-4772.** www.hermitage.restoran.ru. Reservations recommended. Main courses $14–$50 (£7–£25). AE, MC, V. Daily noon–midnight. Metro: Nevsky Prospekt.

Staraya Tamozhnya (Old Customs House) ⍟⍟ FRENCH/RUSSIAN This ornate, top-notch restaurant celebrates French culinary traditions the way Russian aristocracy of the 18th and 19th centuries did. A special truffle menu comes out in January, and the *pot-au-feu* with lobster pops up a few times a year. Keep an eye out for the pheasant with pine nuts and endive. The French cheeses and three-chocolate fondue are always divine. The wine cellar corner is cozy, and a light jazz ensemble plays most evenings.

1 Tamozhenny Pereulok. ⓒ **812/327-8980**. Reservations required for dinner. Main courses $21–$45 (£11–£23). AE, DC, MC, V. Daily noon–midnight. Metro: Vasileostrovskaya.

MODERATE

Kavkaz Bar 🕸🕸 GEORGIAN   For expats and visitors, this is St. Petersburg's most popular spot at which to sample cuisine from the former Soviet state of Georgia. Its Caucasus Mountain spices and fruits are not found in Russian cooking. Try the enormous *khinkali*, spiced meat dumplings you're supposed to eat with your hands; the tandoor-style chicken (chicken *tabaka*); or the eggplant slices slathered in walnut-garlic paste. If you want to try Georgian wine, stick with the dry reds.

18 Karavannaya Ulitsa. ⓒ **812/312-1665**. Main courses $6–$15 (£3–£8). AE, MC, V. Daily 11am–10pm. Metro: Mayakovskaya.

Propaganda 🕸🕸 INTERNATIONAL   This popular restaurant's name and Soviet-style decorations are decidedly tongue-in-cheek, concealing a relaxed, open, post-Communist atmosphere. It's an unbeatable lunch spot and a good choice for dinner, except on weekend nights when it gets crowded. The menu includes Russian favorites with a twist, such as the melt-in-your-mouth salmon *pelmeni* (like Russian ravioli), made with fresh fish blended with fresh greens. Be sure to view the Lenin-themed restrooms. The hall facing the Fontanka River offers an all-you-can-eat buffet lunch for less than $10.

44 Fontanka Naberezhnaya. ⓒ **812/275-4558**. Main courses $8–$20 (£4–£10). MC, V. Daily 24 hr. Metro: Mayakovskaya.

INEXPENSIVE

Street of Broken Lights (Ulitsa Razbitykh Fonarei) 🕸 Kids RUSSIAN   The main draw here is the extensive takeout menu, something unheard of elsewhere in town (other than at McDonald's). The decor and menu borrow from the popular Russian television series after which the restaurant is named, featuring cops and neighborhood dramas. The show and the restaurant are popular among families.

34 Ulitsa Radishcheva. ⓒ **812/275-9935**. Main courses $8–$20 (£4–£10). AE, MC, V. Daily noon–midnight. Metro: Chernyshevskaya.

Stroganovsky Dvor (Stroganoff Courtyard) 🕸 RUSSIAN/EUROPEAN   This cafe is cool, cheap, and convenient, and the atmosphere is so bizarre it's worth experiencing. The two-story restaurant is housed in a huge transparent tent plopped in the courtyard of an 18th-century aristocratic mansion. Customers can use special telephones placed at each table to call in orders—or to call occupants of other tables. Service is friendly and readily available.

17 Nevsky Prospekt (inside courtyard). ⓒ **812/315-2315**. Sandwiches $3–$5 (£2–£6). No credit cards. Daily 24 hr. Metro: Nevsky Prospekt.

EXPLORING ST. PETERSBURG

St. Petersburg was a planned city from day one, and therefore makes sense to most visitors right away. The center of town is relatively compact, and English is increasingly used on street signs and billboards.

SUGGESTED ITINERARIES

If You Have ❶ Day

Begin at **Palace Square** and the **Hermitage,** for an intense morning of history and art that provides context for the rest of the St. Petersburg experience. Next, take your pick from the sights on the **"walking tour"** later in this section, followed by a visit to the **Peter and Paul Fortress** and an evening stroll along **Nevsky Prospekt.**

If You Have ❷ Days

Use your second day to take in the masterpieces of the **Russian Museum,** then visit the eye-catching **Church on the Spilled Blood,** the sculpted **Summer Gardens,** and the prestigious banks of the **Fontanka River.** Shop in **Gostiny Dvor,** then use this evening for a visit to the renowned **Mariinsky Theater.**

If You Have ❸ Days

A third day offers an ideal opportunity to whiz up the Baltic Coast to **Peterhof,** the palace Peter modeled partly on Versailles. The ride itself—on hydrofoil or ferry—is part of the adventure, offering a seafarers' view of the city and surrounding forest. Catch the ferry at the piers on Dvortsovaya Naberezhnaya in front of the Winter Palace.

THE TOP ATTRACTIONS

The State Hermitage Museum and the Winter Palace ★★★   The Winter Palace would be a museum itself even if it didn't hold the Hermitage Museum, one of the world's largest and most valuable collections of fine art. The permanent collection which, among other treasures, includes more French artworks than any museum outside France. Hall no. 185 to 189 are worth a glance even if their labels RUSSIAN CULTURE and STATE ROOMS don't enthrall you. The Pavilion Hall, with mosaic tables and floors, marble fountains, engineering marvels, and a wraparound view, is a favorite for the whole family. The Impressionist and more recent works, including two rooms of early Picasso, are a must-see, Planning is key to any Hermitage visit, and an online tour can be a great preparation. Allow yourself a full morning or afternoon in the Hermitage itself—or a full day, if you can spare it. You won't regret it.

1 Palace Sq. Entrance to Hermitage main collection: through courtyard of Winter Palace, from Palace Sq. ℂ 812/110-9079. www.hermitage.ru. Admission to Hermitage Museum $13 (£7) adults, $3 (£2) students with ID, free for those under 18. English tours for up to 5 people by official museum guides $55 (£28). Admission to other buildings in the Hermitage collection is $7.50 (£4) for each one, or you can buy a $25(£14) ticket that allows entrance to the main museum and 3 others of your choice over the course of 1 day. Main museum Tues–Sat 10:30am–6pm; Sun and Russian holidays 10:30am–5pm. Ticket office closes 1 hr. before museum closing. Metro: Nevsky Prospekt.

Peter and Paul Fortress (Petropavlovskaya Krepost) ★★★   Peter and Paul Fortress was one of Peter the Great's masterpieces. The citadel occupies small Hare's Island (Zaichy Ostrov) across from the Winter Palace, and contains a notable cathedral, the Museum of City History, a mint, an old printing house, a former political prison, and a long stretch of sandy beach packed with bathers in the summer. **Peter and Paul Cathedral** ★★★, named after the city's patron saints and erected in 1723, was St. Petersburg's first stone church. Two highlights are **walking along the fortress's southern walls** (tickets can be purchased for about 50¢ (25p) at the stairs on either end); and watching (and hearing) the **daily cannon blast** at noon.

The fortress is on **Zaichy Ostrov (Hare's Island;** ℂ 812/230-0340; metro: Gorkovskaya). Entrance to the fortress grounds is free. Admission to cathedral and other museums on the grounds costs $4.25 (£2) adults, $2 (£1) children.

From 6–7pm, cathedral admission is free. The complex is open daily from 10am–10pm. The museums and cathedral are open Thurs–Mon from 11am–6pm.

Admiralty (Admiralteistvo) ✸✸✸ Overlooking Palace Square from a distance to the west is the Admiralty, once a fortified shipyard. It is now a naval academy that sadly is not open to the public. It's worth spending a few minutes admiring its 61m-high (230-ft.) spire, topped by a weathervane in the shape of a ship. Stand on the plaza beneath the spire and look toward the city: You're at the nexus of three major avenues—Nevsky Prospekt, Gorokhovaya Ulitsa, and Vosnesensky Prospekt. This is no accident, and is one example of the city's careful design. The building was one of the first in St. Petersburg, built to feed Peter the Great's dream of making Russia into a naval power.

St. Isaac's Cathedral (Isaakevsky Sobor) ✸✸ St. Isaac's mighty, somber facade rose only in the mid–19th century but has become an indelible part of St. Petersburg's skyline since then. The church earned residents' respect during World War II, when it endured Nazi shelling and its grounds were planted with cabbage to help residents survive the 900-day Nazi blockade. Its interior is as awesome as its exterior, with columns made of single chunks of granite, malachite, and lazurite; floors of different-colored marble. If the viewing balcony around the dome is open, it's well worth a climb for the view of the city and of the cathedral from on high.

Isaakevskaya Ploshchad. ✆ **812/315-9732.** www.cathedral.ru. Admission $8 (£4) adults, $4 (£2) children. To climb colonnade, an additional $4 (£2) adults, $2 (£1) children. Thurs–Tues 11am–6pm; colonnade closes at 5pm. Metro: Nevsky Prospekt.

Russian Museum (Russky Muzei) ✸✸✸ This museum should be on every visitor's itinerary, even those who know or care little about Russian art. It's as much an introduction to Russian history, attitudes, and vision as it is a display of artistic styles. Housing 32,000 artworks from the 12th to 20th centuries, the museum is best viewed with a tour guide or by using the English-language audioguide to ensure that you get the most out of its collection before you drop from exhaustion. The most popular rooms are in the Benois Wing, where works by avant-garde artists Malevich and Kandinsky attract international crowds. The Old Russian Wing deserves a good look, too, offering perspective on the evolution of Orthodox icon painting that helps you better appreciate any cathedrals you visit later. Note the Art Nouveau paintings and sketches of set designs for Diaghilev's Ballet Russe. Allow at least 2 hours.

4/2 Inzhenernaya Ulitsa. ✆ **812/595-4248** or 812/314-3448. www.rusmuseum.ru. Admission $12 (£6) adults, $6 (£3) students with ID, free for children under 18. English-language tour for up to 5 with official museum guide $65 (£35) plus entrance fee. Wed–Sun 10am–6pm. Metro: Gostiny Dvor or Nevsky Prospekt.

Blockade Museums Two exhibits, both of them eye-opening and tear-jerking, trace the city's experience enduring 900 days of siege and isolation by Nazi forces from 1941 to 1944. The **Memorial Museum of the Leningrad Siege** ✸ is the more commonly visited, but no less impressive is **"Leningrad During the Great Patriotic War"** ✸✸, a permanent exhibit at the **St. Petersburg History Museum** in a riverside mansion. The hall of children's photos and diaries is especially moving.

Memorial Museum of Leningrad Blockade. 9 Solyanoi Pereulok. ✆ **812/579-3021.** Admission $2.50 (£1) adults, $1 (50p) students and children over 7. Thurs–Tues 10am–5pm; closed last Thurs of each month. St. Petersburg History Museum. 44 Angliiskaya Naberezhnaya. ✆ **812/117-7544.** Admission $3.50 (£2) adults, $2 (£1) students and children over 7. Thurs–Tues 11am–5pm. Metro: Nevsky Prospekt.

Summer Gardens (Letny Sad) ★★   This is the place to rest on a bench after a day of visiting museums, or to escape from the crush of city sidewalks—or to imagine how Peter the Great spent his summer afternoons. Peter brought in marble Renaissance-era statues from Italy to give the park a more European feel. He and his successors threw grand receptions here with dancing, drinking, and fireworks under the endless sun of the White Nights. Summer Palace is open to visitors, its rooms re-created as they would have been in Peter's time.

Entrance from Kutuzov Embankment (Naberezhnya Kutuzova) or Panteleimon Bridge (Panteleimonovsky Most). Park daily 10am–10pm; admission charged during festivals. Summer Palace Wed–Sun 10:30am–5pm. Tickets $2 (£1). Metro: Gostiny Dvor or Gorkovskaya.

Peterhof Palace and Park (Petrodvorets) ★★★   Unquestionably the number-one day trip from St. Petersburg, Peterhof lures visitors with its Versailles-inspired palace, overlooking a cascade of fountains and gardens opening onto the Baltic Sea.

Start with the **Great Palace,** built in 1715 by Jean Baptiste Leblond, and be prepared to squint at all the gold inside. Many visitors say the palace feels too magnificent to live in—and Peter felt the same, preferring **Monplaisir,** a small baroque bungalow close to the water's edge that was the first building in the Peterhof complex. In the lush park, the Monplaisir house, the small red-and-white Hermitage, and the **Marly Palace** (with a carved wood desk that Peter himself made) are well worth exploring, too. Before heading down into the park, spend a moment on the palace balcony to take in the view of the greenery and the **Grand Cascade** from above. Be sure to see **Samson Fountain,** with the biblical strongman tearing apart the jaws of a lion, symbolizing Peter's victory over Sweden in 1709.

Boat trips are the best way to get to Peterhof from mid-May to early October, not least because of the breathtaking view of the palace as you pull up to the Peterhof pier. **Russian Cruises** (✆ 812/974-0100; www.russian-cruises.ru) is well equipped and offers English-language commentary. From October to May the best way to go is by bus. Russian vendors hawk trips on direct buses from Nevsky Prospekt metro station.

2 Razvodnaya Ulitsa. ✆ 812/427-9527. Admission to the palace costs $12 (£6) adults, $6 (£3) college students and children; admission to the park alone costs $7 (£4) adults, $3.50 (£2) students and children. The palace is open Tues–Sat 10:30am–5pm (closed last Tues of each month). Monplaisir and other buildings on the grounds have different hours.

WALKING TOUR	ST. PETERSBURG HIGHLIGHTS

This tour, starting at Palace Square, links key St. Petersburg sights with less important ones. The side streets and embankments are just as crucial to understanding the city as are the palaces, so look at everything, even between stops. Allow 2 hours.

❶ Palace Square

Stand at the Alexander Column in the center and turn around slowly, a full 360 degrees. Each building on the asymmetrical square emerged in a different era but they combine to create a flawless ensemble. Nothing in this view, or this city, is accidental. Imagine the royal equipages pulling into the square, the czarist army processions, the revolutionaries' resentment of all the square stood for—and the Communist-era appropriation of the square for holiday parades.

Walk north from the column to the courtyard of the:

❷ Winter Palace

The palace's now tranquil courtyard bustled with court activity in Empress Elizabeth's and Catherine the Great's days, and with revolutionary activity 150 years later. You can pick up a museum plan while you're here, though a visit to the Hermitage deserves at least an afternoon or a full day to itself. As you leave the courtyard, take in the view of the curved General Staff building across the square.

Head left toward the Moika Canal, then turn right and follow it down to Nevsky Prospekt. Note the uniformity of the buildings along the canal, all in various shades of yellow, and the odd proportion of the wide bridges crossing the narrow waterway. Cross Nevsky and head left, until you reach the columned gray facade of:

❸ Kazan Cathedral

Walking the length of the cathedral's concave colonnade gives you a stepped-back view of Nevsky on one side and a sense of the cathedral's scale on the other. Its modern, secular lines are almost reminiscent of the Capitol Building in Washington, built just 2 decades earlier. Compare this to other Orthodox churches you see around Russia. Even if you don't go in, note that the church's entrance is on the east side instead of facing the street, to satisfy Orthodox church canon.

Cross the avenue again and stop at the corner of Nevsky and Griboyedov Canal to admire:

❹ Dom Knigi

This Art Nouveau treasure is just another building along Nevsky, but worth noting are its glass dome and mystical mosaics. It once belonged to the Singer sewing machine company, whose name is still engraved on the facade. For decades it was Dom Knigi, or House of Books, Leningrad's main bookstore.

Cross Griboyedov Canal and head north along it, past the boatmen hawking canal tours, toward the dizzying domes of the:

❺ Church of the Savior on the Spilled Blood

Built 7 decades after Kazan Cathedral, this church sprang from an entirely different era and worldview. Though constructed during Russia's industrial and economic boom of the late 19th-century, the Church of the Savior harkens back to the piled, etched, color-coated domes of medieval Russian churches. Inside, note the spot where czar Alexander II was assassinated by a revolutionary.

Walk around the cathedral along the outer edge of Mikhailovsky Gardens, stopping to study the undulating patterns of the cast-iron fences surrounding the gardens. Continue to follow the fence around to the entrance to the gardens.

❻ Mikhailovsky Castle & Gardens

The warm coral of the castle makes it look almost inviting despite its grim history. The paranoid czar Paul I had it built because the Winter Palace made him feel too exposed to threats from without and within his court. (Paul was right about the threats, but not about the security of his new home: He was assassinated by advisers soon after he moved in.) Mikhailovsky Castle is now the Engineering Museum.

Circle the palace and turn right onto Italianskaya Ulitsa, heading straight until you reach the Square of the Arts. Take a rest on a bench in this small rectangular plaza, then wander its circumference to study its components:

❼ The Russian Museum

This museum is housed in the triumphantly classical Mikhailovsky Palace (Dvorets). The optimism of the period when the palace was built (1819–25) is reflected in the mock war trophies that top its gates and victorious frieze.

Walk around the square past the Mussorgsky Theater (check out its repertoire of ballet and opera performances on the way), around the Grand Hotel Europe and across Mikhailovskaya Ulitsa to the:

Walking Tour: St. Petersburg Highlights

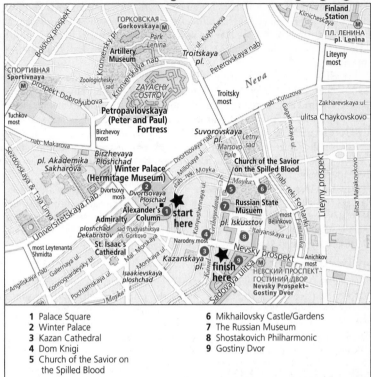

1 Palace Square
2 Winter Palace
3 Kazan Cathedral
4 Dom Knigi
5 Church of the Savior on
   the Spilled Blood
6 Mikhailovsky Castle/Gardens
7 The Russian Museum
8 Shostakovich Philharmonic
9 Gostiny Dvor

⑧ Shostakovich Philharmonic

Built in the 1830s, Russia's premier music hall has staged the country's leading works, from Tchaikovsky's concertos to Rachmaninoff's symphonies. It has hosted conductors including Sviatoslav Richter, and of course Dmitri Shostakovich.

Continue down Mikhailovskaya Ulitsa to Nevsky Prospekt. Turn around and look at the Square of the Arts one more time from this perspective. Then turn left down Nevsky and continue to the

underground walkway at the next intersection. Cross Nevsky through this passage, noting its lively commerce in pirated CDs, DVDs, and software. You'll emerge at:

⑨ Gostiny Dvor

This 19th-century shopping mall has gone through several incarnations. Picture its early years, when it was a gathering place for the nobility looking for gifts to take to balls at the Winter Palace.

SHOPPING

Nevsky Prospekt is the city's commercial lifeline, and **Gostiny Dvor** shopping arcade concentrates all of Nevsky's riches in one two-story prerevolutionary mall. **Upper Nevsky** holds the posher shops, while **Lower Nevsky** (east of Moskovsky Train Station) is less pretentious. **Vernisazh,** an outdoor market across from the Church of the Savior on the Spilled Blood, is the city's most convenient and extensive gift bazaar.

The Baltic Sea coast from Kaliningrad up toward St. Petersburg holds nearly all of the world's **amber.** Amber rings, necklaces, pens, and other souvenirs are widely available in St. Petersburg. **Amber House (Yantarny Dom)** (© **812/112 3013**) on Ulitsa Marata, has a broad and reliable but pricey selection of jewelry made from amber and Siberian stones.

For china and porcelain, try the **Lomonosov Porcelain Factory** (© **812/560 8300**), opened in 1744 by Peter the Great's daughter, Empress Elizabeth I. Its craftspeople designed china for the royal family and nobility. After the revolution they produced plates with Constructivist Soviet art and propaganda slogans. Today it's been reprivatized, and sells both imperial and Soviet patterns.

Eliseyevsky Gastronome (© **812/311 9323**) on Nevsky Prospekt is a reincarnation of a czarist-era shop with a rich selection of teas, sweets, and Russian treats, beneath crystal chandeliers and surrounded by stained-glass windows.

Russian Icon (© **812/314 7040**) on Bolshaya Konyushennaya (near Nevsky Prospekt) has an extensive array of icons on display. They're all recently made, meaning you'll have no problem taking them out of the country, but they follow the same rules icon-painters have adhered to for centuries. The icons are more expensive than those at the monasteries, but the selection is larger.

ST. PETERSBURG AFTER DARK

Most of St. Petersburg's liveliest and richest cultural events take place during the magical summer weeks when there is no "after dark," under the soft, elongated sunset of the White Nights. Of course, this city that considers itself Russia's cultural capital is alive with performances the rest of the year as well. The city's club and bar scene hasn't reached the superlative debauchery of Moscow's, but St. Petersburg's discos and casinos still offer plenty to shock and stimulate a Western visitor.

THE PERFORMING ARTS

Jazz Philharmonic Hall For more traditional shows, head to St. Petersburg's jazz shrine, whose large hall offers balconies and a nostalgic atmosphere. Performances are consistently excellent, with classically trained performers. Shows start at 7pm daily. Check out the Museum of Petersburg Jazz on the second floor. 3 Fontanka Naberezhnya. © 812/164-8565. Tickets $5–$10 (£2.65–£5.30). Metro: Vladimirskaya.

Mariinsky Theater ★★★ Viewing anything in this theater makes you feel regal. The sea-green exterior encloses a five-tiered theater draped, embroidered, and gilded in blue and gold. Top-floor seats have a dimmer view of the performers but a close-up view of the ceiling frescoes that draw you right into their pillowy clouds and floating angels. The repertoire of the renowned and rigorous Mariinsky (formerly Kirov) Ballet features mostly classics such as *Sleeping Beauty* and *La Bayadere*. Tickets purchased at the box office are cheaper than those bought through your hotel, but availability is limited. 1 Teatralnaya Sq. © 812/114-5264. www.mariinsky.ru/en. Tickets $6–$18 (£3.25–£9.75) for 3rd balcony seats; $100–$150 (£54–£81) for orchestra. Metro: Sadovaya or Sennaya Ploshchad.

Peter and Paul Cathedral The cathedral inside the Peter and Paul Fortress is the main hall of the St. Petersburg Men's Choir, which carries on the tradition of its czarist-era founders. A stunning setting for some stunning voices, with performances Monday and Friday nights. Tickets run from $15 to $22 (£7.95–£11.65). Peter and Paul Fortress (Hare's Island/Zaichy Ostrov). © 812/767-0865. Metro: Gorkovskaya.

Shostakovich Philharmonic Two halls, the Bolshoi (Grand) and Glinka (Small), stage symphonies, solo piano concerts, international festivals and competitions, and

Babushkas

The word *babushka* technically means "grandmother" in Russian, but the term encompasses much more, a whole mindset and layer of the Russian population. You'll see the babushka everywhere: guarding a museum, running a coat check, patrolling the metro escalators, sweeping Red Square, or suspiciously eyeing your untucked shirt. She may or may not be wearing the brightly flowered headscarf often associated with the word "babushka" in the West. She may not have grandchildren, or may not be particularly old. But if she has the attitude, she's a babushka.

The babushka considers it her responsibility to keep the world dressed warmly, well-nourished, free of infection, and properly groomed. She'll give you an earful if you're out hatless in winter. She'll huff if you hand her a coat to check that's wrinkled or missing a button—and she may even mend it for you.

If you speak no Russian, you may not notice the critiques babushkas send in your direction. If you understand Russian or if a babushka upbraids you in English, stay cool. You may find it intrusive, but she wants what's best for you, even if she's never seen you before in her life. In other words, she wants you to feel right at home.

more, featuring music by Russian and international composers. The Grand Hall is home to the St. Petersburg Philharmonic but shares its stage with visiting performers. Both halls boast ornate and intricate interiors and superb acoustics, though they're in need of renovation. Mikhailovskaya St. ✆ 812/110-4164. www.philharmonia.spb.ru. Tickets $20–$35 (£11–£19) in Bolshoi Hall; $5–$15 (£2.65–£7.95) in Glinka Hall. Metro: Gostiny Dvor.

DANCE CLUBS & BARS

Akvarel   Several of the ship-restaurants along the north side of the Neva offer dance clubs at night, but this all-glass dockside restaurant/club is by far the sleekest way to party on the water. Door control gets fierce after 11pm; if you come for dinner and stay for the party you'll have no problem passing muster. 14a Prospekt Dobrolyubova. ✆ 812/320-8600. Metro: Sportivnaya.

City Bar   This bar is run by an American and attracts a mixed Russian-expat crowd for its "Amerikansky Biznes Lunch" at midday and its lively bar at night. Beer, martinis, and a Sunday all-you-can-drink champagne brunch for just $12 (£6) are among its highlights. 10 Millionaya Ulitsa. ✆ 812/314-1037. Metro: Nevsky Prospekt.

Fishfabrique   Part of the Pushkinskaya 10 art complex, this is the hippest and most creative place for alternative bands, though perhaps the smallest. Open daily from 3pm to 6am; concerts usually take place Thursday through Saturday. 10 Pushkinskaya Ulitsa. ✆ 812/164-4857. Cover $2–$8 (£1.05–£4.25) for concerts. Metro: Ploshchad Vosstaniya.

Jakata   Consistently hip, and playing a mix of lounge, techno, and trance, this is the city's most authentic and least pretentious dance club. Open daily 24 hours, but don't bother showing up before midnight. 5 Bakunina Ulitsa. ✆ 812/346-7461. Metro: Ploshchad Vosstaniya.

11

Slovakia

by Mark Baker

Slovakia's humble tourism motto, "A Part of Europe Worth Visiting," seems to sum up the country's rather modest ambitions when it comes to luring visitors. Just barely a teenager—Slovakia became an independent nation only in 1993—the country still seems unsure of itself as a nation and what it has to offer. But the motto surely underestimates Slovakia's very winning charms. The mountains, starting in the hills of the Malá Fatra and running east to the Alpine peaks of the High Tatras, are some of the most starkly beautiful in Europe. And it's unlikely that any country in Europe, or anywhere else for that matter, has a castle with the pure drop-dead shock value of Spišský Hrad. Slovakia's youthful capital, Bratislava, has shed some of its hulking Communist-era architecture and fixed up its charming Old Town. The result is a fun, lively, and energetic city that makes Vienna feel fusty and overly mannered and Prague feel forced and overly touristed by comparison. And the Slovaks' humility is part of the charm. The rudeness or arrogance you sometimes find in more popular destinations is absent here. Just let slip in conversation that you've come all the way from the United States, or Canada, or wherever, and the reaction you get will be nothing short of amazement. You'll feel like a real guest.

To be sure, you may have to put up with some relative hardship now and then. Standards for food and lodging, especially off the beaten track, are a step down from western Europe, and even perhaps lower than you might find in the Czech Republic or Hungary. But don't let that deter you. Relax, enjoy the largely unspoiled countryside, take a meal and a glass of wine in a traditional "koliba" restaurant, and let the natural warmth and hospitality of the people win you over.

1 Getting to Know Slovakia

THE LAY OF THE LAND

Slovakia is a compact country, sandwiched between Austria and the Czech Republic to the west, Poland to the north, Ukraine to the east, and Hungary to the south. It borrows a little bit from each of its neighbors. Linguistically and culturally it's closest to the Czech Republic, with whom it shared a common state for more than 70 years. With the Poles, the Slovaks share a deep Catholicism, and here as in Poland, you'll see people lined up at the church door on Sunday morning. Hungary ruled over the Slovaks for 1,000 years until 1918 and the Hungarian influence is still evident, if difficult to pinpoint. The easiest-to-see example might be in the cooking. The Hungarians brought the peppers and paprika, and Slovak goulash has been the better for it ever since. The Austrian influence is also strong but hard to describe. Vienna, for Slovaks,

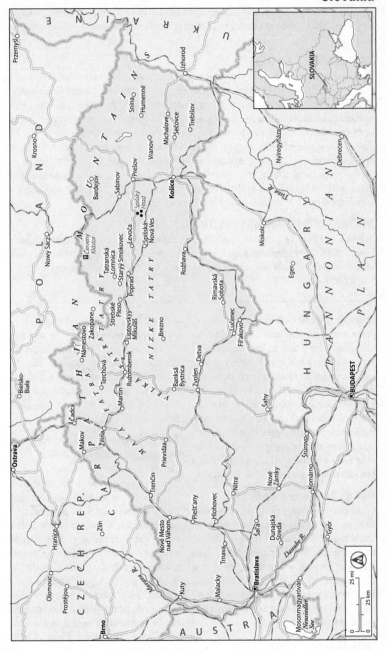

Slovakia

remains the ideal of class and manners, and every time the time a waiter nods as he serves you your coffee or strudel he's echoing a notion of Viennese civility going back centuries.

THE REGIONS IN BRIEF

For a small country, Slovakia possesses a wealth of regional diversity, both cultural and geographic. The western third of the country includes the capital Bratislava and, except for a few hills running north of the city, is relatively flat. It includes the Danube lowlands and much of the border region with Hungary. The central region, running from the Malá Fatra highlands east of Žilina to the country's highest peaks, the High Tatras, is considered quintessential Slovak territory. The eastern third of the country defies description. While geographically it's relatively flat, ethnically speaking it's diverse, including ancient communities of Poles, Hungarians, Ukrainians, and Germans. Here folkways and traditional wooden architecture dominate and religion is very important. A visit here is very much a trip back in time.

SUGGESTED ITINERARY: SLOVAKIA IN 1 WEEK

Slovakia is a compact country, with decent roads and a dense network of trains and buses. The following itinerary assumes you're arriving in Bratislava and have a week to see the country. It's laid out ideally for car travel, but can be easily adapted to train and bus schedules.

Days ❶ & ❷ Arrive in Bratislava

After resting at the hotel, head into the Old Town for a quick "get acquainted" walk. The city's laid-back pace is a perfect way to adjust to time zone changes. On the second day, get a good breakfast and plan on doing serious walking. Start in the Old Town and take in the castle and the former Jewish quarter. Plan on a good celebratory dinner tonight, since restaurant food outside of the capital (with a few exceptions) is a significant step down.

Day ❸ Trenčín and Žilina

Head north and east along the Váh river, first to the enchanting castle town of Trenčín and then farther along to Žilina, the jumping-off spot for the Malá Fatra National Park. If you're traveling by car, try spending the night at one of the places in or near the park; if you're traveling by train, Žilina makes for a more convenient overnight stop.

Days ❹ & ❺ The High Tatras

The High Tatras are about 3 hours or so by car east of Žilina (and about the same

distance by train), so try to get an early start. Once you've found your way to one of the High Tatra resorts, use the Tatra Electric Railway to explore the other small towns. Use the second full day for a long walk in the mountains, keeping in mind, of course, the usual precautions pertaining to mountain hikes.

Day ❻ Option 1, Dunajec raft trip; Option 2, Levoča and Košice

Depending on what you want to do and how much time you've got, at this stage you can decide to spend another day in the High Tatra region or push off farther east to Košice. If you opt for the first and you've got a sunny day, drive or take a tour bus to Červený Kláštor for an exhilarating raft ride down the Dunajec river. If you're ready to head east, follow the road to Košice (about 2 hr. east of Poprad by car). Be sure to stop in Levoča (which can be comfortably toured in a couple of hours) and at Spišský Hrad. Once in Košice, book a room at the Bristol (for a well-deserved splurge) and plan a meal at

Le Colonial. You'll soon feel like the king of eastern Slovakia.

Day ❼ Return to Bratislava

From Košice the return trip to Bratislava will take the better part of a day (7–8 hr.), so start early. From Poprad and the High Tatras to Bratislava, it's about a 5- to 6-hour drive, depending on traffic. By train, it can take equally long or longer, depending on the type of train.

SLOVAKIA TODAY

At press time, Slovakia was in the midst of another gut-wrenching lurch in government, this time from a moderate coalition of centrist parties to a more nationalist, pro-Slovak grouping. And that's how it's been since independence in 1993, with coalitions of nationalists being voted in and then tossed out in turn in favor of more centrist coalitions favoring the European Union and Slovakia's international obligations, and so on, and so on. The new government has the country's more liberal students and intellectuals hanging their heads in shame, but maybe it's fitting for a young nation still finding its feet that the natural yearnings for a strong national identity would play such a prominent role in politics.

The good news is that the shuffling and reshuffling of ministerial seats has not hurt the country economically or culturally. Slovakia is making the most of its entry into the European Union in 2004, and the government has adopted a host of far-sighted economic measures, including a 19% flat income tax, that has led to boom in foreign investment. The economy is now one of the fastest growing in Europe.

A LOOK AT THE PAST

Slovakia is one Europe's youngest countries, dating only from January 1, 1993, and the amicable dissolution of Czechoslovakia into separate Czech and Slovak republics. While many on both sides at the time regretted the split, for Slovaks it represented a chance to realize a long-held ambition of forming an independent state. Slovak history goes back about 1,200 years, but for the entire time—save for a few years during World War II when the Slovaks were allowed a quasi-independent puppet state by the Germans—they were ruled by others.

The Hungarians first conquered the territory of modern Slovakia before the first millennium and ruled over the Slovaks for nearly 1,000 years, until the end of World War I. Slovakia was known on maps from the period simply as "Upper Hungary," and indeed Bratislava even served as the capital of Hungary during the Turkish occupation in the 16th and 17th centuries. The Hungarians suppressed Slovak culture and language, and the Slovaks were only one of a number of ethnic minorities sharing the territory. The end of World War I saw the breakup of the Austro-Hungarian Empire, and provided the Slovaks with a chance to split from Hungary and form an independent state with the Czechs.

The Slovaks profited greatly from the 70-year existence of Czechoslovakia, but there was also a bitter undercurrent of resentment against the authorities in Prague and a festering Slovak inferiority complex. It was only the collapse of Communism in 1989 that first opened the door to the possibility of a separate Slovak state. In 1992, with national politicians in Slovakia calling loudly for independence and Czech leaders fearful of the drag a poorer Slovakia would have on the national budget, the split was sealed and Czechoslovakia was finished. The years since independence have brought both ups and downs. Poor political leadership initially hurt the Slovaks in their bid to join the European Union and NATO, but they eventually achieved both goals.

SLOVAK PEOPLE & CULTURE

With the country's expanse of unspoiled nature, Slovaks, generally speaking, fancy themselves as simple folk, with a taste for fun, rich food, and strong drink. Folk music, while certainly an anachronism, can still be heard in some of the smaller towns and villages. Slovaks are generally known for being gregarious, generous, and loyal. On the negative side, they can sometimes seem stubborn or even hotheaded. Of course, these are generalizations. In reality there are as many "typical Slovaks" as there are people living here.

The vast majority of the population is ethnic Slovak, though a sizable minority of around half a million Hungarians still lives in the south of the country along the Hungarian frontier. There's also a large community of Gypsies, or Roma, spread out around the country, most living in squalor in the countryside or in decrepit public-housing projects outside the large cities. The Roma represent a seemingly intractable problem for the Slovaks. The Roma, with some justification, say they are routinely discriminated against and forced into substandard schools and living quarters. The Slovaks, for their part, say the Roma rigorously resist integration into mainstream life. There's truth on both sides, but sadly no solution in sight.

SLOVAK CUISINE

As with culture, it's difficult to pinpoint Slovak cuisine with any certainty. If you had to generalize you'd be safe in saying it's similar to Czech and Austrian cooking, but spicier, more adventurous, and often better. That means lots of meat dishes, with beef, pork, and chicken popping up on menus most often, but with a fiery taste that's often lacking in the countries to immediate west.

Many meals are built around the ubiquitous halušky, the Slovak equivalent of dumplings in the Czech lands. Halušky are little noodles made of potato meal, flour, and egg, which are then boiled and served as mains or sides. The national dish is "bryndzové halušky," where the halušky share equal billing with a deliciously sharp, sour sheep's cheese, and small chunks of bacon.

Mealtimes hold to the Continental standard. For breakfast (raňajky), Slovaks take a light meal that may only consist of a bread roll with tea or coffee, though hotels and pensions typically offer the standard table of cold cuts, cheeses, and cereals. Lunches are larger and usually served from noon until 2pm. Here you'll be offered two courses: a soup (polievka) and a main dish. Common soups include a deliciously sour cabbage (kapustnica) and vegetable (zeleninová). Mains are usually built around meat of some kind, with pork (bravčové) the most common, followed by beef (hovädzie) and chicken (kurča). You'll usually be expected to order a separate side dish. Potatoes (zemiaky) are the most common, usually served boiled or as fries, or something called "American potatoes," essentially large fries served with the potato skin intact. Dinners are more substantial, consisting of an appetizer, main course, and desert (dezert). Deserts are normally built around pancakes of some sort, usually featuring chocolate and nuts, or fruit jam.

Vegetarians will find Slovak restaurants disappointing. Most restaurants offer salads, omelets, and fried cheese, but few if any meatless entrees. Menus typically include a section called "Meatless Dishes," but these too, curiously, usually contain a piece of ham or bacon.

LANGUAGE

Slovak is a western Slavic language, closely related to Czech. The two are mutually comprehensible. For centuries Hungarian was the official language in much of the territory of modern-day Slovakia, though command of Hungarian these days is limited mainly to ethnic Hungarians in the south of the country.

English speakers are likely to find the language something of a challenge. English is not widely known outside the larger cities, though nearly anyone can muster a few words in a pinch. This shouldn't deter you. Most museums and restaurants and anywhere else you're likely to go will have English information on hand. Almost every tourist information center and hotel will have a least one English speaker. If you know some German, that may help as well.

USEFUL WORDS & PHRASES

English	Slovak	Pronunciation
Hello/Good Day	**Dobrý deň**	*Doh*-bree den
Yes	**Ano/Hej!**	*Ah*-no/Hey!
No	**Ne**	*Neh*
Good morning	**Dobré ráno**	*Doh*-brey *rah*-no
Good evening	**Dobrý večer**	*Doh*-bree vech'-air
Goodbye	**Do videnia**	*Doh*-vee-*den*-ya
Good night	**Dobru noc**	Doh-*broo* nohts
Thank you	**D'akujem**	*Dyak*-oo-yem
Please/pardon	**Prosím**	*Proh*-seem
What's your name?	**Ako sa voláte?**	*Ah*-koh sa vol-*ah*-te?
My name is . . .	**Ja sa volám . . .**	*Yah* sa *vol*-ahm . . .
Nice to meet you	**Teší ma**	*Teh*-shee ma
Do you speak English?	**Hovoríte anglicky?**	*Hoh*-vor-ee-te *ahn*-gleets-key?
I don't understand	**Nerozumiem**	*Ne* roh-*zoom*-yem
How much is it?	**Kolko to stojí?**	*Kohl*-ko toh *stoy*-ee
Menu	**Jedálny lístok**	Yeh-*dahl*-nee *lee*-stoke
The bill, please	**Účet, prosím**	*Oo*-chet, *proh*-seem
Cheers!	**Na zdravie**	Nah *zdrah*-vye
Bon appétit!	**Dobru chut'**	Doh-*bru* hooty-a
Open	**Otvorené**	*Oh*-tvor-en-neh
Closed	**Zavreté**	*Zah*-vreh-teh

2 Planning Your Trip to Slovakia

VISITOR INFORMATION
ENTRY REQUIREMENTS

There are no special requirements for entering Slovakia. Passport holders from the U.S., Canada, and Australia can enter the country without a visa and stay for 90 days. Passport holders from E.U. member countries do not need a visa.

MONEY

The unit of currency is the Slovak crown (koruna), designated as Sk. Bills come in denominations of 20, 50, 100, 200, 500, 1,000, and 5,000 Sk. Coins come in denominations of 1, 2, 5, and 10 Sk. You may also see little-used coins of 50 hellers, which is half a crown. Ten-koruna coins are handy for parking machines and other vending

Major Festivals in Slovakia

The major festivals in Slovakia usually celebrate either religious rites or the country's folk origins. Among the biggest religious celebrations is the annual **Maria pilgrimage** in Levoča the first weekend in July. Unless you're a pilgrim, try to avoid Levoča on that weekend; otherwise you'll find yourself elbow to elbow with 100,000 other people looking for hotel rooms and tables at restaurants. Nearly every village holds a folk festival of some sort or another during the summer months (too many to list here), but the granddaddy of them all is the **Východná festival** in early July in the town of Východná, not far from Liptovský Mikuláš. The **Pohoda Music Festival** (www.pohodafestival.sk) in mid-July in Trenčín is the highlight of the outdoor rock music season, drawing many of the best alternative and independent bands from around Europe and United States.

---

machines. At press time, the exchange rate was about 30 Sk for 1 U.S. dollar, and 54 Sk = 1 British pound.

As a member of the European Union, Slovakia is expected to adopt the euro sometime toward the end of the decade. Many establishments catering to visitors will quote prices in euros and accept them as payment. Some hotels quote exclusively in euros. Major credit cards are widely accepted at hotels, restaurants, and shops. Traveler's checks are less useful and must usually be cashed at banks. ATMs are ubiquitous in both big and small towns. They remain the best way to get cash on the spot.

WHEN TO GO

Slovakia has a continental climate with four distinct seasons. Summers are generally warm to very hot, and have reliably good weather. Winter is ski season in the resorts of the Malá Fatra, and the Low and High Tatras. Ski season starts in late December and runs through March. Spring and fall are generally ideal. The months of May, September, and October bring warm sunny days and crisp cool nights. By the end of October, hotels and many sights start shutting down for the winter.

HOLIDAYS

January 1 (New Year's Day, Day of the Establishment of the Slovak Republic), January 6 (Epiphany), Good Friday, Easter Sunday and Monday (Mar/Apr), May 1 (Labor Day), May 8 (Victory over Fascism Day), July 5 (St. Cyril and Methodius Day), August 29 (Slovak National Uprising Day), September 1 (Constitution Day), September 15 (Day of Our Lady of Sorrows), November 1 (All Saints' Day), November 17 (Day of the Fight for Democracy), December 24 (Christmas Eve), and December 25 and 26 (Christmas Day). Offices, banks, museums, and many stores are closed on holidays, though some stores and restaurants remain open.

GETTING THERE

BY PLANE   Bratislava's regional airport (*letisko*), **M.R. Štefánik Airport** (© 02/3303–3353; www.letiskobratislava.sk) is 9km (5 miles) northeast of the city. **Czech Airlines/CSA** (www.csa.cz) maintains regular air service to and from Prague. Budget carrier **SkyEurope** (www.skyeurope.sk) flies to several European capitals, including London, Paris, Amsterdam, and Rome, and several smaller European cities. Other airlines that fly to Bratislava include Austrian Air and Lufthansa. Vienna's **Schwechat** airport

(© **431-7007-22233;** www.viennaairport.com), 67km (40 miles) west of Bratislava, offers the most flight options, and remains the only option for direct flights from North America. Bratislava is a 70-minute bus ride away (see details in the Bratislava section, below).

BY TRAIN   Regular train service links Bratislava with Vienna (1 hr.), Prague (5-6 hr.) and Budapest (3 hr.). For exact times, check the **Slovak State Railway**'s **(ŽSR)** (© **02/2029–1111;** www.zsr.sk) online timetable (use "Praha" to search for Prague, "Wien" to search for Vienna, and so on). Most international trains arrive at Bratislava's centrally located **Hlavná Stanica** (Predstanicne nám. 1; © **02/18188**), about 20 minutes by tram or 10 minutes by taxi to the Old Town.

BY BUS   The Slovak national bus carrier, **SAD** (© **02/5556-7349;** www.sad.sk), together with the Europe-wide consortium of bus operators, **Eurolines** (www.eurolines.com), maintains regular long-distance bus service from Bratislava to a number of European capitals and other cities, though this service is coming under increasing competition from budget airlines. Bratislava's bus station is at Mlynské nivy 31.

BY CAR   Bratislava lies on a main central European motorway, linking Prague with Budapest. The drive to Bratislava from Prague (320km/200 miles) will take 3 to 4 hours, depending on traffic. From Budapest (250km/155 miles) expect to drive about 3 hours. The drive from Vienna (70km/42 miles) will take about 1 hour, but try to avoid travel on Fridays to miss frequent preweekend backups at the border crossing. Note that you will have to buy a special sticker to drive on Slovak highways. The sticker, available at the border crossings and at major gas stations, costs 150 Sk ($5/£2.75) for 1 week, and 300 Sk ($10/£5) for a month. If you rent a car in Slovakia, the rental should include a valid highway sticker.

BY BOAT   It's possible to travel between Bratislava and Vienna by high-speed catamaran (about 75 min.). Check **Twin City Liner** © **0903/610-716;** www.twincityliner.com). Boats depart from the main dock area on Rásuzovo náb, just behind the Devin Hotel. Fares average about 729 Sk ($25/£13) one-way. Regular ferry service is also available to Vienna and Budapest (about 4–5 hr. away). Contact **LOD** (© **02/529-3222;** www.lod.sk).

GETTING AROUND

BY CAR   Car travel offers the most flexibility, and if your plans are to see some of the countryside away from the main cities, you should consider renting a car. To rent, you'll need a license that's valid in the country of origin (U.S. state licenses are acceptable), a major credit card, and a passport. Slovak driving rules follow Continental norms. A yellow diamond denotes a main road where you do not need to yield to incoming traffic at intersections. At unmarked intersections, yield to cars on the right. Cars on roundabouts have the right of way. Speed limits are 130kmph (81 mph) on highways and drop down to 60kmph (37 mph) in villages and incorporated areas. Speed limits are rigorously enforced and if caught you'll have to pay a spot fine, usually 1,000 Sk ($33/£18) or higher. The blood alcohol limit is zero. Slovakia has very few four-lane, limited-access highways, so prepare yourself for some slow two-lane stretches, where you're usually trapped behind a belching truck or a painfully slow bus. Remember to pass with care and only with a clear line of sight.

BY TRAIN   Slovakia's aging but serviceable national rail line, **ŽSR** (© **02/2029-1111;** www.zsr.sk), is the best way to travel between major cities, including Žilina, Trenčín, Poprad, and Košice.

BY BUS In theory, nearly any city, town, or village is accessible by Slovakia's dense public bus network, **SAD** (ⓒ 02/5556-7349; www.sad.sk). In reality, while the network is dense, service can be sporadic. The timetables are oriented toward commuters and fall off during the evenings and on weekends and holidays. Bus schedules are notoriously difficult to read. Just as you're rejoicing that your bus should be coming in 10 minutes, you'll discover that it only runs on certain days or during certain months of the year.

TIPS ON ACCOMMODATIONS

The number of newer, privately owned hotels is on the increase. If you arrive in town without a room, the best place to go is the local tourist information office. Many of these, including the helpful office in Bratislava, can advise on rooms and book according to your wishes. Failing that, look around for private rooms, usually identified by the word "Ubytovanie" (accommodations) or "Privat" on the outside. These are invariably bed-without-bathroom setups, usually in an unused part of the family home, but are almost always clean and cheap.

TIPS ON DINING

With disposable incomes on the rise, more people are eating out more often and the restaurant situation is improving. The transformation is easiest to see in Bratislava and Košice. That said, you may still find yourself in a small town with relatively few options aside from the ubiquitous pizzeria on the main square and a couple of unappetizing pubs, catering mostly to old guys crouched over beers. In that case, go with the pizza.

FAST FACTS: Slovakia

American Express There's no full-service American Express office in Bratislava, but some Amex services are offered through Agency Alex (Kuzmanyho 8; ⓒ 02/5941-2200).

Business Hours Stores and offices are generally open Monday to Friday 9am to 6pm. Banks are open Monday to Friday 9am to 4pm. Some larger stores have limited Saturday hours, usually 9am to noon. Museums and other tourist attractions are often closed on Mondays.

Doctors & Dentists Phone ⓒ **155** in a medical emergency. In Bratislava, there's a doctor on call 24 hours at the Faculty Hospital (Ružinovská 10; ⓒ **02/4443-2429**). Private dental services are available at Kostková 54 (ⓒ **02/6286–0033**).

Electricity Slovak outlets follow the Continental norm (220v, 50hz) with two round plugs. Most appliances that run on 110v will require a transformer.

Embassies **U.S.:** Hviezdoslavovo nám. 4, ⓒ 02/5443-0861; **Canada:** Mostová 2, ⓒ 02/5920-4031; **U.K.:** Panská 16, ⓒ 02/5998-2000.

Emergencies In an emergency, dial the following numbers: police ⓒ **158**, fire ⓒ **150**, ambulance ⓒ **155**, road assistance ⓒ **154**.

Internet Access Internet cafes are located throughout Bratislava and in all larger cities. Internet cafes generally charge 30 Sk ($1/55p) per half-hour of

Internet use. Many better hotels now set aside at least one public computer for guests to use. A few hotels offer in-room dataports or wireless connections.

Laundry & Dry Cleaning At press time, there were no self-service laundries in Bratislava like you would find in Prague. Many hotels, particularly better properties, offer laundry service to guests (usually for a fee). Failing that, dry cleaners usually offer normal laundry services, but costs can add up quickly.

Luggage Storage & Lockers Railroad stations in large cities, including Bratislava's main station, have storage lockers or an attendant to watch luggage.

Mail The main post office is at Nám. SNP 35, just outside the main gate to the Old Town. The rate for mailing a postcard or first-class letter to the U.S. is 25 Sk (80¢/45p), and 22 Sk (70¢/40p) within Europe.

Safety Crime is generally low, but as everywhere use common sense.

Telephones & Fax Slovakia's country code is **421**. To dial Slovakia from abroad, dial the international access code (011 in the U.S.), plus 421 and then the local Slovak area code (minus the zero). The area code for Bratislava is 02. Other commonly used area codes are: Trenčín 032; Žilina 041; the High Tatras 052; Košice 055. To call long distance within Slovakia, dial the area code (retaining the zero) plus the number. To dial abroad from Slovakia, dial 00 and then the country code and area code to where you are calling. A call to the U.S. or Canada would begin 00-1.

Time Zone Slovakia is in the Central European Time zone (CET), 1 hour ahead of GMT and 6 hours ahead of the eastern United States.

Tipping In restaurants, round up the bill 5% to 10% to reward good service. Bellhops, taxi drivers, and tour guides will also expect a small amount in return for services rendered. Around 50 Sk to 100 Sk ($1.70–$3/90p–£1.85) is usually enough in any circumstance.

Toilets You will find decent public toilets in cities and towns throughout Slovakia. Expect to pay 5 Sk to 10 Sk (15¢–30¢/10p–20p) to use the facilities.

Water Tap water is generally potable and there are no specific health concerns. If in doubt, buy bottled water, which is cheap and widely available.

3 Bratislava

Slovakia's youthful capital (www.bratislava.sk) has transformed itself from a relatively unappealing sprawl of postwar, Communist-era buildings into a relaxed and pleasant medium-size capital in the span of little more than a decade. The city's compact Old Town has been completely and stunningly renovated. Most of the area is restricted to car traffic, and in the evenings, it seems, the whole town converges for a cup of coffee or a glass of wine. Plan on being thoroughly charmed, and you might even consider extending your stay.

Until relatively recently Bratislava (known as Pressburg to the Germans, and Pozsony in Hungarian) was a quiet city on the Danube river (Dunaj in Slovak). It was only in the past few decades, under Czechoslovakia's then-Communist government, that the city exploded in population to the current around 500,000. The Communists were keen on building up the Slovak capital as a way of gaining Slovak support. You can see the results of this rapid buildup in the high-rise residences on the outskirts of town. The largest of these Communist-era housing projects, Petržalka, just across the SNP Bridge from the Old Town, holds something like 150,000 people.

Bratislava has played an important role in Hungarian history. During the Turkish occupation of Hungary, the Hungarians moved their capital here. No less than 11 Hungarian royals were crowned in Bratislava's St. Martin's cathedral (Dóm Sv. Martina) throughout the years.

ARRIVING

BY PLANE

Bus no. 61 connects Bratislava airport with the main train station, Hlavná Stanica. The journey takes about 25 minutes. An **Airport Shuttle** service (© **02/4363-2305; www.airportshuttle.sk**) is available, with prices starting at 400 Sk ($13/£7). If you are arriving in Vienna Schwechat airport, buses run hourly to Bratislava's main bus terminal. The ride takes 70 minutes and costs about $10 one-way and $16 return. Several operators maintain regular car and minibus service between Schwechat and Bratislava (www.bratislavahotels.com). The price for up to four passengers is 2,000 Sk ($66/£37).

BY TRAIN, BUS, CAR, OR BOAT

For details, see the general "Getting There" section on p. 610.

CITY LAYOUT

The area of most interest to visitors is the Old Town (Staré Mesto) and the adjacent Castle area, all lying north of the Danube. For restaurants, accommodations, and most of the attractions, you'll rarely stray from this area.

GETTING AROUND

ON FOOT   The best way to see Bratislava and in the Old Town is to walk. Distances are not far, but wear comfortable shoes, since the cobblestones are not kind to heels.

BY TRAM   Bratislava's tram system is comprehensive, though for traveling around the Old Town and the immediate area, you won't need it. Ticket prices vary by time. A 10-minute ticket, the cheapest, costs 14 Sk (50¢/25p). A 30-minute ticket costs 18 Sk (60¢/35p). A ticket for large pieces of luggage costs 7 Sk (25¢/15p). You can also buy day or multiday tickets. A 1-day pass costs 90 Sk ($3/£1.65). Buy tickets from newsdealers or ticket machines. Validate tickets on entering the tram and hold onto them until the end of the ride. The fine for riding without a ticket is 1,800 Sk ($60/£33). Trams generally run from 5am to 11pm. More information is available on the Bratislava Transport Company website: www.dpb.sk.

BY BUS   Bratislava has an extensive network of buses and trolleys, and these are generally the only ways of reaching the more far-flung parts of the city. The ticketing is the same as for trams. Validate your ticket on entering the bus or trolley. Buses generally run from 5am to 11pm.

BY TAXI   Taxis are relatively cheap and easy to find. Hail them on the street, at taxi stands, or call by phone. Watch that the driver turns on the meter, since dishonest drivers, relatively rarely now, may try to cheat you. Fares around town shouldn't be any higher than 150 Sk to 200 Sk ($5–$7/£2.75–£3.70). Two reputable agencies include **Fun Taxi** (② 02/16111) and **Euro Taxi** (② 02/16022).

BY BIKE The car-free Old Town is easily negotiated by bike, but there are few rental shops around. The rest of the city is less bike-friendly, with trolley buses, trams, and traffic to contend with.

VISITOR INFORMATION

The main **Tourist Information Center** is located inside the Old Town (Klobučnícka ul. 2; ② 02/5443-3715; www.bratislava.sk). The staff is efficient at supplying maps and suggestions of all kinds, as well as helping to arrange transportation and accommodations. The **Bratislava Tourist Service,** also in the Old Town (Ventúrska ul. 9; ② 02/5464-1271; www.bratislava-info.sk) is a separate but equally helpful office, where you'll find plenty of maps and booklets as well as helpful suggestions on what to see and where to sleep. The office runs daily walking tours (in English and German). For a more fun tour, head to Hlavné nám. in the Old Town to catch the little red trolley through the Old Town. Tours last 30 minutes and are great for a quick orientation (② 0903-302-817; www.presporacik.sk). **Nick's Bike Tours** (Medená 15; ② 0915-153-265; www.nicksbiketours.com) offers off-the-beaten-track bicycle and walking tours, both within Bratislava and in the surrounding countryside, from July 1 through October.

WHERE TO STAY

You may experience sticker-shock on arrival in Bratislava. The city attracts relatively few individual travelers and most of the properties are aimed at businessmen on expense accounts and the odd coach tour from Germany and Austria. If you do decide on one of the luxury hotels, bear in mind that it never hurts to bargain. Even the most expensive hotels have been known to slash rack rates on slow nights.

At the other end of the spectrum are private rooms. These, understandably, vary greatly in comfort, cleanliness, and location. Some are real gems, situated in or near the Old Town and presided over by Slovak grannies who make sure everything is spotless. Others are less desirable, in public housing estates in far-flung residential neighborhoods. If you decide to go the private room route, insist on a room within comfortable walking or tram distance from the Old Town. Check www.bratislava hotels.sk for a good general overview of hotels, pensions, and private rooms.

VERY EXPENSIVE

Carlton ✶✶✶ Once the rather dowdy Grande Dame of Bratislava's prewar hotels, the Carlton has gotten a multimillion-dollar face-lift courtesy of the Radisson hotel chain and the result is easily Slovakia's finest hotel. You'll find everything you would expect from a leading international hotel, packed into a lovely 19th-century neoclassical building, along one of the city's leading squares. It's convenient to the Old Town, the river, and all of the city's cultural facilities. The staff will cater to every whim.

Hviezdoslavovo nám. 3. ② 02/5939-0000. Fax 02/5939-0010. www.radissonsas.com. 168 units. 7,200 Sk ($240/£132) double. AE, DC, MC, V. **Amenities:** Restaurant; spa; concierge; business center; shopping arcade; salon; 24-hr. room service; dry-cleaning; nonsmoking rooms. *In room:* A/C, TV, dataport, minibar, coffeemaker, hair dryer, iron, safe.

Devin ✶ A quirky, local alternative to the Carlton if you're looking to spend high-end money, but don't necessarily want a prefab chain experience. The Devin dates from the 1950s and was once the hotel of choice for visiting Communist dignitaries. It's been thoroughly scoured and spruced up since then, but you'll still find a sort of old-school regalness to the well-proportioned rooms, as well as the lobby and reception area. The adjoining cafe is an classic midcentury period piece. The location, just away from the Old Town, along the Danube, is excellent and especially convenient to the ferry docks. Parking and access to the hotel is easy, since the freeway runs nearby.

Riečna 4. © 02/5998–5856. Fax 02/5443–0682. www.hoteldevin.sk. 100 units. 7,200 Sk ($240/£132) double. AE, DC, MC, V. **Amenities:** Restaurant; indoor pool; spa; concierge; business center; limited room service; dry cleaning; nonsmoking rooms. *In room:* A/C, TV, dataport, minibar, hair dryer, safe.

EXPENSIVE

Hotel No. 16 ☆☆ This dark-wooded, cottagelike inn, tucked high above town in Bratislava's tony villa quarter, is one part mountain chalet and another part boutique hotel. The rooms themselves are small but cozy, and ooze rustic charm. That's a ruse. They're wired with every modern convenience you're likely to need, including in-room Wi-Fi and plasma TV screens. Everything, from the furniture to the bathroom fixtures, feels sturdy and well crafted. The relatively remote location affords an illusion of seclusion, but the Old Town is still only a 10-minute walk away. If you arrive in town by plane, bus, or train, take a taxi and don't try to negotiate the twisting streets. Be sure to ask about discounts, since the hotel will cut rates on slow nights.

Partizánska 16. © 02/5441–1672. Fax 02/5441–1298. www.hotelno16.sk. 12 units. 5,700 Sk ($190/£105) double. AE, DC, MC, V. **Amenities:** Restaurant; concierge; room service; dry cleaning; nonsmoking rooms. *In room:* A/C, TV, dataport, minibar, hair dryer, safe.

Perugia ☆☆ This medium-size Old Town hotel offers the best mix of comfort, location, and affordability, and for that reason it's often difficult to get a room. The emphasis is on style. A former baroque town house renovated in the 1990s by a well-known Slovak design team; the modern rooms have original art on the wall. In the summer, the welcoming terrace is often filled with friendly-faced foreigners. The in-house restaurant serves very good Hungarian food.

Zelená 5 16. © 02/5443-1818. Fax 02/5443-1821. www.perugia.sk. 14 units. 5,000 Sk ($165/£92) double. AE, DC, MC, V. **Amenities:** Restaurant; limited room service; nonsmoking rooms. *In room:* A/C, TV, minibar, hair dryer, safe.

MODERATE

IBIS ☆ Exactly what you'd expect from the European hotel chain that has pioneered the market for moderately priced hotels with central locations. Okay, so the lobby and hallways feel a little cramped, and the room is tiny and lacks—well—atmosphere. You're a stone's throw away from the Old Town and you have relative luxuries like in-room Internet and air-conditioning that would easily cost twice as much anywhere else. Note that only queen-size beds are available; no twins or triple rooms.

Zámocká 38. © 02/5929-2000. Fax 02/5929-2111. www.ibis-bratislava.sk. 100 units. 3,000 Sk ($100/£55) double. AE, DC, MC, V. **Amenities:** Restaurant. *In room:* A/C, TV, dataport, minibar, hair dryer.

Old City The only moderately priced hotel located within the Old Town has a few good things going for it. First is location, right in the heart of Bratislava's Old Town. The hotel is also clean and nonsmoking throughout. On the downside, it's a four- or five-story walk up, and the rooms themselves are nondescript. Ask for one of the lower rooms in midsummer, since the rooms just below the roof can get hot.

Michalská 2. © 02/5443-0258. Fax 02/5464-8304. www.oldcityhotel.sk. 15 units. 2,400 Sk ($80/£44) double. AE, DC, MC, V. **Amenities:** Restaurant. *In room:* TV, minibar, hair dryer.

Slovenská Reštaurácia ✶✶ SLOVAK   The ideal spot if you're looking for bryn-dzové halušky and other classic Slovak dishes in a highly traditional setting, complete with waiters in folk costumes, folk music, and the whole 9 yards. If this sounds too touristy, don't be put off. The food is excellent (this may be your only chance to try wild boar) and the clientele includes not only the inevitable tour buses, but also Slo-vak couples looking for good home cooking in their capital city.

Hviezdoslavovo nám. 20. ℂ **02/5443-4883**. Lunch and dinner items 210 Sk–270 Sk ($7–$9/£4–£5). AE, DC, MC, V. Daily 11am–11pm.

MODERATE   ~~LUNCH~~

Prašná Bašta ✶✶ *(Finds* SLOVAK   This well-concealed cozy little garden, just a couple steps away from the St. Michael's Tower, is an oasis of mostly laid-back locals who know good food at good value when they get it. Sit outside on the back terrace in nice weather. There's usually a little combo band keeping things lively in the evenings. Start off with the spicy "Armenian" salad, and then move through the mains of mostly chicken and pork dishes, but more interesting and original than the usual Slovak menu. There's also a nice selection of vegetarian meals. Reservations recom-mended, especially for the terrace.

Zámočnicka 11. ℂ **02/5443-4957**. Lunch and dinner items 180 Sk–240 Sk ($6–$8/£3–£7). AE, DC, MC, V. Mon–Sat 11am–11pm.

LUNCH

Tokyo ✶✶ JAPANESE   One of the few places in town that serves decent sushi. That might sound like a strange claim, but after a week or more in the wilds of eastern Slo-vakia, facing dinner after dinner of stuffed chicken breasts, you might welcome a lighter change of pace. The sushi is pricey by the piece, but a decent range of sushi-maki sets brings the price down to the affordable category. In addition to sushi, Tokyo serves decent Thai food, including staple noodle dishes and some spicy curries (though mild by Thai standards). The restaurant is light on atmosphere, so head here, like many Slovaks do, for a quick lunch instead. Reservations not needed.

Panská 27. ℂ **02/5443-4982**. Lunch and dinner items 180 Sk–300 Sk ($6–$10/£3–£6). AE, DC, MC, V. Daily 11am–11pm.

INEXPENSIVE

The Dubliner IRISH   A friendly Irish-themed pub that remains an expat anchor in the Old Town. In nice weather, grab a street-side table, or head inside to the expan-sive bar, complete with traditional cobblestone flooring. The food runs to pub sta-ples—a kind of fusion between what you might actually see in Dublin and what Slovak taste buds demand. The "Traditional Irish Stew" bears more than a passing resemblance to Slovak "gulaš." A nice mix of hot and cold sandwiches, salads, and standard appetizers like spicy chicken wings. If you're looking to meet up with com-patriots, this is the spot to find them. Reservations not needed.

Sedlárska 6. ℂ **02/5441-0706**. Lunch and dinner items 90 Sk–150 Sk ($3–$5/£1.70–£2.75). AE, DC, MC, V. Daily 11am–1am.

17 Bar ✶ ITALIAN   The place to go for pizza and beer in a casual student atmos-phere. The pizza, served in typically thin-crusted, Slovak style, is some of the best in town. Try the "Diavalo," with spicy Slovak sausage and red peppers. Sit on the terrace in summer or grab a wooden bench inside in winter. In keeping with the largely stu-dent clientele, the service and presentation are casual. Reservations not needed.

Hviezdoslavovo nám. 17. ⓒ **02/5443-5135.** Lunch and dinner items 90 Sk–120 Sk ($3–$4/£1.70–£2.20). No credit cards. Mon–Sat 11am–11pm.

EXPLORING BRATISLAVA

Bratislava is best suited to ambling. There are few "musts"; instead the **Old Town (Staré Mesto)** itself, with its inviting, laid-back mix of restaurants, cafes, and bars, is the primary attraction. The best place to start your exploration is at the main entrance to the Old Town, **St. Michael's Tower (Michalská veža).** From here, walk along the main pedestrian streets of Michalská and then Ventúrska, pausing to admire the detailing on the lovingly restored baroque and Renaissance housing stock. Alleyways fan out in all directions, and the best advice is simply to follow your nose. The core of the Old Town is small and can be covered in a couple of hours. The focal point of the Old Town is **Hlavné nám,** the Main Square, lined on one side by the Old Town hall and the other by a mix of restaurants and cafes. At some point, be sure to pay a visit to the city's cathedral, **St. Martin's (Dóm Sv. Martina),** situated just outside of the Old Town, following the signs. From here it's a short walk below the freeway to the **Castle** side of the Old Town. The hike to the castle takes about 20 minutes. The views out over the Old Town are spectacular, but the castle itself is a disappointment. From here, you can't miss the view of Bratislava's retro-futuristic bridge, the **Most SNP,** which links the Old Town to the sprawling housing project of Petržalka. On your return from the castle, walk through the **old Jewish quarter,** once situated in the area around Židovská.

Cathedral of St. Martin (Dóm Sv. Martina) 🀧🀧   The city's most important church was neutered and neglected by the former Communist regime, who planned the main highway right past the church's front door. That was done intentionally as a way of snubbing religion in the name of modernity. Now the church is making a comeback, though it still feels a little lost and forlorn here. St. Martin's served as the main coronation cathedral for a procession of Hungarian kings and queens during the centuries of the Turkish occupation of Hungary.

Rudnayovo nám. No phone. Mon–Fri 10–11:30am and 2–4:30pm; Sat 10–11:30am; Sun 2–4:30pm.

St. Michael's Tower (Michalská veža) 🀧   A highly inviting entryway into the Old Town. The gate is actually part of the city's medieval fortification system, and you can still see the remains of the moat and bastion. The 50m (150-ft.) tower, topped with a statue of St. Michael himself, houses a small exhibition on weaponry; the top of the tower affords a postcard view over the Old Town.

Michalská. No phone. Tues–Fri 10am–5pm; Sat–Sun 11am–6pm.

Bratislava Castle (Bratislavský hrad) 🀧   This squat, square castle, high above the Old Town, is worth the climb to the top, if only for the fabulous view of the space-age bridge, the Most SNP, in the distance. The castle dates from the early 16th century. It burned to the ground at the start of the 19th century and stood as a ruin for almost 150 years before the Communist government started restoration work (still ongoing) in the 1950s. The historical exhibitions are a bit of a disappointment and you can give them a miss.

Hrad. No phone. Tues–Sat 9am–5pm; Sun 1–5pm.

Primate's Palace (Primaciálny Palác) 🀧🀧   A beautifully restored 18th-century palace that now serves as the seat of the mayor of Bratislava. It was here in 1805 that a victorious Napoleon Bonaparte and Holy Roman Emperor Francis I signed the "Treaty of Pressburg" following the Battle of Austerlitz (now "Slavkov," near the Moravian city of Brno). You can tour the inside of the palace; the highlights include the **Chamber of Mirrors (Zrkadlová sieň)**, as well as a valuable collection of tapestries.

Primaciálne nám. ℭ **02/5935-6111**. Tues–Sun 10am–5pm.

Museum of Jewish Culture (Múzeum Židovskej Kultúry) 𝆕 For centuries, Bratislava was one of the most important centers of Jewish scholarship in central Europe. The area below the castle—now covered over by the highway—eventually became the Jewish quarter, and was once home to as many as 20 schools and synagogues. The quarter survived largely intact until World War II, during which the puppet Slovak government—following the Nazi lead—deported the Jews to the death camps. The Communist government after the war then paved over the remains (in this case, by building a highway over them). The photographs and documents on display here tell the story.

Židovská 17. ℭ **02/5441-8507**. Admission 200 Sk ($6.70/£3.70). Sun–Fri 11am–4:30pm.

SHOPPING ✳

Bratislava, as a modern European capital, has everything you might want or need. In terms of souvenirs, there are a couple of unique shops worth visiting. **Galéria Donner** (Klobučnícka 4; ℭ **02/5443-3753**) specializes in visual arts, paintings, and graphics from the 1950s to the 1980s, including an interesting collection of Communist-era paintings and sketches. If you're looking for more traditional folk art, including textiles, lace, and ceramics, try **Úluv** (Nám. SNP 12; ℭ **02/5292-3802;** www.uluv.sk). **Ten Senses** (Ventúrska 16; ℭ **0903/388-864**) is a modern gift shop in the Old Town that combines commerce with fair-trade community values of social development. Here you'll find Slovak ceramics and textiles sharing the shelf with other quirky gifts from around the world.

BRATISLAVA AFTER DARK

As the nation's capital, Bratislava is the center of Slovak culture. The **Slovak National Theater (Slovenské národné divadlo)** (Gorkého 4; ℭ **02/5443-3890;** www.snd.sk) maintains an active program of high-quality opera and ballet in season (Sept–June). The **Reduta** (Palackého 2; ℭ **02/5920-8233**), just next door, is an excellent venue for classical concerts. You can buy tickets at the box office, or ask at the tourist information office. To find out what's on, pick up a copy of *Kam do mesta,* the city's free monthly, available at tourist information offices and bars and restaurants. The English-language weekly *The Slovak Spectator* devotes two or three pages to culture and is a good source for what's happening.

As for culture of the drinking and clubbing variety, there's no shortage of late-night bars, cafes, and music clubs. Most of the action is concentrated in and around the Old Town, and typically starts around 10pm or 11pm and lasts until 1am or 2am.

Charlie Centrum An all in-in-one alternative movie house, pub, and club. If you get bad weather, check out the excellent movie program here, and the films are usually shown in their original language. Špitálska 4. ℭ **02/5296-8994**.

Sparx 𝆕 A huge disco, cocktail bar, and dance club occupying the site where the legendary pub "Mamut" once stood. The club of the moment. Cintorínska 32. ℭ **0903/403-097**. www.sparx.sk.

Verdict One of a number of generic cafes and drinks places that line the streets of the Old Town. This place is recommendable for its location, at the center of the action, and for a great terrace in summer. The little bar inside can get quite popular after 11pm. Panská 6. www.verdict.sk.

4 Western Slovakia & the Malá Fatra

TRENČÍN
100km (60 miles) N of Bratislava

Trenčín (www.trencin.sk) is a welcoming town that has three things going for it: a picture-perfect, brooding castle; a small grouping of welcoming hotels and pensions at each price point; and a positive attitude. As recently as a few years ago, the town was in steep decline, with its major textile industries facing stiff competition from cheap Asian imports. That's changed as the town has begun to embrace the future and play up some of its cultural attributes. Trenčín is now host to arguably the best open-air alternative and independent music festival in the country, the Pohoda festival (www.pohodafestival.sk) each July.

The city's history dates back to Roman times, when it served as a northern garrison town to protect the empire from Germanic tribes. On rocks below the castle, a fascinating Roman inscription dating from the year A.D. 179 and ordered by Emperor Marcus Aurelius, celebrates a Roman victory over the hordes (you can see it from the first floor of the Hotel Tatra). In the Middle Ages, the town grew in importance because of it position on the Váh River, astride one of the main trading routes linking the Baltic and Mediterranean seas. Trenčín achieved arguably its greatest place in history in the early 14th century as the seat of a renegade kingdom declared by one Matúš Čák. Čák, who made the castle his residence, proclaimed himself the king of the Váh and the Tatra Mountains. His kingdom ended with his death 20 years later in 1321.

ESSENTIALS
GETTING THERE From Bratislava, the drive takes about 90 minutes in light traffic. Trenčín is also easily reached by train or bus from Bratislava or Žilina. Regular bus service links the city to Brno in the Czech Republic and points west. Trenčín's bus and train stations are next to each other and situated about a 10-minute walk through a park from the center of town.

VISITOR INFORMATION Trenčín's **Tourist Information Office** (Sládkovičova; ℂ **032/743-3505;** daily Apr 15–Oct 15 Mon–Fri 8am–6pm, Sat–Sun 8am–4pm; Oct 16–Apr 14 Mon–Fri 8am–5pm) is situated just off the main square. The helpful staff can provide a local map, information on the sights, as well as good advice on hotels and restaurants. While the office doesn't book rooms, they keep a list of accommodations and can make a few helpful phone calls.

WHERE TO STAY & DINE
Outside of mid-July and the annual Pohoda music festival, you shouldn't have any problem booking a room. Eating is a different story. There's not much aside from the (very decent) restaurants at the Tatra and pod Hradom hotels and a bunch of pizzerias and coffee bars along the main square.

Giuseppe The ubiquitous pizzeria on the main square in this case is actually not a bad choice for a simple and cheap meal. The menu includes all of the pizza combinations you'd expect, but the mozzarella with tomatoes and fresh basil stands out because they use real mozzarella. The service is slow.

Štúrovo nám. 18. No phone. Lunch and dinner items 90 Sk–120 Sk ($3–$4/£1.65–£2.20). No credit cards. Daily 11am–9pm.

Hotel pod Hradom ★★   The kind of family-run hotel every Slovak town needs. Clean, moderately priced, fairly modest, and comfortable, with a friendly staff eager to show off all that the hotel offers. The location is excellent on a quiet lane that runs below the castle and parallel to the main square. Choose the Tatra (above) if you're looking for a full-service hotel, but this will do if you're just looking for a clean bed. The restaurant here is excellent.

Matúšova 12. ✆ **032/748-1701.** Fax 032/748-1703. www.podhradem.sk. 12 units. 2,300 Sk ($77/£42) double. AE, DC, MC, V. **Amenities:** Restaurant; spa. In room: TV, minibar, hair dryer.

Hotel Tatra ★★   Nicely refurbished turn-of-the-20th-century hotel retaining many Art Nouveau details. The rooms are a delight, evoking that idyllic time of the "First Republic," the 20 years between the two world wars that both Slovaks and Czechs look back to with such fondness. The location, on the tip of the main square just below the castle, is perfect. Still, the hotel is probably overpriced for what it offers. The reception has been known to cut rates on slow nights. The restaurant is easily the best in town.

M. R. Štefánika 2. ✆ **032/650-6111.** Fax 032/650-6213. www.hotel-tatra.sk. 70 units. 4,600 Sk ($153/£84) double. AE, DC, MC, V. **Amenities:** Restaurant; spa; concierge; salon; limited room service; massage. In room: A/C, TV, data-port, minibar, hair dryer.

Penzión pod Hradom ★   An excellent low-budget pick. The rooms are spotlessly clean and modern. The beds have crisp white sheets and nice big windows. Some open onto the castle above, while others open onto a quiet inner courtyard. The location couldn't be better: a 5-minute walk from the main square or a 15-minute hike to the castle.

Matúšova 23. ✆ **032/744-5028.** Fax 0032/744-2507. www.podhradom.sk. 5 units. 1,800 Sk ($60/£33) double. AE, DC, MC, V. In room: TV, hair dryer.

Slovenská Reštaurácia ★★   This traditional, informal, tavern-style restaurant situated below the Hotel Tatra serves very good food. The restaurant has recently won some "Best of Slovakia" awards. It's good, but that probably overstates the case. The menu is heavy on the standard pork and chicken combinations. The trout *(pstruh)* comes highly recommended. The wine list is extensive; ask one of the knowledgeable waiters for a recommendation.

M. R. Štefánika 2. ✆ **032/650-6111.** Lunch and dinner items 150 Sk–240 Sk ($5–$8/£2.75–£4.40). AE, DC, MC, V. Mon–Sat 11am–11pm.

EXPLORING

Trenčín has a handsome and compact historic core, comprised of two central squares. A modern one, Štúrovo nám, and a more traditional square, Mierové nám., joined by the town's last remaining old town gate, the Dolná brána. Simply choose an entryway onto the square and walk.

To reach the castle, look for steps going up just before you reach the Hotel Tatra toward the end of Mierové nám, or climb the stairs running off Farská ulica. It's a 15-minute climb to the top, with some beautiful views over the Old Town and Váh river valley.

Trenčín Castle 🏰🏰   Worth the climb for the marvelous views and a close-up look at the rambling structures that make up the castle complex. The restored interiors are only accessible via guided tour (though English tours are a rarity behind Slovak and German).

Hrad. No phone. May–Oct daily 8am–6pm; Nov–Apr daily 9am–3:30pm.

AFTER DARK

Trenčín nightlife is laid-back and usually follows one of two patterns. The first is a comfortable meal at the Slovenská Reštaurácia at the Hotel Tatra, followed by a stroll around the central square or maybe a climb to the castle to work off some of those calories. The second option is to have a couple more drinks and line up at one of the clubs that line the main squares. The action starts around 10pm and goes until around 2 or 3am. It is not sophisticated in the slightest, but it can be fun if you're in the mood to dance.

ŽILINA

80km (50 miles) N of Trenčín; 180km (110 miles) N of Bratislava

Žilina is a brawny industrial town that's better known as the home of some of Slovakia's more conservative politicians than anything worthwhile for tourists. On the other hand, it's an important bus and train junction, as well as a major stopping-off point on the main east-west highway, so many visitors find themselves here for one reason or another. And if you have your own transportation, Žilina makes for a comfortable base to explore the Malá Fatra National Park. The town of Terchová, the center of the Malá Fatra region, is a 25km (15-mile) drive down the highway.

ESSENTIALS

GETTING THERE   Žilina lies on the main east-west highway and is a relatively easy drive along some four-lane highway from both Trenčín and Bratislava. Figure on an hour's drive from Trenčín and 2 to 3 hours, depending on traffic, from Bratislava. Žilina is also a major train and bus depot. There are frequent train connections to both Trenčín (70 min.) and Bratislava (2–3 hr.). The train is also the best bet for reaching Poprad and the High Tatras. The train station is a 10-minute walk from the main central square along Národná Street. If you're planning on heading to the Malá Fatra, the bus is the best bet. There are frequent bus connections to Terchová; figure on a ride of about 45 minutes. The bus station is east of the city center, about a 10-minute walk from the train station and from the center of the city.

GETTING AROUND   The inner city is relatively compact and most of it has been restricted to automobile traffic, so walking is the only option.

VISITOR INFORMATION   Žilina's tourist information office (Burianova medzierka 4; ℭ **041/562-0789;** www.selinan.sk) is situated in a private travel agency called **Selinan** on a small street just off of Mariánske nám. They'll generally do their best to help you sort out the train and bus schedules, as well as recommend lodging and dining options. The office is open Monday to Friday, 8:30am to 5pm.

WHERE TO STAY & DINE

Žilina has two decent hotels, both offering the same level of comfort and convenience at similar prices. Book at whichever has a free room. Another option, recommended if you have a car, is to continue on in the direction of Terchová for more rustic lodging in the hills. Most of Žilina's restaurants are clustered around the Mariánske nám. in the older part of town. Though they all have different names and slightly different menus, they all serve the same nondescript food.

Astoria   Similar to the Grand in terms of basic amenities and price, but perhaps a tad less "grand." Like the Grand, it's an older hotel dating from the early 20th century that's been given a modern makeover. The Astoria's slight advantage might be location, especially if you're coming from the train station, which is just down the road. Ask for a room that fronts on the park or toward the rear to avoid busy Národná.

Národná 1. ✆ **089/624-711.** Fax 089/623-173. 24 units. 2,500 Sk ($83/£46) double. AE, DC, MC, V. **Amenities:** Restaurant; limited room service. *In room:* TV, minibar, hair dryer.

Grand ✿   A nicely refurbished, charming, older hotel just off of the Mariánske nám. A thorough modernization in 2004 added the unexpected touch of Jacuzzis and air-conditioning (rare for these parts) in some of the "Lux" rooms. Given the shortage of good places to eat, the restaurant is fine for a meal. The rooms themselves are bright and airy. The helpful reception staff can help you with basic directions if you arrive on the weekend, when the tourist information office is closed.

Sládkovičova 1. ✆ **041/564-3265.** Fax 041/564-3266. www.hotelgrand.sk. 43 units. 2,600 Sk ($87/£48) double; 3,000 Sk ($100/£55) Lux. AE, DC, MC, V. **Amenities:** Restaurant; limited room service. *In room:* Some A/C, TV, dataport, minibar, hair dryer, Jacuzzi in some.

Trattoria Pepe ✿   This is the warmest, cleanest, and most inviting place to eat in the center of Žilina. Unlike the restaurants that line Mariánske nám, this small, family-run Italian restaurant honestly cares about the food and the service. The pizzas are

Malá Fatra National Park

Though it lacks the natural drama of the High Tatras to the east, the Malá Fatra highlands feel more rustic and relaxed. The pristine park is one of the most popular in Slovakia for weekend mountain walks, bike rides, and in winter cross-country and downhill skiing. If you have a few days to spend, and are not rushing to those *other* mountains (the High Tatras), plan on spending a couple of days here. The administrative center of the region is Terchová, a long narrow village about 25km (15 miles) east of Žilina. Here you'll find the main tourist information office (Ulica sv. Cyrila a Metoda 96; ✆ **041/599-3100;** www.ztt.sk) as well as dozens of pensions and private rooms. The tourist office sells hiking maps and can help book rooms.

The European Union has provided funding for an extensive network of bike trails aimed at cyclists of all abilities. Throughout the region, you'll find chaotic, downhill "adrenaline" rides as well as more level trails for simply puttering around and enjoying the views. Pick up the pamphlet *On the Bicycle Across the Jánošík Region,* available at the tourist information office in Terchová. You can rent bikes at the Pension Malá Fatra in Terchová (Družstevná 176; ✆ **041/569-5413**).

a notch above average, with the cheese and other ingredients mostly fresh. The pastas are good. But the real drawing card is the welcoming service.

J. Vuruma 5. (℃ **041/564-3555.** Lunch and dinner items 120 Sk–180 Sk ($4–$6/£2.20–£3.30). No credit cards. Daily 11am–9pm.

ACCOMMODATIONS OUTSIDE OF ŽILINA

Bránica 🐾🐾 *(Finds* One of Slovakia's newest and most luxurious getaway hotels. This is a destination in its own right, with beautifully groomed clay tennis courts, wine-tasting rooms, a full fitness center, and sauna. It's the kind of place you book for the weekend to take some time off a hectic work schedule. The hotel is situated just along the main road between Žilina and Terchová, about 15km (10 miles) east of Žilina. It's possible to reach the hotel by bus (tell the driver where you're going and he'll drop you off at the far eastern edge of the village called "Belá").

Belá. (℃ **041/569-9035.** Fax 041/569-9039. www.hotelbranica.sk. 98 units. 2,700 Sk ($130/£49) double. AE, DC, MC, V. **Amenities:** Restaurant; indoor pool; health club and spa; bike and ski rental; tennis courts; concierge; limited room service; massage; nonsmoking rooms. *In room:* A/C, TV, dataport, minibar, hair dryer, safe.

Chata pod Malým Rozsutcom 🐾 This very modest pension situated about 30km (20 miles) east of Žilina, just beyond Terchová, is one of the most authentic mountain cabins you'll see. The owners have set aside six tiny rooms with bathroom on the second floor of their log-cabin home. The rooms can be chilly at night and hot during the day, but at the same time the experience is enjoyable because of the hospitality you're extended. Even if you're not staying here, stop in for a meal. It's real Slovak cooking in the best sense of the word.

Demkovska 7, Zázrivá. (℃ **0908/785-092.** www.chpmr.sk. 6 units. 600 Sk ($20/£11) double. AE, DC, MC, V. **Amenities:** Restaurant (daily 10am–10pm).

5 The High Tatras & Eastern Slovakia

THE HIGH TATRAS/VYSOKÉ TATRY
150km (90 miles) E of Žilina; 350km (210 miles) NE of Bratislava

The High Tatras (www.tatry.net) are Slovakia's biggest tourist draw, and a visit to the country is not complete without seeing these majestic mountains. It's not the hills' height that's so impressive; the tallest are only in the 2,600m (8,500-ft.) range. But it's the way that they vault, so dramatically and out of nowhere, from the flat grasslands around the town of Poprad to their lofty snowcapped peaks.

The High Tatras are commonly called the "world's smallest Alpine range." That's a reference to the relatively short length of the mountain chain, just 30km (about 20 miles) end to end. The Tatras are actually part of the much larger Carpathian range that begins its rise just outside of Bratislava and then draws a wide arc through northern Slovakia, southern Poland, and into Romania.

The High Tatras enjoyed a brief golden age in the late-19th and early-20th centuries, when the wealthy classes from Hungary, Austria, Germany, and later Czechoslovakia came to ski or to ride out the hot summers in the mountains. Many of the most beautiful buildings, including the two "Grand" hotels in Starý Smokovec and Tatranská Lomnica, were built at that time. The two world wars and the decades of Communism afterward put an end to all of that. These days, the High Tatras remain a popular tourist destination for Slovaks, Poles, and, increasingly, Russians, though it's hard to escape that bittersweet feeling of nostalgia for those good old days.

The Tatras have two main seasons, summer hiking season and ski season in winter. Summer season starts in June, when the trails to the peaks are opened up to the public, and runs through September. The hikes here are some of the best in Europe, and if you enjoy walking, then pick up some maps and gear and plan on staying at least a few days. In addition to hiking, a fledgling mountain-biking industry is taking hold. Ski season, depending on the weather, starts in mid-December and runs to mid-March. The best skiing is situated near Štrbské Pleso, but all three major resorts have lifts and ski-rental facilities.

Most of the best hikes, hotels, and restaurants are clustered around the High Tatra's three main resort towns, all easily reachable by car or electric railroad from the regional capital of Poprad. At the far western edge is Štrbské Pleso. The word "pleso" means "tarn" and refers to the resort's large mountain lake. At the center is the largest resort, Smokovce, divided into "Starý" (old) and "Nový" (new) Smokovec. Starý Smokovec has the largest station on the Tatra's electric railroad, and is a junction for reaching the other resorts. The third resort is Tatranská Lomnica to the east of Starý Smokovec.

Everyone has his or her favorite resort, but of the three I prefer Starý Smokovec. As the main rail junction, it's easier to get around. It's also in better physical condition and feels livelier. Štrbské Pleso is favored by skiers, since the best slopes are here. It also offers some of the best trails to the peaks, if climbing to the top of the mountain is on your list of things to do. Tatranská Lomnica, since it lies on a spur of the electrical railway, is quieter and boasts two of the area's best hotels. One disadvantage is that you'll have to travel a bit to get to the best hiking trails.

One note about the environment: In late 2004, a freak windstorm struck a wide swath of the High Tatras, knocking down tens of thousands of trees in a matter of minutes. The damage was greatest in the area between Štrbské Pleso and Starý Smokovec. The initial reaction was shock, but the authorities have since worked night and day to clear the fallen trees. You'll still see extensive damage, especially in the lower ranges, but the overall beauty of the mountains remains intact.

GETTING THERE

BY PLANE   The Bratislava-based budget carrier **SkyEurope** (www.skyeurope.sk) now flies twice daily from London's Stansted airport to **Poprad-Tatry** field (© 052/ 776-3875), about 5km (3 miles) outside of town. CSA also offers regular flights to the Tatras from Prague, but the flights usually go to Košice airport, with a minibus transfer to Poprad (2 hr.).

BY TRAIN   Poprad is a major rail junction and ŽSR state railroad train service is relatively frequent to and from Bratislava, Žilina, and Košice. From Bratislava, the journey on an express train takes about 5 hours; from Žilina, 2 hours, and from Košice, 2 hours. From Poprad station, the Tatra Electric Railroad runs directly to Starý Smokovec and Štrbské Pleso, about 30 minutes to Starý Smokovec and 1 hour to Štrbské Pleso. To reach Tatranská Lomnica, change trains in Starý Smokovec.

BY CAR   Poprad lies on Slovakia's major east-west highway. The drive from Bratislava follows the Váh river north to Trenčín and Žilina, before turning east. Some of the drive is along four-lane highway and takes about 4 hours. From Košice, the drive is along mostly two-lane highway and takes about 2 hours.

BY BUS   Slovakia's national bus carrier, SAD, maintains regular service from Poprad to many regional cities and towns, including Levoča. You can also use the bus station at Starý Smokovec, just on the edge of the resort in the direction of Tatranská Lomnica. The bus is often the best option for seeing the smaller towns in and around the Tatras. The tourist information offices can help you sort out the timetables and destinations.

GETTING AROUND

BY TRAIN   The Tatra Electric Railroad is cheap and efficient, and serves all of the major resorts. Trains run about every 45 minutes from Poprad to Starý Smokovec and on to Štrbské Pleso and several points in between. Travel to Tatranská Lomnica requires a change at Starý Smokovec. Ticket prices vary depending on the length of the journey. The price from Poprad to Štrbské Pleso is 40 Sk ($1.30/75p).

BY CAR   Excellent roads connect Poprad to all of the Tatra resorts. The travel time between Starý Smokovec and Štrbské Pleso (20km/12 miles) is 15 minutes.

BY BIKE   You can easily rent a bike and move from resort to resort along the main road. The ride from Starý Smokovec to Štrbské Pleso is challenging, since there's an elevation change of about 300m (900 ft.) between the towns. Coming back of course it's all downhill.

ON FOOT   Walking between the resorts is not a viable option. The distances are too far.

VISITOR INFORMATION

The main **Tourist Information Offices,** identified as **TIK,** in Starý Smokovec (© **052/ 442-3440**) and Tatranská Lomnica (© **052/446-8119**), can provide basic information and maps, as well as book accommodations. The staff is also helpful in sorting out basic transportation questions. The **Mountain Rescue Service (Horská Záchranná Služba),** based in Starý Smokovec (© **052/442–2820;** www.hzs.sk), is the first place to turn in the event of an accident. The **Mountain Guide Agency (Spolok Horských Vodcov)** in Starý Smokovec (© **052/442–2066;** www.tatraguide.sk) can provide guides to the summits, or for adventures like snowshoeing and rock climbing. A guide for a climb to the highest peak, Gerlach, will cost 4,000 Sk ($130/£73) for one person and 4,800 Sk ($160/£88) for two.

WHERE TO STAY

The High Tatras have plenty of hotel rooms and outside of the peak Christmas and New Year's season, you'll have little problem finding a place to stay. The tourist information offices can help book hotel rooms and private accommodations. In addition to the hotels and pensions, many families offer private rooms. All hotels boost their rates by at least a third over Christmas and New Year's. The rates quoted below apply generally to the high skiing and hiking seasons.

Very Expensive

Grandhotel Praha Tatranská Lomnica *★★★*   If you're one of those people who love that faded elegance of the early 1900s, with billiard rooms, crystal-chandeliered cafes, and cocktail bars, look no further. The Grandhotel Praha was conceived for a time when the wealthier classes summered in the mountains to escape the heat of the cities. Alas, those times are gone, but the hotel still lives on in its former glory. The Praha went through some hard times under Communism but is now trying to reach out to a new clientele of young professionals and their families. The rooms have gotten a makeover and the bathrooms have been completely modernized. Still, enough exquisite period detailing remains to give aficionados of that *fin de siècle* fantasy something to sink their teeth into.

Tatranská Lomnica 8. ✆ **052/446-7941**. Fax 052/446-7891. www.grandhotelpraha.sk. 98 units. 3,900 Sk ($130/£71) double. AE, DC, MC, V. Electric railroad station: Tatranská Lomnica. **Amenities:** Restaurant; indoor pool; health club and spa; bike and ski rental; concierge; limited room service; massage; nonsmoking rooms. *In room:* TV, minibar, hair dryer, safe.

Grand Hotel Starý Smokovec ✦✦

Like the Grandhotel Praha, the Grand Hotel Starý Smokovec is a beautifully faded anachronism trying hard to win over new customers. The hotel's immense Alpine-neo-baroque facade (how else to describe it?), so au courant in 1906 when the hotel was first built, smiles over the resort like a rich, benevolent auntie, lending a sense of grace and civility to the entire town. The large and comfortable rooms have been completely modernized. Ask for a room with a balcony for a commanding view of the valley. But the real draws here are the public areas, including the picture-perfect, period-piece cafe, restaurant, "Rondo" room, and "Cristal" bar. The location is a big advantage; just a few steps up from the electric railroad station in Starý Smokovec, and with some of the best hikes just outside the hotel's back door.

Starý Smokovec. ✆ **052/478-8000**. Fax 052/442-2157. www.grandhotel.sk. 83 units. 3,600 Sk ($120/£66) double. AE, DC, MC, V. Electric railroad station: Starý Smokovec. **Amenities:** Restaurant; indoor pool; spa; bike and ski rental; limited room service; massage; nonsmoking rooms. *In room:* TV, minibar, hair dryer, safe.

Expensive

Hotel Tulipán/Best Western ✦✦

The only hotel in the area so far to be managed by a major Western hotel chain, and the Best Western polish shows through in staff training and in the modern, no-nonsense-but-comfortable rooms. The property is on the small side, occupying what looks like a big house just outside the center of Tatranská Lomnica, about 15 minutes walk from the electric railroad station. The on-site wellness center is small but spick-and-span. Unusual for Slovakia, all the rooms have computers with Internet access and the hotel is nonsmoking throughout.

Tatranská Lomnica 63. ✆ **052/478-0611**. Fax 052/478-0614. www.bwtulipan.sk. 15 units. 3,000 Sk ($100/£55) double. AE, DC, MC, V. Electric railroad station: Tatranská Lomnica. **Amenities:** Restaurant; health club and spa; bike and ski rental; concierge; limited room service; massage; nonsmoking rooms. *In room:* Some A/C, TV, dataport (in-room Internet), minibar, hair dryer, safe.

Penzión Vila Park ✦

This inviting, smaller hotel in the center of Tatranská Lomnica is particularly suited to walkers and climbers. The owner is a mountain guide, who can help you plan your assault on the peaks or gentler walks along the "Magistrale" hiking trail. Even the facilities seem aimed at purists. You won't find rowdy bars and smoky billiard rooms; instead it's simple, no-nonsense furnishings for those who are here to commune with nature. That said, the prices are relatively high for what's offered.

Tatranská Lomnica 37. ✆ **052/478-0911**. Fax 052/446-7835. www.vilapark.sk. 12 units. 2,600 Sk ($87/£48) double. AE, DC, MC, V. Electric railroad station: Tatranská Lomnica. **Amenities:** Restaurant; bike rental. *In room:* TV.

Moderate

Hotel Smokovec ✦

A cheaper alternative to the Grand Hotel, offering the same excellent location, near the Starý Smokovec electric railroad station, at about two-thirds the price. What you sacrifice is ambience. The simple, dormitory-style rooms were built for sleeping and not for lingering. That said, the standards for cleanliness and efficiency are high and facilities like an indoor pool and wellness center offer good value for money. Ask for a room facing the mountains.

Starý Smokovec. ✆ **052/442-5191**. Fax 052/442-5194. www.hotelsmokovec.sk. 30 units. 2,400 Sk ($80/£44) double. AE, DC, MC, V. Electric railroad station: Starý Smokovec. **Amenities:** Restaurant; indoor pool; health club and spa; bike and ski rental; limited room service; massage. *In room:* TV, minibar.

Villa Dr. Szontagh ★★ A lovely steepled mountain manor offering what you might expect of old-school hospitality: squeaky clean public areas, tasteful turn-of-the-20th-century period furnishings (the first-floor apartments are especially inviting), and a solicitous owner who is only too happy to guide you around the resorts. Villa Dr. Szontagh was one of the first traditional inns to open up in the immediate aftermath of the fall of Communism, and remains one of the best. One drawback may be a lack of special wellness and spa facilities.

Nový Smokovec. ⓒ 052/442-2061. Fax 052/442-2062. www.szontagh.sk. 15 units. 2,200 Sk ($75/£40) double. AE, DC, MC, V. Electric railroad station: Nový Smokovec. **Amenities:** Restaurant; limited room service; massage. *In room:* TV, minibar, hair dryer.

Inexpensive

Hotel Tatry Clean if sterile dormitory-style rooms that are perfectly acceptable if the priority is saving money or if your initial choices are fully booked. The property itself is a charming, ramshackle sort of Alpine-style chalet, with an in-house Slovak restaurant serving standard food. It's popular among students and young families with children because of the prices. A small bunny slope with a tiny ski lift is just down the street.

Tatranská Lomnica. ⓒ **052/446-7930.** Fax 052/446-7724. 14 units. 1,200 Sk ($40/£22) double. No credit cards. Electric railroad station: Tatranská Lomnica. **Amenities:** Restaurant. *In room:* TV.

Panoráma ★ This used to be one of the top hotels in the High Tatras, but somewhere along the line the standards slipped. Now the owners are working hard to update the facilities. Depending on when the work is done, you could get a pretty nice hotel at a very good price. Be sure to request a room on one of the already remodeled floors and away from the construction. Part of the funding to rebuild the hotel is coming from the European Union, and plans are eventually to update the property's classic 1960s-style architecture. The hotel is shaped like an inverted pyramid, which in the heady days of postwar modernism must have seemed like a fun idea.

Štrbské Pleso II/20. ⓒ **052/449-1111.** Fax 052/449-2810. www.hotelpanorama.sk. 91 units. 1,800 Sk ($60/£33) double. AE, DC, MC, V. Electric railroad station: Štrbské Pleso. **Amenities:** Restaurant; health club and spa; ski rental; salon; massage. *In room:* TV, minibar.

WHERE TO DINE

The quality of the food in the Tatras has lagged behind the quality of the lodging. To be sure, the restaurants have definitely improved, and all three main resort towns now have a clutch of three or four decent, privately run eateries. But, sadly, there are still no breakthrough restaurants on the scene. Most of the new places build on the traditional, folk, "koliba" theme and have broadly similar menus that are heavy on the grilled meats, schnitzels, and stuffed chicken breasts. For something different, consider taking a meal at the Grand Hotel in Starý Smokovec or the Grandhotel Praha in Tatranská Lomnica (see "Where to Stay," above). While the quality is not much higher than at the independent restaurants listed below, nothing can match that faded, old-world opulence. The beautiful crystal chandeliers, the perfect seven-pieces-of-cutlery place settings, and that oh-so-proper waiter will have you staring at the chicken breast on your plate with a renewed sense of civility. In keeping with the overall informality of the Tatra resorts, dress is casual. You might want to dress up for the two "grand" hotel restaurants, but clean, casual attire is all that's required.

Very Expensive

Koliba Starý Smokovec SLOVAK A newer version of the "koliba" theme that tries and largely fails to capture the treacly sweet, but pleasant kitsch of the Zbojnícka

Koliba (see below). Maybe it's the toned-down interior or the fact the waiters are not decked out in full Slovak peasant regalia. Still, the food is similarly good, with grilled chicken and trout featuring prominently on the menu. This is also a good place to sample some local game, including venison steak and goulash. And the central location of this koliba in Starý Smokovec is much better than the Zbojnícka Koliba if you don't happen to be staying in Tatranská Lomnica.

Starý Smokovec (just behind the Starý Smokovec railroad station). ℂ 052/442-2204. Lunch and dinner items 210 Sk–300 Sk ($7–$10/£3.85–£5.50). AE, DC, MC, V. Daily 11am–9pm.

Zbojnícka Koliba 𝕽𝕽 SLOVAK   A fixture on the High Tatras dining scene for several years now and certainly the best meal in town during Communist times. It hasn't changed much since then, and it's still pretty good. You'll find all of the classic koliba trimmings here: a picture-perfect cottage setting, a crackling, wood-burning fire in the middle of the room (sending sweet wood smoke out the chimney), spits of roast chicken and pork searing over the open fire, wines served by the jug, and on weekends an irrepressible Gypsy band, keen to play a folk song or two for a small gratuity. It's kitschy for sure, but fun too.

Tatranská Lomnica (just next to the Grandhotel Praha), ℂ 052/446-7630. Dinner items 210 Sk–300 Sk ($7–$10/£3.85–£5.50). AE, DC, MC, V. Daily 4–9pm.

Expensive
Furkotka 𝕽 SLOVAK   You wouldn't expect to find such a clean and welcoming spot so close to Štrbské Pleso's down-at-heel electric railroad station, but the family owners of this traditional Slovak restaurant maintain high standards. There are no standouts on the menu, but staples like fried pork cutlet and grilled chicken range from good to very good. The decent food at modest prices attracts a range of in-the-know day-trippers and local shop clerks on their lunch breaks. The large nonsmoking room off the main bar area is great for families with kids.

Štrbské Pleso (right outside the electrical railroad station, across from the Hotel Toliar). ℂ 052/449-2167. Lunch and dinner items 150 Sk–270 Sk ($5–$9/£2.75–£4.95). No credit cards. Daily 11am–10pm.

Reštaurácia Tatrasport Zampa 𝕽𝕽 SLOVAK   The best food in Starý Smokovec is served at this unassuming set of picnic tables next to a sporting goods shop, just to the right of the Grand Hotel (if you're facing the hotel from the street). From the outside, it looks a place cyclists might go to grab a cold drink before hitting the trails. But don't let appearances deceive. The house specialty, pork tenderloin served in a red wine and bacon reduction, is a cut above the average cutlet. The menu features the standard mix of pork and chicken entrees, plus a "fresh vegetables" section for vegetarians (which means at least 1 night you won't have to eat fried cheese), all at prices that are no higher than average. Tatrasport Zampa is one of the few places around to serve breakfast, which is something to keep in mind if you're staying in private accommodations where breakfast is not part of the deal.

Starý Smokovec 62. ℂ 052/442-5241. Breakfast 60 Sk–90 Sk ($2–$3/£1.10–£1.65). Lunch and dinner items 150 Sk–240 Sk ($5–$8/£2.75–£4.40). No credit cards. Daily 8am–10pm.

Moderate
Reštaurácia Sviš 𝕽 SLOVAK   This relaxed, family-run pub restaurant is a welcome addition to Nový Smokovec, just a short walk west of Starý Smokovec. The clean, blonde-wood interior and the open fire at the center of the room keeps things cozy, especially if it's cold or snowy outside (likely at least half of the year). The roast

pork, a house specialty, is served with sauerkraut and bread dumplings, similar to what you would find in the Czech Republic, but the black peppercorns give the pork an added dimension you won't find across the border.

Nový Smokovec 30 (a short walk from either the Starý Smokovec or Nový Smokovec railroad stations). © 0915/ 937-111. Lunch and dinner items 150 Sk–240 Sk ($5–$8/£2.75–£4.40). No credit cards. Daily 11am–9pm.

Inexpensive

Polská Krčma ✮ POLISH   If you're not planning a trip north of the border, you might consider sampling a plate of Polish pierogies ("pirohy" in Slovak) here at one of the few Polish restaurants on the Slovak side of the Tatras. The "Farmer's Plate" allows you to try a half-order of pierogies, potato-filled dumplings topped with sour tangy sheep's cheese, and a half order of halušky, also topped with sheep's cheese and bits of bacon. The family owners are obviously aiming at the many Polish tourists, but a typical night brings just as many Slovaks and visitors from elsewhere. Located about a kilometer east of Starý Smokovec on the road to Tatranská Lomnica.

A Good Walk

Although the High Tatras attract many serious hikers, there are trails for walkers of all abilities, and some of the most beautiful walks require only an intermediate level of skill and exertion. One of the best of these follows the beautiful, red-marked "Magistrale" trail for part of its length from just above Hrebienok to the mountain lodge at Sliezsky Dom (www.sliezsky dom.sk) and back down to the electric railroad station at Tatranská Polianka (for a total walking time of 5–6 hr.).

Start the hike in Starý Smokovec, from where you can follow the green- or blue-marked trails for about an hour uphill to Hrebienok, an elevation difference of about 300m (900 ft.). If you want to save energy, take the funicular from behind the Grand Hotel up to Hrebienok. From Hrebienok pick up the red-marked Magistrale trail and follow the signposts in the direction of Sliezsky Dom. (Be careful, the signs are tricky; you should be walking with the mountains to your right and the valley to your left.) The walk begins in the forest, and as you move uphill, the large trees gradually thin out and the dwarf pines start. After another hour of gradual climbing, you break through the tree line along ridges just below some of the lower peaks. Here, the views, both up and down, are nothing short of spectacular. After another hour or so, you'll round a bend and see the boxy Sliezsky Dom lodge in the distance. Stop in at Sliezsky Dom for a light hot meal. From here, you can follow the road down to Tatranská Polianka, or if you have the time and energy, take the green-marked trail. The walk from Sliezsky Dom down to the electric railroad station will take another 2 hours.

No matter how long or short a hike you're planning, there are a few rules to follow: Remember to get an early start to avoid getting stranded in an afternoon rain- or snowstorm; always wear sturdy shoes to avoid ankle turns on the descent; and always pack extra water, sunscreen, sunglasses, a water-resistant jacket, and a good map.

Rafting on the Dunajec ✦✦✦

Just to the east of the High Tatras, the peaks end abruptly and the rolling highlands of eastern Slovakia start. This is the border region with Poland, and communities on both sides share a common folk culture and heritage going back hundreds of years. A short segment of the border is formed by the Dunajec river, a surprisingly narrow waterway that zigzags through some breathtakingly rocky crags, with Poland on the left and Slovakia on the right.

Daily from April to October, several tour operators run guided group floats down the river, starting from just outside the small town of Červený Kláštor, about 60km (40 miles) from the High Tatras. These trips are great fun and make for a special day out, particularly for the kids. The floats follow the river about 12km (8 miles) to the town of Lesnica in the Pieniny National Park. The guides are dressed up in traditional "Goral" (highland) folk costumes and can be quite entertaining (most speak only Slovak, but some can also manage a smattering of German and English). The entire trip takes about 90 minutes and costs about 300 Sk ($10/£5.50) per person.

In Lesnica, you can get a drink or light meal at a little cottage restaurant before boarding a bus back to the rafting operator. If you have the time and energy, rent a bike and ride along a little path beside the river back to your car. It's easy to organize a trip from the High Tatras; simply inquire at your hotel or the tourist information office and they can book you on a coach tour. If you want to travel independently, one of the better organizers is **Pltnictvo** on the main road just outside of Červený Kláštor (✆ 052/482-2805; www.nokle.szm.sk).

Horný Smokovec II/17. ✆ **0903/653-555.** Lunch and dinner items 90 Sk–150 Sk ($3–$5/£1.65–£2.75). No credit cards. Daily 11am–10pm.

EXPLORING

Aside from simply hiking, biking, or skiing the hills, there's not much else in the way of must-sees or -dos. If you get a bad-weather day, there are a couple of things worth seeking out.

Museum of the Tatra National Park (TANAP) ✦   A small, easily managed museum that details the founding of the Tatra National Park, with some nice displays of the tremendous variety of the flora and fauna native to the High Tatras. The exhibits include some stuffed bears, Tatra "grizzlies," several of whom are said to be still frolicking around the higher elevations.

Tatranská Lomnica. Mon–Fri 8am–noon and 1–4:30pm; Sat–Sun 8am–noon.

Cable Car to Lomnický Štít ✦✦   It's possible to reach one of the highest peaks in the Tatras, Lomnický Štít (2,634m/8,700 ft.), without ever having to lace up your hiking boots. A modern cable car makes the bracing ascent in several stages from its base in Tatranská Lomnica, though the price can be steep for groups or families. Each car holds about 15 people. You'll be allowed to spend about 50 minutes at the top before making the return. Try to book in advance to avoid waiting and bring a jacket or sweater. It's chilly up there, even in midsummer.

Tatranská Lomnica. Admission 390 Sk ($13/£7.15) (Tatranská Lomnice–Skalnaté pleso) and 550 Sk ($18/£10) (Skalnaté pleso–Lominický Štít). July–Aug daily 8:30–6:30pm; other times daily 8:30am–4:30pm.

SHOPPING

Folk handicrafts, like lace or folk costumes, make for interesting, one-of-a-kind souvenirs. You'll see stands selling these items at all of the major resorts. Look especially in the parking lots, where the stands are set up to cater to visiting tourist buses. One of the nicest places to buy handmade folk items, including genuine folk costumes, hats, and blouses, is **Vila Flora,** in Starý Smokovec (Vila Flora 2; © **0908/321–794**). **Sport Risy** (Starý Smokovec 70; © **052/478–2911**) is a great place to stock up anything you might need for the hike. They carry a full range of high-quality walking and hiking boots, fleeces, caps, and outerwear, and can give good advice on what you're likely to need.

AFTER DARK

The Tatras, with an emphasis on athletic, healthy living, is alas no place to party. The Cristal Bar at the Grand Hotel in Starý Smokovec occasionally books live entertainment in the evenings, so check with the front desk to see what's on. Otherwise, enjoy a slow meal, take a stroll around the town, and then fall asleep with a good book (that's why you came here in the first place).

LEVOČA

40km (25 miles) E of Poprad; 360km (220 miles) NE of Bratislava

Levoča is one of the best-preserved medieval towns in the country, boasting a charmingly tumbled-down square of Renaissance and baroque burghers' houses and a church with a 15m-high (50-ft.) wooden altarpiece that must be seen to be believed. Most of the sights can be taken in during an afternoon, but a cluster of nice hotels and a few recommendable restaurants make Levoča an excellent place to plan an overnight stop. For centuries, Levoča was the leading town of a confederation of 24 towns and villages, known collectively as the "Spiš," filling a large swath of central and eastern Slovakia. The Spiš towns came of age in the 14th and 15th centuries, following a series of devastating raids from East that left the area devoid of population. To resettle the region, the Hungarian kings then in power invited German-speaking Saxons to form towns, and bestowed special trading rights on the towns to sweeten the deal. The Spiš soon became wealthy, and Levoča, which enjoyed the greatest number of these special trading privileges, emerged as the wealthiest of the lot.

Levoča reached its high point in the 16th and 17th centuries, and many of the most impressive buildings date from this time. The highlight of your visit will certainly be the town's beautiful cathedral, St. Jacob's, in the middle of the main square, and its exquisitely carved wooden altarpiece, the work of the local master Pavol of Levoča in the early 16th century.

Given the town's wealthy past, the state of modern Levoča comes as kind of a shock. In and around the beautifully crumbling facades of what were once the homes of the wealthiest merchants in the land, you'll see Roma children running around, mugging for the camera, and occasionally begging for a coin or two. Times are tough in the Spiš region these days, and the brain drain hit these towns especially hard.

The first weekend in July sleepy Levoča is turned upside down when tens of thousands of worshippers descend for the annual Marian pilgrimage. Most of the action takes places at the Marian church, the white building on a hill about a mile outside of town and easily visible from side streets running off the main square. If your visit happens to coincide with the pilgrimage, it probably goes without saying, don't even dream of finding a room.

ESSENTIALS
Getting There
BY BUS   The bus is the only way to get to Levoča using public transportation. The bus station is a short walk from the main square. The regional bus hub is in Spišská Nová Ves, about 10km (6 miles) away. Frequent buses ply the route daily from there to Levoča.

BY CAR   Levoča is on the main road connecting Poprad to points east. The drive from Poprad takes under an hour. Košice is about an hour away to the east.

Visitor Information
The main tourist information office, **SUZ,** is situated on the main square (Námestie Majstra Pavla 58; ✆ **053/451-3763;** http://suz.levoca.sk). The office is a good first stop for brochures on the sites and can advise on hotel and restaurant options. The official town website, a source for basic information like population and various other statistics and links, is also helpful (www.levoca.sk).

WHERE TO STAY
Levoča is blessed with a few decent hotels, including arguably one of the best mom-and-pop hotels in the country. It's best to try to book in advance during the summer, and well in advance if you plan to be here in early July when the pilgrims hit town. In winter, you'll likely have the entire town to yourself.

Barbakan ✦   The Barbakan is less overall appealing than the Satel (below), but welcoming and comfortable for an overnight stay. The hotel occupies three floors of a burgher's house, a block off the main square. The rooms, particularly the doubles at the back of the hotel, are well appointed, with hardwood floors, throw rugs, and roomy bathrooms with big new bathtubs. Whether you choose a double or a single, ask for a room away from the main road. The house restaurant is decent in a pinch, but the food is frankly better at the Satel and a couple of other restaurants around town.

Košická 15. ✆ **053/451-4310.** Fax 053/451-3609. www.barbakan.sk. 12 units. 1,600 Sk ($53/£29) double. AE, DC, MC, V. **Amenities:** Restaurant; limited room service. *In room:* TV, minibar, hair dryer.

Penzión pri Košickej bráne   A no-frills bed-and-bath pension, right next to the Barbakan and about 15m (50 ft.) or so from the main square. The building, which dates from the 16th century, is lovely, but the room furnishings are the standard-issue particleboard beds and desks. The four-bed apartment is spacious and represents real value if you're traveling in a larger group.

Košická 16. ✆ **053/469-9713.** www.penzionkosicka.sk. 9 units. 800 Sk ($27/£15) double. AE, DC, MC, V. **Amenities:** Restaurant.

Satel ✦✦✦ *Finds*   This is Levoča's nicest hotel and one of the best small hotels of any Slovak town. The rooms are spotless, with inviting, modern furnishings and beautiful hardwood floors. Some of the rooms have the original Renaissance-era vaulting. Don't miss the gorgeous Renaissance-arcaded restaurant/cafe in the back. An on-site sauna and small wellness center add to the, frankly, unexpected charms of this family-run inn.

The location, right on the main square, is ideal, and the position away from the main highway means less noise at night.

Námestie Majstra Pavla 55. (C) 053/451-2943. Fax 053/451-4486. www.hotelsatel.com. 23 units. 2,700 Sk ($90/£49) double. AE, DC, MC, V. **Amenities:** Restaurant; health club and spa; limited room service; massage; nonsmoking rooms. *In room:* TV, minibar, hair dryer, safe.

WHERE TO DINE

The range of eating choices is smaller and less agreeable than the hotels, but fine for the length of time you're likely to be here.

Cafet CAFE (R) (*Finds*) An inviting art cafe that serves freshly ground coffee, beer, wine, and soft drinks (but no food) in a funky, arcaded interior about midway up the main square. The cafe's young owner is trying to raise locals' appreciation for high-quality coffee, which he says is succeeding but going slowly. Good luck to him.

Námestie Majstra Pavla 9. (C) 0902/308-631. Coffee 30 Sk ($1/55p). No credit cards. Daily 10am–10pm.

Pizzeria PIZZA This is better than most of the small-town Slovak pizzerias you're likely to run across. No surprises on the menu. You'll find the same combinations of cheese, ham, corn, sausage, bacon, and whatever else they can put on a pizza, but the crust is thinner and crispier than the norm. The main dining area is nonsmoking, and the two tables on the terrace command an inspiring view of the Marian church in the distance.

Veprova 4. No phone. Lunch and dinner 90 Sk–150 Sk ($3–$5/£1.65–£2.75). No credit cards. Daily 11am–10pm.

Slovenská Reštaurácia SLOVAK The nicest spot in town for that traditional Slovak meal, either on the outdoor terrace in nice weather or in the warm, peasant-style dining rooms, complete with wagon wheels on the walls. As you might expect, the emphasis here is on simple Slovak meals done well. The house specialty, a potato pancake stuffed with a spicy mix of pork and beef, is recommended.

Námestie Majstra Pavla 62. (C) 053/451-2339. Lunch and dinner items 120 Sk–240 Sk ($4–$8/£2.20–£4.40). No credit cards. Daily 11am–10pm.

EXPLORING LEVOČA

Levoča is essentially a one-horse town and all of the main sights are perched along the town's oblong square, Námestie Majstra Pavla. The four free-standing buildings at the center form the most important complex of structures in town. Here you'll find the Roman Catholic Church, St. Jacobs (Chrám Sv. Jakuba), as well as the former town hall, the current town hall, and the main Protestant church. Start your exploration from St. Jacobs, with its fabulous wood-carved altar (the only absolute must-see) and move on from there. The Old Town Hall (Levočská Radnica) behind the church is recognizable from its handsome Renaissance arches dating from the 17th century. The original town hall, built in the 15th century, burned in a fire in 1550. In front of the Old Town Hall you'll see a large bird cage–like contraption. This is the so-called "cage of shame," once allegedly used to hold adulterous women. Across the street from the Old Town Hall is the Spiš Regional Museum. Take a stroll on both sides of the square to admire the old baroque and Renaissance housing stock in all states of repair and disrepair.

St. Jacob's Church (Chrám Sv. Jacuba) (R)(R)(R) The richness of the interior of this church is a testament to the town's former wealth and importance. Parts of the church go as far back as the 14th century. The high point is certainly the wooden altarpiece, carved over a period of 10 years by Master Pavol of Levoča in the 16th century. At more than 18m (55 ft.) in height, it's commonly described the world's largest of its kind. Look

Spišský Hrad ✦✦✦

Put this in the "Most Spectacular Castle You Are Ever Likely to See By a Civilization You've Never Heard Of" category. When the Spiš confederation of towns first got rolling in the 13th and 14th centuries, the towns lived in constant fear of devastating raids from the east. To ensure that would never happen again, the Spiš built this enormous castle on the highest hilltop around. Nothing you've seen or read in the tourist brochures will prepare you for the shock of seeing this ghostly white ruin from a distance for the first time.

If you're driving from Levoča in the direction of Košice, you'll catch a first glimpse around the village of Klčov, about 8km (5 miles) away. From that point, you won't be able to take your eyes off of it as the road winds you closer and closer. The view traveling in the opposite direction is even better. At night, it's given a garish blue-white lighting and seems visible from about half of eastern Slovakia.

The castle served the Spiš towns well until the mid–18th century, when it burned in a tragic fire. By that time, the threat of invasion from the east had past and the castle was never rebuilt. Today the castle is a designated UNESCO World Heritage Site. You can climb up to the castle and walk the ruins by following a small road just beyond the village of Spišské Podhradie (traveling from Levoča toward Košice). Alternatively, you can take a bus or train to Spišské Podhradie and hike the 3.2km (2 miles) or so to the castle. **Spišský Hrad** (✆ **053/454-1336;** www.spisskyhrad.sk).

toward the bottom of the altar to see Master Pavol's carving of *The Last Supper.* You are not permitted to get too close to the altar, so buy a photograph of it (in the church) for a closer look. The faces of the disciples were apparently modeled on merchants living in Levoča at the time. Master Pavol's depiction is certainly humorous. St. John is shown sleeping in Christ's arms! Entry to the church is by guided tour only.

Námestie Majstra Pavla. ✆ 053/451–2347. Admission 50 Sk ($1.70/90p). June–Oct daily, tours on the half-hour 9am–4pm. Nov–May tours daily once an hour 8:30–11:30am and 1–4pm. Purchase tickets at the cash desk across from the church entrance.

AFTER DARK

Aside from an after-dinner walk along the square and the side streets, there's not much to do in Levoča in the evening. The town shuts down almost completely by 10pm, and locals looking for action head for the relatively "big city" diversions in Spišská Nová Ves, about 10km (6 miles) away. Levoča maintains an active festival scene is the summer months. Ask at the tourist office if anything special is going on in and around town during your visit.

KOŠICE

100km (60 miles) E of Poprad; 400km (240 miles) E of Bratislava

Košice, Slovakia's second-biggest city after Bratislava, has transformed itself from a smoggy, provincial backwater into one of the country's most attractive urban destinations within the short span of a decade. Much of the credit goes to the former Slovak president, and former Košice mayor, Rudolf Schuster, who vigorously promoted development of the city, including the extensive renovation of the main drag, Hlavná ulica. Hlavná is a stunner from end to end, a 30-minute corso that takes you past the country's biggest Gothic cathedral, its turn-of-the-20th-century State Theater, a lovely little park with a singing fountain, and, in warm weather, a never-ending row of outdoor terraces, packed with stylish coffee drinkers.

Košice has been an important market town on major east-west and north-south trade routes for centuries, and during the 16th and 17th centuries served as a bastion for the Hungarian nobility in their struggle against the Ottoman Turks occupying the Hungarian mainland. Just 20km (12 miles) from the frontier with modern Hungary, the city, in more recent years, has shuttled back and forth between Hungarian, Czechoslovak, and now Slovak sovereignty. The city still has a sizable Hungarian minority, and if you listen carefully you will hear Hungarian spoken on the streets.

GETTING THERE

BY TRAIN Košice is a major rail junction and the ŽSR state railroad train service is relatively frequent to and from Bratislava and other large cities. From Bratislava, the journey on an express train takes about 7 hours. The train station is next to the bus station and is about a 10- to 15-minute walk from the center of the city.

BY CAR Košice lies at the eastern end of Slovakia's major east-west highway. The northern route from Bratislava follows the Váh river north to Trenčín and Žilina before turning east. Some of the drive is along four-lane highway and takes about 6 hours. From Poprad, the drive is along mostly two-lane highway and takes about 2 hours.

BY BUS Slovakia's national bus carrier, SAD, maintains regular service from Košice to many regional cities and towns. The bus is often the best option, for seeing the smaller towns to the east. The tourist information offices can help you sort out the timetables and destinations. The bus station is about a 10-minute walk from the center of the city.

BY PLANE Košice Airport (© **055/683–2105;** www.airportkosice.sk) lies about 5km (3 miles) outside of town The budget carrier SkyEurope (www.skyeurope.sk) maintains regular flights to and from Bratislava. Regular air service is also available to Vienna and Prague.

GETTING AROUND

ON FOOT Much of Košice's center, where most of the hotels, restaurants, and attractions are concentrated, is either closed to cars or allows only limited car traffic, so walking is the only option.

BY CAR It's best to leave the car in one of the city parking lots or at the hotel. Navigating the small streets of the inner city can be challenging and finding a parking spot on the side streets is difficult.

BY BIKE Hlavná ulica has bike lanes running up and down its length, but it may be hard to find bike rentals. Inquire at the tourist information office or your hotel.

VISITOR INFORMATION

The main tourist information agency, **MIC Košice,** maintains two offices in town located on each end of the long main square, Hlavná ulica (Hlavná 2, Hlavná 111; © **055/ 16-186;** www.mickosice.sk). The helpful, multilingual staff can provide maps and guidance, as well as book rooms in private homes, pensions and hotels. The town's official website (www.Košice.sk) is also worth a gander.

WHERE TO STAY

The past year has brought a couple of new entries onto the lodging scene, led by the opening of the Bristol in late 2005. At the low end of the market, several new pensions have opened up, making a comfortable, in-town stay possible on any budget.

Very Expensive

Hotel Bristol ★★★ *Finds* Just what Košice needed: a stylish, hip, and yet still halfway affordable designer hotel, a 5-minute walk from the city's main square and 2 blocks away from the best nightlife. You'll see the difference first in the sleek, clean modern lines of the lobby, with its hardwood floors and smart wicker chairs. The mix of style, comfort, and technology extends to the rooms, which (still unusual for Slovakia) are equipped with separate climate-control settings and dataports. Breakfast is the usual selection of meats, cold cuts, yogurts, and cereals, but the difference is that it's fresh and freshly squeezed.

Orlia 3. ℂ **055/729-0077.** Fax 055/729-0079. www.hotelbristol.sk. 20 units. 3,100 Sk ($103/£57) double. AE, DC, MC, V. **Amenities:** Restaurant; indoor pool; health club and spa; limited room service; nonsmoking rooms. *In room:* A/C, TV, dataport; minibar, hair dryer, safe.

Expensive

Hotel Ambassador ★★ This small, well-run hotel right on the main square is a nice pick if the Bristol is booked. Ring the buzzer on the big wooden door (curiously unmarked) and you'll be ushered into the house's inner sanctum. The rooms actually extend behind the facade into the courtyard at the back, meaning that street noise and commotion are not a problem. The clunky room decor, with big rounded beds, evokes something of the schlock 1970s. In-room Wi-Fi is a nice perk.

Hlavná 101, ℂ **055/720-3720.** Fax 055/720-3727. www.abba.sk. 14 units. 2,600 Sk ($86/£48) double. AE, DC, MC, V. **Amenities:** Restaurant. *In room:* A/C in some rooms, TV, minibar, hair dryer.

Moderate

Penzión Krmanova ★ One of the best of a new breed of privately owned, in-town pensions. Despite the location, near a normally loud arterial roadway, the rooms are generally quiet because the house has thick walls. If noise is a concern, ask for a room overlooking the garden in the back. The modern, pastel furnishings won't win any design competitions, but the rooms are large and clean, and the beds and chairs still feel and smell new. The bathrooms have been completely renovated and some in the larger apartments have tubs. Aside from the rooms, the services are modest. Breakfast is not included in the price.

Krmanova 14, ℂ **055/623-0565.** Fax 055/622-6483. www.krmanova.sk. 13 units. 2,200 Sk ($73/£40) double. AE, DC, MC, V. **Amenities:** Nonsmoking rooms. *In room:* A/C in some rooms, TV, fridge.

Inexpensive

Penzión Slovakia Four cozy little rooms next to the Rosto steakhouse and across from the Bristol. The location, just up from Kováčska Street, where the best clubs and cafes are located, is a major draw. You can't beat it for the price. The rooms, named after four Slovak cities, Bratislava, Žilina, Banska Bystrica, and, naturally, Košice, are clean and roomy, with TVs, big beds, and armchairs. The bathrooms are on the tiny side, with showers. One drawback may be that the rooms, just below the roof, tend to get hot in midsummer. Ask for a room away from the street.

Orlia 6. ℂ **055/728-9820**. www.penzionslovakia.sk. 4 units. 1,350 Sk ($45/£25) double. AE, DC, MC, V. **Amenities:** Restaurant. *In room:* TV.

WHERE TO DINE

The restaurant scene in Košice is improving rapidly. As in Bratislava, the number of eateries is growing and the range of cooking is slowing starting to expand beyond the beef, pork, and chicken trilogy. Most of the best places to eat, and to go out for that matter, are not along the main Hlavná street, but just to the east of the main square, along Kováčska.

Very Expensive

Rosto STEAKHOUSE   Local version of an American-style steakhouse, but less formal, featuring excellent aged beef imported from South America. This place gets crowded, especially at lunch. The grilling extends to chicken, pork, lamb, and whatever else can be cooked over an open flame. They also have a full range of Middle Eastern–style shawarma sandwiches, essentially shaved lamb, chicken, or pork served in a pita pocket.

Orlia 6. ℂ **055/728–9818**. Lunch and dinner items 180 Sk–420 Sk ($6–$14/£3.30–£7.70). AE, DC, MC, V. Daily 11am–10pm.

Expensive

Camelot ★★ SLOVAK   Newly opened in 2006 and already claiming its spot as one of the best tables in the city for Slovak and international specialties. The handsome decor mixes the best of the dark woods and high-backed chairs of traditional Slovak restaurants, with a modern emphasis on clean lines and cleanliness. The "Camelot" theme extends to the menu, and the main courses are named for the Knights of the Round Table. Some combine the traditional Slovak emphasis on grilled meats with international, especially Asian, spices and sauces.

Kováčska 19. ℂ **055/685-4039**. Lunch and dinner items 180 Sk–360 Sk ($6–$12/£3.30–£6.70). AE, DC, MC, V. Tues–Sun 11am–10pm.

Le Colonial ★★★ CONTINENTAL   This popular place, just off the southern end of Hlavná, never fails to impress. Maybe it's the inviting 19th-century "colonial-era" decor, the impeccable service, or the creative turns on traditional Slovak cooking that make it so special. Try the "escalope panee," a chicken breast that's stuffed with sharp-sour sheep's cheese and lightly breaded and fried, served with little bunches of green beans wrapped in bacon. And that's just the start. Like lots of restaurants in Košice, to find it, you'll have to first walk through a rather uninviting little doorway off the main street. Your anxieties will be relieved once you walk into the warm and inviting interior. Good choice for a business meal or a romantic dinner for two.

Hlavná 8. ℂ **055/729-6126**. Lunch and dinner items 240 Sk–360 Sk ($8–$12/£4.40–£6.70). AE, DC, MC, V. Daily 11am–10pm.

Moderate

Villa Regia ★★ SLOVAK   A local favorite and reputed to be the best place in town for bryndzové halušky and other typical Slovak dishes. If you've come from the High Tatras or from one of the outlying areas, you'll recognize the dark woods and heavy tables and chairs as the hallmark of a traditional Slovak restaurant. At their best, and this is certainly one of the best, these spaces run to the cozy and intimate, with the emphasis on food, drink, and close conversation. While the halušky come highly recommended, the full range of pork, beef, and chicken specialties are done well.

Dominikánske nám. 3. ☎ **055/625-6510.** Lunch and dinner items 150 Sk–300 Sk ($5–$10/£2.75–£5.50). AE, DC, MC, V. Tues–Sun 11am–10pm.

Inexpensive

Villa Francaise ✦ BISTRO   A contemporary French bistro, and one of a number of new, trendy, and very good restaurants that are turning heads in eastern Slovakia. You'll find all of the French classics, from steak au poivre and homemade crepes (both savory and sweet) to scalloped potatoes "dauphinoise." After all of those cottage restaurants with wrought-iron swords and wagon wheels on the walls, the simple, funky, retro-'60s decor is a welcome change. The cafe bar serves a full range of excellent espresso drinks, teas, and some cocktails. The outdoor terrace, off a pleasant pedestrian street, is a nice spot to people-watch. Popular with students.

Mlynska 20. ☎ **055/729-0516.** Lunch and dinner items 90 Sk–180 Sk ($3–$6/£1.65–£3.30). No credit cards. Daily 10am–10pm.

EXPLORING

Almost all of the major tourist attractions are along or just off of the main square, Hlavná ulica. A sensible plan is simply to start at one end of the square and slowly walk to the other, admiring the baroque, Renaissance, and neoclassical facades that line the long street on both sides. The southern end of the square possesses the most important clutch of buildings, centered on the **Cathedral of St. Elizabeth (Dóm svätej Alžbety),** the biggest cathedral in Slovakia and the easternmost Gothic church of its kind in Europe. Next to the cathedral on the north side is the Renaissance-style **Urban's Tower (Urbanová veža),** which now houses a small wax museum. On the other side is the **Chapel of St. Michael (Kaplnka svätého Michala),** with its valuable relief work on the portals. The chapel is older than the cathedral and dates from around the middle of the 13th century. Just here as well you'll see the entryway to a relatively recent archaeological find called the **Lower Gate (Dolná Brána).** It's certainly worth poking in to take a look at the fascinating medieval fortification systems that were built here some 700 to 800 years ago.

To the north of the cathedral, walking along Hlavná, you'll see a small park, complete with the locals' pride and joy: a "singing fountain." Just beyond the fountain is another local treasure connected to music, the handsome **State Theater (Štátné Divadlo).** The theater dates from the late 1800s and was built in the neoclassical, historical style that was so popular in Austro-Hungarian provincial capitals at the time. Farther along the square you'll see little gems here and there, hidden behind the day-to-day life of a bustling city. Be sure to take a look at the Art Nouveau facade at Hlavná 63, home to the Café Slavia and hotel of the same name.

Cathedral of St. Elizabeth (Dóm svätej Alžbety) ✦✦   The country's largest cathedral is a master work, both inside and outside. Admire the relief on the north side of the cathedral, and the immense carved wooden altarpiece, one of the biggest of its kind (but still short of the altar in Levoča). The nicest aspect of this cathedral is that it still plays a vital role in the lives of people living here.

Hlavná ulica. Daily 9am–6pm.

Lower Gate (Dolná Brána) ✦   Košice residents remember with horror the mid-1990s, when pretty much the entire Hlavná ulica was torn apart during the city's general large-scale renovation. One of the more unusual finds at that time was this intricate system of medieval fortifications, town walls, bastions, and even sewage systems, now buried underground, going all the way back to the late Middle Ages. Hlavná ulica. ☏ 055/622-8393. Tues–Sun 10am–6pm.

East Slovakia Museum (Vychodoslovenské múzeum) ⟨★   Primarily of interest for the massive collection of gold coins, around 3,000 or so, that were originally minted in Kremnica from the 15th to the 17th century. The coins were hidden during raids on the city in the 17th century and were only discovered in 1935. Hviezdoslavova 3. ☏ 055/622-0309. Tues–Sat 9am–5pm; Sun 9am–1pm.

SHOPPING

If you've been looking for a special wine store that carries the best Slovak wines, try **Cabinet** (Pri Miklusovej vaznici 2; ☏ **055/622-5566;** www.vinotekacabinet.sk). The knowledgeable wine merchants there can guide you through the plonk to some very nice bottles. For something different, try to the 2005 cabernet sauvignon rosé, a recent gold-medal winner at an international wine competition in Brussels.

AFTER DARK

Košice, as the capital of the Eastern Slovak region, is a cultural center, and maintains an excellent program of music, theater, and the performing arts. Spring and fall tend to be the liveliest times of the year and an annual musical festival is held in May. For culture of the cocktails, clubbing, and carousing variety, the center of the action is Kováčska ulica, which runs parallel to the main square.

Cosmopolitan ⟨★   Maybe a notch or two above the competition if you're looking for something a little quieter and more sophisticated. The cocktails here are probably the best in town, and you might even catch a special event, like a champagne tasting or something similar. Kováčska 9. ☏ **055/625-8419.**

Jazz Club   Still going strong after several years as Košice's leading music club. Don't expect much jazz here, despite the name. Disco, techno, pop, and slop are the genres of choice. Also includes an affiliated cocktail bar and decent pizza restaurant. This place can get very crowded on a weekend evening. Kováčska 39. ☏ **0907/103-700.**

Štátne Divadlo Košice ⟨★★   The center of cultural life for Eastern Slovakia, with an active theater, ballet, and opera repertoire 9 months out of the year (the theater largely shuts down during summer). Tickets are available at the box office. Even if you don't see a performance, stop by to admire the handsome turn-of-the-20th-century building, one of the finest concert halls in central Europe. Hlavná 58. ☏ **055/622-1231.** www.skke.sk.

Slovenia

by Keith Bain

I f you've ever wanted to visit a place that few people even know exists (and fewer still can point out on a map), start planning your trip to Slovenia soon; it won't be long before this smart central European country is setting the tone for fashionable travel. With fewer than two million inhabitants, and only recently discovered by a select group of globe-trotters who've tuned into tales of its idyllic beauty, Slovenia is considerably more tranquil and sophisticated than any other destination cast under the "Eastern European" banner, with almost none of the hang-ups associated with its former Communist connections; 15 years after gently wresting itself from Yugoslavia, there's a fresh exuberance

of spirit here suggesting a nation still enjoying its independence honeymoon. Its beauty has drawn comparisons with Switzerland, a country that is twice its size, and while there are similarities, Slovenia's relative anonymity means that you can still enjoy yourself here for fewer euros (although it's certainly not as cheap as other Eastern European destinations). Imbued with fantastic, scraggy mountains, turquoise rivers and silver lakes, vast subterranean caves, and just enough medieval castles to conjure up a fairy tale or two, Slovenia is one of those destinations you wish you could make your regular weekend getaway.

1 Getting to Know Slovenia

THE LAY OF THE LAND

Easy to miss on even the largest of maps, Slovenia is tucked into the armpit formed by Italy to the west, Austria to the north, Hungary to the east, and Croatia to the south. It's pretty much in the center of Europe, about the same distance from London as it is from Istanbul, and more or less midway between Moscow and Lisbon.

THE REGIONS IN BRIEF

Ljubljana is more or less in the center of the country. To the north, the **Julian Alps** on the Italian border form one natural perimeter of the **Triglav National Park,** synonymous with the triple-peak Triglav Mountains seen on the national flag. Triglav's proud peaks add to the splendor of the country's most cherished lakes, **Bled** and **Bohinj,** both defining features on the country's tourist trail. Tucked between Triglav and the Italian border is the fantastic **Soča River Valley,** a tour de force for travelers looking for river and mountain thrills. And stretched along the northern Austrian border is the Karavanke Mountain range, providing rewarding views as you drive anywhere north of the capital.

Slovenia's southeast is defined by its unique limestone formations that make up the unique region known as the **Karst,** a term that has been exported around the world to describe similar "Karstic" phenomena. Squeezed between Italy's Trieste and the border with Croatia is Slovenia's tiny slither of **Istrian coastline,** with fishing ports of distinctly Venetian influence. Finally, more mountains, wine lands, and remnants of a Roman and medieval past are found in the less-traveled east.

SUGGESTED ITINERARY: SLOVENIA IN 8 DAYS

While you could rush around Slovenia and cover it quite extensively in just a few days, I recommend you take things easy and soak up this tiny country's myriad pleasures. Relax in and around its many pleasure spots and enjoy the possibility of adventures both hard and soft. Bear in mind that there are tolls on all highways; these are clearly marked and you can pay with a credit card.

Day ❶ Arrive & Head East

Pick up a pre-booked rental from Ljubljana's international airport, and head east, to the salubrious town of Maribor, where you can stroll through gorgeous squares, lunch at excellent restaurants, explore a vast underground cellar, and enjoy a sundowner at the legendary waterfront area known as Lent: In summer, you may catch some of the excellent entertainment that forms part of the Lent Festival.

Day ❷ Ptuj & the Jeruzalem Wine Road

From Maribor, it's a short drive through gorgeous countryside to the ancient Roman city of Ptuj (pronounced *pit-ooey*), which you can explore in a few hours. Then head out to sample the fruits of the vine along the Jeruzalem Wine Road. Presuming you enjoy a liquid lunch, overnight at one of the wine farms, where you can also enjoy a traditional farm dinner.

Day ❸ The Lakes

Strike out early back toward Ljubljana, but head instead to Bled, some 31 miles (50km) north; you should arrive well before lunch. Book a suite at Vila Bled; you can use the spa at sister hotel Grand Toplice, sunbathe on the private lido, or take one of the private boats and row yourself to Bled Island, where you can

explore the lovely church. Take a relaxed stroll around the lake and drive or walk to the thousand-year-old castle perched above the water, before setting off to explore Lake Bohinj.

Days ❹ & ❺ Soča River Valley

If you're feeling adventurous, start your day by swimming out to the island and back. After breakfast set off north to the adventure resort of Kranjska Gora, which marks the starting point for the route over the Vršič Pass in the Julian Alps. You'll negotiate 50 hair-raising switchbacks in just 16 miles (25km) before reaching the other side—the Soča River Valley. You can indulge your spirit for adventure in Bovec (the best base for skiing on the slopes of the Kanin), but reserve accommodations near Kobarid—either at Casa Hiša Franko (which also offers the most exciting restaurant menu in the country), or at nearby Nebesa, perhaps the most idyllic getaway in Europe. In Kobarid, visit the antiwar museum, and grab a map for the outdoor walking "museums" that you can undertake under your own steam, preferably in the early morning, before temperatures start to rise. Spend your second day white-water rafting and attending to other river- or mountain-bound adventures. At Hiša Franko, ask for a lunch basket and picnic on the banks of the nearby river.

Slovenia

Day ⑥ Piran

From the Soča Valley, it's a 2-hour drive towards the Istrian Coast, connecting with the main highway heading south. En route, stop at the Škocjan Caves, which are a scintillating 2-hour diversion. In Piran, take your time exploring the cobblestone streets and back alleys, cooling yourself in the refreshing waters of the Adriatic before settling in for an evening of seafood at Neptun. If you feel you're up for a party, head over to the nearby resort town of Portoroz where you'll find casinos, nightclubs, and merry-making crowds.

Days ⑦ & ⑧ Ljubljana

The highway leads directly from Piran to the capital; set out after an early-morning swim. Ljubljana has great charm and can be extensively explored on foot or bicycle. Head up to the castle for a good look at the layout of city, then explore Old Town, where you'll find plenty of stunning restaurants. In the afternoon, prioritize the art museums, but be sure to grab a seat at one of the lively cafe-bars lining the Ljubljanica River for sundowners. In summer, try to catch a festival performance at the **Križanke Summer Theater,** perhaps after an early dinner at AS. If you have the energy, prepare for a night of clubbing, or try to visit a selection of the city's best watering holes.

SLOVENIA TODAY

Having emerged from its 10-day war of independence practically unscathed, Slovenia is a country of tremendous stability and calm. One high-ranking E.U. official recently referred to Slovenia as the "good pupil of the European Union," but in fact Slovenia could teach the rest of Europe (and much of the world, in fact) a lesson or two. A country that quietly gets on with the job of improving its position on the world stage, Slovenia consistently administers to all spheres of local life, thereby attracting foreign investment through both industry and—now that the crisis faced by its Balkan neighbors appears to have abated—also on the tourist front.

A LOOK AT THE PAST

Slovenes will tell you of a history fraught by outside rule; when independence was won in 1991, it was after a 1,000-year struggle.

Once the ancient home of southerly Illyrian tribes and Celts from the north, the Romans arrived here in A.D. 100, legendarily traversing the Julian Alps (named, in fact, for Julius Caesar) and creating the trade hubs of Emona (Ljubljana), Poetovia (Ptuj), and Celeia (Celje). Attila the Hun raged across Slovenia from the east, en route to Italy in the 5th century, causing the Roman settlers to regroup at the coast, where the port cities of Capris (Koper) and Piranum (Piran) were created.

Slavic tribes—the ancestors of contemporary Slovenes—arrived in the 6th century, bringing pagan superstitions and an agricultural lifestyle, and finally uniting to form the Principality of Karantania. But it wasn't long before the Slavs were forced to submit to the rule of the Frankish emperor, who converted them to Christianity. From the 14th century, Slovenia fell to the Habsburgs, who stimulated great resentment during most of their reign. War, Turkish invasion, and economic gloom were the ongoing themes in the 15th and 16th centuries. The coastal cities fell under voluntary protection of the Venetian Empire until the end of the 18th century, while the Ottomans repeatedly trampled through the region in attempts to take Vienna.

Germanic culture was encouraged among the elite, while the peasant classes occasionally rose up, determined to replant their Slavic roots. Slovene culture was touted by nationalist movements, and for the brief 4 years (1809–13) that Napoleon made Ljubljana the capital of his Illyrian provinces, the Slovenian language entered schools and government. In the mid-1800s, Slovenian nationalism reached its zenith; amid (largely unsuccessful) cries for nationhood and recognition of a unique identity, the call for Slavic unity could be heard pushing for the unification of all Serbs, Croats, and Slovenes. The second half of the 19th century was a period of industrialization, but this failed to prevent mass emigration by the country's poor.

In 1914, Archduke Franz Ferdinand was assassinated, sparking off World War I between the Austro-Hungarian Empire and the Triple Entente. Dragged into the fray, Slovenia was forced to fight the Italians to protect their homeland. When the Austro-Hungarian Empire collapsed in 1918, Slovenia was partially incorporated into the newly established Kingdom of Serbs, Croats, and Slovenes, which later became Yugoslavia ("Land of Southern Slavs") in 1929; coastal Slovenia was given to Italy.

In 1937 the half-Slovene half-Croat Josip Broz Tito became party leader, and was the man at the helm when Hitler invaded Yugoslavia in 1941. After World War II, Tito headed up the Socialist Federal Republic of Yugoslavia, with Slovenia as one of six states. Tito played his cards right with both Eastern and Western powers, and—unlike other Eastern bloc countries—Yugoslavia enjoyed a fairly open relationship with the rest of the world.

To curb the tide of nationalism from Slovenes who resented their unbalanced contribution to the socialist economy, Tito gave cultural freedoms to minorities, and constituent states had some autonomy. In 1980, Tito's 35-year rule ended with his death in Ljubljana, opening the floodgates of political and economic disaster. Slovenia represented less than 10% of the Yugoslavian population but brought in over 25% of its export wealth, and with Tito's death Slovenes affirmed their desire to break free from their Balkan neighbors. In December 1990 over 90% of the population voted for independence which it declared in June 1991, sparking a short, bloody war with president Slobodan Milosevic. The small Slovene defense force resisted for 10 days before Milosevic was forced to withdraw his troops to focus on Bosnia and Croatia. Slovenia was formally recognized as an independent state in January 1992, joining the United Nations later that year, and the European Union in May 2004.

SLOVENIAN PEOPLE & CULTURE

Slovenes, one of the smallest ethnic minorities on the Continent, are a proud, prosperous people, with a distinct cosmopolitanism that has evolved out of the assimilation of foreign and neighboring influences over the centuries. Seen as former-Yugoslavia's well-to-do sibling, Slovenia is a nation of vivacious, cultured, and gregarious people, and you'll find it easy to meet locals, many of whom speak several languages (typically Slovenian, English, German, and Italian). While city life is energetic and modern, you may also come across tiny bucolic communities where a traditional agricultural lifestyle is augmented with the odd beer festival or carnival, complete with a lineup of cheerful polka bands. For while they're considered a nation of hard workers, Slovenes love to kick back, relax, and party; with life this good there's plenty to celebrate.

LANGUAGE

Most Slovenes you meet will understand English, so you won't have much call to try Slovenian, a complicated and difficult-to-learn South Slavonic language. Using Roman letters, written Slovenian includes three modifications, of the letters s, c, and z, which receive a *hacek* top in order to slur them; thus, *š* sounds like "sh," *č*sounds like "ch," and *ž* sounds like "zh."

USEFUL TERMS & PHRASES

English	Slovene	Pronunciation
Hello	**Živijo**	Jhi-*vi*-jah
Please/"Can I help you?"	**Prosim/Prosim?**	*Pro*-sim
Goodbye	**Nasvidenje**	Naz-vee-*dan*-ja
Good day/evening	**Dober dan/večer**	Do-*ber* dun/*ve*-tcher
Good night	**Lahko noč**	La-*ko* noc
What's your name?	**Kako ti je ime?**	*Kak*-o tee *ye*-may
Cheers!	**Na zdravje**	Naz-*dra*-vee
Yes/No	**Ja/Ne**	Ya/Neh
Thank you (very much)	**Hvala (lepa)**	H-*vah*-la (lee-pa)
Excuse me	**Oprostite**	O-pros-*tit*-eh
Open/Closed	**Odprto/Zaprto**	Od-*pr*-to/Zap-*pr*-to
Entrance/Exit	**Vhod/Izhod**	Vod/*Ee*-zod
Bon appétit	**Dober tek!**	Dob-er tek

2 Planning Your Trip to Slovenia

VISITOR INFORMATION

The **Slovenian Tourist Board** (Dunajska cesta 156, 1000 Ljubljana, Slovenia; ℂ **386/ 1/589-1840;** fax 386/1/589-1841) is incredibly organized, pitching every aspect of the country on its excellent website (www.slovenia.info), from which you can download or order a dozen different brochures.

U.S. travelers can also contact the **Slovenian Tourist Office** (345 E. 12th St., New York NY 10003; ℂ **212/358-9689;** slotouristboard@sloveniatravel.com). In the U.K., travelers should contact the **Slovenian Tourist Office** (New Barn Farm, Tadlow, Royston, Hertfordshire, SG8 OEP; ℂ **0870-225-5305**).

ENTRY REQUIREMENTS & CUSTOMS REGULATIONS

Citizens of the U.S., Canada, the U.K., Australia, and New Zealand do not presently require visas for stays of up to 90 days. Check the Foreign Ministry website (www. gov.si/mzz) for any updates on visa and entry requirements. Visitors to Slovenia are exempt from Customs duty on items intended for personal use; additionally you may import 200 cigarettes or 50 cigars, 2 liters of wine, 1 liter of spirits as well as 50 grams of perfume or .25 liters of toilet water. Visit http://carina.gov.si if you have any queries in this regard. There are no restrictions on cash brought into the country.

MONEY

Until the end of 2006, the local currency was the Slovenian Tolar, or SIT; by midyear it was pegged at about 239 SIT to 1€. Slovenia started using the euro as of January 2007, although nearly everyone displayed both currencies for some time already, and Slovenes have been familiar with relevant values for quite some time. Exchange facilities are widely available, as are ATMs and credit card facilities; you can swipe your card almost anywhere, including at toll road pay points and gas stations.

WHEN TO GO

Slovenia is wonderful all year round, enjoying a mix of Alpine, continental, and Mediterranean climates. In winter, the Julian Alps are ideal for skiing and snowboarding. Be wary midsummer, however; in July, Slovenes take a break from everyday life and head for the coast (of Croatia, mostly). So while it's a great time to see the old towns in the east, the capital is rather quiet, and the coast terribly crowded.

HOLIDAYS

Slovenian public holidays are: New Year's Day (Jan 1); Prešeren Day (Feb 8); Day of Uprising Against Occupation (Apr 27); Easter Day and Easter Monday; Labor Day (May 1, 2); Statehood Day (June 25); Assumption (Aug 15); Reformation Day (Oct 31); Remembrance Day (Nov 1); Christmas Day (Dec 25); and Independence Day (Dec 26).

GETTING THERE

BY PLANE Slovenia's national carrier, **Adria Airways** (www.adria.si), has regularly scheduled flights from 19 European cities. Your best option for a reasonably seamless flight from North America or Australasia is **Air France** (www.airfrance.com), via Paris, which has flights from most major cities, and up to four daily flights to Ljubljana with its short-haul carrier, Régional. Flight time from Paris is about an hour. It's also worth checking out flights with **Austrian Airlines** (www.aua.com) and **Lufthansa**

Major Festivals in Slovenia

The eastern town of Ptuj erupts with life on Shrove Sunday **(mid-Feb),** when 50,000 people assemble for the country's anticipated **Kurentovanje.** This winter carnival has revelers taking to the streets in spectacular Kurent masks and costumes—an outrageous pagan celebration that's become an awesome excuse for a raucous party. For 2 weeks in **late June,** Maribor hosts the **Lent Festival,** one of the most exciting cultural events in Slovenia, attracting great musical acts and supporters from all over Europe. In **mid-July,** Laško holds a weeklong beer festival, probably the best place to experience Slovenia's affection for drinking, polka bands, and live music. **Ljubljana Summer Festival** runs from **July through to the middle of September** and features performances of all kinds— film, theater, jazz, chamber music, opera, ballet, symphony concerts, theater, puppetry. Ljubljana also hosts the **Druga Godba (The Other Music),** an alternative music festival scheduled around **late May;** while in **late June,** you can catch the **Ljubljana Jazz Festival.** In **mid-July,** the popular summer resort of Bled hosts **Blejski Dnevi (Bled Days),** a festival of music, craft markets, fireworks, and a candlelit lake.

On the **last Sunday in August,** Predjama Castle hosts **Erazem's Medieval Tournament,** complete with jousting knights on horseback and costumes from the Middle Ages. **The Cow's Ball (Kravji Bal)** happens at Lake Bohinj over the **(second or third weekend in September);** the cows literally come home from the mountains and villagers set about their drink-fuelled merrymaking. On **November 11th (St Martin's Day),** look out for winemaking celebrations in the country's wine regions.

(www.lufthansa.com). British low-cost airline **easyJet** (www.easyjet.com) flies to Ljubljana from London's Stansted airport daily; the London-Ljubljana flight is 2 hours. **Czech Airlines** has flights from Prague, **Malev** flies from Budapest, and **Turkish Airlines** arrives from Istanbul. You could also consider flying to Venice or Trieste in Italy, and then getting a train or car for the short trip to Slovenia.

BY TRAIN   Daily services connect Slovenia (usually by way of Ljubljana) with larger cities in neighboring countries. Venice (245km/152 miles), Vienna (385km/239 miles), Zagreb (135km/84 miles), and Budapest (491km/304 miles) are all an easy train ride away.

BY CAR   You'll have little trouble driving into and around Slovenia. Be aware that border crossings can get jampacked; there is a great deal of vacation and business traffic passing in and out, and its entry points can get crowded.

GETTING AROUND

BY CAR   Slovenia's size makes driving here very attractive; besides, you'll be able to get into many smaller villages unnoticed by those on trains and buses. Drive on the right-hand side and pick up a road map (from Tourist Information centers at the airport and in Ljubljana). On expressways, the speed limit is 130kmph (81 mph); on highways, 100kmph (62 mph); on secondary roads, 90kmph (56 mph), and in built-up areas, 50kmph (31 mph). Keep your headlights on at all times, wear your seat belt, and do not use your cellphone while driving. Carry your driver's license and insurance documentation at all times. Gas stations are ubiquitous; you can pay for gas using most credit cards. Visit the website of the **Automobile Association of Slovenia** (www.amzs.si) for information about traffic and details of what to do in emergencies. This is also a good place to get the lowdown on Slovenia's complicated parking rules; you can also call their **Information Center** (© **01/530-5300** or 031-646-464). For road emergencies, call © **1987**; you'll get immediate roadside assistance and a towing service if necessary. For up-to-date road condition information, call © **01/518-8518.**

BY TRAIN Slovenia's train network is fairly extensive and reliable; it's also fairly cheap. Intercity ("IC") trains are faster than *potnški,* or slow trains, which stop at every backwater village. English timetables are available at www.slo-zeleznice.si. Usually you'll be able to purchase tickets for domestic journeys at the station just before departure. Ticketing staff is incredibly helpful.

BY BUS Buses are slightly more expensive than trains, but the network is more extensive, allowing access to more remote destinations; they're also more frequent (except at weekends in some areas). Buses are operated by a number of local companies, and the larger towns have stations with computerized booking systems.

BY BIKE Slovenes love cycling and it's possible to rent bikes in most towns for countryside exploration. Cycling is also popular within cities and towns; in Ljubljana, where parking is problematic and distances are quite short, bikes are definitely the easiest and most economical way of getting around. Don't ride on highways.

TIPS ON ACCOMMODATIONS

Accommodations range from average to superb. There's a five-star classification system loosely reflecting the quality of hotels, but it certainly doesn't give a clear indication of price, which is dependent on demand. June through August is considered peak vacation season, when you should reserve accommodations well in advance, especially on the coast; the exception to this is the ski resorts that fill up between December and February.

To avoid high hotel costs, consider staying at a *penzion* or a small, family-run hotel; these might be referred to as *gostišče.* There are an increasing number of upper-end establishments, particularly in resort towns, spas, and in the capital. The country's hostels are among the very best in Europe.

TIPS ON DINING

Generally, you'll be choosing to eat in either a *restavracija* (restaurant) or a *gostilna,* which is more like a tavern with down-to-earth atmosphere. If there's an accommodations attached to the tavern, it will probably be called a *gostišče,* making it a real "inn." *Okrepčevalnice* are snack bars where you can get in-between fillers or light meals. Meat (including horse) and fish feature heavily on the Slovene menu, and—depending on where you are—the cuisine shows some Austrian, Hungarian, or Italian influences; in Ljubljana there are a wide range of international dining establishments. *Note:* Like Italy, many restaurants in Slovenia charge a "bread and cover" charge—in short, a 1€-to-3€ ($1.25–$3.75) cover charge (added to each bill) that you must pay for the mere privilege of sitting at the table. We have referred to this as "cover charge" in the dining sections of this chapter.

TOURS & TRAVEL AGENTS

Based in London, **Slovenija Pursuits** (www.slovenijapursuits.co.uk) arranges reliable all-inclusive trips to Slovenia.

FAST FACTS: Slovenia

Addresses Throughout this chapter, the following Slovene words may occur as part of an address: *ulica* (street), *cesta* (road), *trg* (square), *pot* (trail), and *steza* (path).

Airlines All the major airlines have offices either in Ljubljana or at the airport. **Adria Airways:** Kuzmičeva 7, Ljubljana; ✆ **01/369-1010;** Airport: ✆ **04/259-4339;** toll-free: ✆ **080-1300;** www.adria-airways.com. **Air France:** ✆ **01/244-3447** or 01/242-8403; Airport: ✆ **04/206-1674;** www.airfrance.com/si.

Area Code For Slovenia, dial ✆ **0386.**

Banks & Currency Exchange ATMs are your best bet for getting cash quickly, although credit cards are also accepted for cash advances at most banks.

Business Hours Shops should be open weekdays 8am to 7pm, and Saturday 8am to 1pm. On Sundays, some shops and services may open at 11am and do business until 5pm. Banks usually take a midday break between 12:30 and 2pm, and close at 5pm, and are open Saturday mornings until 11am or noon. Most attractions close on Mondays.

Car Rentals All major international car-rental agencies are represented; rates are competitive and vehicles are in excellent condition; always return the car with a full tank to avoid a 50% surcharge. **Avis:** ✆ **01/583-8780;** www.avis.si. **Hertz:** ✆ **01/239-6010;** www.hertz.si.

Drugstores *Lekarna* are found in all towns, and are open from early until 7 or 8pm. It shouldn't be too difficult to track down an all-night drugstore, or *dežurna lekarna.*

Electricity Local current is 220 volts. Outlets take plugs with two round prongs, typical to continental Europe. Plug and power adapters are necessary for appliances requiring 110 volts.

Embassies & Consulates All embassies and consulates are in Ljubljana. **U.S. Embassy:** Prešernova cesta 31; ✆ **01/200-5500;** fax 01/200-5555; www.usembassy.si. **U.K. Embassy:** Trg Republike 3/IV; ✆ **01/200-3910;** fax 01/425-0174; www.british-embassy.si. **Consulate of Canada:** Miklošičeva 19; ✆ **01/430-3570;** fax 01/430-3575. **Australian Consulate:** Trg Republike 3/XII; ✆ **01/425-4252;** fax 01/426-4721. **Consulate of New Zealand:** Verovškova 57; ✆ **01/580-3055;** fax 01/568-3526; janja.bratos@lek.si.

Emergencies Dial ✆ **113** for police emergencies. Fire service ✆ **112.** Ambulance ✆ **112.** For nonaccident road emergencies, call AMZS at ✆ **1987.**

Internet Access Slovenia has good Internet service, although dedicated Internet cafes are few. Most hotels have in-room Internet connectivity.

Language See "Language" on p. 647 above.

Liquor Laws The legal age for drinking is 18.

Mail Post offices (look for signs that read POŠTA) are generally open weekdays 8am to 6pm, and Saturdays 8am to 1pm; mail service is efficient and reliable.

Maps Good maps are available at the airport, and tourist offices around the country will give you everything you might need to find your way around.

Newspapers & Magazines You'll find heaps of useful tourist publications at the airport. *The Slovenia Times* is published in English every 2 weeks.

Police Dial ⓒ **113.**

Restrooms Clean and user-friendly; you'll pay a very small fee to use public facilities at train and bus stations.

Safety & Crime One of Europe's safest countries, with a below-average crime rate.

Taxes & Service Charges VAT will generally be included in all quoted prices; at hotels, there may be an extra "tourist tax" of around 1€ ($1.25) per night.

Telephones Use a phonecard, bought at post offices and newsstands, to use public pay phones, which are fairly ubiquitous; you can also call from a booth at the post office. Numbers in Slovenia have seven digits; this should be preceded by the two-digit area code if you're calling from a different region.

Time Zone Slovenia is 1 hour ahead of GMT.

Tipping Leave 10% to 15% for all good restaurant and bar service.

Water Slovenia's water is clean and delicious; in some areas, it's considered among the purest water in Europe.

Weather information Dial ⓒ **090-7130.**

3 Ljubljana

In many ways a fairy-tale city, replete with castle, the capital city has as its defining motif a dragon, which you will see on flags that flutter from bridges and buildings (and in the form of a child-friendly costumed character that roams the center during summer). The historic center is imbued with striking monuments and generous squares that suggest good urban planning. Graffiti artists mark these public spaces, often branding historic edifices with such unironic one-liners as "Ljubljana is a beautiful city." And it is. Graffiti aside, Ljubljana has a low-key buzz and an air of exuberance that extends to the artfulness of its buildings, its statuary, and its fountains.

According to legend, Argonauts may have laid the foundations of Ljubljana as they fled along the Ljubljanica River from the Black Sea to the Adriatic with the Golden Fleece 3,000 years ago; certainly the Romans established a city, Emona, here by the turn of the 1st century A.D. With Emona destroyed by the Huns, Slavic immigrants chose to build a city at the foot of what is now Ljubljana Castle Hill; it grew to become what was known 500 years later as Leibach and in 1144 as Luwigana. When the Habsburgs took over, this became their administrative center until they were expelled during World War I. In the mid–19th century the city's economic pull was enhanced when the railroad linking Vienna and Trieste was built through Ljubljana, and much of the city's prosperity came from its tobacco factory.

A university town, with cutting-edge ambitions, Ljubljana percolates with charm. It's long been a cultural center, home to one of Europe's oldest philharmonic societies, and now also to a swinging alternative youth and student culture, drawing international artists from all spheres. It's also the birthplace of celebrated architect, Joze Plečá nik, who almost single-handedly reshaped the city, erecting many of its lovely buildings, and developing its squares and bridges. Best of all, the city is small and compact, so you'll see plenty of it with little effort.

GETTING THERE

Although **Aerodrom Ljubljana** (Brnik 130a; ℂ **04/206-1000;** www.lju-airport.si), located at Brnik, 23km (14 miles) from the city, isn't the busiest place in Europe, there are regular flights arriving from Paris, London, Prague, Zurich, and Frankfurt, as well as smaller regional cities. You can rent a car at the airport from **Avis** (ℂ **01/583-8780;** www.avis.si) and return it when you fly home. Taxis, airport shuttles, and public buses all operate between the terminal and the city, but the best option, in terms of cost and efficiency, is to hop on one of the special buses operated by Adria Airlines. These run from early until midnight and are more or less scheduled to coincide with the arrival of their flights; the trip to the city lasts half an hour, and terminates at the city **bus station** (Avtobusna postaja; Trg Osvobodilne fronte 4; ℂ **01/234-4600;** www. ap-ljubljana.si), which is also the main point of arrival and departure for other Slovene and European destinations. Ljubljana's **train station** (Železniška postaja) is next to the bus station, and has a currency exchange facility as well as tourist information office (ℂ **01/433-9475**). The stations are a 10-minute walk from the center.

CITY LAYOUT

Most of the tourist action is within a small, compact area centered on Ljubljana's Old Town, which straddles a bend in the Ljubljaniker River. For more detail see "Exploring Ljubljana's Center," below.

GETTING AROUND THE CITY

This is a city for walking, and you'll be irritated and frustrated if you try to explore it by car; finding parking—even on quiet days—is hellish. Hotels beyond walking distance of the center usually provide shuttle services, and taxis are very reliable.

BUSES   Decent, comfortable public buses will get you wherever you need to go; the network is extensive and route maps clearly indicate when and where buses are going. Purchase bus tokens from newspaper kiosks and some shops, or deposit the exact fare (around 1€/$1.25 before the official adoption of the euro) into the box next to the driver.

TAXIS   Call ℂ **9700** (and all numbers through 9709) to have a cab pick you up. Alternatively, you can hail a taxi on the street; you'll always find taxis at the station and smarter hotels. **Rumeni Taxi** (ℂ **041-731-831**) is another option.

OTHER   To really get your bearings, consider a 90-minute **hot-air balloon ride** organized by any of the tourist information centers. For a more down-to-earth sightseeing option, rent a **bicycle** (also from tourist information; see details below).

VISITOR INFORMATION

Ljubljana knows that tourism is where it's at, and there's a great deal of literature and assistance for visitors. Right in the heart of the Old Town, at one end of the Triple Bridge, is **Ljubljana Tourist Information Centre** (ℂ **01/306-1215;** www.ljubljana-tourism.si), an excellent source for sightseeing advice; it's also where you can buy the **Ljubljana Card** (around 13€/$16), a 72-hour discount passport that is only truly useful if you are able to use it for reductions on accommodations or car rentals, in which case you'll score major savings. **Slovenian Tourism** (Krekov trg 10; ℂ **01/306-4575/6;**

daily 8am–9pm) provides assistance on the entire country. The train station hosts a **Tourist Office** (© 01/433-9475), and there's an **Airport Centre** (© 051/606-172).

CITY TOURS & GUIDED WALKS

You can join one of the city tours provided by **Ljubljana Tourist Information Centre** (Stritarjeva ulica; © 01/306-1215; www.ljubljana-tourism.si).

FAST FACTS: Ljubljana

American Express Kolodvorska 16; © **01/430-7720**; Monday to Friday 8am to 5pm.

Area Code For Ljubljana, dial © **01**.

Banks & Currency Exchange Exchange is available at banks and also at post offices. If you arrive by train, there's a facility at the station open until 10pm. ATMs are an easy way to draw euros throughout the day.

Drugstores Round-the-clock service at **Lekarna Miklošič** (Miklošičeva 24; © 01/231-4558).

Hospital The city's main hospital is situated at Bohoričeva 4; © **01/232-3060**.

Internet Access If for some reason there's no Internet at your hotel, head for the Slovenian Tourist Information Center on Krekov trg.

Police Dial © **113**. Report any incidents at Trdinova 10 (© **01/432-0341**).

Postal Services Central: Slovenska 32; Monday to Friday 7am to 8pm. Adjacent to the stations: Trg Osvobodilne fronte; Monday to Friday 7am to midnight, Saturday 7am to 6pm, Sunday 9am to noon.

WHERE TO STAY
VERY EXPENSIVE

If you choose to research further you may come across the city's most expensive and, arguably, most glamorous hotel, **Lev** (www.hotel-lev.si), but note that it suffers from an alarming location on a busy central intersection and, frankly, lacks character.

Domina Grand Media Hotel & Casino ⟡ When it opened in 2004, this Italian-owned monolith was heralded as the world's most technologically advanced hotel, offering guest rooms packed with enough electronic gadgetry to make even the most hardened computer geek shriek with delight. From touch-screen pads on the doors (where you can activate an electronic DO NOT DISTURB sign) to computer-simulated fireplaces, it's a haven for techno-savvy travelers and business folk (you can even make free international telephone calls, thanks to the miracle of broadband). Despite the hotel's poor location on a busy city intersection in a building that's more office block than anything else, once you're inside, things don't look quite so bad, particularly once you're away from the cold marble lobby (escalators lead down to the casino and doors open on to a convention center). Guest rooms are spacious, carpeted, and design-conscious, with patterned textiles and dark wood furniture in a style that's probably best described as "formal Italian modernism"; closets and bathrooms are large. Suites are even more wired and spacious, with massive plasma screens against the walls and walk-in cupboards. Guests make use of a shuttle for the center.

Ljubljana Lodging, Dining & Attractions

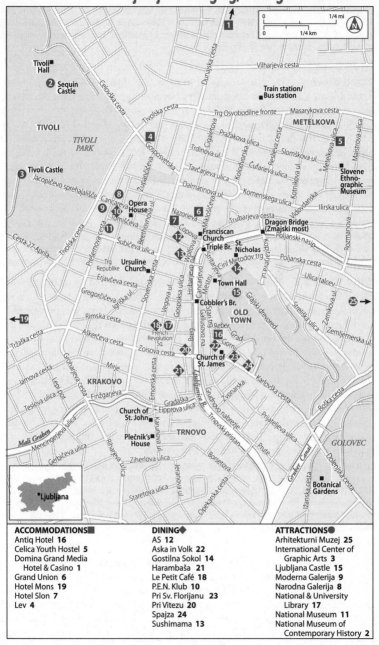

0	1/4 mi
0	1/4 km

Tivoli Hall

2 Sequin Castle

Vilharjeva cesta

Train station/
Bus station

Trg Osvobodilne fronte

TIVOLI

TIVOLI PARK

3 Tivoli Castle

Jacopičevo-sprehajališče

Celovška cesta

Tivolska cesta

Masarykova cesta

METELKOVA

Pražakova ulica

Slomškova-ul.

Metelkova ulica

Maistrova-ulica

5

Slovene Ethnographic Museum

4

Gosposvetska

Trdinova-ul.

Cigaletova

Kolodvorska

Resljeva cesta

Tavčarjeva ulica

Čufarjeva-ulica

Kotnikova ul.

Komenskega ulica

Vidovdanska

Ilirska ulica

Dalmatinova ul.

Zupančičeva ul.

8 Opera House

9

Cankarjeva

Tomšičeva

Beethovnova

11

Miklošičeva ul.

Nazorjeva

Čopova

Trubarjeva cesta

6

7

Dragon Bridge (Zmajski most)

Poljanski nasip

12

Franciscan Church

Triple Br.

St. Nicholas

Rozmanova

Cesta 27.-Aprila

Tivolska cesta

Prešernova cesta

Subičeva ulica

Wolfova

Štritarjeva

Cankarjeva

Mestni

Ciril Metodov trg

Poljanska cesta

13

14

15

Town Hall

Ulica talcev

25 →

Erjavčeva cesta

Gregorčičeva ulica

Slovenska cesta

Vegova ul.

Gosposka ul.

Igriška ul.

Hribarjevo

Trg Republike

Ursuline Church

Stari trg

Gallusovo

Cobbler's Br.

OLD TOWN

Grajski drevored

Streliška ulica

Zarnikova-ul.

Zemljemerska ul.

Rimska cesta

Aškerčeva cesta

Zoisova cesta

←19

Tržaška cesta

Grudnovo

Breg

Reber

Grad

Gornji

16

17

French Revolution Sq.

22

16

Karlovška cesta

Roška cesta

Jamova cesta

Lepi Pot

Gradnikove

Barjanska cesta

Mirje

21

20

Church of St. James

23

24

KRAKOVO

Finžgarjeva

Emonska cesta

Gradaška

Eipprova ulica

Zvonarska

Prijateljeva ulica

Teslova ulica

Gradišče

Church of St. John

Ljubljanica R.

Grudnovo nabrežje

Trnovski-pristan

Prule

GOLOVEC

Mali Graben

Mencingerjeva ulica

Plečnik's House

Rihtarjeva ulica

Ziherlova ulica

TRNOVO

Borsetova

Gruber Canal

Jeranova ulica

Opekarska ulica

Staretova ulica

Botanical Gardens

Ižanska cesta

Dolenjska cesta

Ljubljana

ACCOMMODATIONS ■
Antiq Hotel **16**
Celica Youth Hostel **5**
Domina Grand Media
  Hotel & Casino **1**
Grand Union **6**
Hotel Mons **19**
Hotel Slon **7**
Lev **4**

DINING ◆
AS **12**
Aska in Volk **22**
Gostilna Sokol **14**
Harambaša **21**
Le Petit Café **18**
P.E.N. Klub **10**
Pri Sv. Florijanu **23**
Pri Vitezu **20**
Spajza **24**
Sushimama **13**

ATTRACTIONS ●
Arhitekturni Muzej **25**
International Center of
  Graphic Arts **3**
Ljubljana Castle **15**
Moderna Galerija **9**
Narodna Galerija **8**
National & University
  Library **17**
National Museum **11**
National Museum of
  Contemporary History **2**

Dunajska 154, 1000 Ljubljana. (℗) **01/588-2500.** Fax 01/588-2599. www.dominagmljubljana.com. 214 units. 200€ ($250) double Royal Media; 230€ ($288) double junior suite; 260€–1,015€ ($325–$1,269) suite. Rates include breakfast. AE, MC, V, DC. **Amenities:** Restaurant; bar; lounge bar; casino; business center; room service; wellness center; Thai massage; laundry. *In room:* A/C, TV, Internet, minibar.

EXPENSIVE

Grand Union ⚜ The main contender in a group of three co-owned central hotels, Grand Union is aimed at business travelers, but pins its image to a sense of character and refinement (despite former Holiday Inn connections). Built in 1905, it was then the most modern hotel in the Balkans, with a high-ceilinged sprawl of wide passages and shiny marble floors, behind an Art Nouveau facade. Guest rooms are in two categories: Executive and Business. Opt for the classier Executive part of the hotel if you crave historical ambience; the Business wing is in a less-elegant 1970s building. However, the newer wing includes great views of the castle and the city's rooftops from even-numbered units on the seventh, eighth, and ninth floors. Guest rooms have pale-yellow walls and turquoise carpets; they're relatively spacious with bright big bathrooms.

Miklošičeva cesta 3, 1000 Ljubljana. (℗) **01/308-1170.** Fax 01/308-1914. www.gh-union.si. 200 units. Executive: 177€–283€ ($221–$354) double; 350€–487€ ($438–$609) suite. Business: 164€–283€ ($205–$354) double; 279€–487€ ($349–$609) suite. Rates include breakfast and VAT. AE, MC, V, DC. **Amenities:** 2 restaurants; bar; cafe; pool; fitness room; sauna; room service; laundry. *In room:* A/C, TV, Internet, minibar, hair dryer, iron on request, safe.

Hotel Mons ⚜⚜ Billed as Slovenia's first designer hotel and set at the edge of a thick green forest right at the outskirts of greater Ljubljana, Mons may be a little way out of the center (5km/3 miles away, in the suburb of Brdo), but is well positioned for quick highway access to the rest of the country, and there's a regular free shuttle into the city. Designed by Boris Podrecca, it's a bright glass-encased hotel, the chic modernism counterbalanced by its salubrious garden setting (which you're reminded of by views from practically every window). Guest rooms in pale tones continue the modernist theme; they're smart, comfortable, and easy on the eye. The drawback here is that Mons is attached to a Congress Centre, meaning that from time to time it fills up with delegates; instead of an a la carte restaurant, there's a self-service "market" -themed canteen-style facility, which is great if you're a conference attendee, but ultimately without charm. Rates are very reasonable, and when things are quiet, you might get a reduced rate, even without a reservation.

Pot za Brdom 55, 1000 Ljubljana. (℗) **01/470-2720.** Fax 01/470-2708. www.mons.si/en. 114 units. Jan 8–July 15 and Aug 16–Dec 23: 180€ ($225) double, 335€ ($419) junior suite, 370€ ($463) suite. Jul 16–Aug 15 and Dec 24–Jan 7: 145€ ($181) double, 265€ ($331) junior suite, 335€ ($419) suite. Rates include breakfast. AE, MC, V. **Amenities:** Self-service restaurant; breakfast room; bar; fitness room, sauna; conference center; room service; laundry; city shuttle; airport transfers; billiards; shop; Internet facility; travel agency; jogging paths; bike rental; sightseeing. *In room:* A/C, TV, Internet, minibar, hair dryer, safe.

MODERATE

Antiq Hotel ⚜⚜ *Finds* This brand-new boutique hotel in the heart of Old Town— the entrance is marked by four potted "designer" trees adjacent the fountain on Gornji trg—is a sure winner as the most fabulous place to stay in the capital. Decorated with an assortment of antiques, the interior is like an advertisement for Ljubljana's Sunday market; passages are decorated with mirrors and original framed paintings. Guest rooms are a mixed bag and charged accordingly: Book no. 1 if you want a spectacularly large room with ornate carpets, a carved wooden bed with sumptuous bedspreads and cushions, lovely closets, antique desk, and a seating area with sofa, armchair, and an old ottoman; even the bathroom is big and long, with his and hers basins, a bidet, and a separate toilet. The suite is done out in a more contemporary style with an air-conditioned loft bedroom and downstairs living area with its own kitchen; it even has a private rooftop terrace. On the other end of the scale are a number of small rooms with shared bathrooms for travelers on a budget (just 70€/$88 double). At press time, the hotel was only serving breakfast.

Gornji trg 3, 1000 Ljubljana. ℂ 01/421-3561. Fax 01/421-3565. www.antique-hotel.com. 70€–153€ ($88–$191) double; 185€ ($231) suite. Rates include breakfast and taxes. AE, MC, V. Children under 4 stay free in parent's room. **Amenities:** Lounge; bar; room service; laundry. *In room:* A/C (some), TV, minibar, hair dryer, safe.

Hotel Slon ✦   One of the most conveniently situated hotels in Ljubljana, walking distance from all the sights (although be warned: it's also on the busiest road in town), this Best Western "Premiere" property has a history stretching from 1552, when Archduke Maximilian allegedly stayed here with his elephant (*slon* means "elephant"); the hotel was actually built in 1937, however. Packed full of amenities (most of which you probably won't use), guest rooms are fairly standard and quite comfortable, but you may need to carry your own luggage up to the room.

Slovenska cesta 34, 1000 Ljubljana. ℂ **01/470-1131.** Fax 01/251-7164. www.hotelslon.com. 171 units. 117€–165€ ($146–$206) double; 191€–358€ ($239–$448) suite. **Amenities:** 2 restaurants; breakfast room; cafe; delicatessen; nightclub; Jacuzzi; sauna; gift shop; Internet. *In room:* A/C, TV, tea- and coffeemaking facility, minibar, hair dryer, safe, Internet, Jacuzzi (suites).

INEXPENSIVE

Located in the Metelkova precinct, an area in the old part of town that is experiencing progressive urban renewal, and a heady nightlife, **Celica Youth Hostel** (ℂ **01/230-9700;** www.hostelcelica.com); 17€–27€/$21–$34 per bed) offers a novel stay in what was once part of the barracks of the JNA (Yugoslav People's Army); the most celebrated rooms are converted prison cells (48€/$60 double), given a design makeover by a number of invited artists. You pay for the level of privacy that you enjoy: First floor dorms have facilities shared by 40 people, while on the second floor there's one bathroom per dorm. Breakfasts are a touch better than the usual hostel fare, and linen and towels are provided free of charge. There's a self-service laundry, free Internet, and an on-site tourist agency that organizes trips through the city and throughout Slovenia.

WHERE TO DINE

Considering its size, Ljubljana has huge number of restaurants, most of them good. You'll find plenty of options along the Ljubljanica River, but these fill up quickly at dinnertime, so get there early. If you're looking for a place that tourists haven't discovered (probably because Tourist Information hasn't either), try **The P.E.N. Klub** ✦✦ (Tomisiceva 12; ℂ **01/251-4160**), in the headquarters of the Writers' Society. Near the parliament and behind the Opera House, this Bohemian-styled place is where Chef Miki has local foodies, politicians, and intellectuals in his thrall. You will however need to call ahead to check if it's open, and whether they can find a table for you.

EXPENSIVE

AS ✦✦✦ SLOVENE/ITALIAN   A casual terrace disguises a beautiful interior signaling this restaurant's excellent pedigree. Consistently producing top-notch food and attracting VIPs and celebs, this exclusive joint it the best in town. The menu (for which there isn't much need thanks to on-the-ball waiters) changes according to the seasons, and is often based on whatever owner-chef Svetozar Raspopovic finds when he sometimes pops over to Trieste in neighboring Italy to pick up the day's inspirational ingredients. They might include those he'll use in his famous *pesce tartuffalo,* angler or monkfish filet with tartufi sauce. Although not on the menu, ask to start with marinated shrimp tails. Then order the excellent *tagliata,* made from two different cuts of individually flambéed beef medallions. If you're after fish, opt for the house-blended herb and spice-crusted sea bass; there's also a divine homemade calamari and squid pasta with mushrooms, red pepper, and zucchini.

Čopova 5a, Knafljev prehod. © 01/425-8822. www.gostilnaas.si. Reservations essential. Main courses 16€–26€ ($20–$33). AE, DC, MC, V. Daily noon–11pm.

MODERATE

A great bet for Slovene cuisine with a contemporary edge is **Pri Sv. Florijanu** ☆☆ (Gornji trg 20; © 01/251-2214), where some of the standout options include veal medallions with roasted garlic (accompanied by noodles with truffle oil), and filleted red scorpionfish, served with fresh vegetables and polenta. If you're craving your weekly intake of raw fish, stop off at **Sushimama** ☆☆ (Wolfova ulica 12; © 01/426-9125), a modern place in the heart of Ljubljana; it's one of the top sushi restaurants in central Europe, with a loyal local crowd. Go classic with *miso* soup, followed by *nigri* sushi and *kinako* with a pancake; the sashimi is fresh from the Adriatic. Another interesting option, this time for Balkan dishes, is **Aska in Volk** ☆☆ (Gorni trg 4; © 01/251-1070), situated right next to Cerkev sv. Jakoba. Expect an energetic crowd scattered about the gorgeous little rooms decorated with framed pictures and painted in bright, dramatic colors.

Gostilna Sokol ☆☆ *Value* SLOVENE   This superb upstairs *gostilna* is squarely aimed at tourists, yet it's managed to retain an authentic atmosphere. Wooden tables and stone floors, chunky wood paneling, wine barrels, hunting trophies, and an eclectic collection of paintings contribute to a real country-tavern vibe, underscored by the accompanying funky accordion music. Also, Sokol is a microbrewery where you can order beer made on-site. Dishes are prepared from the recipes of someone's grandmother and include such down-to-earth favorites as game goulash (served with bread dumplings), fried sausage with cabbage, and the very excellent medallions of deer with Mahaleb cherry sauce. Beyond the wide range of grilled steaks, there's also seafood, including a kilogram of grilled trout, and squid stuffed with cheese and ham. Hard as it may be, save room for a taste of Slovenia's traditional dessert, *Prekmurska gibanica,* a rich mix of cottage cheese, apples, poppy seeds, and walnuts.

Ciril Metodov trg 18. © 01/439-6855. www.gostilna-sokol.com. Reservations recommended. Main courses 6€–35€ ($7.50–$44); most dishes are under 20€ ($25). AE, DC, MC, V. Mon–Sat 7am–11pm; Sun and holidays 10am–11pm.

Pri Vitezu ☆☆☆ SLOVENE   This riverside eatery is owned by Slovenia's very own "Naked Chef" contender: Luka Lesar has marketed himself extensively under the brand name "Luke Gourmet," and a number of restaurants are buying into his culinary flair. Specials are chalked up outside the beautiful multithemed restaurant, and are usually based on whatever's freshest at the market (usually straight from the Adriatic coast). Start with a mixed seafood platter or fragrant ginger soup, then order the unforgettable beef filet *a la Calabrese,* prepared with olives, dried tomatoes, and capers. There's a selection of homemade cakes, but don't miss Luka's tiramisu.

Breg 18–20. © 01/426-6058. Reservations essential. Main courses 7.50€–20€ ($9.40–$25). AE, DC, MC, V. Mon–Sat noon–11pm.

Spajza ✦✦✦ SLOVENE/INTERNATIONAL   When the restaurant was featured on Discovery Channel's documentary about Slovenia, Spajza's reputation was sealed. In summer you can dine in the outdoor courtyard, but at night you'll be drawn to the romantic, slightly informal indoor spaces, divided into different rooms. All the seafood is super fresh (it arrives daily from Croatia). Fish lovers could start with octopus salad or the mixed-fish plate, followed by the excellent John Dory, prepared with Mediterranean flair. But it is for its meat dishes that Spajza is known for, with horse-meat the main specialty (*spajza* means "horse"); *špajzin file s tartufi* (horse filet with truffles) is a particular highlight, or so I'm told. For more reserved tastes, there's beef and veal, best topped with local mushrooms *(jurčki),* or—a personal favorite—medallions of venison with wild berries. Finish off with apricot and apple strudel, or homemade lemon cheesecake.

Gornji trg 28. ⓒ **01/425-3094.** Reservations highly recommended. Main courses 10€–46€ ($13–$58); most dishes are under 20€ ($25). AE, DC, MC, V. Mon–Sat noon–11pm; Sun and holidays noon–10pm.

INEXPENSIVE

There's a friendly atmosphere at **Harambaša** (Vrtna ulica 8, Krakovo; ⓒ **041-843-106**), which serves Bosnian pub fare in a space filled with antiques and junk—swords, coffeepots, and copper urns alongside postcards, newspapers, and Sarajevo sports team shirts. Food is simple: *Čevapi v lepinji* (pieces of meat with bread), *sudukice* (Bosnian sausage), and *pola-pola,* a combination of the two, best with *kajmak* cheese. A filling meal with beer and Turkish coffee (served with a cigarette) is under 5€ ($6.25).

Le Petit Café ✦ *Value* FRENCH/CAFE   This ultimate Sunday-afternoon cafe has a popular wooden terrace under a tree right on French Revolution Square; inside it's a little like an intimate Parisian cafe, with posters against exposed brick. It's a fine place for healthy breakfasts made with fresh ingredients, including homemade yogurt; in summer the drinkable lemon sorbet is a great quencher; in winter, sample the mulled wine. The menu is pretty casual, offering salads, pastas, and wholesome sandwiches (only the latter are available after 8pm). Good choices include beef carpaccio with truffles and Parmesan, served on rocket (arugula), gnocchi stuffed with rocket and ricotta cheese, and grilled filet of salmon with Trevisiano chicory and mozzarella. Daily specials are written on the blackboard.

Trg Francoske Revolucije 4. ⓒ **01/251-2575.** Main courses 6€–12€ ($7.50–$15). No credit cards. Mon–Fri 7:30am–11pm; Sat–Sun and holidays 9am–11pm; may close later Fri–Sat.

WHAT TO SEE & DO
EXPLORING LJUBLJANA'S CENTER

If you don't dally in the art galleries, you could see the whole of the city in a single day, starting at **Ljubljana's Castle** (reviewed below), which overlooks the entire city. The best buildings are in and around the finely preserved **Old Town,** a fine mixture of baroque, Secessionist, and neoclassical buildings around a curve in the **River Ljubljanica,** and heavily beefed up by the city's designer laureate, Jože Plečnik. Life proceeds at a gentle, lively pace along and around the Lubljanica, defined by its cafe and bar culture, and on and around the bridges linking the two banks.

A good place to find your bearings is **Prešernov Square,** centered on the statue of France Prešeren, considered the Father of the Nation, and the poet whose words are now the national anthem ("A Toast"). Also here is **Centromerkur,** marked by an Art Nouveau awning over the entrance; this is Ljubljana's oldest department store, in a gorgeous Secessionist building dating from 1903. This is roughly the heart of the Old Town, where young people meet to start their day (often on the steps of the **Franciscan Church**), or the night—often heading one way or another across **Triple Bridge (Tromostovje)** to get to their favorite riverside drinking spot. Across Triple Bridge you can take a left turn (at the Tourist Information Center) to reach the colonnaded covered promenade of the daily **crafts market;** alternatively, after crossing the bridge, continue on Stritarjeva, where you soon hit **Mestni trg,** marked by the recently restored **Robba's Fountain (Robbov Vodnjak),** completed in 1751 and celebrating the confluence of the three Carniolan rivers (the Ljubljanica, the Sava, and the Krka). The fountain is just in front of the **Town Hall (Magistrat),** which you can visit for free; exhibitions are occasionally held in the interior courtyard. Medieval Mestni trg is a defining part of Old Town, as is **Stari trg (Old Square)** at its southern, narrowing end. Together, Mestni and Stari squares form a lively pedestrian cobblestone avenue lined with shops, restaurants, and cafes, and culminating with the massive early-17th-century **St. James' Church.**

As Mestni trg curves east, you'll notice the looming **Cathedral of St. Nicholas** ⊛, An important religious building in the baroque style, defined by its high dome and massive bell towers. Started in 1701, the cathedral was designed by Andrea Pozzo; its interiors are famous for frescoes by Quaglio, depicting miraculous moments in the life of St. Nicholas, the patron saint of all seafaring people. Worth a look are the bronze sculpted church doors, added for the 1996 visit of Pope John Paul II (whose image can be seen looking over the history of Slovene Christianity on the main doors).

Adjacent the cathedral is the **Market** ⊛, another of Plečnik's designs. Just north of the market, crossing the Ljubljanica out of Old Town, is **Zmajski Most (Dragon's Bridge)** ⊛⊛⊛, designed by Jurij Zaninovich and completed in 1901, four fabulously sculpted dragons that adorn each corner of the bridge. Just beyond the bridge, if you head east along **Trubarjeva cesta,** you'll encounter a distinctive student culture, with a succession of cheap cafes, adventure companies, and New Age shops such as the hemp-based cosmetics outfit, Extravaganja. Turn off Trubarjeva into **Vidovdanska cesta,** which soon gives way to interesting **Metelkova,** an area experiencing progressive urban renewal, and a heady nightlife. Formerly the barracks of the JNA (Yugoslav People's Army), the buildings that comprise the Metelkova project have been reclaimed to serve as a center of alternative youth and student culture; the project is famous thanks to **Celica** ⊛, a prison-turned-hostel, known for its artistically renovated cells (see "Where to Stay," earlier in this chapter); nonresidents can call © **01/430-1890** to arrange a visit.

Near the Celica is Metelkova's highbrow **Slovene Ethnographic Museum** ⊛ (Metelkova 2; © **01/300-8745/00;** www.etno-muzej.si), which sheds light on the relationship between humankind and the multitudinous objects that make up our world, be they part of survival, evolution, or everyday existence. You can join the pottery workshops that are held in the trendy-looking studio near the entrance. Or, better still, grab a drink at the cool new cafe-bar (called **S.E.M.**) at the entrance.

Back in Old Town, on the western side of the river, **Kongresni trg (Congress Square)** is a fine urban park named in honor of the Congress of the Holy Alliance, for which it was laid out in 1821. Of note around the square are the **Ursuline Church** (1726), the **Kazina** (a 19th-c. establishment hangout), the *fin de siècle* **University** building, and the contemporaneous **Slovenska filharmonija (Slovene Philharmonic Hall)** ⊛, which is the headquarters of the country's celebrated Philharmonic Orchestra, which traces its root to the 1701 Academia Philharmonicorum, making it one of the world's oldest music societies.

Vegova ulica runs south from Kongresni trg, passing the **National and University Library** (reviewed below), and terminating at the 1929 **Illyrian Monument** (another of Plečnik's contributions), which marks **French Revolution Square (Trg Francoske revolucije).** It's also where you'll find the **Križanke Summer Theater;** formerly the Monastery of the Holy Cross, it's now an outdoor theater venue used during the Ljubljana Summer Festival. The complex was redesigned by Plečnik in the 1950s.

Stretching past the open end of Kongresni trg is **Slovenska cesta,** the city's main road. Just north of the square is the "famous" **Nebotičnik "skyscraper."** Designed by Vladimir Subic, this is the "Rockefeller Center of the Balkans." Commissioned in the 1930s, it was then Europe's tallest residential building. Sadly, in recent years it became Ljubljana's favorite suicide spot, prompting the closure of the upper level to allow for the building of a protective fence around the top-floor perimeter.

West of Slovenska cesta is the gorgeous **Opera House** ☆☆ (along Cankarjeva cesta), worth seeing just for the loveliness of its facade; it was built in the neo-Renaissance style in 1892. Farther west, on Prešernova cesta, are the two main art galleries (both reviewed below), and **Tivoli Park** ☆, where you can visit the **International Center of Graphic Arts** ☆ (Pod turnom 3; ℰ 01/241-3800; www.mglc-lj.si), occupying mansionlike Tivoli Castle (it's a 10-min. walk from Old Town, or you can hop on a bus to Hala Tivoli). The Center hosts excellent temporary programs with diverse themes, from street art and film and theater costumes, to amazing record cover designs. Also in the park is Ljubljana's **National Museum of Contemporary History** (Celovška cesta 23; ℰ 01/300-9610; www.muzej-nz.si), which makes for a possible diversion; exhibits highlight significant moments from 20th-century Slovenia.

Back near the Opera House the **National Museum** (Muzejska ulica 1; ℰ 01/241-4400; www.narmuz-lj.si; Fri–Wed 10am–6pm, Thurs 10am–8pm), where the prize possession is Slovenia's oldest discovered artwork, a 5th-century-B.C. Iron Age bronze urn known as the Vače Situla. The museum occupies a neo-Renaissance palace built in 1883 to 1885; in the same building is the **Museum of Natural History.**

Just south of the museum building is **Trg Republike,** an unattractive square where concrete blocks hide **Cankarjev Dom,** a major space for cultural events and exhibitions. Also here is the **Parliament,** marked by an interesting sculpted relief around the entrance; the figures represent different aspects of social and industrial life.

Farther south of the center is the residential suburb of **Trnovo,** with a small, burgeoning cafe culture that attracts a mixed crowd; it's also where you'll find **Plečnik's House** ☆, behind Trnovo Church (Karunova ulica 4; ℰ 01/540-0346; www.arhmuz.com; Tues–Wed 10am–2pm).

TOP ATTRACTIONS

Arhitekturni Muzej ☆☆　Somewhat off the beaten track, the city's Architectural Museum is likely to be a highlight for anyone interested in learning about the built environment—at least as far as it pertains to Ljubljana's urban planning god, Jože Plečnik. Housed in a 16th-century Renaissance castle, **Grad Fužine,** the "museum" is more accurately a tribute solely to Plečnik, centered on a condensed version of his "Paris Exhibition," which wowed visitors to the Pompidou 2 decades ago.
Pot na Fužine 2. ℰ 01/540-0346. www.arhmuz.com. Fužine Castle Mon–Fri 10am–2pm.

Ljubljanski Grad ☆☆　According to the legends, the dragon slain by St. George lived beneath the hill on which Ljubljana Castle is situated, and around which the capital has grown. Start you exploration of the city up here, where you can climb up one of the watchtowers and admire the whole of Ljubljana, which turns out to be a little larger than it seems when you're caught up in the relaxed sybaritic ambience of Old Town. A gondola-style funicular should be up and running to make trips up to the castle more effortless; at the top, there's a lovely terrace cafe and a good souvenir shop; the open courtyard plays host to many of the events during the Ljubljana Summer Festival. Disappointingly, the castle's **Virtual Museum,** which tells the city's story by means of a plodding stereoscopically projected 3-D documentary, is virtually unbearable; unfortunately, tickets to the **Outlook Tower** ✹✹ are combined with the virtual show, so people feel forced to endure it, despite the patronizing tone.

Festival Ljubljana, Ljubljanski Grad. ✆ **01/232-9994.** www.festival-lj.si/virtualnimuzej. Castle entrance is free. Outlook Tower and Virtual Museum: 3.30€ ($4.25) adults, 2.05€ ($2.75) seniors and students; 4.15€ ($5.25) family ticket. Guided tours: 4.60€ (5.75) adults start at 10am and 4pm daily June to mid-Sept; for private tours call ✆ **01/232-9994.** Castle hours: Oct–Apr 10am–10pm; May–Sept 9am–11pm. Outlook Tower and Virtual Museum: Oct–Apr 10am–6pm; May–Sept 9am–9pm; Virtual Museum screenings start every half-hour.

Moderna Galerija ✹✹   Ljubljana's Modern Art Gallery was designed by Plečnik disciple Edvard Ravnikar. It hosts a lively collection of Slovenian paintings, sculptures, and installation pieces from no earlier than 1950. Standout works include the excellent 1960s surrealist works of Štefan Planinc, and Jože Slak-Doka's graffiti-inspired mixed-media assemblages from the 1980s. There's some eyebrow-raising conceptual art definitely worth checking out, while the quality of temporary exhibitions that are regularly hosted here varies considerably.

Tomšičeva 14. ✆ **01/241-6800.** www.mg-lj.si. 4.15€ ($5.25) adults, 2.95€ ($3.75) seniors and students, 2.10€ ($2.75) children. Free admission Sat afternoon. Tues–Sat 10am–6pm; Sun 10am–1pm.

Narodna Galerija ✹✹✹   Housed in an interesting architectural juxtaposition of two 19th-century buildings linked by a modern structure in glass and steel, the National Gallery holds the country's largest collection of Slovenian paintings, which are surprisingly good. Art enthusiasts will appreciate the thorough survey of the nation's early modern artists, including work by Mihael Stoj (1803–71), Biedermeier portraitist Joef Tominc (1790–1866), and the Slovene landscapes of Marko Pernhart (1824–71) and Pavel Künl (1817–71). Look out for the interesting works of "realist-Impressionist" Ferdo Vesel (1861–1946) and notable 19th-century painter Anton Ažbe (1862–1905). Also here are works by the first internationally reputable female Slovene artist, Ivana Kobilca (1861–1926), whose pale portraits are exquisitely ghost-like. Ivan Grohar's (1867–1911) modernist techniques include excellent use of color, and there are some striking canvases by Richard Jakopič (1896–1943). Galleries of older, classical works include 17th-century Hans Georg Gaiger a Gaigerfeld's *St. George Slaying the Dragon* with a rather sci-fi-looking beast.

Prešernova cesta 24. ✆ **01/241-5434.** www.ng-slo.si. 4.15€ ($5.25) adults, 2.95€ ($3.75) seniors and students, 2.10€ ($2.75) children. Free admission Sat afternoon. Guided tours: Tues and Thurs 11am. Tues–Sat 10am–6pm; Sun 10am–1pm.

National and University Library ✹✹   Perhaps the most important of Pležnik's achievements, the nation's main library is remarkable for the unusual and fascinating design of its exterior walls; part brick, part concrete, and part stone, the red-brick walls are dotted with ancient Roman rocks that appear to be sliding toward the sky. Besides its intriguing design elements, the building is notable for the symbolism of the layout; apparently, the main stairway (as you enter) represents a journey into the light of knowledge. You may be tempted to take a book to the reading room, thanks to its rich furnishings and eye-catching chandeliers.

Narodna in univerzitetna knijižnica, Rimska cesta. ⓒ 01/200-1110. www.nuk.unilj.si. Admission 1.50€ ($1.90). Guided tour 2.50€ ($3.15). Mon–Fri 8am–8pm, except July 10–Aug 19 when visiting hours are reduced.

SHOPPING

ANTIQUES   Ljubljana's **antique flea market** ☆☆☆ unleashes its collectibles on the world every Sunday until 1pm. Strung along the edge of the Ljubljanica from the Triple Bridge as far south as it needs to go, it's a cornucopia of bright and faded memories, including some genuine treasures. It's also a great place to meet locals.

ART & IMAGES   Exquisite photographs and photographic books are sold at **Galerija Fotografija** (Mestni trg 8; ⓒ 01/251-1529; www.galerijafotografija.si), which also hosts impressive exhibitions of international photographic work. Peruse and shop for paintings by Slovene artists at **Galerija Hest** (Židovska 8; ⓒ 01/422-0000; www.galerijahest-sp.si). **Art.si** (Židovska 5; ⓒ 01/421-0123; www.art.si) is the gallery of Andris Vitlinš, which sells bright contemporary paintings.

BOOKS   Two of the nicest bookstores in the country are **Azil** (Novi trg 2; ⓒ 01/470-6438; http://azil.zrc-sazu.si), with an astonishing selection of books dealing with philosophy, art, film, and Slovenia; and **Knjigarna Behemot** (Židovska steva 3; ⓒ 01/251-1392; www.behemot.si). Architecture buffs should pick up the excellent *Architectural Guide to Ljubljana* by Andrej Hrausky and Janez Košel; it features images and commentary on 100 buildings in the city. You'll find it at **Darila Rokus Gifts** (Gosposvetska Cesta 2; ⓒ 01/234-9720; www.darila.com), good for books on Slovenia and its culture.

GLASS & PORCELAIN   Among the rash of touristy paraphernalia at **Darila Rokus** (see "Books," above), you'll find the distinctive "Janus" crystal wine–cum–coffee glass sets, which make lovely gifts. At **Galerija Marjan Lovsin** (Breg 8; ⓒ 01/426-0402; www.marjanlovsin.com) you can buy vases by Tanja Pak, who hails from a family of glassblowers, and is known for her distinctive "Drops" design. Slovenia's foremost **porcelain** artists, Katja Jurgen Bricman and Jure Bricman, are known for having had their unusual and unique porcelain jewelry modeled by Miss Slovenia in 2003. They now have a gallery right near Robbo Fountain. **Porcelain Catbriyur** (Ciril-Meotdova 19; ⓒ 041-499-528; www.catbriyur.net) carries an exclusive range of porcelain cups, bowls, and jewelry.

HOMEWARE & FURNITURE   Antique furniture is available from **Carniola Antiqua** (Trubarjeva Cesta 9; ⓒ 01/231-6397). To ogle Slovene style, visit **Nova** (Levstikov trg 7; ⓒ 01/426-0410/08; www.nova-on.net), an inspirational furniture store and lovely nursery. You'll find gorgeous European-design homeware, ornaments, and simple furniture at **DOM Design** (Stefanova 6; ⓒ 01/244-3460; www.domdesign.si).

FASHION   For the best in Slovenian designer wear, head to **Oktober** (Kersnikova Ulica 1; ⓒ 01/431-6343), where Uros Belantic calls the shots. **Katarina Silk** (Gorni trg 5), next door to Antiq Hotel, is a small boutique with stylish silk garments.

SHOES & ACCESSORIES   Accessorize with a fashionable handmade handbag by award-winning **Marjeta Groselj** (Tavcarjeva Ulica 4; ⓒ 01/231-8984). For eccentric shoes and boots with fancy buckles and interesting decorative motifs, you can't beat the idiosyncratic footwear made and sold at **Obulalnica Butanoga** (ⓒ 041-334-701), a little cobbler's boutique hidden down an alleyway off Levstikov trg; look for the hanging signboard across from St. James's Church. **Leonora Mark** (Kersnikova Ulica 1; ✆ **01/ 431-6343**) uses Murano glass pearls in her 1950s-inspired leather designs.

WINE   Pick up wine from Slovenia's top-rated Movia Estate (owned by Mirko and Ales Kristancic) at **Vinoteka Movia** ✹✹ (Mestni Trg 2; ✆ **01/425-5448**); the intimate wine cellar is not only a sales point, but an excellent place for tastings, accompanied by an informative pitch by sommelier Luka Lukažs.

LJUBLJANA AFTER DARK
LIVE MUSIC, THEATER & OPERA
The performing arts are very much alive in the capital, and in summer there is likely to be street theater, especially in and around Old Town—keep eyes and ears pealed. For cutting-edge productions look out for shows conceived by **Draga Živadinov,** the native Ljubljaniker responsible for staging the world's first theatrical production in a weightless environment, somewhere far above Russia.

Theatergoers should catch a show at the beautifully designed **Slovene National Opera and Ballet Theater** ✹✹ (Cankarjeva 11; ✆ **01/241-1700;** www.opera.si). Performances by its 115-year-old resident company are critically acclaimed (**box office:** ✆ **01/241-1764;** Mon–Fri 1–5pm, Sat 11am–1pm, and 1 hr. before shows).

During the famous **Ljubljana Summer Festival** ✹✹ (✆ **01/241-6000;** www. festival-lj.si), performances of all kinds—film, theater, jazz, chamber music, opera, ballet, symphony concerts, theater, puppetry—are held in venues around the city. Main venues are Ljubljana Castle, and the **Križanke Summer Theater** ✹✹✹ (Trg Francoske Revolucije 1). Križanke is also the venue for **Druga Godba** ✹✹**,** literally "The Other Music," an alternative music festival held in late May; and in late June, it hosts the **Ljubljana Jazz Festival** ✹✹.

Classical music fans should attend a performance of the **Slovene Philharmonic** ✹✹✹, which enjoys a proud 305-year musical tradition; performances are held at the Philharmonic Hall (Kongresni trg; ✆ **01/241-0800**). Look out for straight theater and musicals at the **Slovene National Theater** (Narodno Gledališče; Erjavčeva 1; ✆ **01/252-1511**), although the large, modern **Cankarjev Dom** (Trg Republike; ✆ **241-7299;** www.cd-cc.si) has become the main venue for stage productions.

You can catch **live music** spilling out from the terrace of one of the popular cafe-bars at Triple Bridge, nightly in summer; a fun crowd gathers to take in the free entertainment. If you'd like to get a taste of Slovenia's **alternative music scene,** find out what's happening in the Metelkova cultural precinct; start your investigation at any of the Tourist Information offices, or simply wander along **Trubarjeva cesta** and pop your head into any of the trendy-looking stores, or you can opt to inquire at the **Celica Youth Hostel.**

BARS & CLUBS
You could spend days just cruising for your favorite place to drink; virtually all of these establishments are cafe-bar hangouts equally good for coffee, beer, wine, and cocktails. Some also serve ice cream (**Poet** ✹, on the water's edge at Prešernov Square, is a favorite). Many places also carry light meals, so you can forgo restaurants entirely if you're in a party mood.

Drinking along the Ljubljanica is the most popular activity in town, and **Maček** ✹ (Krojaška ulica 5; ✆ **01/425-3791**), inexplicably obsessed with pussy cats, is *the* favored people-watching haunt. You can sit literally on the water's edge at **Makalonča** ✹ (✆ **040-187-975**), an unusual bar-cum-cafe under the Shoemaker's Bridge on the

Ljubljanica. At night, candles are lit and fairy-lights switched on to add even romance. Electronic vibes set a relaxed mood at **Salon** 𝕶𝕶 (Trubarjeva 23; ℂ **01/439-8760**), a fun lounge bar with a distinctly shagadelic look—padded walls, plush sofas, gold drapes, and dazzling mirror-ball effect behind the small bar. Each summer, the garden of the Writer's Society (behind the Opera House) hosts **Jazz Club Gajo** 𝕶𝕶 (Beethovnova 8; ℂ **01/425-3206**), where you can sit under the trees, or sip your drink in a hammock.

For dancing, hit **Global** 𝕶𝕶 (Tomšičeva ulica 2; ℂ **01/426-9017;** www.global.si, closed Sun–Mon), a rooftop restaurant by day and a sixth-floor club by night. An elevator will whisk you up to the top of the Nama department store to experience Ljubljana's hippest discothèque, where music varies through the week.

4 The Julian Alps

VršičPass in the Julian Alps ranks as the most exciting drive in Slovenia, its hairpin (and hair-raising) bends offering views of soaring peaks that define the northwestern corner of the country. Straddling Triglav National Park, and hemmed in by the Karavanke Mountains to the east and the Julian Alps range to the west, the lakes of Bled and Bohinj are two of Slovenia's most treasured resorts, both an easy getaway from Ljubljana and a great base for all kinds of outdoor adventures. Farther west, along the Italian border, and best reached via the aforementioned VršičPass, is the Soča River and the beautiful valley it has carved. Here, the tiny town of Kobarid retains memories of battles that raged along the border at a most critical time in the history of Europe. Besides sheltering some of the nation's finest restaurants and accommodations, Kobarid makes a fine base for exploring the valley by land or water. In winter, nearby Bovec fills up with skiers who prefer their adrenaline rush dusted with white powder.

THE LAKES

Bled is 50km (31 miles) NW of Ljubljana; Bohinj is 26km (16 miles) SW of Bled

Bled is a lake fit for a fairy tale—complete with dramatically situated cliff-top castle, an island church, and wraparound mountain scenery; the shock of its electric turquoise surface is emblazoned on tourism materials everywhere. Situated in a national park, Bohinj manages to resist the limelight, and isn't as developed. A Swiss hydropath named Arnold Rikli (1823–1906) first developed health tourism at Bled after spending years "studying" the beneficial effects of its water, clean air, and sun. Today, it's one of the most fashionable destinations in Europe, drawing an upmarket crowd from all over the world. It also draws hordes of day-trippers at the weekend, yet the crowds never seem to overwhelm the sheer loveliness of the resort, which offers plenty to do. Popular trips from Bled include the Babji Zob Caves and Vintnar Gorge. Also nearby is the exquisite town of **Radovljica.**

ESSENTIALS

Bled is reached by driving from Ljubljana along the expressway that goes to Jesenice; follow the signs from the Lesce turnoff. **Trains** from Ljubljana stop in the nearby town of Lesce (Železniška ulica 12; ℂ **04/294-4154/7**), where you'll need to catch one of the regular buses to Bled. **Buses** arrive at Avtobusna postaja Bled at Cesta svobode 4 (ℂ **04/578-0420**). The **Tourist Information Office** is at Cesta Svobode 15 (ℂ **04/ 574-1122;** www.bled.si).

The nearest train station for **Lake Bohinj** is at Bohinjska Bistrica, which isn't served by trains from the capital. **Buses** stop at Ribčev Laz, at the head of the lake, right near the office of the helpful **Bohinj Tourist Association** (Turistično društvo Bohinj; Ribčev Laz 48; © **04/574-6010;** www.bohinj.si), open 8am to 8pm in summer. Buses also continue to Ukanc at the far side of the lake.

WHERE TO STAY

Bled's infrastructure is fairly sophisticated, evident in its excessive line up of large hotels, many of which cater to tour buses. Lake Bohinj has fewer options, and most of these are smaller pensions with homely accommodations at good rates; the tourist offices will be able to point you toward such bargains.

In Bled

Budget hunters who you don't mind bunking up and sharing bathroom facilities should consider spending the night at **Bledec Youth Hostel** (Grajska cesta 17; © **04/574-5250;** www.mlino.si), one of Europe's nicest, with a terrace overlooking the lake. Still, it's a hostel; a big step up is quaint and lovely **Mayer Penzion** (Želeška 7; © **04/574-1058;** www.mayer-sp.si), a family-run operation with 12 comfortable en-suite guest rooms right near the lake; dining here is excellent.

Grand Hotel Toplice ★★
Built in 1931, Bled's most opulent hotel is an ivy-covered stone building right at the water's edge. In summer, guests flock to the wooden deck that hovers over the water and affords immaculate views across the lake and up to the castle. Interiors are styled with antiques and Persian rugs, plenty of carved wood, and crystal chandeliers. You simply *must* reserve a lake-facing room (which all have balconies behind shuttered doors) to make the most of the most awesome setting in town. Although bedrooms aren't enormous, they're well proportioned and beautiful, with parquet floors and air-cushioned mattresses. It's all superclassy, and staff are charming. There's also a full on-site spa, with naturally-heated indoor pool fed by thermal waters and a drinking fountain with mineral water tapped straight from the earth.

Cesta svobode 12, 4260 Bled. © **04/579-1000.** Fax 04/574-1841. www.hotel-toplice.si. 87 units. 131€–211€ ($164–$264) double; 261€–601€ ($326–$751) suite. Rates include breakfast. AE, DC, MC, V. **Amenities:** Restaurant; bar; terrace; lounge; golfing privileges; spa w/pool, massage, sauna, treatments; room service; laundry. *In room:* A/C, TV, minibar, hair dryer, safe.

Vila Bled ★★★
One of Slovenia's few Relais & Châteaux properties, this estatelike hotel is set in lovely gardens near the edge of the lake. Originally a royal villa, then rebuilt as a country retreat for Marshall Tito's favored guests in 1947, the hotel has since seen the likes of Prince Charles, William Hurt, and Jeff Bridges. Accommodations are divided between huge suites and fairly small doubles. Reserve a suite for a real sense of being on Tito's VIP list: Decked out with parquet floors, massive windows and big Art Deco furniture, they have a distinctive Soviet atmosphere conjuring up memories of secret meetings in a smoke-filled haze. The 1950s styling includes idiosyncratic period pieces such as chunky telephones and gigantic ashtrays, and everything—from silverware to waste bins—has been monogrammed. The hotel has a private "lido" on the lake (basically a wooden deck for sunbathing), and boats are available so you can row yourself to Bled Island. Do visit the first-floor meeting room, where Tito had his private cinema; the walls feature Slavko Pengov's pro-Yugoslav frescoes dating back to 1947. Even if you don't spend the night, book a table at the **Vila Bled Restaurant ★★★**, offering the best food and service in town; dishes are better priced than you might imagine (mains range from 14€–21€/$18–$26).

Cesta svobode 26, 4260 Bled. © **04/579-1500.** Fax 04/574-1320. www.vila-bled.com. 30 units. 191€–210€ ($239–$263) double; 210€–290€ ($263–$363) suite; 620€ ($775) presidential suite. Rates include breakfast. AE,

DC, MC, V. **Amenities:** 2 restaurants; bar; golfing; Jacuzzi; sauna; massage; aromatherapy; spa baths; tennis court; business facilities and meeting rooms; room service; babysitting by arrangement; lakeside bathing area; rowboats; travel assistance; laundry. *In room:* TV, minibar, hair dryer, safe, fan.

Around Lake Bohinj

Vila Parc ⭑⭑ *(Finds)* Stylish and beautiful, Vila Park is a pitch-roofed chalet-style lodge with roughly cut lawns and a low wooden gate; behind its shuttered windows, there's a certain trendiness that's far removed from the rusticated pensions that dominate Ukanc, at the western end of Bohinj Lake. Opened in 2004, and still gleaming with the fresh appeal of a good idea, guest rooms and public spaces show contemporary style; they're done out in pale blue and mushroom shades, with crisp white linens that still feel brand-new. Each room has a balcony and a lovely en-suite shower. Downstairs, there's a gorgeous wood-floored restaurant and a lounge with hi-fi system, CD collection, and a selection of *National Geographic* magazines; in case you're here in winter, there's an inviting fireplace.

Ukanc 129, 4265 Bohinjsko Jezero. © **04/572-3300** or 041-622-105. Fax 04/572-3312. www.vila-park.si. 12 units. 92€–112€ ($115–$140) double; 152€ ($190) (Dec 25–Jan 4). Rates include breakfast and taxes. AE, DC, MC, V. **Amenities:** Restaurant; bar; TV room and lounge; room service; laundry. *In room:* TV, safe, Internet.

WHERE TO DINE

The best restaurant in Bled is at **Vila Bled** (see "Where to Stay," above). For something more down-home, **Glostnia pri Planincu** ⭑ (Grajska 8; © **04/574-1613**) is so popular you'll have your menu whisked away before you've had a chance to make sense of the Slovenian listings. For a more relaxed atmosphere, head to nearby **Glostina Murka** ⭑ (Riklijeva 9; © **04/574-3340;** www.gostilna-murka.com). Operating since 1909, it offers authentic Slovene cuisine, including barley soup made with dried meat, and traditional pork sausages; veal steak is served with boletus mushrooms; the venison in a juniper berry sauce.

Gostišče Erlah ⭑ SLOVENE Delightfully remote, this relaxed little eatery near Lake Bohinj affords sumptuous mountain views from its covered garden terrace. Menus are on a wooden platter and there's a strong fish bias, with plenty of fresh trout. You can, however, get meatier items, like steak, turkey, or roast sausage (served with cabbage); there's also a mixed grill platter, and even burgers *(pleskavica)* for the kids. Particularly popular is Bohinj's equivalent of surf 'n' turf: the "Ukanc" plate for two comes with meat, pomfret, and vegetables. Remember that Erlah is in the country, so service can be slow—not a problem considering how polite and gentle the staff is.

Ukanc 67, Bohinjsko jezero. © **04/572-3309.** www.erlah.com. Main courses 5.80€–18€ ($7.25–$23). MC, V. Daily noon–10pm.

Planšar *(Value)* BOHINJ This traditional little pension and restaurant is right across from the specialized **Museum of Alpine Dairy Farming** in the small village of Stara Fuzina, just minutes from Lake Bohinj. Renata Mlakak is the lovely hostess, who prepares local specialties that you simply can't get anywhere else. Try the delicious farmer's soup *(ričet)* or cabbage soup *(jota),* both prepared with smoked pork, and the Bohinj cheese and mashed corn with sour cabbage. Save space for homemade *štruklji,* dumplings made with cottage cheese. Renata is also a great source of knowledge about local culture (for many years she worked at the museum) and will happily talk you through the dishes.

Stara Fužina 179, Bohinjsko jezero. © **04/572-3095** or 041-767-254. www.plansar.com. Expect to pay around 4€–8€ ($5–$10) for a hearty meal with beer and dessert. Tues–Sun 10am–8 or 9pm.

WHAT TO SEE & DO

Don't miss either of the lakes (both reviewed below), and allow time to swim if you're here in summer. Both lakes are starting points for rewarding hikes—either right around the lakes themselves or into the valleys and gorges nearby. It may be a serious splurge but consider reserving a scenic flight over the lakes; contact **Alpski Letalski Center** in Lesce (✆ **04/532-0100;** www.alc-lesce.si) to organize a panoramic flight over Bled, Bohinj, and Mount Triglav. Over and above the normal summer chaos, each July sees Bled host **Blejski Dnevi (Bled Days),** a festival that includes music concerts and ends with fireworks and the spectacular sight of thousands of lit candles floating on the lake. Earlier in the same month, there's a highly regarded festival of classical music (www.festivalbled.com). In August, Bled prepares for a lineup of world music entertainments as part of the **Okarina Etno Festival.**

Bled's pseudo-Gothic **St. Martin's Parish Church (Cerkov Svetega Martina)** 🛪 is situated below the Castle, overlooking the Lake. Consecrated in 1905, it is worth visiting for the intriguing interior frescoes by Slavko Pengov (the same artist responsible for the paintings in Tito's former cinema at Vila Bled); in particular look for the clever rendition of the Last Supper, in which Judas has been depicted as none other than Comrade Lenin!

Five kilometers northeast of Bled, the River Radovna has carved the mile-long **Vintgar Gorge** 🛪🛪, one of Slovenia's great natural attractions. Visitors can experience the spectacle of rushing rapids and gushing waterfalls, which include the 13m (43-ft.) Šum Waterfall, by traversing the bridges and walkways put in place since the end of the 19th century, when the gorge was first opened to the public. To get there, leave Bled via Prešerenova cesta, heading toward Podhom (there are plenty of signs), which marks the public entrance; there's a small admission fee. **Babji Zob Caves** 🛪🛪, named for the monstrous-looking "Hag's Tooth" rock formation above them, are some 4km (2½ miles) west of Bled, and require participation in a 3-hour guided tour.

Blejsko Jezero 🛪🛪🛪   Lake Bled is a jewel, pure and simple. Nestled between two great mountain ranges—the Karavanke and the Julian Alps, which tumble into Slovenia from Austria and Italy respectively—there is something indescribably beautiful about the way in which the surface of the water changes through the day, wearing its striking turquoise facade when the sun is brightest, and maturing to a silver-blue as dusk descends. Swans swoop down over its surface, and gondolier-style oarsmen steer their *pletna* across the waters (transporting tourists for an outrageous fee), adding to the fairy-tale idea of the place; occasionally a fierce and noisy rowing regatta changes the energy entirely. To get a good idea of the size of the lake, and to appreciate it from every angle, walk the hour-long route around its perimeter. Adding to the drama of its setting is its darling islet forming a perfect centerpiece: You can row (or be rowed) to **Bled Island (Blejski Otok)** 🛪🛪🛪, but fitter types like to break the "official" rules and swim to it—an utterly invigorating exercise, this is highly recommended if you're a strong swimmer. On the island is the delightful **Church of the Assumption** 🛪🛪, dedicated to both Mary the Virgin and Mary Magdalene, and built on the site where the ancestors of modern Slovenes worshipped an ancient Slavic goddess. The pagan idol was broken down in the 11th century when Slovenes were Christianized. People from all over Slovenia come here to tie the knot on Saturdays, only to discover that the tradition of carrying the bride up the 99 stairs to the church is tough (many grooms, in fact, conduct test runs before the wedding day, in order to avert an embarrassing disaster). Inside the church, look out for the frescoed reference to Christ's circumcision, a

> ### *Tips* Golfing at Bled
>
> Slovenia's top golfing spot, **Bled Golf and Country Club** (www.golf.bled.si), is just 3km (1¾ miles) from the lake, and includes thrilling views; the 18-hole King's Course was laid out by Donald Harradine. Ask your hotel to book your tee time several days ahead of schedule.

seldom seen reminder that Jesus was Jewish. *Note:* If you swim to the island, you won't be able to explore the church unless you ask someone to bring a change of clothing by boat.

Bled. The Church of the Assumption is open to visitors from 8am until sunset.

Blejski Grad ☆   Backed by Mount Triglav and the Julian Alps, the real drama of Bled Castle is its striking position atop a sheer cliff, 138m (460 ft.) up. The castle traces its history back to 1004, and was once the center of an important self-sufficient state measuring 900 sq. km (351 sq. miles), and ruled by the bishops of Brixen. Today it's the most obvious of Bled's attractions, but perhaps a little jaded, housing as it does an uninspiring museum and soulless modern chapel. But there are rewards for making the journey to the top (around 15 min. by foot via three different paths, or 5 min. by car, after which there's still a stiff climb up the final stretch): **Views** ☆☆☆ from the castle ramparts are without equal. There's a restaurant and ice-cream shop at the top.

Rečiška cesta 2, Bled. © **04/578-0525.** www.bled.si. Admission 6.05€ ($7.50) adults, 3€ ($3.75) children ages 4–14. AE, DC, MC, V. Daily 9am–8pm in summer.

Bohinjsko jezero ☆☆☆   Measuring over 4km (2½ miles) long, Bohinj is the largest permanent lake in Slovenia. Because it's inside Triglav National Park, it has been spared the development which has affected Bled, so there's no town on its shores; instead, there are small villages nearby and there's a road connecting its two ends, Ribčev laz and Ukanc, where you'll find a range of accommodations. Visible on the local flag, the **Church of St. John the Baptist** ☆☆, at the head of the lake, near Hotel Jezero, is Bohinj's best-known man-made attraction, mostly built in 1520 and renowned for its interior frescoes. For heart-stopping views of Bohinj and the Julian Alps, take the cable car up **Mount Vogel,** or head for the **Vodnikov razglednik viewpoint.** Bohinj's Tourist Association can suggest walks to bring you closer to the lake's many charms. From Ukanc, you can hike to **Savica Falls,** the best-known of Slovenia's 260 waterfalls, immortalized in France Prešeren's epic poem, *Baptism on the Savica,* published in 1836, and dedicated to his friend who drowned in the Sava a year before. The two-pronged waterfall measures 51m (167 ft.); the gushing water comes from Black Lake (Črno jezero) half a kilometer farther up. There's a small fee to be paid at the entrance to the path leading to a wooden pavilion that offers the best views of the falls.

Bohinjsko jezero. © **04/574-6010.** www.bohinj.si/tdbohinj.

ADVENTURES IN & AROUND THE LAKES

Bled's **Lifetrek Adventures** ☆ (© **04/578-0662;** www.lifetrek-slovenia.com) offers a variety of water- and mountain-based adventures to meet your level of experience. **3Glav Adventures** (© **041-683-184;** www.explore-more.com) targets a younger crowd.

VršičPass: From Bled to the Soča Valley ⭐⭐⭐

Slovenia's best drive traverses **VršičPass,** an awesome journey between Kranjska Gora, just north of Triglav National Park, over Mount Vršič, and down to the town of Trenta. The intense drive takes you through beautiful views of soaring rocky peaks and lush, plunging valleys. It's the most spectacular way of traveling the otherwise short distance between Bled and the Soča Valley, but requires cautious driving to negotiate 50 numbered hairpin bends along the 25km (16-mile) roller-coaster route. At bend number eight, the **Ruska kapelica (Russian Chapel)** honors the 300 odd Russian prisoners of war who died in an avalanche while building the road; near bend 21 is the **cemetery** for the thousands more who died during construction, often starved or tortured to death. There are great viewing sites along the way; the highest point (at 1,611m/5,284 ft.) is **Vršič,** where there's a parking fee. Be aware that the road can be alarmingly narrow; some drivers speed in spite of this. Cows and sheep may stumble across the way; cyclists, too, are ubiquitous, but usually more alert.

Skiing around Bohinj is arguably the best in the country from a scenic point of view. Cable cars whisk passengers from the western end of Lake Bohinj to **Ski Center Vogel,** from where there are chairlifts for skiers wishing to access some of the higher reaches of the Triglav Mountain range. **Alpinsport** (ⓒ 04/572-3486; www.alpinsport.si) is the place to hire an instructor and ski equipment. Besides offering scenic flights, **Alpski Letalski Center** (www.alc-lesce.si) runs gliding courses in two-seater and Alpine gliders, and Cessna flying courses for beginners. If you'd rather feel the wind beneath your feet, ask Alpski to arrange a tandem parachuting jump from 3,000m (9,840 ft.); you'll be enjoying the same perfect free-falling views enjoyed by jumpers during the world parachuting championships. **Pac Sports** (ⓒ 04/572-3461; www.pac-sports.com) is the place to call if you feel like a spot of tandem paragliding instead: same breathtaking views but a lot less scary.

THE SOČA VALLEY: KOBARID & BOVEC

A haven for adventurers, the valley formed by the electric turquoise advance of the Soča—one of Europe's loveliest rivers—is scintillating. This part of the country is blessed with gorgeous mountain views, splendid towns, plenty of well-organized sports outfitters, and a people who are as charming as they are relaxed. It may be Slovenia's least developed region, with a dwindling population of just 19,000 (generally due to overeducation!), but it is likely to provide many of the defining moments of your visit to Slovenia. Kobarid is at the heart of the more exclusive and developed portion of the valley, offering its best accommodations, and two of the country's finest restaurants. Slightly north of Kobarid, Bovec is one of the prime adventure resorts in Slovenia; it's an excellent ski resort and ideal for access to the Soča River, which hosts a number of international rafting competitions. The valley is also great for biking, with extreme cycling races held around Bovec—and given the enchanting topography, a wonderful place to observe from the air.

GETTING THERE

From Bled and Bohinj, the most exciting way to get to Bovec or Kobarid is by driving over the VršičPass, via the Kranjska Gora winter resort; there is also a bus that traverses the pass at a very gentle speed.

ESSENTIALS

Kobarid's Tourist Information Office (Gregorčičeva 8; ✆ **05/380-0490;** www. lto-sotocje.si) is very helpful. **Bovec Tourist Information Centre** (Trg golobarskih žrtev 8; ✆ **05/389-6444;** www.bovec.si) is largely geared toward providing information about sports activities, but will also help you find accommodations.

WHERE TO STAY

Dodra Vila Bovec 🏶🏶   This handsome villa in Bovec offers a touch of class in a town that's generally geared more toward sporty types than those who prefer their adventures wrapped in elegance. It's easily the most gracious place in town, where, after a grueling day on the slopes, you can kick back in a wine cellar, a private in-house cinema, or a library-style drawing room that's perfect for a glass of Slovene wine in front of the fireplace. There's also a smart restaurant where fresh trout is always a sure thing. Guest rooms are big and bright with high ceilings and dark wood floors; crisp white linens and beautiful bathrooms score high points. Should you be tempted to leave the villa's pleasing comforts, your hostess, Andreja, and her staff can help you book a variety of activities, from horseback-riding to sky diving.

Mala vas 112, 5230 Bovec. ✆ **05/389-6400/3.** Fax 05/389-6404. www.dobra-vila-bovec.com. 12 units. 110€ ($138) double. Rates include breakfast and taxes. **Amenities:** Restaurant; wine cellar; laundry; library; sports and adventure activities; rooftop viewing area; computer access; cinema. *In room:* TV, minibar, DVD player, Internet.

Hiša Franko Casa 🏶🏶🏶 *Value*   Just 3km (1¾ miles) west of Kobarid, on the way to the Italian border, Hiša Franko is pure delight—the creative expression of husband-and-wife team Ana Roš and Valter Kramar. Gorgeous, simple, and dramatic, each guest room is designed to a particular color theme, and offers slick comfort. Choosing a favorite is difficult as each unit has a different shape and design, but all offer wooden floors, smart furniture, silk drapes, and plenty of space. Room nos. 9 and 10 share an amazing enclosed terrace with a chill-out lounge vibe, where you can relax on clever armchairs that light up. With the emphasis firmly on relaxation, there are no telephones, and you need to specify if you'd like to have a television or sound system in your room. A recommended outing is a picnic lunch at Nadia River, which has Slovenia's cleanest and warmest water, naturally heated by white riverbed rocks.

Staro selo 1, 5222 Kobarid. ✆ **05/389-4120.** Fax 05/389-4129. www.hisafranko.com. 10 units. Aug 8–Apr 20 and Oct 1–Dec 25: 90€–113€ ($113–$141) double; Apr 20–Oct 1 and Dec 25–Jan 8: 96€–119€ ($120–$149) double. Rates include breakfast. 21€ ($26) extra bed; 7€ ($8.75) cot; 1.10€ ($1.40) tax. 6€–7€ ($7.50–$8.75) discount per night for stays of 3 days or more. **Amenities:** Restaurant; bar; wine cellar; room service; laundry; bike rental; picnic arrangements; library and CD collection. *In room:* Minibar; TV, hi-fi, hair dryer all by request.

Hotel Hvala 🏶 *Value*   What started as a family restaurant in 1976 recently celebrated its first decade. A great three-floor hotel, this is the best place to stay in the center of Kobarid. The spotless accommodations have toothpaste-white walls and straightforward modern furniture. Guest rooms also have balconies and good-size bathrooms, most of which have tubs. While the main focus is on the extremely popular downstairs restaurant, your hosts will take excellent care of you, treating you like a guest in their home, and helping you get in touch with your adventurous side through one of the local activity companies, X Point.

Trg svobode 1, 5222 Kobarid. ✆ **05/389-9300.** Fax 05/388-5322. www.topli-val-sp.si. 31 units. 90€ ($113) double; 125€ ($156) family room; 135€ ($169) suite; 30% discount for children under 12. Rates include breakfast. **Amenities:** Restaurant; bar; sauna; room service; laundry; bike rental; fishing; adventure-activity assistance. *In room:* TV, hair dryer.

Nebesa ★★★ *(Finds* Nebesa means "Heaven," and it isn't much of an exaggeration, with each of the four private guesthouses, overlooking Kobarid and the Soča Valley, feeling as though it's on the edge of the world. Built in wood, with steeply pitched roofs, the little cottages are designed as a contemporary take on traditional mountain hay-houses. All things considered, they're perfect; the minimalist interiors (wooden floors and smart, simple contemporary furniture) draw attention to the large picture windows that frame those astonishing views you get from the lounge and the upstairs sleeping area. Each unit also has a porch, from which you can play god to the valley below. You also have your own kitchen with a fridge that's stocked for your basic needs. Guests have access to a communal dining area and kitchen, as well as a sauna, fitness room (with meditation and yoga areas). There's a sublime help-yourself cellar with on-tap house wine and prosciutto that you are welcome to shave yourself. From up here, you can see Italy and even feel a sea breeze from the gulf; the neighboring property is home to 30 deer, one of which is tame enough to come when called. What's more, your hosts epitomize Slovene hospitality and will introduce you to the truly debonair spirit of the nation.

Livek39, 5222 Kobarid. ✆ 05/384-4620. www.nebesa.si. 4 units. 220€ ($275) per guesthouse; 198€ ($248) per night 2-day stay. Rates are all-inclusive. **Amenities:** Dining room w/kitchen; wine cellar; wellness center w/pool, sauna, and yoga area; laundry. *In room:* Kitchen (fridge, stove, oven, kettle, toaster), hi-fi.

WHERE TO DINE

Hiša Franko ★★★ EXPERIMENTAL You haven't dined in Slovenia until you've tried this hugely innovative restaurant just outside Kobarid. Making magic in the kitchen is Ana Roš, who gave up her career as a national skier when she fell in love, and then discovered a passion for food. Ana's imagination inspires a regularly changing menu, which might include such dishes as "deer filet on a Cuba chocolate with fresh mint, lime, and mushroom" or "trout filet in green tea and jasmine flower crust with an orange salad." If it's available, try the suckling pig, served with rhubarb chutney and almond pâté; it's absolute bliss. As are the desserts, like fresh fig salad in sweet spices and red-wine jus with white chocolate foam and toasted almonds. Running the wine department is Ana's lovely husband, Valter Kramar, who trained extensively at Italy's Gradisca d'Isonzo, and knows his wines. He's been cultivating a stellar cellar for years, so this is one meal where you should splurge on a few of his five-star rated wines.

Casa Hiša Franko, Staro Selo 1. ✆ 05/389-4120. www.hisafranko.com. Main courses 12€–16€ ($15–$20); side dishes 2.90€ ($3.65). Cover charge 2.50€ ($3.15). AE, DC, MC, V. Wed–Sun noon–3pm and 7–10pm.

Topli Val ★★★ SEAFOOD This is one of the finest seafood restaurants in central Europe; no wonder regular diners come from across the border to join in the feasting that's best enjoyed on the small terrace on warm summer nights. Do yourself a favor: Ignore the menu and ask what's hot. You'll be served wonderful creations dreamed up by Vlado Hvala, the patriarch in this family business, who still rules the kitchen after 3 decades. To start there may be fresh scampi with shredded crab, or kabob-style skewered prawns. Then move on to whatever fish of the day is recommended; fresh from the Adriatic, it'll be baked in salt for maximum flavor. If you want to sample everything, share the gourmet platter; it includes lobster, sea bass, scallops, mussels, and fish kabobs. Order a bottle of perfect, dry Brda četrtičFerdinand Belo (2002) to go with your meal. Finish with hot blueberries and ice cream, or the famous *Kobariški struklji*, with ice cream and cinnamon.

In the Hotel Hvala, Trg svobode 1. ✆ 05/389-9300. Main courses 7€–28€ ($8.75–$35). AE, DC, MC, V. Dec–Jan and Mar 15–Oct noon–3pm and 7–10pm.

WHAT TO SEE & DO

Practically on the Italian border, Kobarid is known for the Battle of Kobarid (or Caporetto) which happened here on October 24, 1917, and is considered a key moment in World War I. Pick up a map from the **Tourist Information Office** (Gregorčičeva 8; *C* **05/380-0490;** www.lto-sotocje.si) and set out on the **Kobarid Historical Walk** ⚔⚔⚔, a 3- to 5-hour trail that takes you to some key war sites, and surveys some of the loveliest natural phenomena in the area, including the Kozjak Brook Waterfalls; at one point you'll cross the Soča River on a 52m (171-ft.) suspension bridge. A lovely way to spend the morning, the walk starts at the award-winning Kobarid Museum (reviewed below), considered one of the best of its kind in Europe.

Kobariski Muzej ⚔⚔ Kobarid Museum is an antiwar museum designed to illustrate the senselessness of war. Several rooms, spread over three floors, are filled with war-related paraphernalia, photographs, and excerpts from journals and letters. On the first floor, The Black Room includes horrible photographs of survivors who were savaged by weapons of war. One man shown in profile has lost his nose and upper jaw—left with half his face, he is a dreadful irony juxtaposed with the display beneath of military medals and badges. Nearby, more grotesque photographs of mangled, skeletal war victim corpses are displayed over a number of defunct, "dead" weapons that may very well have been used in their slaughter. Much of the museum deals with the role played by Kobarid during World War I, and some of the displays (particularly those on the ground floor) don't make much sense. There is a 20-minute video, but you'll need to ask when the English version is to be screened.

Gregorčičeva 10. *C* 05/389-0000. www.kobariski-muzej.si. 4€ ($5) adults, seniors, and students; 2.50€ ($3.15) young children. Apr–Sept: Mon–Fri 9am-6pm; Sat–Sun and public holidays 9am–7pm. Oct–Mar: Mon–Fri 10am-5pm; Sat–Sun and public holidays 9am-6pm.

OUTDOOR ACTIVITIES IN THE SOČA VALLEY

Outdoor adventures are usually high on the list of priorities of visitors to this region; in winter there's great skiing, while in summer climbing, hiking, and river-based activities are among the best in the country. One of the top all-round outfits in the Soča Valley is Kobarid-based **X Point** ⚔⚔⚔ (Stresova 1; *C* **05/388-5308** or 041-692-290; www.xpoint.si), which offers rafting, kayaking, paragliding, canoeing, hydrospeeding, canyoning, trekking, and mountain-biking excursions; the company can also set you up with one of five good ski instructors. Ask owner Dejan Luzar about the company's multi-activity packages.

CANYONING   X Point has excursions (all equipment included) for different levels of experience; some outings last up to 8 or 9 hours and cost around 100€ ($125).

HORSEBACK RIDING You can ride Lipizzaners in the Soča Valley through **Pristana Lepena** (www.pristava-lepena.com).

MOUNTAIN BIKING Bovec's bike specialists are **Outdoor Freaks** (Klanc 9a; *C* **05/389-64/90** or 041-553-675; www.freakoutdoor.com). They can rent you a suitable mountain bike and put you onto a number of trails in the **Kanin mountain bike park** (www.mtbparkkanin.com), which opened in 2003.

PARAGLIDING   Avantura (*C* **041-718-317;** bovecavantura@hotmail.com) offers tandem paragliding in Bovec. **X Point** offers first-time courses as well as tandem jumps (85€/$106). Skiers should inquire about a combination package in which you paraglide from 1,800m (5,904 ft.) after being on the slopes.

RAFTING & KAYAKING X Point (see above) offers all-inclusive rafting excursions, with some four rapids (33€/$41 per person, including transfers); you'll spend some 90 minutes on the water. Also offered by X Point, **Hydrospeeding** is a less taxing option, which involves wearing a wet suit and gripping a hand-held navigational board as the current sweeps you down the river.

SKIING & SNOWBOARDING High-altitude skiing in the Kanin Mountains is popular and rewarding. Cable cars take you into the mountain ski areas from **Ski center ATC Kanin** (Dvor 43; ℂ 05/389-6310; 11€/$14), just beyond Bovec. The circular cabin cableway offers hourly departures from the ski center starting at 8am; the half-hour ascent takes you an altitude of 2,200m (7,216 ft.), from where there's skiing in winter (Dec 20 to early May) and fantastic hiking in summer. There's a separate Information Office (Trg golobarskih rtev 47; ℂ **05/389-6003;** Mon–Fri 8am–noon and 1–4:30pm, Sat–Sun and holidays 8am–noon). Note that while out-of-bounds skiing is a possibility, it is dangerous, as navigation in the Kanin is difficult. **X Point** can design a skiing program that takes in three different sets of slopes—on Kanin, Kranjska Gora, and Vogel.

5 The Karst & Slovenia's Tiny Sliver of Coast

An ancient word meaning "stone," Slovenia is where the word "Karst" was first coined, and refers to a rocky limestone plateau that links the Soča Valley to Slovenia's tiny piece of Istrian coast. Here you'll find spectacular cave systems, the best of which are the UNESCO-protected Škocjan caves; nearby is Lipica Stud Farm, where the glamorous Lipizzaner horses are sired.

Slovenia's Istrian coast stretches from the bottom edge of the Karst in the north to the Dragonja River in the south, which creates the border with Croatia; this 46km (29-mile) coastline has been a refuge for people since the 7th century, when the Roman Empire collapsed, and the first olive groves and vineyards were established by people fleeing marauders from the east. During the 13th century, these coastal principalities looked to Venice for protection, and so began 500 years of Venetian rule, a period that has imbued the port towns with a distinctive look and attitude that still today make this region a most pleasant sojourn, and possibly the ideal entry into Croatia.

POSTOJNA & ŠKOCJAN CAVES

Slovenia's "Karst" landscape has hundreds of subterranean caves. Two of the most fascinating (and best-exploited) cave systems are Postojna and Škocjan, both filled with unbelievable limestone formations, and colored by different minerals, the result of thousands of years of rainwater seeping through the surface of the earth into the underground chambers. Over the eons, these drops of water have caused stalactites and stalagmites to mushroom throughout these vast otherworldly spaces where underground rivers, secret lakes, immense tunnels, and rock-hard formations that look like melted wax form the backdrop against which an unusual albino creature has evolved in almost complete isolation from life above the earth's surface.

ESSENTIALS

Postojna is situated roughly midway between Ljubljana and the Slovenian coast. Take the Ljubljana-Koper Highway, and follow the signs at Postojna. **Škocjan** is much nearer the coast, also easily reached using the highway. Trains from Ljubljana reach Postojna and Divača, near Škocjan. There is parking and information at the entrances to both sets of caves.

Stellar Accommodations En Route to the Caves

Postojna can be visited as a half-day trip from Ljubljana, and Škocjan is near the coastal city of Piran. If you're traveling to either of the caves from anywhere in the Julian Alps, consider breaking up the journey with a night at **Kendov Dvorec** ★★★ (www.kendov-dvorec.com), a 14th-century manor situated roughly midway between Kobarid and Postojna. Accommodations are some of the most refined in the country, with just 11 luxurious guest rooms, furnished with smart antiques; doubles range from 126€ to 205€ ($158–$256).

WHAT TO SEE & DO IN THE KARST

Postojnska Jama ★   Visited by more than 30 million people, the famous Postojna Cave has been an official tourist site since 1818; graffiti signatures prove it's been attracting visitors since the 13th century. The largest of the classic Karst cave systems, with a network of over 20km (12 miles) of chambers and galleries connected by passages and tunnels, this is, quite frankly, the Disneyland of caves, complete with a little tourist train, which each day propels thousands of noisy people through an artificial tunnel and into the heart of the cave system. Visitors then divide into groups on the basis of language (a terribly time-consuming process) before being led off on a tour of Postojna's most representative and exotic chambers; there are galleries with such telling names as Beautiful Cave, the Gothic Hall, and the Brilliant Passage. All in all though, it's a remarkable journey, with a second train trip that gets you even deeper into the system. Along the way, you'll also see the unusual "human fish," a salamander-type creature, or olm *(Proteus anguinus)*, that's blind and the color of Caucasian flesh, hence its fanciful nickname. Note that the caves are chilly (46°F–50°F/8°C–10°C), and walking surfaces slippery; bring something warm and wear nonslip shoes.

Jamska cesta 30, Postojna. © 05/700-0103. www.postojna-cave.si. Admission 16€ ($20) adults; 12€ ($15) seniors and students; 10€ ($13) children. Scheduled cave tours Jan–Mar and Nov–Dec 10am, noon, and 2pm; Apr and Oct 10am, noon, 2, and 4pm; May–Sept every hour, on the hour, 9am–6pm.

Predjama Castle ★★ *Kids*   A mere 10km (6¼ miles) from Postojna, the medieval Predjamski grad is dramatically situated on a 123m (403-ft.) cliff carved into the rock face. Legend has it that this was the hide-out of Slovenia's very own Robin Hood, named Erazem, who was more likely a rebellious thieving baron. Erazem incurred the intense hatred of the governor of Trieste, who laid siege to the castle, before cannonballing it and killing Erazem in 1484. Predjama remains a spectacular sight, perched defiantly against its rocky backdrop; very much the stuff that medieval fantasies are made of. Although the castle's curators have given the interiors a whitewashed museum feel, it's worth getting a ticket to explore inside, if only for the exhilarating views from its stone windows and balconies. Today, reliving the pomp and ceremony of the past is the annual Erazem's Medieval Tournament, with jousting scenes and costumes straight out of *A Knight's Tale;* the event happens in August.

Predjamski grad. © 05/751-6015. www.postojna-cave.si. 5€ ($6.25) adults, 3.50€ ($4.40) seniors and students, 2.90€ ($3.65) children. Combined ticket for Postojna and Predjama saves you 2€ ($2.50). Guided tour available for a small fee. Nov–Mar 10am–4pm; Apr and Oct 10am–6pm; May–Sept 9am–7pm.

Škocjan Caves ★★★ *Value*   Far more alluring and peaceful than Postojna, cave exploration doesn't get much better than this. Škocjan is where the first Karstic discoveries were made, and the caves have been spared the onslaught of tourism thanks to the protection of UNESCO. So, no intrusive miniature trains or Disneyland adventure-park atmosphere; here there's a real sense of exploration. Moving through the 3km (1¾-mile) subterranean system (which includes rigorous stairways), you almost sense the voidlike drama of Silent Cave, and become increasingly aware of the subdued roar of the Murmuring Cave, coming from the underground Reka River. Besides spectacular stalactites, stalagmites, and rim limestone pools (resembling those in Pamukkale in Turkey), Škocjan includes what is believed to be the world's largest underground canyon, as well as awesome bridges and drop-away galleries where the vastness of the subterranean world (at one point you're told the parking lot is 140m/459 ft. above your head) undoes everything you think you know about the earth. (*Tip:* While you wait for your tour to begin, don't miss the Belvedere Viewpoint, overlooking a magnificent gorge with a small waterfall.)

Park Škocjanske jame, Škocjan 2, Divača. ✆ **05/708-2100** or 05/763-2840. www.park-skocjan-jame.si. Admission 22€ ($14) adults, 7.50€ ($9.40) seniors and students, 4.15€ ($5.25) children, free for children under 6. Purchase tickets 30 min. before tour. June–Sept hourly guided tours daily 10am–5pm; Nov–Mar guided tours Mon–Sat 10am and 1pm, Sun and public holidays also at 3pm; Apr–May and Oct guided tours daily 10am, 1pm, and 3:30pm.

Lipica Stud Farm & Riding Center ⟨⟩ Lipizzaners, bred here since 1580, are arguably the most intelligent horse breed; certainly their combination of strength and agility has turned them into excellent "dancers," able to perform a number of leaps and pirouettes in choreographed formations to the beat of music. Enthusiasts can visit the stables and watch a **dressage performance** ⟨⟩⟨⟩ (you'll need to call ahead to check when these happen) or arrange to ride one of these magnificent beasts.

Lipica 5, Sežana. ✆ **05/739-1580.** www.lipica.org. Stable and farm tours Nov–Mar 11am, 1pm, 2pm, and 3pm; Apr–June and Sept–Oct hourly 10am–5pm except at noon; July–Aug hourly 9am–6pm except at noon.

PIRAN & THE ISTRIAN COAST
Piran is 120km (74 miles) SW of Ljubljana

Piran is easily the loveliest place along Slovenia's tiny slither of Istrian Coast, drawing inevitable comparisons with Venice which—after 500 years of rule—it echoes in many ways; only here there are no canals—the entire city is built on dry land, rising to a low hill, along which defensive walls are built. Within walking distance of Piran is the modern seaside playground of **Portorož,** with its strutting crowds and concrete resort hotels. Popular with pleasure-seekers and always crowded during the peak summer months, it may be a worthwhile clubbing spot if you grow weary of Piran's more restrained nighttime tavern activity. North you'll find two more Italianate ports, Koper and Izola, neither of which are nearly as nice of Piran.

ESSENTIALS
While it's an easy drive along the highway from Ljubljana, getting into Piran itself can be a nuisance. If you're driving, you'll need to leave your car in the town's parking lot, just beyond the city limits, which is controlled by boom gates; from here there's a regular shuttle bus to transport you between the parking area and the town center. (You can enter Piran with your vehicle, but you're charged rather heavily for the time you spend on its few cramped roads, and you can forget about finding parking.)

Buses to Piran terminate at the **bus station** (Dantejeva ulica), located just outside the town proper; a short walk around Piran Port, along Cankarjevo nabrežje, takes you to Tartinijeva trg, at the town center. Trains from Ljubljana terminate in Koper, 10km (6¼ miles) northeast of Piran. Piran's helpful **Tourist Information Office** is in the

City Hall building (Tartinijev trg 2; ℭ **05/673-4440**). The students who work there can help you with most anything, including trips to **Izola, Hrastovlje,** and **Sečovlje Salt-pans Nature Park,** recommended if you have time.

WHERE TO STAY

Historic Piran is where you should base yourself, but there are no luxurious options here. If you need your pampering there are numerous upmarket modern resorts with spa facilities that line the waterfront at nearby Portoroz; of these **Grand Hotel Palace** (www.hoteli-palace.si) is the best option. Back in Piran, serious budget-hunters may be interested to hear of good-value **Val Hostel** (Gregorčičeva 38a; ℭ **05/673-2555; www.hostel-val.com**), offering accommodations in two-, three-, and four-bed rooms for 20€ to 24€ ($25–$30) per person, breakfast included; facilities are shared, but clean.

Hotel Tartini ⍟ This classic hotel gets a star for its great position right on Tartini Square—which is why it's usually full in summer months. Other than this it's a fairly standard place with a slightly ramshackle feel; the atrium-style lobby was actually once a road, the hotel having been constructed from two separate houses that were on different sides of the street. The best thing about Tartini is the view of Piran's rooftops afforded by climbing to the gazebo above the second-floor terrace where, until recently, there was a pool. Guest rooms are neat, clean, and dull, with furniture that's somewhere between *The Jetsons* and the 1980s. Tartini offers free parking for guests.

Tartinijev trg 15, 6330 Piran. ℭ **05/671-1666.** Fax 05/671-1665. www.hotel-tartini-piran.com. 45 units. 106€–112€ ($133–$140) high season double; 88€–94€ ($110–$118) midseason double; 70€–76€ ($88–$95) low season double; 122€–187€ ($153–$234) suite. Rates include breakfast. Tax 1€ ($1.25). **Amenities:** Restaurant; breakfast room; bar; cafe; terrace; room service; laundry; meeting room. *In room:* A/C, TV, Wi-Fi, minibar.

Max Hotel *(Finds* In a pink four-story building at the high end of the town right near St. George's Church, this is a lovely addition to the local accommodations scene. More guesthouse than hotel, it's filled with thoughtful touches and is more intimate than any other option in town (you're handed a front-door key and reminded of the importance of an afternoon siesta). Some serious stairs lead up to six simply furnished but immaculate guest rooms. These too have pink walls, with small, original paintings and shuttered windows affording great views of the local cobblestone neighborhood (better the higher up you stay). There's a quaint breakfast room downstairs with books and relaxing music: Friendly proprietor Max goes out early each morning to bring home fresh ingredients. Well located, away from the tourist bonhomie, Max is near Piran's nicest beach areas (including a little nudist spot) yet close to Tartini square.

Ulica IX korpusa 26, 6330 Piran. ℭ **05/673-3436** or 041-692-928. www.maxpiran.com. 6 units. 70€ ($88) double high season (New Year and July–Aug); 60€ $75 double off season. **Amenities:** Breakfast room; laundry. *In room:* Fan.

WHERE TO DINE

Avoid the dozen or so tourist-trap restaurants that line Piran's waterfront. If you want a break from the excellent food at Neptun, head for Izola's harborside Ribič.

Neptun ⍟⍟⍟ SEAFOOD Away from the crowds and away from the main drag, Neptun is in an intimate white space with exposed wood beams from which fishing nets are draped. Members of the Grilj family (who've worked the kitchen and tables since 1994) offer a warm, inviting atmosphere, and charm guests with polite reminders that everything is fresh and therefore requires some preparation time. No matter; you'll be provided with homemade bread, sardine filets, and homemade fish pâté while you wait. Ordering is easy: Ask for catch of the day, grilled and served with fried potatoes. Simple, straightforward, and utterly delicious. If you want something slightly richer, consider the "Neptun" fish filet, prepared with cream and pepper, but be sure to leave room for the unforgettable chocolate mousse.

Župančičeva 7. ⓒ 05/673-4111. Most dishes are 7€–15€ ($8.75–$19). MC, V. Daily noon–4pm and 6pm–midnight.

EXPLORING PIRAN

Occupying a horn-shaped promontory, Piran is a rambling rabbit warren of narrow cobblestone streets, back alleys, and squares. Small as it is, Piran is packed with detail, and there's lots to explore even if you do nothing more than wander around looking for emblematic references to Venice, like the famous winged lion of St. Mark you'll find on buildings all over the city. For a full-on view of the town, start at its inland perimeter wall on Mogoron Hill. These **defensive walls** are believed to date from as far back as the 7th century, attaining their present form in the 16th century; today you can climb up the Gothic towers and look back at the town and Piran Bay. Down below, the town's center is marked by **Tartinijev trg (Tartini Sq.),** which celebrates the Piran-born violinist and composer Giuseppe Tartini (1692–1770), whose bronze effigy rises in the center of this marbled public space. At the southern edge of the square is **Hotel Tartini,** while the lovely 19th-century **City Hall,** the most impressive building here, is to the north. To the south of the square is **Piran Port,** where hundreds of boats and yachts are docked in the small harbor formed by a curve in the Piran promontory.

All around the square alleyways lead into a jumbled web of fascinating back streets; facing the square from the northeast is the red facade of the lovely old **Venetian House,** which marks one of the many narrow streets leading up to Piran's quaint tangle of churches, including the lovely **Minorite Convent** and its early-14th-century **Church of St. Francis of Assissi;** in summer, concerts are held in the convent courtyard. Along the northern wall is **St. George's Church,** rising above the sea-facing cliff walls. At St. George's (undergoing long-winded restoration), you can climb the church tower for splendid panoramas, and visit the adjacent **Baptistery.** Then, continuing along Admaičeva ulica, you'll head back down to Piran's concrete **bathing area,** full of tourists in summer. Continuing west, you'll reach the tip of the Piran promontory, marked by the **Punta Lighthouse** and by **St. Clement's Church.** From the lighthouse, the promenade formed by Prešernovo nabrežje leads back toward the **Tartini Theater** at Piran Port, passing a slew of seafood restaurants in quaint Italianate houses on the one side, and the Adriatic's Gulf of Piran on the other; all along this concrete coast, bathers find a spot to sunbathe or dive into the warmish waters.

While there are plenty of places to stop for a drink, the most fun (and least expensive) has got to be the semidingy **Kantina Zizola** (9am until very late), in a corner of Tartini Square. There are a few outside tables, and inside there's a strong maritime theme as well as a photo of Robert De Niro, who apparently stopped by here in 2004.

SHOPPING

Visit the studio of artist and artisan **Marko Jezernik (Studio Šterna;** Bolniška 8; www.jezernik-sp.si) for some alternative reminders of your trip. Besides propagating Piran's alternative lifestyle—"essential," he says, "for the artist"—Marko sells satirical paintings, quirky T-shirts, and books of textual and visual impressions of life inspired by the perfect isolation of Piran; you can also pick up one of his idiosyncratic painted beehive panels. As a spirited nonconformist, Marko opens when he feels like it.

On Tartini trg, in the Venetian House, visit the stylish outlet of the Sečovlje Salt-mine, **Piranske Soline** (© **05/673-3110;** www.soline.si), one of the country's more unusual stores where you can purchase cosmetic salt, salted chocolate, and coarse sea salt, all beautifully packaged.

6 Exploring Eastern Slovenia

Slovenes tell us that a few years back, **Celje,** the country's third-largest city, was the fastest growing in Europe. Whether or not this is true, it suggests just how much room for growth there is east of Ljubljana. Though Celje itself does not hold much to interest the first-time visitor it's worth setting aside a few days in July to visit neighboring **Laško** ✹, a gorgeous town that holds a weeklong celebration in honor of its main product: beer—don't miss this lively festival if want to witness Slovenia's penchant for polka bands, street parades, and all-night merrymaking. Other than this, three destinations beckon: the salubrious riverside university town of **Maribor,** whose citizens seem entirely given over to idling in cafes and soaking up the atmosphere along its tiny waterfront; **Ptuj,** once a Roman stronghold; and, farther east, the vineyards along the peaceful **Jeruzalem Wine Route** (easily taken in as a day trip from Ptuj or Maribor).

There's a congenial air about **Maribor** (www.maribor-tourism.si), Slovenia's second-largest city. Straddling both banks of the River Drava, with its historic center to the north, Maribor evolved as a market town in the early 13th century. Today Maribor is a pleasant university town; its position at the foot of Pohorje Mountain, garlanded by winegrowing hills, giving it an idyllic aspect. The Drava itself has plenty of spots for swimming, fishing, and even sailing, while south of the center, Zgornje Radvanje is a base for mountain activities in the Maribor Pohorje ski resort.

It's worth climbing to the top of the **Cathedral Tower,** located in the historic center, to get a bird's-eye impression from the wraparound viewing platform, then exploring **Vinag Wine Cellar** ✹✹ (Vinagova klet, behind the recently renovated City Castle; © **02/220-8111;** www.vinag.si); comprising 2km (1¼ miles) of subterranean caves that run right beneath the city, the cellar provides storage for up to 5.5 million liters of wine. South of the castle is **Grajski trg,** a pedestrian cafe haunt, where flea marketers operate at weekends. Head south past more shops and bars to reach the city's main square, **Glavni trg,** fringed by lovely architecture and centered on Straub's majestic 18th-century **Plague Monument.** For many, the highlight of Maribor is a ramble along the waterfront promenade, centered on a small, salubrious area known as **Lent** ✹✹, the city's principal docking port before the arrival of the railway in 1862. Lent is defined by its pleasant bars and cafes, but the most famous attraction here is the **Stara Trta,** at 400 years supposedly the world's oldest living vine, and the June **Lent Festival** ✹✹✹.

From Maribor, **Ptuj** ✹✹✹ (pronounced pit-*ooey*) is a short drive along bucolic back roads. Called Poetovio by the Romans, Ptuj (www.ptuj-tourism.si) became a town in 977; with its hilltop castle and cobblestone streets, it feels every bit the medieval stone-walled fortress. Like Maribor, Ptuj straddles the banks of the River Drava; the Romans put greater Ptuj on the map when they grew the population to 40,000, transforming it into one of the largest provinces in the Empire, an important trade point along the road linking the Mediterranean and Baltic seas. Today, the population has dropped to 20,000, but its Roman and medieval heritage continue to lend it considerable charm. Ptuj's Gothic-era **City Tower** marks **Slovenski trg,** at the heart of the old town. Near the foot of the tower is the **Orpheus Monument,** a 2nd-century Roman tombstone used as a medieval pillory to which wrongdoers were tied and ridiculed by the towns-folk. Behind the tower is the Gothic **St. George Parish Church.** Just beyond the church is the **market,** and nearby—on Mestni trg—the century-old **City Hall.** Beyond the square, along Kremplijeva ulica, is the **Minorite Monastery;** ring the buzzer marked "Župnijska pisarna," and a monk will arrive to take you on a tour. In summer classical concerts are occasionally held in the large open courtyard. Several routes lead up to the town's main attraction, 11th-century **Ptuj Castle** ⋆ (www.pok-muzej-ptuj.si), overlooking the city and affording panoramic views of the surround-ing landscape; you can drive or walk up the steep cobbled pathways, or take the signposted steps from Prešernova ulica. Call ahead to book a guide (© **02/748-0360**).

Usually quiet, even empty, Ptuj comes to life each year on Shrove Sunday, when 50,000 people gather for the **Kurentovanje Festival** ⋆⋆⋆, when revelers take to the streets in their startling Kurent masks and fantastical traditional costumes in an out-rageous pagan celebration that is traditionally an attempt to magically stave off win-ter, but is today an awesome excuse for a raucous party.

WHERE TO STAY & DINE

You'll probably want to bed down in either Maribor or Ptuj, and there aren't a whole lot of options. Note that you can also stay along the Jeruzalem Wine Route.

IN MARIBOR   Hotel **Piramida** (© **02/234-4400;** www.termembe.si; 94€–132€/ $118–$165 double) is a bright, modern, professional business hotel just a few minutes' walk from Maribor's main drag. The room rate includes access to a recreational spa (pools, Turk-ish baths, saunas) just outside town. **Hotel Orel** (© **02/250-6700;** www.termemb.si; 70€–86€/$88–$108 double) is a newly renovated, simple hotel in a lovely historic building over-looking the main square.

Maribor has two excellent restaurants. **Novi Svet pri Stolnici** ⋆⋆⋆ (Slomškov trg 6; © **02/250-0486**) is a top choice for seafood from the Dalmatian coast; try the sole *(morski list)* with truffle sauce or share the "Fish Feast" *(ribja pojedina "Novi Svet"),* a seafood platter for two. **Toti Rotovž** ⋆⋆⋆ (Glavni trg 14; © **02/228-7650;** www.mednarodne-kuhinje.com), has a massive subterranean cellar that dates from 1874. The international menu has a strong Slovene bias, highlighted by great choices like filet of red scorpionfish with truffles, roast veal, escalope of wild boar, and grilled squid. Finish with sour cherry strudel, and be sure to order a bottle of local Vinag wine.

IN PTUJ   In a fine building on Ptuj's oldest street, **Hotel Mitra** (Prešernova ul. 6; © **02/787-7455;** www.hotel-mitra-fm.si; 71€–81€/$89–$101 double) is the best accommodations in town (and the only option in the center). Reserve a room on the second floor; those higher up have ceiling windows preventing you from seeing out. The nicest place to eat is **Gostilna Ribič** ⋆ (Dravska ulica 9; © **02/749-0635**), where a seat on the riverside terrace is an ideal place to enjoy a bottle of wine and some excel-lent freshwater fish. Particularly good is the *trout (postrv),* but you can fearlessly try the mixed seafood stew, served at the table.

TOURING THE JERUZALEM WINE ROAD ⋆⋆⋆   Drive 30km (19 miles) beyond Ptuj, to **Ljutomer,** where you can pick up a **Jeruzalem Wine Road** map from the tourist office (© **02/584-8333;** www.lto-prlekija.si). Then head off for gorgeous vineyards and their accompanying cellars; 20km (12 miles) from Ljutomer is the hill-top village of Jeruzalem, so named by the crusaders. From here, set off for **Kog** for a memorable tasting at **Hlebec** ★★ (© **02/713-7060;** www.slovina.com/hlebecmilan/ eng). Owner-sommelier Milan Hlebec will pour noble vintages produced by his family—responsible for some 18,000 vines, including local favorite, *šipon*. You can enjoy a hearty lunch, and if you're not up for driving back, stay the night in the guesthouse, which has good en suites.

Index

See also Accommodations and Restaurant indexes, below.

700 INDEX

RESTAURANTS

POLAND - NO ADDRESS FOR NATI. TOURIST OFF
NO MENTION OF HERTZ OFF
IN TOWN
NO INFO ON LOWICZ, ~~LUBLIC~~,
KAZIMIEZ DOLNY, LUBLIN
LANCUT, ZAMOSC

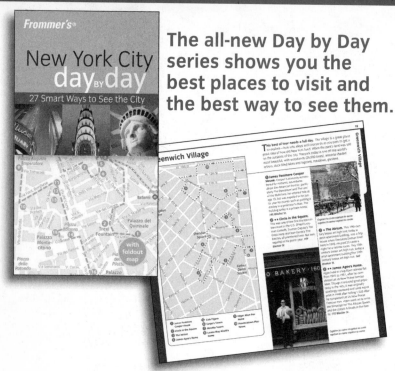

A Guide for Every Type of Traveler

Frommer's Complete Guides

For those who value complete coverage, candid advice, and lots of choices in all price ranges.

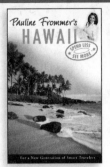

Pauline Frommer's Guides

For those who want to experience a culture, meet locals, and save money along the way.

MTV Guides

For hip, youthful travelers who want a fresh perspective on today's hottest cities and destinations.

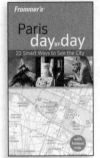

Day by Day Guides

For leisure or business travelers who want to organize their time to get the most out of a trip.

Frommer's With Kids Guides

For families traveling with children ages 2 to 14 seeking kid-friendly hotels, restaurants, and activities.

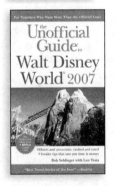

Unofficial Guides

For honeymooners, families, business travelers, and others who value no-nonsense, *Consumer Reports*–style advice.

For Dummies Travel Guides

For curious, independent travelers looking for a fun and easy way to plan a trip.

Visit Frommers.com

WILEY
Now you know.

Explore over 3,500 destinations.

TOKYO — 7766 miles

LONDON — 3818 miles

TORONTO — 4682 miles

SYDNEY — 5087 miles

NEW YORK — 4947 miles

LOS ANGELES — 2556 miles

HONG KONG — 5638 miles

Frommers.com makes it easy.

Find a destination. ✓ Book a trip. ✓ Get hot travel deals.
Buy a guidebook. ✓ Enter to win vacations. ✓ Listen to podcasts. ✓ Check
the latest travel news. ✓ Share trip photos and memories. ✓ And much mo

Frommers.com

New series!

Pauline Frommer's

Pauline Frommer's ITALY
Pauline Frommer's HAWAII
Pauline Frommer's NEW YORK CITY

SPEND LESS ★ SEE MORE

For a New Generation of Smart Travelers

★ SPEND LESS ★ SEE MORE™

Discover a fresh take on budget travel with these exciting new guides from travel expert Pauline Frommer. From industry secrets on finding the best hotel rooms to great neighborhood restaurants and cool, offbeat finds only locals know about, you'll learn how to truly experience a culture *and* save money along the way.

Coming soon:

Pauline Frommer's Costa Rica
Pauline Frommer's Paris

Pauline Frommer's Las Vegas
Pauline Frommer's London

The best trips start here.
Available wherever books are sold.

Frommer's®
A Branded Imprint of ⊕**WILEY**
Now you know.

Fun destinations for all ages!

Let Frommer's take you across town or around the globe to some of the kid-friendliest places in the world. From the best hotels, restaurants, and attractions to exact prices, detailed maps, and more, Frommer's makes the going easy—and enjoyable—for the whole family.

FROMMER'S® COMPLETE TRAVEL GUIDES

Alaska
Amalfi Coast
American Southwest
Amsterdam
Argentina & Chile
Arizona
Atlanta
Australia
Austria
Bahamas
Barcelona
Beijing
Belgium, Holland & Luxembourg
Belize
Bermuda
Boston
Brazil
British Columbia & the Canadian
    Rockies
Brussels & Bruges
Budapest & the Best of Hungary
Buenos Aires
Calgary
California
Canada
Cancún, Cozumel & the Yucatán
Cape Cod, Nantucket & Martha's
    Vineyard
Caribbean
Caribbean Ports of Call
Carolinas & Georgia
Chicago
China
Colorado
Costa Rica
Croatia
Cuba
Denmark
Denver, Boulder & Colorado Springs
Edinburgh & Glasgow
England
Europe
Europe by Rail
Florence, Tuscany & Umbria

Florida
France
Germany
Greece
Greek Islands
Hawaii
Hong Kong
Honolulu, Waikiki & Oahu
India
Ireland
Israel
Italy
Jamaica
Japan
Kauai
Las Vegas
London
Los Angeles
Los Cabos & Baja
Madrid
Maine Coast
Maryland & Delaware
Maui
Mexico
Montana & Wyoming
Montréal & Québec City
Moscow & St. Petersburg
Munich & the Bavarian Alps
Nashville & Memphis
New England
Newfoundland & Labrador
New Mexico
New Orleans
New York City
New York State
New Zealand
Northern Italy
Norway
Nova Scotia, New Brunswick &
    Prince Edward Island
Oregon
Paris
Peru
Philadelphia & the Amish Country

Portugal
Prague & the Best of the Czech
    Republic
Provence & the Riviera
Puerto Rico
Rome
San Antonio & Austin
San Diego
San Francisco
Santa Fe, Taos & Albuquerque
Scandinavia
Scotland
Seattle
Seville, Granada & the Best of
    Andalusia
Shanghai
Sicily
Singapore & Malaysia
South Africa
South America
South Florida
South Pacific
Southeast Asia
Spain
Sweden
Switzerland
Tahiti & French Polynesia
Texas
Thailand
Tokyo
Toronto
Turkey
USA
Utah
Vancouver & Victoria
Vermont, New Hampshire & Maine
Vienna & the Danube Valley
Vietnam
Virgin Islands
Virginia
Walt Disney World® & Orlando
Washington, D.C.
Washington State

FROMMER'S® DAY BY DAY GUIDES

Amsterdam
Chicago
Florence & Tuscany

London
New York City
Paris

Rome
San Francisco
Venice

PAULINE FROMMER'S GUIDES! SEE MORE. SPEND LESS.

Hawaii

Italy

New York City

FROMMER'S® PORTABLE GUIDES

Acapulco, Ixtapa & Zihuatanejo
Amsterdam
Aruba
Australia's Great Barrier Reef
Bahamas
Big Island of Hawaii
Boston
California Wine Country
Cancún
Cayman Islands
Charleston
Chicago
Dominican Republic

Dublin
Florence
Las Vegas
Las Vegas for Non-Gamblers
London
Maui
Nantucket & Martha's Vineyard
New Orleans
New York City
Paris
Portland
Puerto Rico
Puerto Vallarta, Manzanillo &
    Guadalajara

Rio de Janeiro
San Diego
San Francisco
Savannah
St. Martin, Sint Maarten, Anguila &
    St. Bart's
Turks & Caicos
Vancouver
Venice
Virgin Islands
Washington, D.C.
Whistler

FROMMER'S® CRUISE GUIDES

Alaska Cruises & Ports of Call

Cruises & Ports of Call

European Cruises & Ports of Call

FROMMER'S® NATIONAL PARK GUIDES

Algonquin Provincial Park
Banff & Jasper
Grand Canyon

National Parks of the American West
Rocky Mountain
Yellowstone & Grand Teton

Yosemite and Sequoia & Kings
  Canyon
Zion & Bryce Canyon

FROMMER'S® MEMORABLE WALKS

London
New York

Paris
Rome

San Francisco

FROMMER'S® WITH KIDS GUIDES

Chicago
Hawaii
Las Vegas
London

National Parks
New York City
San Francisco

Toronto
Walt Disney World® & Orlando
Washington, D.C.

SUZY GERSHMAN'S BORN TO SHOP GUIDES

France
Hong Kong, Shanghai & Beijing
Italy

London
New York

Paris
San Francisco

FROMMER'S® IRREVERENT GUIDES

Amsterdam
Boston
Chicago
Las Vegas

London
Los Angeles
Manhattan
Paris

Rome
San Francisco
Walt Disney World®
Washington, D.C.

FROMMER'S® BEST-LOVED DRIVING TOURS

Austria
Britain
California
France

Germany
Ireland
Italy
New England

Northern Italy
Scotland
Spain
Tuscany & Umbria

THE UNOFFICIAL GUIDES®

Adventure Travel in Alaska
Beyond Disney
California with Kids
Central Italy
Chicago
Cruises
Disneyland®
England
Florida
Florida with Kids

Hawaii
Ireland
Las Vegas
London
Maui
Mexico's Best Beach Resorts
Mini Mickey
New Orleans
New York City

Paris
San Francisco
South Florida including Miami &
  the Keys
Walt Disney World®
Walt Disney World® for
  Grown-ups
Walt Disney World® with Kids
Washington, D.C.

SPECIAL-INTEREST TITLES

Athens Past & Present
Best Places to Raise Your Family
Cities Ranked & Rated
500 Places to Take Your Kids Before They Grow Up
Frommer's Best Day Trips from London
Frommer's Best RV & Tent Campgrounds
  in the U.S.A.

Frommer's Exploring America by RV
Frommer's NYC Free & Dirt Cheap
Frommer's Road Atlas Europe
Frommer's Road Atlas Ireland
Great Escapes From NYC Without Wheels
Retirement Places Rated

FROMMER'S® PHRASEFINDER DICTIONARY GUIDES

French

Italian

Spanish

THE NEW TRAVELOCITY GUARANTEE

EVERYTHING YOU BOOK WILL BE RIGHT, OR WE'LL WORK WITH OUR TRAVEL PARTNERS TO MAKE IT RIGHT, RIGHT AWAY.

*To drive home the point,
we're going to use the word "right" in every single sentence.*

Let's get right to it. Right to the meat! Only Travelocity guarantees everything about your booking will be right, or we'll work with our travel partners to make it right, right away. Right on!

Here's a picture taken smack dab right in the middle of Antigua, where the guarantee also covers you.

The guarantee covers all but one of the items pictured to the right.

Now, you may be thinking, "Yeah, right, I'm so sure." That's OK; you have the right to remain skeptical. That is until we mention help is always right around the corner. Call us right off the bat, knowing that our customer service reps are there for you 24/7. Righting wrongs. Left and right.

For example, what if the ocean view you booked actually looks out at a downright ugly parking lot? You'd be right to call – we're there for you. And no one in their right mind would be pleased to learn the rental car place has closed and left them stranded. Call Travelocity and we'll help get you back on the right track.

Now if you're guessing there are some things we can't control, like the weather, well you're right. But we can help you with most things – to get all the details in righting,* visit **travelocity.com/guarantee**.

*Sorry, spelling things right is one of the few things not covered under the guarantee.

I'd give my right arm for a guarantee like this, although I'm glad I don't have to.

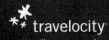

travelocity
You'll never roam alone.

IF YOU BOOK IT, IT SHOULD BE THERE.

Only Travelocity guarantees it will be, or we'll work with our travel partners to make it right, right away. So if you're missing a balcony or anything else you booked, just call us 24/7 **1-888-TRAVELOCITY**

travelocity

You'll never roam alone